To Agnes

REFLECTIONS ON
SUCCESS

Every Success!

Martyn Lewis

FAMOUS ACHIEVERS TALK FRANKLY TO

MARTYN LEWIS

ABOUT THEIR ROUTE TO THE TOP

Lennard Publishing

First published in 1997
First paperback edition published in 1998

Lennard Publishing
a division of Lennard Associates Ltd
Mackerye End, Harpenden, Herts AL5 5DR

© Martyn Lewis 1997, 1998

The right of Martyn Lewis to be recognized as author of this work has been asserted by him in accordance with the Copyright, Designs and Patents Act, 1988.

A CIP record for this book is available from the British Library
ISBN 1 85291 139 5

All photographs in this book are by Martyn Lewis

Interviews transcribed by Linda Prior, Gillian Hall,
Denise Elsdon, Julie Jefferson and Lucy Chamberlaine
Edited by Caroline North, Roderick Brown,
Michael Leitch, Kirsty Ennever and Mike Seabrook
Production Editor: Ian Osborn
Jacket design by Paul Cooper

Printed and bound in Great Britain by Butler & Tanner, Frome and London

Key to portraits (pages 1 and 2)
Page 1 (from left to right and by row from top to bottom): *Jeffrey Archer, Bob Ayling, Barry Norman; Martin Bell, David Blunkett, Richard Branson, Cliff Richard, Paul Condon; Billy Connolly, F.W. De Klerk, Ron Dearing, Noel Edmonds, Tom Farmer; David Frost, Evelyn Glennie, Michael Grade, Richard Holbrooke, Jeremy Irons; Linford Christie, Andrew Marr, George Martin, David Mellor, Georg Solti; John Monks, Nthato Motlana, Tony O'Reilly, Michael Palin, Matthew Parris; Phil Harris, François Pienaar, Cicely Saunders, Ray Seitz, Shimon Peres.*

Page 2: *Yehudi Menuhin, Tony Blair, Terry Wogan, Michael Atherton, Bruce Oldfield; Jack Charlton, Tim Henman, Cameron Mackintosh, Ian MacLaurin, Nick Park; Norman Foster, Helen Sharman, Maurice Saatchi, Anita Roddick, Anthony Hopkins; Barbara Taylor Bradford, Bernard Ingham, David English, John Birt, Sadako Ogata; Nigel Dempster, Mary Robinson, David Bellamy, George Carman, Jackie Stewart; John Major, Stella Rimington, Sebastian Coe, Lodwrick Cook, Judi Dench; Bob Alexander, Sam Chisholm, Rebecca Stephens, Andrew Neil.*

REFLECTIONS ON
SUCCESS

FAMOUS
ACHIEVERS
TALK
FRANKLY
ABOUT THEIR
ROUTE TO
THE TOP

CONTENTS

To the inspiring ladies in my life –
Liz, Sylvie, Katie, Jonie and Jill

'It is not the critic who counts: not the man who points out how the strong man stumbles, or where the doer of deeds could have done them better. The credit belongs to the man who is actually in the arena, whose face is marred by dust and sweat and blood: who strives valiantly; who errs, and comes short again and again, because there is no effort without error and shortcoming; but who does actually strive to do the deeds; who knows the great enthusiasms, the great devotions; who spends himself in a worthy cause; who at the best knows in the end the triumph of high achievement, and who at the worst, if he fails, at least fails while daring greatly, so that his place shall never be with those cold and timid souls who know neither victory nor defeat.'

Theodore Rooseveldt, address at the Sorbonne, Paris, France, 23 April 1910.

INTRODUCTION

For many, the desire for success is the driving force in their lives; some will achieve it through coincidence or luck; for others it requires careful planning and hard work; to observers it stirs differing emotions ranging from envy to admiration. It can be large of scale and high in profile; it can be created in smaller, but no less valuable, nuggets of satisfaction – hidden from the outside world – that come from reaching personal goals.

However success is achieved it generates widespread media attention and private interest – all the more so because there seems to be no set formula for being successful, no real standard for measuring it, and no guarantee that it will be sustained. The interviews transcribed in the following pages reveal the conversational comments, philosophy and judgments of well-known people in many walks of life who are generally considered to have been successful in one or more particular field. They talk freely about the benchmarks of their success, as they see them; the influences of their formative years; any conflict between their professional and personal lives; the thinking and the catalysts behind their achievements; the setbacks and failures, and, more importantly, how they recovered from them; and they offer much good advice for others starting out now in their particular field seeking to mirror their achievements.

My interviewees are not just successful, but thoughtful and articulate about the way in which that success has been achieved. Their fields of expertise range across business, politics, music, stage, films, animation, sport, journalism, diplomacy, travel, the police, the security services, charity, best-selling novels, comedy and television entertainment. Their judgments on success are laced with experience and wisdom – and everyone brings to the table a new perspective, a different balance of core values – and a few surprises too. For some their biggest successes are in the past; for others they are yet to come.

I have long believed that there is, for society, a potentially destructive imbalance between the media's coverage of success and failure. We quite properly analyse and explain disasters, mistakes and inadequacies; we are less inclined to provide interesting analysis of triumphs and achievement. Successful people are more likely to be interviewed when something goes wrong; the hiccups and hesitations on the road to success are considered more newsworthy than attempts to explain why someone has done well. On top of that, many important small successes with enormous potential to improve the fabric of society are ignored because they don't fulfil the media appetite for superlatives. Those imbalances are touched on in different ways by many of the interviewees, including Britain's new Prime Minister, Tony Blair. Making a point which finds wide agreement across the political spectrum, he sees a need to 'pay more attention to celebrating things that are actually working, that are good in society'. He talks of 'many unsung heroes', including those running a voluntary sector project achieving virtually a 100 per cent success rate in putting unemployed black kids through a training scheme and into jobs. No one will ever have heard of them; yet, he says, they are just as important as the bigger success stories which actually do hit the headlines.

None of the journalists or politicians involved in backing these arguments, now being debated in many countries, would ever suggest that the media should stop reporting the negative. That is clearly a nonsense in a democracy; yet it is a distortion of the argument for a more balanced news agenda often peddled accusingly by those who – deliberately or accidentally – fail to see the serious point that is being made, that the media, far from being removed from the society on which they report, have a responsibility to it. Some critics believe that journalism, by definition, must predominantly be about things going wrong; others, perhaps with reputations carved by dwelling on disaster, feel threatened, and seek to nip in the bud any move to present a more balanced mirror image of the world, and perhaps a few are worried that their jobs could be made more difficult. Many negative stories virtually write themselves – the pictures and the words fall into the reporter's lap. It can be a much more difficult challenge to take a positive story, and turn it into really interesting journalism which people want to watch, listen to or read. There is a place for all of those viewpoints in the growing debate. I hope that this book will make some contribution to that, for it asks some questions which many interviewees said had never been put to them before. For instance, although I wanted to hear about their setbacks and failures, I was much more interested in how they recovered from them. So the thrust of the book is to try to improve understanding about success, as well as providing insights into the lives and thinking of people whose decisions and activities touch – or have touched – many lives.

Normally, when a journalist is sent to interview someone who is regarded as successful, the routine goes something like this. First they visit their news information library and read other articles that have been written about that person (some will contain long-standing inaccuracies of a relatively minor nature which were locked in place many years before, and poached and repeated by each new interviewer). They talk to the interviewee's friends, but more usually their enemies (the latter are usually quoted as anonymous sources, affording them a degree of protection seldom offered to anyone else). They perhaps discuss an angle with their editor. Then, preparations complete, they spend an hour or two having a wide-ranging conversation with the interviewee, whom they are probably meeting for the very first (and only) time. When the article appears, the interviewer has picked out the best quotes, and painted around them considered judgments about the subject's life and opinions. These are often very fair; sometimes they are not; the reader has no way of judging. Or it may turn out to be another type of interview where the subject's comments are less important than the reporter's desire to show what a clever, witty writer he or she might be. All of these factors are fully understood by most prominent people who agree to be interviewed; and a case can usually be made for each type of interview with varying degrees of conviction.

But there is another type of interview, seen less frequently in newspapers and magazines – and seldom in books, in which the reporter's questions are merely the catalyst, unlocking the detailed thoughts of the interviewee. Minor editing then takes place to allow for the difference between the spoken and the written word, and remove the natural repetitions that can occur in conversation. The interview is then presented in question and answer format. And that is what you have in this book, allowing you, the readers, to judge for yourselves the detailed thinking and arguments deployed by 67 people who have been touched by success.

Robert Woodruff, a former chairman, chief executive and president of Coca-Cola used to keep on his huge desk a brass plaque on which were inscribed the following words of encouragement for his employees: 'There is no limit to what a man can do or where he can go if he doesn't mind who gets the credit'. So I hereby – and hopefully – give lavish credit to all those without whose help, advice and encouragement this book would not have been possible.

First and foremost – to the interviewees themselves, who found time in their formidable diaries to talk to me especially for this book. To my splendidly helpful and tolerant publisher, Adrian Stephenson of Lennard Publishing, and his team of resourceful editors – Chris Hawkes, Caroline North, Roderick Brown, Michael Leitch, Kirsty Ennever and Mike Seabrook.

To Mark Rowland, Henry Eagles and Vaughan Dagnell at Mentorn Films for generously aiding the transfer of the original digital sound recordings; to Linda Prior, Gillian Hall, Denise Elsdon, Julie Jefferson, Lucy Chamberlain and Felicity Smith, for the care they took in transcribing the tapes; to all at Selwood Systems and Butler & Tanner for turning the manuscript into an impressive volume in record time and to the many who eased my path considerably in setting up the interviews – including Helen Davis, Norman and Liliane Peck, Dick Foxton, Jenny Williams, Jeremy Ractliffe, Anji Hunter, Alastair Campbell, Howell James, Alan Percival, Bride Rosney, Ivan Fallon, Tommy Flood, Ken Dickerson,

Rupert Grey, Jane Erith, Karen Friend, Beverley Kleiman, Colin Browne, Janine Thomason, Steve Brown, David Jones, Alison Burley, Bill Connor, Susan Barrett, Alexandria Wight, Sue Jennings, Peter Jones, Diana Potter, Jan Bates, Rebecca Hogan, Deborah Thackery-Tyers, Jenni Hopkins, Michael O'Brien, Aric Schwan, Jan Felgate, Judy Willett, Jilly Judd, Vera Lamport, Tony Bloom, Yusef Surtee, Beryl Baker, Christian Berthiaume, Eileen Wright, Yona Bartal, Arthur Sherriff, Gill Snow, Roger Bruce, Sara Tye, James Stuart, Valerie Solti, Charles Kaye, Pat Hughes, Ali Hay, Margaret Neilson and last, but by no means least, for their splendid support in so many ways, Sam and Alayne Courtney, Anita Land, Georgina Capel, Brian MacLaurin, Liz Ivens, Fiona Coleman, and – above all – my darling Liz, whose gentle tolerance of every new project on which I embark never ceases to amaze me!

Two of the less obvious requirements for success recommended here are a strong degree of curiosity and the ability to enjoy whatever you are doing. I hope those come together as you are drawn further into the pages of this book, and that you will find new thoughts and perspectives to encourage and help you succeed in reaching your own goals – whatever they may be. Above all remember William Feather's advice that 'success is largely a matter of hanging on after others have let go!'

Martyn Lewis
London, May 1997

LORD ALEXANDER

'The best advocate of his generation' is how the legendary judge Lord Denning once described Bob Alexander. Yet this remarkable lawyer-turned-banker confesses that for much of his life he found it difficult to speak in public. So the rapier-like mind and analytical skills that fought celebrated legal tussles on behalf of author Jeffrey Archer, Australian tycoon Kerry Packer, Singapore's ruler Lee Kwan Yew, the British government and trade unions never once found a voice in that formative debating cauldron, the Cambridge Union. And even now, at the age of 60, he believes he has still not lost all his shyness – 'we all have moments when we feel less sure of ourselves, less sure of the contribution we are going to make'. But, as with many achievers,  that sense of insecurity became a driving force for the tall, gangling youth from Newcastle-under-Lyme, whose parents ran a petrol station and made conscious sacrifices to give their elder son the best educational start in life. The path from the garage forecourt to the House of Lords (he was made a Life Peer in 1988) led him through a Cambridge MA degree and 27 years at the bar, culminating in the chairmanship of the Bar Council when the full force of his courtroom cunning was channelled into laying a framework for the reform of his profession. That was followed by a two-year spell as Chairman of the Panel of Takeovers and Mergers. Then, in 1989 – to the surprise of many colleagues – he walked away from the career at which he had been such a conspicuous success to try his hand at the world of banking, about which, he freely admits, he knew nothing! Out of the blue had come an invitation to chair the National Westminster Bank. Unfailingly polite, courteous and urbane, he talks here of the doubts and challenges of that job switch – 'I'd come home sometimes, and admit I was clinging on by my fingernails. But you can't have a leadership role and appear too shy, whatever you're thinking underneath.' A passionate interest in constitutional reform has given him a seat on Lord Jenkins of Hillhead's Commission examining Britain's voting system. Here he discusses the qualities needed for the legal high-flyers of tomorrow – a passion for fairness and integrity, a logical mind, flair and hard work. He warns that when you achieve success, that is precisely the moment at which you sow the seeds of your own downfall.

Lord Alexander, what is your definition of success?

Success is impossible of definition in absolute terms. All individuals are different and what is success for one individual as a magnificent use of their talents would only be a modest use of talent by another. So much depends on who you are, where you start from, where you decide your place is in life.

So success is a very personal thing and everyone achieves it in their own way. But are there any general principles that will guarantee success?

Success can come in the oddest guises and for a brief hour only. I don't think any general principles guarantee success because there are elements of luck, elements of choosing a career or a lifestyle that happens to be right for you. You can be absolutely thrown by being in the wrong place at the right time, or by someone else's attitude to you. But I think if there are two key elements, they are, in alphabetical order, determination and enthusiasm. Of the two, enthusiasm is probably more important because it's so infectious and it helps you get opportunities.

Can you have too much enthusiasm, so that you are all force and no direction?

Yes, it's perfectly possible, but I think without enthusiasm it's very difficult to succeed even if you're well directed.

To what extent has your success been shaped by your upbringing?

Aren't we all shaped by our upbringing? I think my upbringing was in some ways pretty fortunate. It wasn't over-fortunate in material terms but it was good enough. My father had his filling station and garage. My parents, who had both left school young, believed passionately in education and saved to send my brother and myself to decent schools so we had opportunity. But one thing they also instilled in us was that we should take that opportunity because we knew how much they had sacrificed to give us that chance, and that was a driving force. I also realized that it was quite essential to use my education well if I was to have the chance of getting on in the world, exceeding what they had achieved and moving forward. So I think there was a very strong, almost puritanical driving force. It was a driving force that also created its own uncertainty because I used to agonize over things. What if I didn't do well in this exam? What if I got a low class in my degree? What if no one would be prepared to give me a pupillage at the Bar? Or a tenancy? So as well as a drive to succeed, it created an agony, an insecurity about what would happen if I didn't achieve at every single stage.

So in a sense, insecurity and fear at some early stage in your career helps to drive you towards success. Is that insecurity always there or do you lose it?

The insecurity can always come back. It may be dissipated for long periods when I'm doing well but it can very quickly return if I get into a difficult work situation or if I feel that in some ways my life has become more uncertain. I look at how my life has gone so far and what I really hope is that I can achieve more, either in personal terms or in work terms. I'm conscious I've done well in certain areas, but also, perhaps, of how much better I could have done if I had had a wider degree of knowledge from the beginning. If sometimes one had greater certainty, greater brashness, the possibilities might have been greater but, for me, insecurity was one of the driving forces – there's no doubt about that.

How important a part does parental ambition play in shaping whether a person is successful or not? Do you have to be driven by your parents?

I don't think you have to be driven by your parents, although parental ambition can play a considerable part in an individual's striving to succeed. On the other hand, I'm sure that there are people who have an innate driving force, so whatever the views of their parents they may well have an ambition to succeed. As a parent you have to be very careful about what you mean by ambition for your children. You don't mean ambition in the conventional sense, you don't want them to be a successful barrister or successful businessman. What you ultimately want is for them to be satisfied and fulfilled in the use of the talents that they actually have. In the case of one's daughter, for example, her talent may be to bring up her child at home rather than be a working mother. If a child is not particularly academic, it would be parental folly, and a disservice, to perceive ambition as being to try and change that child. What I hope for my children is that I can look back at the end of my life and see that they're giving where they can in the role that they're playing in life, and they're getting fulfilment from what they're doing.

When your parents advised you to become a solicitor and you decided that you wanted to be a barrister, was there an argument?

No, my parents were thrilled because although they hoped I would become a solicitor, they weren't set on it, they were too intelligent for that. They would have accepted it if I'd become a schoolmaster or if I'd become a writer, both of which flitted across my thoughts when I was young. But when I said I was going to become a lawyer, my father was delighted because he had been helped at a crucial stage of setting up his garage business by a very good solicitor. So he had a respect for lawyers.

When I went on to say that I wanted to be a barrister, they found that hard to comprehend because London, the Temple, the law seemed a long way off to all of us, but I think underneath they were thrilled and they backed me. Although my father had died beforehand, I remember my mother's pride in my becoming a QC. I remember her coming to see me do cases.

It was once said that you were a shy man who shed his timidity only in a wig and gown. Does it help the pursuit of success to be a different person in the public arena to the person you are in private?

No, I don't think it does. In one respect that comment was quite perceptive, as for a lot of my life I found it very difficult to speak in public. I couldn't do it at university. I think in a sense the key moment of my own personal development – and I remember the feeling I had afterwards – was the first time I was sent to court and asked to defend some minor case before the Croydon Magistrates. I achieved an acquittal for someone whom I probably wouldn't have acquitted myself, and this, whether it should or not, gives a barrister considerable satisfaction. I realized that getting up and speaking in a court in a disciplined environment where I had a role, where my turn to speak was laid down by the rules, my turn to question was laid down by the rules, was something I could do in an outgoing way, far more than anything I'd ever done outside the court room. I say in an outgoing way – I don't think I was ever a particularly dramatic advocate, but in terms of competence, fluency, use of language, I did have something, and I could use it in the court room.

For a long time I found it very difficult to take that ability outside, as I'd have liked to do. I only began to do so when I became Chairman of the Bar and had a more public role, in which I had to deal with the press, had to make after dinner speeches, had to make general speeches at conferences. Gradually I began to lose my shyness because in a sense I had to. Then, when I went to my present job, a large organization where I have to meet many people both from the outside world and within the bank, it was for me to put them at their ease. Perhaps because I'd been very shy myself, I could do that better because of my consciousness of it. But I had to take the lead. It's no good me going to a meeting with some junior staff of NatWest and saying, 'Ask me questions' or 'Tell me what you want from the business.' I've got to get the occasion going, and get them going, so I've lost a lot of my shyness over the years.

But not all of it?

Probably not all of it, no. We all have moments when we feel less sure of ourselves than we were, less sure of the contribution we're going to make.

But I have lost quite a lot of it and I don't think the fact that I'm shy comes over very often from my public image. In the job I do it shouldn't because it wouldn't help the confidence of other people within the group. You can't have a leadership role and appear too shy, whatever you're thinking underneath.

The catalysts for losing your shyness – whether they be the courtroom performance in Croydon or the move to NatWest – came, some might think, relatively late in life. Was there any reason for that?

Perhaps if, at school, I'd been a very successful cricketer or a very successful rugby player, and had therefore achieved more and made an impression on my contemporaries, that might have made me feel more at ease with myself. But I can remember sitting in the Cambridge Union and listening to people and thinking, 'I don't think much of what you're saying.' But then thinking, 'I can't get to my feet for the life of me.' Ten years ago I went to the Cambridge Union and spoke in a debate and I very much enjoyed the experience, but then I was a leading speaker with an organized role in the situation and I find that far easier than if, for example, I'm in a group of people and suddenly think, 'Shall I intervene without necessarily being asked?' Once my role is set I find it very easy to lose my diffidence. I also think that the more I experience life and meeting people, the more I actually enjoy socializing, which I do enjoy very much, and I think that helps too.

When was the first time that you thought to yourself, 'I have been a success, I am successful, at one thing or another'?

I'm back at that episode in Croydon. Although I did do quite well at school – I did quite well in exams, I ran film societies, I was captain of school chess, I played a moderately decent, though not exciting, game of cricket – none of that was enough to drive away the sort of inner insecurities of a tall, thin, gangly boy, and I think physical development does have a bearing in this area. At university I had many friends in my college, but the wider area of the university I rather watched with awe – the university cricket team, the university debating society. It was a wonderful period of my life, but it was only when I did that first case at the Bar that I walked out and thought, 'I can do this.' And although I had many periods afterwards wondering how far I would get at the Bar, I didn't really, from then on, doubt that I would do at least reasonably well.

Did you at any stage give yourself a plan for your future career, a benchmark by which you would judge your success or otherwise?

No, I never have. That way you put yourself on tram lines, which you may well fail to stay within and, if you do, it may bring you very little satisfaction. As my practice as a junior developed, I thought I would love to take silk young – that would be a further proof of ability. The list of QCs is published with the person who has been in practice longest at the top and the person who has been in the race the shortest at the bottom, so to be the junior person at the bottom of the silks list was, I think, a further important step in my gaining self-confidence and recognition in the world.

What do you regard as your greatest triumphs?

That depends on how you're measuring them. There are a number of court cases that I look back on with satisfaction, but I think in general terms there are three areas that have given me great satisfaction and they are all in relatively recent years.

First, I do believe that in my time as Chairman of the Bar we managed to change a large number of aspects of the profession and set the pace and framework in which it could modernize itself. I got considerable pleasure from that because, coming to the Bar as a young man from outside, it did seem a rather strange, daunting environment. I thought its basic values, practices and standards were tremendous, but there were clearly areas in which it needed to change, and a lot of those changes have endured.

I also got satisfaction from my time as chairman of the Takeover Panel – an important role, regulating takeovers, trying to do it outside the court system, trying to do it before damage was done and trying to do it in a way which the City and business – not easy constituencies to satisfy – respected. When I went to the Takeover Panel it had had a tough period, there was a question mark over whether it could endure, or whether that form of regulation would have to become statutory. We had a very good team there and we pulled it back very quickly. That was a source of satisfaction.

And now that I've been at NatWest some time I do begin to feel pleased with progress there. NatWest is completely different from the Bar Council or the Takeover Panel. Small organizations are like sailing dinghies – you can pull on the sheets and the sails move, you can get action going fairly quickly. By contrast, NatWest is more like an oil tanker, and an oil tanker which had tremendous difficulties in the first two years that I was there. There were various areas of loss – parts of the business were doing badly, there was a host of issues about quality of management, the way we approached staff, the way we communicated with them, the way we developed, which I found absorbing. So we built a good board and a strong management team. Like all organizations we are in the business of constantly trying to improve and develop, and I'm not saying we're there yet, but I do find it a very different place to the one I came to seven years ago. Now, of course, in that development I played as part of a team, it's not like being an individual advocate, but I know that as a member of that team I've had influence. That's another area that I feel has been very worthwhile.

You're demonstrating the enthusiasm that you mentioned earlier when you talk about NatWest, but to many it would have seemed strange that someone right at the top of the legal profession should suddenly switch professions. Now why did you do that and was it an easy decision to make or a difficult one?

I had been at the Bar for over 25 years. I had been lucky enough to take silk young. I had been in silk as a QC for 15 years. I had had a wonderful range of cases and I had had my period as Chairman of the Bar. I found it difficult after being Chairman of the Bar to go back to arguing individual cases, because you're not judging those cases, nor – in the traditions of the Bar and a practice which I very much respect – are you only arguing those cases you approve of, you're arguing those cases which you're hired to argue. Although I hope I was not showing it in terms of performance, I was finding it more difficult to motivate myself. I had dipped a toe in the waters of the City when I had been part-time Chairman of the Takeover Panel, but when I was approached about being Chairman of NatWest, I was totally surprised and totally unprepared.

It really did come out of the blue?

Completely. The then Chairman asked if he could come and visit me in my chambers one morning. He said, 'You know, I've come to talk to you about the chairmanship of NatWest.' I said, 'Well, from my perspective as a lawyer I can't offer much advice on the rival candidates,' and he said, 'No, what I've come for is to see if you're interested in becoming Chairman, because if so, I believe my board would be united in asking you to.' That struck me as pretty extraordinary. I didn't even know enough about NatWest to ask intelligent questions. I asked if we could talk again in a week's time and then talked to the people I knew in banking and in the City. They said that it was a very worthwhile task because it was one of our largest banks, and banking, whatever image it sometimes has, is actually fundamental to society and has to be done well. It seemed that the opportunities which it offered in terms of involvement in a wider sphere of affairs, economics, banking, the whole structure of a large organization, communication with the public, were very interesting.

What I totally underestimated was my lack of preparation for that job, because at the Bar you tend to think that you see all human life – you argue cases for cricketers, company chairmen, for people who have been dismissed from jobs, for doctors who have been brought before the General Medical Council, for broadcasters and so on, and you tend to think you've seen it all. Well, what you've seen has only been with a particular slant, with a particular focus. What you haven't seen is so much of the wider world and its wider challenges. I found myself pretty much at sea for a time when I went to NatWest. First of all I didn't know the institution well, so I didn't know which levers I should press to get things done. I didn't know which people were abler than others. I didn't know where one's initiatives might be stopped down the line – and there's a considerable expertise in any large organization for preventing what those at the top want to happen from actually happening. At the same time the recession hit before I had completed my learning curve. There was a need for action and however I might have appeared in public, I'd come home sometimes and admit I was clinging on by my fingernails.

So you really had doubts about the job after you had taken it?

Oh, very much so. In my first two years I felt that I might well not have taken it if I'd known how it would be – at least I felt that on some days. On other days I felt, 'This is a terrific challenge and I am determined we shall actually get it right.'

Does the pursuit of success and satisfaction involve taking a risk?

I'm sure it does. This is a fairly high-profile and satisfying job, but clearly it involves risk. But then what about a musician when he adopts a new style of interpretation? What about a dramatist or an artist who goes a different way from conventional acting or painting? Or, in another area, what about all the effort that Rutherford put into splitting the atom? If it hadn't succeeded, then his life's work would have ended in disappointment. So I think wherever you're going, you're actually taking a risk with what you do with your life. If, for instance, I had stayed at the Bar, I would have been taking the opposite risk. I would have been taking the risk of not being fulfilled in later years. So there is a risk either way – a risk in going for it, and a very considerable risk if you don't.

When you felt at NatWest that you weren't yet on top of the job, was there any formula by which you clawed yourself back, so that you built yourself up again to go in to tackle the job the way you wanted?

First I tried to make everyone realize how determined I was, because undoubtedly coming from outside as chairman to a large organization, there would have been some people who would have had a vested interest in making me just a figurehead. I had to establish that that wasn't going to happen and it was hard work. The second thing was that I had to look to the next generation of management. I had to try to make certain I met people in their late thirties, early forties, whom I could identify as being key people, suitable for early promotion and able to contribute to the change in the culture of the organization – which was deeply needed.

I had also to make certain that I learned as much about the business as possible, because unless you know the facts, unless you know what is involved in banking, people can blind you with science. My lawyer's training gave me the ability, when a paper was presented, to look for the traps, ask the questions, and to probe, especially in areas where we were failing. That I think is a priceless part of the advocate's training. The papers I get now are incomparably better, but still I find myself always reading through them, putting a question mark here to discuss at the meeting, or a comment there – 'Where does this lead?' That discipline can always be translated to the business world, I think.

What are your biggest failures and how did you overcome them?

Obviously there were failures at the Bar, but they were failures to win cases – we all have those. I once had the best part of a year when I didn't win a case, and some of them I felt might have been won. Now that's not good for the self-confidence but I think it can be accepted as part of the chances and patterns of a professional life. I would actually regard my inability to take part in debate at the Union, and what you called my shyness, as a failing or a disability, because it really precluded me from ever considering whether I would have liked to have had a political career. I clearly wasn't right for it in that sense. It's quite different being in the House of Lords because everyone is so courteous, you get your opportunities to speak, and there's committee work. But what I call a real political career wasn't open to me temperamentally.

To what extent does luck play a part in success?

It's very important, and not just in the conventional sense that as a barrister you need to get the right cases. There is one key area where luck plays a part. We all choose our careers, whether broadcaster, doctor, or barrister, because of the impression [of that career] we have from the outside and as students. A large slice of luck is needed if it turns out right for you, and if you turn out to be good at it. No amount of hard work can change things if you actually haven't chosen the right slot for yourself. Yet when choosing, you're choosing on insufficient knowledge, you're choosing on instinct, on feel. You're marvellously lucky if it does turn out to be the right choice.

And if that piece of luck does go your way, and you work your way into the right profession – in your case the law – what are the factors that anyone needs to make a success of it? What makes for a really successful legal career?

I believe that you've got to have a passion for fairness and a passion for integrity – that, after all, underlies the law. It's what makes it worth doing. It's better if you have a logical mind, but fortunately you don't need to be the most brilliant intellectual in the world. I've got quite a good intellect but I'm not in any sense brilliant. You do need to be able to analyse and you need to be able to present your case in a very logical and orderly way. I do think you need to have, in many areas of the law, sensitivity to people, sensitivity to witnesses, sensitivity to juries, and also sensitivity to judges. What is the judge thinking? Which of the points you are making are appealing to him? All that should be going through your mind all the time. But of course, advocacy is not just a science, it's got a considerable amount of art to it. It's flair, if you like, that adds to the other qualities. I hope I have already indicated that hard work is important. I used to write out every speech I made. I didn't necessarily present it in that way to the judge, but I'd still write it out in advance. I'd also write out every cross-examination in such depth that if, in answer to some key question, a witness unexpectedly said 'no' instead of 'yes', I'd have a different line of questioning prepared on the other side of the page. I don't think there's any substitute for hard work in that area.

Who are your heroes?

I'll start with one who might be a bit unusual because I think it emphasizes that success is not just in the headlines. I have always followed the Dreyfus case with fascination – the case of the Jewish French officer who was imprisoned wrongly on a charge of treason. There were strong undercurrents of anti-Semitism and he was imprisoned for many years. Yet his family were a patriotic family. His brother devoted all his life to securing freedom for Dreyfus and he persevered in the face of all adversity until he was released. I think that is the most wonderfully admirable quality.

If, as I am, you are passionate about cricket, how can you not regard Don Bradman as a hero? A man, incidentally, of great insecurity, who did not have it easy. He had detractors, even some members of his own team who were unpardonably jealous of him, and he suffered from ill health. Yet he was an Australian icon. In the arts – I've enjoyed the arts in recent years, and I was lucky enough to have a period as a Trustee of the National Gallery – I suppose Cézanne for his influence on the artists of this century. I mean, that is really success, to influence painting across a whole century.

In another area, how can my generation not have Churchill as a hero?

Without Churchill this country might not have fought through the dark days. If I can take a personal hero from the War, it's someone admired not so much because of his considerable achievements but because of his attitudes – Field Marshal Lord Wavell, who wrote that wonderful book, *Other Men's Flowers*. He had the ability of a soldier but the detachment of a statesman, a philosopher and, underlying all, an apparent serenity of spirit. Going back in history, there are so many heroes amongst poets and musicians that it's almost impossible to single one out. Perhaps Mozart and Beethoven – Mozart for what he achieved so young, Beethoven for achieving what he did despite his disability.

Almost all your heroes overcame difficulty at some stage in their lives in order to achieve the success that they had. Is that a hallmark of success?

Success involves striving, and you're very detached. You're in a sense incomplete in terms of humanity if you haven't had to overcome some disadvantage, some disability. I think it may lead to a stronger inner core. I have a sneaking admiration for Oliver Cromwell, not a fashionable historic figure, but a tremendously clear-sighted achiever who, 300 years ago, had the wit to realize that the situation where Parliament could sweep aside every single law if it wanted to, and where there was no entrenched law, was dangerous. That was prescient 300 years ago. I'm not sure I'd make him a hero, but I've got a great admiration for him.

What are the greatest enemies of success?

Believing your own image. I think when you achieve success, that's precisely the moment at which you can sow the seeds of its downfall. You may cease to work as hard, you may cease to analyse what you do critically. That's a tremendous enemy of success. Another enemy is over-confidence. So, at the opposite pole, is not being a little afraid to try, a little afraid to climb the mountain that's before you.

What's the greatest pleasure you've had from the fruits of your success?

We've been lucky financially and we're very comfortably off. I don't mean we are in the mega-rich category, but we do enjoy having a nice home, a house in France, the opportunity to have holidays and to buy our books, to go out for meals without having continually to count the pennies. It would be wrong to pretend that having enough money isn't a valuable aspect of life, particularly if you have had an uncertain financial background to start with. But I think overall it's the interest value of what I've been able, and am able, to do, and what I'm able to participate in. I think being part of events that are happening and trying to take your part in them is one of the fundamental, really lucky opportunities. It was Oliver Wendell Holmes, the great American judge, who said, 'I think that, as life is action and passion, it is required of a man that he should share the passion and action of his time at peril of being judged not to have lived.'

If you could gather before you all the young people who admire your success in either the law or banking, what general advice would you give them?

The first advice I would give them would be not to be over-awed by other people's success because there are people in their generation, the rising generation, who will be equally, and perhaps more, successful. I would say, 'The opportunity to succeed will be there for you. Don't think it's unnatural if it comes and you are able to take it.' I would then say, 'Throw yourself wholeheartedly into the profession or the job that you doing. Try very hard to relate to your colleagues wherever you are, because it's not only our absolute abilities that count, it's what other people think of you, how they respect, and also how they like you. Use, if you can, your personality to the full, and don't try to clone other people too much. You're an individual with your own strengths and talents. While you can try to adapt them and develop them, if you try to change them to match someone else's image, they will actually find you out. Be totally open to the continuous learning process, from what people do well and from what they don't do well. Recognize from the outset that you probably won't achieve all the magic of success that you want to achieve. Recognize also that you can always go on improving. When we all come to the end of our career and life, we will not just be assessing where we have got to in material terms – was I head of this or that, was I the great advocate or whatever – but overall, have I done my bit, has my life been worthwhile for myself and others.' Then I would say, 'Now, that sounds pretty banal but I wonder if there is any other absolute test. What do you all think? I would love to hear your views.'

When your time comes to leave this Earth what would you like people to say about you?

The honest answer is I don't know. It's rather like people's last words. William Pitt the Younger is said to have remarked on his death bed, 'My country, how I leave my country.' But he is also supposed to have said, 'How I could do with one of Mrs Bellamy's pork pies.' I think it's very difficult to put together a ritual and rubric for it. I hope there would be a significant number of people, or even a few people, who will be sorry when I go and who, if someone writes an obituary of me, will say, 'Well, that wasn't a bad life.'

LORD ARCHER

'If you know Jeffrey Archer you like him; if you don't, you probably don't' – a close friend's judgment on the multi-millionaire author who has been described as Britain's most colourful public figure. His chutzpah and unshakeable self-belief have carried him through a series of controversies and setbacks, any one of which would have destroyed a less resilient person. He has attracted high-placed allies and resentful critics in almost equal measure. The New York Times called his second novel 'trash'; yet he has now penned no fewer than 12 best-sellers read by millions of avid fans, and in 1995 signed a three-year book deal said to be worth $20 million. Along the way – the setbacks, which he believes are essential for 'anyone who is going anywhere'.

His writing career was an accident that spilled out of disaster. A failed investment nearly bankrupted him and forced his resignation as one of the country's youngest MPs. In desperation, he turned story-teller (a word he prefers to 'author') to repay his debts. When a newspaper involved him in a sex scandal, he launched a celebrated libel action, winning £500,000 in damages. Later, an inquiry cleared him of much-publicised allegations of insider share dealing.

His early life ricocheted through minor public school, the army, the police, bartending and teaching physical education before he arrived at Oxford to claim a blue in athletics and run for his country. His recollection of some of the detail of his early life was recently questioned in an unauthorised biography. His wife Mary – an eminent scientist – once admitted that he has 'a talent for inaccurate précis'. But he has always been a great persuader too – from the days when he roped the Beatles into an Oxfam charity concert to his tireless fundraising for the Conservative Party and his campaign to help the Kurds. On one occasion he even bounced the great film director Otto Preminger into giving him a screen test. He believes there is nothing he cannot do. He feeds on ideas and enthusiasm. The disaster that led to his successful career also denied him his great ambition – to work his way up the Parliamentary ladder to 10 Downing Street itself. His determined campaign to become the first Mayor of London has met much opposition within his own party. He quotes Proust: 'We always end up doing the thing we are second best at', and says, 'I will go to my grave unfulfilled.'

Lord Archer, what is your definition of success?

It must differ from human being to human being. I don't think there is such a thing as success, in the sense that every successful person wants to achieve more. I remember once sitting next to David Niven in an aeroplane and thinking I was next to one of the most successful men in the world, and we had never met. We had each other's company for no other reason than that we had been put next to each other, and I had a very interesting conversation with him. I talked to him about his books obviously, which had been a massive success, and his films, some of which have become classics, and he said, 'I always look back on my life and think about the parts Clark Gable got, the parts that Gregory Peck got and other actors, and I always remember the parts that I had wanted.' He didn't even remember the Oscar, he said, even the number one on the *New York Times* bestsellers list.

I took that thought away and I think it applies to most successful human beings. I am the natural captain of the England cricket team and have never reached beyond the Grantchester third eleven. I am a natural Olympic gold medallist and just squeezed into the British team. I ought to be Prime Minister, and I am not. So I think that most people think they really haven't made it. The secret of success is never believing you are successful.

And that pushes you to greater and greater efforts?

All the time, every day of your life, you rise and say, 'What a pathetic little object you are, what have you done? You have done absolutely nothing – get up and do some more.' I suspect that for me this is driven, in the sense that mine wasn't a harmful upbringing to have – number one, a tough start, number two, a desire to run for your country, number three, 15 years of working with Margaret Thatcher. In those three, you have a combination which shows you a) that success is fairly ephemeral, and b) that there are a lot of people doing a lot better than you are.

You are not exactly a 'pathetic little creature'. The impression that you give to the outside world is one of immense confidence, riding through everything that life can throw your way.

Confidence is very important. I am bound to say that when I collapsed financially in 1964 and lost everything – was down nearly half a million pounds, which in today's terms is several million – I did lose all my confidence. I wondered if I was capable of getting a job.

How did you pull yourself back from that?

I was greatly helped by Sir Noel Hall, the Principal of Brasenose College, who was then an old man and had retired. He called for me and I travelled down to his home near Henley. He had been a terribly kind man to me when I was at university and remained a friend. I held him in great affection and awe. He sat me down and said that people who are going anywhere have setbacks, it's how they handle the setbacks that decides where they go. Be thankful that you are only 34. And no sooner had he said that I went back, and I remember receiving a letter from someone in the north of England who had also invested in the company that I had invested in:

> Dear Mr Archer.
> Stop feeling sorry for yourself. You may well have had to leave the House of Commons, you may well be in debt, indeed a far larger sum than I am, but I have lost everything, £50,000, not the sum that you have lost, but there is a subtle difference. I am 67 and I can't start again.

And I think that letter of all letters made me say, 'I can do it.' A second occasion, which got me very annoyed, was when I had a tiny little office at the top of Whitehall, where I worked with the company that had collapsed. I went to the pub next door and I heard a conversation between two people on the far side of the room and one said, 'I hear that young Member of Parliament is going to have to resign,' 'Yes,' he said, 'he overstretched himself and made a bit of a fool of himself and lost all his money,' and the first one said, 'Oh, we won't hear from him again,' and I remember leaving my half-finished meal, walking out and saying out loud in Whitehall, 'You will, you bastard.' I think the combination of that conversation and the letter made me very angry. If anything, it was anger that made me come back.

Is a high degree of sacrifice necessary on your route to success?

One hundred per cent. If you are not willing to do 19 hours a day, if you are not willing to fight every inch of the way, you can forget it. That's what I always say to young people who come to see me who want success or want to create success. I admire them so much, I put money into their tiny companies, I watch how they work – they get up at six, they work till midnight, they ring me once a month with the latest position, they drive, drive, drive the way I did at that age. Nothing is going to stop them, they just never give in. You above all need energy and, yes, sacrifice.

Does your wife play an important part on the path to success?

Well, if you are intelligent enough to admit that as 50 per cent of the nation are women, then it is more than likely that half or more of those women are more intelligent than the men. Why should the men be more intelligent than the women? You only have to look at the Cabinet and their wives to work that one out. Well, I have been married to a very remarkable woman for 31 years and it has been a great privilege. I looked upon myself on leaving Oxford as a pretty uneducated man. I now look upon myself as a well-educated man, but then, I have had a tutor for 30 years that most students have not. I would like to believe that Mary's ability as a speaker, her almost entrepreneurial attitude now to the academic world, may well have come from being with me for 30 years along with her ability to use contacts to get things done. So I think in that way, if one side isn't giving to the other all the time, it must break down. I have to say to you that the joke of 'There's a successful woman behind every successful man' is balls. Equally, behind every successful woman there's a successful man, and the two working together is a formidable combination.

It is said that some people on the path to success are faced with a choice of work and family. Do you think that choice does exist and what would your advice be on making the right decision there?

If you are driven you have no choice, if you are motivated in that way and driven in that way you will choose work. I thank God I am married to someone who works 19 hours a day. I would hate to have someone who was sitting at home at six o'clock with the slippers, waiting for me to come home to supper. I said to Mary last year that I intended to take her somewhere this summer she hadn't been for a very long time, and she said, 'Where?' and I said, 'The kitchen.' That, in fact, is a good thing, not a bad thing, because if she was sitting in that kitchen with a meal cooked waiting for me, we would have been divorced within three or four years. It's the fact that she is, in her own way, as driven as I am that makes us compatible, and the answer to your question is both of us, I believe, would have chosen work, and because we both had each other and the work, it's worked wonderfully for us.

To what extent is success a product of your family background, your upbringing, your early days and what happened in those early days?

Mary has always said, and I have a tendency to agree with her, that there is a disadvantage in being brought up in an easy, comfortable home. You only have to look at our Olympic results to see that Britain has become middle-class. I came from a home which was tough, in Weston-super-Mare. It wasn't disastrous, but it was tough. My mother had to go out to work in order to pay the bills when I was sent away to a small school in

Somerset on a scholarship. I think when I was a child you were aware of the lower classes, the lower-middle classes, the middle classes, the upper-middle, and that's all balls nowadays. I mean there's the Royal Family and whoever, and there are those who are genuinely in trouble, then frankly the other 90 per cent are in the middle somewhere, and the old system has gone – and a very good thing it has gone – but Mary has always said it is somehow an advantage to start being hungry, and I agree with her.

Was there any one point in your very early life where you suddenly clicked into ambitious mode?

I always wanted to run for my country – you would have to call that ambitious.

So you had your ambition and later you tried a series of jobs – Sandhurst, Metropolitan Police, bar-tending, schoolmaster, and they worked for a while but then they stopped working. Did you not at any point feel, 'Hang on, I am having trouble finding my métier.'

Oh, yes, some of those jobs only lasted for a couple of weeks.

How did you pick yourself up from that?

I suppose I was so young, I didn't care. I didn't know where I was going or what I was doing. I think I discovered work and life at the age of 26, when I finished at Oxford and came down and looked for a real job, and I don't think that's a bad thing. Looking back on it, if you have a thoroughly orthodox life – you go to school, end at 18, go to university, end at 21, go to the Foreign Office or a bank – I think you are unlikely to find the one thing in your life you ought to do. At the age of 34, it was almost a good thing that I left Parliament with no money, because otherwise, I would never have written a word. I might have become Minister of Transport and written a rather dull memoir, whereas in fact, having been thrown out, I had to get a job. I wonder how many people out there have a second talent that they never discover. Proust said we always end up doing the thing we are second-best at.

So every setback is a potential trigger?

You've got to turn it into a triumph, you should never look backwards. I say it to every child I meet, 'You will make mistakes. Spend the morning chastising yourself and crying, stop at lunch and never look back again.' This comes from the great Bernie Delfont. He stood by me tremendously when my finances collapsed. I was shocked by those who ran away from me and surprised by those who stood by me. Many of those who stood by me, as my doctor pointed out at the time, were those who had been through the same problem or who understood that it was a problem they might face in their life. Someone said to Bernie, 'I hear Jeffrey's collapsed,' and he said, 'Yeah, he had a very bad morning' – such a memorable statement. I know what that sentence means, and I know what it meant to Bernie. Yes, I did have a very bad morning. I actually had a bad seven years, but for Bernie that was a morning.

When you came as close to bankruptcy as you did, and you had to repay all this money, you had to find a way of doing it. Now what made you choose writing, because you could have gone down so many different routes?

I did think about other routes. James Hanson offered me a job as his personal assistant, and I explained that I thought I was going to go bankrupt and that would harm him. He was chairman of Yorkshire Television and I was the Member for Lincoln and I used to fight him every day that I could about the Lincoln Beaumont aerial and the disgrace of Yorkshire Television covering Lincolnshire, and he always won. I never won once, and I assumed he hadn't a very great deal of respect for me as a result, but I was wrong, he immediately offered me a job and he has remained a close friend.

And so I was desperately looking round for things. I did a job on the midnight show on LBC, I did midnight to 4 o'clock at £10 an hour or whatever it was. I was taking anything I could get, and then I suggested to Mary that if I wrote the story of four young men who between them had lost a fortune, one of them an American Rhodes Scholar, etc. etc., and she said, 'Well, you have never written before, you have never written a word before,' and I went away, I went in fact to Sir Noel Hall. He put me up for a month, six weeks, and I wrote the first draft, but I was still looking for what Mary called a real job. When I brought it back and she read it, she thought it was not her style.

So the writing wasn't the rescue package, as it were. The writing was simply something that was hovering in the background while you were looking for a real alternative?

It was an exorcism. I was terrified of not working. I was terrified of becoming a sorry-for-yourself, out-of-work person.

And the theme of the book was the exorcism?

Yes, very much. I remember vividly now, 22 years later, how many pencils I broke, physically broke, when I wrote the words. How could I have been so stupid, I was a young Member of Parliament, promising career, everything going for me, and I gave it away. I remember breaking pencils in half, I was so angry with myself – not with anyone else. I don't blame the people who stole money from me. They were evil people and that's that. I blame myself, it was me who was stupid, and the anger was coming out. I was determined not to write a book saying, 'I've been robbed, it's been unfair, the world's not fair to me!' I didn't want to write that, I wanted to write an amusing book about these idiots who had lost their money, but the fun was getting it back. Maybe, when I had finished the story, the exorcism of it was that I said I will get the money back, but the shock was it was the book that got it back!

And you say, that was a shock. How did you set about getting it published?

I had a very bad start. I mean, a very good start in the sense that I found a wonderful agent, Deborah Owen, terrific lady. David, her husband, told her very clearly what I had been through – and he knew what I had been through – and she was terrific and she read it and believed in it, but 18 publishers turned it down and she got very depressed because the day she read it she said it was a bestseller. Finally, Jonathan Cape published it and gave me an advance of £3,000. So again, neither Mary nor I thought … you know, this is hardly the road to riches. One of the great myths I read of now is that I was an instant overnight success – it's absolute balls. *Not a Penny More, Not a Penny Less* sold 3,000 in hardback and 25,000 in softback and then *Shall We Tell The President?* went into the bottom of the bestseller lists in New York and to number four in Britain, and this was four years down the line. I was still paying off debts, I was still £200–300,000 in debt and it was *Kane and Abel*, six years down the line, that paid for it overnight, because it was sold for £3,400,000 – so suddenly I went from being still in deep debt, running a Mini, unable to pay the bills and living off my wife, to being a millionaire in one day.

During those six years, as well as writing, were you still constantly looking for other things to do?

Oh, yes, I was doing other jobs. I was still trying to do deals and trying to put things together. They weren't succeeding very well. The writing was going better and better so I began to concentrate more on that. But it's hell being in debt. I actually believe that 90 per cent of people's problems are financial. I think if all your financial problems are removed, there aren't a lot of problems in life. If you have a bad relationship with your family or your wife then there's not much you can do about that and you may as well divorce and pack up, but a lot of tension between man and wife, a lot of tension in a human being, is that they can't pay next month's mortgage, that they can't pay the school fees or whatever it is, or they have to cancel the holiday or not buy something.

Why is it that you want to do so many different things? Why not say, 'I am a successful author, I am a politician with incredible political contacts, I am happy to sit on that'? Do you want to run the world?

Yeah, sure, love to. Not going to get that chance, but I'd love to. But many of the other people you have interviewed already will be standing by the side of me, if not in front of me, trying to stop me because they want to as well.

But why do you want to move into different areas?

I am never satisfied. If I ever achieve anything, I always want to look for something else to do and I would be bound to admit that I would give it all up to be a bar-room piano player and singer. What I would like to be doing is what Bobby Schultz is doing at the Carlisle, that's what I would like to be doing. My minor problem is that I can't sing and I can't play the piano – which I consider a minor problem, I'd get over that somehow.

So are you saying that everything you've done is a kind of compensation for not being able to do what you really want?

That's true with everyone. I think John Major would like to captain the Surrey and England cricket teams. I think if you say to most people, 'If you could give it all up to do something else, what would it be?' I bet it would be something totally different. If the world looks at you on the television, it would say he is at the top of his profession, yet most people who reach the top of their profession want to do something else. I am not unique in that way.

When you sit down to write, what's your technique?

You can't sit down and say, 'I am going to become a successful writer.' I am a storyteller by the way, not a writer. In my particular case I like telling a yarn. I have stories every day of my life, all the time. I was in the South of France quite recently on holiday with friends, and when the mother said, 'I must leave now to tell my children a story,' the father said, 'Well, we have got Jeffrey with us, send him in,' and that was such a marvellous, fun challenge. All the people round the table slipped into the children's room, the three children and the six of them stood at the back and I went into the room and the mother said, 'Tell them a story.' And I said, 'I have just discovered that in this house is the smallest monster in the world, now nobody under the age of eight can see him, this is the problem. We have all been looking, but we have just discovered you have got to be under eight to find him. Now this monster...' and I had them for 15 minutes and I was making it up. I am told those children are still looking for the little bastard all over the place!

But what advice would you give to people who want to become as successful a writer as you have been?

Well, a lot of people come to see me and a lot of people write to me, and they fall into so many categories. At the moment I've got one who looks as if she might be the type who wins the Booker prize, then I've got another I think might be able to tell a story. It's tougher now. I think to be fair it's even tougher now than when I joined the book world and they told me it was pretty tough then. A hundred people are sending in books every single week and of the 100, one gets published. Of the 100 that get published, one gets on the list – it's a heck of a battle. And very few people make a living writing, very few people. I mean if you get to the very top you make millions, but we are talking about ten or fifteen people, we are not talking about hundreds, we are talking about hundreds who make a living, we're talking about thousands who survive, but we are talking about millions who write and don't make a living at all, they have to supplement it with another job.

What do you say to all those people out there who think, 'I've got this great novel in me'?

I'm very tough on them. I say, 'You have to go away for at least six weeks to write the first draft.' I always give the example of the distinguished surgeon who wrote to me and said, 'I have written a novel, will you read it?' and I generally say, 'I don't read novels because I get 20 or 30 requests a week,' but this particular surgeon was someone I admired very greatly and so I agreed to read it, saw him and said, 'Did you write this novel between operations?' and he said, 'Yes, how did you know that?' and I said, 'Because there is a good chapter and a bad chapter and a medium chapter and a quite good chapter, a quite bad chapter and an awful chapter and a good chapter and you have obviously written it in a bitty way – you must go away for a long period and write the first draft. You'd find it pretty damned insulting if I announced I was going to do operations between chapters,' and he nodded, agreed and went away, rewrote it and it was published.

What do you regard as your biggest setbacks, the biggest failures in life?

Education. In many ways that may be a good thing, by the way – I look upon it as a very bad thing that I didn't work at school. I wanted to run for my country, I wanted to be a sportsman, I wanted to do other things, and I didn't have masters who kept me in order and made me do it. It was only when I was 26 that I realized after the running how incredibly disciplined I could be and how incredibly hard I could work. In some ways, though, if that had happened at school, maybe I would have gone down a very formal road and become a solicitor and would not have had the very exciting life I have led, so there are always two sides to every coin. I have had setbacks. I've had to leave the House of Commons, but that turned out to be an advantage – setbacks aren't always setbacks.

Do you actually instantly click into gear with a plan for dealing with setbacks?

Mary once said, 'Jeffrey thrives on a crisis. He doesn't like life just going along normally.' And my closest friend, Adrian Metcalfe, whom I adore – we shared rooms at Oxford and he was the greatest runner of my age – once said, 'Jeffrey's problem is he needs a war.' If Britain was at war I would be at my best because I would be given a real job, I would be told to beat whoever it was. I don't know what job it would be but I would be given a real job. I like crises, I like wars. But I don't actually have a technique for dealing with setbacks.

Who are the people, big or small, past or present, whose success you really admire? Who are your heroes?

Well, at an obvious level, Nelson Mandela, Mother Teresa and Margaret Thatcher.

Why?

The thing I most admire about Mandela is the lack of vindictiveness. I just think it's staggering that you can be put in jail for that amount of years and not come out saying, 'Kill every white man in sight, I want them out of my country, kill them by tomorrow night,' which the black population of South Africa would have done if that was the order he had given. What he believed, as I understand from reading his memoirs, was that the only way that you could make that situation work was to make white work with black. So I admire him greatly.

I worked with Margaret Thatcher for 15 years. It was a staggering experience. I remember saying to someone the other day that I adore her and they looked at me with disgust and said, 'You couldn't adore that woman,' and I thought, 'Yes, well you just don't understand.'

What was special about working with Margaret Thatcher?

She is wicked, incredibly, as Dame Edna would say, in a teasing way. For example, I took her to Japan soon after she'd stopped being Prime Minister and I know how she likes these runs, so I went there a week ahead and when she arrived, the plane landed, there was a red carpet, the Foreign Secretary, the Ambassador were there to meet her, there were three cars, outriders, we got up to the hotel. Everything was going perfectly, and she hates things to go perfectly, she loves to have something go wrong so that she can grumble. She adores it. When she got to the doors they were open, when we walked across the hotel the lift was waiting for her with two people standing there, when she got out of the lift there was a British flag and a Japanese flag crossed, flowers all down the corridor, her room had been stripped and Impressionist paintings had been put in. When she walked in, I had said to the girl who was to be in charge of her there, a 35-year-old, very intelligent American, 'You must have a whisky and soda ready for her, she likes Glenlivet and this amount of soda, and that's it really. Don't worry about anything else because that's what she likes.' Then Margaret stormed in, looked round, saw the Impressionists, saw the people standing to attention, saw everything had gone perfectly, sat down and I said, 'Can we get anything for you, Margaret?' 'Yes,' she said, 'I'd like a gin and tonic' and she knew that I had had to run at 100 miles an hour to get that drink. She will never let you have an inch.

I love the challenge of being with her because the only time I have ever defeated her was when she was due to speak to the University of Tokyo and she had sat up all night preparing her own speech – she is the hardest worker I have ever dealt with in my life, along with my wife – and she finished the speech and I read it and I thought it was fantastic. I made a few comments that she did or did not take and then we went to the function where we were to dine with the dons. We were sitting in a corner just checking one or two small things, when the Principal came out and said, 'Lady Thatcher, you would do me a great honour if at the end of the lunch you made a small speech to the dons. We would all, of course, be present to hear you speak to the students, but if you could say a few words,' and then he went away. She went over the top! She was livid because she had got the speech for the kids, yet she hadn't got a speech for them ... and she blamed me, she said, 'You didn't tell me this was going to happen.' Well, frankly, I didn't know it was going to happen, it was obvious that this guy decided that as she was there it would be wonderful if she said a few words. She went through the roof and I waited for her to calm down completely, looked her in the face and said, 'I apologize, Margaret, it is totally my fault, I am to blame, and as that is the case, I will make the speech myself.' She said, 'You most certainly will not,' and she delivered a brilliant speech, ad-lib, about universities. I think I learned discipline and incredibly hard work from her. I remember Mary saying one night when we were on tour with her, 'An incredibly serious woman, that's exactly what Margaret Thatcher is, she is an incredibly serious woman.' I learned a tremendous amount from her, it has been a very great privilege to work for her.

In a sense, has it been a kind of surrogate success for you in the political field to have worked so closely with Prime Ministers? You were forced to give up your political career, but you still have this great hunger for politics?

Yes and no. I have worked very closely with Margaret Thatcher and John Major, as everyone knows, and it helps to be on the centre of the stage and to be working flat out. It has been a marvellous aphrodisiac to win, don't let's kid ourselves, winning four elections in a row, it was fun and worthwhile. But no, it isn't a substitute for the real thing, don't kid yourself. The real thing is having the power and changing things, making things happen, making things work.

Do you make your own luck?

Yes, of course you do. You get up and find it. I have got this kid at the moment I have put some money into, he's a young boy he's 27, 28, he was signing up something by Steven Spielberg last week, something from Disney the week before, he just never stops, he was in the *Daily Mail* last week, he's banging on the door, banging it down. He never opens the door, he kicks it open, and good luck to him. He'll get to the very top and build a massive great company. It's an amazing achievement, I really admire him.

Should we know his name?

Yes, I think that's all right. His name is Nadeem Zahawi, he sits on the council at Wandsworth. This kid works 19 hours a day, he never stops, and he will ring me in the middle of the night and say, 'Have you ever met Lord Hanson,' and I say, 'Why?' 'I need to meet him, I need to meet him tomorrow.' 'Well, tomorrow may be tough.' 'Well, I can do it in the afternoon.' And it's marvellous, I love that enthusiasm. When he grows older he'll realize that James Hanson is actually quite busy. I hope he doesn't, he musn't discover that too early, he must believe that everything is possible.

Does that 'can do' philosophy have to be tempered by what is possible in practical terms, or must you ignore that and break down doors?

You mustn't believe anything's impossible, particularly with children. When children come to me and say, 'I want to do x,y or z,' I put my arms round them and I say, 'And you will, you will achieve, you'll be there. '

Does every successful person need someone behind them encouraging them like that, and do you also need contacts?

Yes.

So how did you then set about building up contacts?

Well, you work hard and you achieve things and people admire you for what you achieve. I'll give you a classic example of that if I may. During my first book, maybe my first or second I can't remember, I was asked to do *Newcastle at Midnight,* so I travelled all the way to Newcastle to do *Newcastle at Midnight* with Barbara Castle who was living up there, and she was the top spot and I had some minor little spot and I got about three minutes. And two years later I was on *This is Your Life* with Eamonn Andrews, which sent *Kane and Abel* through the roof in this country. It went from nothing to number one overnight. In those days 21 million people watched *This is Your Life.* I learned afterwards that the producer of *Newcastle at Midnight* had two years later become the producer of *This is Your Life* and had said to Eamonn Andrews, who had never heard of me, 'If you get this kid on for 30 minutes, he'll give you a hell of a show,' and Eamonn believed his producer. Why did the producer say that? Because I had done two or three minutes on *Newcastle at Midnight* so I had made the contact, to answer your question, without even realizing it and that contact had made his suggestion to this giant, Eamonn Andrews. They used to have very famous people on the show and, as you know, one who was coming up – and they chose me as the one who was coming up. Eamonn, who had never met me, took the risk.

So in building contacts, never dismiss any opportunity however small it might appear?

I would say to young people, if they want you to do Birmingham Radio, if they want you to do LBC, whatever it is, do it, get the experience, go on Sky at 3 o'clock in the morning, watch where the camera is, see what's going on, learn – and by the way be warned, that at every level in life, that person behind the camera, that person who is producing, that person who is your constituency chairman, one day, maybe in two or three years' time, will be a lot higher up the ladder and they will remember if you worked hard for them, they will admire the fact that you worked hard for them. So build those contacts.

But I have another golden rule as well. If I don't like someone or I think they're dishonest, I never have anything to do with them again. I have now reached the stage in my life where I am very aware, I know what I want to do, and I want to do it with people I like.

I also like everybody to be in debt to me. I would like to have done more charity work, more this, more that, so everybody is in debt to me. I have terrible trouble at the moment with Bill Bradley, because I feel in debt to him and there are also a couple of Americans I am feeling in debt to.

Why do you not like being in debt to other people?

I feel then I owe them something. I would much rather the balance was on my side. I would much rather do things like charity shows for them so that if I need to call on them one day, I can genuinely expect them to come to my rescue or come to my help.

I have two or three people I try not to speak to, they only ring when they want something, 'Will you speak here, Jeffrey? Will you give us a set of your books? Will you give money, will you give time?' If they ring on the phone and I pick up the phone I know they are going to ask me for something. I hate them. I like people who ring up and say, 'Free for lunch?' or 'Shall we go to the theatre?' and that's great, that's lovely, I love that and then, when they say would I do a charity show, of course I will, we are friends. But the people who only want something are the ones I despise most.

What have you found to be the greatest enemies of success?

The envy of lesser people who feel they ought to be doing what you are doing, that's a simple one. It must be worse in your profession than mine, because in mine there are enough people who are kind enough to admit that it ain't as easy as it looks to write a book, but my own view is that everybody thinks they can do what you do and you suffer worse. David Frost is a classic example. I've met 10,000 people who think they're David Frost, until they actually get up there and try to do it themselves, and I think David, because he is such a nice person, such a genuinely nice person, has very few enemies. But there are still 10,000 people who think they're better than David Frost, and I have met 9,999 of them and they've told me. But they ain't. He's the tops because he is the best.

So you will always face that. If you dare to succeed you will always have people who say or think they are better than you, and you can't do anything about that. Margaret Thatcher one year won the BBC award for the most popular person in Great Britain, you know, that Sunday thing that they have in the New Year. The same year she won the award for the most unpopular person in Great Britain. She won both the same year.

Have you ever wondered why success arouses such conflicting emotions in different people, from admiration through to the envy you were talking about?

You mustn't give that sort of thing a lot of thought or you will just stop trying to achieve anything.

But it is curious, isn't it, that some people will look at a successful person and say, 'Wow, I really want to be like that person,' the American attitude, and yet others will say, 'I can't stand that person, because he's successful'?

I used to think this was a British disease, but I was in Germany recently and I met the equivalent of David Frost, who interviewed me, and he said he had to travel home in a small Volkswagen. I said why and he said, 'Because they hate success in this country.Of course I can afford a Rolls Royce or a big Mercedes, I can fly out anywhere I like, but I travel home in a small Volkswagen and I dress in scruffy clothes when I leave the office.' So I realized it wasn't just Britain. It's what they call in Australia 'the tall poppy syndrome' and in France it exists in a big way as well. So it isn't just Britain – and the opposite is, of course, the United States, where there is a tremendous admiration for achievement and success.

But where envy exists, is it pulling people down, is it pulling down the ambitions of individuals and of countries to be as successful as they might be?

Oh, very much so, and it greatly harms a country and individuals. I see what John Major has been through as Prime Minister and wonder why anyone wants the job. I still want to be Prime Minister, but I still wonder. I wonder more when I see the way that poor man has been treated. He has been treated disgracefully and a lot of it, most of it, has been envy, and a lot of it has been snobbery, of a degree that I thought went out 30 or 40 years ago.

But would some of it have been due to genuine disagreements over policies?

Well, if you get an honourable man or woman, honourably disagreeing about policies, they will not say, 'Oh well, he left school at 16.' I mean, what a pathetic comment. It's said of half of the greatest people in the world, what a pathetic comment in a modern new Britain. It's even more pathetic in a modern new Britain. What he has experienced over the past few years has shocked me and I know, through knowing Norma very well, that she just finds it puzzling beyond belief that so-called decent, civilized human beings can act in that way. I think it has harmed the position of Prime Minister and I think it has harmed public life, because when I travel around the country now I find our very best young people want to go into journalism, they want to go into the law, they want to go into big business, they don't want to go into politics. Well, Great Britain Limited, frankly, in my opinion, is bigger than anything else, and the best people shouldn't be going into the BBC and ICI, they should be going into politics.

So success in politics requires you to put up with quite a degree of abuse and misrepresentation as well as criticism?

Yes, all of those things, and in some cases just downright ill-manners, which you can't do anything about.

But you've got to be tough enough to ride it?

Yes, and if you get through that and you get through to the other side it can be the best profession in the world. It has no rivals. I mean, any amount of people who aren't in politics say to me that they can see it is the ultimate in achieving, really achieving, something – and of course it is.

Are there any obligations that come with success?

I try very hard with the next generation, to listen to them carefully and to talk to them. A young lady came to see me yesterday who's just qualified as a lawyer in the United States, who said would I be kind enough to give her 15 minutes? We had an hour together, it has certainly been the most exciting hour over the last few months. She's obviously going to go a long way and she's very, very bright, having had a successful career both in the United States and at Cambridge University. She's now taken a junior job in a partnership in Washington. And I am as stimulated by that as I hope she was. I love to talk to someone like that, young, probing me, kicking me but being knocked on the nose herself and still saying, 'You're wrong, you're wrong, I can do that' – great, I love it.

Has success changed you?

I think I'm more relaxed. I think I'm more content in the sense that I don't want anything else, in the financial sense. I have a lovely home, a wife, two children, can travel anywhere I want to, can do anything I want to. So in that sense I'm very relaxed and very easy really. I am not fulfilled and I suspect I will go to my grave unfulfilled, but I don't think that would be any different for anyone else you will have interviewed.

Your books sell in phenomenal numbers, yet you have literary critics who turn round and say, 'Well, not the greatest stuff ever written.' Do you secretly sit back and say, 'Well, maybe I would like to win the Booker Prize'?

I can't win the Booker Prize. I'm not capable of that, I am not a good enough writer. But *The Scotsman* said of *First Among Equals* that it was the finest political novel since Trollope. I am not quoting silly papers, I've got thousands of those. The *New York Times* said the short stories were better than anything Somerset Maugham had ever written – well, thank you very much, I will go to my grave with that.

So what do you say to your critics?

I don't pretend to be a literary genius, but with many of the literary geniuses who win the Booker Prize I never get beyond page 16, and I happen to believe – and I may be wrong – that neither do most people. I think most books on the Booker shortlists are not read by anybody – well perhaps three or four hundred people. Each of my books is read by 10 or 15 million people and I am very proud of that and I refuse to apologize for it. I would rather be read by 15 million people than three or four hundred. It's damned hard work making you turn those pages quickly and making it smooth and making you want to get to the end, and anyone who thinks it isn't is an idiot. Those people who criticize should have a go themselves sometime if it's so easy.

If you could gather together all the young people in the world who either want to be great writers or who want to be great politicians, taking them one at a time, what advice would you give them?

Well, what I do with schools and universities is always answer every question very candidly, but if I was literally giving advice to young people on success or achieving whatever it is they want to achieve, I am afraid I would repeat many of the clichéd things. I would say, 'It's going to be damned hard work and if you're not willing to sacrifice almost everything for it, you will not get there. If you are lucky enough to have originality, and by that I mean talent, you have a better chance if you can combine that originality with the hard work. But never allow anybody to get you down, and never look back. If you make a mistake and fail, criticize yourself, but never look back, and if others are jealous of your success, if others try to bring you down, put them on one side and go forward, because they'll stay behind you, never let them get you down, it's little people who try to get you down.'

That's advice in general terms. Specifically, if someone wants to be a writer?

There are no formulae and there are no rules. Some people write with a pen, some people type, some people use a machine. Don't be frightened of what you want to do, but you have to be utterly dedicated. Do not be a part-time writer, you will not get to the top doing it part-time. You have to have an absolutely clear vision of where you're going and what you wish to achieve. Don't imagine you can write a bestseller. Always remember that Jane Austen lived in a small village and wrote about the people in that small village. What did she have? She was a damn good writer and she was a brilliant storyteller, and that's what got her to the top. It is not surprising, or it shouldn't be, that she is now dominating the world, both in films and in writing – why? Because she wrote about what she knew about, and what she knew about was young women having to find a husband. What an out-of-date subject as we approach the millennium – but three of the four best mini-series or films I have seen in the last ten years have been written by Jane Austen. In the end, do your thing and hope the masses want it, don't do what you think the masses want because it won't work.

And the advice you would give to would-be politicians?

Be absolutely sure you want to do it before you start, because it is crippling and killing in some ways. When people ask me, 'Why do you bother, Jeffrey?' I always say, 'If you ask you can't understand.' So when I see a young person and that's their ambition – and I see people like that all the time – I tell them that at the end of their life they must be able to stand up and say, 'This is what I achieved, not this is what I am.' What you are is irrelevant, but if you can stand up and say, 'I took that Bill through the House of Commons, I changed attitudes on that particular thing, I made people think about that' – that's worth doing. Saying, 'I am Secretary of State for Plumbing and Diabetics' is not what we're here for and if you are, then you're in the wrong game. You must be in it to change the world. When people say, 'God, you'll learn better when you grow older, young man, you can't change the world,' they are called cynics; have nothing to do with them. I am a naïve enthusiast, at 56 I remain a naïve enthusiast, at 90 I will be a naïve enthusiast, and you can stuff all the cynics down the drain because I want nothing to do with them.

When your time comes to leave this planet, what would you like people to say about you?

Generous, kind, loyal, and if you looked at his friends, you would have seen what sort of man he was.

MICHAEL ATHERTON

Captain of the England cricket team is the job players want most and least! Most – because in victory you are carried high on the shoulders of the nation; least – because in defeat (of which there has been plenty in recent years) you are the butt of the frustrations of every armchair expert in the country. Mike Atherton, who became England's 71st captain at the relatively tender age of 25, lasted more than five years on the rollercoaster, in the process notching up a record 52 Tests at the England helm. Who could forget his legendary 645 minutes at the crease in South Africa at the end of 1995 when he spectacularly pulled a draw out of the jaws of defeat? Yet 18 months earlier, his reputation – and possibly his career – had been on the line when the cameras at Lord's caught him rubbing dirt from his pocket into the ball to dry it. After early denials, he confessed all to the Chairman of Selectors, and was fined £2,000. The experience, he said, 'opened up my eyes, I can tell you', and he believes that however much you prepare for being in the public eye, it is still a shock.

Sport was in the family – his father, a teacher, once played for Manchester United. Mike 'did his homework, and played cricket in the backyard'. He admits that he was 'a bit solitary' – didn't have many friends. At Manchester Grammar he broke all batting records; then went up to Cambridge to read history. It was once said that he 'played like a prince and looked like a grocer's boy'. But his untidy, unshaven look has always underlined a steely tenacity – hence the nickname 'Iron Mike'. And he's tough on himself too, taking time out each night to analyse ruthlessly every aspect of his performance. Known as a man of few words, here he opens up to discuss the many facets of that elusive beast – cricketing success. He says it's a very individual game within a team framework, and it works providing you can get the mavericks to play within the team. Qualities needed are talent, a good technique and good temperament, while what finally gives you the edge is preparation, fitness and psychology. He explains why he always carries around a videotape of his best innings; admits he's too stubborn at times; finds the media in Australia far more supportive than in Britain; and concludes that the way individuals respond to setbacks, failures or crises tells you more about them than how they are in times of success.

Michael Atherton, what is your definition of success?

In individual terms, and in a sporting way, success is being the best you can be. The closest analogy I can draw is probably with the British team at the last Olympics. I remember Linford Christie saying that whilst you could look at the medal tally and it might appear that it was not a very successful Olympics for the British, 10 or 12 of the athletes passed their personal best times. Although they did not get into the top three, it was a successful time for them as individuals. So success is definitely being the best you can be. In team terms, winning is not the ultimate thing. Often the result is out of your hands. Certainly as a captain, getting the team to prepare in the best possible way and play to its limit is all you can do.

Yet the world at large equates success with winning. What you're saying is that there is a kind of success, an individual success, in which it almost doesn't matter whether you win or lose?

It does matter in the final instance, but it's not everything. In cricket you may find that you're playing for a team, or captain of a team, that is vastly inferior to your opposition, and that victory, no matter how well you play, is beyond you. Yet if you prepare the best way you can and play to your full potential, then you'd have to regard it as a successful effort by your team. But the problem is that victory and failure, winning and losing, are regarded as all-important by the general public at least, and you tend to take that with you.

How big a part does luck play in individual and team success?

Luck plays a vital part. Obviously, you need the right opportunities, whether it be in background, upbringing or whatever, and you work as hard as you can at your talent to get to the top. But you still need that element of luck. Looking at it from a personal point of view, in 1993 I'd got back into the England team – I was kicking my heels around India, not playing very much – and then we came to the home series against Australia. In the first Test Match, I failed and the team lost the match. We went on to Lord's for the Second Test, and I knew that was the key match for me. If I had failed in that match, I'd have been out of the team and it would probably have been the end of my Test career. I had a bit of good fortune, in that Australia's key bowler, Craig McDermott, got injured. Even then I got dropped early on but I managed to get 99 and 80 in the match and that sealed my fate. Two games later I was made captain, and since then I have had a long run in the team. It's a fine line – I was certainly balancing on that line in that Test Match, and a bit of luck turned it my way.

Do you also think that was partly down to responding to pressure?

That as well. I realized that it was the key game for me, and I've always been good under pressure, being able to cut out all the external factors and just concentrate on the next delivery. So it was partly my good response to pressure, but a little bit of luck helped as well.

How big a part does background and upbringing play in shaping whether someone is going to be successful or not?

I think it's vital. I was very fortunate. My parents sent me to a primary school which was strong at sport – Briscoll Lane Primary School in Manchester – and, again, I had a little bit of luck there. I happened to have a teacher in the fourth form who gave me extra tuition, which enabled me to get into Manchester Grammar School.

Did your parents drive you?

No. My initial introduction to cricket was through my dad, who played for a local club side and would always throw balls to me in the back garden and give me a bit of coaching. And I'd always go and watch him playing at weekends. What they did do, obviously, was push me into studying to get to MGS and that was a vital thing, sportswise. But they were never overbearing or overpowering, and that's one thing I'm very grateful about. I did a bit of coaching at MGS one year to a group of under-12s, and there were a couple of very overpowering parents there. You could tell the effect they were having on the kids, who felt under far more pressure than the other lads. So, although I'm not a parent, I think it's vital that parents don't get too pushy, and just let the kids take their own course.

Do you have a particular set of tactics for dealing with the aftermath of failure?

It very much comes down to your character, how you are individually. Some people will be full of determination to bounce back, others might get to the stage where they want to throw in the towel. Age is an important part in that as well. But it's very much down to the individual response. Usually the way an individual responds to a setback, to a failure, to a crisis, tells you more about them than how they are in times of success. If they show the right attitude and want to fight back, you usually know that that's the guy you want around.

How do you recover from setbacks? Do you go and lie down in a darkened room?

Not really. I'm quite determined. I've not had that many setbacks in my professional career. I've had one or two, and generally it's just been a case of getting on with whatever needed to be done. In terms of the back operation that I had, it was three or four months' rehabilitation, and I just got on with it – didn't think twice about it. A pretty practical response, I suppose.

Have you ever come close to giving up?

No, not at all. It's such an enjoyable way to spend your time. As somebody said the other day, travelling around the world at somebody else's expense is a wonderful thing. And obviously I took the game up in the first place because I enjoyed it. Sometimes you can lose that sense of enjoyment, but I've never got to the point of thinking I'll throw in the towel.

Did you think, when the dirt-in-the-pocket business was rumbling around, that your career might be on the line, and you were staring failure in the face?

No. The captaincy might have been on the line – that was certainly in the forefront of my mind – but not my career. If I had had to give up the captaincy at that point, or been sacked, I would still have had my career as a batsman to fall back on.

Do you think that part of the price that you have to pay for being successful is that when things go wrong there is almost a surfeit of attention focused upon you?

There's certainly a lot of attention when incidents like that boil over, and when the team's unsuccessful, there's a hell of a lot of attention. When you take on the captaincy you know that that goes with the job. It's not something I'm ever overly comfortable with, but I'm probably getting more used to it, and realize that it is part of the territory and I just have to get on with it.

After a bad England defeat, do you ever bump into people who, either directly or when they know you're within earshot, say some pretty unkind things?

Frequently. To be honest, most people are very friendly. If you bump into people in the street it's generally a 'Hello, good luck, well done, hard luck' kind of thing, and on they go. Occasionally you get the odd bore who wants to have a go at you, but you've just got to be strong enough to ignore them.

What are the pros and cons of captaining England?

The plus side is the enormous challenge of it all. Obviously England, since the 1950s, have not been regarded as the top dogs, the best side in the world. The enormous challenge of it, when I took over in 1993, was to try to improve the team's performances, to mould a younger and more successful outfit. The challenge is still there. There are so many facets to the job, every day's a challenge. That is the most enjoyable thing. There are obviously the games that you play and the tactical challenges on the field as well, but the general challenge of producing a decent team is the one that excites.

What are the problems in trying to produce a team that will consistently come up with great results for England?

The problems lie within the structure of English cricket. Our top players are overplayed, in that when they come back from international duty they go straight to their counties. They're under contract to their counties and not their country, so there's this divided loyalty between county and country. I think that's a basic problem. The domestic structure is improving, in that it's become far more competitive over the last two or three years with the introduction of four-day cricket. In the long run that will mean a vast improvement in our domestic game.

You've talked in the past about the importance of consensus, but you've got a very strong authoritarian style, almost a stubbornness. How much control do you like to have as a captain? How much control do you need to have?

You need to be in control of the dressing-room. Cricket's changed over the years. Twenty years ago the captain was probably the sole fellow with authority in the dressing-room. Nowadays there are coaches, managers, various people, but in my opinion the captain still has to be the one who controls the dressing-room because he's the one who takes the players out onto the field, who's with them six hours a day, and therefore he's the one who has to get the reaction from them. I wouldn't say that I captain in a particularly authoritarian style. We try to have fairly interactive team meetings. I certainly load the responsibility for fitness onto the physio, for preparation and coaching onto the coach, and make sure that my domain's really the five days during the game. Stubbornness? I probably am a bit too stubborn at times. That's just a trait of mine. I think it's a good thing occasionally, but it can lead to trouble, and learning when to step back is important.

Do most successful people have difficulty in deciding when to exercise a huge degree of control themselves, and when to stand back and let events take their course or let other people's opinions come to the fore? How do you get the balance right?

It's difficult. I felt, when I took over the captaincy, that the team needed more input, more say. When Graham Gooch was captain, the lead came very much from him, the talking came from him, and I felt that the team's views were a little bit subservient. I felt when I became captain I'd like to get more input from the team. It wasn't easy doing that because for two or three years they'd been very subdued. But gradually, and certainly in the last six months or so, I've been getting far more input from the players. As they get older and a bit more experienced, they should feel freer to give their opinions. The problem is that, when you have captained for some time, people get sick of the sound of your voice, and you just end up repeating the same message over and over again. So if you can find a way of making team meetings more interactive, making the team have a bigger part in the decisions and the way you want to go out and play, that's a far better way of doing it.

Is there a fixed shelf-life for every successful cricket captain?

Historically there's not, in that Allan Border was Australia's captain for a ten-year period, but a) he's an exceptional man, and b) he didn't have the commitment of going back and playing for his county in between times. And certainly the press and the media in Australia are far more supportive than you find here. In terms of doing the job in England, Peter May has captained most – 40-odd games – and nobody's really looked like beating that. I'm mid-30s and Graham Gooch did 30-odd games. I think there certainly is a fixed shelf-life in England, because eventually the honeymoon period with the media ends and criticism starts building – unless your side's consistently successful. You can be captain for a long period of time of a consistently winning side, but if your side's struggling, the pressure tells in the end.

What are the qualities for a) a successful cricketer, and b) for a successful captain?

For a cricketer, you certainly need a good technique when you get to the top level. But most of all you need a good temperament on the big occasions where there are 20,000 or 30,000 people, TV cameras, the media and the general pressure that surrounds a five-day Test Match. Then temperament is the key thing. We've seen so many talented players come into the England team and fall by the wayside, while less talented players – I'd probably call myself one – manage to survive in that rarefied atmosphere. You need talent in the first place, you need good technique, and good temperament is the key. To be a good captain, you need to have the respect of your team. You don't need to be liked particularly, but I think you need to have the respect of the team so that they'll follow you where you ask them to go.

You say you don't have to be liked particularly. Is it possible to be a really successful person with everyone you command being fairly resentful or indeed, hating you?

If you're absolutely hated by everybody, then it's difficult. The key thing is respect, but it helps if people think you're a decent bloke as well.

And how do you deal with mavericks within the team?

I enjoy mavericks within the team. Cricket's strange in that, although it's a team game, so many parts of the job are individual. When you're out there facing the ball you're on your own, nobody can help you. When you're starting to bowl the first over of a match, again you're on your own. So it's a very individual game within a team framework, and it works providing you can get the mavericks, as you call them, to play within the team. I prefer those kind of people in my team – people with a bit of spark, a bit of get-up-and-go about them, people who are not ready to accept the party line and who will question it, but at the end of the day, if they'll go with it, then that's the best combination.

How important is your relationship with the Selectors?

It's most important to feel you can trust the Selectors. The English system is that the captain is part of the Selection Committee.

Do you think that's a good idea?

Three years down the line I'm thinking that maybe it's not such a good idea. It's difficult to say, but it certainly affects your relationships with players. When players know that you have a vote on selection, they're perhaps not so straight with you as they might be, and when you've got to tell players they've been left out of the team, it perhaps affects relationships next time they play in the team. Possibly the Australian way might be better, whereby the captain has no involvement. A lot of things are said in selection that are very private things – things said about individuals – so you need to feel that you've got absolute trust in the Selectors that what's said in the Selection Room remains within those walls.

And do you think you have, on the whole, had that or not?

There have been ups and downs. I've worked with a lot of really good Selectors who've had English cricket's interests bang at heart, and one or two that maybe haven't.

So you have to be aware of the politics of cricket, as well as concentrating on the game itself?

I'm afraid so, and it's one of the least palatable aspects of the job for me. There is a lot of politics, not only within my club, Lancashire, but also inside the Test and County Cricket Board. Whilst I try not to get involved too much, you have to be aware of what's going on, both as captain and as part of a Selection Committee that has changed radically in the three years that I've been involved. I've worked with three different Chairmen of Selectors, a number of Selectors and three or four different coaches. You're dragged into it unwillingly.

Any successful team needs to be fit. Do you think there's been enough emphasis on fitness in the past?

We have a massive emphasis on fitness. I think it was started with Graham Gooch and Micky Stewart. Gooch was captain at 36 and after he'd got past 30 he realized the need to be extra-fit himself. He found that helped his game, so he imposed quite a rigorous fitness routine and regime on the team. We've carried that on, although I perhaps have been less upfront about it. It's been less in the forefront of the news, if you like. We have a sports physiologist, a guy called Ian Riddle who's a Rugby League man. Each player is given an individual fitness programme. So we do have a very strong emphasis on physical fitness, and amongst teams of a similar ability – South Africa, England, India – what finally gives you the edge is preparation, nutrition, fitness, psychology – that kind of thing.

So it really is a total package now, putting together a successful team?

Definitely. The modern-day professional and the modern professional outfit is a full package. You've got the cricket – coaching, technique, your talent. You've got the mind games – the psychology, your temperament. You've got all the physical side of it – nutrition, fitness and so on. It's a whole package, and I think we're a pretty professional outfit.

Can analysing victories lead to a greater chance of you achieving more victories?

Well, on an individual basis, looking at the best innings you've ever played certainly gives you a better chance of playing more of those innings. I always carry around a video of my best-ever innings. A lot of people carry around tapes of when they're doing badly to look at and analyse their faults. I think it's equally important to look at what you were doing well, because you can often forget. Three months down the line you forget what was working for you.

I understand the England team have a video set to stirring music, of all the great moments. How does that help?

That's really just a feel-good factor. We have a number of videos, one of great moments that we've had as a team – that was a short video – and also a video of every individual's finest moments, moments that they've particularly enjoyed, when they've done well, set to their favourite bit of music. The England rugby team do it as well. I'm sure a lot of successful outfits do. It's not meant to be anything more than a simple tonic.

Was your momentous innings against South Africa your greatest success in cricket, or was there something you'd put above that?

From a personal point of view it was my best innings, without a doubt. One of the problems is that I'm not so sure I'm ever going to be able to beat that. That's a problem when you realize you may have played your best innings. The only thing that would better it for me would be to play an innings of similar length and magnitude in a winning situation. That's the next challenge.

You've hit on one of the big problems for successful people – when they are successful, maintaining that success.

It's maintaining the success, maintaining the desire and the motivation to be successful. Certainly there's plenty of desire and motivation for me, because we've not had that much success, and there's plenty of opportunities coming up. There's much to do and plenty of success, hopefully, just round the corner. But certainly, from an individual point of view, and as a batsman, I think probably that was my high point. I'm not so sure I'm going to get higher than that, but you never know. That's the thing, you never know.

Isn't it slightly defeatist to think that was your high point?

You could say it's defeatist, you could also say it's realistic. I'm sure Graham Gooch felt the same way about his 150 at Headingley when he carried his bat against the West Indies. Everybody must do it, they must sit down and say, 'I'm not so sure I can do better than that.' And it may be a depressing thought, but I think you have to be realistic as well.

How do you identify the cricketing talent of the future? When you watch a cricketer in action, a young lad between 10 and 15, how do you know that he has the potential to be a great cricketer?

It's very simple – I don't. I can't relate to how good or bad I was at that particular age and I think you have to relate a little bit back to yourself and your team-mates. That's why I'll never be a coach of young cricketers. Some players stand out, that's obvious, but amongst the general level of things I'd find it very difficult to pick out the one or two that are going to succeed.

Is that because the qualities required to be a successful cricketer change over the years?

Various things change. As you grow up your body changes. Some players are much stronger and bigger at 15 than the rest and stand out a mile, but two years later everybody else has caught them up. The physical advantage they had previously, they might not have two years down the line. As I said, the mind is such a key thing to success – whether a player can stay focused, whether he can work hard in the growing-up years, if you like, and it's very difficult to get to know somebody's mind unless you know them very well. So, there's so much that can change over a period. I would think it's a difficult thing to do.

Do you think there's any difference between achieving success on the cricket field and achieving success in other sports, or in other professions?

That's difficult. In football, there's far more competition, there are far more footballers. Football has a massive influx of money now from Sky and other sources, which makes it the sport that most people want to play. To be a successful footballer is the most difficult thing. But the basics of being successful – of identifying your talent, working on your talent, knowing your limitations, staying focused, staying motivated – I'm sure stand for not only all sports, but for success in other areas as well.

Do you think cricket could ever attract the big money that football does?

No. It's to do with market forces. Very few people come to watch your average County Championship match. You're probably lucky at Old Trafford if you get 1,000 people. Manchester United get 55,000 people every week.

Who are the people that you really admire as being at the peak of success, either past or present?

The one guy I looked up to was Australia's captain, Allan Border. I know the pressures that you're under as captain, and how difficult it has been doing this job for three years – and he did it for ten. Whilst, as I said previously, there were one or two things that were in his favour, I think to keep his motivation and his focus throughout that period – and he won most things along the way – was a phenomenal effort. What's more he averaged 50 against the world's best bowlers in that time and he constantly dug his side out of trouble. He was the one bloke that I always looked up to in cricketing terms.

Outside cricket I've met a lot of people that I've admired. I met Nelson Mandela in South Africa, which was a thrilling moment, and it was amazing to see the attitude that he and his fellow inmates at Robben Island had, the kind of forgiveness that they showed.

What do you think are the greatest enemies of success?

Lots of things are out of your hands. You can have career-threatening injuries, injuries which cause you to lose your place in the team. You can lose your motivation. You can get too wrapped up in the material side of sport. I see a lot of young cricketers come into the England team and do well, but there's a perceived fame and fortune around the corner and that definitely can affect how successful they'll be in the future. Failing to cope with that attention, the material success, is definitely an enemy of success. The George Best syndrome, if you like. If you can keep focused on being successful on the field, then the material things will always take care of themselves. That's the attitude I try to have anyway; I'm sure it's the right one.

In the team sense, the enemies of success are the mavericks who you can't get to play within the team structure. And, of course, the lack of talent within the team, the lack of a world-beater. The right kind of work ethic and attitude is an absolutely vital part of a successful team and its absence is an enemy of success. You don't get anywhere without hard work, putting in the hours.

Do you think that success brings obligations in its wake to others, to society at large?

I feel an obligation when people ring up and ask for interviews. Whether I ought to feel that obligation is a different thing. Generally I'll do things. I won't do everything that I'm asked to do. I try to avoid after-dinner speaking like the plague because I just don't enjoy it. I think the PR side of the job is essential because cricket is competing with a lot of sports for the attention of youngsters, and you've got to try and give it an upbeat message.

Have you set a time limit on being a cricketer?

No, not as such, but I have a particularly dodgy back, so I don't think I'll be playing till I'm in my mid-40s. If I could keep going until 35, that would be absolutely brilliant for me. I'd like to think I could play for England for another three or four years, till maybe 31 or 32. A couple of extra years for Lancashire and then that'll do me fine.

What does a successful cricketer do when his playing days are over?

Obviously, if you're in my position or that of the five or six who are regular England players, you get a reasonable salary and there's no hardship. But there are a lot of cricketers who come to the end of the road with no idea what else to do, and it can be tough. For those well-known ones, the options include the media – writing newspaper columns, Sky TV, BBC TV – but when I see 15 former England cricketers in the tent after the day's play, I say to myself, 'I hope I'm not one of those in ten years' time.' The problem is that when you get to 35, you've finished your career but you don't know anything else, or you've not done anything else. Then it's a bit late to start another career. It may well be that the options are so limited that I shall indeed be hanging around the tent at the end of the day's play. But I'd like to think I could do something else.

What do you fancy doing? There must be something for which your history degree qualifies you?

Qualified for sweet FA. The people who got history degrees with me are doing a variety of things. After all, your degree just tells people that you've got a bit of grey matter, you can organize your time reasonably well, and you can get through three years of university with something to show for it at the end. As I say, I've not had to think about it yet, in the next two or three years I will.

Are you good at managing your time?

Yes. As I said, at university that was instilled into me pretty quickly. I had to do that fairly well, and I still do – time is limited. Cricket is a game that takes six hours a day for five days at a time, so you tend to find there's not much time left over.

Do you think that every successful person has at some stage to sacrifice their personal life in order to pursue their professional career?

For last winter's tour, we asked that no wives and girlfriends come on tour, and that's a sacrifice the guys had to make. We got back in March, so it was a three-month tour – a hell of a long time to be away. But the winter before in South Africa we found that the focus of the tour, the emphasis on cricket, changed somewhat when the families arrived, so this year we asked them not to come. That sacrifice can always be there, particularly for a cricketer who throughout the summer is away for weeks at a time, and then, in the winter, can spend a further two or three months away. That's peculiar to cricket, you don't get it with football. Cricket's strange in that sense, and that's why there's probably such a high divorce rate amongst cricketers.

In pursuit of success, have you ever been driven to do something you wished later you hadn't done?

Cricket is a game where there's a lot of etiquette, rules, regulations. You generally try to stick within those rules. There's a fair bit of leeway out on the pitch, players overstep the line, and I've overstepped it as much as anybody. But as regards the hard and fast rules which you must uphold absolutely, I've stuck to those reasonably well. I've been in the Match Referee's Room and I've been fined a couple of times – once for dissent and once for ball-tampering – but in my own mind I was in the clear in both instances. In the case of the ball-tampering, it was a particularly hot day and I was using the soil in the footholds to keep my hands dry and also to keep the ball dry. I felt that was an acceptable thing to do within the laws and regulations of cricket. The dissent with the umpire was ridiculous, the Match Referee was just after me for the previous offence. So those two incidents have not really bothered me. They only bother me in that I'm the only England cricketer to have been fined in a Test Match.

Do you wish they hadn't happened?

I wish they hadn't happened in that when you finish your career these things are tagged onto your record. I suppose it's like a footballer who gets sent off half a dozen times in his career. It would be nice to look back on a cleaner record, but I'm not too perturbed about it.

If you could gather together, out in the nets or wherever, all the youngsters in Britain who look up to you as being someone they admire, what advice would you give them?

Well it's a trite thing to say, but I think a key thing is enjoyment. You must definitely enjoy the game. As soon as you start thinking about success and where you want to be in ten or 15 years' time, you stop enjoying the game in the present, and that's fatal. You must also identify your talent and work on it. I wouldn't say I slavishly worked at my game, but I did put in the hours as I was growing up. It probably kept me out of the pub, and that kind of thing.

When your time comes to leave this life, what would you like people to say about you?

Well, I will probably be long forgotten as a cricketer.

You really think so?

Yes, definitely. Time moves on.

That's not just modesty?

No, I don't think so at all. It's just the way I view things. I certainly don't give my profession and my career the kind of overwhelming importance that other people give it. We chase a little red ball around and do our best, but it's not a life-or-death situation. And cricket as a career is pretty transient.

Do you think that attitude has helped you, that you don't feel it's a life-or-death situation? Is someone likely to be more successful if they're not fighting for success for its own sake?

That attitude of it not being a life-or-death situation has helped me. I'm fairly laid back about it, and therefore I don't load too much pressure on myself. But I'm sure other people take a different view, I'm sure it helps them if they feel they're fighting for an absolutely vital cause. It depends on the nature of your personality.

You haven't told me what you'd like people to say about you.

I thought you wouldn't get back to it. I don't know. In cricketing terms I'd like to think that I was a batsman who got runs for the team when they were most needed against quality opposition. I know I won't be remembered as the most thrilling player to watch.

BOB AYLING

The decade since privatisation has turned British
Airways into one of Britain's great success stories. Its
obsession with customer satisfaction is reflected in its
advertising slogan – 'the world's favourite airline'. It
is constantly hunting for innovations and ways to
cut costs – a saving of £1 billion over three years is
one target. It invests in a growing network of global
partners – and appears to be on the way to gaining
regulatory approval for a link-up with American
Airlines which could give it 60 per cent of
transatlantic air traffic. Only rarely does it have
cause for regret, as in the so-called 'dirty tricks' affair
with Virgin Atlantic and the allegations of passenger
poaching – when, as Bob Ayling puts it, 'there were
things that should not have happened, and they will
not happen again'. Personally untouched by the

allegations, he took over as Chief Executive of this most entrepreneurial of airlines in
January 1996 – a move which even his strong sense of ambition would not have predicted
when he was forced to abandon school (and hopes of Oxbridge) at the age of 15, after his
father's grocery business went bust. He's said that working in the family shops taught him
how to look after customers' needs; but the background that really prepared him for his
eventual airline career was the law. Being articled to a firm of solicitors helped him to 'grow
up rather quickly', and at 24 he was an equity partner in a City law firm.

Selling his stake to pay off his mortgage, he joined the Civil Service and rose
rapidly – becoming the youngest Under-Secretary at the age of 37. Despite being tipped
for the very top by senior politicians, he felt it was time to move on. Out of the blue
came a telephone call asking him to join British Airways as legal adviser, helping the
company prepare for privatisation. He admits he had no formal schooling for his
subsequent jump into management, instead 'learning by example'. His 'Be Brave'
staff campaign devolved responsibility for decision-making to almost every level.
'Employees,' he says, 'must feel they can make a contribution, or we diminish people
who are very good.' He later drove through job cuts and changes in working practices
at some cost to staff morale, and triggering an expensive strike from which both sides
claimed victory. He has an unnerving habit of bursting in on meetings 'because there
are too many occasions when people sit around talking in an unstructured way.'
Here, he allows us to burst in on the driving philosophy and experiences of the man
who is likely to guide British Airways through the millennium.

Bob Ayling, what is your definition of success?

I believe that people seek success for one of two reasons. There's the selfish personal side, what it means for oneself, and there's the side which is about what other people think and about reputation. I tend to the first side. It's about personal satisfaction and achievement, though I would not be truthful if I discounted altogether the aspect of reputation – but that isn't the drive. I always value feedback, both good feedback and bad feedback – that's sometimes more valuable, but it's only valuable when it actually corresponds with most of what you know yourself. The worst feedback of all is that which is knowingly untrue – you know it's untrue, the person giving it to you knows it's untrue, it's worse than none at all. Success is about making some sort of impact, making a difference, making a contribution. We are all here for such a short time, and to have made a contribution in a way which is helpful and moves life on – that's success.

What happens when the two judgments do not coincide? That what you consider to be successful is not so judged by others and vice versa?

That would be an element of 'unsuccess', because personal satisfaction must have as part of it an element of what other people think, though it isn't the whole picture. That's the interesting thing about it – it's not the whole picture. Sometimes other people can think very well of something a person's done, which the actual person doesn't rate highly at all.

Do you think that your success in running British Airways is very much tied up with the success of the airline as a whole?

First of all I'm not sure I've had a great deal of success so far, because it's too soon to judge. Of course I was doing things before, and I made a contribution, but those contributions have in a sense been acknowledged and are now in the past. Whether or not anyone is successful in doing a job inevitably depends on the success of the whole organization and therefore my own success can never be exclusively, or in any sense wholly, my own – it's the success of the whole organization, in this instance over 55,000 people.

Is there an element of luck in success?

Of course, there's a huge element of luck in life. The one important factor of life that is neglected more than anything else is its randomness – how things can happen that are completely unforeseeable, yet which make such an enormous impact. They can happen for the good or for the bad, you can have good luck or bad.

What were the memorable unforeseeable things that happened to you?

The first random event of importance was my leaving school unexpectedly early, and that was a random thing because my dad had some bad luck. The whole family had some bad luck.

That was when your father's grocery stores went under?

Yes. We knew a solicitor who lived near us who agreed to take me as an articled clerk – and had it not been for that bit of good luck, that random factor, it's very difficult to know what would have happened to me. Something else would have happened that might have been as good, but it would have been different. That first bit of luck, that random friendship, really fixed the next five years of my life, because from the age of 16 to 21 I was being trained in a firm of really very good lawyers.

What did that do for you?

I grew up very quickly. I learned about things – human life, the complexities of human behaviour, which perhaps I might not have learned until rather later on. We had a wide general practice – commercial work, corporate work and a lot of private client work, and at that stage, before the law on divorce had been reformed, there was still a great deal of contentious divorce. The facts of family life that were brought to light in divorce proceedings, and the correspondence that I used to read between a man and his wife, were probably not what people would have thought was good for a teenager to be exposed to. But anyway, that was how it was and I learned about that aspect of life quite quickly, and also about the ways human relations, whether commercial or personal, can go wrong. Secondly, I learned how to get on in a professional firm – how you behave, how you don't behave – and I learned the law, I learned how to practise the law, part of the time at law school, part of the time in the office.

What did you learn about how to behave and how not to behave? What were the benchmarks there?

There were two rules that were required of us all very early on. One was honesty with the people in the firm. I am sure we were told it, but also learned it from the way people in the firm behaved, that was very important. The other was confidentiality – the idea that you simply did not talk about the affairs of the clients of the firm with anyone – friends, girlfriends, parents – outside the office. There is an element of my character, which I know has been criticized (which I hope I am now reforming), which is to be quite close with information. It all goes back to this training: it belongs to someone else – if somebody told you something about themselves, then a) it was a privilege and b) it wasn't a privilege that you broke by telling somebody else. Now that sort of training causes problems later when you need to communicate, tell people things rather than keep secrets, it takes a certain amount of tugging at the roots. That's something I've learned to deal with.

Sir John Nott is quoted as saying that you could have gone right to the top in the Civil Service had you wanted to. Why did you say, 'It's no longer for me, I want to take the commercial route, I want to go into business'?

I suppose it was about personal challenge. I was 37 by then, I think I was one of the youngest Under Secretaries in Whitehall, at least at the time. There were two more levels in the hierarchy and there seemed a reasonable possibility that I might achieve them. But of course it's entirely a matter of luck and the random factor comes in again so whether I actually would have done so or not I can't be sure. But just getting a place in the hierarchy didn't seem, to me, to be completely satisfying, because it isn't the title somebody gives you that matters, it's what you can do. Although officials do have immense influence and can influence events in our system of government it is, at the end of the day, ministers who paint the big picture and decide policy. And I felt maybe if I moved into a different situation I might get the chance to paint a picture of my own.

So having control is an important ingredient in your pursuit of professional satisfaction and success?

I don't think I'm a control freak – in fact I'm a bit lax, sometimes I have to make myself get involved – but, if I have an idea, I then like to see it put into effect, so I will want to persuade people personally that it is the right thing to do.

But in your position, you don't need to persuade – you can tell.

It's much better to persuade people – it's always better to persuade people. If you tell somebody to do something and they don't really want to do it it won't happen, but if you can persuade somebody, even somebody you could have told to do something, then it will happen smoothly and you won't need to be so involved after that. Best of all people should promote and implement their own ideas.

Weren't you tempted to copy your predecessors, Lord King and Sir Colin Marshall, because they had been perceived as successful by others?

No, I wasn't. I learned much from both of them, from Colin in particular, about management and discipline of management. But I think it's very dangerous to try and start being a different person just because you've seen other people behave in a particular way. I think it is very important to know who you are, to be your own person and to try and contribute from that point of view. When you get into a job where there's no one telling you what to do, you might find people giving you advice and, if you've got any sense, you listen to it. All the people who have made a difference, who have made an impact, haven't tried to be somebody else – they've been themselves.

When you became chief executive you had what was described as your big idea, the 'Be Brave' campaign, devolving responsibility. What made you go down that particular route, what made you adopt that as the hallmark of the start of your term as chief executive?

I thought that the organization had become rather centralized and there was a tendency for every decision, however minor, to rise to the top and therefore for people to begin to feel that they couldn't make a contribution themselves. There was a danger that we diminished the people who were really very good, and since they were much closer to most of the problems that needed to be resolved than I was, they were the right people to deal with them. Now that has to be done within a framework and within an environment which is appropriate, there are some things that are not going to be devolved to junior or middle-ranking managers. We try to give customers what they expect or to exceed what they expect and we behave well to other people – that's one of the rules of the organization, and we take careful note if we find people are not doing what they should. And we want our money to be spent in a particular way, i.e. prudently not recklessly. But there are so many things that need not be decided by me, and ought not to be decided by me, that it wasn't a very radical change.

So the principle is, judge managers on what they do and not the number of questions that they pass up to you?

Yes.

But as a manager it is a very fine judgment as to the nature of the questions that are worth dealing with yourself, and those you pass up to a higher level. There's an element of fear that if you get it wrong your job could be at stake.

I hope that isn't the case if people make honest mistakes. I've made lots of mistakes, I hope honest ones, and the people who have suffered as a result have been kind enough to overlook them when they realized they were honest mistakes. The absolutely critical thing about this is to own up to yourself and to other people that something's gone wrong and to fix it. We try to get this ethos into the company, particularly when things go wrong, as they will do. Take the engineering side of the business, which looks after the aircraft. There's an inviolable rule that information is transmitted to the Civil Aviation Authority – there's absolutely no question of it coming up to me or going to the legal department, no question of, 'Is it all right for us to pass this on?' It automatically goes to the CAA. There's an open, transparent relationship with them.

Did you resent not going to university?

I felt I'd missed out, because it actually was a physical separation – my friends went off and did something else.

Is that feeling of deprivation, almost of sacrifice, an important ingredient in making someone more successful than somebody else?

It might be, it certainly was in my case. It doesn't have to be financial success, but you have to achieve something, to show yourself that you can.

Is individual success harder to achieve than team success? Is is possible to be part of a team and be individually a success while your team is not?

I think that's very difficult. The analogy is a slightly awkward one – you can have a cricket team that is unsuccessful yet in it you can have a star batsman. In that sense, of course, cricket isn't only a team game – it is also an individual game. I suppose business is more like that than, say, football where the team becomes more important than the individual. But I wouldn't feel very successful personally if British Airways wasn't successful.

Do you think you can sit down and methodically plan success, to the extent that you iron out all the bumps and hiccups that might occur along the way and say, 'We really are perfectly clear that this project is going to succeed'?

No. I'm not saying it can never be done, but I think that in anything which has human factors involved, as business does, it's very much more difficult. If you're building a bridge – and I don't know anything about building bridges – provided you understand the geometry of the land you're building it on and the stresses and strains, you can do some calculations. I've talked to people who've been responsible for big engineering projects and I've said, 'Are you absolutely sure this is going to work?' and they've said, 'Yes, yes it will.' They are very much more sure than a business person can be, because the factors involved are physical factors, there are physical laws and their calculations can be done on that basis. But if your business is involved with changing how people feel, how they behave, what their attitudes are and how that might affect a whole lot of other people, you can never know at the outset whether you will be successful.

Do you think that after all the expansion and cost-cutting that are priorities for a company such as British Airways, there will ever come a point where you say, 'That's it, we have achieved as much success as we can possibly achieve, from now on it's a question of minding the shop'?

No. Because the demands of air travellers change all the time and will continue to change in the future. What they want, and how much they are going to pay is going to change. The strength of the economies that you trade in will change – that's a very important factor. The British economy may get stronger, it may get weaker relative to other economies. The competition is going to change, the nature of the equipment that you fly is going to change. And those are just a few of the things, without my really thinking about it. Things change every day, every day a competitor is thinking about doing something which is going to have an effect – they hope a negative effect – on the business I run and you have to be awake to that and willing to cope with change. So in a way – and perhaps this is what you're hinting at – the slight problem with this sort of job is that there's never an end to it. You can't ever say, 'Well, we won that case and we'll now hang up our boots.' If you time it right, you could end with a good year, a good few years – but then you might not time it right.

In any company, and I suppose especially British Airways which came from the public sector, bureaucracy is an enemy of success. How do you fight it, how do you stop it clawing its way back into your organization?

I talk about it. I see managers every day, I have a meeting with 15 of them every week. I give them my views and ask them what they think about this particular issue. The important thing with responsibility is to be held accountable for what you do. Bureaucracy is a system which takes responsibility away, because individuals are given clearance by people who are higher up the hierarchy. If you take all that away, it is the person sitting with the problem who actually has to decide what to do about it. It's like the junior controller who took it upon himself to send Concorde to rescue some passengers. Now that had huge expenditure implications but it was clearly the right thing to do – the Concorde was available, there wasn't any other aircraft, so he just dispatched the Concorde, he didn't ask. Certainly there was no reference to me. And, as far as I could tell, to no one else either. Another thing I do is to burst in on meetings, because I think far too many meetings take place where people sit around talking about things in an unstructured way.

Do you burst in to end the meetings?

I burst in to punctuate them.

And they all know that at any time you could burst through the door?

Yes. I think that is fair enough. My own door is open for anyone who wants to burst in, unless I am having a personal conversation with someone about their own position or we've got a board meeting. Otherwise if people want to burst in they can, if I don't want them there I'll ask them to leave. So I burst in to punctuate meetings and make a point, and it's interesting how often people say, 'It's all right, Bob, we're not actually having a meeting here.' The message has got through, even if the practice hasn't changed yet.

Are you really anti-meetings?

I'm not anti-meetings. A well-organized, well-structured, well-run meeting is a good way of transacting business, much better than people sending a lot of notes to each other. But people have got to be disciplined, you've got to think about the issues before you go to the meeting, you've got to speak only when it's relevant, not when you want to hear your own voice, or because you're getting bored. The chairman has a very important role in making sure the meeting works, that there is an outcome which is then implemented, and what irritates me is when a meeting has no outcome, or leads to another meeting with more or less the same people discussing the same thing over again. That's one sort of meeting which I am against. The second sort is where it's just a question of transmitting responsibility to other people instead of taking it yourself.

Who do you really admire, who are your heroes, past or present?

There's one particular man, Sir Michael Kerr, who was a Court of Appeal Judge. I admire him because of his immense warmth of personality, his very giving personality. He's more overtly emotional than many lawyers, he is a most remarkable man. He left Germany when he was about 12 in the early 1930s and moved to Switzerland and then to France. There he had to learn to speak French and went into a French school. At the end of the year, having started with no French at all, he won the form prize. Then sometime later he moved to England and he went to boarding school in England and got an open scholarship to Cambridge. By this stage war was imminent or had just broken out. He was about to take his first-year exams when he was rounded up as an enemy alien and sent to the Isle of Man, and it was only after about a year that he was released. He eventually joined the RAF, rather ironically, but he wasn't allowed to fight in the front line, so became a training captain. Eventually he went back to Cambridge and qualified at the bar. Now any adversity that I've had is nothing compared with that. Despite everything he became a successful silk and then a judge – and a great judge.

With a lawyer's eye on business, is it becoming more or less difficult to achieve success?

I don't think it's more difficult. The circumstances are different, technology's different, business challenges are different. One of the greatest liberating forces in post-medieval society has been trade. It was trade that eventually demolished medieval society, and it will be trade which will eventually demolish the class system. It's trade which gives people opportunities. Apart from sportsmen in modern times, all the people who have had opportunity have risen through commercial opportunities. The freedom to trade is one of the most fundamental freedoms in life and I hope that people go on having opportunities in commerce, in small companies, big companies, international companies or whatever. I am sure they will.

What are the greatest enemies of success?

Success is hampered when spirits are down. It's the human spirit which allows success to happen and, if the human spirit is down, the black side of life overcomes the white side of life. Also people have got to deal with each other honestly and openly. That's not to say you've got to be naive about human behaviour, but deceit and bad behaviour are really the enemies of anything – and certainly success.

It's said we're an envious country, whereas in America they put success on a pedestal, here people knock the successful and envy them.

I'm not sure that's actually right. I think people do secretly admire success. It doesn't matter whether it's Alan Shearer or whether it's a business person. I'm not saying the press don't criticize people and I am not saying people don't read newspapers which contain criticism, but I think we are just as admiring of success. The problem is that we haven't had enough of it. We've seen other countries being successful. If you were born, as I was, in 1946, a whole life has been spent in a period of relative economic decline. I think people like to see a bit of success and they certainly don't seem to begrudge my company its success. Some of our competitors might, that's natural and understandable, but I believe success has a better name than you might think.

Do you feel that success has changed you?

It's changed me in the sense that I feel a bit more fulfilled, and in the sense that I feel, within reason, I only need to be myself. That's one of the privileges of getting a bit older, of course, you learn that.

If you could gather together in one room all the young people who wanted to make careers in the airline business, what advice would you give to them?

I'd give them the advice I give to a management trainee. Just as I trained as a lawyer, all lawyers have other lawyers sitting with them all the time so I have a management trainee who sits with me. They sit with me for a year, and I encourage them to take the opportunity to learn from every experience they have. When I myself was training as a solicitor, every time I sat with one of the partners I learned what they were doing and I pestered them with hundreds of questions until they got bored with me and didn't want to answer any more. You have to learn from other people's experience, and that means you've got to have a certain approach to what they're doing which will make them want to help you. First of all it's a human behaviour thing, you've got to learn that there's a lot to learn and the way you learn is from other people. Just keep on learning and then, as opportunities come along, take them with enthusiasm.

When your time comes to leave this planet, what would you like people to say about you?

Well, my family's important and I would like it to be thought that I contributed to the family and we had a successful family life and, in the same way, that I contributed to the organizations that I've been with, and that my being there has made a difference.

MARTIN BELL

Before his sudden election as an MP, Martin Bell was one of the greatest television war reporters of his generation. An eye for a picture, a way with words, always interesting, never ponderous – his reports were carefully crafted models of film-making, their consistency underlined by his Royal Television Society Reporter of the Year Awards – one in 1976, the other 16 years later – and his OBE for services to journalism. Across three decades of the world's conflicts, Martin was there – in Vietnam, the Middle East, Angola, Rhodesia, Biafra, El Salvador, the Gulf War, Nicaragua, Croatia and Bosnia.

   It is not difficult to find the early influences that pointed him towards journalism. His father was an eloquent Sussex farmer who compiled the very first Times *crossword. He instilled in Martin the importance of being a good listener, and encouraged his passion for the English language, which earned him a scholarship to King's College, Cambridge. Two years' national service gave him first-hand experience of the soldier's life. His entire career in journalism was spent with the BBC, joining their Norwich newsroom as a graduate trainee in 1962, and taking just two years to be promoted to the general reporting pool in London. A remarkable 80 countries and 33 years later, including almost a third of that time as chief North America correspondent, found him still in the reporting saddle – at some cost to his personal life (he has two divorces behind him). His most dramatic television appearance was during the Bosnian conflict, when he was wounded by shrapnel, and carried on talking to millions of television viewers. He explains here his belief that that conflict changed the nature of war reporting, and why he now presses the case for 'the journalism of attachment – reporting which cares as well as knows'. Not all TV news folk agree, but Martin makes his point passionately, and is an experienced voice in the growing debate over the fine judgments that shape the agenda and content of news bulletins. In 1997, he surprised journalistic colleagues by resigning from the BBC to respond to appeals for an 'anti-sleaze' candidate to challenge the then Conservative MP Neil Hamilton in the general election. His victory gave him a baptism in political success. Although this interview was carried out before his decision to enter politics, the kind of values and principles he talks about have already been carried into his new role as an Independent MP.*

Martin Bell, what is your definition of success?

I don't think that success has got anything to do with money – money for me isn't a way of keeping the score, so that's what it isn't. In the end, it is achieving the esteem of one's peers, of people in the same business as oneself.

Does your background or upbringing have anything to do with whether you are successful or not?

Sometimes, I like to think so. I had an extraordinarily serene and happy background which in a way enabled me to live through some very turbulent times later in life, because I know where I come from and I know who I am. But I might be wrong – I might have come from a troubled background and still taken to it easily. I don't think I know myself well enough to answer that.

Tell me more about that serenity that you were talking about.

I lived a very sheltered life until I was 24. I was educated in a series of all-male institutions, which I wouldn't necessarily recommend to anybody these days because it made for all kinds of problems, but my family life was as serene as that of anybody I know. My father was a country writer, he was the compiler of the first *Times* crossword puzzle, he was a remarkable man, as well as a farmer and a man of great eloquence, and many ideas which fizzed and fizzed in his mind were transmitted to me. I learned to be a good listener having the father I had. My mother was quite the most delightful and serene woman I have ever met who put up with a lot and together they made an extraordinary team in a household where I never, ever heard a voice raised in anger. That is a strange background and preliminary to becoming a war correspondent, but that contradiction, that contrast has struck me very often later in life, where most of the voices that I do hear now are raised in anger. It's given me a sense of how important it is to have a serene domestic background, something to hold onto, so that I could come out of those war zones and sit in my garden and watch the oak tree grow.

With parents like that was there a feeling that you had an enormous amount to live up to?

Yes, particularly because they sacrificed. If you have parents who sacrificed, as mine did, then you cannot be an underachiever because it betrays their trust and their sacrifice. They spent money they hardly had, they sent me to a very expensive school and an extremely expensive university and also my two sisters – because the girls, quite rightly, had to have just the same opportunities as the boys – and they made these sacrifices. They did not have a holiday for 20 years, they just worked and over-worked for their children, and the only reward you could really give them was that you shouldn't screw up and you should come through having benefited from those sacrifices, so that was a big motivating force for me.

So you were repaying a debt as you sought success in the journalistic field?

Absolutely. I suppose success for many people is its own reward. I have never believed that you succeed at the expense of others. Journalists are very bad team players. My feeling is that if I am on an enterprise with a lot of other people, then you either succeed together or fail together. But this is a very difficult concept to get over, because journalists tend to be rather driven, egocentric people. I'm driven, but I think I am not egocentric because I learned from my parents, who gave so much, the importance of giving and the importance of love, and love is giving not taking.

And yet, you have come to the top in a profession where there are a great many people who would not have had as perhaps a charitable attitude as that.

It's strange. People imagine that the world of war reporting is full of head-banging maniacs and would-be soldiers and Walter Mittys. The tougher environments – and lately these Balkan wars have been the toughest I have ever faced – have sorted out the men from the boys in a general sense – and I think these days I have to add the women from the girls – in that they have not produced these battle-hardened, uncaring, frontline reporters. I don't think the war has hardened us at all – it has softened us, because we have come so close to the suffering of other people in a way that I never thought I would experience in my time, and I think we have changed the nature of war reporting. Television has as well, in that it now focuses on people, not on strategies and weapon systems and ideologies, but on the people who start the wars, the people who provoke the wars, the people who fight the wars and the people who suffer in the wars, which are very different categories of people, so I don't think it's a tough guy's job. I now argue for what I call the journalism of attachment, which is a journalism that cares as well as knows because if you don't care about what you're doing, you shouldn't be doing it.

But is there a danger of caring so much that you lose the objectivity that is a requirement of any war reporter?

I am not sure about objectivity, because everything I do is filtered through my eyes and my mind and my experience, and that's the very definition of subjective. I think fairness is terribly important, more than ever in the days of satellite television, and it's especially important if you find the side in some conflict which is universally reviled according to the political correctness of the day – shall we say the Afrikaaners in South Africa, the hardline loyalists in Northern Ireland, the Serbs in Bosnia. These are the people I go for, these are the people I try to understand, because they normally hold the key to peace or war. I am not saying that you shouldn't be fair, I'm saying you have to be fair, but you have to understand that this is fundamentally about people and we are not just bystanders, we influence the events that we report on in a lot of subtle ways and some quite obvious ways. If I am standing next to a man in a water queue in Sarajevo at the height of the fighting and the man is wounded, there's nobody else who can take him to the hospital but me. I've got an armoured vehicle so I stop being a reporter and I become an ambulance driver – is that being objective? No, it's participating, but we're people, we are part of the scene we report, and there's nothing I think in the Geneva Convention that disbars us from helping the afflicted.

There was a time when war reporting was considered to be more dispassionate and neutral, a time when you had a whole breed of reporters who would think that they were almost immune from the events that were taking place around them.

That's right, and you could take part in our sweepstake on where the country was that you had just been assigned to. I used to be that kind of person, I used to be pretty well untouched. I went through Vietnam, Biafra touched me a bit, but Vietnam, a couple of Middle East wars, the Gulf War – you would attend it, you would listen to what the soldiers were saying, you would get as close to the front line as you could, you would chronicle it and move on and I was not much touched by any of them. I now see this as a failing. I now prefer this journalism of attachment, in which we have some responsibility, a responsibility which I don't think we had in the old days. People used to read about the wars or see them on television and shrug their shoulders and put down the newspaper or switch off.

What has happened in recent years is a technical revolution, the revolution of the satellite dish, which links up all our tragedies and binds us to them. Now for the first time in history, the means of mass destruction which is modern warfare and the means of mass communication which brings it straight into people's living rooms within hours or minutes of its happening have been brought together. This imposes an extra strain, burden and responsibility on the journalists and I think – this may sound pompous – I think journalism is, or should be, like everything else in life, fundamentally a moral enterprise in which you have to have a sense of right and wrong.

What was the catalyst that turned you from being the old type of war reporter into this new type of correspondent?

It was Bosnia. It was not just that I was wounded in Bosnia and that, for the first time, I was in such a mass of flying shrapnel and metal, it was very, very dangerous for all the journalists, to the extent that very few of us were daft enough to work there. But to be so close for so long to the intense suffering of ordinary people, you could not be unmoved by it, as the soldiers were deeply moved. They were shocked, not only by what they saw, but also, in the UN days, by their inability under the mandate to do very much about it. So it changed us in all kinds of ways. It brought us close to these kinds of soldiers. The usual antagonism between the military and the press did not occur in the Bosnian war unless we felt that they were failing to live up to their mandate, to fulfil their mandate, which was quite often the case.

So you are closer to the people involved in those wars. Does that give you any problems in translating that into the finished reports back home, because there are certain restrictions on how much suffering you can show on television news?

That is a great difficulty. I am at one extreme end of this argument. I believe that we should show much more than we have shown. We are talking about the portrayal of real-life violence and certainly the BBC, for which I then worked, has, in recent years, become more and more restrictive, I would even say timid, in what it is willing to show, because it listens to its audience and its audience doesn't want to see a lot of this. I believe in the end, it may seem a trivial analogy, but it's rather like swearing. If you do it occasionally, if you show some of these extreme scenes occasionally, they will have an impact. If you show them every day, people will become hardened to them and shrug and turn away. But if we don't show the reality of the suffering and pain, then war becomes a great adventure again, which I suppose it was up to the Battle of the Somme in 1916, or it becomes an acceptable way of settling differences. It's not an adventure, and it's not an acceptable way of settling differences, and when I talk about journalism being a moral enterprise, that's one of the dimensions I mean.

And yet, you have to respond to the sensitivities of the viewers, don't you? If by showing the whole truth all the time, you end up with a generation of viewers who don't want to watch war reporting on television, then in a sense wouldn't that be counter-productive?

I think the debate here is not a debate of principle, but one of degree. There are many pictures I've seen of the market-place massacres and other atrocities in Bosnia which I can hardly bear to look at myself, let alone inflict on other people, but there should be, even in a sanitized report, some symbolical picture that shows the horror of it. I managed it on one Sunday at the Ahmici massacre in 1993 – we did it by showing one picture of a burnt, clenched fist. On the second of the market-place massacres, in late August 1995, I did it with a picture of blood being swilled down a storm-drain after the event, which is vivid and just within, I think, the bounds of acceptability. Without that, you can't tell the story.

War is an expression of failure in many ways. Your success as a war reporter has, therefore, been born out of a considerable number of failures. Does that ever trouble you or worry you?

It troubles me a lot. Towards the end of the Bosnian war – if it is indeed over – in the summer of 1995, I was sitting on a hillside called Gypsy Hill. We used to sit overlooking the battlefield, and there we were with our cameras and beside us were the UN soldiers with their blue helmets. They were counting the explosions and we were filming them and I asked myself what good has either of us ever done to bring this war to an end. It troubles me also that I built my journalistic career on the sufferings of others and perhaps I am, in a sense, some kind of a war profiteer as a result. Out of these troubles has grown my moral concern with the responsibility of the job. I haven't resolved it in my own mind, it disturbs me a lot.

Do you think you ever will resolve it in your own mind, or is it one of those imponderables that will never be resolved?

I don't think it will ever be resolved. I know what the arguments are – that somebody has to show what's going on in the world, and all you can do is to do it as well as you can. But if all you show is the carnage and mayhem, it gives a fairly unbalanced picture of the world, and that troubles me as well. I am troubled that the reports I did always included what we call the 'bang-bang' – the undroppable pictures of soldiers blazing away in the ruins – this is the stuff that runs, whereas something about attempts at reconstruction or people helping each other will not necessarily get on and often won't. Another of my doubts is that journalists are so much better at reporting war than at reporting peace. A better way of reporting peace has to be found.

Success as a war reporter must have led you to a certain amount of frustration with those people working in the diplomatic field, and to some extent in the military field, to actually end a conflict, because you must have seen ways in which the conflict might have been ended that they perhaps disagreed with or didn't recognize.

That is true. One of the reasons I didn't go back to Bosnia was that I became deeply angry with the failure to save the lives of up to 5,000 Moslems in Srebrnica last July, in a country where there were 34,000 UN troops mandated to protect the people, and in an area to which that mandate specifically applied. The UN just walked away and these people were summarily executed in the worst single war crime in Europe for 50 years. That made me very angry and I made a speech about it, and the problem with this is that I don't think anger is helpful to useful journalism. Anger blinds the mind and skews the judgment. Indignation is fine in a journalist, it helps kick down the door behind which the truth lies hidden, but anger – no.

On the other hand, we had to learn from these terrible mistakes over three and a half years and finally action was taken, effective action of a force within an effective mandate which we were assured by our leaders was impossible for three and a half years – three and a half years in which 278,000 people died. I am not quite sure what the line is here between just reporting the events and some kind of advocacy journalism, but clearly I'm upset with what happened. I've given a lecture about it and I've banged on about it a bit – but I tried to keep this out of my reports.

How do you successfully control anger in order to fulfil the obligations of producing reports that are as dispassionate as you can make them?

I didn't think I could control the anger successfully, which is why I asked to be excused from Bosnian duty.

Is that because the anger made you feel you were a lesser war reporter?

Yes. But up to that point, a moral sense is important. I don't believe that you should become a campaigning or crusading journalist. I don't like those journalists, they tend to have preconceived notions and find what they are looking for. By contrast, I never made much of an argument in any of my reports, even though I thought we should have intervened much earlier. It was the pictures which made the argument for me. Television is a very cool medium and the understated narrative is what holds the attention.

Coming back for a moment to your earlier career, when was the first time in your life that you said to yourself, 'I have been successful'?

I have always doubted that I am a success. I have lived – and many journalists I know are the same, because we work in such an ephemeral and, if you like, superficial medium – in fear of being found out. It was only at the time of the Bosnian war, and the Croatian war before it, when I really felt that I had mastered the subject and the people and the issues and I felt for the first time, 'Now Martin Bell you are not going to be found out.' It's a kind of negative definition of success, but it's mine.

That earlier feeling about being found out, did it come from the speed with which you moved from one story to another? The rapid transition – you get on the plane, you pick up news cuttings from the library and you hit the ground running with a brief to produce a report for that evening's news and you have only been in the country a few hours. Was that what made you feel a sense of inadequacy, and fear of being found out?

A little bit of that, in those days we did much more of what we called 'fire-brigade journalism' than is done now, where you tend to be given a patch and have to stick to it. But mostly I think my fear of being found out arose from a veneration of my predecessors, the great broadcast journalists like Richard Dimbleby and Frank Gillard, the great print journalists like James Cameron. When James Cameron's newspaper folded, the *News Chronicle*, I was an undergraduate at Cambridge and I cried because this man and his writings had meant so much to me, and I honestly felt I was not a worthy successor to that kind of deeply moral and yet totally accurate portrayal of the world as such people found it. I mean, I'm just Martin Bell, I'm straight out of a university, what do I know about anything?

And yet, success has brought you fame of a quite considerable kind, because you are now recognized as being right at the top of that particular profession. You would appear to be very modest and not to recognize this, but there must have been moments when you thought, 'Yes I've made it.

I know my strengths and my weaknesses. My weakness was that I could too easily cover with words pictures I hadn't got. My strength was I could put stuff together probably faster than anybody else in the business. I did this because I didn't write the stuff down.

Could you explain that technique?

It came upon me when I was the correspondent in Washington. When you're five hours the wrong side of your deadline anyway, and by four in the afternoon you have to have everything together for the *Nine O'Clock News*, you have to accelerate. You don't write it down, but you don't ad-lib it, you work out in your head what you want to say, you look at the pictures, you bounce the words off the pictures because the pictures are the mastertrack, if you like. So I worked this system out – it's fast and also has the advantage that you're not reading a script with these dreadful sing-song deliveries you sometimes get in broadcast journalism, where they hit the penultimate syllable of everything whether or not it's the most important syllable.

I'm terribly critical of other people's work, but I'm equally critical of my own. I look at that and say, 'Did I get that right?' I know how to write fast, and thanks to my father – I think it's genetic – I know how to write well. I also know that I'm not terribly scared in situations in which I might have expected to be scared, but that's not a moral quality at all, that's simply a matter of luck – like having a short nose or a long nose. I've known journalists, I've known soldiers, absolutely speechless with fear – I'm lucky, it doesn't get me like that.

But I do believe that the kind of journalism I did was a very collective enterprise – in television you have to work with each other, two or three people at the minimum – and you can only work in a war zone if you really like each other and you can operate as a league of friends. That's what gave me the strength to carry on – and I was not even the leader of the league of friends, we all took the decisions together.

So there is no such thing as what you might call isolated success in the journalistic profession – it's got to be part of a team effort?

Yes. I always argue that you succeed together or you fail together and you do not succeed at the expense of anyone else, least of all that of one of your comrades in arms. When I was Washington correspondent, supposedly chief correspondent, a succession of allegedly deputy correspondents came through and I always gave them a good selection of the best stories to do, otherwise they would feel resentful and the team wouldn't work. It's got to be a happy team because I've seen so many occasions where it wasn't. I also believe that so many things in life are better created by small teams rather than large ones.

And yet, even now, as you look around the reporting profession, there are people who, in the search for success, are unashamedly trying to carve each other up.

That is true.

Does that go with the territory?

You know what worries me? I competed all my professional life with a downmarket outfit, these days known as ITN. I mean they used to be mainstream and admirable, but they can still pull a few stunts. Now I can understand the ITN people trying to carve me up, although I have never reciprocated in that sense. I tend to help people because it's who I am, but what I cannot understand for the life of me is why the members of the same side should try to carve each other up, which is why I used to like small teams in war zones.

It's called creative conflict, isn't it?

Yes, but I don't believe in it. In fact, I was instrumental in Sarajevo in setting up a pool system in which, during the worst of the fighting, which lasted for three years, anybody's video would become available to anybody else, so camera crews were not put unnecessarily at risk by competing with each other under pressure to go that extra half-block forward where the fighting was at its fiercest. People were being killed like that, and one of the few achievements of which I am really proud is that I put an end to that, and that pool lasted for three years. Nothing like it had ever been attempted before.

Does success breed over-confidence?

I think unearned adulation from other people can. I am very dubious of celebrity journalism, because people so easily begin to believe the propaganda about them. I have seen this in the major stars of American television. They are not only the face of the network – which is fine, every network has its face and you're one of ours and good luck to you, but they also have the power of managing editor, the power to decide what is news today and what is not, who to hire and fire. Whole careers are made and broken by these people, it's the old problem of the actor-manager, no one can stand outside and say, 'Is this working?' And in journalism, too, power corrupts. It's very strange in American television, that here they are, one of the world's great republics, and they run their news divisions on a monarchical principle of the king and his court. Fortunately we don't have that here.

What do you regard as your biggest failures, and how did you turn yourself round to recover from them?

My biggest failure, professionally, was early on in Vietnam, in 1967, when I spent three months at a very critical juncture of the war, and I did not know or understand enough about the war to get out from under the shadow of the Americans. It was logistically easy to go along on their helicopters to their fire bases and their units and report the war from their point of view. I made a mistake, I took the easy option and I don't think there is a single report I did in those three months which I would wish to be kept in the archive. I went back there in 1972 and I'd learned a bit.

So a considerable learning curve at a very early stage?

Yes. And something else, and I don't think that this applies to journalism alone. You have to keep running fairly hard just to stand still. You learn lessons and you think you've learned them, and then something happens and you realize you haven't learned them at all and you've got to learn them all over again. You have to keep at it.

And for those who are seeking success in television journalism, what's the difference between going and covering your first war and covering your twentieth war? What's the difference of approach?

After 20 wars, I had got the fieldcraft right. I would not make so many dumb decisions and I would take fewer risks because I knew much more about what I was getting into. There's a moral dimension now to war reporting which there wasn't before – reporting about people, reporting about the victims of war and soldiers as people. I don't care very much about the weapon systems – I don't think defence correspondents are very good at reporting wars because they don't see them sufficiently as human enterprises or human disasters.

Only the fire power and the latest technology.

Yes. One of the marks of modern warfare is the targeting of civilians who are necessarily innocent people. I tried to be as fair as I could.. I unashamedly took the side of the victims of the war. It makes the war more understandable, and I don't think you can be morally neutral, as between war and peace – there is such a thing as a just war which I accept – but between those who, shall we say, start and prosecute a civil war and those who try to mediate an end to it. I had no doubt whose side I was on, which is why in Bosnia we used to pass information to the UN to help them understand things better, because we often knew things they didn't. I said in my book that I hope one day I'll have grandchildren and these grandchildren will look at me with their eyes aglow and they will say, 'Grandfather, were you ever a spy?' and I shall answer, 'Yes, just once I was, just once I spied for peace.'

Are there any successful moments in your life that you put right at the top of the tree – personal moments when you said to yourself, 'I have achieved something of which I am deeply and immensely proud'?

Yes. One or two of my reports out of Northern Ireland when I was one of the first metropolitan reporters – much spat at and hated by all the sides. It was not an easy time, I'm talking about the late 1960s, early 1970s. But now and again you'd get it right, because it was so difficult to work there at that time. We might be the only people there. But this sense of satisfaction would stay with you for 24 hours. It's very strange, but I've always had the feeling that if you're talking purely of the big report, the report that everyone's going to talk about, then it can actually be rather dangerous and counter-productive. An example of this is the report made by the esteemed ITN correspondent Michael Nicholson in Cyprus in 1974. He got an amazing scoop – he was right there when the Turkish paratroopers fell on him. Every time he goes out to do a foreign story after that, he's under pressure to reproduce that kind of triumph. Maybe we should just amble along at a level of competence and never become too outstandingly successful, because it's hard to live up to, and I think you're judged, in the end, on the sum of your work and the general level and competence of it over many, many years.

And yet there is journalistic saying, 'You're only as good as your last story.'

I don't think that's quite true. You can get away with one or two crummy ones – you have to, I've done one or two believe me – because sometimes you are asked by your editors to produce a story which you don't really think is there because they've got time to fill, and sometimes you'll come up with something that you think is absolutely terrific and you'll find there's no market for it at all.

To what extent do you, as a former journalist, dictate the degree of success, and to what extent is your success dependent on decisions taken by other people, the luck of being assigned to a particular story at a particular time?

You make your own luck. I'm very impressed by that Gary Player quote, 'The more I practise, the luckier I get.' Sometimes you'll be out of the mix and sometimes some great event will happen. I remember Kate Adie going to Tiananmen Square, I think she was amongst the third or fourth wave of reporters to go there and she called me up from Hong Kong, 'Well, this is no good,' she said, 'We've had this story and they're just kind of sending me out to babysit it' – and, of course, she was there when it all happened. The answer is persistence, and you do get some kind of intuition. One of the fascinating parts of being a news executive is being able to spot that little cloud no bigger than a man's hand before it becomes the storm, then you get right in ahead of it and under the storm, and that's the job of a foreign editor.

Do you think there's a difference between success as a journalist and success in other professions?

Some of the qualities are the same. It needs persistence, it needs intelligence, it needs an ability to lead people in such a way that they do not even know they're being led, so that it becomes a joint collective enterprise. Leadership is very important, but not the old 'follow me' kind of leadership, it's leadership by example, they have trust in you. And anything is a moral enterprise, there has to be a sense of right and wrong in just about anything you do.

You mentioned James Cameron earlier, and Frank Gillard. Who are the people you really admire, past or present, who are your heroes?

My two heroes in life are not actually journalists, although I will tell you which journalists I do admire. I admire Christiane Amanpour of CNN who is a terrific war reporter, who never sends her camera crew out where she's not with them – that's the mark of competence and of a decent reporter. I also admire Kurt Schork of Reuters who stuck it out. He stuck through the Bosnian war with a deep sense of commitment to making things better for four years.

My heroes are Elie Wiesel, who understands that good and evil are active forces in the world and helps us and shows us how to deal with them and never to forget, and Václav Havel, the President of the Czech Republic – there is a deeply moral man who was imprisoned for not selling out. He could have had a very comfortable life under the Communist world and he chose to have an uncomfortable life because he had to live with himself – those are my heroes.

Is it becoming more difficult to achieve success in the journalistic profession?

It's becoming easier to achieve a sort of flashflood type of impact. You know there will be stories of immense moment and importance and you just happen to be there and everyone says, 'Terrific.'

When in fact you'd have had to have been pretty stupid to fail?

Yes. I say to myself, anybody can describe a fire fight, it's pretty darned easy – the groups are doing this and that, and it all looks very exciting. But to explain it, to see the battle for the skirmish and the wood for the trees, that's difficult. Why are people fighting, what does it mean, what does this particular skirmish matter beyond the bang-bang? That's the difficulty, to give it some context and meaning, and the mark of a successful journalist is, over a long period of time, to be able to do that.

Success often arouses in some people a feeling of envy. Do you understand why people are envious of success?

I don't think many people envy me, because I am going to the kind of places where they really wouldn't be interested in earning their living.

But you would find a lot of journalists who envy the reputation that you have and would wish to acquire one like it.

I sometimes get a sense that I see myself being imitated, which I suppose is a kind of flattery. But this is human nature – if you are a junior league dogcatcher, you want to become a senior league dogcatcher, don't you?

What do you think are the greatest enemies of success in journalism?

Cynicism. The feeling that, 'Oh, it's just a job,' or it's something that you have to write this way to make the front page. You've got to make it this way to make the top of the television news. I have seen some serious shading of the truth in my time by journalists who should have known better and were too anxious to get their stories in the newspaper and in the television news, taking out some of the facts that should have been put in, going for the sensation, occasionally fabricating stories. This is done out of ambition and cynicism, and I wish I could say the practice has now ceased, but ...

It's still there. But surely those journalists don't last long, do they?

They shouldn't last long, but I've known one case where such a story won a major award. This is not sour grapes, because I was nowhere near it at the time, and the reporter made up a whole legend about an earthquake, and it was known to be a legend and the names were fabricated, and his managers and editors knew it, but when he got that award, the order was not to rock the boat. Journalism is a stable that needs cleaning from time to time.

But are there enough pressures within journalism to clean the stable, or are the pressures such that journalists prefer not to have their own profession looked at in the way that they insist on looking at other professions?

I think there's journalism and there's journalism – there are many tribes. Tabloid journalism, and its television equivalents, are extremely brutal with the truth. Broadsheet journalism, and its electronic equivalent have probably never been better. We've got the worst newspapers and the best newspapers in the world. We've got some of the best television in the world – the worst remains with the United States – but some of it's pretty bad. I think it's getting better, I actually do – the technology has caused us to sharpen up our act.

If you could gather all the young people who are interested in pursuing journalism as a profession, what advice would you give them?

I would tell them that unless they care about what they are reporting, they shouldn't be in journalism. They don't have to care so much as I care about the victims of war, but if they are reporting a football match of Norwich City versus Ipswich Town, they should care about the result and what it means to their audience. They should care enough to get it right and write it as well as they can. I think what I would communicate to them is that it is not just another way of earning a living, it is a rare privilege, and it has to be lived up to.

What advice would you give them about the techniques of successful reporting?

Writing is important, writing is vital. Cut out the surplus words and the tendency to show off and show people how much you know. You're talking to one person in that person's living room, and the language, the mood and the manner of doing it have to be tuned to that – the mood is very important. Analyse yourself, criticize your work, always be critical of your own work, because if you're not, I assure you, plenty of other people will be. It's my belief that a constant mark of good journalism is a certain dissatisfaction with itself as a body.

Are you a better, more successful reporter if you've made some kind of sacrifice at some time in your life?

I don't think you can be very good if you haven't come through a certain amount of hardship, but there's enough physical hardship that goes with the business. I think – and this is another huge benefit and privilege of war reporting – that people believe it makes you hardened and cynical, but it does nothing of the kind. It teaches you what not to take for granted, such as health and survival and peace. I certainly do not take these things for granted, especially after I had my brush with shrapnel some years ago. Every day after that is the first day of the rest of my life, so adversity brings great benefits.

And are failures an essential part of the route to success?

Absolutely. Everything defines itself by its opposite. I can tell you the feeling of being scooped – something that happens to all journalists sooner or later – produces a dreadful sinking feeling in the pit of the stomach, because you zigged when you should have zagged and the other guy's got the story and you didn't. That drives you, it's just normal elemental human competition. It applies probably more to journalism than to most things, but again, like adversity, you learn from it. 'What did I do wrong then? I'm not going to do it wrong again,' and you have to learn and relearn those lessons. So failure can be a wonderful spur to success.

When your time comes to leave this planet, what would you like people to say about you?

That he got it right, that he cared and that he made a difference.

DAVID BELLAMY

At 64, David Bellamy's trademark shows no sign of fading. Words tumbling over each other, he still speaks with the passion and excitement of someone who has just discovered something that will change the world. And, in a sense, he has!

The countless television appearances of the world's most famous campaigning botanist have changed the way millions of people view the life forms on this planet we call home. His latest book suggests that evolution is just a series of grotesque mistakes – and he testifies here that everything that contributed to his success in life happened by mistake.

His original unlikely ambition – to be a ballet dancer – was frustrated by his height and weight. He wisely gave up classes when, at the age of 14, he tipped the scales at 14 1/2 stone. To the despair of his strict Baptist parents, he managed to fail O-level maths five times; and after school just drifted through a series of odd jobs – minding deckchairs, plumbing, crane driving and painting lines on roads. It was while working as a lab technician that friends finally persuaded this rebel to go to college. Five years later he was a don in Durham University's botany department. And there he might have stayed if it hadn't been for the Torrey Canyon *oil tanker disaster in 1969, when John Craven's* Newsround *was looking for an environmental pundit. He was an instant hit – and his love affair with television began. Fame drove him in other directions too. He became a campaigner, joining the protests over the carving out of a motorway across Twyford Down, and being arrested for (successfully) opposing the building of a huge dam in Tasmania. Even more controversially, he risked accusations of 'selling out' by setting up a Conservation Foundation to advise industry how to be greener. Here he tells us that 'the only way to make conservation work is by holding hands with big business and saying, "Look, you can still make a profit out of doing it the right way."' He talks too about success in nature – about the need for 'a top carnivore'.*

He unexpectedly joined Sir James Goldsmith's Referendum Party to run against John Major in the 1997 General Election. To his great relief he was soundly defeated.

David Bellamy, what is your definition of success?

Successs is being able to do, I think, what I set out to do. I suppose, at some point, I said to myself, 'The world is in a terrible mess,' and set my sights on helping people to understand that. At one time, starry-eyed, I thought we would change the course of history and our way of thinking about the world. I'm certainly excited that there are more and more people talking about the things I was talking about 30 years ago. And the green renaissance is beginning, whether we like it or not. We've got Agenda 21 working throughout the world and some of the biggest firms are now trying to put their houses as right as they can, within the limits of the stock exchange, and so on.

Is being starry-eyed an essential ingredient for someone who starts out in pursuit of success in any particular field?

I suppose it is now, but it wasn't so much when I was a youngster. I think you have got to look further than your immediate horizons. My parents used to say, 'Goodness gracious, you get a job with a pension.' And when I got my job at the university, my mum and dad were over the moon. I'd done it, I'd got a job with a pension. It was going to be there for life, a life sentence. I don't think success is having a life sentence, but having a life, a purpose. I'm one of the most privileged guys on earth. I go round the world and I see all the problems – I hate the problems, of course, but I've seen that there are solutions to them – and I meet people. And I've probably seen more plants than any other botanist who has ever lived.

So can you be a success in your life without actually achieving your long-term goal?

Well, what is success? Is success the fact that at the height of my television career I was recognized round the world? Now that was amazing – to me that was everything. That was success. I was sitting in Heathrow Airport not very long ago, and a little girl in a wonderful astrakhan coat came up and spoke to me in Russian. I said, very slowly, 'I am very sorry, I don't speak Russian.' And she said, 'But, Sir, you do on our television sets in Russia.' So there is a very personal sense of success in something like that, but then, to me, real success is internal rather than how you are seen by other people. I have never watched myself on television – perhaps that's why I make such rotten television programmes! I just can't bear the thought of it. Everyone says, 'Send us a copy of your videotapes,' but I don't have any. I suppose the fact that you've got letters stuck on the end of your name means that you are a success to other people, but I wish my mum or dad had still been alive when I got my OBE. That's a personal thing. I think people who look at you and say, 'He's successful' create more enemies than friends for you.

So you're talking about two kinds of success – the public recognition of success and alongside that a sort of deep, inner personal feeling of success. Is that not dependent at all on public recognition?

I think if you get into that success thing, and perhaps I have, you can almost start to think you are God and you are going to change things. You're not God and you're not going to change things. Public recognition is terrific. I love it when I'm on my own on the train. But when I'm with my family I have no peace, no private life. I can't take my family to the theatre or to the Science Museum because I'll be in the corner signing autographs the whole time. It's quite amazing because I don't do that much television these days. And there is another element, which is that success, in so many people's minds, seems to be tied up with money. If I get on the train and go up north, I can be sure someone will say to me, 'Why don't you travel first-class?' Now that really does get up my nose. I usually answer, 'Because you meet a better class of person down here.' Not long ago, the *New Scientist* were interviewing successful scientists, and they wanted to know what my earnings were – more than £1 million, more than £10 million, or more than £100 million a year? And I said, 'Well, actually, if I had stayed in the university as a don, I'd earn more money than I do now.' They didn't believe me, but it was the truth. I make money, but I have to employ an awful lot of people who actually earn that money. But I wouldn't have been better off as a university don in terms of the success of my cause. I'm successful because I'm doing what I set out to do, even if I've not achieved.

Is it, then, important that you don't achieve your long-term goal? Is part of success the fact that there are always various stages and each one drives you on to the next?

I think you need challenges. It would be marvellous if we could turn round the whole world so that no more tropical rainforests were destroyed, no more open-net fishing was carried out, no more children were going to be abused and the world was a wonderful cuddly place. It's not going to be like that in my lifetime, but at least now people are talking about it.

To what extent do you think success is a product of your background and your upbringing? How did your parents influence you and set you out on your career?

Well, my father was from the East End of London. I don't know very much about my mother's roots. She was adopted and didn't know all that much about her own history. I think she came from a much more upmarket end of society. They were both devout Baptists. My father was a pharmacist and a lay preacher, and my grandfather was one of the Spurgeon deacons in the tabernacle. We weren't allowed to look at picture books on a Sunday, and I went to church from the time I was three. I looked up to them enormously.

I think they did fire an ambition in me because my mother wanted me to be a medical missionary. She would have loved to have done that herself but she was lame, and they wouldn't take disabled people. So she transferred that ambition to me.

I think Dad would have liked me to have been a Baptist preacher. And I'm sure I got my gift of the gab from my grandfather – they were both great speakers in the Baptist tradition. I got my love of everything else from Mum. She loved children and so do I. I only have to see a baby and I go broody, just like my mum did. I would have loved to have been a mum. To actually have had a baby of my own would, I think, have been the greatest success in my life. But I couldn't do that, so instead I've enjoyed being married and bringing up children.

I went through an awful period, because I saw people experiencing their roads to Damascus, and it never happened to me. So I thought I must be a very wicked, terrible person. But then I started to see some basic things wrong with the way the church was run, although I didn't criticize – I had respect for my parents.

Were you good at school?

No, I wasn't good at anything. I don't actually think that anyone really stimulated me to think. I mean, I learned French for seven years, but I didn't actually realize that there was a place called France where you spoke the blooming language. For some reason I'd set my sights on becoming a ballet dancer. I don't know why. I'd seen it on television – we had one of the first sets – and I thought it was beautiful. And there were all these children at school who could play the piano or sing or do something, but I couldn't do any of those things. Anyway I had lessons, and I did dance, but by the age of 14 and a half I was this big sissy, and I weighed 14 stone, so I had to play rugby instead. And I used that as an excuse for being a dunce at school. I failed O-level maths a lot of times and I failed O-level art and never actually got that. I left school without the A-levels I needed for university. Only two people ever inspired me at school. One was my English master, Danny Sayer, who was a wonderful Welshman. He said to me, 'David Bellamy, you've got the most amazing command of the English language. Why don't you learn to spell and punctuate?' The other guy was our biology master, Hutchins. They fired my ambition to be a medical missionary as well.

When I left school I got a whole series of wonderful jobs – working in factories, painting white lines down the road, working down the London sewers, being a deckchair attendant. And then I met the woman I eventually married, and I decided that if I was going to marry her, I'd better get a degree. Five years later I was a university don. So from drop-out to don – all because of one woman!

So your wife was the inspiration for that, but how did you manage to achieve it, recover from the inadequacies of at least part of your early education?

Well, I don't think I ever recovered from those gaps. But I did have A-levels in botany and zoology, and I'd managed to get an A-level in physics, but you had to have four at the same sitting, in those days, to be a medic. I never quite managed that until I met Rosemary. She was doing a pre-nursing course and was persuaded by two teachers, George Fluck and Ned Norris, both zoologists, that really she should go to university and read for a degree. I thought, goodness, I've got to do something. And I did, I just plugged away and got my four A-levels at the same sitting. I didn't get into real university because my academic record was so grotty, so I did my degree part-time at Chelsea Polytechnic, and Rosemary went to Queen Mary's College.

Once I got to be a university don it was such fun, bouncing ideas off the top five per cent of students in this country. I never actually taught anyone anything. I would give a lecture and there'd be six times more people there than there should have been at my lectures, and probably no botanists at all because I wasn't teaching botany very well. If there was something I didn't understand, I would set it as a seminar and the students would all teach me. It was a wonderful time, and my 22 years at Durham University were immensely rewarding.

What was your technique? What made your teaching of botany different?

Perhaps it was the fact that when the students came I used to say, 'Look, when I was taught biology I was taught the five characters of living things. But inanimate things can do all these things as well, except reproduce. And I can't reproduce by myself, either. I enjoy doing it with my wife, and together we reproduce. So that means I'm dead. That's a stupid definition for life. Let's find a new one.' And then we did. The first course I taught the students was plant anatomy, and I used to say, 'Look, at the end I'm going to set you an essay. I want you to go in through a plant root as if you were a molecule of water, a sentient molecule of water, and describe to me the root going through the plant. I'll have taught you anatomy, you'll know all about how a plant works, and, OK, so you're going to describe it from the inside out.' Most people didn't do that question, but the ones that did are now very, very good ecologists all round the world. It's a great privilege, that anywhere I go, I might meet former students of mine. I'll probably have forgotten their names, but they'll say, 'Do you remember that first-year course when you made us crawl through that damn plant?' And of course I did that on the BBC with *Backyard Safari with David Bellamy*.

Is there a sense in which the best kind of success, and the quickest and most lasting success, comes to people who think laterally and are prepared to challenge the conventional ways of doing things?

I think so. People listen to you then, don't they? It gets a bit boring listening to the same old thing. I was recently asked by one of America's top advertising agencies whether I would go and tell them why I looked sideways at things and didn't answer like everyone else. I think all they really wanted me there for was to see whether I would advertise McDonald's, but it was interesting to meet these guys who must, themselves, look laterally at things in order to make these amazing adverts.

I think that's what storytelling is. In an awful lot of natural history programmes today they tell the story in the first breath and then spend the rest of the time boring people about it. You've got to craft a story that goes all the way through and comes up with, perhaps, an entirely different answer at the other end. I've put up a series called *Radical Solutions* to just about every television company in Britain, but no one's really interested at all because they just don't make that kind of documentary any more. Remember the great James Burke and all those wonderful two-hour things we used to have on science? They've gone now, which I think is a shame. That's why we're not getting youngsters to become scientists. I don't think every youngster expects to make ten million pounds a year as a scientist, but they do want to be able to spend their lives using this thing between their ears.

There was a wonderful book published last year called *Beauty and the Beastly* by an American scientific writer. She'd interviewed a lot of female scientists, and one of them said, 'You know, it is so exciting to be a scientist today, because we are actually moving to a stage where we think we're answering questions.' And that is what I try to do. I say, 'Look, we don't know how a water molecule gets to the top of a tree; nobody does. Right, the first thing we've got to understand is the plumbing system.' In one of my early programmes for the BBC, we cut down a mature oak tree and killed it by sticking it in a tank of picric acid. As the tree died, the water still went up, and we measured how much was actually transpired. People still say, 'That was absolutely amazing, that was real science.' I think television has missed the opportunity of becoming the great educator of the world. If only education had capitalized on it in the days when the whole family would gather round the television to watch David Attenborough. Those days have passed in Britain. They're there in developing countries – there people all sit round and watch the television as a family – and it still could be an educational force there, but I think we've rather missed the boat in this country. I don't think we're going to create new Magnus Pykes, Miriam Stoppards, David Bellamys or David Attenboroughs now that family viewing's gone.

What do you think are the secrets of your success? Why should you have made it and others not?

I think I've just been immensely lucky. Everything that ever happened to me happened by mistake. In fact I'm writing a book about how evolution is just a series of grotesque mistakes, and certainly my own life has always worked like that. I grew too big, so I couldn't be a ballet dancer, I met my wife and stopped being a drop-out and became a very happy and contented man. And then I was working on marine pollution when the *Torrey Canyon* disaster happened and, bingo, I was dragged screaming from my ivory tower and was stuck on a sewer pipe with John Craven, who was then a junior reporter with the BBC. We've both been on telly ever since.

So that was your big break, and there was an element of luck involved in that, but you'd clearly done a lot of work to gain a reputation that enabled you to create your own luck. You wouldn't have been there if you hadn't had a reputation for being able to talk articulately and sensibly about the issues involved.

I don't know. I wasn't known on television although I'd spoken a couple of times on the radio. I just stood on that sewer pipe, and when John Craven pointed at the stuff coming out of the end of it and said, 'Tell us about marine pollution,' I said, 'Well, the stuff coming out there is shit to you and me, but to a mussel, a filter feeder, it's cordon bleu cookery.' And Paul Fox, the boss at Yorkshire Television, said, 'Sign the man up,' and I just went on making television programmes for both the BBC and Yorkshire Television. That was pure luck. The only talent I ever had was that I could remember the Latin names of plants. That's a pretty useless talent, really, but wow, look where it's taken me – six times round the world this year. If I hadn't had that break of meeting Rosemary, and if I hadn't had that break on television, I might never have been able to do all the things I've done. I've never really worked very hard. We have a working-men's club in our village and they won't let me join, because they say I've never done a bloody day's work in my life. It's true – I haven't. I just enjoy myself.

What do you reckon are your greatest successes, the things you look back on and of which you can say, 'I was at or pretty close to the peak with these'?

I suppose it was helping to save the Franklin River in Tasmania, although I personally had very, very little to do with it. I'd been down there and done some campaigning, and Bob Brown, the most brilliant conservationist in the world, who is now in the Senate in the Commonwealth Parliament in Australia, asked me to go there and be arrested on my 50th birthday. When I was arrested it was in front of seven camera crews, and I was virtually saying, 'Now I will be seen being arrested by 152 million people.' That actually did save that river, but it was nothing to do with me – I was just the ugly face who could get the press there. That's the power you have when you speak through this thing called the television set.

And one of the most amazing things was meeting all the people involved in the protest. There was one very nice young lady called Myrtle, who taught at one of the public schools in Australia. She was really putting her job on the line to come on this picket line, and she hated it. She'd never lived in the bush before, and we were living in pretty bad conditions – land leeches in your mouth when you woke up in the morning, and so on. She came up to me on the day I was going to be arrested and said, 'David, I can't stand this any more. Can I be arrested with you today, please?' And she had dressed herself absolutely immaculately in a Harris tweed skirt, the works. It was a privilege to stand alongside people like that.

The Franklin River debate was a real turning point in conservation and I was invited to talk to Mrs Thatcher. I expected her to say, 'You naughty boy, you've let the country down – a university professor who has been put in jail!' But she didn't, she said, 'There are votes in this green business, aren't there?' And an awful lot kicked off from that. Look at all the picket lines round Britain. And they're not just the hairies – the ferals, as they call them in Australia – they are ordinary people. They're genuinely there because they are worried about what they are handing on to their children.

You could have remained a successful television presenter. What is it that made you involve yourself in this additional hassle of going out and campaigning, of using your fame and success as a platform to campaign?

Well, for a start, money doesn't matter very much to me. I didn't sit there and say, 'Oh, I won't make as much money if I'm a campaigner.' Becoming a campaigner was another of those things that just happened. I took a whole group of students out to West Africa to work on the biodiversity of tropical rainforests long before people were talking about it. We were actually studying the phytosociology, how tropical rainforests are put together. We didn't know the names of the plants, but all the kids in the local schools did, and they would come out and tell us what they called them. And then some of them stopped coming, and I'd say, 'Where's Boco?' 'Oh, he died yesterday.' 'Why the hell did Boco die?' They were dying from malnutrition, because their rainforest and their food had gone. They were given jobs on the plantation or whatever it was, and they couldn't afford to buy Western food. And here we were in the most fecund living system on Earth, right in the tropics, where they should be able to feed an awful lot of people. That's why I became a campaigner. It just shows how thick I am, because most people who take up a cause don't actually have to bury a kid, or a few kids, to get switched on to that cause.

You find that the whole problem is a series of vested interests which really couldn't give a damn about ordinary people. The saddest statistic I've heard is that there are now 358 billionaires in the world, who, between them, own more money than the annual earnings of half the world put together. And do they actually care about that half of the world? I do.

In fact your campaigning has helped your career as well, hasn't it? Haven't the two gone in tandem?

I don't know about that, actually. Certainly since my media campaigning began I have not been allowed to make as many television programmes.

Why do you think that is?

Perhaps it's just that I make rotten television programmes these days! But, as I said before, they don't make my sort of documentaries any more. The ones they do make are rather cuddly ones which say there's nothing wrong with the world.

Is there anything that we can learn about success, about rising to the top of the pile, from nature? Anything that happens in nature which creates a different definition of success? For example, is nature more ruthless than humans?

There is no top of the pile in nature, because success is being part of the evolving thing. I know – I don't believe, I know – that evolution doesn't stop at the organism. What use would you or I be if there wasn't a BBC or other media? Or if there weren't other people nice enough to pay to watch us? That is why, I think, my definition of success is doing what you want to do, and doing it as a part of something else. You can't actually be the tops on your own. If there weren't other people there, you couldn't be top of anything anyway, could you? So you've got to be a part. Basically, it's symbiosis.

That's why, 13 years ago, I set up the Conservation Foundation. I really stuck my neck out and said, 'Look, it's great fun standing on picket lines and stopping things, but we don't have any money. The only way we're really going to make this thing work is by actually holding hands with big businesses and saying, "Look, you can still make a profit out of doing it the right way".' This world itself was dead once. If I'm asked, 'Is there life on any other planet?' I say, 'There absolutely can't be.' Because if you look at all the planets coming out from the sun, they get colder and colder. We should be a blooming sight colder or warmer than we actually are, and the reason we're not is that we've got this great living envelope created by life on this Earth. I'm a part of that. You've either got to say that you like the species you're part of, which means we'll go on trying to cover the whole world with concrete, and it's going to be a pretty awful ending, or we've got to adapt.

The most telling book I've ever read is the *Waning of Humaneness* by Konrad Lorenz. He was the father of ethology, the study of animal behaviour. He hatched some goose eggs, and he knew that although goslings had a certain amount of knowledge already in them, he could imprint some things on them, for example that he was their mum. The first half of this book is the most wonderful exposition of organic evolution. He says that 60 million years ago some little camel-like quadrupeds found the sea full of food and nothing using it, so they leaped in and became the whales and dolphins we now know. Then some primates swinging around in the trees tried the same thing, but they couldn't live in the sea so they became human beings. But the second half of the book kicked me right in the guts because it said that by the end of the century, 64 per cent of the human race will be conditioned, like the goslings, to living in concrete. But they won't realize what's happening. So carry on, Attenborough, making those films for another 50 years, because they let people in the concrete jungle know. And Lorenz said that it's going to be very, very much more difficult to persuade those people to save the world.

So nature is a whole series of important interactions, but we also know that in nature there are some plants which, in pursuit of reaching the top, will actually quietly strangle and choke others, and the same applies as far as animals are concerned. So do you think that, because we're a part of nature, we have inherited some of those unsavoury tendencies in pursuit of our own route to the top?

Yes, this is all to do with the waning of humaneness. What is humaneness and can a humane organism actually survive? You see, if you don't have a top carnivore, the whole system collapses. I've been studying the central

Indian Ocean for a long time, and when I went out to the Chagos Bank 25 years ago there were lots of sharks there. It was the most exciting diving in the world, and the coral reefs were perfectly safe. Now there are no sharks left, they've all been fished out. The Chagos Bank is now in great danger because up come all the parrot fish to eat the algae which grows on the coral and this kills off the coral. If you don't have carnivores, you don't have the system, and that's that. On Kangaroo Island, in Australia, there are now 2,000 too many koalas and they're eating their food out. The Department of Conservation were going to go and shoot the things, and there was a hue and cry, 'Don't shoot the koalas!' So what do you do with them? Do you let them starve to death, and totally ruin their habitat? Do you cull them? Do you sterilize them? Do you move them to a zoo? Of course, if you suggest any of these things there's going to be somebody who says, 'Oh no, you can't do that.' And that is the problem: you can't be top of the pile all on your own. What is the use of being a brain surgeon and earning a lot of money if there's no one to empty your dustbins, or look after the sewage you flush down the toilet?

Ananda Coomaraswamy, whose mum was English and whose dad was Sri Lankan, became one of the world's leading authorities on oriental art and ended up in the San Francisco Museum. He wrote the most wonderful book called *The Sources of Wisdom*, first published in 1911, in which he said that the withering touch of our civilization is that we go along and replace art and craft with mass production. Once you've done that you've smashed up the human world. The illustration that he gave was the caste system. When the Brits got to Sri Lanka, he said, they had a wonderful caste system there, but the Brits said, 'Oh, you can't have Untouchables,' and smashed the caste system to pieces. But, he said, if you had actually studied the caste system, you would have seen that the Untouchable was the guy who worked with soil and built the earth dams which held back the water coming down from the native rainforest to water the paddy fields. When, at the end of the year, all the food was given out, he was given the most because he did the most important job. And that's what we have got wrong, you see. We are never going to sort it out, because are you going to become a brain surgeon if you're only going to earn the same amount of money as the bloke who empties your dustbins? In the world everything has a place, and tooth and claw is the way it is maintained.

Why do think some people rise to the top while others don't?

Well, I would have to query success. It brings us back to those 358 billionaires who have all that money, but they don't actually need it. There's so much money awash in the world at the moment, and people don't know what to invest it in. Yet 100,000 people will die today of malnutrition or from dirty water. There are between 60,000 and 100,000 people being forced today to leave their rural roots for the 'promise' of the throwaway society. I'd like to see those 358 billionaires sitting round a table and discussing what they can do to help the whole world, not just themselves. Was it Ted Turner who suggested that, instead of having a listing of the top 100 richest people, we should have the Miserable Old Buggers awards for the richest people who give away the least money.

But do you think that every society needs people who do strive for the top in order to pull up those in the lower ranks of society?

Talking in botanical terms they, in some ways, are the tall trees. We always think of plants as rather benign, wonderful things, but as soon as a plant unfolds its leaves it is in competition for light with every other plant underneath it. When it is expanding its roots it is in competition with every other plant around it for nutrients. If it doesn't do the job properly, it's had it. Tropical rainforests must be in total balance, so some trees must fall down and die and be chewed up by bacteria and fungi to release the carbon monoxide needed by other plants.

So as far as the plant world is concerned, success is based on a healthy, tough competition that is endemic throughout the plant world – the competitive instinct is there?

I have no answer to that because, of course, I don't believe plants can think. Plants don't know they've got to stop, they just stop. What happens is that all of a sudden the forest starts to use too much energy, too many nutrients, and it goes acid. The trees get fewer and fewer and, until we have another Ice Age, that's it. Humans are the only organism – with the possible exception of whales and dolphins, although we have no proof – which can learn from history, either natural history or people-made history, and perhaps plan a better way ahead. I met the head of Du Pont, one of the biggest chemical companies in the world, and he said, 'Do you know why we've got an environmental policy?' I said, 'No.' He told me he had two daughters at high school and they came home one day and said, 'Dad, people won't speak to us because you run a dirty chemical company. What are you going to do about it?' So now they are doing amazing things and their mission is to achieve zero emission. They will put nothing into the world which will cause any problems. So perhaps it is beginning to work.

And technology is helping that?

Well, certainly technology can do a lot. My main job in conservation is as president of Population Concern, and we really are winning there, because the country which now leads the world in family planning is Italy, followed by Spain. I think we've got to come back to the village concept of things. Well, that's as far as I've got – I'm only 63 and I hope I've got another 20 years to go on thinking – but as far as I can see the only role model we've ever had which has worked in human terms is a unit of about 1,000 people, who have some jurisprudence over what they're doing.

Remember the great Summit in Rio? All those 184 heads of state and their representatives met there, and the reason they went was because they were worried that the world was beginning to collapse about them, and they understood that they'd never sort it out from the top. They said, 'We'll work from the bottom upwards.' They stole the great green slogan which I went into prison shouting all those years ago – 'Think Globally and Act Locally' – and they said that, although local authorities, schools and businesses think that it's a global problem, if we start putting it right from the bottom upwards, perhaps we'll win. And it's very exciting to see Agenda 21 actually beginning to happen all the way around the world.

What are the principles for success? Clearly we can learn from the animal kingdom that you need to adapt, that's one thing. What else?

I think you have to have a pretty broad base of knowledge in the area you're going to be successful in. Lots of gurus have come and gone, but haven't known what they were talking about, so you've got to have basic knowledge. You've also got to be moderately big-headed. I always thought I was a tremendously shy person, and as a youngster in my Baptist community I undoubtedly was. My parents were very good role models, but I knew I was different. It was through ballet and the arts that I discovered there was an extrovert in there somewhere.

What are your biggest failures, and more importantly, how did you recover from them?

I've never had any real failures. I've certainly had disappointments. I get immensely disappointed when someone in whom I absolutely believed, 100 per cent, turns out to be a real basket. But that's his failure, not mine. My failure has probably been as a father, because I've been away too much. My children have grown up in fits and starts, and how Rosemary has ever put up with me, I don't know. I do think I've failed as a family man.

Do you think every successful person has to make some degree of sacrifice in their personal lives to achieve that success in his or her chosen profession?

Well, it's a very good excuse, isn't it? The best thing that ever happened to me was finding Rosemary and being able to marry her, to have a living partnership with her and to produce children. We always said we'd have two children and adopt two, because there are too many people on this earth already, and we ended up having one and adopting four. That, to me, is the absolute joy of my life.

I suppose you do have to make sacrifices, but you don't think about them as sacrifices, you just get on with it, don't you? Sometimes you wonder how you are going to make it up to your family, but you can't. I'm very, very lucky in that I've had a wife who has stuck with me through thick and thin, and has done all the things that I really should have been doing with our children. Perhaps, if I'd have been born 50 years later, I could have been a ballet dancer after all. They have big dancers these days.

You've already mentioned some of your heroes, but are there other people – big or small, past or present, in any field – whose achievements you really admire?

Emily Davison, the suffragette who threw herself under the king's horse. She gave everything for her cause and I'm quite sure that act was a great turning point in the suffragette movement. I've always said there were certain things that would make me do that if I had to, but whether I would have the guts to do it in the end, I don't know. And there's Wangari Matai, the amazing woman who set up the Green-belt movement in Kenya. If I'm ever really down and I am embraced by Wangari Matai, then my batteries are recharged. Petra Kelly, the leader of the German Greens who first put the Green Party into the Bundestag, was amazing too. She didn't commit suicide, as it is assumed. Someone must have killed her. She was too full of life ever to have allowed anything to snuff out her life in that way. And I've mentioned Ananda Coomaraswamy. My dad and mum were very successful. They enjoyed their lives and they both went to their graves knowing they were going to heaven. That's a pretty successful way of living.

What is your reaction to critics? Do you have any kind of inner mechanism that enables you to deal with the slings and arrows of outrageous criticism?

Well, it worries you most when it first starts, but then you tend to say to yourself, 'There's no such thing as bad publicity.' I did get very, very concerned when I opened *The Times* to find a picture of children in the Chinese dying rooms alongside a photograph of myself captioned, 'David Bellamy backs China.' I shouldn't have worried because it got me a lot of job offers in China. I got a bit cross when another paper claimed that Greenpeace, Friends of the Earth, Jonathan Porritt and Anita Roddick said I should get out of Nigeria and Shell because I was causing harm. When I phoned up Greenpeace and Friends of the Earth, they told me they hadn't said any such thing. It was at least partly fabricated by the papers. That hurts.

What do you think are the greatest enemies of success?

Laziness and arrogance. And other people's jealousy. I don't like jealousy, although in some ways your own jealousy helps you to be successful because it pushes you on.

So it's not an unacceptable emotion to be jealous of people who are successful?

I try not to be. I was jealous of people in academia who got more money for their research programmes or whatever. But working in the media I've always tried to avoid jealousy, because no one person really does it on their own, do they? There are all those wonderful technicians who make the whole thing work and cut out all your mistakes.

You have said that money isn't important to you but is it a driving factor with you at all? Does it drive you on a bit?

I don't know what I'd do with it if I had it. I mean, look how I'm dressed. I was given this shirt – I've never ever been out and bought myself any clothes. My wife says, 'You need a new pair of trousers,' and off she goes and gets them. I suppose I'd like money so that I could go to the ballet more often – it's so blooming expensive now. I'd like to be able to go skiing. To take seven people skiing now, you need to take out a mortgage. Basically I think I'm a miser. If I had money, it would probably pile up and I'd be worried about burglars. I don't even know my bank manager – that's how little I care about money. I don't think it's a great driving force.

Has success changed you at all?

I think it has given me a greater drive to continue onwards, rather than go back. I'm 63, and I thought perhaps when I reached 60 that I should retire and give my last ten years to Rosemary. But she said, 'You'd be such a miserable swine, and I wouldn't want you like that.' And, as I said, I think it's made me a worse father than perhaps I could have been. But I'm a damned good grandad, and do spend a lot more time with my grandson than I ever did with my own children.

Is there a downside to success?

I don't think there possibly can be, unless you go over the top and have to be dishonest – and I mean really dishonest – to get your success.

Everyone embroiders stories, don't they? I could have been an immensely rich person if I'd given the wrong evidence about certain things, or advertised certain products. I have been asked to advertise everything. I have done some advertising because I needed to finance the time I've spent on conservation. But now, unless I can put my hand on my heart and say, 'This product will actually do some good and no harm,' I wouldn't do it. I was also offered a directorship of one company and they asked me what sort of fee I would like. I said, 'I couldn't take a fee because people would say I'd been bought.' So they said, 'Well, how about a company car?' My one vice is fast cars. They must have known that and they suggested a Lamborghini. I said, 'How could I be your environmental adviser and drive a car like that?' 'Well, it could be green with a catalytic converter,' they said. I told them they didn't know what they were talking about, and I said, 'No.' My youngest son, who was then about seven, said, 'You bloody fool, Dad.'

But success involves knowing when to say no, doesn't it? You can't bowl headlong down a particular route taking everything that comes your way?

Of course. You've got to know when to say no. Either that, or you've got to be bloody lucky and never get found out!

If you could gather together in one room all the young people who look up to you and want to be as successful as you have been in the environmental field, in the television field, in the lecturing field – what advice would you give them?

Goodness, that's an almost impossible question to answer. I would say, 'First of all, you've got to get a damned good degree, a damned good grounding. But you also have to have something inside you already which really wants to understand plants. I don't think you can be successful without that desire for knowledge. Some might be driven by money; others by knowledge. I think it is knowledge that drives all good scientists. Singers are driven by seeking perfect pitch, dancers by perfecting steps, it all takes a hell of a lot of practice. The practice involved in being a natural historian is knowing your subject. I think everyone who has been successful in making good documentaries really does know what the hell he's talking about. But I don't think there are going to be as many well-paid jobs in the media as there have been in the past.

What would you like people to say about you when your time comes to leave this life?

When he died his remains were recycled to help other plants to grow.

SIR JOHN BIRT

The iron resolve with which John Birt has pushed through difficult and often unpopular changes at the BBC was forged by the ambition of his parents and his early schooling in Liverpool under the Irish Christian Brothers. He describes it as 'a notoriously fierce disciplinarian teaching which took lots of kids from relatively humble backgrounds and propelled them to university'. For him, the university was Oxford, his aptitude for maths and physics pointing towards a degree in engineering. But within days of arriving there he became absorbed by film-making, and abandoned all interest in engineering. Only in his final year did he cram for his finals so he wouldn't disappoint his parents by not obtaining a degree.

By now he knew his only career choice was between films and television. Joining Granada TV as a production trainee, he was editor of the flagship World in Action *by the time he was 24. David Frost headhunted him to produce the* Frost Programme *for LWT , and his rise up the management hierarchy was rapid. He stayed for 17 years – only once tempted outside when he unsuccessfully applied for the job of first chief executive of Channel 4. En route, he devised the cerebral current affairs programme* Weekend World, *and (with Peter Jay) used the pages of* The Times *to underline the importance of journalism's 'mission to explain'. Hence the attraction of the approach from the BBC in 1987 to restructure their news and current affairs. He sacrificed his considerable share options for a period of public service, and soon found himself promoted to the top job of Director-General with a brief to reform what he saw as a 'horribly bureaucratic' organisation. He talks here about how he tackled that task, about what he knew would be 'the almost certain opposition from within and without', and the 'national vilification' that he experienced in moving the BBC 'from a command economy to a trading economy'. He talks frankly of the hostility faced by people trying to succeed in certain kinds of jobs in Britain, and says that 'what pains me most is the impact that has on my family'. Knighted in 1998, he plans to step down before the milennium and seek pastures new. But, he insists here that his job is 'by no means over', and, in spelling out his core philosophy, he outlines the key qualities that will mark out the successful programme-makers within the BBC of the future.*

John Birt, what is your definition of success?

I think somebody in the sort of job that I'm in defines their success in rather personal terms – what is it that you think you're trying to do, and how well do *you* think you're doing? These may not necessarily be the same as how the world defines success. More obvious and simply measured definitions of success – winning the FA Cup, for instance – are not so appropriate if you're running a large organization. In this instance, you've got tens of thousands of people involved in a huge welter of activity, and the world can't so easily measure your successes as sometimes you can yourself.

Which is more important, personal success, doing what you want to do to your own best ability, or the kind of professional success that puts you up there with your head above the parapet, taking all the knocks and the blows, and being publicly recognized for that success?

In my case it's very much the former. I'm driven by purely personal ambitions and want to succeed by my own lights. I'm not suggesting that being recognized in the world as a success doesn't figure at all, because it does with all human beings to some extent or other. Everybody likes to win a prize. It always slightly amuses me when I see a programme-maker with impeccable socialist credentials, win a prize – they're just as pleased as anyone else. There is a competitive spirit in everybody. If I play sport I like to win, so of course that consideration is there, but much more important is to sense that you're doing a worthwhile job – and to believe that you are succeeding in ambitions as you, yourself, define them.

Are there enormous forces trying to shake you off your personal targets?

Yes, there generally are in public life. There probably always have been, but those forces are especially intense today – not just for me, but for anybody involved in public life, especially running a large institution like the BBC, which comes under ever-greater public scrutiny. And of course, almost any kind of activity will attract opposition and critics.

Has control been particularly important for you? Control in the sense that you have a vision, and then, as you set about driving it through, you have to bring in people who think like you and support you?

It's a very good question, but I dislike the word control. No one person can change an organization alone. But you put the question in exactly the right way because I think all the evidence – and I've discussed this a great deal with other people in large organizations – is that you simply cannot change an organization unless all the people that you work with broadly share a vision and a strategy for pursuing it, and agree a common set of objectives. A lot of people are needed to bring about change, and I think a lot of organizations make the mistake of pursuing a programme of change without all of the top people agreeing to it. Then it almost always goes wrong.

Is it particularly more difficult when you're trying to turn around the bureaucratic supertanker which was the BBC? Do you have to be ruthless? Do you have to take some very tough decisions, about which you feel, 'I don't really like to do this, but I've got to if I'm going to reach my long-term goals'?

I think we *were* horribly bureaucratic. There are tens of thousands of activities in an organization like this and every single activity was directly funded. No one person could possibly have known everything that was going on and whether the activities were adding value for the licence-fee payer, or whether they were efficient in their delivery. We have transformed this organization. I emphasize it is not a task I have done alone. We are now delivering far better value for money than in the past. It has, by any standards, been a tough, difficult and very painful job. Just in the last few years, we've made the best part of 10,000 people redundant. We're not the only institution in the country to go through that. The path that the BBC has trodden in recent years is one that plainly has parallels both in the private and in the public sector. We've done it pretty rapidly and I think, by any standards, we've done it pretty well.

We make more programmes and we make better programmes. And we are performing very well in most areas of activity, including the non-programme areas. In the past, we set world standards of excellence in our programmes and in our craft, but not in our management, but I think in areas like finance we have greatly improved our performance, to the benefit of the licence-fee payer. To bring about a programme of reform on that scale is very, very hard work. And it's a job by no means over. I could give you scores and scores of examples, indeed hundreds, where we have needed to sort ourselves out. One was making sure our huge spend on information technology was well spent and was going to lead to better programmes made at a lower cost.

So you can't do all this unless you're prepared to undertake a vast programme of work, and yes, it does require you to be pretty tough-minded because all of this is about changing: changing the circumstances in which people work; changing the structures in which they work; changing relationships. One of the key ideas we introduced at the BBC was to move away from a command economy to a trading economy, where hardly anybody in the organization is directly funded. Almost everybody is in competition with the outside world and has to sell something. That's a profound change for an organization which for the best part of 75 years had acted as a command economy, indeed one that was constantly expanding in real terms throughout its history. Suddenly to say to everybody, 'Sorry, the money's not coming in any longer, revenue is flat, you've got to learn to trade,' was a vast change. And of course an awful lot of people couldn't manage that, and a lot of people voluntarily left the BBC because they couldn't accommodate that scale of change. We've also sucked in a lot of new talents from the outside world, and promoted a lot of young people who had the flexibility to make the change and wanted to acquire the new skills. The sort of people who are managing the BBC now have changed a very great deal in terms of age and outlook from ten years ago. In the process, yes, sometimes you've got to be very decisive – I prefer words like decisive, nobody uses words like ruthless in respect of themselves. You have to be decisive about people and organizations, knowing that in the old order there were groups of people who had worked together for a long period of time, and enjoyed each other's company. They had often worked in conditions of considerable latitude, some would even say luxury. I knew I was going to take decisions which would completely overturn what, for those people, was a way of life. But I only ever did it because I thought that the gain was in better programmes and more programmes for the licence-fee payer, and that's the set of ideas that's always driven me. Although some individuals lose, there are gainers too; the more talented, the more capable, the more able, the more energetic, benefit from a period of change. I'm not surrounded by a lot of moaning minnies, I'm surrounded by a lot of people who've proved to themselves and to everybody else that they can manage change on a major scale and produce something which, at the end of the day, is a lot better than what was there before.

Did you ever have any doubts when the criticism was at its peak, or when a new surge of criticism came along?

It's a terrible thing to say, but no, I never ever had any doubts, which is not to say that you do everything perfectly. I occasionally make mistakes about people. You underestimate some people and you overestimate others, and if I had my time over again I'd do lots of small things differently, but in terms of the overall drive I never had a moment of doubt. I've had more than my fair share of moments of misery, because sometimes, especially when you're bringing about a lot of change, you reach moments where there is a critical mass of opposition, and that's not particularly pleasant. But as long as you know why you're there and you know where your critics are coming from, you also know how to handle it. You know that 99 times out of 100 you come through it. If you have a strong sense of direction, you almost always come out the other side.

Some of the criticisms against you have come from former BBC people - John Tusa called you a vandal, Dennis Potter called you a Dalek. Were you surprised at the vehemence of the criticism?

No, I wasn't. Some artists who work for the BBC come to me and say, 'The work-force has experienced a great deal of pain. They've gone through massive dislocation.' They can remember what life used to be like and they resent the change; they don't like having to work much harder and in much more difficult circumstances, and being insecure about their jobs. And they pass on that unhappiness to people who come to me and say, 'Isn't there another way? Isn't there a better way?' Over and over again, one sits down and tries to explain the basic facts of life; that the licence fee hasn't gone up since 1985 – we've had a flat income. Right across the world you see public service broadcasting in decline, but throughout this period, the BBC has grown and developed. We are still maintaining our classic role of supporting our national culture, safeguarding the quality of the national debate, extending educational horizons. We have very strong networks that are performing extremely well in the marketplace, and yet our programmes are as creative as they ever have been. We're paying the people who work for us at market levels and we've managed to fund the rising costs of sports rights. It's a near miracle. We're a dynamic public service broadcaster in a world where most others are in decline. One has to try to make that argument. Not everybody finds it convincing. People find it hard to reconcile it with their day-to-day experience of the BBC being a harder place to work in.

Some people are resentful for completely different reasons. Perhaps they have been passed over for jobs they want. That happens in any organization. There are a hundred different reasons why people would be opposed to what's happening in the BBC. Some who oppose change are very sincere and pained and others less so, they're more self-interested.

Is it a help or a hindrance to have the image that you have? Is there a way in which it could actually be a help, in that when you say something, people jolly well believe it?

You don't seek an image, though a lot of people think you do. My image before I came to the BBC was very different from the image afterwards. To some extent, your image comes from the circumstances which you operate in.

How was it different?

I certainly wasn't so well known. I was a senior figure on ITV, a director of programmes, but I'd never been involved in substantial controversy. I wouldn't like to say what my image was, but it certainly wasn't what it soon became. I came to the BBC in the middle of turmoil and I was seen, as it were, like a Protestant being made Pope. I was the most senior person brought into the BBC for decades. There was a strong sense within the organization that it didn't need an outsider to tell it what it knew how to do very well indeed.

Image may, of course, come from your personality, but I'd also suggest that it very often comes from the circumstances in which you operate. I've observed it in others; suddenly, by some freak mix of events, they become landed with an image which is at odds with their view of themselves, and then they invest a huge amount of time, effort and sometimes money in trying to overturn it. I would argue that that is nearly impossible – so you shouldn't waste a great deal of time trying to overturn an image. You are, to some extent, stuck with it. I don't happen to believe – and I don't know anybody close to me who does – that my public image bears much relationship to my private personality. But, again, I'm not protesting about that; I think it would be a waste of time.

There's a certain amount of fear associated with your image in the minds of some people. That's got to be a help in driving through radical change.

I genuinely don't like the idea and I don't believe that it's in any part of my make-up. I'm not an aggressive person, for instance, I don't like dirty play on the sports field; I'm not attracted to violence; I don't believe in engendering fear. I strongly believe in trying to bring people along with me. I believe that we have developed, across the organization at the top level, a clear consensus about the right way to go. You can't do that unless you carry your colleagues with you and I believe I have achieved that. I hate people who bully or use the strength of their personality to get their way. That isn't how I operate. I always try to operate through argument and persuasion.

I don't believe fear plays any part, but what I do accept is that I am seen as somebody who, when he sets out on a course of action, means to achieve it. If it's a legitimate objective, I will really fight very, very hard to achieve it. There's a famous BBC saying which is, 'Once the decision is known, we can set about overturning it' – that's very much part of the BBC's culture. I came from a culture where you made a decision after a great deal of thought and then everybody got on with it, so it was a great shock to me to join an organization where they waited to find out what your decision was going to be so they knew how they would set about overturning it. It took me a long time to understand that that was what was going on, but it was. If I'm party to a decision, then I try to communicate to the world that once it's made, we'll all work to achieve it. I'm very intolerant of people trying to overturn properly made decisions.

Do you think that in the past your eye has been so firmly fixed on change that, given the size of the organization, you haven't had the time to communicate your message as well as you would have liked to people on the shop floor?

Well, it's nice of you to try to give us an excuse, but I don't think it's good enough. If you say to me, 'Do you think we have communicated well?' then my answer is that we certainly have not succeeded in communicating with our work-force, in spite of having done a lot of work on it. We've professionalized internal communications – as lots of organizations have. We've spent a great deal of time and quite a lot of money trying to do it. But have we succeeded yet? No.

Why not?

A lot of academic work has gone into internal communication, and I think broadly what that work finds is that of all the things we have talked about, this is the most difficult. I think there is general agreement that the only truly effective form of internal communication is down the management line. The old-fashioned idea that a single person at the top of a company can perfectly communicate with all 25,000 workers is not, in our case, a useful model. What all the professionals and academics advise you, is that the real trick is to be able to pass down, at every single level of the organization, the understanding of the problems that the organization faces, and to ensure that at every level those problems are understood and reinterpreted appropriately. And that takes a very long time. If you say have we succeeded, I would say, 'No, I don't think we have.'

Do you think you're making some inroads into the problem?

Yes. We do surveys of staff opinion and we know a fair amount about how successful or not we are. We know, for instance, that our staff are actually happy in their work. They find it very rewarding and very fulfilling. And they are, generally speaking, quite happy with their immediate management. (That's a bit of a general statement because it varies from area to area across the organization.) But as they look up the organization, they are less and less happy and feel more and more disengaged the higher up the management chain they look, and they find it quite hard to sympathize with the overall problems that the institution faces. As the BBC is a creative organization, I understand that. I used to be a programme-maker too and most of them say as I did, 'I love my programme, I want to get on with it. I don't want to be messed around by having my budgets cut or having to buy things that I used to get for free. All these things are making my life more difficult.' It's perfectly easy to understand why they feel this.

Five years ago, when we started the process of change and introduced internal markets and restructuring, and surveyed staff opinion, the survey showed staff had no understanding of why any of these things were happening. We hadn't communicated that well enough to them. Now when we survey them, we know that they do understand it. They have a good understanding of why the changes of recent years have been necessary, even if they don't welcome them very much. They would have preferred a world without the scale of change that they've had to undergo. That's only human, and probably no organization that's been through the scale of dislocation that we have can, in the early years, have a work-force that's enthusiastic about the experience. Why should they be? I think the thing to work for is the maximum understanding. We'll never reach the equilibrium that people enjoyed in the past, for the reasons we've been discussing. The world is changing too rapidly for that, but I hope that the change will come to be more incremental. In a well-run organization you should be changing the whole time, but if the change is incremental, it doesn't necessitate the huge scale of change that we've had to go through in the last few years – to a very large extent because historically the BBC had not done what it should have done. The need for change had built up and a great deal of action was necessary in a very short space of time. It's a pity that was necessary, but it was.

Let me take you back to your earlier years. How did they help to shape your character?

I emerged more or less unscathed from the Irish Christian Brothers' education, but it was fiercely disciplinarian teaching in a very, very successful school. It took lots of kids from relatively humble backgrounds and propelled them into university – in my case to Oxford. So my background was a combination of a striving family and a tough education. Oxford was the experience that really transformed me, because I arrived at Oxford, in terms of what I later became, completely unformed. I had never read a serious newspaper; I knew almost nothing about politics.

Never?

No. We didn't have a broadsheet paper; we had the *Daily Express* and the local *Echo*, and they were my windows on the world. I had hardly ever been to the theatre. I saw my first art film just months before I went to university – and was very affected by it, actually.

Do you remember what it was?

Yes, it was called *L'Eclisse* – Michelangelo Antonioni. I can remember it as if it was yesterday because of the impact it had on me. And Oxford affected my life, to a greater extent, I think, than anything that had happened earlier.

And affected your ambition, because you had excelled in maths and physics, and you went to Oxford to read engineering; suddenly there was this massive shift in ambition to a totally new world.

It happened within two weeks of being at Oxford. I met my wife straight away. She was an American art student. She knew a lot more about the world of art and the cinema and things like that than I did. I know that somewhere inside me, goodness knows why, I'd had some interest in the cinema. It had always attracted me as an art form, and I immediately started going to the Scala on Walton Street. We'd go three or four times a week to see the great classics of the day, films by Truffaut, Bergman. In my first term I made a film. The college had a film society and somebody put up a notice on the board in my first few weeks saying, 'Would somebody like to take over the college film society?' 'Oh, that's for me,' I thought, and I made very much a beginner's film that first time. But by the end of my first year I was making what was, in those days, a major production, the only major film that was made in Oxford during my time there.

In my second year I made another film, so it was an almost immediate transition from the world I had known. I'd been a reasonably broadly based student at school, but in those days if you were good at science, which I was, and good at maths you were strongly encouraged to do science in the sixth form because it was very much 'the white-heat-of-technology' period: 'If you can do science, young man, do it because science is the future.' I was capable of doing it and in truth I enjoyed doing science and maths in the sixth form. But if I had my time over again I know my real interests are much closer to other subjects.

By my final year, I knew I wanted to go into the film business or into television, but I'd spent two years not studying at all. These days the authorities would not tolerate that, but in those days they were tolerant because they knew I was doing other things. They took the view that I was doing worthwhile things, if not engineering. And in my final year, by which time I was married, I taught myself engineering from text books in the college library every day. I did it mostly because I knew my mother and father would be upset if I didn't get a degree. I taught myself whole areas of engineering like metallurgy and control theory. I count that as one of the greatest challenges I ever had to overcome because I was no longer interested in the subject. The experience was absolute torture.

How important is it at some stage in your career to have: (a) an element of luck, and (b) one or more mentors in your formative years, someone who rides shotgun with you and says, 'I believe in you', and gives you opportunities and tolerates the mistakes while you're building up your experience?

It's very important. I can't believe there's anybody you talk to that wouldn't feel they'd had both luck and mentors. I am certainly very conscious of some critical moments in my life where I've taken one fork in the road rather than another; coming to the BBC, for instance. I could have stayed at LWT and made a lot of money, but I decided to come here.

Why did you decide to do that?

Firstly I think I've always been a risk taker, and secondly, and much more importantly, I'd spent my life in broadcasting admiring the BBC and what it stood for. I often say to people in the BBC, who are very rude about the institution, that I hardly ever heard anybody be rude about the BBC when I worked at ITV. It was held in great respect. It was a bit of a shock to come to the BBC and find that people inside did not always revere it as much as people on the outside. But if you go back to the mid-1980s, the organization was in a lot of trouble. It was deeply riven internally, the Board of Governors was at war with the Board of Management and there was a sense that it was losing its way. So when somebody said to me, 'Come in and be the number two, be the deputy director-general, try and pull the BBC's journalism together with a single management focus, bring it together and make it the best in the world again.' In truth, I didn't pause for thought. The idea of coming to work for the greatest broadcaster in the world, when you've spent your life in broadcasting in this country, there was no contest. And I care much more about that than I care about money. I like money, but it's no substitute for an interesting and rewarding life. And I'm always clear that however miserable the odd moment has been, I've never regretted coming to the BBC.

What are the qualities that you need to be (a) a successful manager within the BBC, and (b) a successful programme-maker within the BBC?

Well, some of our managers are programme-makers. We are the most successful creative organization in the world, and that's because we have managed to attract and retain some of the most creative people in our society. We've done that through developing their careers intelligently, through training them well, by being willing as an organization to take risks and to innovate, and allowing them to do the kind of work that they can't do anywhere else. That's what's produced this unrivalled, unmatched tradition in areas like comedy – *Fawlty Towers, One Foot in the*

Grave, Monty Python, and the contemporary work from Harry Enfield, or whoever. I think that's always been true of the BBC, and I think in tougher times we've had to be even better at that task than we have been in the past.

What are the greatest enemies of success, in general terms?

I guess the enemies would be within. The most successful person can face insuperable odds. But I would say that most people *can* succeed if they themselves want to and have the capability to make it happen.

And do you think that people who want to be successful in life have to, at some stage, sacrifice an element of their family life?

That is one of the toughest sides of it. I think I've worked quite hard to stay in touch with my wider family and to structure my life so I spend a proper amount of time with my immediate family. I don't want to overstate it, because these jobs are punishing and take up a lot of time, but I've never been somebody for whom family life has gone out of the window. I've always invested a lot of time in making sure that days are set aside for different sorts of family activities, and so on. But anyone in a job like mine is not going to be able to devote as much time to family matters as he could if he had an easier job.

There is another problem, which we haven't talked about, and that is the hostility that you face when you do certain sorts of jobs in Britain. Even though I may be able to bear it myself, the thing that most pains me is the impact it has on my family. They are the innocent victims. I have brought it upon myself, but I don't like the fact that my children, my mother and father, my wife, sometimes have to read a lot of adverse material in a paper. It's the toughest price of success. That's the only thing that gives me real pause for thought, and sometimes I feel guilty about it, because although I pay a price, it's massively counterbalanced by the satisfactions that my job brings. Now, I don't want to overstate it because my family also shares in some of those satisfactions, but the only time I ever feel 'This is unfair and unjust' is in respect of my family.

Who are your heroes?

I have any number of heroes in the spheres of the arts and sports, whether it be Jane Austen, François Truffaut or Eric Cantona. But in the realms we are discussing, of changing the way large organizations work, Taiichi Ohno stands out as a visionary for what he achieved after the war at Toyota in Japan. He put his customers first, turned every worker into a responsible manager, collaborated with his suppliers, and in the process produced cars at half the price of his competitors. He led the way in bringing fundamental and revolutionary change to organizations across the world.

If you could gather together before you in a room all the young people who want to make a career in the BBC, what advice would you give them?

I'd say to them that you have to ask yourself honestly whether you've got the creative ability, because this is an organization that, in the end, works with the most able and creative people in society. So look hard at yourself. Have you got the ability? If you've got the ability, then fight to get in and you'll get in. If you've got the determination you'll get there.

Even with the exceptional competition there is these days?

Yes. I think in the end talent will out, and if people fight hard enough, their talent will always be recognized.

When your time comes to depart this life, what would you like people to say about you?

He did his best.

That's all?

That would be an improvement on what I get now! The thing that has always guided me, not just in my time at the BBC, but before, when I worked in ITV, is being on the public-service side of broadcasting. This may sound terribly pompous, but what really motivates me has always been wanting to do good for ordinary people. And that's where my background does make a difference – especially when I was a programme-maker in ITV making programmes like *Weekend World*. I was never making programmes for the elite, I was making them for the kids that I used to know in Liverpool, for my wider family. I have always felt that you run institutions like this for the benefit of everybody in society, and that has been my guiding light at the BBC. I want the BBC to extend horizons, to provide experiences that make the life of every single person in this country better. That's the thing underlying it all. I'm sure the rest of the world has a very different view of me, but it would be nice for my children, and those I leave behind me, if that were recognized. But I suspect that's asking for rather a lot.

TONY BLAIR

On 2 May 1997, just four days before his 44th birthday, he became Britain's youngest Prime Minister this century. Labour were in power with a majority of 179 – the biggest achieved by any party for over 150 years. It was not only an electoral indictment of Conservative feuding and scandal, but a remarkable endorsement of the way in which Tony Blair had – in just three years as leader – thrown out the ideology and dogma of the past, and transformed the Labour Party into a lean, disciplined fighting machine. Trade union domination had been reduced, the party's constitution rewritten, policy-making transformed, and membership doubled. A hefty slice of Middle England, duly impressed, climbed on board to deliver victory. There to cheer was his father, Leo, a former local Conservative politician whose own ambition to be Prime Minister had been curtailed by a stroke when his son was just eleven.

Tony Blair was educated at Fettes public school (the Eton of the North), where he was a bit of a rebel, fond of acting and pop music, and once even ran away. But he did enough work to get to Oxford, going on to take bar exams and join chambers where he met and married a brilliant lawyer, Cherie Booth. He says he never thought that someone from his background and with his politics would ever lead the Labour Party. Indeed, he almost failed to be adopted as a candidate for the 1983 General Election, and remembers 'feeling that life was at an end'. One day later, through luck, the safe seat of Sedgefield came up, and within a month he was an MP.

In 1994 he was catapulted into the leadership unexpectedly early when John Smith died of a heart attack. Here he suggests that most achievement is born out of struggle – it never comes easily; and you're more likely to be successful if you question the assumptions other people take for granted. The greatest enemy of success is the pressure on you not to do things. He says that successful politicians need an ability to get on with people and good judgment; and for a country to be a success it requires a sense of national purpose and unity. His new government's undoubted enthusiasm for reform has been tinged by occasional scandals and media complaints of excessive spin-doctoring. For him, it's 'the big picture' that counts. In this interview, carried out just before his election triumph, he says: 'I will have succeeded if, at the end of it, I have changed Britain for the better, and helped to improve people's lives.'

Tony Blair, what is your definition of success?

I suppose my definition of success would be to have fulfilled your life's purpose and I think that's more than simply personal success. There's a sense in which you have to feel spiritually fulfilled as well and I think, for me at any rate, success incorporates more than just your own individual achievement. I feel, rightly or wrongly, that it has to be about contributing to society or to the world around you.

When do you decide your life's purpose?

Fairly early on, or at least *I* did. Politics to me has never been just a job, it is a vocation. It's something I believe in. It results from conviction, and if you want to do it then you say, 'Look, this is what I want to do. I believe there are certain injustices in our society and I want to see them corrected.' That's then what you set out to do. I've been very lucky in the sense that my life's purpose is about idealism – most people never get the chance to find their life's success in terms of how they can change their country, but I will have succeeded if, at the end of it, I have changed Britain for the better and helped to improve people's lives.

Is there a difference between small-scale success that goes relatively unnoticed by society, but which is very important for an individual, and the large-scale success which comes by sticking your head above the parapet?

Yes, I think there is. When you asked me what my definition of success is, it's not, 'Will I do a good Prime Minister's Question Time tomorrow.' You can succeed or fail every day to a certain degree, but I take it that you mean success at a bigger level – success with a capital S. There are lots of things people do, work that they carry out, that will never hit a headline. Recently, I visited a voluntary sector project to help young unemployed black kids. They are achieving virtually a 100 per cent success rate in getting them through a training scheme. They've all been unemployed and passed through the scheme and into a job, but no one will ever have heard of them, no one knows about it, but that is a big success. People tend to gauge success as something that hits the headlines, but other things, like the example I've just given, should equally be viewed as a success.

We should pay more attention to celebrating things that are actually working, that are good in society. In recent times we appear to have lost the idea of dedication to other people, to public service, and we tend to see success simply in terms of who's made £20 million. That's one definition of success, and I'm all in favour of successful entrepreneurs, but there are unsung heroes who should get a bit more praise.

Do you think that success is a goal in itself, or must it be tied to a particular vocation?

For me it does have to be. For example, if we were to win the next General Election, obviously that would be a success, but ultimately I would only feel I'd succeeded if I'd achieved something with that election victory. People often say to me, 'You've made a big success of your life so far,' and I say to them, 'Well, I haven't really, because the purpose in my life is to go and change things and all I've done at the moment is get myself into the position where I've got the opportunity to do that.' It's not actually happened yet, and the test for me is not how good an Opposition you run, but whether you can run a good Government, which is why this interview may be a bit premature. Success to me is something that derives from what you believe your life's purpose to be.

To what extent do you think success derives from life's accidents and to what extent is it a product of a relentless determination to drive something through?

That's an interesting question. My view is that you don't succeed unless you struggle. I'm a great believer in the fact that most achievement is born out of struggle, that it never comes easily, and one of the few advantages of the job I do is that you get to meet a broad range of people from different walks of life who are, I suppose, highly successful or at least at the top of their chosen profession. With each of them, maybe they're a famous writer or a big businessman, you always think they must be sitting back and thinking life is just wonderful, but actually when you meet them, they're still striving, there's a goal to be achieved. I think the concept of struggle is essential to success in the end.

I'm never quite sure what the interplay is between what is naturally within us and what is the product of circumstance. You can occasionally meet people who, for no particular reason, have been born with enormous drive and determination. They just have it, but usually you find that the person has been aware that they've had something to overcome, that they've needed the edge that comes from thinking, 'I've got to get out there and make something of my life.' When I'm talking about my own life and I think back, I became aware, when my father became very ill when I was ten or eleven, that life can be bad as well as good. There was a sense of insecurity, a sense that life wasn't going to be easy.

Are you more likely to be successful if you do have a sense of insecurity and you feel, despite the perceived success, that you have never, ever succeeded?

I think so, yes. I think that is true in the sense that I don't believe that I will ever think, 'Right, that's it, I have now succeeded.' I think I will always be saying, 'I could be doing more, I should be doing more, I've got to do it better.' Now that's not to say that is always the case, I'm just saying that I think, in the end, very few people I know succeed without a lot of hard work, dedication and application. There *are* people who walk onto the football pitch and are just more brilliant than anyone else at it, or the musician that sits down and just happens to play better than anybody else but normally you find that success is achieved through hard work.

To what extent do you think that success is down to background and upbringing?

If there is natural ability, I do believe that will out in the end, but I think the background helps enormously, it helps to have the support of parents.

Did your parents drive you in any sense?

I wasn't aware of it, but they were immensely supportive to me and certainly I felt, particularly after my father was ill, that our family had to, in a curious way, rebuild itself. Family background is certainly very, very important to it, but it also depends on the people you meet and the breaks you have. I've been very, very lucky in the people that I've met and those that have influenced me.

Did you work as hard as you should have at school?

No, except in the subjects that I really enjoyed, which were English and history. Those were the subjects I loved and I didn't work as hard as I should have, but then I always worked sufficiently hard to make sure I got through the exam. I wasn't daft about it.

Do you think you were lucky?

I think I was very lucky. I was very lucky in getting a good education, I was very lucky because I had parents who encouraged me. I certainly believe that without a good education and very supportive parents I wouldn't be doing what I'm doing today, and that's one of the things that makes me so passionate about educational opportunity and what's happened to the family – these things make such a difference to whether people can succeed or fail. I know perfectly well – it's not that I'm naturally clever or particularly talented – but I had the good fortune to have the things around me that helped me to get on and to do well.

A lot of people say that in every successful person there's a bit of a rebel. Is there a bit of a rebel in you?

Oh yes, definitely.

How does that manifest itself?

Rebelliousness is perhaps not quite the right term. What you need to be able to do is to have the boldness within yourself to think in a different way from how other people may be thinking about something and to take a chance. I didn't rebel in the normal sense, rather by saying, 'Hang on, is the convention correct or not or is it really wise?'

So it's constantly questioning the established ways of doing things that you see around yourself?

Yes, I think that's a very, very important part of making a difference. In the end it's amazing how many things you simply take for granted without ever questioning the premises or the principles on which they are based. We would never have changed the Labour Party if we hadn't stood back and thought from the outset, 'What are we trying to achieve with this Party and are we achieving it? The answer, no. Therefore, we are going to have to change things. Are these changes too terrible to contemplate? The answer, if they're right they should be contemplated.' That's the thought process you go through.

Sometimes, when I've met successful businesspeople, for example, what makes them successful is that, whereas everyone has simply accepted that the context within which they're working is given, they've said, 'It's not given, let's challenge it and maybe we can do things in a different way. Perhaps we should be building this product in a different way altogether.' It's the same with writers or musicians. They just say, 'That's the way it's done now, but maybe that's not the right way to do it at all.'

So what you're saying is that you're more likely to be successful if you push through change?

Yes, if you question the assumptions that other people take for granted, but if some of these assumptions are just there for various reasons, they may be there because it's in the interests of a certain group of people that they're there, or through laziness. I don't think you ever succeed, certainly with an organization, unless you're pushing through change, not change for it's own sake, but by reassessing the assumptions upon which it's built.

The two really important things in my view are firstly, never accept that what people tell you has to be has to be, because you can change what has to be, and secondly, always be prepared, if necessary, to say, 'If there's an integrity about the way I'm doing this, I've got to be prepared to walk away from all the fame and success and say, "That's fine, if that's not what people want then that's their choice."' If you calculate too much you miscalculate. If what you do is set out to be 'successful', you're usually not very successful, because you're pursuing a mirage really. You should have a goal, a purpose. You may end up being successful, but that's another matter.

What I certainly found again in rebuilding the Labour Party was a stage when I was pushing through the notoin of reforming our relations with the trade unions, and people were saying to me, 'This is crazy. You'll finish off any chance you ever had of leading the Labour Party,' and that's how it seemed to me at the time. But in fact it wasn't, the opposite was the case in the end because people out there were saying, 'Actually, the thing did have to change.' There's got to be a difference between determination and obsession. To be determined to do something is a good thing, to be obsessed by it is usually not very good.

When was the first time that you remember saying to yourself, 'I've been successful at something, I am a success'?

I don't think I've ever said that to myself in quite that way. I've done things that I've been proud of, but I don't think I've ever woken up and said, 'Here I am folks, I'm now a success,' and I don't think I'll ever do that. I remember the first time I ever made a political speech, before I ever got into Parliament, at a completely meaningless debate about whether we expelled the Militant Tendency from the Labour Party. The conventional wisdom at the time was that you had to deal with them by political argument and not expel them. I was in favour of expelling them.

Was this before Neil Kinnock's speech condemning the Militant Tendency?

Yes, this was in 1981. I remember feeling for the first time that I could persuade an audience, I could sway them. It was just a strange thing, but it was the very first time I felt, 'I can do this.'

Do you remember that audience?

Yes, in fact some of the people are now in Parliament today. It was the first time I had ever really made a political speech, and I could feel them move, feel them start from one position and finish in another and obviously that lodged with me.

Was it intoxicating?

Exhilarating would perhaps be a better word. I suddenly realized that this is something I could do. Politics of course is about belief and conviction, or at least it should be, but you also have to be able to go out there and make an argument to people and bring them round to your beliefs.

Does every successful person need a mentor or mentors, someone behind them who is riding shotgun to their careers and giving them the right nudges and encouragement at the right times?

I've never had a mentor in that sense. I've had people who, at various stages in my life, have been very influential and important to me, and I've been lucky in that. People I knew at university were important in bringing me round to politics. Derry Irvine, who was then my pupil master, was very important in terms of how he really taught me to think intellectually about a problem, how to analyse problems, which is not just useful as a lawyer, but invaluable in politics and political debate. I suppose John Smith, in terms of getting me into Parliament. It was John who really suggested that I first stand for Parliament and then was a very strong supporter of mine all the way through my parliamentary career, as indeed was Neil Kinnock. I've always been very lucky.

And did you think, when you set your mind on a political career, 'I want to be Prime Minister'? Was that ambition there right from the very beginning?

Absolutely not. I was keen on getting into the Labour Party as a Member of Parliament because I thought, at the time, the Labour Party was in a lot of trouble. I never thought that someone from my background and my politics in the Labour Party would ever lead it, and therefore I never thought that I would be Prime Minister. I suppose there must be people who start out from the age of four saying 'I want to be Prime Minister,' but I certainly didn't. I can't imagine having ever thought that, and it's not that I wasn't determined and ambitious in politics – I just didn't think it would happen.

What do you rate as the key benchmarks of your success so far?

What I'm proud of is of having turned the Labour Party round, and constructed, I hope – building on the work that others did before me – a Party that is a broad-based coalition for progress and justice, something I believe the Labour Party should stand for. We've got away from simply saying we're a trade-union dominated party, and I'm immensely proud of the organizational changes we've made, the expansion of the membership, the involvement of people, but I'm aware always that it's a preparation for something more than that.

Do you think that every successful person has to make some kind of sacrifice as far as their family are concerned?

Yes, you see less of them because you have to work hard. I'm very close to my kids and I see a lot of them and that's great, and I hope it continues no matter what happens, but I would love to see more of them and I can't really because of the job that I do. I do worry in case I'm not seeing enough of them. I think it's good for children to have a father there who's going to talk to them about things and help them grow up. The nature of my job dictates that I spend time away, or get home late at night, and I start to worry that they don't have the influence there that they should have.

How important is your wife to your political success?

Very important. If I didn't have the emotional stability and pleasure from a happy marriage, then I don't think I would be doing what I'm doing today at all.

Some people say it's a full-time job being a politician's wife. Is it, in a sense, going to be any handicap to you having a wife who chooses to continue with her work?

No, I rather like that because I think that in the end she brings a different experience, she's got a different way of working. I also think it's important for her own happiness. She is brilliant in her own right, she's one of the successful people that I admire. She came from nothing and has done so well and I think she would be unhappy if she were not able to use the ability and brains that she's got. Conversely, some people find emotional unhappiness either easy enough to deal with, or even a spur to them. I don't. If I'm not happy in my home life, I'm not happy at all.

What are the qualities needed to be a successful politician, first of all as an ordinary, working politician, secondly as a Leader of an Opposition, then as a Cabinet Minister and then as Prime Minister? Are there subtle differences in the qualities needed at every stage of the process?

Obviously, it helps if you are articulate, which is one of the reasons why so many politicians have been lawyers. The ability to analyse a problem and get to grips with it very quickly is extremely important, because politicians often have to work at very great speed. I think it helps enormously to get on with people. If you don't like people there's not much point in coming into politics. There was that character in the Georges Duhamel novel, who loved humanity in general, just hated people in particular, and I think you've really got to like people, because you meet a lot of them. But the thing I always look for in any politician is judgment. The world is full of highly educated, intelligent fools, people who have all the qualifications, but if you ever put them in charge of anything then disaster swiftly ensues. By contrast you can get people who do not have great qualifications but who have an instinctive shrewdness for what works and what doesn't – those are the qualities for an ordinary politician.

For a Leader of the Opposition, well, it all depends on the state in which your Party is in. For me, obviously, it was essential to transform the Labour Party. My view was that the Labour Party is basically a great political party, but was living in the past and had to update itself and become a proper, modern centre, centre-left party, so to be a Leader of the Opposition you've got to make an assessment of where your party is. Why is it in opposition? That's the first question you've got to ask yourself, and you have to be able to answer it very honestly. If there's fundamental change required, then do it and get it through.

And to do that, do you need determination, ruthlessness even?

You certainly need determination and occasionally a bit of ruthlessness, although that's a tough word for what is actually taking the decisions that need to be taken.

Control, total control?

People sometimes think I'm always controlling everything that happens in the Labour Party and it's probably not a bad thing that they think that I do, but I don't. I don't think that that is what's important. For me the big change in the Labour Party was to make the connection between organization and ideas. My view of the Labour Party was that its organizational structure was wrong, because too much control was exercised by small pressure groups, small groups of activists, and that distorted the development of its ideas and its policy and, therefore, the achievement of its ideals. What I've wanted to do, in ideological terms, was to get the Labour Party to a set of values – we're not a class-based party that believes in a particular economic prescription that is good for all time, we're a party of values. Our values are community, justice and a fair deal – basic simple values – and so then, in organizational terms, I wanted to allow the Party to develop those values into policies and programmes.

We broadened the way the Party took decisions, we consulted the whole of the membership, we doubled the membership. Now you've got a leader that's accountable to a broad-based Party, not just a small group of activists, and the Party, by being broad-based, is accountable to the local community and to the country. That was the essence of the transformation and, when I look back on the Labour governments of the past, what has always been their bane are small groups of activists that haven't actually had that much support in the country or even in the Labour Party, but have ended up trying to run the show. Now all that's had to change, so when you said, 'What do you need as Leader of the Opposition?' I think you need a pretty clear appraisal of why it is you're in opposition and not in government.

And what are the qualities needed for a Cabinet Minister?

To be able to take decisions sensibly. This is where good judgment is obviously extremely important, to distinguish between what is important and what is ultimately not important. As a Leader of an Opposition, you're in a position of executive responsibility, and the great thing is always to decide which battles to fight, and which not to fight – you have to keep your eye on the big picture. We want the big picture. Don't drive me off into all the little highways and by-ways. What are we actually trying to achieve here? It's the same for a Cabinet Minister and for a Prime Minister, you've got to have a very clear set of objectives and goals, you've got to know what you want to achieve and you may get side-tracked one day and diverted another, but you've always got to get back on to the path you want to travel.

What qualities do you need to do that?

You need first of all to know where you're going and secondly, you need to have an absolutely clear determination to get there and not let things stand in your way.

Can you be blown easily off course though by the day-to-day twist of events?

Yes you can. The real test is not to allow that, you have to lead your agenda. It's very difficult to try to mould an agenda without being in government. Newspaper coverage matters a great deal, but because you're not in government you're not announcing things and you've got to think of new ways of getting up the same message. It's a bit of a game from time to time in the way that that happens, but you've got to do it because you're trying to make an impact on the agenda.

In government I think it's completely different. I think the day-to-day headlines do not matter that much, what actually matters is having a clear set of objectives and seeing them through. It's not dissimilar from having to change the Labour Party. I set myself certain clear objectives when I got into the Labour Party: rewrite the constitution, double the membership, transform the policy making, re-order the relations with the trade unions – we basically did those. I didn't know how I was going to do them, and from day to day I got knocked off course by this or that, and then I'd have to go back and deal with it, but you are still always on the same track.

When Macmillan was asked what was the biggest problem he faced as a politician he answered, 'Events, dear boy, events.' I think that's wrong. It is true in one sense, but in the end, if you allow events to determine your agenda, you've had it. The difference between Government and Opposition is that in Government you wake up every morning and say, 'What shall I do today?' In Opposition you wake up every morning and say, 'What shall I say?' There is a big difference. I am essentially, by nature, a doer.

Every successful person has to face criticism and in politics criticism is often meat and drink. How do you personally deal with criticism, some of which you may consider to be unfair?

I get upset about criticism when it impinges in an intensive personal way, particularly on the family, but in general you've got to live with a certain level of it. Some of the criticisms are valid – it is possible to get things wrong, and you should always acknowledge that, but never take the criticism so seriously that it paralyses you. I tend to take the view that today's newspapers are tomorrow's fish and chip papers for most things, but if the people make a serious criticism and I think it is done in a serious way, then I will listen to it. I think it's important to listen.

And yet very often that criticism, if it is widespread in the media, is shaping public opinion and politicians are dependent on public opinion?

Yes, that's true, but you've then really got to decide the degree to which you're simply going to bend with that and the degree to which you will try and reshape it.

Do you think some bending is sometimes necessary?

I don't think you should ever bend on basic fundamental beliefs and convictions. You may decide you are going to do it in a different way because of particular criticisms that are being made, but in the end, I wouldn't want to remain in politics unless I felt I could make a difference in the way that I wanted to make a difference.

Would you like to change the situation where the media often home in on short-term solutions and choose to ignore the long-term picture?

I suppose everyone in politics would love to change it, but I think it's a pretty hopeless endeavour frankly. People will always look for short-run solutions, and usually painless solutions as well, which is part of human nature. But as a political leader, you've got to have long-term objectives and keep to them.

Do you sometimes wish the media would take a longer view?

Yes I do, but I have to say that I don't think there's the remotest prospect of that happening and in a sense, to be fair to the media, what they would say is that the politicians are often playing on the short-term themselves which is true. We live in the world that we live in. That's why I think that when, earlier this year, we published our priorities for government, although it didn't really get much publicity, it was a document of which I was very proud. It really set a compass for government for us. We know the tests by which we want to be judged and what we're trying to do and I think that we are better prepared for government in that sense than we've ever been before because we're not promising the world the day before yesterday. They're very clear, specific objectives and priorities, and I think that's a very good thing for us to have done.

What do you rate as the greatest enemies of success?

Complacency and the pressure there always is upon you, certainly if you're in an executive position, not to do things. I found the greatest battle I've had in changing the Labour Party is that people will always find reasons for not doing things. You would have a very easy, happy life if you didn't do anything, but you would end up not taking the decisions that are necessary – that is the hardest thing. It must be the same if you're turning round a company or a football team, people don't like it; we're all conservative with a small 'c', in not liking change. Change is a problem, and if you give in to that, then you don't get the thing done, it's very simple really.

Do you think that politics has an ability to absorb both success and failure, so that both are forgotten in a very short space of time? More so than in any other profession perhaps?

Yes, I think one of the things you learn, certainly in politics, is that on a day-to-day basis you're only as good or as bad as your last performance. It all passes pretty quickly. You've always got to realize too that if you're in the public eye, most people aren't even aware of something that to you seems to be a catastrophe. I remember meeting – I won't say who it is because I wouldn't want to embarrass them – but I met someone who's in the public eye the other day and I'd been completely blissfully unaware that they'd been fighting some great titanic battle within their particular organization and had the most terrible time of it. I was asking them how they were and they were saying, 'It's been absolutely awful,' and I didn't know what on earth they were talking about. But for them, and I can imagine this myself, when something terrible happens they think the world's about to come to an end, but most people out there are just getting on with their lives and not really worrying about it.

So your advice to potentially successful people would be, don't be too mesmerised by what people write about you?

Don't let that get to you. There's a bit of you you've got to keep to yourself. One of my ambitions as a politician is to end my political career by still remaining a human being, and that is a very difficult thing to do, but I aim to achieve it. In the end, you've got to have a bit of you that's you and everyone else can just disappear on that front. You're *you* in the end, so never end up thinking you've become the property of your public persona because you haven't, you're still your own person, or at least you should be.

What do you rate as your biggest failures and, more importantly, how did you recover from them?

Well, Cherie used to sing the old song, 'Pick yourself up, dust yourself off, start all over again,' and there have been times when I've had setbacks when that's what you have to do. I couldn't get into Parliament for a long time, because I was out of kilter with the way the Party was at the time in the early 1980s. I was getting very, very frustrated and going for selections and failing to get anywhere and thinking, 'This is hopeless, I'm never going to make it.'

Did you ever consider giving up the quest to be a politician?

No, I didn't.

Why not?

Because I was absolutely set on it. I was living in London, I was a London barrister, which wasn't a great starting point for most constituencies, and I'd actually decided to move back to the North-East, because that's where I wanted to go back to represent if I had the chance. The election was called in 1983 and I was in an absolutely desperate state. I could see what was happening to the Labour Party and I just felt I couldn't make it anywhere. I was on the point of going into the Party headquarters and saying, 'Look, if any seat comes up, it doesn't matter how hopeless, I'll just go in and do something, knock on the doors or whatever.' The Sedgefield seat came up through a completely fortuitous set of circumstances at the very last minute. It was the last seat anywhere in the country to select its candidate.

And if it hadn't been for the luck involved in that, you might not be here today?

No, I certainly wouldn't. I remember going up to Sedgefield on 10 May, the election having already been called. I was selected and by 9 June I was in Parliament. All that from the feeling on 9 May that life was at an end. It just shows you that the breaks can happen.

Are there any other particular failures that you're prepared to admit to, where you can tell me how you turned a potentially disastrous situation into a triumph?

I don't know that there are big things that I can think of. In a sense in the changes that we made in the Labour Party. There was a point in time when we felt, particularly on Clause 4, that it was possible the whole thing could go wrong. I remember we started, in early 1995, with quite a lot of problems. People were coming out and asking, 'Why are you doing it?' Then we took the decision to go on the road, to go to the Party membership. I said, 'We've had enough of all this. We've got to go out, we've got to communicate, we've got to tell people the reason why this is happening.' We just set up a whole series of meetings throughout the country where Party members could throw anything they wanted at us and it really was one of the odd situations in which you could actually feel the thing being brought round. Suddenly people understood why it was necessary, why it was absurd that you had a party constitution with a whole lot of beliefs no one ever liked, rather than a proper, modern constitution through which we could express our beliefs. There was certainly the potential to fail very badly on that. A lot of people were saying, 'For goodness sake, play it cool. Don't hype it up.' I thought in the end that if we didn't start getting out and telling people what we were about then it would just be back to the old days of rustling up a few votes here and there by the old deals – that was just not going to work.

So that was a moment when you felt you were staring failure in the face and you had to get up and do something about it?

I felt I'd just been letting the thing drift without really going in and hammering it out, and once we turned it around we turned it around.

If you are successful in Government or in Opposition you are subject to a considerable number of pressures. Are there any ground rules for when you stand firm and when you compromise?

Yes, you never compromise on basic objectives. If the objective is fundamental you don't compromise on it. If the compromise involves doing something wrong, then don't do it. I think all politicians know the difference between a tactical compromise and a strategic retreat. A tactical compromise is fine; strategic retreats – no, don't do them. And if you end up doing them, you end up paying a far heavier penalty in the end than you ever think.

How important is public perception as far as political success is concerned?

It is important. Communication is an essential part of political leadership in the information age. You have to be able to communicate. The public is always cannier than we think. It's not just about communicating what pops up on the *Nine O'clock News* every night, it's actually developing a story for people about the country, what you think is wrong with it, what you think you can do to put it right. That's what is more important in terms of communication.

Is there something deep-down inside the British psyche, the British character, that makes us almost not want success and indeed envy it when it occurs in others?

I think people are a bit suspicious of success.

Why?

I don't know. I think we're very understated in many ways. We don't like to be too demonstrative, we're very slow to be roused, but once we are the world had better watch out. I think we should celebrate our success a bit more, the successes that we do have as a country or individually.

How would you set about changing that attitude towards success?

By giving us some national pride and saying, 'Look, this is what we can still do in the world.' I sometimes think that we feel our position has changed so much since the Second World War, since the loss of Empire, but actually Britain has an enormous amount to contribute in the world. We are achieving and can achieve an enormous amount.

How do you portray that though in the teeth of an often cynical media?

Well, if the media is cynical about it, you go over their heads. Appeal direct to people.

As you did with Clause 4?

Well, you *can* do that with people. You can go direct to the public, in more ways than people think. Also, as I say, the public are always cannier about these things than we think – they make an assessment on a far more considered basis than we politicians, or indeed the media, like to think.

Are you ever concerned that success for you, as a politician, inevitably means failure for another politician? Is there room for what you might call a generosity of spirit or is it a no-holds-barred approach – let's get the enemy at all costs?

I hope there is a considerable space for generosity of spirit. I don't hate the Tories or the people that I'm fighting – I believed they should be removed from Government, but we're all in this together, and I think there are points in time when it's very important to try and have a sense of solidarity with your political opponents, as this country has shown on occasions in wartime. We often forget that during the Second World War Winston Churchill was the Prime Minister, but the Deputy Prime Minister was Clement Attlee and Labour and Conservative actually worked together. A lot of the war effort couldn't have been achieved without the Ernie Bevins of this world, as well as all the others, so I think that generosity of spirit is essential. However, I felt that after 18 years it was not unreasonable for us to say, 'You've had long enough.'

Have you ever thought your political opponents were being successful, that they were doing something right?

Yes, certainly. Throughout most of the 1980s I thought that as an electoral and campaigning machine, the Conservatives were better than we were. I do believe, however, that that has now changed.

And in terms of principle?

They had, at that period of time, however much I disagreed with their policy and politics, a clear sense of purpose. My basic attitude is learn from wherever you can. I will look at ideas from some of the think tanks that are connected with the centre right, as well as the centre left. It doesn't mean to say I accept them, but to me it's what works that matters; it's your values and priorities that make the difference.

And to achieve success would you always put principle before pragmatism?

Well, I hope so. The only honest answer for any politician to give is that they hope so. I certainly believe that what we've done in the Labour Party so far, the changes we've made, have been principled changes, and I hope the same will be true in government.

You've said several times that focus groups play an important part in finding out what people want. To be a more successful politician do you then give people what the focus groups say they want?

No. To be blunt, there's a lot of nonsense talked about focus groups. For years the Conservatives had Saatchi & Saatchi, they had focus groups, they had private opinion polling, they had big advertising campaigns and everyone said, 'Very sensible professional group of people.' The moment the Labour Party starts doing it everyone asks if focus groups are designing our policy. To be serious, I've seldom come across any findings from a focus group that told me something I didn't know already. In the end, if your own instincts as a politician aren't much good then you don't get very far. These things are like opinion polls. What they can do is give you a snap-shot of opinion, but they should not influence how you develop policy, although they may show you that you need to do a bit more persuasion in places.

Is there anything you would like to see changed in the system of government in Britain to give the country a chance of becoming more successful? For example, is five years for a parliament too limiting? Does it drive you into short-term priorities?

It would be a bold step to come out and say I was in favour of 15-year terms. No, I don't that matters so much. What I do think – this may seem a small change, but I think it is quite an important one – my experience with legislation, when I was dealing with it directly, is that a lot of legislation is passed through the House of Commons that is defective and faulty because it is not properly considered. It's considered on a ridiculously partisan basis, there is very little preparatory work done by those that are making the decisions, the MPs are often extremely ill-informed about the legislation that they're passing and therefore completely in hock to the government machine and the government machine itself is often driven by considerations that it shouldn't be. I favour the far greater use of special standing committees and trying to make the political process resemble what is the reality today. At least then there would be areas of public policy and public life in which there's a broad measure of agreement with regard to the objectives that are to be sorted. The problem with Britain and its political system is that you've got very-nearly-now 21st-century politics with a 19th-century parliamentary system.

Does Prime Minister's Question Time mitigate against success because it feeds short-term sensation, what's been called the 'soundbite' culture?

Yes. It may be bad for the public to watch, but I can assure them that it's just as bad to participate in. It's just a ritual, I'm afraid, but it's a ritual that we all go through and something needs to be done about it. The basic idea of Prime Minister's Question Time was to hold the Prime Minister to account, but no one can seriously argue that that's what it's about at all. It's 15 minutes of politicial jousting and knockabout.

Who are your heroes, past or present?

I think in political terms, Lloyd George, Ernie Bevin, Attlee – in that great period of government. In broader terms, I was asked the other day about some of my favourite writings and poetry and I mentioned Dietrich Bonhoeffer who was a pastor in the Second World War. I think many of those people that fought then in the Resistance, in circumstances of not just the most acute danger, but when they thought civilization was about to end, I think their courage was quite extraordinary. And I suppose some of the people you have down on your interview list. If I had a political hero in a broader sense, Nelson Mandela would fit the bill.

You once said, 'Everyone has doubts and worries.' Even the most successful people?

I don't know, maybe some people are completely untroubled by doubt of any sort, but I think they're slightly unusual and maybe slightly scary. I think you shouldn't lose the essential sense of humility.

Do you have any frustrated ambitions outside politics?

Oh, I'd love to have done a whole range of different things. I loved acting and music when I was younger, and when I was very much younger, professional football. I'd love to have run a business or a voluntary organization. The trouble is you can only do a certain amount in one life, but yes, one of the good things about the job is to meet a whole load of people from different walks of life and it's fascinating to see what they've done and what they've achieved, but I'm lucky to be doing what I'm doing.

What are the qualities that you think you need for a country to be successful?

A very close sense of national purpose, to know what we are trying to achieve as a country. A close sense also of national unity – something that is not just there for a few of the citizens, but it's there for the whole country to share in. When I talk about one-nation politics or, one-nation society, what I actually mean is that you don't really have pride in yourself as a nation unless it is a pride that extends right down, all the way through the layers of society. That's what I think is important for a country, a sense of national purpose and a sense of national unity.

What would you say to all those young people out there who want to be successful in their careers? What advice would you give them?

I would say don't pursue success itself. Ask what you want to achieve and go out and achieve that. If you fail occasionally, don't get put off because it happens to everybody. Have the strength, as I said, to be able to walk away from it if you can't do it on the right terms. Don't overcalculate, pursue it as what you believe in or what you really think you can do, and if you do that then you've got a better chance of being successful. Recognize, too, that the way that some people measure success is not always what success should be about, and if you're doing something in your local community centre for elderly people on a Saturday afternoon, then maybe you've achieved just as much as some guy who's taking home £5 million a year from running a big business.

What would you say to those young people who want to pursue a successful political career?

Well, only come into politics if you've got really strong convictions and you want to carry them through. Don't come into it because you fancy yourself as a star in the Houses of Parliament or think, I'm going to be Prime Minister or whatever, because you'll end up either by being a failure or a pain in the neck to everyone. You've got to decide that it's something that really, really motivates you. Realize that a lot of politics can be very tedious and often very irrelevant to what you really believe in but in the end understand too that it's important, that it matters. However much people like to throw stones at politicians, in the end the more politicians who come in – whether they're Conservative or

Labour or whatever they are – with some sense of idealism, the better.

One last question, when your time comes to leave this life, what would you like people to say about you?

He tried to make Britain better, he tried his best to do that. You can do no more than try your best, and the goal is to improve the country. It's as simple as that.

DAVID BLUNKETT

'I want to be judged on equal terms,' says David Blunkett, 'to be seen to be doing a good job, and for people to forget that I can't see.' Born blind to elderly Methodist parents on a Sheffield council estate, he was sent to a special boarding school at the age of four, and suffered the trauma of his father dying in a works accident when he was 12.

There is a neat irony in the fact that the man put in charge of the Labour Party's education policy left school at 16 without any qualifications. His headmaster told him that O-levels were unnecessary, as his prospects were few. The options offered were piano-tuning or light engineering. Believing that 'you either drive yourself forward or you go under', he worked for the Gas Board by day, and enrolled for evening classes. Driven by ambition and plagued by moments of despair, he obtained not just the O-levels he'd missed, but three A-levels that took him to Sheffield University. Drawn to politics by what he calls a combination of anger and arrogance, he became the youngest member of the city's council at the age of 22. Eleven years later he was leading it. Immensely popular with Labour activists, he became the first non-MP to be elected to the party's National Executive Committee for almost forty years. Inevitably, he entered Parliament in 1987, and five years later joined the Shadow Cabinet as health spokesman before taking over the education portfolio. He admits he 'sometimes got up people's noses' in his early days when opponents labelled him a rabid left-winger. Despite mellowing along with New Labour, he proudly retains what he calls 'a healthy pig-headedness'. He believes that 'the strongest people are those who can admit that they made mistakes'. Blind people need, more than most, the ability and enthusiasm to keep going when life seems bleak. For David Blunkett that means late nights and weekend working to catch up on all his documents in Braille or on tape while his friends and colleagues might be relaxing. Now in his early fifties, he is living proof that blindness is no handicap to success and achievement – if you want them badly enough, and provided you never take no for an answer. This interview took place just before he became Secretary of State for Education and Employment in the new Labour government.

David Blunkett, what is your definition of success?

I think my definition of success is to feel and know that you have fulfilled your potential, whatever the obstacles and the difficulties placed in your way, so that you can't look back and say, 'If only I hadn't been blind, if only I hadn't failed to complete that qualification, then I would have been whatever.' I think success is being able to see, through good and bad times, the light at the end of the tunnel. I suppose getting there takes tenacity, and an ability to sustain what you believe in, and your integrity. Those are the things I try to hold to.

Have you always been driven?

Yes, I think I have. It stems from my childhood, and the difficulties I faced. I had to go to boarding school at the age of four. My parents didn't have any choice in the matter, because that was the way in which schooling for blind children was organized, on a residential basis. There was the trauma of finding yourself in a dormitory with other children for the first time, and learning to clean your teeth and wash yourself, and having just your little locker with your own small collection of personal things. I had to deal with my dad's death in a work accident when I was 12. In those kinds of situations you either go under or you drive yourself forward, and I drove myself forward.

What was it that stopped you going under? There will be some people under similar pressures who succumb, who do go under. What would you say to encourage them?

There's always a brighter propect just over the horizon. Even when you get to the top of a mountain and find another valley and another mountain, you need to keep believing that you can do it. Never take no for an answer; always believe that what you are aiming for can be achieved if you just put in that extra effort. You see this in people who have been in the most disastrous circumstances – marooned with aircraft crashes in the middle of the Andes, for example – and who have managed to struggle through, to hang on to life in situations in which all of us, me included, would just give up, lay down and quietly go to sleep in the snow. But they don't, and for those of us who have never experienced anything as challenging as that, the ability to keep going when life looks bleak and to have a new enthusiasm for each new mountain you must climb is very small beer.

Do you think you are more likely to be successful if you have known sacrifice or failure somewhere along the line?

I think you become steelier. To use an expression from the Sheffield steel industry, you have gone through the furnace and your mettle has been tested, and after that things don't daunt you. Having succeeded against the odds, other difficulties become a challenge. They often involve you in having to struggle to overcome them, but they don't dishearten you. I suppose it depends on what kind of person you are, because some people, having succeeded against the odds on one occasion, have had enough. It must be something in the blood that drives you forward to want to do that extra mile.

Did you always want to be better than everyone else?

No, I wanted to be as a good as them. In politics there is a fine line between wanting to be one up, and genuinely just wanting to be able to do a first-class job, and to be able to do it on equal terms. I have examined my conscience on this on a number of occasions. I genuinely want to do a good job on equal terms. I don't have a burning ambition to somehow be seen as better than other people, but I don't want to have people saying, 'You're doing well despite the fact that you can't see.' That little tail on an apparent compliment is actually quite disastrous. I want to be seen as doing a good job and for people to forget that I can't see.

So that would be the ultimate tribute as far as you are concerned?

Yes. When people do forget that I can't see – even though sometimes it can lead to them forgetting to tell me something I need to know – I count it as a tremendous compliment. I suppose what drives me most, and the reason why I put in the hours I do, is that I don't want anyone ever to say that I would have done better if I had been able to see. Whether or not I do a good job has nothing to do with me not being able to see. In politics they don't suffer fools gladly, and you don't get to a position of potential authority, or potential cabinet posts, unless you can do the job. I know that in my bones. There's not a lot of sympathy in politics, and I wouldn't want it. The tribute is just being there.

But you undoubtedly have to work harder because you are blind.

Yes, I do. I have to be prepared to put in the time to deal with material in Braille and on tape which I would easily be able to skip-read in print if I were sighted. I am fortunate in having good friends who are prepared to assist me, I have excellent staff in both Sheffield and London, and I did negotiate after my first year in the House of Commons a package of support which is essential – the equipment for Brailling – the software as well as the transcriber – and the staff who were able to operate it. That was a crucial, practical step in enabling me to do my job. The *quid pro quo* of that supportive measure is that I am willing to put in extra time very late at night and at weekends when I would much rather be doing something else. It makes me slightly aloof, a little distant from my colleagues, because when they are having a chat in the tea room or in the bar, I'm stuck in my room making sure I'm on top of things. But it's the only way I know of working whereby no one can ever say I didn't read a report, or that I don't answer essential correspondence, because I can't see.

So being successful is tougher because you are blind?

Well, I hesitate before answering that question, because I think being successful is tough for anyone. I wouldn't pretend that other colleagues don't devote long hours to it because I see the time and energy they dedicate, the commitment and the sacrifices they make, particularly people like Tony Blair, as leader of the Party. What I am doing is not as exceptional as sometimes, when I am very fed up, I would like to think. But there's no doubt whatsoever that having to do that bit extra makes me different. It sometimes diverts me from what I would call networking politics – keeping in touch with people – which in the end may not make any difference to the public, but would certainly make a difference to my relationships with other politicians.

Do you think it is possible for people who are not blind to understand the degree of effort you have to put in?

I think it's possible for those who actually see it at first hand to appreciate what goes on. My closest friends do, but I don't think people outside realize. It's not from lack of interest or intent, just that people find it very hard to understand the practicalities of using alternative methods to gain access to information or for dealing with correspondence. I don't ever talk to them about that, because the moment you start to express it, you do two things. First, you lay yourself open to ridicule, or to being suspected of not really working on equal terms and of bemoaning that. Secondly, you are actually revealing your inner self, how you are coping, and in doing that you are raising the issue of your blindness – you are starting not to work on equal terms, saying, 'Well, you don't understand how I feel, you need to appreciate this in greater detail to fully comprehend the commitment that I am making.' The moment you do that, you put yourself in a vulnerable position and an unequal one.

Is it important to you that you should not be placed in a vulnerable position? Do you have a kind of front that you put on, which is the David Blunkett we see in public, as opposed to the David Blunkett that exists in private?

I suspect there's a bit of that in all of us, and I try to be honest with myself about it. There is a front which denies there is any dfficulty, there's a front that tries to ensure that I always find a way around a problem, and there's the David Blunkett who sometimes resents the fact that a practical helping hand is needed. I don't resent it when friends help, but I resent it when people make a particular point of it. For example, by pointing me to the right door, or preventing me from going into the wrong room, in a way which is clumsy. It's not their fault, it's just that they don't really know how to do it.

And it's possibly an indication of a sense of weakness on the part of the person who is offering you guidance, because they don't quite understand what you are feeling?

Yes. I suppose if I was in a psychiatrist's chair, I would say that there are two sides to it. There's a danger of my being oversensitive to it because I don't want my dignity pricked, and on their side, there's a danger of helping in a slightly paternalistic way. Some people find it genuinely quite hard to accept that someone who is blind can work on equal terms with them, and I understand that. I only hear that second-hand. People have told me that when I first entered the House of Commons, there were colleagues who didn't actually believe that a blind person could work on equal terms and could not be persuaded otherwise. I hope there are a lot fewer now.

A great deal of politics depends on the chance encounter, the casual acquaintance. Is it difficult, or indeed impossible, for you to initiate those introductions because you can't see a person in the corner of the room to whom, it might suddenly occur to you, it would be good to talk about something in particular?

You are not as socially adept, that's absolutely true. You have to find ways round it. I don't spend enough time thinking about that and working out ways of doing it. I nearly said I'm too busy, but that's pompous – I'm occupied with selling the cause, in articulating what I believe in, in producing the policy material. But as you say, if I go to a reception where there's a buffet, I can't look across the room and see who I want to speak to. I can't catch somebody's eye. I can't think, 'It would be a very appropriate moment to raise that with this person,' and therefore I can't walk across and say, 'I wouldn't mind just having a minute with you,' or even just be affable at the right moment and make somebody feel good. Politics is … well, I don't suppose politics is any worse than anything else, except it's writ large, but making people feel good is part of the oil that keeps the machinery going, and I am not too good at that, I have to admit. So I have to work out other ways of retaining respect and esteem. That has to be done by doing my job well publicly, and handling the policy development well.

Going back to your earlier life, when was the first time you said to yourself, 'I am a success, I have been successful at something.' Maybe back in your teens, maybe even before?

It's very hard to recall. I had a sense of achievement from little things. I used to take satisfaction from being able to hit the bullseye hung on my back door with my bow and rubber-suction arrow. Often I just used a point on the back door as a target, which upset my mother even though she was very tolerant about it.

How did you do that?

Well, I used to place the target, or agree with myself whatever point of the door the target would be, and then I'd take steps backwards and then I'd practise. It was an example of the tenacity I spoke about earlier, just plugging away at something and getting some satisfaction out of being able to do it. It was overcoming not being able to see, it was finding an alternative way around a problem.

I suppose I was pleased to achieve things that in hindsight were a bit crazy. I once agreed to meet a schoolfriend of mine outside Stamford Bridge for the quarter-final of the FA Cup, when Chelsea were playing Sheffield Wednesday. I came down on the coach on my own from Sheffield. My mother was horrified, but God bless her, she didn't stand in my way. I couldn't see and my friend could only see a tiny bit and we arranged to meet outside the main gate! By some miracle we found each other. I just sort of lifted my voice and said, 'Tony,' and he said, 'I'm here,' and in we went. We got somebody to show us to our seats, and we persuaded the people sitting behind us to give us a commentary. The whole thing was an adventure – finding the right coach at the bus station, getting off and going to the toilet, having a coffee and chatting to people, getting off and finding Stamford Bridge. I found it all very interesting. I remember to this day asking someone for directions on my way back – I had parted company with my friend, who was going home to Surrey. The person detoured round me because he was too busy to help. It has stuck with me ever since, and that's a long, long time for something to stay in your memory. I thought how making just a little time for each other can make all the difference.

What makes someone who is blind want to go to a football match when you could probably have listened to the commentary on the radio?

Pig-headedness, I think. Football is tribal, it isn't merely about the game, it's about the camaraderie. It's about belonging, it's about a sort of identity with the team. I was brought up on a council estate a couple of miles away from the football ground, way up on one of the famous seven hills of Sheffield. I could hear the match when I was at home and wasn't going to the match, I could hear what was happening in the ground. I could tell when there was a near-miss by the sound the crowd made, I could hear the goals when we'd scored and the sigh of horror when the visiting team scored. So it was in my blood, and I just wanted to be there, and I still do. Now I go with friends. Two of my three sons have season tickets, but I don't make them do the commentary – they want to be with their friends. I enjoy it, and I don't get enough time to go as often as I'd like to now. I often have to listen to the match on Radio 5. They do good commentaries – when they are not having to commentate on Arsenal versus Sheffield Wednesday, which is always a disaster for Sheffield Wednesday.

If you are aiming to be successful, is pig-headedness a help?

Yes, no question about it. The ability to keep going when anyone else would stop, sometimes to the point of irritation as far as other people are concerned. The line between healthy pig-headedness, which sees you through, and stubbornness and awkwardness, which makes other people's lives a misery, is a very fine one. I think Margaret Thatcher crossed it.

You went to a school where the headmaster didn't believe in O-levels, so at the age of 16 you found yourself without any formal qualifications. You then went on to become extremely well qualified with A-levels and a university degree and so on. Did you do that because you felt that qualifications were at least part of the passport to success?

Yes. I was faced with quite dramatic choices, really, some of which were wrong for me and which I knew I had to avoid. Some would have been satisfactory but would not have allowed me to develop my potential in the way I wanted. At 16 I was given the option of doing a commercial course which involved Braille shorthand and typing, which I decided to take up because I thought they were good skills, and I still do. Secretarial skills are one of the most underrated accomplishments – personal-assistant skills will never be replaced by e-mail and voice-activated word-processing – and I knew they would be helpful to me. It was that, piano-tuning – I like music, but I was no good at that – or light engineering, which I didn't want to do. They were really the only three options offered to me. I suppose the second really major challenge from which I got satisfaction, which I actually felt made a difference, were those first O-levels. I went to evening classes for a year, and I took a couple of O-levels at a time and I got them. That was probably a seminal moment for me because it was then that I realized I really could do it. If I had failed, I might have backed off, I might just have decided that I wasn't up to it. There are plenty of people in life who tell you not to risk disappointment, not to try too hard, in case you fall flat on your face.

What attracted you to politics in the first place, and then what made you think you could actually become a politician?

I think two things got me into politics. The first was anger – anger at the inequality and injustice I saw around me – and the second was an arrogance that led me to believe that I could do something about it, that I could actually change the world. I believed that it was possible by getting involved to change things, and that I had something to offer. The anger just came from experience – my dad dying, and my mum struggling for two years to get compensation, us having literally no money in the house at all, and the unfairness of that. And the fact that I grew up in an environment where people worked extremely hard has rested with me. I believe very strongly in good rewards for hard work, and I don't suffer fools gladly. People didn't where I was brought up – the peer-group pressure on scroungers was enormous. But people were not well rewarded for great craftmanship or long hours, and I thought that was unfair. I learned a lot from history as well. I had a teacher who encouraged me, and as I learned about what had happened in the past, my experience was placed in some sort of historical context. The fact that very few things are new – they might be new in a particular time or place, but they are not new in terms of what has happened previously – got me interested in political philosophy. In the end I read political theory in institutions at university, and I had the chance to read and to think at the same time as being a local councillor. I believed that a new government could change things, and I joined the Labour Party in 1963. We had the white-hot heat of technology, we had Harold Wilson offering something new and there was a vibrancy in the community.

I came in on all this at the age of 16, and I started to think that I could take part in it, I could do something. I have to say that I was rapidly disabused of the idea that anything was going to change overnight, or that I was going to make a difference to the world without a great deal of hard work and struggle. Standing outside an old community hut waiting for the local branch secretary to bring the keys on a very wet night with about five of us present was a rude awakening, and I wondered what I had let myself in for. But to see that through, and to carry on, and to continue to believe that you can do something... I suppose you have to come back to that word 'tenacity'.

You talked earlier about needing to have a certain arrogance. Do you think that all successful people have an ego, something that almost at times defies the odds to say, 'I am the greatest'?

They have a touch of it. They have a little sample of it somewhere about their person, even the saintliest people.

Even though some pretend they don't?

Yes. Take someone as great as Mahatma Gandhi. I'm not an expert on him, but if you examine his life and what he did and his relationships with other people, even there there was that touch of ego. But it's a question of degree. How much do you believe you are right? How much do you believe you have got the answer? And how can you temper that with an ability to listen to other people, leaven it in a way that makes you an acceptable person to be with? It's interesting, isn't it? All great leaders believe in themselves, they have enormous confidence in what they stand for. They have to. But the best ones are prepared to leaven that with the wise words of those around them.

And do you think that every successful person must have some moments of weakness when they question what they are doing, when they may be forced to think it through a little more carefully?

Yes. I think all people, no matter how confident they appear, or how successful they are, have an inner self, have doubts and moments when they reflect on where they have got it wrong. The strongest people are those who can admit to themselves that they made mistakes, and can sometimes admit it to the world as well. It is a sign of weakness if you *always* believe that you are right. But in politics this is very difficult, because it isn't always understood. If you admit that something's wrong in the wrong circumstances, it could well unseat you, pull you down. It's a cruel and difficult world, and you know it is when you work in it.

One of your opponents in Sheffield said you had a short fuse, that you could get very upset if you didn't get your own way. You have yourself admitted that you were a bit bumptious. Is this one of the characteristics necessary to your success? Do you have to drive things through sometimes in a way that is not as tactful as you might like?

Yes, I do. I plead guilty to that charge, but less so now than ten, fifteen years ago.

You've mellowed?

It's partly that I've mellowed, and partly because I am much more content. I am much easier with myself and I can find other ways of getting my way rather than losing my cool.

But is that because you have achieved success?

I think it's partly that, but I haven't climbed to the top of the ladder. I shall be happy when I am actually able to try out the things which up to now I have only talked about. But I suppose it would be foolish not to concede that I have been successful in my position, and I am comfortable with that, and it makes things easier. I was both angry and a little intolerant of people before, and I suppose that intolerance of others' failure to see, and not suffering fools gladly, helps in some circumstances to drive things through. And if you believe in something then you mustn't waver, you have to carry it through.

And that may have been a factor in your success?

Yes. I think sometimes I carried it too far. Sometimes I really did get up people's noses, and you have to balance that because you must persuade people. I remember a councillor, now long retired, who said to me at the end of a very difficult meeting of Labour councillors, 'You won the vote. You won the debate. But you didn't persuade me of the argument.' That's rested with me, because it seemed to me that really to have won, I needed to have won him over. I often didn't do enough of that. In politics you ice-skate, you move rapidly, and sometimes you don't spend long enough securing the ground and ensuring that you have genuinely convinced people.

Politicians are keen to present the right image to the world at large. Have you ever allowed yourself to be moulded by the image-makers?

I'll try to give you an honest answer. I've shied away from the most obvious manifestations of that. I have declined to go on courses where they explain to you what colours you should wear, and whether you should shave your beard off, and things of that sort. I've been arrogant enough to believe that it is not necessary to imitate other people in interview techniques, but to try to be myself. But I have listened to people who have said to me, 'You are far too serious on television. You've got to smile and laugh a bit.'

I've responded, 'But I can't smile if I don't feel smiley, I can't grin. I will just have to be myself.' Then they say, 'Yes, but sometimes you are not yourself. We know you as someone with a sense of humour and a twinkle, but when you are doing a soundbite you look so fierce that people will think, goodness gracious, what on earth is this man all about?' I do listen, but I can't mould myself, I can't be what I'm not.

What do you regard as your biggest failures, and how did you overcome them?

In the political arena I think my biggest failure, which I have mentioned already, has been not understanding that I had to win people over, and not spending enough time on that. For instance, when I left the leadership of Sheffield City Council, I had not ensured that the kind of programme we were developing would automatically carry forward rather than simply being overtaken, because I hadn't thoroughly convinced my colleagues that the direction we were going in was right. I am not just talking about my fellow councillors, but about senior officers at the council. For instance, we'd been aiming for decentralization, devolving power, activity and participation to the community, I had only just begun the process and started to get people involved, so that they could see it was crucial that the community played a part in changing their neighbourhood rather than just having things done to them. I didn't complete that process at all, and it slipped away.

I suppose in my personal life my weakness, if that is what it was, was not wanting to be left on the shelf, and therefore feeling that it was necessary to form a relationship and get married at a time when it might have been better not to. But good things came out of it – I have three sons of whom I am very proud and whom I love dearly.

Do you think politics is such an all-consuming business that most politicians are forced to make a choice between their careers and a family life, and most choose politics?

I don't think that's universally true, but I think it's substantially correct. Many of us are driven and prioritize politics, and that changes our relationship with our families. It doesn't necessarily destroy it – there are people suited to such a set of circumstances who can cope with the lifestyle because they have two quite separate personalities and lives. But I don't think this situation is unique to politics. All people who are wholly committed to their work, whether they are an executive of a major company, or a broadcaster, if I may say so, have enormous responsibilities outside the family which put a strain on their relationships. The majority of us struggle to keep the balance right.

Do you think it would ever be possible to have the correct balance in politics?

We could if we could change the nature of politics. There's one overriding problem – not enough people are involved and participating in democratic activity, and those of us who are therefore take on too much, and as a result, we often exclude other people. And we make politics so boring that you really do have to be really driven to turn up to some of the meetings. Berlinguer, who used to lead what were then the Italian communists, was known as 'Iron Arse' because he just sat through every damned meeting going, to the point where other people would have the pants bored off them. The consequence of that was that he was always in the right place at the right time, or the last one there, and he who writes the minutes writes the world. So it can be a sort of self-fulfilling prophecy that we put people off because of the way in which we order the procedures in politics. In one sense, the changes in the Labour Party have brought a breath of fresh air into this. People are now much more interested in trying to be more social beings than they are in interminable meetings which merely end up alienating people. We haven't got it right yet, but at least there's a move in that direction. We have got to find new ways of communicating and being with each other, otherwise we will drive away good people, because they want to live another kind of life – they want a bit of fun, they want to enjoy themselves.

Who are your heroes? Who are the people, past or present, who are up there on your pedestal, the people you admire?

There is a man called Ron Ironmonger, who was eventually knighted for services to local government, who was the leader of the Sheffield council when I first joined it at 22. He was both decisive and courageous in leadership and he was also prepared to be tough. I saw both sides of him, but I admired the man for his commitment to his city, to what he believed in, and for his skill in pulling people together. He had no ambition to be a Member of Parliament, or to move anywhere else, but he just wanted to give to the area. I have a great deal of affection and time for him. On a wider front, I am in danger of repeating what anyone else would say, but nevertheless I'd choose someone like Nelson Mandela who, it seemed to me, had very little to hope for or to cling on to for so many years. When we move from star to star we move from opportunity to opportunity, and there is something that offers hope around the corner. What unites someone like Mandela in prison with people in deep poverty who retain the will to continue, is the belief that there will be a tomorrow. I suppose that, in politics, if all I could do was offer people a tomorrow, so that they had something to hold on to, to work for, to inspire them, to give hope to their children, that would be worthwhile in itself. There are a lot of people – because of unemployment, because of the sameness of their lives – who see no prospect of change tomorrow, or the year after, and whose despair is reflected in the lives of their own children. I think that is the most dangerous aspect of our society today.

What do you think are the greatest enemies of success?

I think cynicism, and a kind of debilitating ... I nearly said lack of ambition, but it isn't that – it's a kind of debilitating detachment from life around us. I suppose the symptoms of clinical depression are the most obvious analogy, although, of course, that is something that nobody can help. What I mean is people who have failed to stay part of the community, identifying with the neighbourhood, the people around them, and have literally retired into a selfishness which means that they don't care what happens to anyone else around them. They have just switched off. Sometimes they are driven to it, but very often it's just a kind of detachment. I am back to where we started – success doesn't have to be recognized publicly, it doesn't have to be something that is applauded, it doesn't have to take a bow, it can be fulfilment in a job well done, or a family well brought up or in the care of someone else. That is fulfilment.

What is the greatest pleasure you have had from your success?

Well, like all politicians I enjoy scoring a goal. I enjoy achieving something that takes us a step forward, not just downing an opponent boxing-style, but actually having created something. I am a great believer in the positive, so developing a policy paper, getting it through, having the argument accepted – particularly finding a solution to what has been deemed a pretty insoluble problem – I find really satisfying and I have had a fair amount of that over the last two years. Grant-maintained schools were supposed to be a great insoluble problem for the Labour Party, and things like how we were going to deal with the funding of higher education, employment-rights issues, the question of what we were going to do about a training levy. They all seem very trivial in retrospect, just as once you have passed an exam it always seems to have been easy afterwards, but very difficult at the time and those have brought me satisfaction, but in the end it's all small beer compared with the question of whether you can deliver.

The great satisfaction would be delivering something to my constituency. People have put their faith in me, and have given me so much, and by doing something for them. I hope I can do it for the nation. I believe passionately that education, skilling and employment are the keys to everyone's personal success because they are enabling. It's not me doing it, it's me facilitating them doing it. I believe with everything I've got that if we can make a difference, then that will be worthwhile, and then I really will rejoice. If you ever have the chance to come back, I'd like to be able to open a bottle of champagne and say, that was worth doing, even if I achieved only half of what I wanted to.

If you could gather together in one room all the blind people in the world and advise them on how they could become as successful as you have been, either in politics or in their own chosen profession, what advice would you give them?

As I said earlier, I would tell them, never take no for an answer. Believe in your own talent, and have confidence that, if you stick at it, if you keep at it, you can do it. You won't have set out on this unless you know it's feasible. I won't drive a bus and people will be pleased to hear that I won't fly an aeroplane – actually with modern technology it would probably be as safe with me as with most pilots, but people wouldn't take the risk! You know what you can do, generally. Sometimes you don't achieve it, but if you don't go for the high jump, you've no chance of getting over the bar. You have got to have a go, and if you get the knock, pick yourself up and brush yourself down and have another go. That is success, because even if in the end you don't make it, you've given your best. That's all I can say, really, and it applies to everything. For example, a blind person might find it difficult to make a meal for himself or even to pour a kettle without scalding himself. It doesn't have to be anything clever, it is whatever that hurdle is that you have set yourself.

What would you like people to say about you when your time comes to leave this life?

I'd like them to remember me for having integrity. I'd like them to remember that I really did mean what I said, and that I wanted to do it for other people. I'd like them to say that in the end he wasn't really so stern after all, that he did have a sense of humour, that he was personable and that he tried. If you try then you have little to worry about. I think people judge each other quite harshly, and if you've actually had a go, and you've succeeded, at least in part, against the odds, then you've cracked it.

BARBARA TAYLOR BRADFORD

She is said to be the richest British woman after the Queen. Her books have sold over 54 million copies in 88 countries and 38 languages, spawning movies, audio-tapes and videos. She specialises in heroines who overcome adversity to make something of their lives, and modelled the first, Emma Harte in A Woman of Substance, *on many characteristics she sees in herself – ambition, drive, determination, dedication, discipline, a penchant for hard work, that Yorkshire understanding and a canniness about money. Barbara Taylor was born to a disciplinarian father and a quiet mother who instilled in her an enormous self-confidence and a love of books. She knew at the age of seven that she wanted to become a novelist, and sold her first short story to a magazine when she was ten. Aware that she had to 'live life a little', she left school at 15 for a £2-a-week job in the typing pool of the* Yorkshire Evening Post. *She tells here how she sneaked a story she'd written into the paper, and then, through enthusiasm and personality, persuaded the editor to give her a reporting job. By 18, she was editing the women's page, and two years later was in Fleet Street, going on to work for the London* Evening News *and* Woman's Own.*

Moving to the USA in 1963, she developed a regular column on interior designs and lifestyles which was syndicated to 183 newspapers. Reviving her story-telling ambitions, she started writing novels, but abandoned her first four through fear of failing and an uncharacteristic loss of confidence. She was in her early forties when she finally clicked into gear with the blockbuster hit A Woman of Substance, *and has been turning words into multi-million dollar fortunes ever since. She talks here about how the marketing and publicity flair of her film producer husband, Robert Bradford, turned her into an international celebrity and hits back at those critics who have questioned the literary quality of her work. She describes how she gets her ideas, creates the main characters, and then makes them interesting by giving them a problem 'because if there is no problem, there is no story'. Then comes the research, when the plot, and the main characters' life and background are locked into place. Her advice to all those who want to write a best-seller is to have tunnel vision: 'You've got to want to be a novelist more than anything else – it's got to be your obsession.'*

Barbara Taylor Bradford, what is your definition of success?

I think my definition of success is to have achieved what I wanted to do as a child, and that was to become a novelist. I didn't know what a bestselling novelist was in those days, so I have to say, just a novelist. The fact that I have achieved it, in a sense against great odds, to me defines success. I knew at the age of seven that I wanted to write books.

Why did you know so early?

I don't know. It's something that has always fascinated me, and it particularly fascinated my mother and father. I was an only child, and a little spoiled, I suppose. My mother was a voracious reader and I can only think that my love of books came from her, and from the fact that she read to me and taught me to read when I was four. I started writing in school exercise books, little stories a page long, when I was seven, and I sold my first short story – which, again, wasn't very long, I think it was all of three or four pages of childish handwriting – at the age of ten.

You sold it at the age of ten?

Well, I didn't know I was going to get paid for it. We sent it to a magazine called the *Children's Magazine.* My mother loved this story, which was about a child wanting a pony and getting it, so she made me copy it out neatly, with no ink blots or anything, and she sent it to this magazine. Nothing happened, but then, three months later, we got a postal order for 7s 6d, and they said they were going to use the story. Lo and behold, they did – eventually – but it didn't take up much space in the magazine. I think my destiny was sealed that day, when I saw 'Barbara Taylor' in print.

Was it seeing your name in print that made you think that this was the career for you, or was it the postal order?

Oh, it was definitely seeing my name in print. I was very good about that postal order. I bought my father some hankies from the local haberdasher and my mother a green vase, and put the rest in my money box. In those days you could get quite a few things for 7s 6d.

I think you will find, if you talk to writers who are as successful as I am, that they did start as children. I didn't suddenly say to myself at the age of 40, 'I want to be a novelist.' I had always wanted to be a novelist, and I always kept my eye on the hole in doughnut, if you want to put it that way – I always had tunnel vision, seeing where I wanted to go. I left school at 15 and got a job in the typing pool at the *Yorkshire Evening Post* knowing that I had to earn a living. I had enough common sense to know that you couldn't sell novels at the age of 22, or indeed 26. I think you have to live life a little bit before you can really write novels. I did that job in the hope of becoming a journalist simply to mark time.

In the space of two years you went from being a copy-taker in the typing pool to becoming the editor of the women's page. That is a remarkable transition by any journalistic standards. How did you do that? Was it just sheer ambition that drove you forward, or did you have any tactics, any plan? Or was it luck?

I think it was a combination of talent – because you have got to have the basic talent, and even at that age I had that going for me as far as my writing ability was concerned – drive, and a lot of ambition. I have always been a very ambitious woman, and I wouldn't be sitting here like this today if I hadn't been. But luck came into it too, and my first mentor.

Who was your first mentor?

He was the editor of the *Yorkshire Evening Post* at the time. His name was Barry Horniblow, and he had been brought up from Fleet Street from one of the Sundays – I can't remember which one any more, but he was very famous. The *Yorkshire Evening Post* was a broadsheet at the time, and it was losing money. He was brought in to transform it into a tabloid rather like the *Evening Standard*. In fact, I think it has gone back to being a broadsheet now, but for a long time it was a tabloid. While I was in the typing pool I kept doing little stories and sending them in, but nothing happened. Then one day I wrote a little feature story about a woman who lived locally, in Upper Armley, where I grew up. All the children thought she was a witch. She lived in a tumbledown, dirty old house with a lot of cats and dogs and she was very witch-like – she always wore black. Her name was Old Polly. I had discovered that her brother was in fact one of the richest men in Yorkshire. I tried to interview her but she banged the door in my face, so I talked to the neighbours. Everybody hated her because she was really very dirty and she really was a recluse. So I wrote this story and I dropped it on the sub-editor's desk along with some copy I had taken as dictation. Although I was in the typists' pool, for part of the morning they sent me over to the editorial side of the paper where I wore earphones and sat at a typewriter. A reporter would come on the phone and say, 'Oh, hello, this is Frank Shire,' or Keith Waterhouse, or whoever, and he'd ask, 'Who is this?' And I'd say, 'It's Barbara Taylor.' 'Oh, hello, Barbara, take my copy, I'm down at the CID,' or at the court, or whatever. And I would take it down and then take the sheets to the sub-editor.

So this piece had not been commissioned by anyone in the newspaper? It was written on your own initiative?

Yes. I had written a few other little items, but nothing had ever happened to them. But this one appeared in the paper.

With your byline?

No, I put Barbara Taylor on it, and typed it up in the way that I typed up the reporters' copy. And it appeared! But it just said, 'By a correspondent'.

And they didn't know it was you who had written it?

No, not until the chief sub, Edgar Craven, who had to list the stringers to be paid, said, 'Who's this? Could this be a stringer in Doncaster or in Wetherby? Who is Barbara Taylor?'

Somebody said, 'Wait a minute, I think Barbara Taylor is one of those copy typists.' Then, about three weeks or a month later I was summoned by the woman who ran the typing pool, whom I loathed. I'd told her, 'I'm going to be a reporter one day,' and she'd said, 'Oh, they all think that when they come here, but it never happens.' I'd thought, 'You wait and see.' Anyway, she said to me, 'What have you done? The editor wants to see you.' I said I hadn't done anything, because I hadn't. Now, I was all of 15 and a half, no make-up, and hair down to here, and I looked very innocent.

So I went to see Barry Horniblow, and he looked at me and he said, '*You're* Barbara Taylor?' I don't know who he thought was coming, but I suppose they'd told him I was just some young woman. What he didn't expect was a child to walk in. I was so nervous, I lost my shoe under his desk and was trying to get it back. He asked me, 'Why are you wriggling?' When I told him I'd lost my shoe under his desk, he got down and gave it to me. He was very nice. He said to me, 'Do you want to be a journalist?' I replied, 'I don't want to be, sir, I am going to be.'

Good line!

And I meant it most sincerely! And he said, 'Well, have you written anything before?' I told him I had written for the *Armley and Wortley News,* which was a weekly paper, and written this and that. He said, 'Oh, I would like to see those things some time.'

This was, I suppose, 10 a.m. My lunch-hour started at 12 o'clock, so instead of going to the canteen which I normally did, I took a tram all the way to Upper Armley. My mother was startled. I got my clippings book and she asked me whether I wanted something to eat. I said, 'No, no, no!' I was back at the newspaper at 1 p.m.

The editor's secretary was another old ogre like the one in the typists' pool, so I knocked on his door. There was nobody around. Horniblow happened to be sitting there having a sandwich. I said, 'Mr Horniblow, I've brought my clippings for you to see!'

So what was that? Was it ambition, was it youthful enthusiasm? What motivated me? Or was it seeing an opportunity? I think it was his enthusiasm, and the fact that he was thrilled that this young girl was so eager, excited, fresh. And, to digress for a moment, he was not liked, first of all because he was extremely good-looking. He had silver hair and wore wonderful Savile Row suits.

Why should he not be liked because of that?

I think the Yorkshiremen up there in those days saw him as a Fleet Street fellow who had been brought in because they weren't good enough to revamp the paper. And certainly he was charming and very suave and sophisticated and smooth – you never saw him with his jacket off and his sleeves rolled up like everyone else in the newsroom – and he was a damned good journalist as well, so there was a lot of resentment. So I think that my enthusiasm appealed to him. Of course, when he asked me how old I was and I said 15 and a half, he looked very shocked. Anyway, I gave him the stuff and he asked, 'When did you get this?'

I said 'Well, I went home in my lunch-hour.'

'Did you have lunch?'

'No, I didn't have time because it's half an hour there and half an hour back.'

He ordered me a sandwich from the canteen, and I ate it in his office. From that point I suppose I never looked back. That is the story of my life, though. People have often taken to me. Of course, I was very pretty, that goes without saying at 15 and a half. I was very fresh and blonde and green-eyed and all that, and had a Yorkshire complexion. But it was my enthusiasm that captured him, not my looks. It was my personality, my desire to do this work. We had a long talk over that sandwich.

So it was energy, enthusiasm, making a good impression, and the element of luck, which you created for yourself in many ways. You created the opportunity by looking for a way to beat the system and slipping your copy in with the other stories.

And also I had the smartness to go home for my clippings at lunchtime, to strike while the iron was hot. Something told me to do it straight away. I don't remember thinking that – obviously, it's a long time ago – but something did make me go home. My mother never forgot that. And it was lucky that the secretary was out to lunch because she was very possessive of Horniblow. What if she had been there? She might have taken my book and never given it to him.

Tell me where this confidence and this drive came from. To what extent did your parents push that into you? To what extent did they create the drive and the confidence that you clearly possessed from your very early days?

Well, I think the confidence did come from my parents. I was an only child, as I said, and there wasn't a day in my mother's life, right up until she died, when, if she spoke to me or saw me, she didn't tell me she loved me. Whenever I saw her. So when I was living at home that was every day. She also told me I was the prettiest, the most talented, the best at everything. I'm not, of course, but she gave me that self-confidence.

Was there never a cross word?

Oh yes. My father was quite a disciplinarian. He would tell me, 'You are not going to get anywhere if you don't work hard.' And my mother would say, 'You can do anything you want in life as long as you stick at it and don't lose sight of your goals.'

Being an only child is in some respects a terrible burden, because your parents pin all their hopes and dreams on you. There are no siblings to share any of this load. So it was almost a case of having to succeed because I couldn't let them down. But the confidence came from their belief in me. And my mother always said, 'I want you to try, because I really want you to have the kind of life I think you should have.'

Which was?

To be very successful at whatever it was I wanted to do. Well, of course, they knew I wanted to write.

You said you saw journalism as a means to an end. Did you always, throughout your journalistic career, see writing the big novel as the ultimate target?

Yes. When I gave my mother a finished copy of *A Woman of Substance*, she looked at it, leafed through it – even though she'd read the manuscript – and she had tears in her eyes. She said, 'This is the fulfilment of your childhood dreams.'

Let me take you back to before A Woman of Substance *was published. You'd had four goes at writing a novel?*

Four or five. I think it was four, yes.

So you had moved to the United States, where you wrote a syndicated column on interior design and lifestyles which was syndicated to 183 newspapers. You had a good career going in journalism, but you still wanted to write this novel and you'd had four dry runs with unpublished novels. Were they part of the plan, or each time, did you think, 'This is it, I am going to get this published'?

No. I'd also written six decorating books, but I never lost sight of the fact that I wanted to be a novelist. By this time I was about 40, I guess, and I thought, if I don't do it now I'm never going to do it. That was when I started on *A Woman of Substance*. But preceding that period, for about five years from around 1968, I would every so often start a novel.

And this was in between all the other things you were doing?

Yes. But I would get to either page 125 or 210 and stop and say, 'Oh, no, it's not right, I don't like this.' I'd lose confidence. It was the material, I think. I actually found three of them recently, when we were moving. I don't know what happened to the fourth. And they really weren't bad. I think if I'd given one of them to somebody halfway through, I would have had a contract. I don't know what the problem was. Maybe it was fear of failing. And they were suspense stories. I realized when I started *A Woman of Substance* that suspense had been the wrong genre for me.

So you had been trying to write the wrong kind of novel, and you realized that. A lot of people who would like to be writers sit down and put pen to paper, and someone says, 'Well, in literary terms it's not good enough. It doesn't read well, it doesn't flow well.' Are you saying that you've got to get the right subject for your style as well?

I think you have to, yes. The last book of those four was called *The Jasper Cipher*, and it was based on a true story, on some facts I had gathered from a titled woman in Spain who had been very close to Eva Peron and had been with her when she died. This woman told me a fascinating story about how Peron himself had hounded her for many years because he mistakenly believed that when Evita was dying she had given her friend the number of a Swiss bank account in Geneva.

So I had built a story around this, but one day I was working on it and I just realized that it wasn't right. I thought, 'I don't like this, I'm not sure why, but if it's not working for me, it's not going to work for the reader.' So I just stopped. I got out my yellow pad, and said to myself, 'All right, what do you want to write about?' I thought for a while, and I realized that I wanted to write about England, specifically about Yorkshire – a big, old-fashioned saga about a woman who makes it in a man's world when women weren't doing that. And I thought, 'Yes, that would make a good novel – a book about a woman who becomes a woman of substance.'

I knew straight away that that was a great title, and I wrote down the title *A Woman of Substance* and never changed it. A lot of people didn't like it, but now that phrase has passed into the language. People are always talking about women of substance. So in a funny sort of way, I think you have to know what subject you can write about and write about well, but you also have to know – and a lot of people don't understand this – what the public wants to read about if you want to be a commercial novelist.

So do you do research to try to find out what the public are interested in? How do you actually sit down and say, 'Right, this is going to be the great subject for my next novel'? Are there tactics, is there a plan? Do you look at it dispassionately, and think, 'Well, this is what I believe the public will respond to'?

There is detailed research, but that comes latterly. What usually happens is that I get the idea, and that is the only bit of inspiration there is for me anyway in writing a novel. And when I get the idea, it comes instantly, just like that.

Where do the ideas come from?

I don't know. Observation, I suppose. I watch the television news a lot. I watch CNN constantly. I'm a news buff. I read the newspapers and a lot of magazines. I am aware of what is going on in the world and what people are interested in filters into my brain, and I think that's how the ideas formulate in my mind, from everyday happenings and everyday realities. When I wrote a book called *Everything to Gain* I had suddenly realized that I lived on a day-to-day basis with violence, through television, especially in America. There were so many murders and car-jackings and so on that I suddenly thought, what would happen to a woman if she had a really wonderful marriage and that was her career – the marriage and the children – and it was all ripped away from her one day? And that novel became a big TV movie.

So, having had the idea, you sit down and write?

No, I don't actually do that. Having the idea is just the beginning, because then I have to get my protagonist, my main character, whether it's a man, like Maximilian West in *The Women in His Life*, or a woman like Nicky Wells in *Remember*, who was a TV journalist and was in Tiananmen Square. It wasn't about her career, but I wanted to show her working. Anyway, the protagonist comes to you as soon as you get the idea for the story – it is almost as though something bursts in my head at the same time. I get two thoughts. Then I have to say to myself, 'What makes this man or this woman interesting enough to be written about? What is it about them? What's their problem?' Because if there is no problem, there is no story. You have to have conflict, drama, almost melodrama, even, and emotional content as well.

So now you have the basic outline of the plot and the characters. You've worked out what they are going to be. Is it then that you sit down to write?

Then I do the research, if there is any research to do. First I figure out the plot and the main character's life, background and past history, because I have to know who he or she is and where he comes from. And I have to figure out the plot because I must know the end. If I don't, I can't ever start. Then I must have the title before I can begin – all strange idiosyncracies. Then I do any research that has to be done, and do it very quickly, within weeks. If I can't do it quickly, I start writing anyway, because I think people can research a book for ever and never write it.

When you start writing, what are the disciplines you impose on yourself? What is your routine when the words start to flow?

I get up early when I first start a novel. I am up every day at about 6 a.m. anyway, so I'm always at my desk by 6.30, often earlier. Usually I start in longhand every morning, unless I have a half-finished page typed.

Even if there is no inspiration there, you just feel you have to do it?

I have to. How else do you get a long, complicated book finished? Sometimes I'm slow starting, and sometimes it's not what I want. But I think if you don't get something down every day, that's how writer's block occurs. Touch wood, I have never had it, because I do get something down. At least then you have something to rewrite the next day.

Do you do a lot of rewriting?

Yes, I do. Basically, I start at 6.30 for the first few months, and then I begin to get up about 5 a.m., and sometimes even at 4.30, because I am always afraid of missing the deadline. And I never know what might happen in the story that I might not have anticipated, and which might make the book longer or more complicated, or if I will come up against something I have not thought out.

Are there moments when, halfway through a writing session, you will say, 'Hang on a second – this is wrong. I am going to go in a different direction from the one I planned'? Or, 'Here's an idea that I must pursue with my characters'?

Yes, that often happens. I often get new characters I didn't think I'd ever have or need. That is often because you can't have a lot of thought processes and inner dialogue, with just one character thinking things. With popular fictions you have to have dialogue and movement. So sometimes I need minor characters who I call 'messengers', a cook or a chauffeur or an assistant to whom the protagonist can pass information. Because you are always passing information to the reader.

A lot of successful people feel that there is a basic conflict between their family lives and their professional lives. Many, given the option, choose the professional life in order to achieve success, and the family have to make sacrifices. Have you ever found yourself in that conflict, and if so, what are the priorities for you?

Well, I have never had a conflict, because Bob has always been my most ardent supporter. Of course, we are in business together now, in a sense, because he produces all of my books for television or feature films, and in a way he manages my career. He looks after the advertising and the publicity, and manages all the other things involved.

There has never been a conflict because he was a movie producer when I married him, and he was always travelling the world and making movies then, and I was only on location with him some of the time. And we don't have children. I am not one of those people who regret it. So I didn't have children – too bad. I would have liked them but it didn't happen, so I must move on. Bob has always understood that I need my work tremendously, that it is my gratification, and for my own self-satisfaction, and to express a talent.

Could you have been as successful as you have been without him? Did you need that infrastructure there to make you as successful as you have been?

I think I would still have been a successful novelist, but I don't think I would have been an international celebrity. If we forget writing for a moment, I have become a very big name everywhere in the world, and I think that is because he made me a star. The writing of the books he had nothing to do with, but marketing and publicity he has. And there is another thing – Bob is a very good sounding board for me. He has always been involved with scripts and storyline and producing, and he has a wonderful eye for detail in a story. And when I finish a book I will listen to his advice, So, in a nutshell, I don't think I would have been as big as I am today if I had not been married to Bob.

Do you believe that there is no limit to a person's potential for achievement?

I don't think there is a limit, but you've got to work very hard. When people say to me, 'I want to be a novelist, but I never have the time,' I always tell them, 'You've got to want to do it more than you want to do anything else. You have got to want to write that novel more than you want to go to the movies, to the theatre, to a party or out to dinner. It's got to be your obsession.'

So success involves a certain sacrifice?

Yes, it does.

In terms of your personal lifestyle?

Absolutely. There are moments when Bob and I hardly get to talk at all. He's very busy, he goes to his office every day and I'm writing, and we snatch a moment in the morning. If we are going out to dinner, sometimes he has to phone me during the day just so that we can talk! And then when we come home at night we are tired. Being successful requires a lot of work. It sounds funny, but you have to work at your success. You can't stop, because if you do, somebody will overtake you.

It has been said that in some of your novels there are no mundane details of everyday life, that you create a sort of aspirational fantasy world.

Well, that's not true at all, and anybody who says that has not read the books. Often all reviewers do is look at the dust jacket. *Act of Will*, for instance, is about a woman who is a nurse in England in the 1930s and the 1940s and who has a truly hard life. For *The Women in His Life*, I did research into the Second World War. I went to East Berlin three times to do research. I also looked for old books and pictures to see what Berlin looked like in the 1930s. Even so some snotty reviewer on one of the Sunday papers said that the book was inaccurate. I wrote to him and asked him to tell me what the inaccuracies were, but I never had a reply because there were no inaccuracies. The bombing of Oxford Street, for example, was researched, and I am very proud of my research. After all, I was a journalist and I'm very factual.

How do you react to that criticism? Does it get to you, or do you have a kind of mechanism for overriding it, or brushing it away?

I brush it away. It does irritate me, and it makes me mad at times. I feel that if they haven't read the book, they have no right to criticize. Bob is a marvellous leveller for me. He says, 'Did they spell Bradford right?' If I say yes, he says, 'You start worrying the day they are not writing about you.' That's why ours is such a wonderful relationship. He dismisses all that as junk. He says, 'What was it your mother used to say to you? That they'll be wrapping up tomorrow's fish and chips in today's newspaper?' He won't let me get upset about it. But I feel that if they haven't read the book, they have no right to criticize.

What if they have read the book and still criticize?

Well, that's fair enough.

Do you take those criticisms on board?

No. If somebody doesn't like what I write, that's fine, but millions do. The public love me, so that's all that matters in the end – those women and men out there in 88 countries go out and buy Barbara Taylor Bradford books in 38 languages and watch the movies and buy the audios and the videos.

What do you say to those critics who question the literary qualities of your work?

I don't think the books are literary in that sense. If they were they wouldn't sell what they do sell. It's popular fiction, but it's damned good popular fiction, because I put a lot into it. The research is accurate, the writing style is very clean, straightforward and quite lyrical at times, especially if it's descriptive stuff. I think the books are jolly good for what they are, for pleasurable reading. I'm a lot better than most other people on the bestseller lists. I'm not going to be coy or modest – it's silly. I know that I'm better than most popular writers.

How do you prevent success, repeated success such as you've had – and I'm not thinking necessarily in your terms, but in terms of repeated success in general – from going to your head and influencing your behaviour?

I don't know about anybody else, but for me great success, as a novelist, came to me when I was in my forties, and I am a girl from Yorkshire with my feet on the ground. And I understand that success can be ephemeral. Bob always says, 'You are only as good as your last movie,' because he thinks in terms of movies. I am only as good as my last book. I think it's a lot to do with my upbringing, my marriage, my personality. I'm a very natural person and I don't play the star. I've taken success in my stride. I am not big-headed about it at all.

Does there not come a point for every successful person when they have to start reining back and saying, 'I've done enough now,' or do you think that driving force will carry you almost to your grave?

Well, I think it carries you on. I always joke that I am going to die at the age of 92, and like Custer, with my boots on, only I won't be carrying a sabre, I'll be at my typewriter. I go to the country most weekends and that is very quiet. We see a few friends up there, and I pull back a bit – we have holidays. But I still have all of this stuff going around in my head, and I really think they'd take me away in a straitjacket if I didn't write books and get all that stuff down. Irwin Shaw – the American novelist who is dead now – once said to me, 'You know, novelists don't need psychiatrists, Barbara, because we have our typewriters. We get all that junk in our heads into that machine.' And I think you will find that another writer I admire greatly, Pat Conroy, feels the same way. He is always recycling his family turmoils in his books.

The titles of all your books reflect the success ethic. They are all about success and achievement, aren't they, in one way or another?

They are not always about success in the sense of monetary or business success, but they are about overcoming adversity. *Act of Will*, for example, is about a woman striving to give her daughter a better life than she's had. *A Woman of Substance* is Emma's substance of character as well as the substance of money.

So is it possible for people to be successful in small ways, without having to aim for the kind of heights that you have reached, and without putting either money or a formidable workload as a top priority?

Yes, I think there is success on every level. It would be silly to say that there wasn't. It is also a matter of people's expectations. I suppose that as a child I was force-fed so much by my parents about success that I can't stop. You really would have to lock me up and throw away the key if you wanted me to stop, because my success is something that gives me great satisfaction. I have a friend who has a small linen business. She doesn't need to work – she is married to a wealthy man – but she loves old linens and spends a lot of time hunting for them and washing and ironing them. She's become very successful, and her work gives her an identity apart from just being somebody's wife. There again, a woman who has a family and a good family life is successful too. There are many levels of success – it all depends what it is you want. I'm just competitive by nature, and if I'm going to write novels, they have got to be bestsellers. But I wasn't aware of that when I started.

What advice would you give to people who say, 'I'd like to write a bestseller, too. I want to be Barbara Taylor Bradford'?

Well, first of all, forget the word bestseller. If you are going to set out with that in mind, you won't do it, because it is the wrong motivation. You have got to want to do the work. It's got to be telling the story that is important, and creating those characters, and being a novelist. That has to be the driving force. You can hope it is going to be a bestseller – why not? But don't try to do it unless it is absolutely essential to your wellbeing.

Who are your heroes? Who are the people, past or present, you regard as being really successful in life, and why?

Well, Winston Churchill, of course. He is my great hero. And Napoleon, although he didn't end up too well, did he? But for a time he was tremendously successful.

Doesn't your husband call you 'Napoleon'?

Yes, he does, because he says I am very bossy. I call him the General, or Bismarck – he is German-born – so he retaliates by calling me Napoleon. For a long time, Margaret Thatcher was a great hero. I felt she did an awful lot for England. I'm going for strong women – Elizabeth Tudor, Madame Curie, and Catherine the Great was a great queen, if you really know the story and don't swallow all the garbage written about her love life which is, for the most part, invented.

I am trying to think of somebody else who is alive – isn't that awful? I might add Barbara Bush. I'm very involved in something called the Literacy Partnership – do you know, 90 million Americans can't read – and she's done an awful lot to try to help people to learn to read.

Do you think that if you are successful there is an obligation to put something back into society?

Absolutely. As I said, I am very involved in this thing called the Literacy Partnership – I am going to Houston soon to read from one of my books at a Barbara Bush Foundation event. And I'm involved in City Meals on Wheels. There is a big luncheon every year at which we raise more money, and I am very active in that. I am on the board of the Police Athletic League, which was started about 60 years ago by policemen trying to get kids off the street. We now have about ten centres in the New York area where children can come after school and they are given reading material. It is somewhere for them to go in the afternoons. Police Athletic League have always had athletics, which is where the name comes from, but now we also concentrate on teaching art, music, film and so on. And we do a women's lunch every year when we honour three important women, and sell tickets for it. Those are my three main charities. I do things for the Variety Club of Great Britain (the Yorkshire branch) and for various other charities in England as well.

Have you ever felt like giving up? Just saying, that's it, I've had enough?

Never! I couldn't! What would I do?

Have you ever been confronted with failure?

We all have little failures of some kind or another.

How do you overcome those?

By moving forward and saying, 'Well, I will do better tomorrow.' I might, for example, fail with an employee – in a small way, I employ quite a number of people. Both Bob and I do, either at the office, in town or in the country. I'm always saying to them, 'This is why wars start. You don't communicate properly with each other!' But I say, 'I am going to continue.' I am very positive. My glass is never half empty, it is always half full.

What do you think are the biggest enemies of success?

Becoming swollen-headed, full of self-importance. I hate that. People can get pretentious, I hate that too. A lot of people who achieve success too young can't handle it properly and are inclined to treat people badly. They might speak to waiters rudely or treat their help badly. And the staff can't answer you back really, especially in an office environment. And I think that's bad. You can't treat people badly. The other day I was complaining about somebody to my secretary, and I said, 'I know you think I am too tough.'

She replied, 'No, you're not. You treat everybody the same, whether they are your friends or people who work for you.' I was very proud that she said that.

You might find that a lot of people reading your words now – probably more so in Britain than in America – are saying, 'She's too big-headed, she's too confident. Nobody can be that confident in themselves.' What would you say to people who think like that?

Well, of course I have moments of doubt. When I am writing, I think, 'Is this book going to work? Maybe it won't. How can I make it better? What if my publisher doesn't like it? What if it flops?' I am a terrible worrier, you know. I worry before I start, then I worry when I am writing, then I worry when it comes out. Are the public going to like it? Is this going to be my first non-bestseller?

But I know what I have achieved. I've done many things in my life and an awful lot for a lot of people. And that's what I try to point out if somebody starts flinging the subject of the money I have earned in my face, as if I shouldn't have earned it. There is nothing wrong with earned wealth, it is unearned wealth to which one might reasonably object. What about the work it provides for the people in the publishing industry? What about the movies that Bob has made in England based on books of mine? All the crews he has employed, and the actors and the stars? BBC Radio Four broadcast *The Women in His Life* in eight episodes over eight weeks. That employed 54 actors, not to mention all the other people involved. I don't deny that I earn a lot of money, but don't fling that at me as if I am stealing it.

People might feel that I am big-headed, I don't know. But I don't think I am. I think I am very natural. I am honest and straightforward – what you see is what you get.

Has success changed you? Are you the same Barbara Taylor Bradford as the 15-year-old who worked in that newspaper office?

Well, obviously I am older. I've matured, I'm tougher, and I've grown up in a very sophisticated world, so I'm different in that sense. But in a funny sort of way, I don't really think I am all that different. I was very natural then and I am very natural now. I take my work seriously, but as for the success, well, I can't really take that seriously, I can't let it rule my life. There are obvious changes, of course. I haven't lived in Yorkshire for 43 years, and I have lived in the States for 33 years, so I'm probably very Americanized, in many ways. But I still feel very English inside, very much the girl from Yorkshire.

What is the greatest pleasure you've had from your successful career?

Probably my greatest satisfaction was being able to give my parents *A Woman of Substance*, because they were so very proud, and it was a fulfilment of their dream, too – and knowing that what I set out to do I have done, and done well.

And is public acclaim important?

No, not really. In America I am not recognized in the street, though people might look at me twice. In England I am, especially if I use a credit card and they see my name. But it's not like being an actress – I don't have that high a profile.

But you don't consider public acclaim an important factor in your success? You like people to buy your novels, but you don't particularly care for being put on a pedestal by the public?

No, that's unimportant to me. Of course I want people to read the books, because why would I sit writing for months on end if I were not going to have readers? But public acclaim as a celebrity is of no consequence to me whatsoever. In fact I almost wish it would go away sometimes.

Is there a downside to success?

I think the downside is that people do intrude on your privacy – newspaper interviewers, for example. Of course, you permit it, because you are publicizing a product. The downside is that you've got to be on show a lot when you are out in public, especially if you are doing a book tour. But, as I said, I don't have the kind of high profile an entertainer would have. That must be terrible, like living in a fishbowl.

And you would like to keep your profile the way it is?

I have to do the interviews because I have to sell my books – and everybody does it today – but I don't want to be constantly in the public eye, no. I do need some privacy, I don't want to be always stared at.

What advice would you give to all those 15- and 16-year-olds, in Leeds or elsewhere, who are just setting off on a writing career and have the same kind of ambition you had to write a great novel?

Don't give up. After all, I was pushing myself as a journalist for a number of years, and I think journalism is a good place to begin. In any case, there are not many child prodigies writing novels and selling them at the age of 20 or 25, as we discussed earlier. Learn about writing, and honing your craft. Learn about life and about people, what makes them tick. Don't let rejection get you down – those rejection slips you get when you've submitted something and it is returned. Stick at it. And believe in yourself. Shakespeare put it better than I can, 'Unto thine own self be true.' If you really want to do it, then you must do it, and one day you will get there. As my mother used to say, 'You must have tunnel vision.'

When your time comes to leave this life, what would you like people to say about you?

That's a hard one. I think, 'Her books gave us pleasure.' A lot of readers write to me and say, 'You have given us so much pleasure. We have loved your books. They have touched us. They have moved us. They have entertained us. They have taught us things.' That's what I'd like them to go on saying.

RICHARD BRANSON

One of Britain's richest, most high-profile entrepreneurs launched his business career from a telephone box at the age of 15, because the teachers wouldn't let him have a phone of his own. With his father's blessing, Richard Branson then dropped out of public school to launch Student, *a national magazine for young people. By 19 he was in the record business, and Mike Oldfield's* Tubular Bells *album made him his first million. Other signings included Phil Collins, Boy George and the Sex Pistols. It was the beginning of the Virgin empire, which now stretches into most corners of the world and embraces his own airlines, hotels, megastores, railways, cinemas, radio stations, soft drinks and financial services. Daredevil attempts at balloning and powerboating records have fuelled his natural flair for publicity. Fiercely defensive of his empire, he launched legal action against British Airways over 'dirty tricks' allegations that they were poaching his passengers.*

He admits there have been a few close moments when the dividing line between success and failure has been very thin. But the bank manager who once pulled the plug on him when he overstepped a £3 million overdraft must have been more than a little put out when Branson sold Virgin Music to Thorn EMI for £510 million in 1992. He angrily went out of his way to buy back shares in the Virgin Group after an unsuccessful flotation on the Stock Market in the mid-Eighties. Condemning 'the fickleness of the City', he extols the joys of being a private company again. 'I'm very naughty,' he confesses. 'At times when I could live happily ever after, I will throw my life, my family and my business partners into turmoil by getting into another survival battle.' He believes the key to success is being able to motivate people and looking for the best in them. As befits a boss usually seen in a sweater, there is no dress code in his companies. He writes regularly to all his staff, and encourages them to write back. A scheme for allowing staff to take unpaid leave is a model he believes other companies should follow. Here he offers an entrepreneurial idea for a 16 year-old starting out in business today, and remembers his mother's ban on watching television: 'She would make sure I was doing things rather than watching other people doing them.'

Richard Branson, what is your definition of success?

I suppose success is achieving what one sets out to achieve. My particular definition is getting a group of people around me, inspiring them, motivating them and then setting out together to achieve something. And trying to be proud of what one creates – proud of the people you have around you and, ultimately, proud of yourself as a result.

To what extent is success a product of your background and your upbringing?

I was fortunate in having a mother who brought me up in a particular kind of way and her determination was that I wouldn't spend time watching television – I wouldn't spend time watching other people playing football, going ballooning. She would make sure that I was doing things rather than watching other people doing them. And I think that upbringing has helped me get where I have got. My father is the opposite. He is very laid back and very unambitious, a very lovely man who wanted to be an archaeologist, but was pushed into being a lawyer. And they balance each other well, but my mother can never stop, and I think maybe I've got a little bit more of my mother than my father in me.

Do you remember the circumstances in which you told your father that you wanted to leave school, and his reaction?

I was about 16 and I'd started a magazine at school called *Student* which was sold around other schools and colleges as well. My headmaster told me that I either had to get on with my schooling and give up the magazine or leave school and do the magazine. I chose to leave school and do the magazine, and I remember walking around the garden one day with my father, telling him that I was thinking of leaving school, and trying to get his blessing on it. He was remarkably understanding, I think, because he'd been pushed by his father into doing something he didn't want to do, and had spent his lifetime doing it. He basically said, 'At least at 16 you know what you want to do in life,' which is quite rare. 'Give it a go,' he added, 'And if it fails, we'll try to get you into some school to finish your education.'

Did you ever think, when you were leaving school at 16, that you could be doing the wrong thing? At a time when all the pressure was on getting A-levels and moving on to university, did you think, 'I might be blowing it'?

Strangely, I didn't. I decided what I wanted to do and I didn't particularly enjoy the academic way of life – all this knowledge was being crammed in, in a slightly unreal way, in my opinion. I wasn't really learning any French, the way it was taught, or Latin – and I couldn't see any point in learning that anyway, nor could I see any reason for religious studies. When I actually listed the subjects, I thought that my day was being taken up with things which weren't leading me anywhere. So getting out of school, getting down to London, getting into a basement, exploring life in what I felt was a much more real way, made sense and was something which I never really look back on. It was a wonderful sense of freedom.

And your first business was started from a telephone box?

I was not allowed a telephone at school, understandably perhaps, and so I had to use the school telephone. I would ring advertisers and try to persuade them to take advertising in the magazine because that was the only way I could think of to fund it. It took me a year or so, but I managed to get about £5,000 worth of advertising committed to the magazine, and used that as the means of getting the first 50,000 copies printed. I had to learn the art of bullshit, I suppose, telling National Westminster Bank that Lloyd's Bank were advertising when they weren't necessarily. And vice versa. Playing one advertiser off against the other. I can't remember how I learned it, but I stumbled into it and soon learned that people will most likely say no unless they feel they are going to miss out, and then they come along quite quickly.

Do you feel when you're setting out in any business venture that an individual can only bring a certain amount to the table and that you do need others to come in and fill the gaps, to make it a rounded package, as it were?

The absolute key to success is being able to motivate people and looking for the best in people. All of us have our faults and strengths, but too often people look for faults rather than strengths. If you're a leader of people you've got to put people's faults on one side and draw out all their good points. To a large extent you have to ignore their faults, because the moment you start highlighting faults you're going to lose your relationship with those people and demotivate them. I think adults are no different from children. I've got two young children and believe in bringing them up with the philosophy that you praise them – lavish praise on your children and they will flourish, in the same way that watering plants lets them flourish. The same applies to adults. As the chairman of the company, I myself love praise, I flourish under praise, and criticism often makes you feel, 'Is it really worth it all?' Praise is absolutely critical.

If you have a project and you want it to be a success how do you counter adverse criticism and comment that comes your way, that could actually affect the success of the project?

Virgin's philosophy is that we won't go into a new business unless we feel that it will bring better value for money, that the quality we will provide is better than other people are offering, that we have got the best people, and that we are going to enjoy doing it. If you've got those ingredients right, then any criticism is, most likely, undeserved, and the public will see that criticism for what it's worth. Our philosophy is that we don't ever want to see the Virgin name damaged and we will go to extraordinary lengths to make sure that the products we produce and the services we offer are exceptionally good. If at some stage we were to decide to go into something just for making money's sake or to make a quick buck, and we got criticized, then the public would soon see that we'd messed up and that would damage everything else that we'd done. But as long as you make sure that you believe in what you're doing, then the public sees through unpleasant criticism. The public are no fools in the end.

So money is not the be-all and end-all of business success?

I suspect you won't find any entrepreneur you've interviewed ever saying that money is that important in his or her life. I started off as a teenager editing a magazine. I wanted to bring a magazine out, I wanted to change the world, as most teenagers do, and I never considered that I'd one day become an entrepreneur. I only became one in order to make sure that my magazine survived. I had to deal with the printers, the paper manufacturers, the advertisers in order to get the magazine out, and I had to learn the art of survival. I became an entrepreneur by mistake. Ever since then I've gone into businesses, not to make money, but because I think I can do it better than it's been done elsewhere. And, quite often, just out of personal frustration about the way it's been done by other people. Take the airline business. I used to fly on other people's airlines, and thought the experience was a very unpleasant one. It was obvious that people in the airline business ran it extremely badly and didn't take the customer into account whatsoever. I felt we could create the kind of airline that I'd like to fly, and if you create the kind of business that you'd like to experience, then quite often it will work. And because I fly a lot and experience a lot, I'm always looking at details and striving to get them right. That's perhaps the best reason for going into a business. What money brings you is the freedom to spend time in the day doing what you want to do rather than what somebody else wants you to do. It enables you to indulge in fantastic challenges, fantastic ways of testing yourself to the limits, which maybe you couldn't do if you didn't have those resources.

You talked about your airline. How important is the bottom line there? You went through a year when you were losing quite a bit of money and you're now back in profit again. Obviously that must be a factor, when you lose money like that on a project that is close to your heart. Do you ever have any doubts that you've done the right thing?

When we went into the airline business nearly 14 years ago, people thought we were absolutely mad. What's somebody who runs an entertainment empire doing going into the airline business? My closest friends thought I was mad as well. But I felt that I could afford to do it by protecting the downside. I could buy one plane, and I could do a deal with Boeing whereby, if my vision was proved to be mistaken, I could hand that plane back at the end of the first year. This gave me one year to try it. And fortunately that first year proved reasonably successful. It proved that people wanted the kind of airline that we were going to create, and so we went on to buy a second plane, and a third. But all the time I tried to make sure that, should this vision not work out, we could one day close it down and not have it bring all the other companies down as well.

Throughout the 30 years of building companies, there have been quite a few close moments when the dividing line between success and failure was often very thin, and there have been occasions when I've had to persuade that last bank to keep everything going. And having somehow managed to come through, I think we're that much stronger as a result. You'll find there is not one entrepreneur who started from scratch, without any financial resources, who hasn't come very close to disaster, and an awful lot of them fall by the wayside. There are very few that actually go through their lifetime without having had a spectacular bankruptcy or having had something go horribly wrong at some stage or another. But each of those experiences makes you that much stronger and makes it that much less likely that it's going to happen in the future.

So if you have failed at something or come close to failing at something, that puts you in a stronger position to be successful?

Yes. Life is one long learning process and I suppose what's fascinating with Virgin is that we go into many different areas, and we're learning all the time. I see running Virgin almost like a new university course every two months.

You went public for a couple of years and then you were deeply disillusioned with your love affair with the City. Why did you want to go public in the first place? And why did you think it hadn't worked?

I think one has two evils to consider. One is having to deal with banks – and banks can be very tricky people to deal with – and the other is having to deal with the City – and the City can be very tricky to deal with, too. We had a very successful company, what turned out to be the most successful independent record company in the world, Virgin Records, and yet banks were always playing up with us, despite the fact that we had acts like Phil Collins, Peter Gabriel, The Rolling Stones, Janet Jackson. The banks couldn't comprehend the value in these artists who go on year after year after year. We thought that maybe the City would be more understanding, so we floated the company. We got a valuation of £240 million for it. Our profits that year were £15 million then we doubled our profits to £31 million – but the October 1987 crash took place the day that we announced our results, and instead of our share price doubling to £500 million in value, which I think it should have done, it collapsed, showing a market value of about £75 million. So I had 50,000 members of the public who were showing a paper loss, all our artists were showing a paper loss, my friends, my neighbours, my family were all showing a paper loss, and there was a danger that we'd lose our reputation, which is everything. So I felt that if we gave everybody their money back and we went private again, we would keep our reputation intact. By going public we'd actually put a value on the company, and we could then go back to the banks and say, 'Look, this is what the company's worth,' and we could bow out gracefully. That was one of the best decisions we've ever made. It gave us a taste of what life was like in the City, and also of its fickleness, its short-term thinking, and it made us realize that it wasn't something which we'd ever do with one of our top companies again. It made us appreciate the joys of being a private company.

To what extent does all the extra-curricular activity in which you indulge – the ballooning, power boating and so on – have an effect on the business?

Up until about the time we launched the airline – 14 years ago – I used to follow my parents' philosophy and that was, 'Whatever happens in life, remain a private person. Let your businesses speak for themselves, avoid doing interviews, avoid projecting yourself.' And I remember I met Freddie Laker over lunch and he said, 'Look, if you're going to compete with the Pan-Ams and TWAs and British Airways, and you haven't got the advertising spend, you've got to get out and use yourself to promote the companies.' And believe it or not, I was quite a shy person. I was not very good at public speaking, in fact I was pretty dreadful at public speaking, and I had to overcome that. But I believe that if you do something in life, you've got to do it well. I try to throw myself into this new world of promoting our businesses with a vengeance. So I thought that if journalists are going to turn up for an inaugural flight, they're not going to want a boring picture of me in a suit, they're going to want a picture of me with a captain's outfit on. That would have a better chance of getting a front-page picture, with our airline being projected well as a result. And ever since then, that is the philosophy we've taken, and because of that the brand name has become one of the top 100 brand names in the world. In a business sense, there's no question that it's helped Virgin and the other companies enormously. On top of that, I love personal challenges as well, and have great difficulty resisting a challenge. If somebody says to me, 'Well, maybe technically we can get a balloon to fly in the jet stream and maybe we can be the first people to cross the Atlantic,' that, personally, is a great challenge, and if I'm going to do it, I might as well kill two birds with one stone. I'm not going to have British Airways on the side of the balloon, Virgin will be splashed across its side.

I would do these challenges, I think, whether I was running a company or not. I'm very lucky to be in a position where I can do them, but they do help put Virgin's name on the map around the world, and they do have a rub-on effect on all the businesses. Amongst, say, young people who buy Virgin Cola, it gives an image which Coca-Cola could never manage to get across.

Is there a danger, though, that it means you *are Virgin? And if anything were to happen to you, that the companies might suffer as a result?*

I think that would have been the case if something had happened to me a few years ago, but Virgin, as a name, is now stronger than my own name. Virgin is synonymous with fun, good value and quality and all the things that we've set out to achieve. It will outlive me for many, many years to come. And on top of that, I hope that if I ever get run over, Virgin will benefit from a sympathy vote, if nothing else!

You said you were shy at one stage. How did you overcome your shyness?

I had two good friends, one was actually Gavin Maxwell who wrote *Ring of Bright Water*, the book on otters, and the other a man called Gavin Young who's *The Observer*'s war correspondent, and I remember over lunch one day they said, 'Look, if you're doing an interview, just think of yourself sitting in a front room talking to a friend,' and that helped a lot, rather than thinking of an outside group of people listening to you. I remember Tony Howard, the BBC commentator, when I did my first interview – aged 17 – on *The World at One*. He sent me a tape and one tape had all the er's and um's he'd cut out, and the other tape had left all the er's and um's in. Without the er's and um's I sounded relatively eloquent. But I think because I'd left school before I'd got properly educated, and because I'd had to go out and educate myself by getting out and interviewing people and being in the real world, I hadn't had the benefit of being well read. It was a very different kind of education. That does handicap you in certain circumstances, particularly when it comes to making speeches. I remember making a speech on the steps of University College in the late 1960s – Tariq Ali spoke first, wonderfully eloquent, about student revolution and then Danny Cohn-Bendit stood up and then I stood, and after about 30 seconds I forgot my words and disappeared into the crowd and just thought, 'Thank God nobody knows who the hell I am!'

You talked earlier about the importance of the people who work for you enjoying themselves. What would you say to those businessmen who look constantly at the bottom line, who take a hard-nosed financial approach to their companies and enjoyment doesn't really come into the equation, because it is the dividend to their shareholders, it is the way that they can save costs, that matters at every stage of the process? Are they making a mistake?

Yes, I think they are. They would most likely make a lot more money if they took a completely different approach to things. If you think that somebody who works for a company spends 80 per cent of their life at work and maybe only 20 per cent of their life at home, how sad it would be if that 80 per cent of their life is a miserable one. It ought to be a happy one, it ought to be something special, and it ought to be special from the switchboard operator right up to the chairman. I think it's up to chairmen to realize this and to go out of their way to make sure that people are enjoying their jobs. For instance, if you take a switchboard operator, you know if she answers the phone and gives her name she's immediately a person, and if the chairman rings through to the switchboard and has a minute to talk to the switchboard operator instead of just asking them to put them straight through, they're even more of a person. It's communicating with all your staff and making sure that even if they've got little problems, someone's there to deal with those. I try to deal with it by writing to them every month or two months, giving them my home address and encouraging them to write to me if they've got problems. I get about 30 or 40 letters a day, and try to make sure that those are the letters that get answered first. And in a bigger sense, if a company has financial problems, most companies will look at dealing with those problems by laying people off, that'll be the first thing that they will think about doing.

But that's the stereotyped way of doing things. At Virgin, we've attempted to avoid that, and a few years ago when Virgin Atlantic was in the depth of the recession, the Gulf War, and the British Airways attacks on us, we had too many staff and we wrote to all the staff asking for suggestions as to what we could do about it. About 400 people wrote back saying they'd love to have unpaid leave for a while and then come back when the company was stronger again. That was so successful that we now have introduced, on a permanent basis, unpaid leave for people who want it. And at any one time in the Virgin companies we have about 500 people on unpaid leave, which means we are actually employing 250 more people than we would have done as a company otherwise. If every company in the country were to do something like that, the amount of people on the dole would be cut down dramatically. I think other companies need to look at imaginative ways of avoiding demoralizing their staff, rather than taking the easy option.

Another trademark of your company is the dress code. Ninety per cent of companies would require their male employees to come into work in a collar and tie because that somehow gives the impression that they are creating a better business environment. You've deliberately said no to that. Why and how do you feel that that contributes to the successful atmosphere within Virgin?

I'm the last person who would require anybody to wear a collar and tie. I've been fortunate that ever since I was a teenager I've been running my own company, and I therefore have never had to conform to what somebody else would expect me to conform to. Personally, I find it more comfortable in the winter months to wear a sweater and in the summer months to wear a jacket. I've never found a tie particularly comfortable. Therefore, we've made it clear to anybody working for Virgin that they should dress as they feel comfortable. And interestingly enough, quite a number of people actually feel more comfortable in a collar and tie, and they wear collars and ties and suits, but I think the vast majority of people who work at Virgin find that dressing in casual clothes is something which they prefer to do. Maybe more companies should consider that. I was in Los Angeles in a large company the other day, and they have experimented with letting people wear casual clothes on Fridays, and they say people seem to work twice as hard when they dress as they feel comfortable. They seem to get more done. I can't quite understand why companies carry on insisting that their employees have to conform to such a large extent.

Do you have any general rules for maintaining the quality of your products and ensuring that right through all the companies you are reaching a certain standard?

I don't have any rules as such, but I think what's critical is attitude. For example, take myself as chairman of the company. It would be easy for me to think, 'We're successful now, we've made some money, we've got something which everybody respects, I'm just going to lie back, go to sleep and enjoy what we've created.' The moment you get into that frame of mind, your company is going to start slipping. What you have to do is get on a flight, say hello to all the staff, spend time with all the staff, have a little notebook in your back pocket, listen to all their comments, write all their comments down, get out and talk to all the passengers, greet them all, listen to them, write all their comments down. Even after 14 years I will always come back with about 30 or 40 new suggestions, new ideas, down to the tiniest little details like the size of the salt sachets, or the shape of the new blouse. It's all these little things which, if you make sure the next day you follow up on and get changed, make for an exceptional airline or company over just an average airline or company. When I watch directors or chairmen of many companies going out and talking to their staff I find that they will listen and they will nod, and I know that there is no way they can remember more than one or two suggestions. If they don't write them down or they don't follow up on them, they're not going to get anything done. The most frustrating thing for people working for a company is when they see the same things wrong day after day after day, and they can't understand why the management aren't putting them right. That's when people leave companies, out of frustration at things not getting sorted out. People work for companies because they want to work for something which is the best company in the world. They want to be proud of working for the best company in the world, they want to contribute to that. If it is the best, then they're going to be smiling, they're going to be happy, and the customer who comes into contact with them is going to have a great time. You can lose that very easily, and you've got to keep at it the whole time.

What were your greatest failures and how did you recover from them?

We've come very close on a number of occasions to failing. In a sense we perhaps got too close to one bank, in the early days with Coutts and Company. I remember the day that I came back from the inaugural flight from Virgin Atlantic, finding my bank manager sitting on my doorstep – we'd gone just over a £3 million overdraft facility. And he told us that he was going to bounce the cheques on the Monday, and this was Friday. This was for the airline. I got up and showed him to the door and told him he wasn't welcome in my house. I was shaking with rage and we managed to scramble some money together, so that we were only £200,000 over the limit, then we managed to scramble more money together from our various companies around the world, and cover the £200,000 on the Monday. And by the Friday we'd been to various other banks and we'd increased our overdraft limit from £3 million to £30 million. It just showed that one bank manager was willing to bankrupt, not just Virgin Atlantic, but all our Virgin companies. And yet another bank, looking at exactly the same set of figures, was willing to lend ten times the amount. And so I think that not relying too heavily on one bank and one bank manager is a good rule to learn.

You've talked of the team spirit amongst the Virgin companies, but at the end of the day someone has to be in charge. Do you have to be, to a certain extent, ruthless and even arrogant at times in order to drive through what you want?

I don't think so, strangely. I think that people have the idea of an entrepreneur being the sort of stereotyped person who treads all over everybody and bullies their way to the top. There certainly are people like that, and they have managed to get away with it, but they generally get their come-uppance in the end. I think that the alternative way of finding good people, motivating them, giving them the benefit of the doubt, and trying to draw out the best in them is a better way. At Virgin, we desperately try not to sack people. If somebody is not working out in one area, we think, 'Maybe if we moved them into a different area, their good points would be better used.' Obviously there are occasions when we do part company with people, but we try to make sure that that is the exception to the rule. It's something which I hate doing and feel incredibly uncomfortable about.

But when it has to happen, it has to happen. You can't carry any passengers.

No, ultimately, you're right. If somebody is literally a passenger then obviously we have to part company.

And what about someone who threatens your position at the top?

I suppose I'm fortunate that because I own the companies and we're not a public company that situation wouldn't happen. But the important thing is that there are times when you get really frustrated by somebody, or somebody does something which really angers you. You could have a flare up with that person, and fall out with them and say that you want nothing more to do with them. But basically the world is a very small place, and I find that there have been occasions where I've forgiven somebody for something, which perhaps some people wouldn't have done, and two years later that person's cropped up in another field, and I have needed them for something completely different. They appreciate the fact that one treated them in that way, so good comes of these things. We were proud of the fact that in 20 years of running a record company, we never lost a major artist. They appreciated the way they were dealt with and always re-signed their contracts. A different approach, a harder approach, would have meant that we would have fallen out with a lot of those artists. They would have left to go to other record companies and the company would have been the poorer for it.

Who are the people whose success you really admire? In any field, past or present.

President Mandela, of all the people in the world, is the person I most admire. His forgiveness is the most wonderful thing, given the way he spent 25 years in prison. And not just him, actually his whole Cabinet are remarkable individuals who've come out and are now working with the people who kept them in prison. They have managed to unite a country that was so divided before, and I can't think of any better example.

Anyone whose success you particularly admire in business?

There are quite a few people. Somebody like Anita Roddick – who in fact we're just going into competition with, so she's maybe not quite so happy with me at the moment – she's built a tremendous company in Body Shop, and she's stood by what she believes, and I think created a special company with good, well-motivated staff. An interesting person who is not so well known is a guy called Archie Norman who used to run Asda. I admire him because when he once came to see me and asked permission to go and meet all the staff at Virgin to see how we ran our company. He took a day off, and went and saw our people, and I'm sure after seeing Virgin he went off to look at other companies. I think for a chairman to take the time and trouble to go and examine how other people are doing things and to see how he can motivate his own staff is quite a rare commodity.

Could someone, a 16-year-old, setting out now in the current business environment, achieve the same kind of things you have achieved? Is the potential still there?

Yes. I suspect that the best thing for them to do would be to try and indulge in their hobby. If for instance they play tennis, they might find that there needs to be a sort of tennis ball delivery service amongst all the tennis courts in the area, so they could get the names and addresses of all the people who play tennis there. Ideally it should be something which they have a passion for.

The important thing is that they don't think, 'Right, how can I make a lot of money? Let's go into something to make a lot of money.' It's got to come from the heart.

What do you think are the greatest enemies of success?

If you start becoming aloof and start losing touch, that obviously is a great enemy. I think one of my deep dangers in life is I have great difficulty saying no, and therefore there is a danger of spreading oneself too thin. That is a danger that one has to watch for all the time.

Does success bring obligations in its wake, to society as a whole?

Success must bring obligations. If you're in a position to change things and you feel that things are not being done well in society, then one should try to use that position to change things. It's also business sense. For example, when the Gulf War took place and there were thousands of refugees pouring over the borders, we brought in a number of planes to help those refugees. It meant that the staff who worked for Virgin felt they weren't just working for a money-making machine, they were working for a company that *did* care and *could* set out and do something. And so I think that caring can actually pay for itself, and that if companies do more than just function as businesses, the staff can feel far prouder of working for those companies than if they're solely money-making machines.

Has success changed you at all?

I'm sure it has, but I don't actually feel that different from when I was 15 or 16. Even then I was running the student magazine and then having the Student Advisory Centre and the student this and the student that, and now I'm running Virgin, it's Virgin this and Virgin that. So things have not changed that much, they've just got a little bit bigger and I've learned a little bit more over the years. But it's still much as it was in the early days.

What is the greatest pleasure you've had from your success?

I think it's being in a position to empower, to get up and fulfil dreams and get to know people, and have the pleasure of collecting a great bunch of friends over the years. It's been a fascinating number of years.

And if you could gather together, in one room, all the young people in the world today who want to be like Richard Branson in 20 years' time, what advice would you give them?

I think the definition of success must be whatever one's doing in life, do it well, enjoy doing it, and do it with a smile – whether you are the switchboard operator, the carpet cleaner, the window cleaner or the entrepreneur. Life is short – just get out there, enjoy it and throw yourself into it. If you're one of those people who throw themselves into it and do it with a smile, I suspect you'll find you'll move up in the world far quicker than those people who think, 'What on earth am I doing this for – what a drag it is, I wish I was doing something else,' and show it on their faces. You want to be one of those people who stand out from the crowd by being the cheeriest, happiest person around.

So is happiness a core ingredient of success?

I think it is. When I see somebody with a genuine smile, who's cheerful and throwing themselves into what they're doing, it's such a pleasure and I think it gives pleasure to everybody else. And sometimes it's not easy for those people – sometimes they're under an enormous amount of stress. But they are definitely the people who will go places in life.

Some people would say they are happiest when they have actually achieved success, but you're saying, 'Be happy on the way to that goal'?

Yes. Sometimes it's not easy, but you've got to lift yourself above the norm and this is one way, I think, of doing so.

One final question. When your time comes to leave this life, what would you like people to say about Richard Branson?

I don't know, I suppose something like, 'He treated people well,' or something. I think it's how you deal with people that matters most in life, how you bring up your children, and the friends you have around you.

GEORGE CARMAN

They call him 'the silver fox', in deference to his gently advancing years and the forensic cunning with which he dissects the evidence of those who stand in the way of his legal triumphs. His mood in court varies with his purpose – from the deadly to the avuncular. He knows how to slide in the knife and when to draw gently back – a skill summed up by one newspaper in the headline 'Excuse me while I take you apart.' He celebrates victories with champagne – and has broken open the bubbly on behalf of the former Liberal leader Jeremy Thorpe, Coronation Street actor Peter Adamson, Elton John, Richard Branson, Jason Connery, Ken Dodd, the cricketer Imran Khan and a succession of grateful newspaper editors. He is not infallible – the occasional defeat has been inflicted upon him – but his reputation as a leading libel lawyer is as formidable as the huge fees he is said to command. He says he owes much to his mother, an ambitious perfectionist from a relatively humble background whose influence on her only child was strong. Educated under 'the pretty harsh regime' of the Irish Christian Brothers, he was beaten at school for not eating his porridge, ran away, but had to return, thus learning that he couldn't be too much of a rebel. He trained for the priesthood – until he found he liked girls – and went up to Oxford for a first-class degree and 'three of the most stimulating years of my life'.

The urge to make a living by speaking in public was strong. Cutting his debating teeth on a soapbox at Hyde Park Corner, he contemplated journalism, the Foreign Office, and even politics, before settling on the law. He eked out such a meagre living on the Northern Circuit that, at times, he couldn't pay his gas bill, but found poverty a great stimulus to working hard. Then came his big break. He went to London to defend the manager of a Big Dipper which had collapsed killing several children. Carman got him off, and the famous solicitor Sir David Napley, who was also involved in the case, decided that 'if he could do that without much of a defence, he was worth watching'. Three times divorced, there is today a sense of loneliness about George Carman, but, as he approaches his seventies, he shows no sign of retiring. 'The successful person,' he says, 'is usually discontented – he always wants to reach the next peak.' Normally a reticent man, he is here unusually frank about his legendary courtroom approach and technique.

George Carman, what is your definition of success?

I think success is the satisfaction of using whatever talent or skill you discover that you may possess to help other people or to give pleasure to other people, either at a time of crisis or at a time when they are relaxing. But it is essentially the satisfaction of knowing that you have made some contribution, however modest, to the general welfare of society.

In the course of doing that, have you got to have a certain ambition for yourself?

Yes, you have. Unless you are a saint, and everything is done solely for non-selfish reasons, people usually have to be driven by ambition to achieve a significant success.

To what extent has your success been shaped by your background and upbringing?

No doubt, profoundly, like everyone else. I started from a fairly humble background and, as a boy, I was determined to try and succeed, not knowing of course the exact path to success at that time.

So success itself was a general ambition rather than a particular profession or a career path that you saw opening up before you in those early days?

I think initially that was so. I was determined to try and do something worthwhile with my life and something different from what other people around me were doing.

What was it about the other lives that you saw that made you want to be different?

Well, in the arrogance of youth, those lives were insular, they were limited in outlook, they were very content with their position, and the successful man is usually a discontented man. He always wants to reach the next peak.

As far as your parents were concerned, did they have ambition and drive themselves and did they transfer that to you?

My dear father was not a highly ambitious man. He was an auctioneer and he had a modest furniture business, but he was a man who was easily satisfied, placid in temperament and fairly easy-going. My mother was quite different. She was an Irishwoman and she was temperamental. She was ambitious and she was a perfectionist. And I think her own standards somehow touched off on me.

Did you ever rebel against her desire to transfer her ambition on to you?

No, I think it stimulated me. Never once did I find that in any way offensive or disagreeable. On the contrary she was for me a very profound support, both as a child and as a young man. Unhappily she died when I was only 24 years of age.

You went to boarding school at the age of eight, was that a help or a hindrance in shaping your desire for success?

Well, it was a pretty harsh regime. The Irish Christian Brothers weren't noted for their gentleness, necessarily, but the beginnings of discipline at that age were probably, in retrospect, very good, because another secret of success, of course, is self-discipline, which you have to achieve. To start as soon as possible is perhaps no bad thing.

But you didn't like that discipline at first. You actually ran away from school?

Yes, I did. I was beaten for not eating the porridge that was put in front of me, and I ran away, but I had to go back and face the music – which was to eat the porridge next time round.

What did that teach you – the fact that you did run away because you felt you couldn't take any more, but then had to go back and face up to it – what did you learn from that?

I suppose I learned that you couldn't be too much of a rebel, that you had to conform if you were to succeed. Some people succeed without in any way conforming. I am afraid I wasn't such a person.

Your ambitions drew you towards the priesthood at first. Why?

I was an altar boy as a young child, and of course very much influenced by the priests I met. They seemed to be kind men doing a tremendous job and they became heroes to me, whom I admired, so I went away to be a priest at about 14 years of age.

But you changed your mind at 16. Why?

A number of reasons. I have a frivolous answer to this question, but it is at the same time quite a serious one. I realized I liked girls and it is interesting that nearly half a century later the problem of married priests is resurrecting itself. But a second reason was that I was beginning to entertain doubts about some aspects of the Catholic theology, the principal one of which, curiously enough, was the besetting problem of birth control. I realized that population was an important problem for the world, and I thought the Catholic position on it was intellectually untenable.

So having decided not to be a priest, what were the options that you considered?

I considered journalism, the Foreign Office and the Bar.

Why did you turn down two of those?

I'm not sure I had any natural gift for writing, and I'm not sure I would have fitted into any civil service administration – I would not naturally have adapted to the collective corporate discipline.

So was it simply a process of elimination that drew you to the legal profession, or was there an actual enthusiasm for it?

There was a positive enthusiasm to earn a living by speaking, in some way or another, in public. I was very attracted by debate and very attracted romantically by the lives of famous advocates.

Had you done much debating at school?

Yes, I took every opportunity to debate and indeed later on, I think at about 19 or so, when I got into Oxford, I actually spoke at Hyde Park Corner on a soap-box in support of the Catholic Evidence Guild as it was called. I very much enjoyed speaking to a tough crowd in Hyde Park. I think I did that about half a dozen times.

What do you remember about the cut-and-thrust of the crowd at Hyde Park Corner?

Well, the hecklers were quite terrifying, because they were pretty seasoned campaigners, and I recall very much the enormous stimulus that it gave me to be able to speak, albeit rather badly at the time, no doubt, and the sense of achievement from conveying a message to a large indiscriminate group of people.

Do you remember any times when a heckler put you down?

I am sure the hecklers got the better of me many times, but that would be the exact incentive to try and improve and learn how to deal with them.

You say you were attracted by the lifestyle of the great advocates. What was it about that which attracted you?

I think their individuality. The Bar is a profession which is highly individual, which significantly depends on personal performance in each case – as the phrase goes, 'You are only as good as your last case.' Also, in many cases there is a tremendous sense of drama and of course a great deal at stake for the litigant. It was those features that attracted me then and attract me now.

You like the sense of drama? Do you find that stimulating?

Yes, a courtroom case is sometimes like a military campaign. There is ebb and flow in the battle and it may take a long time to achieve success, or you may see the case slipping away from you. So there is that drama of not knowing what the result might be, and of having to fight for the result throughout the case.

You went up to Balliol at Oxford. It might be said you were a provincial boy arriving at this great university. Did you arrive as many do, with something of an inferiority complex?

No doubt I felt very diffident. I hadn't got the self-confidence of some of my contemporaries who had been to the major public schools, but I had the privilege of meeting a lot of very interesting people. William Rees-Mogg was one of my contemporaries at Balliol. Dick Taverne was another. These people have all made great success in public life in this country and I found the whole thing absolutely stimulating. They were three of the most exciting years of my life and I have been eternally grateful to Balliol for what they did for me. They opened my eyes to a broader world. They opened my eyes, I hope, to a degree of culture. They taught me the importance of endeavouring to achieve success academically, because they demanded very high standards. It was a college which, then as now, expected its undergraduates to do very well. And it had an international element. We had a lot of Rhodes scholars from overseas at Balliol, so at a young age I was meeting some bright young men from America, Australia and so on, which broadened my horizons. Furthermore Balliol was a politically active college, so I got involved and interested in politics and debating at that time.

Was there something special about Balliol, and about the atmosphere at Oxford, which instilled the success ethic in you even more?

Well, Oxford University, like Cambridge, still likes to think it is one of the great universities of the world. It has an immense history. It has produced, I suppose, a large number of Prime Ministers and other people who have made enormous contributions to public life. And so, yes, you felt that you were a very small, modest part of a very great organization and that more than average things were expected of you. It imposed standards of excellence in the hope that you might achieve some of them.

When you left Balliol were there many options open to you for the start of your legal career?

I don't think there were any options at all. One had to get on with the job, start at the bottom and slowly, painfully and remorselessly try to make your way up the ladder.

Do you remember your very first job?

Yes, I remember going down to the Old Bailey to speak in a courtroom for the first time, being terrified out of my life and taking advice from an older barrister in the robing room before going in, about what I might say. But I felt very, very nervous indeed.

Even though you had built up a kind of confidence, even though you were used to debating, was it the fact that it was the Old Bailey that made you nervous?

No, it was the fact that I was in a courtroom, as a young man, wearing a wig and gown and actually addressing a judge for the first time on something serious. The solemnity of that occasion, and the fact that the responsibility for what might happen to the defendant rested upon me, totally inexperienced, was rather awesome. You don't lightly forget that first occasion.

How long did it take for the nerves to disappear?

They never do, and if they did there would be something the matter with you. You should always be nervous before you go into court. The important part, of course, is not to be nervous once you start.

And what is the secret of that? How do you make the transition from being nervous before you go into court to not being nervous as you walk through the door?

By constant practice and by improving yourself and your preparation over many years. It is a gradual process of learning confidence.

Your early days in the legal profession were on the Northern circuit when money didn't exactly flow like water. Were you particularly hard up?

Pretty hard up. The final demands for the gas bill would come in and I couldn't meet them. I didn't have a motor car until I was 26 or 27 years of age. After four years at the Bar I was earning just as much as a Manchester bus driver without overtime, so I wasn't exactly affluent. But poverty is a great stimulus to working hard.

Do you think that these days maybe some people have it too good, too quickly?

That is always the comment of the older generation, isn't it, but I am afraid I have to say I think there is a grain of truth in it.

When did you first discover that you had a way with juries?

Well, I don't know whether I discovered it and I don't know exactly what a way with juries is. I like to think that I am an all-round advocate, capable of addressing judges as well as juries. But I found great excitement in learning the art of communication with ordinary men and women who determine cases as a jury.

Your big break came when Sir David Napley brought you to London for what was known as the Big Dipper case. Sir David said that the chap didn't have much of a defence but you got him off. What do you remember about that case?

Well, the facts are that I was brought down to London not by Sir David but by a Manchester firm, and met Sir David, who was defending someone else in the case and had instructed a QC in London. But he was there most of the time and paid me a compliment at the end of the case. I cynically thought I would never hear from him again. But I *was* to hear from him again, in important circumstances, later.

What were the circumstances of the Big Dipper case? It was a catalyst in your career, was it not?

In that case it was important to take a fundamental decision whether any of the defendants should give evidence. I persuaded the Queen's Counsel who was appearing with me, co-defending, not to call any evidence. We didn't, and the jury acquitted because the prosecution simply hadn't proved the case. I think that strategic decision was the principal feature of that case, and of course it was repeated a few years later in the Thorpe trial.

Can you just summarize what the Big Dipper case was all about, for those who mightn't be aware?

A number of children were killed because the big dipper ride was defective and came off the rails at Battersea Funfair in London. Of course, it was an emotional case because it involved the death of young children, and the manager and the consulting engineer who were supposed to look after it were both charged with manslaughter. I defended the manager and was able to point out that he was really rather poorly paid and ill-equipped to supervise the finer points of the big dipper. But clearly the jury started off with a prejudice against both because they were looking for a scapegoat. Whenever children are killed, people look for someone to be responsible for that fact.

You successfully defended the accused in the Big Dipper case and then moved on, as you say, to the Jeremy Thorpe case, for which you were brought back down to London. When was the point where you felt, I'm on a roll, this is it, I've started to make it?

There is never one point in the professional career of a barrister when you can say, I am on a roll, because there are peaks and troughs, but that was the first case which attracted enormous national and indeed international attention. I had defended, for example, years before in Manchester, people like George Best, so that got a certain amount of parochial interest, if not national interest. But the Thorpe case was a major challenge and the acquittal of Jeremy Thorpe and all his co-defendants was something that made me realize that my professional career might be changing its course a bit. I made the decision to up sticks and leave Manchester to start practice full-time in London.

You talked about the encouragement of Sir David Napley when you came down to London. Does every successful person need a mentor at some stage in his career, and was Sir David your only one or did you have others who backed you at key moments?

I don't think people succeed without very carefully watching others who have already done so. You learn from your elders and betters. I learned an enormous amount from watching more experienced barristers, from being led, as a junior counsel, by Queen's Counsel and trying to learn from them. And I am sure that in any walk of life you don't really plot your own way to success without learning an enormous amount from people who are more experienced than yourself.

What is your formula for being a successful lawyer?

Hard work. Dedication. A passionate commitment. A belief that a great responsibility rests upon you in terms of the client, and a constant vigilant self-criticism to see how you can improve.

You have been married three times. Do you regard your personal life as a failure?

I don't regard it as a failure. I think that is an over-simplification. I am sure the failure of those marriages ultimately is something for which I bear responsibility, but nevertheless, one shouldn't regret that fact. I look back on the positive features. I look back on what I learned from them. I look back on the fact that much happiness was mixed with the unhappiness that eventually emerged. So life is not all good or bad. It is a glorious mix and I am not prepared to confess to failure in my personal life although it could have been very much better if I had been able to work at it harder.

You've talked about the formula for being a successful lawyer. What do you bring to the table that enables you to rise so much higher above the pack?

I don't think I have risen so much higher above the pack. There are lots of very distinguished Queen's Counsel whose names don't necessarily get into the national press because they are not in high-profile cases of public interest. But insofar as I and others become successful at the Bar, it is, I believe, the result of a never-ending, passionate commitment to the profession, a belief that it is necessary to try to succeed at all times. You must make yourself the most stern critic of your own performance and always look ahead at the challenges that you still face.

There is an old lawyers' saying that 'It is not enough that I succeed, others must fail'. Does it concern you that what you see as success must inevitably represent failure to somebody else?

Well, I don't believe that an English football club goes home and laments the fact that the other club has lost. It is important to be gracious in victory but equally it is not something to be ashamed of. It is very much a sort of English fashion to decry success to an extent. Not so elsewhere in the world. One should be proud of success but humble with it if humanly possible, and always generous towards your opponents.

What do you regard as your biggest failures and more importantly how did you recover from them?

As a young man I think I was too arrogant, intolerant of lack of recognition, intolerant of not getting enough work, impatient, over-dogmatic, too critical of other people's imperfections. I think growing up is a very long process. It certainly has been in my case, if I can claim to be grown up by now. I think to battle against your own failures is a lifelong task and you should review your own failures periodically and continually try to get rid of them.

What do you regard as the most successful moments in your life? Not the obvious ones that the world knows about, but others that were important benchmarks where you felt, perhaps, an enormous sense of triumph?

The case that sticks in my mind above all others is defending Dr Leonard Arthur, a consultant paediatrician, in the early 1980s. He was a dedicated doctor charged with the murder of a Down's Syndrome baby. It was a case charged with great emotion, where the law and medicine were on a potential collision course. The jury came to understand the level of this man's dedication and the agonizing decisions that doctors have to make in these circumstances. My own contribution to the case, such as it was, was personally very satisfying, in that eventually he was acquitted and able to resume medical practice.

Do you think you can sit down and methodically plan success or does luck play a huge part in whether you make it or not?

Maybe others have methodically planned success. I did not. I think luck plays a significant part. I am an optimist. I believe most people get some breaks in life. The important thing is that when the tide in the affairs of men rises, you have to take it at the flood, to paraphrase Shakespeare.

And yet you methodically plan your cases, in fact you are famous for putting in a huge amount of detailed groundwork, perhaps more than might be necessary?

That may be, because experience teaches you that you can rarely be overprepared and to be underprepared is to expose yourself or, more importantly, your clients, to unnecessary risk. So preparation is everything.

Do you think you have ever gone too far in a cross-examination?

Oh, I'm sure I have. A cynic once said that Christopher Columbus went too far, but I am sure I have gone too far on occasion in a courtroom, and regretted it, and that is a very good example of where you hold a post mortem and say to yourself, 'Don't ever do that again'.

When you look at a jury, can you tell now what each person in that jury is thinking, and the way in which they are likely to react to the evidence before them, and does that then shape your approach to the cross-examination?

You certainly can't tell what the jury are thinking. It would be a gift from divine providence if you could. What you can do is be very sensitive to their reactions in court, their body language, the way in which they might talk to each other, their facial expressions, and try to apply common-sense standards of decency, of fair play, because essentially that is what juries concentrate on in the courtroom. The English, as I have said, are a tolerant people, and juries develop an immense sense of fairness in trying a case. So what you try to do is concentrate on being fair to the witness. You may have to be hostile but you have at all costs to be fair. If ever you are unfair you will lose the jury and that is the last thing you ever want to do.

And do you change the way in which you conduct a case depending on your observations of the jury's body language?

You may. You may misread it, but importantly you may change the emphasis or tone of the cross-examination by the way in which the witness replies to your questions. It is very hard to describe. It is rather like an elephant. You know it is there but it is hard to describe it. With a witness you know whether he is going down well or badly with the jury. If you are cross-examining and he's going down too well you might switch tack and move in another direction where the witness is more vulnerable. If the witness is going down badly, then you pile on the agony.

When you suddenly realize, in that quick moment when the jury come back with their verdict, that you have won, what emotions go through you?

The adrenaline naturally flows. You feel very grateful for the verdict. You feel very relieved for your client and you feel you have achieved one more victory. It is a great sense of satisfaction and relief, but you must get over it pretty quickly and get on with the next case.

What are the core principles for achieving success?

The core principles for achieving success are – a persistent determination not to be defeated by temporary setbacks, constant analysis of your own imperfections and endeavours to improve them, a constant review of what you have done to see where you have gone wrong and to see how you can put it right, a passionate commitment to something that you profoundly believe in, in my case the value of the professional work of a barrister, and above all else a decision that this is to be perhaps the single most important thing in your life, not the achievement of success, but the achievement of deploying what talent you have in the interests of others; success should follow that.

In pursuit of success have you ever done or been tempted to do anything that you later wished you had not?

I have certainly been tempted and, I hope, avoided the temptation but I have no doubt that I tried to make myself known as a young man and was probably very obnoxious in the process. But I haven't, so far as I know, set out to engineer success by any means other than trying to do the job properly.

When the media attack and criticize people who, because they are successful, have stuck their heads above the parapet, do you think that a lot of that criticism is unfair, or is it justified? Are successful people fair game for attack?

To use the time-honoured phrase, if you can't stand the heat, get out of the kitchen. If you make any kind of mark in your own life or in the life of the country, of course you are a legitimate target, but that doesn't mean you should be subjected to personal abuse or vendetta, or to ill-informed or badly-based criticism, but you shouldn't be over-sensitive to criticism.

Is there a downside to success?

Yes, successful people aren't always very happy people. They are restless people, they are people driven on remorselessly, never to stop. They sometimes get work totally out of perspective and out of context and they make the great personal sacrifices which we have already talked about.

Are there any people, big or small, past or present, whose success you really admire?

Yes, in the political world I greatly admire the way in which Margaret Thatcher started from the position that she did and ended up exactly where she did. The contribution that she made to international as well as domestic politics was a formidable example of self-discipline and constant self-improvement. Quite an interesting study for successful people to follow is the world of the arts. When you have the privilege of listening to a very great artist like Yehudi Menuhin or watching a great actor you realize how much hard work has gone into the achievement of the finished product, and that stimulates you in your own work.

Is it becoming more or less difficult to achieve success in your particular field?

In my particular field, like any other, there must always be room for people who have enough talent and are prepared to be sufficiently dedicated throughout their lives to achieve success. They will achieve it if they have sufficient determination.

Do you have any formula for weathering criticism, or some kind of inner mechanism that enables you to withstand the slings and arrows that the outside world might chuck your way?

The important thing is to have a broad back, to recognize or be reminded constantly of your own imperfections and shortcomings. That's rather healthy for people. I am sure it's healthy for me and so one ought almost to welcome criticism, one should welcome occasionally a sharp or adverse comment, it is good for the soul. To be told you were a great chap all the time would be very bad news indeed.

What do you think are the greatest enemies of success?

People who are too easily content or become too easily satisfied with their lot. People who are not prepared to dedicate themselves to achieving the best out of the talents that they have been given.

Do you think success brings obligations in its wake?

It certainly should. I believe people should try and put a little back into the lifetime in which they have achieved that success rather than simply take the rewards.

Do you yourself have time to do that?

In a very limited and humble way I try and do it. I have spoken a lot at universities, at law societies, on student occasions and I hope in that small way that I am able to make some contribution to the lawyers of the future.

Has success changed you at all?

I suppose it has, as it inevitably changes everybody, but deep-down I believe I am the same boy who emerged from the background I did. When I visit the North I feel perfectly at home. I don't believe you should allow success to go to your head, if the phrase can be forgiven. The important thing about success is to keep your feet on the ground and be very grateful you managed to achieve a measure of it.

What is the greatest single pleasure you have obtained from having had a successful career?

If it be true that I have commanded some respect from my own profession, then that has given me the single greatest pleasure.

One of your colleagues, a QC, said 'Inside George Carman there is an essentially lonely person'. Do you feel that is the price you have had to pay for your success?

I think that is a perfectly true and valid comment. As I said earlier, some men are all-rounders, but I don't think I am. I think I had one talent. I have tried to make the most of it, but I wish I had had a few more.

Imagine you could gather before you, in one room, all the young people who hold you up as a role model. What advice would you give them?

A fixed, deep commitment and dedication to put their professional work above all else in their life and never to be deterred by any adversity they meet.

When your time comes to leave this life, what would you like people to say about you?

I don't know what they actually will say. What I would like them to say is, 'In spite of all his faults he was a fairly decent chap and had some talent as a barrister.'

JACK CHARLTON

A gritty, rock-like determination and refusal to compromise blew into Jack Charlton's soul from the streets of the mining community where he kicked his first football. 'Street football taught us about competition,' he says, 'and you've got to want to win to compete.' The game was in his blood. The legendary Jackie Milburn was a cousin, and four uncles played soccer professionally. Always in the shadow of his more talented brother Bobby as far as both the game and their mother were concerned, he had to work that much harder to reach the top. But reach it he did, turning out alongside Bobby in the team that brought the World Cup to England. He remembers the early encouragement from his parents – his mother made shorts and shirts from the blackout material everyone put over windows during the war. He left school at 15 to follow his father down the pit, then briefly signed up to be a policeman. But it was a spell in the army that gave him a chance really to develop the footballing skills that won him a first-team place at Leeds United and 629 League appearances for the club.

The man who was capped 35 times for England never thought he'd be good enough to join the national squad. That master tactician and England manager Alf Ramsay explained to him, 'I pick players that fit the pattern of play – not necessarily the best players.' Attention to detail was another lesson he learned – this time from Leeds manager Don Revie, whom he believes was the most important influence on his career. 'I don't believe in luck,' he says, 'the better you get the less luck you need. And you've got to be bloody-minded about the game.' His reputation for being very much his own man has earned him the respect of fans the world over. He moved into management, putting the pride back into first Middlesbrough, and then Ireland's national squad – but he's still bitter that he never got the chance to manage England. He argues that footballing success is different from country to country because expectations differ; talks of 'the changing nature of the game because football is becoming a business' and comes up with some ideas for creating the young players of tomorrow.

Jack Charlton, what is your definition of success?

It is very difficult to say exactly what success is. Footballing success in England is different to footballing success in Ireland, or even in Scotland. It's a case of what the general public and what the people who support you expect. In Ireland, success was getting to the World Cup finals or to the European Championships. It was giving the players and the fans the opportunity to have a crack and be part of a huge competition. In England it seems that unless the team wins all the time, they're not successful. The expectations in England are probably a lot higher than they should be, not only in international football but in the European club competitions as well. People are never really happy with our performances. Although we're competing, we're not competing in the way that a lot of people think we should be. In other words, we should be winning.

But in any competitive sport, isn't a measure of success the extent to which you win?

Not necessarily. It can also be a question of what people expect you to achieve. The small clubs have their own ambitions and expectations. How far will they go in the FA Cup? Can a Third Division team actually get to the FA Cup Final? Most people would say, 'No, we can't, but it would be great if we got Man United in the fourth round, or if we got to the quarter-finals.' A lot of Third Division teams have enjoyed this type of success over the years, so their level of expectation is about right.

But if you are a national team, do people not expect you to win for your country?

That's usually right, but the Irish never really expected us to win. They wanted to compete and be part of the occasion. That was all they were after – that's the way I felt about it anyway. When England enter a World Cup or a European Championship, we expect to get to the final or win. The Germans, the Italians and the Brazilians are all disappointed if they don't win. Because they've achieved success before, they are expected to achieve it all the time, which, at this level of competition, is almost an impossibility.

That high expectation of victory, where does it come from? Does it start with the media, does it start with the supporters?

I think it's a question of what they've achieved in previous generations. Leeds United, in the days before Don Revie, had never really achieved anything. Then they got into the Cup Final, won a European competition and won a First Division championship. Don's success was in building a team that was capable of winning and then going on doing so. At the moment they are not happy in Leeds because they're not winning anything, and this reflects in the number of people that go to the games.

If football is starting to be more of a business than a sport, will that change the nature of the game?

Almost certainly. When you've spent a lot of money, you've got to justify it and you've got to get it back through the gates or whatever other businesses you run, like selling shirts. I hear it's not unusual for a football club like Man United or Newcastle to sell 350,000 shirts a year. There is also the enormous revenue from television. But it's only the few clubs at the top that benefit. They are the ones people are really interested in seeing and who can guarantee the large television audiences, which the television companies like Sky and ITV need to justify what they charge for their advertising.

But if the income that the clubs get from television and from shirts and other sales is used to buy players, doesn't that help them become more successful?

Of course, but when you're in a league situation, not everybody is going to be successful all the time. If you just want to compete at that level, you've got to spend money whether you can afford it or not. Lawrie McMenemy would tell you that at Southampton they haven't got a prayer. With the amount of money they generate there's no way they can compare with the likes of Manchester United or Newcastle. They haven't got the following, they haven't got the chimneys round the ground, the number of people to attract to the games. Densely populated areas will always produce the best teams, mainly because more people will come to watch them. The more money they generate, the more they can spend on new players, and the more important it becomes that they win something.

Are there core principles for establishing and running a successful football team?

There used to be a story going about that if a team were in the First Division and they wanted to get into the Premier League, the manager would say to his team towards the end of the season, 'Look, we just need one little push for the last month and we'll get into the Premier League. Then we'll be able to sell loads of season tickets and buy some new players for next year.' Now this used to be a joke, it's no longer a joke, it's a reality. That's exactly the way it works. There was talk, when Sunderland got promoted, that Peter Reid would be given £10-12 million to keep them in the Premier League. Peter's not spent the money yet, and whether it's there for him to spend is another matter. But that is the expectation, that the finances will be forthcoming. The thing that worries me is that we're not producing enough good players in this country to fulfil the need that we've got. So we are going abroad and it's costing us an enormous amount of money – not in transfers as much as in the amount of money that people now get in wages. If you believe what you read in the papers, we're talking about £15-25,000 a week. It makes you wonder whether it's right.

You said we're not doing enough to create the new young players of tomorrow, how could we set that right?

That's very difficult. When I was a boy we went to school and we played football for our class, we played football for our house and we played football for any one of the three teams that represented the school on a Saturday. All the kids played football, and the ability to control and kick a ball was learned at a very early age, because that's all you did, play football. Now there are so many distractions for young people. They've got television, they switch it on as soon as they come in and just sit there. The only time that kids ever really get taught anything or get to play or, even more important, practise is when they are supervised by someone. They may get someone in from outside to coach them one evening and maybe they'll practise on another, but they should be practising on Monday, Tuesday, Wednesday, Thursday, Friday, Saturday and Sunday. And not enough kids get a chance to play. We've got comprehensive schools now where there are probably a thousand boys and yet they've only got three or four football fields – they should have 30. And they should have coaches in there, in the schools, who do nothing else but teach our national sport, or whatever other sport a kid wants to play. The only way you improve is to practise and play.

Is a really successful football player born or can you learn to be successful?

The basic talent has to be there in the first place. I was born into a family of athletes. All my uncles and my grandfather were footballers and they also did a lot of professional sprinting. Bobby and myself, and our other two brothers, were all brought up in a family where football was our game. Everybody in the North-East played football. They practised it and they played it on the streets, and they played it all day on a Sunday. In fact, the only other thing you had to do was dash home to hear *Dick Barton, Special Agent* at a quarter to seven on the radio. Which was normally the time your parents would want you in anyway.

It worries me when I see all the foreign players coming in. Are we doing enough with the younger kids to encourage them to learn and practise on their own, rather than just being taught by other people? I can't remember a day when I didn't go to school with a tennis ball. On the way you'd knock it against a wall and it'd come back to you and you'd control it. And then you drove it to somebody else across the street and you dribbled against somebody – a pal of yours that was going with you to school. In other words, you played all day, you practised all day, and you got better because you practised. Simple.

On a personal level, to what extent do you think a person's success is due to their background and upbringing?

I think your background and your upbringing are very important. We were brought up in a family that was all football, so I was never going to play anything else. I was given a football and football boots when I was a kid. My mother made us shorts and shirts from the blackout material that we used to put up at the windows during the war, and she would knit us football socks. We were always going to be encouraged to play football and it was very single-minded. What we learned in the North-East, particularly, was competition. You must be able to compete. The game doesn't give you anything. If you want to win you've got to battle to win, and you've got to tackle and you've really got to want to win. The idea of winning is very important.

And that instinct to win came partly from the competitive spirit that surrounded you, and partly from your parents as well?

That's right. My father was a boxer. He actually won the money to buy his wedding ring, through illegal boxing down in the back streets – bare-knuckle stuff. I don't ever remember talking to my father about any fights he lost, but I heard all about the fights he won. I don't think my father was deliberately teaching me to be competitive, but what he was instilling into me was that we don't discuss it when we lose, we discuss it when we win. My mother was very much the same. She would come and encourage us whenever we played for our school team, or whatever team we were playing for, whether it was a class against a class or a house against a house. We would be encouraged to win.

Was there a moment, at whatever age it might be, when you said to yourself, 'I am going to be a success at football'?

I think it was probably when I went into the Army. In those days you had to do two years' National Service, and it was very easy in the Army to let things slide. Fortunately the Army were very good at spotting if you'd got any ability in sport and they would get the best out of you. When I was training in Carlisle I was picked to play for the Northern Command after only six or seven weeks in the Army. Then I was posted to Windsor where they made me captain of the football team in the Horse Guards – we had three or four young pros that played with me in that team. The Army gave you the time and the opportunity.

And it was then that you felt, 'I could be good at this'?

Yes. I was grateful for that opportunity because had I not been able to play football, except at the odd weekend when I could get home to Leeds, I would have found it very difficult to practise. Luckily the Army encouraged me to take charge of the team and to train them. In fact I was really the manager of the team. I was expected to achieve something and we won the Cavalry Cup in Germany. We also had a good run in the Army Cup, and because the regimental team was doing so well, we were allowed time to prepare and train and work. When I came out of the Army, at 20, I remember coming home after a match with one of the Leeds lads on the train, and he said to me, 'If I don't get in the reserves by the end of the season, I'm going home.' This was in the September when I was de-mobbed. And I said to him, 'Well, if I don't get into the first team by the end of the season, I'm off as well.' It was a different way of looking at it. He wanted to play in the reserves and I wanted to play in the first team. I got to play in the first team, he played in the reserves and he left after a couple of years. It was just a question of different attitudes, but I also had this great fear that I might be a failure at football and would be sent home to Ashington.

How did that fear start?

The fear started for me, and many others, the moment you left home at 15 or 16 to join a football club. Lots of lads who didn't make it were sent home. I never wanted that to happen to me. It was like a personal shame that you hadn't made it and now you'd come back. People would ask, 'What's he going to do now?' I worked very hard between 16 and 18 before going into the Army, and then I worked very hard in the Army to make sure I was still a good player when I came out. It paid off and I won a first-team place at Leeds that first season after I was de-mobbed. So I got a good start. It was years later when Don Revie came along that I got involved with really learning the game and then developed as a good pro – I was always thought of as a good pro.

Does every player need a mentor, like Don Revie was for you?

Yes. Don Revie was certainly a mentor for me, as were Les Cocker and Sid

Owen, who were the trainers at that time. Looking back, the amount of aggravation I must have caused them was ridiculous.

You mean Don Revie actually said to you, at one stage, 'You're spoiling it for the others, with that chip on your shoulder'? Did you have an attitude problem?

Yes. I suppose I did. It was mainly to do with coaching. I started going out to schools and learning to coach. I was taking lower teams and going to Lilleshall to get my badges. But at Leeds United, there was no real coaching until Don Revie took over. Nobody did anything. You ran up the long side of the field, you walked the short side. You played five-a-sides or six-a-sides or seven-a-sides on the car park which was then just gravel and shale. You never went on the main field to play. I made the point that I didn't think the teams prepared themselves the way that they should, and that was what caused some of the problem. When Don came, he introduced a totally professional attitude. All my arguments with the club went out of the window. Suddenly we were well prepared, we were informed, we worked towards a game, we worked after a game. It was a professional approach and that suited me fine.

Didn't you think that you were good enough to be an international footballer, despite all the confidence that you had and all your ambition?

I wanted to be a better player and I wanted to play in a better team. Instead of playing in the Second Division of the Football League, occasionally going up to the First Division and then getting relegated again, I wanted to play in a good team and win things.

And you didn't think an international place might be yours at any stage?

No. My brother was an international player. We all expected that, and it was always going to be the case. But it never entered my head that I would ever be good enough. Only when Leeds started to win things at home and in Europe, did I have thoughts that maybe I would get a cap. I never thought I would end up with a World Cup winner's medal, never thought that I would play 36 times for England, or whatever it was, never thought I would play in two World Cups. To this day I still think that I wasn't that good a player.

How much did luck play a part in your success?

I have never believed in luck. You might be lucky today but unlucky tomorrow. Luck is something you work for and you achieve by work and preparation, by going about your job and doing it in the correct way, by listening to the right people, by being a professional at your job. The better you get, the less luck you need to achieve success.

Alf Ramsey recognized a talent in you. What did he say to you when you asked him why you had been picked for the team?

'Well, Jack' he said, 'I have a pattern in my mind of the way I want the team to play, so I have picked the appropriate players to fit the pattern. I don't necessarily always pick the best players, Jack.' In other words what he was saying to me was, 'You will do the job the way I want the job to be done, playing your natural game.' I would be playing alongside Bobby Moore, who was a totally different centre-back from me. I didn't play from the back. The ball came to me and I got rid of it. I never tried anything around the 18-yard box. I've always believed centre-backs are there to compete and to defend. The real people who do all the work in front of you are the midfield, and you've got to pick up whatever they don't handle. You've got to spot whatever's happening in front of you and deal with it. But you never put yourself at risk, you never put your defence at risk by trying to be a player. When people say to me, 'Oh, that centre-back, he's not bad but he's not a great player,' my response is, 'Well, he'll do for me, he's a good one-touch player.' The ball comes in, you get rid of it.

So you were right in terms of attitude, in terms of your style of play. You were in the right place at the right time. There must have been an element of luck, in that you just happened to be right for the plan that Alf Ramsey had in mind?

You can call it luck in getting to play for England if you want. You might also remember that we got to the Cup Final that year, that we'd won the League Championship and we'd got to the final of the FA Cup in '65. Leeds United was a club that was on the up and up and one that everybody found great difficulty in beating. We had a lot of good players, and Jack Charlton and Norman Hunter were a formidable pair of centre-backs. Remember not only did I play for England, but Norman played for England as well. We were good at defending and good competitors.

You've always had a healthy sense of aggression in your game. Is that an important ingredient in every successful footballer's life? And what other characteristics would you add?

You've got to be bloody-minded about the game. You know that you've got to win the ball, and when you tackle, tackle as hard as you can. Sometimes I would play against a centre-forward and I knew he wasn't going to cause me trouble because he was frightened of me.

You applied for the job as England manager before you moved to Ireland to take over the Irish team, and you didn't get a reply. What did you think when there was no reaction? Did you have any sense of failure at that point?

No sense of failure, just disappointment. I would have liked an interview. I saw some of the people that were interviewed and I thought, 'Hell, I'm a staff coach with the FA. I've played and managed in every level of the game, with the exception of international football, and I never got a reply to my letter.' And I never found out why, not to this day. The annoying thing was that the message suggesting I apply came from two members who were on the Committee at that time. I've never been someone that's applied for jobs, I've never applied for a job in my life, I always felt that if they want you they'll come and get you. But in this case I did apply and I didn't even get an answer.

Any feeling of resentment?

No, not resentment towards the English national team or to the English public, just to the guys that made the decision and never replied.

Then you were invited to become manager of the Irish team and made a huge success of that job. What was going through your mind when you were training the lads who were going to play against the team that you would have liked to manage yourself?

It never occurred to me. The main point of being an international team manager, and a manager of any club, is that your loyalty lies with the club you're with. I wanted desperately to beat England with the Irish in 1985. In fact news of the England result from Poland was probably my worst moment in Irish football. We had just beaten Turkey 3–1 in Istanbul, and we sat there and waited for the England result. We heard that they had got an equalizer, five or six minutes from the end, and that the Poles had been disallowed a blatant penalty. So we were out of the competition. I suppose I would have felt the same no matter which country had put us out, but it happened to be England.

How did you take that? Everything was hanging on that moment and there must have been a huge sense of disappointment. When that happens, what should be your approach for pulling yourself round and going back into the fray again?

At Leeds United we lost a lot of competitions in the final and we lost the league championship on many occasions on goal difference. Don Revie used to say, 'If we haven't done it this year, we'll just have to do it again next year. We've got to get on with it, and eventually we'll win everything' – which we did, with the exception of the European Cup.

What do you say to the lads to turn them round from that immediate sense of disappointment or failure?

You can't be glum with them. I walked into the dressing-room in Istanbul and they were still sat there. It was about half an hour after the game by the time I'd finished with all the press conferences and television interviews that you have to go through, and not one player had taken his shirt off. They were sat there with their heads in their hands. It's not my style to go and pat them on the head and be sympathetic. You don't say, 'Right lads, pick yourselves up. We've just got to start again.' You just say, 'Come on, let's get back to the hotel, let's have a pint or two tonight and we'll drown our sorrows. We'll join in the party and we'll have a singsong. We've done our best, and if you do your best nobody can ask more. Anyway it wasn't our fault. We won our game, they were lucky.'

What do you regard as your biggest successes, your biggest triumphs?

Whatever pleases your public. If the public are happy, you're happy. I had four great years at Middlesbrough. The first year we won the Second Division by a mile and really pulled the crowds in, then we had three good years in the First Division. Those were great years. Next I went to Sheffield Wednesday and took a club that were in fast decline and brought them back to within goal-difference of promotion to the First Division, and we got to the semi-final of the FA Cup. We created a team again at Sheffield, and I enjoyed my days there. We would have liked to have won more, but the public were happy, because they could see that the club was getting better. Then, when Howard Wilkinson took over, he just carried on and won the Second Division, no problem, the following year.

So the judges of success are the public?

Yes. It shows in the way they treat you, the way they talk to you, the way they approach you, the way they want to talk football with you. Basically, the public are the people that you want to please.

What are your biggest failures and how did you overcome them?

My greatest disappointment was the match in Liechtenstein which we had to win if we were to qualify for the European Championships that year. We drew a game that we might have won eight or ten nothing, nobody would have been surprised, but the ball just wouldn't go in. That was a great disappointment because I could see the repercussions. Then there was more disappointment when we lost at home to Austria in a game that normally we would've won comfortably. We really never got over that Liechtenstein match, and we failed to qualify for Europe. Our last chance was to beat Holland in a play-off at Liverpool, but I never really felt we were strong enough on the day, or had enough confidence to beat the Dutch.

As a manager, do you need total control to achieve success? Must you be there pulling all the strings?

Yes. But you don't have to do everything yourself. I went to Middlesbrough with a list of requirements that Don Revie had suggested to give me total control of the club, although I didn't really want it. I would never interfere with somebody who was doing his job correctly. But I always wanted to be the boss, the one that people get an immediate decision from rather than having to wait for a board meeting.

And you made it a condition that you wouldn't even go to board meetings?

Well, I didn't go to many in my career as a manager. If they asked me specifically to go to a board meeting I'd go, but they were usually on a Tuesday or a Wednesday night, and there were football matches on a Tuesday and Wednesday night.

So it wasn't a matter of you not being prepared to sit down and argue the toss?

No, it wasn't necessary. I said to the directors on many occasions, 'If you want to talk to me about the game or you've got a point you want to make, come and sit in the office with me and talk to me about it. Don't wait until we get to a board meeting, when eight of you all want to have your say, and we finish up with a big argument about something that we could have sorted out in two minutes if you'd come and sat and talked to me.' I like to think that the people within the football clubs that I worked for thought of me as the boss.

Do you ever feel that there is a conflict for any successful person between the demands of their professional life and their home life? And that in order to succeed you have to make sacrifices?

Yes, that goes without saying. You've got to make sacrifices. People had this thing about me, that I was away fishing all the time. It was a myth. I made a joke of it, but it wasn't true. You can only enjoy your pastimes when the game allows you. Mondays or Thursdays were days when you could sometimes get the training out of the way in the afternoon, and you might be able to get off for a couple of hours to do a bit of fishing or play a bit of golf. But more often than not it was up and down motorways, sitting in cars, going to football matches, getting away just before the end so you could avoid the traffic and then driving home for four hours. It's not an easy life, but you can't prepare teams if you don't go and see them.

And what can your family do to give you back-up and support?

Well, just that. My wife never questions where I am going. If I say I've got to go to a match in Birmingham, I'll go to a match in Birmingham. We've got three kids and Pat brought them up. I saw them as much as I could, but I was in and out. In football you know where you are going to be at the weekend, but you never know where you're going to be during the week.

Success in others arouses conflicting emotions. Why should that be?

I don't know. Envy is something that you've got in-built in you, whether you like it or not.

But is envy a driving force encouraging you to do better?

Take my brother Bobby, I've never begrudged him anything that he achieved. Never occurred to me. Maybe I envied him a little bit in the back of my mind for being a better player than me, and playing for England. Maybe I envied him because he played in an area of the field where you didn't have responsibility to the same degree as a defender.

So did that drive you on?

Maybe it did, I don't know. I suppose I'm envious of Terry Venables, now he's got the Australian coaching job. Apparently I had been linked with it for weeks and, although I wouldn't have taken the job, I still felt a bit envious. Maybe it's because I'm still thinking to myself that I should get back into football and that was a job that might have suited me. It's the same feeling when somebody gets to the Cup Final and you watch them walking out in front of the team. If you've never led a team out at Wembley, you feel envious.

And that's a driving factor?

Yes I think so.

Can the media influence whether you're successful or not?

Oh yes. I mean if you are prepared to listen to them and take any notice of them, but you don't.

What do you think are the greatest enemies of success?

I think the enemy of success is probably success itself. You've got to learn to live with it, and in learning to live with it you've got to learn live with the press as well, because they won't always say good things about you. You've got to ride out the criticisms. I have had a good relationship with the Irish because I never bought the Irish papers. If we played a match on a Sunday, I was home in England on a Monday morning, so I never saw the reports. I never read what they said about me or what I'd done wrong. I mentioned this to a journalist once and he started sending me cuttings from the paper in a brown paper envelope. I quickly put a stop to that. It's best if you don't read anything, good or bad, just get on with the job in the way you know that it's got to be done.

But it's impossible for every successful person to isolate themselves from what people are saying about them.

Yes, in England that's very apparent. Look at the history of English managers over the last ten years and see the disastrous way they've been reported in the press – Graham Taylor, in particular, and also Bobby Robson to a certain extent.

Do you think that affected their ability to be successful?

I think they always had this worry in the back of their mind. In Ireland I was treated with great respect by the general public and by the press, in most cases, and I loved the job. I wanted to do the job, I wanted to be part of it, I wanted to join in, I wanted to share their happiness in whatever results we had. All you ever see about the England team are criticisms. That's not good enough. I really enjoyed it when England beat the Dutch 4–0 at Wembley. I was at the game, and my thoughts were not about the way the players felt, I was thinking to myself, 'The press can't knock them after this, they're going to have to write something good for a change, because everybody's played magnificently and they've beaten one of the best teams in the world.' I was actually thinking about the press before they'd written a word. That's how much they are a part of the game now.

So they do affect you, whether you read the papers or not?

Of course. If you want to get rid of the manager of a football club, it's not the directors that get rid of him, it's not the public, it's the influence that the press have on the public that will do the job. If the press start saying he's not good enough, then the public start saying it and, although the manager may get a vote of confidence from his chairman, he knows he's on his way. Once the press have turned on you, you may as well go.

Has success changed you as a person?

No. I'm still like I used to be – perhaps more so. I'm the same chap in the pub as I am when I appear in public. I can never change. I can't act and I don't tell lies. I enjoy people. I enjoy talking to people. I enjoy taking the mickey out of people and having them take the mickey out of me, having little laughs and little jokes. I like people to like me. I'm sure I have my off days, when I get up in the morning and I don't feel right and I might shout at somebody – it's usually the family. But I still think I would like to know me if I wasn't me.

What is the single greatest pleasure you've had from your successful career?

The greatest pleasure is walking down the street, like today, walking across London. I walked up from St James's Palace, through the town and it was raining, and although I'd got my coat up round my neck 30 or 40 people tapped the person they were with and said, 'That's Jack Charlton.' Instant recognition is a great reward.

If you could gather before you all the young people who want to have a career in football, what advice would you give them?

Nothing comes easy. Nothing is given to you. Whatever you do, you've got to work for it and earn it. Whatever reward you get you've got to know that you've had your input into that success. There's no substitute for hard work. And if you want to be well known or well liked, you have to put yourself out for people.

When your time comes to leave this life, what would you like people to say about you?

That they liked Jack. Sometimes you go to funerals where you don't know the guy very well, but you've felt you should be there because of his influence on what you've done. Other times a close friend dies, and then you'll travel halfway round the world to be there, and you turn to the guy next to you and you say, 'I liked him, he was a good pal of mine.' I would like people to say, 'Jack was all right, I liked Jack'.

SAM CHISHOLM

He was by far the highest-paid executive in British television. He believed in taking risks – and founded his career on one. He gave up what could have been a comfortable life running the family farms in New Zealand to do his own thing in Australia. His marketing skills drew him to the attention of the legendary tycoon Kerry Packer, who wooed him to Channel Nine TV and soon promoted him to run it. Over fifteen years, the Chisholm formula built it into the country's biggest, most successful TV network. For most people, that would have been the career peak – the job to see them through to retirement.

Then Rupert Murdoch came knocking with an irresistible challenge – to turn around the 'absolute nightmare' of the loss-making BSkyB satellite broadcaster. Finding a company that was run 'by the staff for the staff instead of a company run by the management for the shareholders', he began with a 'scorched earth policy'. The new edifice he rapidly constructed was all about teamwork – 'a champion team will beat a team of champions any day'. But there was never any doubt about who was boss; his blunt, no-nonsense approach generated a certain amount of fear. 'You've got to run scared rather than take it all for granted. Insecurity and doubt are enormous motivators – every successful person has them.' In tandem with that, he has always believed that the best ideas come from the ground up, and in order to respond to them properly, a leader must be accessible. All telephone calls to his office – wherever they came from – were returned within 24 hours. The formula worked. When Sam Chisholm took over, Sky was losing £12 million a week; eight years later it was making profits of £7 million a week. Strangely for an executive who had a TV news channel in his stable, he maintains that 'there is no upside for businessmen in giving interviews to the media'. But here, in a rare personal exception to that rule, he talks of the key benchmarks in the rise of the Sky network; why it's important to take risks and make mistakes, and what will mark out the successful TV stations and executives of tomorrow. He defends a pay cheque that once topped £4 million-a-year; and says you can 'be a success with just average ability if you back your own judgment and have a lot of courage'.

Sam Chisholm, what is your definition of success?

My definition of success would be to enjoy every aspect of your life.

And what are the qualities that are necessary to achieve that?

It takes different qualities in different fields. To be successful and to enjoy your personal life is almost the antithesis of what you have to do in your business life – the secret of success there is persistence. To be successful in your personal life and to enjoy it, you need a credo that is quite the opposite of the requirements for conventional business success.

Can you not enjoy business success as well?

I think you do enjoy business success, but you need two different sets of rules.

Tell me what those rules are.

In your personal life it's to be able to relax and enjoy the things and the people around you, that's the secret of success – to have a genuine *laissez-faire* attitude towards it.

And in your business life?

Well, it is certainly not to be *laissez-faire* or to sit back and enjoy everything around you – the secret of success in business life is persistence, that is how you get there. This is the definition of the workaholic – the workaholic is a guy who has a prescribed formula he knows works. He could probably do it at half the speed and rely on his innate skills, but he's too scared to do that. Success in business is about winning, and the way that you win in business is you don't leave anything to chance. You could say to yourself, 'Look, I could cut a few corners here in order to get what I want,' but you don't, you simply leave nothing to chance. That's how you're successful in business, in my view.

Does that mean that you have to make some sacrifices in order to be successful in business?

I think it does require sacrifice, because you have a sense of duty. You've got to learn to put everything ahead of yourself, you can't say, 'I really want to go and play golf today, the hell with getting the Premier League deal.' When you're in pursuit of what you do, you put everything else aside, you put yourself in the background.

And yet a lot of businesssmen would happily take a day off to go and play golf to relax and might even use golf as a means of achieving that deal?

Well, they may do, but I don't know many successful people who are scratch golfers.

You said that you could do it at half the speed. There are a lot of businessmen out there who would say, 'We do it at half the speed so we can get a better balance between our work life and our personal life.' Are you really saying that's not an option?

Well they're more courageous than I am. I'm not saying that they're wrong. I had a discussion with Gerry Robinson, the chairman of Sky and the chairman of Granada, and he has a different attitude towards business from mine – I'm not sure that he isn't right, but it's to each his own. He has to work things out for himself, so that he kicks the goals for himself. That's his way – my way is leaving nothing to chance, to cover every option, every base, every angle – that's what's been successful for me in business and I've found what I think is a successful formula in my little world and I am too scared to vary that.

A lot of people who know you might express surprise at the concept of Sam Chisholm being scared?

Not scared in the conventional sense. You've got to run scared – that's what leadership is about or success, call it what you like. If you take it all for granted and think you can walk up the Thames, that's the beginning of the end.

So you're saying that every successful person has to have a degree of self-doubt?

Absolutely. Insecurity and self-doubt are enormous motivators.

Are they the driving force?

I think they are. If you're an intelligent leader, then you've got to have self-doubt. Once you start believing you know it all, that becomes self-deception, and that's the start of the end.

What about those many people – and you are among them – who come across as being incredibly assertive and appear to have an almost limitless supply of confidence. Are you saying that inside every person who comes across in public as being immensely confident, there is bound to be an element of self-doubt?

I believe that. All the people I know certainly have a self-doubt factor.

Do you ever play on that in negotiations?

No. You know it's there with most intelligent people.

You talked earlier about sacrifices. What personal sacrifices do you think you have made in pursuing your career?

I've made enormous sacrifices. I haven't had the opportunity to spend the amount of time with my family that I would have liked.

Tell me about your family.

Well, I've got a wife and a daughter. They live in Australia, although they do spend time in Britain. My daughter's a journalist, working in the features section of a Sydney newspaper. People like me have to take on the assignments that come our way in life and we have to go where these assignments are. That's how guys like me earn their wages.

And the family didn't come with you from Australia?

I was just speaking to a friend of mine in Australia who's sitting at an outdoor restaurant in 75 degrees, barbecuing a steak for himself, and I said, 'I'm sitting here in a howling gale.'
   The hours I work are long and demanding. A good executive must be accessible all the time. One of the great things about leadership is accessibility and there is simply no point in saying people can't get hold of you. That in itself requires enormous discipline, so if you have your family around you it is trying for them. It is easier for me and easier for them and easier for everybody in my life to have their own independence.

So you are better able to focus on what you're doing without having family problems to deal with?

It's not a question of family problems. Everybody that knows me understands and respects what I'm trying to do and they allow me the latitude and the space to do it, because they know I enjoy what I'm doing. I am obsessed about what I do.

Where did that obsession start? Was it there right at the beginning?

I don't know. I think I've always been a bit that way, but you don't sit down and analyse yourself that closely.

To what extent do you think a person's success is due to their background and their upbringing?

I don't. To be a success you need average ability, if you're above average it's good. You need to back your own judgment and have a lot of courage – when you tell somebody to go to hell you mean it. Most people have average ability, most people probably have above-average ability, but most people don't back their own judgment, most people don't have courage and most people when they tell you to go to hell don't mean it. They say, 'I'm sorry, I didn't mean it' the next day. If you look at most leaders, you'll find that most of them are prepared to back their own judgment. Most of them have got tons of courage and when they say, 'Sorry, no,' they mean it.

So an element of stubbornness, almost bloody-mindedness?

No, I don't think it's stubbornness. You've just got to back your own judgment. You are your own best guide. An example of that was when we went into pay-per-view boxing. We got an enormous amount of criticism in this country for doing things that had been operating in other parts of the world for 20 years. We priced the Bruno–Tyson fight at £9.95 and I said to myself, 'Would I pay £9.95 to see this fight? Yes, I would. What does everybody think? Would you pay £10?' Everybody said yes. You've got to have the courage against the face of the masses. All the papers said it was an outrage, but you've got to have courage in what you believe.

It's often very difficult for people to do that in the teeth of what can be overwhelming media criticism. Do you have any kind of formula for riding through that kind of criticism when it comes?

You *make* it successful. You set about it, you leave nothing to chance and you make it successful. We got a world-record buy-rate for that fight.

Did you have any sleepless nights when you took that decision? Did you think, 'If this all goes wrong then my career could be hanging in the balance'?

No, you don't think about it that way.

But a lot of people would.

In which case you've got to put it all on the line all the time. If you start thinking about your career, then you start taking life insurance, you don't make those brave calls – you are the guy who doesn't back his judgment, you are not the guy who has courage.

What do you say to those people who are always looking over their shoulder as they move up the career path and being ultra-cautious about what they do, and perhaps being hesitant about taking decisions, because the easiest thing in life is not to take a bold decision, but to go for the status quo?

You try to prove by example that it can be done. It's all about making bold calls, putting everything on the line, and seeing if it can work.

Let me go back to your early days. Your father died when you were eight. Do you remember your father and mother as being people who had ambition for you, who were driving you?

No, I don't. We were brought up in an era where it was important to be seen as a success. My daughter has a completely different perspective of the world to me. Her generation has a more rounded view of the world, I was brought up in an era where success meant more than it should. People today would not make the sacrifices that my generation would make.

After school you went into the family farming business, and then you gave that up and decided it wasn't for you. Why was it not for you?

The solitude. I'd spent all my life at boarding school and then I went away farming and I thought, 'I don't want to spend all my life in splendid isolation.' I'd been to a very good school and had quite a good upbringing, I'd set out on a routine path, and I decided to see whether I could succeed on my own. That's when I went to Australia.

You had no university background, no formal training in anything. Do you believe that getting on in life is a matter of instinct?

I think you work it out as you go along. Success isn't something you can plan. I'm sure most people you have interviewed would never have expected to be the success that they are. When I left school, I remember the headmaster saying, 'The chances of most of you becoming successful are remote because you've been to a good school and had a good upbringing, and that will mitigate against you.' Most successful people haven't had a particularly good education and don't come from particularly good backgrounds. The people who are the real successes are the people that have gone out and had to defy the laws of convention to get there.

How big a part does luck play in the whole equation?

A lot.

Being in the right place at the right time?

You need a bit of good luck, but I also think you make your own luck by virtue of your endeavours. If you work away and leave nothing to chance, then you create your own luck.

And does it help to have a mentor, one or two people who ride shotgun to your career, who believe in you?

It's all about teamwork, that's the key to it. A champion team would beat a team of champions every day. I've been very fortunate in my life to be part of such teams – the television network in Australia I worked for was an amazing team. Everybody thought that television in those days was cyclical, there always had to be a winner and a loser, and it all went in cycles. What we demonstrated was that if you applied yourself and you had all the rules, stuck to them and left nothing to chance, if you were obsessive at what you did and prepared to make the sacrifices, you could keep winning. The network is still winning today because that has carried on. If we look at Sky here in Britain, it has been a phenomenal success. That's because it's got an incredible team of people and a great ethos – that's made it successful and I am just part of that team.

When you came to Britain, what were the problems you identified with Sky Television?

Well, the problems were almost insurmountable. At this stage there were two businesses, BSB and Sky. Then, of course, the merger took place and we set about ascertaining how much money we were losing and how to get the company going again. There were problems in every area and looking back on it, it was an amazing experience. It was an absolute nightmare at the time and something you'd never want to do more than once.

So big, bold decisions were necessary?

I explained to the people at BSB that this appeared to me to be a company run by the staff for the staff, and that it was now going to be a company run by the management for the shareholders. It was a new experience for them. I was quite open with all the management and all the staff and said, 'We've got to take this company back before we take it forward and the quicker we take it back, the sooner we'll be able to push it forward.' It was a scorched-earth policy and, as it turned out, it was good judgment because when the Premier League contract came up, we were in a position to be a serious bidder for it.

I rang Greg Dyke at ITV – I had known him previously from TVam – and I told him that Sky was going to bid for the Premier League contract. He laughed at me and was dismissive. He said, 'You might have been a big dealer in Australia, but you're a non-eventer here.' I said, 'I think that's probably right, but we are very determined and you shouldn't underestimate us.' And he did. I then went and saw Will Wyatt of the BBC and he gave me his word that he would stick with us through thick and thin and he did. It was a great credit to Marmaduke Hussey, the chairman of the BBC, because they were tested at great length by everybody to break this relationship and they would not. We went on and we won the Premier League contract. ITV lost it because they simply underestimated Sky.

And how important was that Premier League deal? Was that the big catalyst that set you on the profits trail?

Yes. That was the turning point of the company. That brought it of age.

Was it a gamble for you doing that?

An incredible gamble. We were betting the company on it. If we had missed that, Sky would have staggered on, but it would never have been the success that it is. That's why I've said that the relationship Sky has with the Premier League is one of the great corporate romances of our time – it has been that important.

You were betting the company on it. Were there any sleepless nights?

Yes, on the night the Premier League contract was decided. I suspected that ITV were up to something. Everything went quiet on the Friday. I'd spoken to Rupert on the Friday night and said, 'Everything's too quiet, I am suspicious, they must be doing something.' On the Monday I said to Rick Parry, the chief executive of the Premier League, 'I think something is afoot.' We had set out the rules with Sir John Quinton, the chairman of Barclays, and the chairman of the Premier League. This was a knock-out contest, everybody had put their final price and that was that, it was all over. But initially, Sir John Quinton had laid out the rules of engagement, a fight to the death. When I left the chairmen on Friday, I turned round and said, 'Do you think this is our last bid?' They said, 'Yes.' I said, 'Well it isn't, don't assume that because it may not be.'

The chairmen's meeting was on the Monday and we talked constantly over the weekend. I said to Rupert, 'I think something's going to happen,' so he said, 'OK, let me know.' Then, on the Monday morning, I said to Rick Parry, 'Don't go down to the chairmen's meeting in case something happens. We're still in the ring bidding.' Sure enough, Trevor

East, who was then working for ITV, was handing out the envelopes at the door with his final bid as the chairmen went in, in the hope that we couldn't get in behind that. At this stage, they realized that we weren't to be underestimated. As David Elstein says, 'Anybody who doesn't think that Sky has Plan B when they're dealing with them, doesn't know Sky.'

Anyway, Rick Parry rang and said, 'There's another bid going in.' I had no clue what it was. It was 9.00 a.m. and Rupert was in New York, so it was 4.00 a.m. his time. I woke him up and said, 'These guys are putting a bid in at the door, just before the door closes they're pushing their final bid to each chairman.' He said, 'What can you afford?' I said, 'I think another £30 million.' 'We should put it on the table,' he said. So I faxed through a higher bid to have the final word.

Then Rick Parry called to say we'd won. I rang Rupert to tell him and he said, 'That's absolutely fantastic, congratulations. I thought you were going to ask for another £30 million.' I asked him whether he would have given it to me, and he said, 'Without question.' That was the sort of backing we had and when you're in the sort of battle we were in, what makes success the joy that it is, is that you've got everybody with you on the team.

And for you that was the moment when you suddenly realized that after all the pain and anguish you'd been through, it was going to work?

That was when everybody got together and had a million drinks! That's when everybody realized the pain had been worth it, that we were able to take the company forward, that there was a future for everyone.

You've talked about the team spirit that you've created and you've been quoted in the past as saying that creativity from the bottom up is particularly important. Tell me what kind of chemistry makes a successful television executive. What are the ways in which you play running a company?

Television is 99 per cent perspiration and 1 per cent inspiration. It is attention to detail. It is sitting down, whether it's a news script or whatever, and it's attention to detail. The whole thing is far more precise and much tougher than most people think. Most people think the television industry is like a dream factory – everybody swans around in flash cars and sips champagne and spends their life having lunch at Harry's Bar. The people who work inside it know what a tough business it is. You go into the news at 6.00 p.m., not one second before, not one second later, when the floor manager cues you. It's exactly on the button and it is absolute precision, and that extends right through the company.

A good television executive needs a few qualities – he needs extraordinary discipline, he needs to have visual literacy, where he can look at things and understand them visually, he needs a lot of imagination and good instincts. He's got to try to work out what he thinks his constituency wants, he's dealing all the time in trying to communicate with a vast audience that he really doesn't understand because, by and large, in television most things fail. You will get *Coronation Street, M.A.S.H.,* the *Cosby Show,* but it's very difficult to achieve success in television – there is no prescription. Putting a lot of money into it doesn't work.

The television executive is a far more savvy, rounded individual than most people give him credit for. He is genuinely a good programmer, he is genuinely nagged by self-doubt – these are the guys that have the sleepless nights.

And what about the people who've developed reputations as good programme makers, but are then moved up through the management structure so that they are out of touch with the day-to-day running of the programmes?

Well, I think good programmers are like talent. I don't think they make good managers. It is almost an art to be a good programmer.

So if you want to be successful in television you should first choose very clearly whether you are going down a management route or whether you're going down the programming route?

Yes. My experience is that managers can have a feel for programming, but not much. They think they can – all managers think they're fantastic programmers, and one of the great strengths in television, in my view, is knowing your weaknesses and a lot of people don't. A lot of people think, 'Here I am running this, I must know more than I think I do.' The capacity for self-deception in our business is staggering. But if you are a programmer and a very good programmer, and this is mainly in terrestrial television, you should just continue to become a better programmer, and if I were an employer who had a good programmer I would pay him more than anyone, I would pay him much more than I would pay a knock-about television executive. He can't be replaced, there are so few of them – they are the real estate of our business.

So you think taking brilliant programme makers and moving them up through the executive echelons is actually not a good idea?

I think it's a tragic waste of talent. An executive's a fairly ordinary piece of merchandise, a programmer is unique, he's an artist.

The rewards of success have been very good for you. You are the highest-paid television executive in Britain, and one of the highest-paid in the world. What is your answer to those critics who say that however good you are, nobody's worth that amount of money?

It's not for me to judge. I don't put the value on myself, that's not decided by me, that's decided by the remuneration committee. Somebody has to put a value on me.

And what do you say to those people who claim it's an almost obscene amount of money? Do you think they are part of the anti-success ethic?

I think there probably is an anti-success ethic, that's the politics of envy. People don't say that to me incidentally, but if anybody did, I'd say, 'Nobody would say that to me if they knew the sacrifices that go into it.' I don't think any amount of compensation can really make up for committing your life, which is what you do. I've spent six years here in Britain at Sky, to almost the sole exclusion of everything else. If the company wasn't successful then you'd say, 'Yes, that's a respectable argument,' but the fact is that I didn't get paid this money until the company was successful. If the company had been a failure I suppose I would have been on the unemployment lines. I don't suppose anybody would come along then and say, 'The way the shareholders have treated you is obscene.' It's all predicated on success, so when the company became successful, I became successful and so did everybody else.

When you are very successful, you stick your head up above the parapet and you're very much in the public eye. Some successful people live at the centre of a kind of publicity whirlpool. You've consciously decided not to do that – you very seldom give interviews. What advice would you give to successful people about playing the media, about when you decide to give interviews and when you don't?

There's no upside in giving interviews.

No upside at all?

In my view, no. I don't feel the need to do interviews and profiles. To sit down and read about yourself must turn your head eventually, I wouldn't recommend it.

Yet you're running a news operation that feeds on other people doing precisely that?

Yes, now I understand that. If you're a politician or suchlike it's necessary, but for a businessman, if you've got things to say and you inform your shareholders or if you've invented a brilliant new product, then that's fine, but doing profiles of yourself is not something I'd recommend.

Has it been integral to your success not to have done it?

I think it's given me a lot more time to concentrate on the job at hand.

What do you regard as your biggest mistakes or failures, and more importantly, how did you recover from them?

I think my biggest failure is not taking more care of myself in terms of my health. I shouldn't have smoked, but I did. When I was a young guy people didn't know that smoking was a bad thing, in fact it was fashionable. It was only a few years later that everybody suddenly decided that smoking had horrific consequences and at that stage, for an asthmatic, it was too late.

And anything in business terms?

There have been so many mistakes. In Australia, the biggest mistake I made was with regard to the programme *Beyond 2000.* The Beyond Group came and offered their programme to me and I said no to it. It's since been wildly successful. In England, the biggest mistake I ever made was to say no to Thames.

For what?

Well, we could have bought Thames after they lost their franchise. We could have bought the production company and Pearson bought it, for virtually the cash inside the company. It would have been a wonderful asset to Sky.

How soon after that decision did you realize that you had made the wrong move?

As soon as Pearson bought it.

And how did you then set about recovering and countering that loss?

I haven't yet.

What are the enemies of success?

The enemies of success are conceit, complacency, arrogance, laziness, lack of application, and lack of focus.

Is there a downside to success?

Yes, the sacrifices. You don't get anything for free – you don't become successful by lying in a hammock all day.

Have you ever done anything, in pursuit of success, that you later wished you hadn't?

Never, no. I may have been even more successful in some areas of my life over the years had I been prepared to cut a few corners, but it's been absolutely critical to me that I've adhered to a set of very, very strict principles.

Have you ever felt like giving up?
No, I haven't.

There's always been that constant drive forward?

Yes, I'm still trying to get it right.

Who are the people you admire for being really successful? Who are your heroes, either past or present?

I don't really have heroes. There are a lot of people that I admire, but I admire them in a whole range of areas for the most idiosyncratic reasons. I'm completely unconventional in that sense. I admire people for the things that they do, or for their attitudes towards life.

What do you say to people who envy success in others?

I'd say, 'Go and take a long, hard look at yourself in the mirror. You might not like what you see.'

Do you think success brings obligations in its wake?

Yes, I do. I think you should be a force for good.

And every successful person should put something back into society?

Yes, I think you should if you can. I think you've got to be a giver not a taker.

Any frustrated ambitions of any kind?

Yes, there are a lot of things that I've missed out on that I'd like to do. I'd like to see more of the world, I would like to spend my life in something other than a car, a hotel room, or a plane. I would like to take life a bit easier and see the wider world.

Has success changed you at all?

No, I don't think it has. I think I'm still a pretty ordinary guy.

What's the greatest pleasure you've obtained from having a successful career?

What I've been able to do for other people's careers, and their lifestyles.

If you were to gather together in one room all the young people who look at Sam Chisholm and say, 'I want to be like him one day – make a career in television, make a success of it' – what advice would you give them?

I'd go back to the set of rules – believe in yourself, back your own judgment, have courage – it is an amazing industry, companies like Sky are going to be like the railways were at the turn of the century. These are going to be the great conglomerates, and are going to sweep the world. The whole communications business is going to be just an absolute explosion and if these guys get into this today, and if they're prepared to apply themselves, Lord knows where we'll all be.

You say, 'Lord knows.' I'm going to ask you if you know where we are going to be in 10 or 15 years time. Paint me a picture of the television scene in Britain in 10 to 15 years time, maybe technically, in terms of the number of companies, the programming mix. Who are going to be the main players in the living room?

Well, they are going to be programme providers. The one thing you do know you're going to have – and that's why people should keep investing a lot of money in it – is a news service. Sport will be a huge factor, there will be thousands of channels, your television set will have become, I suspect, the focal point of your house – it will all be voice-activated as your house will, you won't press buttons and do all that sort of thing, everything will be done on voice command. You'll probably have a relatively short working week. You certainly won't all get in cars and career back and forth like we do.

More opportunity for watching television?

It won't be just watching television, I think everybody will have a lot more leisure time. Lifestyles will be more balanced. The television set will be a resource in your house as much as it will be an entertainment vehicle. People first bought television way back to be entertained and informed, its role now is as an information source. You're seeing discovery channels and such like, people have an insatiable desire to be informed about what's going on.

So what is going to be the successful television company of the next century? What are the main characteristics?

Well, in this country it will be British Sky Broadcasting, it will become the influential broadcaster in my view.

You would say that, wouldn't you?

No, everything will come through this system. You see it in America now – direct TV are putting up these small dishes and taking down your television aerial. The world will go into digital broadcasting and I think that companies like Sky will become the delivery vehicle.

And the future of the BBC and ITV?

They will have a phenomenal future because they've got huge reach. The BBC will always be there, it will have changed I suspect, but it makes a fantastic contribution to the country and will continue to prosper. There is a school of thought that says it will become a sort of cultural artefact, but I disagree. It has produced a lot of good programmes and, I think, it will continue to do so, it's very much part of the culture of this country. I think it will change, but everyone will have to change.

How will it have to change?

It will need to provide a lot more services to its customers, because as the world fragments and becomes inter-digital, there will be a lot of BBCs – you'll be able to watch the news at 6.00 p.m., you'll be able to watch it at 7.00 p.m., 7.30 p.m., so what will happen is you, the customer, will dictate. You won't rush home and plonk yourself in front of the television to see what Martyn Lewis has to say to you at 6.00 p.m. – Martyn Lewis will tell you what you want to hear when you want to look at it. That's what will happen to the television business, it will become a commodity like dishwashing liquid. You'll use it when you want it.

If it became possible, would you want to take over big slices of ITV, or even take over the BBC?

No, I don't think so. We try to create and change. We will try to work inside structures. We don't try to do things by acquisition, we try to do them by energy. What I've missed out in all this is how big a factor energy is in success. Energy is a huge factor.

What is the potential for politicians to affect the success of television in years to come?

Not much.

They are almost an irrelevance?

They're not an irrelevance, but the airwaves belong to the people, and broadcasters should never forget it. These are the airwaves that belong to the people and the people will be the single biggest factor – you can't have good television by dictate.

But it also means that you mustn't drive relentlessly downmarket. You actually have to have responsible programming, which reflects your responsibility to society.

Absolutely, and the self-regulations generally tend to take you upmarket. If you've got a set of rules, you try to work out ways to get around them. You've seen this with censorship. As soon as the censor set the rules, you were always trying out ways to get around them, but then, when self-regulation came in, everybody treasured it so much that the standards of television lifted dramatically.

When your time comes to leave this life, what would you like people to say about you?

I think in business I would like people to say he always put his team ahead of himself. In my private life, I would like people to say he always put others ahead of himself, because I do.

And what about that famous slogan you have on your desk at Channel 9?

To err is human. To forgive is not my policy.

LINFORD CHRISTIE

The best sprinter that Britain has ever produced came from a background where he had 'just enough, and sometimes nothing at all'. Early days were in Jamaica, brought up by his grandmother who gave him the Pentecostal faith that remains strong to this day. At the age of seven he joined his parents who'd come to seek work in London, and remembers how 'eight of us lived in two rooms with a cooker on the landing'. He ran his first race at the age of eight, but it wasn't until secondary school that the victories started to flow. His big break was being spotted by Ron Rodden who became his coach, and Andy Norman of the British Athletics Federation, who told him that he 'could be the best, but would have to work at it'. And work at it he did, developing not just a physique of steel, but a mental approach and resolve to match.
'When my opponents are having a day off,' he says, 'I'm training, because that gives me a day on them.' Such effort brought him the 100 metres gold medal at the 1990 Commonwealth Olympics; but a year later, when he could only manage fourth place at the World Championships, he wanted to give up. The press wrote him off as too ambitious; some athletics luminaries told him he'd never be world-class, and he himself wondered if he was too old. A flood of letters from the public, urging him to give it one more go, changed his mind. Rodden, his 'Rock of Gibraltar', worked on his weaknesses without neglecting his strengths. The following year, he took Olympic Gold with style.

He has waged a long-standing war with sections of the British media – most recently fighting and winning a high-profile legal action against a journalist who had accused this passionate anti-drugs campaigner of taking drugs. The press are far too critical, he adds provocatively, 'because they're failures themselves. A lot of them have never achieved anything in life, so they try to discourage others.' That sense of annoyance certainly doesn't seem to have fractured an inner confidence so strong that he is still prepared to argue with the computer decision on false starts that disqualified him from the 1996 Atlanta Olympics. His support system is fortified by making sure he keeps around him 'people who knew me before I was successful'. He has no time for sycophants. Now with his own sporting management company, splendidly named Nuff Respect, he here passes on advice for handling rising success. 'Work as a contender,' he says, 'never as a champion, 'cos as a champion there's nowhere else to go; as a contender you always want to get there.'

Linford Christie, what is your definition of success?

Success is achieving whatever you set out to do – your own goal. Getting to the very top against all the odds.

Do you think success is dependent on getting to the top?

Everyone has his own idea of how far he wants to go, what he wants to achieve. As long as you attain the goals you set yourself I think it can be classed as success.

How do you find out what you're capable of?

You never do. I believe that you never stop learning, and nobody is an expert at anything at all. Being an expert means there's nothing more you can learn; I think you can learn something new no matter how many years you've been doing anything.

Why do you think your success came relatively late? Was it to do with attitude or what?

No, it was just destiny, I think. I've been in my sport a long time. I've seen a lot of athletes come and go. The guys who were really good at a younger age when I was around all disappeared a long time before me so I think I came into the sport at the right time, when athletes could actually make a good living from the sport rather than having to go to work and come home and train; when athletics came into the mainstream, as it were.

So there was an element of luck in that?

I think the only luck in athletics is not being injured. No matter what shape you're in – you could be in the best shape of your life – you can't prevent injury. You can take precautions against it at best. People say, 'Good luck,' but I believe your destiny is mapped out.

When you say you believe destiny is mapped out, do you mean that everyone has a path in life which is pre-ordained?

Yes, I do believe that. But I also believe that you can change things, depending on, I suppose, your faith, your belief ...

And what else can help you to change things?

Your attitude towards life. A lot of it could also be your attitude towards God: I believe there is a God. Those are what I would say are the major factors. You could go through life not caring about anything else and just let it go, but as with everything you have to work at it; and the harder you work, the more you are able to shape life for the better.

Can you say how much of your success is due to your faith in God and how much is down to your actually getting out there and doing the hard, physical training necessary?

They say God helps those who help themselves. It's easy just to sit back and say, 'OK, I believe in God and just let it run and see what happens.' But you've got to work at it, and I believe that as long as you believe in yourself, God will help you. But a lot of people have always found it easier just to blame everything on God and it's just not that way at all. The Bible tells us to give unto Caesar the things which are Caesar's and unto God the things which are God's. I accept that.

But do you think that people need a certain basic drive to make them succeed, and if so where does that drive come from? Why is it stronger in some people than it is in others?

It's hereditary, I suppose. Successful people are people who are hungry, people with a little bit of fight, people who decide, 'We're not just going to sit back and let things happen for us, we're going to go out there and work for what we want.' Those people make a difference in life, not just for themselves but for others. The people who say 'I'll just chill and let it all happen,' are the ones who fall by the wayside.

Do you have any formula for overcoming the obstacles and difficulties that life tends to throw in everyone's path?

Once you set out to do something, just get out there and do it. You can't let anyone or anything stop you, because I don't believe in failure. Failure doesn't come into my vocabulary at all.

If you believe that, what happens to you when you fail?

I just put it down to the fact that, on the day, your best wasn't good enough. You've always got to come back. If you believe you've failed because others are better than you, you'll never be the best, and the day you believe you can't come back, failure has got you.

So even what happened at the Olympics didn't put you off in any way?

Not at all. You win some, you lose some, and you never appreciate what it is to win unless you lose, because having lost you come back and you win and that makes the victory that much sweeter.

What was your reaction when you were disqualified? How did you feel, knowing that you'd trained all this time for the Olympics, then suddenly you were disqualified because you'd come out of the gate a bit too fast once too often?

I very rarely make false starts. When it happened, to be blunt, I was totally pissed because I knew I didn't false-start.

But the computer said you did.

What was happening was they were refusing to accept that I could react so quickly. Who are they to say that? You can't limit progress. No one can say that a reaction time can never be improved beyond a certain point, and nor can a machine. Man made the machine, so therefore, isn't man greater than the machine? The starter didn't think I false-started, it was the machine that said I did.

But if the machine can identify false starts more closely, shouldn't we go along with that? Why should a human have better judgment than a very precise machine?

Everything is capable of error, that's why machines will never totally replace human beings. When a machine goes wrong you need a human being to fix it. Here we have a machine telling me that the signal that goes from my brain, the moment I hear the gun, to my feet cannot be transferred so quickly, that it's impossible for me to move as quickly as I actually do move. How could a machine tell me that? That's utter rubbish.

So what you're saying is that human success ought to be judged by humans and not by the ever more sophisticated machines that humans invent?

I do believe that, because who makes the machine? Man makes the machine. To me it's like idol worshipping. People make these effigies and statues, then bow down to them. But who's the greater? Isn't the maker of the statue greater than the statue? So why should I make a statue then start worshipping that statue?

Nevertheless of course the machines are there …

They're there to help, not to be totally depended on. Machines have no common sense and that is one of the great things that we as human beings have, and there are times when it has to prevail.

Have you now changed or adapted the way you start because of the presence of these machines?

Not at all. Nothing will change, because that's just my natural reaction. What can I do?

But it means that you could be disqualified again, doesn't it?

If that's what it means, then that's what it means. I can't hold myself back because there have been times when people have had a quicker reaction than I have and got away with it. It just depends on the other guy, or the other machine, or which machine they use. Life is risks. You've got to take risks – that's what makes people successful.

So no regrets about what happened at the Olympics?

No. There's nothing I can do about it, it's no use having regrets, and given the circumstances all over again I would still do the same thing.

And yet way back in 1991 when you took fourth place in the world championships, you wanted to retire at that point and had to be talked out of it. Why did you want to give up at that point and what was it that made you come back into the sport?

I wanted to give up because at the time I think I was underestimating my ability. I once said I was going to be Olympic champion – and I was written off. A few press guys told me I was too ambitious and would never be that. There were people in athletics at the time who told me I was crazy and was never going to be a world-class sprinter. Then I ran 9.92 which then was the fourth fastest time in the world – and nobody cared. I felt that I had run as fast as I was ever going to, but when I should have been happy about it, everybody thought, 'You didn't get a medal.' So I decided maybe all the things they said were true, maybe I was too old, maybe I wasn't good enough and maybe I should give up.

But a lot of members of the British public wrote me letters saying, 'Barcelona is just a year away and we've bought tickets to come and watch you run because we believe you can go out there and stuff everybody, so please give it one more go,' and after thinking about it for a while, I spoke to my coach, my family and people around me, and they said, 'What have you got to lose?'

So I decided to put everything into it, to train hard. I sat down with my coach, we looked at my weaknesses and strengths, and we decided to work on the weaknesses without neglecting the strengths, and the rest is history. That's why I believe that in order to be successful you've got to work to build up your strengths, without neglecting to work on your weaknesses.

So encouragement is important, the encouragement you had there from members of the public; but when you talked about the discouragement you had earlier from critics telling you that you couldn't do it, was that in fact a help in achieving your ambition because when people tell you you can't do something, with your make-up and temperament, you want to prove them wrong? Does it in a sense help a successful person to have someone there at the back telling them, 'It's impossible, you'll never do it?'

I don't know. My grandmother used to say, 'Encouragement strengthens labour.' No matter who you are, when you've done something you want people to tell you you've done well. Then you can say, 'Now I'm going to go out and do better.' You've got to be encouraged without getting over-confident. You've got to accept criticism, but if people are telling you all the time that you're no good, you're useless and such things, well, you can work against that to a certain point, you can say, 'I'll show them,' but if someone tells you the same thing every day, eventually no matter who you are or how strong you are, you'll start to believe it.

And who was it telling you this?

I had it from the media, and from the people who actually ran the sport. A lot of the people who ran the sport were telling me, 'Change your event, you're never going to get through.' You see these as the people who know what's what. They're talent scouts, they're out there to recognize talent, so if the top coaches in the country are telling you you're never going to make it, well, who should know better than them?

You've often criticized the media for the way in which they persistently knock achievement. Why do you feel that the British media are overly critical?

They're failures themselves. So because a lot of them have never actually achieved anything in life, they try to discourage others. Of course, we're all guilty at some point in our life of criticizing. But if it's constructive, it's for the good of the person, it's something they can learn from. But our media are not constructive, and they're too opinionated. They believe they're reporting what the public wants to hear, but the public wants to hear what's gone on, not the reporter's opinion. They're supposed to report the truth, the facts as they see them, not as they think them.

But aren't they entitled to come to a judgment after reporting the facts?

They never report the facts. If it was the facts they were reporting, why have they been sued so often? If they claim that they're reporting the facts why are they always complaining about the compensation they have to pay out? If you believe that you're not doing anything wrong you shouldn't be worried about the consequences.

Is there a big difference between the media in this country and the media in other countries, in the way in which they treat athletes?

I think there is a big difference. I've been to Australia. Now Rupert Murdoch is one person who is responsible for the way the media in our country report or distort things; but you should go to Australia and see the way they write up their sport. Australian athletes win their national championships and they are hailed as Olympic champions. They play Aussie rules football – as the name implies, no one else plays it; but the Australians are proud to say that they are the world champions in Aussie rules football. They are encouraged by the press to go out there and succeed. Meanwhile our newspapers discourage us, they are forever trying to tell us that to be successful is wrong and that we should despise those who are successful. What hope are we giving the youngsters? We should be out there telling them it's good to be successful, you should be proud to be successful. Only then will we have the champions that the newspapers are complaining that we don't have.

There are those who say that if you pop your head above the parapet and into the public arena, then your whole life is open to scrutiny.

My dad always says, 'The higher the monkey climbs, the more his backside is exposed.' You can go along with that to an extent, but when people are climbing your fence and chasing you around ... everybody has to have a private life, everybody has to have time out, time away from the track or wherever. If the roles were reversed on the editors of some of these newspapers they wouldn't be able to take it. If you start taking pictures of photographers they panic. People must realize that we're human beings, with a right to time apart.

Let me take you back to your early days. To what extent do you think that your success is a product of your background and upbringing?

I come from a background where we never had anything in abundance: we had just enough, and sometimes nothing at all, but we always loved each other, we were always there for each other, and that background would naturally play a big part in the way things have happened. My grandmother was the leader of the clan. In all the years I've known her I've never heard her say a bad word about anybody. I've always wanted to be like her, and that's one of the reasons why I have a problem with the way the media criticize people: these people don't know me and we have so many Linford Christie experts out there, it's unbelievable. If they think I'm so bad, why are they trying to cash in on me? They're making money by forever knocking me – and others, in all sports – in the papers and in unauthorized biographies.

Was your grandmother ambitious for you, was she ambitious for the whole of your family, did she want you all to achieve?

She didn't differentiate between us at all. She loved us all equally and as far as she was concerned we were all going to be doctors. She always said you should put your hat a little bit higher than you can reach, so you will stretch on tip-toes. We can't all be doctors, but we can all try to be and I think that's more what she meant than anything else: you should always try to be the best you can be.

You came to Britain from Jamaica at the age of seven to join your parents.

That's right.

Tell me a little about those early days.

My parents came here because they wanted to make a better life for us. When I arrived there was myself, my mum, my dad, two sisters, a brother … I think there were eight or nine of us altogether. We were all living in two rooms and the cooker was on the landing. My dad was earning less than five pounds a week, out of which he had to pay the rent, support my mother and send money to Jamaica for us, and he still had to save up to pay our fares. But we were happy.

What was his job?

When he came here he worked in a place called British Bathworks. They made big enamel baths. Then he worked as a porter in the BBC for many years until he retired. That to me was success. On less than five pounds a week he did all that, supporting six kids as well as himself and my mum.

It must be quite difficult to keep a family on the rails under those circumstances.

Well, Dad managed that and on top of all that they bought a house in West London. We lived on Loftus Road when we first came here, then we moved to Stowe Road, which is about a mile away We were only young kids and we couldn't understand why Mum and Dad had to leave at seven o'clock in the morning and why we wouldn't see them again until seven o'clock at night. But we brothers and sisters were there for one other, and when Mum and Dad came home they were there for us, and so here I am today. I believe that's success. Sometimes you take it for granted when you sit back and enjoy a good life. I'd say the younger generation take that for granted. But what our parents went through so that we could have what we've got today – I'd say that's as good as anything achieved by the civil rights movement when they were fighting to get black people the right to vote. For me there can't be a better success story than that: to come to a land where you know no one, where the culture and everything else is different, to go through all the trials they went through and overcome all those obstacles. Young people nowadays find it hard to get up and move out of the home, or to another country – I would find it very difficult if I had to move to another country and start another life without knowing anyone, it would be very, very difficult.

Was racism a factor in those days? Has that had any influence on your life?

As they say, 'Seen it, done it, still wearing the T-shirt.' I've been through all the obstacles of racism, but that could never keep me back.

Did you feel you were having to fight the system?

Oh yes. I believe the majority of black people who have made it have had to work damn hard, we've had to overcome a lot of obstacles.

Have they had to work harder than white people doing equivalent things?

Yes, I do believe that. Some people say it's wrong of me to say that but I do believe it. But you can't let the fact that someone doesn't like your colour keep you back. I'm proud to be black. If I was white I'd be proud to be white. Whatever colour I was I'd be proud. I didn't ask to be this colour, it's the colour God made me. Whatever you are, you've got to be happy with that. The only difference between us is what you can see on the outside; on the inside we're all the same. We all bleed the same, and we're none of us going to live any longer than the others. You've just got to make the most of life. To go round thinking that because you're black you're not going to get a job ... that's just too small a chunk in your life to worry about.

Do you recall the first incidence of racism at your school?

It was when a little girl in primary school told me that her mummy had told her not to play with the blackies. That was the first time I realized I was black. I think I must have been about eight. I went home and told my parents, and the strange thing is my parents never told me to go back and call her any white names or anything else like that. And when I had my little white friends come to the house my parents treated them the same way as they treated us: if the ice-cream van came round and Dad couldn't afford ice-cream for two of us, none of us would get any. That's the way our family was and still is.

So after you'd had that taunt from the girl, did you feel, 'I'm going to have to try harder, I'm going to have to redouble my efforts in order to succeed in life'?

No. I suppose it hurt a little bit thinking back on it later on, but it didn't make me think anything different at the time. It was just an incident, you go on until the next incident comes along, and you deal with that. You can't allow something like that at seven or eight to be anything because it wasn't the little girl. It was her parents.

Did you feel that you had to try that bit harder because of your colour?

I suppose subconsciously you do, but it's not something you think about. At any rate, I don't think about it. I really don't go through life thinking, 'Gosh, it's because I'm black.' I know I am and more shame or more fool you for wasting time not getting on with your life – or for trying to hold me back because I'm black. If I'm the man for the job and you want to give it to someone who's less qualified, who's losing out, you or me? That's how I look at it. Certain people in athletics have said to me many times, 'Here you are, always successful, what success you'd have had if you were white – you'd have had twice as much.' But hell, I'm happy with what I've got. I've been the fastest man in the world, and I haven't done it because I'm black, I've done it because I worked hard, because I wanted to get there, I wanted to achieve and I think that's the difference. We have many white guys who say, 'I'm going to be the fastest white guy in the world.' Well, the fastest white man in the world only ran ten seconds, so who cares? I want to be the fastest man in the world, whether he's black, blue or white. I want to be faster than anybody, so it doesn't matter what colour I am. If you're racist towards me I'll tell you there and then, but I'm not going to hate a whole nation because I have an incident with one person of a different colour or creed. I've got a problem with that one individual. That's how I was brought up.

When did you win your first race?

I started running when I was about eight and I honestly don't remember winning any races. I think the only race I ever won when I was younger was when I was trying out for my primary school team and even then it was only because of the staggering, although I didn't realize it at the time! I felt that people were saying I cheated because I had a head start, but it was just the teachers who put me on a stagger. Later on in life you realize that it all evens out anyway. I ran when I was at secondary school, and I won races then. But it was something I enjoyed, and still enjoy, because it gives me the chance to pit my ability against the next person's.

So you are instinctively very competitive?

Oh yes. Yes, indeed.

And when was the first time that you thought you might make a career of it?

Well, it wasn't until my coach, Ron Rodden, and Andy Norman, who was a promotion officer at the time, both told me I could make a career of it, I could be good at it. Prior to that it had never crossed my mind. I was running races and I didn't get paid for it; and to be honest, I could still go out and run and win races without being paid, I'd have been satisfied with that. It wasn't until they told me what I could do that I started working hard and seeing results. But once you start doing that, then you want to work harder, obviously you want more results. So I went out and gave it everything I had. I believe now that if you're not going to do anything to the best of your ability you shouldn't do it at all.

You talked about encouragement from Andy Norman and Ron Rodden. Do you think that everyone on the path to being really successful needs a mentor, someone who sits beside you and says, 'Yes, you can do it', someone who instils a kind of belief in your abilities?

Yes. My faith is strong, but not enough to move mountains. There have been times when I've doubted myself, and that's when Ron gives me that little push, tells me of course I can do it, I've done it before; and at the end of talking to him you think, 'Damn, I am in good shape, I've done all the work and I am the best. I can go out there and do it.' You need that. Everybody experiences self-doubt.

So you think that every successful person, no matter how successful, has to have some kind of self-doubt?

Unless you're God. Every mortal person has self-doubt.

Is that a driving factor?

It can't be a driving factor. Sometimes you think you've done your best and then you pick up a newspaper and read that it was rubbish. Then you need someone who can see you for what you really are and be your Rock of Gibraltar, give you support. Now I've got not just Ron but many people around me who are like that and I'm becoming more and more immune to all the criticism I get.

Do you think coping with the media is part and parcel of being successful, of being at the top. Is it a price that every successful person has to pay?

You may joke with your friends, but I don't class these people as friends and I don't have to take their jokes. What is a joke to one person is death to the next. I can't accept their kind of jokes, talking about my genitals, Linford Christie's lunch-box and so on, trying to bring a lunch-box to a photographic shoot. That's an embarrassment for me. I'm trying to escape from that kind of stereotyping, from the notion that I'm good for nothing but running on a track. I have a lot more to offer than that.

You don't feel that all the things you see as indiscretions by the press are part of the price that a successful person has to pay?

I don't see why there should be a price I have to pay. I'm the one who's gone out there and been successful, why should I have to pay a price? Some people sit back and say that's the way life is, but it isn't. If I sat back and accepted it, how far would it go? I don't make racist jokes and I don't accept them. If I sit back and allow someone to make a racist joke, whether it's against me or someone else, and laugh at it, I'm encouraging racism. So I stop it straight away.

Do you think every successful person needs an element of ego, even a touch of arrogance?

Confidence is sometimes mistaken for arrogance. I believe that if you sat down and analysed every successful person you'd see they have an air of grace around them, an aura. You need that, you need to be head and shoulders above your opposition, you need to make others believe that you're better than they are. It's been said many times to me by other athletes that when I walk into a room they can see the difference between me and the other athletes. It's one thing to be able to run very fast, but you've got to have something to back it up. People like personalities. If you run and you're boring, then no matter how well you run, who really cares? You've got to have a bit of personality behind it, and that's how I am – I have got what I believe is personality. It entails making your opponents realize that when Linford Christie's in a race they can't afford to be in 80, 90 per cent shape, they've got to be 100 per cent, all the time, even 110 per cent, because if I'm even 90 per cent, they're going to get beat. That's the message you've got to send to your opposition, and if they call that arrogance, so be it. I call it confidence.

What is the physical regime that a potentially successful athlete needs to follow?

First of all you've got to have talent. That's the most important part of being a successful athlete. In sprinting, for instance, if you haven't got that twitch fibre, no amount of work, nothing you do, is going to make you run faster.

So you need the talent, you need someone to identify it and then once that has happened, what else?

You work hard, you don't not work hard. That is how I work.

How tough is it?

It's very, very hard. A guy from the *Mirror* once wrote, 'What does Linford Christie know about hard work? He goes out there and runs for ten seconds or just less and he makes more money than most of the mums and dads out there?' He couldn't be more wrong. People only see me run when I run for ten seconds. I train seven days a week and between three and six hours a day. When my opponents are having a day off I'm training, because that gives me a day on them. I don't let up, I believe I have to be in the best possible shape I can. I've also got to look good, because one of the most important parts of being an athlete is to look the part. If you look like an athlete you scare the hell out of everybody else and that's half your work.

And fear is a factor?

It is. We're all scared, every single one. Anyone who tells you he's not afraid when he goes out there has never been successful. You're afraid of losing, you're afraid of not being successful, but at the same time your opposition are just as frightened of you as you are of them. You've got to make them believe that they're more afraid of you than you are of them.

What would you say to young people looking up to you and saying 'We want to be like Linford Christie?' What advice would you offer them?

I always say the money factor should be the last thing on your mind – don't think about the money, do it because you enjoy it. The more you enjoy something the harder you work at it, the harder you work at it the better you become, the better you become the more money comes in. That to me is the only way to do it. And always, always work as a contender, never as a champion, because as a champion there's nowhere else to go, as a contender you always want to get there.

Do you feel as a successful athlete you are also under an obligation to put something back?

I think you should feel the obligation. If all the people who have made it in our sport just got out and did something else, who would the youngsters coming in have as their blueprint? The people who run our sport are old, and they're not going to be around forever, so we need the young people in the sport to keep the interest going. In the Bible it says, 'Young man, I call on you because you are strong.' Old men dream dreams and young men have visions. We need to get rid of some of the dreamers and then, with some of the youngsters contributing their vision, the sport can only get better. If we only take from it, the sport will eventually get weak and fade away.

What are the biggest enemies of success?

Failure! Not being successful has got to be the biggest enemy. Complacency also. Complacency is a big enemy and no one can teach you how to overcome that, you've just got to learn for yourself. And always accept losing, because if you don't know what it's like to lose, you'll never know what it's like to win.

Is there a downside to success?

The critics! The media.

Anything else?

No, there's no other downside that I can see. There'll always be obstacles, of course, but I think you can overcome those.

Who are the successful people you really admire?

I have a lot of respect for people who have made it against all the odds. I respect people like Richard Branson, people who started out with nothing and have made something. I also respect all the foreigners, immigrants who have come from wherever they've come from to a land they know nothing about, and have made a success of it instead of sitting back and hanging on to society and making out that they are owed something – people who get off their backsides and go out and get what they want.

Athletes have a limited life on the track. Is there success after your running life finishes?

Well, my running life has been finishing for a long time. There is success for some of us, the ones with the personality. There is always something for you to do. I believe I was born to succeed: if I wasn't an athlete I would be just as good at whatever I chose to be, I think it's just my destiny to be successful.

You have a company, 'Nuff Respect'. Why that name?

We were trying to find a name for it, and often when Colin Jackson, Sue Barrett and myself were walking up the road people were saying, 'Nuff respect to you guys, nuff respect.' It's a street phrase for when people appreciate you for what you've done. I'm a man of the streets, which is one reason why Joe Public can identify with me. I didn't go to a public school, my parents never had an abundance of wealth, they're working-class people. I rate myself as a working-class person and the average person I deal with is working-class. I made sacrifices and got down to some bloody hard work and I've made a success of myself. I had no great tools to work with, but I just worked hard and they can see that with a little bit of hard work and a few sacrifices, they too can be like me.

So when your running life finishes, Nuff Respect is going to be the engine that fuels you to a different kind of success?

I hope so, but I don't limit myself to Nuff Respect, though at the moment it's a brainwave that Colin Jackson and myself have had, and it's working. We are a miniature Mark McCormack group, but the way our work-force is organized, there's no bosses and no workers: we are people. I treat everyone the same and everybody treats me the same. There's no difference between the workers here at all. We manage, we do sports management, event managing, we're jacks-of-all-trades and masters of many.

Has success changed you at all?

I hope not, and according to my friends it hasn't. Every now and again when there's a group of my friends round I ask them 'Do you think I've changed?' Because I don't want to change and none of them, unless they're lying to me, has ever said that I've changed at all. I have always been me. Success has made me a bit more cautious of people, a bit less trusting, which I think is a shame.

You said you hoped your friends weren't lying to you. Is there a danger when you're very successful that people can be sycophantic and tell you what they think you want to hear?

Not my friends. The people I have around me are the same people I had before I was successful.

Is it important to keep the same people?

Very important. So many people, once they've made it, forget their old friends and move on to new ones, then find that those friends are only around because the person's successful, and once he starts to fade away, the new friends fade away too. I'm not saying you can't make new friends, but you need the old faithfuls around you first, the people who were there at the beginning, because they are the people who keep your feet firmly on the ground and make sure that you don't get big-headed.

What's the greatest single pleasure that you've had from your successful career?

I'd say the MBE. We're all out there to be recognized, if anyone tells you he's not doing what he does because he wants recognition, it's not true. We're out there to be recognized, and to receive the MBE, that shows that someone out there somewhere is watching what you're doing and appreciating it. When I get the knighthood I might have a different answer but for the moment the MBE will do!

What would you like people to say about you when your time comes to depart this life?

The only thing he couldn't beat was death. That's it. Nothing else.

SEBASTIAN COE

On the athletics track he broke 12 world records, including the 1500 metres, one mile and, most famously – in the 1981 World Championships – the 800 metres (which remained unbeaten for over 16 years). The most important advice he has to those who would follow in his tracks is 'find a good coach who looks long-term, can help you plan strategically and remove some of the pressures'. He thinks budding athletes also need strong parental support – and in his case both roles conveniently combined, because his coach was his father, Peter. From being just a good, national-standard 800-metre runner, he suddenly became the focus of a surge of public and media interest. Leaving on the desk his degree from Loughborough University and the applications for management training courses
it had spawned, he moved on to the 1500 metres gold and 800 metres silver at the 1980 Olympics – 'the culmination of ten years of hard slog'. The early Eighties saw a frustrating and depressing time when he was hit hard by illness, but he pulled himself back for the 1984 Olympics, becoming the first man to retain the 1500 metres title.

By now, perhaps unwittingly, the preparations for his later career in politics were starting to drop into place. He became Vice-Chairman of the Sports Council and the athletes' representative on the IOC; while his outspoken opposition to the use of drugs in sport earned him a place on the Health Education Authority. Left out of the 1988 Olympic squad, he switched into the Parliamentary race, becoming MP for Falmouth and Camborne in the 1992 General Election. He believes politics is 'the stuff of life', coming alive in the constituency 'where you can really achieve things'. But he thinks the House of Commons 'sometimes isn't the real world', and is critical of the way in which single-issue pressure groups are 'beginning to clog the system, often stopping individual voices from being heard'. Here he compares success in athletics, 'where I could control the variables', to politics 'which is much more brutal'. He recalls attacks on his strategy for a race in which he finished third, and explains how that race was, in fact, 'the single most important contribution that any race made to my career. What drives successful people along,' he explains, 'is that perfection is always around the corner.' The unexpected too – he lost his parliamentary seat in the 1997 General Election, finding some compensation in being appointed chief of staff to the new Conservative leader, William Hague.

Sebastian Coe, what is your definition of success?

I think being asked to define success is one of the most difficult questions you'll ever ask anybody because inevitably the answer is a personal one. I tend to define success not as a product, but as a process. It's all wrapped up with the pursuit of excellence. I don't think you ever sit back and suddenly say, 'I am a successful person,' because what tends to drive 'successful people' is the fact that perfection is always around the corner. I try to identify what I thought success meant in terms of my previous career in track and field, and I think it's best summed up by the point that I retired from athletics when I felt that I was probably not going to run any quicker. That didn't mean whether or not I was going to win races, because for two or three years after I'd retired, if I'd stayed in the sport, I probably could have won races. That tells me that my own personal definition of success was actually running quickly, being a better athlete than I was this time last year, and I got to the point in my career when I suddenly realized that I wasn't going to be a better athlete. There were no unturned stones either physically or mentally that I could look under and say, 'OK, that may help me to be better.' I had turned them all over, and at the age of 34 I decided that the challenge wasn't there. That was interesting because I had always thought that I was motivated by just wanting to win, and I suddenly realized at a crucial point in my career, that wasn't just what it was about, it was actually an amalgam of so many other things. That's why I think it's a process rather than just an individual product.

Having achieved the success you did in athletics, you could presumably have moved on to any number of areas – why politics?

Politics is something that has always interested me. I don't mean it to sound quite as precocious as it probably does, but I knew I wanted to enter politics when I was about 14 or 15. I wasn't quite sure how that would be identified, whether it would be party politics or political journalism or whatever, but politics has always fascinated me.

So was athletics a means to an end?

They are different issues here. I've read profiles of me, and some have inferred that I left athletics and went into politics in the way that some footballers buy fish and chip shops or nightclubs. In fact, politics was something that actually interested me far more than sport. I was vice-chairman of the Sports Council and still have an active role with the International Olympic Committee, but I got dragged into that because of my competitive background, and because I had been very outspoken on the drugs issue in the early 1980s when it wasn't that popular to be quite as outspoken on drugs as it is now. I was the first athlete to address the International Olympic Committee back in 1981 in West Germany and it tended to flow from there. But I never had any intention of having a career in sport – sport for me was something that I loved doing. When I left Loughborough in 1979, I was actually applying for jobs, but the year I graduated also happened to be the year I broke the world records and suddenly my whole career took a completely different path. But like fellow undergraduates or recent graduates in my year at Loughborough, I was concerned about management trainee courses or whether I was going to go into journalism or something like that. I never thought I would spend the next 10 to 15 years of my life actively involved in sport.

What was the catalyst that made you decide to have 15 years in sport?

The success of 1979, which was the watershed year in my career. In pure athletic terms it probably wasn't, but it was the watershed year in terms of the general public and the media. Up to that point, I was known as a good national-standard 800-metre runner in the UK, capable on my day of winning medals at championships. But then I suddenly broke a world record and that attracted a whole cluster of people that are not desperately interested in track and field or the nitty-gritty of 800-metre running and the science of it – they see you as somebody who's broken a world record. Therefore, there was a media interest and so from 1979 onwards my sporting career took me way beyond sport, it went into a whole group of different areas where there are very pleasant but inordinately different types of pressures.

While you were achieving as much as you did in your athletics career, did you have this constant feeling that you were being forced to put politics on the back-burner?

There were occasions when sometimes I baulked a little bit, not externally, but I sometimes sat back and thought, 'This is a lovely lifestyle, but actually it's a very narrow one and it's not ultimately what I want to do.' The only career planning in real hard terms I made was after 1984 when I successfully defended my Olympic title in Los Angeles. I was 27 and I then sat back and I suddenly thought – I remember thinking about it on the way home – that really up to this point I'd had a remarkably lucky and privileged career. I had successfully competed in two Olympics, I'd broken world records, I'd had a couple of frustrating years in terms of injuries, but by and large I'd been blessed, and that from this point on anything else I did in track and field was a bonus, it was to be enjoyed. But I did have to think that it was going to end at some point. I wanted to get out at the right point and I wanted to put some things in place so

I accepted the vice-chairmanship of the Sports Council. I chaired the Olympic Review Group which looked at the whole issue of Olympic funding which was very time-consuming – certainly 1985 was so time-consuming that it actually took the edge off my performance on the track in a couple of key areas. I had now come to terms with and was recognizing that track and field was very enjoyable and provided a wonderful lifestyle, but it did have to be in tandem with something a little bit more constructive.

What is it about politics that gives you a buzz and why the Conservatives rather than any other party?

The simple answer to 'Why Conservative?' is it is a philosophy that I am most comfortable with. I doubt whether there's a single active politician who doesn't at some stage in their career sit down and ask themselves that question, particularly at times when they may be out of sorts with the direction in which their party is taking them. The simple answer is that it is a philosophy that comes very naturally to me. There is a more mechanistic answer to why politics, of course. I've given this answer before and been accused of being cold-blooded about it, but when I became vice-chairman of the Sports Council, my responsibility, along with the other vice chairman and the chairman, was to make sure that sport got a good shake of the dice. I spent a lot of my time at that stage of my career sitting down talking to senior civil servants, sports ministers, even the occasional secretary of state and I recognized that there were in that situation, albeit a narrow area of activity, some buttons to press and some to leave well alone and I pushed this point quite hard because I don't think sport ever quite realizes this – that politics of course is the stuff of life. If I make the argument to a secretary of state that I want more tennis courts, more indoor facilities, better running tracks, then I am also making those arguments in the face of 101 other interest groups who will be making arguments for better hospitals, better defence systems, better roads. So I'd better make those arguments pretty well and I'd better rally as many usable facts and arguments as I possibly can. It was the first time the Henley Research Centre was brought in to support the fact that there are more people involved in sport actively, as an income producer, than in petrochemicals, coal mining, the car industry and agriculture put together. It's the third largest retail activity in this country – a few years ago it was calculated at £33 billion a year.

Having said that, I realized at that stage that I was interested in politics and that I'd actually quite like to do that on behalf of a constituency. That's where I get a lot of pleasure, for me politics comes alive in the constituency where you really can achieve things. The House of Commons is an interesting place and I grew very fond of it, even in the four years I was there, but sometimes it's not the real world. But what really made me decide on politics was that period as vice-chairman of the Sports Council, just watching the system of government. It's a red-blooded issue as well. You can't go into it and just survive on the simple love of the mechanism, because if that's the case you're better off being a civil servant. You've actually got to believe in things.

Did you enjoy the cut and thrust?

Yes, I did, immensely.

Did it sometimes get too tough? Did you sometimes feel, 'This is a pretty ruthless business'?

There were boundaries beyond which I wouldn't step. It's the same in sport – sport is a very tough business, but there are plenty of people who survive very well in sport, make a huge contribution, but also know there are natural boundaries beyond which common courtesy tells you that you don't step. That's the same in politics and the vast majority of Members of Parliament know where those boundaries are.

Having seen politics from both sides, first as a lobbyist and then as a member of the government, do you sometimes think that it is getting tougher for the ordinary person to push through an idea successfully and get the ear of the people who govern our country?

There are two things here. I wouldn't quite define the Sports Council as a lobby group because it's almost an executive arm – albeit at arm's length from government. The one thing that is a problem and is beginning to clog the system, is that the single-issue lobby groups are very much more skilled in the way they can achieve their results. They're very, very much more skilled in communication and the way they disseminate information and the way they can muster campaigns.

You're saying that they have huge PR machines while individual MPs do not?

They have huge PR machines. Lobby groups have the ability to deliver to every individual Member of Parliament up to 2,000 stamped-addressed cards that require nothing other than a signature at the end of a well written piece of prose, whether it be on hunting, or landmines, or whatever, and I see that as a problem. I don't see that as a way of allowing the will of the people to get to their elected representatives, because for every one of those cards that comes in – and they all have to get responses – you are actually taking time away from the real hardpress cases that constituents come to you with, because your whole office is submerged for a week in trying to deal with the massive lobbying that goes on.

So are you saying that it would be better if single issues came up from the constituencies, without the support and back-up of national pressure groups?

Yes. I recognize that the lobby groups are a part of the democratic landscape. It's been something present from the 1960s onwards – the Americans with Ralph Nader and such people developed this culture very much earlier than we did. But we've got to be very careful that we are not so swayed by their campaigns that they have everybody jumping around when in fact it may not represent anything other than a very slick PR machine – we've got to be very careful to see through that sometimes. *Brent Spa* is a classic example – it was demonstrably bad science putting a company in a position where they were forced to do something which any independent scientist told them was wrong, but suddenly they've got a 20 per cent reduction in their income on the forecourts of their garages because Greenpeace or whoever it was suddenly got on to this bandwagon. If you are a single-issue lobby group you have a responsibility to make sure that you're not playing fast and loose with the actual facts of an issue.

So is the sheer volume of single-issue pressure groups' activity is actually affecting the degree of success of ordinary people around the country, in putting forward their points of view and having their arguments heard in Parliament?

That is often the case. MPs are often swayed far too much on all sides of the House. Members are often put under a great deal of pressure by single-issue lobby groups and sometimes there is a tendency to panic when hundreds of cards are received on something that appears to be the will of your constituency, when in fact those hundreds of cards may only represent a very, very small part of what people are genuinely feeling.

Let me go back to your early days for a moment. To what extent do you think your success has been due to your background and upbringing?

I don't think you can divorce the two. My father happened to be my coach, so I speak with some feeling about this. I hate the word ordinary, I hate people talking about ordinary people because we're all rather ordinary in our way, but I suppose I come from a fairly average family. I have two sisters and a brother. My father always had great aspirations for all of us and his view was always, 'I don't mind what you do, if you're going to empty dustbins just do it and as well as you possibly can – be the best dustman around.' There was never any pressure on us. My mother was a repertory actress for many years in Worcester and Birmingham. One of the great things they brought to my career was probably more balance in my early years than I would have had otherwise. They were in a position to say, 'This is important,' as my father was coaching me and training me, but they were also never slow in saying, 'For God's sake get a life, go out and do something else for a bit.'

Is that quite important to have someone in your early days, whether it be in your case your father, or in other people's case a mentor, who guides you through the particularly difficult decisions and keeps you on the right track at a crucial time in your career?

Yes, absolutely. In sporting terms it is a vital contribution. I've got very good friends who are coaches, and when they have a youngster come to them and ask them if they could be coached by them, the first thing they ask is to see their parents because they want to know what kind of support, what kind of background there is – whether the parents are basically interested in what their children are doing. Any coach will tell you if they've got parents on board then they're already halfway down the road. Any teacher will tell you that if you've got parents that are interested in their child's development, then that child's progress is certainly likely to be helped rather than hindered.

Is it possible for parents to be too ambitious? Can there be dangers in parents wishing their own ambitions on their children?

Yes. Some of the worst scenes I've ever witnessed in sport have been from the touchline of under-11 football matches or under-11 rugby matches watching youngsters who have a very good instinctive feel for the bounds of responsibility and what is acceptable on the pitch, being egged on by parents screaming all sorts of things at them. A parent/athlete relationship, coach/athlete relationship is vital – when it works well it's wonderful, when it works badly it can be tragic.

Is a degree of sacrifice and failure necessary to achieve real success?

Yes. Nothing in sport, nothing in life that is good and successful is produced overnight, therefore it's a long, long road. I first competed in 1969–70. and ten years later I was at the Olympic Games, so those were ten years of hard, hard slog. I think anybody who loves what they do tends to think of it not as a sacrifice but as a way of life.

When you were up at the top in 1982–83, years that should really have been your best years, you were either injured or ill. That must have been pretty mentally debilitating for you. Did you ever consider giving up and if not, why not?

I didn't consider giving up although they were deeply frustrating and sometimes very depressing years. For about a year I was soldiering on with an illness and nobody seemed able to tell me what it was. I remember reading in various tabloids that I was cracking up mentally and I remember reading one piece where they brought in a psychologist to psychoanalyse me, my family and the whole thing. In fact it was quite amusing. My sister was quite a successful dancer and the summation of the article was that this was a typical two-child family where the attention had been focused on a boy and a girl. We read this with great laughter at home. My mother wrote a nice letter to the paper – actually it didn't get published – saying that she enjoyed the article, thought it was interesting, but there was only one minor point – would they like to explain what the other two in the family were thinking about at this point. There were some quite miserable articles. I remember one paper described me as being as friendly and approachable as Frank Sinatra on a bad night. When I got it right, having been helped by a very good team of doctors, I came back to the Olympics in 1984 and in the six-month build-up to that one of my training partners used to keep the articles in a scrap book and if ever he thought that I was wandering a bit in training he would just leave them out, lying around the house I shared with him. It worked. This was feeding off stress, and stress is actually important. People talk about stress but don't actually know what they mean by it. We all need stress, stress is a big contributor to creativity.

What is the difference between here and America in the way that success is treated?

If you do well in America you are looked up to and if you repeat that success, then that is even better. The one thing I've always tried to say to youngsters in athletics is that it is not about whether you can do it once, in a way that's the easy bit. It is clichéd to say this, but the hardest bit is to come back next year and do it again and again and again – real success is consistency. I sense this in American businesses as well, that if you work in an American business you actually don't begrudge the people at the top earning very high salaries because you know that you are part of a successful business and if they're doing well, the chances are that you're going to be doing well. In fact we are perhaps getting to that now, but there's still a bit of a divide in the UK on that. Furthermore, the Americans value coaching so much more highly. The high-school coach in a small-town American community is an important person. I speak with good experience on this one – my closest friend's probably one of the most successful high-school coaches ever in the history of cross-country in America, a guy called Joe Newton from Chicago. I stayed with Joe before the 1984 Olympic Games. Joe is looked up to like the local preacher and like the local police chief, he is a fixture in that community because he's seen four or five generations of youngsters through his college. They all come back to him, they keep in touch with him wherever they go. Some of them are in very senior, very influential jobs in America, but when they come back to his college in their forties and fifties they still refer to him as 'Coach'. Coaching is a very important part of life there, but in the UK I don't think we've ever properly understood the role of coaching in the process of pursuing excellence.

So would you like to see the coach being treated in this country as one of the fathers of the community, as someone people look up to?

Yes. The work, the unsung work that is being done, the length and breadth of this country, by coaches who are giving up hundreds of hours of their year free of charge – it's almost like having a paternal arm of the social services, yet people just have no appreciation of it.

How would you elevate that position in the community?

First of all I'd fund it properly. We are beginning to do this, and thank goodness the National Lottery has now moved from capital funding to revenue funding, appreciating that facilities are important but also that you've got to get people in those facilities who are in a position to influence – and you can only do that through revenue funding. One of my objectives in the 1980s was to try to upgrade the political status of sport. When I first joined the Sports Council people openly referred to those civil servants who were working in sport in the DoE, which was then the sponsoring ministry, as being in 'the toy department'. Then we had a Prime Minister who had probably put more thought into sport in this country than any single politician for many years. Raising the game was probably one of the most important pieces of government thinking on sport since 1945. So for those of us who were battling away in the 1980s it's a bit of a culture shock suddenly to have Prime Ministers and Leaders of the Opposition standing up talking about sport in coherent ways.

When you have been confronted in your life with exceptional criticism or failure, how have you overcome that?

It has certainly been my belief that what motivates me is a physical love of running. The worst thing anybody could say to me today, tomorrow or next year would be, 'Sorry, your ankles are too far gone or your hips are too far gone to be able to go out and run.' But also, when I was still competing, I had the belief that it wasn't simply about winning – of course that's important, and the miles and miles of bashing the roads in and around the Peak District and the hills of Sheffield for years and years wasn't simply about just going out because I enjoyed doing it, because if that was the case I would perhaps have done it two or three times a week. I wouldn't have done it three times *a day*. Winning *is* important, but it really isn't and wasn't the only thing that mattered. Testing myself, asking questions that only I could answer in terms of my career and whether I could actually improve as a runner and do things that nobody had done before – they were important. My father was exactly the same. He transformed the way 800-metre running was done by working with me and I think we both quite enjoyed challenging the orthodoxy of the sport.

And did you accept you would have to take criticism?

Yes, sure, we had to. The year 1978 was a classic example. We had a lot of criticism for the way we both decided I would run the 800-metre final in Prague. I was still a relatively immature athlete. I was suddenly in a final against some of the household names in Europe including the great Ovett, and we looked at this absolutely coldly and said, the chances are I'm not going to win this by sitting in there and being outkicked by athletes who at this stage in their careers are quicker than me. The only way I stand a chance of either winning or getting a medal is going out and making it hurt for them. I took the first lap in the fastest time anybody's ever been through in an 800-metre race – well under 50 seconds, nobody had run that speed before. In fact Steve Ovett said to me that if he'd looked at the clock following me round for the first lap he'd have probably stepped off the track. In the end I came third. We had a lot of criticism, but we both flew home from that championship knowing that we had learned more that day about my capabilities and, by implication, the capabilities of those athletes around me, than we had learned on any single occasion previously. What we learned we put into practice throughout the winter, and 12 months later I was back on the track breaking the world record at 800 metres. Now to say a successful outcome is only if you win would be ludicrous, because the single most important contribution that any race has made to my career was the race in which I finished third. You've got to be very careful about those assessments.

Success for you in athletics involved taking risks. Can you afford to take that same level of risk in politics?

There are greater strictures. Athletics was a very individual sport. We would, of course, go to a games as a British team, but at the end of the day it was up to me what I did, the races I chose to run in, and how I approached them. Politics is a much longer game, it's a marathon not a sprint, and of course there are more strictures. There are inevitably more strictures when you are in a team hopefully all pushing in the same direction. Sometimes it is not as easy to be an individual in politics as it is to be in sport.

But did you have a technique for riding through political criticism? There was a poll of MPs and you didn't come out of that too well. Did you say, 'That poll got a lot of publicity, what can I do to counter this'?

No, because I've got rather long in the tooth and a bit cynical, having dealt for so long with another form of the media. You read the article and learn that out of six hundred and something MPs they'd only polled ten, and they then didn't go on to say which side of the House those ten were polled from. In fairness, Glenda Jackson came in for exactly the same criticism. I'm slightly too long in the tooth not to recognize that if you want to put a headline with Coe and Jackson in it then the chances are you are giving credibility to a bogus piece of journalism – it's not something that you should get wound up about. I got rung up on the morning of my 40th birthday at home and I was just planning to go to a football match that afternoon and I didn't realize it but my wife had organized a surprise party for me that night. I was preparing to go and I got a phone call from a guy from the *Sunday Times*. 'We've done a poll and you've come at the bottom of it for competence, have you got anything to say?' I said, 'Certainly not.' I put the phone down and I did think for a moment, 'Do I really need this on my 40th birthday?' Then I got in the car and went off and watched Chelsea lose, so I had much more to complain about at the end of the afternoon.

If I had thought that there was some truth in the article, that I was genuinely doing a duff job or that I was in some way failing my constituents, if I thought, 'Perhaps that's what colleagues do think,' I would have been concerned. But I was probably arrogant enough to think that I was not doing a bad job and what the paper had said was not what the average Member of Parliament thought, any more than the average Member thought that about Glenda Jackson at the time.

Who are the people you admire for being really successful?

People who consistently achieve, not just the one-off characters. Someone like Steve Davis, who for ten years dominated his sport. Daley Thompson, who first won a decathlon in 1978 and dominated his event until he retired. People who actually not just do it well, but do it differently, who bring something to an area of activity that's not been done before.

One of my great heroes, not simply because he was born on my birthday, is Lord Nelson. In political terms, in the post-war period you certainly have to look at someone like Churchill, and Margaret Thatcher in the way that she dominated politics – they dominated the scene by sheer will and determination.

Is it possible to have a successful career in any field without having to make considerable sacrifices in your personal life?

I think it's how you define sacrifices. I've always tended to think that if you are genuinely enjoying what you are doing and it is giving you personal satisfaction, you don't look at it as a sacrifice, you look at it as part of the process. You could argue, and I think with some justification, that's a rather selfish view. I recognize that I enjoyed immensely my time both as a junior member of government and as a constituency Member of Parliament, but I also recognize that I probably saw my children on fewer occasions then than the average professional person in this country. I would like to have spent more time at home, I would like to have been able to devote more time to them, but I couldn't. So you could argue that the pleasure, the enjoyment, the intellectual stimulation I got from being in Parliament was at a certain cost and I could genuinely define that as a sacrifice.

Is there any difference between success in sport and success in politics?

The same amalgam of successful ingredients has to be there. In sport I was able simply to say, 'Right, this is what I want to do, this is where I'd like to be. I'll set out a coaching schedule, I want to be running this speed by 1975, I'd like to be at the Olympic Games by 1980.' Ostensibly, that was under my control, all the variables were very much easier to control. I could choose the races. I could choose where I wanted to race, when I wanted to race. Politics is very different, because ultimately your career pattern, at its most basic, will be determined by the way the majority of people in the constituency vote. In a way it's very much more brutal. I hoped my contract would be renewed. It wasn't. From my experiences so far, I think it would be a very frustrating process to sit down, as some have supposedly sat down in the past, and say, 'Right, I'm in the mid-1990s, by 20-something I want to be in Downing Street.' I don't think it works like that. That ultimately leads to frustration. I also make the genuine point that you can't look at life in politics as simply being a member of a government or on a front bench. Some of the best contributions and sometimes some of the ablest people are actually sitting on the backbenches, making massive contributions.

What do you think are the greatest enemies of success?

An undervaluing of your own potential. Sometimes people are a little bit scared to stretch themselves because there is always that fear in the background that they might not succeed. But that's part and parcel of the process, there's no certainty of outcome if you pursue excellence, and sometimes you are going to over-reach yourself. Sometimes just lack of ambition. I've worked with youngsters who have got physical and mental gifts but they don't believe it themselves. The hardest task of any coach is to get youngsters to believe in themselves, sometimes to paint the picture for them, to excite them, to show them just what lies beyond the horizon.

What advice would you give to all those young people who have looked at your 800-metre and 1,000-metre world records and said, 'Hey, I want to do that one day'?

You've actually said it – it starts with saying, 'Hey, I want to do that.' There's nothing much more I can say because that's all I thought 15–20 years ago. I looked at Alberto Juantorena or Brendan Foster and said, 'Hey, I want to do that' – though I wasn't quite sure how I was going to do it. I was lucky, I was helped. The best bit of advice is to find yourself a good coach who thinks long-term and can help you plan strategically and remove some of the pressures at a time in your career when you're probably not intellectually or physically capable of dealing with them. It's a psychologist, it's a father, it's a valeting job, all wrapped up into one thing, but find a good coach who looks long-term. It's like a rose, you don't whip a rose into shape, it has to be nurtured, manured and all sorts of things. It's selective, sensitive, targeted coaching.

And what advice would you give to young people wanting to get into politics?

If you want to and you think you can make a mark, it is one of the most satisfying jobs that you can possibly do. The results are not always successful, but you'll get an insight into people's backgrounds, people's surroundings, different problems that you'll probably get in few other walks of life.

Is it becoming more or less difficult to achieve success?

We run the risk in politics of wringing out individuality if we're not careful and I don't mean that in terms of just having to follow the party line, I just mean in the types of people that we would be encouraging into it. The last couple of years have put a lot of pressure on people who have come in with slightly different backgrounds. We seem to accept readily that teaching or law or banking is not an unreasonable background to come in from, but we're slightly nervous about anybody who would want to come into politics from sport or, from Glenda Jackson's point of view, from a theatrical background. The great thing about Parliament has been the breadth of interest and background from which people have come into it. It would be very, very damaging if you just had career politicians coming in who have done their time in student politics, become researchers, and then just thought of it as a career path. You've got to come in with some kind of background. I'm not sure I'd let anybody in under the age of 30.

In pursuit of success, have you ever done anything you wished later you hadn't done?

I can't honestly say I have. That's probably a very self-satisfied thing to say, but nothing obvious comes to mind. I'm sure that in an hour's time, thinking about this, I'll think of a whole list of things, but there's nothing that has been too cataclysmic.

What's the greatest pleasure you've had from your success?

I don't wish this to sound too mushy, but probably the pleasure it's given close friends and family. That success, winning races, Olympic Games, things like that, has given them an enjoyment that they deserve, because their contribution was a massive one.

When your time comes to leave this life, what would you like people to say about you?

He gave it a go.

SIR PAUL CONDON

Britain's top policeman says his children joke that he was never young – he was helicoptered in as an adult! A disciplined schooling in which 'theft and vandalism were unknown' sent him into the wider world at 15, hungry to earn a living. Joining a small industrial publisher, within just four years he was managing director, in charge of forty people. But the police force had always been in the back of his mind, and he signed up for 'the Met' a year later, going on the beat in the old gangland areas of the East End. After taking just two years to pass his sergeant's exam, the police magazine The Job *tipped him as a rising star. From the National Police College, he won a scholarship to Oxford and took a degree in law. Rising rapidly through the ranks, he became, at 46, the youngest person ever to be put in charge of the Metropolitan Police – at a time when London had the most crime and the worst detection rates in the country.*

He talks here in detail about how he set about turning that around with 'a quiet revolution in the way the city's police were managed and organised'; about the devolving of power down through the ranks, and the introduction of performance targets for every police station; the benefits of pitching recruiting at an older age group; the introduction of 'tension indicators' to monitor constantly the mood on the streets, and the part they played in dealing with what was probably his worst crisis; about the 'terrific colleagues from the ethnic communities coming through to senior ranks'; and the time he came closest to resigning. He reveals his message to new recruits: 'You have awesome powers to ruin people's lives. To exercise those powers you need honour, integrity, courage and restraint in large measure. Your purpose is to improve the quality of life in our communities, to provide stability and tranquillity.' He has controversially gone public with an admission that there are '250 corrupt officers' in his force who must be weeded out, and publicly apologised for the failure to pursue leads in a racial murder case. He believes that success doesn't happen naturally in the public sector 'because it's so easy for inertia to prevent change', and you need the determination to fight that. 'Changing big organisations involves leading them on journeys they don't necessarily want to take,' he says, so 'as a leader, if one of the measures of your success is popularity, you're on a hiding to nothing.'

Sir Paul Condon, what is your definition of success?

To define success is difficult in the context of policing. I want to talk about qualities rather than just what people achieve, so, for me, a successful constable is one who is honourable, courageous, professional and in touch with his community. At more senior levels, it's displaying leadership, achieving things and so on. But I find it harder to define leadership in the police context than I would if I were running a company. Everyone has a different view on what success means in policing terms. It certainly isn't just about the number of arrests or traffic tickets issued.

So there is something special about policing, about the qualities needed to be a good policeman, at all levels, which is not there in other sectors of society?

I want to focus on policing. When I brief the young officers coming out of training school, I tell them, on their first day, they have awesome powers to ruin people's lives – by arresting a member of your family or one of your friends, they could ruin that person's life. So, on behalf of society, we exercise awesome powers, up to and including the lawful right to kill, in certain circumstances. To exercise those powers, I'm looking for qualities of honour, integrity, courage and restraint, which have all got to be there in large measures. I believe they are present in many other professions, but in policing, if they're not there, then the Police Service would be in awful trouble.

And do those qualities change, depending on who is Commissioner?

No, I would like to think that those qualities are enduring – certainly if I look back over the history of the Metropolitan Police Service I think there have been, in my terms, excellent Commissioners. There has been courage and bravery and dedication throughout the whole history of the Met, at all levels. So, I don't think there is a fashion to those issues. In policing, they should be enduring and ever-present.

But the emphasis that you bring to some of them, and the priorities that you have, are different from those of other Commissioners. What are you doing that is different in a bid to achieve success?

I hope it's not just the fashion of the time in which I happen to find myself as Commissioner. I've probably put a greater emphasis on our performance, as a Police Service, than some colleagues. I don't think you can have a Police Service which merely talks about qualities, as I've done earlier. We're there for a reason, we're there to improve the quality of life of our communities, we're there to provide stability so that people can get on with their lives – private and commercial – we're there, with other partners, to keep crime to an absolute minimum, we're there to ensure public tranquillity. So, I think I'm ruthless with myself and with colleagues about measuring our performance, talking about what we're doing, acknowledging our failures, which takes us into discussion of quite tough areas: what it means to be policing a multi-cultural, huge cosmopolitan city, for example.

When you became Police Commissioner, the Force had the lowest detection rate in the country. What were your tactics for changing that, for turning it round?

I've always had a three-stage approach to these issues. One, define what it is you're trying to do – and with the Met I said what we were doing was not good enough, and I defined some standards which we aspired to. So, say up front what it is you're trying to do. Two, do whatever is necessary to get you into the best organizational shape to deliver. So we went through a quiet revolution, in terms of how we were managed and organized. A lot of senior ranks have gone – 300 senior posts have gone. We had too many layers, too many managers, too big a hierarchy. So, define what it is you're trying to do, get in the best organizational shape to give you the best chance of delivering. And then, three, measure. I honestly believe what gets measured, gets done. And we've been pretty ruthless with ourselves. So I would like to think you can go into any Met police station, any department, any unit and examine their performance, and have a pretty good idea as to what they're doing, where they've come from, and what they're trying to achieve.

But is there an element of successful policing that can't be measured? Time spent, points scored. Are those the sole criteria by which you judge whether someone is successful or not?

A lot of our measures are *qualitative* measures. One of the most important indexes, for me, is how Londoners feel about their Police Service. Once a year we have huge surveys carried out for us on Londoners. How do they feel about the Met? What do they want the Met to do? How do they feel about quality issues? And I'm pleased the latest survey shows that – bucking the trend in public life – confidence in the Met has gone up by four per cent in the last year to around about 60 per cent, a level of confidence that most professions would eat their hearts out for. So, I think Londoners are recognizing that we are trying to do things for them which are not just about number-crunching. It's about quality, it's about feel, it's about style, and our style is very much about partnership.

Do these surveys also enable you to trace back the improvement in your position, in the public eye, to specific things that you have done, specific actions you have taken?

Yes, they do. If I were looking for reasons why I think we have improved public confidence, it would be that a number of years ago we said to Londoners, 'What are the crimes which worry you most?' And they said, burglary, and being robbed in the streets, mugging. We have addressed both of those issues. I've just had the latest results on our Eagle Eye Campaign. For the first time in many, many years, there has been a drop in street robberies in London, and there has been a significant reduction in people having their homes broken into. And I think Londoners acknowledge that, and most of them appreciate it. So staying in touch with what people feel they want from their Police Service is vital.

When you're effecting changes, often of a quite dramatic nature within the Force under your control, you've got to carry people with you. Sometimes there will be painful decisions to be taken, and you have to persuade people of the value of those decisions. How do you set about that? Do you have any particular tactics?

I would say, initially, you can't always achieve that, so part of being Commissioner – part of being leader of *any* organization – is a recognition that if one of the measures of your success is popularity, you're on a hiding to nothing. If you're changing big organizations, you have to acknowledge that there will be a time – perhaps for all the time – when you are taking the organization on a journey that it doesn't necessarily want to go on, and then you must have the confidence – or the arrogance – to see that journey through. Hopefully, as you approach that sort of destination, to continue the analogy, people will understand why you've set out on the journey. But if popularity is a measure of success, then it's a very dangerous index to lock yourself into.

It helps that I think we've got the best people ever coming into policing. Our standards are higher than they've ever been, our performance and productivity are better than they've ever been. But if the measure is, 'Are people happy bunnies?' Then no, not everyone is a happy bunny.

What have you changed about the recruitment?

The average age of the recruits in the Met, at the moment, is 27. We tend not to take youngsters. I think policing is so demanding, to take someone (as I was) at 20 years of age, a country lad, then put them on the streets of a big city that he doesn't know anything about, is a hell of a challenge

– probably too much of a challenge for most people. So we've deliberately pitched our recruiting at an older age group. They've got life skills, they've got common sense, they've probably got a partner, a house, some kids, they're not looking for aggro, they're looking for fulfilment and achievement. We've pitched a lot of our recruitment at Londoners. We want people who understand, who've got an investment in the future of London, and we've worked very hard to draw black and Asian Londoners into the Met. This is a multi-cultural city. It will become even more so over the next ten years. I need a Met that's in touch with black and Asian Londoners, so we've worked very hard to get more ethnic recruits, and with some success.

And what argument would you use to the black community – where quite a few have been traditionally suspicious of the police, and there has been a degree of hostility – to get them to come forward to join police ranks?

I recently did a phone-in on a radio programme that goes out mainly to black Londoners in South London. And one of the questions was about this very issue, and the answer I gave, and I believe it very sincerely, was, 'Don't believe all the mythology, don't believe all the rumours.' If *you* are concerned about policing, if *you* are interested in policing, show the commitment, come forward – either be a Special Constable first or come into the regular service and influence our future. Influence the future of London. Don't criticize from the outside, come and get involved on the inside. In the longer term, I'm optimistic. We've got some terrific colleagues who happen to be black or brown, coming through to senior ranks. In specialisms they are role models, they are succeeding, quite properly, on merit. Time will take care of the issue. But I'm impatient, I want it *now*. I'm not prepared to wait for another three or four years, I'd like to see more ethnic Londoners in the Met as soon as possible.

Is that generally another quality you need to be successful, a degree of impatience?

Yes. And arrogance and self-confidence, which you can disguise as impatience, but it's believing that, as the boss, you really know where the organization is going. And when I've been asked what's the one big thing, as a leader, you can give to an organization, my reply is – vision. This is where we are going, and this is how we are going to do it.

As a rule, do the media have a fairly dramatic effect on your ability to be successful in certain areas?

Yes. I think when the history of this period of time is written, then I think there will be an awareness there has been a huge transfer of power, away from the democratic process to a small number of people in the media – people who can determine the news, set the agenda for the news, put a spin on a particular aspect of news. I'm not saying that's wrong or I always resent it, but as Commissioner I need to understand it, and work with it. I met a lady a couple of years ago whose father was Commissioner in the 1930s. She said that during the whole time he was in office as Commissioner his name appeared in the media only twice – the day he was appointed and the day he retired. Now I have no wish to go back to those days, but if I look at how my time is spent, I would say a good 20 per cent, at least, of my personal time is spent on the media side of policing.

Don't you accept that in a democratic society, and in a society where there is a huge evolution in communications, the media have the right to be sceptical, to question everything that happens and probe and dig for motives?

Absolutely right, and I'm the fiercest defender of that. Part of the reason I'm a policeman is that I believe passionately in democracy and I believe passionately in rights of free speech and rights of assembly and so on. It's just occasionally I feel there is a sort of nasty, rancorous hunting-in-a-pack on an issue, whether it's to make or break an individual, or to put a spin on a story which will make it more attractive, and the facts are not going to get in the way. Only rarely do I feel that, but it is there on certain issues, and I think it arises from the media's quest for circulation. If that descends into real pandering to xenophobic feelings or racist feelings, it can get rather ugly.

What have you done to try to stop those kinds of reports actually appearing?

We have a very vibrant communication strategy. I have some very good people, at all levels of the organization, who work with the media. And we get, by and large, a very good deal in terms of people understanding who we are and what we're trying to do. And I wouldn't want to overstate this point, but just maybe a couple of times in four years I have sensed an ugliness around a story which I thought was not edifying for the media concerned, and not in the public interest.

We talked about your fight against racism, and one of the early problems that you had to deal with was the Joy Gardner case – a black immigrant who died while being arrested. When you heard about that story, what was your tactic for dealing with what could have been a pretty explosive situation?

In those cases there are a number of legal processes which must be unleashed immediately – an investigation into what took place, the involvement of the Police Complaints Authority, the preparation, eventually, for an inquest, and so on. We gave all these vigorous and full support. There was a feeling that this was a hugely significant issue for the Metropolitan Police Service and that we should do everything in our power to make sure that everyone understood what was happening, had confidence in our procedures, and so on. In doing so there are always victims, not just the person who has died but their families, the police officers involved and their families. So one doesn't go into that sort of situation lightly, but it was obvious from the first second I got the news about that issue that it was hugely significant.

Was it an immediate feeling of crisis?

Not crisis in the sense of something that could not be dealt with. There was an immediate feeling of significance from the factors involved – a woman, the early reports of what allegedly had happened, the fact that someone had died, the fact that police officers had been involved in that situation. So it was not just making judgments as to whether everything had been dealt with properly or not dealt with properly it was also the significance of all of those factors coming together.

And the use of restraining techniques, some of which you hadn't heard about?

Yes. We have something called tension indicators, which we monitor throughout London. And they tell us the mood on the street, they tell us what people are saying, what people are doing.

How do you establish those?

Every police station reports on them. They are things like assaults on police, violence, crowd disturbances, people gathering, what informants are telling us, and so on. But our tension indicators told us that once the news of that incident hit the streets, tension indicators in London changed dramatically. And I have no doubt that we were within hours of serious disturbances in a number of locations in London.

So what did you decide to do? Do you have a plan ready to swing into action?

Clearly a plan was swung into action, which was about doing the right thing in terms of investigation – a communication strategy to tell key opinion-formers what we were doing, to be open, to share what we were doing with Londoners, and within 24 hours those same tension indicators had dropped almost back to the level before that incident. So that told us that Londoners acknowledged that here was a significant issue, but that it was being dealt with properly.

Can I take you back for a moment to your very early days? You were brought up in a council house and went to the local school. What kind of school was it?

It was a secondary modern school, in a fairly new building. It had a very happy atmosphere – and I don't think that's me looking back through rose-tinted spectacles.

What did your parents do?

My father was a paint sprayer, had been a Serviceman during the war, had come out of the army. His trade was spraying cars. It was a very loving household, I had very supportive parents. At school – and I don't think I'm censoring my memories – I don't remember any one of my friends, or *anyone* from the school, being arrested for stealing or for vandalism. Certainly it was before drugs. There was not much money around, it wasn't idyllic in the sense of being a privileged background, but I had a very happy childhood.

What was different about that school? What kind of things were they doing that would have had an influence upon you?

I'll start at a slightly different point. In the middle to late 1950s England was still coming out of austerity. A lot of my teachers were former Service personnel. Some of the people teaching us were heroes. Although it was a decade after the war, I think there was still a lot of that discipline in the post-war atmosphere – people who'd been Servicemen now in teaching, parents who'd all been in Service cultures. That's not a disguised plea for National Service. I just think it was a different time, which it would be impossible to reproduce. It was a particular time in our history and I happened to experience it at a particular age. I think most schools would have been like that – school uniforms, caps, discipline.

You left school at 15?

Yes. Feeling the world was my oyster. I couldn't wait to start work and get involved and do a whole range of things. I can conjure up the vision of myself, like a video, actually leaving school on that final day in 1963, with a tremendous sense of excitement.

And then you went to work for an industrial publisher.

Yes I did ...

You were the manager by the time you were 19, in charge of 40 people ...

Yes. My own children jokingly say that I was never young, that I was helicoptered in as an adult. And I know what they mean, in the sense that I was given responsibility at a very early age, and hopefully responded to it in a positive way. I've always felt the need to fulfil myself in whatever I've done. And I was very lucky to work for a company which gave me lots of opportunities as a very young man. And I hope I didn't let them down. I enjoyed every minute of that.

So you had these opportunities, you were enjoying life, why did you decide to leave?

At 20 I suddenly thought to myself, 'Is this what I want to be doing for the next five, ten, 15 years, the rest of my career?' And I decided it wasn't. I'd almost tried to join the police cadets at 16 when I left school, but I thought I'd work in the private sector first. It was a decision to learn something about the world. I'd never spoken to a policeman, I'd never been in a police station, I had no family connection with policing. But at the back of my mind, as a teenager, was the notion that to be a police officer was a good thing to do, and at some stage I would return to that notion. So I did that at 20. I thought, 'Now is the time,' and I thought I could fulfil a number of things. I could see what it was like to be a police officer, I could move to London – I was brought up on the South Coast. I wanted to see the bright lights. And it all came together at 20 and I joined the Met.

Was it difficult to join the Met? Did you need an element of luck?

There was luck in the sense that I applied, heard nothing for ages and then one day I timorously rang up and said, 'Forgive me for asking, but, are you ever going to respond to my application to be a policeman?' and they were honest enough to say they'd misplaced my application and said, 'We'll write to you, we want you to join fairly soon.' So, but for that phone call, you and I wouldn't be talking in this context.

And what would you have done?

Who knows? I guess, because at that point I'd got the notion of policing in my mind, I would have applied to another Force.

You were then on the beat in Bethnal Green, which was the old gangland area. Was that a tough time?

Actually, I started at Leyton, which was a bit further out in the East End, but I took to that, I hope, like a duck to water. I loved it. The excitement of going to work, not knowing what you were going to face, no personal radios, no computers, very few cars. You had to talk your way into situations and out of situations. If you got involved in a punch-up or whatever, it could be quite a while before you got help. And so I think young police officers, at that time, very quickly built up confidence, a personal style, an ability to communicate. I had a wonderful three and a half years on the beat as a constable.

By the time you'd finished that, you had decided you really wanted to make a career within the Police Force. Did you have any master plan? Did you say to yourself, at that stage, 'I am going to be Commissioner of a Police Force'?

When I joined the Met, I was aware there was an accelerated promotion scheme. I was aware there was a graduate scheme, and I thought, 'Yes, I'll have a go at those when I can.' I took the sergeant's exam when I had about two years' service – which was quite young to do that – and was selected for the accelerated promotion scheme. So from about my second to third year of service, I knew that I'd been accepted for that scheme. But I had no grand design to be Commissioner or Superintendent, or whatever. I remember in training school, in the first couple of weeks, one of my instructors saying who he was and that he was an inspector in the Metropolitan Police with 11 years' service. And I thought it must be wonderful to be an inspector, but in terms of horizons, nothing beyond that, at that stage.

Taking it a step at a time?

Yes. And by that time I had met my wife and we married in 1969. So I had the excitement of my family life – with my wife and children – running alongside the excitement of my professional life.

At the age of 23 you were identified by the police magazine, The Job, *as a star of the future. Did you think, 'This is it. The world's my oyster'?*

No. The Police Service is a great leveller. If anyone's head gets a centimetre too big, they soon bring you down to size. I was just trying to do my best in an organization with a lot of talented people. And there was a feeling, as I guess in all walks of life, that a group of well-motivated young colleagues were moving up through a service together. I've had the joy of feeling that. I have contemporaries who are Chief Constables, I've got senior colleagues in the Met, you know, we've been PCs together, sergeants together, inspectors together, and that's very reassuring. But I never had a sense, at any stage, of being personally selected to be drawn through to the most senior ranks in the service – just a feeling that I was in there with a pack who were moving through the service.

What do you regard as your biggest failures, and how did you recover from them?

I take the loss of police colleagues very badly. As Commissioner, my task is to lead the Met through difficult times, through dangerous times, as safely as possible. Now since I've been Commissioner I've had those three phone calls, two happened to be in the middle of the night, one during the day, where the second you answer the phone, you know it's going to be bad news. And to be told that a police officer has been shot to death, stabbed to death, just the feeling in the pit of your stomach, of failure, that never goes away. It's reinforced when you meet the families, when you go to the funerals. It's absolutely soul-destroying, particularly if there are children involved. And it's as if the emotions of the service, the whole grief of the service is focused through whoever is the boss. Not in the sense of blame, but in the sense of recognizing the emotion of the occasion. And I'm not ashamed to say that I cry at those funerals, even if I've not known the officers involved. You always think, 'If only. If *only* we'd been able to do this, if *only* we'd had slightly different policies on that, if *only* we'd had better officer safety programmes at an earlier stage.' So there is a very dramatic sense of loss which edges into a sense of failure.

And in the immediate aftermath of that, are your decisions driven, to a degree, by anger?

No. I think anger is one of the emotions that you have to park at a very early stage as a cop if you're going to stay sane, and if you're going to stay fair and balanced. You cannot allow the baggage of anger to mount up and go forward with you. A resolution which came out of the early losses for me, as Commissioner, was a profound sense of determination to improve officer safety, which we have done through protective vests, longer batons, handcuffs and officer training. I was pleased to report in 1996 that there had been a dramatic reduction in assaults on police since that programme. During the previous year, the figures stay in my mind, we had a 16 per cent drop in assaults on police. And in human terms, that means a drop in about 500 to 600 hundred officers being assaulted. Now you think of all the saving in terms of distress, emotion, injury for them and their families. So, it's pleasing to achieve that.

The Police Force, like every other public service organization, has to operate within financial constraints. Have those, in any sense, inhibited your success, and have you ever been tempted to resign or threaten to resign in order to achieve your goals?

You should never play fast and loose with threats to resign. You should only threaten to resign if you're prepared to resign.

Has that ever happened to you?

The closest I got to it, I guess, was probably in my first year when there was a major review of police pay and conditions which had very good recommendations, and these have helped improve the service. But there were some which I felt would have totally undermined the service – to do with pension provisions, age of service, the thought that police officers would have to serve on until they were 60, on the streets, before they were eligible for pensions. I could not have presided over those recommendations if they'd been implemented. I would have been put in a very difficult position. I never threatened to resign, but I think I would have had to have thought very seriously about my future.

But, no, in a democracy it is right that the level of resources, the laws, issues like that, are determined by Parliament, by the government of the day. My job is to implement those decisions. Like all public services, I could do even more with more money, but so could education, so could social services, so could health. We've got to be realistic, it's grow-up time about resources. We can't endlessly pour money into any of our public services, so like everyone we're about providing value for money, making the best use of our resources. But if there was an offer for another £50 million, I'd willingly take it and we could do even better than we are doing now.

What do you regard as your greatest success?

I find that very difficult. After four years as Commissioner, I'm proud of a whole range of things that we have achieved with Londoners. We were about to go though a million crimes a year in London in 1992–93. We're now down to about 830,000. We've dramatically reduced the number of burglaries, we've got on top of street robbery, we provide the best emergency response service in the world for a big city. And I'm proud of all those things, and the policing world still beats a path to our door. In the last couple of weeks I've had delegations from the Ukraine, Australia, Egypt, Russia, South Africa. They come to Scotland Yard because they think we're one of the benchmarks for excellence in policing around the world. And I think their trust in us is justified and I'm immensely proud of, if you like, stewarding the Met for a small number of years and then handing over to someone else. If we get it right, people's lives are better, if we get it wrong, that would undermine the whole stability of our society. So it sounds a bit arrogant, but it's a good feeling that we're not doing a bad job and it's a job that makes a difference to people's lives.

What do you think are the greatest enemies of success?

Complacency, inertia, human nature. There are people who can, if they are in the right place at the right time, achieve niche success, almost regardless of who they are. In public-sector activity it is so easy for inertia to prevent change, and to achieve success in the public sector in particular, you have to have a determination, a resolution, and a commitment. That can be exhausting for everyone concerned, including yourself, but has to be there. Success doesn't happen naturally in the public sector, you have to work very hard.

Has success changed you at all?

Yes, and probably for the worse. Certainly power corrupts us all. Corrupt is probably too pejorative, but power changes us all. And I think there is a shelf-life to being something like Commissioner. I've said that I'll be Commissioner for a minimum of seven years and I've done four. Much beyond seven years, I suspect, probably wouldn't be right for the organization or for the public or, ultimately, for me. There is a shelf-life to top jobs which is about excitement of the acquisition of the post, the vision about what you're trying to do, the excitement of doing it, the sense of achievement. But one can outlive one's stay, outlive one's usefulness perhaps by doing things for the 15th time. In policing, demands are made upon us by the changing nature of the world around us, so I think there's probably a ten-year maximum for me. I've put the first review point at seven years into my Commissionership. Much will depend on how people feel at that point in time about me as Commissioner, what we're achieving.

But part of success is knowing when to stand aside?

Knowing when to stop or when to change, when to take on other challenges.

If you could gather together all the young people who look up to you and say, 'We want to be like Paul Condon,' what would you say to them?

Well, first of all may I say, and it's not just modesty, but I think there are a whole lot of youngsters who would say, 'When I grow up, the *last* thing I want to do is be like Paul Condon the Commissioner.' Firstly, I am very, very optimistic for the future of this country. I am hoping that the Millennium celebrations will be a focal point for regeneration of confidence, of optimism, of looking forward. I don't say that in a party-political sense, I say that as someone who believes passionately in the future of this country. I think we've got some terrific youngsters growing up. Their attitude is about being true to themselves, having ambitions, being public-spirited, being good neighbours – a whole range of things which can sound trite and small-scale. I don't think there is a big idea of regeneration with regard to the good things in our lives, it's about getting lots of *little* things right. I am, as you've gathered, an optimist, and I look forward to the future – part of that looking forward is having confidence in many of the young people who will inherit the mantle of public service and lead big organizations into the future.

When your time comes to leave this life, what would you like people to say about you?

I think it will be something like, 'He lived his own life to the full and he didn't miss the opportunities that were given to him. And that in terms of policing he helped move the Police Service on in a way that was both necessary and right.' And I would like to think that, certainly in terms of the Metropolitan Police Service, I will hand over to my successor a Metropolitan Police that is in good shape, in tune with its public, and seen to be doing a good job.

BILLY CONNOLLY

'I am,' he once said, 'a millionaire who used to sleep in Preston railway station.' The humour of Billy Connolly has a rare, magic quality that carries it across international boundaries. His technique is to make people look at all aspects of everyday life afresh, highlighting both the incongruous and the obvious in the most unexpected ways. He always had an ability to make his schoolmates smile, although his own early life wasn't exactly a bundle of laughs. His mother left their Glasgow working-class home when he was four, and his father wanted to put him into an orphanage. Instead he went to live with two aunts, where he endured 'violence and humiliation', and was constantly told how worthless he was. Not surprisingly, he now  believes that a difficult upbringing is just as strong a base for success as a good one. By treating you less well, your parents may 'set off a desire for acceptance within you, and going into the world to achieve this acceptance and approval starts to shape you'. Leaving school at 15, he wanted an engineering job in the shipyard, but 'the guys with posh accents got those', so he ended up a welder. The Territorial Army licked him into shape as a paratrooper, but by now he was getting gigs as a folk singer – even doing a European tour.

Gradually he put the guitar aside as audiences responded to his sense of humour. Nicknamed 'the Big Yin', he began to pack the clubs north of the border. And there he might have stayed if the interviewer Michael Parkinson hadn't taken a chance and given him a national break on his top-rating TV chat show. He's never looked back – going on to develop a parallel career as an actor in films and television. An American mini-series, **Billy**, in which he starred, was cancelled after 13 episodes, but he never sees setbacks as failures. 'A big ego is an absolutely essential ingredient. You've got to believe in yourself, because every day people will give you great reasons for not doing something. Like the hula-hoop, all new ideas are bizarre!' He has waged a vigorous war with his critics: 'They don't know anything,' he says, pulling out a Roosevelt quote, 'they've never tasted the dust in the arena.' His advice: in comedy, you need to be continually successful. 'Forget the standing ovation tonight, because being funny tomorrow is quite hard.'

Billy Connolly, what is your definition of success?

I've tried really hard over the years to understand what success is, and it's like trying to understand what comedy is or trying to understand what wealth is. With success, you're never actually there – wealth is the nearest correlation you can get. Nobody thinks they're rich. I've met billionaires, but they don't think they're rich. And success is the same, you never seem to be quite there. You know you're a bigshot, but Clint Eastwood's bigger than you.

Success is the drive to do more, no matter how apparently successful you become?

Yes. It's an elusive, almost a mythical thing, success, almost like a wisp of smoke. It's like wealth. When you are a wee boy you think maybe it would be lovely to have £100, you know, and when you're a big guy you think maybe £1,000 might be rather pleasant, and then £1,000,000. But once you get all these things you think, 'Well, it's not quite what I thought it was.'

So the successful person is never content?

Never content. It's a series of little hills, the top of which you get to and see another wee hill, and then you get to the top of that one and see another hill. It's a constant. It's isn't a finite thing. It's an elusive constant.

And do you need the break – the big break?

No. I think the big break is in the hands of media people. For instance, in my story the biggest break for me was Michael Parkinson. But then, Michael had heard about me, that's why I was on his show. I was working, I was filling theatres everywhere. Jimmy Reid, the Upper Clyde shipyard guy, mentioned me to Parky, taxi drivers had mentioned me to Parky and so on. But an outsider would say, 'Oh, he came on Parkinson – *booff* – an overnight success.' Well, it wasn't quite like that.

But you do need to be constantly successful if you are going to be a successful person. You need to be good again and again and again and again, particularly in comedy. Being funny isn't the most difficult thing on Earth, but being funny tomorrow is quite hard. You have to forget the standing ovation tonight and start again tomorrow and be exactly as good, if not a wee bit better, because now you have to please yourself as well. You have this discipline driving you, to please yourself too and impress yourself.

But why do you need to do that, because some people might think it's enough just to have a standing ovation every night?

I really don't know. And I've spoken to many many people, some of whom have even quit because of it, like Jim Carrey in America – he quit because of the standing ovations and got out. He said, 'It was just driving me towards Las Vegas and I wanted to be a film star, and film stars don't need standing ovations. I need something else.' So I can understand that completely. You set a standard for yourself and it's in a constant state of change. You set the standard to achieve, then you set a higher standard, and then a higher standard, like an athlete. I don't know where that comes from, though, I don't know what instils this in you.

Is it perhaps something to do with background and upbringing?

I think it must be, and I don't think that if your background is good – inasmuch as if your parents behaved really well and did all the right things and invested the right amount of money and energy into you – that it will work. It can work in the opposite way. If they didn't do all the right things it can be the making of you. They may, by treating you less than well, set off a desire for acceptance in you, because they didn't accept you and didn't love you, as you see it, the way you thought you could have been accepted and loved. You may then go out into the world trying to achieve this acceptance and approval from the world that you didn't get before, and it starts to shape you. In show business I know there are a lot of guys like me, their background is very similar to mine, they were unhappy people or badly treated people. Some of them, as in my case – which is the most difficult of all, and I know several people like me – their lives looked okay from the outside. All my neighbours would be amazed if I told them what my life was like, it baffles them completely. 'Your father was such a nice man and your auntie was so kind to bring you up,' and blah blah blah. But they didn't know that they were always desperately unhappy people, behaving the way they did.

How bad were those early days when you were growing up?

Well, to me it was awful. Other people would have found it dead easy, I think, but to me it was terrible. My auntie leapt in when my mother left and my father had us, and he was going to put my sister and me in a home, then this auntie leapt in and said, 'They should be brought up within the family.' So two aunties brought me up, but one was in her early thirties and one was in her twenties and after about three or four years they bitterly regretted doing it, because their lives were kind of finished.

They were saddled with this ready-made family and they took it out on me. And she was very violent.

Violent?

She was very violent indeed. She was into humiliation. She liked to humiliate and that was the most harmful thing. Just being constantly told you were worthless, every day of your life. And it had a profound effect on me and my self-esteem and it's taken me till now to get over it, and that was a result of trial and error. I've tried all different bits and pieces from all the alcohol and dabbling around with various bits and pieces, to religions and philosophies and having a look around to see what's going on. I've come to a kind of semi-conclusion about being okay, about what would pertain to be normal.

You left school at 15, went into the shipyard.

I had a big smile on my face when I walked out the school gate, I didn't look back either. I remember saying to myself, 'Don't look back, don't look back,' I just walked right out the gate and away.

A lot of people think you need qualifications in order to be successful and yet, what is particularly interesting, is that you walked out of school at a very early age. Do qualifications matter?

I really believe that they do matter when it comes to taking you to the next step. Qualifications at school matter to get you into a decent university. And qualifications from there matter to get you to your next step, if that's the way you want to go. But I've always felt that people with qualifications make good employees, you know? And people with imagination make good employers. And most of the successful people in the world are successful because they had a good imagination and you get that, really, from the public library and not from school. You get it more from Sir Walter Scott than you do from your teacher. You get it from literature, I think that's where the secret is. The public library system was so brilliant. I grew up without television, until I was about 13 or 14 we didn't have a telly. Radio was very popular, but the wonderful thing about radio is that you can listen to it and do something else. People in Glasgow would read, knit and listen to the radio at the same time.

But the public libraries were incredibly popular and you could join as a wee boy, an infant, and you'll be over in the infant section and you were driven to be in the bigger boys' section and get their books. Then you would qualify when you were older, and you'd get this kind of teenage ticket because you weren't quite a man yet but you'd get into this teenage section, and then you qualified as a man. Now you qualified as a man at about 14 in the public library system, and it was brilliant because you could then get to this exalted stage of being able to order a book and they'd get it for you, or you'd go on the waiting list for a book. Now all of my friends were in the public library and it was considered a great thing to have read the necessary books. There was a list that you had to have read, then you got to the stage where you could hire the books, and buy your own books. I remember buying Steinbeck, it was probably in the library, but it was ahead of what I was doing at the time, and I just got lost.

So you were being driven from two ends of the spectrum. You had a home life where you were told you were worthless, then on the other hand you had this competitive element starting in the public library, this desire to acquire knowledge. You went into the shipyard at 15. You wanted to be an engineer, you ended up a welder.

That's right. I'll tell you the strangest thing about that. I was speaking to Gus MacDonald, he was an apprentice in the same shipyard, an engineer. He's now the head of Scottish Television and various other bits and pieces and he looks like being the President of Scotland – buying up all the newspapers and God knows what! I remember him well because he led the apprentices' strike. I didn't put it down to religion. I was brought up as a Catholic and Gus was a Protestant, a typical Scottish Protestant family, ours was a typical Irish immigrant Catholic family, and he said the engineering section was totally Protestant, unless it was an apprentice who was outstanding at school and all that, and then they would grab him. I remember when I was interviewed to be an engineer and there was a posh guy next to me, he'd been to a posh school but he couldn't even point to an engineer this guy, while I had two engineering certificates from school before I left. This guy was posh, but the most outstanding thing I can remember about him was he had a Boys' Brigade badge on his blazer and he was swept in to be an engineer. This man couldn't point to a spanner, but I was sent off to the 'black squad' as they called them, the welders.

Did you resent that?

I deeply resented it.

Was that another driving force to say, 'I can beat the system'?

No, it didn't instil that in me, it instilled a kind of darkness in me, that you've got no chance no matter what you do. People kept saying to me,

'It's a Protestant country,' and I never knew what that meant, and I still don't know what that means. Does it mean that Catholics have fewer civil rights? What are you talking about, you? If you don't know what you're talking about, shut up.

You had some rows in the clubs when you didn't exactly mince your words.

That's right. I've had a lot of trouble. There's a joke about me being thrown out of a club in Blantyre. It's not true but I don't deny it because I don't like to disappoint people who think it's true. The story goes that some baddies stole a television from this social club. They broke in and stole the telly, and the following week I was booked. They put a crucifix in the place where the television had been in the little alcove where the television lived. Christ was being crucified in its place and apparently I came in and said, 'I see you've got the guy who stole the telly.' It wasn't me, but I'm glad they think it was me, because I'm very capable of that.

What do you think are the ingredients of successful comedy?

I wouldn't really know. The ingredients for successful comedy are so many and varied. You get people who are very very happy, like Ken Dodd who is a kind of joke machine, he's a driven joke machine, or Frank Carson, another deeply happy man who's extremely funny live. He is the opposite from me, he is very fat and a jolly, happy man who's never had a problem in his life, and then you get me, this troubled thing, trying to be Hank Williams but who will settle for comedy. Then you get to Rowan Atkinson and John Cleese, these very dark, middle-class people, who don't appear funny at all when you meet them, and then when they do what they do for a living you're on the floor unable to breathe properly. So I wouldn't think there is a recipe for it.

You said different styles and different characteristics, but you are always coming up with something new.

Yes, always. There's this peculiar drive that Hancock and people had, and I think I have myself. I'm not likening myself to Tony Hancock, just this drive to constantly push the boat out further and further. And to be inventive, to perhaps be funny with things that weren't funny before. To be brave. For instance, if you are in a room full of people who are disabled, say, make fun of disability, or in a room full of military people, make fun of the military. Just to confront instead of just concede all the time – 'You're a wonderful, wonderful audience. It really is a privilege to stand before you.' Well, I don't know who the hell they are, so they get what I've got on my mind, and so I push and push and push.

But do you ever feel, 'I'm pushing too far'? Do you ever feel that there comes a point beyond which you cannot go and where, in a sense, your imagination runs out? You feel, 'That's it. I've had it.'

Well I don't know about that, but I do know that when I'm on stage and I'm building, I don't know what I'm building to, but I'm heading in a certain direction and adding and subtracting and doing that inventive thing, and sometimes I can feel people getting uncomfortable.

How do you feel that?

They make a noise.

Not shouting, 'Get off'?

No, not like shouting, 'How dare you,' or anything like that – they shuffle. An atmosphere comes about the room. There's a kind of silence. They get more quiet and they kind of cough. Do you know what I think it is – I think you start hearing them. Silence is fine, but when you hear them it's a bit like after-dinner speaking. When you can hear them coughing and whispering to each other, you're doing it wrong.

You once admitted to being incurably vain. Is a big ego an essential ingredient in your success?

Yes, but you can learn it, you don't need to be born with it. It can come along, because it happened to me.

How do you 'learn' an ego?

You can learn this vanity. The beard was the first for me. The vain step was the beard. I grew a beard because I thought I looked great with a beard and I grew my hair to look interesting. It was all purely to attract attention. Previous to that I always thought I was plain and boring because I was encouraged to think that way by my auntie. I had this desire to be interesting and worthwhile and I taught myself to be so. I would like people to meet me and leave me saying, 'What an interesting guy!'

But there are people who would say Billy Connolly is interesting regardless of how much facial hair he's got, how long his hair is, even how he looks.

I guess, but that came later. I kind of invented myself. In those days I was just telling jokes and singing funny songs like everybody else and stealing stuff from other guys. And if I couldn't steal it I would create something that was similar and I think that's the way people do it. It's the only way I've seen anybody doing it.

Having created your initial success with this particular image, you then took a very important decision, to shave your beard off. In other words, change your image. Was that gambling with success?

I've never believed in image. Your image belongs to other people, it doesn't belong to you. Images are a received thing. David Bowie is the absolute proof of that. His image just constantly changes. You can cut your hair a certain way, or shave a certain way or wear certain types of clothes, but that's not image. Image is the way that you are perceived by everybody else, and a big mistake is for people to let their image control them. I had always said that I would cut my hair easily, because when you've got a beard and long hair you can't see it. You're the only one in the world who can't see it. You're on the wrong side of it. And I thought I would cut my hair if I had a reason. And I would shave if there was a good reason, but I'm not going to do it just to see what my chin looks like, because it was 25 years since I'd seen my chin and I'd forgotten I'd got a dimple like Kirk Douglas. I was kind of curious. I thought, I wonder who lives in here under all this stuff? I thought I was a boy and then there was this hairy thing, and I'm going to remain this hairy thing until the day I die. I think I should have a look and see who I've become, see what my face is like. And then along came the film *The Big Man* with Liam Neeson and the director said, 'The beard will have to go because you're playing a kind of bookmaker's assistant, a kind of slimy character, and you're too hippie, you're too Save-the-Whale, so I think we should give you a bad haircut and take the beard off.' And I said, 'Great.' I couldn't wait. I just couldn't wait to do it. The reason had come. At the time it was almost a kind of holy thing. You know, the reason had appeared.

And of course it engendered a fair amount of publicity.

Ohhh, it got loads of publicity. It was the first time in many many years I actually worked with the newspapers. I did this to stop them chasing me down the street trying to get a picture of my chin. I invited a newspaper to watch me being shaved, the *Daily Mirror*, I think it was. I said, 'You can be the only one if you put money in this charity,' and they did. And so it took all the weight off me, it stopped people chasing me along the street. I had eight or nine inches off my hair and my beard was gone, and they took the picture. Now that happened on Sunday morning. The picture wasn't to come out until Monday morning, so I had Sunday night to myself, as this other guy. I'll never forget it. I flew up to Glasgow and no one knew me on the plane, not one person. Then I walked around Glasgow. I went along Argyll Street and two policemen came towards me and one of them gave me an old-fashioned look, you know, but then just walked on. They didn't know me. And I'm used to people saying hello to me every day of my life. But not one person did. It was lovely.

Did you long for more of that?

No, I didn't long for more at all. It was just a fact of life. It's one of those things, like when you're famous, you've got a famous face and you go on holiday to a place you've never been before, Indonesia or something. And you walk along the street and say to your wife, 'I keep forgetting, I keep thinking I've forgotten something.' You feel uncomfortable, something isn't right. And then you realize, nobody's looking at you. You say, 'That's what's different,' and then once you realize that you relax completely. Then two or three weeks later you come home and you come out of Heathrow and everybody's looking at you and you get all upset – 'What are they looking at?' It happens again in reverse. It's not a desire to be stared at it, it's just that your normal is so odd.

When you shaved the beard off, you were moving into the acting profession.

It was just for that specific film. I didn't have any ideas about moving in and changing direction.

But you have gone on to do various other acting roles, with varying degrees of success. Did you consciously say, 'I'm successful in one area, therefore I think I can be successful in another'?

No, it was a thing I'd always wanted to do from the beginning. I used to tell people I'd become a welder to escape the worst effects of homosexuality. When I told my father I wanted to be an actor, he said, 'They're all poofs, you cannae do that, they're all homosexuals.' And then I said I'd like to be a steward. The guy next door to us was a steward in the merchant navy and I said, 'I think maybe that will be good,' and he said, 'Oh, you cannae do that,' he says, 'they're all homosexuals these guys.' Eventually I became a welder. I never met a gay welder, I must say. Oh, no, I think I did. I think I did, yes. On reflection.

When you were doing the mini-series, the sitcom Billy *in the United States which flopped after 13 episodes – did you actually get withdrawal symptoms? Did you think, 'My goodness my whole career is threatened here'?*

No I didn't. I was dying for it to end.

But how did you pick yourself up from the public criticism that was clearly associated with the series coming to an early end?

Well, the criticism was in Britain. In America it wasn't like that and that's where I lived. See, in America, 13 episodes of a series is quite a successful thing. It doesn't have the same connotations as here. And what had happened to it in America was one of those things that happen to lots of people, more so perhaps in the record industry than in television. You're signed to do a thing, you do it, and while you are doing it, the executives all change upstairs. And so there's no one there who was part of signing you, and they all have their own ideas. So they drop you and put their own ideas in. It's a perfectly normal part of the whole thing. I didn't like *Billy* by the way. I was in a series called *Head of the Class* and *Billy* was the spin-off, I was the teacher and this was me further along the line. I didn't think the writing was very good and it didn't show me at my best. But that's OK, it's all part of the learning thing and that was my third year in television. I wanted to be on the road again.

So it was part of the learning curve, just like your failure to become a folk singer way back in the early days. Do you have a technique for recovering from setbacks?

My technique is my vanity. But I didn't see them as failures at all. None of them were failures.

Despite this wealth of criticism.

Yeah. They don't know anything. The critics don't know anything.

So you need that self-confidence. That particular attitude.

Yeah. It's them and us. They do not know what I do. They don't know how I do it. They don't know how I arrived at it, and given a million pounds they could not do it. So how can they criticize it? They don't know what it is. Because if I don't know what it is, they don't. I saw a quote once by one of the Roosevelts. It was about critics and the line I remember was, 'They've never tasted the dust in the arena,' and that's the big difference between me and critics. They don't know what I do, they don't know how it feels. And if you watch them when they get on telly on *What the Papers Say* for instance, they're a mess, they haven't a clue, they're twee.

I've always thought with critics that their biggest failing is that they face the wrong way when they come to the theatre. Their job isn't to say whether I'm good or not. Of course I'm good, that's why there are 3,000 people in the room. Their job is to say what effect I've had on these people, because they are not qualified to say whether I'm good or not.

You're saying it's not the effect on the individual critic that matters, it's the effect they have on the audience you're trying to entertain?

Precisely.

So critics really ought to be market researchers.

Absolutely, and usually they influence people who weren't at the show, which is a crime in my opinion.

You've gone further in your dislike of critics, taking on the whole of the Scottish tabloid press. But isn't part of success having to take what you see as other people's unreasonable comments and behaviour on the chin?

No.

You don't think it should be?

No. Why should I? I've never seen this written anywhere. People keep saying, 'It's par for the course,' it's 'the price of fame'. Oh yeah? Nobody showed me the menu, the tariff, what was this price? What are you talking about? And it's a load of little middle-class boys with their Highers who thought they were going to do well and they don't like people like me doing well. Because their mummy told them if they worked really hard they would be successful and I went screaming past them and that makes them unhappy.

Why do you think that successful people in general are a target of critics? Is it because, perhaps more so in Britain than in America, these critics feel that good copy is knocking copy?

Yes. It's because it's easier to write funny knocking copy than it is to write funny copy in praise of someone. It's because they are not really clever. There's a lust for failure in this country, a desperate lust, especially in Scotland. If you can make up for lack of success in yourself with hatred of success in someone else, that'll do.

But the media are very often the vehicle by which other people learn about successes and failures in others. So they are an important conduit in terms of shaping opinion. Do they matter in that sense?

They do matter in that sense. There was a period in British television, and children's television on Saturday mornings in particular, where it was considered funny to throw green slime over famous people. And I don't think putting down successful people should be encouraged.

It's going back to the humiliation.

Yes, that's right and constantly criticizing the famous and saying, 'Mick Jagger's old.'

But then everyone says it's only fun.

Of course they say it's only fun. It's only fun in Scotland to say that the English are awful and they're terrible, it's not racism it's fun, fun, fun. No, it isn't fun. It's not fun if you are English and somebody's kicking your arse in the street in Edinburgh. It's not fun, it's not funny and the papers know it's not funny. They encourage it, in exactly the same way as the newspapers here in England were criticizing football rowdyism. When football rowdyism stopped so remarkably at the European Championships, they tried to create it by doing that '*Achtung*' and all that anti-German crap they did. I thought the media was really found out by all that. They were caught with their trousers down. They were sad to see football rowdyism go.

What advice would you give to anyone wanting to be successful? Should they take on the media, as you have, or should they rise above any criticism?

You don't need to take them on. Just don't talk to them. That's what I do. It looks like a huge confrontation. I haven't taken them on. I used to. I used to punch them and stuff like that, but there's too many of them, and they kind of like it. You know when you punch them, they'll take pictures of you doing it and then the whole game starts again. So I stopped punching them and kicking them and stuff, and now I don't talk to them at all. And that just seems to be worse. It looks like a massive confrontation. To anyone who wants success, I would say, 'Don't overrate the media, they are not as powerful as they seem.' I am living proof that they are not as powerful as they would like to think they are. They cannot end your career, only you can end your career by listening to that junk. But the main thing about success is that almost every successful person I know – me, Sean Connery, all those guys – if you looked at their career when it was over, or from the stance it has achieved, if you looked back it is the most unlikely story on Earth. Look at Sean Connery, he was a body-builder, you know?

And a milkman.

He was the milkman but he was Mr Scotland the body-builder, and the chorus in *South Pacific* were too effeminate and the guy said, 'Look, do you know they are singing "There's Nothing Like a Dame" and they are lisping. Get me some men.' And they went hunting for men and Mr Universe was on and they found Sean – 'He's manly, get him in.' Then he was in *Darby, O'Gill and the Little People* and Cubby Broccoli's wife was in the movies out of the rain, sees him and says to Cubby, 'I think I've found James Bond.' I mean, if you wrote that people would say, 'Oh, come on, you'll need a stronger story-line, you know you'll really need to work harder at this writing.'

So luck is seriously important?

I don't know if it is luck or application – taking what comes along and making the very best of it. And your goodness will shine through it.

But you need the breaks, don't you?

You create the breaks. Good poets are published.

Sean didn't create those breaks, did he?

He did by taking the job and doing it really well and then other people said, 'Oh, I like that,' and they take the quantum leap. He's playing an Irish gardener with elves in the garden, she took the break of saying, 'That's James Bond' and tells her husband. Well, in my case, I believe sincerely that good poets are published, and people love singing good songwriters' songs. There's millions of songwriters but not many good ones, good plays are performed and people cannot wait for good comedians. There are not enough. There are millions of comedians but a good one just screams through the way. Every generation there's a hero in the pop charts, like Paul Simon, somebody writes the right song, and wacko. Your idea will always seem bizarre, all new ideas are bizarre. The hula-hoop was bizarre. All good new ideas are bizarre. The trick is to hang on to your original idea, it hit you with such power because it's good. Listen to it, it's telling you, you know, it's telling you what to do. Stick to it. That's when you need a wee bit of courage and that's when things like vanity come in handy. It'll give you some strength and belief in yourself. Well, call it vanity, maybe it's not vanity, but it's just the ability to be able to look in the mirror and like who you see. Stick with your idea, don't be swayed left or right, because all of these left and right movements will dilute it, television will dilute it. They'll say, 'Well, I like your idea but would you take that bit out, they will find that offensive.' This great beige 'they out there', they don't exist. Americans talk about the Midwest and Kansas: I've been there, nothing offends them, they want to be treated like everybody else. Stick to your original idea, it's like a chariot, it'll take you wherever you want to go.

What do you regard as your most successful moments, not necessarily the ones the world knows about but the ones you privately regard as benchmarks in your life?

I made an album with Gerry Rafferty. We were performing in Ramsbottom and made this extraordinary album, just the two of us. This would be in '69, '68-ish I think. The end of the '60s, maybe the early 70s. I'm not very good with dates.

When you were trying to be a folk singer?

I was trying to be a singer-songwriter-folky. I was always funny on stage at the same time. Gerry was far superior to me, as a musician and a writer, and still is, but I thought that as time went by I would get better, and I did, but so did he and the gap never closed. In my way of thinking I thought we would become the same thing, but he remained the better. But we made this beautiful album with this sensational sleeve. I always wanted a lovely album sleeve. Jethro Tull had wonderful album sleeves and I wanted one like that. I didn't want to be making a funny face or be a folky standing by a river or something like that. John Burn in Scotland painted this beautiful primitive picture of me and Gerry, me as a sailor and Gerry as a hockey player, with all these animals and a big banjo. I remember thinking, 'I'm becoming the thing I've always wanted to be.'

And then, some time later I was on my own and hearing the voice, 'Ladies and gentlemen, welcome to Carnegie Hall. Will you please welcome Billy Connolly.' I thought, 'Well maybe I'm here.' And lo and behold, I wasn't there at all. But it felt like being there, you know? Because now, success at the Bottom Line in Greenwich Village is much, much more important to me than success at Carnegie Hall. I know a lot of duffers who've played Carnegie Hall but you can't be a duffer at the Bottom Line. They'll eat you alive.

Are you ever frightened of success coming to an end?

No. I live the same life today as when I wasn't successful. Of course I have mushrooms in my breakfast and I drive nice cars and that's all very pleasant, but the things that make me happiest are fishing and playing my banjo and I didn't need success to do that.

Is there a difference between success in your profession and success in other professions?

No. It's the same thing. It's being driven. It's the same as inventing the hula-hoop, really. Writing a song and inventing the hula-hoop's the same thing.

Are there any people, big or small, past or present, whom you really admire as being on the pinnacle of success? Who are your heroes?

Bob Dylan. He's the ultimate hero to me. He does it completely and utterly his own way. Takes no prisoners at all, it's his way. him! He is the ultimate for me, for all the right reasons. His output just continues at an extraordinarily high standard. He doesn't play it anybody else's way. He keeps changing direction, only because the new direction makes him feel more comfortable than the last direction. And he goes on and on and on. His critics go up and down, they live and die and disappear, and he goes merrily forward.

And he sits above any heroes you might have in your own profession?

He sits way above all my comedy heroes. Because I also find him very funny. But in comedy Chick Murray was my hero – the Scottish comedian. And Max Wall. But none of them was as funny as P.G. Wodehouse. He was the funniest man who ever lived. Nobody ever made me laugh out loud like P.G. Wodehouse. We were going on holiday, Pam and I, some years ago, to the Caribbean and at Heathrow I bought those Penguin P.G. Wodehouses, all the Jeeves stuff, and I said, 'Look, tell me what you think of these.' And one of the great things in my life was hearing Pamela just roar – she's got a great laugh, Pamela, it's kind of bell-like – to hear her scream with laughter when she was reading the Jeeves stuff, you know, *The Clicking of Cuthbert* and all these things. And I thought, 'It's as funny as I thought it was.' And Stephen Fry has P.G. Wodehouse's autograph, 'To Stephen Fry from P.G. Wodehouse.' I could have killed him when I saw that on his mantelpiece.

Do you think it's becoming more or less difficult to achieve success in your profession?

It's not becoming more difficult at all. Channel 4 and all those little production companies have made comedy kind of muddy. You know, they go up to Edinburgh Festival and get all those people they think are alternative and stick them on the telly, when they actually should be out working. Those boys aren't ready for television, you know. They should be working, they should be going round and round and round honing what they do. Somebody once said to me that they haven't been booed enough but I don't hold with that one, you don't need to be booed or be treated badly. But what they haven't had enough of is honing, going round the country and saying, 'I think I'll put this bit first tonight instead of last night's and see how this works at the end' – you don't know why it's working but you know it works better, and 'I'll make this bit shorter and maybe make this bit longer, I'll take half of this story and put it in that story and see what...' And that's what makes you good.

What are the greatest enemies of success?

Lack of belief in your original idea. Dilution of your original idea is the enemy of success. It's that terrible thing where you can read 12 crits of yourself, 11 are good and one is bad, and you choose to believe the bad one.

And what's the greatest pleasure you've had from the fruits of your success?

Buying school uniforms. It's the ability to book my children into the school I want them to be at and buy the uniform and the kind of things that they need just to be ordinary, just to get on with it, which is the ultimate for me. You know, the blazer and the proper summer uniform and the shoes, so they can go through life without difficulty.

You of course got heavily involved in Comic Relief *with visits to Africa and the moving documentaries we saw on the BBC. Was that because part of achieving success almost requires you, as an act of conscience, to give something back.*

I've never thought that way about it. I've often thought though, I like the Jewish way and the Mormon way of looking at things, where a certain percentage of your income should go to the public good, everybody, you know, from labourers to me because the percentage system works it out.

People would say that's more taxes.

Yeah. But you need to do it on your own. To discipline yourself to do this is a very good idea, I think. And I think the Jews have got it right – a percentage of your income should go to the public good. And I've always had a deep suspicion of the bow-tie brigade, the public display of wealth, auctioning a football, blady blah – although it achieves great things, and one guy in particular who does that brilliantly is Jimmy Tarbuck. He has raised thousands and thousands of pounds that way. But it doesn't really suit me, I don't really fit in and so Red Nose Day is very good and

Amnesty's *The Secret Policeman's Ball* was very good, because all you do really is go to work with your peers and because they couldn't normally have afforded to put you all in the same building at once, it became a great event and I've loved doing it. Actually doing what I do to raise the money is much better than sticking a bow tie on me and putting me at a dinner at the Grosvenor House because I don't do that and Iwouldn't do it very well.

Has religion played a part in your success?

Yes. Well not in my success. Of course it has, it's played a part in my life. In my early life Catholicism was really important to me and it isn't any more. Christianity isn't any more. I like Jesus but I have my own sort of theories about him and I like Francis of Assisi, he was my hero. And you'll notice in Christianity the more Christ-like a person becomes the more distrusted they are by the Christian institution. They hated Francis of Assisi, they like embroidery and pointy hats and golden shepherds' crooks, that was more their line. And if you go to the Vatican it's stuffed with pagan stuff from wall to wall, it's all Roman pagan gear. But I must have learned something from it. I know that as a child I found great solace in it.

And yet you don't now?

I would now if I put myself to it. I used to like Benediction. I used to love the incense and the hymns and all the paraphernalia. And I loved confession, it was a great feeling. I remember as a child when I'd been to confession, I remember thinking I was made of glass and you could see right through me, you know? It was a lovely feeling. And in those ways I have learned from religion. I didn't embrace Buddhism but I learned meditation from Buddhists and I sometimes go up to the Buddhist monastery, up at the Borders. The Tibetans and I have a great pal up there, a great friend called Lama Yeshi. He's a wonderful guy, Tibetan, and he's so brilliant you know. He's so intelligent and happy.

Do you go to him and others because of the pressure of success?

No, I go to him as an alternative, because success doesn't bring pressure on me, I like it. I like success. I like fame.

So it's a clear alternative.

Aye. Sometimes when I'm troubled. When there are things I can't get out of my mind, or if I can't relax, or if I can't apply myself. I go to Lama Yeshi and say, 'Why is that, why do you think that is?' He's like a psychiatrist and the answer is always right in front of you. It's always too close, it's never obscure. I'm always hoping for a really obscure answer. I'm always hoping he'll say to me, 'Well, the trouble is you know you're a very rare case, Billy. And you need a rare solution and we should go to a river in Tibet and drink of the waters.' But it's never like that.

What advice would you give if you could gather before you all the young people on the first rung of the ladder of your profession who really want to become as successful as you have been? What would you say to them?

Believe it. Believe it properly. Just work on your belief. Every day people will give you great reasons for not doing it. There are a million great reasons. As a matter of fact, in showbusiness success there is no good reason for doing it except money and that is obvious to everybody else except you. I was thinking about this the other day, I was at a wedding, I was just a guest, and it always terrifies the top table at weddings when you're a guest and you are a comedian and they have to make the speeches and they've got their jokes ready, and they're sweating. And I was looking at them speaking, and they were all delightful of course, and there was an ordinary guy making a speech which was ten times more impressive than a comedian doing one, except the paper was shaking and the nervousness. And it just reminded me what a silly thing walking onto a stage is and getting a light on you. What a strange, strange thing it is. It's so incredibly unnatural, even to the person doing it it's unnatural. So what I would say to the kids is, 'Enjoy the oddness of it. Don't let the oddness of it make you not want to do it, turn all of that round and be encouraged by its weirdness, because that's what is going to make you good.'

What would you like people to say about you when your time comes to leave this planet?

He was a good laugh. That's what I would like on my gravestone – 'He was a good laugh'.

LODWRICK COOK

Brought up during the Depression in small-town Louisiana where hot water came from a kettle on the wood-burning stove, 'Lod' Cook started as 'an engineering trainee digging ditches' and worked his way up through ARCO, the world's seventh biggest oil company, to become its chairman and chief executive. What is even more special about him is that he is a role model for those who believe that successful companies have a strong responsibility to the communities in which they operate. So pioneering education programmes, inner-city job development and environmental projects are all firmly on his agenda – an involvement which has earned him the friendship of four US Presidents, laden him with honours in his native USA, and earned him
a rare honorary knighthood in the UK. After four years in the army heading a 70-man platoon in Germany, he completed an engineering degree and opted for the oil business, going to night school to pick up an MBA.

His big break came when the owners of the Trans-Alaska pipeline gave him a key role to help bring the oil on-stream. America was in the midst of an oil crisis. They were all systems go when a vital pumping station burnt down. Lod got to hear of a new drag-reducing agent, and, to the laughter and scorn of pipeline experts, ran some tests to see if it would help oil flow faster. It did! The DRA not only increased capacity by 50 per cent, it saved him having to build another four pumping stations. His reputation was made. He flourished by being different. He pushed management responsibility down the line – 'If you make people feel they matter, and can influence decisions, you get a better job.' He placed new emphasis on marketing in a business that had been all about volume. He developed a new cleaner-burning petrol to help tackle pollution in Southern California – and, in a shrewd PR move, offered the formula to his competitors. Now elevated to Chairman Emeritus of ARCO, he talks of the role of both praise and fear in shaping success in a company, and advises: 'Communicate, keep people informed, make sure you know where you expect them to go, and show appreciation for what they're doing.'

Lodwrick Cook, what is your definition of success?

Success is achieving a degree of recognition in a particular field, achieving the satisfaction of becoming good at what you set out to do. I don't measure it by fame and fortune, although many people do. But it is wrong to use that as a way of keeping score. A teacher, for example, can be highly successful. I think people know what real success is. It involves a sense of accountability both personally and professionally.

So really you are talking about two kinds of success – there is a kind of inner success within yourself where you achieve your own objectives and then there is the success that is the judgment upon you by the outside world. And you are saying the former is probably more important than the latter?

They are both very important. People do measure it in terms of celebrity, and if you don't live up to society's values, in many ways you're not viewed as successful either. But there is also this inner success that comes from knowing that you've given your best, given your all and reached a goal you've set for yourself.

Do you think that people can have an ambition of just wanting success without having a clear idea of the field in which they want to be successful?

I think so, yes. You can be a driven personality, and wander in different directions until you either stumble on something or get lucky or focus eventually. I'm always wary of people who say, 'I've had my life planned, in five years I'll do this, in six I'll do whatever.' I don't mean to say you shouldn't be goal-oriented to some extent, I think goals help lift you to the next level. But most successful people really haven't a complete plan for success when they start out. I had high expectations, and that's a valuable ingredient in success, but there are people who are just driven by energy. To some extent all of us pick and choose a little bit along the way. I have a little symbolic way of talking about success to young people. I use the word 'POWER' to demonstrate what I have in mind. We have within ourselves a power to succeed if we unleash it. It includes things like persistence, which is the P. The O stands for optimism. I've rarely met people who've succeeded at anything who are negative and pessimistic. The W, there's no substitute for that, it's work. Lazy people are rarely successful in anything. E is education. It prepares you for success. It may be formal, it may be various things. The R is risk-taking. Success always involves the taking of some risk, albeit calculated, not foolish. Risk may include moving some place, taking on a new assignment or betting everything on a particular course of action.

To what extent do you think your success is due to your background and upbringing, going way back to the early days?

People do say sibling ranking plays a part in success, and I was the first-born of the family. But even more, I was raised in a small southern town where I was the eldest grandchild, which reinforced that sense of expectation in the family. It was sort of a heavy load to bear sometimes because I was expected to be good. I was expected to achieve. Education was paramount because that's the only way you could pull yourself out of that environment. Back in the early 1900s my grandfather sent all his children to college from a small country town, which was unheard of in those days. So education was very important. With uncles, aunts and others all pushing in that direction, it could have crushed me, but as it was, it motivated me. We all come into the world with a certain amount of talent. I was fortunate to be channelled by family first and then by friends and mentors later. I think mentors are very good in your life to help you along, and that's the reason I feel it's important to give something back to young people, and to educational and youth institutions.

You said that the kind of expectations that the family had could have crushed you. Do you think that there are times when parents and grandparents want too much for their children, and so can actually prevent the creation of the conditions that would lead to success for that person?

Yes. There are many examples where children can't bear up under it, or have a strong parent whom they try to emulate and simply can't, because they don't have whatever it took the parent to get there – you see it a lot in celebrity families. But beyond that you see a lot of driven parents who want to live their lives through their children. Fortunately my father didn't want to do that. He certainly encouraged me, but he was more of an intellectual – a student, a chess player, a very inward type of person. My personality comes from my mother, and she wasn't driven to achieve through me because she continued to succeed in her own work till she was past 80. She was always trying to improve herself and be successful in her own right. But the spirit, the inspiration was there. So I had a nice mix to balance the pressure from the family. I was raised in a strong southern Baptist household, so I was told I had to be good all the time. That led me to develop a sense of mischief. Fortunately it didn't get me into too much trouble. It might have pushed me the wrong way, but the mix was OK. I was lucky.

You trained as a mathematician, but you went into the oil industry. Did you want to go into the oil industry from an early age, or was it simply something that happened? Was it just a job that came up and you were lucky enough to get it?

Most kids really don't know what they want to do. They're influenced by people they know, family, or by things they see or read about. We happened to have an oil well drilled on our farm, and fortunately, or unfortunately, it was a dry hole, but it got me to thinking about the oil industry. I had a first cousin married to a petroleum engineer, who told me about what they did. Maths was easy for me in high school, and the two things seemed to fit. My high school had five seniors in the graduating class, it was so small. And, of course, we were living in the segregated South at that time, but even if we had included the black children in the community it wouldn't have been very large. Nowadays, of course, they are integrated.

Were you top of the class?

I wasn't even in the top forty per cent – two girls were one and two. I was third in my class, which means, of course, that there were only five of us. Anyway, I went to Louisiana State University and soon learned that to be a good engineer you really had to devote all your time to that. There really wasn't much time for campus politics, for the social side of college, which is very important, I think. And so I decided to switch to maths, which freed up time for these other things. When I eventually ran for campus vice-president, I had already worked at a number of jobs to earn some money, I had joined a fraternity and been active in a number of organizations, I had also been active in the ROTC – in fact I graduated as a distinguished military graduate. All this was a conscious decision: I knew I wasn't growing as a person studying as an engineer, and for me, coming from a small school, all these other things were like a *smörgåsbord* of things to choose from, and I wanted to try a little of all of it. And I'm glad I did.

But at the back of your mind you still felt that the oil industry was there, although you were keeping your options open in case something else came up?

The oil industry was there but the Korean War was going on, so I knew I had to serve some time. I was in the Ordnance Corps, which, again, built on my maths, because that led into missiles. I had three extremely interesting years in Germany after the war as a young lieutenant. I headed up a 70-man platoon on my own, and gained tremendous experience. But I felt that the peace-time army couldn't provide the pace I wanted, so I went back to LSU, finished my engineering degree, and went to work in the oil industry.

Take me through some of the key benchmarks of your career?

When I got out of LSU as an engineer I was interviewed by the Atlantic Refining Company, a predecessor company of Atlantic Richfield. They offered me a job when I was dating a young lady who lived in Louisiana, and I wanted to continue that relationship, so I reneged on an offer that I had accepted from Atlantic and went with a company in Louisiana.

So you put love before career?

I put love before career that time, and we were married for 19 years and had four wonderful children. But after about a year of that company I realized that it was a pretty stagnant place to be, and I looked ahead. My boss had been there ten years still doing the kind of things they were asking me to do, and that didn't sound very exciting. So I made a change out of the oil industry, back to my home town nearby, where my father worked for a trailer company. I went to work there and started off as a marketing assistant. But I soon realized that that was not a good decision; it did get me out of the company I was unhappy with, but it was a family business. They had one daughter and she was already married and so was I, so I didn't see much future for me there. Atlantic ran an advertisement in the paper for junior engineers to go to Venezuela. So I sent a letter in; never heard from them. Finally I went to Dallas, their headquarters in Texas, to see what had happened. They'd lost my letter. But the fellow there remembered me. He had interviewed me on campus, and they weren't angry with me for having reneged on their initial offer, so they hired me as an engineer trainee. But they said, 'You don't want to go to Venezuela, you want to stay here and become part of the domestic organization.' And they were right. So I started as an engineer trainee, digging ditches. Here I am at 27 years old, college graduate, former army lieutenant, having to start at the bottom – the bottom of a ditch, no less.

Did you resent that, considering you already had quite a bit of experience under your belt?

I would have if I hadn't had a prescribed schedule. They had a training programme for engineers. I knew I'd only do certain things for three months and then move on to something else. And I also knew that I'd need to get a feel for the industry. I needed to understand it from the bottom up: that was the whole purpose of the programme. They don't do that any more. It's unfortunate, because I think it gives you a better understanding of what goes on out there. The first week I almost passed out with the heat and they took pity on me, because I wasn't in terrific shape at that point. But after I'd been on the programme about six months, they brought me in the office, into the accounting end of the business for a while. Then they asked me to go to LSU to help them on a recruiting trip, so I could tell potential recruits about the company. I went and enjoyed it, and they said, 'You seem to like this kind of thing,' and asked me to go to Dallas as an administrative assistant to the manager of the personnel department. I realized that I wasn't the greatest engineer in the world; that my interests really were in getting people to do things. I was a bit of a salesman. I had enough engineering to get by, but to get into the office and deal directly with personnel problems was what appealed to me. So I did, I went into the job and learned some things along the way.

What are the characteristics you need for a successful negotiation, in general terms?

Like anything else, where you're trying to lead people to a common ground, a certain leadership capacity, persuasion, the ability to look ahead of where you are. If you move too fast you know it won't work, you've got to let them think they got there on their own, and that they have got more than they thought they were going to get. Then, sometimes it's important to let your anger show in negotiations, but you must only show it if you're firmly controlling it. A guy I once worked for in labour relations used to say that a little theatrics is not a bad thing in negotiations, provided you don't let your emotions get out of hand.

So your time on the pipeline, with the various negotiations and other activities it entailed for you, was a key defining period in your rise up though the company. You were then marked for high office; you became Chief Executive and Chairman of the company, and in 1988 you were on the cover of Forbes Magazine *which said that ARCO was the best-managed US company in the oil business. What were your criteria for making ARCO successful? You were unconventional. You have talked about ARCO flourishing by being different; you yourself were described as a kind of noisy maverick. What did you mean by 'flourishing by being different'? A lot of companies would go with the flow.*

First of all our company saw the coming crash in oil prices that happened in 1985-86. We saw it in 1985 – people other than me; I wasn't CEO at the time. And we set about restructuring the company dramatically; I was named CEO and led that. I was given the assignment to sell off most of the businesses that we no longer wanted to be in. We finally understood that while we might be good in the oil business, we couldn't necessarily be good at everything else.

Is that a big risk for a company that is successful in one field, to think automatically that it can expand into another? Is that always a mistake, or more often than not a mistake?

You have to be very careful, because it doesn't necessarily follow that you can be good in one thing and automatically move to another. The conglomerate concept worked in a couple of cases but finally got out of hand in the United States, perhaps over here too. You see success stories, you certainly have the Hansons of the world that put things together and make it work, but a lot of times it doesn't work. In time it tends to come unglued and you have to kind of reinvent the company. In our case we made some bad decisions and had to undo them. I felt very strongly that we should focus on what we were going to be, and that was a hydrocarbon company. And I was very focused towards profitability. The oil industry, traditionally, had been orientated towards volume, towards drilling and exploring and discovering, and that's very exciting, but it doesn't mean much if you don't make money and get good returns. I wanted to instil in the company a new idea of profitability in different pieces of the company. A lot of times it got blurred. One piece of business was carrying another piece. I wanted to get a marketing mentality, a kind of proxy for profitability, into every piece of the business. For example, the people producing the oil weren't selling it, they turned it over to another group who sold it. I wanted to put the selling, the bottom line, the ringing of the cash register with the people producing it, so they'd understand what they were trying to do – to make money. I was very marketing orientated. Not just pumping gasoline, but thinking about selling yourself, your product and your service at every level of the business, and creating profit centres and accountability for that.

So what you were actually doing was pushing management discretion down the ranks, but closely monitoring the results? You had a sort of free-wheeling chain of command. Was there a risk that this would go too far? You were allowing tank truck drivers to set their own routes, you told drilling directors, simply find oil and don't mess up? Was there a risk involved with that?

The tank truck drivers had some flexibility, and we did push the pricing decisions down further. But we still had controls, you can't run a big company without good financial controls. I tried to give more authority further down the organization. At the same time we had control of legal and environmental matters. It was the right kind of sharing of communications, but we tried to make people think of it as their business, that they were participating in the business rather than just hired hands. If you make people feel that they matter and can influence decisions, you get a better job. But you can't give away the store, you have to check. In a big company where everything's grouped together, a single part of it can get hidden, as it were, so you can't identify what it's contributing. If you spread it out so you can look at it, sometimes you find a much better way of doing it, and that happened as we went along. For example, you've got to keep your costs down – especially in a commodity business like ours, in which all the prices are dictated by what happens in the Middle East. On the West coast, for example, we became a low-price major oil company. We had a major brand and a low price. Then we went from having ten per cent of the market to, today, over 20 per cent. We went from third or fourth to number one. We made money. Our margins were good, our profitability was good, and then eventually, of course, we went to clean gasoline. We became convinced that the Clean Air Act was pushing Washington to look at alternative fuels, and we felt that the fuel of the future was cleaner gasoline, that to revamp the automobile and the refining industry, to move to automobiles running on some blend of methanol, was a mistake. The costs would be enormous, and the rest of the world probably couldn't afford to follow. But if you could find a cleaner variant of what we already had, then you could take it to Mexico or somewhere similar and they could clean up too. The catalytic converter in automobiles has certainly been a great step forward in cleaning automobile emissions. So we started working on a reformulated gasoline to go towards still cleaner emissions. We did this spending our own money, announced it, and pushed it within the oil industry and in Washington.

And stopped the legislation going through?

That's true. That was the consequence of it because we thought it was a mistake. And we slowed it down and stopped it. We used ethanol, and methanol, in gasoline blends, it's an alcohol to help the burning. But to convert completely ... nobody comprehended, nobody even thought about it, nobody had tested this, and those fuels have emission problems as well. Even electric cars have emission problems because you've got to generate the electricity somewhere, you've got to get rid of the batteries, and all that sort of thing. So I think one of my greatest achievements in our company has been leading the fight for cleaner fuels. And we were at the forefront of that, a lot of our people played a role in it.

Having achieved this great success with the new fuel, with a modified fuel, you then offered it to your rivals. Now that would not seem to be a sound commercial decision.

The technology wasn't so unique that they wouldn't have been able to get there by other routes. It was important also in the political circumstances to have the industry together on something that would be a better solution than what was being proposed. That was beneficial to us as a company. We wanted to encourage that to happen, try to see the country move in that direction, which it did. We wanted the rest of the world to do so. There are 400-500 million automobiles in the world today, over 200 million of them in the US. If you can help clean up a fraction of that, with all that stuff moving around in the atmosphere, it would be useful.

You consciously chose to take ARCO down the environmental route. Did you do it because there wasn't any option, and because you saw it as successful PR, if you like?

Certainly there were elements of that in it. The movement was there. It was translating itself into political actions and into rules and regulations, some of which were wrong and needed to be changed. At the same time we wanted to be constructive. I don't adopt the theory that a company has no business doing things within its community – with young people and education, or what have you. I think you can be a constructive force. The same thing with the environment.

What about the argument that comes up in quite a few companies, that your first obligation is to your shareholders – if they want to help the community, fine, let them do it, but you as a company really have no need to get involved? There are a great many companies that feel that way, as well as, of course, a growing number that are adopting your argument of going into the community and helping in what way they can.

You must have balance. Certainly your first duty is to your shareholder. And the most important thing, obviously, is to think about economic reward for investors in your company. On the other hand you also have to help protect that opportunity to make money, which is where working within the community comes in. The Milton Friedman argument, that your only responsibility is to make money for your shareholders, is one extreme. At the other extreme, although obviously you can't be a do-gooder in everything out there, you can make a difference. In any case shareholders themselves today expect you to be a good citizen, especially when it comes to the environment. Otherwise you may be pushed in an entirely different direction that would really damage your shareholder.

What part does public relations play in success? Is it a key part in any successful company?

Community relations, public relations, I think are important. How you react to a disaster is very important. We saw that in the Exxon spill. You can't just hand public relations over to the expert, the CEO has got to be part of it too. In hindsight, if the Exxon CEO had gone to the scene quickly, it would have helped. His lawyers advised him otherwise, and you can't go down two paths. But my point is, public relations has to be something the company feels strongly about from top to bottom. And the public dictate the ground rules. They dictate the environment you're going to work in, and it may rise up and bite the hell out of you if you don't understand it and work with it as you go along.

Political contacts have always been important for you as well, talking to the right people at the right time. Has that been an integral part of your success?

You can't operate in today's world without participating in the political process. When I became CEO of ARCO I had a simple formula that I talked to employees about: '5P + M = NA'. NA was New ARCO, and M was marketing. 5P stands for politics, philanthropy, planning, profitability and people. All of those are vital. With politics, every day something political in some country of the world affects you. Laws are being passed, governmental decisions made – you've got to keep abreast of those and have your say. I think we're entitled to have our say about things. People won't always agree with us, but we have a right to say them. And you need to raise money for people within the new rules – the people that you feel are sympathetic to the free enterprise system and to business, irrespective of political party. I've raised money for both parties. I tend to raise more for the Republicans because they tend to be more sympathetic towards business.

Do you have any formula for recovering from those moments when you're down, or from failures? How do you pull yourself back?

You do have to do that. Exercise is always good, for relieving stress and renewing you. I'm an optimist, so a rest or some diversion, the family or something that gives pleasure can bring you to realize what's important in life, and things that have you down begin to pale beside more fundamental things, like family and relationships. And you have to assume that you're going to have your knocks and pick yourself up and go on. That's not to say you don't feel badly about them, almost crushed maybe, at times, but I usually can shrug them off. I think prayer, too, is a great renewal for people who believe in a higher being, which I do.

What do you think are the core qualities needed to be successful?

We've already discussed a lot of them, but I would add the need to communicate, to keep people informed, to make sure they know where you expect them to go, and to show appreciation for what they're doing. Praise is a great tool in leadership and there's not enough of it. You can't overdo it. People also respond to criticism – if it's given correctly. A sense of humour is awfully important too. It's helped me at times to deflect antagonism or hostility, or to lighten up a meeting. You don't want to be continually cracking jokes, but I think President Reagan has shown the value of being able to tell humorous stories to make a point, and he was able to deflect things that way. You can lower the level of intensity sometimes in a situation.

By and large people want to like you and if you give them an opportunity they will. That will enhance your ability to get things done, which is, after all, what leads to success and good leadership. There are people who use fear to motivate people. In the long run I don't think that works. I'm not suggesting that it's not useful at times, but it's like the Pattons against the Bradleys in terms of US generals in the war. Patton used fear. Bradley had a more inclusive way of doing things, a participatory kind of leadership, which seems to work better for me. Lastly, there is pure personality. Take President Clinton for example. Whether you agree with him or not, he has a tremendous personality, great charm. That affects people. Even if they disagree with him, at least they listen to him. He's a very bright man too, for that matter. As another example, one of the leaders who had the charisma that a lot of great leaders have was Mikhail Gorbachev. I couldn't understand a word he was saying, but it was just great to be around him.

Who are your heroes?

I'm a bit leery of giving somebody hero status, because we're all human and have our faults and I don't want to be too disappointed, but certainly there are a lot of people I admire.

If I was seeking a role model today, it would be some combination of President George Bush and President Jimmy Carter. Two totally different personalities, but they have great strengths. President Bush is such a class act in all that he does and he does everything so well. President Carter is an excellent role model for combining drive with compassion. I didn't get to know Ronald Reagan, whom I admire greatly, until after he was in office. I'd met him many times in the White House but didn't really get to know him personally until later. Certainly he has a great sense of optimism, which I believe in, and a great focus on what he believed was necessary to do at different times.

Winston Churchill's a hero of many of us, and I also admire a great deal about President Truman and Margaret Thatcher. Of course, my mother's enthusiasm for life and self-discipline continues to amaze and inspire me.

Do you think it's becoming more or less difficult to achieve success in the business world?

It's different. There's entrepreneurial success, the Ted Turner kind of success that's more an individual success, as against those who go through the corporate structure to become successful. It seems to me that there are more things to work on. Technology has exploded, creating all sorts of opportunity in areas that didn't exist when I was growing up. On the other hand there are more entanglements and governmental complications in business. I'm involved in a couple of small businesses – I've started one with my nephew – and I see how difficult it is for a young person to get going. The capital requirements, the taxation that comes on you very quickly. A Chief Executive today has many things to deal with that they didn't have to deal with, say, 40 years ago. There wasn't a great environmental challenge 40 years ago. Legal challenges today are enormous compared to 40 years ago. You have to have a much broader-gauge person to run a big corporation than you used to. But there is greater opportunity today.

So is it more or less difficult?

It's more difficult, but with more opportunities.

What are the greatest enemies of success?

Ego. Getting too wrapped up in your own self-importance. Thinking you've got all the answers. Thinking you can do everything and you don't need people. Some people get too arrogant and push the envelope too far, legally perhaps, or financially. Once again it's a matter of retaining balance.

In pursuit of success have you ever done anything that you wished, in retrospect, you hadn't done?

Nothing of any major consequence. I have occasionally offended individuals that I didn't mean to, and when I've realized it I've gone back and apologized. Most of the time it was unintended. I don't think I'm a cruel person. But you forget sometimes that as a CEO you can be intimidating to people, and a cross word can really be devastating to them. I've had that happen. I was just flailing out a bit when I shouldn't have, and it had far more of an impact than I ever intended. I have gone back and apologized to people who worked for me when that happened. I don't mean I lost my temper, I just was a little more critical than I should have been. And coming from a CEO, that's not good.

What do you think is the biggest change in your life as you've become more successful?

I think it's the realization that you're capable of doing a lot more than you ever thought you could. And the feeling that I don't live up to what I could have done. Maybe that sounds arrogant, but I don't mean it to. When I think back I could have done a better job. I don't have a lot of regrets about it, because I feel it's been a good run, but I have learned that there is hardly any limit on what you can accomplish. I never thought that I would become friends with the people I have. Presidents, princes, you name it. And I haven't done that to have a list that I can brag about, it's just been a natural kind of evolution. And it has convinced me that if you want to you can reach for the stars.

Obviously not everybody can have the same results that many of us are fortunate enough to have. I feel privileged that I've had these opportunities. I go back to LSU and speak to young people. I helped put up a building down there, the Alumni Centre. President Reagan told them they ought to name it after me, which they did, and they got me to put a lot of my memorabilia there. It isn't for the purpose of exalting Lod Cook, but they said, 'This would let young people see that some of these things are possible and you ought to share it with them.' So I've done that, in the hope that I can just help a few people to see that this is possible. And there are a lot of people, a lot brighter than I am, who can come out of my home state or a country town and who knows what they can do. The realization that you can do so much, it really is unbelievable; unlimited.

If you had before you in one room all the young people who look up to you as an example of the kind of success they would like to achieve, what advice would you give them?

Set your sights high, prepare yourself, emotionally and educationally, and work hard. There's no substitute for work – hard work. Anybody that thinks they can do it on an eight-to-five schedule is kidding himself. That means you're going to have to make some sacrifices. And then you just attack it with great zest. Success comes from watching what works for other people, trying to adapt some of that – and adopt some of it. Role models are important as long as you don't get consumed by notions of heroes. Be open for discovery; don't have a fixed notion of the path, have some idea of the kind of things that appeal to you, because you're going to do things better if you get a kick out of them. I get a kick out of working with people, out of teamwork and persuading people and leading people to get something done, and that seemed to work for me.

When you do finally pass off the great stage of life, what would you like people to say about you?

He made a difference. I always kid people that on my headstone they'd write, 'Gee, what a guy!'

F.W. DE KLERK

He is the only politician this century to have
achieved the ultimate political success – working
his way to the very top of his country's
government – and then to have voluntarily given
up that power to satisfy the greater long-term
interests of that country, because 'the alternative
was a tremendous conflict with devastating
consequences.' But F.W. De Klerk also explains
here for the first time how the arrival of President
Gorbachev and the subsequent change of strategy
by the Soviet Union made it all possible; and
how, when support for his efforts appeared to be
slipping, he staked all on a referendum which
ended up giving him the necessary mandate to
amend the constitution. He and Nelson
Mandela shared the Nobel Peace Prize, and after
the election he became a co-Vice-President in President Mandela's government of
national unity. A new spirit of co-operation filled the land. Two years later, after
coming under vicious attack from the white Afrikaans community for 'selling them
out', he resigned in order to 'give South Africa a strong and vigilant opposition'.
More recently he apologised to the Truth Commission – the body investigating past
misdeeds – for his National Party's policies and record under apartheid. This
interview, carried out while he was still in government, concentrates on the
'realistic idealism' driving this remarkable statesman.

'Politics,' he says, 'is public service – a commitment to achieve something that is
not for yourself – and a politician who strives for success just to achieve a
leadership position won't last long.' He believes that 'to be a winner, you really must
understand and look at circumstances through the eyes of your opponents', because
'in the final analysis, nobody can claim to be the representative of the absolute
truth'. He concedes that the politician's success relies on 'responses from others', but
'if you are constantly involved in just reacting, then you lose the initiative, and the
initiative is an essential part of success in politics'. Spelling out his core principles
for success, he warns budding politicians against becoming 'small power cliques
within a party'; and he discusses the sense of disillusionment across the world that
has left politicians 'at an all-time low in modern history', blaming that, in part,
on the power of television and 'the boredom of economic prosperity'. He also showers
praise on the 'Mr Nobodys' who are the backbone of his nation's success.

Mr De Klerk, what is your definition of success?

A sure definition of success would be to set clear goals, to know where you want to go and then, through hard work, to achieve those goals. I would say that success, whether it's the success of an organization or an individual, centres around what can be called the five Cs – core-values, commitment, competition, communication and co-operation.

You are in a very interesting position because everyone assumes that in politics you are in pursuit of power, that you are in pursuit of rising to the very top of your profession, which you did. But then came a point where you made a sacrifice. Is sacrifice part of success?

Generally speaking, yes. You cannot achieve success without hard work and hard work entails some sort of sacrifice, specifically in your personal life. When it's neglecting your family, there is sacrifice on their part as well. You are not participating in the amenable things in life as regularly as the average office worker has the opportunity to do. In other words, you don't have the same amount of spare time. But in a more specific sense success needn't always go hand in hand with great personal sacrifice. In my case there was an element of it. I could have clung to power, I could have remained President for another ten years using the army more and more, continuing to circumvent sanctions. But as a country we would have been moving towards a tremendous conflict which would have had devastating consequences. Therefore I well knew when I embarked – and my party with me – on the course that we did, that in all probability it would result, at least in the first round, in us taking second place, and in another party becoming the majority party. And there was an element of sacrifice in that.

Did you ever think twice about giving up the top job?

No. While I held the job, I was totally motivated with regard to what I was doing and I never had any compunction. Obviously, in one's life there are times when you get so frustrated that you ask yourself, 'Is it really worthwhile?' But I haven't had that problem to the extent that it de-motivated me.

You were talking about the concept of setting yourself other goals and the fact that you were now heading for a new target that would represent a new kind of success. Tell me more about that.

The new target is to become the biggest party again. Not just for the sake of becoming the biggest party, but to ensure that the values for which we stand and the fundamental principles in which we believe will become the core-values and principles of the new South Africa. And we sincerely believe that the majority of South Africans actually share those values with us. The first election in which all South Africans were able to participate was fraught with historical stances. People voted with their emotion. They regarded this election as the culmination of a conflict which had been continuing for centuries in South Africa.

Already now it is clear that people in a normalized situation, irrespective of their race or colour, are asking as all voters do, 'What is in it for me? Which policy will secure the best future for my child?' And in that sense normalization is creating a fluidity in South African politics earlier than I really expected.

When you conceded defeat in the General Election you talked about achieving what you wanted to achieve, the target you had set yourself some four, four and a half years earlier. But when you achieve one target, is that enough, do you not have to move on to other targets?

Absolutely. That is my philosophy. Life becomes meaningless if you don't set yourself targets. It depends what you do in life. If you are involved in politics, then you are involved in public service. You have a commitment as a leader to achieve something that is not for yourself. A politician who just strives for success in order to obtain a leadership position invariably won't last long. A politician in a leadership position needs to be infused with realistic idealism. It's what I want to achieve if I become leader which is important. Not everything centres on merely becoming the President or Prime Minister.

In the course of your political career, have you known failure?

Yes, I've known failure.

Was that difficult to accept?

Failure is never pleasant, but I believe problems are there to be solved. So when you have to admit to or recognize failure you must decide how to change that into success. For instance, in a series of by-elections just before the referendum, my party was sliding back, we were losing by-elections in our own heartland and it was suddenly questioned whether I still had a mandate to negotiate the new constitution within the framework which we had put forward in the 1989 elections. I sat down and decided for myself, without discussing it with anybody, that if at a last by-election, which took place in February 1992, if after putting everything that we had into that, we had another failure, that I was going to call a referendum to ask for a clear mandate on the main issue at stake. I did so and I've never looked back – we gained a two-thirds majority.

You used a key phrase there, you said you took that decision without consulting anybody else?

Before I announced it I consulted, but in my heart of hearts I decided that we would continue to fail unless we did something which would really change the mood of the electorate.

Are the best decisions taken by you yourself sitting down and working things out within your own mind, then driving through the decision you take? Or are they taken by sitting down with many people, many committees, many consultations? What's the best way to achieve success?

I'm a great believer in teamwork. I'm a great believer in bringing your main advisors together when you face a serious problem. Then you can give a lead on the direction in which you think the solution lies, then have a very open discussion and a very thorough debate, canvassing all viewpoints. But in the final analysis in politics, the leader has to formulate the consensus and has to accept the responsibility for the decisions.

And sometimes the decision will come first, in the sense that you will decide what you want to do and then you will pull everyone else on board, but on other occasions you might have the consultation first and then come to the decision. How do you decide which to do?

Well, it depends upon the nature of the problem, but I have experienced quite often that although I felt fairly convinced that A should be done, after the consultation A fundamentally changed to B. So even in cases where you as a leader take a decision, if you expose yourself to this consultation process and if you listen carefully you get good advice. You must then have the insight to amend the initial decision taken in your own mind. I served under a leader before – no names, no pack drill – who had the habit of listening to the advice of certain advisors, actually taking a decision and then consulting other advisors. When I become President I decided never to do that. During my office as President, I never allowed a Minister to make a deal with me and then merely took it to Cabinet to have it validated. I'd listen and say, 'Thank you for preparing me, I'll think about it, but let's consult the whole Cabinet.'

You have had one tremendous international triumph as a politician but have there been any moments when you felt a deep sense of triumph that we perhaps haven't heard about?

Apart from the obvious highlights, no. The result of the referendum I would highlight as, maybe, the most important feeling of achievement that I've experienced because, as I said, my party and I were sliding, and to have changed the current with such a dramatic effect was a wonderful political achievement and provided the key to everything which has happened since.

Anything on a personal level?

On a personal level let me relate one anecdote. As a young MP, after about three years in Parliament, I was heavily tipped to become a Deputy Minister and there was some inside information that the Prime Minister – we then had a Prime Minister – had already decided to appoint me. My own father, who had been a minister under three former Prime Ministers, was actually privately invited to be there when his son's appointment as Deputy Minister was announced. And then something happened and Treurnicht, who later became leader of the right-wing party in South Africa, was appointed.

I suppose some senior advisors convinced the Prime Minister – who is now dead – that he could not by-pass him and that it would cause problems in the party. That was a tremendous disappointment, but then two years later the Prime Minister made me a full Minister directly – I've never been a Deputy Minister. That was a sort of atonement which gave me a great feeling of gratitude and satisfaction.

Does that mean that it helps to appreciate success better if you have experienced a kind of failure before?

Oh yes, I've no doubt that it is a process, in the way that when you take iron and you put it through a process it becomes steel. There is an Afrikaans word that describes that process as a process of becoming stronger through trial.

Does it concern you that what you might see as success inevitably means failure for somebody else?

It doesn't concern me in the sense that in politics one is involved in a cut-and-thrust situation. There are winners and there are losers. It's like in boxing or in any sport where you fight to win. But I've had a sense of compassion for losers, under circumstances where I have won. Because losing is not easy and it's painful.

Is that a handicap in a politician or a virtue?

I think it's a virtue. It's a virtue to understand that in the final analysis nobody can claim to be the representative of the absolute truth. And I find it important that at times in politics you must really fathom and understand your opponent's viewpoints. Also, to be a winner, you need to really understand and look at circumstances through the eyes of your opponents.

As a politician have you ever sat down and planned a successful sequence of events? Or do you find that you have to respond to changing and unpredictable circumstances much more often, and that it is very difficult as a politician actually to say, 'This is my plan and we're going to drive it through'?

I think it's absolutely necessary at all times to have a plan. And to have a strategy. And to have clear goals and say, 'Well, how am I going to achieve those goals?' If in politics you are constantly involved in just reacting, then you lose the initiative and the initiative is an essential part of success in politics. Obviously as you implement a plan, circumstances beyond your control quite often force you to adapt your plan, to become reactive for a while, but whenever you are in a situation where circumstances or your opponents' strategy forces you to admit that you've lost the initiative, then you must come back with a new plan, and you must grasp the initiative again. Initiative is fundamental in politics. The most important plan in my political career was the plan prepared and decided upon in the run-up to 2 February 1990, and the biggest success was the effective implementation of that plan within the time-frame that we had set for it.

Can success be achieved just by hard work or do you need an element of luck?

I don't think luck in itself is an essential element. It does occur and when it occurs it is a bonus. In our recent history I wouldn't call it luck, nor would I call it fate, but a tremendous change in the rest of the world did create for us a window of opportunity. I would not have been able to do what I've done in the five years of my presidency if the Iron Curtain hadn't come down and if the Berlin Wall hadn't fallen, and if the Communist world, and specifically the USSR, hadn't stopped being a threat. The USSR had a strategy, aimed at gaining more than a foothold in the whole of Southern Africa. They were backing the ANC and the PAC to the hilt. Until the Iron Curtain came down and until the power structures of the USSR and the Communist block crumbled, those two organizations were instruments in the hands of a world power with an expansionist policy in Southern Africa.

When the Iron Curtain came down, suddenly they were political movements – involved in terrorism, yes, but political movements nonetheless – made up of South Africans focused on gaining political rights in South Africa, and although they remained dangerous, from a security point of view, the whole scene changed and we could take the risks that I took.

So your success was dependent in the very beginning on the lucky throw of international events?

Well, as a Christian I won't call it a lucky throw. I would say the intervention of God Almighty. But not dependent on that – even then we could have failed dismally. It was a trigger, it created a window of opportunity, where the challenge was firstly to see it and secondly to use it.

Do you see political success as being very different to success in other fields such as sport and business, or are there core similarities?

There are core similarities but there are also fundamental differences. In essence success in politics depends upon your capacity to get a response from millions of people. For an athlete, success depends upon his or her own speed, fitness, guts and whatever is needed. The politician needs those as well, but the politician's success relies upon responses from others. To a certain extent, I would say business is more similar to politics in that sense.

Are there people, big or small, whose success you admire? People in history, people that we might not have heard of, or people who are well known to those who will be reading this book?

I have no sort of folk heroes who for me were specific role models but in politics I'm deeply interested in Churchill's life, I find him a fascinating man. Further back in history I think Bismarck was a remarkable man because he succeeded in creating a form of unity and co-operation, and indeed a nation, from a great diversity of people who, although they had one language, were killing each other around every bend and corner, who had been at war with each other for decades if not centuries.

And you've done the same job here.

To a certain extent that is what we are still trying to achieve. I think we've laid very good foundations and I think we are making good progress to achieve that, yes. To build a nation. In our case it is more complex, because it will forever remain a nation of great diversity with 11 languages. There is not only racial diversity, but there is also ethnic and cultural diversity.

I also have great admiration for Mr Nobody who starts a small business on his own, and who through sheer determination and acumen and hard work makes a success of it and builds it into something really worthwhile. I have great admiration for handicapped people who overcome their handicaps and who show by tremendous example to everyone around them that you needn't be sorry for yourself in this life. You must take what you get and nonetheless rise above the setbacks.

Could you do your job if it wasn't for the Mr Nobodys of this world?

No, they are the backbone of the nation.

Is it becoming more or less difficult to achieve success in your particular field?

Well, in my specific circumstances, it's more difficult at the moment. In politics, the size of your support base has a deciding effect on your influence and on your capacity. But the challenge is once again to start from this support base, which is not negligible and which is the most representative support base of all political parties in South Africa.

More than 50 per cent of the people who voted for the National Party, which has the baggage of the past to carry, were people of colour. My party has become a truly non-racial party and if I look at the four main population groups there is a good spread of them, even 600,000 to 1,000,000 black South Africans voted for the National Party. So in my specific case at the moment I would say it is more difficult.

In general terms is politics becoming a more difficult profession?

I think at the moment, yes. Across the world I perceive, if I read and look at TV, a sense of disillusionment with politicians. I think politicians, generally speaking, are going through a sort of all-time low in modern history. There is a tendency to look for something new, to the extent that the ruling party almost disappeared from the scene in a recent election in Canada, being left with only four seats. In Italy, what used to be the centre has totally disintegrated. In Britain I have great admiration for Mr Major whom I regard as a friend, and I also have great admiration for Mrs Thatcher. But notwithstanding the fact that there is good government, there seems to be a sense of disillusionment there as well.

Why should that be?

I think it needs a thesis to really analyse that. No doubt modern communication has a great impact on this, the power of television, the global village concept. It is changing attitudes across the world. Economic prosperity I think also plays a role. In many countries there is not much idealism left. Running the country is really maintaining the country – it is not leading the country to new horizons. If you have the highest living standard in the world, if you have a full democracy, if everything is running smoothly, if there are no signs of danger on the horizon in the sense of a war, then it becomes quite a boring matter just to govern a country and to see that things are ticking over. Fortunately, we still have horizons and mountains to climb and tremendous challenges ahead of us, which infuses a sense of idealism into politics. I think those are a few of the factors.

If you could gather together in one huge room all the young people in politics today and offer them advice on how to make a success of their lives, what would you say?

I would firstly say that if you are in politics just on the basis of ambition and if your main interest is just advancing yourself, then you are on the wrong track and you won't make a success. You must dedicate yourself to realistic ideals, you must dedicate yourself to values and you must become a team man. Individualism does not serve a cause well. A cause needs individualists, but even these individualists can make themselves more effective by working together with colleagues. I would warn them against becoming part of small power cliques within a party. And I would like to instil in them the sense that being in politics is a calling. It's not just a job.

When your time comes to depart this life, what would you like people to say about you?

That my contribution has made a significant difference for the better, for all the people of South Africa.

LORD DEARING

'A likeable lad, but below average in the class' was the verdict at the age of 13 on the highly successful civil servant and businessman charged with reshaping the education system in England and Wales. That early school report was one of two 'short, sharp shocks' that changed his whole attitude – the other being when his father, a clerk at Hull docks, was killed in a German bombing raid. Ron Dearing believes that 'a really disturbing experience helps make you what you are'. Months after that remark by his form-master, he had risen from 23rd to 2nd in the class, claiming top place the following term. Lack of funds forced him to leave school at the age of 16 to work as a clerk in the local labour exchange; but, with correspondence courses making up for the education he missed, he soon passed an intermediate degree in economics and won a scholarship to Hull University. A thirty-year rise through the ranks of the Civil Service found him second-in-command of the Department of Trade and Industry.

When he took over as Chairman of the state-run Post Office in 1981, he confessed that he'd 'never even run a coffee shop before', but says 'the trick is believing you can do it – and then doing it'. He explains the 'island culture' he found in his new job, and how he tackled it by 'being constantly on the move' and refusing to be ruled by systems. 'You've got to have a vision,' he says, 'I never come to work to deal with the in-tray!' He dismisses those who rule by fear, believing that business leadership 'is about getting people to want very much to do what you want to be done'. Briefly Chairman of lottery organisers Camelot, his legendary success in reconciling different viewpoints had by then taken him into a series of key government roles aimed at improving the educational system. 'Education,' he says here, 'is about helping all pupils. We must stretch the most able, but for those who are getting nowhere at school and feel themselves failures, we've got to find ways of helping them to become successes within their own framework.' He explains how the drive should come 'from engaging people's enthusiasms'. With a twinkle in his eye, this highly successful man admits to no actual failures, but says that personally he doesn't rate highly much of what he does, and is intensely critical of it. 'At every stage of life, I felt that what was called for by the job was more than I had to offer.'

Lord Dearing, what is your definition of success?

Success is being able to say at the end of your days, 'I lived on the edge and I did what I could.' It means that you were fully engaged in life, gave it what you had to give, and can feel at the end of your days, 'Yes, it wasn't a bad shot.'

Living on the edge must involve a sense of risk.

Oh yes. It means being stretched and taking the risk of failure.

And does it mean always being stretched?

No, to have lived life well, there have to be moments of peace, and that comes from family life – even when the grandchildren arrive!

To what extent is success a product of your background and upbringing?

It's difficult to say. I think the inescapable element is you, who you are, what you are. Of course, that's moulded by environment and upbringing. My upbringing was quiet and unperturbed until my father was killed in the Second World War when I was ten, and that shook the quiet world I lived in and made it a world of changing experiences. I think that, in a sense, was the beginning of living on the edge because there wasn't the security of family life any longer, and there wasn't a home for a number of years. So the death of my father was one of my moulding experiences. A ten-year-old isn't used to taking many responsibilities. My mother went to work, and I was evacuated to live with someone else, and so for five years we were separated. I moved between three families. However welcoming people are, a youngster still feels a guest, a touch alone.

But there was one specific challenge in my early years. When I was 13, a kindly man, my form master, wrote of me: 'A likeable lad, but below the average in the class.' Now I'd never really thought about achievement, seriously, except on the sports field, and he didn't have that in mind. What he said brought me up short – it was a powerful phrase in that it really did change my whole attitude. That year-end I'd come 23rd in the class. The next term I was second and ever after that, the one above that. It was just the flip side of the coin. I was still successful on the sports field, but now there were other things that mattered as well. I suppose the need to do things well is built in me. And having got an extra dimension to my values, thanks to that man, I no longer did my homework two minutes before I took a test, I did it a bit longer before.

Does everyone need a trigger, like that shock to your system, at some stage in their youth, in order to give them greater potential to be successful?

I think it's immensely helpful to have a short, sharp shock like that. I had two – the death of my father, and then this comment, perhaps just at the right time in my life. And sometimes, you don't take risks unless you're forced to. If you're comfortable and doing all right, you plod along. If you suddenly get the sack – bump, you're forced to take risks. In America it's part of the culture that it does a person good to have had one failure on his record. A really disturbing experience helps to make you who you are. I make no general rules about it – if a person has too much failure, that too is destructive. But adversity, if it doesn't break you can make you, and I've been very lucky. I've had no such disasters, but as I said earlier, for most of my time, even in the Civil Service, I was conscious of living on the edge and doing things where I was close to failure.

But you've never actually known failure itself? Not in any way, shape or form?

I can't think of something where I have had to say to myself, 'Oh, I failed.' I'm very self-critical, I do not rate highly much of what I do, and I am intensely critical of it. But in terms of those outside me, I guess it hasn't looked much like that.

So when you do look at something and say, 'I could have done that better,' what is your frame of mind, for making sure that you do improve?

I always aim to do something well, as well as I can. When I was a clerk, at 16, when I was a young, very junior executive, at every stage of life I felt that what was called for by the job was more than I had to offer. I have always felt, gosh, I wish I could have done more.

You rose, over 30 years to the top of the Civil Service. Are there any secrets to that particular success? How do you become a successful civil servant?

I reached one from the top when I was 45. You need a certain amount of brain-power. Another element is courage – what was once described by my chemistry master as a characteristic of the British, the ability to sit tight in a hot corner, and I have been in some. A further element is to be able to empathize with the minister or secretary of state, whoever he or she may be, and whilst giving that minister honest advice, doing it within a framework of understanding his philosophical approach and what he or she is trying to do. Some people say, 'You're turning your coat,' or they may think that. But when you take on the job of being a civil servant, what you're doing is saying to the minister, 'I work for you. I'll do my best to help you put in place the policies you were elected to deliver, and it isn't my right, because I haven't been elected, to tell the nation what should be done, you've earned that right.' I think that has helped me to gain the confidence of ministers, who sometimes wonder whether a civil servant is working for them.

In 1980 you went to the Post Office to be chairman. In how bad a state was the Post Office when you arrived, and how did you set about turning it round? Particularly when you said you'd never even run a coffee shop before.

Well, no, I hadn't as a matter of fact, and here's one of the tricks, for me. It didn't occur to me that I couldn't do it. The trick is believing you can do it, and then doing it. Perhaps that's the most important thing.

But does that mean that everybody must think they can do everything? Or have you got to have a realistic appraisal of your own abilities?

It's a balance between the two. I can't jump to the moon, but if you start out with the belief, 'Can do, will do,' you find that those two words 'can' and 'will' are immensely powerful in enabling you to do things. A lot of life's a trick of confidence. I recently opened a speech with the words, 'I'm a con man – no expertise in this but here goes,' and I often think of myself like that. You convince yourself, by experience, that you can do it, so perhaps that was one of the things that enabled me to go into the Post Office thinking, 'I can do it.'

Now then, how about the state the Post Office was in. The Post Office's main problem was that it was an island culture, to which people committed themselves for life. Within one frame of reference, their history, they were superb, but there were some things they were missing through being an island culture. And things were not very good. The general forecast was, and I quote from the union side, we are going to face serious redundancies. That was the view of the University of Sussex, which had been employed to advise the Post Office. Prices had been shooting through the roof. The people were good, they were excellent, but they'd got themselves into a real jam. Rules and regulations ran the Post Office.

Rules and regulations are what people used to think you had to have in order to achieve success, but that's not the culture now. What has replaced them?

Well, first of all, it's necessary to break down big organization. Big organizations are run by rules and regulations and hierarchies, and the current thinking is to kill them off. The big firm is best run as a collection of smaller firms. The world is changing so fast that two years is a long time. We have to be constantly on the move. But rules are anti-change, rules are what cement you into the past. In my seven and a half years at the Post Office I don't think I looked at the manual of rules once, and perhaps that was another element in helping me to get somewhere.

So it's the free-form approach to success – to take your coat off, sit down in the office, and not be driven by rules, but accept the winds of change and try to manage them as best you can on an ad hoc *basis. Is that the way to do it?*

You've got to have a vision, but you mustn't be ruled by systems. My in-tray, for years and years and years, has never been what I came to work to deal with. I come into the office each day minded to deal with specific issues, and if there is time I get round to looking at the in-tray. In other words, if you want to create change, you've got to take initiatives and make things happen, rather than respond to the system.

So that means a longer-term strategic approach, keeping your eye on the ball and not being buffeted by the winds of daily requirements?

Certainly you've not got to be blown over by the exigencies of the moment – you're required to grasp the tiller and control direction.

And yet those exigencies may actually be throwing up problems that do need to be dealt with and do need your attention.

Absolutely, and you have to deal with them. You've got to survive. If something horrid has happened – and such things do happen all the time – you deal with it. But you have a guiding star. When I joined the Post Office, at the end of the first week I said what I thought our policy ought to be and we stuck to it for the whole of the seven and a half years. Perhaps I had no better ideas and I'd spent my penny in the first week, but you've got to have some clear sense of direction. You don't need to articulate it in detail, you don't need to be precise about the exact compass point, but simply decide that you are going this way, rather than that way.

In the work I have done in education, which has been something that's come very late in life, I've always been in the business of listening to people, but there have been some underlying themes in my mind which have always been very influential in the way I want to go. For example, education is about helping all, and I stress *all* people to develop. We must stretch the most able, but for those who are getting nowhere at school and feel themselves failures, we've got to find ways of helping them to become successes within their own framework.

What do you reckon would be the ways in which you'd turn around people who are perceived, at the moment, as being failures, or maybe see themselves as failures? What are the planks within the educational framework that can help them in this?

First, to think of them and respond to them as individual human beings in their own right, within their own terms. Second, instead of imposing your view of what they should be capable of doing, find out what they actually are capable of doing and what interests them. You've got to catch alight, generate some enthusiasm. I am talking here about people of, say, 13 or 14, who've got nowhere, sitting at the back of the class, lost and possibly disruptive. It's no good saying, 'You must master your grammar, you must master your mental arithmetic.' You can't start from there if they see it as a desert. You've got to say, 'Now let's have a talk, let's see where we are. What are you thinking about? What are you interested in?' And if it's throwing a dart – I'm talking about an extreme case – at a dartboard, we'll start from there, as a basis, which isn't a bad thing for mental arithmetic for example. Or a motorbike – they'd want to read the manual in no time at all, so they can know how to do something with the motorbike engine. And I argued, when I joined the schools' world, that we ought to kindle enthusiasms, provide more opportunities for those types of 14-year-olds, through freeing up more of the curriculum, to enable people to do what they can, which they need for their own good. The drive comes from engaging their enthusiasms. I learned in the Post Office what an immense amount of talent there is in people who have no academic inclinations or abilities to learn that way. They can be immensely creative – intuitively clever in other directions. I learned to respect people a lot.

So there is no one who's intrinsically a failure in life?

It's hard to say no one. But I believe, and to some degree I know, that somewhere in the vast kaleidoscope of talent of which we have a little bit of this or a little bit of that, there is almost always something. A person may have a gift of friendship, a person may have a gift of laughter. There are things on which you can work and help a person to get some fulfilment out of life. And one of my great concerns is to avoid having within our society a percentage who come out of school, fail, move into unemployment and failure, and can't engage in society. They're outside society and we can't afford that, for social reasons, for economic reasons, as well as having a bit of feeling of care towards those people. I suppose that's my greatest personal concern in education – to help the losers become winners.

There are certain core threads that run through success in education and success in industry, but is there a difference in that with education you have quite a few years to get it right, but industry want results quickly. They haven't got the tolerance to ride shotgun alongside someone who is maybe potentially successful, but will take a while to get there.

There is a difference, undoubtedly. One of the things I learned in business was, if you make a bad mistake – I'm talking of a chairman/chief executive – it can take the business two years to recover from that. I tend to say there are one or two things, three at most, you do in a year that really matter. If you get those right you make the business, if you don't, you break it. In education there's always another day, another opportunity. Learning is for life and part of the job of schools is to set fire to people's enthusiasm for learning, for their own sake. And one of the successes of our society is the extent to which people come back into education in the middle years, having got nowhere when they were young. They become excellent students, they have something to offer from their experience. This happens a lot.

And, of course, your life mirrors that, doesn't it, because you left school at 16?

My mother got her house back after the war when I was nearly 16 and the natural thing to do was to help the family's bottom line by earning some money. So I went to work at 16, at the local labour exchange, which was a rich learning experience in itself. I was there for nearly three years.

And you saw all the hopefuls going in looking for work?

I saw the unhopefuls, with no chance of work. Hull was a city with high unemployment and there was a crowd of men who hung around the labour exchange all day. It was their social centre, hoping for a job, and I met the not-so-young hopefuls as well. But sometimes you went away with a good feeling when you'd got somebody a job – that was really rewarding.

But seeing those who hadn't got qualifications struggling to get work, was that what drove you back into the academic world to get qualifications?

I finished school at 16, but I signed up for a correspondence course immediately and began the long treadmill of part-time work to gain various qualifications. All the time between leaving school at 16 and going to university at 22, I was engaged heavily, and I mean heavily, in part-time education, and then I had two years at university doing a degree. I think that was as hard a period as I've lived through.

We've talked through the ingredients for a successful education, we haven't really touched on the ingredients of a successful business career. Everyone says that business is the engine that drives the world's economies and it generates the wealth that enables us to do all kinds of other things in life. Is there any set formula for being a successful businessman?

Absolutely not. I just marvel at the differences between people who have got to the top in business. Of course, they must have good judgment – and that doesn't necessarily mean clever, it means having a sense of where the opportunity is. It also needs a lot of drive and a lot of self-belief. It means getting a lot out of other people. To be successful at the top you depend massively on the success of other people, and there are very different ways of getting it. Some do it by fear, and that is a very powerful driving force.

An acceptable one?

Not to me.

But acceptable in general business terms?

I wouldn't say it was acceptable in general business terms, what I'm saying is, in some people it is a way of getting results and I've no time for it. Others do it by helping people to give the best of what they have. I used to say that leadership is about getting people to want very much to do what you want done, and there are different ways of going about it. I think people who work with me probably see I have a great deal of enthusiasm for whatever it is, and I seem capable of generating my own personal enthusiasm for almost anything. I think if you gave me a barrow and a brush to sweep the gutters, I would develop an enthusiasm for it. And others catch light from that.

I wander around talking to people and developing a community of friends who are strongly committed to a common goal. And if one can generate a vision collectively, and generate a commitment to it, things really happen. I never think of myself as a good manager, I often think of myself as too disorganized a person, but others see what I'm doing and they see I give a lot to it.

So enthusiasm can drive you forward without all the necessary ingredients in place?

Yes. Enthusiasm can drive you forward, but it's a good idea to know where you're going.

Is there any particular technique for achieving a successful consensus in a company, for bringing people together and resolving all the different forces that are at play, particularly in big organizations?

I think, from experience, the first thing is to have listened to other people and understood them. Often, if people feel they have been heard with respect and understood, you're halfway to persuading them to go where you want to go. The second is to let the debate take place, and the third is, then to give leadership – showing in what you say that you've understood and respected what they say, and providing it isn't barmy they'll go with you and you will have a consensus. I'm not one of those who despises consensus. I feel that if you have a consensus, you get greater momentum than if you get grudging acceptance. One of the strengths in Japan is the way they work to develop a consensus. It's not imposed from the top, things start from the bottom, and there's a huge commitment to the consensual views – not the culture of Britain of the 1980s when the emphasis was on leadership, but you can have leadership with consensus, and some people are very gifted in getting a positive, creative consensus.

Quite a few outstandingly successful people left school at 16, if not before, some with virtually no qualifications. Might that indicate that success has really nothing whatsoever to do with a good education?

Again we're talking about the definition of success. Let's put it in worldly terms. You don't have to have a lot of education to be successful. But, by golly, your chances of being successful are much greater if you've had the benefit of a good and continuing education. Can we just talk more about education for a moment? Perhaps the most important part of education is to develop the capacity to be curious. It certainly stimulates you, and possibly having an active sense of curiosity is the entry to good ideas which are the foundations of success. I think that as a society we have nowhere to go except to declining standards of living unless we invest in ourselves through education, throughout life, but in a form that's relevant to the individual.

So no boxes?

No. We mustn't categorize people when it comes to this. There are things they have to master. We have to help them, however late in life it is, to master facility in the English language, because it's *that* that we use to think, and what you do need is to be able to think.

We need people with the imagination and the drive and the courage to be great entrepreneurs. They don't have to be highly educated, but they need very highly educated people to help them to realize their ideas.

So the very types of education are going to be crucial in laying the groundwork for our national success, but you still see the opportunity for the wayward spirit to become successful, for the person who bucks the system, the rebel almost?

Yes. Those are the people who really make things different, the rebels with an idea, a determination and a passion.

How will you judge whether you have been successful in reshaping education in England and Wales?

Somebody asked me three years ago how I judged that, and I had to reply that it will be years before the effects show through. It's impossible for me to say yet. The changes in the National Curriculum, the changes to the tests have only just taken effect. I think, hopefully, there will be two contributions. One is to give back to the teachers more of the ability to shape what happens in their own classroom and thereby to have more commitment and enthusiasm, and therefore improve the quality of the teaching. The other is having an inclusive vision of education, challenging and responding to the whole range of talents. I want to stretch the most able. I want to have rigour and all those things that are so important, but we can't afford a society in which 20 per cent leave school without the standards of an average eleven-year-old in their national language and in mathematics. We must lift those into being effective and successful learners, and if, looking back, I feel I've made a contribution, especially to that last one, I shall be well pleased.

What do you regard as the most successful moments in your life? Not necessarily the ones that the world is aware of, not necessarily the obvious benchmarks of your career.

First, when I heard I'd got through an examination I never dreamed I'd get through. It was in the civil service and I was about 23. It was a rather tough one. Second, when Mrs Dearing said, 'Yes.' That was rather nice.

Because you'd had quite a job persuading her?

Well, of course. And then we had our two children – both of those were marvellous moments, and I hope they won't mind me saying, but both of them were adopted. I remember particularly well when we went to get our first child, Erica. We brought her home from the Adoption Society and we offered her a bottle and nothing happened. She wouldn't take it, and the bairn began to bawl. We were desperate. We rang up a friend who'd had a child who lived about ten miles away, and those friends came to our house and the baby took the bottle. It was a great moment in my life when we got over that.

At cricket, a good square-cut, a good forcing shot on the on-side, the occasional goal at soccer – they were great moments. There have been other great moments. I remember at the marriage of one of my daughters we had country dancing where you have a caller and you do your best to respond, and I cannot remember enjoying myself so much as I did in that hour, making a fool of myself.

What are the greatest enemies of success?

Losing confidence, losing energy, drifting. None of those things is compatible with success. And also losing your health, which I came to the threshold of doing, and I should have known better. Those are my warnings.

Does luck play a part in success?

Yes. Somebody said to me once, 'You make your own luck,' and there's an awful lot of truth in that. Let's put it this way, there is chance, there is good chance and there is awfully bad chance. When this man said, 'You make your luck,' he may have meant when something lucky has happened, you seize it, you use it actively, and that makes a lot of difference. Recognizing the opportunity and using it, I suppose a lot of greatness has come from that.

Who are the really successful people whom you admire? Who are your heroes, past or present?

Albert Schweitzer, a man called Jesus, in my younger days one or two cricketers and footballers ... I tend to think – maybe this is a bit silly – the man in the street. I remember seeing a woman with a bag full of shopping at a quarter past five, bustling in a queue at the bus stop to get on the bus to go home and feed her family. I had a lot of respect for that woman. There are an awful lot of people like that woman, and there are men as well, I dare say, whom we should respect for the way they go about their lives and for what they give to other people. If you were talking about politicians, I admired Mrs Thatcher, I can't say I enjoyed her company all that much, but she's a great, courageous person. And John Smith.

I'd settle with the two names I first gave you as particularly heroic characters. They're in the same trade in a way, separated by two millennia.

You were chairman of Camelot when they won the franchise for the National Lottery. Do you think there's anything unfair about becoming financially successful without working for it?

I don't want to have a critical view of someone to whom wealth came by inheritance. I don't think envy is a good part of life, it weakens, makes life third-rate. But I admire the people who've got it and got it by contributing, rather than exploiting, if I may put it that way. I think I admire those who in becoming wealthy have made others wealthy, by the nature of what they chose to do. And when individuals do things like creating an enterprise from scratch, creating a lot of jobs for people, providing good products and services for people, I have no envy but only delight in the success of those people, and wealth is part of their reward. So be it. Perhaps, may I say, the National Lottery also gives us a chance to put funds behind people in a way which the State cannot do to create new images, for example, on the sports field and in the arts. It gives us a great opportunity to build things up. We desperately need it.

Is there a downside to success?

Yes, the one we talked of earlier, the dangers that come from spending too much time living at the edge. It is, in a way, like a magnet which draws you away from your family. You cannot resist it. It's like a boy with a bag of toffees, he can't resist having another one.

If you could gather together every youngster in the country who wants to be successful, what advice would you give them?

I would repeat, perhaps at slightly greater length, four words I gave you – 'I can' and 'I will'. Believe that, say to yourself, 'I *can* make something of my life, I *can* be a success, and I *will*,' and then if you believe that, you will be a success.

And if you are a success, does that bring obligations to society in its wake?

Yes. Share your blessings with society. You'll do that almost accidentally in your wake. You'll create success for other people. If you become very wealthy, you can have the joy of giving some of it away. And somebody once said, 'It's better to give than to receive, there's more joy in it.'

One final question. When your time comes to leave this life, what would you like people to say about Ron Dearing?

He did what he could.

NIGEL DEMPSTER

'Lead a blameless life – and if you can't lead a
blameless life, get your story in first.' That's the
advice of the doyen of Britain's gossip
columnists, talking here about both the
achieving and the reporting of social success.
Not surprisingly, he sees success in terms of
'being written about'. He is unashamed about
intrusions into the private lives of those who
aim for the peaks: 'If you seek success, then what
comes with it is that you are known to the press,
and they won't stop when the bad times arrive.'
He points out that there is a way rich and
powerful people can very easily stay out of the
media: 'Do not, at any stage of your life, deal
with journalists, and do not seek publicity.'
But, of course, to the great relief of gossip
columnists the world over, many do, and he highlights 'a new area of flaunting
going on in Britain', pointing out that most of the successful people that fill his
columns have public relations advisers, which in itself 'makes a statement that
they're worthy of press attention'.

Nigel Dempster is an Australian who arrived in Britain at the age of five, and
found it 'a cold, chilly, class-oriented country'. Describing himself as 'very much of
the middle classes', he endured a 'rather unhappy education' at prep and public
schools, leaving at 16 because he wanted to 'get into the maelstrom of the world as
fast as possible'. He worked in Lloyd's of London, meeting people 'who were of some
use to me at a later date'. Moving to an unpaid PR job, and living off a weekly
allowance from his father, he met journalists and was attracted to their world. He
applied for a job with the William Hickey gossip column in the Daily Express, and
was accepted. Being at first 'shy and tongue-tied', he had to work hard at a job
which involves 'going up to total strangers and asking them outrageous questions'.
New York beckoned, and he worked there until his draft papers for Vietnam arrived
– at which point he returned rapidly to London and the Hickey column, switching
to the Daily Mail five years later. His formula for success in this most cut-throat of
professions boils down to 'enormous knowledge of what's going on in the world –
see when people are passé and when they are rising – see what your readers'
aspirations are, and be one of them, and remember you are dealing with rich,
powerful people who have recourse to expensive lawyers'.

Nigel Dempster, what is your definition of success?

I think it's fairly obvious that when you've made it, you become well known and famous in terms of being written about. Also you have the bonuses of success, such as cars, houses, flashy women if you want them. I would say that success is someone being applauded by his peers – someone like George Best in his heyday – someone who is so obviously better than anyone else in their field, whether it's the armed forces, business, the sports field or whatever. It becomes self-evident because you rise to the top. You achieve success by being acknowledged by your peers as the leader in your particular field.

Are there any circumstances in which you could be successful without attracting public acclaim and attention?

Oh there's an infinite number of Nobel Prize winners who are never written about, in fact I'd be hard-pressed, even if offered millions of pounds, to tell you who won the Nobel Prizes for the last 20 years. They are all fairly esoteric academic or even medical people who've discovered the cure to this or the enzyme for that, who are never remarked upon. You can also be enormously rich and never be remarked upon – many people have billions yet have never been written about because they didn't acquire their money by a public method.

Do you think it's possible to be successful in a quiet way with your family, just beavering away, doing something at a much smaller level, without attracting a huge amount of attention and for that to be a success in its own right, or does success always have to be associated with public acclaim?

No. If you flaunt it obviously you're going to, shall we say, excite the interests of the public, but there's no need to flaunt it. There's a whole new area of flaunting going on in Britain – the rugby football teams. Up until recently, they were all amateur, but now they're professional and people have been crawling out of the woodwork who one's never heard of before and are sponsoring rugby teams with anything up to £6 million. I can only assume they are doing that to make a statement, to demonstrate that they've made a lot of money. I've hardly heard of some of them before. Certainly I've heard of Sir John Hall in Newcastle because he already owns Newcastle United, but such people as Ashley Levett of Richmond or Nigel Wray of Saracens have, in the past, enjoyed a certain anonymity, and by getting into the public arena have now forfeited that.

You're not talking at all about the kind of people who don't inhabit gossip columns, who don't arrive fairly regularly on the front pages, or indeed any pages of newspapers. What about the person who might be, for example, an architect, or someone who works in a bank and who has got different targets that don't involve public acclaim – they simply are very content and regard themselves as being very successful in doing their job well and going home at the end of every day?

Success on that level is a very minor success, rather like being centre-forward for Tranmere or Accrington Stanley, which I don't think exists any more. I think you can be a successful architect, but if you are *the* architect, like Sir Richard Rogers or Sir Norman Foster, then you have to be in gossip columns – they don't mind it at all.

I think that if you do aspire to an anonymous life, you're rather like Mr Pooter. Unfortunately, if you are a banker of note you become a Hambro or even a Lord Alexander of Weedon, the head of NatWest, and you cannot avoid the trappings of success which is making yourself known to the public because that then adds to your success. I think on a certain level there are successful people, but they're probably down the echelon a bit.

Do you think that people should have the right to be successful in a prominent way and yet stay out of the gossip columns? Do you feel that all of them are your prey, as it were, if they stick their heads above the parapet and start being really successful?

If you've got a PR, and most of them have, then you're making a statement that you are worthy of press attention. I don't know of anyone who has made money or who is a success not having a PR. Back in the 1950s and early 1960s my good friend, J. Paul Getty, who died in 1976, actually had a PR to keep him *out* of the newspapers – that doesn't happen any more. People now have PRs to get them into the newspapers. There are a lot of people who are enormously rich and powerful who do not excite the attention of journalists, and it is very easy not to do so – very simply do not, at any stage of your life, deal with journalists, do not deal with the media, do not seek publicity.

Looking at you personally, how much of your success as a gossip columnist is down to your background and your upbringing?

Well I don't have much of a background. I come from an Australian family and arrived in this country aged – my mother says it was six, I think it was five. I found this a very cold, chilly, class-oriented country even at that age. I went to a prep school in Devon where my headmaster just by chance happened to be the grandfather of Sophie Rhys-Jones, who is about to marry Prince Edward – or not as the case may be. I then went on to another boarding school in Dorset called Sherborne. None of that equips you to be a gossip columnist because I'm very much of the middle classes. Coming from far away and seeing a strange socially-divided country, I acquired an interest in what went on, and through that I acquired an interest in people. You cannot work for a newspaper unless you're interested in people and you certainly can't work on the gossip column unless you know who people are, what they do, where they fit. Obviously it's become less homogeneous, but up until the 1960s Britain was a homogeneous society, going back a thousand years. Now it's less so, in which case you cast your net further and wider, but at the end of the day a journalist carries with him as much as he can in terms of information, and how that information is acquired has nothing to do with background.

Apart from the knowledge, what other breaks or help did you have in rising to the position that you have achieved? Did you have a mentor, and was there an element of luck?

I would say that I just met a lot of people at the right time. I left school just before my 17th birthday.

You didn't go to university?

There was no point, although in our day people used to crawl round Sherborne and say they'd come from a certain college and a certain university and would you like to go there, and you said, 'No, thank you very much.' University was just an elongation of a rather unhappy education as far as I was concerned. I had already been in boarding school for ten years, and I didn't have any urge to go on for another two years at Sherborne and then further my education by another three. I felt that you had to get into the maelstrom of the world as fast as possible, and at exactly 17 I joined Lloyds of London, then I went into the Stock Exchange. During that year or two, in the late 1950s, I chanced to meet people in Lloyds – which is an insurance stock exchange and therefore, obviously, about money – who were of some use to me at a later date because I knew their faces, I knew who they were. Many of them are now heads of merchant banks, heads of colleges at Oxford and Cambridge, heads of this, heads of that and that was totally fortuitous. It wasn't planned, it just happened.

How did the move into journalism happen?

I decided I didn't want to stay in the City having spent a couple of years there and having learned as much as I wanted to learn, which was that it was a male-oriented society. Really it was very dreary, an extension of school, and so I was looking in *Queen* magazine in 1960 and there was a lengthy article with coloured pictures on PRs. These were the days when Jocelyn Stephens ran and owned *Queen*. I wrote to the five PRs mentioned and one wrote back. He was called the Earl of Kimberley and said, 'Would you like to come and see me?' So I went to see him in South Audley Street and he said, 'I've got a job but I can't pay you any money.' So I wrote to my father, who had retired and lived in Jersey, conserving what little money he had by being a tax exile, and he said that he'd give me £15 per week for a period of, I think, six months. So I went to join Kimberley who had various clients including Sam Bronston, who was the producer of such films as *King of Kings, El Cid, Fifty-five Days in Peking, The Fall of the Roman Empire* and was very big in the movie business. He also had Smirnoff. We launched Smirnoff vodka on an unsuspecting British public. He had various other clients as well and because of those clients, one met journalists and because Kimberley was who he was – apart from being a peer, he had been much married and I think he was getting married for either the fifth or the sixth time – journalists used to come knocking on our door, so I met various journalists and got to know them because they obviously wanted something from me. One of them, a man called Robin Essor, who was then running the William Hickey column at the *Daily Express* – he's now an editor on the *Daily Mail* – said, 'Why don't you come and join me because you could make a lot of money?'

Was money a driving factor?

Not really. Kimberley had decided to go into tax exile in Jamaica with his latest woman and so there was no job – I had nowhere to go. I knew Max Aitken because I used to sail down at Cowes quite a lot and I said to him, 'Do you mind if I go for an interview with your newspaper?' He said, 'No. I'm not going to help you but go ahead.' So I went for an interview and I got the job and in the autumn of 1963, I joined the *Express* on a full-time basis.

Did you have an enormous amount of confidence right from your younger days? Or were you, like some successful people, quite shy at first and the confidence grew in a bid to overcome shyness?

I'm still very shy. Part of this job is being able to go up to total strangers and ask them outrageous questions. Robin Essor said to me, 'I'm going to make you work six days a week but you'll get an extra fiver,' so I worked six days a week for £30. The first job he sent me out on – I was 20 or 21, I suppose – was to a gallery opening. There was a man there called Sir John Rothenstein, who was then head of the Tate Gallery I think, who'd brought along a very, very young girl called Marina Warner, and my photographer said, 'Come on, we'll just *have* to get this couple.' John Rothenstein was in his sixties or seventies and Marina was in her teenage days. I was in a room full of total strangers and I had to talk to them, which I hated doing. I had to ask her who she was, then I said, 'Have you got any famous relations?' She said that her grandfather was Sir Pelham Warner, the cricketer. I said, 'What does your father do?' and she says, 'He's totally anonymous, he runs a book shop in Cambridge, blah, blah, blah.' The next day the *Express* wrote a story about Sir John Rothenstein and Marina Warner and said who she was. Since then, of course, she's become very famous. She's married and divorced William Shawcross, she's written more books than I've ever read or can read, especially because they are very intellectual. That was my very first job, my very first interview, and it was hateful.

Did you think at that stage that this was going to be your eventual career, or did you see it as just another stage of a life that had seen several careers?

No. In the late 1950s there were very few careers. You were basically told you could either be a banker, an accountant, a stockbroker or even an insurance broker, and that was it. Advertising was very much frowned on in those days, people never went into advertising if they could help it, and people certainly didn't go into journalism because it was grubby, lower-middle class, for grammar school boys at best, and you were very, shall we say, regimented into doing something which required getting up in the morning, putting on a suit and going towards the City. So at every stage, whilst I was enjoying myself at the *Express*, I always assumed that I'd end up somewhere back in the City. Then Robin Essor resigned in, I think, July 1964 and I decided to go and live in New York, so I went to New York.

And when did you come back to run your own column?

Well, I got to New York and was having a tremendous time when I discovered there were two sides to having a green card. You had to go to the American Embassy in those days and get an immigration card and to be an immigrant you had to say, whether it was truthful or not, that you were going to live the rest of your life in America and God Bless America, blah, blah, blah, and the Consul, Eugene Coffey – who once worked on the *L.A. Times* – said to me, 'You're just the sort of person we want in America.' I could see why because the other people there were all bikers, who arrived at the Embassy in leathers. He went on, 'But I've got to warn you there's a thing called the Vietnam War that's hotting up a bit and we're basically going to induct anyone who's between a certain age and another age if they're single and in your case there's a problem, because you can't be an officer unless you're an American citizen.' I said, 'Well, I'll take my chances.' I never believed they'd call me up but after less than a year I was drafted. I was working then for John Mills who owned Les Ambassadeurs in London and he owned, or said he owned, El Morocco in New York – in fact it was owned by the Mafia, but I only discovered that at a later stage. So I said to him, 'Look, they want me to join the American army,' and he said, 'Under no circumstances!' and as he was something to do with TWA, he smuggled me out of America on a TWA plane, and I didn't go back for ten years.

And was it at that point that you developed your own column when you came back to Britain?

No, I came back having had a narrow escape from Da Nang and other places and got back onto the *Express*. The then editor of the William Hickey column was called Richard Behrens. I worked there for five years and I discovered at the end of those five years that I was doing pretty much 80 per cent of the work. There was a staff of perhaps eight people there and I thought that this was quite wrong. At that time the *Mail* was sinking fast and was about to merge with the *Sketch*. The *Sketch*'s editor was David English, who used to be my foreign editor at the *Daily Mail*. He decided to start a gossip column and employed Paul Callan who was an old friend of mine who used to run the *Londoners' Diary* which was part of the *Express* group. In August 1971, three months after the *Mail* had been grafted onto the *Sketch*, Callan and I joined the *Mail* and started a gossip column.

Do you enjoy it?

I think as far as the newspaper's concerned, I'm selling part of this great newspaper. When I started, my column used to be one page out of 28, now it's one out of 82 sometimes. All you're doing, all any journalist is doing, is making that newspaper more eminently saleable to the public.

What inherent qualities do you need to be a successful gossip columnist?

You've got to have an enormous knowledge of what's going on in the world, you've got to see when people are *passé*, you've got to see when people are rising, you've got to see what the aspirations of your readers are, you've got to be one of them. I think that it would be terribly difficult being a gossip columnist who was a) well bred, and b) well educated – in fact almost impossible. You've got to see instinctively, which is something you are born with, it's not something you learn, you've got to *see* what a story is. The great Dino de Laurentiis, who made a fortune from Italian films like *La Dolce Vita,* went off to America and took over a studio, and whenever he was shown one of his films he knew whether it was any good because his bum would start twitching, and that was his criterion for success. The same is true for a journalist – when you see a story, if your bum starts twitching you know it's a story, whether it's a front-page story or a sports story or whatever.

How much work goes into your news gathering? Typically, what would be your main lines of inquiry when you come into the office in the morning?

It's like a conveyor-belt with no end to it. If you get off the conveyor-belt, it's very difficult to get on again. Stories are just a running item. I spend a week being very active, I go out a lot – not necessarily to parties, in fact very seldom to parties – but I put myself around. I flew to Melbourne for three days to write a column because you've got to meet people, you've got to find people, you've got to keep expanding and increasing your stage.

And do you become friends with the people you're writing about?

I would say that 95 per cent of my friends are those I had prior to becoming a journalist. There are a few who have become friends through journalism, but basically they are in the media themselves, I mean advertising people, movie people, people like Andrew Lloyd Webber – who's a friend and would be a friend even if I wasn't a journalist. I think he'd be a friend even if he wasn't a composer.

One of the criticisms of gossip columns is that you often write about relatively obscure people, of whom the average reader has seldom heard, and probably couldn't care less about. How do you answer that kind of criticism?

It's totally untrue. People have got this fantasy that I write about the Royal family – I can't remember when I last wrote about the Royal family.

But they're well known. What about minor lords that don't matter to the average reader but perhaps are there just because they have a title?

We don't write about them. The *Express* used to – Lord Beaverbrook had a fantasy that everyone wanted to know about titled people so he could only envisage his column including people who were titled, and if they weren't titled then you had to make them titled – it was called 'standing them up'. We don't do that – the only peers we write about are peers who've got enormous affluence like the Duke of Westminster. We don't even write about the Earl of Lichfield. It's one of those jibes that people in *Private Eye*, who know no one, put out about gossip columns – that they write about obscure people.

What is social success? Is it totally dependent on wealth?

No, there's a famous story of the Duke of Marlborough and Sir Charles Clore. Charles Clore became enormously wealthy and took up sporting pastimes including shooting. He wanted to go to Blenheim, which has got a finer shoot than in his part of the world, and he was finally invited by the late Duke of Marlborough. Charles took along his loader, a director of Holland and Holland, a very fine gunsmiths, and at the end of the morning drive they went off to a lodge for lunch. Charles went up to Marlborough and said, 'Bert, I wonder if I could ask a favour? This loader, he's not really a loader he's a director of Holland and Holland.' Bert saw exactly what was going to happen and said, 'Really, Clore, you've had that man all morning teaching you how to shoot, now I suppose you want him to teach you how to eat!' Sadly, class in this country is still mired in the past, few people make it into the new areas. Money doesn't come into it.

Do people seeking social success often ring you up to try to plant stories about themselves, and how do you respond to that?

No. No one would ever dream of doing that because they know they'd be laughed at. There are PRs out there who occasionally want their clients put into the public press, but they want it in the City diaries. When I came into this business at the *Mail*, gossip columns were on their knees, they were finished, and it is only through my dedication, application and making my gossip column interesting and competitive that gossip columns have suddenly become the vogue again. This has spawned many imitations, the best being the City gossip columns – *The Times*, the *Telegraph*, the *Independent* have all got them and the Sunday papers as well. And of course there are now gossip columns for pop, for show business, for estate agents, and so on. There are gossip columns for every part of our life and at the end of the day if people want to get into those other areas they can – show business PRs are at it all the time – but people who want to get into the *Mail* diary or a diary which is on a decent newspaper are going to find it jolly difficult because they'd be laughed at.

Are there occasions when you would regard it as justifiable to intrude into privacy?

There's no such thing as privacy. I mean private people are private people, and if they're private they don't come into my sights. I'm only dealing with people who are very much involved with the public and who have in the past traded with journalists and who are known to journalists. The good thing about this country is that people have been brought up with gossip, they've been brought up with being written about, they're knowledgeable about it. It's only lately that people have turned against newspapers, people like Prince William who's convinced that newspapers or the media broke up his parents' marriage – he can't see that they were totally incompatible, but one day he will. As far as I'm concerned people can and do remain private. We don't intrude into privacy.

When you occasionally, as people do, get something wrong, how do you react to that? How do you react both inside yourself and professionally?

Getting it wrong is one thing, being unable to prove it is quite another, and this is the Richard Ingrams defence to libel. When it's getting it wrong in terms of being unable to prove it, you apologize, it's very simple.

And it doesn't concern you that the apology might be somewhat lower-profile than the actual accusation or original story?

As you quite rightly deduced earlier, a lot of our stories appear with the compliance of those involved, so it's very rare that we take on someone and get it wrong because we're taking on people with the full knowledge and proof. I think I've had one libel writ in the last two years.

How do you avoid falling prey to malicious information fed by people who are giving it to you simply to try to do someone else down?

We don't deal with malicious people. I know who's malicious, I can see it a mile off, and it's part and parcel of what comes with being a journalist – you can differentiate between truthful and untruthful stories. And also, all you've got to do is make one telephone call.. The *News of the World*, whose methods I don't approve of, now employ as many private detectives as they employ journalists, so if something's going on – and let's remember the *News of the World* tends to deal with *EastEnders* people and footballers – they send out their private detectives with cameras who come back with a dossier on people with their pants down, scarpering between one terraced house and another at odd hours, and that dossier is then given to a journalist, whose job it is then to go and confront the star of *Emmerdale* or *EastEnders* or Tottenham Hotspur and say, 'Look here, it's a fair cop.' I don't approve of that, but there are very few ways that you can't prove a story. Obviously Royal stories are fairly difficult, but they're now much easier than they were. There were stories in the past which you could never ever use about the Royals because you can't ring them up. You can't actually ring up the Queen and say, 'Look here ...'

How do you react to criticism?

I don't think anyone does criticize. The only people who do criticize gossip columns are those who are jealous of them and those who don't appear in them. Gossip columns are a force for good, not a force for evil. They also add to the gaiety of nations, as another great person once wrote, and at the end of the day they are an integral part of the newspaper inasmuch as they reflect yesterday's news and can look forward to tomorrow's. But best of all, if they get a story which is maybe six months or a year old they can write it, which you can't do on, say, page one, and gossip columns can actually refer back saying, 'This happened a year ago, and isn't it funny.'

What do you regard as your biggest failures and, more importantly, how did you recover from them?

Biggest failures? You're so protected in a newspaper that it's almost impossible to fail. In fact, it is impossible to fail because you've got colleagues, sub-editors, lawyers, editors, people around you, all of whom are giving you advice and saying, 'I wouldn't do that, don't do it.' I don't think I've ever written a story that I regret. Obviously if they're wrong you do regret them and you apologize and that's the end of it. It's like in life, if you hit the wrong person, you say, 'I'm terribly sorry,' and you get a smack back.

But if you were really down for one reason or another, how would you recover? If you've had a bad day, for example, how do you pick yourself up to sally into the fray again?

It's very difficult to have a bad day, but were you to have a disappointing day, the whole thing about journalism is that tomorrow, as Vivien Leigh said in *Gone with the Wind*, is another day. By 4.00 p.m. people are reading evening newspapers and you're preparing the next day's newspaper. There's always an onward factor. I write six columns a week and, therefore, one's got a perpetual aim, which is tomorrow's column.

Who are the people, big or small, past or present, whose success you admire, and why?

I admire Anita Roddick's success because she's done something which was almost impossible. She's actually enhanced the business she's in, she's probably a pain in the arse, she's married to a lovely man who's a tremendously good polo player – which I also admire because it's an esoteric sport – and she's made a local garage owner who invested a few thousand in her business so rich that he travels the world like the Flying Dutchman on his yacht. I admire Peter de Savary, a buccaneer who's done terrible things in his life – and he's the first to admit them – yet he bounces back. I think you've got to admire people who bounce back and just say, 'Damn it, I've lost £200 million, I'll go and make another £200 million.'

Do you think that people in public life ought to take any notice of what is written about them? A lot of them say that the only way they can survive and remain successful is by ignoring most, if not all, that is written about them.

I think everyone in the Royal family, if they were to take heed of everything that's written about them, would have killed themselves a long time ago. The *Sunday Mirror* invents Royal stories literally week by week. One week's invention was, 'Edward and Sophie to part' because they can't stand the heat. Nothing could be further from the truth. It's the same newspaper group which invented 'Princess Anne pregnant at 43'. They dream up Royal inventions. If I had a thousand pounds for every Royal story they'd made up I'd be a very rich man.

In pursuit of success for your column or yourself, have you ever been driven to do anything that you later wished you hadn't done?

I don't regard myself as successful. I only regard others as not having achieved what I've achieved.

But that is a definition of success.

Up to a point. I don't see myself as being out of the ordinary, I see myself as an excellent journalist and it just so happens that gossip occasionally excites and attracts other people to stare in on us and see what's going on.

But have you ever done anything that you later wished you hadn't done?

No, I've never employed any sneaky devices. I've never put bugs under beds, I've never taken infra-red photographs. All of our stories are gained fairly and squarely and it's part of the great game that we're all taught about in this country.

Given your caveats about whether you are successful or not, is there a downside to success?

I think your privacy tends to go, i.e. your public life becomes much more open to inspection. There was this poor man who spent all of his life getting to the head of some building society and then it was discovered he was having his lawn mown by the building society's gardener, and from then on his life was made a misery because round his surburban house in Tonbridge were the world's press. That is bad. But against that, at least he should have been aware that if you seek success, then what comes with it is the fact that you are known to the press. Therefore they will make you known to the public, and they won't stop when the bad times arrive.

What advice would you give to successful people for dealing with criticism from whatever source it comes or whatever kind it might be?

The first advice is to lead a blameless life, but if you can't lead a blameless life, get your story in first.

Success in others arouses conflicting emotions ranging from admiration to envy. Why should people react in such different ways to other people's success?

The British have always done so. The British don't like people to be successful. I think now the lottery's come it's changing slightly, because everyone's doing it and if you win money on it then you're just someone who has won money on the lottery, but if you make money like Lord King did at Babcock and then become head of British Airways, you don't tend to get plaudits from others, because they think there's something slimy, something wrong, they think there's been chicanery in the past. The British people are envy merchants, I'm afraid. They don't enjoy people having money.

What do you think are the greatest enemies of success?

Flaunting it. You can flaunt it if you live abroad but you can't flaunt it if you live in England. By flaunting it I don't mean going to expensive restaurants – that is not seen by the masses – but driving around in posh cars. I don't think you can really be flash. Buying a football team, for instance, is not seen as a good thing. Alan Sugar, the poor old Amstrad man who bought Tottenham Hotspur, had his whole life ruined by it as far as I can see. He'd be better off selling dishes off the back of his car in Whitechapel Market.

But are there any inner qualities in terms of attitude that are generally enemies of success?

I think that if you're successful in this country you want to keep damn quiet about it. You want to buy a house with a high wall, and then you can live a very good life within your private fiefdom. Once you buy a house in, say, the High Street of a dinky little Cotswold village in Gloucestershire, you are suddenly open to people throwing things through the window, etc. The attitude to success in this country is two-fold. First of all, people would like it to be them, but because of the impossibly bad education here, they know it can never be. There are people out there who are barely literate, who are innumerate, and they can see other people being successful but they know they never can be, whereas in America, from the day you start shining shoes, there's always the thought that maybe you can be a success.

Do you think it's terribly sad that we should have that attitude in Britain, and does it mitigate against our country ever having real long-term success?

I think that despite everything people will get through – like Alan Sugar, there will be those who will profit and who will get through to the top. Having said that, no one's going to make the sort of money they made in the Margaret Thatcher years ever again. We are now in a decline.

But doesn't the fact that you still have the odd person coming through prove that some people from some quite poor backgrounds can actually make it in the kind of society we have in Britain today?

I never said you can't make it, I'm just saying that the opportunities are getting less. And also that when they do get through, by some quirk of fate, then they are reviled by those from the background they've come from. They're not appreciated. Alan Parker's a tremendous movie-maker, who's just done *Evita* with Madonna. If he went back to Islington where he was brought up, he'd be jeered at and booed instead of applauded – it's pathetic and sad.

Do you think success brings obligations in its wake?

Everyone that I know who's made a lot of money immediately gets a charitable foundation like Sir Donald Gosling of National Car Parks. I think you've got to give a lot of money away, and the sadness about Britain is that so many things that should come from the government depend on charity. You've only got to see the begging letters that I, in my small way, get to realize how much and how many people depend on charity, when they should be getting it from government-sponsored agencies.

Has success changed you at all?

I still do exactly what I always used to do. I work harder than I ever worked. I find that today, to stand still you've got to work harder than you ever envisaged. I never thought that at the age of 55 I'd be working six days a week, eight, nine, ten, even 15 hours a day, which I am.

What is it that drives you on? Presumably you could retire if you wanted to?

I don't think I could retire because I'd be bored.

What is the greatest pleasure you've had from having a successful career?

I think being able to drive around in my own car and park outside the office. It's as simple as that. When I started off I used to have to take a tube at 6.00 in the morning to the City and on the way back I used to fall asleep so often that I used to end up in Hendon, which is the wrong end of the Northern Line. I find now that I can at least manage my own life in my own interests and, for example, go and watch my own horse win a very good race at Sandown and be able to write about it in the column.

Two final questions, if you could gather together before you in one room all the young people who want to be gossip columnists, who want to run their own columns, what advice would you give them?

I don't believe there are people who want to become gossip columnists or even journalists. I think they want to have what journalists have. There are many people in this country wanting things without being able to achieve them. They want money, cars, big houses, they want this, they want that, but they don't know how to go from A to Z. People want to be journalists or they want to be on the telly, they want to be one of those named children's presenters on BBC or ITV, but they don't know how to get there. Now it's no good going to media classes and all the rest of it, it doesn't get you a step further. I think that, like me, if you have got this innate ability to be a journalist it will come to the fore whatever you do, but at the same time you've got to have some sort of education. It's no good coming from a background where you've got no education and expecting to be given a job in journalism. There are people who apply here aged 19 or 20 who can barely read or write, and in that you find great sadness.

But what if someone is clear about that route, has had a burning ambition from quite an early age to be a gossip columnist – what advice would you give them, assuming they have all the levels of literacy, enthusiasm, energy and determination that is required?

Give me a call. There are people who have burning ambition and who make it. Gaby Roslin is one such person. You can see several examples. Paula Yates is another. I first met her when she was 15, she was brought to lunch by her mother, Helene Bosman. Paula always had the urge to make it and, in her terms, she has. There was never in my mind, or her mind, any doubt that she wouldn't make it. You can spot these kids but you also see kids who think that making it is getting to the top without putting in any of the spade work. People don't realize that I've been at it since the age of 16 and I'm now 55. I've had a National Insurance card and I've worked every day of my life since I left school.

As you survey the social scene – all the people you've reported on with their weaknesses, their foibles, their great triumphs, all their ups and downs – are there any general criteria that you could apply to successful people?

Yes, first of all diligence, secondly application, perhaps the same thing, and thirdly a fantastic ability, at dark times or when they could be enjoying themselves, to work hard. I think everyone who puts in 18 hours a day, seven days a week is eventually going to triumph one way or the other, whether it's in a minor or a major way. There's no get out in this world, if you don't put in the work you don't get anything out of it.

Do you think that a degree of sacrifice as far as family and personal life are concerned is part and parcel of being a successful person?

Enormously so. You can't marry at the age of 18 and still expect to be married at 40. It doesn't happen. It's better to get your work done and then marry – perhaps even a trophy wife. I don't mind trophy wives, I see them all the time.

When your time comes to leave this life what would you like people to say about you?

That he did his best. I just hope that what one puts down about people every day informs and amuses. That is as much as one can hope to do.

DAME JUDI DENCH

'You are only as good as your last performance. Success in acting is very ephemeral – it can't be judged as clearly as in other professions.' That is the view of Judi Dench, one of the giants of the British theatre, following firmly in the footsteps of her great heroes, John Gielgud and Peggy Ashcroft. But the judgments of others on her four decades in the profession are more certain: 'No other actor of her generation is able to appear so spontaneous on stage ... she alternates between success and triumph.' In demand too for television comedy and films, she nevertheless insists, 'I always get frightened about not being in work, wondering what will be next. Fear is food to me. I'd hate to think I knew it all. I'd hate to get to the point where I think I know how to play a part.' She would not advise reading all the reviews – something she used to do as a student 'and then go and have a good cry!' Certainly in her early days she had her fair share of cruelty to overcome. A director advised her, 'You can't call yourself Dench – a name like that won't do!' At an audition, a producer commented, 'You have every single thing wrong with your face.' And one notorious review of her first big role – as Ophelia at the Old Vic at the age of 22 – said, 'She stepped out into the limelight, tripped over her advance publicity, and fell flat on her pretty face.'

It was all part of the theatrical shaping of this devout Quaker with a sense of fun who, despite her fears, has never stopped working. Drama was in her blood. Her father, a Yorkshire doctor, and her Irish mother were both 'keen amateurs'. She trained as a stage designer, convinced herself she 'didn't have the imagination' for that, and was persuaded by her brother to study acting at the Central School of Speech and Drama. She remembers being 'a bit half-hearted about it' until, after two terms, praise for a mime she was called upon to do changed her life. 'I suddenly started to realise what I wanted to do and why.' Now she has embraced virtually all the great roles including, most controversially, a brilliant Cleopatra at the age of 52. More recently, she wowed London's West End with her performance in Stephen Sondheim's A Little Night Music, delighted millions in the TV comedy series As Time Goes By, and revels in becoming the first female 'M' in the Bond films. Her portrayal of Queen Victoria in Mrs Brown won her (not for the first time) a BAFTA Best Actress Award – and an Oscar nomination. Her advice to today's young thespians is: 'Do as much as you can in all media, watch people – how they use their craft, and don't talk about it, just do it.'

Dame Judi, what is your definition of success?

It's a very ephemeral thing, success. You are only as successful, I believe, as the last thing you have done. People's memories are very, very short, and I don't think you can say that a person is successful all through their life. They do some things that are more successful than others. Even if you get wonderful notices for doing a play, it doesn't necessarily mean everybody sees you as a success. Success is a very ephemeral word for actors.

Despite the cumulative effect of all the successes you have had, you still regard your success as based on how good you are in your latest production?

Yes, I do. Whether you are going to be in work depends on whether people want to come and see you. I always get frightened about not being in work, what will be next. But then I have always felt that way so maybe there's something in me that has to have that fear.

Do you think that fear might be an important factor in your success, that everybody has a kind of hesitancy about what they do, fear being partly a product of that, which is a factor in driving them on?

Yes, I am sure that fear is food to me. I just know that the more I do, the longer I go on in the profession, and I have been in it 40 years now, the more doubtful I get about myself and the more unconfident I get. But I suspect that's something that I need, a part of me. I'd hate to think I knew it all; I'd hate to get to the point where I think, I know how to play that part. I've never done that, and I don't expect it is ever going to happen.

But a lot of people would say, there is no reason for you to become less and less confident, because the more experience you have, the more you know about how to be successful.

And the more people expect of you, and the more is the shortfall.

So is your judgment of success inside yourself or is it what the critics, what other people, what the audience say about you, or is it a bit of both?

I don't think it's inside me, because I have never applied success to anything that I have done. Some productions have been more successful than others, some parts have been more successful than others. And I don't think that you can judge success on whether the critics will like it; you can only ultimately judge success at the end of each performance, whether you feel that the audience had been told the proper story that night. Then you can come home and say, 'Gosh, it was a really good night tonight.' But then the next night you do it, you come home and you think, 'The whole thing was a disaster, none of it worked.' Success is not at all an ongoing thing in my vocabulary.

What do you think are the qualities you need for acting success?

You need energy; it's no good being tired all the time, absolutely no room for that. You need a tremendously heightened sense of observation and a photographic mind, like a book of photos. And you have to be resilient and not be depressed or downhearted when the tricky and the ghastly things happen, because you have got to go on and do the work. It's no good being too affected by one bad notice. You have to go on and you have to have a belief in your director, the belief that what you're doing is as truthful as you can make it.

Can you learn all those attributes or qualities, or are they instinctive?

You can learn them, and you must never think that you know it all. I have never done a part, ever, where it hasn't thrown up some kind of problem that I hadn't thought about, where I haven't thought, 'Crikey, how am I going to do this?' When I was first at the Vic, I used to stand at the side of the stage and watch everything every single night. I think you can never can stop learning about the business, because actors are so varied in their ways of working. When I became a director, I suddenly learned a lot more, especially about actors' attitudes towards directors. I must have been terrible to direct, but I am better now because I have more sympathy for the director. There are many things you can teach yourself, but you can't teach yourself to have energy. If you are at all lethargic and get tired easily, don't even think about acting. But some things are instinctive. I mean I only ever wanted to be a designer. I trained as a designer and then quite suddenly, quite dramatically, I thought, 'I don't think I can be a designer.' And I changed, seemingly overnight. I went to Stratford, when I was at school, and saw *Lear*. There was this extraordinary and wonderful set just like a huge rough saucer on the stage, and the middle of it was a cave and a throne and everything just turned around. I was only used to the curtain going up, the curtain going down and then a change of scene. I was really terribly simple-minded and I thought, 'Oh, this is the kind of theatre I believe in,' but then I thought, 'I don't have the imagination to think that way.' I am better at it now, I have learned from working with a lot of wonderful designers.

But despite that, you still went on to pursue a career in design until there was one particular point where you said, 'Right, I'm switching out of that and I am going to be an actress.' When was that point?

I can't remember when it was, but I suspect it was to do with the fact that my brother Geoffrey had only ever wanted to be an actor and went to the Central School. He kept telling me all the things that they were doing, and it was probably something that he said that made me think, 'Maybe I will have a go and see whether I can get into the Central.'

Was it a risk for you at the time?

I don't remember feeling it was risky but I do remember being a bit half-hearted about it. I just thought I'd have a try. I didn't think, 'Oh, I am going to be an actress.' I didn't think that at all. I thought, 'I will just see how I get on.' Even when I got in I wasn't your typically keen drama student. It wasn't until the end of my first or second term when Walter Howard, who was the head of productions there, suddenly gave me the most incredible notice for doing a mime. We'd been warned that we were going to be asked to do a mime but it had completely gone out of my head. That shows you how lax I was. Suddenly one morning, we all sat down for a lecture and he said, 'OK, it's the day of the mime.' I had to do something completely off the top of my head and I got this incredible notice saying, 'It was so spare and so economical and ...' Well, it changed my life.

What do you regard as your greatest successes?

I have no idea. I really don't know. There are certain parts that I have done that I feel prouder of than others. I feel very proud of the fact that I played Juno in *Juno and the Paycock* with an all-Irish cast. I can't say that I am totally un-Irish as my mother came from Dublin and my father was brought up there, but it was a terrific experience for me to do that play with a really Irish cast. I learned an enormous amount from it and adored doing it. At the same time I was doing *A Fine Romance* for television with Michael, which was quite hard work.

I was pleased that I got away with Cleopatra, because everybody had expressed their surprise. They laughed in my face about the fact that I was going to play it at the age of 52. As I said to Peter Hall, 'I am a menopausal dwarf. You don't want this playing Cleopatra, do you?' People were very openly scornful. I felt that I climbed a big mountain with that part and absolutely loved playing it.

So there are lots of things that I have liked doing for different reasons. It wasn't just a question of whether they were successful. *Juno* and *Antony* were acclaimed not just by the critics but by people who came to see them. But when I did *Romeo and Juliet* for Zeffirelli I got completely panned. Nevertheless I loved doing it and learned a huge amount. I was very young at the time.

One of the critics once said your professional career alternates between success and triumph. Have you ever known what you consider to be real failure?

Oh yes, I certainly have. That *Romeo and Juliet* for Zeffirelli. Out of all the reviews, I got only two good notices; they completely disregarded me in one paper, never mentioned me. It was very difficult, but what was wonderful was that I had a whole year at the Vic and longer, in order to get better at it. And in the first part I ever played, Ophelia at the Vic, I was heavily criticized, and so was the Vic, for having taken on a virtual schoolgirl, straight from the Central to play Ophelia. I think a couple of critics gave me a good notice, but the rest were very scornful.

There was another review which said, 'She stepped out into the limelight, tripped over her advance publicity and fell flat on her pretty face.' Now you were just starting off in your career – how did you react to that? How did you gird your loins to enter the fray again after that review?

Because of Michael Bentall, because of John Neville and because of the people around me. They said, 'Don't read that, read this.' And there were a couple of very nice notices. So I looked hard at those. I was walking on at the time, too, in other plays. I was playing the first fairy in the *Dream*, I was walking on in the *Henry VIs*, and I was playing Juliet in *Measure for Measure*. So I had a very full rehearsal period which helped to get me over it. It was worse at the end of the year, the end of my first season at the Vic, when we were all going to America. Michael Bentall called me in and said, 'You're not going to play Ophelia any more.' That was terribly hard. He said, 'Do you still want to go?' and I said, 'Of course,' and I went playing Maria in *Twelfth Night* and the Princess of France in *Henry V*. After six months in America, we were invited to Yugoslavia with *Hamlet*, and Barbara Jefford, who had taken over as Ophelia, had to go to the Vic, so Michael said, 'Now you have had six months away from it, you've had a lot of experience, you've played to lots of audiences, I'm going to give you this part back for Yugoslavia. And it was the most incredible two weeks in Yugoslavia; they just went absolutely mad. It was worth waiting for and worth gulping back the tears and getting on with it.

Were you tempted at the time to say, 'You are not giving me the part in America, so to hell with you, I am not going to America'?

Oh no. Maria in *Twelfth Night* was a wonderful part and I also enjoyed playing the Princess of France; anyway I wanted to go with all my mates. It paid off because then I went back and did more seasons and eventually Juliet, and Cecily in *The Importance of Being Earnest* - wonderful parts all the time.

Why do you think you have been thrown this chain of terrific parts right through your career?

This is not fake modesty, but I think that a lot of it is that you're in the eye. If you're employed or around, people see you and you become the 'in' thing. So a lot of it is luck. Luck plays an enormous part. I am not good at choosing parts. I am hopeless at saying what I want to do, so I have to wait for somebody to say to me, 'You know, here's a terrific part.' Another complication is that I won't read anything. I don't know why. I just don't want to read a part, I like somebody to tell me the story. On one occasion Howard Davis asked me to play Mother Courage. He said, 'I will come round and tell you the story.' After he had finished, I said, 'Oh, that sounds rather good.' When it came to the first day of work, I was furious with him because what he had omitted to say was that she is in every scene and never gets to sit down for a single minute! So now I am a little more careful; not always, but I will sometimes read a part.

Is it tough to stay at the top?

If you think of it as the top I think it would be impossible, but I like the expression 'jobbing actor'. It is somebody who keeps in work, and that is all I really want to do. I want to keep in work, I want to keep up the best standard I can, I want to learn more and I want, if possible, to have the biggest challenges given to me. I want to be asked to bail out the sea with a thimble, or a sieve; I love those kind of jobs and I love doing something that's really really different. That's why I love doing the situation comedy, *As Time Goes By,* with Geoffrey Palmer and the others and then going to the National at night to do *A Little Night Music,* and then doing the Bond film. I don't know whether that's staying at the top. It's keeping in work, and that I do like.

Are there any really big challenges left? Is there anything you want to do that you have not yet been offered in the acting profession?

I don't know; I have no idea what I ought to do. I just hope that there are parts for me. I remember reading not long ago, 'What is Maggie Smith going to do in *Juliet*: the wheelchair part?' I thought, 'Christ, not wheelchair parts yet.' I just hope that people go on writing good plays. I am going to do a new David Hare play this season at the National. I hope people are going to write parts for people who are getting much older. I am going to start playing grandmothers now.

You've collected many awards in the course of your career. Do you regard them as benchmarks or are they ships that pass in the night?

They are ships that pass in the night. They are there in your home and you think it was wonderful getting that recognition for doing something that people enjoyed. And then it's on to next thing.

Going right back to your early days, to what extent is your choice of career and your success in it a product of your background and your upbringing?

I don't know. I think my attitude towards a lot of things is driven by the fact that I am a Quaker.

And you became a Quaker at quite an early age.

Yes, after I had gone to boarding school. I chose to go to this boarding school, and I feel that perhaps it wasn't really by accident, although at the time it was only because I liked the uniform. Being a Quaker suits me well. Michael and I both come from very close families and I think there is no substitute for that.

How important do you think religion has been in your success?

I don't know about religion as regards success, but I know how central it is to my attitude to things and to being in a company of people. It's there subconsciously and it's an incredible strength to me.

What are the qualities, the characteristics that it brings to you in your life?

I think you have to ask somebody else that. I am not sure, it's just something I can't do without.

You once said, 'Even if you take the most difficult path, it is the right one.' What did you mean by that?

I think the things that happen to you are inevitable and everything is a learning process. However hard the knock or however hard the path is that you have to follow, there is ultimately some good, something you have to learn through it. I remember my father saying to me, 'You will find that you will want certain things to happen for you. Don't be surprised if something totally different happens, maybe that's the way it should be.'

You have also said that you are a team player, you would never do a one-woman show. Why do you feel so strongly about that?

Because I wouldn't know how to get ready. I know there's an audience out there, but I have to get ready with the team. I like to see other people getting ready for the same show; it's something to do with all of us presenting this one thing, this kind of present, to the audience. I would find it very, very difficult to do this on my own. I have been asked to do so on many occasions and they've said, 'Oh, but somebody can be in your dressing room while you are getting made up.' It's not the same. There's something too solitary about it for me.

Is there any reason why you have always retained a central part of your life within the subsidized theatre?

That's where you get to play lots of very good parts, and not the same part every night. It is very nice to be able to play two or three plays all at the same time and not every night - you might do a matinee of one thing and an evening of the other. We used to do that at Stratford. It's very exciting and it's terribly beneficial to the actor. Sustaining a performance, night after night, in the same role, is very difficult.

Do you think that you are a better actor or actress if you have known sacrifice and failure along the way?

I think you are a better actor or actress whatever you have experienced. The more you have observed, the more you have gone through, the more you know about knotting wigs, the more you know about the business of designing, the more you know about stage management, the better actor or actress you will be.

Who are your heroes?

I have just recently seen quite a lot that Alec Guinness has done, his is an extraordinary career, and there's Dame Peg, and others who are not necessarily very well known. I watched *Rebecca* not long ago, and I saw Millie Fox who I have known since she was a little girl. I thought she gave the most exquisite performance, beautifully judged. She got very criticized for it, but I thought it was wonderful. And Derek Thompson, who's in *Casualty*, is such a good actor. I have never met him but I saw him on television in *The Price*, where he was an IRA man; I thought he was a Northern Irish actor. That's always happening to me; you go and see a performance that just takes your breath away. So it's an ongoing thing. But there are no giants up there that you look up to. Well, maybe there are, but I am in my sixties now, my giants are getting very, very old. Sir John Gielgud, of course, is around still.

What do you say to young people entering the acting profession now? What advice would you give them?

It's very difficult now because the work isn't around, but I would say, 'Do as much as you can in all media.' I was very lucky in that I went to a huge company where I was surrounded by the most wonderful actors and I stayed there from 1957 to 1961 and I watched all that was going on around me. It's so important to watch people, how they use their craft. Nowadays a lot of young actors want to make a big name for themselves in films, so they might do a bit of television and they do a bit of film. But when it comes to projecting in a theatre, they don't know how to do that. It is sad, but without the reps where do you go to train? I don't know. You need to get as much experience in everything as you can, and watch everybody. Even watch somebody whom you think can't do it, and make up your mind why you think they can't do it. That teaches you something. Everything teaches you something.

What do you think are the greatest enemies of success in the acting profession?

Believing you are one, I would imagine. I think that's a disaster. If you believe you're a success, crikey, I should think it will come up and get you by the ... tail!

Are there any other unsavoury qualities that actors and actresses should avoid?

Yes, talking about it! You shouldn't talk about it. It's the kiss of death. You hear actors talking about acting and the theatre and it's a big switch-off. Just do it.

Have you ever felt like giving up?

Yes. I wanted to give up when my daughter was born. I would have given up and just been a housewife and painted and done things at home. But Michael said, 'No don't do that.' He said, 'It would be awful, you wouldn't like it.' And I suspect, in a way, he's right. But now it's lovely having a young daughter who's an actress.

What is your view of those people who judge whether an actor or actress has been successful? Do you generally like and respect the critics or do you think that they are an unnecessary hindrance, that they are part of the fabric of society but in fact they don't actually help the acting profession as much as they should?

Someone said, 'Critics, they are like eunuchs.' They watch it being done but they can't do it themselves. I respect some critics, but you always know anyway if there is something wrong with your performance. While there are critics whom I admire and trust, I trust my director more, and my other actors, and the play. I trust that most. And my audience. And my own instinct. I never understand the role of television critics because they usually write a notice after something's gone out. People have made up their own minds by then. In theatre work, if you make the critics your benchmark you can run into a lot of trouble, because notices are so split. You know in yourself and your director knows how the performance has worked, and you just go on getting it better.

So is it best to ignore the critics?

I read them in the two papers I get but I won't go out of my way, as I used to as a student, to buy them all and read them all and then go and have a good cry.

If you weren't as tough as that, as resilient as that, if you were a young actor or actress getting these notices pasting you to the wall as it were, what advice would you give to help them ride through that?

I would say, 'Look into yourself, talk to your director, really re-examine yourself.' But if you're so affected by them that you can't go on, don't read them. Just do the job and work at getting it better.

If you are successful, is there a downside to it? Are there disadvantages built into your success?

Well, I suppose that if people regard you as a success, and you don't fulfil their expectations of you, I should think that's a downside of success. But I do think that success is how other people regard you.

The moment I think, 'Oh, this is it, I've made it,' the man with the bucket of ice-cold water will come and dash it in my face, because that's what's always happened. I don't like to think about it. I don't like to think ahead, except that I hope I get another job.

What is the greatest pleasure you have had from your successful career?

The people I have met. The opportunities to meet people, and the friends I have made. When we had a very bad fire that destroyed the top two storeys of our house in Hampstead, Michael and I, and Finty, were completely snowed under with letters and gifts from friends and from a lot of people we didn't know. It was a very difficult time for us and it was everyone's support that got us through it. So much so that I have kept absolutely everything that was sent to us, every letter, because I thought, I may not read them again, but I am going to look at that box and remember.

Some people think that if you are successful, that inevitably means a degree of sacrifice as far as your personal and family life is concerned. Is that true in the acting profession?

Well, success has a lot to do with ambition, and I don't really have any ambition. I just want to go on doing the job and doing it as well as I can and learning as much as I can.

Isn't that ambition in itself?

I suppose it is, but I have never, for instance, wanted to be a huge film star in Hollywood. I have always turned down the opportunity to go to America. I was there for six months with the Vic and I haven't been back since 1959. If you really want to be a big name in Hollywood I can see that some things might have to go by the board. You may have to decide very early on what is more important, a family life or your career. For us, because of our close family background, the most important thing is family; career comes second.

And yet on the stage the show must go on, so in a sense can an actor or actress ever put their family before their professional life?

When our daughter was little I didn't do any television. When she was having a bath and going to bed I went to the theatre. When she got to an age when she went to school, then I started doing television and didn't go to the theatre, so that I was there at the end of the day. I did that as much as I could. In actual fact all the time she was growing up there was only one occasion when Michael and I were away from her both together, and on that occasion she flew out to Bangkok to be with me. I would always discuss it with the family before I made a move on a job.

So if there was an element of sacrifice involved you would get their approval for that?

Or we would somehow work it that we didn't have to make that sacrifice.

When your time comes to leave this life, what would you like people to say about you?

That I had a good sense of humour. Just that.

NOEL EDMONDS

'In career terms, the secret of success should remain a secret. I'm always baffled by people who let their own "Coca-Cola recipe" out into the open.' But this presenter, whose programmes have long commanded slices of peak-time television, comes pretty close to that, revealing the frustrations, the rejections, the luck, the friends, the foresight, the career-threatening setbacks, the moves and the deals that marked his route to the top. Born in Ilford, he made his first public appearance at the age of 9, reciting 'The Postman Cometh' in a junior talent contest at Weymouth Pavilion; and, as a teenager, went on to build a makeshift studio in his own bedroom, recording his own programmes and optimistically sending the tapes off to radio stations. His

upbringing was modest, rich in love and support, and 'education-packed', with his father a head-teacher, and uncles and aunts in the profession as well. 'To fail in exams would have been to let my parents down.' He was not happy at his public school, but left with 10 O-levels and 3 A-levels. He turned down a place at Surrey University when offered a £300 a year job at the pop station Radio Luxembourg; but the controller didn't like him 'laughing when he read the news', and he left before he could be sacked.

His career through BBC Radios One and Two began as a teaboy and rocketed to DJ superstar status. But he'd always made it clear that he was 'not a music jock, but more interested in the communication power of the medium', and television beckoned. Initially he found the transition difficult, but his audience-pulling power was such that the BBC were prepared to listen to his new ideas, and allow him to share control of them. He explains here how, as a presenter/businessman, he came to negotiate a partnership with the BBC for his House Party *and* Telly Addicts *shows, working with their overseas sales team to exploit them around the world. He analyses why* House Party *has been so successful, and talks about the day an earlier show was taken off the air, and he faced what he thought at the time was the end of his career. A key part of being a successful presenter, he says, is that you always have 'other strings to your bow'. He offers advice to young hopefuls on how to fill the gap: 'Work hard, be true to your own principles … if you start thinking you're successful, you're probably on the way down rather than the way up.'*

Noel Edmonds, what is your definition of success?

I don't think I have got a concise definition of success because you feel successful in different ways on different occasions. For example, family happiness, an achievement which is terribly minor, learning to fly and getting your pilot's licence (which is something that is only relevant to yourself because it is a very lonely thing to try and achieve), or maybe staying on a horse slightly longer than your six-year-old daughter. Success for me is not about material possessions, it is not about acquisition of wealth, I think it is about a balanced outlook on life.

But can you only say that because you happen to have considerable wealth?

In career terms I think the answer to your question is that success, and the secret of success, should remain a secret. I am always baffled by people who let their personal 'Coca-Cola recipe' out into the open. I think your own success is something that should be analysed by others and defined by others. If you start to consider yourself successful, then you're probably on the way down rather than on the way up. From my point of view there have been certain milestones in my life where I have thought, 'Oh yes, maybe I am successful,' but there is no one element to success, there is a mixture of things, such as knowing your weaknesses, perhaps even recognizing your weaknesses more than your strengths. If you liken it to the Himalayas, someone is going to invent an even higher Everest by the time you get to the summit, so I don't think you ever fully achieve success.

Tell me about your background.

I was the only child of two educationalists, and had aunts and uncles who were teachers as well. I grew up in an education-packed environment. It was a very modest upbringing, but rich in love and support. The result was that I always felt I had to achieve things, not just for myself but for my parents. Therefore I got all my exam results at school. Failure would have been a disaster, because I would have felt that I had let my parents down. My education took me right through to the very brink of university, and I think I would have gone if my father had stood up and said to me, 'I have not worked this hard, I haven't backed you this much to have you turn down university.' If he had said that, I would have gone simply to please him.

But he didn't say that?

No, he was quite remarkable about it, bearing in mind that in the 1930s, when he could have started a career as a barrister, there wasn't a grant scheme and his parents didn't have the resources, so he had to turn down university. And, although he had a very successful life as a secondary school headmaster, and did many things outside of school, including publishing books, I think deep-down inside he resented missing that first, very important launch pad. In the 1930s, going to university was a very important thing to achieve, so to have your only son turn round at the door of university and say, 'I'd rather go and be a disc jockey,' required some guts on his part.

But you were giving up one potential launch pad, a launch pad recognized by parents throughout the world, for what you saw as another kind of launch pad?

Oh yes, I never doubted that radio offered me the chance to capitalize upon what meagre talents I had.

Did you ever think, 'I am really blowing it by not going to university'? Did you ever have doubts about that decision?

No, I didn't have doubts at the time. I was 18 years old, you are arrogant, you know everything then, don't you. And the optimism shone through – it was probably my first major blinding flash of uncontrollable optimism – and away I went with my father's words of encouragement ringing in my ears, 'If you want to do well in radio, make sure that you're the best.' I went into a dream environment as a newsreader with Radio Luxembourg. That was my university.

It is unusual to have a career plan set in concrete at an early stage.

Yes, I have often wondered what it was that motivated me when I was a teenager. It's very easy to paint a picture of a slightly lonely young chap in his teens. I went to a public school with a thousand boys. I was medium at everything – I got into the football team when someone got run over by the school bus. I did not excel on the playing fields of England, and all my O-level and A-level passes were pretty much down the middle. I went to a six-days-a-week public school, and I wasn't happy there, I didn't particularly enjoy it. I didn't live very near to the school, so there were very few other people going through the same purgatory as I was. There wasn't much to do on a Sunday, other than swot or muck about with go-karts and things like that. So, when radio came along in the form of pirate radio ships, it had the same significance to me as the arrival of The Beatles to anyone who could play a guitar.

And you had already had some kind of rehearsal for that in your bedroom?

Well, it is back to painting a picture of a very lonely person, who used to make up programme tapes, and I don't like to go into this too much because it makes me worry about myself. There I was making up programmes, spinning the discs and trying to play around with jingles, and then I came across this fantastic guy on Radio London who was doing it on a ship and doing it to millions of people – that was Kenny Everett – and whilst I was playing around with tapes I found him a massive inspiration.

Was he a role model, a sort of hero?

Yes, because he was the first person that I'd come across on radio who was producing material that was clearly far more interesting and significant than the records themselves. I liked his anarchic style. I was fortunate that I finally came up with a tape that one day found its way to Radio Luxembourg and I got my first job.

The principle of there being a kind of radio that is more important than the records themselves is criticized in some quarters. How do you react to that?

It's never bothered me because it's how you present your product. I made it very clear to the audience in my days at Radio One that I wasn't a music jock, you know, I wasn't a Bob Harris, a John Peel, even to a certain extent an Alan Freeman, someone who had made their radio career involving the music and knowledge of the product. I have always been more interested in the communication power of radio and, now, television. That was the thing that sparked me off as a teenager. Yes, sure, I thought it must be quite nice to be famous, it might help you with the girls a bit, because I was quite a shy sort of person, and it's quite a good way of breaking into a conversation if they know more about you than you do about them. But it wasn't a fame-driven thing. It was the opportunity to really get into what I now understand to be the art of broadcasting.

I remember seeing a picture of Radio Caroline, the studios, and being completely aghast when I realized that an engineer sat there on the other side of the glass while you were doing your thing, because I was used to doing it all by myself in the bedroom. The idea of performance as something distinct from what I saw as a communication thing that tried to stimulate the audience just filled me with horror. And, although I've learned to master certain fears in that area, I am still terribly reluctant to be described as or put into the role of a performer.

What was your first audience in your bedroom?

I used to just play them to myself, although I had quite a few mates who were also into radio. The enthusiasm to play around with the tapes spilled over into hospital radio. It was still an embryonic thing in the hospitals of Essex in those days, but generally speaking I just used to muck about and fine-tune things, make up new gags and try them out on friends and relatives. My dad would go, 'Yes, I suppose that's funny.' I did not have a lot of encouragement in those early days, but despite that, I had this incredible will to send tapes to radio stations all round the world. I used to write to the BBC and they would send me little bits of paper about how to be a cameraman or how to be a producer, absolutely anything other than how to get on in front of the microphone. So that was all a bit frustrating, but I got the big break in the end.

Was there any luck involved in the big break?

It was an incredible set of circumstances. I was committed to what I wanted to do. I had no doubt in my mind that radio was where I wanted to be, but I just didn't have any way of achieving it. There were no such things as commercial radio stations. We just had the BBC Light Programme – which in 1967 was just about to turn into Radio One – but there was only Brian Matthew's *Saturday Club* and *Pick of the Pops* on a Sunday. The BBC didn't want people like Noel Edmonds coming out of Ilford, they had the pick of the broadcasters from around the world. When you consider that, it was an incredible break that somebody on the pirate ship kept this tape of mine, it then went to Radio Luxembourg where a man called Tony Windsor was working, and he remembered it and a year later he phoned me, while I was repairing a car and about to go to university. He said, 'Would you like to come to Radio Luxembourg and do an audition?' I did, and it started from there. But I had almost given up.

But, alongside luck, you had this incredible persistence, this almost relentless determination to take every conceivable avenue to explore the career on which you had set your heart.

Yes. I can remember my father saying to me that I didn't suffer fools gladly, and I suppose that's true. The type of people I have very little time for are the ones who dream but aren't prepared to put the effort in. I had a dream, and I had a target to aim at. I have always had this motto that every day you should try very hard and then just try that little bit harder. Maybe, sometimes, it makes me a slightly intense person and probably very difficult to work with, but I really do believe that it is not worth doing something unless you can do it to the best of your ability.

So, while you were taking steps to seek that moment of luck that set your career moving, you were also sowing the seeds of the business side of your career.

I used to buy and sell go-karts, and that was simple because at the age of 16 I wasn't allowed to drive. My parents were very good, they used to take me off to an old airfield and let me have a go at driving their car, but with my 17th birthday looming, I hadn't got enough money to buy a car so I used to buy and sell go-karts in an attempt to raise the money. Fortunately, I got my driving test quite quickly. I had £90 and I bought a Mini van. I was one of the few people driving to school in the later stages of my A-levels. I also used to do some gardening. I remember filling the back of the Mini van with Dad's lawnmower and all his tools, and going off around Gidea Park in Essex and doing the gardening for people. I was a bit cosmetic in terms of gardening, but after all, what people want to see is nice edges and nice stripes up and down the lawn.

Did you get well paid for that?

Yes, I got very well paid, although I was incredibly naive. I didn't realize that there was one woman in particular who was paying me extremely handsomely and I think she had an ulterior motive. But it's taken me some years to realize …

An ulterior motive?

Yes, I did seem to spend more time having coffees with her. Nothing improper occurred, more to my regret now. I think looking back, 'My God, I was naive,' but I did very well and I was able to maintain the Mini van.

Does everybody need a mentor to help them in their early days?

Yes, I think you do. I think you do need someone you can look up to and someone who can guide you through the dark moments. I tend to be very good at putting disappointment away. I have got a very selective memory and the painful things have become well removed, but, if I delve around a bit, I have to be honest and say I was going to be sacked from Radio Luxembourg because I just didn't fit in. I was laughing while reading the news. I was doing daft things at three in the morning and thinking that the chairman couldn't hear me. I don't think I was the Chris Evans of the time, but I was certainly not quite as disciplined as one might think I ought to have been.

So, did you get the boot?

Well, I jumped before being pushed, then spent a year to 18 months on a fraction of the salary back home, living with Mum and Dad.

Doing what?

Well, in the late 1960s, when Radio One was created, everyone wanted to be on it. They had not only an A-team but a B-team and reserves a-plenty, and I was the tea-boy. I hung around a lot, I made programme trailers, I did competitions that went out on air and prayed that people would get the 'flu, which they did every now and again.

How did you get that job?

I went to see a fellow called James Fisher, who was then Head of Presentation of Radio One and Radio Two, and told him my background and my limited experience, and James liked me. I have been very fortunate that I found people at various important stages of my life who have given me not only advice and assistance but also friendship, and James Fisher is one of those people.

In between leaving Radio Luxembourg and joining Radio One, you must have felt a bit depressed. How did you turn yourself around mentally?

I'd love to come up with a really fanciful response to that. I think it just comes down to belief in yourself. I know I can't do certain things. However much I enjoy broadcasting, I have to accept the fact that I wouldn't make a newsreader or a serious political commentator. There are many jobs within broadcasting I simply couldn't do, but what I have always felt I could do is communicate with people. It probably comes out of my upbringing. My father taught me the basic principles of being a teacher. You can have the greatest knowledge in the world, but if you can't make the pupils and the people that are listening to you pay attention, you're not going to get anywhere. I have been very fortunate. The thing that has come up time and time again in my 28 years of full employment in broadcasting, is the fact that for some reason an awful lot of the public just want to see me having a good time.

Did you find the move from radio into television difficult?

I found the transition from radio to television difficult, but because I am a team-player it wasn't the struggle that I think a lot of people would find today. You have to bear in mind that in the early 1970s, when I was making that transition through *Top of the Pops*, and then latterly through children's television, the opportunities in television were fairly limited. But, if people did like you then they would offer you all sorts of different things. At one time I was doing a programme on stress for BBC 2, I was doing *Top of the Pops*, I was doing *The Motor Show*, and a boat show down in Southampton. Now, if you did all that today, I think you would burn out very quickly, but I was able to put the reins on it, pull it back and just pace it slightly. And, of course, being able to do that with your career is terribly important.

I now run an artists' representation company, and what I am saying to a lot of the younger people that we represent is, 'Look, yes, I know you want the Porsche today, but why not wait till the day after. Why not slow all this down, because otherwise you are just going to burn out too quickly.' For a lot of people in broadcasting, we live in a disposable world where people say, 'Oh, the format's dead, it's too serious, it's dead.' Why should it be? Why shouldn't people last a long time? I think *you* are part of the whole success thing. It's about trying to build up enough self-confidence so that you can operate to a different time-scale to other people.

Unusually, for many broadcasters, you produce as well as present your shows.

Yes, I was fortunate that when the *Multi-Coloured Swap Shop* came along, it was a new style of television for the BBC. What didn't occur to the people on the sixth floor was that this individual was going to be given so much power. We were doing two to two-and-a-half hours of live television, and, of course, it was structured, but the actual content wasn't entirely known. You could guess what was going to be the outcome of certain things on the show, but we made it up as we went along. By the very nature of it they were having to follow what I was doing, so I was sort of producer/director and, to a certain extent, editor. Those roles were filled correctly by very experienced people, but because it was live, I had an enormous amount of control. And, with *House Party*, I love the fact that I am in control. I always liken it to getting the opportunity to go up at Wembley and collect the FA Cup. You would look stupid if ten other people hadn't turned up for the game, and you wouldn't win by yourself, but every single Saturday night I am the lucky bugger who gets to pick up the Cup. I also liken it, because I've got such an enthusiasm for motor sport, to the role of the Formula One driver. There is all the effort and the massive levels of trust that exist between designer/engineer/pit crew, but it all goes to worms if the driver goes and stuffs it on the first corner. I feel very much that way about a lot of the work that I do – I bear quite a load of responsibility in order not to make the efforts of others just simply dissipate and drift away.

How important is it that you actually have the business control of your own ideas, and how did that start in the BBC? How did you achieve that?

Well, I will take you back to the first thing I said, that the secret of success is to keep it a secret. I have always been quite good at noticing the things going on around me. I don't mean this unkindly, but I do find it fascinating to look back on the people I was at Radio One with and where they are now. And there's one or two of them I have got incredible sympathy for, because they didn't deserve to be chopped away. But with a couple of others I think, 'Well, didn't you see the writing on the wall?' and 'How long did you think you were going to carry on doing this?' In the 1980s, when I did a lot of work in the States, I saw how the big names owned the programmes that they were presenting and, in many instances, were producing them. It wasn't because I felt particularly vulnerable, but I could see that there were going to be very big changes on the British radio and television scene. And you don't have to be that brilliant to think, 'Well, it could well go the way the American market has gone.' I just wanted to have a little bit more strength around me, if you like. I've been grateful for that foresight, and I think I've read the changing broadcasting scene from a performer's point of view reasonably well.

So you go into the BBC and you say, 'I've got this terrific programme idea, this is how it's going to work.' And the BBC says, 'We love it.' Do you then say, 'If it's my idea, I control the whole thing, I control the merchandising,' etc., etc. But the BBC reply, 'Well, yes, that's fine, but we're not going to transmit the programme unless we get a slice of the action.' What's your response to that, how do you keep control against the arguments of broadcasters who want to control what they transmit?

Well, I'm sorry, but that set of circumstances doesn't exist and it has never existed. In the case of *House Party*, which was the major property of the Unique Group, I went to Jim Moir who was then the Head of Entertainment and said, 'Look, I'm doing this show called *Saturday Roadshow*. It goes out on Saturday nights and gets a respectable figure, but we're being beaten by ITV and I think if we were live and we had a different format that would change. I think we could add 2 million viewers.' And he said, 'OK. All right. You've thrown down the challenge, but where's the programme?' So I went away, and with my wife Helen I cooked up what is the *House Party*. The role of the founding producer Michael Leggo was also fundamental. It's actually an extension of what I was doing on the radio, because I had a fantasy programme set in Perkins Grange with the Radio Four newsreader Brian Perkins and Martin Wainwright of *The Guardian* reviewing the papers, and we used to play music and have gags. The show was set more to words than to music and it was set in this fantasy residence – we took that as the core thing.

So the *House Party* came about simply because the BBC fell for my argument, a very strong argument, that there should be this format. We did have some tussles early on, because there was, and to a certain extent I think there still is, a frame of mind in certain management areas that anything outside an artist's contract is merely cream on the cake, but we now make a major contribution to the show in creativity and in resource management and, therefore, we have a partnership production. With *Telly Addicts* we own the format and we also have an input to it there, and we have a major input into the other show *Telly Years*. So, the BBC are benefiting as well. We work with their overseas sales teams to sell the formats around the world, and we help them with the exploitation of the intellectual properties that are within the programmes. It's a true partnership, there's never been a situation where you walk into an office with both guns and say, 'Right, this is what I want.' And I actually think that the BBC would never fall for that. I remember in the very, very early days someone said to me, 'Remember, you'll never be bigger than the smallest part of the BBC,' and that thinking has done me very well.

What makes Noel's House Party *such a successful programme? Do you know? Have you sat down and analysed it very carefully and do you, as a result of that analysis, tweak and change the ingredients as you go along?*

I know exactly why it's popular, but I am not sure why it has been so *hugely* successful for so long and I don't take that for granted. I think when we stop trying to answer that question we have a serious problem. We analyse it all the time, maybe over-analyse it. I am very self-critical and I work very hard at making sure that everything is just right. It was and remains a very simple concept, a single format, i.e., old house set outside a fictional village, Crinkly Bottom, and that's a vehicle upon which you can put different loads – the different games, the different features. I also wanted something where well-known people came to the door, because I felt that the age of the public entertaining the public could be coming to an end, and I believe that very strongly now. And so we've had some of the biggest names in the world come to the door. The show, therefore, has a status. That's not a new idea.

When Morecambe and Wise were having problems, and had gone to ITV, they started to involve the Glenda Jacksons and the Peter Cushings of this world doing strange things, and, of course, that's what we've got on the show. More than anything, it's back to what inspired me all those years ago, it's about communication, and it really is an interactive show. I know it's a terribly overused word, but it's an accessible show.

Is there a general principle that you should embarrass, but not humiliate? Are there any core principles like that running through the programme?

Yes, it's always really annoyed me if some stuck-up newspaper critic has ever said the show seeks to embarrass people. We just don't do that, and I think if I didn't have that gland that seems to fire up and prevent me going overboard, I don't think I would have been successful. I think at some stage you have to be able to say, 'No, that's wrong, this is uncomfortable.' I do a show, a special show, once a year, called *Christmas Presents*, and it goes out on Christmas Day. It's now after the Queen's speech, and a number of people that I respect in the industry have said, 'It's a tradition now.' We deal with some very sensitive stories – a lot of people, regrettably a lot of the children that have featured in the past, are no longer with us. You're dealing with sensitive issues, you're dealing with the raw edge of human emotions, and I think every single Christmas we pull the camera away before it gets cloying, before the viewer feels uncomfortable. I think we achieve that with humour as well. There is some shocking humour around, and personally I don't actually feel comfortable with shocking humour.

Do you always know how far you can go, and when to stop?

Yes, I think so, but I think that's probably a product of age. I think I have to admit that in the past I probably had to learn the hard way about where the cut-off point is.

Is it because of the unfairness with which some people regard success in this country that you actually said second-best was where you felt more comfortable. Your exact phrase was, 'It is better to be a comfortable number two than an over-exposed number one.' What did you mean by that?

I actually said that at a time when Terry Wogan appeared to be on everything. He had his chat show and he was winning Showbiz Personality Awards, and I couldn't quite understand what Terry's great success was. That's not a dig at him, but he had been elevated to a position where no one seemed to be criticizing him.

It was his way with words, presumably.

Yes, it was his charm, his character, he was in the right place at the right time – for the *Eurovision Song Contest*, for a number of programmes he was doing. And in all the popularity polls and whatever, I seemed to be Avis to his Hertz, and, you know, Avis will try harder.

And so, in a sense, you are saying that was a kind of self-justification for what was happening?

I would like to think that there was a bit more thought in it than that. One of the things which I think is very important is to have other strings to one's bow, which is the reason why, ten years ago, I set up the Unique

Group. I wanted to develop business ideas, not purely from a financial security point of view, but just so that people would know I could do something else. I've got a very good team of people there and I am very happy to admit to them that, 'Yes, I'm trying to prove something now.'

To what extent do you think appearing on television successfully is dependent upon looking right?

I think it's not so much about looking right, I think it's how you look at the viewer. I know for a fact that I do not have a great broadcasting voice. I come from Essex. You know, it's difficult enough to get the voice out of my nose, to get it down to Auntie sort of blandness. And in television terms, I am not a great looking person, but I am very recognisable, which is another reason why I've stuck to the trademark beard. I am probably one of the most recognized and recognisable people in the country. Now, that has an advantage, it also has a disadvantage, but in terms of what I do on television, it's definitely a plus.

Obviously, every presenter is different and brings something special to the table, and there are some things that are unique to them, but are there any basic core principles in being a successful presenter?

I think the principles have changed over the years. One or two hold through the passage of time. I don't think you can work hard enough,I don't think you can be grateful enough to the people that make it happen for you. Experience is what you're left with when everything else has gone. You are not as clever as you think you are. There is always somebody else who has got another spin, another twist on something. One of the things I love about the *House Party* is on a Friday afternoon when we sit down and we go through the scripts with genuinely funny people – the really talented scriptwriters. We look at every line and we try and twist them around. Is that a better tag? Does this work better? I laugh all Friday afternoon. These scriptwriters sit there with straight faces and go, 'Oh yes, that's really funny,' and that's their way of laughing. I wouldn't want to be one of them, but I don't think there's anything wrong, whatever the job is, in working 10 per cent harder than you think you can, being more committed than you think you are able to be, and being incredibly grateful for every single opportunity you get.

What do you regard as your biggest failures, both in your career and in your personal life, and how did you overcome them?

Well, undoubtedly, because I do like to see the job through, the failure of my first marriage was, and still is, a huge disappointment. However, as someone who feels it is more important to get out of a bad mistake, and to recover from a problem in a positive way, to turn a negative into a positive, even that has just turned out to be the best thing that happened to me. It was at a period in my life where I was really concentrating on my work and was in my mid to late thirties. Then I met this extraordinary woman called Helen, we now have three beautiful children, and the period of our relationship has been quite the happiest period of my life. I have been able to put more emphasis on my family than my job.

I do actually feel great sympathy for people who find success and financial security later in life. They may not be in a position to thank their parents because their parents have gone. Maybe they have paid the ultimate price in terms of their family relationship. For me, however, things have actually stacked up very well.

Let me ask you about something that I know that you don't like talking about, but which is clearly a major moment in your life. You'd had this incredibly charmed career, and then on one of your programmes a member of the public, Michael Lush, is killed performing a stunt, and you resign immediately from the programme and you do virtually nothing for a year. Now, at that point, you must have seen everything that you had worked for in your career vanishing rapidly. How did you pull yourself back from that incredibly difficult moment and gird your loins to go out there and be even more successful?

It's still something which I find very difficult to talk about. This year is the tenth anniversary and I think about it a lot. I know, for obvious and quite proper reasons, that that accident has changed the way in which the industry operates. It was an incredible thing to have happened, because the BBC is not a flippant organization, all the systems are in place there and yet this accident occurred and somebody lost their life. In the context of an entertainment programme, that was something which I needed two or three years to understand, and which, even now, I have failed to come to terms with.

What is amazing is that I think it actually strengthened my relationship with the British public, because the only thing to do was stand up and be counted. And although at the time certain newspapers wanted to twist things around I think, generally speaking, the message came over. It wasn't my fault, but I felt responsibility. If the engines fail on a jumbo jet it's not the captain's fault, but he is responsible. He is responsible for what is then going to happen afterwards. I was given enormous support by Bill Cotton, who was then the managing director of BBC Television, and I remember going in to see him the day after the accident and the day that we should have been doing the show. There had been talk till late in the night that maybe the show should be rested, I had no appetite for it at all. And it wasn't a knee-jerk reaction, I felt very calm about it.

Helen and I went into the Television Centre, and we walked in and Bill was there, and he walked right past me and up to Helen, sat her down and he said, 'You've only just got married, haven't you?' We had. She didn't marry me because she's a gold-digger, she married me for 101 reasons, but she had every right to think I was still going to be successful, and within six months of us getting married I could see the end of a career. Bill talked to her for about ten minutes, during which he said, 'I want you to know that the BBC will support you and your husband for as long as it takes us all to feel that we are comfortable with the way forward. I know that you ladies worry about money and this, that and the other. All contracts will be honoured and we will deal with this in a professional way, and when the time is right, we will talk about new shows, but I know Noel's come to this decision.'

Now, I don't know how he knew, but I was all set to say, 'I've got to resign.' So, in fact, I never actually had to resign, and we shook hands on it. We met the following week very quietly and privately and we talked about it. It was a hugely difficult time which has probably been, along with the death of my father after a long illness from cancer, the most difficult thing for me to deal with – to find that optimism, to see how I could turn this negative into a positive. And, as you can probably tell, it's still there, it's only just beneath the surface. It's just very, very difficult, but maybe, maybe it's part of the maturing process in life, maybe it's given me other strengths.

Do you think that it is one of the important ingredients of success that you have experienced either some form of failure or some form of sacrifice at some stage in your life?

Yes, I'm absolutely certain that's the case, and I don't think happiness in life comes down to how you deal with success, I think it's about how you cope with failure – that's probably my most important creed.

Who are the successful people you really admire?

I admire anybody who works like mad. The work ethic is something that I really do believe in. I have got a number of heroes. They tend to be people who are associated with things that I either like or have engaged in. Jackie Stewart is somebody who I've admired greatly over the years, not just because of his skill as a racing driver, but at a time when it was not popular to do so, he really did push track safety. A lot of people who should have known better were saying, 'But you're racing drivers. Every year one of you gets killed, but you don't have to do it.' And then he's made the transition into an international business person and I shall be rooting for him with his new Formula One team. A lovely thing he did last year – he was due to appear on a show which I was hosting, then couldn't make it and cancelled at very short notice – in fact to announce his Formula One team. Ford had brought the date forward and he had to be in Detroit. He phoned me seven times, we missed each other and I eventually got him in Japan and he just said, 'I wanted to apologize to you, because I've seen print where you have said very nice things about me, and I wanted you to know I just don't turn things down.' And I thought, 'God, he's gone to all that trouble.' So he shot up in my estimation even further.

Alan Whicker I admire enormously. I just think he's brilliant, he's made a niche for himself. I do like people who can make a niche for themselves. David Attenborough is another, and then the other evening I was watching David Frost and thinking, 'You know, there's a man who can't sing, he can't dance, can't really act very well, but he's been in television a long time.'

Does success bring any obligations?

Oh yes. I've always felt huge responsibilities for being in the public eye; I take personal conduct very seriously. I don't drink and drive, I never would get that near to it, I simply do not drink and drive. I take my flying very, very seriously. I recognize that, for some people, maybe I'm a role model and therefore I feel it is important sometimes to engage in clear messages about drug abuse and that kind of thing. I think if you are in the public eye and you have the opportunity to energize other people, it's a good thing if you can. I've never been one to feel that you have to do charitable things because you're famous, because you're successful.

And yet you do.

I do them because I want to. A journalist once said to me, after I'd launched my charity Airborne where we fly disabled children, 'Is this Noel Edmonds putting something back?' And I said, 'Bollocks, that's like I've nicked something.' I haven't nicked anything. I've just worked very hard for what I've got. It's not putting something back. What it's actually doing is creating an environment in which I, and a lot of other people, can care. And that's what I want in society.

A few years ago I tried to launch a retail initiative where we were selling mineral water and giving money to the Woodland Trust, and it principally failed because we had a major recession. I hope one day to explore that again, because all of us who enjoy a degree of success have a wonderful opportunity to make it possible for other people to care more.

If you could gather together all the young people who admire you as a role model and want to become as successful as Noel Edmonds, what advice would you give them?

I think the advice that I was given is still sound. I think you need to work harder than other people expect you to, be true to your own principles, and not put other people down on the way. Success is a ladder but it doesn't mean you have to stamp on other people's hands in order to get to the top.

What's the most important thing a young person can do setting out now on a television career?

Be patient. Constantly review your own performance. Be extremely self-critical. Try and get yourself into a programme in the area where, if you have them, your communication skills will shine. I think there is a great shortage of skilled presenters and interesting people. We're in an era of shock television, where people need to be shouting into microphones, sticking their face into the camera hood. Be yourself. If you can be yourself in the public arena then you will be comfortable with yourself when you fail. Fail on your own terms, don't fail on something else.

When your time comes to leave this life, what would you like people to say about you? How will they remember Noel Edmonds?

If people are kind enough to remember me, I think it is for something that happened and for which I wasn't responsible – Mr Blobby. I do not want anyone to look back on the life of Noel Edmonds and say, 'He brought Mr Blobby to this planet.' Because I didn't. It was a man called Michael Leggo, it was just me in the costume, it wasn't my fault, I'm sorry.

So, what would you *like to be remembered for?*

I'm not sure that people would really bother to remember me, and I'm not trying to be falsely modest. I suppose there is a difference between what you're remembered for and what is an epitaph.

A one-liner.

He was a professional.

SIR DAVID ENGLISH

'He made grown men cry – but it worked.' A colleague's comment on the doyen of Fleet Street editors, who, in 21 years at the helm, firmly established the Daily Mail as the voice of Middle England.

He was always as tough on others as he was with himself, a meticulous attention to detail giving him little time for anyone who accepted work which was 'not great, but OK'. His entrepreneurial instincts and eye for a good page layout were on early display at grammar school in Bournemouth, when a shortage of comics after the war inspired him to make his own – and rent them out to other pupils! Torn between careers in journalism and architecture, his mother got him a job on the local paper, and he never looked back. At 20, he was in Fleet Street, reporting first for the Daily Mirror, then travelling the world for the Daily Express. He says he never actually had an ambition to be an editor, but sought promotion through 'irritation and anger that people above me were interfering with my work and damaging my efforts'. Denied the job at the Express, he grabbed it at the Daily Sketch, becoming the youngest editor in Fleet Street. Two years later he was running the Daily Mail. In this, his last major interview before his untimely death, he explained his tolerance of 'enthusiastic people who get things wrong', and recalled his own biggest mistake, the day he thought he was finished – and what saved him. He talked of the 26 free-sheet newspapers he built up in his spare time, selling them to Rupert Murdoch for so much money he became 'independently wealthy' – and how that gave him added confidence and authority as an editor. He dispenses advice to journalists – 'Remember you don't write for yourself, you write for other people'; to news editors – 'Be constantly cynical – never accept anything at its face value'; and in general – 'Recognise the recurring failures of your character and personality, and fight them all the time.' Knighted for services to journalism, he sailed energetically through his mid-sixties with a clutch of chairmanships – Associated Newspapers, ITN, ITV's Teletext News Service, cable TV's Channel One and the Editors' Code Committee, which sets the ethical professional standards for the newspaper industry. It's as though he was driven by the rule that guided him through the job of which he is most proud: 'As editor, you've got absolute power – the minute you relax, you're vulnerable.'

He was due to be made a Lord in the very week that he died.

Sir David, what is your definition of success?

Success is personal fulfilment, doing something that I've wanted to do. I've succeeded in achieving that and it has given me a great deal of pleasure.

Was that a long-term aim or were there a whole series of successes that bounced through your career?

I wanted to be fulfilled as a journalist and at every level in journalism I found that fulfilment, starting as a local paper reporter. I wanted to be a very good reporter, then when I became a national newspaper editor, I wanted to be the best national newspaper editor. So at every level my aims and ambitions were fulfilled within this particular discipline.

When did that seed of journalistic ambition start to grow?

It sort of grew, like Topsy. I went to a very good grammar school and was good at English, history and art, and probably didn't start thinking about a career until I was 14 or 15. I was interested in being either an architect or a newspaper man.

So what swung the balance? Could you easily have been an architect?

Well, this was the late 1940s following the end of the Second World War and in my home town, Bournemouth, there had been – as in any city in Britain – no building since 1939, and I was quite interested in modern architecture. The most modern building in the town was the *Bournemouth Echo*, the local newspaper office and that stood out like a beacon for me – I was fascinated by it for architectural reasons. From that I got interested in the paper as a whole. We were a great newspaper-reading family and all through the war we had three papers, the *Mail*, the *Herald* and the *News Chronicle*. My mother knew people on the *Echo*, so I got a job in the building whose interior I was so fascinated to see, having studied the outside, and I just took to it like a duck to water.

A degree of early nepotism, your mother knew someone on the newspaper?

That's how small towns work. I may say that at that time there was never any difficulty about getting jobs anywhere, that was the difference between my generation and the generation now – there was full employment. Incidentally, the *Echo* building is still there, though the newspaper is about to move out to a new building. I asked its general manager what was happening to the building, and I am very happy to say that it's listed, so will remain for a long time to come.

Did you have any doubts in those early days that journalism was the right career?

Not after the first two weeks. I thought it was incredible. At that time there were a lot of movies in which 'knight errant' journalists were the heroes, and so in my very youthful teenage way, I saw journalism as a romantic, highly idealized job.

Did journalism live up to those ideals? Do you still think it is a glamorous job?

I think it has been glamorous for me for much of the time. It's still glamorous, but as we know it's also tacky and sleazy. It's a curate's egg. But on the whole, I still have that high opinion of journalism, that it is absolutely fundamental to democracy and the right kind of national life. Although journalists as a tribe can do bad things, they can do some essentially very good things as well. I don't know where we'd be without them.

Have you always been ambitious or did ambition grow as a talent was perceived and developed?

My ambition was strictly layered. I had a progressive ambition to be the best reporter when I was reporter, the best feature writer, the best foreign correspondent. I didn't have an ambition from the outset to end up being a national newspaper editor. I never had an ambition to be an editor, as a matter of fact.

So there was no long-term plan, it was simply taking what opportunities were there?

Yes, that's a typical good journalist's attitude. Every assignment was important to me and whenever I sought promotion it was because of the irritation and anger I felt that the people over me were not actually seeing the things I wrote in the right way, as I saw it, and were interfering through their editing and damaging my efforts. That drove me to get on top and make sure it was done the way I thought it should be done.

That's the eternal journalist's cry, isn't it? You create this baby – your report – and then someone else hacks it around.

That's absolutely true, but they can also improve it. A good editor can take something and improve it, a bad editor can mangle it and butcher it. I quickly realized that in journalism, as in any other profession, there were people with varying degrees of talent. Sometimes people got into positions of power for which their talents were not fitted and they weren't confident at their job. Sometimes they would be over me. There are just as many people who ruin copy as there are who improve copy and I could tell the difference early on from underneath.

Can people still rise up to positions to which they are not entirely suited?

It happens all the time. The art of being a good editor is to keep the percentage of the Peter Principle very low. That's what I did as an editor. I managed to have the judgment to pick the right people for the right job and not over-promote people and under-promote people.

Does every successful journalist need a mentor at some stage in their career, someone who's prepared to ride shotgun alongside them and have faith in them while they make their mistakes?

I think that applies to far more than just journalists. It applies to almost every profession. I suppose my most important mentor was a man called Herbert Gunn, who was editor of the *Evening Standard*, and later editor of the *Daily Sketch*. He was an anglicized Scot, very decisive, very polished, very good looking, very charming, very ruthless, very clever. I was an assistant editor under him at the age of 27 and we got on very well. He was then about 53 – that generation gap very often works with mentors, doesn't it? – and saw that I had energy and imagination and drive, encouraged me a great deal, and was very tolerant of my mistakes.

I remember on one occasion, I'd heard, or I'd read in a medical magazine, that an American drug company had invented a drug that would coat the lining of the stomach and prevent drunkenness. I decided to run a consumer test on this and we got seven sets of twins and fed them with vast amounts of drink. In each pair, one had the pill and one didn't. In order to monitor this I'd taken a great number of *Sketch* writers with me – we did it at the Waldorf Hotel. Anyway, it turned into a completely and utterly drunken evening. Journalists, like homing pigeons, will go back to their offices. I'd taken the doctors involved for a drink at midnight – I hadn't had a drink and neither had they – and I said, 'Would you like to see the newspaper we're printing now, it's very interesting?' and they said, 'Yes.' As we went round the corner to the *Daily Sketch*, there was a huge fight going on in the middle of the road and to my horror I saw it involved about six of my reporters and five of the senior editors – the reporters had come back to the building and set about wrecking it, and the editors had had to sort them out with fisticuffs. I should have been fired the next day, but Gunn forgave me and said, 'Well, that's a great lesson for you, never give free drink to your reporters because they will always come back and set fire to the office,' which is what they tried to do.

How much tolerance do you now give to people on a similar learning curve?

I give exactly the same tolerance to enthusiastic people who get things wrong. I was very forgiving of genuine mistakes. I was very intolerant of laziness and slipshodness, but not of over-enthusiasm – over-enthusiasm I would always forgive, as I was forgiven. I think that's very important.

Going way back to your early days, were there any formative moments at school when you realized, 'I am a success at something,' and the seeds of an ambition were formed?

Well, I was always entrepreneurial. There was a newspaper shortage for many years after the War, you couldn't get children's comics, and I used to spend hours producing my own comics and then renting them out for a penny a time. I used to write everything, and being quite good at art I used to be able to do the illustrations as well. That was formative, in a sense, because it did turn out that I was a very good newspaper lay-out man and I was able to design newspapers.

Being an entrepreneur and selling those comics, did you consider business?

No. I was never very interested in making money as my primary goal. I've made quite a lot of money out of journalism but it was a side-effect. I was there for the fun and impact of journalism.

Can money ever be totally ignored? Is it not a factor in some people's success?

It certainly is because it does give you freedom. I realized this quite early on in my career, because being an editor is a bit like being a football manager. There's always a lot of tension in newspapers between the management and the creative editorial people, and management and publishers have power over an editor in the sense that they appoint him, and give him a high salary. The editor then moves his lifestyle and his family's lifestyle up several notches and is then committed to that salary which can be pulled away like a rug from underneath him. Sometimes that can impinge on an editor's independence and he will sometimes compromise in order to protect his family and lifestyle.

I felt that if you were going to be an editor you had to be true to yourself. You had to be truly independent so that at the drop of a hat you could resign and walk away over a matter of principle. In order to do that you had to have money, so I decided that I would make money so that no one could ever blackmail me by threatening to remove my salary since I would always have money in the background. So, again through journalism, I set out in my thirties to make money and, with a friend, I started – while still working on the *Express* – a free-sheet newspaper which

I eventually built up into 26 newspapers over several years and sold to Rupert Murdoch for quite a large sum of money. That made me independently wealthy and I do think it did make a huge difference in all those years of editing. I had nearly 22 years at the *Daily Mail* and two and a bit years on the *Sketch*, but for a quarter of a century I was never frightened of losing my income from being an editor because I knew that it wouldn't affect my lifestyle. Thus I could afford to be very independent and stand up to a board of directors over matters that I felt were important. I didn't have to do it very often, but I think the fact that this financial independence was there at the back of my mind gave me a tremendous sense of confidence and authority in what I was doing.

How big a part does luck play in success?

An enormous one. I've thought about success a great deal and talked to my children about it, and I think it results from talent, then application, then timing, then luck – not necessarily in that particular order. You certainly have to have luck in whom you meet and in being somewhere at the right time. It's incredibly important, but you can't quantify it. But you still have to have the talent and the drive as well.

What happens when you have setbacks? At one time you went for the editorship of the Express *and were turned down. How did you deal with that?*

I'm not sure that's right, that I went to the *Express* and was turned down. But I certainly rose very quickly. I was a foreign correspondent on the *Express* for a long time and then I was brought back to Britain for fast-track executive grooming. I rose to being number three on the *Express* when just 35, then I was acting number two, and what happened was – and this shows, I think, you've got to be a gambler to be successful – I was offered the editorship of the *Daily Sketch*, the smallest paper in Fleet Street. I was offered that because Rupert Murdoch had started the *Sun* tabloid, and clearly there was going to be a tabloid battle. So to run the *Sketch* was real gamble, and at this point the *Express* said to me, 'Don't go and do that, we will make you the next editor of the *Express*,' and I said, 'I don't want promises, will you make me the editor of the *Express* now?' 'No, we can't do that because we've got an editor but you are going to be the heir.' I thought about that and I thought, 'No, an editorship in the hand is worth any number of promises,' so I went from the *Express* – which was then the most powerful paper in Fleet Street – to the *Sketch* which was the most insignificant. But it gave me a platform to show what I could do and as a result I then became editor of the *Daily Mail*. There was then an attempt to merge the *Express* and the *Daily Mail* and I was chosen by both sides to be the editor, had that merger gone through.

What are your biggest failures and how did you recover from them?

There are two types of failures. There are the recurring failures of your character and personality, which everyone must have, otherwise they wouldn't be human. The thing is to recognize and fight them. I certainly know what my failure was as an editor – I was a perfectionist, I expected everybody to work to a high level as the norm. I only acknowledged it if they didn't reach a high level, when I would be extremely critical, or if they did reach a superbly high level, when I would thank them. I did not, in my view, thank the people who performed consistently well over time. I took that for granted. I did correct that failing because I learned over time that I didn't thank people enough for what they did. Furthermore, I sometimes made judgmental mistakes on stories – not often, but when I did, I did it in a big way.

It's been said that you have a capacity to make grown men cry, particularly in the morning planning conferences. Is it necessary, particularly on a newspaper, to create this kind of tension, almost an atmosphere of fear? Do you get a better newspaper through that?

I did tend to drive people as I drove myself – never to accept the first thing they did, nor the second, nor the third, but constantly to try to improve. Sometimes in a morning conference, perhaps I would be short-tempered. I learned to contain that a bit, and of course you mellow with age. But on the other hand, I would be enormously enthusiastic about and grateful for brilliant ideas. I'm a bit black and white on things. I don't know that I made too many grown men cry, but I do know that I had a pretty sharp tongue.

Is ruthlessness one of the ingredients of success?

It's hard to be successful without being ruthless because, after all, what is ruthlessness? It's cutting to the point, it's getting everything superfluous out of the way, and sometimes it's being destructive for the greater constructive good. Again, it's something that has to be controlled. As I've said, I was tolerant of mistakes if they were genuine mistakes, but I was never tolerant of people who cut corners for laziness. And I couldn't bear slipshod journalism – I was nasty about that.

To what do you put down your longevity as an editor? Two decades is a tremendously long time by British media standards to be running a newspaper. Why were you able to do it while other newspapers' editors came and went?

First of all I loved doing it and I wanted to go on doing it. Secondly I think

I was unique amongst editors – Andreas Witham-Smith is an obvious exception – in that I created the particular paper I was editing. The tabloid *Daily Mail* was a new creation that grew out of the broadsheet *Daily Mail.* It was my baby and so I had that love for it. In addition I couldn't see a life after editing – though in fact, it's turned out that there is one and it's very enjoyable – so I wanted to go on doing the job and I had worked out fairly early on that every four or five years you had to go into retreat with an almost religious intensity and rededicate yourself to your tasks, so that you would never be cynical or bored and say, 'Oh, well, this is the fourth general election we've covered,' and so be lacklustre about it. I could rededicate myself and find within me all the enthusiasm and freshness that you need when you first become an editor.

How do you do that? Rededication is an interesting concept, particularly in journalism where there is a touch of cynicism that says, 'I've seen it all before'?

I used to say to myself that one mustn't say that I've seen it all before because nothing is ever the same however much it is repeated. It's always different, and you have to look for the difference and find it. My job, I thought, as an editor, having seen something before, would be to give guidelines on how we would approach it. I would still look for freshness in it myself, see freshness in others' reporting and seize on that. So there was never any tiredness in anything we did. If you approached an issue in that frame of mind, it worked because you did find new things. You did dig deeper into the story, you did do it better the third or fourth time. My self-induced technique of doing that always worked, so I never got bored.

Did you have a set formula, a set list of principles which, as far as you were concerned, shaped the paper? Or was there an evolving set of principles, and if so, how did they evolve?

I think we did have a set from the beginning – this was as much Vere Rothermere's idea as mine. The *Mail* is the paper of middle England, there had to be a voice of middle England, and I come from middle England – that was the first thing. Secondly, I've got a very curious mind and I'm interested in many wide-ranging things, and I was able to translate that into interesting articles. Thirdly, I thought the paper should always be honourable and I thought we should not give way to the trendiness that brought four-letter words into print and we have never used obscenities in the *Mail,* even in other people's direct speech – we're old-fashioned and use asterisks. I did have a lot of trouble with younger journalists who wanted to scatter four-letter words through their articles because they thought it made an impact. I thought that was boring and cheap. I used to say, 'We're not going to do this, and you may think that

I'm an ancient, dull person, but the fact is if we do it we will lose sales and our job is to increase sales. They would accept that, so that was a standard of value. Fourthly I always thought that in our reporting we should be both hard and accurate. Certainly we would angle things in feature writing and in our political attitudes. I genuinely believed in Mrs Thatcher and I truly felt that the Labour Party in the 1970s and 1980s was a severe danger to our country and its way of life. And we kept saying so. But that was not dishonourable, that's what we on the paper felt, so we fought very hard for those views, just as the *Guardian* would say very much the opposite. That's one of the great things about British newspapers.

Do you think all newspapers are political in the end?

I don't think they can be successful unless they are.

Do you have to have an opinion on every issue?

No. To have an opinion on every issue is possibly boring. We always see newspapers as a personality and if you've got a friend who's got an opinion on every issue that friend swiftly becomes a bore. But if you've got a friend who's got decisive views on certain issues and they're interesting and well argued, that's fine. So we don't have a view on every issue and often we will print contradictory views. People forget that the *Mail* was against Heath and for the miners in the early days of the three-day week, we've never been totally consistent in our views. But we were pretty consistently for Mrs T, I must admit that – but then, so was the country.

When you say you haven't been consistent in your views, is that a weakness?

No, because to be absolutely consistent is not opening your mind. I think if there's a problem with modern England – and to some extent the newspapers are a part of it – it is coming at everything from a political viewpoint, and I believe that is wrong. I think you can be a wet on some issues and a dry on others and to some extent we were like that. We would sometimes surprise people with our views, which were really the views of a bunch of people editing a very successful, commercial national newspaper, led by me, representing their constituency, in a sense, representing the people that bought our paper.

How do you decide what middle England wants? Did you have a whole series of focus groups reporting back to you, or was it basically gut instinct?

It was all gut instinct. I don't believe in focus groups. You can pick an awful lot up from your friends. The bulk of my friends are not journalists.

I have some very good journalistic friends but I have always believed that you have to have friends who are not journalists to be a really rounded human being. You couldn't live totally in Fleet Street.

Some journalists make journalism their total life. Are they lesser journalists because they don't have as much contact with people in other walks of life?

It's hard to speak for them because all people are different. When I was sent to America first, to be an American correspondent, most of the British correspondents there lived in a little enclave in New York. But I was married with two kids and I wanted to live in the real America and I bought a house in the suburbs and made many friends. I beat a great number of my competitors simply because I lived with Americans and learned and picked up so much more, so had a much wider range to write about. That was an interesting lesson. I don't say I picked my friends for that reason, but I always thought that you should not have all your circle of friends from your profession. I don't think that's a good thing. I have a very catholic range of friends and I try to get away from Fleet Street in my spare time, and that has made me a better journalist.

Is there a danger that successful journalists can become isolated?

Yes, because it's such a competitive business and we all spend such a long time together, just as I think MPs can become isolated. What is talked about in Westminster and Whitehall and Fleet Street may often be of very little interest to the rest of the country and I think newspapers can actually bore their readers with some of this.

Have you found it difficult to make the transition from a working journalist to a wider managerial role?

I had to learn a lot at first but then I got absorbed and fascinated and now I'm enjoying it, I can't believe my luck. At the end of my career I've got all the freshness of new disciplines, and new things and new challenges which I think keep me pretty young, and I'm really grateful.

Have you ever, at any stage in your career, felt like giving up?

No. And I've never wanted to do anything else. I've rarely had a day that I haven't enjoyed. I've had some hellish days, but I still enjoyed them.

Have you been able to resolve the age-old conflict between family and work? Many successful people say they couldn't be successful unless they had made some degree of sacrifice at some stage as far at their family were concerned.

I know this sounds Pollyanna-ish, but I never really faced that problem. I have a terrific family, I made a brilliant marriage when I was young to a wonderful woman and it's been a fantastic marriage. I never really sacrificed too much of my family. I was notorious for taking very long holidays. In my view you couldn't work at a newspaper unless you worked for a minimum of 12 hours a day, as I did, so I didn't see my wife and children much in the evenings, but I always saw them at weekends. And I would take eight or nine weeks' holiday every year, and I would argue to the board that this was a very good investment because I had to recharge my batteries all the time in order to keep up a high level of performance, and that was a way of doing it. We were a family that did things together – we used to sail in the summer and ski in the winter and the family has held together. They understood the hours I worked and we made it work by slicing it that way, so I don't think I did make any sacrifices.

Did your wife know what she was going to let herself in for when she married you?

I doubt it, but then how many of us do know what we're letting ourselves in for when we get married? We were only in our twenties.

Is it important to have a strong partner who complements you and helps you?

It depends on the individual – it was for me. The luck was that I married someone who is perfect for me in this job, and therefore this company was very lucky that I found someone like that. She was never jealous of the newspaper, she always loved it, and she kept my feet on the ground, which is very important when you're editing for people out there – you must not lose touch with them. Everyone is different, but my personality was such that I needed that rock person in my life, and that has made it easy to do all this.

In pursuit of success some people go for total control; others say, 'We'll have a fair amount of consultation,' or 'We'll make it a team effort.' How do you get the balance right between the two?

I was more of a total-controller, I must admit, and it goes back to what I said earlier – I think I rose up the ladder because I wanted total control over my own copy and if people damaged it, that would anger me. So when I became the editor I felt I would have total control and if I failed it would be entirely my own fault, it wouldn't be because I had delegated it to someone who had then let me down. But you can't do that for 22 years, night after night after night. So I got a group of like-minded senior people around me, but not so like-minded that they wouldn't argue with me. I was very lucky that I had a deputy who would always argue with me and whom I would listen to. He retired quite a while ago but he's still a very good friend. I was lucky that I had people like that who would challenge me, so we would reach our consensus and agree on certain things, then take our sections and do it. But I would always want to do everything myself at some stage, so I would always lay out certain pages, but not always the same pages. I would always rewrite certain things, sometimes the key editorials. Being the kind of shirtsleeves editor that I was, I would control things very much and set the necessary standards. I'm sure I made people very fed up most of the time but on the other hand I could sometimes go back afterwards and say, 'Look, I took that away from you, but I don't think I did it all that well.' I used to drive home with various pages in my mind. The presses would be running and I really could see the columns of type and the headlines and the way the pictures were. I'd done them about three times but I could still see flaws in them. Then I would get home and get on the phone – this was before car phones – and say, 'I think that picture was in the wrong column, and if you look on column three, there's a paragraph where the wording is wrong.' I exercised that level of control, but I believe that's what good editors should do, and certainly I encourage all the editors to do it here, and they do.

Is this restlessnes a vital ingredient in creating a successful paper?

It's absolutely fundamental that you keep polishing and get things right. I was always very critical of journalists and departmental editors working for me who would say, 'It's not great but it's OK.' That's when I used to make them cry because I would explode with rage – that kind of phrase would drive me mad. I would be very angry with people who would put things in the paper where there were still glaring inconsistencies and mistakes and questions unanswered, and I would remove those people if they didn't improve their game. That's how I survived.

Is another factor in survival identifying those who are a threat to your position and doing what you can to get rid of them?

I never thought there was anybody who was a threat to my position. I know that sounds very arrogant. I chose people who were very good journalists. They were all loyal to me and I guess I made an unwritten pact with them that as I advanced they would advance with me, and that at the end of the day I would help their careers. I believe very much in internal promotion. When I've promoted good people I never saw them as a threat, I just saw them as great journalists. I knew I was good, so I didn't feel threatened, that's the point I'm trying to make.

Who are your heroes? Who are the people you regard as having been successful, either past or present, in any field?

I have to say that I thought Mrs Thatcher was absolutely brilliant, immensely successful, so she is definitely my number one heroine – for the same dedication, for the same will, for the same vision of seeing something clearly and not letting yourself be put off track and working so hard and not accepting second best and yet being flexible enough, certainly in her early days, to move position when it was right to do so. I never agreed with her about Europe, but on everything else I agreed with her. I have to say this sounds close to home but Vere Rothermere is one of my heroes. I've known him since he was very young, when I was on a rival paper and he was a deputy circulation manager. I liked him and I think that's why we were able to work together. I also think he had a vision for newspapers and it's been great to see him build this empire. It's difficult to be part of a dynasty. Lord Northcliffe was a genius and all the following generations are measured against him. I think Vere's the first one really to measure up against the founding father.

Is it becoming more or less difficult to achieve success in the field of journalism?

It's becoming more difficult because of the multi-media world in which we live. It was quite simple when newspapers dominated. I wanted to see the world so I wanted to be a foreign correspondent. Now kids go backpacking, they never did that when I was young, I went round the world as a newspaper man, I went to a lot of difficult hot spots but that's what I wanted to do. Then you could be a newspaper star because it was a primary means of communication. Newspapers made great stars in those days and they had big circulations.

Returning to your question, I think newspapers are terribly important now, in that sense we're bigger than we were 20 years ago, but it's quite hard to get into newspapers. For one thing we don't have the size of staff. When I took over the *Daily Mail* it had 660 journalists working on it, now it has about 330. Everything's downsized, to use the jargon, so it is a bit harder, but it's just as much fun if you make it.

Success in others arouses a wide range of emotions, from outright admiration to deep envy. Is there something unique about Britain that makes us less capable of acknowledging success than, for example, in the United States?

I know it's thought to be a prevailing fault that we're riddled by and inhibited by our so-called class structural system. But I've never believed it. I lived for a long time in the United States and for some time in Europe, and I think that Britain is a very mobile society. It's very, very easy to be successful in this country and we're just as flexible as the Americans. Americans admire success more than we do. I suppose one of the reasons we haven't done – and this is one of the reasons why I was, for much of my life, very anti-left and very anti the Labour party – was the socialist ethos which was used politically, that if people were rich they could only become so by making other people poor. That is not right economically – successful people actually drag society up with them. That's now accepted in the modern Labour Party – I don't find that Tony Blair, for example, has any of those old views. It was a post-war phenomenon when we went through austerity – people were generally envious of post-war success, perhaps because there was thought to be an 'under-the-counter' nastiness about it. So we've had this anti-success thing in this country which was terribly, terribly destructive. But I think that's going now, I hope so anyway.

Is there a downside to success?

It doesn't always bring happiness and fulfilment. It did in my case, but one has met many successful people who are deeply unhappy. You can be a success and happy or you can be a success and deeply miserable, just as you can be a commercial failure and happy or deeply miserable. I don't think the two things are necessarily connected.

Some successful people say that the media tend to shoot at them in an unreasonable way and don't understand what they're doing. How do you, as a newspaperman, answer that?

There's some truth in that. If you get into the public domain, you're likely to have the spotlight on you and be questioned, and if you make mistakes you face a huge amount of criticism. And often it can range into the personal. It's happened to me – I've made one or two mistakes in editing, including one very big one, and there was a great cry for me to be severely punished and crushed. I was subjected to a media barrage, because the thing about the media is that we are not one unified force, we are all desperately fighting each other, and if you make a mistake, you don't get any mercy from your peers. So I know what it's like to face criticism – some of it fair, and some of it unfair.

What was that big mistake?

This was a big story I did early on in my editorship when there was a Labour government and British Leyland was a nationalized company. Someone brought us a lot of documents that showed that there was, with government connivance, a slush fund and huge amounts of bribes and kick-backs were being given to third-world countries in order to buy British Leyland goods. The corruption was extremely widespread and much of the story was right, except for forged documents pointing to government connivance. But I think we went with it at that stage, because there were similar inquiries into similar corruption in both America and the Netherlands. Anyway, the final story wasn't checked and we did libel many members of the Callaghan government who then saw it, quite rightly, as an opportunity to destroy both the *Daily Mail*, which had been a thorn in their side, and me, as editor.

Why didn't they manage that?

For two reasons. First of all Rothermere decided that he wouldn't have me removed as the editor and his view was, 'Look, you've made a tremendous mistake, but you'll be a better journalist as a result of it, and as you built the paper up you will be much more dedicated to rebuilding it and repairing the damage, if I keep you on, than any newcomer.' My view was – you asked me earlier whether there was any day where I'd wanted to give up – I didn't want to give up journalism but I thought, 'I'm pretty well finished here, I shall have to go to America,' because I was under a furious personal attack.

How do you react to that?

Well you resist, but nonetheless, in this case you find that the tide of opposition grows, the mob on the doorstep gets bigger and bigger and when you go to work, you face the barrage of 'Are you resigning today?' Labour members of Parliament tried to get me arrested and tried for sedition. It was a very big story – the lead item for about four nights running on BBC news. Their argument was that we hadn't made a mistake, we had deliberately forged documents in order to try and bring down the government. They were accusing me of plotting to bring down the government, which I hadn't done, of course.

What was inside your mind when this was going on?

The knowledge that I'd made a mistake but had not plotted to bring down the government, but also of course it was more subtle and complex. Mixed up with that was the fact that when I printed that stuff, I thought it would bring down the government. But I kept resisting. I'm mentally very tough, obviously, otherwise I couldn't have done this job, but it was beginning to get to me. I did resign but it wasn't accepted. I said to Vere, 'Look, I can't take it, I can't put my family through this, it's better that I go. I can go to America and restart my life.' I gave you his response earlier. He took me into the wind, as it were, ready to stay and face it all, and I did take it all. And it got easier. It ended with the BBC doing a *Panorama* on me. They wanted me to go on it. I said, 'I can't face it.' They said, 'Well, we're going to do it anyway, we want to know all about you, we're digging into you, we're going to go into everything.' The BBC can be pretty tough too, so I went on and faced a tough interrogation, but I got through it and that was the end of it, in a funny sort of way. I cleared myself through *Panorama* in a sense – at least I cleared myself of the charge that I had plotted to bring down the government.

I established in fact that I had been incompetent, which is the truth, and from that day I never made another mistake about a forged document. Rothermere was right. I'll just give you this anecdote – *Stern* magazine came to the *Mail* with the 'Hitler Diaries'. By that time I knew everything about forgeries, I'd made myself an expert on ink, paper and everything else. I was determined that I would never, ever be caught by a forgery, and I told *Stern* that these were forgeries and that we wouldn't buy them. I said, 'Look, I went through hell, you are going to go through hell.' But no, they were true believers and they sold them to *The Times*. So I rang up the editor of *The Times*, Charlie Douglas-Hume, and said, 'I'm ringing you now as a fellow editor and telling you they are forgeries.' He responded, 'You don't know what you're talking about, you're just envious because you didn't get them. We've had them absolutely authenticated by no less than Lord Dacre [the historian Hugh Trevor-Roper], you didn't get them, too bad!' When they were finally published Rothermere said to me, 'Why didn't we have them?' and I said, 'Because they're forgeries.' 'Well, I hope you're right,' he said. 'I am right,' I replied – though I was beginning to lose my nerve a bit, then I thought, 'No. I am right,' and of course within 24 hours, I was shown to be right. So you do learn from your mistakes.

What do you think are the greatest enemies of success?

Megalomania and vanity. They cloud your judgment and your humanity.

What is the greatest pleasure you've had from your successful career?

I've often thought about this, and this is something that I am proud about, it's shown that you can do something worthwhile as a newspaper man. I'd been in Vietnam a couple of times for the *Daily Express* when the war was won and had very much liked the Far East and Vietnam, and when the North was on the point of over-running the South, there was huge concern that those who'd supported the Americans should get out. There was a Christian organization I knew of that arranged adoptions of Vietnamese war orphans in Britain. Communications were shut down and they had 100 children trapped in Vietnam who had homes arranged here and for whom the paperwork had been done. The organization went to the British government but the British government would not help them. Then they came to the *Daily Mail* and I said I would help because I saw it as a wonderful story, because I liked Vietnam and because I wanted to help this organization, being a Christian myself. It was only two or three days before the final fall of Saigon and we couldn't get an airline to help. I finally found British Midland who said they would give us a Boeing and they would fly to Vietnam, though they wanted the money upfront. Eventually we went into Vietnam and got those children out. They were all adopted and they've all grown up to become wonderful young people. They went back to Vietnam last year. Some of them have done amazingly well, and I thought, 'That started as a sort of newspaper news exercise, which turned out to be a wonderful exercise in humanity.' I get letters regularly from the families and the kids. It was something that the paper and I did, of which I'm very proud.

Has success changed you at all?

It must have done, but then, age changes you. Certainly success has made me much more confident and, I guess, more demanding in everything in life, but it's made me realize what is achievable. You try to drive your own children to be successful, but not madly successful. I do set high standards for them when we talk about things – life, work, attitudes.

If you could gather together all the young people who admire your success and want to follow a journalistic path, whether as writers, broadcasters, or as management people within a newspaper, what advice would you give to them?

Half of it depends on your own enthusiasm. You've got to want to do what you're doing, so you need to know what excites you most and stick to that – that's the first thing. The second thing is to go the extra mile, never accept second-best. And when you've done your work, you really have to edit yourself – you have to read it again, examine every adjective, look at every sentence and see if you can improve it. And when you've done that, do it again, and, as I've said, even when you've done that, you still think about it in the car or on the train going home. Another thing is attention to detail. Then there's thinking of the reader and trying to think, 'Is this message getting through? Will this be understood?' It's not just writing for yourself, it's for other people.

And in practical terms, what should they do? If they are leaving school now, should they go to university, should they do a training course for journalists, should they go and do something else and then come back to journalism?

That's hard to answer because we are all individuals. There was no journalism school when I came into journalism – you got onto the local paper as a trainee. Now people get degrees in journalism. I guess in today's world you should have a degree. That's the first thing. Secondly, I do believe that every journalist should learn shorthand, despite the fact we've got electronic equipment. There's a discipline in it and that's very important. I sit on the Press Complaints Commission and when a perfect piece of shorthand is produced, we all know whether the journalist is lying or not – so that's vital. Overall, I think you get your training and you do as much work as possible and then it's almost up to you. If you've got this tremendous urge to get writing, I see nothing wrong with trying to get on to a paper immediately. You may later regret that you didn't go to university but I never regretted it, because I've regarded Fleet Street as a university. However, it's a matter for each individual.

Do you think that everyone who is successful has an obligation to put something back into society?

I certainly feel that as far as I'm concerned. I really have involved myself in trying to complete the circle. I've got very conscious memories of when I came into this business and of the people who were my mentors and of the people who helped me. I do feel obliged to help young people and I've gone out of my way to do so, and I've found it very rewarding. I think I'm by no means alone in that an awful lot of people of my age who love this business do that. I find it very rewarding, talent-spotting 21 year-olds and giving them jobs. It's commercially rewarding too, because we get them into our group. We've always been journalistically led and we've always gone for the highest talent, so it's not just *pro bono*, it makes good business sense.

When your time comes to leave this life, what would you like people to say about you?

That he wasn't as bad as they said he was.

That's all?

No, I think I would like them to say, 'He was a good editor, a good journalist.' I am a bit preoccupied with this occupation! I wouldn't want any highfalutin things said about me, but I would quite like journalists to say, 'He was pretty good and frankly he ran a tough ship, but he wasn't as bad as they say he was. His bark was worse than his bite, and he actually did lead people rather than drive them.'

SIR TOM FARMER

Tom Farmer is one of Scotland's most inspirational business leaders, and a model for all entrepreneurs setting out from relatively humble backgrounds. The schoolboy who cleaned cookers to make some extra pocket money is now the multi-millionaire chairman of Kwik-Fit, the UK's biggest tyre and exhaust-fitting business, with a network of more than a thousand depots, and expansion onto the European mainland well under way. Success for him has come through maintaining a 'can-do' attitude – a sensible belief that everybody can achieve something. The youngest of seven children, he was brought up in a stable home and neighbourhood where people encouraged each other to 'do that wee bit extra'. Leaving school at 15 with few academic qualifications, he was rejected by the Navy because of colour-blindness, so worked his way up in civvie street from stores boy to van driver to tyre salesman. It was annoyance at not being paid his commission for three months that prompted the decision to quit and set up his own discount tyre store.

Five years later, having put in what he calculated to be 'the equivalent hours of someone who had worked until they were 65', he sold the company for enough money to retire to California. He was just 28. But he couldn't stay still for long, and soon decided to return to Scotland armed with new ideas of specialisation which were showing signs of success in the USA. Starting with exhaust systems, he created Kwik-Fit, and the motoring public flocked to a company that quickly established a reputation for taking on the more established names, and cutting the bureaucracy and time-wasting out of some of the most common maintenance chores. He saw that the more the business grew, the harder it would be to make changes. So he broke it down into a series of smaller units, each with their own 'entrepreneurial manager'. He has mellowed over the years, accepting that not everyone is driven by the same intensity and that success can also be achieved by someone 'reaching their own comfort level'. He believes his days of pushing people beyond their capabilities and limits are over. A devout Catholic, he is heavily involved in many community projects, chairing a major anti-drugs programme, buying an island just to save it from developers, and rescuing Hibernian Football Club. Life, he says, is a conveyor-belt, and you can't just sit there and watch the opportunities flow by.

Tom Farmer, what is your definition of success?

For me, it is to maintain a 'can do' attitude, but that doesn't mean believing that you can do anything in the world. If somebody asked me if I would be able to run a four-minute mile, there would be no point in my saying, 'Yes, I could do that.' But if they were to say, 'Would you run a seven-minute mile?' then I know that's within my capabilities and, if I put some extra effort in, I could be successful. People who have this can-do attitude are people who want to learn. They never hesitate in asking, 'What do you think, what are your views about this?' and they never hesitate in approaching people who have achieved some degree of success. They are always trying to find out, 'Why did you do it, why did it work for you?'

Sometimes I go back to the area where I was brought up in Edinburgh and I go to church. Afterwards in the church hall, everyone is sitting around having a cup of coffee and you are look about and think, 'How is it things worked out for me differently from all the other lads or girls?' I think it's self-belief, not a stupid self-belief, just a sensible belief that you can achieve something. Of course, one of the biggest influences in your life is the environment that you are born into. That's something you have no control over. I was very fortunate, I was the youngest of a family of seven, my mum and dad encouraged us in every way, always to do that wee bit extra. I was brought up in a terrific neighbourhood. It was a nice stable type of neighbourhood, it didn't matter if it was the policeman or the postman or whoever, they were always encouraging young people, chastising them when they had to, but also praising them. That all helps to develop you.

Is it more difficult to create that kind of environment today?

I think it is much more difficult. I often think about it and I talk about it with Anne, my wife – we were brought up together and went to the same school. We look at our own two children, Sally and Jordan, and we think about their upbringing. Sure, they are fortunate that things are going quite well for us and we have always lived in a nice house, but perhaps they have missed out on the neighbourhood feeling. They have been brought up in a neighbourhood where people don't necessarily relate to each other in the same way, people don't rely on each other or help each other in the same way – it's a bit more insular now.

When was the first time that you really thought, 'I have been a success, I have been successful at something'?

I would like to be able to remember winning a race or doing something special but there was nothing like that in my childhood. I didn't particularly shine at school but I enjoyed it.

You left at 15?

Yes. I wasn't particularly involved in the sports scene or anything. I was a bit of an independent spirit – I think that's part of my success.

Were you a rebel?

No, I wasn't a rebel to the extent of fighting against things. I was independent and again I think that was part of the upbringing that we had with my mum and dad. I was always trying to do things after school. I would either be working in chemists' shops or doing newspaper rounds, then I started to buy second-hand bicycles and put them together and sell them. I suppose the time I really thought I had been successful was when I got a job as a sales rep and part of the package was that you got a car. That was very important. I was 21 years of age and for me it wasn't the money, it was having this car which no other young person had in our neighbourhood. To me that was a real outward sign of success.

So, to a certain extent, were you driven by the desire to make money to build up a reserve of money, to be seen to be successful in the eyes of your friends and colleagues?

I was very fortunate to have been born with an independent attitude, the sort of high energy which breeds enthusiasm and a can-do approach to life. One thing I have learned is that it is very difficult to create high energy within a person, but those that have it can easily waste it. I had energy and enthusiasm in all the various jobs that I did, and I moved up from being a stores boy to a van driver and then a van salesman. They were always jobs that were relatively independent – you were out on your own. As a van driver it depends how quickly you do your round as to how many calls you can make, and it's the same as a sales rep. I enjoyed my job, and even in my late teens and early twenties. I was earning more money than my friends. The decision to start working on my own was brought about by a feeling that I had been let down in the job I then had. I thought to myself, enough is enough. I'd put in as much as I possibly could and I'd been let down, so I just wanted to be on my own. I went and found a shop in Edinburgh, and because I had quite a good reputation in the trade people backed me. One supplier gave me 100 tyres on sale or return, somebody else gave me some equipment and said pay for it when things are going well.

The real sense of achievement was being on your own and knowing that whatever success you got was totally dependent on yourself. Of course that changed when you began to realize that if you really wanted to be successful in a big way then you could only do it with a team.

You asked me if it was the money that drove me, and I have to say that without the financial gain, I don't know that I would have been as enthusiastic. It's a material world we live in, you need financial rewards, and a better standard of living. But there was also a desire for recognition, and especially so today.

Recognition by whom?

Other people, whether it be the media or your peers. I remember somebody saying to me once, when I was about to sell the first business, 'You're really doing quite well, you've got this nice house and things are going well for you, what do you really want?' And at that particular time the Motor Show was at Earls Court, and there used to be a row of booths for all the tyre manufacturers which they called 'Tyre Alley'. I remember saying to someone, it must have been about 1967, 'You know what I would really like, I would like to walk down Tyre Alley and have people say, "That's Tom Farmer".' Everybody has a little bit of vanity and there's nothing wrong with that – recognition came into it as well. There's a tremendous satisfaction in that.

Did you find it difficult to delegate in the early days?

It's probably the hardest thing that I have ever had to try to master. I think I have done it relatively well. We couldn't have almost 1,000 sites and operate in Holland and Belgium and have the size of business we have if we didn't have people who are in positions of authority and responsibility who are held accountable. But in the early days it was very very difficult. There was a learning curve. I learned a lot from talking to other people and the one thing that really came through strongly was that you must always recognize the difference between delegation and abdication. So many people make the mistake of thinking that just because they've handed something over to somebody, that's delegation. Well, it's not, of course. The real art of delegation is to hand over something to someone but also to have a clear understanding of how and when they will report back to you. They will get fed up if you are continually asking them questions and you yourself will get frustrated if you feel there's a lack of information coming through. It's not easy.

What was your first real business?

Real business? At 14 years of age I was buying old bicycles for a few pounds, doing them up and selling them for seven or eight pounds, that was a business. And when I was 15 I used to go out in the evenings after school cleaning cookers. I felt that too was a business, but I suppose my first real business was Tyre and Accessory Supplies which I started in 1964. At the time the government were about to abolish the old retail price maintenance whereby the manufacturers had always been able to stipulate the price at which you sold their products. I decided to open my own place and sell at discount prices. That took off very well. It took off because I got a bit of exposure in the media about the fact that I was giving discounts. In those days I was regarded as a bit of a pirate, giving discounts and taking on the manufacturers.

That was quite a revolutionary step in those days. Did you take a gamble with the law?

The Bill was already going through Parliament so there wasn't much chance of actually ending up in court. Things were about to change, so it was a calculated gamble, a tremendous opportunity to offer discounts and sell at the lower prices. The business took off in a big way and I needed help, so I asked some people I had known at school to join me.

Was that important to have your friends on board?

It made it easier in those early stages. We were all of the same age, we were all single, there was an unbelievable bond, you would never describe it. We had a tremendous relationship, this group of lads. We worked together and we played together, the hours didn't matter. Then we all started going out with our girlfriends together, we all married about the same time, we had families about the same time, there was a tremendous spirit. It made an unbelievable difference to have really good close friends working with me.

Why's that?

Well, we'd already built up a relationship over the years and I think the strength of our friendship was that we trusted each other implicitly. That's so important in business – working together, trusting each other.

Are you saying that your success in those early days might not have happened if you hadn't been able to bring your friends on board?

Without a doubt. I didn't have any experience of having people working with me or employing people. I had never been a manager or anything like that, so when the lads joined me it was just like a club. We all took the same wage, it was very democratic. Everybody came on a promise. The only time we stopped work would be a Friday night when we'd finish by 9 o'clock, get washed up and we'd all go to the local dancing. It was that type of relationship.

What was it drove you on? Was it money or was it taking on the establishment in your profession or what?

It wasn't money as such. We were taking £12.10s a week out of the business and were working so many hours that you didn't need a lot of money. There were really a couple of things. Firstly it was tremendous fun, you were doing something which was a bit adventurous, taking on the establishment. Secondly there was the awareness that you were actually succeeding and the customers were flowing through the door in bigger and bigger numbers. It was like being at the front in the race – you always wanted to be the winner.

OK, there you are in your mid-twenties, your first company a great success. You decide to retire at the age of 28. What was going through your mind that encouraged you to take such a drastic decision?

At the time it didn't appear drastic because I had put a lot of time into building up the business. There are two things that drive you on, one is the need for financial security and the other is that you must enjoy your job. I had financial security and I was no longer enjoying my job, there was no challenge. I calculated that I'd put in the equivalent hours of someone who had worked to 65. So I decided that I would just stop working.

Then you go to San Francisco and you have a wonderful time, but a few years later you are drawn back to set up your business again. So after what you have just said, what was it that pulled you back and made you feel you couldn't stay away from the business environment?

Hoagy Carmichael is supposed to have said the only problem about retirement is that you can never take a day off. I no longer enjoyed not being able to work. It really was Anne, my wife, who spotted it. She made it very clear one night when we were having dinner. She said, 'We got married for three things, for richer, for poorer, for better or for worse, in sickness and in health.' She leaned across the table, took my hand, squeezed it and looked me in the eye. 'There was one thing I never married you for and that was to live with you seven days a week, 24 hours a day. I think we have to do something.' By that time I had come to the same conclusion and so we came back. When we met up a couple of days after I'd been back with the original team of people who had helped me develop that first business, the only question was, 'Now you're back, what are you going to do?' That was a tremendous feeling.

And where did you get the idea for what you were going to do?

In America I'd seen the growth of specialised businesses. There were changes in the restaurant business, changes in the various service industries, and changes in the automotive industry. There were specialist paint shops, specialist gearbox people, specialist brake people, and specialist exhaust people. Back in 1964 we had started a business specialising in tyres and hadn't considered going into any other area apart from accessories. This time I decided that we would try to concentrate on exhaust systems. We discussed the idea and I was lucky to come up with a good brand name, Kwik-Fit. And that stemmed from when I used to go out in the evenings and clean cookers. I used to put a little advert in the paper, 'Kookers kleaned as new'. It was just to attract people's attention. So that was how Kwik-Fit was born.

Do you have a technique for overcoming the hiccups and setbacks that you must have faced along the way?

In any business there are always setbacks, and we've had them. Fortunately they have never caused us tremendous financial worries, more operational concerns. The best technique is to ensure that everybody in the team has the opportunity to sit down and talk about how best to overcome the problem. I have learned that three heads are better than one and ten heads are better than three.

What was your worst problem, was it expanding too quickly in the '80s?

Yes. With 50 places in 1980 there was nobody like us, we were the king of the castle. We decided to expand and very quickly went from 50 to 200 and found that we didn't have the managerial expertise, the training programme and all the other things that are necessary to handle that size of business. We were good operators, but we needed expertise in the financial field, in the marketing field, in administration and personnel. We covered all these areas but not in the depth that was needed. We were fortunate that we were able to put things right not by heavy investment but by bringing in good people who had the experience that we lacked, and it allowed us to carry on doing what we were good at.

You are hugely dependent upon customer satisfaction in your business. You introduced computerised tele-sales. Can you describe to me how you check on customer satisfaction?

It is really difficult to find out whether you are giving the customer what they want. For instance I fly up and down to London regularly and if somebody were to ask me, 'Are you satisfied with the service that the airlines provide?' I would probably answer, 'Yes, I am very satisfied.' However, if they said to me 'Is there anything that we could do which would improve our service to businesspeople like yourself?' I would come up with a number of suggestions. We found the same. Asking the question, is the customer satisfied, isn't enough, you have got to try and dig more out of them. So we have set up a tele-marketing operation. Last week we telephoned 27,000 customers.

What was the most unexpected little thing you picked up?

There was a lady who said, 'I think your boys are wonderful, everything was fine. However, can I just say one thing, when we ladies visit the ladies' room, we like to have a mirror, and there was no mirror in your ladies' room.' Within two days the manager of the centre phoned that lady and told her, 'By the way, next time you come in, we've got your mirror.' She was over the moon.

As your business grew, you broke it up into smaller units. Why was that?

The bigger the company, the harder it is to make changes. Each outlet's a small business on its own. The centre manager has got to be entrepreneurial, he has got to understand that the success of that outlet depends on how well he or she motivates their team. By keeping each unit as a small business on its own, people then are going to take more pride in it. It's a formula that's worked for me and I shall keep working on it.

You have been said to object to the term 'shop-floor workers', why?

To me that's the last generation's language. What we have in our organizations are people. Shop-floor worker was a term used to differentiate between the people on the shop floor and the so-called managers, but for me there is no difference, not in our organizations. There used to be the old management chart with the chairman at the top, then underneath you had the board of directors and then the managers and at the bottom the thousands of people who actually created the wealth in the organization. It shouldn't be like that. These thousands of people are the front line troops. In our organization, it's very simple, if you don't work at the front, your job is to support the people who do. You're only there to support. I'm part of the support team, the divisional director responsible for the south of England is a part of the support team, our financial director is part of the support team. We've got to support these people to enable them to do the job. So any terminology that in any way sets them aside or could be perceived to be talking down to them is wrong. Let's recognize that these are the people that create the wealth.

How do you break down the hierarchical barriers that tend to exist within any company?

We are fortunate. We are a 25-year-old company and this approach is a part of our culture, it's always been there. But as the business grows, one of my hardest jobs is to make sure that doesn't change. I think that most businesses today have developed into this way of thinking, there isn't the old 'them' and 'us' anymore. It's just 'us' and its only by us working together as a team that we can actually achieve anything. Of course, in that team people have different responsibilities, different influences on the success or the failure of the organization, and that is recognized by different reward systems. There are people who because of their responsibilities will draw a higher salary, but this in no way creates a culture of them and us. It's all us.

One of your directors said that if someone's not up to the job, Tom Farmer will find a suitable place in the company for them rather than fire them. Is that a strength or a weakness?

I think it's a strength, other people say it's a weakness. What I think he meant was that sometimes we've put somebody into a job which they weren't really capable of doing because it suited us to do that. When that happens we have the responsibility to make sure that we put it right and we try to find the right slot for that person. This way people recognize that the company doesn't let them down and they develop a trust in you, a loyalty to the company. But at the end of the day everyone has a job to do and if they don't do that job properly or if they are not making the effort, then there's only one way to handle that and that is to look the person in the eye and say, 'It's about time we parted company.' I don't think you should ever put up with people not giving their best. One of the biggest problems in our own organization and many others is the failure to look someone in the eye and just say, 'You ain't cracking – what's the problem?' Sometimes you'll find out that there is a problem, but in a lot of cases the real problem is that they just have not put in enough effort and when that happens they have got to go and go quickly.

Are you capable of pushing people a little too hard at times?

Yes. Not consciously but I believe we all work best under pressure provided at the end of the day there is an end to that pressure. The real thing I suppose is to make sure you identify when that pressure should come off. Sometimes I have been able to sustain the pressure longer than somebody else and haven't recognized that. One person who taught me that more than anyone was my son. He said to me, 'Dad, you know you've got to watch it, everybody's not like you. You live for your work, you've just got to appreciate that other people work to live. Sometimes you can really put too much pressure on a person.' I tell you, children are pretty smart.

Can success be achieved just by hard work, or is there an element of luck? Do you need that lucky break for real success?

There are tremendous opportunities for all of us. It's like that Bruce Forsyth show where the prizes came out on a conveyer belt. You had to remember them and the more you could remember, the more you won. Opportunities are like that in business, and in life in general. You can measure your success by how often you reach out and grasp them, and you must watch out that you don't just sit there and let those opportunities move on by.

I never really know the meaning of the word 'luck'. There's the Gary Player saying, 'The more I practise the luckier I get.' Certainly I know that the harder I work, the more successful I've been. But you can also work very hard and waste a lot of time. I can remember hours of work I've put in when it wasn't hard work that was necessary, it was being smarter that was necessary, and to be smarter you've got to sometimes take time off and sit and think. You need what I call shower thoughts – when you are standing in the shower and you can think about things. You're constantly looking for ways to do things smarter rather than working harder. In our organization it wouldn't be possible for me to ask people to work harder because they already put their heart and soul into it, but I can say, 'Let's work together to find smarter ways of doing this.' That's an important part of being successful.

Is it becoming more or less difficult to achieve success these days?

What is success? I have a friend who's a Cistercian monk, he's 70-odd years of age and he hasn't got anything in this world. He would tell you that he has as much success as anybody else in the world. People sometimes say to me, 'Tom, I don't envy what you've got. I feel I'm more successful than you because I've got all that I actually set out to get, I don't need anything else.'

So there are two levels of success – there is the comfort level where you've achieved what you want, having worked hard for it, and then there is the other level where you are continually driving on to do more. Is it important to recognize those two?

Yes, in every way.

What are the greatest enemies of success?

Complacency. If I try to identify where I missed an opportunity and why did I miss it, it was usually because a degree of complacency had set in at that particular time. For me that's the biggest danger.

Who are the people you admire most, who are your heroes, the people who you judge to have been really successful, either past or present?

In business there's a man called Robert Woodruff. He was the man who built Coca-Cola. He had tremendous clear thinking and the real secret of his success was that you should never tamper with a brand.

Has success changed you?

It must have done. A friend once warned me, 'Whether you like it or not, the unfortunate thing is that if you are financially successful there will come a day when buying a new suit or buying a shirt will not give you the same kick as it does now.' You have got to make sure that you don't get spoilt by success. Of course it changes your way of life, but I've been very fortunate in that I have been surrounded by a lot of people, and in particular Anne, who have reminded me to keep my two feet on the ground. You have to make sure that the changes don't separate you from your friends and other people you like to be associated with.

What is the greatest pleasure you've had from your success?

Business-wise, the greatest pleasure I get is being recognized as being the person who started Kwik-Fit. Anne and I went away for a few days recently and we went up to the North of Scotland. We stayed in a country hotel in the middle of nowhere and the gentleman who owned the hotel actually came out to greet us. 'Mr Farmer,' he said, 'I'm delighted to meet the number one Kwik-Fit fitter.' I couldn't have thought of a better description.

If you could gather in one room all the young people in the world who want to make as much of a success in their lives as you have in yours, what advice would you give them?

If it was in our industry maybe I wouldn't be too keen in giving them advice because they could be competition. I've never accepted the expression that says you have to live with competition. For me the competition is there for one reason, to take away my customers and I'll fight it as much as possible – the important thing is that you fight honestly. I'd come back to what I said earlier, you must have this tremendous belief in yourself and this can do attitude, because you can do it, you can achieve tremendous things.

And what if the circumstances of your own particular life tended to pull you down, to drive you down, how do you maintain that can-do approach?

I could only answer that if I'd actually experienced it. There have been occasions when things haven't worked out, when I had a nervousness that something was happening that I couldn't control any longer, but that was only for a very short time because I have this tremendous confidence in myself and the team of guys. I always knew that, whatever the problem, we could overcome it.

You are a devout Catholic. How big a part has religion played in your success?

We were brought up in a very strong Catholic environment. It was a very important part of our life, not just the going to church but the social side – the boys' club, the girls' club and going to school together. It still remains a very important thing and a lot of good friends are clergy. People ask me whether you can be successful in business and still operate within the principles of Christianity. I reply that the only way you can have a long-term successful business is if the principles of the business run parallel with the principles of Christianity. In business you can make short-term profits by cheating people, by exploiting people, whether it's a customer or the people who work with you or your suppliers. But the really successful businesses, the really big ones, Shell, C&A, Marks and Spencer, John Lewis have all been built on very sound principles. The most important Christian principle is that you love your neighbour. That doesn't mean that you love them in the way you love your family, but you respect them, you don't let them down, you don't do anything to exploit or cheat them. It's exactly the same in business.

When your time comes to depart this life, what would you like people to say about you?

What I would like would be, 'Tom Farmer, he tried his best.' That's the best compliment that anybody can give, that you tried your best.

SIR NORMAN FOSTER

Destined to become one of the great international architects, this son of a Manchester factory worker left school at 16 to work as a town hall clerk. It was 'inconceivable that anyone from my background would go to university'. But, as a teenager, he'd pored over architectural books in the local library, and, after National Service in the RAF, took an administrative job in an architect's office, where he realized that 'perhaps he wasn't quite so dim after all'. With no grant to help him, he paid his way through Manchester University by taking any job that was going – selling furniture, making crumpets, driving an ice-cream van and working as a bouncer at a cinema ('a real irony, because I'd been bullied mercilessly at school'). He went on to Yale to  *study under the great James Stirling, and there met another rising star, Richard Rogers, with whom he formed a promising partnership, working out of his wife's flat. The two men have long since gone their separate ways, but between them they dominate a world architectural stage that is big enough for them to dismiss any suggestions of rivalry.*

The clean straight lines of Norman Foster's Modernist approach dominate skylines from Tokyo to Stansted Airport, challenging convention in both design and engineering. Whether remodelling the Reichstag or Wembley Stadium, giving central London a new look for the Milennium, or completing the new £2 billion Hong Kong Airport, the largest construction project in the world, he drives his team hard. Having come within a hairsbreadth of failure, he accepts there is an element of fear in his office: 'If you take any task seriously, then you are going to be fearful for its outcome.' He believes that 'the only way you achieve quality and high standards is by inspiration, by attempting to set examples, and by creating the spirit of a shared endeavour where everybody, from the chairman to the cleaner, wants to have a pride in what they're doing'. Here he talks about how the architect has to understand but also challenge and question the nature of a brief, and the need to have the courage to admit you haven't got it right – even at the eleventh hour. He reveals the approach that delivered some of his most admired projects, and, above all, advises that throughout all the difficulties and obstacles, you should never be 'prepared to sit around and take advantage of the many excuses that present themselves for failing'.

Sir Norman, what is your definition of success?

I've never thought about it, but I don't think it's a static thing. I'm floored by the question. I was about to deliver in full flow the various definitions of success in a field like architecture. Is it winning awards? Is it getting a good press? Is it a client who comes back to you a second time? Is it seeing a building where people are actually happy?

I think that the only thing that touched me recently, when I think I came close to having an element of success, was when a television unit followed a project from its beginning. It was a rarely publicised home for mentally handicapped in the Forth Valley. There was a lot of involvement with the patients and with the people who were looking after them and it talked about the architecture and then, when the architects had long since gone, it ended up with a postscript by the doctors and the nurses. They said that they had never seen patients so transformed – patients that they'd looked after for years, in one instance for 17 years – they'd changed dramatically. They put that down to the patients' surroundings, yet the basis of that project was really not to do something special, because the budget and the timescale were not unusual. What made it what you might call a successful project was that it had taken all the ingredients that normally produce excuses, and somehow the combination of energy, hard work and the quality of teamwork, of people pooling their resources and having a shared vision of what the priorities were, on that occasion delivered.

If you and your work are in the public eye, is it possible to be successful without having the critical acclaim of the outside world and of the media? Is there a kind of inner success that satisfies you, which might not satisfy the outside world?

I think success is probably the wrong word. A building involves a vast number of people – people who make it, commission it, vet it, or audit it, and an incredible number of parties have to be satisfied from the Fire Authorities and Health Authorities onwards. It's a very complex process. You're aware of all the things below the surface, so outside the building itself is like the tip of an iceberg. Here in our offices you see the total body of everything that comes together in a project. There have to be occasions when you feel you've justified your role in a project while it may receive criticism and doesn't appear successful to the outside world.

On the other hand, maybe you're in possession of so much insight and information on a project that you know in your heart of hearts it could have been better, despite its being received very, very well. So you can really end up disatisfied, even though people are saying very nice things about it. Nowadays, there is more interest in architecture and therefore more criticism, but that has to be healthy, that has to be positive. The fact that this country is open to the involvement of architects from outside Britain is very good for everybody.

How do you deal with criticism?

You can only do what we do if you're inherently optimistic. If you weren't you wouldn't even try, because the task is so awesome. Every building is a one-off, an extraordinary complex network. A building evolves over a long period of time. The people who may have started that project commissioned you, and in a way they are the true patrons, the true creative driving force. It is they who make it possible for an architect to achieve anything worthwhile which goes beyond the humdrum, anything that might improve the quality of life. That's where it starts, but over the period of the project you could have changes – the people who shared the idealism of that project could have moved on and been replaced, and this happens quite frequently. The new people might have a completely different point of view, they might deliberately want to sweep clean, challenging and changing the course of a project, so it demands tremendous staying power. In the end, we all are very human and that does affect you – you develop a kind of armour against such circumstances. You develop a thick skin. In the end, the most important thing is your inner self, knowing whether you did it as well as you could have done – and I say 'you' in both a personal and a collective sense.

Do you ever have any inner doubts about any of your projects? Do you ever think, 'Maybe I have got this wrong'? Or is the secret of your success that you ride across any doubts that might crop up?

I'm suspicious of snap judgments. Even the most short-lived buildings (and some are deliberately short-lived) are around for quite a long time, and they have a major influence in the public domain, they dramatically affect the lives of everybody who inhabits them. So it's very important for us to test and to challenge, and I think that that is an important aspect of what we do as architects. In a way, it's not architecture, it's more a response to the client – the client tells the architect what the specific needs are. It's unusual to challenge and penetrate that client domain – if the client is a bank then it's the world of banking, if a ship owner, it's the world of ships, what makes ships tick and the docks they arrive at. If it's an airport, the brief involves all the infrastructure of airlines, security, and all the things that lie behind the scenes. That generates the need for an architect to understand, but also to question and challenge the nature of the brief. That process may indicate another way of doing it, another way of looking at that kind of building, perhaps reinventing that particular building type. Occasionally a client says, 'I have to have this plant operating this time next year', and it's a mission impossible. But even so, you pace that time so that you allocate as much to challenging and questioning.

Hopefully, if you revisit a building, although things might have moved on over 20 years – the outside walls for example may have been overtaken by more sophisticated technology or the plant that drives the building may have changed over time – essentially, the diagram of that project is right. When you look back at what you've done, the question you as k is, 'Was the strategic design right – did we get it right?' That is the acid test.

If during the project you realize that you haven't got it right, you need the courage to admit that to yourself, and share that knowledge with everybody involved. And then, at one minute to midnight as it were, you turn it around and get it right, because you have enough knowledge to allow you to act very, very quickly. That can be totally unnerving, but it has happened and I am sure it will happen again in the future.

With what projects in particular?

I can remember one project – the Sainsbury Centre, where we realized very, very late in the day that we could transform that building so it would be significantly better, but that meant tearing up a lot of work and throwing it away. It meant burning a lot of midnight oil and I remember one meeting with the consultants who shared that responsibility. It was asking very real sacrifices and one of those consultants – a very close friend as well – said, 'I think you're right, but I think we're so far down the line, I think that that direction should be for another building,' and I remember saying, 'There may not be another building – we have to get it right for this building.' It was the right thing to do. It was unnerving at the time, but it transformed that building in all kinds of ways.

As an architect, do you feel that you are only ever as good as your last project, or can you develop to such a stage in terms of your international reputation that you can ride out the occasional criticism – indeed, in the nature of things, do you have to expect to do so?

In the world of building there are so many variables, there is the potential for so many things to create difficulties. Every building is a one-off. We did a major project which is an ocean-going motor yacht which cruises around the world and does three tours every year, one in the Caribbean, one in the Far East and one in the Mediterranean. It moves at 35 knots, it generates its own electricity – it's a floating hotel, it's a restaurant, it's everything, it's unbelievably complex. Yet against all the odds, with all that new technology, it's an extraordinary success story. On the other hand, I can show you a traditional building with absolutely traditional materials which two years after completion will start to have a problem with water penetration that challenges the best brains in Britain. When you're operating at a scale where you are doing some of the most complex buildings in the world – Hong Kong Airport is the largest construction project in the world at the moment, it is one room under a single roof of 45 acres, it is on an island, on land that was made in three years and this building, which is bigger than Heathrow (which evolved over somewhere between 50 and 60 years) is being created in just three years – that poses problems of logistics, of management, of the way that materials come together, of quality control on a scale which is totally new. There is no parallel, it involves for example the largest glazing contract in history. You can guarantee there are going to be problems. Buildings are designed by people, made by people, lived in by people, and we are all imperfect. All you can do is use all your energy, experience, expertise, research, tap the experience of others, be very, very open, ask all the questions a lot of people might be embarrassed to ask, and when you feel you know everything, assume you know nothing and then listen to, engage with, the experience of others and finally back your judgment.

After you've had a great deal of experience as an architect, does there come a point when you say, 'Look, I've cracked it'?

That must be the most dangerous point in the world. If you ever allow yourself to feel that, then alarm bells should be ringing in your head and red lights flashing around you.

But isn't it safer to hang on to success and maintain success by reproducing something you know works, rather than always pushing forward the boundaries and going for new challenges?

I can't even give the same *talk* twice. Seriously, I do every talk – whether it's to a group of students or whether it's the kind of presentations that one might have to make to people like Royal Fine Arts Commissions or Planning Committees – as if I've never given a talk in my life before, and I think I can honestly say that if somebody comes into this office and asks us to do a project it would be the same. For example, the Mayor of Santiago de Compostela contacted us. We went out, met him, he came here. He loved the Barcelona Tower that we did, the communication tower, he a had a similar problem with his city, which is a pilgrimage city defiled by the most ugly communications mast overlooking the main square. Santiago is a pilgrimage city – you approach the spire of the dome of the cathedral from afar – and we started from scratch as if we'd never done anything like that before. Obviously we had knowledge of the subject from before. The mayor assumed a tower but we didn't – the project is a platform, so it doesn't intrude into the skyline. You do not need a tower there because Santiago is special – it's special because of the elevation, because its whole catchment area faces south and has the ocean to the north. So I think if we ever feel we know the answer and think it's just a re-run, that's the time we should give up.

Let me take you back to your early days. You were the son of a Manchester factory worker and you left school at 16. To what extent do you feel your success was shaped by your background and upbringing? What were the formative forces in your early years that shaped (a) your ambition, and (b) your desire to be an architect?

I found myself in Manchester a couple of years ago. The university gave me an honorary degree. I was with a very distinguished group, some of them very famous politicians, and they really put me on the spot because they insisted that I should make the speech on behalf of all of us who were receiving honorary doctorates. That was an intimidating prospect, but I touched on my days as a student in Manchester. I said that at the time I really thought I was poor, because ours was a very poor family and I didn't have a grant, so I had to work to pay my way, to earn money for fees, and I said it has taken me a very long time to realize that I am very rich. I had incredibly supportive parents who were very loving and very caring and in that sense I was left entirely to discover a direction. Once I'd discovered that, I was so driven by it, I had so much passion for the idea that I could do it. I think that testing yourself to the extent that finally you do what you want to do does involve a particular degree of commitment, and sacrifices often go with it.

When was the moment when you actually decided, 'This is what I want to do'?

I must have been about 21 after National Service. I left school at 16, and I think that my parents were instrumental in persuading me to take a job in the Town Hall. I think from their perspective – and I can understand it looking back – that was the ultimate in respectability and had the stability they'd never been able to achieve in their own lifetime.

What kind of a job was that?

It was in Manchester Town Hall in the City Treasurer's Office. I would be a clerk during the day, doing wage rounds, carrying vast sums of money around – it would unthinkable now – making up wage packets, collecting petty cash from outposts around the city, from the parks department, the public lavatories, the day nurseries and so on. Making tea in between for my superiors, and studying commercial law, commercial general knowledge and bookkeeping at the College of Commerce in the evenings.

I guess what then happened was that I didn't feel comfortable in that environment and I think I knew in my heart of hearts that really I wasn't the stuff that local government administration is made of. I wasn't filled with a burning ambition to become the next City Treasurer. Then I went off to do National Service, which was compulsory at that time.

I'd always been interested in architecture. As a teenager I used to inhabit the local library and read quite sophisticated books on architecture – original works by Le Corbusier; one book, *In the Nature of Materials* by Henry Russell Hitchcock on the work of Frank Lloyd Wright – they're the kind of books that I would have on my shelves now and go back to as reference works, but I was discovering them back then. It's very difficult to describe the background where I was brought up. For example, it was inconceivable that anybody would go to university – an honest day's work was manual work and anything else was considered as opting out. It was really only after National Service that I realized that it *was* possible to go to university and I eventually went into an architect's office using the fact that I'd had two years in the Town Hall – it was really on the contract side, contract administration as an assistant to the contract administrator. During that time, I really plucked up the courage – which took a great effort – to try and engage architects and those studying architecture in conversations about architecture, with much trepidation and a great deal of humility, and I realized for the first time that although I'd never been to a school of architecture, I was quite well read on the subject. I asked one person what he thought of Frank Lloyd Wright and he looked at me blankly and said, 'Is he at the College of Art?' I realized then that perhaps I wasn't quite so dim. It was out of that that I got a place at Manchester University, but I couldn't get a grant. Manchester Education Authority funded the College of Art and you could become a registered architect by qualifying there and then taking the exams, but I'd done enough research to know that the University was better, and at that point I wasn't going to compromise, even if that meant earning my way though university.

How did you earn your way through university?

I sold furniture in a department store on Saturday afternoons, I made crumpets overnight in bakeries, I drove delivery vans, I worked in garages under cars covered from head to foot in grease and oil, I worked in cold stores heaving crates of frozen ice cream, I sold ice cream from little vans around the housing estates, I was a bouncer at a cinema throwing out teddy boys and being confronted with knuckle dusters (which was a real irony because I'd been bullied mercilessly when I was at school). I did anything and everything. I also travelled every summer to Italy or to Scandinavia, because pretty well every year I'd win a cash award for academic achievement. For example, I won the RIBA measured drawing prize which was given to me by Sir Basil Spence. That was £100, which in the late 1950s was a lot of money.

You talked about being bullied at school. Was that a factor in shaping your determination to succeed?

I've no idea. I've never really thought about it. Possibly I was bullied because I was the odd one out.

Why were you the odd one out?

My parents sent me to a small school which was not a state school, although eventually through the eleven-plus I went to a state high school. I came from literally the other side of the tracks, so at this rather quaint little private school I was the odd one out, and then when I got back home, as far as all the kids who lived around me were concerned, I was again the odd one out because I didn't go to their school. I guess an element of that continued at the high school that I went to, which was again in an area which was essentially a middle-class area rather than a working-class area.

You got your degree, you then went off to Yale to study under James Stirling and it was there that you met Richard Rogers and set up Team Four, working out of your wife's flat. Then you famously split up. Has that rivalry between you been a driving force, pushing you to accept ever greater challenges?

I certainly don't see it that way and even if I turn myself inside out to try and see it that way, I can honestly say I don't.

But there is a competitive instinct there, isn't there? You want to be the best.

The world is such a big place and I genuinely don't think we're in competition. I think that we've gone in quite divergent ways, although I know that it's a kind of fashionable game to link us and to draw comparisons. But if you look at the buildings and you look at the way in which we work as architects, we are in fact very, very different, and we're very different as individuals. Maybe it's the very difference as individuals which brought us together and maybe it's the fact that there are aspects of Richard and his qualities and his background and the kind of person that he is that I respect enormously. I think that's paralleled in the way that Richard sees me and in the way we came together. America was fantastic for both of us, again in rather different way. We certainly benefited and shared extraordinary insights through the work of other architects like Frank Lloyd Wright or Mies van der Rohe or the West Coast school of architects with Charles and Ray Eames, and also the whole thrust and optimism and dynamic of America was liberating for us in different ways. When I went to the States I really felt at home for the first time because I wasn't the odd one out. You can imagine that to go through a university – particularly at that time a place like Manchester, a very traditional university – and not have a grant and be essentially a part-time student doing a full-time course, was pretty rare and unusual. But in America it's absolutely normal to be working your way through university or to be borrowing money to study.

And were you touched by the success ethic in the States?

I thought it was terrific. I still do, and I'm very, very grateful to America and to the education that I had there. James Stirling was a visiting critic, but the combination of people like Paul Rudolph and Serge Chermayeff and Louis Khan in Philadelphia, a whole range of individuals and influences was, I think, formative. At Yale the head, Paul Rudolph, at a snap could instantly mobilize the whole school on a design, so that in the first year the masters class had 24 hours in which to design, say, the toll booth or the toll station at the end of a turnpike motorway. You were then left with your own resources, you backed your judgment and then presented your scheme to a wider jury which Paul Rudolph had invited and some would be quite awesome in terms of their reputation. All this – the idea that you were in a forum and you presented your work – was totally new, because at Manchester, which was a very traditional university, you handed your work in and three weeks later you got it back with a mark, no explanation sometimes, just the mark, and that was it. There was very little in the way of dialogue.

Richard's background was completely different, he came out of the Architectural Association, it was a completely different world. When there were student uprisings and so on, there was nothing to rise up against, because they'd had a very mature relationship with those in a teaching role. I think that in the same way we derived different things from our experience in America. It brought us together and we shared – and I think still do share – a language in which in relatively few words, or by looking at an image, we can have an exchange of ideas. That was something that I think was part of an extraordinary creative period. When we went our different ways, that was for a combination of reasons. It was rather like some pop groups which come together and contain within them the seeds indicating that later they will go their own different ways and perhaps form different groups or be solo performers. The same thing happened to us, we've gone in a divergent direction professionally, but when we come together it's as friends and with that shared experience, although we still have things that we disagree about – it's not rivalry. I think we operate in different places. Sometimes we do come together to compete for the same project but that's quite rare.

In building up a successful architectural career, does it help to court controversy in terms of designs?

Being different for the sake of being different is a stupidity, a madness, and I think there are, in some of the more fashionable 'isms' of the world of architecture, certain movements which cultivate that, and create a rather mysterious language, which I have to say I don't understand. I think architecture is about very down-to-earth issues, it's the stuff a building is made of. If, when you examine the challenge of the combination of a client, the needs of the people who will use that building when they're going to work in it, live in it, and the site on which that building will be built, you honestly believe that the solution to those challenges is something different from anything that's been done before, then in the course of that you are challenging the status quo. That's going to excite controversy and debate. You might be going back to something that in the past was considered quite traditional, but people have forgotten that that tradition even exists. You might be using materials in a way that they haven't been used before in a building but perhaps they've been used in a different context – you might, in a sense, almost be reinventing that building type.

Are there new challenges to come? Must you constantly be looking for new ideas and challenging the status quo in order to be really successful?

I think you have to take the word 'successful' out of it, because that implies that you do what you do for something which is out there. I think you do what you do for the sake of it, but in the process of doing it, you may challenge an entrenched view. For example, going back to an earlier point about the little home for the mentally handicapped, we challenged the idea that the mentally handicapped had to have a room off an institutional corridor. We demonstrated that like everybody else they could have a front door. Now that is, in a way, almost reinventing the wheel, but maybe you have to be – I don't know what the word is – perhaps *naïve* enough to contemplate that route of action.

Is it possible tto retain the degree of control you used to have?

In many ways I feel much closer to everything. In one way I feel I have a lot of contact with the people that we work for, and I do perhaps more drawing now than I've ever done before, but over time a number of things have happened. I think that we've evolved the kind of spaces that work for us. We don't have separate little rooms, we're all together in this very, very large room, so just walking from one end of this room to the other involves you with people working on projects together, just stopping here, stopping there, or somebody stopping me as I go past. Also, if I look across there I'm seeing new generations coming through the practice and I'm seeing my partners averaging something like 25 years' experience, and I think we all learn together, we all evolve together.

That means you have to surrender a certain degree of control. You have to delegate a bit more than you would have done in the past?

I think it's sharing. It's very different from design by committee. Also we're very mobile and although we all travel a great deal, we still have every Monday morning around this table, we have our meeting here in the heart of the office, so I think a lot of it is about communication. But yes, it *is* different from those early days. But it is a balance because to do projects at the scale that we've been talking about and also to retain the flexibility at the other end of the scale. To be as equally obsessed, if you like, with the design of a door handle, bringing to it the same degree of care and concern and love, needs a balance between conflicting pressures. So to be, in a way, mobile enough, compact enough, dynamic enough to be able to respond to a larger project, to be able to cope with the bureaucracy of projects at that scale, but also to be able to control them down to fine-scale detail – that demands a continuous balancing act.

And what about personal qualities that you bring to your firm's success? You're ambitious, some people say you're ruthless, some people say you're driven – what do you see as the main personal qualities that you bring?

In a way you have to point the microphone at some of the people around me and get those answers from them. I think that nothing we do can ever be achieved by the image of somebody directing like a maestro at the head of a large orchestra – it can never happen like that. The only way you achieve quality and high standards is by inspiration, by attempting to set examples and by creating the spirit of a shared endeavour where everybody genuinely wants to have a pride in what they're doing and developing that – right from the head of the board of a company that you may have as a client, right down to somebody who is cleaning the building site. To get, for example, a shared endeavour and concern about the quality of the surface of the concrete as it comes out.

You can never get anywhere in this field and I suspect any other field of endeavour by barking at somebody or by this image of being ruthless. Everybody will tell you to push off, and quite rightly.

And yet you have to have a certain amount of drive. One employee said that there was a certain amount of fear in your office because you were always working to these tight deadlines. Is there any truth in that?

I think there's probably a degree of truth in that, because I too have a degree of fear. I have a degree of fear because of the people I'm responsible to. I think that if you take any task seriously then you are going to be fearful for its outcome. We are all against Murphy's Law.

Who are your heroes? Who are the people you regard as being hugely successful, past or present, in your profession or outside it?

I think you look up to people who've created buildings that have endured, which have qualities which inspire you, and as you visit them you're moved by them. So it's anybody who's done that, and they may or may not be named. You may step into a most magnificent barn or a totally anonymous structure and be completely awed by it, or you may read the exploits of anybody who's responded to challenge whatever those challenges are, whether they've been the heroic engineers of the past, the bridge builders, the monument builders or people who've made extraordinary achievements – epic flights and suchlike, I suppose. Anybody who's stretched themselves.

Do you think that it is necessary to experience a degree of sacrifice and failure in order to be really successful. Are you fortified and strengthened by that?

Well, I suppose it must be the yin and the yang. Unless you've experienced unhappy times, then you have no measure of what happiness might be. Unless you've experienced bitter disappointment, then there could be no pleasure in being successful. In a very competitive world, you pitch your design skills against others and then somebody decides who wins, and so, to that extent, unless you know what it's like to lose, then there's no satisfaction on those occasions when you win.

What do you think is the greatest pleasure you've had from your success?

Perhaps the ability to be at home and look forward to coming here to the office, and to be here and to look forward to going home. Being fortunate to have an extraordinary wife and to have found that degree of personal happiness and be fortunate enough to have colleagues that I really look forward to being with.

Do you think that every successful person has a conflict between the priorities of their home life and the priorities of their professional life and that most successful people end up giving priority to the professional life?

I think it's a tall order to find the balance between different worlds and I would agree that the challenge is there between the two worlds that you mentioned. For me there's another world as well, that of some of my private passions, and the challenge is to get the balance between those private passions, my home life and my professional life. I think that true happiness is getting the balance right, even though it's always in danger of jumping out of one box or the other. But I feel very privileged to be able to say in this conversation that, wonderfully, they're not in conflict.

What about your aviation, your flying – is that a great combination of work and pleasure?

No, there's a degree of frustration in that. When I started flying sailplanes, it had no dimension beyond pure personal pleasure, working the elements, gaining extraordinary insights into nature and experiencing a great personal challenge in terms of harnessing the, how can I say, solar energy if you like, lift and sink to get from one place to another and not land out in a field but complete the task. In one sense I've been very fortunate, in that in aviation terms I now integrate flying into a professional life in such a way that I couldn't do what I do as an architect if I didn't fly as a professional pilot, that's the only way that I could get around Europe and be here in the morning and back in the evening. But the downside of that is that I hanker more and more after pleasure flying, using light aircraft just for the pleasure of it, and I think that I have to work at that balance. I also enjoy cross-country skiing.

If you could gather together all the young people in Britain who look up to you as a role model, what advice would you give them?

I'd try to put into context some of the things that look like difficulties and I think I'd try to point out that what appear as incredible obstacles looked at in a different light could be really powerful incentives, and that really if you genuinely, passionately believe in something, if you really want to do it, then you're going to do it anyway, you just have to have enough conviction and want to do it enough, even though the situation appears at times hopeless. And that's not just true of somebody starting out. In the life of this office, it's been through absolutely appalling times and it's put a very brave face on them. It's been through economic recessions. But we've gone beyond the boundaries of this country, we've not been prepared to sit around and take advantage of all the many excuses that present themselves for failing.

What do you mean by that?

Well, in the recession we had no alternative but to cut back, but at the same time we were prepared to take massive risks, so far as it's possible for an architect to act as an entrepreneur and to back a judgment.

Risk is important?

Everybody talks about the success of Hong Kong Airport. Nobody talks about the time that the office went through a massive series of cutbacks because it was hit by the recession and then does Hong Kong Airport and invests everything in a competition against consortiums from around the world who had expertise and great financial backing. Now what would have happened if we'd *not* won Hong Kong Airport? That was a risk.

Would you have failed, because some of your friends have said you've come very close to failure?

I think that if you really push the boundaries then at times you must come close to failure.

How do you recover from it?

I think it's a battlefield in those circumstances and you fight to win.

One final question. What would you like people to say about you when your time comes to leave this life?

That he did his best.

SIR DAVID FROST

'Don't be boxed into any particular part of television,' he says, *'feel you can spread right through it.'* No one has succeeded in doing that to quite the same extent as this presenter of the BBC's Breakfast With Frost *and* ITV's Through the Keyhole. *From satirist to serious interviewer, from chat show host to documentary maker, from film producer to author, from bidder for TV franchises to businessman running his own group of companies, he has for over three decades earned a unique place in the affections of viewers on both sides of the Atlantic. His 'rather chaotic and frantic' schedule (at one time he was flying to the USA and back every week) is driven by his belief in 'the reverse of Parkinson's Law'.*

Instead of work expanding to fill the time allotted to it, he is convinced that 'your time expands to allow you to fulfil all the things you want and are sufficiently determined to fulfil'. The only child of a Methodist minister, he was brought up feeling that 'everyone has a duty not to waste time, opportunity or talents'. He walked across to neighbours to watch television because his family 'couldn't afford one of their own'. After a 'gap year' as a lay preacher, he went on to Cambridge, joining the famous Footlights revue, where he remembers feeling 'instantly at home' on their first appearance on local television. He hosted a twist dancing competition for ITV and worked the clubs as a stand-up comic, which is where he was discovered by Ned Sherrin and, at the age of 23, offered his big break – presenting television's first big satire show That Was The Week That Was (TW3) *for the BBC. He advises: 'Keep looking for new frontiers and trying new ideas, and just because a new idea doesn't test market very well doesn't mean it's wrong.'*

Way back in 1964, a newspaper predicted he would have 'a short life and a sad decline', and there is occasional sniping at his interviewing technique as 'too soft', but by asking tough questions in a nice way he often gets more out of his guests than the more aggressive interviewers, producing the quotes that generate new stories or drive old ones forward. He says here that 'success, like ambition, has a slightly negative connotation in Britain', but criticism 'comes with the territory – you've got to take the rough with the smooth'. And do take risks – 'if you think you've got a 50-50 chance, go for it !'

Sir David, what is your definition of success?

There are two sorts of success. There is success in the eyes of the world, i.e. success as a measure, and then there is success in your own eyes. True success, I suppose, needs to combine both. By that standard, of course, you could have a situation where many great artists, Cézanne for example, were not recognized in their own lifetime and so I suppose never knew that first, outward success. So although Cézanne would not qualify on the first basis, he would on the second in the sense that he was a success in his own eyes.

The reason I divide the two types is because I think that success has a slightly negative penumbra at times in Britain, as ambition does. These words are sometimes seen as rather superficial. For instance, if anyone asks what makes you a success, one always wants to say, 'First of all that's not my judgment that's your judgment and it's very nice of you to say that, but I am not claiming it.' As you know, in America ambition is an unarguably good virtue, but in this country ambition can be taken to mean a ruthless search for success regardless of principle or conviction – it is a more negative word. So I would say success divides itself into two. Some would say that what the world deems success is not necessarily success at all in the long term, for example, the pot-boiler author who sells millions of copies but who will be forgotten in 50 years. Then there is success in the sense of your own assessment of what you've done. That comes back to fulfilment.

Your upbringing was Puritan – no Sunday newspapers, no TV, no alcohol. Did you react against that and was it a factor driving you to achieve success?

I think it was a factor in terms of not wasting time and talent and so on. Of the three things you mention, the Sunday newspapers and the alcohol were my parents' principles, the lack of TV was much more a Methodist minister's lack of stipend, as they used to say. We couldn't afford a TV set and so I watched my first TV on a Saturday night across the road with neighbours. But that was a financial consideration – I don't think my parents were ever opposed to TV. They were opposed to alcohol and, for a while, to Sunday papers, although they came round to that. The Methodist Church has since come around of course, it is no longer a teetotal church. The curious thing about my life, in a way, is that I never really rebelled, I never really rebelled against God or the Church particularly. I was ahead of the Methodist Church in embracing the concept of wine but they later followed. But I never really truly rebelled against my upbringing.

What was it in your upbringing that shaped your success?

The main thing was this factor of time and talents – the duty of people to use whatever time and talents they have to the full. It was a Puritan ethic of my Puritan parents. They weren't puritanical in the sense of censorship or whatever, but Puritan values played a very big role in me driving myself. Allied to this was a very happy home life which was the perfect sort of basis for this rather chaotic and frantic life that I have led ever since – there was a solid bed-rock.

Another thing – and I think this is something that parents either do or do not give their children – was that my parents imbued me with a tremendous sense that anything was possible, you can pull off anything if you try hard enough. My parents basically convinced me that I could do almost anything. The two things they forgot were swimming and singing and I have no confidence in either, which makes me think that the confidence I have in everything else does come from them.

I think that an insecure childhood must have a very, very strong effect. Mind you, an absolutely hopeless childhood, an absolutely splintered childhood can also affect people in one of two ways – it can give them an enormous drive, or leave them as a basket case. You meet two people from tragically broken homes – one's made their life work, one hasn't. So there's still a personal factor in there. I'm not suggesting that people who don't have happy childhoods and a happy home cannot achieve later, they can; but I think it is a tremendous help to have the feelings of confidence and self-confidence that a happy childhood gives you – it's a tremendous plus.

When you went across the road to watch TV for the first time, did you say, 'That's for me'?

I loved it instantly, but though I think if there was a 'that's for me' moment it came a bit later. I remember going to their house, I would have been about 13 or 14, and it was therefore the mid-'50s so just prior to the start of ITV. I think the shows on alternate Saturday nights on BBC had Benny Hill and Dave King. The 'that's for me' moment came later when I was up at Cambridge and I was in the Footlights, the university revue and cabaret society. There was a programme called *Town and Gown* on Anglia TV hosted by Dr Glyn Daniels, who was at that time still a great national figure from his BBC show *Animal, Vegetable and Mineral.* This was Anglia TV's weekly obeisance to Cambridge, because they were based in Norwich. It was a weekly programme and they wanted a Christmas edition in December 1959. The producer, Michael Jeans, wanted to do a spoof edition of *Town and Gown* and Peter Cook and I wrote it. It was a parody of all sorts of TV programmes and the day we went in to record it, I felt instantly at home, so that was the 'this is for me' moment, December 1959.

And from that moment was your desire to be a success in television all-consuming?

I think the crucial thing about success is that it should be a by-product. There are certain things in life that are better if achieved as a by-product. For instance, I don't think you can say, 'I am going to be happy.' You do the things you believe in or enjoy and you are happy as a result. But you can't say, 'Right, my object in life is to be happy,' because that way you somehow focus on the chimera rather than the reality. And likewise I don't think I ever thought, 'I want to be a success,' because the word has that partially negative penumbra. I think you set out to do things, and hopefully as a by-product of those things, people conclude that what you have done has been successful. However, I don't think you can go hell-for-leather for success, because I think that's self-defeating. Success should be a by-product of doing the things you believe in and the things you enjoy.

Do you accept that the most successful people have got to have an element of planning in their lives?

Yes. You can certainly plan for achievement or you can plan for the future rather than specifically for success. For instance, I can remember I had done *That Was The Week That Was* and its follow-up programme *Not So Much A Programme, More A Way Of Life*, and I thought, 'What should I do next?' It seemed to me that there were two things. One was to follow up the humour or satire of *That Was The Week That Was* with another programme which was based on intelligent humour but which was more contemporary than topical and more social than purely political – and that became *The Frost Report*. And having seen Jack Parr and Johnny Carson in America, the other thing was to do a form of talk show but then I wanted to do a talk show with a participating audience, a talk show where the audience were more than visual wallpaper, and that hadn't really been done here at that stage – it hadn't been done in America either – but it was a combination of the talk-show idea and the participating-audience idea that I worked on with Tony Jay. Now those two ideas came from a moment of clear decision-making about what I ought to do next. I didn't think of it in terms of success, but in terms of how can I move on, how can I find some new frontiers, etc. And that was a time when I did plan ahead.

In general, though, I think that life is improvisations upon a theme, so I don't think that everything is necessarily a result of good planning. There are opportunities that come along, which you didn't know would come along. So on the one hand you have a guideline for the type of thing you want to do and believe in and the sort of things you enjoy, the sort of things you are looking to do, but on the other hand you've always got to be ready for the unforeseen opportunity because we all need luck, we all need opportunity, and a lot of the time the test is how you respond to these opportunities.

And yet you could have said at one stage, 'I'm successful as a satirist, I will therefore stay in the business of satire and won't take the risk to move on to serious current affairs and business ventures.'. Do you require a sort of leap of faith in order to do that? Do you have to say, 'I'm taking a gamble here, but it's worth doing because I simply can't stand staying in this single area in which I am a success'?

Yes, that's absolutely right, you think to yourself, 'If I just stay doing what I've done so far, even if it were only for two or three years, then I will calcify like X or Y. You've got to take the risk, you've got to take the gamble. I suppose it's not so much gambling as risk-taking.

How do you judge that risk?

You have to think you've got a sporting chance of pulling it off, even if the odds are against you. Other people can say, 'Don't do that,' as they have said at various times, you know, the odds are 20-to-1 against, but if you think you can beat those odds, if your private assessment is that you've got a 50-50 chance, then go for it. I think that's the key.

Is a degree of sacrifice neccessary for people to be really successful? Have you had to experience some degree of sacrifice, possibly even some degree of failure, in order to be truly successful?

I don't think that I have, attractive though it is to say I've sacrificed and so on. I don't think that I can claim to have had this enobling experience of major sacrifice. I suppose the only sacrifice, if any, was that I have worked very hard, but that's not really a sacrifice because I love it. I remember when I was commuting to the States every week, people said, 'Bloody hell, he really is pushing it,' but I couldn't really claim that to be a sacrifice, because I was enjoying it. The only sacrifice I suppose would be the working hours, which have been all-embracing at times. But then one of the most basic factors is that you do enjoy your work. I have a more-or-less endless get up and go, but it is always for things that I enjoy doing. If I was doing something that I didn't enjoy ... my nightmare would be to be a dentist, gazing into people's decaying mouths all day. But if I was a dentist I'm sure I'd start working at 9.30 in the morning and be exhausted by ten o'clock because I would loathe it

There are two qualities which are underestimated in terms of making for a successful life – two rather prosaic things which I have only ever seen mentioned once. Dr Anvon Rupert of the Rembrandt Empire in South Africa – he is 80 this year – brought out a book on leaders and leadership and one of the people in the book quoted two qualities which struck an echo with me – the vital qualities of energy and enthusiasm. Now they sound rather prosaic words but they are absolutely basic because if you enjoy what you do, you love doing it and so on, that gives you a hell of a step up over people who don't enjoy what they are doing. Obviously health is a vital factor, but the factors for success are summed up, it seems to me, in those words – energy and enthusiasm. They carry with them the sense of conviction that what you're doing is the thing you want to do or that you believe in.

In pursuing success a great many people are forced to make a choice at some stage in their lives between work and family. How have you approached that?

I suppose by delaying the family bit to have the fun of it now. Timing is essential to all these things and there were one or two terrific ladies along the way who were more keen to get married than I was. I wasn't ready and I was intent on achieving some things in America. At that stage the career dictated the timing in a way, although one wasn't consciously making a career decision, one just didn't feel ready to settle down and get married. Now as it happens that was no sacrifice at all because I ended up by marrying the woman I had fallen in love with more than anyone else. So the timing worked out superbly. I was able to play the field and then to have this glorious experience of fatherhood at the age of 44. And so that worked out fine for me. I am not suggesting that's the pattern everyone should have, because friends of mine who got married very quickly and are now grandparents, are very happy. I guess in that sense the timing thing just creeps up on you – you are just ready at a particular point.

Are there times now when you feel, 'I'm going down a particular career path, I am pursuing a particular project, and by golly I wish I could spend a bit more time with the family'?

Well, if I get that feeling I try to adjust my schedule. One of the things about being self-employed is that, to a certain extent, you can plan your own schedule. Although a number of people point out that you lose the alibi of 'I've got to be at work', because obviously your wife can say, 'You haven't got to be at work, it is your decision to go to work' – though if you are fulfilling a contract somewhere else that's not entirely true. However, one of the most interesting things to me is that you're doing six things, let's say, and you are absolutely full up, and then a seventh project comes along which you really want to do, so you take it on as well, and you can never analyse which of the other six projects gets less time. You can't say, 'I spent 16 minutes less on project 3, thus hollowing out 53 minutes for the next project.' It just happens. I've always thought of it as the reverse of Parkinson's Law. Parkinson said that your job expands to fill the time available. I think it's the other way round – your time expands to allow you to fulfil all those things that you want, and are sufficiently determined to fulfil. And that's where the family comes in. If I go home an hour earlier because I want to see Carina and the boys, to use an Americanism, I prioritize. I'm doing as much as ever but I'm spending much more time at home than I ever did before I was married and before I had children. So where that time is squeezed from God knows, but it happens.

You have experienced criticism, as all people in the public eye do at some time in their lives. How do you respond to that criticism within yourself? I mean, when someone talks about you rising without trace or sinking without trace, or they actually criticize you for perhaps not interviewing as toughly or as strongly as others might, how do you react to that? How do you pick yourself up when there has been a particularly wounding barb or criticism? How do you go back out and start battling again?

I think that 'rising without trace' is a fascinating phrase. I think it was Kitty Muggeridge who said her husband Malcolm always used to say that after *That Was The Week That Was*, 'David Frost would sink without trace, instead he has risen without trace', and that's become a memorable phrase. I quite enjoy it. I did a programme on the Resurrection of Christ last year. The title was *The Easter Enigma* and someone said, 'Why don't you call it *Rising without Trace?*' But to return to your question, there are two basic things. The first is the old philosophy – I don't know who said it first, Henry Ford or whoever – 'Never explain, never complain.' Ned Sherrin summed me up on one occasion I think, when he said, 'David always learns from his mistakes without ever admitting he's made any.' As for not complaining, you don't rush into print, you don't write disgusted letters to the editor every two minutes. If something is written about you that you don't like, you've got to reckon that it comes with the territory, you've got to take the rough with the smooth. But on the other hand you sometimes glean something from it, from reading stuff like that. Obviously it is sometimes rather disillusioning to read stuff which is completely untrue, and where, by a bit of checking, somebody could have found it to be untrue. But I think when you go into the public arena – not public life because that sounds like politics or the civil service – you've got to reckon that that goes with the territory. It's something you should try and inoculate yourself against, which I think I've done pretty well over the years, I'm reasonably inoculated, but not totally.

What about the failures in your business career? For example, when TVam collapsed. And you had a marvellous phrase as you stepped into a Bentley after losing the franchise round for ITV – remind us what that was.

That's right, that really stuck in people's minds. A friend of mine was saying he saw it on TV that night in Japan and roared with laughter. I said, 'I was always taught at school that the important thing is not the winning but the taking part. I didn't believe it then and I certainly don't believe it now.' Well, that was just an ad-lib way of dealing with that. I mean, that was a blow.

How did you cope? You obviously place a lot of store on succeeding in every business project you go in for. When you get a major reversal, a rejection like that, how do you come to terms with it?

I think there are two things. I think you've got to have a feeling that – well maybe the biblical version is a bit over-optimistic, but all things work together for good to them that love God, and out of every setback there's an opportunity. In general I do believe that, so that, for instance, the loss of the franchise, the outbidding of TVam paved the way for *Breakfast With Frost* on the BBC. It was a question of thinking, 'Well, what opportunities can one draw from this?' and *Breakfast With Frost* has been an incredibly happy experience. And yet that was an oppportunity which might not have arisen.

But you've got to be hungry for the opportunities and constantly aware of what other opportunities are out there.

Absolutely, because I think that's the important thing – it is the question of luck and of opportunities. The key thing is to be open to opportunities, and to be looking for them. We were talking before about the combination of planning and improvisations on a theme. Another good example of that would be that if in 1980 – I think it was in 1980 – you had said to me, 'In a year's time you are going to be involved in breakfast TV,' I would have said, 'Rubbish, there is no such thing in Britain.' Then it was announced by the IBA on a 'maybe' basis. They were advertising for a breakfast franchise. Suddenly I was into that. I hadn't planned to be, but I saw the opportunity when it came along – as did others – and I went for it. That is life on an improvisations theme rather than setting out a clear career path. For instance, I'm doing a CD Rom series in the States at the moment. Until two or three years ago I would not have known that I was going to do that, because there was no such thing.

Who are your heroes, past or present?

Most of all Nelson Mandela, for all the reasons that are so clear – for the ability to be wrongly incarcerated for 28 years and yet to emerge as he did. I asked him the question that must occur to us all, 'How on Earth did you manage to emerge from that level of injustice without bitterness? Was it, as some have said, that you were converted to Christ in prison?' And rather than fielding it in a it-is-very-kind-of-you-to-say-so way, he said, 'David, I would like to be bitter, but there is no time to be bitter, there is work to do.' It was just a marvellous reply. And then, of course, following on from that, the sheer skill with which he went about achieving his dream.

The second hero I would pick was also someone I interviewed – an unknown man called Major Dudley Gardiner who worked for the Salvation Army in Calcutta. I met him in 1967. I went out there because I was doing the Oxfam appeal that year in the form of a newsletter. I was going out to Bahir and Calcutta and he was at the Salvation Army feeding centre in Calcutta. He made meals for people who came to the centre in the morning, then he went on an incredible food run, on which I accompanied him one afternoon. It was fantastic, he had been doing it for years, but the really amazing thing was he did it with a form of gangrene. He had to bathe his legs at the end of the day because they were both swollen just by his being on them, but he ignored it. The most extraordinary thing about him, however, was that although he was working for the Salvation Army he was not in fact a believer. He was an agnostic – I don't think he was an atheist – but he certainly didn't believe in God. And he said to me, this hero, 'You know, the only problem with this job is it's so boring.' Now I'd never met a hero who found his own heroics boring because most people living a life of self-sacrifice like that are empowered and are uplifted by their faith, either in God or in their political views – and here was an agnostic, sacrificing his life and saying the trouble is it gets so boring. I had never heard a hero say that, so he was a real hero to me.

What's the greatest pleasure you've had from the fruits of your success?

I think having enough money to live a life and provide a life for Carina and the boys that is comfortable. I don't own any yachts or anything like that. When you talk about money then you're talking about money, as someone said, as a tap and you know if you turn on the tap there will be some water there, although through the years there are times when the odd project goes wrong and you can be financially endangered. I also think that knowing you have done the very best you can do, and that it seems to have worked. Then there are cases where programmes here had an effect – back in the 1960s a programme we did on Ronan Point led to the government policy over buildings being completely changed.

If you could gather together all the young people who were entering broadcasting today, what advice would you give to them?

One of the most important things about being an interviewer is to have been born with a sense of curiosity. In my case it is a sense of curiosity about what makes people tick. I suppose this is a rather useless comment to this particular group you've just assembled, because that's something you're born with, but if you were born with it at all, it is a quality to cherish, in whatever branch of broadcasting you're going into. If you've got it at all, develop it – I think that would be tremendously important.

Another thing, I think, would be not to get tunnel vision about one sort of television or one sort of radio, because throughout my life I have found that some of the most rewarding areas are hybrids. The talk show with a participating audience, where one day it's Ian Smith from Rhodesia and the next day it is Sean Connery. The thing that keeps people on their toes is one of the qualities we have with TV – television can surprise you much more. Unpredictability is something that needs to be maintained and indeed fertilized in terms of TV – unpredictability, in terms of keeping people a little more alert, a little more awake, a little more aware. Don't be boxed into any particular part of television, feel you can spread right through it.

The other thing is to keep looking for new frontiers and to keep looking to try new ideas. The fact that a new idea doesn't necessarily test-market very well is meaningless. When I expanded to do 90-minute interviews with one person on my talk show in America, people thought I was crazy because normally you have five people in each show, and no one had more than one segment. Now if I had test-marketed that, it would have test-marketed very badly – it was something the public had never experienced before, so they couldn't really comment on it. I know you can do a survey, a series to evaluate ingredients – a nun and a dog and a de-frocked priest or whatever – but there you are dealing with known ingredients and people can give a known response. But just because you've got an idea that doesn't necessarily test-market very well, doesn't mean you're wrong. If it's a new idea it may be the thing which should be pursued more than anything else.

When your time comes to depart this planet, what would you like people to say about you?

In general I think I would go back to my father and say, when it really comes down to basics, if I'm thought of as half as good a father to my children as he was to me, then I would be very happy.

EVELYN GLENNIE

Classified profoundly deaf at the age of 12, Evelyn Glennie went on to become one of the world's outstanding percussionists – and the first to go solo full-time. Born into a close farming community north of Aberdeen, she had 'the luck of a normal, stable, consistent home background', and a very good percussion teacher who took the time and trouble to introduce her to 'vibration'. She talks about how she coped with gradually becoming deaf; of the 'dangerous time' when a careers adviser said that for her to enter the music profession was an impossibility; and of the hearing specialist who advised her to become an accountant. Defying them all with her stubbornness and sense of adventure, she avoided a special school for the deaf by winning a place at the Royal Academy of Music, where no one believed it was possible to become a solo percussionist, let alone play forty instruments in the course of a single concert as she does now. She reveals the secrets of her technique: how she creates her own 'sound colours'; how taking her shoes off 'makes her feel more connected to the sound'; the way she places speakers against parts of her body 'to determine the basic tempo, dynamics and interpretation of a piece of music'; and the 'wonderful, vibrating type of chair that enables me to experience the layers of sound. When I perform, I depend on my touch, my eye and my imagination. I just involve my whole being.'

She explains how much she owes to her husband, sound engineer Greg Malcangi, who 'taught me how to use my time, and expand as a person' instead of simply feeling that to become a better musician she had to practise six hours a day. She calls launching herself on a solo career the 'big experiment – it's about walking on a tightrope when you are not sure what is going to happen'. Constantly questioning her work after every performance, she believes that 'the more you progress, the more critical you are – that is part of being successful'. She draws a distinction between the public success of good performances and the private success of achieving happiness, and offers this advice to other deaf people, their families and friends: 'Explore and experience all sorts of things, so hopefully a seed will be dropped somewhere.' It is a measure of the inner strength of this remarkable woman that she asserts, 'If I suddenly had both my arms chopped off now, I know I'd cope.'

Evelyn Glennie, what is your definition of success?

I think my definition probably changes as I grow older, but at the moment my definition would be achieving something that is satisfying on a personal level. For me there are two aspects of success. There is the very private, personal side of success where happiness has to be achieved. In order for happiness to be achieved, I think that you have to go through all sorts of unhappiness to find out what makes you happy. But then there is what the public see – 'Evelyn Glennie success' – and that means, for me, performing in live situations, recordings, doing something that communicates with people, and allowing them to feel something emotional. They see me as a successful person, but of course this is only one aspect of what I do. There are a great many ways to achieve that particular performance, at half past seven on 29 August 1999, or whenever it may be. All sorts of things may have to be dealt with behind the scenes. I really feel deep down, though, that success means being satisfied in something that you are doing, but always seeing a road ahead where you know that you can grow, where you can expand, so that you are not just literally going to stop dead.

And have you ever had to make sacrifices, as far as personal success was concerned, in order to achieve professional success?

Well, I am married and one of the most important aims for me is to stay married, and for this companionship and relationship to develop and to be healthy. If I can manage that, then that's a very important success. But of course this means that two people have to compromise a great deal, every single day. In my past, I just thought about music, about what I wanted to achieve as a musician. That meant that I didn't go out to pubs, discos or nightclubs. I had a very shallow and poor social life, I suppose, because I wanted to get up first thing in the morning and go to bed as late as possible, so that I could really practise and prepare and develop. But in my mid-twenties or so, I suddenly realized that I didn't know very much about anything apart from my profession, and so I felt very, very empty, and quite stupid, really. That was when I met my husband, who made me aware of books to read, of things to see, of how to use television, how to use my time and how to expand as a person. I didn't need to expand as a musician in dealing with my instruments, but I needed to expand as a musician, full stop – and that meant going out to a museum or an art gallery, or going for a walk down by the river, or watching a television programme. Things like that, so I could then begin to pick up on ideas that would help me interpret music – and music, at the end of the day, is usually related to a story or an incident, or it could be colours or a certain emotion, or whatever. I needed to experience more general emotions than simply feeling that in order to become a better player I had to practise six hours a day.

If you had expanded your experiences much earlier in life, would that have detracted from the dedication that has led to your success?

I had a balanced and normal upbringing on a farm, just north of Aberdeen, where music was not at all pushed. I don't come from a musical family, so music for me was just a hobby and we had no idea at all that I would ever become a professional musician. This meant I could develop in a very natural way, at a pace that I could cope with. It wasn't until I decided, 'Right, I am going to be a professional musician and I want to specialize in solo percussion,' that I ploughed my heart and soul into this one thing. And that is normally the way I work. If I have a particular interest or if I have a desire or an idea, then come hell or high water I go for that – nothing else matters. I do feel that having this natural, steady and supportive upbringing, and then having this complete and utter dedication towards music where I thought of nothing else, was a good thing, because I was able to get the actual mechanics of playing the instrument out of the way. I was able to do solid groundwork. It made me independent and it made me realize that this was really what I wanted to do, so now I don't have to worry so much about the mechanics of playing, I don't feel as though I have to lock myself in my rehearsal room for hours on end. I can actually take time to sit in front of the television or do some painting or read a book without feeling guilty about it.

How did you reach the decision that you wanted to be a musician? Did it evolve, or did you say with a sudden flash, 'That's the career for me'?

It was fairly sudden. Music was a very important hobby of mine, as a schoolchild, then around the age of 15 we were presented with careers people who talked to us about what we might want to do with our lives, and helped us to identify the subjects that we wanted to specialize in, for O-levels and Highers, as we have in Scotland. Music was one of my subjects, but I actually wanted to go in for art. A lot of my cousins are artists. However, I also wanted to find out what sort of standard I was as a musician. The Grampian Region is not exactly overflowing with percussionists, so I didn't know how I stood in the percussion world. I auditioned for two institutions – the Royal College and the Royal Academy of Music – both in London, and lo and behold the places were open to me, which was a great surprise.

Why was it a surprise?

I had absolutely no idea that I would ever possibly reach the standard to get in. I thought you'd have to be a great player to get in. Of course they are looking for potential and how they can allow each individual to grow. So this put me in a dilemma where I still had to do my Highers, in order to do the degree course at one of these colleges. I decided there and then that I would only study music if I could specialize in solo percussion. I completed my school exams and chose the Royal Academy, and stayed there for three years, graduating at 19. I knew in my first year that I would stay for no longer than three years. It was just a gut feeling I had. The only way I could really learn my craft was by getting out there and doing it – having the experience of constructing programmes, finding the repertoire and learning it. All those things I did on my own because the system, if you like, and the tradition of the Academy, was not geared towards a solo percussionist.

When you took the decision to go to the Royal Academy of Music, you did so at a time when you had become profoundly deaf. A lot of people would say that music was the last career you should have contemplated. What made you think you could do it?

To be a musician there is a huge degree of risk anyway. But as far as I'm concerned, I am very single-minded. I am rather stubborn, which is a North-Eastern trait. Nevertheless, I think I had had enough years before I studied at the Academy to realize that there is another way to experience music, and so I felt fairly confident and, in a way, comfortable with sound. My whole profession is geared towards sound. That's what I do, I just play around with sound. In a way you have to forget you're a percussionist, clarinettist or pianist, or anything like that. You are just a sound-maker and you translate that sound into some kind of emotional feel for the audience. The challenge with being a solo percussionist was that there had never been a full-time soloist before. In the Academy library there were only two percussion concertos. Now, in my own personal library, I have over 300, so the repertoire is out there, but it was just a case of finding it, and of course, more and more pieces are being published and recorded.

Everything I do, I do in a very focused way. I'm not distracted by other things. For example, at the moment I'm learning the Highland bagpipes and this is wonderful because it's bringing me back to the Scottish traditional music that I was brought up with. For me it means a lot more if you can actually participate, as opposed to being a passive listener, or experiencing the music by reading books. That isn't enough for me. Also, unlike many percussion instruments where you have a stick or mallet to detach you from the instrument, you actually have direct contact with the bagpipes. You have the chanter in your mouth, you have your fingers on the chanter, you have the bag there, under your arm, against your tummy, against your chest. You have the drones leaning against your shoulder and so on. So you're experiencing all sorts of different feelings and things that are so different from anything that I experience with percussion.

But how can you create a sound that is recognized by those of us who have a full sense of hearing? What technique do you have for identifying those sounds to yourself and reproducing them with such purity?

First of all, I depend on imagination. I create the sound and the feelings – for example, if I'm playing a piece that has a slightly subdued feel about it or a sad feel, a dark feel, I think about dark sounds. I think about sounds that could be broad or sounds that could be thin, that kind of thing. So I'm not thinking, 'Oh, well, I am in A minor or C major or E flat minor or F major, or whatever.' I just think about the actual touch that I want to use. And perhaps touch is the most important sense that I use. If I play very loudly – fortissimo – on a timpani, and use exactly the same weight that I've used on that timpani on a triangle, it's going to be totally out of place – do you see what I mean? It's a case of treating these instruments as a child would, with no preconceived ideas. When I look at the instrument I think, 'What is it made of?' I look at the shape of it – whether it's a thick shape, a solid shape, a thin shape, a fragile shape, whatever, all the things that the eye sees, and you can then use that to determine what kind of sound is going to be produced from the instrument. Therefore I would experiment by using different sticks – very heavy sticks, big sticks, very light sticks, thin sticks, and so on, and then maybe just my hands – skin on skin. Suddenly you are beginning to create your own sound colours, and this makes it all very individual to you.

Sometimes one can go along to a concert and think, 'Oh, I love the sound of Yehudi Menuhin,' or 'I love the sound of Itzhak Perlman,' or something like that. Well I don't just rely on that. It's their *interpretation* of music that means so much to me, and that can only really be detected in a live situation, as opposed to through recordings. If I see movement, I can hear it, so sometimes I want to tease my audience by playing so softly that they can actually see the sticks move but they are not hearing anything. They think they are, but they are getting this *mood* that's so important.

But what do you hear? How do the sounds translate themselves into your mind? Is it vibration?

It's a combination of things. It's a combination of actually hearing them through the ears – I do have residual hearing, so I make use of that when I can. But also, I use what the eye sees, which is very important. The imagination also plays a very important part, because the sound is formed in your imagination before you actually produce that from the instrument, but nevertheless, the sound that is produced depends on that instrument. Tingly instruments such as triangles, cymbals, glockenspiels, gongs – those sort of things that have very high frequencies, and when you strike them, they have a very long duration of sound afterwards. You can work out the actual stroke to use in order to play those instruments and to achieve the sound you want, but what happens afterwards is hard to know. So sometimes you do need someone to say, 'Oh, look, the instrument is still ringing on,' or 'You have a thick, thick sound after you strike it, but then it really deadens quite quickly.'

But this is just one aspect. Sometimes I feel things. I love to take my shoes off – this makes me more connected to the sound. This is common to many musicians. For example, the wonderful violinist, Anne-Sophie Mutter, loves to wear dresses that allow her shoulders to be free, to be bare, so she can pop her violin on her shoulder because she just loves to feel connected with the instrument, in the same way that cellists have the cello in a position which allows their whole body to resonate with the instrument. The same with the double bass and so on. It's no different from percussion. If I'm playing a bass drum or timpani, I feel that in the lower parts of my body. If I play higher instruments, I will feel that, perhaps through my chest, my neck, my cheekbones, my scalp, and, of course, a lot comes through onto your fingertips. So over the years I've begun to determine where I feel these vibrations, but these are only felt and understood from my own instruments. For example, I have instruments that are stored in different places throughout the world, but all of those instruments are of the same make – the same make of marimbas, tom-toms, bass drums, and so on. So I know how they speak, and that's really important because you may have two marimbas (which are basically like overgrown xylophones) of exactly the same size and the same make, but they might be just slightly different, because they are made from natural wood.

How do you take on board recordings of other people's music?

Well, I have a wonderful vibrating type of chair that when you sit on it you can adjust it, so that you experience the layers of sound – the bass sounds, the brass, the woodwind, the strings, whatever else is there. This is something that I hadn't been able to do before – before it was just this cacophony of sound, a balloon of sound, if you like, so this chair has been very important to me. But I also used to pop the speakers between my legs, against my tummy, against my chest, and this allowed me to determine the basic tempo, the basic dynamics, the basic interpretation of a piece of music. Of course, you can't determine whether a performance is really good and you can't determine the actual subtleties of what's going on in the performance, but that doesn't matter because at the end of the day, most of the repertoire I play is not recorded.

I need to be inspired by all sorts of musicians, in order to play my instruments. I love going along to trumpet master-classes or piano master-classes or speaking with other instrumentalists to find out what makes them tick as musicians. What do they have to do in order to play their instruments? What's involved in the actual mechanics of playing? I use a lot of the ideas I get from them. Sometimes when I'm playing I think, 'Wow, I really want this part to be like a trumpet.' Or if I'm playing the marimba, 'Oh, wow! I really want this to be cello-like.' But you can only determine that when you have actually been with another instrument.

When you were little, how did you come to terms with your growing deafness?

Well, fortunately I had a very unfussy upbringing. My family were very concerned about my loss of hearing and after perhaps a year to two years, I was too. Initially I had no idea that I was actually losing my hearing. I just thought something wasn't functioning properly, but that it would get better. And so, over a period of time, two or three years or so, I was able to adapt without actually realizing that I was having to do anything. I was beginning to look more closely at people in conversation, I was beginning to be a little bit more choosy with whom I spoke because of the ease of understanding them. I was beginning to become more involved when I was playing the piano, because I started on piano and moved to percussion at the age of 12. I was becoming more involved with my instruments, as opposed to just literally playing them in a standard way. That wasn't enough for me, I needed my body to respond to the instruments. All of those things were dealt with in a fairly instinctive way and I think most people who do lose a sense just find that they naturally adapt without thinking, 'Oh, I must now look at people.' It just doesn't work like that.

If I'm in a social situation, perhaps in a pub or at a reception, I find those occasions very, very tiring. They are very frustrating because all sorts of people are talking, they need your attention. And there is this background noise that I can also pick up, but quite often I don't know where the sounds are coming from. In fact you can hear an awful lot, but it's just a jumble of sounds. That is why I got rid of my hearing aids because they were giving me volume but not clarity, and really you need clarity of sound in order to understand it. The less you actually hear through the ears, but the more you involve your body, as it were, like a resonating chamber, the more personal the sound is – and this can really help with your co-ordination, with your balance and just basic control over dealing with the sound.

Was there a point when a doctor said to you, 'You are going to be profoundly deaf and we can't cure you'?

Well, yes. When I was 12 years old I was kitted out with my hearing aids and my phonic ears and so on. Sometimes the medical profession can be very black or white. If you've gone through umpteen tests of one sort or another and the results are not so promising, they will have to say, 'Right, you are deaf,' or 'You're *profoundly* deaf,' or 'You are blind,' or whatever. This can be quite a shock, because to the general public, deafness means silence, blindness means darkness, if you're in a wheelchair you cannot walk. It's as black and white as that. So it was very disturbing, certainly for my parents, when this statement was made. 'You are categorized as profoundly deaf, therefore you will not be able to do...', this, that or the next thing. And we thought, 'How can this be?' I walked into this room, maybe an hour or two before and I was able to do these things, and now suddenly we have this bit of paper that confirms, with all the test results, that I am profoundly deaf, therefore I cannot do these things. It just didn't make sense, so my father, who was a very shy, quiet person, simply said, 'Look, you'll progress as you're doing and we'll just cross the bridges as we come to them. We'll just deal with what we have to deal with when it arises, but we cannot possibly have one individual saying "Evelyn cannot do something", because this individual has only known her for x number of hours.' And that's how we dealt with it. Of course, there were very frustrating times, especially when I was depending on volume, when I hadn't understood what sound was about, hadn't understood that there is another way to approach music. There were two years or so when I became completely frustrated with wanting everything to come through the ears. I thought, 'That's the only way you can hear.'

I did have a very, very good percussion teacher at school – which was unusual in those days – and he introduced me to vibration. I would place my hands on the wall of the music room and he would play two timpani. He would ask me, 'OK, are you feeling anything? *Where* are you feeling it? How much down the palm of your hand are you feeling it?' And then he would tune another drum and gradually I would begin to determine the pitches through the palms of my hand, by popping my palms on the wall. This, for me, was a revelation. I had no idea that this was possible, and neither had he. We were just groping in the darkness, we were both experimenting, but that important seed determined whether I could deal with music or not.

So that was immensely encouraging, that you had a mentor like that. Are mentors important in the creation of success?

Very important. Certainly my inspirations have been people like the late

Glenn Gould, the Canadian pianist, the late cellist, Jacqueline du Pré, James Blades, who is in his 95th year now – they have been tremendous inspirations for me because they were all great communicators. They forgot themselves as instrumentalists. They created art and this art was visually stimulating. You could *see* the sound – the music just flowed from them. But more than anything, they were all willing to experiment. Jacqueline du Pré, there is absolutely *no* one you can compare her to. The same is true with Glenn Gould and James Blades. This kind of individualism was really important to me. It suddenly made me realize that I could literally do anything I wanted with my instruments, there were absolutely no barriers at all. I deal with a lot of new music and most of the music that I play stems from the 1950s, so it means that there are very few recordings to hang on to. And there are very few percussion concerts to go to, in order to learn. So I have got to rely on my instinct. I think, 'This is how I want to do it,' while knowing that I may have ten more performances of it, so there can be ten different interpretations.

When you were going through the key stages of your early career, what other professions did people advise you to go into? Were you being put into a box, as it were; were people not prepared to think that certain careers might be open to you because of your deafness?

Certainly. I think the most dangerous time of all was when I met a careers person at school who simply said, 'Well, you just cannot go in for music,' and that's quite a statement to make to any individual. And my doctor, the audiologist in Aberdeen, said, 'Well, why don't you become an accountant?' Looking back now, the knowledge these people must have had was quite scary, and to make those blunt statements is dangerous, because, heavens, if you're gullible, you might well take those in and think, 'Oh well, I can't be a musician,' or 'Maybe I ought to be an accountant,' and so on. So you end up doing something that just isn't natural to you.

But did you not think, 'These people are experts in their field, they must be right?' What made you so determined to almost prove that they were wrong?

I have no idea. I really don't know. I think it's just part of my make-up to do what feels right to me. I have always conducted my life like that. You usually have a gut feeling towards things, and it really did not feel right to follow their instructions. As a full-time student at the Royal Academy of Music, people advised that I should be an orchestral player, and again this didn't ring true with me, it didn't feel right, and so I couldn't follow that. Even now, if someone asks me to do something that isn't for me, I just will not do it.

What have been the biggest challenges to which you've had to respond as your career has developed?

I think, strangely enough, it's the repertoire, the percussion repertoire. It's all about being a solo percussionist. It's about walking on a tightrope where you are not sure what's going to happen. It's one big experiment, really. It hasn't been done before, there is no tradition of it, we don't know where it's going to lead to. So, everybody is learning. The concert organizers who book me and put on these concerts are learning. I'm learning, as far as structuring a programme, knowing what might be successful with an audience. The record companies are learning because they don't know what might sell, and so on. It's like a domino effect. But this is part of the fun. You expect yourself to fall flat on your face sometimes, but you pick yourself up, I'm learning from those mistakes. So it is that – not my deafness which is personal, something I deal with every single day of my life. By contrast, people have paid to be at those concerts so you've a huge responsibility, and at the end of the day you want to be asked back at those places. The hardest thing of all is knowing that everything you do is going to be written about, is going to be in the newspaper the next morning. Although I'm most critical of myself – always have been and probably always will be – nevertheless you still have to deal with the fact that these concerts are, nine times out of ten, reviewed and you have to deal with that as well.

How do you deal with that? Do you feel that because you are deaf, the critics give you an easier ride?

Absolutely not. Critics are critics in that they review the concert. They do not take into account whether you are deaf or blind or anything like that. If you stand up on a platform, you have to perform. I think in this day and age people really don't take into consideration your background or whether you are young, old, rich, poor, black or white or you are standing on one leg or you are blind, deaf or whatever. If you produce the goods, that's what it's about. Of course my deafness is referred to in several of the reviews, but not many, because I don't mention it in my concert biographies. So many of the people who attend the concerts are quite simply seeing this musician who's a percussionist – that's how I like it to be.

Why is it important that people put your deafness to one side in making a judgment about you?

Because I feel that my statement is through the music. How I achieve that music is, in a way, my secret. It's me, it's part of me. My deafness is part of Evelyn Glennie, in the same way that I have brown hair or I'm five foot two. It's part of me and I don't want people to think, 'Oh, well, she must be doing something unusual in order to achieve the performances she does.' I don't know if I would be a different player if I had hearing in a conventional way. I play in a way that feels natural for me and that involves *every* sense I have. When I perform, I depend on my touch, I depend on the eye, I depend on my imagination, I just involve my whole being, it isn't just *one* sense that I involve.

You've said that if you were suddenly to get your hearing back now, it would be a greater handicap than being deaf. What do you mean by that?

My knowledge of the results that have happened to other people who have had implants of one sort or another is that they have been able to receive a greater sound palate, but it's not something that is truly remarkable in that it doesn't change their lives. I think my whole sound-world is to do with my whole being. It isn't just to do with one sense, and I feel that if I was suddenly to perceive more sounds through my ears, and if they were not as pure as I remembered them to be, then I would not be happy. It would be more of a handicap than it is now. I'm in total control of what I want to do now with my instruments because the imagination plays such a big role. I could be wrong, but again, it's this gut feeling, I just don't want to have my hearing changed.

When was the first time you said to yourself, 'I'm a success'?

I've never said that. I don't think I ever could. The nature of what I do – and I think many, many people are in this situation – is that you strive to be better, you strive to improve, you always see an avenue that you want to explore. Part of the fun, in all of this, is finding new things, discovering things. I don't think that I could ever say, 'Well, I am successful,' or 'I am a success.' Every time I walk off the platform, I think, 'Why didn't I do that?' or 'What happened there? I should have done that.' You torture yourself, so how can you be a success if you're asking those questions?

So is that part of being successful, that in a sense you're never content with what you are doing? You never feel you have achieved as much as you, inwardly, would like?

That's very true. I look at the past ten years of my professional career and although I understand that I have done a lot, there are many things that I think, 'Wow, I really ought to have done that' or 'Why haven't I done this?' So I think the more you progress, the more critical you are. I do feel that is part of being successful.

Do you sit down and plan for success? Do you say, 'In order for me to keep achieving, I've got to have a set programme,' or do you, in a sense, expect certain things to come your way, to happen for you?

I'm very much a planner. I keep aims and goals in mind, with a timescale, and so on. I always have been like that, and I think most of the things I have done have been planned. Of course, you have to create your own opportunities, I think that's really what today is all about. I think that we are all so exposed to knowledge now, through technology, that it is a matter of using one's imagination in order to achieve what you really want. You have to take the plunge to do things, become more daring, and not necessarily play safe or copy others. It is being *you*, so I think if I can be entirely *me*, then I'll have been successful, because I know that I will have done or tried things that have felt right for me, even if they haven't worked – it's knowing you've had a go. I don't think I could just sit expecting things to happen, but of course when those things do happen, it's very, very nice.

Does luck play a part?

I think it does. I've always gone through life trying to be as prepared as I possibly can, which I think is important. Trying to be as flexible and versatile as possible so that should something unexpected arise, I can take advantage of that. You have to feel confident enough to take advantage of things, and there have been things that have happened to me, I'm sure, that have been totally unexpected or have just been lucky.

Who are the people that you admire, past or present, whom you regard as having reached the pinnacle of success, in any field?

It's a very difficult question because I know that the people who have achieved success will be highly critical of themselves. I can name many people who seem successful to me, but there could be an area of their life that needs attending to or that they don't feel happy with. I think we all have that – we are all, I suppose, disabled, if you like, but we're not dysfunctional. We all have something to keep working at. So it's a very hard question, and it's impossible for me to pick certain people out. There are many people who have inspired me, but I cannot say, 'Wow, that person is the ultimate success story.'

Do you think that we should be in the kind of world where people never say that, because everyone is always trying to move a little bit further, no matter what degree of success they achieve?

That is very true. We all need a pat on the back, we all need to be told, 'Oh, that was good,' or 'Yes, that meant something.' This is why things like awards are important to me, because they are stepping stones. They allow me to think, 'Now I want to try harder.' The awards are not meant to say, 'There, you've done it.'

Is it becoming more or less difficult to achieve success as a musician?

The more you progress, the harder it is to progress or even to stay still. I think that a lot more energy and imagination are needed – I keep going on about imagination, but I feel it's so important. I feel many things have to be worked on a lot, to keep you stimulated, to keep you fresh, to make you an inspiration for younger musicians coming up.

What do you think are the greatest enemies of success?

Standing still. Complacency. How can we achieve success in absolutely every single aspect of our lives? I want to be successful in my marriage, my music, my profession and many other different ways.

Do you think that success brings obligations in its wake – either within your immediate circle, or in the wider society at large?

I think so, and this can be quite dangerous. People expect a lot from you if they see you as successful, they expect many things outside your profession as well. It's this word 'expect' all the time. That's why I think that privacy is extremely important to hold on to. I also think that having new aims, being seen to try things, even often being unsuccessful at something, is important. At the end of the day we're all human beings and we all try out things that don't work, but it is important to do that. But, yes, I feel there are many obligations.

There are hundreds of thousands of young people out there who are born deaf, or, like you, become deaf and who may think that life is going to be pretty tough for them. What advice would you offer to give them a chance of becoming, in whatever field it may be, as successful as you have become?

Well, that's quite a responsible question, in that it needs a very responsible answer. I'm not directing this to the individual who may happen to be deaf, but also to family members, to teachers, to friends, all sorts of people like that who deal with a deaf person. Keeping an open mind is vital. I think that these people have to explore and experience all sorts of things. They must experience art, or cooking, or music or watch television, or go to the theatre, whatever it may be. Because at the end of the day we are not all going to be musicians, the seed or the interest is just not there. I have a brother who is a born farmer and that's all he would ever want to do. No matter how much music we present to him, he will not be a musician. So, I think these people should go out of their way to experience all sorts of things, so that hopefully a seed will be dropped somewhere, and they think, 'Wow, I'm really interested in art, or I'm really interested in journalism,' or whatever it may be, and they should cultivate that. We have to forget that these people cannot hear, because we should not think in such a black and white way. You may have two profoundly deaf people side by side – one may hear a lorry go by, while another will hear a bird singing. We have to treat them as individuals.

And leaving the deafness to one side, what advice would you give to those young people who want to be as good a musician as you have become?

Versatility is extremely important, so is flexibility, imagination, taking every opportunity that comes your way, creating opportunities. Learning from your mistakes is important, though it's quite hard sometimes not to become despondent because of them. And really, following what you believe in as a musician. Sometimes that can be hard, sometimes it can take a long time to suss out. You are always faced with people who know better, or think they know *you* better as an individual and sometimes you've got to say, 'This is what I think is right and this is what I do,' and not be embarrassed by trying something that hasn't been done before. So it's finding your own voice. It's like playing your instrument, you eventually find your own sound.

When your time comes to leave this life, what would you like people to say about Evelyn Glennie?

I hope people will recognize that there was only one Evelyn Glennie, and she really gave something to the world that could only be associated with her. That could be something that is outside music, it isn't just dependent on my instruments. If I suddenly had both my arms chopped off now, I know I'll cope, I know I'll find something that will bring me happiness, first of all, but will also then be transmitted to other people. I know that, it's there, it's in my system. This kind of giving, this assurance of what the human is capable of, of what *you*, as an individual, are capable of – this, I think, is very, very important.

MICHAEL GRADE

The world of broadcasting misses the perpetual cigar, brightly coloured socks and braces, forceful views, scheduling skills and panache that were the trademarks of a man who was at the top of British television for the best part of three decades. His sudden announcement early in 1997 that he was quitting as chief executive of Channel 4 – one of the best jobs in the business – stunned the industry. In what turned out to be a valedictory interview, he talks in detail about the various forms of success in television, and his own career moves. Born into a family of entertainment moguls, his mother walked out when he was just 15 months old and he was brought up by his grandmother. He left school at 16 disillusioned with education – 'it completely *knocked the stuffing out of me' – and his uncle, Lew Grade, got him a job as a trainee sports reporter on the* Daily Mirror, *His father's illness led to him successfully taking over the family talent agency, selling stars and ideas to TV companies like LWT, which eventually signed him up to become Director of Programmes. Next stop was Hollywood, where he spent three years, first as president of a TV company, then as an independent producer, before returning to Britain as Controller of BBC1 and, later, BBC TV's Director of Programmes.*

His approach is based on experience and gut instinct. On people: 'My skill is in recognising talent and letting them get on with it' and he dismisses control freaks who take all the decisions themselves. On programmes: 'You're paid to know what has got absolutely no chance, and to make more right than wrong judgments.' But 'it's the public who decide whether a programme is a success or not'. On tactics: 'I've never planned the next move – it's always just fallen into place. I saw a lot of careers at the BBC destroyed by people who were plotting their next three moves ... they'd abandoned their day-to-day responsibilities, so other people were doing their work and being recognised for being successful.' He explains how he came to the famous decision that delivered a record 30 million viewers for EastEnders *one Christmas Day. He reveals why he left television for pastures new, and predicts that those who want to be successful in the next TV era will have to be 'sharper, quicker and hold their nerve longer'.*

Michael Grade, what is your definition of success?

I think success is getting the approbation of people you admire, perhaps emulating their achievements. It starts with looking at people whose opinions and achievements you respect and then trying to get close to what they have achieved, and hopefully getting a pat on the head from them saying, 'You're one of us' – that's success.

To what extent do you think success is due to your background and upbringing?

A very great deal. Different things motivate different people. By the time I was born and was conscious of being on the planet, my family was fairly successful and never wanted for anything, so I wasn't driven by hunger and poverty and deprivation, as my father and uncles had been – that was their motivating force. I think what motivated me was the desire to emulate their achievements.

So in a sense you didn't need ambition to achieve success, yet you do have ambition. Where did it come from?

I think it comes from a deep admiration for what the family has achieved. My father and my two uncles set the targets and achieved them and it seemed the most natural thing for me to want to try to follow in their footsteps. So it wasn't a financial motivation, and although I have done very well, I've never made the kind of money that they've made. I'm not complaining, I earn a very, very good living and I'm very happy, but I am not motivated by money, I am motivated by a need to one day be mentioned in the same breath as they are. That's what motivates me.

When was the first time that you said to yourself, 'I have been successful at something'? It might be going way back to your early days.

We always have milestones, every chapter in my life so far I've had a little milestone. I think the first one was at prep school. I was made head boy, quite surprisingly because I got it a year earlier than I would normally have been expected to, so that was nice. Then I didn't really have another until I got my first by-line in the *Daily Mirror*, that was also nice, and so on. All through my career there have been lots of little milestones.

Have you always been someone who wanted to achieve, or was it a need that grew up later, perhaps out of family circumstances such as your mother leaving home when you were very, very young?

No, I'm not conscious of that. I've never planned my career, I've never been ambitious in a stereotypical sense. You read about people being ambitious and so on but I've never been ambitious in that way. My ambition has always been to be the best at what I'm doing. I've never plotted the next move, it's always just fallen into place. What I've learned is that progress and ambition are satisfied if you are a success at what you're doing. Opportunities open up, people notice you because you are successful and offer you the next opportunity. It's no good sitting here plotting: in five years time I'm going to be chairman of ICI and I'm going to be this and I'm going to be in the Cabinet – it's nonsense, it just doesn't happen that way. You get unfocused, you stop looking at the job you're actually doing. I saw a lot of careers at the BBC destroyed by people who spent all day plotting their next three moves. They were amazed when it didn't work out the way they planned, and that was because they had abandoned their day-to-day responsibilities, so other people were doing their work and being recognized for being successful.

When you got that first job at the age of 17, it was a clear decision to go for a traineeship on the Daily Mirror *rather than going to university and furthering your education. Why did you take that route?*

I got very disillusioned with education. I was slightly above average, bright, I wouldn't say I was a scholar or anything like that, but I could do anything: maths, Latin, English, Greek, German, you name it I could do it. But when I moved from prep school to public school (I went to a public school called Stowe), it completely knocked the stuffing out of me and I just gave up on education after that. The classes were too big, it was a miserable environment. I left after a year, and hadn't learned anything. So I then went to a London day school, St Dunstan's College, and did the minimum necessary. I had a very liberal father who didn't push me, he believed in you finding your own level in these things. I suppose he indulged me to a certain extent, but I don't think it did me any harm.

Was your first job in a sense a product of who your family happened to know?

Oh, unquestionably, yes. There was no way I would otherwise have got the job on the *Daily Mirror*. In those days the union said that you had to go to provincial newspapers and do an apprenticeship for several years before you could possibly join a national newspaper. That was all short-circuited because of my family's friendship with Hugh Cudlipp and their shareholding in ATV which was the family television business in those days. So it was entirely influential. I'm not saying it wasn't something I wanted to do, but I was very lucky to have that opportunity.

Has that changed? Can you still get on in the media and television by knowing somebody, or has it got tougher?

There's no doubt that people get the opportunity to get jobs because of who they know and because of who their parents know and so on. The difference today is that they don't last very long if they're not good at it. People can open the door for you, you can get in the shop window, but if people ain't buying, you're out. Nothing now will protect an underperformer, or an unqualified person, or a person who's not making progress, irrespective of who they are – unless the family owns the firm.

After the Daily Mirror *you went on to join your father in a theatrical agency because he had been ill and wanted someone to take over the business eventually. Having started your career as a columnist, did you feel that somehow you were being deprived of a potentially successful career?*

Not at all. I knew that the prospects of being a sports writer were very limiting financially and all the rest of it. I had already started a business in Fleet Street, a sort of embryonic Mark MacCormack-style business, which was one of the earliest sports promotion companies of its day. There were two or three of us in Fleet Street who had been looking at this: Terry O'Connor, who was the rugby and athletics correspondent of the *Daily Mail,* John Bromley who worked with me at the *Mirror* and I. They could see its potential and they talked to me about it, we identified a small business which we bought into and we were busy building it up when my dad became ill and everything changed. If that hadn't happened, I think I would have ended up in a sports promotions business.

Did you identify any principles for running a successful agency?

Just work harder than anybody else, and that's what I did. I would drive up to Blackpool and back before the M1 and the M6 were connected. I would do a morning in the office, drive to Blackpool, see two shows, drive back. That was a typical day. I just worked all hours that it was possible to work. Always available to the clients, always there, always around, always supporting them, doing things for nothing, building up goodwill, just working harder than anyone else.

Then you were drawn to television. Why?

The foundation of the family was basically variety theatre, the Palladium, the Talk of the Town, seaside shows, Blackpool, Yarmouth and so on, and I could see, very early on, that television was the key to all that, that television was a much more interesting business, and I began to care more about the television side of things than the variety side. And television was so important to the clients. I started having ideas for television shows and selling them to different companies and then one day, London Weekend Television said to me, 'Save the taxi fare and come and work for us,' and that was a big decision – it took me a year to decide.

Did you give up a lot of money to do it?

Yes. I had a third share in a very successful business, and my own freedom, but the job of being an agent is a miserable job really, you've got to have the temperament for it because you're always in the middle, always trying to get two ends to meet and usually one end or the other doesn't want to meet the other, so you're forever 'piggy in the middle'. It's an exceedingly frustrating business. It had been a fantastic apprenticeship – I had had a wonderful time working with Morecambe and Wise and Tony Hancock and all kinds of wonderful people. But I realized I wasn't going to do that for the rest of my life – and I loved television, I really wanted to learn about television.

And what did you learn about succeeding in television? Are there any principles, either on the management side or the artistic side or indeed on simply the programme-making side that guaranteed success in television, or is it always a little elusive?

My great belief is that if you think you know what is going to be a success you're deluding yourself, because you don't decide, the public decides whether a thing is a success or not.

But aren't you paid to make judgments?

I was going to come on to that. What you're paid to know in this business, if you're good at it, is what has got absolutely no chance whatsoever of succeeding, and if you can weed that stuff out, you've got a chance. That's the key. You hope that you make more right judgments than wrong judgments and then, if your batting average is OK, you're a success.

You have developed a considerable reputation as a scheduler, how do you make so many good judgments, what is the secret of that?

Well, scheduling is really only window dressing. And if you take that department-store analogy a bit further, the key person is the buyer, who decides what to order for what season. Somebody then has to put it in the window in an attractive way that catches people's eyes as they pass the store, but the key person is the person who makes the judgments about what to buy to put in the window in the first place. A scheduler can't make a silk purse out of a sow's ear, the key skill is picking the right programmes and making sure they're executed well enough. How do you do that? Pick very good people and leave them alone, that's always been my watchword really. My skill, if I have any skill, is in recognizing talent and letting them get on with it.

Is that a general formula for success, to actually pick the right people?

Yes, absolutely. If you are a control freak and you make all the decisions yourself, how do you know if the people who are working for you are any good or not? If you're second-guessing them all the time, if anything goes wrong you can't fire anybody, you can only fire yourself. So I work absolutely on the basis of giving people as much responsibility as possible, even more responsibility than they actually want to take. Just to take a situation, when I arrived at Channel 4, and someone came to me with a problem, the words most often used were, 'What do you think? What's your recommendation?' Then you get them used to thinking it out for themselves. Certainly you want to encourage people to come in and say, 'I'm not sure which way to go on this,' that's a different matter, but nine times out of ten people will push the decision on to you if you let them, and you must never let them – they've got to learn to flourish on their own and stand on their own two feet.

And what about the checks and balances in that system? You could give someone their head, let them hammer on down a particular route and suddenly you find it's too late, that they've got a programme, it's about to be transmitted and at the last minute you suddenly realize they've made some terrible mistakes along the way.

Well, then you've got to let them fail.

But if you actually take the approach that you allow people to fail, isn't that abdicating some responsibility for the success of your organization?

No. People work within a certain framework. There are checks and balances along the way, people have to pitch their ideas for a particular budget and so on, but essentially you've got to find out, and the only way you find out if people know how to fly the plane is if they can fly it on their own. It's no good giving somebody a test as a pilot and the instructor flies the plane and at the end says, 'Yes, you're a good pilot, there were no incidents on that flight.' You've got to let people fly on their own, you have to. If they make too many mistakes for the wrong reasons, the wrong kinds of mistakes, then they are obviously not up to the job, so you get somebody else in.

After LWT you went to Hollywood. Was that because, in show-business terms, that appeared to be the place where you could achieve a pinnacle of success?

Lots of reasons. I was at a point in my life where I wasn't earning enough money. I'd just got divorced, I wasn't earning enough money really to take care of my kids the way I wanted to take care of them. I had a considerable debt, I had no prospects. In those days ITV didn't pay the kind of money they pay today and my last Christmas bonus at London Weekend Television was a packet of shortcake biscuits and a bottle of whisky from Marks and Spencer, a far cry from the share options and all the rest of it that exist today. So it was partly that, and partly that Hollywood came looking for me, in particular a creative genius called Norman Lear. The opportunity to spend a few years working with him was absolutely dazzling to me. So all of those things came together at that moment in my life. 'I really fancy this, I'll have a go at this,' I thought. And I had done everything I could for London Weekend Television, we'd got the new licence, got extra air time, I'd gone as far as I could have gone with LWT.

But then after a while in America, your dreams turned to sand and you started looking for other things to do?

No. I'd run this television company very successfully for three years. I had made the transition. But I decided that the corporate thing was driving me crazy because I had eight sitcoms on the air, eight in development and I was reading six drafts of each show every week. I was reading something like 100 sitcom scripts a week, and you start to go a bit crazy at that point. They didn't want to lose me so they offered me a huge deal as an independent producer within their company which I took. I set up a 13 million dollar mini-series with CBS as an independent, that was my first project which I sold very quickly – that was Jeffrey Archer's *Cain and Abel*. Then I embarked on a career as a producer in Hollywood, but I really missed broadcasting and I missed England, and the kids and everything else. And at that moment the BBC took a flyer and said, 'Why don't you come home?'

Did you feel that that part of your life had been in at least some way a failure, that you had tried America, and for whatever reason it hadn't worked, and if so how did you recover from that feeling of failure?

I honestly didn't feel it was a failure. I wasn't there long enough. I feel that I succeeded as the president of the company that I was running. In fact, after I left, the television side of it was sold for half a billion dollars to Coca-Cola, so I think I did a pretty good job for them. Then I took the independent production route and started on a highly successful note.

There were a million producers in Hollywood trying to sell mini-series. I sold one in the first few weeks and got it made, so I didn't feel in any sense I was a failure. I did miss England and I missed the kids and I missed broadcasting. The thing about Hollywood is that the rewards are great, but the work is very narrow. I missed news, I missed documentaries, I missed the arts, I missed the theatre, I missed all those things.

So what drew you to the BBC? Was it the public-service ethos or what?

Going back to broadcasting and having responsibility for such a wide range of output. And the BBC is the BBC, there was an enormous attraction for me to go back to running a network. At LWT I hadn't really run the network, I'd run the weekend bit of it, but it was still a federal system, nobody actually gave you the whole train set to play with. At the BBC you get the whole train set. You could only run things by committee at ITV which is not quite the same. It's also a nice thing to have done, a few years at the BBC.

Then after a few years the Channel 4 job came up. To what extent were you driven to that by a feeling that you could no longer do what you wanted in the BBC?

It's a complicated story. I think all my life, when I've not been self-employed, I have always chosen who I wanted to work for. If I'm going to work for somebody, I'm independent and arrogant enough to make a decision about who it is I want to work for. I chose to work for John Freeman and Cyril Bennett at London Weekend Television and then Brian Tessler – a very good decision. I chose to work for Norman Lear, I chose to go to the BBC and work for Stuart Young. I didn't work for Alistair Milne, for whom I have very little respect, I worked for Bill Cotton and Stuart Young, they were my protectors, if you like, at the BBC, they were my sponsors. I had three wonderful years working with the BBC. Then, as John Freeman once said to me, 'Always remember, Michael, the BBC's a very funny place,' and I didn't quite know what he meant until the end of that three years. Then the politics and the BBC changed – Stuart Young died, sadly, and a new chairman came in, plus a new director-general, and the whole thing shifted. I woke up one day and looked around and said, 'If I was being offered a job to come and work for these people, I wouldn't want to work for Duke Hussey. What am I doing here? Bill's retiring, I want to get out.'

But when you saw that 'writing on the wall', did you think, 'This is a disaster'? How do you recover from the sort of emotional hit that you take when you realize that something on which you've set your heart is not going to be possible?

I never set my heart on anything.

But you must have set your heart on rising as far as you could within the BBC?

Well, I'd got the managing director's job, which was the next stage. They'd given me that.

But there are other jobs above managing director.

Yes, the director-general job, but I had applied for the director-general's job. Bill Cotton advised me, 'You'll get an hour with the governors and you are not going to get the job, but you'll have an hour with the gloves off with the governors. Since you've got a lot to say for yourself, if I were you I would apply and have an hour with the governors, it won't do you any harm at all.' So I did. I'd no ambition at that time. If I had stayed on as managing director no doubt the ambition would have arrived, but it was an alien culture, to tell you the honest truth.

How important is image in the creation of success? You've got your trademarks – the braces, the red socks in Hollywood and so on – and you generally have a very upfront image, has that been a factor in your success?

No, I've always been in the business of attracting audiences, audiences in a theatre or audiences on television and because of my name and everything else, if I can get the coverage in the newspapers for my channel, for my programmes, I'll take advantage of that. It's an opportunity you exploit. Image, I think, follows personality, image reflects personality. I'm an extrovert, I enjoy being accountable, it doesn't bother me. I like actually getting out there and explaining what we do and why we do it and I think I was possibly the first channel boss actually to welcome that kind of examination and take the mystique out of it all and be quite prepared to go and argue the toss and be accountable through debate, articles, interviews and TV appearances. I think that's healthy. I'm quite proud of what we do, so I don't think the 'head-down' approach is very helpful.

Do you think, as a golden rule, it helps to have an ego?

Everybody has an ego, every single person has that thing that you call ego, it manifests itself in different ways. Being reclusive, a hermit, and never being photographed, that is ego in a way, isn't it? You're setting yourself aside from the rest of humanity. So everybody's got an ego; you have to have it in control. What you mustn't do is believe what you read. If people are telling you how wonderful and successful you are, for

God's sake don't believe it and also certainly don't believe it when they tell you you're crap.

Do you think that, particularly if you're in the media yourself, you can consistently ignore what the critics say, or does a little of what they say become a factor in your desire to continue the success of the channel that you're leading?

You almost need a plan for dealing with the media, particularly in this industry which is under scrutiny all the time. You should never allow the media to distort your decisions so that you're making decisions because that's what you think will get the good headlines tomorrow. If you want to run that kind of business, then you should go into politics.

Do you think that pushing at limits of taste and acceptability is part and parcel of the development of any successful television channel?

No. Innovation, yes, but just pushing at the barriers of what is acceptable for the sake of it is not acceptable. But whatever the business – whether you're Sainsbury's, Harvey Nichols, Comet Warehouse or Channel 4 – you keep growing by innovation. Innovation implies high risk, and with high risk comes failure, so you've got to be prepared for that, but if you don't risk, then your business goes stale very quickly.

And what do you say to those people who might have failed somewhere along the way, how do you pick up those who might not be as resilient as you in resisting the criticism or indeed in understanding it, how do you set them back on an ambitious path?

The first thing is to examine what created the disaster in the first place. You're describing a disaster scenario. The question is, was it a foreseeable mistake? Have you been misunderstood? Was it the right decision and you've just been misunderstood? Or did someone make a calamitous mistake along the way? Did the market turn against you unexpectedly? You have to examine the reasons for the disaster. If it was a ghastly piece of judgment then you have to take the responsibility and you have to go. There's no question, you have to resign, that's the only way the business can recover. If, on the other hand, you're still convinced it was the right decision and people have misunderstood you, you have to explain that to your people very clearly and you have to get them to believe with you that you're still on the right course, no matter what they throw at you.

You won a great battle in achieving a change in the funding formula which had seen large c hunks of your revenue being handed over to ITV. How did you succeed in that, what were your tactics for doing this?

The difficulty with that particular issue was, leaving aside that there were big vested interests ranged against us, that the natural position of the government is always to do nothing if they can avoid doing anything at all. This is not a criticism, this is a fact of life – they've got so many things to attend to that the only things they will actually find legislative time for are those that they absolutely have to do because there is some political downside, some real disaster scenario if they don't act. That's the way they assess their priorities. With Channel 4's funding formula I knew at the beginning when we sat down and made the decision to try and change it that there was no political downside, I couldn't go to the government and say, 'Unless you do this Channel 4's going to go broke,' because that was demonstrably not the case. So we decided that the only clout we would have in this was to shout and shout and shout and go on shouting and run a campaign that would just not go away, so they couldn't possibly ignore us because we just kept coming. And every time they battered us down we just kept coming and in the end it was, 'Oh God, we've got to do something to get this channel off our back!'

Was it letters, lunches?

It was everything. It was every speech I made. Every time Channel 4 or anything to do with television was mentioned in the papers, we'd find a way to write a letter, get an article in, bring the funding formula in. Endless lobbying, bombarding people. Just everything we could think of to raise the subject, and it worked in the end. We created a political downside, we just weren't going to go away. They were amazed, they couldn't believe how we kept this campaign going, because we had mistimed it very badly. When we pressed the button to go with the campaign we were expecting a Broadcasting Bill in six months' time, but it got delayed by a year so we were then left trying to keep this balloon up in the air for 18 months, which was pretty hard going. But we managed it and in the end that worked for us.

Was there a downside to that successful campaign, because a lot of people said, 'Well, if you're making so much money, let's privatize the channel'?

That was a calculation at the beginning, but the fact is we couldn't go on. It was demoralizing for our producers, our suppliers and the staff to work as hard as we were working, being successful, and then to give everything away to the shareholders of ITV. The money wasn't going into programmes, and we couldn't let that position pertain. We knew we were risking running the privatization issue again, but we took that calculation and we figured privatization would be an easier issue to win than the funding formula because it's more demonstrable. But what a disaster it would be to privatize the channel.

Do you think a successful person can ever resolve the conflict between family and work?

No, I don't think you can ever successfully resolve it, because it's a matter of day-to-day, week-by-week, year-by-year management. You have to manage your time in order to meet all the obligations that you have, and it's very difficult to do that.

Do you feel that your personal life has been sacrificed to a certain extent?

Oh, no question, yes. I've been married twice, unsuccessfully, or partly successfully but ultimately unsuccessfully, neither of those situations was all bad or all good. I'm a workaholic to begin with, and if things weren't absolutely right at home I would just throw myself more and more into work instead of dealing with the problem at home. I would run away from the problem. Work is an easy gratification for me. You're appreciated, you're the boss, everybody 'loves you' – or they say they do.

What do you regard as the most successful moments in your life? Perhaps some which the world wouldn't necessarily be aware of?

I think the most satisfying on a tiny microcosmic level was the first Christmas *EastEnders* when I was running BBC1. We'd nursed this show. I didn't invent the show, I inherited it, but I marketed it and nursed it and scheduled it and got it on the air in the right shape and Julia Smith, the then producer, came to see me. I was running BBC1 and she said she wanted to do a one-hour *EastEnders* Christmas special on Christmas Day. I said, 'Oh, Julia, it works in the half-hour, can't we break some new ground here somehow, I'm not really mad about doing a one-hour ...' And then I suddenly had a flash of inspiration. I said, 'I'll tell you what we should do, here's what's never been done before, why don't we do two half-hours on Christmas night. Do one episode at 6.30 with a cliff hanger, and one at 10.00.' And her eyes lit up, she said, 'That will work because the storyline I'm working on for Christmas is Den and Angie splitting up.' I said, 'Let's do it,' so we did it and we got 30 million viewers on Christmas Day. The product was brilliant, but that was just one of those flashes of inspiration that you have now and again, a tiny story but it was fun at the time.

Is it becoming more or less difficult to achieve success in television with the fragmentation of channels that is coming up? Is it going to be a much, much tougher environment overall?

You've got to be sharper, you've got to be quicker, you've got to hold your nerve longer, but I think there are fewer and fewer people who are going to be able to take risks, and I think as long as Channel 4 continues to innovate and take risks, they'll be fine, because nobody else is going to do that.

What are the greatest enemies of success?

Complacency, a feeling that we've cracked it, we know that we've got the code now, we know how this works. You don't, you absolutely don't. You know, you start putting the money into research and development and marketing and those things, but they are the things that kill your business. And closed minds – you've got to be open, you've got to get out and about, you can't be locked in your office. I don't do any business in this office, I do the business getting out and about in the theatre, going to movies, meeting people, talking to writers.

Do you think success brings with it any obligations to society as a whole?

Yes. I feel an obligation personally to put back whatever I can, which is very little in the great scheme of things but it makes me feel better. I've done various commissions, I did a report for the Home Office on fear of crime, I've just sat on the NSPCC commission on child abuse which was two years' work. I do a lot of charity work, Jewish charity work, I go to little synagogue halls and I talk to the old people about TV and things. I do whatever I can.

So what do you say to those people who don't?

It's very, very shortsighted because in the end what we want is a healthy thriving country with as little poverty as possible, with good feeling about the place. Industry and business can make a contribution – they can't change things individually, but if we all make a bit of a contribution we can make it that bit better. That makes the climate for business better. So it's very shortsighted, very unfair and very selfish of those businesses that don't contribute to the community in any way, shape or form to live off the backs of those businesses that do, and I've got no time for them.

If you could gather before you in one room all the young people in Britain who want to get into television, what advice would you give them?

It's an expanding business, it's a glamorous business, it's an exciting business and there are more and more opportunities for youngsters, skilled or unskilled. What I would say to them is, 'Because there are so many of you and so few opportunities compared to the number of people who want to take them, when you meet somebody like me or anybody who's in a position to give you a job or to steer you in the right direction, you've got to have thought very, very hard about why you want to get into television, what you want to do eventually. You may never get there, you may even want to be a sound engineer and you end up as a newsreader, you never know how it's going to work out, but you've got to have thought harder about it than anybody else. And be able to talk coherently and articulately and instinctively about why you like television and what you get out of television and, particularly, to be able to converse about programmes, what you like, why you like them, shows you don't like, why they don't work for you. You need an ability to show that your mind is capable of analysis, of evaluation, and those kinds of things.

On the whole is it going to be more or less difficult to be successful in television in the future?

There are going to be more opportunities, therefore there could be more failures and hopefully some successes. So far everybody's eventually succeeded. GMTV, LWT, BBC2, they were all disasters to begin with, TVam too. I think you are going to find that there are going to be a lot more disasters, more people folding up in the future, but out of that will come some successes. It will be like any other business, it will be like magazines. There's a new one launched every week, some of them stick, some of them don't. It's going to be like that in broadcasting.

When you have been so successful yourself at climbing to the top of the television industry, why give it all up? Why change professions?

Channel 4, of all channels, needs to re-invent itself almost annually. That is what is expected of it. For the last year or so I have been concerned about getting stale. I would never have taken any other position in broadcasting, but when the opportunity presented itself at First Leisure it concentrated my mind. The decision made itself. I hope I have done the right thing.

One final question. When your time comes to leave this planet, what would you like people to say about Michael Grade?

Basically, all things considered, he was a good thing in the end.

LORD HARRIS

At 13 he was selling rugs from a stall in Peckham market; by 53 he'd built up two retailing empires and had a seat in the House of Lords. An only child, Phil Harris threw himself into sport because he was 'hopeless at reading and writing' and had to learn everything by heart. (In fact, he didn't discover he was dyslexic until one of his own sons was seven.) He left school at 15 when his father died of cancer, and took over the three shops that were the family business. 'Everyone said we would go bankrupt, so the pressure was on me to do well.' Setting himself a series of targets for opening new shops, he built up the firm into Harris Queensway, by 1988 the largest carpet retailer in the world. His sales director, asked whether Phil Harris's secret  was to use the carrot or the stick, replied, 'Both – he hits you with the carrot!' Harris now admits that he got carried away by the 1980s takeover boom, making no fewer than 38 bids, and diversifying into retail areas he 'should have left to other people'. That made him vulnerable to a takeover himself; despite putting up a strong fight, he lost the company – although personally walking away with £70 million must have been some compensation. But, refusing to sign a 'no competition' agreement, he started again, building up a new company, Carpetright, from scratch. Knighted for services to business and his long-standing passion for politics (he and his wife, Pauline, are prodigious fund-raisers for the Conservative Party), he was later elevated to the House of Lords where he pursues interests in education and health that grew out of his extensive charitable work.

His family motto is 'whatever we make, we give 20 per cent away.' He offers here his formula for motivating people with more than money: 'You make them enjoy their job, give them responsibility, and make sure they can work within their capabilities. He describes the qualities needed in his business to be a boss; the best career path for someone joining right at the bottom, and the priorities for setting up a retail business today. He talks too about being 'very, very worried' when he was attacked for using a legal loophole (since closed) to purchase a huge number of shares in the BT privatization. He accepts the blame for 'more than one wrong decision' in his choice of people, and remembers the early lesson in teamwork his father taught him when he was injured in a cricket match.

Lord Harris, what is your definition of success?

I always say to people, 'Work hard, play hard and enjoy life.' Putting it another way, I think you have to work hard, be able to motivate people and remember the most important thing about life, whether you're building a business, working in schools, health, or even in politics, is that it's all about people, and being able to motivate other people.

You said, 'Enjoy yourself.' But there's often a conflict between successful people, who are incredibly motivated to work, being able to spend enough time enjoying themselves – spending enough time with their family. Is there an inevitable conflict between work and play for people who want to be successful?

I agree with that. I get very few holidays. I'd like more. And one of my big regrets in life was when I was young I didn't spend enough time with the family. My grandchildren see more of me now than my daughters and sons did. But, if you enjoy what you're doing, you will be successful.

You left school at 15. You were, on your own admission, hopeless at reading and writing. To what extent were those handicaps in establishing a successful career?

I think they were handicaps. What I really wanted to do when I left school – no one believes me – was to be a lawyer. But, being dyslexic, there's no way I could have been a lawyer, because my English was terrible.

Did you realize you were dyslexic?

I didn't actually find that out until my youngest son, who was seven at the time, went to be tested and he was hopeless at school, and quite good at maths, and they found out he had a high IQ but couldn't read or write. Then I realized I was dyslexic – I was also good at maths – and that's why one of the reasons some of the work we do today, with colleges and schools, is to help the dyslexic.

Did that give you anything approaching an inferiority complex, because you felt there was an area of life in which you were, apparently, not good?

Not really, because dyslexics usually have a good memory, and so I could learn things by heart. It was easy to learn things, but hard to put them down on paper. But I started playing cricket, football, tennis, and enjoyed life that way, because I was quite good at them.

To what extent do you feel your present success is a direct product of your background and upbringing?

Without doubt my determination comes from it. When my father died, I was 15 and everyone said the family business would go bankrupt, so the pressure was on me to do well. That gave me my first determination, which was to get to ten shops, then 20, then build up from there. I've always said that you're better off to be born lucky than rich, and I was lucky.

You started off with the three shops that your father left you. To what extent did that give you a much better start than someone starting from scratch?

Well it did and it didn't, because in those days there were death duties, which took quite a lot of money away from us, then within three years my mother died, so we had a second lot of death duties. I can tell you that, the first year I was in business, our profit for the year was exactly £890. The previous year, when my father ran it, it was nearly three times that. So we were not a rich family, but I was lucky, and I think I was lucky because I had the determination to do it, and what's more, I had to work.

I was also very lucky to marry my wife when I was only 18 and she was just 19. She built up the family, while I built up the business.

The support of your wife and family is a vital factor in success?

Oh, no question. Your wife has to be with you; she can help you all the time. My wife never got in the way of business, and she looked after the family. She took them on holiday when I couldn't.

John Kitching, your managing director at Carpetright, once said that you use fun and humour as a management tool. What did he mean by that?

Well, I think when you're working and when you're going round the country seeing people, obviously you're serious on the business side and you have standards – and we like to set very high standards – but also, you should enjoy doing it. Going out for a drink with them in the evening, taking them out for a dinner, that sort of thing.

And are you able effectively to separate the two?

I like to think I can. Unless there are problems, such as when you go to a shop and they are not operating to the required standard, then of course you carry on working in the evening. But if everything's well, you let the people enjoy life and relax with you.

People have spoken about your inspirational enthusiasm, your lack of pretension, your boundless energy, your toughness. Which of those is most important in building up a successful business? Or is there another factor?

Number one is energy, number two is toughness. But there is another thing – fairness. You've got to be very fair with people – and you can be tough and fair.

What do you regard as your biggest failures, and how did you recover from them?

My biggest failure was in 1988 when we were taken over. It was my biggest disappointment, and still is. People say that it was well planned and I planned it, but I didn't. I loved that company, I didn't want to lose it. The City said that my management team was not strong enough, but that team produced profits of over £50 million over a year. They wanted me to bring people in – experienced people – but when they actually joined us, they were not, in my view, as good as the people we'd already got. That was my biggest disappointment, because if I had been given another three years, Harris Queensway would undoubtedly have been sorted out, to a slightly different format than it was, and we would have been successful.

To what extent are you dependent, as a businessman, on the opinion of the City?

One is definitely dependent, to some extent on the City. But the City expects more and more from you; you tell them you're going to make *x* and they put *x*+. It actually drives companies up too fast, too high, making it more difficult for people. The City people set their goals too high. With Carpetright we tell them what we think we're going to make and we stick to it, and, touch wood, every time we've just slightly exceeded budget, or their figures.

In the 1980s you were on the acquisition trail; was that a mistake?

There's no question. We had too many take-overs – in three or four years we took over about 12 companies, some very good, some not so good. But remember, some such as Harveys were very successful. Where we did go wrong was to move into electricals, we were not very good at that. We should have left that to those who are brilliant at that particular business. Another problem, which I didn't cotton on to and I should have done, was when I built up the furniture business; the big problem was that we couldn't get deliveries. It's a cottage industry – manufacturers making a 100–200 suites a week – whereas with carpets, however big you get, the manufacturers can simply turn the machines on more and produce the goods required. In furniture they can't, and that was my big mistake. I don't think Harveys, in which I am a majority shareholder, will make that mistake.

Which is more important in driving people to success – the carrot or the stick?

You need to use both. You need to make them happy, make them want to be successful, but if anything goes wrong you need to hit.

Even in the failure of Harris Queensway you achieved a kind of success because you walked away with £70 million. Now a lot of people would have said, 'That's it, I've made my pile, I'm perfectly happy to retire.' You didn't – why not?

Because I was 44 years old at the time, far too young to retire. I didn't want to be taken over and I thought there was still a great opportunity in carpets or textiles. I've said I want to do 50 years in retailing, so I've got 11 years left. I went away for two weeks and sat down and said, 'What do we want to do?' That's how Carpetright got formed and we built it up from that team to what it is today.

What did you think as you watched your old company, Harris Queensway, under the new management?

It was very sad. I knew they were doing things wrong. Not everything was perfect in the old Harris Queensway, but in the last six months of my being in charge we made £25 million. In their first six months, the new regime made a profit, and then went into loss. It was a new team coming in trying to do different things. They had two rights issues of over £18 million, so they had enough cash, and furthermore, when I left it had £25 million in the bank. It was still a very good business, but they didn't go about it the right way. The main thing was that they had a good team of people there when I left, but they didn't motivate them enough. And they brought in new people over them who didn't know anything about furniture or carpets.

What do you regard as your biggest successes throughout your business career?

My first large-scale take-over of Keith Royle's, in 1974. We bought 24 shops for £750,000, which we borrowed from NatWest on 1 September and paid back on the last day of December the same year.

Were they surprised?

Very. And when it came to buying Queensway two years later, we borrowed £2 million and again paid it back very quickly. I don't like debt.

How important is borrowing in setting up and expanding a successful business?

You do need it, but in retail, because you get credit from suppliers, you don't need it quite so much as you do in other businesses such as manufacturing. But you have to look at cash flows and see how cash flows work through.

Do you think that success should involve some degree of sacrifice or failure along the way? Are you likely to be more successful if you have experienced that?

As I said, my parents dying when I was very young made me more determined. Then the failure of being taken over made me more determined to get back. You mentioned I had £70 million when I left, but on the very day when we were taken over, I was still there until the last minute trying to fight and put a management team together. On that basis I got up to 185p per share, then Gulliver offered 190p and I decided my heart mustn't rule my head and therefore I had to let my company go. I remember my young son was in school in Boston and I had to phone him up and say, 'We've been taken over,' and I told him how much we got, and we talked about that. He came back to me, and I will always remember it, with, 'What would your father think about your being taken over?'

Do you recall the lesson your father taught you at a cricket match?

I was very close to my father. I was about 13 at the time, and we were playing cricket at Dulwich in the first round of a Cup match and we were all out for about 25. I was very lucky to get just over half the runs, and we won. I had a whitlow on my finger – the scar's still there – and at the end of the match I said, 'Dad, will you take me to hospital to have it seen to?' But he said, 'You're captain of the team, you've got to go back with the team,' and he drove off, so I went back with the team. He took me to the hospital later. So I learned from that experience that if you're a captain or a leader, you stay with the team, no matter what.

And that is a principle which has carried on right through your business life?

Yes. The two great lessons in my life were what my father taught me, that day – when you're with a team you lead them in good times and bad times. And second, what my son said, 'What would your father say about being taken over?'

The sense of team spirit is one way of running a business, but some believe you've got to be a control freak to do it successfully. How do you get the balance right between the two?

I'm as tough as anybody, but I'm tough and fair. And that's the difference – being fair to people. To give you an example, if I find a manager who's not up to it, but then I find out his wife is very ill at home, there is no point in knocking him then. You knock him when you find out he's over the problems. And normally, in retail, if a manager goes wrong it's usually due to betting, drink or family, and the point is to find out which of the three it is. The first two have to be dealt with very strongly. The third is more difficult, if say, someone's very ill. If it's that, you've got to forgive a manager who performs badly and help him through his family problems.

Do you still serve behind the counter?

I love it! One of my biggest thrills recently was when we bought back the shop that I first worked in – in Penge – and I served there from nine in the morning till two. I must say that by two o'clock I was very tired.

You do that on a regular basis – why?

I do it on Saturdays on a regular basis. I go to all the new stores when we open them, and if there are customers there I speak to them – see what they like, what they don't like, see if they like the range, get a feeling for what people want.

And what do they tell you? Do they recognize you?

Very few do, thank goodness, but if they do we talk about what they like in the shop and what they dislike.

Does what you learn from those Saturday sessions translate through to decision-taking in the Board Room?

Yes. Every Monday morning, first we go through the sales figures, then we look at the advertising for the week. Thirdly we consider what changes we are going to make that week, and finally we discuss where we're going generally that week.

Do you recall the very first time that you ever said to yourself, 'I've been successful at something'?

No, I don't. But I do say to my wife Pauline, quite regularly, 'Aren't we lucky to be able to see the Queen, aren't we lucky to be with a Prime Minister, aren't we lucky to be able to go to Chequers or Downing Street or Buckingham Palace?' And we both say to one another, 'I couldn't believe, 35 years ago, that this would happen.'

Do you think that's one of the fruits, the rewards of success?

Yes, of course, and it's also being able to give your family what they want. But also, there's the other side of it which is to be able to give help help people – dyslexic children – to help a hospice or a hospital.

Do you think that anyone who is successful in business has an obligation to put something back into the community?

No question. We have a family motto – whatever we make, we give 20 per cent of it away. And I hope my children are carrying on in my footsteps with different charities from mine. I believe by doing that, it helps your luck.

You've mentioned luck several times, is it an essential part of success?

Yes, it is. One kind of luck is being in the right place at the right time. It was, for example, fortunate that I could start Carpetright again in a recession, as that gave me opportunities to get stores and to get people. I couldn't build Carpetright today, with the economy the way it is, in quite the same way that I did in 1988. So you do need luck.

How would you set about building a business empire today?

Have a clear identification of what you want to do, get a good management team, make sure you've got a good cash flow in the business, or you've got enough cash available for what you want to do, and add hard work. There's no difference whenever you're starting. It's about people, motivation, and a clear idea of marketing, and marketing yourself and the business.

If someone was joining Carpetright, now, indeed joining any other High Street retailer, what do they need to do in order to be successful?

It's going to be hard work. They've got to have vision and they've got to want to get on and want to get to the top. They should want to get into a sales director's or managing director's post. And everyone in our business has that opportunity. Also, I'm a great believer in enriching people around you. If they're successful they get rich – our managing director of Carpetright is worth probably £6 or £7 million, and, please God, in two or three years' time, he'll be worth £10 million.

What about people at shop-floor level? Do they get a slice of the action?

When we floated Carpetright, we gave people share options. Everyone who'd been with the company for two years, whoever it was, got share options. And many of the area managers now have a quarter of a million pounds' worth of stock, which I'm very happy for them to have. If we do well, I want them to succeed with us.

Do you think that is a core part of a really successful company, that everyone feels they have a share in its financial success?

Yes. I believe it's all about sharing, all about helping, and the better we do, the better I want them to be.

What do you think are the greatest enemies of success?

Jealousy from people who haven't made it. I find that very disappointing.

Do you think that people understand the extent of the risk that entrepreneurs take?

We take risks, but, of course, we get the rewards for it as well.

As you became more and more successful, was there a danger that this might encourage a kind of arrogance? Do money and success make you more unfeeling, as it were, to the rest of the world?

I can only talk about me, and my answer is no, not at all.

Because you have a huge amount of money, did that encourage you to take risks, to go to the margins on business decisions, in a way that you would otherwise not consider? You know, one thinks of the underwriting in the first British Telecom privatization. In retrospect, would you have done it exactly the same way?

Six months before anyone knew what the price of BT was going to be, I was at dinner with Gerald Ronson, who took two and a half million pounds of underwriting. He said, 'Would you like to buy half of it off me?' And I said, 'No, it's too much for me, but I will buy a quarter of it off you.' So I did – we paid quite a lot of money. But remember, it was six months before the price was agreed. When I took it I didn't know I was going to get it, I didn't know there was going to be a restriction. People say I was questioned by many people in the DTI. But I have never been questioned. The press picked it up and made out I was in trouble, when I hadn't done anything wrong at all.

And how did you react when the press were criticizing you over this? Did you get a really low feeling, and if so, how did you recover from that?

I was at a sales conference with a lot of my staff, and when I read on a frontpage that I was in trouble, I was very, very worried. I didn't know what I'd done wrong, and I didn't see that I had done anything wrong. I went straight away to my lawyer, who told me I'd done nothing wrong at all.

Did you still feel a kind of sickness, because of the media's attitude?

No. I honestly thought, 'Have I done something wrong?' I could understand the moral side of it, where an ordinary investor could only get 800 shares, and I got however many it was – 250,000. I could understand that, but on the other hand I did take the risk six months earlier, and no one would have said anything if it had been a flop.

Are there any general principles in business for riding through such times?

They make the good times better, and that's why I said at the beginning, you should play hard, work hard and enjoy life. I didn't enjoy that time. I didn't think I did anything wrong, and I still don't. But people out there think I did something wrong, and it's one thing that annoys me.

Have you any frustrated ambitions?

I want to help hospitals, spend more time helping hospitals. And I want to be the biggest retailer in carpets in the world – no, I want to be the most profitable carpet retailer in the world.

As far as your charitable work is concerned, to what extent should things like hospitals be dependent upon people like you, and to what extent should they be dependent on the Government? Is it a mix? Should it be one or the other?

I actually think the mix today is perfect, but I do believe people should be generous and people should help others. We're lucky because we've got money and people with money should help those without it.

Has success changed you at all?

I hope not. I'm still the same. I like being at home. It must change you to a degree – I now look to buy art and horses. Show jumping is one of my hobbies, and I go out there to win. If I didn't have money I wouldn't be able to do that. That's changed me, but I don't think it has changed me much. If I went back and lived in a small house again, it wouldn't worry me at all.

So you could happily live your life, having experienced success, if you went back to having nothing tomorrow?

I would be happy to have a nice house with enough money to have holidays and a nice car. Just Pauline, myself and the children and the family, that would make me happy. I think where I would be disappointed is not being able to give money to charities, which I enjoy doing.

What's the greatest pleasure you've had from all your success?

Being able to give money to charity. The Hospice Movement gives me a lot of pleasure. There's a charity called NABS, which looks after advertising people in Peterhouse. It gives me a lot of pleasure to work with them, as does helping babies through Birthright. All those things. Recently Pauline and I opened a children's ward in a hospital at Lewisham. It gives me pleasure seeing people happy and giving them the best service available.

One point we haven't touched on, which I think was my greatest achievement, and it's the thing that really I will always look back on with pride, was being able to restructure Guy's Hospital. There was a management team there that was very fixed in its ways, and to actually convert it, with 8,000 staff, into probably the most successful hospital in the country in two years was, I think, my greatest success.

What was wrong with Guy's when you took over?

There was no one motivating the people, there were few areas of responsibility. Give people responsibility and let them get on with it, and you motivate them to be successful. And when they are successful, you give them the credit.

To what extent does success open doors that would otherwise be closed?

Success has helped me to be able to get into politics, in a small way. As I said, it's helped me to be able to meet people, and to be able to do a lot of things that I wouldn't have done otherwise. It's been a great life doing that.

You had a knighthood, now you're in the House of Lords. Do you feel that the whole concept of successful people being rewarded by their country with awards is an essential part of the fabric of success?

I was very, very proud when I got my knighthood, it was probably one of my greatest days. Going into the Lords was different. I've gone in as a working peer, to talk about what I believe in regarding health and education, and I hope to play an active part in those areas.

When you sit in the Lords and you look at the splendour that surrounds you, do you ever think of the boy from Peckham?

I think I'm very lucky to be there. But having got there I want to play an active part to make sure that other people get a better chance.

What advice would you give all the young people in Britain, who want to emulate your success?

Have a clear idea of what you want to do. If you want to be a lawyer, for example, it's hard work and you're really working for yourself most of the time, and then you need a secretary or an assistant to help. If you want to be a retailer, have a clear vision of what you want to do. If you want to be a property developer, you've got to spend time going round the country learning the business. So there are all sorts of different ways. If you want to be a manufacturer, you've got to know the field, you've got to look forward ten years and ask yourself, 'Is that product going to be selling ten years down the line?' There's no point in looking at something that's going to be out of date next year. So it's all about looking forward, hard work, building a team with you, and enjoying it.

When someone walks into your office looking for a job, how do you know that they're going to be successful? And how do you weed out those who will not be?

I'm a great believer that if the chemistry between two people is right, you give them a chance and you work with them. I think if someone's not going to be successful, or won't enjoy working with you, or doesn't like the job he's got, you're not helping him if you keep him on. You actually help him by moving him on so he can find another job elsewhere.

When your time comes to leave this life, what would you like people to say about you?

I would like them to think, he's made a contribution to public life and he's been happy.

And those are more important than running a successful business?

Oh yes, because making a contribution to public life means you've helped many more people.

TIM HENMAN

He picked up his first racket at the age of three; by the time he was six, 'I knew it was what I wanted to be involved in.' At ten he had his first year of proper coaching, before being talent-spotted by David Lloyd, who offered him a scholarship at his tennis school. When he reached 18 he was ranked 774 in the world. Five years later, he was in the top 20 via the Wimbledon quarter-finals and a stylish victory in the Sydney Open; and in 1998 became the first Briton for 25 years to reach the men's semi-finals at Wimbledon. Now, he carries the hopes of a country hungry for home-grown tennis heroes. Behind him is a strong tradition – his family has produced Wimbledon players across three previous generations, and his great-grandmother was the first woman to serve overarm there – although he denies he was driven by a desire to follow in their footsteps. Success for Tim Henman is 'definitely not about winning', but 'trying to fulfil your potential – giving 100 per cent at all times'. Twice it looked as though his career might be brought to a premature end – first when a damaged elbow put him out of the game for two years from the age of 11, and then three years ago, when he broke his leg in three places. Another potential setback came when he hit a ball in a fit of temper and it struck a ball-girl. As a result, he became the first person to be disqualified at Wimbledon for 120 years, enduring press coverage which made him feel awful – 'as if I had murdered someone'. He explains here how he dealt with that, and 'came out of it a better person'.

He breaks down the qualities needed for a successful tennis player into the technical, physical and mental sides; he discusses how he psychs himself up for the fray; the need for a set plan not only during the match, but before it as well; the mental resilience needed when you are on court. He says he is aware of the pressure on Wimbledon's Centre Court, 'but it doesn't affect me – I go out there to play for myself. The moment you start thinking about all the people who want you to win, and their expectations, your focus is taken away and you are going to struggle.' The 'healthy competition' with his rival, Greg Rusedski, he considers 'definitely important', and he regards jealousy as the big enemy of success: 'If I knew someone was jealous of me, I wouldn't let it affect my performance, because then if there was a battle to be won, they would be winning it.'

Tim Henman, what is your definition of success?

I think in the area in which I am involved, success is very much a personal thing. For a player there are obviously different levels. It is all about trying to fulfil your potential. If, at the end of the day, you can look back over your career and say you have given it 100 per cent at all times, and you believe you have fulfilled your potential, then I think you can say you have been successful.

Curiously, you are not saying that success is about winning?

No, definitely not. There have been times while I have been growing up – and I am still growing up, and still learning about my profession – when the way I have performed has been more important than the result. In some of the matches I have played, that has been the key thing. I may have ended up losing the match, but if I learned something from that, then it has probably been a successful day for me.

So the benchmark is actually learning and improving? When you come off the court, if you feel you have learned something and improved your game, then that for you is a successful match, whether you win or not?

Yes, very much so. Now, as I move higher and higher up the rankings, and the improvements I can make become smaller and smaller, then I am going to start looking more at the end result, but I think when you are learning, performance is very important. The learning curve then is huge, and if you can stay on the up, that is success.

To what extent do you think your success so far has been due to your background and upbringing?

Very little. A lot of people focus on my family's involvement in tennis, and I do have a tennis history – I am aware of that. My parents both played the game, and I was fortunate that they had a tennis court at home, and that is where I started, playing with them. But from the age of about six or seven, with no influence from my parents, I knew that tennis was what I wanted to be involved in. And at that age I was probably too young to appreciate what my grandparents and great-grandparents had accomplished in the game, so it was very much my own decision. As I grew older I became a little more aware of my family's history, but the idea was already firmly in my head by that stage.

When was the moment that you said to yourself, 'I want to go with tennis. Tennis is going to be my obsession. I like tennis more than anything else'?

It was a gradual thing. I didn't wake up one day and say, 'Tennis is going to be my profession.' I started very, very young. I was probably hitting tennis balls when I was three. Obviously I wasn't making decisions then, but, you know, it was then and still is very much my hobby. It is now my occupation as well, and what I get paid for, but as I played more and more, I realized how much I enjoyed it. By about six or seven I was aware of professional players. I had been to Wimbledon, I had seen Bjorn Borg play. I think it grew on me and it is probably still growing on me. I played other sports until I was 11 or 12, but I had already known for a long time that tennis was what I was going to be involved in.

So you knew, or thought, that you were good at tennis. However, to take a decision to pursue it as a career, other people have to think that you are good as well. Who were the people who told you, 'We think you ought to concentrate on tennis.' Were there mentors along the way?

Obviously, my parents realized early on that I had ability. I had good hand-eye co-ordination and they saw how keen I was. So they played an important part when I was very young. They just wanted me to be happy, and they didn't need to be Einstein to work out that I was at my happiest on the court. When I was about ten, I had a year of my first proper coaching, with Onny Parun at the David Lloyd Centre. He was a big influence early on, because that is an important age. It is when you begin to learn your trade – the techniques of different shots. And it was there that David Lloyd first noticed me. He was setting up his own tennis scheme, and offered me the chance to take one of his scholarships. So my parents, Onny Parun and David Lloyd were pretty key people at that stage.

What do you do to make sure you surround yourself with the right sort of people, to take all the other pressures of life off you so that you can concentrate on tennis?

You have to learn as you go along about what's best for you in terms of preparation for matches, and about relationships. David Felgate, my coach, and I have worked together for nearly four and a half years. We have a very good relationship on the court, and we are great friends off it as well. I think that is very important. I have noticed, probably in the last year or so, when I started to make my mark in the game, that suddenly more people want to be involved in what you are doing. So it is important to have a group of people around you on whom you can rely, whom you trust, and who understand you.

There are various stages in success, rungs you reach as you move up the ladder. After you have achieved one particular goal, how do you stop yourself saying, 'OK, that's great, I have done that. I can wind down for a bit now'?

There have definitely been cases of people becoming comfortable and thinking that now they have reached a certain target, that might be enough for them. It is up to the individual how high his or her ultimate goal is. In tennis terms, the ranking system goes down to about 1,200 or 1,300. Some people might just want to break into the top 500, or the top 100. The top 100 is really the benchmark by which players are gauged. I have worked towards all those, stage by stage. I have worked towards being in the top 100, the top 50. The top 20 was my next target, and I can assure you that it won't be my last. I think it is important to set goals.

What do you think separates the really top tennis players from the rest?

In technical terms, in the way they hit the ball. Somebody at the very top, like Pete Sampras, has a huge serve which is probably going to be his major weapon. But a lot of the time, when you really analyse it, the difference is mental. It is their ability to play the key points well, and to come up with a great shot at exactly the right time. If you were to see a whole line of players from rankings 1 to 100 practising hitting the ball, a lot of them would hit the ball very, very well and you wouldn't really notice much difference between them. At the end of the day success boils down to the belief and confidence the individual has, and his or her ability to play the big points.

In terms of mental attitude, what is your approach when you go on to the court for a big match? How do you psych yourself up for it?

I have a routine. In tennis it can be difficult to predict when you are going to play because you follow on after previous matches, and so you never know when the match before you is going to finish, but I will probably practise an hour and a half before I estimate I am going to start. Then I go back to the locker room, have a shower and a bite to eat if I feel I need it. Then I go back to the changing rooms to get everything organized – to sort out my rackets and make sure my grips are OK. Then I just generally have a think about the match to come. There might be something my opponent might do to think about, but usually I just concentrate on my own performance. I think I have got to the stage where if I can perform to the best of my ability, then I believe I have a good chance of beating virtually anyone in the world.

And if you are to play at your best, is it important that you follow that chain of events and then get straight out on to the court?

Definitely. The vast majority of my best performances do occur when I get into a routine. It might be just very, very simple things – getting up at a certain time, having a car to pick me up and take me to the tournament, having my practice court booked. It is certainly no coincidence that it is when you don't have a routine – if things get rushed, you get side-tracked and your mind is on other things, perhaps on some business off the court – that your performance suffers. This is something I have learned about myself – how important it is to have a set plan before the match as well as during it. And if you can stick to that plan, it will give you your strongest opportunity to play your best tennis.

You damaged an elbow at the age of 11, which knocked you out of the game for almost two years. Then, in Singapore 1993, you snapped your leg in three places. For a lot of people, both those injuries would have spelled the end of a tennis career. How did you overcome those obstacles?

Well, there was no guarantee that either the elbow or the leg would mend 100 per cent in the way they did, so I suppose there must have been an element of good fortune to it. But mentally, I always remained very positive in each case. I didn't let them get me too down too much. Obviously, I was very disappointed, because if I am injured I can't play tennis, the thing in life I enjoy most. I think the people I had around me were also very important – they supported me and probably pulled me through it just as much as did my own mental strength and determination to get back on the court. But those were certainly not easy times.

During your teenage years you were very slightly built – someone described you as almost scrawny. Did you feel that that was going to be a handicap, and that you would have to put on some weight at some stage or another?

Not really. I always knew that I probably always would be slight. There is not really any chance of me ever becoming overweight.

I know it is important to build up muscle, and in the last 18 months or so it is something I have been working on. I am on a big drive to become fitter and stronger. If you look back at my record in 1996, I made six semi-finals on the tour but was not able to get further, and it was definitely not a psychological thing. So I need to be at my peak when I am playing the better players in a tournament, having won three or four matches already.

I think it is probably more important in tennis to have height rather than bulk. You don't really see too many people below 5ft 9in. There's Michael Chang, of course, and there have been others who have coped, but I think it is an advantage to be tall. And that has never been a problem for me. I only had to look at my father, and and my two elder brothers, who are both over 6ft, and, going back generations, there hasn't really been anyone short in my family.

When you are behind in a game, out there on court, with the pressure and the tension of the crowd, how do you psych yourself up to hit back?

You definitely need a mental resilience to be able to deal with that situation. You also need belief in your own ability, to be able to say to yourself, 'Well, things are probably not going as well as they could do, but I know that I can turn them around.' Much of it is about what goes on between your ears.

Have you ever felt like giving up?

Never.

You've never felt even a twinge of doubt?

No. I suppose that is what people think is a little scary, maybe even a bit odd. But even when I was injured and had long spells away from the game, when some people might have said, 'This is probably the time to start looking to move into a different field,' I didn't think about giving up. I have always enjoyed tennis so much that I think even when I stop playing, when my career is over, you will still find me hitting balls.

What about the criticism that came in the wake of that 1995 incident when, right out of character, you hit a ball in a fit of temper and it accidentally hit a ballgirl. Didn't that cause you any self-doubt?

Not self-doubt. If I knew deep-down that I had a bad temper, and that that was something that was going to happen again, and I was going to have to be careful about it, then maybe I would have had doubts about it. But that wasn't the case. I think most people who know anything about tennis, sport or about life in general understand that accidents happen, and that's what it was. I just had to go out there and deal with it.

I faced the problem head on. I dealt with the press. I had a pretty lively press conference after the match, and I said, 'Accidents happen. I'm very upset that this is the way the match finished, but at the end of the day, life goes on.' It was a pretty big thing, it was the first time somebody had been disqualified at Wimbledon in 120 years, and I think the fact that I am British probably made it worse. So my only worry at that stage was that this shouldn't be my career highlight, that I wasn't going to be remembered for being disqualified from Wimbledon. It will always be there, but I think the more and the bigger the achievements that I can put above it, the better.

Did you ever think that it might have been the end of your career in terms of having the British public on your side?

It's funny how it all ended. It happened on Wednesday evening and on the Thursday at Wimbledon I felt awful, as if I had murdered somebody or something. It wasn't because of people's reactions – between that Wednesday and the end of the tournament I must have had between 500 and 750 letters from the public, and not one of them was negative. Every one of them said, 'I think it was an awful decision, I don't think you should have been disqualified,' or words to that effect. So obviously that was a big morale-booster. The reason I felt so bad on the Thursday was the coverage in the newspapers. It was blown out of all proportion, really. There were big headlines saying that I had hit the ball so hard I could have killed the ballgirl, and things like that. But then, come the Thursday afternoon, it was all sorted out with the help of a big bouquet of flowers, and by Friday everyone was saying I was the nicest guy. It is amazing how the situation evolved. Looking back on it, I don't think the media could have a better opportunity to be as negative about me. And in the end I think I dealt with it, and maybe I came out of it a better a person.

What are the qualities you need to be a successful tennis player? What ingredients make up the ideal tennis player, the player who has everything?

I think you can break it down into three categories. First, there is the technical side of your game – your forehand, your backhand, your volleys, your serve. Then there is the physical side – your movement about the court, your speed, your agility, your stamina. Thirdly, there is the mental side – your determination, your ability to stay calm under pressure, to deal with adversity and to overcome any nerves or incidents on the court. If you are strong in all three of those areas, then you are going to be a pretty tough opponent.

So are there some occasions when you say, 'Oh, no, not tennis again – I can't face any more of that'?

It's not a question of not being able to face it, but there are times when you say, 'OK, tennis isn't on the agenda here. It is not going to be a talking point, it is not going to be discussed.' But I don't have to force that on myself. There are plenty of occasions, even when we are in the middle of a tournament, when we might go out to a restaurant or a bar and let our hair down and just generally switch off. And I think it is very important that you can do that, to maintain your peace of mind and keep yourself keen. If you play too much there are times when you become stale, and you are not going to practise and train as hard and as intensely, and that will end up affecting your performance.

Does it help to have a rival in your own age group working his own way up the ladder at roughly the same level. You have Greg Rusedski, for example. Does his presence help? Is it a driving factor?

I think that has definitely been important in my career. If you look back to when Jeremy Bates was playing some of his best tennis, I think he would probably admit – and certainly a lot of other people would say – that he had the ability to go further in the game. But he never really had anybody British close to him in the rankings to push him higher. And I think that is where Greg has been very relevant to me. At the end of 1995 I finished 99th in the world, which was a benchmark I had been working towards, and, if you were to take Greg out of the equation, I would have been British number 1. But suddenly, with him ranked 50 spots in front of me, there was another target to work towards, and now I have overtaken him. So it is definitely a case of healthy competition. I am sure he will be as keen to overtake me as I will be to stay ahead.

British tennis in general has not had the greatest century. Do you believe in what Tony Pickard, the former Davis Cup captain, called the pyramid effect, whereby standards in British tennis can be raised by one player doing particularly well and pulling up the rest?

Definitely. I think there are a lot of other factors involved, but certainly something we've lacked in British tennis is a role model, if you like. In other sports you have top British golfers and footballers, you have Damon Hill in motor racing. And there are many others. When youngsters are growing up they see you live or on television, and they do say, 'When I grow up I want to play golf like Nick Faldo.' In tennis it's something we just haven't had. The perfect examples are Borg in Sweden and Boris Becker in Germany, people at the pinnacle of the game who have really brought tennis home to their respective countries. And it is fair to say that it has taken off – in both those countries they have tennis players coming from all angles. So I think this pyramid effect is very important. At the base of the pyramid you have the grass roots, and they are very important too. I hope we are going to be working at both ends of the pyramid.

Are you working at the base of the pyramid?

I think it is fair to say that I am working at both ends, yes. Obviously, playing in the tournaments and moving up in the world rankings, I am at the top of end of the pyramid, and I hope the youngsters will watch me play and that I will be able to influence people to follow in my footsteps. But then, at the base of the pyramid, there are grass-roots schemes. I am working with the Midland Bank on one of them, which involves taking tennis to schools in all areas and trying to show the youngsters that what I do is a lot of fun, and providing the necessary coaching. So I hope I am working at both ends.

Are you overawed by the responsibility of being at the top of the pyramid?

Not at all. I am conscious that I am helping to promote British tennis, but when people ask me if I worry about the expectations or the pressure they are putting on me when I play on Centre Court at Wimbledon, and there are 15,000 people willing me on and obviously on the edge of their seats at times, my answer is that I am aware of it, but that it doesn't affect me. When I go on to the court, for most of the time I am out there to play for myself, and I think that is very important. The times when I am not playing for myself are obviously in the Davis Cup, when I am representing my country, which is slightly different. But the moment you start thinking about all the people that want you to win and their expectations, your focus is taken away and you are going to struggle.

Is the way you play dependent on, or affected in any way, by the expectations that are now riding on your shoulders?

If you use the expectations as a positive, I think they can raise your performance. I said that I don't pay attention to those expectations, but I am aware of them – you can't blank them out of your mind totally. I noticed that at Wimbledon in 1996, when suddenly it was my face that was on the front page of virtually every newspaper, and although I didn't read the newspapers, or watch pieces about myself on TV, it was impossible to avoid to some extent. But when you have got, as at Wimbledon, 15,000 people cheering you on, you really want to go out there and give them something to cheer about. So I think that definitely raises my performance.

Do you think there is any formula for recovering from the moments of failure that affect everybody who is successful in one way or another?

I think it is important that people do realize that in everybody's career, whatever profession you are in, there are going to be times when things don't go the way you want. You have to believe in your own ability so that you know you will come out of a slump. That slump may last for only two or three weeks, when you play badly in three tournaments and then things turn around, but you also have to be aware that it might go on for two or three months, or even six months, and obviously that is going to be demanding. So you must have the mental strength, the determination, to continue working in the belief that you will come out the other side.

Is there anything that Britain could do to give more youngsters a chance of being as successful as you have been at tennis?

I think schools play a very important part. You could say that tennis is competing against football, rugby and cricket, and at the moment it isn't on a par with those sports. If maybe the country as a whole could make tennis more of a major sport in schools, more people would play the game, from the very lowest level. And the more people who play the game, the better. It would improve standards and that would move up right the way through to the top of the pyramid – the professional game. At the moment I think we have about 40 men players with a world ranking. I am sure that if we had more people playing the game those numbers would increase and the standards would get better.

Who are your heroes? Who are the people you regard as being incredibly successful, either past or present, within tennis or outside it, and why?

In terms of my profession, when I was growing up, Bjorn Borg was an influence. He was my role model. I saw him at the top of the game when I was very young and thought I would like to follow in his footsteps. When he retired, probably earlier than anyone would have expected, Stefan Edberg was somebody I looked up to. But that was a different scenario, because he was living in London and practised at Queens, so I was able to learn from him on the court when we practised together. Those two have been role models for me, and you only have to look at their records to see how successful they have been.

What do you think are the greatest enemies of success?

I think at times there are always going to be people who are jealous of your success. I can't say I know anyone in particular like that, but maybe there are people that are jealous of the success I am beginning to have now. Nobody likes it, but I think if you are aware of it and can almost understand it and accept it, it won't affect you. If I knew somebody was jealous of me, I wouldn't let it affect my performance, because then if there was a battle to be won they would be winning it. That is probably an example of one of the negatives of success.

Of course, jealousy can drive people to greater heights, can't it?

I think in a way that is something that is involved in a healthy rivalry. In the rivalry between Greg Rusedski and myself, for example, I suppose there is an element of ... I wouldn't call it jealousy, more competitive instinct. But when I have a good result, or he has a good result, the other will say to himself, 'That is what I want to do.' That might be interpreted as jealousy, but it is a kind that spurs us on, and we go out and work that fraction harder, and hope that that will show in our results.

Has success changed you at all?

I think it is inevitable that success changes you to a certain extent, but to what extent is the question. I think I have different standards and obviously I am older and wiser, and I have learned a lot from the experiences I have had. But when I am away from tennis I would like to think that the people I've known for my whole life see me as the same person.

What do you think – in general terms, not just in tennis – are the qualities you need to be successful, as far as attitude and temperament are concerned?

I think a lot of it does boil down to your own desire. I firmly believe that if you really, really do want something, and you have the attitude that you are going to go out and get it, in the vast majority of instances you will be able to do it. This is a tennis-example again, but take David Lloyd. He wasn't a great tennis player by any means, but he went into business with no qualifications at all, very little money, and little financial help. What he did have was an enormous desire to achieve his goal, and that goal was to produce very good tennis centres, and now leisure centres, throughout the country. And he has succeeded. He desperately, desperately wanted to do that, and I think if you have a similar attitude, you are already a long way towards getting what you want.

What is the greatest pleasure you have had from your success?

I think the greatest moment I have had was Wimbledon in 1996. If I had to pin it down to one specific moment, it was beating Kafelnikov on Centre Court. He was French Open champion, and Wimbledon was the next Grand Slam event. I was a British player, and it was my first time playing on Centre Court – the match had a lot of elements which I look back on with a great deal of satisfaction. If you remember the situation, I had been two sets to love up, then he got back to two sets all, and was up in the fifth. There were match points against me before I turned it around. That was the moment, that split second after he hit his final backhand into the net. The crowd's reaction was really something special.

Has there been particular pleasure outside tennis that has come as a result of your successful career?

Financially, it is obviously very rewarding, although that's not the reason why I am in the game. But in my early tewnties, I am pretty fortunate to have some of the possessions I do and to be, at the moment at least, as financially secure as I am. Taking the financial aspects away, I am very content with my life at the moment and I think that is probably the most important thing.

If you could gather together all the young people who look up to you as a role model, and who want to become as good as you have become, what would you tell them they should be doing now to give themselves a chance of achieving that?

If they want to be good players, a lot of time and effort has got to be put in, so it is vital that they enjoy what they do. If you can enjoy what you do, and go out on to the court and give 100 per cent at all times, no one can ask anything more of you. And if you do that and you can look back at the end of the day and say, 'I put in 100 per cent and I made 150 in the world,' then I think you have been successful, because you've fulfilled your potential. It is the same if your potential is to be number 1 in the world, and you have done that by putting in 100 per cent all the time.

Does it involve sacrifices? Perhaps not being able to do as many of the things youngsters normally do as they grow up?

I suppose there are instances when I might have missed out on something like going on holiday with my family or going to a few parties because I was away playing in tournaments. But I can't think of many occasions like that. I would like to think that I am becoming a good tennis player, but at the same time, I would like to think that I am a pretty normal 22 year-old. I don't think I have been affected in any way.

This is an incredibly premature question, but when your time comes to leave this life, what would you like people to say about you?

I think pretty much what I said about being successful. I would like to think people would say that I gave all I had got at all times on the court. Off the court, I would like people to say that I was a very approachable, normal, down-to-earth kind of guy.

RICHARD HOLBROOKE

Known in the White House as 'Hurricane Holbrooke' for being 'highly effective but unpredictable', this 56-year-old American has a place in history as the man who successfully negotiated an end to the war in Bosnia, ensuring that 'people are alive today who otherwise might not be'. Here he reveals his approach and tactics – 'a kind of relentless harassment of the parties into concessions that they were not ready to make unless pressured by the United States with the credible use of force'. He spells out the complexity of the negotiations, the problems with allies as well as with the warring factions, the difference between lying and bluffing, and the contrast between the American and European styles of diplomacy. Denying accusations of bullying, he says, 'You have to match the circumstances and style to the situation, and the method to the moment.' The son of 'idealistic parents – refugees from Nazism who verged on pacifism', Richard Holbrooke grew up in 'the liberal, progressive hothouse that was New York in the 1940s'. He won a university scholarship to study science, but 'just couldn't cut it', so switched to history, aimed for a journalistic career, and when turned down by the New York Times, *accepted a job offer from the State Department.*

His diplomatic skills took him to Vietnam, and then on to the US delegation at the Vietnam peace talks in Paris. He took leave from the foreign service for four years to be managing editor of the magazine Foreign Policy, *before Jimmy Carter made him the youngest-ever Assistant Secretary of State. At just 36, he was in charge of East Asian and Pacific Affairs. At the end of the Carter presidency he set up his own consulting firm before joining Lehman Brothers as a managing director in 1985. As a banker and diplomat he has travelled to over a hundred countries, and earned numerous awards for public service. President Clinton called him back to his old job – only this time looking after European and Canadian affairs, and his skill as chief negotiator in the Dayton Peace Accord ended the savage conflict in former Yugoslavia. His diplomatic shuttle continues, taking him to the troublespots of Kosovo and Cyprus. Here he spells out his formula for a successful negotiation: the importance of bringing people onside, and discusses the 'bureaucratic games played with great viciousness'; the 'fatal and very common' internal divisions in your own team; working with the press and 'the most famous planted leak of our time'.*

Richard Holbrooke, what is your definition of success?

I don't think about success in macro or global terms so much. Everybody understands success in a short-term sense. But for larger goals in life, one can only look back afterwards to decide whether one succeeded or not. A lot of things that aren't clear until later define success. People start out looking for a specific goal in life and think that if they don't get it they haven't succeeded, and then later they may look back and say, 'I *did* lead a successful life.' I'm not even sure about the concept of success as a way to judge one's life. One ought to think about achievement and fulfilment and feel good about oneself. But I do not want to define success in narrow terms such as one might do in sports.

I would also point out that there are very successful people who are very unhappy for some reason or other – personal, psychological, genetic – and there are very unsuccessful people who are quite satisfied because they know they did their best. For me success is best defined, I guess, as having done one's best and left something behind which makes a difference. In the most recent phase of my life, it's the fact that I played a role in ending a war, that people are alive today who otherwise might not be. I don't think that the Dayton Agreements were perfect and no one knows the flaws in them better than those of us who negotiated them. But we succeeded in ending a war, and to me that is a success.

What were your tactics to make that a successful negotiation?

Persistence. A kind of a relentless harassment of the parties into concessions that they were not ready to make unless pressured by the United States with the credible threat of the use of force.

Did you have to be ruthless?

I don't know what that word means in this context. I wasn't ruthless, I was determined and tough. Ruthless implies to me that you'll sacrifice principles for the outcome, and we never did that. It implies that you don't care about other people, and we were operating out of exactly the opposite motives. So although I've read the word ruthless in the press, I've never understood it. I consider myself a very compassionate person. Much of my life and work has been devoted to refugees, for example.

A lot of people talk about your incredible combination of charm and bullying at the same time. How do you do that?

I don't know. I'm delighted to hear that I'm charming. I'm appalled to hear I'm a bully. I never thought of myself as either, but what the press refers to as bullying is really the fact that as a negotiator my job was to represent the United States. And you can't represent the United States unless you are strong, and represent it with authority. The European diplomatic style is much more consensual, much more relaxed, and much gentler, and I must say in the case of Bosnia it was not very effective. So I didn't consider that bullying. I worked in Asia for most of my career, and in Asia no one ever accused me of bullying because you just wouldn't act that way with the Asians. You have to match the circumstances and the style to the situation, and the method to the moment. In Bosnia I may have acquired a reputation for bullying, but that was only because a certain approach was necessary.

Is it fair to say that every diplomatic negotiation contains an element of the carrot and the stick?

I very consciously approached each issue on a carrot-and-stick basis with incentives and punitive or costly measures. I agree with that.

Were there times in the course of the negotiation when you had to bend the truth, as it were?

I'm not even sure what truth is in the Balkans. I'm not sure what your question refers to.

There was a newspaper article which suggested there were times in some negotiations when you actually had to lie.

I don't know about lying, but there are times when you have to bluff.

What's the difference?

Lying is saying something which just isn't true. Bluffing is when you leave the person you're negotiating with uncertain as to what you would do if he doesn't go along. It's the same as poker. You don't say that you've got a royal straight flush in your hand, you let people think it. And the most important element in diplomacy is that you are not perceived as a liar, or bluffer, because if you are then you lose all credibility. So I didn't lie in these negotiations, on the contrary I think we acquired a reputation for telling the truth, which was, 'If you don't do this, we may resume the bombing.' And we were credible, those weren't empty words. But I can't think of any time during the negotiations when I lied, I really can't. And I don't think any of the articles written about the negotiations would suggest that. But there were a couple of times when we had to bluff. The most notable was when we went back to Belgrade, on 13 September 1995 and NATO was running out of bombing targets, and the bombing would probably run out of its own accord within about three days. If the Serbs had known that, we would not have been able to negotiate the lifting of the siege of Sarajevo. So we let them think that the bombing would continue indefinitely unless they lifted the siege. That was not lying, but it was essential they did not know that NATO was thinking of stopping the bombing unilaterally, because we would have lost our bargaining chip. But that was not a lie.

Was there something about the Bosnia negotiation that made it almost more difficult than most other diplomatic negotiations that the world has seen over the last few decades, in the sense that you were dealing with particularly intransigent people?

I don't know if they were particularly intransigent. Anyone who's worked on the Arab/Israeli problem can tell you about intransigence. Anyone who's negotiated with the Chinese can tell you the same thing. What made the Balkans uniquely difficult was that there were three parties in shifting alliances and coalitions with each other. That's number one. Number two was that we had to co-ordinate with our allies in Britain, France and Germany, and the rest of the EU and NATO, and that was exceedingly difficult. And number three, that we had to deal with Russia as a member of the contact group. For the first time since World War II, the Russians were part of an international effort with the West to solve a problem, and we and the Russians had different points of view. And very often the United States and Germany found themselves facing a coalition of British, French and Russian views – a line-up which was unprecedented in the last 50 years, but it happened quite often. Germany and the US stood, for example, for continuing sanctions against Serbia, when Britain and France joined the Russians in advocating lifting them. That's what made it difficult.

And as far as the Serbs were concerned, what attitudes did they bring to the negotiating table?

One has to differentiate very carefully. Milosevic was the only authoritative voice for the Serbs. The Bosnian Serbs, whom he despised but had a great deal of influence over, were hard mountain men, isolated, provincial, really brutal. Milosevic was a cunning ex-Communist – with the emphasis on Communist, not ex – who, in style, is very reminiscent of many Communist leaders of the Brezhnev era – tough, ruthless, detached from human beings to a considerable degree, cunning and smart, and actually somebody that one can negotiate with. You can negotiate with him, you can't negotiate with the Pale Serbs. They are pretty close to insane, and they have to be dealt with through sheer force. Not ruthlessness, but real force.

It was obviously a help that you had Milosevic wanting to deal at the end of the day, but how did you counter the effect that those mountain men, as you called them, were having on him?

Well, at Dayton, in particular, he kept the Bosnian Serbs upstairs in the second floor of his quarters while he was downstairs, and just kept them out of the negotiations. He wouldn't tell them what he was doing. Every few days the head of the Bosnian Serb delegation would send me a letter saying, 'Could you please tell me what you're discussing?' I'd take it to Milosevic and say, 'These guys are on your delegation, what do you want to do with this?' And he'd take the paper and literally drop it into the wastebasket.

Wasn't there a risk with that?

No, it was up to him to deliver the Bosnian Serbs. Now he did deliver them on some parts of the Dayton package, particularly the military provisions, but he has not delivered them, to this day, on the political provisions.

Leaving Bosnia aside, are there any general principles that tend to make a diplomatic negotiation successful?

First I think you have to figure out what your goal is. There are two different kinds of negotiations – ones in which your own interests are very much at stake, and ones in which you're really in the position of arbitrator. Bosnia was the latter case, most of the time. It wasn't important to the US whether there was a three-person Presidency or a seven-person Presidency, whether there were 36 or 42 people on the National Assembly, you just wanted them to agree and you facilitated it. But there were other times, like the Rules of Engagement for the NATO troops, which were literally matters of life and death to the United States, and to our NATO allies. So the first thing you have to do is decide what your goals are. The second thing you have to do is decide what the goals of the parties in the negotiation are, and to what degree you can find things that are acceptable to them. Now negotiations involving the recourse to force as a last resort, or maybe even not a last resort, are very rare. Bosnia was a unique example of that. There have only been a handful of negotiations in the last 30 years that have involved the use of force as a recourse. In your average negotiations, like the ones I conducted with the Chinese over normalized diplomatic relations, or the trade negotiations I was involved in with Japan, or even the relations with Marcos, those issues are not at stake. But you do have to figure out whether you have options, and then you have to position yourself. If you're negotiating on behalf of your country, at least – it's different in a private situation – you have to position yourself so that your country can survive any outcome.

What are the typical difficulties that would stand in the way of a successful diplomatic negotiation?

Internal divisions on your own negotiating team are fatal and very common.

On your own negotiation team?

Sure, because in the Government – I'm only talking about the Government now – you represent so many different interests. In a trade negotiation, for example, you're representing foreign-policy interests, the trade interests of the nation and the trading interests of individual groups. I was involved in textile negotiations with the Chinese, where the textile industry, by law, had its own representatives participating in the negotiations. Their interests were very specific to them. So internal divisions in your own team can be fatal. Second, you can always miscalculate. Third, you can run up against an opposite number in the negotiation who's just not rational or is not prepared to make a deal. I've seen, time and time again, countries act against their own long-term interests. Most dramatically, in 1977–8 I was the chief negotiator with the Vietnamese and they threw away an offer from Jimmy Carter on normalization of relations, which was quite astonishing. They never got a better offer since, and they did it because they completely misread the United States politically and they were locked into a sort of revolutionary romantic view of their own Communist heritage.

Are you an ambitious person?

Well, I've been so described so ...

But you're not denying it?

I don't see what's wrong with ambition as long it's harnessed to some sense of purpose. Not just self-advancement. And my ambition was to achieve things, to accomplish things, to leave a legacy behind. My father, probably, was the greatest influence on me in that regard, because he always had great hopes. He was an immigrant, a refugee from Bolshevism. He believed in the United States, and he wanted me to achieve something. Now his dream for me was in the field of science, but that was his hope, and that was very influential.

What was it about your upbringing, as a youngster, that helped to shape the kind of drive that you've got? You've talked about your father, but were there any particular principles attached to your upbringing, any particular ways in which they brought you up, that looking back you can now see generated a drive to succeed?

Well, they certainly gave me some core values. They had a reverence for human life, and they verged on pacifism, in a sense, since my mother was also a refugee from Nazism. They really were very idealistic. I grew up in the hothouse of New York in the 1940s, a very liberal, very progressive era. So, there was the combination of these elements and the sense that one had to do something useful. They believed deeply, I think, in the idea of progress. In the 1940s, almost everybody believed in progress.

Do you think that's something that's gone away now?

Oh, sure. There's a very interesting book by Robert Nesbitt, called *The History of the Idea of Progress.* I would say from the 1700s until very recently, most people believed that human beings were getting continually better, that their lives were getting better, and above all that technology and science would somehow solve problems. But it turned out that every solution created new, unforeseen problems. The whole concept of unintended consequences, which is now quite conventional wisdom, was not widely understood then. My parents were very much of the generation who believed in progress, despite the fact that they had lived through these terrible upheavals that had torn their home countries apart, despite the Holocaust. They believed particularly in progress in the United States, and that the United States could spread those values around the world. Those were very idealistic beliefs.

If that has gone, why has it gone? Are there forces at work stopping the world in general, people in general, being as successful as they might have been in the past?

As I said, every solution created a problem. For example, the tremendous drop in infant mortality, which is one of the greatest achievements of the last century, and the tremendous increase in human longevity. The average life expectancy has risen from the mid-30s to the mid-70s, or more – fantastic. But it has contributed to other problems – the problems of an ageing population, the problem of overpopulation. Pesticides, which were widely seen as a way of killing malaria, and so on, ended up creating environmental deserts. There has been the degradation of the environment, and the ozone layer. So many miracle solutions turned out to have problems. But I still believe that one can deal with these things. Also, I think we've learned over time that there are some fundamental aspects of human nature – a capacity for self-destruction, for hostility, based on ethnic or racial characteristics, a propensity towards violence, domestically and in personal lives, genetic defects in a small, but significant number of people that create rogue elements in society – which are inherent in the nature of certain people. Bosnia, in a sense, is the proof of this.

Do you think that the inherent irrationality on the part of some people who you are trying to bring to the conference table can be overcome by diplomatic negotiation, or is there an impossible element about every tough negotiation?

In the case of Bosnia I repeat what I said earlier – you can't deal with the Bosnian Serbs without recourse to the threat of use of force. It's just not possible, that's their nature. And so bombing for peace is, in a sense, a necessary approach. That's a very unusual situation. There are very few places on Earth where that kind of approach is necessary, but it certainly was in Bosnia. The propensity of some human beings towards violence or irrationality or racism is not changeable. It exists in our country. There's plenty of racial hatred on the streets of New York, but it has not erupted into any kind of racial conflict of any significance in over a quarter of a century, even though many people worry about it year after year, because each time it was threatened – as it was in the famous incident in Crown Heights about five years ago between Orthodox Jews and blacks – the community leaders got together and said, 'We've got to stop this.' In Los Angeles, in April 1992, the situation fell apart, briefly. An anarchy ruled the streets of LA and the city looked a little like Sarajevo. It was the same month, incidentally, that the two things exploded, and I felt they were very similar. But unlike Sarajevo, the leaders of the Los Angeles ethnic communities got together and said, 'This is insane.'

One last point – it's very wrong to throw up one's hands and say that such issues as Bosnia are simply the result of ancient hatreds. This is wrong. The Yugoslav tragedy of 1991–2 is a direct result of huge mistakes made by the Big Four – Woodrow Wilson, Clemenceau, Orlando and David Lloyd George – at Versailles in 1919. They created a single country – then called the Kingdom of Croat Serbs and Slovenes, subsequently called Yugoslavia – out of parts of the Austro-Hungarian Empire, parts of the Ottoman Empire, and some other loose ends. In the name of self-determination, Wilson and his colleagues created a country that did not have self-determination. It didn't make sense then, it doesn't make sense now.. And the attempt to hold it together was only successful when it was held together by external force, or internal police-state methods. And so the origins of today's tragedy in the former Yugoslavia lie in Versailles, and in that odd high-water mark of American moralism, Wilsonianism. Woodrow Wilson thought he was creating something that fulfilled self-determination, but in fact he was either ignorant or wilfully cynical; he created a system that couldn't work. It survived for 70 years, but it was fundamentally flawed and after 70 years of survival it just exploded like a pressure cooker building up. There should have been a negotiated divorce – a velvet divorce like the division of Czechoslovakia into two countries, or the Soviet Union into 15 countries – a long time ago.

As you look back over your diplomatic career and the things that have happened, some of which you were involved in, some of which you were not involved in, do you feel that there are a large or a small number of occasions where short-term expediency has been put to the fore, and long-term potential for lasting solutions has been sacrificed?

That's a very good question, and the answer is, almost always, negotiators go for short-term expediency. I did it, to a certain extent, in Bosnia – to end the war, to stop the killing was my highest priority. And to do it we created a structure which is fundamentally flawed at its core. For one thing, we had to allow to entities of what the Dayton Agreement calls a single country each to have their own military, which clearly creates the seeds of a future problem. For another, we could not get the two sides to agree on a really strong, stable, single government at the centre. We knew that, but stopping the war was a higher priority. Time and time again negotiators go for the short-term solution.

How do you stop that?

You can't stop it. Nobody can see 60–70 years into the future. When I say that the Big Four at Versailles, in 1919, created the seeds of Yugoslavia today, I am not saying that in 1919 you and I could have done any better. Seeing 70 years into the future is not possible for any human being.

Looking back on your career, did you, right from the early days, want to be a diplomat?

No, I wanted to a be a scientist first. I went to Brown University, on a full maths-physics scholarship, a National Merit Scholarship. Then I realized that I was not going to fulfil my father's ambition and win a Nobel Prize in physics because I just couldn't cut it. When I got to advanced integral calculus I switched to history, and then my second goal was to be a journalist with James Reston and Harrison Salisbury and Edward R Morrow as my role models. Going into the State Department was a complete accident and one that my mother – my father had died by this time – felt was insane.

So why did you do it?

In high school – this is an example of luck – in Scarsdale, a suburb of New York, my best friend was named David Rusk, and two years after we graduated from high school his father became Kennedy's Secretary of State. I knew his father very well, and the family had been like a second family to me when my own father died. So suddenly, for the first time in my life, I knew somebody who was very famous and very important, and he said to me, 'You really ought to think about the Foreign Service as a career.' So, at his suggestion, I took the Foreign Service exam, passed it and got into the Foreign Service while he was Secretary of State, although I want to stress, because of your previous question on mentors and protégés, that that was a completely regular exam, and he had nothing to do with it. But I would never have taken it if it weren't for Dean Rusk. I wrote an article about Rusk when he died because that is a perfect example of serendipity, or lucky opportunism, or whatever you want to call it. What happened was a pure accident. My whole career was an accident. I wanted to be a journalist, and I'd worked for the *New York Times* – odd, isn't it, Martyn, that anyone would want to be a journalist?

Yes!

I worked for the *New York Times* two summers in a row, in 1960 and 1961, in Paris and in New York, and I wrote to James Reston – who was then the leading journalist in the United States, the *New York Times* Bureau Chief in Washington – asking for a job with him on the *New York Times*. He wrote back and said there weren't any. At that exact moment I was taking this Foreign Service exam, mainly because Dean Rusk said I ought to consider it. So the *Times* turned me down and the Foreign Service took me in. I had no other job. I was out of college. They were offering me $5200 a year starting salary, which was a lot of money for me. So I took the job.

So you did it because your main ambition had fallen by the wayside?

Ambition would be too strong a word. I had been editor-in-chief of the Brown daily newspaper, and the thing that I thought would be the most fun to do was shut out for me at the *New York Times*. I could have gone to other newspapers, or gone into television and had a completely different career. But I did it because it was a job offer, and I did it with no great understanding of whether I'd do it for five years or 30 years.

And was there a feeling of disappointment as well, that you hadn't got something that you were going for?

Not really. It wasn't an obsession with me. If I'd have been obsessed with being a journalist I would have gone to the *Washington Post* or to CBS, or somewhere. Furthermore, I never lost the option. Ten years later I left the Foreign Service and became the editor of a magazine – *Foreign Policy Quarterly* – and three times later in my career the *New York Times* did come back and offer me jobs. But by this point I felt – no disrespect to you, Martyn – that being a participant was more interesting than being a chronicler.

I think you're right!

There was a moment which I always remember when I really decided that I didn't want to be a journalist. It was in 1968 when we were in Paris with the team negotiating with the North Vietnamese, and once a week we went over to the conference centre on the Avenue Kléber to meet with the North Vietnamese for sterile, public propaganda meetings. There was a lot of excitement about these talks, and when we came down the stairs each Wednesday, reporters would wait for us at the bottom, and Averell Harriman, the head of our negotiating team, would say something quite routine in order to give them something to write. Early on we came down the stairs in a driving rainstorm, and some of the big hitters in American and European journalism were waiting in it, as Harriman doled out this rather meaningless stuff which we had to give to the press. I remember listening to that, and having just sat in the room when Harriman had said, 'Well, we've got to give the press something, what do we give them?' and various people had made suggestions. I thought, 'These great reporters, whom I respected and admired, are not reporting what's important, they're just reporting this stuff that they themselves are demanding, which doesn't mean anything.' So I thought, 'It's more interesting to try to affect policy than to report what isn't even the reality.'

Can the role of a journalist affect the success of a negotiation? Can a critic, perhaps not in full possession of the picture, say the wrong thing and affect the course of a diplomatic negotiation?

There's no question that the press plays a major role in the process. Leaks can be devastating, and working with the press in a productive way can be very useful. I think that was the case in the Bosnia negotiations.

In other words you would use the press?

We used the press, but only because the press wanted to be used. We never held formal press conferences, and I did not have a press officer with me in the negotiations. But they would wait for us in hotel lobbies and they would say, 'Are you optimistic or pessimistic?' and we'd say, 'Well, we're making progress,' or, 'We've reached a stalemate,' and because that was the only source of information, it would either create a sense of momentum or pressure. A bad leak can really have an effect. The most famous leak of our time, which had a tremendous effect on American politics, occurred in February 1968 when the *New York Times* reported that General Westmoreland had asked for another 206,000 troops for Vietnam. This leak, which was accurate, hit Washington with a power that you cannot even imagine. It had a tremendous effect on the New Hampshire Primary, which took place four days later. It brought Bobby Kennedy into the race. It created an uproar in Washington and it contributed substantially to Johnson's decision to pull out. That was clearly a leak designed by people inside the Government to stop what they thought was an insane policy decision. There have been other leaks, but that was probably the most famous planted leak of our time.

Do you have any kind of inner mechanism for dealing with criticism when it comes?

I hate criticism, who doesn't?

But how do you deal with it? I mean when you get a particularly unfair or nasty piece of criticism which rocks you back on your heels, how do you gear yourself up to go back into the fray?

It depends on what the criticism is. Some of the criticisms I've read about myself have merit. I've been told that I'm too impatient with people, that I don't 'suffer fools gladly' so I see the merit in that, that I've been rude to people, and I try to improve. Then I read in the papers that I'm not part of a team, and I know that's coming from somebody who has got their own rivalry going for their own purposes, because the facts are quite the contrary. Four or five times in my career I've forged very strong teams and held them together. I deal with each criticism on its own basis. The most annoying thing, of course, and this has happened to all of us who've been in public service, is when you pick up a newspaper or magazine and you read a story which is just not true, which never happened.

The best example of this was when the *New York Times*, one of the world's great newspapers, printed a story saying that I was cut out of Bosnian policy decision-making, and was strolling in the Rocky Mountains on a vacation with my wife. At the exact moment that the story was printed I was on a plane from Colorado on my way to Washington and Bosnia, to begin the diplomacy. And here was this big story in the *Times* saying I'd been cut out of the policy. If the reporter in question had called my office that day, my secretary would have said, 'He's on his way back to Washington.' It wasn't a secret, we just hadn't announced it yet. But the *Times* printed it. I read the story, if you can believe it, while I was changing planes in Denver on my way home to take over the negotiations. The *Times* never printed a correction, and the story became part of the internet database about me, and it appears all the time. It was just wrong, and it wasn't just minor league gossip, it was an erroneous story with consequences. At the same time that newspaper's coverage was in general very, very good.

Did that weaken your negotiating position?

No, no. It didn't have an effect because it was self-evidently wrong. Within 24 hours the press was reporting that I was on my way to Belgrade.

But it could have had an effect?

It did have the enduring effect, to this day, of creating an impression that I had been cut out of the process. Every story written since then, by every other journalist, involves their going back into their databases where they see this story in the *New York Times* and they say, 'Well, Holbrooke was cut out and fought his way back.' It's now part of the mythology of what happened in 1995, but that's not what happened. But since the *Times* never printed a clarification, or a correction, and since journalists under deadline are lazy and accept the fact that if the *Times* print it, it must be so, it's now become part of the story-line.

Do you have any huge regrets about moving out of the diplomatic world, in which you had been successful, into what for you was the relatively new territory of banking?

Oh no. I left the Government in February 1996, solely because I was recently remarried and I'd made a personal commitment to my wife, and she couldn't leave New York and move to Washington because of her children. Otherwise I would have stayed in the Government. And yet the decision to leave, made entirely for personal reasons, was transforming and liberating. Since then the President and the Secretary of State have asked me to undertake several missions to Bosnia and elsewhere, and they have been very supportive and I've been able to stabilize my personal life, and create more of a financial cushion. So here's an example of where circumstances create an accidental process which works out. I want to stress that I would never have left the Government if it weren't for the fact that my wife couldn't come to Washington, because I like public service, but leaving the Government a good thing for me personally.

What do you think are the greatest enemies of success?

First of all I want to stress again that success does not automatically go to the smartest person in the room. It's a combination of a sense of timing, self-control, willpower, analytical and strategic skills, experience and luck – I want to stress luck again.

What stops success? What drags you down?

Bad luck. A person can just get caught in something that he or she can't control.

But is there a characteristic, an attitude within a person, that can actually work against them?

Yes. If a person has a defeatist attitude towards setbacks, that's terribly damaging. I think everyone in life who wants to achieve something should anticipate that he or she will face obstacles, and that not every obstacle can be overcome. To have one's personal health is critical. If one's sick, in any way, it becomes an almost unbearable burden to carry, although there are some very brave people – Franklin Roosevelt, for example – who have overcome physical handicaps. But willpower is the most important component in overcoming obstacles. And the more one seeks to achieve, the more likely one is to encounter obstacles. I don't know if this is true in the sciences, but it's certainly true in the arena of public policy and business. In the field of the creative arts, literature and painting and so on, the obstacle is public acceptance of one's work. Think of all the masterpieces that were only discovered after the artist's death. Think of a man like Van Gogh who never sold a painting during his lifetime. He was not a success, and yet he was one of the greatest painters in history, and he died not knowing that. That is an extreme but real case, as we all know – it's not a movie script, it really happened. And so one has to persevere in the face of obstacles.

Can you have success too early?

Yes, sure. It's better to have success in mid-life, rather than too early or too late. But each discipline creates a different cycle of success. Performing artists tend to have success much earlier, but not always. Women's beauty in movies is so important that they're likely to burst out early and then wonder about a second act or a third act. Julia Roberts is a perfect current example of somebody who was spectacularly successful early and has trouble handling the success now. In literary arts it can come at any time – late or early. In business it can come early or late. In the sciences, history shows that it usually comes fairly early. But in politics, in public life, in diplomacy, success usually comes latest of all. In your profession, journalism, it usually comes fairly early, though rarely in one's twenties, it's usually in one's thirties or forties. In public life it's rare that it comes as early as it did to President Clinton or President Kennedy – those are very, very unusual circumstances.

If you could gather together all the young people in the world who look up to you as a role model, what advice would you give them?

If you go into public service you should go in to make a difference. There's no point in going in to be another bureaucrat. There's a very delicate balance between process and outcome in government. You need process to keep the thing going, but you need to focus on making a difference. There are incredible problems in the world – the destruction of the environment, famines – usually man-made famines, I might add – refugee problems, unresolved political issues like Ireland and Cyprus and Kashmir. Work on those to make a difference. There are problems in the inner cities in Europe and the United States. Don't go into government just for the job. I'm talking now only about public service.

If you're a private citizen, you can still make a difference by spending part of your time on public-spirited work, and one of the most interesting phenomena of the last 20 years is the tremendous rise in the importance of the NGOs – the Non-Governmental Organizations. As governments of the world have become more and more bureaucratic and more and more stalemated, NGOs have become more and more important in specific issues.

Has success changed you?

Maybe it's made me more relaxed because I've achieved something and made a contribution that is measurable, and, whatever happens in the future, will not disappear.

One final question – when your time comes to leave this life, what would you like people to say about you?

That he did his best.

That's all?

Yes, that's fine, just that I did my best and made a difference.

SIR ANTHONY HOPKINS

A Hollywood Oscar, countless other acting awards and a knighthood for services to the performing arts mark the career of this Welsh baker's son, who confesses, 'I was driven to succeed because I was so ashamed of myself.' The shame came from being hopeless at school. A slow learner – and possibly dyslexic – he was called an idiot, a moron, and became something of a loner. Then, one day, he accidentally wandered into a play rehearsal at the YMCA, was roped in for a one-line part, and did it so well that the director conceded, 'You've got something, boyo.' So, at 17, he successfully auditioned for the Welsh College of Music and Drama. Then came two years' National Service as an army clerk (which he loathed), and brief spells off and on stage with theatres in Manchester and Nottingham, where he was advised to get proper training as an actor. Accepted for RADA, he remembers being 'rebellious, lazy, undisciplined – not a good student – but I had energy', and left as a silver medallist. Later, at the National Theatre, he was understudying Laurence Olivier when the great man fell ill, and, as Olivier admiringly put it, 'he walked away with my part like a cat with a mouse between his teeth'.

Although the theatre laced his early career, he says he felt 'rather uncomfortable' in it. Ever since an early, star-struck encounter with fellow Port Talbot actor Richard Burton, the movies had been his great ambition. He made his film début at the age of 30, as Richard the Lionheart in The Lion in Winter. America beckoned. He spent a decade in Hollywood working in films and television – and wrestling with a drink problem which, with the help of Alcoholics Anonymous, he has now beaten. His fifties have given him some of his finest roles – in Silence of the Lambs, The Remains of the Day, Shadowlands. The early anger has been replaced by what a friend called 'an aura of peace'; but the drive and the restlessness are still there. In this wide-ranging interview, he quotes Olivier's advice to young thespians – 'Imitate the great actors – be a thief, be a magpie' – and adds some of his own – 'Risk destruction, risk being a fool, risk criticism.' He talks of how he faced going back on stage after a mauling from the critics, and the difference between a bad stage review and a bad film review. But, above all, he advises, 'Don't hold back. Give it everything you've got. Hold onto the dream.'

Sir Anthony, what is your definition of success?

Some people say there is no such thing as success, and that it is all relative. That may be so, but success to me is about conquest. Overcoming adversities and limitations in oneself, whilst also keeping a balance and a sense of humour. Having perspective, a fair balance in life is the most difficult part of success. It's not easy for me to be content. I can't rest on my laurels for long, try as I may. But I try to balance it with a fairly normal life, in the abnormal life I seem to live as an actor. That is it, in a few words – triumph, conquest, achievement, overcoming.

Are you driven?

I am. And I think the foundation of it is based on shame. I had an idyllic childhood. I was the only child, born in Margam, a rural part of Port Talbot. I have an extraordinary memory – it's a gift or a curse. I can close my eyes and flash back to any date in my life, back to about the age of two. I remember clearly the colours, the smells, and it's a wonderful exercise. It moves me deeply because I'm not obsessed with the past, I'm empowered by it. I can remember every stage of my childhood. It empowers me because I like to glance back, go back, ruminate, walk down the back lane of my father's bakery – I do all that. And it puzzles me because there were parts of my childhood which I feel ashamed of. I was hopeless at school, just hopeless. I was called an idiot, a moron and an ox – all those things. I don't look back with any regret at that. Some years ago I used to be a little bitter, but now I look back and I think, I overcame a lot and I compensated, and I was driven to succeed because I felt so ashamed of myself. I probably was a slow learner or a slow starter, maybe dyslexic. Maybe I was just different. Academically, things were alien to me – I didn't know what they were talking about. To this day the only slight regret that I have is that I'm not a fast reader. I'm an avid reader, but a slow one. And I used to regret not having been to university, but I don't live for the regrets anymore. I think, 'I've done this because I had to overcome limitations in myself.'

When did the idea of acting first come into your mind? Was it there in the background, from a very early age, or did it just suddenly appear and you said, 'This is the career for me'?

Just briefly I wanted to be a pianist. I played the piano, but I had no real talent for it. I can play reasonably well as an amateur, but my technique is appalling. I was an artist, I suppose I was artistic. I could draw, I could paint, I could play the piano, but that wasn't enough to go on, wasn't enough to make a career, and I certainly didn't have the talent, the staying power, or the concentration. Maybe there was an attention disorder syndrome, or whatever they call it now. Maybe I had a small attention span. I couldn't master anything, I could never finish anything. And there's a tendency of that in my adult years – I still can't finish certain things. Sometimes I can't finish a book or a piano piece. My hopeless school record did worry my father and my mother. My mother had faith that there was something in me, my father was a little more pessimistic, a born worrier. And yet he had a very positive, vibrant energy in him as a man. But naturally he worried and he used to say to my mother, in all good heart, he didn't mean any harm by it, 'There is something very wrong with the boy.' Of course, I'd picked up on that. But I came from the same town as Richard Burton. I remember in the early 1950s Burton suddenly made a couple of films in Hollywood and my mother had seen him in *The Lady's Not For Burning* with John Gielgud in 1949. I think that percolated down into my subconscious somehow, and I just wanted to get the hell out. Not out of Port Talbot, there was nothing wrong with Port Talbot – I just wanted to get out of the landscape of my own inner world because I felt bereft, very empty, very lonely and very troubled.

You wanted to get away, you were driven to get away from an atmosphere in which you felt success had not happened for you?

Yes. It was nothing to do with the geographical location, I wanted to get away from myself. And I remember very clearly whenever Burton came home it was a big event, because it was a small town. My father then had a baker shop in Taibach and the girls in the shop would say, 'Oh, there's Richard Burton!' He'd pass in his Jaguar, it was very romantic. And I'd had somewhat of a dream of America when I was a child, because American servicemen were around then. What I could do was read encyclopaedias ferociously and I knew facts that weren't of any use to me in school. I knew things like the height of the Empire State Building. The American dream was part of the factor in my drive at a very early age. I remember going up to Burton's sister's house in Caradoc Street, and I knocked at the door, praying to God that he wouldn't be there. I just wanted to ask for his autograph. I went into the living room, it was a Saturday morning, and there he was, this movie star, shaving – with an electric razor. I'd never seen one of those before. He signed an autograph and asked, 'Where d'you come from?' I said, 'Just down the road, my father's got a baker's shop.' His sister added, 'He's Dick Hopkins's boy.' 'Oh, yes, I used to work in the Co-op across the street from your father's place in the shoe department. I was hopeless.' And I thought, 'There, he was hopeless, just like me.'

And sitting at the breakfast table – they'd just finished breakfast – was

Sybil, Richard's first wife. I didn't know Richard, I only met him once after that, but Sybil and I have become friends over the years. They were off to the international match, it was an England–Wales match. 'Going up to Cardiff,' he said. 'Do you play rugby?' I said no. 'Well, you're not a true Welshman, then.' But I shook hands and I walked down the Incline, as it was called, in Taibach where my father's shop was, and the Jaguar passed me and Sybil waved. And Burton was driving. I remember standing there on the Incline, thinking, 'I've got to be like that, I've got to get out, I've got to get out, I've got to get out. I'm gonna do it I'm gonna do it.' I had no idea I was going to be an actor, I just wanted to be rich and famous, and I didn't know how.

And did the acting come because the association with wealth and fame happened to be Richard Burton, an actor?

Yes. He was charismatic and a shining light to the people of Port Talbot and South Wales. Our first big movie star. We had Emlyn Williams and Hugh Griffith, but Burton was Hollywood. It was like having it stamped in the brain, 'That's what I wanted to do.' I wasn't sure if I wanted to be an actor, I just wanted to be something. I have a theory that at a certain age, you implant certain visions and images in your mind and inexorably you're drawn towards that, if you want it and desire it enough. To be successful you have to desire it deeply, and believe in it and have deep faith in it. I wasn't aware of what was happening then, but in 1955 when I was 17 I went to the YMCA because my father told me, 'For God's sake, get out and make some friends.' I was a real loner. So I went to the YMCA with a friend of his, and there was a little amateur acting group. I didn't want to be in the YMCA playing snooker, I didn't know how to play anything, I didn't want to see other kids. I wandered into this hall and there was a play in progress – a rehearsal, it was an Easter play, a religious pageant. And the director, Cyril Jenkins, said, 'What do you want?' 'Can I watch?' 'Yes, sit down there now, be quiet. Do you want to join in?' They needed an extra, a saint, so my mother gave me a bed sheet to put over my head as some sort of costume. I had one line – 'Blessed are the meek, for they shall inherit the Earth.' I remember standing on the stage, and I thought, 'This is it.' And Cyril, a great old guy, said, 'You've got something, boyo, you've got something!' So I joined. I was just about to leave school in July 1955 and my mother read something in the *Western Mail* advertising a scholarship for Cardiff College of Music and Drama. I wanted to be a musician and I wasn't interested in acting, but I wasn't sure. Anyway, I tried an audition and ranted and raved through *Othello*, which I'd never read. I just did one speech at the end, the bedchamber speech, and I was accepted into the college. But I was far too young.

How old were you?

Seventeen. I didn't have the sort of staying power or the concentration. But I felt I had some sort of presence, some energy, some electricity, something. Then I went into the Army and did my National Service for two years, which was hopeless. I loathed it. It was just a complete waste of time, though I look back on it now and can see it wasn't so bad, because it taught me a lot of self-discipline. I was a clerk in the Army, bloody hopeless. But I seemed to be like a cat with nine lives, always landing on my feet, always getting away with scrapes. Somehow I survived in this very cushy job for two years. I couldn't type a letter properly and the chief clerk used to type all the letters for me – I don't know why he employed me. I came out of the Army in 1960 and I got a job in rep in the Manchester Library Theatre, and I had no idea what I was supposed to be doing. I had a job as an assistant stage manager, and soon I was advised by the director, who said, 'I'm going to let you go, but you've got something, a presence on the stage, a lot of power, but you're dangerous. You hit that actor on stage and you mustn't do that.' I was a pretty hefty guy and I had to attack this man on stage, and I nearly killed him, because I didn't know how to do it – I had no technique. 'You don't seem to know what you're doing, but you've got power. Go off to one of those posh drama schools.' So I applied to RADA and I went there for two years.

What did RADA do for you? Was that when you thought, 'I not only want to be an actor, I can actually do it'?

Yes, but thank God I didn't have the luvvie approach, I was rebellious, lazy, very rough around the edges. I wasn't a good student, but I had energy. A few of the teachers there recognized it, but constantly berated me for my lack of discipline. I went to voice classes and tried to avoid fencing and movement classes, and all that.

But do you think energy is a substitute for lack of discipline? Can it actually take over and drive you through in a way that wouldn't otherwise be possible if you lack discipline?

I think it's a force that will get you to a certain point, but if you don't master or discipline energy it can burn you up like rocket fuel. But I came in contact with two very extraordinary teachers, Yat Malmgren and Christopher Fettes, who now run the London Drama Centre. I was very taken with their teaching. It was simply a psychology of movement. I was absolutely fascinated and riveted by this theory of the dissection of the human personality. I became fascinated by the process of acting. I joined the Leicester Rep.

I think energy does have a lot to do with it because I remember going for an audition, my first job. I was in the pub on the day of the audition, having a couple of pints of beer on this beautiful sunny day in July in 1963, and suddenly remembering that I had to go to this audition. I rushed down to Westminster, I ran all the way down the Tottenham Court Road. It was in a church hall near Westminster, a recreational hall, and I walked in there just about on time, dying for a pee. The director was there, and I rushed in and demanded, 'Where's the loo?' I came out and he said, 'Right, I want you to play Undershaft in *Major Barbara* and Bolingbroke in *Richard II.* I said, 'Oh, don't you want me to audition?' He said, 'If you want to. But I saw you last night in *Waltz of the Toreadors.* I think you are a wonderful actor and I'd like to give you a job.' I said, 'When do I start?' 'September.' Then I said, 'Undershaft, what's that?' I didn't know what the hell that was. I discovered later that it was a man in his sixties. So my first major part in the theatre was playing Undershaft, and I was 25, full of pep and vinegar, energy, anger and rage. I was millions of years too young for the part, but somehow it worked. I remember basing the whole thing on my grandfather, a great firebrand. And I remember people in the audience saying, 'God almighty!' I knew I had found some furnace – some core within myself, an energy and firebrand passion. But, of course, that's not enough to be an actor. Then over the years, through discipline and work and experience, a lot of experience, I gradually honed it down. But I don't regard myself today, as a technically accomplished actor at all. I'm very uncomfortable in Shakespeare. I'm rather uncomfortable in the theatre for some reason. It's not my favourite place, that's why I chose to be in movies.

Does every successful actor model the roles he or she plays on a particular person, or can you pluck pieces of personality from a whole variety of people you have known and weld them together into someone who is new and different? Or has it, on the whole, got to be homing in on one particular person?

I don't really know. I know that there are many really fine actors, especially the American breed of American actor – like Paul Newman – they just play their own personality. A British example would be Sean Connery – and within that range they're wonderful. I wish I could do that. I can't. I'm not comfortable playing myself. I think I just have to be what they would call 'an old-fashioned character actor'.

The last line of your biography reads, 'For Tony, it's still either black or white, up or down, all or nothing.' Is there no contented, mellow in-between?

No. I'm a little more mellow than I was ten years ago, or maybe twenty years perhaps, but not much.

Is it a product of achieving great success, of getting the Oscar, the knighthood and so on, that you become more confident and that some of the fear that you've said was there, melts away?

Yes, it does. Something I have discovered recently, over the last year or so, is that it is necessary to let go. I tell myself to relax and let go. That's very hard for me, very hard for a high achiever, for someone who's driven. It's hard for me to let go because there is a fear of being still.

Why is that fear there?

I used to feel that I was 15 moves behind the game before I'd even got out of bed in the morning.

Is that a basic insecurity, maybe going back to your early days of not achieving at school?

Probably. You spoke of everything being black or white, but I can see middle ground now. I'm a little more moderate than I used to be. But I hover between slothfulness and workaholism. I think that's a common thing amongst people like myself. People who don't have a moderate way. I'm either watching mindless television, or trying to do everything, playing the piano, reading books and trying to write a symphony all at the same time. I can't actually sit quietly here in the chair looking out of the window. I catnap a lot, I sleep during the day, in the afternoons – half an hour or twenty minutes. On a film set I always take half an hour to sleep, because I think it rejuvenates and it's good for one. And then I'm out like gangbusters. I've just been doing a film and I had severe back problems in my upper vertebrae. It caused an excruciating and deeply depressing pain, and I had to be tremendously active, being chased by a grizzly bear, actually fighting a grizzly bear, climbing up and down rocks, going into ice-cold water, and I wouldn't be defeated by pain.

So what you're trying to do is discipline the energy and the enthusiasm and create some form of order out of them, otherwise is there a danger that you could go over the edge, as you did in the early days?

Yes, I think you can go over the edge, become derailed and reach a point of no return. You just either blow your brains out or have a complete breakdown or something. I've never really approached that area – I've never got that far.

You've come close to it.

Oh, you mean the dreaded booze problem? Yes, it's a pretty dead and boring subject. I drank just to pacify things, to keep me calm. I'm just glad I don't have to do it any more. These twenty years have been the best. I've been restored

Why do you think so many actors put their success at risk by becoming alcoholics or drug addicts or whatever?

Most people I know who are either alcoholics or drug addicts are very high achievers. People who are attracted to the music profession, or the acting business, or high finance, or high prestige jobs – I'm generalizing – are drawn towards achievement and are just slightly damaged. They are people who need, like myself, to achieve to compensate – to conquer.

Even though there's a basic flaw in there somewhere?

Maybe people who are very content just get on with their lives and are very happy, have the wisdom to accept themselves and say, 'I'm fine, I'm happy with my life.' That's wonderful. But there are others who say, 'I'm not content, I've got to have more.' I like to examine them and I like to listen to people's conversations and find out what their little flaws are, not because I want to use them against them, but because it's fascinating to me. The flaw is, there's a feeling of inadequacy. I worked with Laurence Olivier some years ago, and he said to me once of himself, 'If I hadn't been an actor I'd have gone raving mad.' There was a man, a very complicated man, a very powerful man. The grit in the oyster that makes the pearl of success has to be there.

Let me ask you about other potential factors in success. You talked about Sir Laurence Olivier. One of your big breaks that carried you up the ladder of success was as his understudy in Strindberg's The Dance of Death, *and he said in his autobiography that when he fell ill you walked away with the part of Edgar like a cat with a mouse between his teeth. Now does everyone, perhaps especially in the acting profession, need a lucky break like that?*

Luck is something magical. I really do believe that there is a force in nature, and all we have to do is tap into it. Tap into the centrifugal force of our own psyche which is connected to something immortal and infinite. I have no doubt about that, because I'm connected in my way. I only found it by accident. I think you also have to be ruthless. I remember that time when I went on stage, I didn't register I was going on stage 'to take over from Olivier'. But once I'd got that confidence I thought, 'Right, I'm just going to *go for it*, go for broke, I've got nothing to lose.' I go for broke, and think, 'There's no turning back, go for it.' It's like that victory salute at the Olympic Games, that's my gesture, that's my psychological gesture. Risk destruction, risk being a fool, risk criticism. And of course, the more successful you are, the more bullets are fired at you.

But you need luck as well, do you? Or do you make your own luck?

You make your own luck. There's something magical in it, I believe that once you've made a decision, if it's a bold decision, some force within you says, 'That's what you want, that is what you're going to get.' And it will push you. And as they say, be careful what you pray for, because sometimes you get things that you don't really need and will be bad for you – I'm not talking in a religious sense, I'm talking in a metaphysical sense. I think every human being is invested with such infinite power and we've hardly tapped into our potential.

When was the moment when you realized this?

I've had many moments of realization and I still get them. Whenever I find myself in a very lucky situation, the situation of success or, in a job, in work, even sitting here at this moment being interviewed I think, 'Isn't this extraordinary?' I was such a dunce at school and here I am being interviewed about a book on success. I remember in December 1973, just before Christmas, my wife and I were shopping around in Beverly Hills for a Christmas present for someone. I remember standing outside the shop and I was in pretty bad shape then. I was drinking very heavily, very hung over, very confused – and I remember looking across at the Beverly Wilshire Hotel. I thought, 'I'd love to live out here,' and I visualized myself doing it. I knew that something was working for me, and I thought, 'Wouldn't it be nice if I could give up the booze as well, but, no, maybe that's not the problem, I just want to be happy; I want to be content.' Then, in August 1975 I was in New York. An agent phoned me and said, 'Would you like to come and spend some months in Los Angeles, we'd like to represent you?' I said yes. We had an apartment on Wilshire Boulevard, and one Saturday morning I was walking, pretty hung over, down Wilshire Boulevard, trying to shake off the hangover. I went into a book shop and when I came outside I thought, 'Oh my God, I stood on this pavement two years ago, dreaming of being here. This is weird.' It had all happened. And then I thought, 'Now more will happen.' A few months later I kicked the booze and from then on my whole life started to change by leaps and bounds, because I realized I'd contacted something which was primal and big in myself. And I've never looked back.

You talked about several people in your life, several key people who touched your life in a certain way, ranging from the chap in the YMCA right through to Olivier. Do you think that in order to be really successful, everyone in the acting profession needs a mentor, or series of mentors, who are prepared to ride shotgun with you, at perhaps difficult and unsatisfying stages of your career, and to give you the big breaks?

I think so. Yes. Olivier gave me a big break at the National Theatre. I'd just come out of rep, I'd had an audition at the National. I was playing walk-ons and after about three weeks I got very angry about all this and I thought, 'I don't want to play walk-ons for the rest of my life, in wrinkled tights, standing holding spears.' So I went to the casting director and asked, 'How do I get a part in a play?' She said, 'You've only been here three weeks!' 'I don't care, I'll go back to rep, I'm not going to hang around here.' And I think she covered a smile and said, 'Well, I don't know.' Then later she left a note saying, 'Sir Laurence is going to come and see your understudy rehearsal.' At the time I was understudying Albert Finney in *Love for Love.* And he watched this rehearsal and I remember he came forward, and said, 'Good, but I think I can give you a couple of tips. Why don't you imitate Albert, you know, he's a very good actor. I've stolen all my life from Dame Edith Evans, Noel Coward, John Gielgud. Be a thief, be a magpie.' Anyway, a few weeks later he gave me a part in his production of *Juno and the Paycock*, a very nice little part – one page, that's all it was, called 'the Mobiliser'. I was due in rehearsal and I'd worked on this little scene and come up with some things that seemed to be quite dramatic – a sudden change of voice and so on. And it was a curtain scene, at the end of an act. So I did this something which was quite dramatic and I knew it had an effect, because you have to smell that effect, you have to sense that, you have to know when you're good, and I thought, 'This is good, this is exciting.' When we broke for lunch, Olivier said, 'Tony, I just want to say that's terrific, it's wonderful what you did, but don't do any more than that, though, don't develop tricks.' Then he gave me *Three Sisters*, Andrei in *The Three Sisters*, and he seemed to like very much what I was doing. We were all affected by Olivier at the National, all us young actors. He had such a style, such charisma, and we all used him as a role model.

Everyone has a mentor, I think. Look at Robert De Niro and Martin Scorsese. De Niro would have done it without Scorsese, I'm sure, but Scorsese was there to model him. It's like John Wayne and John Ford. Ford said to Wayne, 'I'm going to make you into a big star. I can do it, you just do what I tell you and you'll become a big star.' He saw in Wayne the potential of a giant American movie star and made him into one.

So, as an actor, are you heavily dependent on the abilities of your director?

If you're marked for success and you want success enough, and you have the talent for it, I think you have to be very wary and have eyes in the back of your head to watch out for bad directors. Because they will destroy you – they'll make you look a fool. And you have to make a stand very early. I remember my first job in rep was with a notoriously sadistic bully of a director, and he started to pick on me. I stood on the edge of the stage one day and said, 'Don't you ever talk to me like that.' Somebody said, 'You'll never work again,' and I countered, 'I don't care.' I've stood up to people who've tried to break me, and I will break them before they'll break me. I wouldn't put up with it. I was told, at an early stage, you can't go through your life like that. I said, 'Screw them. Nobody talks to me like that.' And I won't be put upon. There have been a few of that type, but I've also had some wonderful, positive directors. I did work with a particularly tough director, John Dexter, but he turned out to be a very constructive director – one of the best stage directors I've worked with.

How much control does a successful actor have in the movie business?

I've worked with some wonderful directors recently, and I don't want to come on set and tell the director what to do because it's not my business. I don't know what the role of the director is except to point the camera in different directions and make the film work, and make the scenes interesting, and so on and so forth. So I don't come in and tell the director where to put the camera. No actor should do that and I think they're shooting themselves in the foot – act, that's what you're paid to do, don't direct. But it's a negotiation. I'll say to the director, 'Could I try this here? I've got this idea, can I try that?' If a director's wise he'll say, 'Yes, let's have a look at that.' I say, 'OK.' And then the director says, 'If you do that there, then it's going to screw up that bit there.' And if you're sensible enough, you'll say, 'Oh, yes.' So it's keeping open, and flexible. In recent years I've come to appreciate what directors have to go through and the enormous task they have. And if you are smart enough, you'll listen to the director because they're the boss. Some years ago I thought the other way, I didn't trust them at all, but I don't think it's smart at all to come on and bully a director. You can have a wonderful relationship with them.

What were your biggest failures, and how, more importantly – this is the real nub of the question – how did you recover from them?

I've had my share of those moments. When I was doing the Shakespeare at the National the critics took quite a few pot-shots at me, and later I did a show in the West End called *M. Butterfly*, which the critics savaged. I remember that particularly, going on stage on the second night, which is always a depressing night when they've said whatever they've said. It's tough and any actor who denies that is a liar. It does affect you, that's why I don't work in the theatre any more. On film you can get away with it. As soon as the critics tear a film to pieces you're not even there any more. It's just a pile of celluloid they're looking at, so it doesn't have any effect on you at all. It's nice to get a good review for a film, but if not, well, tough, I've got the money in the bank and that's all that matters. But on stage it's a harder task because you've got to go on with the knowledge in your head that you're not liked, or you're wrong in the part. But you've got to readjust. If you're in a six-month run, as I was, then you have to readjust very quickly and get on with it, do the best you can, and keep it fresh all the time. I remember doing *Lear* and it was tough. David Hare had done a good production, but I just couldn't match up to it. I knew that I was in big trouble, and I spent 25 performances trying to pull it all together for myself again. Fortunately I had some wonderful actors to work with – one was Michael Bryant, and I said to him one night, 'I'm going to have to change it a bit, do you mind if I work on each scene as we're going through it, night after night?' And he said, 'No, do what the hell you like.' And I gradually had to remould it and reshape it and bring it down, because I'd started off too high, and I had to reinvent it for myself every night. And after about 25 performances, I remember somebody from one of the papers revisited it and gave me another review saying, 'He's done it, and he's really changed the performance and brought it to a level which is now comprehensible and has really begun to scale heights.'

So you respond to some criticism as well as trying to ride through other criticism that you believed to be misplaced?

Yes. I think you can tell with a good critic that they've got a point. But there are savage critics who just hate everything, and those are the ones I won't even read if I've been in a play. I see their name and just look at the first word and I throw the paper away. I know that they just want to rip things apart, they want to tear it down. Two or three critics I know don't like anything I do. So I avoid them.

Why do some people admire success and others find it a source of deep envy and resentment?

I don't know. To be fair, I don't think it's just a national thing in this country, it's a trait in a lot of human beings to resent and envy success in others. Maybe it's a feeling of inadequacy, of being threatened. I remember when I stopped drinking in the early years, when I came back here a few of my old drinking pals didn't speak to me again. I think they felt a little threatened – or probably thought I was a bore. I think success threatens some people.

Are resentment and envy driving forces in success? Can jealousy drive you to greater heights?

It drove Iago to self-destruction, and the destruction of a number of people. I think jealousy and envy are corrosive. I've felt envy and I've been jealous. I'll be honest, I've felt jealous of other actors. I don't feel that any more, but I used to in the past. Laurence Olivier said some very truthful words to a very good actor who shall be nameless. They were in a play together. This actor had got rather mediocre notices or reviews while Olivier had great reviews. The actor was sitting in his dressing-room on the second night when there was a knock at the door and Olivier came in. 'Sorry about the reviews,' he said, 'But remember, there's one thing about getting a bad review – you make a lot of other actors very, very happy.'

That reminds me of a story I once heard – a parable. There was a saint who'd spent 40 days and 40 nights in the desert and the devil sent all his little henchmen and trainees out to get him. So they got to this saint, danced around him, tied him to a tree and tempted him with power, riches, anything he wanted, for 40 days and 40 nights, but they were beaten. They all crawled back into their hole in the ground and the devil was on the floor laughing his head off. He said, 'No, you got it all wrong. Go back and tell him that his brother's just been made Bishop of Alexandria.' And I thought, 'That's so true.'

Is there a downside to success?

I don't give much credence to looking at the downside. I'm compulsively energized. I think probably lurking underneath me, is an area of depression. I've had depressions. I had a severe one about a year ago, lasting a few days. It was quite unaccountable. I'd been directing a film in North Wales and I felt rather down. Then I started feeling guilty about feeling depressed, which made it worse.

Some people say that if you're successful, you should never be depressed because you're on a roll?

Yes, but sometimes you wake up in the morning and look in the mirror and see the boring old face looking back at you from the shaving mirror saying, 'It's you again.' You can't live on highs, it would be madness. I always feel good when I hear that people who are very successful sometimes have moments of doubt. I think, 'Good, join the human race.'

There was a wonderful car bumper sticker in California that said, 'Happiness is knowing that your doctor smokes.' Everything tells you nowadays, 'Don't smoke, don't drink,don't breathe,' and so on – and in the end you can't eat, you can't breathe, you can't do anything. Then suddenly you find that people do smoke and have a secret drink, or whatever and you think, 'Good!'

Who are your heroes?

I don't think I'd use the word hero, but I admire Kenneth Branagh. I think he's fearless, and he's driven by an enormous desire for success. I think he's very successful. He's suffered from the critics because he's very successful. Olivier was another. Gielgud is an enormous hero of mine.

I rather admire ruthless people – Picasso was one. I played him recently, and somebody said to me in an interview, 'He's such a monster with women.' I said, 'Yes, but they adored him because he was a single-minded visionary, a genius, and revolutionized the face of art, changed art.'

So do you believe that every successful person has to have a touch of ruthlessness in them somewhere?

Absolutely. I don't mean being cruel to other people or taking advantage of somebody else's misfortune or achieving at the cost of somebody else's career or life. I mean ruthless with oneself, ruthless enough to make sacrifices. One of the negative things that I would say about myself is that although I have a lovely daughter, I haven't been a good father. I don't think I'm the ideal husband because I'm always away. My wife and I talk about it constantly, and she has accepted that I'm very restless. We have a good arrangement in our lives because I am restless and she's not.

How important is it to have another person who is there like a rock?

It's very, very important. My wife is a rock and a very calming influence in my life. I haven't been a great husband at all. I'm ruthless, arrogant. She says I'm not, but I just want more and more and more. But she can laugh me out of seriousness. She can calm things down by saying, 'It's not really necessary to do that, is it?' Sometimes I'll talk her around to my way of thinking because I know I have enormous courage, but I won't do anything just to defy Jenni's opinion of what I should or shouldn't do. I'll just say, 'I think I can do it, and as long as you don't mind I'm going to go ahead. You may not approve.' She'll say, 'OK, that's up to you, but don't complain afterwards.' I say, 'Fine.' If you can't take a joke you shouldn't have joined, that is her philosophy. Sometimes she'll read the script and say, 'I don't think you ought to do that.' Then I'll read it, and say, 'Yes, you're right.' Ninety per cent of the time we're in agreement on that. She's a remarkable woman; very patient and very forgiving.

What is the greatest pleasure you've had from your success?

Well, I've travelled all over the world. I love getting on aeroplanes, going to America, travelling to new locations. I love film sets. I love getting up in the morning and going to a film set, getting changed, getting ready, going on set and doing it. And, at the end of the day, getting in the car and going back to the hotel.

Your pleasures are bound up with your profession?

Yes, but I don't live it day and night. I don't sleep it or eat it. I finish on the film set and I go home and read a book. I usually eat alone in a hotel. I like to go to a restaurant, take a book and read, then go back to the hotel, go to sleep and I'm up the next day. I'm not consumed about the part. The other pleasures come from just being alive. I was in a restaurant last night and people came over for my autograph. I'm not embarrassed by it, I love it. If people want to shake hands, I love it. Anyone that says they don't is a damn fool because if people want to say hello, shake hands and ask for an autograph, they keep me in work. So I hope I'm as gracious and as polite as I can be and say, 'What's your name?' and sign it. It is a part of the merchandise, it's a part of my life.

What are the core principles that people need in order to be successful?

Well, the paradox of it all is humility. That's a difficult one, but humility is the essence of success.

Can you be ruthless and have humility?

Yes. I don't mean cloth-cap-in-hand humility, sackcloth and ashes. That's not humility, that's disgusting self-abasement. I mean the humility to understand that, 'But for the grace of God there go I.' I say that to myself most days. I'm no holy Joe at all, I'm not a religious person, but I do think that. I ask myself, 'How the hell did I get here?' I look at photographs of myself as a child and think, 'Who is that and who is this now? How did this happen?' And the only credit I can take is that I worked a little hard for it, but there was also the good fortune of tapping into something in myself which made me what I am. I think it's gratitude really, though it sounds such a wet word – gratitude to oneself or circumstances or destiny or fate that one is what one is. And acknowledging that. It's also being fair, being well mannered, all those old fashioned things that are so despised. I used to fight with people, I don't do that any more. Just being pleasant to people, being gracious is, I think, so essential.

And never forgetting where you came from?

In my mind I go back to Port Talbot over and over again. This morning I was back there, going over the past. It moves me because I can go down the back lane, back to the school, and I can go up to the side of the mountain and into Margam Woods, and I can remember it so clearly. It reminds me all the time where I come from. When I go back to Wales – my mother lives there in Newport – I always drive down to Port Talbot and go up all the streets where I was as a child and sometimes just sit outside the house where I was born. I'll sit outside my grandfather's house, looking and thinking, 'How did this happen?' I remember knocking at the door of my grandfather's house one day and the owner came out. I said, 'Excuse me,' and she said, 'Oh, it's Anthony Hopkins!' I said, 'My grandfather lived here, I don't want to bother you.' She said, 'Come in, come in and have a cup of tea, sit down there and I'll call the neighbours in.' So just touching base, touching where I came from, is important. I'm not doing it as an exercise in humility, not at all, I'm fascinated by it. I don't know why I am where I am. I'm very grateful to be what I am today. I am today what I've always wanted to be, and that to me is a sort of humility, in a way.

What are the biggest enemies of success?

Doubt. I saw a young student the other night, a very talented young man, yet so tortured, full of self-hatred and anger and rage. And I said, 'The only advice I can give you is, whatever your rage is, use it, but be prepared to let go of it because it will eat you alive, it'll destroy you.' He said, 'Yes, but...' I said, 'Cut that out. You're a "yes, but" merchant and it will kill you. The "yes, buts" of life can cut our dreams to ribbons. Be bold. Boldness is power, magic.'

Do you think success brings any obligations in its wake to society as a whole?

Yes. When you're in contact with an abundance in your life, it's necessary to tithe it out, to give back. I'm not Mother Teresa, I don't have that kind of courage, and I'm not a good person. But one principle is that if you give away, more will come to you. Give it away and let it circulate. Whether it's money or whether it's success, let it circulate. The moment we block it we get a hardening of the arteries of the soul. One of the greatest ingredients of success is saying 'yes' to life.

And participating in as many aspects of life as you can, and that includes putting something back into the society from which you have created your success?

Yes. Putting it back, whether it's through the work or helping out. Whether it's helping to feed the homeless or, as I do, trying to help some young kids who can't get grants to get into acting schools. I'm involved in the ecology of Snowdonia. I sometimes feel that I live a rather narrow existence and should live a wider one, but then one can be spread too thin – that's not productive at all. One has to make certain choices. There are some people who are multi-faceted, like Richard Attenborough who is involved in countless charities. I'm afraid I can't do that. I have to have a limited scope, a limited field in which I can work. I make choices, then concentrate on those choices. There's nothing selfless about what I do. If I give out I'll get more back. But then we get into the areas of definition – what is selfish and what is selfless? Is there a selfless act? Maybe Jesus Christ was selfless.

Has success changed you at all?

It's given me more confidence, and more happiness in my life. I think I started off as a troubled child with a propensity for unhappiness and depression. In school as a young kid, I was miserable and lonely. But what it has brought me now is this wonder, a sense of surprise that I am where I am now. It's given me a sense of, 'I've done it all, I've done everything I need to do.' But I still want to do more.

Is it more or less difficult to be successful in the acting profession now?

Much more difficult. We don't have as many regional repertory companies as we used to have, which were great training grounds for young actors. In 1961 when I went to acting school I earned £7 a week, which was just about enough to survive on. Now there are young kids who are trying make their way who are enormously talented, but finding it almost impossible to eat, to survive. It's iniquitous that public spending has been cut back so much, and especially on the youth of this country. It's a monstrous injustice. I wish there was more awareness. I don't know what the future is. I am still optimistic, I'm not a pessimist, but I do see that it is hard for young people today.

If you could gather together before you in one room all the young people in the world who want to be successful actors and actresses, what advice would you give them?

Hold onto the dream. I saw a production the other night at the Drama Centre and some of the kids up there were just wonderful. I went into this big communal dressing-room after the show. I said, 'You were fantastic.' I could only give them my enthusiasm, just give a couple of hugs. I want to say, and do say to them, 'Just go for it. Have the courage of your convictions; go all out for it 100 per cent. Don't hold back; give everything you've got. And if you've got '*it*', that charisma and the peculiar star quality, there's nothing to stop you. Have more commitment and more faith and belief in yourself.

And if you haven't got 'it', *can you work at it? Can you actually develop it?*

I don't think so. I saw Richard Burton being interviewed by Dick Cavett years ago and Cavett said, 'How do you account for your success?' He said, 'I don't really know. I look at my face, it's quite an ordinary face. I've got quite a good voice, nothing special. I know actors in England and America who are probably much better, technically more equipped. It's something to do with the chemicals of the body or psyche. It's just one of those peculiar things. I can't account for it at all, except I was very, very angry as a young actor and I just knew what I wanted, and I went for it.'

When your time comes to leave this life, what would you like people to say about you?

He wasn't half-bad.

That's all?

Yes, that's it. I don't want them to say he was good. He wasn't half-bad, he was OK. My epitaph would be, 'That's all, folks.'

SIR BERNARD INGHAM

He failed his eleven-plus through extreme nervousness and lack of confidence. Thirty-six years later, when Prime Minister Margaret Thatcher asked him to head the Downing Street press office, he became the official interface between government and media through a key era in British politics, responsible for an estimated 5,000 briefings to the lobby, and 30,000 more to individual journalists. He outlines his approach to the pressures and problems of his Downing Street job with revealing anecdotes and robust frankness. The man once nicknamed 'Mrs Thatcher's personal rottweiler' says he is his own severest critic. He was brought up in the small Yorkshire town of Hebden Bridge by parents who 'hammered into me I should always be true to myself'. He turned out a bright pupil, but left school at 16 because, in those days, 'the working classes were not accustomed to sending their children to university'.

Starting as a junior reporter on the local paper, he worked his way up to the Yorkshire Post *and* The Guardian, *but never really grew in confidence until he joined the Civil Service. He 'took to it like a duck to water', working with several departments before arriving at No. 10, and finding it enormously valuable to see how civil servants approach a problem – 'the inquiring mind behind the sceptical mind that tests everything in a way journalists don't understand'. And he goes on to argue that the journalists' approach, based on 'a lack of understanding of the way government works', actually makes it more difficult for a government to achieve success. He concedes that democracy would be 'almost a basket case if journalists took everything a government said as gospel', and admits that there were many times when he couldn't tell the whole truth. But he also argues that what he calls 'the electric frontier' between government and media contains 'too much suspicion, with the conspiracy theory taken to ludicrous lengths'. He outlines ways in which politicians and journalists can and do collaborate, but also explains why, in the end, he believes 'you cannot trust a journalist'. He talks of the need to deliver with 'integrity of purpose'; and the doubts – 'There is not a day when I haven't gone to work believing that if I made a mess of it, I might be out on my ear the same night'.*

Sir Bernard, what is your definition of success?

Success is feeling that you have fulfilled yourself, and that you are happy about it.

And to what extent is your ability to achieve that a product of your background and upbringing?

I don't think I could feel happy if I were doing something I positively hated, and therefore the extent to which my background enters into it is, I suppose, that my parents were always hammering into me that I should be true to myself. That is reflected in my feeling that success is to feel pretty well fulfilled in what you're doing. I'm not saying that you don't have reservations about anything – of course you do, nothing is absolutely golden all the time – but, taking an overall view, you have to feel happy with it. If you do, I think you're very successful indeed.

Do you need a mentor, some regular form of encouragement, as you go through life? Is that a key part of a really successful person's career?

I don't go too much for all that. I think the support of your family is important – there's no argument about that – but beyond that, it is nice to have the approbation of your colleagues, but I don't think it is the key factor. Well, it certainly has not been so for me. The key factor for me has been whether I myself have thought I was doing a good job. I am, I think, my own severest critic, and I always suspect other people's comments about me. I frequently believe they're being far too kind!

But can you totally ignore external criticism or praise? Aren't you affected by it in some way? Isn't your career shaped to a certain extent by outside forces making a judgment about what you do and how you do it?

Undoubtedly your career is shaped by the judgments people make about you, because, let's face it, they recommend you for jobs – or not, as the case may be. Your peers and your superiors take a view of your worth and your abilities, and you can't ignore that contribution to your perceived success or failure. But I think that if you spend your life buttering people up, especially in the political field, simply for personal advancement, then you're not going to get very far, and you're going to be a very disappointed person. Politicians are all thought to be narcissistic, and wanting to be lauded to the skies, and undoubtedly my job as a press secretary was to support them and make them feel good. But when you have to give real, hard advice, then, quite frankly, you'd better be honest about it, and you'd better not be there just to please people. You are there to set them right, as you see it. And they appreciate that. I would much rather be known as a person who was tough but honest with people rather than somebody who smarmed all over them.

Is that toughness a Yorkshire trait, or do you think it's a characteristic of the Ingham family? Is it something that is handed down from generation to generation?

I think it's been handed down from generation to generation. Some people would say that it's an immense lack of tact, but I don't think that is fair. We all know when not to say the hard thing, even though you have to find a way of saying it. But there is a tradition of plain speaking in my family, and I certainly caught the bug, while at the same time recognizing that you aren't there to gratuitously make people feel uncomfortable or depressed or hurt or whatever. You have to observe many social niceties, but in a professional area there has to be some pretty plain speaking. Otherwise some of the politicians for whom I worked would not have respected me.

To go back to your early days – you failed your eleven-plus and left school at 16. To what extent did those events inculcate within you the feeling that you had to prove the world wrong?

None at all, really. My eleven-plus failure was certainly an absolute trauma, because everybody thought I was going to pass. I was always in the first three in the form and so on. But I knew in my heart of hearts why I failed. You may laugh now, but I was of an extremely nervous disposition, and I suffered badly from asthma. The nervous tension of doing the examination put me in bed for about a week, and when I learned the result it was just as bad. I was just a bag of nerves, and the asthma was a manifestation of that. So I didn't feel I had to prove anything in that sense, especially since I went on to prove myself immediately. My parents scraped together the money to send me to grammar school and I was never out of the top five in the A form there. Leaving school at 16 wasn't unusual in my day. In west Yorkshire, during and immediately after the war, the working classes were not accustomed to sending their children to university, because of their limited horizons. So you didn't feel as though you were being deprived of anything as a result of your 'poverty'. In any case, we weren't all that poor, though we certainly weren't rich. So I don't kid myself that I felt that I had anything to prove in life. Let's face it, when I became cub reporter on the *Hebdon Bridge Times* my parents thought I'd achieved an enormous amount. Far more than they'd ever done, and far more than they'd ever expected of me.

How did you overcome your nerves?

I don't know, to be absolutely honest. My lack of confidence and my nervousness held me back, I think, as a journalist – certainly in my early thirties, when I was on the *Guardian*. I was absolutely overwhelmed by its reputation as a writers' paper, and, frankly, I tried too hard. Worrying about it all nearly made me ill. Then I went into the civil service, with some trepidation, and suddenly I found I was surviving. From then on my confidence built very rapidly indeed. All I can put it down to is the fact that I changed career, not intending it to be a permanent change – I'd only meant to do it for two years. In this entirely new environment my confidence grew apace and I found myself taking to the world of politics – not party politics, but the politics which are a part of the civil service – like a duck to water. Undoubtedly, my 12 months at the Prices and Incomes Board were my university, and I learned a great deal there. Then suddenly Barbara Castle hired me as a speechwriter. It took me 24 years to get back to journalism!

What was it you learned? Here you were, in your thirties, and by your own admission still very nervous, still unsure. What were the factors the civil service was able to bring to bear which somehow gave you the confidence you didn't have before?

Well, first of all, I was operating in a milieu I found I thoroughly enjoyed. You weren't there to tear people down, to write for effect or perhaps even slightly distort the news for journalistic licence. It was almost like going back to my weekly newspaper, where you were there to establish the facts, to have great reverence for the facts, and to understand more deeply the problems the country was up against. I learned a great deal about the way in which Britain was run. After years of reporting local government in its various forms – courts, all kinds of events, civic events and so on – I thought I knew what made Britain tick, but it wasn't until I got into the Prices and Incomes Board that I realized how things were at national level, as distinct from local and regional. This was an enormous piece of education.

It was also enormously valuable to see the thought processes of civil servants at work, to see how they approached a problem – the inquiring mind behind the sceptical mind that tested everything in a way journalists simply don't understand, the way they weighed things up and looked at them from every conceivable angle, and the way they identified problems. The other thing I learned was how politicians take the work of the civil service staff and present it in political terms, in a way which is designed to persuade people. This was an absolutely wonderful, wonderful education – my degree, as I say. I think it was rubbing up against these first-class brains – I'm not saying there weren't first-class brains in journalism, but they had a different approach – that gave me real confidence.

Do you think that the journalistic approach based, as you say, almost on a lack of experience of the way government works, actually makes it more difficult for a government to achieve success?

Yes, I do, and one of the most depressing things about being chief press secretary at Number 10 for 11 years was how little interest most journalists took in the processes of government, how government develops policy, the painstaking care that goes into it. I fully accept that sometimes all this painstaking care is brushed to one side when people make a political decision because of pressures or whatever, but I think the classic example of the way – the cynical way, you might say – in which journalism dismisses government formulation of policy is when somebody leaks a document. Some politically motivated civil servant leaks a document to Robin Cook, via the *Guardian*, and what does the *Guardian* do? This document contains options going from one extreme to another, but the *Guardian*, knowing very well that those in the middle are the most likely, goes for one of the extremes as the news story. That's just laughable to a lot of people in government, and it made my life as press secretary very difficult with civil servants. They know exactly what they're doing by rehearsing the options, and they said, 'How can we take these people seriously?' It was a very good question, but I had to – I was working with them. I was there not to declare war on the press, but to keep the lid on it.

So how did you set about keeping the lid on it, knowing that some journalists have almost a predisposition in their approach to a particular story? Did it mean that you had to be robust? Did it mean you had adopt particular tactics for dealing with the media?

I had to be robust with both civil servants and journalists. Journalists had to be told the error of their ways, and I never hesitated to do that, but equally, civil servants had to be told, in no uncertain terms, 'You may not like it, you may think that this is a travesty of reality, but the fact is they are there, and they're not going to go away. And we have to find a way of dealing with them, and you have to allow me to deal with them.' I had great rows with civil servants who felt that the only people who really mattered were them, and that I was just a sort of servant, and I would say, 'You grumble like a bear with a sore head when things are going wrong, but you do nothing to help me when they are going right. You put too many obstacles in my way for me to create capital with the media during the good times.' You've no idea of the rows I had internally in the civil service trying to represent the interests of the media. If you want to define my success, I would hope people recognize that here was a chap who, given a job to do, would do it, and he wouldn't brook any interference.

Did you consider, at any time, that you might have to be less than forthcoming with the truth in order to put across a particular point of view regarding government policy?

Of course. There were many times when you couldn't tell the whole truth. It may well have been that people didn't know what the whole truth was.

Did anyone stop you from doing it?

Well, I knew how far I could go without compromising the politicians' perfect right to timing, determining the pace of politics, or how we should disclose things. And the media knew that, too. The game we played in the lobby was that they would seek to ask the question which would force me to be more frank than I should have been. They knew exactly what they were doing, and I knew exactly what they were doing. It was an unequal contest, because they knew I could not afford to be caught lying, otherwise I would have lost my credibility. And they fully accepted that I couldn't tell the whole truth. Indeed, I've seen old-fashioned lobby correspondents write in journals, 'He can't tell the whole truth, we all know that, but that doesn't mean to say we aren't going to try to get him to spurt it out.'

Did you ever spurt out anything which you didn't intend to reveal? Were you ever trapped, or did you have an off-day, perhaps, and something came out?

Yes, I can tell you about one instance. I had a very off-day – rather fortuitously for the government – when I lost my temper with the Sunday lobby and told them, during a run on the pound, 'This government is not going to throw good money after bad defending the pound.' That caused mayhem for a short time, but the government then raised interest rates, decisively, as it should have done earlier, and the whole problem was out of the way. Actually, it was rather good for the government that I did drop this clanger.

But immediately afterwards you thought perhaps you'd gone too far?

I knew I'd gone too far – no doubt about that!

So how did you recover from that?

I didn't really have to do anything. The government raised interest rates.

But inside you knew you had gone too far and your superiors knew that too. Were there any repercussions?

Yes, there were. Having got the story, the media were then hunting for my head and suggesting that I might be fired over this, or, reluctantly, commenting that it looked as though I might survive. The fact is that a press secretary is liable to drop clangers from time to time, like all of us. And he has to be protected, as Willie Whitelaw said, when he does. Obviously, you can't make a profession out of dropping clangers. Of course I went too far when I said that it was being so cheerful that kept Francis Pym going, and when I described John Biffen as 'that well-known semi-detached member of the cabinet'. But people never ask why, because there was a reason, and I didn't make a habit of doing this. People alleged that I spent all my time slagging off ministers, but it's not true – they can only point to three cases. Pym and Biffen had both done something for which the lobby wanted them fired, and I was trying to defend them by explaining the kind of people that they were. The third case was when Geoffrey Howe became, after much negotiation, Deputy Prime Minister and his acolytes sold the press a load of hogwash about what being Deputy Prime Minister entailed. I told them what being Deputy Prime Minister meant – that is, the job Willie Whitelaw had done – and was then accused of undermining Geoffrey Howe.

When you were press officer at Number 10, was there an essential conflict between your view of events in the world and that of journalists, whose job it is to be sceptical of virtually everything, especially politicians? And is that healthy?

I think that a democracy would be grossly unhealthy – indeed, I think it would be almost a basket case – if journalists took everything that a government said as gospel. Not only would that mean that the government had a monopoly on ideas, but of course there would be no vigour, no rigour, no interest, no spark left in your journalism. When I went to Number 10, I'd already spent 12 years patrolling the electric frontier between government and media, and there were many more volts flowing by the time I got to Downing Street. But that's only to be expected, you can't resent it at all. I spent hours talking to Marlin Fitzwater, press secretary to Presidents Reagan and Bush, who feels the same way. I think the frontier is too electric these days, too suspicious. The conspiracy theory is now taken to ludicrous lengths. It is all a question of degree, but one thing is absolutely clear – you are not going to have an easy time on that border between government and media, and you shouldn't have, either.

And is there an essential and permanent conflict between journalists wishing to achieve success and politicians wishing to achieve success? Does there always have to be a deep tension between the two?

Yes, I think there does. They do actually collaborate to a remarkable degree, bearing in mind the amount of tension that exists between them.

In what ways?

Well, politicians will collaborate with a journalist to put things down on the order paper, to give the journalist privilege for making allegations. I've seen that. The Opposition will most certainly collaborate with friendly journalists to zap the Government if they can. One Right Honourable Member will feed a journalist stuff about another Right Honourable Member, or even friend, to do him down. I've known that, too. However, at the same time, journalists cannot be relied upon not to zap the collaborating politician if they get a story about him. Journalists are in the business of stories, they don't care where it comes from as long as it's a story.

So any leaker or informant is playing with fire?

Of course he is. Anybody who talks to the press is playing with fire. You cannot trust a journalist. This is not because journalists are inherently untrustworthy – of course most are not – but they inhabit a world of enormous pressure, and frequently that pressure makes them do things that they would not otherwise wish to do. It is not only press secretaries who are under pressure.

What do you think are the qualities necessary for the three careers you have pursued in life? First of all, Number 10 press officer, then perhaps separately from that, or maybe not, a civil servant. And thirdly, a journalist.

I think integrity of purpose. You've got to know what you're there for, and when you know what you're there for, you've got to pursue it with integrity, and not be put off by anybody.

Are there any qualities peculiar to one job that wouldn't apply to the others?

Press secretaries and civil servants have to have a very high degree of integrity, otherwise they'd be dead professionally.

What was the first time you remember saying to yourself, 'I have been successful'? It may go back to your teens, maybe even further.

I think I felt successful, in my own terms, at every stage, but I've always realized that it might not last if I didn't perform. And there is not a day when I haven't gone to work believing that if I made a mess of it, then I might be out on my ear the same night. I think you might say that that's a typical working-class attitude. But when I went to grammar school I felt I'd recovered from a débâcle, and therefore that I was relatively successful. And when I got on to the *Hebdon Bridge Times*, and by the age of 19 I was editing it in all but name, I thought I was pretty successful. But I would have felt more successful in my time on the *Yorkshire Evening Post*, and for much of my time on the *Yorkshire Post* and the *Guardian*, if I'd have had more confidence in myself, because my work was probably better than I thought it was. Sometimes I did worse work through nerves and lack of confidence than I ought to have done considering my capabilities, so my twenties and thirties were not uniformly successful in my own eyes. For the rest, I think, by my own standards I improved with every department I worked in, from Prices and Incomes to the Department of Employment, the Department of Energy, and then Number 10.

Your brother Derek said that when you live in a small town, nothing is right by older folks and when you are told so at every opportunity you begin to think and behave as if you're useless. That remark will strike a chord with a lot of people whose parents and environment were tough on them, and who are maybe discouraged from having confidence in anything as a result. Now should that attitude be there for people to react against or go under, or is there a way in which we could change it to give people much more optimism than we do, and at an earlier stage in life?

My parents used to make me extremely angry and we used to have real arguments over Sunday lunch. Their attitude was, oh, we're only working people, we can't expect any more. That was one of the most depressing attitudes I could imagine, but it was very widely held. A neighbour of ours told my mother, when she sent me to grammar school, 'There's no point in doing that, he'll end up in't mill like rest of them.' People really did feel they were trapped, and indeed they couldn't expect anything more, and I think that was bad. But I think now we have got over that, to a degree. There is now no limit to what people can achieve – if they can strum a guitar very well or kick a football, or box, or whatever, they are immediately lifted into the stratosphere. These days they can even do that by winning the lottery. There is much greater mobility between the classes now. Where I think the problem lies nowadays is perhaps in the narrow-minded approach of certain communities, local communities, maybe, which are very introspective and may resent people getting on. There was a great deal of resentment, certainly in west Yorkshire, if people got on, which is what my brother was carping at, but I think perhaps the greatest deficiency now arises from broken families in which people are never going to have a certain kind of encouragement at all because one parent is missing.

You touched on envy. To what extent do you think that we in Britain make it more difficult for people to succeed because we envy success, and because some of us try to pull down successful people? It's said that in the United States, for example, the success ethic is much stronger.

I think that there is some truth in that. People do resent others getting on, but if you look at the gossip columns in the United States, there is a fair amount of resentment there too, really, I think it's human nature. I suppose it is a question of degree, perhaps it's our culture. We do resent success, and we can't handle it in the way many other countries can.

What's stopping us handling it well?

Some people would say our class system, but there again, that's breaking down today, and there is a vast amount of mobility. It may be that we're a fairly sour people, and we need to get the sourness out of ourselves.

How do we do that?

Well, I think it's about time we recognized that Britain is the one place on Earth people love to come to. They covet the kind of life we have. We can see all the warts but the vast majority of people can come here and feel that they can walk the streets comfortably. Nobody really wants for anything, and, by and large, it works. There's too much litter around, but that situation is better than it was, and Britain is a friendly place, on the whole, if not as friendly as I would like it to be. What is more it's perfectly clear that Europe is frightfully jealous of us. I've been to 31 consecutive European Councils, and I don't think we shall ever be forgiven for twice either beating them, or liberating them, as the case may be. There is an enormous inferiority complex in Europe. Furthermore we have the language of the world.

But we haven't been used, since the war, to talking ourselves up. We were bankrupt then, and we have been on a steady decline since. Before we had an empire, we were the world's great manufacturer, a great trader – we are still the world's greatest trader, proportionately – but we've lived on a diet of failure, certainly up to 1979.

Sooner or later somebody is going to have to stand up and start being counted on the issue of the success of Britain. It's going to be very difficult for a politician, because he or she will be seen to have a vested interest. It is the people who will have to stand up and say, 'This is a pretty bloody good country.'

Do you think politicians think about the fact that their own success inevitably involves a degree of failure for their opponents?

Yes, and I think they love it! They want to keep their opponents unsuccessful in those terms. I suppose the most potent question is, if you do keep an Opposition unsuccessful for a long time, like 18 years, will they ever be able to govern again? There is an argument, I suppose, for letting the other side have a chance, but it is an enormous risk. Politicians actually want to succeed and they don't mind too much if they stay in office for a long time. But I think, to be fair, they have to continue to achieve while they're in office. You can't stay in office without success as it is perceived by the people. And it's a pretty stern test, actually.

And in your job at Number 10 you would have had a key role in putting over that degree of success to the people?

The degree of the Government's success is distinct from party success. Now, you may say, what is the dividing line? But I could only speak for the Government, and tell you what the Government had done. I couldn't say, 'This is what the Tory Party has done.' But certainly, I would have sought at every opportunity to try to present the Government as more rather than less coherent, and more rather than less successful, yes.

Do you think that for successful people there is inevitably a major conflict between their professional working lives and their home lives?

To a degree. Nobody is very successful without effort – unless they're incredibly lucky – and that effort inevitably reflects upon their home life. As someone who has now spent 48 years working hard all the time, I'm the first to admit that I don't go out socializing in the way other people gallivant about. I can't, because I'm working. And I'm terribly proud that I've made a success of my fourth job, as a self-employed chap.

But do you occasionally think that your family has suffered a bit because of this?

I know the family has suffered a bit, and I try to make it up to them in a whole variety of ways.

What do you reckon are the most successful moments of your life? The moments when you feel you were really at the top of the tree?

As a journalist it was when I wrote something good that really made me feel as though I'd captured it all. I remember once, when I was on the *Yorkshire Post* in the 1950s, I went to a town's meeting about some problem which was hilarious, and it just gelled and I managed to write a wonderful piece, which was printed word for word. On another occasion there was a hell of a fire in Halifax and I just walked into it, one of these things you do as a journalist. I just went into a telephone box, having made a few inquiries, and dictated the front-page lead. I felt so elated, and I knew it would be a success. That really did a great deal for my confidence.

And on the political side?

Well, you've no idea the sense of achievement I derived from getting Mrs Thatcher from the door of Number 10 on a Friday afternoon to Port Stanley in the Falklands for 6 p.m. on a Saturday without anybody in the press finding out. And I didn't lie. I didn't tell the whole truth, but I didn't lie. That was an enormous professional achievement. Another was to write my book in three months. I never thought I could do it, but I did, and my family suffered for that, because I really had to concentrate. I had to average 1,000 words a day, like Trollope, that's what my publisher said. They might not be the same 1,000 words as Trollope would have written, but if you average that you'll get there. I made my deadline with a week to spare.

So you need rigid discipline?

Absolutely. I simply couldn't afford to relent. And those three months included the research and everything.

What do you think are your biggest failures, and how did you recover from them?

Well, obviously, for reasons I've explained, the eleven-plus was a failure. Another was to stay in Halifax for seven years on the *Yorkshire Evening Post* and the *Yorkshire Post* and not to have moved earlier. That was a measure of my lack of confidence, I think. But why should I grumble now? I can look back and point to various mistakes, but I can't honestly say that, overall, I have made any big ones since then, because I've not been allowed to make them. I've been moved on. You could argue that if I was concerned about my reputation I should have left Number 10 much earlier than I did, but nobody was offering me anything better or more exciting.

Would you have gone if you'd had such an offer?

I'd have thought about it if I'd been offered something really great, because Downing Street is a very wearing place to be. They did try to move me out to the Central Office of Information after five years, but I just wasn't interested. And Mrs Thatcher wanted me to stay on, so I stayed on. Inevitably, you do get tarred with the same brush and clobbered far more the longer you are with a minister. But I don't think staying on was a mistake, really, because I did thoroughly enjoy it and I felt fulfilled doing it. What is more, I wasn't slipping up, generally, on the job by over-familiarity, and that, in a sense, was a great achievement. I think it was frequently a mistake to hammer the press as hard as I did, but there were no bones broken really. Indeed, after 11 years they gave me a party!

Some people might not believe you really mean that, because you obviously revelled so much in the jousting and the combative nature of your relations with the press, that for you to say that you might have been a bit tough on them might not wash in what was Fleet Street.

Well, it might not, but don't forget that I had to be concerned about keeping the bridge between government and media open and in a good state of repair. If you're chucking rocks across it too often then that can make life more difficult. There were occasions when I went over the top, and that made relations more difficult. One mistake I made at Number 10 was to try out, with the best of intentions, the idea of bringing in small groups of political correspondents to have a closer, more relaxed chat with the Prime Minister. It fell at the first hurdle because of the jealousies that exist. People realized that a privileged few had been in and that damaged relations. I never repeated that – it didn't help, and we had to recover from it and repair the bridge.

Who are your heroes? Who are the people you regard as being really successful in life, past or present?

All those who have had to work at it. Or alternatively, all those who have been landed with it and have worked at it very hard, and have continued with enormous integrity to do their job. After all, if you're the monarch, there must be many, many temptations just to jack it in, but the Queen doesn't. I admire iron discipline in doing a job. Margaret Thatcher had an absolutely iron discipline. What I don't like is seeing people throw their gifts away. Michael Heseltine has thrown many, many gifts away, through his stupidity over Westland, and so has Tony Benn. Enoch Powell has clearly thrown away great gifts which could have been used to the benefit of the nation.

What do you think are the main enemies of success?

Temptation, I suppose. A lack of application, a readiness to take it for granted, a failure to work at it. Success, in my view, is a very transient thing unless you work at it.

And does success bring obligations in its wake?

Yes, and one of them is to maintain performance.

And any obligations to the wider world?

You are not working just for yourself, you cannot work just for yourself. If you do that you will not be successful. You have to work for a country or a community or a family, or whatever. Working for yourself is not my definition of success.

Has success changed you at all?

My brother says not, and he's a very severe critic. I suppose it's refined my accent a little, although you can still tell where I come from.

Have you become more confident?

Oh, incredibly more confident, yes.

Can anything shake that confidence now?

If I make a bloomer, yes. 'You stupid person,' I say to myself, 'you'd better watch it.'

Is it important to have within your family, among the people you really trust and love, a degree of criticism? Can a really successful person achieve success without some kind of criticism?

No, you can't. If your family fails to keep your feet on the ground, then I think you're on very, very dangerous territory indeed. My family will ensure that I never become too big-headed.

If you could gather together all the young people whose ambition is to achieve your degree of success, what advice would you give them?

Work, apply yourself to anything that you do; be honest about it, be straight about it. If you don't feel it is right, don't do it. Give people the benefit of your candid advice, on the basis of your professional knowledge and experience. If you do that, you will not go too far wrong.

And when your time comes to leave this life, what would you like people to say about you?

That he was an awkward old so-and-so, but that there was something to what he had to say and he was straight.

JEREMY IRONS

This stylish Oscar-winning star of Reversal of Fortune, The French Lieutenant's Woman *and* The Mission *says, 'As soon as you stop risking, something dies in your work, because you have to have the bravery to fail in order to have the possibility of succeeding.' The youngest of a chartered accountant's three children, he was sent off to boarding school where he won his rugby colours, headed the cadet corps, became a prefect, played both violin and clarinet – but failed his A-levels. He also collected theatrical prints and read theatrical biographies, and after an inauspicious round of London auditions, and a spell as assistant stage manager at Canterbury's Marlowe Theatre, he joined the Bristol Old Vic. He left rep – to 'try to get a West*  *End show or a film', joined the BBC children's programme* Playaway, *and then, more promisingly, was given the lead in* Godspell *as John the Baptist. His first film role was a minor part in the 1980 film* Nijinsky.

A year later came the big double break from which he has never looked back – starring roles in the hugely popular TV drama Brideshead Revisited *and the highly acclaimed film* The French Lieutenant's Woman. *He argues that the public's perception of him is inaccurate: 'Seeing me in a film makes them feel things about me which bear no relation to me personally.' He has always been an observer, a watcher, and wants to remain an outsider: 'I think theatre and drama at its best is something that should kick against the pricks, stir up the silt and make people examine their complacencies.' He believes it is 'terribly important to know your own value in proportion to other people's'; he advises how to get under the skin of a character – 'I have to find something that touches me' and talks about 'the constant battle as an actor to change employers' perceptions of you'. He suggests provocatively that 'the media is the greatest enemy to successful people and to society'. He believes it is harder today for young actors to get 'the broad base that supports them', and urges them to understand that 'there are peaks and troughs in a career, that the public is fickle, that fashions change, that people get bored and like new faces – which is why in order to be truly successful in my terms, it is important to know what you want from life.'*

Jeremy Irons, what is your definition of success?

I think any definition of success has to be a personal definition and not a definition from the outside. In other words, not a definition of a watcher looking at me saying, 'He is successful,' but a feeling from within myself that I am successful. If you believe, as I do, that you should try to find your equilibrium in life, then I would feel successful if I was in that state. Some call it happiness, some call it contentment. I call it balance.

Is that in any way dependent on what the outside world says about you?

No, that bears no relation at all to what the outside world says about you, except of course that if you are what I laughingly describe as 'an artist', you are a sensitive being and you are affected by everything around you. So if they say nice things about you it gives you confidence, if they say nasty things it attacks your confidence. I work in a world of illusion. I film, I do plays, I create illusions or am part of that process, and I am therefore viewed partly as an illusion. Most people, who think they know me, see me on a very large screen in a cinema or in their sitting room, and that makes them feel things about me which bear no relation to me personally and how I am. So their perception of me is inaccurate, I know that, whether it be good or bad. Therefore their judgment of me is not to be considered.

Where do you think are the major inaccuracies in the public's view of you?

That I am a film star. That I am therefore a rich, larger-than-life person who lives a very glamorous and fast life. That's one perception. Another perception is that I am very English and cold and arrogant and cool, all the typical English qualities.

And you are saying there is no hint of truth in any of that?

I think I am made up of a myriad of colours which I use both in my work and in my life. Real people are much more complicated than the characters one is asked to play in most drama, and I probably am much more complicated than people imagine me to be. I think we all are. We tend to live in a world of black and white values, a tabloid world of soundbites where there is not really time to get to know anything very deeply, whether it be a political problem or a person, and so we tend to categorize people fairly simply, which is why something like this book might be quite interesting.

The parts that you play are layered. Do you choose particular kinds of characters?
Is part of the secret of your success the choice of parts that you make?

I don't think the secret of my success, if there is a secret, or if indeed I am successful...

You doubt whether you are successful?

Sometimes I am successful. I am like a darts player. When I hit the bull I am successful, but that is only for that dart. Then there are the other darts which miss the bull.

Is that common to the entire acting profession?

I think we are made up of the sum of our work. Fortunately, people tend to forget about the work that is less good and remember, the things that are appreciated. Now those characters, those films, those plays are appreciated because they happen when they happen, and they are seen by whom they are seen. One of the secrets of life is timing. If I look at the work I have done, it answered a need that was there at the time, I think.

So you were in the right place at the right time?

I think so. You see a lot of people who aren't. There are often people who are ahead of their time, sometimes film-makers are ahead of their time and aren't appreciated by the general public. But if you get the timing right, then you can be appreciated. You see it with politicians; the right person at the right time in the right place.

And as you go through life, trying, can you make your own luck, or are you almost totally the victim of circumstance?

I don't know if you can make your own luck. All my life I have been lucky, until recently when I had three disasters – wham, wham, wham – hit me, and that made me question whether I was a lucky person still. I think luck can come and go.

What were those disasters?

They were personal disasters. They were all things which, just for little reasons, made three big things happen. Two deaths and a very near death – two road accidents and a dog being killed. Three things which needed coincidences to happen. You suddenly feel someone's pointing at you, maybe. But up until then I had always felt very, very lucky.

How did you pull yourself back to the equilibrium you need in order to move forward?

I am doing that at the moment. I know intellectually what I have to do, and your asking that question reminds me again. When I was a student I would be driving the car and it would be running like a dream – I used to look after the engine in those days – and I would think, 'God, this is wonderful, this motor car.' Then I would think, 'Wait a minute, it's going to break down soon', and sure enough it would. The philosophy I developed to deal with those setbacks was that it was a toughening process, that every bad thing that happens to you toughens you, it hones you. I think that what happened to me recently is that things had been going very well for me for too long. Perhaps I needed to be brought up short, to be honed further. Do you understand what I mean?

Mandela is a classic example. What would he have been, had he not had those years of imprisonment? Would he have been such a great man? Would he have had such time to strengthen his resolve, to think? I somehow doubt it. So in a much lesser way I welcome the difficult things in life. The things that go wrong, the things that don't work properly. As far as performances are concerned, I am almost happier with a bad review than a good one, as if a good review makes you relax your stomach muscles, yet you know that the fist is going to slam in at some point, so you need to be ready for it.

Is there an area, as an actor or an actress, where you can be so consumed with a succession of good reviews that you lose the ability to toughen yourself – you become soft and therefore your potential for future success is compromised?

Yes. Though I would put it a little differently. What happens is you lose your nerve to risk. The more you are praised and appreciated, you cannot but help believe it a little bit. However much you have that little 'I-don't-believe-it' element in you – you cannot help thinking, 'I must have something that works. People come and see my work, they like it. They all say I am great.' But part of you knows that that's all rubbish. It's just the various things that come together over which you have no control. So what you are encouraged to do is not to risk, because you don't want to lose acclaim. You don't quite know what it is, but you try to keep doing the same thing, not rocking the boat, making the same sorts of decisions about what you do, working with the same sorts of people, in case everything tumbles down and you are seen for what you are, which is a charlatan.

Do you think everyone is a charlatan in some way?

I think many people feel a charlatan, except those who are extremely self-convinced. That, then, is the danger, and of course as soon as you stop risking then something dies in your work, because you have to have the bravery to fail in order to have the possibility of succeeding. And if you are watching your tail all the time, and worrying about what people will think, you will never really do great work.

What if you take the risk and it doesn't work?

If you've done it for the right reasons, then you just say, 'Oh well, it didn't work.' The worst thing is if you do something for the wrong reasons and it doesn't work. If you do it for money or you do it for the fame, or you do it because that is what you think people expect of you, then you can't excuse yourself, you have to say, 'I didn't believe I should have done it – I should have listened to myself.' I suppose that is who I try to listen to. I try to listen to my instinct. I am not a very intellectual person, but I try to listen to what my body and my mind tell me and do that, often not knowing why. There are days when you think, 'I would love an orange.' Your body's telling you it wants an orange. OK, why? Maybe it's because you haven't had an orange for a bit. In a way I accept my work like that, so sometimes if people ask me to do a job I say, 'I don't want to do it, but ask me in a year's time if you haven't done it by then, because I might have changed my mind.'

So it is the instinct of the moment?

It is. I suppose I am sometimes a little cannier than that. For instance, with *Brideshead* I knew that I needed a television series to get my name known. I wanted something fairly classy and I thought *Brideshead* might be that. And it did, and more, and at the same time I started making films, so the two things really built together.

Going back to your childhood, to what extent has your success been shaped by your background and your upbringing?

I was brought up with a great love of the countryside, the sea, sailing and riding, in the Isle of Wight. I was the third child. My brother and sister were at boarding school, so I spent a lot of time on my own. Then I went off to boarding school and probably continued on my own. I have never been a group person. I didn't find that most people I was at school with were the sort of people I could open up to. I went through that until I was about 17 and then left and knew that I wanted to be in a career which kept me outside the stream, so to speak. I wanted to be an observer, a watcher, someone who could pack his bags and move on without anybody noticing or minding. I thought acting would give me that, and indeed it has done. It's allowed me to remain an outsider, and it's strange that now that I am, so to speak, becoming middle-aged and successful, people are asking me to sit on committees and be on boards of governors. That's what I became an actor to get away from. And yet, I find myself thinking I should be giving back, and that is a way of giving back. But there are other ways, of course, of giving back, and I try to choose them. I want to remain an outsider. I think theatre and drama at their best should kick against the pricks and make people examine their complacencies. So my instinct is still not to join the club.

Do you regard life as going through a series of stages, each of which requires you to act in one way or another? Is there a real Jeremy Irons or do you wake up and say, 'Today I am going to put on this particular character'?

I think there probably is. I hope there is and I hope that is what you are getting now. When I talk to the media my instinct is to protect myself, to cover myself with a persona, (a) because they expect something interesting, and (b) because I don't, in a way, want them to see my nakedness. And yet this sort of interview is different because it is more considered. I suppose to a certain extent one girds one's loins to do various things, and if that is covering oneself and becoming slightly different, if that is acting, then yes, maybe I do that in any situation where I am not completely comfortable. And that means most of the time. Going back to your previous question about my upbringing, there was (a) that feeling I wanted to remain outside, and (b) I had a very hard-working father who was a chartered accountant; he was a bit of a workaholic and from him I learned what hard work was all about and what commitment was all about.

Later on, when I had left theatre school and I was working as a stage manager at the Old Vic in Bristol, I used to get asthma from all the dust around. I remember sweeping the stage after the show and going to bed at one o'clock, and then at five o'clock every morning I would wake up with wheezes and take ephedrine, which you used to get then, and I would drift off in wonderful sleep and wake around nine. I remember doing that night after night. Fortunately I grew out of it, but I remember talking to the principal of the theatre school and I said, 'This is not what I joined the theatre for. I am sweeping the bloody stage, I am holding up the scenery, I'm painting stuff. I can't do this. I want to act.' There was a pause, and then he said, 'Soldier on Jerry, soldier on.' And that was the best advice I have ever had. Just keep going; the ones that keep going, get there.

Does it help in the acting profession to have gone in on the ground floor like that, to have experienced what it is like when you are not the star, when you are just part of the supporting cast? By cast I mean all the back-up team and so on, who are involved in the production. Do you think you are a better actor because you have seen it from the grass roots?

I don't think you are necessarily a better actor. I am sure you are a better person, a better professional, because you understand the workings. Remember that book, *Zen and the Art of Motorcycle Maintenance?* It is something I am a great believer in: being aware how it all works. Sitting in this room, I can't upholster, but I can do almost everything else that is required to make this room, and so I can see what's gone into it. And it's the same if you are working on a film or in the theatre; having gone through the workings, you know the value of everybody's input, not just your own value. You know your own value in proportion to the others, and that's terribly important. It makes you humble.

And because you know all that, does that at times make you want to take total control, perhaps even from the director?

Not in theatre. In film, if you lose confidence in the director, that can happen. I have just directed a 50-minute film about Bosnian refugees for Channel 4 Children's Television. It is written by a Dutchman called Ad de Bont and called *Mirad – A Boy from Bosnia.* It is basically two people telling a story. I wanted to find a visual way of, so to speak, illustrating, or just allowing the viewer to have something to watch while he was listening to the story. That was interesting. I have been saying for a few years that I must direct, because I love the process of a group of people being together telling a story. There is no story that needs more people than a film story: the designers, the carpenters, the voice coaches, the movement coaches, the actors, the electricians, the riggers, all those people who are really good at their jobs, all doing their best, all working longer hours for less money than they should do, because they care. When that happens it is the most wonderful thing – it's rather what I want to happen to England; if only we could find someone to make us care. The fact that I happen to be an actor in that process is relatively unimportant to me. I just love being part of it. A director may be asked more questions than other people, he has to supply cohesion. If, when you are working on a unit as an actor and things are not going well, you do tend, as I have in the past, to overstep your bounds as an actor and try to step in to help. But it's tricky.

Did you win?

It's not a question of winning or losing. It's a question of making the work as good as possible. The actor can never be in full control because he is not there at the edit. The actor's function is to create the raw material for the director to knit together into a film. You depend on his talent enormously.

Did you think of giving up acting at any stage?

I was giving myself until I was 30. I knew I wasn't very talented. At theatre school I showed no talent. I could wear clothes well, which is quite useful on the stage, though I remember someone saying to me, 'Don't turn sideways because you disappear, you are so thin. Try and keep front on to the audience.'

But when you were scrubbing floors, when you were playing the guitar outside cinemas, when you were working as a gardener, as you went through all these different jobs which you were doing while you were trying to be an actor, did you not think to yourself, This is a hopeless cause? What was it that made you think that you could still, despite all that, make it?

That period of working as a domestic and a gardener was when I came to London. I had been acting in the provinces for three years and I knew I had to do either a film or a West End show, because I had seen colleagues who had continued in the reps and I could see that it was very difficult to hold down a marriage, which was something I wanted in life. It was very difficult to hold on to a mortgage because you were always having to rent a second home in the provinces, and I thought,' I don't think that way is for me – what I must do is to get known in London.' I came to London but I didn't have work, so I went down to Lisson Grove to the dole office. But as I stood waiting in line, I thought,' I cannot bear this. I am able to do almost anything. I have my wits, I have my health, I have no dependants. I have no right to be standing here asking for a handout.' So I left. Didn't pick up my cheque, didn't even sign on. I joined up with a domestics agency, and I would go and clean houses, meanwhile auditioning all the time, sometimes getting the jobs, but not accepting ones that took me out of London. Auditioning is a horrible thing, it's like acting cold, but I thought, 'I just have to do this – I hate it, but I have to do it.' And eventually after about six months of doing that and keeping body and soul together by house cleaning and gardening, I got a job in *Godspell*, which was a new American musical coming to town. That began to get the ball rolling for me in London. But I always knew why I was doing that gardening. I was doing that gardening so that I wouldn't have to go off and do acting jobs that I didn't rate just to earn money.

So you had to take a stand on principle at some early stage. You don't as an ambitious actor or actress, accept anything that's going for you, anything that comes along, regardless of how menial your circumstances might be at the time?

No. Somebody once said to me, 'Imagine you are carrying in the palm of your hand a jewel. It's what you have, it's your talent. It might be big or it might be small, whatever, but that's what you have, and you have to guard that and not be profligate with it, not show it off, guard it and polish it and use it when the time is right.' So, don't do things just for money, don't do things which will destroy your confidence or your *amour propre* or your pride, if you like. Because standing on stage and saying, 'I am,' demands a certain amount of pride.

You can see those actors who have hung on to that and those actors who have lost it. Early on, I didn't want to do commercials. Later in my career I remember being offered, just before I did *Brideshead*, enough money for a day's work to give my son a private education.

What was that?

It was a television commercial, for sherry I think. I had already done one – the first commercial I ever did – and everybody said to me, 'You were great in that commercial.' I thought, 'Too many people have seen this.'

Too many?

It was, after all, only a commercial – they were not saying, 'You were great in that play,' it was, 'Great in that commercial.' As an actor when you walk onto a stage or through a door into a casting office or onto a screen, you are the sum of all work that that audience has seen you in. Now if a lot of people are saying, 'I enjoyed you in that commercial,' then there is much too much of that in your aroma, too much of the smell of that commercial, to mix metaphors. So when I was asked to do a sequel, I said no.

Later, I was talking to my producer on *Brideshead* about this, and he said, 'That's very interesting. The lady we wanted for Lady Marchmain had just done an After Eight ad, and the powers that be at Granada had decided not to use her.' So I realized the importance of choice.

How important are your wife and your family as a contribution to your success? A lot of people feel that their job is in competition with their family; some people choose to give their job priority, others their family. Do you feel that there are any failures there, any sacrifices that you had to make in order to be professionally successful?

I try to avoid regret. It seems, like envy, such a destructive emotion. I think I would have liked more children and I think had Sinead and I not been so busy professionally in our thirties and for the next 15 years, we might have had more. So that is a slight regret as I get older, but as for regret about not being with my children enough, I don't have that, because although I go away for long periods, sometimes I take them with me. In the past, when they were younger, it was easier to do and we had great experiences together. I am sorry that as an actor, I am probably rather more self-absorbed than I should be, and I am perhaps a little more selfish than I should be. I thrive on difficulty, and the difficulty of running a marriage and a family or trying to hold it together probably feeds me. Sinead has always said to me, 'If you had an easy wife you would be bored.' So if I had an easy marriage and an easy job, a nine-to-five job, home every night, I probably would be bored.

But it is important, whatever job you do, whether it is acting or not, to have the right kind of family support – is that the key ingredient of success? Whether it be the difficulty that you thrive on or whether it be someone who is basically making sure that supper's there when you get home in the evening.

I don't think that if I was a single man without a family I would be able to go out and fight the way I do for my work. My home and my family are like a castle, and when I am there I pull up the drawbridge, and then when I go off to work the drawbridge comes down and I come out on a brilliant white charger at speed, drive into the enemy and create havoc. Then I gallop back in and pull up the drawbridge and think, 'God, I did it!' If I didn't have that castle and that drawbridge and that wife with a long white whatnot sitting in her tower waiting for me, I don't think I could be brave enough.

So you are summoning up courage when you go out to act, then you are breathing a sigh of relief when you come back home to a familiar environment?

Yes. I feel I am going into no-man's-land when I am creating a character – I find it very difficult.

What is the secret of getting under the skin of a character?

I have to find something that touches me. I remember when I played von Bulow, the character was difficult because he was alive and physically known and physically quite different from me, and not always likeable, an enigma. I had two televised interviews of him which I ran and re-ran, and suddenly, after watching it in the sitting room, I came out and said to Sinead, 'That's who it is, it's Dad!' Had that happened to him for whatever reason, had he been put into court and accused of trying to murder his wife, that is how he would react. He would use his charm, and of course I am very like him. So I thought that's how I would be. And slowly the process of metamorphosis began.

So you need that moment of identification, the recognition of something in a character. That is probably one of the reasons why you got the part in the first place, because people saw a certain similarity.

Perhaps, although it is hard to see a similarity between me and Claus von Bulow. It is the fact of an actor's life that people ask you to do things because they have seen you do similar things before. It is a constant battle to try to change people's perceptions of you.

And yet, the perceptions that got you work in the first place hold good for keeping you in work and keeping you successful. Why should you want to change this perception?

Because I don't like treading in footsteps that I have already trod.

But isn't there a tendency to characterize actors as being suitable for certain types of parts. Should every actor fight against that, to go on being successful, to maintain success in their lives?

There are horses for courses. Take an actor like the late David Niven. He played the charming Englishman all his life – he was a charming Englishman, a delightful man, witty and funny and liked. That's not for me, because I'm not witty, funny or nice. I get bored. I don't like telling stories and going to cocktail parties and being the life and soul of the party. I am only charming when I am nervous. There is a line in *Brideshead* where Anthony Blanche says to Charles, 'Charm is the great English blight. It spots and kills everything it touches.' I remember when I was rehearsing a play with Harold Pinter, after about a week's rehearsal he said, 'Jeremy, do you think there is anything more to this character than charm?' There was nothing charming about the character at all! I think I have whittled away at my natural charm, really from very early on in my career, because I distrusted it, I disliked how it made people think of me – the lightness in it. I have a feeling that is why I have become a little bit spiky, which I never used to be. I want to get away from that 'charming Englishman' image that I once had.

Are you ever tempted to put a layer of charm back into your public persona, having achieved with it what you have?

I think it's lost for ever.

Not as we are talking now.

Perhaps it's there; but going back to the question about whether you can actually get out of the mould in which people see you, I think you can to some extent. I could never be in competition with Bob Hoskins or Sylvester Stallone, but I can try to widen my brief as much as physically possible. After *Brideshead* and *French Lieutenant's Woman* I waited a year before I worked, and I then played a Polish builder.

Was that out of choice?

Yes. All I was being offered were charming Englishmen and I knew that would be my graveyard – playing Noel Coward all my life in the West End, or Terence Rattigan. I have got to find something quite different. So eventually I accepted this part. I spoke no English, just spoke Polish. Some years later, at a party in Australia, I met Werner Herzog, an German director. He said, 'You are Jeremy Irons?' I said yes. He said, 'No – you are not, you are English!' I said, 'Yes.' He said, 'Jeremy Irons is 'Polish.' I said, 'No, he's not, actually, it's me.' I thought, That's great, that's really being European and confusing them.' I suppose it is my instinct to keep an audience interested and to want to try not to let them know what to expect from me. Perhaps it makes me less successful.

Less successful?

Yes, because I think really successful film actors are actors who trade on what an audience loves in them.

Who are your heroes? Who are the people you really admire, past or present, as having been incredibly successful?

People I admire I have never heard of. That is why I admire them. I admire all those people who have done their best and never been thanked for it and never been recognized. I don't admire those people who have had public acclaim, because that's enough; anyone can be brilliant if they are being applauded. I admire those people that we don't know about and yet who are doing great work.

Who do you think are the most successful actors and actresses of all time?

I used to look at Laurence Olivier and think his was the fullest career. When he came into the business, it was a very fertile time, a time when movies were fertile, when theatre was very fertile, and if you read his biography or you know him at all – I used to know him a bit – you are just staggered by the bulk of work and experience he had. And yet, you read him saying, when he was making some movie in New York in the 1960s, 'If I had my time again I would have done it differently,' and you realize how unhappy he was and you think, 'Well that's not the answer.' So, ten years ago I would have said Marlon Brando, but now I look at Marlon Brando and think, 'Is that the man I want to become?' No. I think probably the person is Ralph Richardson, because he didn't have the stature of a leading man and yet would move audiences tremendously. He had the humility, at the age of about 70, when his lines were beginning to go, to accept a contract at the National to play as cast, which meant they would give him whatever parts they wanted. That's what you do when you are starting out. He had the humility to do that. He never lost the child-like quality that I think actors must always hang on to. He never took himself too seriously. I think that probably he was loved by his wife all his life. He rode a motorbike, strangely enough, like me, and I think Ralph is the guy.

Do you think that for all actors and actresses it is impossible to maintain a pinnacle of success? In a sense, does every actor and actress in some way or other end up as Marlon Brando has?

I think so, and not just actors and actresses.

But it is particularly hard to bear with actors and actresses, because you have hit the heights in such a spectacular way – anything after that can be a let-down.

Depending on your attitude, yes. I think you have to understand that there are peaks and troughs in a career, that the public is fickle, that fashions change, that people like new faces, people like youth, people get bored; on your side, you change, you get bored. Of course things can't remain the same, which is why I think in order to be truly successful it is important to know what you want from life. And if you have that, then whether you are on the screen or on television or in the theatre, it doesn't matter, because your life is all right. That's the secret. I sometimes look at these money guys and think, 'You've got that because you like the fight, but now you are very rich, do you still have that fight?' Maybe some do, maybe Maxwell went off the side of that boat laughing, maybe he had a great time. I don't know: maybe those riches become like a millstone round your neck.

It is an interesting question to ask, 'What is success?', because our youngsters need something to look up to. What is it these days? It's not our politicians – they are made fools of nightly on television. Not our monarchy – that has been made a fool of. Is it our rich people? Is it the transient success that people get from doing soap operas on the telly, or being in rock groups? I don't think there is anything for our kids to look up to, and until we can create a society which has leaders valued by all of us as being people that we should emulate, then I think our youngsters will be directionless.

How do you think you achieve that? You talked about the small people you admired. So there are successes happening. There are role models. They just perhaps don't have the prominence that might give young people a chance to say, 'That's what I want to be, that's what I want to do.'

Maybe we have to think in much smaller terms, because certainly our social institutions seem to have collapsed. The family has been taxed out of viable existence for most people – well, the two-parent families have been – teachers have been laughed out of court, politicians have been laughed out of court, the church has become completely irrelevant. So where are the structures that bind us together?

And yet there are people we still look up to, who we regard as being successful, right across the professions.

I wish you were right.

Why are some actors successful and others not?

I think some actors move an audience. A performance depends on the audience and their receptiveness, but I think there is an element of communication between an actor and the audience beyond the words. I describe myself as an actor, and it is my job to pass the writer's message through clearly to the audience. I think some actors are just better transmitters, so to speak. How they are in their personal lives also adds to it, and so if they are interesting people they are more likely to be interesting actors. For some actors, even though they are very intelligent or they have done huge research or they look wonderful, something blocks that transmission between the seed of the author's idea and it getting into the audience's hearts or heads.

So what advice would you give to young people in the acting profession. What should they do to end up as successful as you have been?

I think if they believe they have talent, they must nurture it, like a gardener with a plant: watch it, weed it, cultivate it, and not listen to anybody else. Rather, listen to everybody, but filter what they say: decide whom you believe and whom you want to listen to, and keep nurturing and nurturing that talent and doing everything to encourage it to grow and strengthen. Don't look for easy success. Try to decide where you are aiming for in 40 years and how you will best get to that, and then, of course, soldier on.

When your time comes to leave this life, what would you like people to say about Jeremy Irons?

Well, I don't know if they will say it, but I would love them to say, 'He stirred the shit.'

SIR CAMERON MACKINTOSH

At the age of 19 he was a £14-a-week cleaner and stagehand at the Theatre Royal, Drury Lane. He sees that as part of an essential learning curve that turned him into a showman now widely regarded as the most successful and powerful theatrical producer in the world. At school, where his productions earned him the nickname 'Daryl F.' Mackintosh (after the great Hollywood producer), he lied about relatives being ill so he could slip off to the theatre. He went to study management at the Central School of Speech and Drama. Clearly bored by 'too much theory', he was asked to leave after one year, took a holiday job in a West End theatre, and did it so well he was asked to stay on. He was producing by the age of 20, which he admits was 'probably too early'. A full year's work on Anything Goes *went down the drain when it folded after just two weeks. He recalls 'sobbing in the stalls bar' until the impresario Lord Delfont came up and said, 'If you get through this, you will survive in our business.' Another effort – a stage production of the radio hit soap* Mrs Dale's Diary *– left him £15,000 in debt, and he stopped producing for a while.*

But he learns 'as much from my failures as from my successes', and before long he was back in business with the box office hits Oliver, My Fair Lady *and* Oklahoma. *The public flooded to see his production of* Les Misérables, *despite initial bad reviews, and* Phantom of the Opera *reinforced his reputation for spectacular staging and effects. Some put part of his success down to a phenomenal talent for PR and marketing. But he says here, 'You can only market something that the public want – if it's a turkey you can't sell it.' So what makes a successful musical? 'I never react to ideas, I react to the author's realization of that idea. You have to smell the story through the music.' He urges aspiring producers to 'fly by their instinct and passion – never put the show on for the audience, always put on what you believe. Do it as well as you can, and then, if it's good enough, the audience will follow.' He says that success should never stop you taking gambles or 'you kill the very thing that made you successful in the first place' and 'anyone driven by the critics makes a big mistake'. His advice to young hopefuls is to 'get experience of as many aspects of working in the theatre as possible. I know several producers who used to be teaboys!'*

Sir Cameron, what is your definition of success?

Success is something I never think about. I've always wanted to follow my heart, and my instincts that something I want to work on is original and worth the years of work that I know lie ahead to bring it to fruition. I suspect that one of the reasons why I might be a success is because I've never wanted to define it. When I was a kid and I told everybody I was going to be a producer, they all looked slightly suspiciously at this little bombastic child. My idea then of success was to have a show put on in London one day, and if it was really terrific, maybe one day on Broadway. But I didn't quantify what that success was.

In fact the few odd times in my life when I started to be successful in financial terms, for example during the 1970s, when shows actually started to make money, as opposed to losing it, I would think, 'Oh, well, I might make an amount of money, and that will pay off this debt or that debt.' But usually my fortune-telling was so hopeless that I discovered that I was trying to bank on things that actually weren't going to happen. And after a couple of times of doing this I thought, 'Don't worry about what it might make. If it makes it, fine, but don't try and foretell what your fortune is going to be.'

So do you think it is a handicap to say to yourself, at the start of your working life, or even earlier, 'I want to be a success'? Is it much better to have a clear focus on a particular career path, and if success comes, then it is incidental?

That's true. What I think you need is a wish to succeed. Achieving success is an unquantifiable notion – indeed, success carries with it an aura of money and power, and things like that, which – certainly for me – would be detrimental.

And yet you have money and power.

Yes, but I'm usually the last one to be aware of it, it's only when I have to dig my feet in and say, 'I'm not prepared to do this.' I'll have an artistic fight. And then I suddenly read that I'm described as an 800-pound gorilla or Mack the Knife. I think, 'God, that's what some people think of me!'

But money and success give you the power to, as you said, dig your heels in and take key decisions, be in control of key decisions, to an extent that you wouldn't otherwise be?

Money obviously gives anybody independence, and independence allows you to be a free spirit. Certainly when Andrew Lloyd Webber suggested to me, in the mid 1980s, that we went public together and floated, I did look into it. The final reason I didn't is that I thought, 'Actually I've got more than enough money, and what I don't want to ever have to do is sacrifice my independence.' Because even when I was working for other people, for very short periods of time, I've always managed to retain my independence. I've been blessed with that all my life. I've really been able to do what I've wanted, and, when my younger brothers were living in much nicer accommodation than me and had houses and cars, I still insisted on not spending personally more than I had – even when I was producing big musicals like *My Fair Lady* and *Oliver!* in the West End, I lived in a £7-a-week flat.

Why did you do that, when you didn't have to?

It was very important to know that, if the worst came to the worst, I could live, and pay my phone bill, on a hundred quid a week. I had my wits about me, I didn't have to earn £500 a week, or £300 a week, pay a mortgage, run expensive cars. I could still catch the tube. I lived in the heart of the West End, I could get to the theatres, I could get to auditions.

For much of my time during the 1970s, I couldn't afford the rail fare to go and see my shows. It was too expensive so I'd pile into my car and drive four hours to Cardiff or Liverpool, or six hours to Glasgow, and see my show. It was the only way I could afford to do it. I was knackered at night and I used to find myself drifting by the side of the road and having to have a kip for an hour or two. But that was all part of growing up and part of having to stretch a pound to be a fiver, because I didn't have it. When I was starting, I was doing some tour, *Murder at the Vicarage* or something like that. When I lived in Maida Vale, I had to go to Lisson Grove National Insurance Office very early, in order to get there immediately it opened to get my dole money, because I knew that the actors would be there at 9.30 or 10 o'clock, collecting theirs. And I had to get out before the actors saw their producer was also on the dole.

Is that something every successful person ought to find a way of doing, to keep their feet on the ground? Because the danger with success is that if it happens to bring a high degree of prosperity, you could lose touch with your roots.

I would hate to say that about everybody, but I know that for me it's absolutely vital. My fortune has been made by the general public, and I know damn well that to pay £30 to see a show of mine in the West End, or on tour, is a vast amount of money to some people. A lot of them will have to judge what they are going to buy in their groceries that week, what they'll spend on clothes. The theatre is a special occasion like an anniversary dinner, and they save up for something like that. I do feel that if I don't occasionally go shopping for myself and don't know what the price of milk and butter is, I could easily forget what it is that ordinary members of the public have to cope with in order to keep me in the style I'm accustomed to. As far as it's humanly possible, I try and do what everybody else does.

Are there any general characteristics of a successful person?

I think I should ask you that question. You're the person that's actually been interviewing successful people.

But do you identify any? Because successful people talk to successful people. Are there any core characteristics that you could identify?

The very successful people – entrepreneurial people like Steven Spielberg or David Geffen, or of course Andrew Lloyd Webber – have a genuine passion for what they're creating. The thing that actually makes us get up in the morning to create success, I think, is very similar. We do it because we genuinely, honestly believe in it. That's the spur.

It's either there or it's not?

Yes. Particularly in the theatre, the people who've always been successful from time immemorial, are those who've got up in the morning and have had to do what they do. And they do it whether they've got no money or they've got huge amounts of money, they're driven. It's a calling. I've always thought that that moment for me, when I was eight, was when Julian Slade, instead of patting me on the head and saying, 'What a nice little boy, here's my autograph,' took me on the stage to show me how the magic piano was mimed to match what he was playing in the orchestra pit. And how the magic flying saucer was actually wired, and how the trees moved. It was my Road-to-Damascus moment.

And originally you didn't want to go to watch this musical – Salad Days *– at all?*

No, I did like going to the theatre and all of that, but I thought singing and dancing was cissy, until the magic piano in the show got me dancing as well. And then, of course, from that moment on I was singing and dancing wherever I was – rather embarrassingly, in shops sometimes.

How did you meet Julian Slade?

When I was still seven I'd been taken – about three months after it opened – by my aunts to see the show and I absolutely loved it. And then on my birthday, my mother and my aunts took me back. By that time I had understood that the man playing the piano in the pit was Julian Slade, who'd written it. So I just walked down the aisle and said who I was. He just said, 'Hello, I'm so glad you liked it,' and started chatting with me. 'Would you like to go backstage? Would you like to see how it all works?' and that's how it was.

Was your passion for musical theatre encouraged at school?

Well, it was allowed at school. In fact my school, Prior Park College in Bath, had an incredible reputation for staging plays, with a wonderful old drama teacher called Hedley Goodhall, but the year I went to Prior Park they stopped it, because they'd run out of money. So, as soon as I was able to, when I was about 13 or 14, I started the Prior Park Review, and my nickname at school was Daryl F. Mackintosh, after the famous film producer Daryl Zanuck. And so my earliest programmes were, 'Daryl F. Macintosh presents the Prior Park Annual College Review.' I used to start selling tickets at a cut rate on the first day of the autumn term. And so I would raise enough capital to be able to hire things – lamps for the stage and so on.

So the entrepreneurial instincts were in evidence at that early age?

There was no doubt what I was going to do. Everybody knew it. And I used to invent things – I had more dying aunts who were terminally ill, my housemaster said, than anyone else in the entire school. Curiously, their illnesses occurred whenever there was an interesting first night in Bristol or Bath or, occasionally, London. And I used to have to go mournfully, and they went, 'Somebody else is dying in the family?' 'Yes.' 'Enjoy it,' they'd mutter.

When you left school, you went to the Central School of Speech and Drama, did a management course, and you were asked to leave after one year. Now why was that?

They asked me to leave because they could see that in theoretical classes – the history of drama, and so on – my eyes would glaze over. All I wanted to do was get the show on, and also they had some teachers then who felt that stage managers should be very stern and use tremendous discipline, whereas the way I used to get my shows on was sidle up and charm everybody. They didn't feel it was the way that you should do it. And one teacher said to me, 'You've got the smarmy ways of a front-of-house manager,' and I said, 'Oh, well, that can't be helped.' So they said, 'We can't teach you anything else, you're not interested in all the historical side, we reckon that you should just get on and go into theatre.'

Did you regard this as a setback?

No. I thought, 'I'm going to go into the theatre.' So I went on holiday and whilst on holiday I said, 'Well, I've been telling everybody I'm going to be a producer but I wasn't expecting to do it this year – I'd better go and get myself a job.' So I went back to London and walked round all the West End theatres in order of the shows I would like to work on – the ones I would deign to actually watch from the wings. Sixteenth on my list was *Camelot* at Drury Lane, which I'd already seen and I wasn't that taken with. I went in one morning in August. 'Have you got a job?' 'No.' So I was walking back down the street, about to go to the next theatre, when the prop man ran after me and said, 'We've got a holiday job – will you do eight shows a week?' Most people only wanted to do seven, not the mid-week matinée. I said, 'Of course,' so I went in. It was a two-week job, but they thought I was jolly good and they kept me on permanently. And then I ended up loving *Camelot* and working on the show. I worked in most of the back-stage departments, and when it was coming to the end of its run, and there was going to be a tour, I wanted to be one of the ASMs, but there was a problem. In the famous joust scene there was a sort of mechanical horse, like a pedal car, with a Camelotian horse on top. And one time I had gone across the stage, during a peformance at Drury Lane, I hadn't looked properly, and I'd hit the proscenium arch and got out of the horse, in front of 2,000 people. So they reckoned that I was a little short-sighted, or certainly too short, so as a result I never got the job on the tour. But at the same time I discovered that they were going to do a tour of *Oliver!* and one Friday night I rang up Ann Jenkins, who was the general manager for producer Donald Albury, and I said to her, 'You've got to give me this job, I want this job, I love *Oliver!* I must have this job!' And she said, 'Well, all right, darling,' she said, 'come round and see me on Monday morning.' On the Monday morning I spent from ten till one o'clock just telling her what I was going to do.

Is there a limit to the amount of chutzpah that you can use to push yourself and push your ideas, when you're right on the bottom rung of the ladder?

I don't think so. That long conversation with Ann Jenkins obviously impressed her, because that afternoon she sent me a contract round without ringing me, I didn't know I'd got the job, she just sent it. Four or five months into the run, I wrote her a very impertinent letter saying, 'I've enjoyed this immensely, I've learned everything I can. But I want to leave and do another show now.' And she wrote back, 'I'm very glad you've learned everything you can, but you haven't learned everything you can, you haven't learned to live out a contract. That will hold you in good stead, I'm not letting you out.' And, of course she was right.

Did your parents play an important role in encouraging you in your career or did they, at any stage, think, 'My God, we've got a son who wants to go into the theatre, what an appalling prospect, it's so full of risks'?

My parents backed me completely. My mother was a little concerned at the beginning, simply because it was the theatre and she had less experience of it. My father has always been a terrific supporter of me and my brothers, Robert and Nicky, partly because it is in his nature to do it, and partly because he was a brilliant jazz musician. He had to make a choice in the early 1950s, when the 'trad jazz' thing exploded, of either running the family business or being a jazz musician. He couldn't burn the candle at both ends, doing gigs up in Birmingham and coming back to run the business. Because he had to give it up himself and only played semi-professionally, I think he always wanted us to do what we wanted. There was never any question that he supported me to do that, and did everything he could to help me to go to Central.

What do you regard as your first big break?

The first big break! Well the first thing that actually made people realize that I might not be just another touring manager was undoubtedly *Side by Side* by Sondheim. That was a show which I didn't even see, though I was a slight catalyst to it coming on, in that Ned Sherrin had rung me to borrow the set of a show I was trying out in Brighton. He said, 'I want to do this show, which Julia McKenzie and Millicent Martin had put together with David Kernan, can we use your set?' I said, 'Fine.' A few days later I'd heard it had gone very well and soon every producer in the world went to see it. Most of them loved it but said it would close during the previews because who'd want to see Sondheim anyway? Eventually I sent two friends of mine, Christopher Biggins and one of my old backers, George Borwick, to see it. I was staying at another producer's flat in the Dakota Building in New York, and in the early hours of the morning I got a call from them, absolutely pissed, at the showcase party saying, 'It's marvellous, it's marvellous,' and they explained to me. They said, 'You must do it.' George, who never used to give me more than £200, offered me £1,000 for it. I said, 'Tell me what the show is,' and he told me it was a collection of songs. Then I said, 'Well, what's the set like?' 'It's four bar stools and two grand pianos.' 'I'll do it,' I said. And that's how I came to do *Side by Side* – and that show went around the world. And I'd been doing *Godspell* at the same time and that took off, too.

Let me ask you about Anything Goes *because you had a bit of a nightmare there when everyone walked out. It was, to put it bluntly, a financial disaster. How bad was that for you and how did you recover from it?*

Well, the basic nature of the failure of *Anything Goes* was that I was far too inexperienced.

Trying to do too much too early?

Yes, though my instinct wasn't completely wrong. I'd been bowled over by the score, but it taught me something later – it doesn't matter how good the score is, if the book's no good, the show isn't going to work. Not in these days unless it's a star vehicle. But I had originally decided to do the show – a small show – to go to the Duke of York's Theatre, where it might have had a better success, but on the wide open plains of the Saville Theatre, a big 1,500-seat theatre, every weakness in the show was exposed. And it just wasn't well enough done. I'd got some very good people involved, but the end result just wasn't good enough. It had taken a year's work to get on so when it came off in two weeks, I was absolutely heartbroken.

Did you feel, 'End of my career'?

No, I didn't feel that, because Richard Mills – he was running the theatre for Bernard Delfont – came to see me as I was in the stalls bar sobbing, and he said, 'Look, Cameron, you may not want to hear this now, but if you get through this, you will survive in our business, and I have to tell you, 25 years ago I had an almost identical conversation with Bernard Delfont, in exactly the same place. Take this in your stride.' And so, I did.

And it was after that, and the failure of a musical based on *Mrs Dale's Diary*, I decided I needed to get more experience. I thought, 'I cannot carry on as a producer for the moment,' so I took off, and I went and got a job as a company manager and publicity manager of *Hair*. I was still working in the theatre, but I was working for someone else.

And was that a tough decision to take?

No, it was a very easy decision. I knew that I'd gone as far as I could at this stage. I had probably started to produce too early. My original game-plan, when I strode into Drury Lane as a stagehand, was I'd do stagehand for a bit, then I'd become an acting ASM, then I'd become a DSM, then I'd become a stage manager, company manager. By the time I was 25 I'd be ready to be a producer. The fact is I was producing when I was 20.

How did you recover from those two failures?

I have a natural bouncy resilience – that's the nicest way of putting it, anyway! But the fact is, my family, an ordinary middle-class family, didn't have a huge amount of money, just enough to bring us up nicely, send us to public school and take us on holiday. And yet, we always knew that we had a comfortable home to go to. Therefore all the things that went wrong, particularly with *Anything Goes*, left me assuming that this was the sort of thing that usually happened. You know, the sets did fall down, the leading lady did run away, so I knew no better, I just thought, 'I'll chalk it up to experience.'

In general terms, do you believe in trying to sell as many tickets as possible before the show opens? Because some commentators say that that is what you do.

No, I don't. But they say that because they don't know what they're talking about. The fact is that once Andrew Lloyd Webber and I became known to be successful, that's what the press think we do. Of course, when anyone becomes successful in any sphere, you get your followers. *Cats* eventually opened with a £400,000 advance, which was good, but not fantastic. It was only two to three months backbone business. *Les Misérables* opened four years later with a small advance at the Barbican and then only £300,000 when it transferred to the Palace after eight weeks. Even though it did actually sell out at the Barbican. Even *Phantom of the Opera* only opened to £1 million, and that was with Michael Crawford who was already a very big television and stage star at that point. Then those shows went through the roof – and when the next two shows, at the end of the heady 1980s at the height of Thatchermania, people were throwing money at anything. The shows were *Aspects of Love*, which was Andrew's show, and *Miss Saigon*. They both opened to a £5 million advance, which was a lot of money.

Another thing that happened in this country, and it didn't really happen until *Phantom* proved to be an enormous success, was the phenomenon of the ticket tout. People were suddenly smelling that the theatre wasn't just something for the élite, but actually there was more money to be made scalping theatre tickets than there was for the Cup Final. The Cup Final happened once a year, but these shows were on eight times a week and they could make a fortune. And then suddenly tour operators discovered that they could have a fantastic business, and all they had to do was actually buy – legally or illegally – a block of tickets to one of these hit shows, and that they could put package deals with airlines, hotels, trips to London, and they could make a business out of it, and a new business built up marketing theatre breaks.

And that really coincided with your shows coming onto the stage?

They built it out of our shows. You look at any Sunday paper now, you look at many papers all around the world wherever our shows, or shows like ours are on; it is a completely different business that never existed before the mid-1980s. And that kind of frenzy was made by speculators not the general public, and caused these enormous advances to build up.

Do you go along with the view of one commentator that word of mouth makes a show critic-proof?

It does occasionally happen.

In other words, you can have a show that you believe to be good, the critics don't believe it to be good, but the audience are with you rather than the critics, and can override persistent criticism within the media?

That did happen with me with *Les Misérables*. The initial reviews were not good. We got four or five people who really stood up for it, but a lot of the reviews were very unselling reviews. However, the public, for some reason, voted with their feet. Most musicals open to 50-50 reviews, it's just the nature of the game, particularly if a musical is different from something the people have seen before. It's only the musicals that are traditional, like *42nd Street* or an *Annie*, that people go, 'We know what that is and therefore everyone can embrace it.' But I think that's been the same ever since Puccini and Verdi were at it, that's nothing new.

What makes a successful musical? What qualities, what ingredients do you need?

I never react to ideas. If you were to come and say, I would like to do a musical version of *Les Misérables* or *Possum's Book of Practical Cats*, I'd go, 'Fine, good luck to you.' I wouldn't do it. What I react to is the author's realization of that idea. A hell of a lot of shows – The *Phantom*'s a very good example – are in the public domain. *Les Mis* is in the public domain, there are four other different musical versions of that show around. Anyone can do *Martin Guerre*, there have been three *Martin Guerre* musicals in the last 18 months. All completely different.

What really makes them special is the author's viewpoint of the source material. Alan Jay Lerner was one of the first people approached to turn *Pygmalion* into a musical. He and Fritz Loewe worked on it for six months. Every single famous composer from Irving Berlin to Rodgers and Hammerstein were offered it, but they worked on it and they couldn't get anywhere with it. Oscar Hammerstein met Alan Jay Lerner at a benefit one night and said, 'How are you getting on? Dick and I couldn't do it, it just defied us, it doesn't belong on the musical stage, it's got no ingredient that is right for musicalization. It's a terrible idea, don't do it.' So then it languished. I mean nobody else wanted to do it, and suddenly, out of the blue, four years later, Lerner realized all the stumbling blocks were in fact the way into it. And very quickly he rang up to see if the rights were still available, and they were. And once they got the idea then they completed it over the next 18 months.

So you're actually saying the important thing is the story and the way it's written? The music is secondary?

The music is, of course, vitally important, but as Verdi said, when asked the secret of a great opera, 'A great libretto.' As Oscar Hammerstein also said when asked, 'What are the ingredients of a musical?' 'The book, the book, the book.' Particularly in a musical play as opposed to a musical comedy, in that both the music, lyrics and the book all have to have dramatic qualities. You have to smell the story through the music. I mean if you listen to *Les Misérables*, in a foreign language, you can still feel the story. That's what I responded to when I was first brought the original French concept album and I listened to three or four tracks.

What's the attraction of looking for a new show, alongside the revivals that you've been responsible for? Why try to do both when you could have, to be blunt, a more comfortable life just working on revivals?

Who says revivals are much easier to do? How many successful revivals have there been? There haven't been many.

So you think every musical, whether it is established or whether it is new, represents a challenge for the audience of the day?

The thing I can tell you about doing a revival, and particularly of a great show, is that it's bloody hard to wipe away the rosy-coloured memory people have of the original. What you have to try and do is recapture the spirit of the original because, quite frankly, you wouldn't be reviving it if the original wasn't any good. I'd say, 'What would Dick Rodgers and Oscar Hammerstein do now? They wouldn't try and do a Madame Tussaud's version of it, they would try and reinvent to get back to what they originally had.' And that's what I try and do with all the revivals, but, for every one that works, there's a hell of a lot that don't work, because they are just embalmed theatre.

Have you ever known failure?

Yes, of course.

How do you cope with it?

I accept it. I've learned as much from my failures as I have from my successes, because you should always learn from everything that you do.

But never be put off by those failures?

Absolutely not, because if you don't take a gamble, and every time you put on a show, or you write a book, or anything in the arts, particularly if it's something new, you're taking a gamble that some people are not going to like or appreciate it. If you don't do that, you kill the very thing that made you successful in the first place. I hope that if I get to the stage where I'm really frightened of failing, I'll have the good sense to stop.

How important is control?

The importance of control is being able to get the best out of everybody else. As a producer I can only talk about my job.

But do you believe in teamwork, in people coming together and chipping in ideas?

Absolutely. If you're employing really talented people, then it's madness not to allow them to take wing. What I find has happened to me a few times in my life is that I've had to exert extreme control because the directors want to do everything. Sometimes I find directors try to have an overbearing influence on a show. But on the other hand, unless you have a really strong director who can stand up to somebody like me, the show isn't any good either. So it's a balancing act, with quite a few arguments. Argument is good for theatre, because otherwise it makes theatre into a conveyor belt.

What's your view of the critics? What part do they play in determining whether a show is successful or not? Can a single comment make or break a show?

I don't think a single comment can make or break a show. We're very lucky in this country that we have 12 to 15 major critics, of which probably half are the key ones who highly influence the public's opinion of a show opening. And therefore the chances are that there will always be a divergence of opinion – which reflects the sort of rather eccentric nature of the British, anyway. We like to be idiosyncratic. But just as there are several examples of shows succeeding despite the fact the critics weren't wild about them, there are also examples – *City of Angels* was a good one recently – of the critics raving about a show and the public taking no notice of them and not going to see it, because they felt it wasn't for them.

So, in a sense, although you notice the critics, you're not driven by their comments?

No, I think anyone that is driven by a critic's comments makes a great mistake. However, often the criticisms are valid and are worth thinking about. The only time that I feel that the critics are wrong is when they come and criticize the show they expected to see, as opposed to the one they've actually seen. I think their job is to react to what they're seeing, not the book that it's based on, not the film, not the play they might have written themselves, but actually what the people have done there.

What are the greatest enemies of success?

I think self-satisfaction, belief in one's infallibility, misuse of power.

Has success changed you at all?

It must have changed me a bit. But the only reassurance for myself that I haven't changed too dramatically is that I still have exactly the same friends, mostly the same people that have worked for me for 25 or 30 years.

What's the greatest pleasure you've obtained from your successful career?

The greatest pleasure is partly growing up with people and enjoying the fruits of all our labours, and having fun doing it. I would say 90 per cent of all the time I've been working, we've all had a great laugh, and it still is a laugh. That's fantastic. And the other thing is knowing, if it doesn't sound too immodest, that my own passion and determination that what you see in London is mirrored anywhere else in the world. It has raised the standard of musical theatre around the world dramatically. Touring shows in America are no longer shabby copies of the Broadway original. And people can, with justifiable pride, say in Norway or Sydney or Copenhagen, 'Our production of *Les Misérables* or *Phantom* or *Saigon* is better than the one I saw in London.' That, to me, is the great satisfaction.

Who are the people that you put on the top of the tree, the people that Cameron Mackintosh admires for being successful? Past or present?

Certainly Steven Spielberg or David Geffen. They believe in what they do, and they are truly innovative artists. Steven's managed both to transform popular film-making, and at the same time achieve artistic greatness.

So from that, can we assume that innovation and risk are key ingredients in every successful person's life?

I think so, and originality – a love of doing something original. I have to say, I don't think about it that hard, I just go and do it. When Willie Russell was once being interviewed, and asked how he wrote his wonderful plays, he said, 'I don't know and I don't want to know, because if I did know I might stop doing it.' And I endorse that immediately.

If you could gather, in one room, all the young people in the world who say, 'I want to be as successful as Cameron Mackintosh,' what advice would you give them?

To work at anything that they felt that they could do, in order to gain experience. By working in the theatre, you find out what your talent is. Get experience of as many aspects of working in the theatre as possible, even if they have no intention of going down that path. Because you never know when it will be useful and it's always a terrific advantage, as a producer, not necessarily to do someone else's job as well as them, but to know what their job is and therefore to understand what concerns they have.

Could you do almost any job in the theatre?

I could do most jobs in the theatre. Some I would actually do rather well. I was a very good stage manager. I'd be very good in the box-office, I was a good flyman and a prop boy. There are lots of things I wouldn't be good at. I'd be no good at pressing wigs, putting on make-up, I wouldn't be a good actor, I tried it once and knew I was terrible. But you talk to somebody in a different way if you know what their job is. I can talk to carpenters, I can talk to orchestrators, even though I make the most appalling racket myself as a singer, and I can't really play a musical instrument, but I have a sense of what their craft is about.

And also, whilst you're doing this, you learn a lot about yourself. You learn about what your tastes are, and taste applies to every aspect of the theatre. Whether it's how the poster looks, to how the lighting is, to what the scenery does, to how the actors perform, and the secret ingredient of a successful producer is the ability to have an original taste.

You need to know what your original voice is, and that's the most important thing. There are a number of producers who do something that's good, but being good isn't necessarily enough. A well-produced show isn't nearly as important as a highly original show that for some reason captures the public's imagination.

And on top of that, do you need to be aware of the wider world outside? The requirements of marketing, of finance, the whole paraphernalia?

Yes, but I don't think there's any mystique to marketing. It is called show business after all, so you actually have to have a knowledge of business.

You can only market something that the public want. You can nudge the public, you can remind the public, but as so many Hollywood blockbusters have proved, time and time again, if it's a turkey, you can't sell it, even if it's Thanksgiving.

Do you think the principles guiding a successful show are changing, in line with public taste and fashions? Is it going to be as easy to put on a successful show as it might have been in the heyday of the 1980s?

I think that it will be just as easy and just as difficult. Look at what's happened in New York. A small show – well it's not that small, it's got about 20 people in it – called *Rent* has come from off-Broadway, it's taking a fortune on Broadway now. It cost $2 million to put on, as opposed to a *Phantom* or a *Miss Saigon*, which cost $10 million. You can't get a ticket, the public are flocking to see it and it looks set for a long run with many other productions. This is the first time for the show's producers who previously ran an office booking theatrical tours.

So the opportunities will always be there for people who come up with the right idea and are prepared to take a bit of a risk, a bit of a gamble, and believe in what they do?

I think so. But of course it is not us producers or directors that are the key to this. You have to be able to spot talent. The secrets of a healthy theatre are brilliant, original writers. All you can do, as a producer, is to spot that what they have created is something original and get the best out of them. Make their work even better than the author dreamed of. Realize their dream and do it in the best possible way. Some Americans try to laugh off the British invasion of musicals as only shows with scenery. But no one goes to see musicals for scenery, they go to see musicals because they're a good musical.

Is there a downside to success?

There can be, if you become public property, which is probably the biggest curse of success at the end of the 20th century. It is very hard to keep a private life if you're in certain areas of success. I have to say I'm not someone that suffers from that. The only publicity I do about myself is in connection with my shows. I keep my home to myself and my private life to myself, because I'm selling my shows, I'm not selling me.

But are there times when you've been tempted to go down the personal publicity route where you feel that the publicity for your professional product was maybe struggling a bit?

No. I mean where it's necessary, you know, because I'm a showman as well as a working producer, I sometimes have to do interviews when I don't feel I want to do interviews. I know it's part of my job. Sometimes I am the hook that you have to pin the story on, and I know that.

So your advice to successful people would be, 'Try to limit the publicity and the media attention to the actual reason for you being successful, rather than your personal life'?

No, I'm not going to give anybody any advice. All I am saying is I don't want everyone to know who I am, it doesn't give me any buzz. I enjoy the fact that I have all the benefits of success, in that I can do virtually anything that I want to, and the greater benefit of my privacy is that I can enjoy it, and I can just be an ordinary person.

And do you think it is possible for successful people to separate the two in the way that you have?

Well I've managed it, and I'm not particularly bright.

Not particularly bright! Do you really feel that?

I don't think I'm particularly bright. I think I have good common sense and I have good intuition, but I'm not all that clever. I have a talent, but lots of people have talent. My talent happens to be something which is quite individual – well, very individual – and quite rare, but I'm not an intellectual, I'm smart in a street sense, I have good common sense and instincts. But I'm not exceptional, except in the area of what I do.

When your time comes to leave this life, what would you like people to say about you?

He was fun, we're going to miss him. He's produced some great shows and they will be remembered long after he's forgotten.

LORD MACLAURIN

Tesco's Ian MacLaurin is rightly proud of how he chose the management team 'of different personalities' that helped him take the supermarket chain from 'a pretty cheap and cheerful operation that was going down the tubes' to 'the best retailer in the UK, if not in Europe', with profits of three-quarters of a billion pounds. He believes in delegating as much as possible: 'It's very frustrating for bright people in an organisation to be hamstrung because the chairman has to sign everything off.' So his management style is relaxed, with everyone on first-name terms, and they 'do things together'; he dislikes rigid hierarchies; his office door is 'always open' because 'the most humble person in this organisation is the most important'. He describes how his board of directors
was 'very carefully chosen', so they haven't had to put anything to a vote during his 12 years at the top. 'We discuss things, and at the end of the day come to a consensus.' In employees he looks for loyalty and dedication, and believes that 'success breeds loyalty, because people like to be involved with a successful company'. He is convinced that if all his people are happy and well motivated, then 'everything else looks after itself. They look after the customers, if the customers are happy they spend money, and they look after the shareholders'. He says you must 'never launch a new initiative and not follow it through very professionally', and he talks of the vital feedback he gets from a whole series of customer panels: 'Retailing is about detail, and it's about listening to your customers.'

Ian MacLaurin recalls how, after two years' National Service in the RAF and a spell as an engineering apprentice, a chance encounter with Tesco's founder, Jack Cohen, led to a job offer and 38 years with the company; how he had 'no hesitation' in taking on the founding family in an historic challenge which was the catalyst for today's success; the 'temporary blip' when they got 'the people factor' wrong, and tried to make everything too mechanical; and what the future holds for success in retailing, with 'more job-hopping than ever before'. Now well into his retirement job as chairman of the English Cricket Board, he is charged with putting the team more regularly on a winning track. 'The first thing I asked for,' he says, 'was the strategy plan, and they didn't have one.' They do now – but turning round English cricket is proving a much trickier proposition than revitalising a chain of supermarkets.

Lord MacLaurin, what is your definition of success?

I suppose in our case it would be the 130,000 people who work for us. It is their success, because they've built Tesco – it is their families' success and their children's. We are responsible for their livelihoods, and they have built our success with us. I feel pretty proud about that.

So as far as you're concerned, success means the success of everyone in the company?

Yes. My personal success is minuscule compared to the company's, and the responsibility that I and the board of directors have for our people, our 12 million customers a week and our suppliers.

And in the order of priorities – customers, employees, and so on – who comes first? Shareholders?

They're all interrelated. My first concern is my people, because if they are happy and well motivated, then everything else looks after itself. They look after the customers – if the customers are happy, they spend money, and they look after the shareholders. So I suppose that's the order.

What makes a good employee? Can one generalize?

It's quite difficult, especially with a very big organization like this. One is looking for loyalty, for dedication – there are an awful lot of qualities. Loyalty, I suppose, is what I look for more than anything. We try to reward it by the various means at our disposal – we've been talking about profit sharing and that sort of thing – and our staff turnover, for a very large company like this, is very small indeed. And, of course, success breeds loyalty, because people like to be involved with a successful company.

How do you set about encouraging loyalty?

However big you are, I think it's an attitude of mind, from the top of the organization downwards. I intensely dislike rigid hierarchies and the 'yes sir, no sir, three-bags-full' mentality. My office door is always open. If anybody wants to come and see me about anything at any time, they therefore feel free to pop in. I think you've got to try to get the team spirit going right the way through. And if you're going to run a team, you've got to be a team player. The most humble person in this organization is the most important in my book.

But there are many people running large, successful companies who would say that that is impossible. You've got to have a kind of hierarchy, and there has to be a chain of command, and a chain of dealing with problems and complaints, because the chairman's door can't always be open to the most humble employee.

Obviously there are levels of management, and they deal with whatever they have to deal with, but it's a matter of your philosophy. I run a big team of people, all of whom talk to each other. We're all on first-name terms, and it is quite a relaxed management style – we do things together. I've been chairman for 12 years, and we've never had a vote in those 12 years about anything. The board directors are carefully chosen, and we sit down and discuss things. At the end of the day we'll come to a consensus.

Are you, in any sense, a control freak? Do you like to put your stamp on all the decision-making processes?

No, I don't think I do. I'm very keen on delegating responsibility to other people. At the end of the day the buck stops with me, and I am responsible to the shareholders, but it is very, very frustrating, I think, for bright people in an organization to be hamstrung because the chairman has to sign everything off. I don't authorize everything – I have to do a bit of that, but I delegate as much as I possibly can.

That requires you to choose the right people for management. What qualities do you look for in a senior manager?

When I started, some years ago, formulating the team that took Tesco from a pretty cheap and cheerful operation to what it is now, I looked at various people we employed. I was looking for people who were bright, intelligent, worked hard, and who had vision for the future. I thought they would share my vision about what we could do with this pretty awful company. And I considered their interests too, because I think the worst thing you can possibly have is a lot of very like-minded people. I chose a managing director, David Malpas, who was a graduate, and somebody else on the trading side, who wasn't a graduate, and who had very different interests. We started with a team of about 20, and got it down to about 12 in the end. Of those 12, ten people have been very instrumental in the transformation of this company. And they are all very different personalities. Some love sport, some the opera, some the arts. We bring the best out of each other, and we make up a very formidable team. Above all, they've shared my vision of becoming the best retailer, certainly in the United Kingdom if not in Europe.

So there is this sense of contrasts, of people who are very different coming together, all bringing something different to the table. What do they have in common?

That vision of being the best. They are competitive. They immediately bought into the changing of Tesco, and the excitement of developing it from something that was very downmarket into one of the best-controlled businesses you'll find anywhere.

What tactics did you have for turning Tesco round? Was there a grand plan?

Oh yes, there was quite clearly a grand plan. Before we changed the company years ago, the profits were going down by something like £2 million a year, and the business was going down the tube. I was faced with a family running the place which wasn't prepared to change. We had an historic vote on coming out of Green Shield Stamps, which I was fortunate enough to win by 5-4. The decision was clinched by the vote of a non-executive director living in the south of France, who wrote to me, 'Dear Ian, you have my vote. I can't stand the sticky little things.' After we won the vote, the wonderful founder of the company – the chap who took me on, Jack Cohen – came into my office and shook me like a little rag. 'It's all your bloody idea,' he said, 'and you know what's going to happen if it fails.' I knew quite well what would happen if it failed, but we put down the plan to start transforming the business. We had nearly 1,000 stores, now we have 550 and a profit, at the last count, of £685 million.

Was getting rid of Green Shield Stamps the key at that point?

It was the catalyst. We were spending a lot of money on them, but the customers didn't want them. They merely served to underline the cheap and cheerful nature of our business. The retail business moves very fast, and we weren't moving at all – or if we were, it was in the wrong direction – so we had to make a very, very big statement, and a big effort to tell the consumer about the new Tesco. We did 101 things, but we got our price structure right, and we did a much better job in the stores, and we started to move the business away from that bad profit performance.

Was it a gamble to dispense with an idea which had in the past been immensely successful for you?

Life is always a gamble. As a retailer, you take a decision based on your gut feeling. My instinct was that we had to do something. I had already given nearly 20 years of my life to Tesco, and I thought, 'Well, I'm not going to waste those 20 years. I want to do something with this business.' If we hadn't won that vote, Tesco would probably not be where it is today.

You believe it was as crucial as that?

Without a doubt. The figures tell you that Tesco was going out of business. The family were sitting there with a reasonable shareholding. They didn't really care too much, they were using the business as their own business, and were enjoying life. Jack Cohen was in his upper seventies at that time, and was still involved, driving everyone nuts.

Let me take you back to your early days. Were you always ambitious?

Yes, I suppose I always was, and still am. I was so lazy at school it was untrue, but I was ambitious on the sports field. However, I don't think I've ever been ambitious in the personal sense, for what I would get out of it. I like to be successful, and we have been successful here.

Could you have been successful at other things, do you think?

I don't know – I've never done anything else. But I would like to think that I could have done something somewhere else with the skills I have brought here over the years.

So the desire to be successful was a driving force, but you didn't necessarily have a driving ambition to be successful in a particular sphere?

No, certainly not. I came here by absolute chance. I went into the Air Force – I spent two years doing my national service there, and when I came out I worked as a trainee with Vactric, the control equipment company. I met Jack Cohen at the Grand Hotel in Eastbourne when I was playing cricket. I played a lot at that time, at quite a high level, and I used to go down to Eastbourne with the Old Malvernians cricket tour. We changed for dinner every night and wore the Old Malvernians flag in our buttonholes. Jack Cohen used to stay at the Grand with his family, and one night he saw these 20-odd young fellows in dinner jackets in the Canada Bar and he came over and talked to us. He said, 'Do any of you young fellows want a job?' And he gave us all cards.

I didn't want a job, but I thought he was a very interesting chap. He was very personable and talked a lot about his business. So I phoned him up and said, 'You gave me your card in Eastbourne – you won't remember me.' He said, 'Oh yes I do,' but of course he didn't. Anyway, I came up to his office and had an interview with him. It was quite bizarre because all I wanted to do was to find out a bit about the business. Jack asked: 'What are you earning?' I told him I was earning £900 a year. He said, 'Well, if you join me I'll pay you a salary of £900 a year, but I'll pay it to you for six months. Then I'll review it, and if I like you and you like me, I'll give you £1,000 and a company car.' And I joined. It was my burning ambition, in those days, to earn £20 a week. In 1959, if you could earn £20 a week you had arrived in a very big way. The company car was actually very useful, because at the time I was driving an old Morris Oxford van, with one seat – driver's. My wife-to-be sat in a deckchair in the back. So the company car was a certain attraction!

Have you found, as you pursued your professional career, that there is an inherent conflict between the demands of work and the demands of family life? Have you ever got the right balance, or is that impossible?

I don't think I've ever got the balance right, and without a very strong home life I don't think I could have done this job at all. Ann, my wife, has been absolutely amazing, and you take a lot of things in life for granted, and you plough on until something happens to stop you in your tracks. About seven years ago, we were coming home from London one night and Ann said, 'I've got a lump in my breast.' She said, she'd see a doctor the next day – she's a physiotherapist – so she had all the tests, and they were negative. But the surgeon said, 'I don't like ladies going around with lumps in their breasts, so come in and I'll just nick it out.' So she went into hospital, had it taken out, and they found that she had cancer. She underwent all the radiotherapy, and all that stuff, and came through it. It was very debilitating, but she came through it brilliantly, and, touch wood, she is fine now. But it was a time in my life when I thought, 'What the hell have I been doing? I work my cotton socks off for my family and kids, and suddenly Ann might not be there.' Something like that really brings you back to appreciating life, and the things outside work. And it did change me quite a lot. As chairman of a company like Tesco you're very much public property, but I told Ann we would do only two evening engagements a week. I'd do one, and she would have the option of doing one herself if she wanted to. And that's how, by and large, we've continued since.

Did you change the way you ran the business, the level of your involvement, as a result of that?

No, not the business itself. That is theoretically nine to five – of course, it's a lot more than that, and people call on you to do things outside business hours. We have to talk to our shareholders, so we have dinner parties for the major ones, and that takes up some time. There are 101 things – shall I go and speak here, shall I do this, that or the other? And suddenly you find you've got a full diary, and four, five nights a week you're out doing something, and you're up again at 5.30 the next morning to get into the office by 7.30. So that was what changed, thankfully. I'm grateful that we had that warning.

In the early days, you were employed by Sir Jack Cohen, but there came a point where you felt he was going in the wrong direction. Was there a conflict there?

You've just got to have the courage of your own convictions, and when you see something that is wrong, you've got to pursue it. You only had to read the papers then to know that we were in trouble. I did owe Jack a huge debt, but I did an awful lot for him as well. He gave me my chance, but I resurrected this business for him and for his family, who are all extremely rich now because of our efforts. There does come a time when you have to take decisions, and that was a pretty major one. But I had no hesitation in taking it.

And there comes a time when business priorities demand that you take action with which your friends don't agree?

Well, my colleagues on the board agreed with what I wanted to do – it was the family who didn't want to do it. Times change, and while Jack Cohen was one of the most brilliant retailers this country has ever seen when he was fit and well and young, when he was not well, and in his mid-seventies, you had to question his judgment, and I think it was gravely flawed.

I am about to retire from Tesco, and I think, with the pace of change in business, that after 12 years as chairman it's the right time for me to go. I shall miss it like mad, because I've done nothing else for the last 38 years, but it is right for the business that I should let the new chaps take over.

Is it important for a successful person to know when the moment has come for him or her to move on and hand over the reins to somebody else?

Yes, absolutely vital. I'd like to stay and remain chairman until I'm 100 or whatever, but I couldn't, because I've instituted the rules which say we have to go at 60, and I would not wish to break those, because I believe very firmly indeed that you can take the responsibility of a business like this for so long and then you should go. I have selected the new team which will take over from me, and they're doing extremely well, so it will be a very painless handover of power from me to the new administration.

A lot of successful people would say, 'Hey, we've got the business going, we've set it up, and we're going to stay in charge for as long as we possibly can.'

That argument can be flawed. We're having a very good run at the moment, but things do change very quickly. A classic example was us giving up stamps all those years ago. I could see the business moving on, and I'm sure that now the younger people are more adaptable in running this business over the next ten years, with all its international aspects, than I would be. We've taken Tesco on from being merely a very big player in the United Kingdom, and we've bought businesses in France, Hungary, Czechoslovakia and Poland. Now the vision will be developing those countries. And that's why younger people should do the job.

What do you reckon were the biggest hiccups – or failures, perhaps – along the way, and, more importantly, how did you overcome them?

When we launched our plan in 1977, the whole thing moved up a gear very quickly indeed, and we had some problems closing down stores and getting the right sites for the new ones, but we overcame them. I suppose one of the most difficult things was when, probably four or five years ago, we decided to centralize everything, our computer programmes, and so on. We took out a lot of the personal involvement, and tried to make everything mechanical. It took us 18 months to realize that this new style of management just didn't work. Then we put the people factor back in, we got the stores moving again, and enthused the staff again, and after that temporary blip we moved forward.

Was it difficult to pick up the people factor after what you had gone through?

Not really. The people were telling us, 'Look, you've got this wrong and you ought to listen to us.' And our customer panels were telling us we'd got it wrong as well. So we introduced new procedures and away we went, and everything was fine.

You mentioned customer panels. To what extent do you think your success is attributable to getting the right feedback from your customers?

Feedback is vital. Retailing is about detail, and it is about listening to your customers. We launched our Clubcard two years ago, and I think we've got ten million Tesco Clubcard members now. We've got a bank full of information about what they buy, when they buy it, what they don't buy. Virtually every day of the year we have a customer panel somewhere, and we listen to the customers and ask them what they want of their store. And they tell us. We need to incorporate that feedback into our policies, in the design of our new stores, and that's ongoing.

The innovative ideas that you and the team have developed have obviously contributed to Tesco becoming what it is today. What is the extent of the challenge involved to stay successful? Can you ever afford to say, 'We're going to sit back for a year and let things ride,' or is it a real furnace of evolution?

I think it's a real furnace of evolution. We've got a shopping list of probably 15 to 20 initiatives we are looking at, of which the Clubcard was one, and we're ticking these off. But what you must never do is launch a new initiative and not follow it through really professionally, because the customers will come back to you very quickly indeed and say, 'Now listen, you've launched this but it's no good and I'm unhappy about it.' So it is an ongoing process. You can never take a year off and say, 'OK, let's just capitalize on this.' You've got to keep moving ahead. If you don't, then other people will catch up with you and maybe overtake you. The pressure we have now is to stay number one, having got there. It's all about innovation and excitement, enthusing the customers and looking after them better and better.

What part has luck played in Tesco's success?

Well, you always have to be a bit lucky, don't you? What part in percentage terms, I don't know – 10 per cent, 15 per cent luck, I suppose. But you can make your own luck in life, and I think that if you get the right philosophy and the right idea, and you follow that through, and you keep checking back to make sure you're on the right track, then you can take a lot of the luck element out of it.

You beat Sainsbury's and became the number one retailer. Did you aim for that as a matter of pride, simply for the sake of winning? Or is there something about the marketplace itself which gives you added clout if you are number one? What does being number one bring to the table?

It brings huge satisfaction to the people who work here. There is nobody in the organization who wasn't absolutely thrilled when we overtook Sainsbury's, because before we had always been the second-class citizen. And we had to work very, very hard to change people's perceptions of Tesco. One of the most difficult decisions we ever had to make was whether or not to change the name of the company. You might have this vision about creating a fantastic business, but you still have that name Tesco up there, which to people of my generation means unattractive little shops. It's quite interesting that now we have more customers between 20 and 40, while Sainsbury's have more between 40 and 60. My children's generation don't have a problem about Tesco at all, because they don't remember the old shops. They just think Tesco is a very pleasant, nice place to shop. But we had to live through the transformation with that same name.

Why didn't you change it?

The advertising agents who worked with me at the time were quite specific about it. They said, 'Look, Tesco has a wonderful reputation for good value – there is not a better brand name in that respect. What you've got to do is to change the public perception of that to persuade the public that Tesco represents not only good value, but also excellent fresh foods, wonderful wines, wonderful everything.' That's why we stuck with the name.

And now, of course, you're trying to bring a business sense to the world of cricket. You have been reported as having been fairly awesome in negotiations with the BBC and BSkyB. What were your tactics in making those negotiations successful?

I was only part of the team. Brian Downing chaired it, and did so very ably. We needed to strike a good deal for cricket, and we were able to do it because BSkyB wanted the Test matches and so did the BBC. The deal brought something like £70 million into the game over a three- or four-year period. But I don't think I was awesome in that at all.

I'm now chairman of the new English Cricket Board, and my main job is to preside over a winning England side. That's very important if we're to enjoy the same revenues in the game. I've set out my stall, with the chief executive, Tim Lamb, and we're going to be talking to the counties, and I hope that with them we will be able to formulate a new cricket programme which will ensure a winning England side.

Do you recall the first thing you asked for when you were offered this job?

Oh yes, I asked for a strategy plan, but they didn't have one.

Have you found any resistance to your attempt to run the sport on more businesslike lines?

No, there's a willingness there, and they're very intelligent people. They're all successful people in their own right. It's early days yet, I'd like to think that I'll be able to say to them, 'Look, I can lead you somewhere.' And if they buy into it, that's fine – if not, I shall be fired.

Who are your heroes? Who are the really successful people, past or present, whom you admire and look up to?

Two of the most splendid people I really look up to, and whom I thank for everything I've been able to do, were two masters who taught me at Malvern. One was the cricket master and the other the soccer master. They taught me at a very early age about people, about man-management and the skills of running a team – how I should conduct myself, how to lead a team and appreciate teamwork – which has stood me in great stead. Both of them are very dear to my heart.

Dennis Saunders taught me geography and ran the soccer side, of which I was captain for two years. George Chesterton also taught me geography and ran the cricket team, and I was captain of that for two years as well. They were fantastic times for me.

If you don't have a mentor, are your chances of success diminished?

Well, I don't know about that, because there are many, many people who have made huge successes of their business life, probably without mentors. Everybody is an individual, and you remember things right through your life that are important to you. I have no doubt at all that those formative days when I was a 16 year-old schoolboy, those mentors were very important to me, and I've never forgotten the lessons I learned.

Can you be successful without having that certain something that appeals to people, and that enables you to elicit a positive response when you appear on television and do all the PR that someone at the top of an organization has to do? Charisma is part of the equation, is it not?

People have to respect you. You can't buy respect, you have to earn it by what you do and your attitude to people. I think that's important. I would like to think that people feel I'm not a bad person to have around here, that I'm approachable and I care for them, and that I'm the captain of their team.

When was the first time in your life you said to yourself, 'I've been successful'?

I don't think I've ever asked myself that question, or ever said I was successful. You're only as good as your last set of results, to be quite honest. And that's the pressure of running a public company. If I fall down, then at some point the press will write off Ian MacLaurin very quickly. 'He's lost his way, he's too old.' And so on.

Do you accept that you've ever had any failures? And how did you recover from them?

Well, I've had failures when I've put people into certain positions and they haven't fulfilled my ambitions for them, and it's probably partly my fault that they haven't.

Is that the biggest difficulty of a successful businessman? To make the right judgments about people?

I think it's probably the most important thing that I was able to do at Tesco – getting the team of people together and judging people. I think I have a good nose for people.

Have you ever made a bad judgment about someone?

I suppose you can be very trusting of people, and a few will let you down. I can think of two or three people I've brought on and given a big opportunity to do well, and they've either fallen down or they've moved on to another job after you've put your trust in them. That's very upsetting.

Do you believe that there are some people who are promoted above their own level of competence because they were very good at one particular job, but couldn't handle the next level?

Yes, I have no doubt at all about that, and I think you're seeing it more as business moves along and gets more technically complicated. And there are probably quite a lot of people in quite senior positions who, if they were true and honest with you, would tell you that they were really struggling to keep up. Technically, the business world has moved so fast over the last ten years or so that it is very difficult for people to keep fully up to speed the whole time.

So would those people be more successful if they acknowledged their limitations and were prepared to talk to their company about them?

I think they should do that, and if you've got a good human resources director, the major part of his or her job is to place people and watch how they perform in any particular area of the business. That is very important.

Does every successful person have an ego, and is that good or bad?

It's inevitable. They all have a bit of an ego. I suppose it's good. It depends on how people cope with it. But you don't get where you are going unless you believe you're quite good.

So self-belief is a core factor?

Yes, self-belief is very, very important.

In a world context, the way your particular profession is going, is it becoming more or less difficult to achieve success as a retailer?

Oh, much more difficult. Wherever you look, the big successful companies are becoming fewer and fewer. Whereas 20 years ago you could probably name 20 or 30 major British retailers, now there are probably only seven or eight. So the competition merely to survive is huge.

What are the next big steps in retailing?

I think there's going to be a move away from one's core business into other forms of stores.

Poaching on other people's territory?

No, not necessarily poaching, but rather adapting your skills to smaller areas. John Gummer has come up with PPG6, which is a planning rule, which means that there will be no more, or very few more, out-of-town shopping permissions given. So in the UK we've developed something called Tesco Metro, which are smaller stores in city centres. We've also got a chain called Tesco Express, which are small convenience stores on the edge of a Tesco petrol station. We're going back and looking at where we can actually fill in pieces of the jigsaw. And that will go on alongside our international ambitions.

Can you ever see retail purchasing being conducted completely from the armchair, on the Internet, so that nobody ever needs to go into shops?

We've got that now. We're running a scheme in Ealing, where we are now on the Internet. And there was a recent article, in the *Evening Standard*, I think, by somebody who said he hated shopping at Tesco on a Saturday, but now he could do it on the Internet, so thanks very much. It costs him a fiver and it's delivered to his door. It'll be a small percentage, in my view at the moment, of the total shopping basket, but it is going to happen. We have done huge business in the last few years over the phone lines on Christmas hampers, wine and flowers, and that sort of thing.

Looking 30 years ahead, maybe 50, do you think the successful retailer won't have any premises at all outside the management offices, and a couple of warehouses? That they won't actually need shops at all?

No, I think people like shopping. For a lot of people it is their only contact with others. There will be a certain segment of the population which will be very happy to use the Internet, and to pay a premium for having their goods delivered, but people are retiring earlier and earlier, they're living longer and longer, and the shops are opening longer and longer hours. It is somewhere to go. And they're not only places to buy groceries – people can go to a coffee shop and have breakfast or lunch; they can do what they want to do. They can fill up their car, they can have it washed, it's all part of life. What we have to do is to make sure that what our stores offer is attractive to the customer.

Do you think that the widening gap in business in general between what the individual on the shop floor earns and what people in the boardroom get is acceptable, because you are taking more risks? What's the justification for high rewards for success?

If people have actually created something, like we have here, from a company that was virtually bankrupt, I have no problem at all about them being paid very well for it. That's a lifetime's work. I can tell them that when I took over the business they were among the worst-paid people in the retail industry. Our staff turnover was way over 100 per cent – it's now down to 30, and that's mostly students – and they are the best-paid retail staff in the country. Their benefits package is as good as that of any other company in the United Kingdom, and we're looking after them to the very best of our ability. They've got shareholdings, save-as-you-earn share schemes, dentist schemes,

BUPA schemes, they've got good pensions, they're running right up in the upper quartile of retail wages, and we've brought all of that about as the company's developed. I'm pleased about that, and I'm proud of it. If I don't have the goodwill of the staff, and they don't want to work for me, I've got no business.

Should there be any limit at all to the rewards of success?

Yes, there should be.

How do you quantify that?

Well, I think it needs to be judged on the size of the company, but I do think you get to the stage where there are some very, very crazy salaries. And it's up to the remuneration committees of the companies concerned to keep control of it.

What are the greatest enemies of success – the internal or external forces which drag people down and might prevent them from being as successful as they could be?

The main one is a lack of attention to detail. If you swan along with something and you don't actually work to get the foundations right, then the chances are that the end product's not going to be any good. You've got to be very diligent in getting right the fundamentals of whatever you do, otherwise you might well fall down. And whatever thoughts you have about the future, whatever business you're in, you've got to make sure you keep checking back to make sure that you're on course. You can't build anything on unsure foundations.

Are there obligations on every successful person to put something back into society?

Absolutely. If you look at a company like Tesco, and you see the money that we take out, we are duty bound, both personally and as a company, to put a lot back as well, and we do. We have a tremendous charity budget here, and give a lot of money to children's charities. Personally too, you've got to try to put things back in some way or another – by helping local educational establishments, by being a governor, or a chancellor, or whatever. You can't just swan along in your own little sphere – you're a public property. I have to do all sorts of things, and that's fair enough. It goes with the job.

And you accept both that and the high profile that success brings? Do you think success would be easier if one didn't have a high public profile at the same time?

Probably they always go together. Success, in a business like this, automatically turns you into a high-profile person. People write about Tesco and the chairman certainly twice a year, and probably more often than that.

So any successful person, or would-be successful person, has to be prepared for that?

I think so. There are people who have inherited a lot of money and keep a very low profile. But in business, you are going to be pretty high-profile.

And how should a successful person ride the inevitable criticisms? Is there a kind of internal formula for not allowing yourself to be knocked around by the critics too much?

If you can look in the mirror every day and feel that what you're doing is right, and you don't have a conscience about it, that's probably as much as you can do. I've tried to balance my life, and tried to give something back, but it's up to the individual, at the end of the day, and his or her conscience. It's the way you want to live your life. I suppose I've always had quite a strong religious belief, and that's helped me. I've always felt very comfortable with my religious upbringing – Church of England – I'm much involved with the local church, and I find a comfort there.

Which extends to the boardroom?

Yes, of course it does. It's reflected in the way you react to people, I think. I like to be a Christian, I like to do things right, and I don't like to do bad things.

But success isn't always associated with strong moral principles, they are not a requirement?

Not necessarily, but I think they help. Again, it's up to the individual, how the individual wants to live his life.

Have you any frustrated ambitions?

Yes – I never played cricket for England!

But you're now going to be running the sport.

If I can get that right, I suppose it will be a bit of a consolation!

Has success changed you at all?

Somebody else ought to answer that question. I'd like to think that it hasn't, but inevitably it has to have done in some ways, because it changes your lifestyle a bit. So it would be foolish to say that success hasn't changed me at all. For example, when I started off I never thought I'd have a holiday home in Spain, and without success, I wouldn't have that.

What is the greatest pleasure you've derived from having had a successful career?

I think seeing the business where it is today. Being number one, and the fun we've all had out of it. That's given me tremendous pleasure. To have come from nothing to where we are has been extraordinary.

If you could gather together all the young people who say, 'I want, one day, to run a huge retailing operation,' what advice would you give them?

First, they ought to join Tesco if they haven't joined already! Secondly, they've got to have a good education. If they've got a good education, and they come into a business like this, they've then got to prove to us that they are all-rounders, not just dedicated to one particular area. They've got to spend a lot of time in the stores, because that's what a retail business is about. It's understanding stores, understanding customers, understanding the excitement of the store, and everything that goes with it. They would have to show themselves to be very good team players, and build themselves up from there.

Does it pay not to be too ambitious? Should they try to get into a company at a certain level, or should they accept any job that's going?

Initially they should accept any job that's going and take it from there. Obviously you have to be ambitious and I'm all for that, but there are different kinds of ambition. If you are a team player as well, you can move up. You get some people who are very, very ambitious, too ambitious for their own good, and they fall by the wayside because they are so self-centred and want success at any price. They won't get it, because they'll be rumbled somewhere along the line and people will say, 'Look, this is not the sort of person we want in this organization.'

In a world where cost-cutting seems to be very much in fashion, and where Business in the Community predicts that everyone will have four totally separate careers, for each of which they will have to be retrained, how do you encourage the kind of loyalty which, you said earlier, was the backbone of Tesco's success?

By the way you treat people. One of the sadnesses we've seen over the last few years is the 'delayering' of companies. Not so many years ago we probably had eight levels of management, now we've got about four. And one of the sadnesses of that was that a number of people who worked very hard for us were retired early. We retired them well, we looked after them financially, but their self-esteem was greatly dented. That's a problem. In a company like Tesco, there is only a very small chance that you'll go all the way from the bottom of it to the top. I'd be very surprised indeed if someone who is a young graduate trainee here today becomes chairman, or chairwoman, in 30 years' time. It might happen, but I doubt it. It's more likely that people will get to a certain level and then move on somewhere else and go up a notch, and then to a third company and up another notch. I don't think I'd necessarily agree with the prediction about four different careers, but I think you are going to get more job-hopping than we've ever had before. Indeed, we've already got it now.

One final question. When your time comes to leave this life, what would you like people to say about you?

He was a good guy. I'm pleased to have known him.

JOHN MAJOR

*You should seek success not for fame or position,
he says, but in order to do something that is
worthwhile; and he likens politics to walking –
you keep putting one foot in front of the other and
eventually you get there. For John Major it was
quite a journey from his family's two rooms in the
deprived London suburb of Brixton to six and a
half years as Prime Minister. He was just 12
when his elderly father's garden gnome business
went bust, forcing a dramatic reversal in their
lifestyle. Preferring cricket to homework, he left
school at 16 with only three O-levels, and was
unemployed for several months before becoming a
bank clerk and eventually moving into PR in the
City. His parents were far from the 'pushy' type,
but made sacrifices to give him opportunities.*

*From the first political stirrings at 13 came a 'step-by-step' rise through
Conservative ranks. He says here his ultimate aim was to be Chancellor of the
Exchequer, and, having achieved that, it was 'touch and go' whether he stood for
Prime Minister after the ousting of Mrs Thatcher. But at the age of 47, just 12
years after entering Parliament, he moved into Downing Street.*

    *At one point in those early days an opinion poll suggested he was Britain's most
popular Prime Minister ever, and, in the teeth of a deep recession, he unexpectedly
won the Conservatives a further term in office. During the five years that followed,
his delivery of the strongest economy in living memory was overshadowed by a bitter
civil war in his party over Europe, the breaking of an election promise not to raise
VAT, the forced withdrawal from the Exchange Rate Mechanism (which he
concedes was his biggest political failure), the controversial re-organisation of the
National Health Service, and an unprecedented flow of sleaze and scandal. Some
commentators accused him of a lack of judgment, of being a manager rather than
a leader; others saw him as a master tactician who 'was dealt a losing hand and
had some extremely disloyal colleagues'. This interview, which took place before
John Major's overwhelming 1997 General Election defeat, provides a revealing
insight into his approach to the job. He talks about his toughening after that 'first
difficult period when you think you will never recover' and measures out the
differing layers of qualities needed to be a successful MP, minister and Prime
Minister.*

John Major, what is your definition of success?

I would define success in terms of achieving something for the common good or above people's expectations of you.

And that could happen at any level?

Of course. Very much at any level. The head of a major company who turns that company from poor results to being a world-beater is clearly successful, but so is someone who has great difficulty in learning to read but does so and then puts that to good use. His success is just as great.

So what differentiates those people who achieve success in a quiet modest way from those who achieve success in a dramatic, more public way, who stick their heads over the public parapet, as it were?

Well, it is a reflection of people's personality. Some people crave success to bring fame, others seek success to bring results.

Do you think that people can or should seek success for the sake of success or should they achieve success almost accidentally by being determined to pursue a particular avenue, a particular career?

The two run together. There is nothing wrong in seeking success. Everest was there. Hillary wanted to climb it. He did. That was a success, driven by a perfectly natural human emotion. But seeking success purely for position, I don't find that worthwhile. You should seek success in doing something that is worthwhile.

To what extent has your success been shaped by your background and your upbringing?

I honestly don't know. I can't be dispassionate enough to give you a proper answer to that. Certainly my background is different from many people in politics, but it's hard to know to what extent, if at all, it contributed to my political career.

Are there any key benchmarks in your very early life? I mean, for instance, the move into Brixton when you were 12 and all that meant to you, or maybe as your sister Pat has talked about, coming home from school having been bullied?

I never quite understood where my sister got that from. I wasn't bullied at school. I read that story, and the way the press reported, it with astonishment. My sister is older than I am and I don't know where she got that story from. I don't ever recall being bullied at school. I think there are some benchmarks. Certainly moving from Worcester Park to Brixton was one, but there were others. I remember coming home from school one day having come second in some exams and my father saying, 'If you had worked a little harder you would have come first.' I remember that very well.

And a feeling of disappointment?

Yes, I think so, don't you? Yes, disappointment, and embarrassment that he was right. But I don't want to make him sound as if he was a harsh, unkindly man. He wasn't, and he didn't say it in a harsh, unkindly way, but the point was made. He clearly thought I had done reasonably well to come second, but I had done reasonably well without a great deal of effort and if I had a put a little bit more effort into it I would have come first.

Did your parents have ambition themselves and did they transfer that ambition to you? Were you a focus of their ambition, did they want things for you?

They were not pushy parents in that respect. Of course they wanted me to do well and they were concerned that I did, and they were prepared to sacrifice quite a lot so that I had the opportunity to do so. But pushy parents – no, they were not.

When was the first time in your life that you said to yourself, 'I have been successful, I have become a success'?

When I was captain of my primary school football team, not having been appointed by my teachers, but elected by my fellow footballers.

Was that the early politician coming out, wanting to be elected?

No, at the age of 11 I wasn't contemplating politics. At 13 I was, at 11 I wasn't.

As you look back on your career now, what do you think were the most formative benchmarks that helped you get to the position where you are now?

That is not easy to answer. In terms of politics, personal experiences give you a determination to try and achieve something. Being unemployed and things like that did so too, although I wasn't unemployed for long, months not years. I was very young and I was single, so I didn't face the difficulties that other people do. But it leaves its mark. It leaves its mark if it was something you didn't expect to happen, and I didn't. Beyond that, I think the benchmarks then were how I moved from where I was to where I wanted to get. There was no sudden transformation, it was step-by-step. In politics it was running the Young Conservative branch, getting into the Senior Association, taking an increasing number of executive offices there, contesting a local election and losing, contesting another local election and winning, becoming chairman of the housing committee, losing my seat, fighting and losing a parliamentary seat twice and eventually getting a winnable parliamentary seat. Then in parliament it was just moving systematically through every job I was given: Parliamentary Private Secretary, Assistant Whip, Senior Whip, Parliamentary Secretary, Minister of State, Chief Secretary, Foreign Secretary, Chancellor, Prime Minister. It was a step-by-step progression. Politics is like walking. You keep putting one foot in front of the other and eventually you get there.

But did you think, right back in the early days, I want to be Prime Minister? Was that one of your feelings when you went into politics?

No, it was not. I always had a hankering to be Chancellor of the Exchequer. The decisions of the Chancellor are central to how people prosper in this country. If economic management is successful then it opens up opportunities and improvements in living standards that are impossible if economic policy is a failure. For that reason I was always attracted to the Exchequer.

So when the job of Prime Minister became vacant or the vacancy was about to occur, did you think automatically, I'm going to go for it, or did you have to be persuaded?

I didn't automatically feel, 'There is a vacancy, I am going to go for it.' I was persuaded to do so by colleagues. I thought it was too early. I was enjoying myself at the Treasury. I had been there for a year and it was a job I had always wanted. The timing wasn't convenient, either in political terms or in family terms. Norma and I had teenage children approaching examinations. It was touch and go whether I stood. I might well not have done and supported someone else.

A great many successful people feel that they have had to make sacrifices in their family life in order to pursue a particularly successful career. Do you feel that in some sense your family have had to make sacrifices because of the way your career has progressed, for the success you have achieved?

Yes, undoubtedly. But my family have been underpinned by Norma, so I have been very lucky. When I first got in the House of Commons we made the decision that we would have our family home in the constituency so we were not mobile. We had a family home that was safe and secure. We agreed that when I was in London during the week Norma would stay at home with the children so there was stability. We took that decision. We never deviated from it. It did mean for years that I was in London from Monday to Friday or Monday to Thursday night, as the case may be, and Norma was in the constituency, but we thought that was right for the family. But that certainly was a sacrifice. It meant I personally missed too much of the children growing up. We made the decision because we thought it was the best decision for the children and I think it was.

So a strong partner is an essential ingredient in any politician's success?

Oh, more value than anyone can possibly know. Absolutely.

What is your definition of a successful politician? What are the qualities that are needed to be (a) a successful politician, (b) a successful cabinet minister, and (c) a successful Prime Minister?

Well, they are not necessarily the same. To be a successful politician, how do you measure success? If you measure success simply by progressing to senior positions, that is not necessarily a successful politician. One of the best examples of a successful politician is someone who has developed a particular empathy with his constituency, the people across the parties whom he represents. There are many examples of that on both sides of the House. People who have had a constituency and built up a majority; people of whom the electorate in his or her constituency will generally say, 'I don't agree with everything that he does, but I think he is a good Member of Parliament.' I think that is a successful politician.

A successful Minister is a different proposition. He may or may not have the first qualities, but he certainly has to have the capacity to absorb huge amounts of detail, and to pluck from the detail the right path forward. And by the right path forward I do not subscribe to the view that all he or she needs is some eccentric vision. That may be a view held by some, but it isn't my view. I think he not only needs to know where he or she wishes to get but he needs to be able to determine how to get there and how to take people with him. There is nothing successful about having a wild and reckless vision that you can't carry out because you have set up huge blocks of opposition or because you fracture your party in doing so.

And a successful Prime Minister?

Judge him by results. Look at his impact on the country. Success sometimes should be measured by the things that do not happen as well as the thing that do happen – the impositions that might have been laid upon this country if the Prime Minister hadn't done something, the impact on this country if difficult decisions hadn't been taken. So there are two measures of a successful Prime Minister. Firstly, what has happened to living standards and the quality of life in the country, and secondly, what might have happened if he or she had not taken the decisions that they did.

You have had a considerable amount of criticism – you personally and your policies – from the media. What is your reaction?

I went through the pain barrier a long time ago. I am not influenced by it now.

Were you at first?

It never influenced significantly any of my policies. If at all, only at the fringes. It is not a pleasant experience when you first have the full ferocity of the media directed at you, and people find it quite a shock. I have become hardened over the years and I am more easily able to put it to one side and ignore it now. The best antidote is meeting the people who write it. They are ordinary people. They are doing a job. Let's be clear about what they are doing, they are trying to sell their newspapers.

Do you think that the role of the critic is overplayed in Britain. Do you think that the media tend to go for instant judgments whereas any politician, particularly a Prime Minister, is involved in the long term, and does that make it more difficult for you to be successful?

Of course. But that is not only true of politics, it is equally true of theatre critics, it is equally true of sports critics. Look at the way some of England's sportsmen are treated by their critics, and yet their critics couldn't remotely perform to the same level. Neither would they have the understanding of what actually determines that footballer's, that cricketer's, success. So it isn't just unique to politics. But I do think the criticism is often too concerned with what makes a good story and a good headline and too little concerned with the extent to which any government, whatever its majority, whether it's large or small, tends to be hemmed in by the realities of politics and the realities of international politics in particular. I don't think there is as much understanding of that amongst critics as there used to be some years ago.

You have talked of a toughening process about being Prime Minister. What is that toughening process?

Well, it is experience really. The first time you go through a difficult period you think you will never recover from it; the second time you know that you will. Subsequently, you know it is a difficult period and you will come through it, and if you are doing what you believe is (a) right or (b) inevitable, then you become more philosophical about it, and I certainly have done so.

What do you think are the greatest enemies of success?

Envy and malice, I think.

Can you remember the very first time in your life when you said to yourself, 'I have been a success'?

When I started working in the City in 1959 I earned £260 a year, £5 per week, and that went up progressively. And I remember it was quite an occasion when my salary eventually passed £2,000.

Does politics have an ability to absorb success and failures so that in time both are forgotten – memories are short?

Politics more than any other trade. I mean the capacity to review what a politician did with hindsight is complete. The number of politicians who have been regarded as successful in their time, but less successful with the benefit of hindsight, or indeed the reverse, is legion. That is partly because over time you discover, as papers are released, precisely why a politician did something. We saw a practical illustration of this recently with the release of some papers concerning President Eisenhower. He ran into terrible trouble because he let the Russians get into space first. Papers released subsequently indicated precisely why he had done that and why it was in America's interests to do so. But that was many years after the event, and that happens often.

Is there a feeling of resentment on your part at the instant judgments that the outside world comes to?

No, not resentment. I have got my job to do and they have got theirs. It is frustrating sometimes when people run stories which are just patently wrong or untrue, but I have learned to bear that and I think all my successors will have to learn to do so as well.

What do you regard as your biggest failures, and more importantly, how did you recover from them?

In politics, it was when we came out of the Exchange Rate Mechanism. I had taken us into the Exchange Rate Mechanism to bring inflation down, as a counter-inflationary measure. As a counter-inflationary measure it worked, but when sterling came out of the Exchange Rate Mechanism it was a huge political setback. Economically it may yet be judged as a success because of what it did to inflation and what that did for the economy, but politically it was a failure.

A Prime Minister faces tremendous pressures perhaps from colleagues or the media to tweak or change the direction of policies. Are there any ground rules for when you stand firm and when you compromise?

Well, it is a question of events. There is a fashion these days that you should make your decision instantly and having made that decision it should never change. In some circumstances that is right. But politics isn't a static profession, circumstances change, events change. If events change and you don't change your mind that is not strength, that is just pig-headedness. If events require you to make a change the strong thing to do is make the change if events make it necessary to do so. There are no hard-and-fast rules about this. It is determined by the outcome you seek and the action you need to take to achieve that outcome. The important thing is the outcome, whether you have achieved that which you sought to achieve and which you believe is in the national interest.

How important is public perception as far as political success is concerned?

Well, it is very important, and public perception is often very negative. I don't just mean now. If you run back over the past 20 or 30 years' budgets, some of which have been very good, some average, some not very good, almost all of them immediately got a negative public perception. I don't think it is deeply felt, but there is too often a negative reaction to political or other events.

Is there something deep down inside the British character that makes us not want success and indeed to envy it where it occurs in others.

No, I don't think the British envy it. I think we are a kindly nation and a tolerant nation. Kindness and that tolerance is instinctively British and I have not seen it matched anywhere else in the world. But among too many people there is a tendency to regard the glass as half empty rather than half full.

How do we change that, is it possible to change?

Yes, I think it is. It is partly because, from 1945, for a very long period, we were in decline from Empire. If you want to see the British nation really buoyant, really confident, really successful, it is when they can see they are doing better than other people, when they can see there is a success – when we won the World Cup, when Virginia Wade won Wimbledon, when Torvill and Dean were mopping up the world titles. And I think we are moving into such a phase now because it is evident to anyone with eyes to see that economically we are outstripping our competitors in Europe. When that happens, while we will still have the tendency to say, 'Yes, well we are quite lucky and we are doing quite well', there will nevertheless be a great inward pride that Britain is doing well. Then, I think, people will say that the glass is half full rather than half empty.

When you were faced with criticism, when things happened in the Conservative party – and it has had more than its fair share of things going wrong over the last five or six years – were you ever tempted to throw your hands up in the air and say, 'Right, that's it, I have had enough'?

Never for more than a second. You would have to live with doing that and that isn't very attractive. If you have got a problem, you don't walk away from it.

Do you think you have been unlucky in the last five or six years in the way in which events have thrown themselves at your feet?

I don't think of it in terms of luck. Some of the events that have caused us the most difficulty have been a direct result of international economic conditions, and these have had a particular impact on us. Of course, in the United Kingdom, what has changed the whole flavouring of politics over recent years is that we are in the middle of one of three greatest debates the British nation has ever had on policy: the Corn Laws in 1840, Tariff Reform at the beginning of this century, and 'Whither the European Union and what is Britain's role in it?' in the 1990s. Only three times in 150-160 years have we had debates like that. On this occasion we have the debate when there is a media that is more pervasive than anything that existed in 1840 or 1910, and it has also coincided with a parliamentary majority that is very tiny. So, self-evidently, this has been a debate unlike anything we have seen before.

Did you feel that because of the size of your majority success was often outside your grasp?

The history of the last five years would have been different if I had had a majority of 100, and not a majority of 20 – of course, 20 and shrinking and a very small majority for the last few years. On the number of votes we got in the 1992 election we should have had a majority of 60 or 70, but the distribution of the votes meant we had a majority of only 20. Now if I had had the much larger majority the history of the last five years would have been quite different.

We talked about failures earlier, what do you regard as the most successful moments in your life?

Politically, the fact that we have moved from a medium- to high-inflation country to a low-inflation country. That is a sea-change in attitude which if maintained – it could be thrown away – is the biggest single economic change in this country for 50 years and one that is wholly beneficial. Providing it is maintained historians will look back 40 years from now, and say that was when it happened, in the early years of the 1990s. It was turbulent, it was nasty, it was very difficult, it caused immense pain and harassment politically at the time, but it was the right thing to do and it was done.

Do you think the judgment of historians on your premiership will be different to some of the judgments that have come along in the last few years?

I think inevitably they will be. Whether they will be better or worse only time will tell, but they will certainly be different because people will have a proper perspective to see what has happened. You don't have that perspective in the ebb and flow of day-to-day politics, when the story of the morning has changed by lunchtime and changed again by the evening and is quite different the next day. We need a diet of sensation to feed our media at the moment and if the sensation isn't there, then the media manufactures the sensation. Most of this artificial sensation, whether created by politicians or the media, is short-term and irrelevant to the long-term interests of the country. The long-term direction of the country can only be perceived over time. And I think what people will see when they look back is firstly the inflation change, secondly the extent to which the health reforms become bedded down, thirdly the very dramatic changes that we have made in education, and fourthly the fact that we have carried through the changes in the armed forces that have enabled us to arm them with the best equipment in the world and be sure that we have got the most professional army in the world. They are all long-term strategic changes, and we have delivered all those and others as well, but they are not apparent to people just looking through the daily headlines.

Nevertheless you have to deal with the short-term sensation in the media. Does that stop you being as successful as you would like?

It is very time consuming. A huge amount of time is wasted dealing with short-term stories that may be wholly and utterly absurd or just untruthful. It is time that could have been better used for long-term preparation or indeed long-term discussion with our partners in Europe and beyond Europe about things that are fundamental to Britain's national interest. But we are a democracy and a democracy requires that politicians are accountable, and therefore its politicians must account for what is happening on a day-to-day basis, and there is no escaping that.

Are you ever concerned that success for you as a politician must inevitably, because of the nature of politics, mean failure for somebody else? Is there a generosity of spirit there, or is it 'no holds barred, let's get the enemy in our sights'?

I'm not a no-holds-barred politician, I genuinely am not. They do exist in politics. Some people are prepared to damn the other side, whatever they do, and assume their side is right, whatever they do. I don't belong to that school of politics.

Have you ever thought the Opposition was doing something right?

Not often, but yes, of course. No party has a monopoly of wisdom. There are times when the Opposition is right. And as a politician you also realize there are some things governments can do if they are Conservative that Socialist governments couldn't do, and the converse is probably also true. There are different things that are politically possible and serious politicians understand that.

Would you like to see anything about the system of government changed in this country to give Britain the potential to be more successful? Do you think, for example, the five-year term is limiting in the sense that there are always short-term priorities and it is very difficult to allow the long-term priorities to take precedence?

No, I think the five years are right. I think a seven-year presidency, as in France, is too long and I think three years, as in some other countries – Australia springs to mind – is far too short for a parliamentary term. On balance, five years is about right. In an ideal world I would have far fewer Members of Parliament, but I don't see how you can easily get from 650-odd Members of Parliament down to a much smaller number, I think it would be extremely difficult to achieve. But there are parliamentary reforms that we can look at in order to modernize our procedures and ensure that the time we spend debating is spent debating the issues that really matter and not the trivial matters that so often dominate our attention.

Do you think that Prime Minister's Question Time has outlived its usefulness and mitigates against success because it feeds that short-term sensation that you were talking about?

No, I don't think it has outlived its usefulness. It's very time consuming but I think it is right that the Prime Minister should be answerable to the House of Commons. I do think, however, that many of the questions put to me are absurd questions to put to any Prime Minister. There are many trivial questions on points of detail that, across the whole wide sweep of government, it would be absurd really to expect me to know. There is also the extent to which the time is just used for juvenile points-scoring. I don't think either of those elements are helpful, either to the opposition or to the government, and I suspect the perception of the country of Prime Minister's Question Time is pretty negative. It's a good show, and people rather enjoy the show, but I don't think many people admire the exchanges all that much. If there were more sensible questions asked, and if it were not such a bear-pit, then I think it would serve more use. But having said that, I do think the Prime Minister should be in the House of Commons answering to his peers and I wouldn't change that.

Who are your heroes?

Every time I have answered a question like that, it has been psychoanalysed by some loopy psycho-babbler who has produced absolute nonsense which then gets in the cuttings and is used in the most absurd way. So I will go beyond politics, if I may. People like Stephenson: the engineer rather than the author. Robert Louis Stevenson is a great author but he wouldn't have been the one I would have picked. I think most people know my love of Trollope, but Dickens was a great author as well. If you really want a proper definition of success, to have chronicled your time and your age in the way that Dickens did or Trollope did or Jane Austen did, is truly astonishing. If you wanted success in the face of every probability, look at the astonishing novels of the Brontë sisters, whose power of story exceeded anything they could have experienced in a tiny vicarage in Yorkshire. That is astonishing success. But I admire people who have achieved the sort of things I could never have done. I couldn't have designed The Rocket. I couldn't have designed Brunel's bridges. These were real pioneers. Whoever originally conceived the Channel Tunnel, the guy who built the first aeroplane, the man who was either brave or incredibly foolish enough to make the first parachute jump, these are people one can only admire. They have done what no one had ever done before.

Do you see yourself as being like any of these people?

I'm a politician. I follow a long line of politicians and I precede a long line of politicians. But some people do what others had never considered possible, and that is really worth admiring.

Does success bring obligations in its wake?

Yes, of course it does. If you have success you have obligations of many sorts. You have obligations to make sure the success is put to good use, and if success brings you fame you have obligations to the people you meet. And that is true whether the fame is political fame, business fame, showbusiness fame. I think you have a particular obligation to other people.

Has success changed you at all?

Well other people would have to make that judgment. I don't honestly think so, but I'm not best placed to make a judgment.

What is the single greatest pleasure you have had from your success?

I don't think there is a single greatest pleasure. I think it is an accumulation of things. If I hadn't been in politics, I would have always have wondered what it was like. But I think it's an accumulation of what I have been able to do over the years and the opportunities that have arisen, not just for me but for other people.

What do you think are the qualities that you need for a country to be successful? You once talked about your ambition of a country at ease with itself.

And I wouldn't change that. I think there are several things you need. You need a sound and growing economy. All other things spring from that. You cannot afford the health, education, defence, police, fire and other services unless you have a successful economy, so that is the first thing you need. The second thing you need is a fair distribution of the quality of life. One of the things I am most pleased about in recent years is the extent to which there is a much better distribution of the quality of life across the United Kingdom. Many of the unemployment blackspots of a few years ago have now seen unemployment fall dramatically. Scotland is an example; there are still small areas which are blackspots but not for generations has Scotland had unemployment down at the UK average. Parts of Wales that have traditionally had high unemployment have now seen that disappear because of inward investment. Those changes are important and have given me a lot of pleasure.

If you could gather together before you in this room or any room all the young people in the world who say, 'I want to be a successful politician.' What advice would you give them?

I would say to them first, 'Why do you want to do it, and what would you do if you did do it?' Depending upon their answers, if they genuinely wish to get into politics I would encourage them to do so. I would also say that they would need hard work, persistence and luck, good health, but not necessarily in that order.

And the most successful route for a political career – what should they be thinking of doing?

It would depend. There are many different routes. I am not in favour of the professional politician who has done nothing but politics. I am not in favour of the guy who has had no real experience of life. I don't believe that politics is a career where you try to get elected in your twenties, you win a seat in your thirties and you continue through your Ministerial career until you reach a suitable retirement age, without touching the outside world at all. I would much prefer people to go out and try to find themselves a career, take an interest in politics in a voluntary fashion, and then decide when they have secured a career and secured some experience of the world whether they really want to enter into politics, because by then they will have something to offer. It isn't just a question of being a Member of Parliament, it is a question of having Members of Parliament with experience and something to offer the country and Parliament once they are elected.

When your time comes to leave this life, what would you like people to say about you?

He did his best. He tried to understand people and he did what he thought was right. I think if they were able to say that, it is as much as any politician can ask.

ANDREW MARR

'A newspaper is not a democracy ... but an editor should be tempered by wise and outspoken people internally who have strong and alternative views.' Thus the judgment of Andrew Marr, who won plaudits as a perceptive and thoughtful political commentator before being elevated for a time to the editorship of The Independent *while still in his mid-30s. His newspaper was a relatively new kid on the block too, still trying to break through to higher circulation levels in the teeth of fierce competition from the more established broadsheets. Apart from the perpetual journalistic quest to keep the writing fresh, the most visible trademarks of his young editorship were unconventional lead stories, ground-breaking longer headlines, eye-catching photographs and even the occasional front-page drawing. For*

him, success is 'the buzz from something well-made or well-done', with 'a grand pot-pourri of elements' – pace, style, balance, narrative, the ability to inform and make you think. He calls his Scottish education traditional and tough – 'I was always a lousy sportsman, and therefore the only way to get on was to be highly articulate and argumentative.' At Cambridge, where he got a first, he recalls being 'a wild, red-bearded student leftie'.

He started – and then abandoned – a PhD, and 'footled around various jobs, including working in a bookshop'. Among many rejected applications was one for a Thomson Regional Newspapers' training course, but at the last minute someone dropped out, and he was offered the place, going on to rise through The Scotsman *and the* Economist *to the hot seat at* The Independent *in just 14 years. He believes that 'dogged determination and rat-like cunning' are the trademarks of a successful journalist, while political correspondents need 'an even stronger awareness of charlatanry, and the mixed motives for being told things'. He explains here the difference between 'essential scepticism' and 'destructive cynicism' in journalism; and why there's nothing wrong with envying success – 'Envy is a great goad – it can be quite creative, reminding you what you've failed to do yourself, and may well be the motivating force for doing better.' This interview was carried out towards the end of his first year as an editor – a job he has now left to return to the role of political columnist that made his name. He advises budding journalists: 'You have to care, be fully engaged, persistent, determined, hard-working and focused, have basic moral principles, indulge in utterly ruthless self-criticism all the time – and don't do a course in media studies!'*

Andrew Marr, what is your definition of success?

Good work, I think, above all. Wendell Berry, the American writer who's a great hero of mine, emphasizes the buzz you get from something well made or well done, as well done as you can do it. A successful day is when you've made a good newspaper or written a good newspaper column, and I guess a successful career is when you have done that day after day for a very long time.

And how do you judge whether it's successful? Is it a judgment within yourself or is it that of others?

Certainly in journalism I think all of us would say that it is an internalized judgment. People will make criticisms of the paper and I'll take on board criticisms of the paper or column, but for myself I will be utterly depressed and deflated by a paper if I think it's not what it should be. One has to be one's own most severe critic.

Are there any particular criteria for what makes a good newspaper?

A good newspaper should make you think, genuinely argue back against it a bit. It should be comprehensive enough that you feel that you know everything that's important about the previous day. It should have a good variety – in other words it shouldn't be monotone, and that means the pace of stories, the style of stories, the balance between stories and pictures, the balance between mono pictures and coloured pictures, between different styles of writing should be sensible. Good narrative writing, good descriptive writing, good polemical writing has got to be there. It is, inevitably, a kind of grand *pot pourri* of elements, and if you've got all the right elements and if they are in harmony or balance, then you've got a good newspaper.

If you are trying to create a successful newspaper, can you do that purely based on your own judgments and your own criteria, or are you subject to external forces within the newspaper industry?

First of all, I'm lucky in that I genuinely don't have a proprietor sitting at my shoulder saying do this or do that – I'm undirected in that respect, so that's one outside force I don't have. A good newspaper is one which reflects the personality of its editor, but in which that editor is tempered, less by outside buffets than by wise and outspoken people internally who have strong and alternative views and are able to rein one in and put a quiet hand on one's shoulder – as somebody did the other day – and say, 'You made a mistake on the front page, you should be taking this story onto the front page, don't you see?' That particular person was right and I altered it. However I think there does need to be a central guiding force in a newspaper. I don't think a newspaper is a democracy. That's what the editor is there for.

The Independent *has had quite a chequered career and you were involved in it right at the beginning, although you went away during the middle part of its development. To what extent do you feel that the* Independent *has had a rough time in trying to be a successful newspaper, and what have been the tactics, as you perceive them, for dealing with the slings and arrows of outrageous fortune?*

I think almost all the way through (except for a very brief phase) the *Independent* has been the cuckoo in the nest. It's been the paper that everybody else was slightly resentful of, breaking up the old pattern. In the early days it was kept going by sheer fun and *joie de vivre* and a feeling of us all being involved in this terribly exciting new thing. As you said, I wasn't there for the middle part, but I think there is still a strong feeling of it being something special; that it's a paper that isn't controlled by any other group or mogul in its day-to-day operation. It has its special *esprit de corps* and a feeling that we're doing something valuable and we are not the *Guardian,* we're not *The Times,* we're not the *Telegraph,* we don't want to be any of those things. We feel there is something called an *Independent-*minded, *Independent-*person and reader, and the same goes for journalists.

How important is the sense of renewal, the freshness of ideas that must keep bubbling to the top at a newspaper?

One of the things that seems to be happening generally in society, is acceleration, it's the dominant thing that we experience all the time. Change seems to happen faster and faster and I think we're now in a period where newspapers are changing the whole time. The old idea that you redesign the newspaper, you find the form and then you've sat back for five years or ten years and it has worked is quickly becoming outdated. Here we're going to have to rethink the paper two or three times a year. It doesn't mean you change the paper dramatically all the time, but you are always asking yourself, 'Is the front page right? We're boring ourselves on page 5, we should be doing something else now.'

Was that done enough in the past?

No, it probably wasn't, but then no newspapers did. The *Independent* found a formula very early on. Looking back at the early papers, they weren't that great on pictures. It's now got a reputation for having, in its early days, wonderful black and white photographs, but that was something the paper stumbled upon six months into its life, then started to develop. A lot of the best things you come across by accident and you think, 'That was good, let's try it again today and see if it carries on working.' But I think the basic answer is energy, intellectual energy and vigour, and one of the reasons that editors change more often than they used to is that people inevitably get tired and stale, and unless an editor can remake himself or herself every few years, then probably the answer is to get rid of the editor and get a new one in, keep the sense of renewal going.

Let me move on to your personal success. To what extent has your success been a product of your background and upbringing?

I think quite heavily, in the sense that I went through a pretty traditional, and in some ways a rather tough education in Scotland. I was always a lousy sportsman and therefore the only way to get on was to be highly articulate and argumentative, and I was.

Did you set about achieving that, or was it something that came naturally?

I've always been articulate – that's the polite way of putting it. I've never been able to shut up and I was always a garrulous, talkative child, but also I think I was lucky in just being before the really big onset of television. Going to boarding schools where televisions weren't allowed, I read and read and read. I'm an obsessive reader so I did a lot of reading and a lot of talking, and there was the tradition of a debating society, and so on. So I was expected to read newspapers and be aware of current affairs and write essays about current affairs at school, and that helped enormously.

Do you think you were driven more to attempt to succeed by the fact that you weren't good at something, that you weren't good at sport?

I think that's absolutely right. People who find things come easily to them early on I have great sympathy for, because I think it's very difficult to keep pushing. If, when you're young, you've got money or are immensely talented at things that give you social success at school and university, I think it's quite hard to have that inner drive to keep going. You need the grit of the oyster, you need to be a not-entirely-happy or formed personality to be successful.

You went on to Cambridge. Were there any factors there which shaped your ambition or guided you in a particular career path, or had you decided by then you wanted to be a journalist?

No, I hadn't decided. At Cambridge I was an identikit lefty student politician. I did a little bit of student journalism, cartoons actually rather than writing, and wanted at various points to be an academic or a politician – I really didn't have a strong idea about journalism. I was very lucky, I started a PhD, gave it up in the first year and basically footled around looking, applying for all sorts of different jobs, including working in bookshops.

So the PhD was basically filling in time while you looked for something to do?

I got a first and I got offered the chance to do a PhD and I thought, 'Yes, I'll go on and be an academic writer, writing mainly about literature and modern literature.' I thought that was what I wanted to do. But it was the early 1980s, and whatever you felt about the early 1980s there was a real sense of things happening, there was a buzz and I thought, 'I can't stick in a university library during all this, I want to get out and do something.' I was very lucky because at Thomson regional newspapers training course which I'd applied to and which had rejected me, a place came up because somebody was going to be the *Scotsman*'s trainee and then went off for another job at the last minute. So unexpectedly they had a spare place and I got it. I got in under the wire, as it were.

When you were rejected first time round, what was your reaction? You'd been to university, you'd got a first, you must have felt on top of the world and here was someone telling you, 'Sorry you're not right for us.'

I was rejected by lots of people, but then again it was the start of the recession and lots of people were getting rejected for jobs and I was a wild, red-bearded student lefty, so I don't think it was very surprising. I think they were probably quite right.

What do you think makes for a successful journalist, and are there any differences between that and a successful political journalist?

I was trying to remember the old phrase we were taught at training school, I think it was a mixture of dogged determination and rat-like cunning. A good journalist is someone who is basically very conscientious about getting at the truth and determined and dogged and has to be able to write well too. There are lots of people who have several aspects of that, but at the end of the day can't produce something in prose that anyone would want to read. In political journalism I think you need to have an even stronger awareness of charlatanry and the mixed motives for being told things. It you're at Westminster, people will come up to you and befriend you and tell you the most fascinating and wonderful stories and you learn a few times, usually the hard way, that they've told you that story for a very specific reason, and they've told you two-thirds of the truth because they're trying to get at somebody else for reasons you don't quite understand. There are a lot of complicated webs of intrigue and manoeuvre behind every story at Westminster and the thing about politics is you have to be specially alert to why people are telling you things, as well as noting what they're telling you and making a story out of it. And you have to be fast, because it's a very fast-moving place when it's working well.

In a recent editorial, you said, 'If you want a job as a journalist on the Independent, *don't bother going to do a course in media studies.' Why did you say that?*

Well, media studies, in the words of the deputy of the paper, Colin Hughes, is becoming the new sociology, it's the slightly soft-option degree, and I think the trouble with media studies is that it's analysing the media, it's looking, in a cerebral or intellectual way, at what is a trade. It gives you lots of interesting theories about communication and the philosophy of communication, but what it doesn't do is teach you to write clearly and fast and accurately and vividly for a mass audience, which is what journalism tends to be about. If you look at people who've won young journalist awards recently, they're as likely to come from departments of geology or history or science or mathematics as from media studies. Given the increasing complexity of the world, if I'm offered two identical graduates, one of whom has done media studies and the other who may be fluent in French, or know a lot about science, having done a science degree, then I'll think there's added value in that second student – somebody who not only knows about how to write, but also knows a bit about a particular part of the world that will come in useful at some time.

There's a debate going on at the moment, particularly in America, about the difference between cynicism and scepticism, and the role that those ought to play. Are you a better journalist by being cynical?

No. Cynicism is corrosive. It's right the way through the culture, it's deeply ingrained. We could have an interesting philosophical argument about whether it's part of the ultimate inheritance of the enlightenment, that the rationalist and scientific belief in probing everything ultimately ends up with corrosive cynicism.

The difference between the two, in journalism, is that scepticism is utterly essential for good journalism and cynicism is utterly destructive of good journalism. Cynicism means you don't believe anything you're ever told, in which case, why bother reporting any of it? Why should your reader read it if it's all untrue? If it's all malign, then there's no point in journalism. Scepticism is, of course, the duty of the political journalist – to stand at one stage removed and always have part of the mind disengaged, however much one is impressed by a politician. I think the best political journalists are all excited by and enthused by politicians at different times, and admire them. If you regard John Major as utterly rotten and useless, or if you regard Tony Blair as an utterly cynical sham, then frankly, reporting British politics at the moment is a pretty miserable business, which you are not likely to enjoy and, therefore, not likely to be very good at. If, on the other hand, you think to yourself, 'Part of the reason that Tony Blair is saying this or that is for this or that tactical reason,' and when John Major presents himself as a kind of rugged outsider who has had a tough life, that's not the whole story – realizing that is scepticism, that's fine, that's what we are all about. It's when you say, 'These people are rotten and useless,' that it's cynical.

Is it too early to ask you what you think makes a successful editor?

Yes. There are lots of successful editors around of one kind or another, and they're all very different. There is almost nothing that unites – Paul Dacre and Andrew Neil, they are very different. Editing is very hard work. You have to work extremely hard, you have to think about the job all the time – except when you can cut off at weekends with family – you have to be relentless about quality and you have to pick yourself up very quickly after something has gone wrong and brush it aside and keep moving forward. You have to be reasonably good with people – you have to be prepared to sit and listen to people and work with people that you don't necessarily get on with or whom you may disagree with and help them to improve what they're doing.

Probably more than any other profession, journalism creates a conflict between work and family. You can't be a really good journalist unless you put in all the hours that God gives you, and yet you've got a family and a balance in life that you need to preserve. What advice would you give for resolving that?

The golden rule is to have a clear perimeter fence around your family life. Exactly where you peg that perimeter fence differs with different people, but if you don't have it and you're doing a job like this, then the family life will be swamped. The very simple rule I made, that I don't do anything job-related at the weekend, means declining absolutely fascinating invitations to, for example, important conferences that matter for the newspaper, or would-be summits to discuss the future of this or that as regards the *Independent*. You make yourself extremely unpopular by not going to these. But if you don't safeguard weekends, they would start to get eaten away as well, and you'd not see the family at all.

But you have been tough about that perimeter fence?

I've been very tough about it, I don't let it get trampled.

But for many successful people on the way up, it must be increasingly difficult to achieve that perimeter fence. If you are in serious pursuit of success, have you got to make those sacrifices in family terms at some stage, on the understanding that it's part of a deal that you hand something back whenever you've done all of the tough work and things get a little easier?

You have to be very careful about striking any such deal. You can't say, 'Right, well, I'm terribly sorry, I'm not going to see the children for a few years, but after that we're going to be so successful that I'll be back.' Things aren't like that. Saying that means you're a driven person who puts work over family and after that particular phase in their career, something else will come along which will be equally fascinating and important and necessary. In the end, if I thought that my children were being seriously damaged by not seeing enough of me, I would give it up and do something else. There is a trigger mechanism that would let me say, 'The job now comes second, the family have had too tough a time.'

Who are your heroes?

All my real heroes would be artistic or literary – Picasso, Proust, Tolstoy, the giants. In terms of journalism, the people I admire most of all are still the great journalistic writers and maybe that makes me a bit odd in the sense that I don't really have editorial heroes. I could very quickly trip off the tongue the writers I admire the most – I wouldn't call them heroes because that's elevating them too much – Matthew Parris, Boris Johnson, Polly Toynbee, Alan Watkins, Tony Bevins, they are the people I admire for their journalism, probably more than anybody else. Suzanne Moore and some of the people we've now got here are people I really admire. By and large I deeply distrust hero worship. I don't think that's cynicism, I think that's scepticism.

No politicians come to mind?

If you say you hero-worship a politician, that's too dewy-eyed or open-eyed.

Who do you regard then as being a successful politician?

I would put, I suppose, fairly obviously, Blair up there, and there are people that I really admire as politicians and operators on the Tory side. Major is a great operator, but in the end he's not a great leader, he's not given his party or the country a kind of clear sense of where we're going, which is what a great leader should be doing. I've got a huge amount of admiration for Ken Clarke and for Michael Heseltine and, when he was in power, for Douglas Hurd – they were all the kind of people I admired a lot. I admire anyone who has also retained a certain independence of mind and spirit, the Claire Shorts and the Frank Fields of this world and I admire Ashdown for the absolutely bloody awful job he's got – it's utterly thankless, and he plugs away. These are a lot of people I like and admire, across all parties, they are not clustered in one particular area or another.

What makes a successful politician?

That's very interesting. Some of the old clichés are true – stamina, luck, being able to sleep at night for four hours and wake up fresh as a daisy the next day – these are all very important because being a politician is a relentless job that can expand perpetually in all directions. But in addition, what a politician has to be able to do is to be able to tell a story, to be able to say, 'This is how the world is and this is what it means for you and this is what it means for the country,' in a way which causes people to nod and say, 'Yes, that's right, that's true. I recognize that and because I recognize that, I would accept the fact that taxes have got to go up this year or that unemployment is taking a long time to go down or I'm going to work a bit harder. I'm going to change my behaviour, however modestly, because this bloke, despite, say, my dislike of the way he behaves with his wife, is, in the end, telling it as it is.' It's that sort of primal story-telling which is I think central to political success.

Can you be a successful politician by being an opportunist and simply seizing the right moment at the right time on a fairly repetitive basis?

Oh yes, Bill Clinton is an absolute examplar of that kind of success. You can stay in office, you can do deals with powerful people, you can buy yourself flattering coverage in certain newspapers or books or whatever, you can have that success, but you won't be looked back on as a great figure and your reputation will crumble quite quickly, because you won't have changed anything in the end. Bill Clinton, for instance, is a phenomenally successful campaigner, brilliant on the stump, and he has ridden and survived scandals that would destroy lesser figures; he has this extraordinary mesmeric power to bind people to him and make them believe him. But in the end there is a right-wing conservative agenda in American politics at the moment which has nothing to do with Bill

Clinton. He has become merely the servant of the ruling or the dominant ideological agenda of his time. He's not changed a thing, in fact he may have slightly slowed down the pace of change. There's nothing fundamental he has done which wouldn't have been done had somebody else been in power.

Can you be a successful politician by having a vision and then attempting to drive it forward or to a certain extent, do you stand a better chance of being successful as a politician if you are simply very good at responding to events?

If your dominant idea is entirely against the grain of your times then you're not going to be successful, however brilliant and powerful you are. If you are, as Enoch Powell was, deeply hostile to the big state but the year happens to be say, 1955, when the big welfare state was still in its heyday and building up, no one's going to listen to you. You have to be in tune with the mood of the times, but you can shape that mood. One of the very interesting things about Blair is this moral crusade, the remoralizing of communities. Now he makes himself very unpopular within elements of his own party, but there is no doubt he is taking the lead, saying, 'This is something we should be doing.' But there is also no doubt that Blair is helping to articulate and shape that for quite a lot of people who would be alienated by it if it came from the Conservative leader.

Do you think there's a difference between success in different professions or are there any general core principles?

We've come back to what success is. If success has anything to do with good work, as I think it does, then the core principle – whatever you're doing – is that you have to care and be fully engaged while you're working, in what you're doing. I think you need to have basic moral principles – a purely Machiavellian road to success will end up with a ruined reputation one way or another. I'm an optimist to the extent that I believe that, but I think to be successful you must be persistent, determined, hard-working, focused on what your job is and believing in it. I think if you are utterly cynical about what you're doing then you won't be a success.

What are the greatest enemies of success?

Indolence, ill health and, I suppose above all, lack of focus or lack of concentration. Successful people are the ones who know where they want go and keep moving in a straight line, and if they are knocked off and they fall by the wayside, they pull themselves back up and carry on going. Sometimes that doesn't bring you success. Clive Sinclair's been knocked off his route to success several times and has climbed doggedly back on and probably hasn't got success in most people's view in terms of being a successful inventor.

Success arouses different emotions in people ranging from admiration to out-and-out envy. Why do you think that is? In Britain, is it partly to do with our national character that we are much more envious about success than they tend to be in America?

Funnily enough, I'm not that much against envy. It's one of the sins that I have a fair amount of time for. I've done a couple of books and I was deeply envious of the success of other people in the same field at selling more copies or many more copies, or getting better reviews. I'm envious of colleagues and friends who have written novels and done rather well with them. The reason I'm envious is that I would like to do that too, and their success showed up what I wasn't doing and reminded me of the failures of what I'd done, or the reason that book wasn't a success, or that I never actually had the guts to really try and write a proper work of fiction or whatever. So I think envy is a great goad. It can be quite creative, reminding you what you've failed to do yourself, and may very well be the motivating force for doing better. I'm reading the second volume of John Richardson's *Life of Picasso* at the moment, and if it hadn't been for the fact that Picasso and Matisse, at a clear, very important point in their careers, were deeply envious of and hostile towards one another, prowling into one another's studios, looking at what they were doing and trying to do better, then neither would have been anything like as great as they were – they required that mutual spur. When we're trying to be nice about anything, we call it competition, but they required that envious struggle between them, and I think, therefore, when it's working quite well, envy is simply about reminding oneself that other people have done much better, and being irate, essentially at oneself for not working harder.

But we are talking here about a little envy, because too much envy could become a destructive force that actually foils your bid for success.

Yes, too much envy, if it curdles and becomes self-pity, becomes destructive. Self-pity is probably a much more corrosive and dangerous thing than envy. All vigorous and competitive societies include quite a lot of envy. People complain about the politics of envy but the politics of envy aren't all bad. If it hadn't been for the politics of envy we probably wouldn't have had any progressive legislation at all, so even there I'm not resolutely hostile to envy. Self-pity and feeling, 'The rules are bent against me so I can't possibly succeed,' or, 'The world hates me,' I'm going to go and eat worms – those are the really dangerous things for success.

Does individual success bring any obligations to the wider society?

If it's monetary success it brings the obligation to pay higher taxes, and to give to charity as well. If we're talking about success as power, then power obviously brings obligations to treat people decently, to try not to be too much of a bully, and to deal relatively honestly with all one's contacts. If we're talking about success being good work, doing something supremely well, then it doesn't bring any more obligations than you've got already, as a citizen or whatever.

Has success changed you at all?

Apart from doing interviews about how successful I am, you mean? No, I don't think so. I don't actually think of myself as being particularly successful. When the *Independent* has hit circulations of upwards of 300,000 to 320,000 and everyone is saying it's a remarkable success, and the paper is making a mild profit, if that day ever comes – and, I hasten to add, I'd been editor over the period that we're talking about – then I'll think I'm successful in doing that. I'll think, 'That was a job that needed doing, it has been done well and, for all my failings, faults, and ups and downs, I have achieved that.'

If you could gather together in one room all the young people in the world who actually want to be journalists, what advice would you give them?

That's very difficult. I think, just indulge in utterly ruthless self-criticism all the time – that's the most single important piece of advice. Be your own harshest critic, because if you are, that means that you will be ruthlessly trying to improve your own game, to improve the way you write and the way you report, and if you do that, then everything else will follow – stories will follow, the scoops will follow, the well-written pieces will follow; the reputation for always being eager to pile in and do something, that will be there too, and no editor will refuse you in the end.

And when your time comes to leave this life, what would you like people to say about you?

I don't know. I think I take the slightly Shakespearian view that you live on in people you've known and your children, and if they are mildly better than they would have been, then that's the best thing. I don't think journalists should have memorials or stones. I think it is, or should be, a fame-repellent business.

SIR GEORGE MARTIN

The man who discovered the Beatles and became one of the greatest record producers in the world had to give up piano lessons as a child because his parents couldn't afford them. Besides, as his mother explained, 'music was not a career for a decent gentleman'. So he set his sights on aircraft designing – and just after his 17th birthday, with World War II well under way, he signed up for the Fleet Air Arm, learning 'all sorts of new disciplines'. When demobbed, he used his ex-Serviceman's grant for three years' study at the Guildhall School of Music – after which he settled for a job in the BBC music library because it gave him 'the freedom to compose and play his own songs in the evenings'. Then, out of the blue, came an offer of a job with Parlophone EMI, where he produced virtually everything from Mozart to jazz – and even Enid Blyton's Noddy *stories! His rise was meteoric. At 29, he became Head of Parlophone – no one that young had ever been in charge of a record label before – and worked with artists such as Peter Sellers, Spike Milligan, Charlie Drake, Michael Flanders and Donald Swan.*

It was envy of the success being enjoyed by his friend Norrie Paramor with the newly discovered Cliff Richard that drove him to take a chance with the Beatles when every other record company in London had turned them down. Attracted at first by their charisma, he admits it took time for him to 'get into' their music! With other singers like Cilla Black and Freddie and the Dreamers on his label, 1963 saw records he had produced hold the number-one slot in the hit-parade for no fewer than 39 weeks. When EMI rejected his attempts to obtain a share of royalties for producers, he left to form his own company, Associated Independent Recordings (AIR) – still his pride and joy. The Beatles went with him, and he never looked back. He rolled into his 70th year as active as ever – adding to his laurels an outstanding version of Dylan Thomas's Under Milk Wood, *the ambitious* Glory of Gershwin *album, the archive-rich* Beatles Anthology *– and a richly deserved knighthood. Here, he talks of the self-doubt, the troughs of despondency and the 'dreadful, seductive pressures' in the music business; of his regret that visual images have become all-important, so that 'people listen with their eyes instead of their ears'.*

Sir George, what is your definition of success?

I think success is probably achieving what you want to achieve, without hurting anyone in the process. You go through life trying to do what you can, as best you can. And if you strike success, you get applauded, and if you hit failure you get all the downside. If you're lucky you have more of the success than the failure.

So it's not a good idea to say, 'I want to be successful', without having a very clear idea of the area of life that you wish to be successful in?

I suppose every young person has the ambition to be successful, and that, in most young people's eyes, means being rich and famous. They don't realize this isn't all that it might appear. Of course it's better to have more money than less, and of course it's nice to be wooed by people and flattering that people recognize you. But true success is getting to a position where you are at peace with yourself, where you know that whatever you have done has been good for other people. Success for me also means a successful family, having the people around me that I love and having that love returned.

Is there not an inevitable conflict though, between someone pursuing a successful career and someone who wants to have a successful family life? How do you get the balance right between the two?

It's very difficult and the first time round I didn't. My first marriage ended in failure. I got married too young. I was engaged when I was 19 and in those days I was a very ambitious young musician. When I started at Abbey Road I was seduced by the business of recording. It was a fascinating business, and I loved it. I worked extraordinarily long hours and that, obviously, had some effect upon the marriage. It wasn't the only reason the marriage failed, but it was a contributing factor. And when I married again, I married a lady who had been in the business and understood it, and she had all the tolerance that was necessary to cope with the extraordinary hours that I kept. With the Beatles, we sometimes worked right through the night and into the following morning, but she understood this and supported it, and without her I would not have been successful.

To what extent is success a product of your background and your upbringing?

I suppose it was imbued in me by my parents. They weren't very well off, but they were good people and both were very hard-working. My father was a carpenter and my mother came from a rather better family than my father, but being poor she had to work awfully hard. She herself was quite talented and always wanted her son to do his very best and urged me on at school. I went to a state elementary school to begin with, and then I got a scholarship to a Jesuit college, St Ignatius in North London. I left school when I was 16 and I didn't go to university because the war was on. But by this time I was running a dance band, which again I was encouraged to do because my parents thought the music was lovely, although they weren't musicians. There was no music in the family, I just had this natural talent.

So the interest in music was there right from the start?

Well, it was a curious thing. We always had a piano in our household, I can't remember the house not having a piano. My sister, who was three years older than I, was first taught by an aunt and then had lessons for two years, but we couldn't afford lessons for two children, so I missed out. But I would imitate what my sister did and I really cannot remember not being able to play tunes on the piano. I was playing when I was four or five, making up little pieces.

From those early days, did you sense that music could be a career for you?

No, I didn't. I just ran a band and earned some money – it was a lovely hobby. And my parents never considered music because it was like the acting profession. It might be fun to do amateur dramatics, but my goodness, it wasn't a career for a decent gentleman. My mother said, 'Do something really solid, take up a profession. You're good at maths, you're good at drawing, architecture sounds a good idea.' My father went along with that, and I was certainly very interested in design. In fact, what I wanted to do most of all when I was in my teens was to be an aircraft designer. And when I knew I had to go into one of the Services, I knew I loved flying, and I loved boats too, so the Fleet Air Arm was a natural choice. I signed up when I was 17. I didn't tell my mother and she was absolutely shaken, when I went home and told her.

When you came out of the Fleet Air Arm you went to the Guildhall School of Music. By that time was the ambition to develop music firmly set within you?

I had a kind of fairy godfather in the shape of a piano professor called Sidney Harrison, and I'd corresponded with him all through the war. Someone had heard me playing one of my own compositions and had advised me to send it to the Committee for the Promotion of New Music, and Harrison was it. That was the beginning of a lifelong friendship. He wrote back with two foolscap pages of criticism of the composition. He urged me to learn more about music, to co-operate with the Marine Band

and write bits for them. At the end of the war I came out and had no job to go to, so I went to see Sidney Harrison and he said, 'You've got to take up music.' I said, 'I can't, I've never had any training.' He said, 'Yes you must, it's your talent, you must use it. I'll arrange an interview for you at the Guildhall School of Music. You must see the Principal and play him your compositions.' So I did. He listened to them all and agreed to take me on as a composition student. I got a grant, because I was an ex-serviceman, and studied for three years.

How important is a mentor in the life of a successful person?

In my case it was terribly important because Sidney put me on the right lines, was a great source of encouragement, and did it for no reason except that he wanted to help. And I couldn't pay him back, I've never been able to pay him back, except maybe by helping young people myself.

When you came out of the Guildhall School of Music, you worked in the BBC Music Library. Were you right at the bottom of the ladder?

Oh, absolutely. It was a job to give me money during the day while I played music in the evenings. And it was very little money indeed. I looked after manuscripts and scores so, if the BBC Concert Orchestra wanted a particular work, I had to look it out and make sure all the parts were there. It was a library job.

How did you get the break with Parlophone EMI?

My fairy godfather again. It's a strange story, but Parlophone was a very small part of EMI in those days, and all the offices were at Abbey Road Studios. The fellow who ran Parlophone was a chap called Oscar Preuss and he did it more or less by himself. He had a secretary, but no production assistant, and he was looking for one because he was 60 and needed some help. He spoke to his friend Victor Carne, who was at that time operatic producer for HMV and a great friend of Sidney Harrison. Victor, in turn, asked Sidney whether he knew of a young chap, with some musical talent, who might want a job at EMI. He gave him my address and out of the blue I got a letter asking if I would be interested in an interview for a post at EMI? So I cycled along, in my old naval greatcoat, to the interview and got the job at £7 4s 3d a week. That was 1950.

So then you found yourself at Parlophone, making Noddy records.

Well, all sorts of records. To begin with I was put on the classical end of

Parlophone, and because I'd taken up the oboe at the Guildhall, I was put in charge of a group called the London Baroque Ensemble, which specialized in woodwind music – things like Mozart's *Serenades*. We had the most wonderful musicians, and so when I started producing it was just supervision of the musicians. But, after a while, you begin to realize that you can influence things. I worked with people like Adrian Boult and Charles Mackerras and, at the same time, Oscar was off-loading more and more stuff onto me. It was a label that did everything – classical music, jazz, children's records. I did little Noddy along with all the other things.

Did you ever feel, 'Why am I doing this? I want to do bigger, better things?'

To begin with it was a job which gave me more money and, again, enabled me to play in the evenings, and it was a kind of stepping stone to the ideal of being able to write music for film or concert performance. But as I got into it I became more and more fascinated by it and from 1950 through to 1955 I learned my craft. What's more I was losing my ambition to be Rachmaninoff II, and began to realize that I was probably better at telling people what to do rather than doing it myself. By 1955 I was doing virtually everything for the label. Oscar reached the age of 65 and retired and I thought someone else would be brought in above me. To my astonishment they gave me the job and I was head of Parlophone, at the age of 29. No one that young had ever been in charge of a label.

Did achieving such high success so early change you in any way?

No, because it was all a gradual process. By 1955 I was already making my own mark in records. I had started recording the top comedians, which became one of my specialist areas. I worked with Peter Sellers, Spike Milligan, The Alberts, then Charlie Drake, Bernard Cribbins and Rolf Harris. I went to watch Michael Flanders and Donald Swan – I thought they were marvellous, and I made their albums. Later on I recorded the *Beyond the Fringe* people, Alan Bennett, Dudley Moore, Jonathan Miller and Peter Cook.

Then the Beatles came along. They had been rejected by everybody else. What made you think that the Beatles were worth running with?

It was in January 1962 that I first met Brian Epstein. I had a number two record with Jim Dale and I had a number one with the Temperance Seven – 'You're Driving Me Crazy' – but I was still looking for an easy way of making hit records. I was very envious of my friend and co-producer on the Columbia label – Norrie Paramor. He had a young guy, Harry Webb, who became Cliff Richard, who seemed to be a great hit. It seemed almost effortless for Norrie – all he had to do was find a half-decent song and because of the following for this chap, he had hit after hit. I th ught, 'I must try some of this.' So I was looking for something special, a d the reason I met Brian Epstein was that I had received a phone call rom a music publisher friend who worked for EMI, called Sid Colema .. He'd met Brian because Brian had taken a tape into HMV Oxford Stre t to get some discs made for demonstration, and he had confessed to Sid that he'd seen everybody in the recording business and he was very dispirited. Sid said, 'Have you been to EMI?' And Brian said, 'Yes, I've been round there and they've turned me down.' He said, 'Well, did you see George Martin there, he runs the Parlophone label?' He said, 'Parlophone, never heard of it.' Sid said, 'It's a kind of jazz-comedy label.' Brian knew he'd hit the all-time low, he'd been turned down by HMV, Columbia, Decca, Phillips, Pye, everybody, and he didn't know where to go. So he said, 'If you can fix up for me to see him, I'd be grateful.' Brian turned up with these records that he'd had cut at HMV and gave me the name of the group that he had, which I thought was a terrible name, the Beatles – what an awful pun that was. Anyway I listened to it. The stuff was not very good, but he was so enthusiastic about his boys, as he called them – they were going to be good, they were going to be big.

The quality wasn't very good, the songs weren't very good, the performances were rough, but there was something there. It was quite intriguing, a different sound. It certainly wasn't Cliff Richard, it was a bit rough and ready, but raw. So I said to Brian, 'Look, I can't judge on these demos, if you want me to be seriously interested in this group – the Beatles, do you call them? – well bring them down. Where are they, Liverpool? Bring them down to London and I'll listen to them in the studio.' He groaned. He'd gone this route before, and now he had to go back to the Beatles and tell them that they had to come down again and go through the same routine. They had a booking in Germany so we didn't fix a time until a couple of months later, and it was no skin off my nose. I thought it was an interesting possibility, but it was nothing vital. When they eventually came into the studio, I spent three hours with them, and I fell in love with them. I thought they were terrific. I didn't fall in love with their music at first, I had to get into that, but as people they had great charisma. And they knew me and they knew all the records I'd made. They were great fans of the Goons and Peter Sellers, and people like that, and we hit it off right away. They were very cheeky, which I quite liked. There's the well-worn story about George Harrison. After the first take, I brought them into the control room and said, 'Look, this is what we've done with your sound, have a listen to it and tell me if there's anything you don't like.' George looked at me and said, 'Well, I don't like your tie for a start.' That's absolutely true. The others pummelled him and said, 'You don't do that, he's an important guy.' I thought it was terribly funny.

So you liked them personally. But you can't allow your personal feelings to cloud your professional judgment, or can you?

I had a gut feeling about them. My rationale was, if they have this effect on me, they are going to have a similar effect on people when they perform, if the music is good enough.

So to the extent that luck plays a part in success, the Beatles might never have happened if it hadn't been for that meeting with you?

Yes, it's probably true to say that.

So success is therefore dependent, not on innate talent, but on the breaks and the luck that you get, as you proceed through life?

You've got to be lucky, but you also tend to make your own luck. As you go through life, you come to a crossroads or a fork in the road and you take one way or the other way, and you try to judge which is best. Sometimes you take the wrong one, sometimes you take the right one, but the opportunities are always there. If you grasp them, then you get success. It's pretty nebulous stuff, but it is true.

Just after you gave the Beatles their big break, you had a major row with the company you were working for, and you walked out. What was that about?

Money. In fact, it was a long time after that. I left the company in 1965. I'd been thinking about leaving EMI before the Beatles came along. I actually signed a new contract in January '62, for three years, but I was reluctant to do so. For years I'd been saying that the people who made the records ought to have a commission. The artists got a royalty and the salesmen got their commission but we got nothing. Things finally came to a head in Christmas 1964, after we'd had a tremendously successful time. Everybody got their Christmas bonus, which I think was about four days' pay – EMI were not renowned for being generous – but I didn't get mine. I couldn't understand, there must have been some mistake, so I rang up the accounts department and asked what had happened to it. They said, 'Oh, you don't get one now.' I said, 'I don't? Why not?' 'Well, you're over the £3000 limit. You're in the management class now, you are getting £3200 a year, people at that level don't get bonuses.' I was furious. That year we'd had number ones all over the place, we'd made millions for the company and I got no lousy bonus. So I was really rather angry.

But then you took the decision to go out on your own. It was based on anger, but there must have been a consideration of the risk involved?

It was a gamble, but I insured myself to some extent. I was so determined to start my own production company that I invited three other people to join me – Ron Richards, my assistant at Parlophone, John Burgess, the assistant of my Columbia mate, Norman Newell, and Peter Sullivan, who had been assistant at HMV and had gone to Decca. They were all hit-makers, so between us we formed a pretty formidable combination. They were younger than I was, and I thought, 'They could carry me into my old age.' It wasn't to be, but Peter recorded Engelbert Humperdinck and Tom Jones. John Burgess recorded Manfred Mann, Adam Faith and John Barry. Ron Richards had the Hollies. We had quite a team of hit artists between us. So we formed our new company and I thought, 'If the worst comes to the worst, I can always get another job somewhere else.'

What do you regard as your greatest successes?

The Beatles, obviously, come pretty high on that list in terms of financial success. Even recently, I've been astonished to see how well *The Beatles Anthology* has sold. Each double album has been number one in America, within a 12-month period, and so far we've sold about 14 million albums. I also like to think that what we did in terms of making sound imagery, all the comedy work that I did with Peter Sellers and Peter Ustinov and those kind of people was successful. I think that established a form of recording which, to me, was invaluable in making a Beatles record. I think that the studios that I've built have been a big success too. Air Studios in Hampstead is the last I'll ever build, but I think it's probably the best studio there is and I'm rather proud of it.

How about failures, and how did you recover from them?

Well, the biggest failure in my life, I suppose, was my first marriage. The children of that marriage had to bear the brunt of that and I have always felt guilty. But you mustn't look back too much. Of course I've had lots of little failures. You record someone and think they are going to be great and they don't happen. Everything is a mixture of failure and success, and you just have to make sure that the successes outweigh the failures.

What were the precise processes by which success came about for the Beatles, because you told them at first what they should do, but then you said it got round to the stage where they started telling you what to do. What was the balance between those two?

The success came by picking the right song and making the right arrangement for it. In the early days the success was in a succession of singles. The first album was done in a day, and it was just a recital of their songs. Success didn't really happen until that magic moment when we knew we were number one in America.

From that moment on it seemed they were able to write better songs each time, and they wrote different songs each time. They didn't write the same song over and over again. There was a big change-round about the time of *Rubber Soul. Rubber Soul* and *Revolver* are a couple of my favourite albums, and I suppose the apogee of it all was *Sergeant Pepper* – that really was painting pictures in sound. Certainly their genius was manifest by this time, but they still needed direction and shaping, and we had become a very solid team. On the floor of the studio there were five people involved, the four Beatles and myself, all with good ideas, exchanging them, considering them and rejecting them, but every voice was equal.

Don't you have one person who is in control in an operation like that, who takes the final decision? Or can it evolve in the way you suggest?

It evolved very happily with us because, generally speaking, I would lean towards the person who'd written the song. He and I would be the decision-makers, but we would listen to the other people's ideas. So if it was John's song, he and I would decide how it would be, with input from the others. The same applied if it was Paul's song, and so on. Later on, there was an unhappy time with John who didn't like production techniques too much, but he was going through an unhappy time anyway, a very druggy period. This was a time when he was also fighting with the others, but generally speaking our co-operation was a very happy one. And when, eventually, we came back and made the final record, *Abbey Road*, it was like the old days and John was his old self.

What are the pressures of success?

Exhaustion. You have to pace yourself, you have to have a good constitution, you mustn't burn the candle at both ends. There are dreadful pressures on the young nowadays to experiment with drugs, and I can't impress upon young people enough how dangerous these are. They are such a seduction and they are so destructive.

You once said, 'Our civilization builds up idols and icons and then tears them apart when it discovers they're not idols any more.' What did you mean by that and is that an inevitable part of success?

Yes, because everything's a bit of a myth. I was talking to Paul about this once, and we were discussing our past and looking at the images of 1964 and '65 and he said, 'You know, it's like it happened to other people, isn't it? It's like we're watching puppets, it is us but it's the images that other people see that aren't us. We know what we are because we're just human beings. You know, the Queen goes to the toilet like you do.' It's true, we're just human beings.

How did you avoid the tearing apart process? Because that's never really happened, has it?

Again, I think my wife had a lot to do with it. I think that she could see when the strain became too great and she was able to warn me that I must pace myself and take it easy.

You've also said that all creative people go through a period of self-disgust. What did you mean by that and how do you recover?

The process of creation, I suppose, is very much a lonely affair and you can get yourself into a situation where you get carried away with your own thoughts and you think you're brilliant and then you suddenly realize that you may be kidding yourself, and you start worrying about that and saying, 'Am I what I think I am?' You have moments of self-doubt and they, in turn, can become tremendous troughs of despondency.

So how do you pull back from those?

I think you have to take the broad view. You have to look at yourself and say, 'Well, in the end nothing really matters. Absolutely nothing. What are we, for heaven's sake? We are tiny grains of sand in the universe, we are so insignificant and yet we're worried about whether our record's going to make it to the top ten or not. In a few years time, all this will be forgotten, we're just a passing bit of dust.' If you can take that view, it certainly brings you down to earth.

Is it a very difficult view to take, because at the time your priority, your obsession, if you like, is this particular musical project you're working on?

Of course, but you've got to level yourself. You've got to get things in perspective. Nothing is really that important. Very few of us are prime ministers about to go to war with another country. Most of the decisions we take are very personal ones and they only affect the little people around us. They are not big deals.

To be able to think like that, do you have to have a kind of inner calm, a sort of equilibrium which enables you to ride across those troughs?

I think you have to have an inner calm, I think you have to try to adopt it and many people have different ways of doing this. George Harrison is a great believer in transcendental meditation and many of the cults of the Far East. When I was ill he came to see me and brought with him a lovely bunch of flowers and a little wooden carving of the god Ganesh, the elephant one. And he said, 'Put him by your bed and look at him before you go to bed and you will be all right.' He had this enormous belief. Well, Ganesh is still by my bed and that's fine.

And did you look at it every day?

I do look at him from time to time, but I'm a Christian and I do believe in God. I think if you have that faith it helps.

Has religion been a part of your success?

Religion's a nasty word to me. I hate organized religion. I think most of the religions have failed. The Church of England has some very good people in it, but as an organization it's not too good. And the Roman Catholic faith has got so many paradoxes in it that it doesn't serve most people. You've got to build up your own inner faith.

Is it more or less difficult to achieve musical success now?

It depends what you mean by musical success. In the pop world it's a much bigger lottery than it used to be and I don't think music has got a great deal to do with it. Visual image is the most important thing. People now don't listen with their ears, they listen with their eyes. We are so conditioned by the television screen that anything visually attractive that comes on it is accepted. And if the image is right, then records will sell.

So what appears on the screen can override the musical quality of a record. In other words, a bad record can sell because of a great image?

Absolutely. This is one of the reasons why we don't have the sort of music that is likely to last very long. In the early days of the Beatles, although they had charisma and a good image, it wasn't the vision that sold, it was the sound they were making. But I don't think Michael Jackson would've been as big as he is without the benefit of his videos.

What are the ingredients of a successful song?

It's so difficult to give a formula for it. If I knew the answer, I'd be writing them all the time. A memorable melody, a meaningful lyric, attractive harmonies that don't go down the well-worn route, and a very catchy rhythm. I think those are some of the ingredients, anyway.

Is it more difficult to write something that is new and original because, in a sense, every sequence of notes has been written before in some form or another?

That's true, but that's always been true. Gershwin had the same problem. The notes were still the same 12 notes on the scale and he came up with 'Summer Time' – nobody had thought of that one before. And when Paul woke up and played 'Yesterday', no one had thought of that one either, but he thought they had. No, I don't think it's any more difficult than it has been, but it is difficult.

If you were setting up a really successful group or singer now, how would you go about that?

Well, being very cynical about it, it would have to be a manufactured job. I would choose a group of people who were very attractive to look at, whether male or female. I would get them choreographed so that their movements were very attractive, also hip, and would appeal to young people. I would find a song that was well written and with a good hook. I would get them to sing it well, and if they didn't sing it well I'd even substitute really good singers who could, and pretend that they had done it. Then I would sell it, market it mercilessly until it became a hit. That's being very cynical.

Who are your heroes?

I've got lots. I was with one of my heroes yesterday, Sean Connery. I think he's such a magnificent character. He's got enormous charisma. He is Mr Scotland to me, he's done a lot for Scotland, and I think he ought to be Sir Sean Connery. He's just one of my heroes. There are lots of people in America that I've never met, whom I regard as heroes. I think Goldie Hawn is wonderful.

Those are present-day people, anyone in history?

The inevitable Winston Churchill. He was a hero, because I remember, as a child, everyone being moved by what he did. There aren't many politicians who are heroes, and a lot of my heroes are people who aren't well known, people with great courage who've gone through some dreadful times. They've coped with grief, or they've coped with disability and setbacks with great cheer. There was a woman, for example, in my village, who is now dead. She was crippled almost from birth and she was in a wheelchair all her life. But she raised children and she always had a smile on her face. She had nothing. We used to take our children down to her cottage and she was always full of life and so delighted to see us, and the sun would shine. When you went to see her and spoke with her, you felt better for it. She was a wonderful woman. There are people like that.

Success in others arouses conflicting emotions, ranging from admiration right through to envy. Why is that?

I suppose some people think that success is not deserved, in which case their envy becomes rather rank. In this country we do tend to have a kind of envy in our make-up that is none too attractive.

What do you think are the greatest enemies of success?

Probably sloth, indolence and a lack of care for other people.

Do you think success brings obligations to the rest of society in its wake?

No question about it. I think that the whole point about success should be to set an example to other people, and to help other people. I think without that, it's empty.

Has success changed you at all?

I hope not. I don't know, you'd have to ask other people that.

What's the greatest pleasure you've had from your success?

Being able to enjoy the trappings of success. Being able to take my wife out to dinner in a nice restaurant without having to worry about whether I can pay the gas bill or not. That's one of them. And also having a good circle of friends – people are everything.

If you could gather together all the young people wanting to make a career as you have, what advice would you give them?

Master your craft. Whatever it is, whether you're a carpenter or a soprano, master your craft. Work hard and learn and take advice from the people who know. Being an apprentice, you've got to learn your trade, whatever it is, in any walk of life. And then, along with that, be true to yourself, don't go astray. Always ask yourself if you're doing the right thing for yourself and for other people. Don't do things just because other people do them, don't be led astray. Follow your own path, keep going at it and don't let go. Keep persevering. It's the people who give up who fail. The people who succeed are those people who are tenacious, who hang on and say, 'I can make it, I will make it.'

And what about singers, people who are in front of the microphone – what advice would you give to them?

Well, obviously try and do your very best. Try not to get nervous, try to listen to yourself rather than to other people, don't worry about what other people are doing and listening to, don't be distracted. Don't, while you're performing, think, 'Is he looking at that mole on my left cheek?' It's easy for me to say this, and this is why being a producer is easier than being a performer, but I remember what it was like when I played the oboe at a music exam. I was so nervous that my fingers began to sweat and the sweat ran down the keys of my oboe and my fingers slipped on the keys, which made me make mistakes, which made me more nervous, which made me sweat more. It's very difficult to overcome that kind of dreadful fear.

But how do you overcome it?

I didn't. I gave it up and did something else.

But from what you have observed of artists out there, a lot would go through that same kind of nervous tension.

Everyone does and it doesn't matter who it is. If you talk to Kenneth Branagh, Emma Thompson, Anthony Hopkins, they will all admit that they get scared witless sometimes – they all do. But you take heart from the fact that everybody goes through it and say, 'I'm going to overcome it as they did.' And you just have to buckle your belt a bit tighter and stiffen the sinews. It's a discipline. You've got to learn it, you've got to really drill it into yourself.

When your time comes to leave this planet, what would you like people to say about you?

He went an awful long way on a very thin talent.

What do you think they will say?

I've no idea. I hope they will say he was a nice man who loved other people. That's what I'd like it to be.

DAVID MELLOR

'You have to put a brave face to the world, sometimes appearing too tough and too determined, or you would be swept away by the tide of events.' That is a rare hint of inner self-doubt by a controversial former politician who worked his way to the top, was brought down by 'being reckless in my private life', and has since built up several successful new careers. David Mellor has always presented an immense aura of confidence and resilience to the world at large. His enemies call it arrogance; his friends see it as the public armour for a brilliant, analytical mind. He himself thinks that every successful politician requires a degree of abrasiveness and 'a granite-like ego'; although public success is 'more than just seizing a few of the glittering prizes that life has to offer – it has to be about making a contribution or making a difference'. His mother was from 'a lowly background', but became 'one of the movers and shakers' in a small south coast town, encouraging her son's ambitions as he moved from grammar school to Cambridge to a career at the bar, and then in 1979 into Parliament as the Conservatives came to power. Earning rapid promotion, he became a junior minister in two government departments, then Minister of State in three.

He ran John Major's successful campaign to take over from Mrs Thatcher as Prime Minister, and was rewarded with a new government department – of National Heritage – widely considered to be tailor-made to embrace his passions for classical music, opera and football. He won plaudits from many in the worlds of television and the arts for the way he set about his task. Two years into the job, the tabloids exposed his affair with an actress and forced his resignation. He has since created a portfolio of new careers, becoming a consultant 'selling British companies overseas', a radio presenter of sport and classical music, a writer of newspaper articles and a wittily self-deprecating after-dinner speaker. He here analyses his failures; reveals how he fought back; argues that 'if every adulterer in Britain had to lose his job, heaven knows how many professions would be denuded of serious talent'; attacks the 'value system of the press and media which is often found wanting'; and concludes that, for a whole variety of reasons, 'it is going to be more and more difficult for politicians to be successful', while 'the most able people won't consider politics a sensible option'. He lost his seat in the 1997 landslide that brought the Labour Party to power.

David Mellor, what is your definition of success?

My own personal definition of success would be two-fold. Success has to be viewed both in private and public terms. In private terms, success is leading a happy and fulfilled life, hopefully being able to fulfil your obligations to those who are dependent on you, and getting some joy out of the human companionship and friendship that life brings your way. In more public terms, success has got to be viewed as more than just seizing a few of the glittering prizes that life has to offer. Success has got to be about making a contribution. I learned this very young from my mother, who from a lowly background became, by the time of her death in our small town, one of the movers and shakers of most of what went on there, and she always said to me that there had to be an element in your life where you actually give something back. If you've been handed out some talents, you've got to make some use of them and you've got to obtain fulfilment through making a contribution or making a difference. I would immediately say on both of those terms I think I have still got a lot of hard work to do to consider myself a success, but, you know, there are odd indications that that has been possible in the past and, hopefully, will be more possible in the future.

You talk about a need to make a contribution, but have you also got to have a basic drive to want to get to the top?

Yes. Drive is one of the essential engines in society. Successful societies are those which don't regard drive, this striving to be different, as something to be deplored and repressed, but as something to be stimulated. As C.P. Snow said of education, 'God gives you a hand of cards, education teaches you how to play them.' We've got to help people play their cards to maximum advantage, and then harness the success of individuals to a greater good.

Are you better able to cope with success if you have known some degree of sacrifice or failure at some time in your life?

Yes. I don't think anyone's life is onward and upward. Adversity makes you discover more things about yourself and then you discover the truth of another old proposition – the blow that doesn't break you makes you. Most people who have achieved any real success in their lives have had to do so through the exercise of great determination and of willingness to overcome obstacles. The key element is having the resilience to cope with the blows and somehow turn them to your advantage.

Do you think that blows are inevitable?

Yes. A philosopher once said that the life that has not been tested is not worth living. It's entirely unreasonable to expect that life will deliver you everything that you want. What life will do is play tricks on you. If you're determined, life will offer you things, provided obviously you are able to harness your own aspirations to what your own capabilities permit you to do – and then, just when you think everything's all right, it will deliver you a blow. The question is, how do you cope with that? And do you turn that to your advantage, do you somehow change? What is also fundamental and, I think, the most difficult thing, when you are actually participating in something, is to stand back and see how you are doing and make judgments that are not just pure gut reactions to the problems of the moment. Some of the people who are truly successful are able to give their life some kind of purpose by always having a clear objective in view which is never obscured by the hurly-burly of day-to-day events.

Are you able to control the circumstances in which you are tested?

I suppose up to a point you can, but it's extremely difficult because tests come in all manner of different ways. In my own life I was one of the youngest people to obtain Cabinet office, and I could have remained in the Cabinet had I not been reckless in my private life. Now I could have controlled that. But equally, we could wake up one morning and find a lump or a bump and go and see a doctor and find that it's terminal cancer – you can't control that. I remember a distinguished political journalist once saying to me that the intensity of the light that shines upon you in politics is so bright it shows up even the most hairline of cracks, and if there are any weaknesses those will be discovered. My weaknesses were in my private life, something I have now striven to put in the past. Other people's weaknesses are, for example, that they ultimately get a job that they can't handle, or they find themselves in a set of circumstances out of which they cannot escape.

The world of politics is extraordinary now. Issues are large and complex and the gulf of understanding between those that make decisions and those that have the decisions imposed upon them has never been wider. It's a paradox – we have an information-led society and yet, I suspect, even a lot of highly intelligent people who read the papers and watch the television have very little grasp of the problems which, say, the Prime Minster has to grapple with – over Europe or over the post-Cold War world. It is inevitable in this kind of political situation that nobody will build a political career without hiccups and we add to our difficulties by our preoccupation with people's private lives.

As you moved up the political ladder and became more successful, was there a danger of this breeding a kind of over-confidence?

Undoubtedly. You don't pause to think, and assume that the rules apply to other people – but then that's true of life as a whole. It's also the case that some of the people who are seriously successful are those who are able to be totally single-minded. I think there are quite a lot of other people with the ability to be very successful, but who are nevertheless unable to get all that they want out of life out of one particular activity. Take for instance the world of business. A senior businessman once explained to me that he knew a lot of people who were wonderful at their business, but they weren't actually very good at anything else, they weren't actually very distinguished people, they were just extremely good at the one thing that they could do. That is why we are always thinking that people who make a success in business would actually be the best people to come in and run the country, but whenever they have been given the chance, severe limitations are seen.

Can that compartmentalized success be an illusion and a danger if you are not a rounded person?

You need to be a rounded person in politics, because you have to understand the ebbs and flows of society and, in particular, you have got to have that essential humanity that allows you to continue to have bonds with normal people and an understanding of how normal people react, even though by the nature of your own career and success you have been placed in an abnormal position. I remember reading a lot of Howard Spring novels when I was younger, and there is one allegedly based on the career of Ramsay MacDonald, which tells of the politician who comes out of the back streets of Manchester and becomes very celebrated, and he comes back to speak in his home area as a statesman. Someone at the back of the audience says, 'Isn't it wonderful that he sprang from the people,' and the person sitting next to him said, 'Yes, and hasn't he sprung a long way away from them?' There is an essential element of truth in that, and indeed many of the politicians that we most admire and respect in the past – people who had what Denis Healey called the 'hinterland' – wouldn't necessarily have survived in today's politics.

For example, Winston Churchill would have had great difficulty in today's political climate – his drinking habits and various other things would have done him down. Look at Gladstone, Disraeli, Lloyd George,

Palmerston – all were able to lead rounded lives, even do things in their personal lives which were not actually commendable, but it didn't have the impact on their public life that it does in today's world, and of course, the danger of that is that you get a very narrow, completely disciplined politician. While people think they want complete discipline, I'm not sure that they really do, because complete discipline can lead to obsessiveness, to a definite growing apart, a fundamental chasm between the politician who is perfect – those on the wrong side of the great divide if you like – and people who sometimes exhibit their humanity through their frailties.

So the way things are going, is it going to be more difficult for politicians to be successful?

Yes, in all kinds of ways. The first point is that it's going to be more difficult for able people to consider politics a sensible option. A real problem in politics today is that a number of the people who are going into it are not out of the first division in terms of ability, and yet never have there been greater demands placed on politicians to display exceptional ability in the key jobs. I think it was William Deedes who said some years ago in one of his columns that most of the talented young people that he met wanted to go into the media rather than into politics.

I am not here as a great advocate of adultery, but you know, if every adulterer in Britain had to lose his job, heaven knows how many professions would be denuded of their serious talent, and when you look at what politics offers, a lot of able people are going to say no because they are going to realize that there isn't a lot that it has to offer them. Those who want a public profile will find that just as well in the media. A politician has to live, has to keep a family, but there will always be some politicians whose political convictions are so strong that they are willing to seriously undersell themselves commercially compared to what they would earn in any normal profession. I think it's wrong that politics should be the exclusive preserve of the glinty-eyed idealogue. Up until recently, Members of Parliament were only paid a salary equivalent to that of a senior secretary. Even now, after all these rows, they are paid what a junior middle-ranking executive gets and that isn't going to attract the right people into politics.

There is another very great problem, which is that politics isn't seen as very glorious any more. I think that people have a sense of politics – because of the excessive scrutiny to which politicians are subjected – as somehow not a very honourable calling, not a very worthwhile thing to do. Never before has politics required bigger people, and never before has it seemed to be attracting smaller people.

One of the major disincentives to politics these days is how difficult it is actually to feel that you have done more than manage a continuum maybe a little better than the other guy would have managed it. It's difficult to feel you are actually making a decisive difference and when one looks at world affairs, one sees the world drifting. A lot of the idealism that we all felt after the collapse of Communism has disappeared, and while it's oversimplistic to blame the politicians, it's hard to see any of the world's leaders who have really stamped their authority on the life of their country, and the question is, is it because circumstances do not permit that to happen? Or is it because the people who are grasping the palm today are not the exceptional people who used to be attracted into the greatest game of all?

Does it concern you that what you as a politician might have seen as success would be judged as failure by others?

It's extremely difficult to gain the recognition of success in politics that you would get somewhere else. I can only give you a small and rather pettifogging example because this happens to be my experience. For instance, although I was a Minister for 11 years, I find the reason members of the public come up and want to talk to me about things and greet me in a friendly way in the street, even if I don't know them, is a result of the fact that every Saturday during the football season I do a programme about football, which is a source of entertainment for most of the people who have been to a football game that afternoon – if they have got a long drive home, they tend to listen to my programme. That is perceived by a lot of people as much more of a success than my political career. Inevitably where politics is concerned, particularly in a polarized society like ours, a lot of the population will feel entirely detached from, and even angry about, what a politician might have done, even though that politician might think what they have done is a success because it represents for them the turning of an idea into a reality through legislation or some other form of change.

When did you first say to yourself, 'I have been successful'?

I must be very honest and say that one of the reasons I have been able to cope with life's highs and lows is that I am not complacent about myself. You have to put on a face to the world, and I've certainly had to do so, and you have to appear to be tough and determined, even sometimes too tough and too determined, but otherwise you would just be swept away by the tide of events. I have never ever woken up in the morning and thought complacently of myself as a success. Even when I look back at the highs of my life, going into the Cabinet, setting up a new Department with no idea that that was going to be for a relatively short duration, I simply saw it as another burden one had to discharge in order to try to place one's talents, to use one's talents more widely rather than being purely self-serving in one's goal.

So you're saying that reaching the top of the tree as Secretary of State for National Heritage was a burden?

Oh undoubtedly. I think a nice strand of opinion has recognized that in terms of the arts and sport and so on I have a genuine commitment to do something – I would like to think that had I not been foolish in my private life, I could have made a difference there, but I can tell you absolutely beyond question that what one was doing was taking on a burden. One could be exhilarated by taking on a burden, but let's be under no illusions, what one was doing was simply presenting oneself with another opportunity to run one's reserves of energy down to the lowest possible ebb by striving as mightily as one could to get these things right.

Politics is not an easy job. When I was a kid I assumed how grand it would be – a politican coming down addressing a lot of people, people all coming to see him, holding meetings and doing interviews and all that sort of stuff, but you soon realize that actually the real job at the top of politics requires a huge amount of effort.

But is it compensated for by this huge kick of getting to the top, staying at the top and wrestling with the problems that you have at the top?

Up to a point, but frankly, I have never spent a day thinking how much I would like to be back round that Cabinet table.

No regrets?

No. I regret the circumstances under which I lost office and at a certain point I would like to go back and prove that some of those who had a good opinion of me were justified in that. This comes back to something I said earlier – a serious political career is about giving, not taking. When you are, in effect, forced to turn more in on yourself and give more priority to sorting out your own personal life, as I had to do, you are actually able to work for yourself whilst carrying on with your duties in the constituency. The role of backbencher, when you have been used to working all the hours that God gave as a Minister, is not a very exacting task, particularly if you've got a good staff, so I was able to redeploy my time into worthwhile business activities, with blue-chip companies trying to sell Britain overseas, to broadcasting – I've done over 200 programmes presenting on BBC national radio – I get a kick out of that, and out of writing articles to express my views. In terms of my own personal fulfilment I can get a great deal, in the sense that one is busy and engaged. One's brain is a muscle, and the more you use it, the more you can do with it. I am busier today than I was when I was in the Cabinet. The only thing I would miss is the opportunity when I look at certain issues, and I think to myself, 'Well, maybe if one had been able to see out a proper period of time I might have made more sense of some things than has been made of them.' I don't say that arrogantly, I simply say that one has to believe that, and it was heartening when even one or two of one's opponents were kind enough to concede that fact. But there is nothing to be found around the Cabinet table that is so special that anyone need have any sense that only there can one get the special buzz and the special kick.

Coming back to my underpinning theme, we must be careful not to make politics too unattractive a career because politicians do matter.

What do you regard as your biggest failures?

I suppose if I had played my cards in a more sober way, I might have been a senior Cabinet Minister, and there are a number of people who would say it is therefore a failure not to have achieved that. I also think that in the course of political life one probably was too consumed by one's public duties and too little concerned with one's private obligations. That's something I have been very determined to address. I haven't been able to live up to all of the things I would have wanted, but I have a very good relationship with my ex-wife, a very good relationship with my kids – they want for nothing and I am trying to build a good relationship with my new partner, we are very happy together. All of these are things where I am trying to redress past failures.

Have you got a technique for recovering from failure?

You have just got to be tough and determined. I tell you what was a great help. If I had been a paedophile or if I had mugged an old lady, or if I had done something thoroughly dishonest, I would have hated myself and I would have thought I couldn't have lived with myself. But there is this old shaving mirror test. I am not proud of having had an unsuitable mistress, but in the great course of human history, and in the great course of human wrongdoings I do not think that that ranks very highly. I felt a lot of the people criticizing me had led lives infinitely more carefree in that respect than I had, and I was determined not to allow that to crush me. I was the author of my own misfortune and I have no self-pity, but I also feel that people made a huge meal of it and indeed I think that's what a lot of the public tell me.

Somebody once said to me, 'When you think of all the scope you were given in an area that matters, an area of culture which by your own inclinations you are exceptionally well-suited actually to getting right, shouldn't you feel angry with yourself that you threw away that opportunity to make such a great difference?' I suppose that is the best point, and one of the reasons why I would like to return to public life is that, at some point – and I am talking years ahead now – one might have the opportunity of doing that job properly.

Do you feel that your difficulties and the publicity that ensued attracted more people to listen to you?

I don't know. When I started, one or two people said it was sort of a Vicar of Stiffkey-type performance, but I actually think we've outgrown that now. I have been given the opportunity through my writing, my broadcasting and other things I do to become a personality that at least is of interest to a wide range of people, even if not always for the right reasons. Also, none of us can choose our gifts. I guess if I had been asked what gift I wanted, I might have chosen a more substantial gift than the one I have been given, but what I have been given is a certain amount of intelligence and ability to express myself with clarity and I like to think that if I go and speak at a dinner for a charitable cause or whatever, hopefully I will give people a good time, I will make a speech that will amuse them, or they will think has some other substance. There's no point in doing it otherwise and I suppose one gets invitations because that is the case.

And is there any type of attitude you can have that makes you more likely to be successful? I mean, you had a reputation for being a little abrasive – is a touch of abrasiveness necessary?

There is a danger with politicians if they're too emollient, because emollient people are always willing to compromise. Mrs Thatcher was abrasive, but thank God she was, for a lot of the things she did in the early 1980s addressed the palpable decline of Britain over the previous 20 or 30 years – excessive trade union power, ridiculous taxation arrangements, a whole host of things we knew were wrong with Britain. But she did it because she would brook no opposition and because she was abrasive. Politics is not like the management of a company, politics is about something where, in the end, although not all that often, you can bang the table and say, 'I don't give a damn what you say, it's going to be done.'

Can you sit down and methodically plan success, are there any core principles for achieving it?

You always hear of some people who have their little bits of paper mapping out their life. I've never done that – maybe I would have been better off if I had. Success is about trying to create a framework within which you can do what you're capable of to its best advantage.

And you have to recognize your own capabilities in order to do that?

Yes, because success is not just a measure of public opinion. A lot of the people that I meet, that I consider successful, are people that you've never heard of. I recently sat in my advice centre on Saturday with a man in his early seventies of whom no one has ever heard except in our area. He's a success because he has shown that you can be a local councillor not simply for your own ego and you can do a huge amount of good, and our community is lucky to have him. There are a whole lot of people doing what others would regard as ordinary, humdrum jobs but who are a success because they do it brilliantly well. I think life is about trying to work out in your own mind what you can do and then doing it to the maximum advantage and, hopefully, that maximum advantage is not only to yourself – there is some advantage to other people.

And does luck play a part in success?

Of course. But I do believe one thing. In the end there is only one piece of bad luck that really matters and that is when you wake up one day and you don't feel well and you go and see a doctor and he says, 'Sorry old boy, but this is it, it's cancer …' and you can't do anything about it. One thing I am absolutely convinced of in my own life is that whatever other little self-inflicted wounds we impose on ourselves, provided you keep your health and strength, and have people around who continue to believe in you, then there's very little that you can't achieve. Sometimes I think what you achieve becomes of more value because your own value system is changed as a result of what happens. Everyone takes a very superficial view of politicians and they assume that if you become Prime Minister you're a success and if you don't you're not – it's infinitely more than that. I think that the success we should be speaking about is some balance in life where an element of personal satisfaction is achieved by bringing out what lies within, and actually achieving what you have the potential to achieve, very much tempered by the fact that empty success, shorn of any degree of any personal happiness, shorn of any degree of giving as against concentration on self, is not really a success, it is neither very estimable nor does it stand up to too much self-scrutiny.

Who are your heroes, past or present?

I am not a great hero worshipper. I think we live in a society where people shower a little bit of achievement with huge, excessive hype, and I am not very taken in by that, neither do I think it very commendable. We are obsessed with hype over someone who just happens to be able to speak other people's words quite well – the film star, soap star-type phenomenon – and there is a huge element of superficiality in this. But because I am keen on the arts I would, for instance, look up to Beethoven. Here was a man who led a pretty miserable life, afflicted with all manner of illnesses including what for a musician must be the most ghastly thing, to lose his hearing, so that when he conducted, I think it was the *Eroica* symphony, someone had to turn him round to the audience so that he could appreciate that they were actually applauding. When you look at that extraordinary achievement of Beethoven with his wonderful music that has depth and substance and real balm to the soul, there isn't a bar of self-pity in anything Beethoven wrote, and yet God knows he had more to be self-pitying about than almost anyone one can think of. I admire that because I know that if I lived a thousand years I couldn't write a bar of what Beethoven did and I think that one of the reasons why I am so wedded to the arts is that quite often in the arts you get that tremendous personal achievement, that ability to make a difference, that ability to lay down a body of work that will go on being appreciated for centuries. Maybe that was once possible in politics, but I don't think there are going to be many people of the 20th century who people are going to be able to admire unequivocally in the way that I admire Beethoven.

You don't have any political heroes?

Do I have political heroes? I turned up to hear President Mandela when he spoke to both Houses of Parliament because I do have a deep respect for him. It would have been so easy for him, after being locked up for 30 years, to come out spewing bile and hatred over those who treated him really most cruelly, yet when faced with the test, he has made national reconciliation his primary goal. It's not the fault of politicians necessarily that they can't always display that largeness of spirit, but when the opportunity comes it's important the politician is able to seize it. Churchill did and I think Mandela in recent times has done so. I admire a great deal of what Mrs Thatcher did, but equally, I'm afraid, there were lots of other things about her that temper that admiration a bit. That's the other problem about hero-worshipping politicians. We know so much about them that it's extremely difficult. If I had known about Beethoven's personal habits I probably might have disliked him in a way I can't now – all I see in Beethoven is a man who produced great and unforgettable work in the midst of torment and despair, occasioned by ill-health and a significant element of neglect. With politicians, particularly these days, it's extremely difficult ever to get to the point where the credit side is so much bigger than the debit side that you are able to say, 'That is a hero.'

Why does success in people right across all professions arouse varying emotions in different people, ranging from admiration to outright envy?

I suppose it's a cliché that in America, if a man drives by in a Cadillac, the man in the street is likely to say, 'Well, I'll have one of those one day or my son will,' and in Britain someone goes by in a Rolls Royce and some of our people are inclined to say, 'Yah-boo sucks!' That's a generalization and not true, but …

Does that still happen, do you think?

No way of knowing, but I think that in society the values that we get are often propagated by the organs of popular opinion, the press and the media generally, and their own value system is often wanting – the sort of slobbering over relatively trivial entertainment people and the continuous attacks on the Royal Family which undermines an institution. I look at Prince Charles – I don't know Prince Charles well, but I have met him frequently enough to have a view of him and to listen to him, and I think that compared to most previous Princes of Wales, as far back as you can go, he is a sensitive man committed to the public good with some genuinely worthwhile ideas on a range of issues that he has, with great courage and eloquence, put forward. What has happened to him is terrible. The way in which people have turned venom on him for inadequacies in his personal life is tragic.

Do you see parallels with yourself and what happened to the Prince of Wales?

No, I wouldn't presume to do that, but I just think it is an unfortunate phenomenon that the Prince of Wales is probably one of the most accomplished people for a number of centuries that is likely to become King of this country, and yet he will become King, unless things radically change, with more people feeling concerned about him than should ever be the case. When you actually look at some of his predecessors, they had all of the faults that people now pillory him for, with none of his many virtues.

You of all people would not deny the press the right to report. You are talking about a question of degree?

Yes. I have never been a zealot in stopping people knowing what, in a free society, needs to be printed, but this obsession with the tawdry side of people's lives, people's sex life, this kind of prurient turning us all into peeping toms, is deeply unattractive. I will defend Britain to the hilt with sceptical foreigners about most of what is part of the British way of life because I know full well that Britain has been a stable, worthwhile country for centuries whilst others have had far more profound traumas. Britain still remains a place that a whole lot of people come to when they can choose to go anywhere in the world. However, I think the British press is the most difficult thing to defend. I had a very distinguished diplomat taking me through the front pages of the British press and then showing me a couple of quality international papers and saying, 'This is what the rest of the world is talking about, and this is what you're talking about,' and contrasting the two in such a way made it very hard to defend.

If you could gather together all the young people thinking of entering the profession of politics now, what advice would you give them?

I would advise them, whatever rubbish and garbage they have read about politics and politicians, to remember that in a democracy it is absolutely vital that a fair proportion of the best and the brightest make a career in politics. In the end, however frustrating and difficult it is, there is no path more worthy than trying to give good government to people, because whatever other jobs people do, there is no job that can have such profound effects, when done well or badly, on a whole lot of innocent people, than that of a politician. Above all I would say to them, 'If all you're doing is going into politics because you see it as a great stage for ego, think twice, politics has got to be about giving. A lot of what you will get out of it will be stress, strain, reading awful things about yourself ...' People have got to be quite clear that they have an inner desire to be of service and a genuine set of commitments that are sensible, measured and appropriate for our country, and that is the basis on which a political career should be sought.

You say, 'Don't go into it for the ego,' but you are not exactly a shrinking violet.

You have got to have an ego to go into politics, there's nothing wrong with ego. It's a question of what lies behind it. Is the ego merely the tip of the iceberg, and the rest of the iceberg consists of something that needs to be thrust forward, or is ego all that it is and the ego merely covers an emptiness? You come back to the old cliché – do you want to be someone or do you want to do something? You need an ego for both, but if your ego is only about being somebody, then it's not worth it and you'll do no good.

When your time comes to depart this life, what would you like people to say about you?

It's impossible to say something that wouldn't sound emptily pompous and, as far as I am concerned, I am going to try and get a few more things under my belt before I even attempt to say that, and I hope I have got the time to be able to duck that question without needing to feel that it's something I have to address immediately.

LORD MENUHIN

The musicianship of Yehudi Menuhin has captivated audiences across the world for a remarkable three-quarters of a century. The Japanese have officially dubbed him 'A National Living Treasure' – probably the most all-embracing of the many superlatives woven around his astounding talents as a violinist and conductor. He believes that success, when it comes, 'is only a small segment of a small link in the process of growing, of living, of time, so you can't afford to wait – it merely means you have the satisfaction of knowing you are on the right track'. He spent only half a day in school, during which he says he learned nothing; so from then on he was taught at home, surrounded by 'devoted parents, sisters, friends and teachers'.
Smuggled to his first concert at the age of two, he demanded his own violin just a year later and, at seven, made a sensational public début with the San Francisco Orchestra. He says his quarrel with today's educational establishment is that 'they don't first of all teach the quality of listening, instead it's all about ambition'. The very word 'success' he describes as loaded, 'because it implies the end of something rather than the beginning, and you don't work for success – you work for fulfilment and achievement'. Crucial to that is 'an environment that encourages eagerness, keeps one's curiosity awake, provides support, clears the way so one's mind is not occupied by trash'.

He talks here about the crisis in his playing technique – the time when he had to 'go back and learn to play all over again'. He confesses to personal failings, but won't concede to any professional failures: 'I've had a few bad reviews, but I'm my own severest critic, I don't depend on others.' He talks of how a composer is 'more than someone who puts notes together – he has to have a theme, a motive, structure and meaning, and must communicate a whole range of human thought and emotion'. As for his extensive humanitarian work, he has deliberately used his success as a musician to give himself a public platform for 'my mission to give voice to the voiceless', to try and help create a more positive, inspired and courteous world. Among his words of advice for budding musicians are these: 'The road to success is not direct. Go straight from A to B and you'll miss the sights and encounters – you'll learn much more if you take the circuitous route.'

Lord Menuhin, what is your definition of success?

I think there are at least three kinds of success. One is success in terms of being at peace with oneself, in good health and being able to think – and to act on those thoughts, if possible. Another is success in terms of one's life's main objective – one's profession or one's work, whether one is a scientist or a musician, whatever it may be. And the third, of course – and the least valuable – is success as defined by other people.

Why do you think that is the least valuable?

Because it doesn't affect oneself, and it can be quite off the mark. Usually it is based on appearances rather than reality.

But if that is persistent and wrong, it can still affect you, can't it?

Maybe. There's too much stress on success in terms of material achievements, and there is any number of books about how to become rich, how to cheat, how to work the casino numbers, and I don't know what else. That really doesn't interest me. Personally, I'm more or less in control, and not too dependent on … what shall I call them? Escapes or enticements. But a great part of success will always depend on two things which are out of one's control – our genetic heritage, and our good luck. I am lucky enough to have had both of those. I had wonderful parents. My mother, who died only recently, was quite extraordinary. She lived to be 100, so the genes are strong. My father's are, too. He died about 15 years ago. I've had marvellous and incredible luck, and devoted parents, sisters, friends, and teachers. What more can one ask? These things contribute enormously. Probably the major part of one's success is due to these factors.

And you see those relationships as luck rather than something that can be cultivated?

Well, genes, obviously, are inherited, but so too is the environment provided by parents, teachers and so on, and that is very important. An environment that encourages eagerness, keeps one's curiosity awake, provides support, clears the way so that one's mind is not occupied by trash, which is unfortunately the case today for many people. In my case it has been music that has occupied my mind and thoughts and with which I have tried to be a help in a sad world. I've always had a great component of compassion and a desire to be of help. I loved literature and poetry and had a great deal of fun, I played badminton and tennis and ran round the parks as a very young boy and walked a great deal.

Later I turned to yoga. Our mental and physical environment, our sensations – listening, tasting, seeing – are very important.

Many people grow up without good experiences and their senses have been atrophied. Life is quite a different matter for a child who grows up in a world where it hears only traffic noise and road drills, than it is for one who grows up with sounds that have signal value, like a mother's voice, a father's voice, and so on. And there are others whose sight is blinded by bright lights and cannot see subtleties, and those whose noses have no opportunity to smell the extraordinary and delicate odours nature has provided, like lavender or the smell of the sea. These are factors which contribute to a satisfying or successful life, or an unsatisfying or unsuccessful one. I'm infinitely grateful for my own experiences.

Let me take you back to those very early days. You had, in many ways, a unique upbringing. Was it of a kind that could not be repeated today?

It would certainly be more difficult. In those early days – it was, after all, a long time ago, 75 years – the California law did not demand that every child be sent to school, but my parents dutifully sent me with the best intentions. When I came back at lunchtime on the first day, my mother asked me what I had learned. I said, 'Actually, nothing.' It was a pleasant enough school, on top of the hill behind our house in San Francisco. There was a park between us and the school. The teacher was talking, but I didn't really bother much about what she said. I was at the back of the class, being the newcomer, and there was a window high up on the wall, and a branch of a tree to be seen through the window. I was just looking there, hoping that a bird would alight on the branch, and that's how I spent my first morning.

So my mother, wisely, said, 'Well, I don't think you are school material.' From then on we were taught by my parents or tutors, wonderful people. In France I had Pierre Bertaux for some years, a very brave man. He was in the Resistance and condemned to death by the Nazis some three or four times. Then he became the Chef de la Sûreté, which is the head of the police in France. He looked like a brigand – his father, too. So I had the advantage of great people – Georges Enesco, who, along with Bartok, were the greatest musicians I've met. I have met Stravinksy and Prokofiev, and I think they were very great, but as human beings they fell short of Enesco and Bartok.

And do you judge that simply on musical talent and ability, or has there to be something more?

There has to be something more, which the music reflects. A composer is more than someone who puts the notes together. Naturally, he has to be a master of his craft, he has to have a theme, a motive, a living cell in any work which then develops. It has to have structure, but it has to have meaning, too. It must communicate the whole range of human thought and emotion, or at least part of it, depending on what you're dealing with. If it's a great symphony, it's pretty well the whole range, if it's a wonderful little waltz by Lehar then it's a part.

Today we're more aware than ever that there is another dimension to life which is beyond ourselves. Never has it been more important for human beings to reach out and communicate with others, and to do their duty by others, not only in one's own country, but for humanity at large, because issues today are global, and we're all one family. And you see that in every sphere. Now banks and industry are sponsoring music. Audi, the German car manufacturer, are doing so much for music it's really quite amazing. They paid for my last trip to South Africa – for the orchestra, and the choir, and everything. And they have sponsored a young black African I found who played the cello beautifully and who is now studying at my academy in Switzerland. They run music competitions in London and do a great deal for festivals, and SAMET, the South African Music Educational Trust.

Do you think that every successsful company, as well as every individual who is successful, has an obligation to put something back into society?

Absolutely. It has occurred generally after some generations. There was the rubber baron who started it – and then Carnegie, Rockefeller and Ford founded institutions of wonderful worth. But I think now such obligations come down to every individual. My quarrel with the educational establishments, in many places, is that they don't first of all teach the quality of listening. Instead it's all ambition. Of course, gathering knowledge is one of the main functions of the human species, I think, but beyond that there's communication between ourselves and within ourselves, through music and dance, and this is ignored. I had a long talk to discuss this with Gillian Shephard, and I brought with me the woman in charge of education in Her Majesty's prisons, and another lady who runs my music project in England, Susan Digby, who's had great experience in choral training. We take folk-singing and dancing to these terrible schools where violence prevails, and within a short time they become harmonious schools where the children are happy and trusting. There is no mystery to this, it is simply that a part of those children has not been developed from their earliest years – before birth, in fact. Our ears are formed in the womb, at 11 weeks, long before sight. And when we're born, it's hearing that develops first, and hearing is a global experience which penetrates us and enables us to communicate.

Seeing doesn't necessarily enable us to communicate. Music is the universal language of sound, whereas I would say that mime is the universal language of sight.

You were taken to your first concert at the age of two, and you have spoken movingly about how you remember the sound of the violins. Then, at the age of three, you demanded your own violin for the first time. To what extent do you have to catch talent early, and how early? Can it develop in later life, or if you want someone to be really successful, colossally successful, do you have to grab that talent at an early stage?

I think that's the wrong approach. You don't catch talent, it's there. You offer every child the whole gamut of opportunities. But you can nurture talent. Take medicine. You begin learning medicine at the age of what, 16, 17, and then you try to cram in an enormous amount of knowledge. Medicine should begin at the age of two, or earlier. The touch of a mother's or father's hand on a child is therapy. Music is therapy. If a child is taught to help with his hands – whether it is to soothe someone who has a headache or to feel, to massage – that is the beginning of medicine. It is medicine at its purest – eagerness to comfort, to help. It's compassion. Then it becomes practical.

Mathematics, too, can begin at the earliest age. After all, language begins early, doesn't it? And that comes from listening. We speak and think in response to listening and to what happens within us. Reading and writing are visual skills, and much more superficial. They are not nearly as important, because if you try to read and write without having listened, you will base it more on visual order than on a natural, organic order. People will be put into categories and ordered around as if they were papers or books in the library.

So you believe that the seeds of any potential talent can be identified and nurtured from as early as two or three?

Absolutely. But too often this is ignored, and children are dragged out on to the streets, where they have no example. They're brought up without example, and often without interest.

When was the first time you remember saying to yourself, 'I am a success'?

I've never said that, nor would I dare to say it. I look for the satisfaction of accomplishment, of achievement, not for success. When I give a good performance, or when I listen to a recording I've made that satisfies me, or when I see children happy, of course there's a sense of achievement. But with my children it is a very modest one, first of all because most of the work was done by my wife, and secondly because their creativity and their work on it is their own. I am not responsible for it.

Do you believe that the acknowledgment that you have done something well spurs you on to greater heights?

A grateful audience, which one feels shared those few minutes of music-making, and was moved by it, is a great spur to further music-making. But the word success, to me, is loaded because it implies the end of something rather than the beginning. 'All right, he's successful now – what else?' No doubt the computer tycoon Bill Gates is one of the most successful people in those terms. But I don't think he would stop there. He would go on, not to earn more success, but simply to achieve his aim and his life's ambition. There's a difference there. If your aim is merely success, it's a very limited one. You don't work for success, you work for fulfilment and achievement, I think.

So the aim is to do the best you can, and if that results in success as well, then that's fine?

Yes. That's all the better. Success is certainly a wonderful feeling, as long as it's not degraded by what is associated with it. Words change meaning. For instance, liberty has become licence, and freedom has become the freedom to exploit, or to start wars, or to do all kinds of horrible things – or take drugs or sell them, whatever it may be. And in the same way the word 'success' has come in people's minds, and certainly in the media, to mean, 'He's made a lot of money.' And I absolutely abhor that criterion.

But isn't making money part of success? Shouldn't you feel that, if you have done what you wish to do in order to lead a fulfilled life, and that has led to success, then there automatically ought to be some financial reward?

Of course there's nothing wrong with making money. I know many so-called self-made people, who might never have gone to school, but who have made money and are using it beautifully. They are people I respect and love, and I can think of a few I admire. There was one I heard of recently in Switzerland, a Jewish fellow who decided that there was a huge market in all the Mohammedans who wanted to go to Mecca every year but couldn't get there from India and other poor countries because it was much too expensive and difficult. So he organized transport which was within their means, and made a fortune on a faith strange to himself. He saw the opportunity and did very well. I think that's legitimate, I don't see anything particularly reprehensible there. He is a man of genius, who presents himself in an ungainly cap. Meanwhile, his son has been to business school and is very respectable, but probably doesn't have the genius of the father.

So there are really two kinds of success here. There is the success that comes from intrinsic talent – the genetic environmental factor you were talking about – and then there is the success which comes from hitting upon the right ideas at the right time?

Exactly. And that may lead to wealth. Take Henry Ford. I met him when I was a boy, and he was a funny fellow. Absolutely frank, absolutely at ease, and when he was asked some historical date and didn't know it, he just said, 'Well, I can ring up any university and get the answer.' I don't think Thomas Edison or the Wright brothers ever made a fortune. Many years ago I met Braithwaite – I think that's his name – at the Royal College of Science, and he showed me the linear railway, which he had invented. It is the most wonderful railway in the world. No moving parts, any speed, and in a vacuum it can achieve aeroplane speeds. They're now building one in Switzerland, in a straight, semi-vacuum tunnel between Lucerne and Lugano. But I don't think Braithwaite is any the richer for it.

Is that because very often the people with the ideas don't have them at the right moment, or in the right way?

Or their ideas are pounced upon by people who know how to process them. England has not supported its great minds. Take Braithwaite. There are no underground vacuum tunnels between London and Edinburgh, which would have been perfectly logical.

Let me bring you back to your music. You had a crisis in your playing technique during the war. How did you recover from that?

Actually I never stopped playing, and most of the time I played very well, but I had to relearn it, or, more accurately to learn it for the first time. In a way I played well because of the wonderful examples I had around me, but instinctively, intuitively. Now I had to analyse it. Actually a good part of my life has been spent in analytical thought about violin-playing, society and music. When I take a new score, I go through the the same process. The first time I really understood a work was long before the war on a trip between Perth and Durban, on the Blue Funnel Line. The ship was called the *Nestor*, a coal-burning ship, and the voyage lasted three weeks. I was 19, and I decided I knew nothing about music. I played the work and decided, well that's no good, I must understand it.

But here you were, acknowledged by the world as a child prodigy, and suddenly you were saying to yourself, 'I know nothing about music'? That seems an extraordinary thing.

It's no more extraordinary than someone who has charted the stars and knows where they are – or those which can be seen, at least – but doesn't know anything about them, about gravity, or their life, or their birth and death, or black holes. We have lived with the sun for billions of years, but we knew nothing about it until quite recently.

So is this constant questioning of yourself very important?

Very important.

And when you came to the judgment that things were going wrong during the war, what did you do about it?

It wasn't a judgment, it was a sheer discomfort. Violin-playing should be easy. To make it easy you have to think about it and analyse it. I had made it very easy from the very beginning, intuitively. And then, under the pressure of many concerts – sometimes two or three a day – and for the period of the war, I didn't practise, I didn't rest, I didn't refresh myself. I just went on and on.

And that refreshment is very important?

It's very important. So, by the end of the war I was really in a poor state, my first marriage had broken down. I had to get out of that state...

How did you do that?

Well, what I did not do is what many people probably would have done – taken a year off. I never believed in that. I believe in just pushing through and going on. I developed my own exercises – breathing, balance, 1,000 exercises in connection with the fingers, the arms, the hands and the neck. I discovered the whole concatenation, the interdependence of the whole body and the mind, and gradually built myself up that way – shored myself up in the way they build an underground railway in a busy city.

What do you regard as your biggest failures, and how did you recover from them?

Well, that's a very good question. I don't actually think you do recover. When you fail you must correct and do better next time. I did draw positive value from failure, because I think if you survive, then you're better off for it. Failures can be put in different categories. There were human failures, in terms of relationships, people who maybe I treated unjustly or condemned, as one does, and towards whom I didn't behave with sufficient understanding.

And were those failures with people who were very close to you?

Sometimes, yes.

Was that something that came out of your great success and the adulation you received? Does that somehow change you as a person?

No, I think it was because I was immature, that it was part of the penalty of not having mixed with my contemporaries a great deal. I did have friends of my own age, and have done throughout my life, but perhaps school gives you a little more of that experience, I don't know. Then again our children have been to school, and all of them have divorced or separated, so going to school is no guarantee that you will be that much wiser. I really don't know. What hurts me most is that there are people whom I didn't understand sufficiently or whom I hurt. There are not many, but there are a few. I was impatient, perhaps. I remember I even wrote my parents a few critical letters, but then, we're getting them from our own children now. That's part of life. Parents must be ready to accept it.

And were there professional failures? How did you recover from them?

Actually, I've had no professional failures. I've had a few bad reviews, but one can't go through life without a few of those. I never read them anyway, but once in a while I hear about them, or they're shown to me. I do take them seriously, because the reviewer has usually been wrong about the reason. He couldn't fathom the reason. He hasn't known the circumstances in which I lived or played, or what I had had to fight for, or what I was struggling against. They can't know. But while a reviewer may not know the reason, he can judge the effect, and so from that point of view reviews can be salutary. Yet on the whole I've been my own severest critic, which one should be. I do not depend on others to tell me that I've played out of tune, or anything like that.

What do you think are the greatest enemies of success?

I think pride in success is the first great enemy.

Shouldn't you take pride in doing something well and being judged to have done something well?

Yes, but you shouldn't waste time on it, because if you sit back on your laurels you're finished. Life is an ongoing process, and it cannot be interrupted. It's like that wonderful poem by Schiller in which a king says to his friends, 'Look at everything that's at my feet. All these are my slaves, my vassals, and all this is subject to my will. You must agree that I'm a happy man.' And, of course, that very night, the whole lot of them are slain. Success is only a small segment of a small link in the process of growing, of living, of time, so you can't afford to wait. You have to continue your work and your life. It merely means you have approval, or encouragement, or the satisfaction of knowing you are on the right track.

Did you ever feel that your talent was drowning in a sea of fame and publicity?

No, because that never really meant anything to me. Fortunately, I was inured against it by my parents from an early age. Whatever people said, whatever notoriety or fame I gained, it was never allowed to intrude into the family routine, into our work, our studies. And it does not affect or have any value in one's personal ambitions or relationships. It's useful to keep a career going, and to fill the concert halls, and it is encouraging to know that people are looking forward to hearing you and have faith in you. Otherwise publicity is only useful, from my point of view now, to help me to propagate certain ideas I have, and I even seek a certain amount just to do that.

So you're using the fame that you have acquired through music to give yourself a public platform for your other ideas?

Exactly, whether they concern education or politics, as does, for instance, my project to enable people of a given culture to be represented as a group. There are political parties to represent the opinions of people and countries and the boundaries of countries, but people themselves are not represented in their own terms. There are seven million Muslims in France, who are not represented. There are a few Turks in Germany who have become German and have a vote, but the others are not represented. Gypsies are not represented in Romania. These are people without a voice. As I've been giving voice to the violin, and to music and to works, I've come to the conclusion that my mission is to give voice to the voiceless, whether it is a violin, whose voice depends on its being played, or something or somebody else. We must all recognize that democracy is not yet perfect. It has advanced to a point of considerable representation, but the next stages are, I think, the representation of people in their daily work, their worries, their anxieties and their opinions. We don't hear those. We hear political opinions, which represent ready-made party lines – we don't hear the opinions of people.

Who are your heroes? Who are the people whom you regard as being the most successful or to whom you look up?

Stephen Hawking – I think he's extraordinary. Normally we think of success as health, wealth, happiness, all bundled together, but that's a very naïve image. You can be a success and die a pauper and illiterate. You will have gathered wisdom – very often reading and writing destroys memory if we don't pay attention to it. Memory comes from another source, from listening, thinking and recalling. The bards and historians of African tribes remember all the details of their tribe's ancestry and history, their migration, their collective and personal property and relationships, and in their way they are incredibly successful. They are living computers with all the knowledge of the past – looked up to, revered. Every evening they recite or tell the history of the wars and successions of the tribe. We don't have people like that today because we can all read and write.

I think a great man, though I know he had his weaknesses, was Charles de Gaulle. Winston Churchill was a great man, too, and he also had his weaknesses. I don't think there is anyone who is without blemish or without weaknesses.

So every really successful person inevitably has a flaw somewhere?

Yes, a weakness of some kind.

And what happens when that flaw is exposed to the world at large, and that person's reputation takes a knock?

I don't think that should make any difference, I really don't. To expect perfection from people is unrealistic. We can revere them and we can love them, but real love, in the final analysis, embraces their very imperfections. It has to. My mother was successful, and she had her faults, God knows. But she was absolutely wonderful and I completely admired, respected and loved her. Churchill didn't get along with de Gaulle. That is a great pity. It would have changed the course of Europe if England had joined the Community earlier. But everyone has some prejudices.

What about successful people who make bad moral judgments in their private lives?

Well, that happens.

And is it acceptable?

It has to be. I hate judgmental people who gather together to point the finger at someone. Jesus said the right thing, 'Let him who is without sin cast the first stone.' On the whole I am fairly balanced and I don't often lose my temper, but one thing that makes me very angry is people judging someone on his personal morals. Like this moral business about politicians and Members of Parliament and priests. We have high ideals and we must keep them, but we cannot be expected to live up to them 100 per cent of the time. When we err, it is salutary to be able to admit it.

What do you regard as your greatest success?

The trust people have in me. Wherever I go round the world, I meet people who are already well-disposed towards me, who listen, from whom I can learn and who are willing to share their thoughts with me. I'm very, very lucky.

What advice would you give to a young musician, starting off at the bottom of the ladder who wants to achieve success in the musical field?

You must love music, and if you have a beautiful voice you must cultivate it, but success is incidental and a secondary factor. If you are after success, you must go the long way round. The road is not direct, the traveller going from A to B will learn much more if he takes the circuitous route. By the time he gets to the good bits, he'll have learned quite a lot. Go straight from A to B, and the chances are you'll miss the sights and encounters. I believe in taking the long way round. I like the detour, and I often make it a habit to start off going in the opposite direction, to be sure I've got to know the landscape and the situation.

In practical terms, is there anything specific a young musician should do?

Of course, he should apply himself to his music. He must first learn to do it, and then he must do it with care. He mustn't overstrain, or work too hard, but he must work with absolute commitment, and continuously. If he feels tension, he must learn how to get rid of that tension. He must work wisely, but absolutely without giving up, just continuously.

When your time comes to leave this life, what would you like people to say about you?

That he was a good fellow.

JOHN MONKS

He remains surprised that he has reached the top of the trade-union movement, because at one time the peak of his ambition was 'to live on a bit of dual carriageway in North Manchester in a semi-detached house with a car'. John Monks is not someone who is motivated strongly by a sense of personal position, preferring to 'choose a cause rather than a career path'. It has always been his top priority to be 'a good community person'; so he rejects 'the dead-end idea that success is only achieved in terms of what you do for yourself and your family'. It was, he says, 'a quirk of fate' that took him into the TUC for virtually the whole of his career. The son of a parks superintendent, he went to technical school rather than grammar school. From the University of Nottingham, he  *became a junior manager at Plessey. Disagreeing with the handling of an industrial dispute, he joined the TUC because a friend had got a research job in the Labour movement, and he thought, 'If he can do it, so can I.'*

Talked about as a possible general secretary as far back as the late Seventies, he was groomed by 'a group of supporters who sought to ensure that I gained the necessary experience in different parts of the organisation to put in a strong bid when the vacancy came up.' He talks here about 'the historic problem of the unions getting on the wrong side of public opinion', and believes that success for the TUC depends on putting right some of the impressions thus created 'so we are seen as a constructive and positive force'. He says that 'the problem today is that we're only representing the relatively privileged', and worries about employer hostility making it 'difficult to reach out to the insecure, the low-paid and the casual workers'. He attacks big shareholders like the pension funds for putting short-term thinking before long-term investments, and is convinced that success for the TUC is bound up with Britain being fully part of a standard-setting European Union. He discusses what makes for successful relationships with managements – '84 of the FT's 100 leading companies are heavily unionised'; the approach of 'a new generation' of TUC officers; the move to the contract culture – 'by the year 2000 only half the workforce will be employed full-time in steady jobs'; and 'the whole new learning experience of negotiating redundancies'. He remains driven by the belief that 'the main obligation of the successful is to those who are not.'

John Monks, what is your definition of success?

I don't think I'm particularly ambitious in a personal sense. I want to be a good family person, a good community person. I see myself as an active citizen, both locally and through my job, in terms of the opportunities it provides to help in some particular causes, but I haven't got any vainglorious ambitions to leave my mark on history. I see my job as essentially to raise the respect for people at work, to reinvigorate the image of trades unionism so that it is viewed as an attractive element of society, a natural partner of people who are trying to improve the lot of the community – that's governments, and employers in particular. So the challenge I have in my time as general secretary is maybe to put right some of the impressions created in the past by trades unions and position us so that we are seen as a constructive and positive force. But on a personal level, I'm pretty content to live quietly, comfortably and to do my bit in the community, and I am very fond of my family.

To what extent do you think success is a product of background and upbringing?

It's a product of both those things, and of luck. I would say, looking back at my own history, that luck has played a big part in it. You meet somebody at some stage, and they say, 'Have you thought about doing that?' or 'What about this?' and you think about it. You think, well, that's probably quite a good thing. I ended up at the TUC through the most odd convergence of circumstances. I had a friend who had done the same university course as me, and he got a job at the Labour Party as a researcher. I never had considered that I was remotely qualified to work for a union, or in the Labour movement, but then I thought, well, if he can do it, perhaps I can. A few months later I got a job at the TUC. It's those little quirks of fate which so often determine whether or not you take a particular direction. I think it's more difficult for young people today, because that was an era of full employment, there was a choice of jobs. It wasn't marvellous, but I think it was better than it is today.

Before that you had been a junior manager at Plessey. What made you decide that that was not for you? Did you decide that you couldn't be successful at that?

No, I think I could have been successful at that. I went into Plessey rather idealistically, expecting it to be one of those companies at the forefront of the drive for more exports. It was the 1960s, Harold Wilson was Prime Minister and the message was export or die. We had recurrent balance-of-payments crises – we've still got them, but no one seems to care at the moment, they've gone on the back-burner. Anyway, it was an idealistic move that put me into manufacturing and export manufacturing in the first place. What I found there was disappointing. I found a company which probably – this is only a guess – spent at least 80 per cent of its time on internal politics. You didn't want to get the blame for things that went wrong – and quite a lot went wrong.

You're not saying there's nothing like that in the trade-union movement, are you?

No, I'm not saying that, but I would certainly say that the proportion of time within the TUC one spends on sorting out internal relationships is infinitesimal compared with what happened at Plessey. There was a defining moment for me – I was working on a contract that was delayed by a late delivery from a supplier, and in those days the penalty clause did not apply in the case of an act of God or a labour dispute. The production manager provoked a labour dispute by sacking a shop steward, and when I went to see him about it he said, 'Well, he's a nuisance, get rid of him. And by the way, it will get us out of the penalty clause, and we can settle it after two weeks.' I didn't think that was right. I thought, well, if there are two sides to industry – and that's not a concept with which I've ever been particularly happy – then it's time I joined the other side. That incident coincided with this friend of mine getting his job at the Labour Party.

You say you've never been happy with the idea that there are two sides in industry, and yet you went into the trade-union movement when the two sides were clearly defined – there was a high degree of confrontation in those days. As you worked your way up through the movement during that era, did you at any stage have doubts about whether you had chosen the right career path?

I didn't choose a career path – in a sense I chose a cause, and the cause was to tackle injustice at work and the kinds of abuses I'd seen at Plessey. I was strongly motivated by employers treating people badly, and being unfair, careless and arbitrary in their actions, and I still am. I've always been on the side of those in the trade-union movement who have not seen things in an adversarial way, but have sought to get inadequate employers to raise their standards to match those of the good ones. My approach to employers has always been pragmatic and tolerant, so I never felt I was adversarial, although I'm certainly a doughty opponent of the bad employer. So I didn't join the TUC for a career – if you want a career, you'd better go somewhere else, because the trades-union community's not really big enough to accommodate careers. But it does need highly motivated people who work hard, loyally and consistently. After that all sorts of luck and personal factors come into it, so it is difficult to give anybody advice on how you would follow a particular route to become the General Secretary of the TUC.

Were you surprised when you became General Secretary, or was it something that you felt you had been moving towards?

I am surprised that I'm General Secretary of the TUC, even today, three years into the job. But it was talked about as a possibility in the long term, probably as early as the late 1970s, and I had a group of supporters who sought to ensure that I gained the necessary experience in different parts of the organization to put in a strong bid when the vacancy came up. In a sense, then, I can't say it was a surprise. I'm not being immodest, but a significant degree of grooming went on to make sure that I was prepared for it, and I'm grateful for that. There were one or two people who thought I should have gone for it earlier on. I didn't think I was ready.

Was that modesty on your part?

I don't know. Diffidence, perhaps. I am not motivated strongly by a sense of personal position. I suppose everybody says that once they have reached the top of their particular tree or ladder, but really I am not. I thought there was a natural order to things, and at that stage there were other candidates in front of me who needed their opportunity. I gave them every bit of support I could at that time.

Do you think it is still possible for the trades-union movement to achieve collective success, or are you increasingly representing a large number of individuals, all with different aspirations for different degrees of success?

Well, things certainly have changed considerably. By the year 2000 we estimate that only about half the work-force will be employed full-time in steady jobs. The rest will be temporary, on contracts, or part-time in some way, and working on a much less secure or more flexible basis, depending on which way you look at it, than was the case before. I never forget that everybody is an individual with his or her own aspirations, life pattern and set of circumstances which makes him or her unique, but I do think that in large organizations in particular, it's a mistake simply to look at people as individuals. There are rules which govern ICI or Rover or McDonald's or Marks & Spencer. Those rules are set by the management. They may be set after some consultation with representatives of the workforce, through trades unions, or they may be set by the management alone. Whatever the case, those rules are important, as is the ethos of the company in applying them. The job of the union is to recognize what's collective and what's individual. We're the friend of the individual when he is in trouble, or hurt, or sacked, or being treated unjustly in some way or another, but we also seek to influence the rules which apply, the contract structure which might be in force in, for example, an insecure contracting-out-type operation such as you find in many parts of the media at the moment. We attempt to find where those collective decisions are taken. Employers often try to pretend that there are no collectively set rules and they're all individual negotiations. So we are all seeking to emphasize the collective rules – sounds a bit Soviet, doesn't it, in this day and age? – perhaps communal is a better word for it. In any society or any group you need a certain set of standards. I'm always looking for those standards, and who has set them. And they're the people the unions need to be talking to.

Do you think the rules are always better when they are formulated by agreement between management and a union, or is it possible for a management to be so in tune with what you are saying that it can actually set them without any reference to a trade-union structure?

There are companies who would claim that they can do it, that they don't need unions – Marks & Spencer and IBM, for example. These are companies which are at the leading edge of their particular sector, the market leaders. They spend an enormous amount of money trying to ensure that they do things better, in their eyes, than the unionized part of their industry. In a sense that is a back-handed tribute to the trades-union world – to keep out the union, to show that the workers don't need it. Marks & Spencer think that they treat people better than some of their major unionized competitors, such as Tesco. I don't think they always succeed, however.

Do they succeed most of the time?

Well, everybody knows what a good company Marks & Spencer is, and their reputation is high, but the reputation of Tesco, now the number one supermarket in the country, which is heavily unionized, is also high. Indeed, Tesco has been one of our great success stories. It has developed from a rather small, tatty supermarket on every high street to overtake Sainsbury as the leading supermarket in the nation, and that was done with union support and co-operation. I think where companies like Marks & Spencer and IBM run into problems is when a major change becomes necessary which involves redundancy. Then all these warm words about how well they treat their workers, how they care for them from when they start to when they retire, begin to taste sour to the employees concerned. Redundancy provokes disbelief and cynicism. The banks, I think, are going through that experience at the moment.

I would say that the union really comes into its own when these unpopular, difficult decisions have to be made. Tesco had to make these decisions as well. Transforming from a scruffy supermarket into a superstore involved a lot of job changes, and some people left, but the union, and the terms on which all that was done, helped them through that difficult adjustment. New management and workers have a relationship which was forged in difficult times. I don't think Marks & Spencer have gone through that kind of experience. Perhaps they have not needed to. But with IBM's redundancies at the moment, we are certainly aware that by trying to keep their ethos intact, they are probably having to pay out more than they would have to under the best union agreement they can find in this country. They might have done it a little bit cheaper if they'd done it with the union.

Was it difficult for the trades-union movement to evolve from a position where you fiercely protected every single job to sitting down and negotiating with employers on the basis that perhaps quite a number of jobs would have to go?

It has certainly been a whole new learning experience for the unions. The great growth of unemployment really started round about 1979–80 in the recession that saw 3 million jobs axed in manufacturing in the most heavily unionized part of the economy. By 1983 union officers had become full-time redundancy negotiators. Their job was the rules, the terms, who went, who stayed, what job opportunities there might be for people who went. The recent recession of 1990, during which another million jobs in the factory sector of the economy went, has seen a lot of that as well.

But I don't think, if we are honest about it, that unions have ever been good job-protectors, though there were certain sectors where unions were very strong, and where employers found it virtually impossible to shed any labour. We're not aware that there are many sectors like that left now. Mostly, I think, unions have been partners in the job-shedding process by agreeing the deals. We would have liked to have been more effective in stopping employers from shifting away from the steady-job concept to the contract-job concept. I don't object to people choosing to work on a subcontract basis – I think it suits many talented, more enterprising people to work like that — but I do think that for the average and below-average sort of person it is a very insecure basis on which to bring up a family and to play a full part in society. I worry enormously about the way the labour market is going, not so much for the talented workers, but for the people who get packets of work here, parcels of work there, but who for the rest of the time are going to struggle to pay their 25-year mortgage.

Is there a possibility that the movement could end up representing only those at the bottom end of the scale in society, and that you wouldn't be truly representative of workers at all levels? Given that membership of trades unions is in decline, how do you see the unions responding to the new mood and new attitudes, and pulling themselves forward to be successful in the next decade or so?

The current figure is 6.75 million, but it was 12 million in 1980. If you look at the profile of union membership, we are not representing the people at the bottom, we are representing those in the middle and just below the middle. The typical trade-union member today, we were quite surprised to find, has at least one A-level and is likely to be a teacher, a professional in some public service, or quite a highly skilled person in an aircraft or motor-car factory. The less skilled, casual jobs in the high streets, and in hotels and catering, which have seen a tremendous growth in employment, are not the areas that we penetrate. The employers, by and large, are pretty hostile and they want to keep control in a way that's unfettered by any reference to collective agreement. I would say that our problem is the opposite, that we're representing the relatively privileged, those in steady jobs, those in full-time work, those who work for big blue-chip companies or in the public sector. We're finding it very difficult to reach out to the insecure, the low-paid, the casual workers. We have very little public policy support in terms of legal opportunities. We've got plenty of employer hostility and a general climate where, in certain high-street operations I could name, to say, 'By the way, I'd like the union to speak up for me on this particular matter,' results in even greater insecurity. It's a quicker way to your P45 than actually being slung out in one or two companies that should know better.

Do you think the fact that the unions are not more representative means that they have, in a sense, failed?

I'm very much aware that we need to be more representative, that our mission is to help the underprivileged and those who are suffering from exploitation, and that at the moment we're struggling to help them. As I said, much more we are dealing with people who are relatively secure – in parts of the public sector in particular they may be low paid, in parts of the private sector they may be a bit less secure, but in relative terms they're a lot better off than their equivalents in non-union Britain, if I can put it like that. Reaching out to non-union Britain is very much central to what I'm trying to do in the TUC at the moment, by persuading workers of the advantages of union representation, and by saying to employers, 'I think you'd do better with a union, because at the end of the day workers won't invariably believe that you've got their best interests at heart all the time. You don't have, if you are honest about it – you've got other interests that you have to take into account.' We have to reach out, too, to the government of the day, to tell them that unions have a constructive part to play in helping to deal with change, and in giving people a bit of security during change. Those are the fundamental audiences the TUC needs to be addressing now.

Do you feel that the targets are moving too quickly for you? There was a report from Business in the Community recently which predicted a world in which virtually everyone would have at least four totally different careers, for each of which they would have to be retrained at different stages of their lives. That is a long way away from the old cradle-to-grave mentality that a great many people have grown up with.

I think the speed of change is bewildering for many people. A minority thrive on it, the majority are afraid of it, particularly when they take on obligations – wife, mortgage, children – in the knowledge that if they lose a job they are likely to have to take a step down in the living standards they can sustain. From the union perspective, too, I think we find it difficult to cope with the speed of change, and at the moment we are very keen to ensure that the generation of union officials which probably came out of large factories and the public services understand what's happening in retailing, hotels and catering, the different work cultures which exist there. For people of my age in the trades-union movement – I'm 50 – and there are plenty of them, that was not our world. Our world was large plants, engineering, shipbuilding, the public services, nationalized industries, and so on. Grappling with split shifts and the heavy emphasis on service is a different world, so we're struggling along with everybody else to keep up with the pace of change. But I think it's a great mistake for others to say, just because we're struggling, 'Well, the unions haven't anything to offer.' In fact we've got polls now indicating that nine out of ten people think that unions are essential, that 5 million extra people would join if there was a union at their workplace, that employers, in too many cases, behave badly and don't treat people fairly. All the conditions for people returning to unions are there except one – people are not convinced that they'll remain secure if they join a union, that membership will benefit and not penalize them. There are enough employers around who will say, 'If you're a union member, watch it. And if you're a union activist, I might not want you to work for me any more.'

To what extent would increasing the membership of the trades unions, regaining those people you've lost and attracting new ones, depend on having the right legal framework delivered by the government?

I think it's important that public policy, which comes from the government of the day, has a friendly and constructive view of trades unions. One of my regrets in my time as General Secretary has been that it proved impossible to persuade John Major and his senior colleagues to alter the Thatcher view of unions. She was the one who called us the 'enemy within', which was a great insult to the trades unionism which was viewed by many as crucial in the war effort 50 years ago in terms of mobilizing the resources of Britain. After all we achieved a higher degree of mobilization even than Nazi Germany, with all the authoritarianism that they were able to deploy. She insulted the sacrifice of many people from the union world in the world wars of this century. But this idea is still around in Conservative circles, and it's one I bitterly resent and find offensive.

Are you actively hostile to shareholders? Do they take too big a slice of the cake?

I'm not hostile to shareholders – after all, many shareholders are workers and trade-union members as well, and they play an essential part in raising capital. Where I think the present system is unbalanced is that increasingly the shareholders are the pension funds of big companies or life-assurance firms. They're very professional, they compete for business and they drive very hard bargains with particular companies, and I am sure that they are encouraging the rather short-term outlook prevalent among many British firms at the moment and discouraging businesses from making long-term investment in people, through training, and in new equipment.

I am certainly one of those who takes the Will Hutton view of the world, which says that a better balance is needed at work, otherwise more and more resources from companies will go to the shareholders. I'm not talking about great big fat-cat shareholders, but ordinary beneficiaries of pension funds or life-insurance companies. In a sense those of us who have such investments are all cutting our own throats by putting pressure on the business community to deliver rates of return on an annual basis which are twice as high as those in Germany, higher even than in the United States. I think we are siphoning too much money which should be seed-corn money into current consumption.

The businessman Tony O'Reilly put forward an interesting theory. He said that because so many ordinary shareholders have their money tied up in companies, and because so many pension funds which represent the interests of workers are now playing such a big part in the running of companies, this evolution has in a sense created the kind of world of which Marx would have approved, because it is really giving power to the people. The people are actually now controlling, through pension funds, the companies they work for.

If only that were true! I think it's a bit of a flight of fancy to suggest that the individual shareholder is controlling anything. They may be benefiting from the very competitive abilities of the fund managers to screw the most out of the shares they own and to demand these very high rates of return, but in a sense it goes into one pocket and probably goes out of the other, and jobs are threatened. I think there's a general shift of resources towards shareholders from employees. I look, for example, at the current British Airways exercise in which they are cutting the pay of regional staff, and I think, 'Who's the beneficiary of that?' It is simply to ensure that British Airways' shareholders, many of whom are the workers, by the way, benefit through improving their shareholding. I just don't think the balance is right, and I'm one of those who believes that companies build their reputation in the end on the commitment, skill and loyalty of the people who work for them. I'd like shareholders to sit back a bit and say, 'We'll take a long-term view of our investment.' I think we'll do better in the long term if we do that rather than engaging in this very aggressive buying and selling, and applying this ruthless pressure on companies to cut costs, which means to cut jobs in many sectors, and which has produced all this downsizing and restructuring and delayering, some of which is necessary, but a lot of which is merely a response to keeping the share price up.

You don't accept the argument that if we – and I'm not just talking about Britain, but about other countries as well – are to compete with low-wage countries, particularly in the Far East, it is increasingly important that we enter an era where wage levels are lower in order to put more people into work?

I'm sure we will not compete with the developing world in terms of low wages and I don't think we should even consider it. We are an advanced industrial nation, we're the oldest industrial nation in the world. Our destiny is to maintain ourselves as a highly skilled, high-quality, high-added-value country that demands a good education and training system, good relationships at work and between unions and employers, and a sense of co-operation in a very competitive world. We won't get that by cutting the wages of people who are perhaps already relatively low paid, and, in some cases, living in poverty. We won't get that by thinking we can compete with nations where maybe £5 a week would be an enormous salary – and in many cases, it is less than that. We need to start showing the sense of social cohesion and care for the less able in society that the Asian countries are beginning to display. The thing that always strikes me most about Japan, for example, is that when children go to school, the gap between the less able and the most able closes. Their education system's great success is what it does for the less able, while certainly not holding back the able. Ours is not like that – our system accentuates differences and varying rates of development, and far from narrowing, the gap widens very quickly. So I think cohesion, added value and high skill are our routes to the future, and I'm unhappy that the Conservative government tended to market Britain as a cheapskate place, an offshore island of Europe. We haven't got a minimum wage, we haven't got the social chapter – come to Britain and you'll get things a lot cheaper than you will in France and Germany. I think it's a pretty unworthy way for a country to act. Perhaps that will change now.

Even if we ended up delivering more jobs at the end of the day than we would if we were part of a European structure?

I think we'll deliver more jobs at the end of the day by being fully part of a European Union. Because it would be the world's biggest economy, if you see it as one entity, it would tend to set standards for the rest of the world. The United States is number one at the moment and sets the standards for the rest of the world, and these are pretty red-blooded capitalism and maximized shareholder values. Workers' rights come pretty low down on the American list of priorities, and I think the kind of example they've set, say, in Russia, where the people are slaves to the American fashion, has been unfortunate. The capitalism that has thrived there has been of the worst kind. The European Union is rather different, isn't it? It has some very successful companies, it also has a system of workers' rights, and unions play a part in that, and it has welfare states. I think that's the model for world development, and a more cohesive one than the American example. I'm not being anti-American – they've got a tremendous record of job-creation, Europe is nothing like as good – but I think the challenge to America is to look after those of its citizens who are missing out on the economic growth. After all, there are 30 million people with a third-world standard of living in the United States, particularly around the city centres and in some of the deep-South rural states. Europe has a narrower gap between rich and poor, and the sense of social solidarity is much stronger. We have got the task of creating jobs, and I think we can do that if we're competitive in the first place. But at the same time we must look after those who are perhaps not able to look after themselves.

So success for the British trades-union movement is inevitably bound up in Europe?

I'm sure it is. We must hope that Britain follows the European way. The European way is itself changing, and we can contribute to making it rather more flexible, rather more responsive to change. We've got many strengths to contribute towards Europe, as well as lessons to learn. I think what we need to pick up from Europe is better training and education, and to re-learn a sense of social cohesion. I'm sure the European direction, rather than the American business-school direction, is the right way forward.

In Britain, some unions have changed and evolved rather faster than others. Do you feel that those unions considered to be the dinosaurs of the movement are holding back things as a whole with their reluctance to change as quickly as you might like?

I don't think we've got any dinosaurs. We've got unions in sectors which perhaps haven't changed much – not every area of the British economy has gone through globalization or the information-technology changes which have completely transformed the nature of people's jobs. There are still lots of basic jobs – cleaning, collecting rubbish, working in hospitals, portering – huge areas which have not changed anything like as much as many people think. Just because the world of some unions and subgroups of workers hasn't developed in this way it does not mean to say that they're dinosaurs. It can be a tremendous shock for just about any group when a major change comes along like a tidal wave.

At the moment in the financial-services sector, bank workers who thought that the deal was a job for life and showed fierce loyalty to their particular bank, which was the contract which bound them to their employers, are now being told, 'We want to shut a lot of branches, we want to get rid of a lot of you. We'll do that on reasonably good terms, but there's no job for life, nothing like that.'

We note the impact on morale, the sense of violation felt by many of these traditionally very loyal workers who are certainly not regarded as militant trade-unionists of the traditional British kind. It's very unfortunate to see that huge change. People find it hard to adapt, and most of them believe they'll be worse off as a result. And I would say, based on the experiences of the last 15 or 16 years, that they're probably right. They won't get jobs as good as the ones they are losing.

Can you paint me a picture of the ideal relationship between a trade union and the management of a company? Is there any firm in Britain that has achieved it? If not, which company would come closest as far as you're concerned, and what further steps would you like them to take?

A lot of companies come very close to the ideal relationship. I won't name them because next week they could have some problem, because they have fallen short of the ideal, or because something has happened externally and they're finding it a struggle to deal with. I'll just mention sectors – the steel and motor industries both now have conspicuous examples of success where perhaps they didn't a few years ago, and areas like chemicals and pharmaceuticals have been as consistently successful. We are very proud of the joint achievements of unions and employers in those sectors. I would say that in Britain 84 of the 100 leading companies listed by the *Financial Times* are heavily unionized. People talk about the decline of union membership, but in fact it's a reflection of the decline in employment among those top 100 companies.

Are those 84 successfully unionized?

Yes. Almost by definition, if you're in the top 100, that's going to be the case. Among the top 50 something like 44 companies are unionized. So big, corporate Britain, by and large, is union Britain.

I would say that the ideal relationship is one in which managements have respect for all workers, and recognize that from time to time employees will need independent representation, and that that's the job of the union. They should be aware that they need to take workers with them during the process of change, and that they need to agree certain rules. They don't cheat on those rules, they don't take short cuts, and basically they try to stick to the agreed path. The temptation for any management is always to do things quickly because of external pressure – to take short cuts, and perhaps to depart from standards from time to time. The union's job is to make sure that doesn't happen.

Should a trade union respond very quickly to external circumstances which affect a company's market or its profitability?

You have to remember that trades unions are reactionary bodies. I think it was George Woodcock, a predecessor of mine, who told a group of managers that unions were not reactionary in the sense of being regressive or slow, but because they reacted. They were the sum total of their members' experience as expressed through the different democracies of the unions. Vic Feather, another predecessor of mine, said to another group of managers, 'When you're complaining about your workers not adapting to change, remember that they work for you and I work for them.' Unions find it difficult to be in the vanguard of responding to change, but there is now a whole core – a generation, really – of union officers who have been through every kind of change you could possibly envisage. Anything which has ever been thought of in the Harvard Business School or by American business gurus, they've been there and they've handled it, by and large. They've sought to do their best for the workers, whatever the circumstances. These people now give an awful lot of advice on a day-to-day basis to employers who might be going through a change for the first time. The district secretary in whichever town it is will have been through it with the firm down the road, and will know the pitfalls, the advantages, how not to do it, how to do it and so on. One of the key jobs of union officers is broadening that kind of experience, which many individual company managements just don't have.

But at the same time you accept that managements have the right to manage? You have just talked about the unions having a kind of policing role, just keeping managements on their toes. Where does the balance lie between those two?

I think it's important for managements to recognize that there are no rights around – what there are are duties and responsibilities. The responsibility of the management is to manage the resources they are given in the most efficient way, to ensure first the survival of the enterprise and thereafter its growth. Any manager, from the Archbishop of Canterbury to the general secretary of the TUC or the boss of IBM, has the same basic responsibility, but the sense of commitment and of common endeavour is something that you need to share. You do that through a unionized sector, through agreements with the unions about how you will do things. You do it by consulting people, by making sure they know what's going on, and by encouraging high morale. That's the kind of management I warm to, the people who take this approach rather than saying, 'I'm the manager, what I say goes, and if you don't like it, you can bugger off.' That's not much of a right, is it? And it's not the proper way of doing things.

What do you regard as your greatest successes?

The time from which I got most satisfaction – I don't know whether it could be classed as a success or not, but I thought it was tremendous – was, funnily enough, the early '80s, when unemployment was going through the roof and I was involved with the Manpower Services Commission in setting up various schemes for young people and unemployed adults. There was a lot of union concern that these would be cheap-labour schemes, substitutions for people paid at the union rate. I went on the road selling these schemes in south Wales, in the north-east of England, in Lancashire, Yorkshire, Scotland and so on, building up a core of union officers who were evangelists for these opportunities. I think all of us involved really enjoyed that, and got a huge kick out of seeing a lot of people do well on those schemes. One of the sadnesses of the subsequent years was that each successive scheme became cheaper and cheaper, with fewer resources per head, and the degree of satisfaction the unemployed have got out of them has deteriorated. But they were good schemes – YTS, the Community Enterprise Programme, the Community Programme – and I think they've a part to play in dealing with unemployment in the future.

Do you think it will become more or less difficult to achieve success in your particular field, as a trades-unionist?

I don't think it will necessarily become more difficult. A cynic might say that the only place we can go is up. As I have said, the conditions for trades-union growth are there. The key is to demonstrate to people that unions are a good thing. They're a great cause – they've been a significant factor in Britain in the last 100 years, and the challenge to make them as significant over the next 100 is a very exciting one. We've got a lot of really good people trying to do that at the moment and I think the ball is at our feet.

What do you think are the greatest enemies of success?

Ego, I think, is a major one. The idea that success is achieved only in terms of what you do for yourself, and maybe your family, is a pretty dead-end route to human satisfaction. I think being always aware of the respect and regard in which you are held by your fellow men and women is the key to a fulfilling life. That's a strong personal motivating factor for me, and the people who are aware that they need to impress and win the affection and regard of a wide range of their fellows are the ones I respect in society.

How do you resolve conflict between work and family on the road to success?

It's very difficult. The hours people work are enormous now. British males work the longest hours of any occupational group in Europe, and I am no exception to that. I'm not sure my wife would totally agree with me on this, but I think we have managed it. You need to ensure that you spend plenty of time with each member of the family when they need it. You're probably going to get a lot less time for yourself, but that doesn't really matter. Aiming for a balance between work, a family and the community is, I think, the ideal way to approach these things.

Could you have achieved what you have without the back-up and support of your wife and family?

I don't think so. I'm proud of my stable and affectionate family life. If my private life were in turmoil, I don't think I would have the peace of mind to concentrate on my job.

If you could gather together all the young people who want to be successful trades-unionists, what advice would you give them?

First, I'd say, you all want different things, people go different routes, and I think that's right for society. Society should be diverse, individuals are diverse – there are many things that need to be done, and I like to see people do things well. My advice is to be clear about what you want to do. Don't be afraid to ask for help, don't be contemptuous of our history – learn about it, reflect on it, discuss it and always be motivated by the fact that we're on this earth to improve the lot of mankind in general, not ourselves alone. We pass this way but briefly, and we make a small mark on the world, but it should be a positive mark, and one about which people can say, 'Well, he did OK. He was OK for himself, but he was OK for others as well.' I'd like my own epitaph to be something along those lines.

And your advice to workers who see in prospect a world where there are perhaps not enough jobs to go round?

Don't despair. I'm an optimist about the working world, and about the things that need to be done. There's a tremendous amount that still needs to be done to improve our environment and the general condition of the world. I look around and see squalor, and idleness alongside it, and I think, 'Can't we put those together, and get the idle to put right the squalor, improve the buildings and structures of our communities?' I'm sure we can do that. We've had tremendous success in the post-war period, now we've got to cope with the developing world in a much more purposeful way. We must not deny them access to our markets, we've got to help them do well. We must not compete with them in the low-tech areas, we've got to seed those areas and go upmarket and take advantage of our education, training and skill levels.

I'm an optimist about people, and my message would be optimistic – we can change things if we are determined, if we're honest and if we set ourselves high standards. That's what I want for the trades-union movement, and that's what I want for others as well.

And would you say that everyone who is successful in obtaining and holding down a job has obligations to the wider community, to society as a whole?

I believe the main obligation of the successful is to those who are not. In our moments of greatest triumph, we should remember those who have not been fortunate enough or talented enough to go down the same path. This sense of obligation is something that should be very strong in all successful people. It is absolutely crucial to the health of our society.

One final question, which you pre-empted slightly earlier, but let me put it more directly. When your time comes to leave this life, what would you like people to say about you?

I'd like them to say two things. First, that he improved the lot of working people through raising the game of the trade unions of this country. Secondly, on a personal level, I would like people to say, 'He was straight, honest, friendly and constructive in just about all he tried to do.' If they can say that, I'll be well pleased.

DR NTHATO MOTLANA

Few in Britain will have heard of this urbane, civilised man, yet he bridges the gap between the poor and powerful in South Africa in a manner which offers real hope for that country's future. Voted Businessman of the Year in 1993 by both white and black business leaders, he has also developed a formidable reputation as a civic leader. 'The desire to achieve is very, very important,' he says, 'I've often wondered what some of us would be driven by if there hadn't been an apartheid system and white oppression.' With his father a poor peasant farmer, 'the idea of reaching High School was a dream that one thought could never be realized'. But he worked hard, earning one scholarship after another, and finally made it to university where he took a degree in medicine. He daringly set up his own practice in Soweto at a time when 'the apartheid government would arrest you for being self-employed'.

As secretary-general of the ANC Youth League, he served two jail terms and was banned twice for his political activities. He says he has 'always passionately believed that the government is there to create the environment to enable business to prosper'. But when he started his first company some 30 years ago, such a move was 'almost impossible for blacks'. It was a factory making school clothing for black children, and it failed after a few years because he was 'undercapitalized, and lacked management and marketing skills'. Undeterred, he found many other ideas to back, among them the country's first black-owned pharmaceutical company, and its first black-owned private hospital. A long-time friend – and for many years personal physician – to Nelson Mandela, he is also a kind of business ambassador for South Africa, and quotes with relish what the Chinese government told him was the formula for their economic recovery: 'Devotion to education, a work ethic and discipline.' He explains that white corporate South Africa (and some overseas companies) are now looking for black partners, but, to his regret, 'we still lack finance, management skills and basic education'. However, he hopes all that will soon change, provided they avoid the jealousy factor! His message to the people who think like that is: 'Instead of asking why Dr Motlana seems to be so wealthy, ask, "How did he get there?", and come and see if I can help you get there too.'

Dr Motlana, what is your definition of success?

To me success has always meant that, having striven to achieve something, you finally do so. I can recall that one of my first desires, ambitions if you like, was that I should matriculate. I had been born in a rural village of poor peasant farmers and the idea of reaching high school was a dream that one thought could never be realized. When I finally got to matriculate, I got a good pass and from then on it became a question of scholarships, of one scholarship after another. It was a great moment in my life when I was finally admitted to university but I regret that my first ambition was to be a lawyer.

You regret?

Well, yes and no. My first choice of profession was law. There was a time when many black South Africans thought that law was a way to fight the 'system'. Throughout my life I have been motivated by the desire to change the system, to fight white rule, and it really determined the course of my life. It was always, 'How the hell do we get rid of this oppressive system?' I know it sounds trite today but, while a lot of our people thought of a career, thought of making money, some of us were motivated by one thing – to get rid of the system. And the example of Mandela and Tambo, who had a very successful law practice and were involved in that struggle, inspired a lot of us. But nobody would give a scholarship to a poor black to do law, because lawyers were always regarded as troublesome people. So I went into medicine. I had the choice of three scholarships, three grants to go into medicine, so I became a doctor.

Is that one of the secrets of success, that you must have a mission, a driving ambition, in one particular sphere or another?

I believe sincerely, completely, utterly that that kind of ambition, the mission, the desire to acquire, to achieve something, is very, very important. I've often wondered what some of us would have been driven by if there hadn't been an apartheid system and white oppression. A colleague came to see me one day and I asked him what was his problem. He said, 'I'm leaving South Africa.' I said 'What? A black man, professional, a doctor, you're leaving this country? Why?' 'For the sake of my children.' And indeed he left South Africa, settled in Canada, became a professor of paediatric psychiatry. His children are all medical doctors. I have never once thought of leaving South Africa. I knew the struggle against oppression, against apartheid, against poverty was here. There was no way we were going to win the struggle unless we were here. At the coalface.

Did anger play a key part in your drive to succeed in your mission?

Anger played a part. Very early on, as a student, as a member of the student representative council at the University of Fort Hare, I became well known as somebody with a very short fuse and when I addressed public meetings, I would explode and swear at the enemy. In fact when Mandela's comrades came back from Robben Island, they were fond of reminding me of a protest meeting, just outside the place where Mandela and others were tried. I addressed the meeting and used the most vulgar terms, which at that time could have got me thrown into jail. I was just a student then, but I soon realized that anger tends to cloud your thinking. It was better to be aggressive rather than angry, so I used to be very aggressive.

But you've channelled that aggression into other areas?

Into, hopefully, productive avenues. I mean, I was always good at organizing a group of students, or whatever, during my days as the secretary-organizer of the ANC Youth League. I'd go out on a Sunday afternoon and I'd find a lot of my peers watching a football match and I'd get so bloody angry. I would say to myself, 'There is a struggle going on, you know. We need to get together to plan how to overcome apartheid, how to overcome oppression, and here we are watching young people playing football.' But I got to realize that watching football and playing football is essential for the development of our people. We don't all have to be plotting how to overthrow the system to succeed.

You've become one of the most successful businessmen in South Africa. In 1993 you were voted Businessman of the Year, a judgment that covered the white community and the black community together. Did you plan your business success?

Again yes and no. I got involved in business about 30 years ago. There are people who think that black success has been predicated on the fact that the ANC is now a dominant partner in the Government of National Unity, but I got involved in business many, many years ago when it was almost impossible for blacks to do so.

Tell me a bit about that. What was your first business?

My first business was an attempt to create the first black-owned factory for the manufacture of clothing. I've always thought that black business being equated with the old woman selling bananas on the street corner is nonsense. I had watched a friend of mine establish a business empire. He was an ANC chap who died a millionaire by selling school uniforms to black children, you know it's compulsory for black children to wear school uniforms.

I was really driven by black poverty. I started my working life as a general medical practitioner in Soweto and my patients couldn't pay even the two rand that I charged them. I watched the immigrants who came to South Africa from Lithuania and from India with only the shirts they had on their backs, and in no time at all they were running around in BMWs and Mercs and I asked myself, 'Why is it that we are so poor?'

I got to know about the laws that dictated that we must remain poor. Denying us access to bank loans, denying us access to training, denying us access to premises, denying us access to everything. So my first attempt was to start a factory to manufacture school clothing for black children. And I failed. It failed after about four or five years because we were under-capitalized, we lacked management skills, we lacked the correct premises, the marketing and so on. And of course competition from the Indians and white South Africans was very strong but I had been aware of that all along. Since then I have started many, many other businesses. I continued as a doctor, so I didn't run the businesses myself but my *modus operandi* would be to identify a particular commercial opportunity and set the wheels in motion. For example, one day we got together and agreed that there was an enormous demand for generic medicines in South Africa but the cost of these medicines was too high, so we decided to start our own pharmaceutical manufacturing facility. There was also a demand for hair-care products which my people love so much. They often want to stretch their hair, they want to look lighter because to be light is to be privileged. Why didn't we do something about it? I mean the white companies handling these products were just printing money.

So we started the first black-owned pharmaceutical company in South Africa called Africhem and I was its founder-chairman. We had a young man who had trained as an organic chemist in Germany, he was the managing director. And it started off very well. I got a few doctors to contribute capital because we couldn't raise bank loans. We couldn't even find premises from which to operate and the marketing was very difficult, but we persisted and that company lasted for ten years. After ten years, again, it collapsed and that has been a common story. I'd get guys together, we'd form a company, we'd raise the capital, we'd find the premises, we'd go on for a few years, but there were always too many factors working against us. My most successful undertaking has been in the building of the first black-owned private hospital in South Africa. It is a facility with 235 beds – it's still operating, therefore it's successful. We've given employment, we've created wealth; I've not gained much from it financially but it is a source of great pride to me.

Did you ever consider giving up?

Never. I am not like the doctor who said to me, 'I'm going to settle in Canada. I'm sick and tired of this place. My children cannot get proper education, I can't even build proper consulting rooms in Soweto, so I'm off.' My response to that attitude has always been, 'You must be mad. This is our fatherland. We have to battle until it is free, so that our children can get proper education and so that we can build proper consulting rooms.' I've never once thought of giving up.

You don't seem to be the sort of person who thinks that the government ought to provide. You believe in people going out and providing for themselves and creating their own wealth?

I'll always believe that the government is there to create the environment to enable businesses to prosper. I recall when I was at medical school, Joe Slovo and his wife Ruth came in to organize us into the Young Communist League. I've always rejected Marxist-Leninism as an economic system, not because it's not smart, just because it didn't appeal to me, and I've always thought that the free-market system that allows people to do their own thing, without hurting others of course, is the way forward. And I'm not saying this because there was a fellow called Gorbachev who virtually rubbished Marxist-Leninism. I've been saying this from the age of 20 when I was at medical school. I've always believed that.

I was among black business people who were invited to a conference in Montreux, Switzerland and there were some who wanted to confront Thabo Mbeki, the Deputy President, and protest that the government was not doing enough to give blacks power in business. I stopped them and said the government may not be doing enough because we blacks have not come up with proposals that make sense. I've had no business training, I'm a doctor by profession, but it occurs to me that we should go to the government and say, 'Look, here are areas in which we as blacks can make a difference, can add value, please make it possible for us to go forward, provide soft loans if necessary, premises if necessary, the necessary training.' We should not go to the government and just say, 'Give us the power.' They can't do it. We can only get there with programmes that we've worked through and which make sense.

Do you need total control to achieve success?

No, no, no. I've never believed in total control. I believe in consensus, we should go forward together. I don't believe in personal control if that means dictatorship.

Can you sit down and methodically plan success?

I don't think so, but I do think that to be successful you must plan. Some successes are unexpected and come without being planned, but if you are looking to succeed a plan is almost always necessary.

And luck as well?

Luck has been defined by smarter people than I am as the moment when hard work and opportunity coincide. I've never believed in luck. I've always believed in hard work.

Are there any core principles for success?

I remember touring South East China in 1993 when I was still Mandela's doctor and used to tour the world with him. We were near Shanghai, with the Deputy Foreign Minister of the People's Republic of China, admiring those derricks going up, their wonderful building plans and the miracle of Chinese economic recovery. We asked what were the reasons for this Chinese success and the Deputy Foreign Minister said, 1) devotion to education, the Chinese work hard, 2) a work ethic, and 3) discipline. If you combine these three things it's an almost sure recipe for success.

Who do you admire? In the past, in the present, who do you think has been really successful?

There have been very many successful people in South Africa and I've always admired the De Beers, the Oppenheimers and so on. I have also enjoyed reading of the lives of Paul Getty, the Rockefellers and the Rothschilds. But in politics my inspiration was one largely unknown young black man called Anton Lembede. Anton Lembede was the first black to acquire an LLM in law and was actually the founder of the African National Congress Youth League. I'd argue that we have got where we are politically because of the influence of the Youth League led by people like Mr Mandela, Oliver Tambo and Anton Lembede, whose influence on the ANC turned it round from a debating society into a fighting organization. Sadly Lembede died in his early 30s – a great tragedy. But many of my generation were inspired by that young man.

Is there any limit to the success that can be achieved in South Africa?

I think in South Africa the sky really is the limit and, given the necessary motivation, black South Africans can certainly make it and that is my message to them every time I speak to them.

Many people admire success but there are some who are envious of those who are successful. What do you say to those whose primary emotion is envy when they see someone who has made a success of their lives?

Mr Justice Dumbuchena, the first black Chief Justice of Zimbabwe, had a phrase for it, 'PHD'. PHD does not stand for Doctor of Philosophy. It stands for 'Put Him Down', and this is a syndrome from which some of us are already suffering but fortunately I was well prepared for that. When I was nominated for top businessman of the year, my co-nominee was one of the most successful merchant bankers in South Africa and he warned me about this thing you were talking about, the jealousy. The poppy that sticks out higher than all the rest attracts attention and criticism. My message to these people is, instead of asking, 'Why is it that Dr Motlana seems to be so wealthy?' put the question the other way, 'How did Motlana get there?' Then come and see me and let's talk, let's discuss how I got there and how you can also get there. And it's beginning to happen. I get lots and lots of visitors to my office and what do they say, 'Dr Motlana, please tell us how do we go about it.' Then we form partnerships and I direct them to black groups who can advise them. I serve on the SBDC, the Small Business Development Corporation, I serve on the DBSA, Development Banking of South Africa, so I can tell them where to get funding and help.

So it is part of your success that you should help others to be successful as well.

Absolutely. I have to take my community with me. It's not enough that one man like myself has succeeded, it is necessary that that success is spread among all my people.

If you could gather in one huge room all the people who admire you and want to achieve what you have achieved in life, what advice would you give them, what would you say?

First of all I'd pass on the message of the Deputy Foreign Minister of the People's Republic of China, I'd tell them that nothing in this world comes easily, there are no free lunches, you have to work for it. I'd tell them about the need to plan. Hard work. Basic education. Work and work hard, success only comes with hard work. That's my message to my people and I repeat it every time, and I think it is beginning to sink in.

When your time comes to leave this life, what would you like people to say about you? What would you like them to think about you as a person?

That as a community worker, both in politics and in business, Nthato Motlana tried his best.

ANDREW NEIL

At the helm of the Sunday Times *through much of the 1980s and 1990s, Andrew Neil had probably the highest public profile of any British newspaper editor this century. It was a double-edged sword which helped him both to grow formidably into the job and, ultimately, to lose it. A fellow journalist once wrote, 'It is by opposition and confrontation that he is defined. His job is to provoke, to be out there irritating people and demanding responses.' Those he has taken on include the Oxbridge establishment, the monarchy, the National Union of Teachers – and the print unions, when his key role in moving News International's news titles from Fleet Street to London's Docklands brought him 'lots of death threats' and round-the-clock bodyguards. He talks here of how that industrial conflict nearly made him give up – and of the 'mistake' of a libel trial when he really thought he was set to lose everything he'd worked for. This feisty Scot from a middle-class Presbyterian family attributes much of his success to the 'world-class education' he acquired at school and university in Glasgow. A degree in Politics and Economics took him into work for the Conservative Party, from where he was head-hunted by the* Economist.*

His leap to the top job at the Sunday Times *was huge. Only 34, he had never edited a national newspaper before. He recalls, 'Everybody was against me, the atmosphere was hostile and brutal, I felt if I wasn't as ruthless as they were, I would lose.' He concedes his people management skills were not a great success. He talks too about the falling out with his boss, the media mogul Rupert Murdoch; and he develops his dramatic vision of the future world of work, and the qualities and changes of approach required to be successful. For tomorrow's journalists that means being not only inquisitive and passionate, but multi-skilled as never before – a view he embodies in spades, having laced his career in print journalism with a wide spectrum of presenting work across television and radio. Broadcasting gives him the public profile, but it is newspapers that offer the power. Which is why just after this interview took place he took on the job of Editor in Chief of a group that embraces three Scottish newspapers and* The European. *Always hunting for ways of doing things better, he complains that 'Britain is the only advanced country in the world where it seems a crime to try too hard, and where ambition is regarded as a flaw.'*

Andrew Neil, what is your definition of success?

I think success is having a sense of satisfaction in whatever you're doing. You can measure success by many ways depending on what activity you're in, but in terms of success for an individual the criteria are – does it give you personal satisfaction, have you got a sense of achievement, a sense of a job well done, are you happy in your work? – given that work has become so important for most people today. At the end of the day, or week, if you can say, 'That's been a good week, I've achieved what I wanted to do, things are going well, I feel happy with myself, I have a sense of achievement within myself,' I think that is a good definition of success.

Is the judgment on whether you are successful or not dependent on your own views or is it shaped in some way by the outside world's perception of whether you have been successful or not?

It is shaped by the outside world to some extent, but the outside world can misjudge you in the short term and you can get it right in the long term. You have also got to be honest with yourself, and I think people who are successful do tend to be honest with themselves, they can be their harshest critics. If you know what you're doing it doesn't matter what the short-term judgment of the outside world is. You can live with that provided you have confidence in yourself and a clear-cut definition of what you're trying to achieve. In the long run, of course, you might hope that the outside world catches up with you and accepts that what you were trying to do has been successful. Obviously your own view of yourself is shaped by what others are saying, but you don't want to let them influence you too much, because quite often the view of others is uninformed, malicious, distorted or has its own agenda. At the end of the day we are all subject to the judgment of the market and to our peer group and to consensus opinion.

But is it difficult to keep to that particular track when there is an overwhelming and persistent weight of criticism coming your way? How do you differentiate the malicious and the ill-informed from criticism which may have some justification?

You have to assume that about 90 per cent of it is malicious and ill-informed, but you also have to trust certain other people's judgments. When you're in a position of power and influence, you are responsible for running the show and an editor of a newspaper has almost dictatorial powers, in a way that a manager or chief executive doesn't necessarily have. You can't run a newspaper by democracy or by committee, you have got to get the paper out, so you have got to have confidence in your own judgment. But you've also got to be willing to listen and you have got to decide which opinions you will trust and which views you will take into account, even when they are not palatable. You need to build a body of people around you whose judgment you trust. You will not always follow their advice, but you take it into account because you believe it's given with the best of motives.

And what if the guy who's telling you that you're wrong, who's giving you advice that you trust, wants your job?

I have always taken the view that the more people who wanted my job the better. But this can be a problem for some people – they find it hard to live with a team of very talented people. The world is too tough and too competitive now, and the other people you are up against are too smart for you not to hire the best and the brightest, and at some stage some of these people should get your job. You should never overstay your welcome, you should move on and do something else. People don't have a lifetime contract on the same job any more and I have always relished the fact that there were three or four people in my team who could do my job and were probably after it as well. You've also got to let these people have their share of the limelight and take some of the credit. If someone in your team gets the credit for something, by reflection you get the credit as well. I learned more than anything else – and it took me a while to do so – that the team is all important, a really strong team which is not afraid to disagree with you, full of people who want your job and one day will get it. That's healthy – they might start to plot against you if they think you are going to be there forever, and although you may be able to see these plots off, there is nothing more destabilizing or debilitating than office politics.

Are we entering an era where people will be successful in four, five, six, seven different ways, perhaps in different careers in the course of their lifetime?

Before one might have gone to university, then become a graduate trainee at the BBC or IBM or wherever, and essentially for the rest of your life you were in that company, but I think the pace of technological change is such that that isn't going to happen any more. Change used to come in major waves and between them were periods of quiet. We now live in an age of constant waves. In the old industrial days, if you happened to take over at the peak of one wave you could survive ten, twenty, thirty years to the next. I remember my father being made redundant from the Territorial Army in the late 1960s after he had been with them since the end of the war in 1945. He had been in a period of quiet, and then there was a huge upheaval. Nowadays companies are constantly lapped by wave after wave and I think that puts a premium on agility, on creativity, on adaptability, and when you take all these things together it also puts a premium on a regular change of personnel, the best and the brightest taking on more than one challenge, not settling for one company for the rest of their lives.

What advice would you give to those people who have grown up in a world where there really has been a kind of progression, a ladder towards success?

They have to realize that nothing is forever, and that if they pursue one single goal and one single ladder of achievement they will never be successful in the exciting businesses of the future. If you do concentrate on doing just one thing all the time and doing that well, you will constantly be overtaken by newcomers coming in and doing it better or doing it differently, or by the changing structure of the market place. The days of people peaking in their fifties and sixties are gone. I think people will now peak earlier and might then go into a trough which will be difficult for them. If they think, 'I'm only 40 and my best days are over,' they will need a strong psychology to realize that needn't be so, they might have a quiet period and then move on to something else. Adaptability will count for a lot. There was a certain security in the old system – provided you played the game, and were dedicated to being a company man or woman, you could eventually, with a bit of luck, make it as high as you could go. Security and predictability were what the Industrial Age was all about. We don't live in that age any more and we must now take the rough with the smooth. A career will be much more like going on a diet now – you sometimes lose weight then put it on, then back down again.

Which means, of course, a different kind of balancing act with your finances?

Yes, it does. It means that you cannot count on incomes always growing in real terms and so you have to be careful that when money is coming in that you don't squander it. It will put a premium on individual financial planning to make sure that your lifestyle doesn't suffer during the quieter periods and that you don't have financial worries at a time when you need to be thinking what to do next – getting educated in the latest information technology, for example. So financial planning in these circumstances becomes a lot more sophisticated, and, another feature of the Information Age, it becomes much more tailored to individuals. It used to be that when you joined a company there was effectively one pension scheme for everybody. By contrast we are going to move much more into individually tailored financial packages, what they call in Silicone Valley 'a cafeteria of compensations', from which you choose the things that most suit your individual needs.

But it is quite difficult for everyone to have a cafeteria of compensations available to them. I wonder whether, in the process of this dramatic change that is already upon us, there are not going to be an awful lot of people falling by the wayside. What can politicians do, what can governments do to stop that happening and prevent the growth of a huge, disaffected underclass?

A major problem in the Information Age is that society will become a bell-curve. There will be 10 per cent at the bottom who lack the cognitive skills essential in an Information Age, who will have trouble speaking the two languages you have to speak – English and computer. Then there will be a vast majority of people in the middle, who live better lives than they did during the Industrial Age. More will work for themselves and there won't be as many working under terrible conditions, doing tedious jobs on assembly lines. The office girl today, for example, has far better working conditions than the kitchen maid 50 years ago. The same will apply to 80 per cent of society. Then there will be the final 10 per cent at the top who will be very rich, the Bill Gateses, the Rupert Murdochs, the people who really do well out of the Information Age. The real problem lies with that 10 per cent at the bottom. Nobody quite knows what to do about them, especially if that 10 per cent mirrors the evidence now beginning to come through from America. They are not there because they are disadvantaged, because they are discriminated against, or because they never got a start in life, they are there because they lack the basic cognitive skills to prosper in this kind of society. They are the consequence of the meritocracy, the ones that fall through the net, and it is among them that most of the social problems arise. They become an underclass. When I first brought the phrase 'underclass' to Britain in the late 1980s, Mrs Thatcher said there was no such thing as an underclass in Britain, and the left said that the underclass was just another name for the poor working-class. The underclass is not a degree of poverty, some underclass people actually have more disposable income than ordinary working-class folk. The underclass is a type of poverty which takes you out of the norms of society altogether. Working-class people in the 1930s had the same aspirations and norms and values as middle-class people, they just didn't have the same amount of money and the same amount of opportunity. This underclass is in a different category altogether and what happens to these people is one of the problems of an Information Age.

Do people who are successful have an obligation to the underclass?

Yes, I think they do. They have a moral obligation to try to do something about it and I think they have a self-interest to do something about it as well, otherwise they are going to end up living in gated communities, as they call them in America, and these underclasses will be herded into reservations, in effect, which we now call ghettos or sink estates, from where the crime will break out and from where the fear in the rest of society will come. So for both moral reasons and for reasons of self-preservation, more and more effort will need to go into helping that underclass, and we should be able to do it because the Information Age is producing people who are not just rich, they are mega-rich. Some individuals in computing and the media are worth up to $18 billion, more than the GNP of a small country in Latin America. So I think, 'What can you do with $18 billion?' I am moderately well off already and I am not desperate for that much more money, and I think that the mega-rich should use their surfeit of money to get involved and sort out the problems of the underclass.

You came from an ordinary background in Paisley. To what extent has your success been based on your background and upbringing?

I think that it's a necessary element in the success that I've enjoyed. There is something within you that makes you motivated and want to get on anyway. You either have that or you can develop it, regardless of background. But I was lucky to have a number of essential building blocks which gave me a solid base. Firstly there was a good family life with *two* parents, the value of which we are only now coming to appreciate, regardless of the background that you are from. Secondly I was fortunate to have one of the best educations that you can have and one that many people in England would have had to pay a great deal to get. I had a very good school and a very good university. Thirdly I had a strong moral base with the influence of the Church of Scotland and Presbyterianism. I think I benefited very much from the combination of family, the Church of Scotland – which helped to give you a moral compass and also reinforce that sense that you can help yourself – and an education system which was essentially open to talented people regardless of background and gave them a world-class education as a result. These three reinforced each other – the family, the church, the school – in producing a feeling that if you wanted to get on in life, you got yourself a decent education and you worked hard. There was nothing you couldn't achieve even if, initially, you were held back because you didn't come from the right background. There were so many examples of people who 'didn't come from the right background' who got on that it didn't matter that others might try to stop you – you knew you could get on.

When was the first time that you said to yourself, 'I have been successful'?

Because the school I went to was so success-oriented, or at least academic-oriented, I often felt that things were going well in that I was doing well in exams. The competition was tough, there were a lot of other bright kids in the school and I was never first, but I was up there with the leaders and I felt, 'If I carry on like this, things are going to work out well.' Every time you feel that, of course, the next challenge arrives. When I went from my local primary school in the middle of the council estate to the grammar school in the centre of town, that was a huge challenge. I felt I had been successful at the primary school, but then, instead of being the big fish in a small pond, I became a small fish in the big pond. In the six years that I was there, all seemed to click into place then came university, which is another huge challenge and you think, 'Is this going to work?' It did. Next came the world of work and, again, every time you think you are being a success another challenge comes along. When Alastair Burnett gave me my first major job at *The Economist* in 1973, I felt that that was another huge challenge, because although I had had a successful track record behind me at school and university, each level of success or challenge widened the net of competition. Now I was moving from Glasgow University into a magazine that was largely dominated by some of the best and the brightest from Oxford and Cambridge, so there was a doubt in my mind – 'I've done pretty well so far but am I up to being in their league?' Then you find that you are, and when I moved from *The Economist* to the *Sunday Times* I remember in that transition period being very worried, too. I had done *The Economist* for ten years. That had turned out to be a success and some of these Oxbridge firsts turned out to be not as bright as they thought they were. But the *Sunday Times* was a world-famous newspaper and I had never even worked in a newspaper. I think that it's important, as you become successful and take on a new challenge, not to assume that you are necessarily going to be a success. Doubts about your ability to do something are healthy.

How great were those doubts, a) when you were asked to go to The Economist, *and b) when you were asked to go to the* Sunday Times?

The doubts were greater when I went to the *Sunday Times*. Because I was much younger – I was only 24 – when I joined *The Economist,* I had the arrogance and enthusiasm of youth. It seemed a natural progression to go to somewhere like *The Economist.* I had done a degree in politics and economics, I had worked in the Conservative Research Department and for 18 months with Peter Walker at the Environment Department. For a 24-year-old I was relatively well informed about the ways of Westminster and about some of the big issues of the day, and I felt that although I was moving into a far tougher environment, I would probably be OK.

The jump from *The Economist* to the *Sunday Times* was huge and it caused me a lot more worries because it meant moving into an area that I didn't know much about. As *The Guardian* pointed out about three times when the announcement was made, I had never even worked on a national newspaper before, never mind edited one. I knew I was moving into a hostile environment as well. They didn't like this new guy coming in from the outside, and I didn't know how I was going to be able to handle Murdoch as a proprietor either. I had a great fear that I would be caught in a vice between a demanding proprietor on the one hand and surly staff on the other.

So given all these doubts, why take the job?

Because the challenge was so great. I did, though, have my one and only anxiety attack flying from Denver to New York in that transition period. I got a nervous churning in my stomach. I couldn't quite work out what it was but clearly, in retrospect, it was the subconscious worry of the job looming a month ahead at the *Sunday Times.* Although it did worry me and I was very apprehensive that when I went there it was just going to be a disaster, nevertheless when someone offers you, at the age of 34, the chance to edit one of the world's most famous newspapers, you have to take it.

Are there any areas of your life, professional or private, that you regard as failures?

I think my people-management skills were not a great success. Dealing with creative people, I found it very hard to indulge them and to have time for their egos, and I tended to be too slow to praise success and too quick and too harsh to criticize failure. Although too much ego-massaging goes on, you do need to do some of it, people do feel the need to be appreciated. And if they have done something badly or wrongly, you can be too brutal in telling them that. People are all fragile to some extent and I think I was sometimes too ruthless. It partly came out of the period when I first went to the paper and knew everybody was against me. The atmosphere was pretty brutal to begin with, and I felt that if I wasn't as ruthless as they were, I would lose. The problem was that as I began to win and build a team more in my shape and more to my liking, I didn't soften the edges quickly enough. Of course the whole dispute over the move to Wapping and the new practices soured relationships with the staff again. But by 1990–91 I had been in the job about seven or eight years, and I should have loosened up and lightened up earlier than I did. I think even the people at the *Sunday Times* would admit that by 1992, '93 or '94 the change in my demeanour had resulted in a change in the whole atmosphere at the paper, in that it was a happier, friendlier place in which to work. If I were doing it again, or were in a similar position, I would be keener to inspire and help rather than criticize all the time. That's not to say that some people don't need a bollocking every now and then – we all do – but I overdid it.

Are you more likely to be successful if you have a mentor, someone who, at the right time of your life, decides that you are worth backing and supporting?

I think it does help. Sometimes it can be your father, but in my case it couldn't, because although my father was a lovely man and I loved him, he was a gentle, unambitious man, a simple man in the nice sense of the word. He'd left school at 15, he didn't have a university education and he knew nothing about journalism so he couldn't be my mentor given the area that I was going to go into. So I was fortunate to meet someone like Alastair Burnett who was doing what I wanted to do – which was to be a print journalist and a broadcaster – who spoke with great authority on many subjects, who took time to encourage talent, who had a great sense of humour and who had certain standards about writing and journalism that I thought were worth following. I always remember when I got something wrong in an article and he gave me – as only Alastair could do – a gentle bollocking, he was too gentle a man to make it too harsh. I said, 'But it's a scoop, Alastair, I just got that one little thing wrong.' But he said, 'Yes, but if you can't get the small things right, how can we trust you for the big things?' Things like that, and the fact that he would take the time to care. In the middle of the Wapping problems, when I had two bodyguards with me almost everywhere I went and received lots of death threats, when the whole of the British establishment was essentially against what we were trying to do, I would get home at about ten o'clock and I would watch him on *News At Ten* and the phone would ring at about 10.30, almost within 30 seconds of his being off air, and he would say, 'I thought if you were at home I would come round and take a drink off you,' and he would come over and stay until one in the morning. The fact that someone who had given me my first major job was still, ten years later, prepared to come round and just lend his support, really mattered to me. I have tried to do the same with some of the younger journalists I have worked with because I know how important Alastair was to me.

You talked earlier about wanting to make a career in print journalism and in broadcasting, but the broadcasting took a while to come. Was print journalism a means to an end in the sense that it was a route to broadcast journalism, or was it something that you got great satisfaction out of in its own right? Could you happily have lived in a world of print journalism without making a break into television?

Print journalism was both an opportunity and a springboard into broadcasting. I got into broadcasting because of what I was writing. It began because I did a special survey of Scotland for *The Economist* which was picked up by BBC Scotland and STV. I went up to defend myself against the outraged Scots. That was seen by someone doing *Tomorrow's World* and so I started doing that. I have been better known until recently for the print journalism, particularly for the *Sunday Times*, but I have always done broadcasting even when I lived in America. I made four documentaries for the BBC and did the *Today* show regularly. In fact the balance now is more in favour of the broadcasting than the print, but I am not saying that it will always be like that, it could easily swing back the other way.

I get great satisfaction from doing both. When I did *Nationwide* in the late 1970s, covering their economic and trade-union stories, I was reporting on the same things for television that I was writing about for *The Economist*. For *The Economist* I was writing for 20—40,000 people at the core of the British Establishment, for *Nationwide* I was often broadcasting to up to nine million people. It was a great challenge to take that information from *The Economist* and recycle it in a way that my mother could understand. Doing that helped me understand what I was writing about for the Establishment. I did not fall into the trap like one editor who, when asked by a sub-editor what a paragraph meant, said, 'That paragraph was written for four people, and you're not one of them.' I have never been that kind of journalist.

Though I didn't realize it at the time, my working in both television and the press only reinforces my argument that we should no longer think that there's a narrowly defined route to the top in any career. I think the ability to be what is now fashionably called 'multimedia' is very important for journalists and we should think of ourselves simply as journalists rather than print journalists or broadcast journalists. We are communicators and we should be skilled in all these areas.

When you went to America, you left the Sunday Times, *albeit at the time apparently temporarily, in order to go for what you clearly perceived to be your big break in television journalism. It didn't work out. Were you really taken aback by that and how did you pick yourself up after Murdoch had said, 'Look, we are not going to run with this programme.' How did you then say, 'I've got to pick myself up, enter the fray again and try to re-establish my success'?*

I didn't perceive it as my big break in television, I would have been amazed if it had worked. What I did perceive was a lucrative move away from the *Sunday Times*, which is what it was. I had been with the paper for over ten years by then. I was getting restless and didn't want to outstay my welcome, and what's more Rupert Murdoch was getting restless at having a too independent-minded editor, too much of a celebrity. That was one of the things that used to annoy him more than anything else, whereas I rather relished the celebrity status or even the notoriety.

Do you think it helped the paper?

Yes. I think it made the paper enemies as well as friends, I don't think there was any doubt about that, but it also meant that the paper had to be read. What's he up to next? Who is he out to destroy these days? So even its enemies had to read it. I enjoyed the controversy, the public argument, being on TV and radio defending my position, even if it did make me enemies.

Rupert Murdoch didn't like that and decided to take the view that editors should be seen and not heard. The big problem was, he wanted me out and I was happy to go but I didn't know what to go to. He came up with this idea, which I always regarded as a long shot, of being the Mike Wallace of Fox's answer to *Sixty Minutes*, Mike Wallace being its most famous reporter. That always struck me as a long shot, but given the way the deal was constructed, it got me out of the *Sunday Times* and it offered a lot of money, so it was worth a shot.

From the moment I got to America I began to put into place what I called my parachute. I signed a contract for a book, *Full Disclosure*, which is now published. I began to talk to the BBC about doing some programmes, I spoke to *Vanity Fair* about becoming a contributory editor to them, I began to talk to other editors about doing columns and so on. I had insisted, as the price of going to America with Murdoch, that not only would he pay me a lot of money if I wanted to leave, but that he would also have to give me a two-year contract to write a column for the *Sunday Times*. So I was well aware of this risk, there was no starry-eyed view of what lay ahead.

As I got more involved and saw the potential for a different type of television news magazine, I did become more enthusiastic and it may well have worked. It wasn't that we failed, it was worse than that – we weren't even given the chance to fail, in the end the programme wasn't allowed on air. Fox just took a decision that it didn't want to have any news magazines at all and still doesn't to this day. I always knew that as a result of going from the *Sunday Times*, which I effectively controlled, into this big Fox network in which I would just be one of many, I would be buffeted around. So I knew I had better have a parachute or a safety net, and that's how it worked out.

How important is control to success? Because you have moved from being in total control to a position where you were a jobbing reporter, seeking work where you can. Do you feel that you have an opportunity to be more successful as a freelance, being a servant to many masters, than being your own master at running a single organization?

There are two forms of control. One is when you are in control of an organization, and if you do it well it gives you great satisfaction. There is nobody more in control than a newspaper editor, and that's why editors sometimes work well in other roles, because they are used to getting things done right away, the tyranny of the deadline forces them to do that. The tyranny of the deadline also gives you great power to control. People can't argue with you too much, you've got to get the paper out. That's one form of control which I thoroughly enjoyed and I am glad to have done it. But the relentless nature of a newspaper means that although you are in control you are still a cog in a wheel and you have to keep turning.

The other kind of control, which I now enjoy, is control of my own life. I am not the servant of many masters. Because I work for a number of people, I am the one in control because there is no one single person who is essential to my lifestyle or financial commitments, and I am now contracted to work for four, five, six, seven people, and if one of them wants me to do something that I don't want to do then I just won't do it, and I don't have to, because the monthly mortgage payment doesn't depend on them alone, someone else will probably come in and fill that slot anyway. I now find that although I am no longer in control of an institution, I am now in control of my own life as I never have been since my days at university, and I have never felt more at peace with myself. But somebody could offer me a great institution tomorrow and I would change again.

Were there any times when you felt like giving it all up?

There were a couple of times, and I suppose that's when the quality of the people around you is most important, because they can help to lift your spirits again and rally round you. In the immediate aftermath of the move to Wapping, when most of the staff had turned against me and the move and it was such a brutal fight, I felt I was fighting a battle without an army or at least with a most reluctant army. But then Murdoch stepped in and made it clear that if the staff wanted to take me on then they would take him on as well, and that made them step back.

Were you tempted to resign at that point?

Well, I just felt that I was losing it and that the confidence of the staff had gone. They were miserable. I felt I had almost no support in the paper and that I was in a very difficult position. I am not sure that, at the end of the day, if they had gone ahead with their motion of no confidence, even if they had voted that way, I would not have bashed on without them because I was so committed to the fight. But it was certainly a low point, I did think that I might have to resign.

There was another time when I came very close to it and I think I would have had to resign if the events had gone the way that I feared. This was in the libel trial against Peregrine Worsthorne who had written an editorial saying that I was unfit to be editor of the *Sunday Times* because of the Pamella Bordes episode. She had briefly been a girlfriend of mine in the summer of 1988, and then about six months later it had been revealed that she had been a highly-paid call girl. I fought the libel case on the basis that since I was single and she was single, I could only be unfit to be editor if I had known that she was a call girl, and I had not. It was unfortunate, it was embarrassing, it was unlucky, but I didn't see why it made me unfit, and I fought this libel case to establish my integrity and good name and also to take on a man whom I regarded as a pompous windbag for writing all this. In retrospect it was a mistake, because the consequences of failure were not worth the risk of success. His piece had annoyed me and hurt me. It had been a serious attack and there was always the risk of the allegation being brought up again in the future. If I had lost, the financial cost would have been huge and all my enemies would have had a field day, which would probably have made it impossible for me to carry on as editor. On the upside, if we beat them, we beat them and that was the end of it. It was a lottery – I won in the end but I just won and no more, and it could easily have gone the other way.

And you did consider what might happen if the verdict went against you?

I remember the jury went out in the morning at about 11 o'clock and I had a deadening feeling in the pit of my stomach about the consequences of defeat. I went to the RAC Club and I just sat there on my own in a side room sipping mineral water. I couldn't eat anything, I could barely swallow the water. I didn't want to be with anyone. Through the trial I'd always lunched with some of my other editors because I was still editing the paper and I needed all the time I could find, but that day I didn't want to be with anybody at all. My driver dropped me off at the RAC and I sat there until about 2.30 and contemplated the consequences of defeat. It would be the end of my career as a newspaper editor and I would have huge legal bills to pick up as well. I would probably have had to sell the house or re-mortgage it, and, frankly, just to put Peregrine Worsthorne in his place, it wasn't worth it, it was too big a risk. To have risked all that was a big mistake.

So you had a horrifying few hours when you actually saw all the success that you had achieved just vanishing out of the window?

Yes, exactly, everything I had worked for – all the hard work, all the slings and arrows, all the long hours, all the risk-taking and so on. It brought back to me something that I have always felt, and it's something that still keeps me on edge and still makes me competitive – you can never take anything for granted. Maybe if you were born into something or if you inherited something and it has been in the family for hundreds of years, you have a different attitude, but if everything you've got has come through your own work and ability and dedication, with some lucky breaks along the way, then I think you feel that nothing is forever, that you can't count on always having it, that things can go badly wrong.

Out of this, have you developed any ground rules for advice you would give to people for dealing with an unexpected moment when everything you have worked for seems suddenly and dramatically threatened?

The first thing is to try to avoid getting into a situation like that by not taking decisions in anger. I reacted too viscerally to too many things. Sometimes in a creative business that's quite useful – if your gut instincts are right, that's helpful. But at other times you'd be better, metaphorically, to go and lie down in a dark room on your own for a while, then come to a decision. If you write a letter in anger, don't post it that night, wait and read it again in the morning before you send it, because you might take a different view. I would often dash off memos to people because they had done something that really annoyed me and later on I would regret that I had been so hostile. If it is something that really threatens you, take longer to make the decision. You don't have to react right away.

Some people say it is by opposition and confrontation that Andrew Neil is defined, and his job is to provoke, to be out there irritating people and demanding responses. Is that an essential ingredient of all successful journalism?

I think to irritate, to provoke and to oppose is a big part of journalism, but I don't think it's the whole story. It was certainly a big part of journalism in the 1980s, which was more of a confrontational than consensual decade. A simple maxim is that good journalism is publishing what powerful people don't want to be published, and all the rest is really PR, even scoops are often public relations exercises because some company or politician has given you the story. The best kind of scoops are those that everyone is trying to stop, whether it's publishing *Spycatcher* or revealing Israel's nuclear arsenal as we did in 1986–87. There's a chapter in my book which I called, partly tongue in cheek but not entirely, 'Ruining the Sunday Breakfast of the Rich and Famous'. But I don't think it's just that, although that was what got me the most publicity. There were also things, as a journalist, that I believed in and fought for and stood for. I believed in the creation of a dynamic market economy, I believed in the breakdown of our class system, I believed in social mobility, I believed in educational opportunities for ordinary people, I believed that the collapse of the family explains why we have now got an underclass, I believed in a multi-racial Britain and that most of the people of different colours and cultures who have come to this country are really a great asset – there were lots of things that I believed in. Whether you agreed or disagreed with the paper, it stood for something, it had an agenda for Britain which I think was a positive one.

Do you make your own luck on the path to success?

You do make a lot of your own luck but you have to have lucky breaks as well. When I got my degree in 1971, I didn't know what I was going to do and I thought, like many others, 'If you don't know what to do, then do another degree.' But I also stood for election as Chairman of the Federation of Conservative Students and I won. That was quite lucky because that gave me a job in the Conservative Research Department and propelled me from university into the heart of Westminster.

But otherwise we may not have seen Andrew Neil, journalist?

I think that's right. Also I was lucky that Alastair Burnett was editor of *The Economist* when I applied for a job, because up to then it had tended to recruit almost exclusively from a few specific colleges at Oxford and Cambridge. The fact that Alastair came from Scotland and still had a house in Glasgow, where I had gone to university, was very lucky. A more English Establishment character might not have even given me an interview.

I also think that if Lord Thomson had still owned *The Times*, I would never have made the move to the *Sunday Times*. It needed someone like Rupert Murdoch to take the risk of appointing an unknown 34 year-old to be its editor, so although you can make your own luck in the sense that you can position yourself to take advantage of opportunities, I was also very lucky someone like Murdoch owned the paper at that time. The cards have to fall the right way.

Who are your heroes?

Well, although she and I never got on all that well together, I must say, as time goes on, Margaret Thatcher has become a bit of a hero. I suppose we live in an age of political pygmies now, and she begins to look more and more like a giant. Although she often used to infuriate me, I think basically what she stood for was right and this country is a much better place for it. John MacIntosh, the Labour MP, was also one of my heroes, he was an academic and he was a social democrat ahead of his time. He and I were about to write a book together when he died far too young. Thomas Jefferson is my hero among American Presidents, because he combined great statesmanship with a huge intellectual grasp of the issues. He was the philosopher king in many ways and also had a view of the devolution of power. He was the one that coined the phrase, 'The best government is least government'. If your mentor can be your hero, I would also put Alastair Burnett up there as one of my heroes.

What do you think are the greatest enemies of success?

The main enemy of success is a conservatism that takes the view that it's always been done this way, that there is no conceivable better way of doing it, and even if there is we don't want to know about it, because we are comfortable doing it this way. I think that's the kind of attitude that took hold in Britain – and looked like it was going to take hold of America as well in the 1970s, but didn't. It made us think that we built the best ships in the world, the best cars in the world, the best machine tools and so on, when we were still making them the way we had done in Victorian times and the rest of the world had moved on and started to make them better and more efficiently. That is the real enemy of success – an inability to conceive of other better ways of doing something. It applies whether you are running a company or running a country.

If you could gather before you all the budding young journalists in the world, what advice would you give them?

I would advise them to have one foot in print and one in broadcasting, to master the skills of both. I would advise them not to go to an American school of journalism, that would take away all the creativity they ever had. I would advise that if they haven't got an inquiring mind then they shouldn't be in journalism, because what makes a great journalist above all is that spirit of inquiry, being interested in things and being enthusiastic about something. If they haven't got that they shouldn't go into it because all they will end up doing is writing diaries sneering about people or compiling frothy feature columns. If they want to be real journalists they should be inquisitive, they should feel passionately about things and they should, in this age, be multi-skilled – able to write and edit tape and broadcast.

When your time comes to leave this life, what would you like people to say about you?

I think, 'He was his own man. We might not have agreed with him, but he believed in what he did and he wasn't in anybody's pocket. He cared for his country and for those around him.'

BARRY NORMAN

He says he 'just drifted' into presenting BBC Television's Film *'72 programme, never thinking it would be his big break. 25 years in the job made him almost a national institution, his style gently ribbed by impressionists, his weekly verdicts helping to fill or empty cinemas across the country. Having judged more than 10,000 films in the course of duty, he knows more than most what makes a successful critic. What's needed is 'honesty towards the audience and the medium you are criticising'. As for the old chestnut that many film critics have no practical experience of movie-making, he has a robust reply: 'To have worked in the film industry would have been a handicap, because then you'd have too much understanding of the difficulties, and*  *would make too many allowances. You've got to think of the person who's spending his money to see the film.' On the other hand, he is critical of 'a kind of brutishness about the British press', where some critics know nothing, but just use criticism as a showcase for their own cleverness.*

The son of the distinguished film producer and director Leslie Norman, Barry says he owes his own drive to achieve to his parents' inspiration and his genes. From public school he went to learn the journalist's craft in Kensington, Johannesburg and Harare, before becoming a gossip writer on the Daily Sketch. *He knows what it's like to be on the receiving end, and describes how he reacted to criticism when he started presenting the* Omnibus *TV programme; and how being kicked out as showbusiness editor of the* Daily Mail *turned out to be 'quite the nicest thing that ever happened to me'. He says, 'I hadn't had the nerve or the capital to freelance until I was forced to,' and then he found out he was 'capable of a hell of a lot more than I had ever realised'. So, from deep experience, he offers suggestions for dealing with unfair criticism: 'the worst you can do is to try and hit back – for a while you think it's going to dominate your life for ever, yet within a couple of days you've forgotten about it'. He offers advice on how to set about becoming a film critic, and the qualities needed – 'hard work, innate talent, an element of ruthlessness, an eye for the main chance, never take anything for granted – and tell the truth.' His quarter century with the BBC was rewarded with a CBE – and an offer he couldn't refuse from Sky Television!*

Barry Norman, what is your definition of success?

It's something that is far more visible to the beholder than it is present in the mind of the person who's supposed to be enjoying it. It's somebody else's idea of how well you're doing. It's very rarely your own idea because if you're any good at all, you never actually feel a success. It's their conception, not yours.

So are there two kinds of success – the success which is the judgment of the outside world and the success which you feel about yourself?

Yes, that's not a bad definition. People look at money and fame and say, 'That guy's famous, he's rich, therefore he's successful.' Yet you can be both famous and rich and not actually feel successful. I know that I feel that whatever I do is never quite as good as it should be. I've always lived by writing, but nothing I've ever written – and I've written some good stuff in my time – has been as good, in its finished form, as it was in my head before it went through my fingers and on to the word processor.

You're suggesting that within everyone who is really successful there ought to be a mechanism that says, 'However good you get at what you're doing, it's not enough'?

Yes, I believe that, because the great enemy of any achievement is contentment. As soon as you get contented, you think, 'I'm the best at what I do, therefore I'm OK.' But as soon as you feel like that, you're not the best at what you do any more. You should always aspire to do that little bit better next time.

Are you saying that deep down inside people who appear successful and supremely confident, there is probably an element of self-doubt?

I would hope so. I don't think I'd like to meet somebody who has no self-doubt whatsoever, they would be intolerable. You've got to have self-doubt, I think that's what keeps you going and helps you achieve this curious status called success.

To what extent is success a product of your background and upbringing?

I don't know. In my own case, I suppose, it is a product of background, because my father, Leslie Norman, was a very distinguished film producer and director. He left school at 14, able to read and write and add up, and that was about it. He came from a very poor background in London and then climbed very high. In my eyes, my father was a great success, in his eyes, he was not – he thought himself a failure. I spent hours trying to talk him out of this belief, but he felt he had not really achieved anything like what he wanted to achieve. What my father had achieved, from that background, told me that with a much better background – a pretty good public school education – I could achieve some of the things that I wanted.

I think it's genetic as well. Whatever drive I have, comes from my father and my mother, because her background was similar, and she became a film editor at the time they met and married. Both of them had a desire to achieve something, and, in their case, to get away from their background. Mine, I suppose, was – though I have never really thought about this – to justify the care and attention my parents had put into my education.

What do you think makes a successful critic?

The first thing is honesty. Honesty a) towards his audience or his readers, and b) towards the medium that he is criticizing. For instance, there are many occasions when I'm writing a review of a film, and I think of what seems to me a funny joke. So I put it in, but then when I'm reading it through afterwards, I realize my joke has diminished the film in a way it didn't deserve. So I take it out and tuck it away in the back of my mind, because I know a film is going to come along that will *really* deserve this joke, and I'll use it then. I won't use it if it gives the wrong impression of a film.

The other thing, I think, is that as a critic you've got to know the subject about which you are talking. You must measure everything you see against what you perceive as the best of that particular genre. You must always bear that in mind. You must not get sloppy and say, 'Oh, well, this isn't nearly as good as, for example, *The Lady Vanishes*, but it's all right, so I'll say this is a good film.' If you know it's not a good film say so. Say, 'It's OK, *but* it's not as it ought to be.' Also, to some extent, you should have a knowledge of how movies are made, and of the people making these things – what they've done in the past, what they're capable of.

But the main thing is honesty, because all criticism is subjective. When anybody goes to see a movie, if he takes his mind with him, *he's* a critic, because he's going to come out with a view of that film – why he thinks it's good or why he thinks it's bad. The difference between that kind of critic and the professional critic is that the first guy, who may have paid his money to see the film, may have only seen five comedies in his life, so he thinks the one he's watching is brilliant because it's the best of the five. But if I've seen 2,000 comedies – which is quite likely – I have better yardsticks by which to measure it. This is the basic difference between the professional and the amateur.

You talked about the importance of knowledge, but there is a view of critics that they haven't actually been players in the area that they criticize. For instance, you have not been an actor or a producer. Is that a handicap for you, or an advantage?

Neither. In a sense, it's immaterial. If you go into hospital to have your appendix out, and the doctor takes your spleen out by mistake, you don't have to have been a doctor to know that he's done a bloody awful job, do you? It really is as simple as that. I think to have worked in the industry would be a handicap, because then you'd have too much understanding of the difficulties, and would therefore make too many allowances. You've got to think about the person spending his money to see the film, and whether he's being short-changed. If you've worked in the industry and you know the problems, you're probably going to be a lot kinder towards whatever you're reviewing, and that's a bad thing. I don't think you should be cruel, but nor do I think you should be kind.

Do you think that some critics are tempted, particularly these days, into a very cynical world where writing for its own sake, regardless of the product that they're criticizing, becomes the important thing? Do some show off what they can do, rather than offer a genuine criticism of whatever it is they're criticizing?

That's absolutely true, but then this is true of the press generally. There is a kind of brutishness about the British press – the tabloid press particularly, but I think it's also creeping into the so-called quality press. I think it's worse in television criticism, because people come into it often knowing absolutely nothing about it at all, and use it as a showcase for their own cleverness – much more than people reviewing theatre, classical music or the cinema. By and large people reviewing the older established art-forms do actually know something about it, but an awful lot of people writing about television have no idea what they're writing about. I remember when I was doing *Omnibus*, and the critics didn't like it very much, I found myself blamed for all kinds of things, which anybody who knew anything about television would know had nothing to do with me whatsoever. I was just introducing a film made by others, a film which I had no part of. But the critics who disliked that film blamed me for it. I don't think a film or theatre critic would make that mistake, he would know who was actually responsible. Criticism probably provides a very good opportunity for the smart-arse to get his point of view across at somebody else's expense.

If you are someone trying very hard to be successful and you fall victim to the criticism of this smart-arse, how do you recover from that? How do you recover from what might be a very unfair attack on you, when only you know it's unfair and the world thinks it perfectly genuine?

How do you get over it? My initial reaction, particularly if I think it's unfair and unjust, is anger. I go around kicking things. And if the offending critic happened to hove into view, I would probably punch him, or her, regardless of sex. Then after a while I calm down and just let it fade from my memory, because it always does so. For a while you think this incident is going to dominate your life forever, yet within a couple of days you've forgotten all about it. The worst thing you can possibly do is try and hit back, particularly with newspaper critics, because *they* always have the last word. The best thing to do is ostensibly to ignore it because that upsets them most of all. If it deflects you from your career, then you shouldn't be doing it in the first place.

To what extent should a successful critic take account of the likely feelings of the person, or people, that he's criticizing?

You should never be deliberately offensive. It is quite trendy to do that now, but I think it's unfair and quite unnecessary. You should be aware that what you're saying is probably going to hurt a person, but you're doing it because you feel you have to, rather than because you're getting any kind of malicious glee out of it.

Does it worry you that a few well-chosen words might destroy a year's work, two years' work?

No, I don't think so, because I don't think that my well-chosen words are going to destroy the work. I think the work has already destroyed itself, or the people who made it have destroyed the work before it gets to me. I don't think a critic, certainly in this country, has anything like enough power to destroy something. There are certain films which are totally critic-proof – Arnold Schwarzenegger movies, Stallone movies, Jean Claude Van Damme movies. They might be quite good passable entertainment, cinematic junk food, but they're not great movies.

I don't think anybody ever sets out to make a rotten film, there's no reason why they should. But it happens, and when it does, somebody's got to recognize it, and say to the public, 'This film is rubbish.' You may feel regret on behalf of the people who made it, but nevertheless, that is what you're there to do. The other thing one has to bear in mind is that the critic is obviously a parasite, because a critic can't exist unless somebody else has created something. But there are parasites and parasites. There is the kind of parasite that cleans wounds, eats away damaged flesh and makes sure gangrene doesn't set in, and that, I think, is the critic's function – to do all that, and with luck to help or encourage people to do better next time.

Do you think that there are some film-makers, actors and actresses who genuinely learn from criticism rather than simply resent it?

Yes, I think there probably are. I remember that there were two bits of criticism directed at me for things I'd done on television, from which I did learn. When I read them, I was startled at first, then I thought about it afterwards and said, 'Yes, that's right.' One was Clive James. A long time ago I wrote and recorded the voice-over commentary for a film – I'd had nothing to do with the making of it – but I was asked to write the commentary, so I did. The makers gave me the notes from which I wrote the commentary, then recorded it. And Clive, reviewing it, quoted a really ghastly bit of purple prose that I'd put in and just dryly said, 'As Barry Norman permitted himself to say ...' I read that and winced. I actually wrote to Clive to say, 'Thanks for pointing that out, I'll make damn sure I don't write anything like *that* again.' And as far as I know I haven't, so that was a salutary lesson, because if that had gone on unchecked, God knows what kind of stuff I'd have written for television.

Another one was when I was with *Omnibus*, which was not the smartest career move I made, though I spent a very enjoyable year there. What happened, as Peter Fiddick – in *The Guardian* – pointed out, was that one of the problems was that my style was not in tune with the style of the rest of the programme. In other words, *Omnibus* was being made by the kind of people that always made middle-aged, middlebrow, middle-class arts programmes, and I was trying to get away from that. I realized that Peter Fiddick was right. Now that meant that I had to change, and that was the time when I decided I wanted to get out of *Omnibus*.

With hindsight I should have turned down *Omnibus* in the first place. What happened was that it had been off the air for a few years and they decided to resurrect it. And its new editor asked me if I'd be interested in doing it. So we had a chat and he said, 'What we want to do is a different kind of arts programme, which will take its style from you.' He probably meant it, but the weight of BBC tradition overwhelmed us all. And that was why I was going one way and the programme was going another, and it wasn't working. Had I been less naïve perhaps, and realized that what he'd said was never actually likely to happen – probably it wasn't feasible – I would have said, 'Thanks very much, I'm hugely flattered, but find someone else.'

So be careful where you jump, and know when to rein back as well as when to move forward?

Yes, but this is a difficult path to tread. In my own experience, the greatest thing that ever happened to me was when I was made redundant as show business editor of the *Daily Mail*. The *Daily Mail* merged with the *Daily*

Sketch and they kicked me out. I was very cross and deeply offended at first, but it turned out to be quite the nicest thing that ever happened. I suddenly realized that because of my redundancy money I had time to decide what I wanted to do. And because I was now a freelance journalist, I was having to take all kinds of different things, and I used this as an opportunity to try as many things as possible, to find out what I could do and what I couldn't do.

What you're saying implies that since you set out on your career path, you really haven't had an opportunity to pursue all the different options. It was only something that came later in life, when you had this enforced redundancy, as it were?

Absolutely. Up till then I had been a newspaper journalist. I was happy enough to be the show business man of the *Daily Mail,* but I always felt that there were other things I might do as well. So when the opportunity came to try the other things, I leapt upon all those that came my way. For a good few years I did all kinds of things just to see whether they worked for me. Sometimes they did, sometimes they didn't, but in the end I realized that I was capable of a hell of a lot more than the *Daily Mail* had ever realized I was capable of – more than *I* had ever realized. If the redundancy hadn't happened, God knows what would have happened to me. I'd probably have just stayed on, then faded away into total obscurity.

You got your big break with Film '72. *Did you regard* Film '72 *as simply another thing you were trying out, or did you sense from the beginning that this was something that was your real* métier?

The former. It was just something else I was trying out, because by that time I was writing a weekly column in *The Guardian* – for want of a better word, a satirical column, mostly about politics. A few months after I'd been made redundant, my friend Bernard Levin – one of the nicest men who ever trod the face of the earth – phoned me up and said, 'If I were you I'd get in touch with Alastair Hetherington, the editor of *The Guardian.*' And I said, 'What on earth for?' And he said, 'Well, I haven't told you this, but when you were made redundant I wrote to several editors saying, if you're taking on any of these redundant people from the *Daily Mail* I would recommend Barry Norman as being least likely to be drunk all the time, sick over your carpet, or rape the managing director's wife.' So with this encomium, Alastair Hetherington had suggested to Bernard that he would be quite interested in talking to me.

So I went along to see him, and what he was looking for was a holiday relief leader writer, and he took me on. This went on for about two months, I think. I was going in three times a week and writing leaders, mostly the light leader, the fourth leader, which was the funny one. I drifted towards those very early on. Then Hetherington said, 'I can't really afford to keep you on any more,' and *that's* when I suggested I do a column. They accepted that, and instead of doing three leaders a week, I did a weekly column. It wasn't remotely connected with show business. It was mostly about politics and social and current affairs.

At the same time I was doing television reviews for *The Times*, I was writing sporting profiles for *The Observer*, and I was doing all kinds of stuff for women's magazines. So when I was asked if I would go in and try out for *Film '72*, along with a load of other people – in those days they were rotating the presenter every six weeks, trying to find new faces for TV – I just thought, 'Interesting gig.' And I'd swiftly come to the conclusion that journalism was no longer a matter of 'either or'. It wasn't newspapers *or* magazines *or* radio *or* television, you could do *all* of those things. The more experience I got, the better. I just drifted in, feeling that this could be interesting. Not for one moment did I think, 'This is my big break and if I blow it I've had it,' which is probably why it worked out quite well, because I was comparatively relaxed.

And what did you think of television?

I enjoyed it very much. What I enjoyed about it was the freedom. This programme is one of the few places on television where the presenter can say exactly what he likes, within the bounds of libel. Nobody in the BBC has ever said, 'You can't say this,' or, 'You must say that.' The bit I enjoy most of all is writing the script. I don't mind sitting in the chair talking to a camera, but it's one of the least enjoyable parts of it.

Do you feel now, after 25 years, that you have been pigeonholed quite happily, having tried so hard to avoid that at earlier stages of your life?

Though it's inevitable, it's still a little bit irritating. I'm not pigeonholed in my own mind because in those 25 years I started several radio programmes. I was a presenter on *Today*. I started a programme called *Going Places*, which, when we started it, was quite a hard-hitting current affairs programme about all forms of transport. I also started *Breakaway* about holidays and travel, and what not. I was the first presenter of the *News Quiz*, I did a current-affairs programme about the computer industry, I did the Olympic Games for Channel 4 in 1988. So, while I don't pigeonhole myself, it's understandable that the public will only be aware of the place where I'm most visible, which is talking about films. I've written eight or nine novels as well, which have not exactly been bestsellers, but they've not done badly and have given me a great deal of satisfaction. I think I would feel worse about being pigeonholed if I had just happily stuck with doing the one thing all this time – but I didn't.

And is it generally a good piece of advice for a successful media person not to allow himself or herself to be boxed in?

That depends on the individual. My advice would certainly be to try as many things as you possibly can. I think, in the end, you're extremely fortunate if there is one thing at which you are regarded as the expert, because that becomes, in a sense, the day job, and around that you can do all kinds of other interesting things. This is what I've done, not really through planning – it's just the way it's worked out. And as far as I'm concerned it could hardly have worked out better.

After reviewing more than 10,000 films, are there any clear criteria that you can lay down for making a successful film?

The criteria for making a successful film are terribly simple. You need a very good script, a very good director, a very good cast, a very good crew, and that's it. If you've got all those things, you've got a great movie. The trouble is, getting all those things together is very, very difficult.

Can you get away with having one or two weak links in the chain?

You might. I mean there is something else, a kind of chemistry that happens in movies. The greatest example of this is *Casablanca*, which if you analyse it is not actually a very good film at all. It's based on an entirely false premise – the idea of an escape route in the Second World War, through Casablanca, is rubbish. No such thing existed. But something happened with that film. Bogart and Bergman should not have made a great team because they were entirely dissimilar, but they did. Everything came right – but it did have a good script and it did have a good director and it did have a good cast and technically it was very well made. And it just also had that little extra thing that nobody can define. A kind of chemistry that either happens, or doesn't happen, on a film set. And if it happens, then you've probably got a classic. If it doesn't happen, and you've got all the other things in place, then you've at least got a very good film.

Do you think a person can ever be really successful if they don't make some sacrifices as far as their home life is concerned? How do you get the balance right – indeed, can you, if you're being really successful?

It's very difficult for somebody who's actually involved in the making of a film because they do have to make sacrifices. They might have to go away for months at a time, a sacrifice if you've got a happy home life. And quite often, of course, it causes the total break-up of a marriage. It takes a hell of a lot of understanding on the part of your husband or wife. They've got to be extremely tolerant of the demands that are made on you. So you probably do have to skimp on your home life and the attention you pay to your family in order to keep going. It's not desirable, but I think that's the way of it.

But it helps to be successful if you have someone back at home who is giving you a lot of support and a lot of help when you need it?

Well, on the assumption that I am successful, then I owe a hell of a lot to my wife, who has always been extremely supportive in every possible way, and is my best friend. That's been absolutely vital.

Who are your heroes?

My heroes generally tend to be writers rather than film-makers or great sportsmen and athletes. I have tremendous admiration for them – as a little boy, if somebody had said to me, 'Look, wave a magic wand, you can be anything you like, what would you want?' I would have said, 'I'd like to open the batting for England at Lord's, and I'd like to be centre-forward for the England football team.' The writers I admire a lot run from Shakespeare to Austen, to Dickens, to Elmore Leonard today, and Raymond Chandler. Not so many people in the show business world. Laurence Olivier was a man for whom I had admiration, respect and affection. Not too many other actors – directors like Steven Spielberg, Martin Scorsese. David Lean was another I had respect, admiration and a liking for. And writers like William Goldman, who wrote *Butch Cassidy and the Sundance Kid* and *All the President's Men,* Joseph L. Mankiewicz, and another writer-director, Billy Wilder.

What do you regard as your greatest success?

I think having had a very good and happy family life is my greatest success, because that's the ballast of my life. Without that, God knows what would have happened. If I hadn't been married or had a family, I might have been richer, more famous. But I don't think I'd be any happier, which is a fairly important aspect of life. Contentment is to be avoided at all times, but you should grab happiness as it comes along and cherish it when you have it, that's very important. My family life has given me that.

What do you reckon were your biggest failures, and more importantly, how did you recover from them?

Biggest failures! I must have had plenty. I suppose, in a sense, getting made redundant seemed a failure because, if you resign from an organization, and they accept your resignation, what they're saying is, OK, we think we can get along without you. If they kick you out, which is redundancy, what they're saying is, we think we can get along *better* without you, which is a big insult. And I do remember feeling deeply insulted, although they were quite good to us at the *Daily Mail,* because they let those of us who were going to be made redundant hang around the office, using the phones, typewriters and the stationery to get ourselves new jobs. I went into work every day and I did nothing, overcome by absolute lethargy, which was really worrying. My confidence had gone.

How did you recover from that?

I think it came the day I actually had to leave the office – the umbilical cord was cut. There came a day when we were not expected to go in any more because the new paper would be taking over, the new tabloid *Daily Mail* took over on a particular Monday from the broadsheet which I'd been employed on. And then the realization came that if anything was to be done, I was the only person who could do it. The world doesn't come beating a path to your door – you've got to go and beat on its door. That was the way I overcame it. I think it took me a few days of very hard thought, in that first week of being at home with nothing whatsoever to do. It was really alarming, a quite terrifying prospect. And I thought, 'This is ridiculous, something's got to be done otherwise we are going to lose the house, we're going to be out on the streets.' I actually locked myself in my study and started thinking of things that I could write and then getting in touch with people to sell them these ideas. And I went out and did that and it seemed to work, because by the time I was asked to do *Film '72,* I was doing much better financially, and as far as job satisfaction was concerned, than I'd ever done before. I was really happy as a writing journalist at that time, which is another reason why I wasn't all that concerned whether it worked or didn't work on *Film '72.*

Does success bring any obligations in its wake? If you are really successful do you have an obligation, of any kind, to society to put something back?

I believe so, very much, yes, and I try to do that. It sounds awful saying this because it's what Harry Secombe once described as 'doing good by thunderous stealth'. I do try to help out with charitable organizations. I don't have very much to do with big national charities, they can get all the people they need, because they are mostly centred in London and most of the famous live in or very close to London. What I am very much inclined to do is to help out the smaller local ones, where they can't persuade somebody to come out from London into, say, Hertfordshire – since I live in Hertfordshire, it's easier for me to do whatever they want me to do. And that I will do, because it is a question of putting something back. I've been extraordinarily fortunate, you know, I've had a marvellous time and it behoves you to recognize that you have been fortunate and there are others who are not nearly as fortunate as you are, and you ought to do a little bit for them.

What are the greatest enemies of success?

Complacency is one, arrogance – no, arrogance often goes along with success. Complacency is the big enemy of success, because I think as soon as you become complacent your success is going to go out of the window.

And the qualities you need for success, you mentioned arrogance – what about ruthlessness?

I'm sure in many cases that is true. Fortunately I've never had to exhibit that. I don't know, I say that, but then probably I have at times, when there have been discussions, not necessarily with the film programme, but with lots of other stuff I've done on television and radio, about the way a thing should be done, and there comes a point where you put your foot down. But that's probably being ruthless and saying, 'I don't care, *I'm* going to do it this way.' So I've probably done that, so there probably is an element of ruthlessness.

Other qualities?

Oh, hard work, some innate talent doesn't come amiss, you need a bit of that. Having an eye to the main chance, I think, making sure that if an opportunity were passing by, you're aware of it and not looking in the opposite direction. Being in the right place at the right time. That is something you can't always manage, but it's terribly helpful if it does happen.

Has success changed you at all?

I don't know. I don't think so, because I was well into my thirties before anything remotely resembling success was visited upon me. And I think, when that happened, I'd knocked around a lot, I'd had lots of ups and lots of downs, and I'd also seen lots of people become successful and then vanish. So I never took anything for granted and never assumed, even when the programme went on and on and they kept renewing my contract, that this was going to continue. The idea of it continuing for 25 years would have seemed nonsense to me at the time. So I never took anything for granted, and also having a very solid family background kept my feet firmly on the ground the whole time.

What's the greatest pleasure you've had from your success?

I suppose it is the knowledge that I don't, now, have to do anything I don't want to do – that is the greatest thing.

If you could gather in one room all the young people in the world who want to achieve the level of success that you've achieved as a film critic, what advice would you give them?

Well, as regards advice about how to set about getting such a job, first of all I would urge them to go to university and read English. Because the most important thing is to be able to handle the English language. Also, go to a university where you can do some kind of film studies – and most universities are offering those now. That's the background to it.

My other advice would be to see as many films as you possibly can, to review them for yourself alone, sit down and write what you think about it and why you think it was good, why it was bad. To read other critics, successful critics – Graham Greene, for instance, wrote a marvellous book of film criticism, well worth reading, also Pauline Kael, and there are lots of others. But whatever you decide, when you are actually writing or talking about any film, you must tell the truth about it. The audience is not stupid, and knows when it's being lied to. Once the audience knows that, you haven't got an audience any more.

What contribution do you think critics have made to the world in general?

I go back to my earlier notion of the critic as a parasite. I *do* think criticism is important. It isn't simply entertainment. It is important and I think people should take notice of critics. Not of all critics – the public will fasten on to a critic who seems to reflect their views. There are people who watch me because they think that my views are very similar to theirs, but lots of other people watch me because my views are totally opposite to theirs, and they will avoid the films I recommend and rush to the films I pan. I think people involved in the entertainment industry – film, theatre, music, television – should take notice of the critics that they personally feel are sensible and intelligent, because the critic, to an extent, is the standard-bearer, in the sense that the critic should know what the standards are, should know what is good, what is excellent, what is acceptable, what is not acceptable. And he should be consistent, always using the same yardstick. People involved in creating films and plays and so on can actually learn something from the critic. I think, finally, that the critic is a much more useful person than those who are criticized would readily concede.

When your time comes to leave this life, what would you like people to say about you?

I'm not sure. I think I'd like people to say that I'd done the best I could, certainly. And that I told the truth.

TONY O'REILLY

'The world is eating out more often, and we're
going to be at the picnic' – Tony O'Reilly, spelling
out here one of the six areas in which Heinz, the
corporate colossus he headed, is striving for world
leadership. In the world table of business moguls
there are few, if any, who can match his stylish
combination of intellect, wit, marketing acumen
and colossal wealth. Quite an achievement for
an Irish lad told at school he was illegitimate,
after his father, a customs official, was found to
have had a secret first wife and family! He recalls
here how the discovery at the age of six that he
was a talented rugby player created 'a great
appetite to be the best'. That was fostered by 12
years' education with the Jesuits; as he famously
once put it – 'we were tops at everything,
especially humility'. At 18, he played his first rugby international, and won a
scholarship to study law at University College, Dublin. Coming top of his final
year, he used his legendary try-scoring reputation with Ireland and the British
Lions as a springboard for a business career.

From masterminding the successful launch of Kerrygold butter, he never looked
back. During his 17 years with Heinz he had, amongst other deals, rescued and
revived Waterford Crystal and Wedgwood China, and built up an international
newspaper empire. Now into his sixties, his manic energy has been slowed only
slightly by an illness and the efforts of his second wife, Chryss Goulandris, who
comes from a Greek shipping family whose wealth matches his own. Success for him
means 'a standard of competence, and striving for, but not always achieving,
excellence'. He believes that the companies successful in the long-term are 'those
with good-quality brands which are recognised by an ever-increasing public around
the world'; that the biggest single enemy of success is 'a lack of curiosity'; and that
sacrifices are inevitable – 'there is this contradiction in life between achieving great
goals and, mostly inadvertently, hurting someone in the process'. He talks about
the community work which successful businesses can stimulate, but also thinks they
give something back by creating first jobs and then wealth for investors and the
huge funds that control workers' pensions. Just to show there is no limit to
ambition, he reveals how he was all set to audition for the lead role in the epic movie
Ben Hur – until a black eye intervened!

Tony O'Reilly, what is your definition of success?

My definition of success is to run competent organizations, day-in, day-out, across both time and distance. That has been the key to the way I've tried to live my life – competence, and striving for, but not always achieving, excellence throughout the world.

Are you being overly modest in saying just competence rather than excellence?

No, I think people run away from competence – competence is a universal word that you could apply to a great number of companies. A company like Coca-Cola is competent in that if you take up their product anywhere in the world, you always get the same product – that's not brilliant, that's not unique, but it's very competent, it's very universal. What we strive for in all the companies with which I'm associated is a standard of competence, which applies globally. We don't always achieve it. We try to, we *expect* to, but we certainly don't always manage it. In all my enterprises, Heinz, Waterford, Wedgwood, Independent Newspapers, we are trying to create an awareness of our symbols around the world, to stand for competence, excellence and universality. So that what you buy in Tokyo is what you would buy in Piccadilly Circus in London.

Do you think that, for your companies and for the others that you mentioned, what you say is always appreciated by those people Nigel Lawson used to call 'the teenage scribblers in the City'?

I think every teenage scribbler in the City recognizes that the battle has turned, that Karl Marx would, in a strange way, be very happy with the world today because we have created a world in which ownership of the means of production and distribution and wealth is in the hands of the common man. For example, I had an extraordinary discussion with a very literate worker in America, who was on the strike committee at a particular company. I said, 'How is your company doing?' 'You know, having a tough time,' he replied. I told him I could see he was at loggerheads with the company. He said yes. Then I asked, 'Is your pension fund invested in that company?' He said, 'No. I would not let a pension fund of ours invest in a company that would have *me* for a worker,' – which is a wonderful inversion of the old Groucho Marx joke. We are getting to a point now where every day on the New York Exchange, 75 to 80 per cent of all decisions are taken by pension funds on behalf of the vast unseen blue-collar masses of America. And that's the way it should be.

It's right that those pension funds ought to be exerting the kind of boardroom pressure that they're now starting to?

Yes. I cannot imagine anything that will make boardrooms more accountable than the pressure of ownership being invested in the hands of the vast majority of the workforce in America. It's the new form of capitalism, but it's the right way.

To what extent do you think that your success has been a product of background and upbringing?

I think very significantly. The fact that I'm Irish has been both an enormous catalyst to me and has also guided my sense of both destiny and commitment. At first I wanted to succeed in Ireland, so I launched Kerrygold on the world market to make Ireland and Irish dairy products the sort of symbol of excellence that they have since become throughout the world. Then it was Heinz – and happily I got to the top of Heinz over 25 years ago, in 1973, and I was President of that company for 23 years and have been CEO since 1979.

When you became the head of Heinz at such a very early stage of your career, did you suddenly say to yourself, 'I don't quite understand how I got here?' Or was there a rationale – were you able to work out how you'd done it?

It's quite clear how I got there – through the success of Kerrygold and through the success of the Irish Sugar Company.

So you have to have one or two big early successes which then drive you on.

Yes. And that of course is at a time when you were really putting virtually all your capital – because your capital is really only yourself at that stage – at risk. If you fail then, when you try again, people remember your failures.

You've been described as being someone with manic energy, with an ego – are those necessary to be successful?

Certainly manic energy is. To be described as having an ego is, I think, something that is meant as a compliment by some, but generally is meant to be negative, even pejorative in the minds of others.

Do you understand that?

Yes. The ego I have is not so much a personal ego as a belief which is, I think, apparent in last year's annual report of *The Independent* about why Ireland is going to be important. Why would a little country of five million people be important in a world that is as large as it is? It's going to be very important for countries to define themselves according to their competence and their excellence. They have to decide what they stand for. Ireland stands for writers and poets, beautiful scenery, kindly people, Guinness, for Kerrygold, for Bailey's Irish Cream, for Waterford crystal – happily – and, we like to believe now, for 'Independent Newspapers Around the World'.

In the 1960s, when you were given an option to join either Fine Gael or Fianna Fáil – the two main political parties in Ireland – or pursue a career in business, you chose a career in business. What made you think running an international company was more important than running a country?

Two things. Number one, money and independence, a very obvious first which I think everyone considers – money brings independence. And second, the feeling I had that perhaps I might be able to play for Ireland wearing a green jersey on a much wider stage than I could otherwise here in Ireland. And it proved to be very much that way. I tended to be rather more influential, in a sense, *outside* Ireland than I would have been had I been *in* Ireland – not necessarily to the Irish, but to the world at large.

And as far as your immense drive and energy are concerned, your cousin once wondered publicly some time ago whether there was a kind of compensatory mechanism at work in you because your parents did not marry until much later in their lives.

I've often heard that. I've certainly reflected on it myself, but I have to say that it is one of those things that is fashionable to say but quite untrue. I lived with my parents throughout my life and they were inordinately loving and caring. Indeed, at rugby internationals, anyone who sat near my mother took their life in their hands, because she was likely to hit them with a newspaper if they said one word of criticism about me. My parents were ever-loving right to the day of their deaths, so I had never had any feeling of exclusion or uniqueness because of that background. I think my half-brother and sisters who were, in a sense, denied my father's daily presence which I was not, probably suffered more than I did. I never really discussed it with them because I'm really fond of them and it's not a topic that one would discuss. But certainly for every day of my life I had a father and mother in attendance at all my failures and all my successes – which is a lot more I might say than my children ever had. Gavin tells the great story that he first met me when he was 13 years of age. And he said I looked at him rather peculiarly and the first words I ever uttered to him were, 'Your name is Gavin, I gather – can you read a balance sheet?' I think it's apocryphal, but anyway that's the story.

That raises an interesting point – do you feel that most successful people have to have made some degree of sacrifice as far as their family life is concerned?

There is no doubt that everyone has only 24 hours in the day. If they want to be a great philosopher, a great thinker, a great writer, a great pianist, a great businessman or a great athlete, they're going to have to make a very singular sacrifice at some stage during their life. And people around them are going to suffer, because life is a collective enterprise and yet excellence, supreme excellence like Michelle Smith in winning those wonderful gold medals for Ireland at the Atlanta Olympics, is all about monastic living for a period of years. Now obviously, during that period somebody suffered. Yet we all shared in her triumph, so there is this contradiction in life between achieving great goals and hurting people in the process – inadvertently at times mostly, but nonetheless hurting people as you make for the try-line, whatever that is.

Do successful people ever get the balance right between work and family?

I think it often happens when it's too late. I must say personally that Chryss O'Reilly, who has taught me a great deal in the past five years, has brought to my life a tranquillity and a capacity to disengage that I lacked in the manic years when I was making the whole thing happen. I would say business was really an extension of rugby to me in the early days, it was another game to be won, and that's the way one tends to think in terms of short-term goals. But what I now look back on – and look forward to, I might say – is life in the round, the things that I miss if I'm to achieve certain goals. I think I'm at a stage in life now where I've made enough of the goals to be able to say selectively, 'Well I don't want that, goddamn it, I'll let that go. I will not strive for that.'

And the choice of your partner is crucial in that.

Absolutely crucial. You cannot travel alone in these matters.

Let me take you back to the early days of your life. When did you first think, 'I've been successful – this is my first success'?

When I was about six and my mother came to watch every single game I ever played in my life. She came to watch a game in which I was scrambling around with a lot of little boys aged seven to eight – I was six because I was the youngest boy in the school at the time. She went over to the trainer at the end of the game and asked him how the game had gone without revealing who she was. And he said simply to her, 'The red fellow is the best.'

And she passed that on to you very quickly.

I think it informed her life because she was a young woman with this young child and suddenly there in rugby lay a path to the sea – both, I assume, for her, but especially for me.

And did that then create a hunger in you for more success?

It created a great appetite – I wanted to be the best at rugby, obviously, I wanted to be the best at cricket and at tennis and so on, and I wasn't, but certainly I was pretty good at *all* these sports, and sport as such was a great means of expressing my aspirations for excellence. And by the time I was 15 I was perhaps the youngest provincial schools player in Irish history. By the time I was 18 I was a very big local schoolboy star. That very year I played in the schools final on 17 March 1954 and I played my first international against France after only three games of men's rugby on 21 January of the following year, so at 18 it was all terrific stuff.

In a sense, did any of that go to your head?

No, I was curious. There were two 'me's. There was the me who was actually experiencing the running and the playing and the passing and the success and the failure and the miss-tackles and so on, and then there was the curious me looking down upon the active me saying, 'Isn't that extraordinary? I never really realized he had it in him. There he is out there playing against that... well, let's see what the next game will bring.'

How much of what you are was shaped by the Jesuits, by your upbringing?

Well, I went to the Jesuits when I was six and left when I was 18 so I had 12 years of them. It's hard to know, but I do not believe that any child could have had a better education than I had from the Jesuits and from my parents. The combination of the day school and of being at home part of the time, and therefore mixing with boys from other schools, was the right combination. I've always been concerned that my boys – we have three boys and three girls – who went to a Jesuit boarding school, lacked the sort of home life that I had. But they turned out very well and all three are thrusting, aggressive, humorous, good-humoured guys today who are, in a way, my pals.

Going back not quite as far, you had become a very big rugby star, you were setting off on a business career and you went and auditioned for Ben Hur. *Now why did you do that, was that part of a feeling that you really could achieve anything?*

No, the old *Ben Hur* story, which has pursued me through life, is rather simpler than that. You may remember the famous Mario Lanza story where they auditioned for tenors all over the world. In the case of *Ben Hur*, as I understand it, they were having a *Ben Hur* competition in almost every country in the world. Noel Purcell, who was the great leader and star of stage and screen here in Ireland, knew a guy at MGM and he said, 'Listen, I know a fella in Dublin and he's your man for *Ben Hur*. His name is Tony O'Reilly.' And so he set up this famous audition on the Monday after the Ireland–England game at Twickenham, and unfortunately on the Saturday Ireland were defeated 26–0 and I had received this most enormous black eye in the game. By Monday my eye was completely closed and in fact I never took the screen test at Pinewood.

So you weren't beaten by Charlton Heston because you were never in the race! Would you have liked to be in the race?

In 1956, when asked what was my main ambition in life – to be Charlton Heston or to be a great rugger player? – I said, 'My ambition in life is very simple. To qualify as a solicitor and to play rugby for my country.' They were my ambitions then and looking back, I think they were entirely justified.

How big a part does luck play in success?

Well, I think Harold Macmillan made the comment that the greatest policy-maker of all is the force of circumstance. You call it luck, I would call it the force of circumstance and there is no doubt that the force of circumstance in my case has played a very big part. I have been around when things happened, but as you go on through life, you learn there are certain things you can do very well and other things you don't do as well, and so you gravitate towards those things that you do do well and away from those that you don't. For example, I love music but I will never be more than an average piano-player.

But you'd like to be a great one?

Of course, but it may well be that I'm a better-than-average maker of money or businessman, call it what you will, so you play to your strengths. As you go on through life you begin to divine. When you're 12 or 14, everything is open to you, and then life and election and geography and time and religion and place begin to play their parts and you say, 'Well, here I am, let's play to our strengths.'

Whom do you most admire – who are your heroes, past or present?

I admire Winston Churchill – I think he was a great man. I think he was a symbol of Britain, I think he led Britain through the war in a way that no other man could have done. He was at his best in adversity – not too good when things were going rather well, his career exemplifies that. I admire Seán Lemass very much in Ireland, a great, pragmatic Taoiseach; I admire Jack Lynch enormously; a wonderful, worthy, independent, candid man who, in a strange sort of way, was above the fray and knew what Ireland needed at a time in 1969 when things with Northern Ireland were very difficult indeed.

On the sporting front, I admire Cliff Morgan enormously, I think he was a great player, the greatest player of my time certainly – and Jack Kyle, of course, a very fine player. I admire lots of the players of those times – McKay, McCarthy and O'Brien, that great Irish back row of the early 1950s. Of the players who played with me, I enormously admire David Hewitt, I think he's quite a genius of a player, and Andy Mulligan and Niall Brophy, and Mick the Kick, the famous Mick English and so on. All these were very good friends and very good players, but what I admire most is the sort of Corinthian way in which they approached the task of being rugger players and we're all friends today. Now I hope that 20 years from now, the players of today who are playing for money will be able to say of their fellow players, 'I like Fred because Fred is a good chap.'

Most of your heroes are friends?

A lot of them are, yes.

You tend to go more for living heroes than those in the past.

I must say I hardly knew Lemass and I never knew Churchill, obviously, so they would not be contemporaries. Of the earlier generations, I admired very much William Ewart Gladstone, the Englishman who did more for Ireland, I would say, than anyone except for John Major. I think that the younger Pitt, who was Prime Minister at 24 and died at 47, had an extraordinary career. To be Prime Minister of Great Britain so young at a time when Britain was engaged in defending itself against Napoleon, in winning the Battle of Trafalgar was extraordinary. Yet when Britain's allies were defeated at Austerlitz, he died at 47 feeling he was a complete failure. In fact, looking back on his career it became evident what a great success he had been. Recently I was at a dinner party where someone advanced the theory that longevity is the politician's final revenge. Another chap disagreed. He said every politician that has lived a long life has outlived his usefulness and has died dishonoured by his age. And he instanced of course Kennedy, Michael Collins here in Ireland, and people like Martin Luther King, people who were killed in the prime of life and therefore will always be in the prime of their life for the generations to come.

If Churchill had died at the age of 65, before the Second World War, none of his success would have happened and his reputation would have been totally different.

Had he died after the General Strike of 1926, he would have died reviled and had he died after the Dardanelles campaign of the First World War, he would have been the worst administrator in the Admiralty ever. Harold Macmillan has always had the last word. He once said, 'You know, the worst thing about getting old is to get old very young, and I've done that.'

You once saved $100 million at Heinz by removing the back label from the bottle. Can one good idea lead to a spectacular career, or has there got to be much more?

There have to be very many daily activities amounting to confidence, because every day throughout the world there are thousands of people working against you – in terms of cheaper competition, commodity price increases, in terms of increases in wages, decreases in productivity, whatever it may be. Therefore, just to stay even you have to have a degree of cost-cutting to at least keep your gross margin and, where possible, to improve it.

However, in every business there have to be moments when you are presented with something which is an entirely new vision of the future. In my view, Al Lippert and Weight Watchers presented that to Heinz about 20 years ago when Heinz bought Weight Watchers. Today weight control around the world is a universal phenomenon. People are concerned about their weight. The first thing they do in the morning is weigh themselves. They jump on the scales and say, 'God I mustn't have a dinner like last night or I'm dead.' We have tapped that rich vein of weight control throughout the world. This year there are six areas in which Heinz will strive for world leadership. Number one, food service – the world is eating out more often and we are going to be there at the picnic. Number two, baby feeding – the mother is concerned about the food she gives her child, and we can supply the quality audits that are not present in homemade foods – more than any other person in the house, her child is most important to her. Number three, tuna – we are the world's largest tuna company and tuna is growing because it is regarded as a protein which is good for you and good value. Number four, pet food. Number five, condiments – the Heinz ketchup that you see around the world, a universal icon of excellence. Number six, weight control. If we hit world dominance in all those six – hold on to your jock strap and buy Heinz!

Is it becoming more or less difficult to achieve success in business?

It depends upon what business you're in. In the world of communications and the Internet and software, it is becoming easier. In the world of harder franchises, it is becoming more difficult for small companies to compete with the big ones – Heinz, Proctor or Coke or Pepsi or Ralston.

In terms of attitude, what are the biggest enemies of success?

I think a lack of curiosity is probably the biggest single enemy of success. I don't know Bill Gates, but I would say he must have been a very curious young man.

What are your greatest pleasures from the fruits of success?

I would say music and reading, both of which I indulge in. I have more time to do so than I had previously, thanks to Chryss.

Do you think there are a great many obligations that come with success? If you are truly successful have you got to put something back, and if so how do you do that?

I started the Ireland Funds 20 years ago and we have raised $80 million for peace and culture in both parts of Ireland. The Funds are now a very important network for Ireland overseas. I also believe in supporting education and am heavily involved with various schools and universities. In rugby football, I admire enormously what Tom Kiernan and Sid Miller are doing at the moment. I admire enormously what Vernon Pugh is doing in Great Britain. But success in business also gives something back by creating jobs and wealth for investors and pension funds.

What do you regard as the most successful moments in your life, not perhaps those that the public would know about, but moments where you privately felt an enormous sense of satisfaction and success?

A very public moment of success was breaking Ken Jones's world record for a Lion by scoring in the last minute of the last Test in New Zealand in 1959. But the interesting thing about it was that I had equalled his record four matches previously, and then failed to score in the next three games and all through the final moments of this final Test. And so to score the last-minute try was terrific. It was a great moment of personal satisfaction for me. That, plus the South African scoring record of the 1955 Lions, were two of the precious possessions that I have.

Privately, I take very considerable pride in the way that my six kids have buckled down to the business of life, and they've all wobbled and wavered on the way. I say to every parent, 'Don't despair, don't give up, don't dissolve, don't stand on the high ground, get down and live with them in whatever trench they have dug themselves and stay with them.' My ex-wife Susan, the mother of these children, is a tremendous believer in that. She's a great friend of theirs and they absolutely adore her. I suppose if we have any satisfactions in life it is having children who have a reasonable sense, a reasonable compass, about how life operates. I would say ours are sensible children and that's a great personal and private satisfaction of mine, and of Susan's.

Do you think that individual success is harder to achieve than team success? Are you a team player?

I tend to be. The name of the plane that I have is 'Collegiality' and I believe in it, I believe that Heinz is a Collegium of Cardinals.

But at the same time, it takes one person to do the driving.

Yes, but only after due reflection, after due consultation and after due exaltation, and after due counselling by these curial figures of the cardinalate. I would say that's true of rugby. You learn early from rugby football, that life is about community and it's about getting it from others.

So you must be part of a team, you must consult, but at the end of the day you've got to take the decision.

I'm afraid that that's the way life has been, yes. You take the decision and you get a great deal of the money from the process, or the glory from the process or get fired, whatever it may be. The fact of the matter is, however, that three generations of managers in Heinz have left Heinz and have left with not less than £25 million *each*. And that must cover 15 key players, all of whom played with me. They were keen players, all pretty damn good, and I benefited hugely from my associations with them.

There are some people – and it's said more so in Britain than in America – who are envious of success. What do you say to those who harbour envy of the truly successful?

First of all, I don't think there's great envy in America about business success. I don't think Bill Gates is envied, nor is Michael Jordan and these people are earning $50 or $60 million per year. British society tends to be one which was originally bound by class, and therefore, if I heard your accent without in fact talking to you, but just overheard you, then asked you one question, what school did you go to, I would know in those two experiences a great deal about you. I would not know that about an American, and until Britain gets away from that society bounded by class, or until excellence and competence become the criteria – and they are increasingly becoming the criteria – then Britain will hold itself back in the world leadership stakes.

If you had to gather in front of you all the young, aspiring businessmen in the world, what is the best advice you could give them?

I would say, 'Number one, learn law and accounting. Number two, don't be afraid of failure. Number three, be curious. Number four, be respectful but independent, and number five, good-bye and have a hell of a time doing it.'

What would you like people to say about you when, at the ripe old age of 100, you finally depart this planet?

I'd very much like it if they said, 'He helped put Ireland on the map.'

SADAKO OGATA

'I wish the politicians were more decisive in taking action – it was easier during the Cold War because there were clear enemies' – a typically trenchant comment from the formidable, diminutive Japanese lady who, as the United Nations High Commissioner for Refugees, has successfully tackled one of the most active diplomatic roles in the world. She talks here of how her appointment coincided with an 'unprecedented change in the nature of conflict', and how she is dealing with that. Her staff has been extended to 5,000 to try to deal with the root causes of the problems that test them in some 200 trouble spots – 'I'm used to dealing with cause and effect, and just dealing with the surface was not good enough for a UN agency.' She also

argues that the United Nations allows too much 'mission creep'. It 'needs a narrow focus, should be more selective and prioritise'. Sadako Ogata was brought up in 'a rather liberal family'. Her father was a diplomat, and much of her education was in China and the USA. She admits she didn't begin to work hard until university, where she discovered a natural academic bent.

The early 1950s saw the start of an opening up of Japan's closed society which had traditionally placed women in a subservient role. New opportunities appeared, and 'I and my friends just took advantage of them'. She married one of Japan's top international bankers, and, as her children grew up, was able to extend her career through a series of university and diplomatic posts. She was 63 when the UNHCR post was offered to her, and thought by then she'd had 'the range of experience' to make it work. But she confesses, 'If I'd known how difficult it was, I don't know if I would have taken it.' Success for her is simply 'doing your task well'. She is careful not to try to do something impossible, or aspire to be something unreachable – 'it came step by step'. She also warns that 'if you get conceited, you think that you can do things without thinking about others who really support you'. As for her talks with various warlords, she says 'we have to deal with very difficult people and very difficult situations, but we must never give up'. She thinks the job has made her 'tougher and more short-tempered' but she is not above using some feminine wiles in some negotiations. 'There is an advantage in being a small woman.'

Sadako Ogata, what is your definition of success?

Success to me means doing your task well. If you've done it well, you've succeeded. The problem is, how do you define your task? I've defined it more or less as what has been given to me as I've proceeded in life. I've never tried to do something impossible, or aspired to something unreachable – it came step by step.

And yet success involves taking on major challenges that might appear to some people to be out of reach. What gave you the confidence to take on one of the toughest jobs in the world and succeed at it?

If you're referring to my appointment as high commissioner of refugees, I must say I didn't know how difficult it was. I took it because I felt I had the experience. I had taken up assignments in the UN since I was on the Japanese delegation to the General Assembly in 1968. I'd done several general assemblies, I was appointed minister in the Japanese delegation to the United Nations so I had done UN diplomacy full-time for nearly four years, I was Japan's first representative to the Human Rights Commission, and so on. I was on several independent commissions, dealing with reform and humanitarian affairs within the UN, so I thought I had enough range of experience to try it.

But you didn't know how difficult it was going to be. If you'd known then how difficult it was would you still have taken the job?

As it has turned out, if I'd known how difficult it was, I don't know if I would have taken it.

You had to be persuaded to take the job. You didn't want it at first, did you?

I never wanted or looked for it. It just happened, and I think a lot of things in one's life happen that way. My predecessor suddenly left the post and there was an urgent search for candidates. The Japanese government was asked if they had any candidates in mind and they approached me.

So luck played a part?

I think there is always luck. I must say I have been a lucky person.

What was your approach when you took on the job, how did you set about it? What criteria, if any, did you have for tackling this particular task, bearing in mind the experience that you brought to the table?

I knew I had to fund-raise. I knew I had to convince governments to fight for refugee protection. I knew about all these things in a general way. But what turned out to be a very unprecedented challenge was the fact that my term of office coincided with the post-Cold War period – there was a lot of change in the nature of conflict and how you dealt with it. For example, refugees in the traditional sense became fewer and fewer. There were relatively few refugees fleeing persecution and leaving their country of origin to seek asylum in another country. My time in office has seen more internal conflict of an ethnic, religious and cultural nature spilling over into neighbouring countries than at any other time. When this happens it becomes an issue of international security. It is not easy to give asylum to refugees, even on a temporary basis, or set up camps and deal with them. The result is that the asylum countries begin to suffer from the massive inflow of people.

And were there any general principles for dealing with these problems?

Oh yes, there were certain guiding lights that existed with the office. I had a mandate from the general assembly that set it up. There was lots of wisdom in the office – we had very experienced people. You require a lot of common sense to do the job, and by the time I was high commissioner, I was old enough to have a lot of common sense.

Have you always been ambitious, have you always been an achiever?

Yes, I think I always wanted to get things done well. Even when I started a new sport I would really concentrate to the point where I became pretty good at it.

Is that something that's peculiar to you or is it part of the Japanese character?

I think we are more achievement-oriented people. But at the same time I don't think I was that competitive. I was never trying to compete against others, I was competing against a goal, I think. The Japanese are very conscientious people – we want to get our tasks done well.

To what extent was your success due to your background and upbringing?

I think my background and my upbringing certainly added to what I was able to do. I was brought up in a rather liberal family. I grew up abroad, in both China and in the United States.

Was your father a diplomat?

Yes, and my mother also grew up in a diplomatic family, so thinking about diplomatic relations was a natural thing in my family. My father was also very educationally minded. He always bought a lot of books for me and encouraged me to study, and although I didn't really study very hard until I got to graduate school, I did all right at school.

Didn't you have a lot of difficulties though, because in the Japan of the first part of this century particularly, the role of women was considered to be, if you like, subservient, looking after the man and yet here you were being encouraged to be an independent woman. Did you have to fight against the system in any way?

Well, I did not think I would become a career woman when I graduated from college. It was then, upon the encouragement of my father, that I went to the United States to do graduate work. The early 1950s was a time of opening for Japan, it was a liberalizing, democratizing atmosphere. A lot of my friends went to study abroad too, opportunities were opening up for us and we just took advantage of them. I didn't immediately set out looking for a career as young people do today. I knew I had the option of continuing with academic work.

But did you feel, as a woman in Japan, you had to fight harder, you had to be that bit better than everyone else in order to achieve?

Perhaps, but my academic work was good – whether it was done by a man or a woman, it was good. Because I was an academic, it had to be good.

What do you think are the qualities needed to be a successful person?

You have to produce good-quality work – if it's writing, good-quality writing, if it's a task, you have to produce good-quality tasks.

Is it possible to be successful once and then to coast on one's reputation?

That's a danger facing any man or woman, Japanese or English. If that happens to you, it's the time you should retire.

What do you regard as your greatest success?

As time passed, the more I did. After I graduated and got my doctorate, I wrote my first book, then I had my family to bring up – so I was always doing a little bit more every time. I didn't make a major jump until I went on the Japanese delegation to the United Nations for the first time in 1968. It was the first time I had left the children, I was away from home for three months. It was a pretty big job and I found myself doing rather well. I enjoyed it too, meeting lots of different people, trying to think of policy options, proposing policy alternatives as a delegation and so on. I didn't continue full-time straight away, because there were family constraints, but I did what I could. I was also teaching part-time. I didn't have to work, and it wasn't until my second child went to school that I got a full-time post as a university professor. Little by little I went into administration. The next big jump was when I became a full-time foreign service officer, having been taken to the foreign ministry as minister to the United Nations. That was quite a jump for me. I was posted on a full-time basis in New York.

Is there any one particular event, one particular achievement within your career, of which you are particularly proud?

The biggest jump for me was when I became High Commissioner for Refugees. The job encompassed enormous difficulties – it started with Northern Iraq, then the Horn of Africa, and then former Yugoslavia.

Was there any particular personal moment when you felt, 'I've made it'?

Well, with regard to my own office, it is very difficult because we could not get on top of the situation quickly, but finally we were able to deal with this great outflow of people and bring them back. After that, I was determined to get a strong agency with the capacity to deal with emergencies. Emergency response teams didn't really exist in the UN up till that point.

Do you see your job at the United Nations High Commission of Refugees as tackling these problems of infrastructure in countries as well as just delivering aid? Why did you carry the job forward into another dimension?

I think it was because of my training as a political scientist. I'm used to analysing cause and effect, and just dealing with the surface was not good enough for a UN agency. During my tenure, the agency's budget and staff have doubled. That's a heavy responsibility, and you have to justify it. One factor for this was definitely circumstantial – the end of the Cold War and the great changes that were taking place in national politics.

Do you feel that it was quite a struggle to achieve what you did against the legendary bureaucracy of the United Nations and against the opposition of a great many leaders throughout the world?

Yes. We always have to face opposition, be it from the donors or the refugee-producing or refugee-receiving countries. But when we are coming up with proposals for a solution, we usually get support.

And how do you react to criticism?

You do have to bear some criticism – of course, some is completely unfounded, although there are times when you have to take it seriously.

When you met the war lords in Somalia or in what used to be Yugoslavia, did you have any particular negotiating technique or approach?

Sometimes, but a lot of the negotiating was done by my colleagues. It is essential to get results, and those results usually mean alleviating the suffering of the people, the victims, the refugees and so on. I'm not doing something for myself, we do what we do for a vast number of people who are very weak and need organizations like mine to help them – that is the objective.

What's your attitude when someone thumps the table in front of you and says you can't have something that you want? How do you react inside, what are your tactics for getting round that person?

Well, because I am a woman they don't do that kind of thing. They don't thump the table, and it's very rare for them to shout at me, even in the most difficult circumstances. I try to get round them through persistent argument. That's one advantage of being a small woman.

Can you remember any occasions when someone did shout at you?

Not people I'm negotiating with. When I was growing up my father would have bursts of temper at times.

Do you think it's right for parents to be strict in certain ways with their children?

I think so, yes. There is such a thing as discipline, and discipline from your parents is ingrained in you for the rest of your life. If the parents don't teach discipline, who else will?

Is that part of laying the groundwork for a successful person?

I don't know. You can't make children do what you them want to, but you can talk to them and hope that some of your values will be understood.

What do you regard as your biggest failures, and how did you recover from them?

Big failures? I think I've passed most exams I've taken. I once failed a driving test, and that was quite a shock, but I went away and practised more and got through. There are lots of small failures in everyday life, but I must be fortunate in that I don't remember any devastating things happening to me. I only remember the happy things in life.

Everyone has setbacks in life. How do you recover from them?

You have to try to sleep well. Often if you're tired, worn out, depressed and so on, a good night's sleep will put you back on the right track.

A lot of successful people find a conflict between work and family and some people say that in order to be really successful it does involve a degree of sacrifice for your family. Do you agree?

Yes. By the time I took the High Commissioner's post, it was the first time I had really been posted on my own for a long period. Up till that point, I had only had the time to fulfil temporary assignments, but by then the children had grown up and were working, and my husband was no longer in a very pressing line-management post so he had a little more leisure time. Relatively speaking, it was an easy time for my family. I think that is what a woman's career is all about – you cannot leave the family, not because of the obligations a family brings, but because it's a very central part of any woman's career.

Is your ambition endless? Is there nothing you wouldn't do? Would you like to move on to the top job if it became available at the UN?

I am quite happy with what I have at the moment. If anything else comes along, I'll have to think about it, but I would like to think that at some point I'll stop running around all day and think through what I've done, and write a book or two. That would make me feel very happy.

Who are your heroes, the people you regard as having been extremely successful?

I wouldn't say I have heroes, but there are people I admire a great deal for what they have done. Most of them are my teachers, I admired their approach to research. I admired another teacher for the way she tried to bring people out of themselves. I admired my parents for different reasons. Most of those I admire are those close to me.

What do you think are the biggest enemies of success?

At times you can be your own worst enemy. If you get conceited, you think that you can do things without thinking about others who really support you.

How do you stop becoming conceited if you are on the path to success?

By keeping your eyes and ears open. If you only hear good things about yourself, that's bad. You have to know where you stand, and that's not easy. When you're at the top of an organization, you have to get the feel of what it's all about.

You run what is known as a 'mean ship', you are very tough, demanding, and sometimes even said to be 'dictatorial', and yet your staff love you very much indeed. How have you managed to achieve that? How have you managed to do both?

I don't know.

You must have thought about it?

You have to take decisions, and be responsible for those decisions.

Are there any decisions you would like to take to be even more successful as High Commissioner for Refugees? Decisions which you have been unable to take because people have stopped you or have frustrated you?

Sometimes I would like to blast some people, yes. We have to deal with very difficult people and situations and we can never give up.

On the whole, do you tend to win more than you lose in those kind of negotiations?

In the long run, yes, otherwise my office wouldn't survive.

Do you think your office is becoming more or less successful in dealing with the world's refugee problems?

Definitely more successful. There are more refugees, and more refugees of a more difficult kind. A good example of this was in Rwanda recently. We had two million Rwandan refugees, many of them women and children, who were part of a regime that carried out genocide. The problem is how to go about protecting these people. That's not easy.

Do you wish that politicians around the world, leading politicians, were more understanding of the problems?

I wish the politicians were more decisive in taking action. I cannot take politicial decisions of the kind that would undermine my humanitarian mandate, and I wish somebody else would do that.

And you've found the politicians reluctant to take some key decisions?

Yes, but I understand there are various political considerations involved. If I work with a political leader I have to look into the country's strategic interests, domestic opinion, and so on, and that tends to stifle decision-making. It was easier during the Cold War because there were clear enemies – that situation no longer exists.

Do you think there is any prospect of politicians becoming more decisive in responding to the new world order that is being created?

I don't think so, because that kind of decision-making is not necessarily required in industrialized countries or in a democractic process. If you were to look at decisive heroes in history, you would find that they usually appear during times of crisis. Despite the problems in various countries, the world is more settled today.

What is the greatest pleasure you have had from your success?

I always get pleasure from doing things well.

And is there any particular thing you've done well where you remember saying, 'This was one of my finest moments'?

This year I received the Félix Houphouët-Boigny Peace Prize, which is an African prize. I felt good about that.

Is that because Africa contains some of the toughest problems you have encountered?

Yes, I think so. I was also able to put the prize money into a teaching fund for African students and as a result at least 50 students will be able to get secondary education – that's pretty nice.

Has success changed you at all?

I don't know. I think that this job has made me a lot tougher and maybe even more short-tempered, but I would not say that that is as a result of success.

If you could gather together before you all the young people in the world who want to effect changes to make it a better world in the way that you are seeking, what advice would you give them?

They should learn by themselves, be solid in their understanding of what the world demands and move forward step by step.

Does that mean they shouldn't have a long-term goal, a great ambition?

I don't mind them having that, but there is usually a gap between what they can achieve and what they should be thinking – this gap can sometimes undermine people's efforts.

How could the United Nations, as an organization, become more successful?

I think it needs to redefine its mission. It needs to know what it is capable of achieving. There are a lot of mission creeps.

What do you mean by that?

Well, if you look at the UN programmes – they involve everything from deep-ocean and outer-space exploration to free birth. I don't know whether the UN should do all that, they should be more selective and prioritize what they can do better as a universal organization. They need a narrower focus.

What areas do you think that narrow focus ought to concentrate on?

Peace and security are still the main missions of the United Nations. That is what is was established for. But nowadays the nature of war has changed – it is now internal. I think the UN does have a role to play in these situations – as a mediator – but it is a role that needs to be defined. The UN has to stand for humanitarian interests and has to maintain the security of the people. It needs to be forward-thinking.

When your time comes to leave this life, what would you like people to say about you?

That she did well.

BRUCE OLDFIELD

The man who has dressed some of the most beautiful women in the world believes that success is all about 'staying there'. That was just one of the lessons he learned the hard way. Certainly, his early life was far from easy. A Barnardo's baby from just a day and a half old, he grew up with a foster mother in Durham – 'in those days one of the few black kids in the North-East'. Seven of them lived in a tiny two-up, two-down house with a 'no-flush' lavatory out the back. They were, he says, very poor, with the accompanying very low career expectations. Maybe that was what drove him to be an early entrepreneur – organising lunchtime discos, getting refunds on empty bottles, selling chocolate biscuits at break and doing an evening paper  *round. Throughout his schooldays he was a rebel and a troublemaker, once being sent back to Barnardo's briefly when he was caught pinching sweets. But he doesn't believe in lingering regrets. 'Feeling sorry for yourself is a total waste of time – just get on with it.' Which perhaps explains why, after living with a stutter that lasted until he was 20, he developed an inner confidence so strong that, in his early career, he was (he confesses) 'the most arrogant prat known to man'.*

With just two A-levels that were not good enough to take him to university, he first tackled a teacher training course; then, helped by a Barnardo's grant, found his true vocation at St Martin's School of Art – fulfilling his foster-mother's early prophecy that he would become a fashion designer. He left without a degree when offered a show in New York – and promptly fell flat on his face. As he puts it, 'I went out in limousines and came back on the bus.' It was a salutary lesson in a profession where designers 'sometimes hang on in there by their fingertips'. Two decades of fame later, he nearly came a cropper once more when the recession threatened his company with bankruptcy. Applying drastic surgery, he sold his much-loved flat and most of his empire apart from the original shop in London's Beauchamp Place. Expansion had taken his eye off the core couture business. Almost ten years on, he's not making that mistake again. So new merchandising operations in London and overseas are funded mainly by licensing deals in which someone else puts up most of the money, but he keeps full control. Not surprisingly, his advice now to budding fashion designers is: 'Learn about the business side.'

Bruce Oldfield, what is your definition of success?

I think it has to be staying there – getting there's important, obviously, but staying there, not being a one-night wonder, which is the great danger in fashion.

It is easier to achieve sudden success than being successful for some period of time?

Exactly. As soon as I left college – I left St Martin's in 1973 – I got all of the press coverage and my first show was in New York four months later, and I didn't even get a qualification, a degree. Then it was two months in New York and back on the bus, because the things hadn't sold well enough. Americans don't invest very much in time, they want things to happen straight away, and if they don't you're out and the next one's in – it's a conveyor-belt. I came down with a bump and I coasted for a while. My career's gone up and down, up and down, up and down, but it's always been a question of keeping yourself in front of the press and the public, always in the best possible taste of course. And just hanging on in there, sometimes by your fingernails.

At your very first success in New York, did you feel that this was it, you had arrived and that you were going to be on the top forever, so that when you came down to earth with a bump, it was all the more dramatic?

No, I think my feelings were, 'What am I doing here?' I suffer from a distinct lack of confidence in what I do, I always have.

Is that a driving factor?

I think so, because it does make you try that little bit harder. You look at other people's work and you think, 'Oh, goodness, that's so good, why didn't I think of that?' But then you have to look at yourself and think, 'Well, I did something like that,' or, 'What I've just done is just as nice.' All the time, you're questioning.

What did it teach you when you came down to earth with a bump the first time?

When I arrived in New York, I had gone first-class, and was picked up by a limousine, taken to the Plaza, where I stayed for about a week – it was very, very glamorous. A few months later, I was going back to JFK on a Greyhound bus.

Why did it go wrong?

Well, I was just a young kid straight out of college. I knew nothing about commerce – I just designed the stuff, they were supposed to market it and make it into a saleable range of products. I remember quite distinctly, the president of the store, a very clever woman, coming into my office saying, 'That's wonderful,' and I said, 'Will it sell?' Even at that point I was aware of commerciality and the fact that if you didn't sell, then you were on a hiding to nothing. I knew also that there was an onus upon me to create something that was different, and that I think is the problem with fashion – because it happens twice a year, it's quite a drain and a strain on one's nerves. It taught me not to rely too heavily on the press, because usually you find that if the press like the collection, it won't sell.

Really? You would go as far as that?

It's pretty much the case. We've seen it so many times where the press have said, 'Fantastic!' – perhaps because one's played a bit to the gallery and there's not enough commercial sense there. It's quite interesting – people say that the English fashion industry produces creative people, but the businesses don't go anywhere. If you look at the French and the Italians, they put the most crazy things on the runway just to grab media attention and it works, but if you go backstage or to the showrooms, there you have the most basic commercial goods. Whereas what happens in England is that young designers come up, and put up all the eye-catching creations for the press, but that is actually all they've got. They haven't got the commercial stuff in the back, so of course the businesses go nowhere.

So the really successful fashion designer has to have one or two products that are going to grab press attention, but beneath that there has to be a core of products that people actually want to buy and wear for almost every day use?

Yes, that's exactly right. I do wish a few other pundits had realized this about 20 years ago. They could have taught me a few things.

If praise from the media isn't a factor, how do you sell a collection? What are the factors that persuade people to buy your work?

That's very difficult. There is a school of thought at the moment that editorial means very, very little, that it is advertising that sells. It used to be that people didn't respect advertising too much, but they felt that having editorial pages, being chosen by the fashion editors was far more influential on the consumer than advertising. But now the advertising pages are so good. Firms such as Gucci and Armani produce in their ads the dream that they want to spin, and I think the consumer finds it far more credible than the editorial.

Does that worry you?

Well, no, because every business relies on selling more than once. If you only sell to a consumer once, then fine, you may have a good season, but actually you want to have two, three or four good seasons, and to achieve that the consumer has to go back. The product has to have integrity otherwise the customer just doesn't go back, and if he doesn't go back, then you're lost.

Do you ever sit back and wonder about the extent of your success?

Never. Success doesn't really come overnight, it's always a series of steps that you make and at each step you arrive, you say, 'OK, that's done, next step, that's done, next step …' It's a cumulative thing, so it's only on occasions where for example, you get an OBE, and you go to the Palace that you think, 'That's special.' So there are special times when you think, 'Well, I haven't done badly really,' but it's not something you spend a lot of time thinking about.

So perhaps a really successful person never feels that they have actually made it because there's always a hunger to move on to the next step?

Yes, exactly. I've got so much going on at the moment that I'm totally over-stressed. I think I have learned to delegate in the last few years, but only because, say, six years ago, things were so horrendous. That's when I learned to type, because I didn't even have a secretary. My computer skills are handy now.

A lot of people would find that strange, someone as successful as you not having a secretary.

We just had to cut back. Six years ago I completely changed track. I had a business which was bulky and mismanaged. Basically I got rid of it and restarted, that was at the beginning of the recession. I was doing everything, which was good because I really got control of things again.

To what extent do you think your success has been a product of your background and upbringing?

I think it's probably got a lot to do with my background. I was brought up by a woman who was a dressmaker, so it was almost inevitable.

Do you think it was her imposing her ideas on you, or were you separately, for other reasons, deciding at that early stage that you wanted to be a fashion designer?

I don't think it was her and I don't think either of us made a conscious decision because her expectations for us children were quite low.

And she was your foster-mother? You were sent to Barnardo's when you were one-and-a-half days old. Did that have an effect on your life, looking back?

What you've never had you don't really know about. I have foster-brothers and foster-sisters and half of us would say it did have a deleterious effect, the other half would disagree, but I think you either make something of yourself or you moan about it for the rest of your life. Feeling sorry for yourself is a total waste of time, you just have to get on with it. But by the same token, I don't actually say to myself, 'Think positively about your background, just take it in your stride.' It's not a conscious thought.

Was there a foster-father?

No, there was no father, so there was a single woman bringing up boys.

Were you all adopted?

We were all fostered, we weren't adopted. There's a difference. The fact that we were fostered and not adopted meant that she was being paid – now we know that she wasn't being paid very much, but nevertheless she was being paid – there was always a feeling of 'What value did the system put on us?' Also, there was always a threat of being sent back to the home. I don't think children in normal families have parents with any recourse to send them away. I don't know what the equivalent punishment would be. And I remember, when you were sent back to the home, they would say, 'You'll end up in Borstal,' or, 'You'll be made a ward of court.' There were always such threats, if you caused trouble, which I did constantly.

You were a trouble-maker?

I was dreadful, yes. It was just that they expected so little and I expected so much. I wasn't going to drop down to their level, I was going to maintain my level, so there were always remarks like, 'Who do you think you are and why do you think you're any different from the rest?' And those negative forces, I think, always made me rebel.

And they didn't pull you down at any stage?

Oh, I wanted to react against them and I did. When I left Spennymoor, County Durham, and went to Ripon, I was put into quite a different environment, into a Barnardo's Home with 24 boys and, having passed my eleven-plus, I went to the local grammar school. I was the only one at the local grammar school – even the superintendent's son didn't go there, much to his annoyance. This is why he didn't get on very well with me, this is why he was always saying, 'Who do you think you are?'

So there was resentment amongst some of the others that you were going to this grammar school?

Oh yes, and also there's a classic resentment because the grammar school's different – the secondary modern school didn't wear uniforms and we did, so we were the snobby grammar school twits and they – well, I can't remember what we called them!

But you were starting to feel cocky at this stage?

Oh God, yes, I think even earlier than that. My inner confidence in my abilities manifested itself at quite an early age.

During your schooldays you had a stutter – now why should someone who was so confident have a stutter?

A stutter is more of a physical thing, it's not being able to get your words out fast enough, I think you can be confident in your abilities and still be nervous.

How long did it take you to get over those nerves?

Oh, I still have them, I stuttered until I was about 19 or 20. It was terrible, it really was, and the problem with a stutter is that you spend a lot of time worrying about it.

Did your stutter affect your relationship with other pupils?

It probably did. I'm quite a self-contained person, I have very few friends. I have millions of acquaintances, you can imagine in my business, and in a way that's probably why, by the end of the day, I don't actually want to be with people. As an example, I've just had my portrait painted by a friend, who's a very good painter and although he and I get on very, very well, we could only fit it in at the end of the day, by which time I would be thinking, 'I do not need this,' and I would sit there fidgeting. He would say, 'Get in your position,' and I would think, 'Oh, just go, go.'

I need my own space and I've always been quite isolated and self-contained, not needing people around me. And in contrast to many fashion designers, who have their cliques, though I have people I employ,

I don't surround myself with others. I don't do anything by committee. I type up exactly what I think, then I might put it to somebody, but I really don't have a lot of patience for consensus of opinion. There's a consensus of one – I say what I think, what I want and then let somebody comment on it and add to it. Coming to a group and making group decisions is hard for me unless I've already made my position quite clear.

Going back to your schooldays, did you resent authority?

I really hated Spennymoor Grammar School, but Ripon Grammar School was a completely different environment. It was the best thing that ever happened to me. And I don't think I did rebel against authority there because I thought that it was fair. It was a very liberal grammar school, whereas Spennymoor was more focused on boys going out into industry.

Have you had mentors in your life?

I have had a few, usually they're women. There was the headmistress of Ripon Grammar School, who took me slightly under her wing. When I only got two A-levels, which meant I couldn't get into university, she said, 'Apply to teacher training college.' I didn't think I wanted to go to teacher training college, but anyway I applied there and I got in.

You'd abandoned your earlier ambition to be a fashion designer?

Well, no, my early ambition to be a fashion designer was never really followed up because, one, it was not the kind of career for a boy, absolutely not, and then of course I was told, 'Get your qualifications, get your O-levels, get your A-levels, then get a degree.' Something to fall back on – everybody's looking for safety nets.

Do you think that approach stops a lot of people pursuing the career they want to go for?

Absolutely. I think that people do get a bit bogged down by their parents' notions, or by the perceived wisdom of 'you need to have a qualification'. I did not have any qualifications in the end. I completed a three-year course in teacher training, but I didn't do the one-year's teaching which you have to do to get the proper diploma. I didn't finish at art school – I did one year at Ravensbourne and one year at St Martin's and I left in the second year – to great rapturous applause.

By that time I had been a student for five years. I was 23 and I was sick of it and I had won the Sarga Mink competition, which is the fur competition, which practically every student in fashion in the country did. Then I was the overall winner in 1973, then part of this promotion for the launch of Charlie – a Revlon perfume back in the 1970s – and for that I had to put together a collection, myself and a girl called Paulene Mucha from St Martin's. We were asked to do six designs each. That was all in that second year at St Martin's and so when it got to June I just thought – and I'd had so much press – I thought, 'Why not leave? They aren't teaching me very much.' I felt I could learn much more by being out. One month later, Geraldine Stutz, the President of Bendels, arrived in my street in Brixton in a huge white limo and this doyenne of New York fashion came up the stairs, curled up on the chair and murmured sweet nothings in my ears, and, of course, I said 'Yes.' Also I was making clothes for Bianca Jagger so I was down there on Cheyne Walk in Chelsea with Mick Jagger and Ryan O'Neal running in and out and Marisa Berenson, I was thinking, 'Hey, I like this!' It went totally to my head, I was probably the most arrogant prat known to man. But the New York experience did bring me slightly back down to earth. Although I don't think it necessarily dented my total confidence, it probably scratched the surface a bit. But it didn't do any serious damage. I think it just makes you stronger, makes you think, 'I'll show you.'

And then you had this marvellous progression until you hit the rock of the recession at the end of the 1980s. What went wrong there?

We, as a company, were always under-capitalized, rather like all the young designers – they leave college and start a business without a business partner, without proper finance, and so on. A business needs to be properly marketed, you need an advertising budget, you need to be able to put on shows using proper models, you need a lot of investment, and in England fashion is not considered to be a very serious game. If you want to do anything where quality is a major part of it, of both design and product, then you've got to console yourself with the fact that you are always going to remain very small. You either make one-offs for individual clients, sell to department stores or open your own retail outlet. All of these separate moves cost a lot of money and it's where the investment is required. We found some investors through the Business Expansion Scheme in the early 1980s which enabled us to open the first shop in Beauchamp Place, which has always made money. But in order to make the name bigger it was necessary to do wholesale and to sell to other stores, broadening your base, but also requiring more money. If you're doing the Winter 1997 collection, for instance, you order the sample fabrics in October 1996, make the samples by the end of January 1997, present them to the stores in March, produce the goods and deliver them in July and get paid – if you're lucky! – in September–October. That's quite an investment in time and money with no income, only outlay!

So you rely on sales and good turnover to fund that?

Yes, and once you start making a lot of clothes, then you can start making money if, like any business, you keep a very tight control on it and watch it. The other way of expanding your business is to go into licensing, which is what all the Americans do, where you find a partner who will produce things under your name for you and market them and sell them on to the shops. But they must do it in a way which is consistent with your reputation, your name and your standing and the quality that you are known for. That's when it all falls to pieces. In the mid to late 1980s I had a lot of licensing deals – shoes, tights, furs, glasses, jewellery, shirts, endless things – and in a way what we were trying to do was to build the core of Bruce Oldfield product, every label said 'Bruce Oldfield for somebody'. The companies that we were dealing with weren't big enough or competent enough really to run the course, so when it got to 1989–90, everybody was feeling the pinch and a lot of those companies suddenly thought, 'Hey, our core business is suffering here, let's get back to it, get rid of all these licensees.'

So how close did you come to disaster, to bankruptcy?

How close? I had a meeting with all of my good lawyers and accountants and partners, because I had partners and they were saying, 'Basically, we think it's time just to pull the plug,' and I said 'No.' I'm not trying to sound like a martyr, but I did feel that I'd just been given my OBE and it says on this document, 'To our trusted and well beloved Bruce Oldfield'. 'Well,' I thought, 'it wouldn't be thought trusting and well beloved to go bankrupt.' Quite often bankruptcy is used as a simple device to get out of trouble when you know, if you really dug your heels in, you could actually trade out of it. So I said, 'No, no can do.'

What steps did you take to save the business?

I just closed everything. I retrenched so tightly and sold my flat and moved to Battersea – that's not such a big deal but there was a psychological thing about moving from SW3 to SW11, you know, especially when you're on the river bank and you're looking at SW3 longingly for three years. I finally got back. I just got rid of everybody that I didn't need. We got rid of all of the things that were just draining the company. It was very, very hard to come back to doing just couture again, which is what I did.

So, as you became more and more successful and the company expanded and the staff grew, in a sense you took your eye off the financial ball?

I think I took an eye off the financial ball and also off the core business, the part of the business that had always been most successful, which was the couture and the limited ready-to-wear that we did through Beauchamp Place. That was always successful – it was doing all those other things that caused the core, the real business, to take second place.

Is it true that the more you charge in fashion, the more successful you are seen to be?

Everyone is always saying that couture is dead, but I find that the couture side of the business is the most profitable, it's the one that's growing. Throughout the recession the turnover and the profitability of this company rose 20 per cent per year. I was continually raising my standards and therefore my prices, but it just didn't seem to matter – people were still buying it. This season, I've got quite a lot of things that are up in the £7–8,000 range which we sell 10 or 12 of per piece – that's a lot of the business on one frock. And at Beauchamp Place, we can do £34,000 in a day without really having to work terribly hard.

So why move into ready-to-wear?

Well, I finally got to the point where I wasn't challenged enough – this was about a year and a half ago – so I sat down and I decided on a plan to expand the business again because it was time. My business was solid because the company was profitable again. I didn't want to be just a little couturier for the rest of my life – it's very nice but I need more challenges than that. I need to be out there, I need to be doing things. So it seemed obvious that I'd got to get back into ready-to-wear, but I only wanted to do it through my own retail outlet, so this was the business plan that I put together, and I found two partners that were very keen to go with it, but what I did was grant the licence to them. You see, I own this business completely, 100 per cent, and I own all the trademarks and all the copyrights completely. All I do is I license it out.

So the way you're making money now – apart from the couture business which is your own – is to license your name and your reputation to others?

Yes, and keep full control, unlike in the 1980s when we were licensing the name to a company to manufacture something. I'm not doing that at all. What I am doing is, I've started this business which is like a joint venture. Because I'm part of the business, I have a stake in it – the ready-to-wear business – but I also license my name to that particular business and I am paid by that business and I get a royalty from that business, but I could withdraw my name from it. It's a very, very strict retailing concept.

But you've cracked the funding now because it's your partners who are putting up the money?

Yes, my partners put up the money. To show good faith I have also put in some money myself.

So where it is possible, one of the secrets is to get other people to put up as much of the money as possible?

Yes, but you have to guide them, because they will all say to you, 'You must come up with the concepts for this, that and the other,' which is fine.

How much control do you exert?

I exert a lot of control, and I have to. At the moment the operation is quite small because I've got Beauchamp Place and I've got Brook Street.

As you expand, are you going to have to delegate more?

Yes, I'm going to have to rely on the partners in the joint ventures that we set up overseas because I can't be there, and in Melbourne, where the next shop is about to open.

So is the potential there for things to go wrong because you are not holding the reins as fully as you have been used to in the past?

There's always a potential for things to go wrong, but because these people are putting in all of the money, they're going to be watching their investment as well. This is the secret too – you have to make sure that they are going by the standards which you've set and that they always maintain those standards. That's always the danger in our business – allowing standards to slip. I will actually pick up dog-ends outside the shop in full view of the staff, just so that they see me doing it, and go in with them in my hand and say, 'Can we get rid of these please?' The next day you go, there are no dog-ends, probably a week later the dog-ends are back, so you've got to do it again, and that is the problem – people are sloppy. They don't learn, they don't take an interest because it's not theirs. That's why with partners for the venture abroad, hopefully they will see that it's theirs and that it is incumbent upon them to maintain standards. Success lies in paying attention to the detail. Not only the business detail, also the visual detail, because that's the thing the customer sees first.

We're talking about attention to detail in all kinds of ways. You aren't a little pernickety in devoting so much time to detail?

It's not only the visual thing. For instance, I constantly get detailed analysis about how things are selling, size ratios that are selling. We may find that we are not selling trousers and you think, 'Why?' The answer is that people are coming purely for special-occasion things and on a special occasion they don't think they can wear trousers. So cut down the trousers for the next season – we have to have some because it is a trouser season and the press will want trousers – but base most of it on skirts. It is that kind of detail.

Does luck play a part in success?

I don't believe in luck. Luck is something that you can manipulate, I don't think it's something that just happens. People say, 'You're so lucky!' and I say, 'You can make your luck, you can position yourself.' There probably is an element of luck somewhere, but it's mainly you manoeuvring yourself into a situation where luck just happens to be.

Are you driven by money?

I have never really been driven by money. Somebody read my hand the other day – it was a client – and she said, 'You must be very, very careful about somebody looking after your money, I see something very funny here.' I'm not money-driven, I don't know what drives me. Actually, I want to succeed, I want to be Georgio Armani, really.

Are you after a level of respect from your peers or from the public?

I think it's both of those things and also financial stability. I think it's recognition and stability.

You are stable now, why go on and want more?

It's probably because I haven't got anything else to do. I haven't got a wife, child, or lover, so I might as well get on. I wake up early in the morning, so I'm quite happy to speak to Sydney or Melbourne or Tokyo, it's no skin off my nose. I'm happy when I'm engaged in this, the cut-and-thrust of it, thinking about it. I like the business side and I like chasing something and getting it.

And work is your life then, your total life?

Yes, sad isn't it?

Do you think it's sad?

I think it's a little sad, yes, but I think that we all have a capacity for certain things. I have the capacity to bang on and on tirelessly about developing my business and I don't feel that I'm missing out on anything else, particularly.

Is it becoming more or less difficult to achieve success in your particular field?

I think that now, opportunities for me are arising on an almost daily basis. The opportunities that come in from all parts of the world are quite staggering because I've suddenly repositioned myself and said, 'OK, yes, I do couture but I also manufacture very nice clothes for a wider audience, what do you think and any ideas?' And they seem to be coming.

What do you think are the greatest enemies of success?

Jealousy, over-reaching yourself, over-reaching your capabilities. I think the English press don't help. They are very negative about success. They encourage it to be given, then they sort of say, 'He's getting a bit cocky, we'll have to sort him out.'

Why do you think they do that?

I think it's that puritanical, English streak. It's quite funny actually, that Britain is so much more entrepreneurial since the 1980s. Entrepreneurship is not a dirty word, but I think it was.

But do you feel the press goes further than just keeping people on their toes in a healthy sort of way?

Yes. The press can be very vindictive. Touch wood, they have never been so to me personally, I've always had a reasonable press. I find that if you over-expose, you start to see them turn – there's a sting in the tail.

So the important factor in success is judging when to push and promote yourself, your ideas, your products, and when to pull up the drawbridge?

Yes, and sometimes you have to pull it up really fast, if you see the signs. I saw the signs earlier this year, when there were two or three pieces that came out where I was mentioned in a not particularly favourable light, and that was when I said, 'OK, stop.'

What is the greatest pleasure you've had from your success?

Independence. Getting the OBE was a recognition that I was OK at what I did, that I'd got there, that I'd done something.

If you could gather together before you in one room all the young people who want to make it in fashion, what advice would you give them?

A lot of things, Don't believe in your own publicity. Go and work for somebody else and learn about the business side of the industry – please don't start on your own unless you've got someone with some business acumen and finance behind you. I think those are the two most important things. Another very good piece of advice is don't get too involved.

And as you move up the ladder, what are the core ingredients of a successful fashion business?

Being correctly financed because it does cost a lot of money. Not only are you manufacturing, you've got to put yourself out, you've got to maintain an image to the public through public relations, advertising, marketing and fashion shows. If you want to produce perfect things in this country, stay small.

You're not doing that, though?

But, you see, I am because I am keeping hold of the core business, which is my couture business – that's where I'll always be found. The other part is delegation.

When your time comes to depart this life, what would you like people to say about you?

Something along the lines of 'He tried hard.' That could mean one of two things – he tried hard but he didn't do that well, or he tried hard and didn't he do well and look what happens when you try hard. It's a nice open-ended, ambiguous epitaph, don't you think?

MICHAEL PALIN

'*Michael Palin as a success is like a set of clothes that are hung on me from the outside, and I never feel quite comfortable with that*' – *his own verdict on the several careers of the amiable satirist from* Monty Python's Flying Circus *who went on to find differing degrees of further success as a dramatist, author, serious actor, film producer and, most spectacularly, as a presenter and writer of much-acclaimed BBC travel documentaries. He argues here that 'too much success in a particular field restricts you', and 'I want to avoid being pinned down because it compromises my freedom.' Comedy was at first 'like a thing you did at the end of the day when you'd done a real day's work', and he 'never, ever dreamed it would be something from which I'd*

earn a living'. He describes how he needed the encouragement of someone with 'a much more focused idea' of what to do, because on his own 'I don't think I had the courage, single-minded determination, perhaps even the ambition to do it'.

He recalls a Sheffield childhood 'without much money' and a cantankerous father who was 'reluctant to accord praise' and his first paying audience at the Oxford Union (admission – sixpence). Leaving behind Python *and the many works it spawned, he moved on to a series of films including* The Missionary, A Fish Called Wanda, *and* American Friends. *His performance in the Channel 4 drama series* GBH *enhanced his reputation as a serious actor. And, starting with* Around the World in 80 Days, *much of the 1990s were spent making the hit documentaries that took him to every corner of the globe. Famous for never losing his temper, he recalls here the reaction of the Monty Python team on the one public occasion he did so, and, perhaps surprisingly, says that 'a certain amount of anger is all part of what makes you keep going and keep trying things'. He talks about why he never thought the Monty Python shows were successful; how he lost out in a famous television confrontation; the way he dealt with the failure of his West End play* The Weekend. *Going back to his early successes, he offers tips on how to write good comedy: 'It has to have a bit of a shock, a bit of a kick in it.' A writer must have a dark streak, a good gut feeling, and 'an ear for dialogue and for the rhythm of a joke'. And in general, 'Success is down to you. Listen to people, learn by example, never be too proud to go and do anything, and be persistent – never, ever give up.'*

Michael Palin, what is your definition of success?

Something that happens to other people! I'm very wary of using the word to apply to myself. It can mean so many different things, according to different areas of your life, that it can be quite incompatible sometimes – success in business or in your career can be accompanied by total failure in your domestic life or whatever, so I suppose I would narrow it down to having, in some small way, achieved a set task and achieved it successfully. That can be as small as you want, it can be an article written or a day's filming done well – that would be a success to me.

But that's only one part of it. I suppose, spending another successful, happy month married would be a success in a way, but I would tend to place things like that in other areas. I think big success is something that is always ahead of you. As soon as you say, 'I've got it, it's there, I can take hold of it,' I think that's the time to worry, which is why I say I think it always happens to other people rather than to me.

So in a sense, no one is ever truly successful, because there is always something else driving you on to greater and greater things.

Yes, if you are talking about success in terms of your public achievements, I don't think there comes a point where you say to yourself, 'That's it, I've done it, I've been successful so now I can stop,' because success creeps up on you in so many different ways. I would never have thought when we did the *Monty Python* shows, for instance, that we had been successful. We'd had a lot of followers, we'd got along well with a lot of people, we'd done basically what we wanted to do, but there were very rough edges, there were things that weren't, we felt, directed properly and hadn't been put across the way we wanted them to be put across. So I would have said that was a qualified success, something to be worked on later. Now, 30 years on, people look back on *Monty Python* and say, 'That was wonderful, that was marvellous, you will never do anything better than that in your life.' Well, if that's success, it's just as well I didn't stop there.

Are you saying that at the time Monty Python *was such a triumph and receiving such critical acclaim, behind the scenes you and some of your colleagues thought that it could have been better in some ways?*

I would question the use of the words 'triumph' or 'critical acclaim'. At the time, we did get a certain amount of critical attention, but we were still considered to be relative upstarts. There were many qualifications in people's appreciation of *Python* and it was never a ratings triumph, nor was it something, to start with, that exported or anything like that, but certainly we all felt we could do better, and in fact as we began to settle into the show so the discontent began to show and various members of the team decided they'd had enough at various stages and wanted to go off. So to talk about success in terms of six people is just multiplying the problem and I would say that at the very point where *Python* was at its most successful it was beginning to break up. I think that happens very often with that elusive concept of success – just as you've got it, it slips away.

Was there a feeling among the team that they could achieve greater success for themselves individually, in a different field, than they would by staying with Python?

I am not sure what everyone wanted to achieve but they wanted to achieve something that was their own, yes, certainly in the case of John. I think he felt restricted in a group of six and wanted to do something where he would be in a group of two, himself and Connie, and went off to write *Fawlty Towers.* John's certainly not the sort of person who would say, 'I know I will be successful if I do this,' it was just a question of making himself feel easier and happier about the way he was working, which I suppose is a prerequisite of doing what you want to do. If you're doing what you want to do, generally you stand more chance of doing it well and being successful than doing something you don't want to do.

And is part of it wanting to be in control, exercising a degree of control that you couldn't exercise when you were part of a team of five or six people?

Yes, control is absolutely the key. Personal responsibility for what you are doing is absolutely vital, and I think that was the case in *Python,* and I think that was the problem with John. I felt at the time that we had a degree of control which only existed because of the group of six, if any one of us had been taken out of that group we would suddenly have had less control.

Did you ever think that comedy would be your first success?

No, I didn't really. Comedy seemed to me always something slightly unofficial, it was a bit like a hobby, it was like a thing which you did at the end of the day when you had done a real day's work, that's when you had some fun and had a few laughs. The idea of actually making a living from writing jokes and playing comedy never really occurred to me. I always had an acute funny-bone, a sort of over-developed sense of humour, so I enjoyed humour and I enjoyed making people laugh and I was able to do that, but I never, ever dreamed that it would be something from which I would earn my living and also earn a certain standard, a certain level of public acclaim. I suppose the first time was when I stood up at the Union in Oxford and did cabaret with my friend, Robert Hewison, and people laughed – not many, but they did laugh. Some stayed and didn't walk away to the bar, so that's what I mean, that's a small success.

And up to that point, you had been doing serious acting?

Well, I'd not been doing anything really for a public audience apart from school plays and things like that, and this was really the first time that I'd been persuaded to do anything in front of a paying audience. They didn't pay much – sixpence an evening.

Did that gave you an appetite for being on the stage, or was it always there? Have you always been someone who liked the buzz of an audience?

I enjoyed performing. I suppose in many ways you can't say you enjoy performing without assuming that you enjoy performing to an audience. You don't really do it on your own in your back room – some may do! Yes, as early as I can remember at school I enjoyed having an audience there to laugh at me, but then so do many people who have now become bank managers or founded car-hire firms or whatever. People were able to tell jokes and people would laugh and there were always people who could attract a crowd around them. But certainly it was through humour that I realized I could stand out slightly from the crowd, which is quite important when you're at school. I was able to do the voices of the teachers and that sort of thing, things that my colleagues couldn't do – so yes, it did need an audience. I wouldn't say I had an insatiable need to be in front of an audience, in fact I was quite content to become whatever I was going to become, working in advertising or a journalist or something like that. It was only that somebody – Robert Hewison, whom I met in my first term at Brasenose – saw what I could do, enjoyed working with me and had a much more focused idea of how this could be enjoyed by other people – so said let's put it on stage.

Did you require someone as a catalyst to make you decide that you had a future career in comedy as opposed to being a bank manager or whatever?

Yes, I think I did need a catalyst.

Why wouldn't it have happened on its own?

I just don't think I had the courage or the single-minded determination, perhaps even the ambition. You've got to want to do what you are doing desperately, that's how you become successful, and at that time, it was just one of many things that I wanted to do. I also enjoyed playing football, straight acting, amateur dramatics – that sort of thing, I enjoyed reading and writing. It wasn't an absolute primary thing – I've *got* to go on the stage – so someone did concentrate my mind on it.

Do you think everybody needs a mentor at some stage in their career who shapes and guides them to future success?

I think it's different for different people. I think there are some people who seem to be born with that ambition as part of their make-up, part of the way they are. Others – and I think they are the more fortunate ones – share it in some way or need someone else to bring something into their lives to either focus it or to push them in a certain direction. I think it can take many shapes or forms. I don't think it's always obviously beneficial – sometimes you will meet somebody you will have a terrible time with, you will get into some relationship that doesn't work out, and that induces in you the feeling that you will do it your own way next time around, which is very important.

There seems to be an element of surprise on your part that you have been successful and yet with the many things that you've done, one would assume that deep down there is actually a very strong desire to be successful at a whole range of things.

I like to take something on and do it as well as I can, but obviously there's a bit more to it than that – I like to do it better than anyone else would do it. Now finding out what you do best is a very important thing, and I found what I do best is being Michael Palin. I've fitted into various categories at one time or another. I wrote a play, I've written a novel and I hope I will write more, but I never feel myself as a novelist or a playwright. Even when I see 'Michael Palin comedian', I don't altogether believe in it. That's only part of the picture. In the end what I do is just what I do, I have a great curiosity for all sorts of things about life, about creative life, I suppose, about writing, about acting, about journalism or whatever you would call the documentaries that I do. I take them very seriously, but on the other hand I don't have that absolute overriding single ambition to succeed in one particular area, which I think you probably do need if you are going to be truly successful. I tend to dissipate my efforts and energies, but that's the way I am and that's the way it will always be, part of my butterfly mind. I'm easily led into something I think will be interesting, but I think what I bring to it is my own form of consciousness about something.

There have been several points in your life when you could have sat back and said, 'Right, I've done it now. I don't need to work any more. I can ride on my reputation.' Why didn't you do that?

I have a low boredom threshold. I do find if I've worked on something and got it right, whether it be a comedy series or a documentary idea or a book or whatever, I don't want to repeat it endlessly. I want to avoid being pinned down. That compromises my freedom.

Or does too much success in a particular field bore you?

It restricts you, that's all. I think if you are particularly successful in any field, if you are not very careful you will get taken over by that particular area and the people in that particular area. If you are so good at what you are doing that people say, 'You're indispensable, we need you, without you we cannot do this, that and the other.' I don't think I'd like to be in that position, but again that's me rather than a general comment on success. I really wouldn't want to be pinned down. I feel I want to know everything which is almost impossible, but that's the aim. Maybe that's why I just have this low boredom threshold, why I avoid putting all my eggs in one basket. It may be just basic insecurity, but I prefer to think it's deep curiosity and restlessness and a feeling of always wanting to work. I've tried the idea of taking six months off and it never works, within six hours I'd be involved in something else, grumbling all the time.

In a sense, notwithstanding the ambition that you've had, has success almost caught you by surprise? Has it been a kind of accident that has left you slightly bewildered at how and why it all happened so quickly and in the way it has?

Success is something I always feel is applied to me by others. Michael Palin as a success is like a set of clothes which are hung on me from outside, and I never feel quite comfortable with that.

To what extent do you think your success is shaped by your upbringing?

I think your success, everything about you, is shaped very strongly by your upbringing. I had certain advantages in that I had a reasonably settled upbringing, but it was also quite bracing in the sense that there was very often a tension between my parents which I noticed and which, I suppose, stopped me from becoming complacent. There was always a kind of dialogue going on between them. There was a feeling that they weren't entirely on each other's wavelength all the time, so you had two sides, you had a father and a mother rather than them being a unit. I think that was quite useful, it made me see two sides of everything. My father had a bad stammer, which I think has left a residue of concern in me for people who, for what I would regard as no fault of their own, do have some disability like that, which really must be quite crippling. That's something that's always been in the back of my mind, a concern for people in that same sort of situation. I didn't have a very affluent upbringing which is probably a good thing. There was always that feeling of being pushed; it was rather important that you passed your exams and got a grant and that sort of thing. My mother had a great strength and great equanimity which helped a lot, she was a real bedrock.

Another interesting thing is a comment made by Barry Took in relation to *Python*. He said I was 'an outsider' in the sense that I came from Sheffield, or words to that effect. I wasn't born and brought up in a comfortable metropolitan world in which you were expected to go on to the stage or write a book or whatever. I came from a different background and had to adjust and I think I've brought something quite fresh, in the sense that all the *Pythons* brought something fresh to our humour and we were all provincials.

You once said of your father, 'He was a difficult man who made me very unhappy when I was young.' Did you have to keep trying to prove yourself to someone who, at an early age, was perhaps not giving you any impression that you might be successful because you were having rows with him?

We didn't have rows all the time, and I have some very fond memories of him which, I suppose, is always the way. One doesn't hate somebody unequivocally and I wasn't always unhappy. There were times when I was more concerned about his lack of contact with my mother than actually about what happened to me, but I was aware – and in my sister's case it happened as well – that for some reason he was not that encouraging of what one might want to do, and certainly not very flexible about the range of options available to you in your life. It was as though his own life had not worked out quite the way he had hoped – he'd been to Cambridge and become an engineer but ended up doing a rather ordinary managerial job. So he was reluctant to accord praise either to myself or my sister, and that might have helped in making me more ambitious.

I think what it did do is to make me feel sorry for him in certain ways. I loved him as one does your parents, unless they are absolute brutes to you and he certainly wasn't that, and I loved him enough to want him to do well and I wished he had done better. I could see certain things in the way he approached his work and life which made it difficult for him. His cantankerousness would come out sometimes and I would think, 'Well, that's not the way to do it.' Maybe I learned a certain ability to compromise from that and I tried to listen to and understand other people, which is very important, too, in getting on.

So a lack of anger and ability to measure life in a calm way – it helps you in success, it helps you to be successful, to have that equanimity about you?

You're using the word 'successful' again, and I am not sure I would put it like that, but I am helped by having what they call a strong foundation, in the sense that if times are hard and difficult I have a certain self-belief which is always there somewhere, even if you've opened a play and ten out of eleven reviews have been highly critical, you have got to find somewhere to go, and I think I've got that, which I probably inherit from my mother. I do have quite a bit of anger in me and you have to learn to recognize and control it because anger is loss of control. Firmness, strength of mind, all of these other things that get close to it and determination, defiance and downright bloody-mindedness are all rather important. You can get to that level, because sometimes you have to get like that before you can get your way, but to fly off the handle – which I do every now and then – I always regret. But a certain amount of anger is all part of what makes you keep going and keep trying things.

There is a story, I think it was with Python, *that for the first time in 11 years you lost your temper and everyone applauded, everyone was so pleased to see that happen. How did that happen?*

Well, if you ask my wife she would say that it wasn't for the first time in 11 years, so John slightly exaggerated. Basically it was a scene in which I had to play the character called the Mud Eater – not a promising part to play. It was in *Monty Python and The Holy Grail* and I had to crawl across a vat of mud across the bottom of the frame while other people came in. It was all right the first two or three times, but then I said, 'That must be it, surely that's it,' and they said, 'A rather nice sun's just come out and we're just getting a nice glint off John's helmet,' so I said, 'All right, fourth time.' So I crawl across. I said, 'That must be it.' They said, 'No, no, it's just that they were too close to each other.' So the fifth take goes through, and I say, 'Right, please, that's it.' 'No, just one more, because now the clouds have come over and we've got to shoot it once more.' So we do it once more all in cloud and it was at the end of that – although I think they said John got one of his lines wrong – that I erupted. I said, 'You've got six takes, I am *not* doing any more,' and I threw myself in the air, fell in the patch of ground, wriggled over and kicked my legs in the air. There was a moment's complete silence and then there was spontaneous applause from John and Graham, who had been doing the scene. They were just overjoyed to see me in a bad mood, but it wasn't the first time in 11 years, it was probably the first time John had seen me like that in 11 years.

When was the first time in your life that you can remember saying to yourself, 'I'm a success, I have been successful at something'?

Very tricky that, because I can remember certain specific instances. There was one, it must have been the year of the Coronation, 1953. I used to do, for some reason, a series of ad-libbed performances based on the Coronation, that's all I can remember, at school during the break, and I can remember on two or three occasions just a few people came in, and then more. In the act, I improvised what would happen in the Coronation if one of the participants was taken short. It was very schoolboyish, but people found it hilarious and in the end there were 15 or 20 people crammed in this little room. I don't know if I felt successful then, but I certainly felt elated and I felt that I had done something well and people kept saying, 'Could we do some more of those?' and I think I remember saying, 'No, that's it, I've run out of material.'

Another time I suppose would be when I heard I'd got into Shrewsbury School because it was very, very important to my father that I continued the family tradition and got into Shrewsbury, and at that time it was very, very important to me as well. It was a hard exam and no one from my prep school had ever got into that school before. On the walls of the prep school dining-room were the crests of various schools that boys went on to, and a lot of them were crests that had been there a long time, but there were no Shrewsbury School crests, and when I saw the Shrewsbury School crest go up on the wall, then I knew I had been successful.

What are the main ingredients that you need to be a successful comedy writer?

Apart from a sense of humour, you've probably got to have a good ear, that's what it goes back to. What helped me in writing was the fact that I was a performer, because comedy writing is very much about the rhythm of a joke. Just one extra word, an 'a' rather than a 'the', can be crucial to the way a line works, so you have to have an ear for dialogue and for good rhythm.

Is that something you're born with or can you develop it?

I seem to remember being able to imitate other people to comic effect from very early on, so I don't know whether my parents induced that in me. My father was quite funny, but I don't think it was that, it must have been something that was in the genes somewhere, I should imagine, in the same way that other people can do calculus or whatever. I didn't really have to work at that. Maybe you can develop it, but I don't think you can. It's one of those things like acting – you've either got it or you haven't.

You can work on technique, but actually the gut feeling, which is also very important in comedy writing, is something that's deep down and that's what distinguishes average comedy writers from good ones.

If you are a good comedy writer, do you have to wait for a major catalyst, as Edinburgh was for you, or can you sit back and say, 'If I believe in myself, eventually I'll make it, I'll get that lucky break'?

No, I wish it were like that. A lot of people ask me, 'How do you do what you're doing?' I have to say that a lot of my achievement, my success if you like, comes from being in the right place at the right time, meeting the right person. A certain amount of that is to do with my own ability to make friends with certain people and to get on with certain people, but a lot of it is just other people seeing something in me. I probably wouldn't have done it on my own and I always say to anyone who asks, 'Try and get a partner, it's so important.' I have got three children, all of whom are very funny, have got great senses of humour, yet none of them as far as I know is going to be a comedy writer in quite the same way, and I'm not sure why that should be. They've got the potential there but maybe they haven't met the right person at the right time, maybe they didn't come from the right circumstances in the first place, or go through the right upbringing. Maybe they've seen what I do and decided, 'No, that's what Dad does, we don't want to try that.'

Maybe they've seen the insecurities in the job. In comedy writing you are only as good as your last joke, and when we first started writing it was a pretty grim business. You'd write 50 jokes – I was writing with Terry Jones then – in two or three days, send them all to David Frost and one would be used and that would be slightly changed, and you'd be so depressed and think, 'Maybe I can't make people laugh, maybe there's some magic thing there I don't have.' And of course that was a time when I had just got married and so the ten guineas I got paid for each joke was very important. If I only got paid ten guineas that week, that wasn't good, that wasn't going to pay the bills. If I managed to get three or four jokes accepted that was 40 guineas, that was great. If they sold it to Denmark, that was 40 guineas. So you know it was very insecure to start with and even when we did *Python* no one was quite sure where *Python* was going to go and *Python* did not pay a lot of money – it was BBC regulation fees. Then when we'd finished the *Python* series, we'd made money out of doing the books but that was about it, and that was beginning to run out and really what were we going to do after that? There was no one saying, 'Now you've done *Python*, you *will* do this, you *will* do that.' You had to sell yourself to someone else, that's always been the way.

Is that one reason why you moved into different areas?

I was aware after *Monty Python* that I couldn't go and do *Python*-style stuff again. There were two issues. One is, had we done enough *Monty Python* by that time? John would say, 'We've done enough, we can't do any more.' I would say, 'Yes, we could have done another couple of series and it would have been very funny,' but once the will's gone, then it all breaks down. All I knew was that I couldn't recreate that sort of humour at that sort of level without the other five. So I went back towards acting and something deliberately more straight which turned out to be the *Ripping Yarns* – I wanted them to be very different from *Python*. They really started the strand of slightly quirky comedy acting that I've done since then, in things like *The Missionary* and *American Friends*.

To what extent is your home life an important ingredient in your success? Some people have to make a choice between a home life, a family and their careers. Have you ever had to make that kind of a choice?

No, I don't think I have directly. I feel the greatest success is bringing up my family and keeping the family together. I don't mean that to sound like some enormous kind of struggle because it hasn't been, they're great. But it is a certain challenge and that is more important almost than anything else I do, and it's a cornerstone of the work I do and my ability to go off and do other things. If I felt I *had* let them down then I would feel a failure. I'm not saying I'm a success because I haven't let them down, but I would feel a definite failure if I had let them down, a failure greater than I would feel in any professional work I had done, so they are vitally important.

Do you think you could have achieved what you have achieved if they hadn't been there providing you with solid back-up?

That's tricky. With creative work, you don't necessarily always have to be happy to do it. I was listening to Eileen Atkins reading Virginia Woolf's diaries on Radio 4. Virginia Woolf said, 'Writers are unhappy people, people who are happy are wordless,' and then spoilt it with some slightly snobby comment about the lady at the bus stop in Potters Bar. But I know what she meant. I think you can do very good work whilst your circumstances are not necessarily very happy. You can see that in people's creative lives. Some of them have very unhappy domestic lives, very unhappy relationships and still come out with brilliant plays and brilliant bits of writing.

I am not sure if it's like that with comedy writing. You've got to have a dark streak, but you've also got to be fairly amenable to the world, because that's what comedy is about. I'm not saying that I wouldn't have written something very good if I didn't have the family, that's not the question. The answer is the family was more important to me than anything I wrote, which is probably a daft thing to say, but it is.

What have been your biggest failures and how did you recover from them?

Some of them I have probably expunged from my memory as one does, something that's been so awful, but I have had to deal in the last two or three years with something that was judged a failure in the most brutal way possible, which is a play called *The Weekend.* I don't regard it as a failure, and that's not just writer's oh-the-critics-have-got-it-wrong attitude. I think there were certain reasons why it didn't work as well as it should have worked. Be that as it may, the play opened in the West End and was gunned down by the critics and when things appear in the papers which basically say, 'You've no talent at all for this sort of thing,' then you have to deal with that as best you can. I find that I cannot deal with it by ignoring it – I think that's very dangerous. People say they don't read the critics, they don't talk to anybody – that, I think, is almost inconceivable. You are in the public arena, writing something about life, and you've got to know how life itself responds to what you have done. So I think it's just very, very important to get down to the basis of what people are saying and why they're saying it. I didn't shrink from reading the reviews – even though I read them at a distance to start with!

And this was something you had put a lot of effort into?

Not enough effort, which is probably part of the reason why it didn't work, but that's another matter. But yes, I had invested a lot of effort over the previous few months putting it all together. All I'm saying is that it was a play that had been around for about ten years or so and that maybe I should have done extra work on it, but be that as it may, I had worked very hard up to that date, and also I felt very responsible for a group of people – maybe ten people in the cast and 15 or 20 others. I felt, 'The last thing I can do is disappear, I've got to go and face them.' So I went straight back the night after the reviews and we talked it through and we had a great party two nights afterwards and decided, 'What the hell, we all liked doing it, we are going to make the best of it.' So that was my way of dealing with it.

You accepted that the critics were right. You didn't say, 'They're wrong and we're going to drive this through.' If you're doing something artistic and in the public eye, do you have to accept the majority view of the critics?

I certainly think you have to give the critics due regard. It's like an article in the newspaper. You may say it's just a critic's view, but it's an article that has your name at the top and it has things about you which if you read in the *News of the World* you would say, 'God, how dare people say that,' so yes, you have to have some due regard for what they say.

In this particular case I felt they were half-right, there were things they put their fingers on that were wrong with the work, and I learned from that and that's terrific. I've found throughout my career that certain critics know what they're doing and they are very skilful practitioners of the art, they know their terms of reference and they're generous and supportive of the particular kind of area you are working in. So 50 per cent are fine, from the other 50 per cent I think I was being given a bit of a slap on the wrist for things that were slightly beyond my control, viz my perceived success in other areas, and that attitude, 'Look, he's done a television documentary, he's done plenty of things, come on, what more do you want? Don't just walk in here to our little club called the West End Theatre and think you can just do it by putting your name to a piece of paper,' and that was hard. There's a bit of envy in that which I could cope with, which helped me understand it. But it's still hard and still makes you very frustrated and potentially very angry.

You addressed the problem with the party two days later, but how did you turn yourself around to say, 'I will move on to my next challenge'?

It was difficult because I was actually writing a novel at the time and that really did suffer, I just couldn't concentrate on it. My mind was always on those people going into the theatre every night and doing their bit, saying my words and all that sort of thing. So the way I dealt with it, I tried to write and I thought, 'No, this is ridiculous, I'm not going to be able to get this done,' so for a while I just faced up to what was going on. I used to ring the theatre and talk about the returns the night before, attendances and all that, and of course they were often very much better than you thought they'd be, sometimes they were worse, and really I think all my energies at that time were directed to seeing that the play completed its run, that people knew it was a good play, that we made the best of the good things that were said about us, so I would do a bit of extra advertising, that sort of thing.

The family were very important there because my wife, not being in the theatre, or even in show business, said, 'Why do you let it worry you, there are far worse things going on, people are having a terrible time.' She's a bereavement counsellor and she said, 'I've been meeting people who are almost terminally unhappy and you are just unhappy because you don't get 100 per cent audiences every night.' So that was important, and also the other thing was that I do have a group of very good friends, mainly the *Python* team and one or two others who are very good critics. I am very glad that those friendships remained in place and they could say they didn't like the play and we could talk about what they didn't like, but it was very important to have opinions from people whom I respected very much because of what they had done as well.

In Monty Python *you had jokes about some people who had failed. Were you able to laugh at yourself over the fate of your play, or was it particularly difficult because for the first time you were being affected by what some perceived to be a major failure?*

I'd like to think I didn't lose my sense of humour. It was under stress at that time, but I always had not only my own family but also friends who I could go out with, and we could laugh about whatever we wanted to laugh about. It's like the Londoners laughing during the Blitz, the war spirit, it's very good, and with the cast and crew we had a wonderful time and I think our relationship was as good because the play was deemed a failure by the critics, as it would have been if it had been deemed a great success. It's an odd thing, but that's what happened and I think that's directly because we chose a good cast and because everybody fought together. We all said, 'We'll do the best we can,' and that's important.

Does discipline play an important part in success?

It does with me, yes. I don't think it's everything, but you may have the most brilliant thoughts in the world and write the best jokes, and if there isn't someone there telling you you've got to have them delivered by a certain time, you have to have the book in the shop by a certain time, you've got to have your photocover done at a certain time, it won't happen. Those things may irritate you but they are very much a part of it.

Do you think there is a very fine line between failure and success?

I think if you are serious about what you are doing and if you are anxious to get it right and if you're a near-perfectionist – which I think most very successful people probably are – then there is a fine line, because you can always see a way of doing something better, and also when you do get a little setback you do feel, 'Now how could I have avoided that, why did that happen?'

There was one occasion when we had made the film *Monty Python's Life of Brian* and had run into some fairly predictable flack from some Church groups, and John Cleese and myself were asked to go on television to debate the pros and cons of the film with Mervyn Stockwood, then Bishop of Southwark, and Malcolm Muggeridge, chaired by Tim Rice. We worked very hard, because we took it quite seriously, but we knew we were going to get some trouble and we had to work out our ground – that the film was not directed against someone's faith, it was against the authoritarian nature of the Church through the ages, etc., arguments that we had worked up and believed in. When we got there we found we were completely bamboozled by Muggeridge and Stockwood, who were both extremely skilful television performers and really played to the audience. I think the idea of a bishop getting the better of the *Monty Python* people seemed to work very well.

I remember thinking, 'This is terrible,' and I was so frustrated, we couldn't put across our points, although John had got in some quite good lines. It was very interesting because at the very end Mervyn Stockwood said something to us, on camera, which was to the effect, 'Well, I hope you make your 30 pieces of silver,' and you could feel the audience just go, there was a silence. They had taken his jokes up till then, but that was one attempted gag too many and it was very interesting to see a bishop censored, if you like, by probably a very secular congregation. It was as if he'd stepped out of line. So I came out of that studio quite shaken up; it was certainly not what we had expected.

Did you think that you had blown a bit of your reputation, as it were?

I felt it was under review. There were people who wanted to say we had all gone too far. But when you are writing comedy which is as thought-provoking and as irreverent as *Python* was, that's just an occupational hazard – I wasn't too worried about that.

Did you think that success should be thought-provoking?

Pretty much so, because comedy generally is a reaction against something. It's not just an underlining of something, it has to have a point of view. You make a joke usually because you are in a situation where for some reason something has gone wrong or there's some tension. That's usually what jokes are about, it's about a situation you have trouble dealing with except by making a joke, so I think comedy is about conflict most of the time.

So it's always testing the boundaries of life?

It's a way of testing the boundaries of life. You don't have to. You wouldn't say that *Dad's Army* was ever testing the boundaries of life and yet it's extremely funny – but that's using conflict very well between the characters, you like all the characters and it's not really saying the F-word or showing anything really rude, that wasn't what it was about. I think sometimes comedy is a way of stepping up to the barrier and having a look over, because taboos are only set up by a kind of cultural consensus and that has to be continually reviewed, and I think people are perhaps saying things about the Church now that we would barely have dared to have said in *The Life of Brian*.

Good comedy has to have a bit of a shock, a bit of a kick in it really. The surprise element is very important and either you get that just from creating good characters who sort of bounce off each other, or you have to step off-line and say, 'Look, we are going to have to talk about something which other people don't talk about.' If, on the other hand, that's *all* you do, I think that becomes fairly boring.

Who are your heroes in any field?

I have a fondness for those great explorers, some of them misguided perhaps, but their courage was always something which struck me very, very forcibly. People like Captain Scott and the travellers who went through the North-West Passage, and I suppose even lone yachtsmen, someone like Sir Francis Chichester. When you actually think what he did and when he did it – I have always admired him because I know that it was incredibly difficult. I would never have had the courage to do that. And to do it, let alone come back and retain a certain amount of composure at the end of it.

In my own field, in comedy and acting, well there are all sorts of people. I would say, as script writers, Galton and Simpson, as actors, people like John Le Mésurier, whom I always thought was a wonderful actor, and Peter Cook as a writer and performer. It's quite a long list. Spike Milligan at his best. Then I suppose, I admire people like David Attenborough in the best possible way. I know him reasonably well and David always seems to be one of those people who does what he does with enormous skill and efficiency and without ever becoming prey to his own reputation. He is enormously popular, he is enormously successful, but always seems to be exactly the same whenever I meet him – the same curiosity about everything, the same bustle, the same sense of wanting to listen to everything and talk about everything, and that's good.

Is success in your field becoming more or less difficult to achieve now?

I think the terms or the definitions of success change. I suppose you could say when we – and I use 'we' meaning the *Python* people and Terry and Robert Hewison and all the people who left Oxford in the mid-1960s – when we were coming out there were, as far as I can remember, two or maybe three television channels, and that was it really. Now you could say that that made it much harder to be successful. You could say it was easier to be successful because you needed fewer people, whereas nowadays there are many more areas in which aspiring comedians can come before the public, like pub theatres and all that, which are a much bigger thing than they ever were. Then, there are also many more television channels and there are going to be many more as we go on. So in a sense, I think it's become easier in one way, in terms of the amount of access available to people, access to the public, but more difficult in the sense that I have the feeling now – and that may just be me being an old 53-year-old – that there are fewer special performers than there were.

If you think back to the *Dad's Army* performers, if you think back to Tony Hancock or *Steptoe and Son*, there was something very, very special. You watched them and they were not comparable with anybody else. It seems there are a lot of people now who are comparable with each other, a lot of whose comedy seems to be based on parody, pure and simple. I think there are fewer of those unique performers than there used to be in the old days, and I am not quite sure why that is. I think it's partly that people are more sophisticated nowadays, techniques available to people are more sophisticated. When we did *Monty Python*, Terry Gilliam had to do his animation by cutting things out by hand, which was amazingly successful – that was the basis of his technique. Now he'd probably have a computer screen, he'd be able to do full, moving animation, and I don't know if that would be as good because he wouldn't have to think quite as hard. That's the sort of area where I think technology doesn't always improve comedy.

Has success changed you?

Well, I've got a bigger office, I've got a very big office. The financial side of success in the sense that I am pretty comfortably off, that's great, I think that probably makes life a lot easier, it takes away a level of tension, but on the other hand, all the other problems are still there. With the family, there's always problems amongst us, there are always things that happen, your children and what they feel about you and all that sort of thing, those sort of considerations are still the same. I would say that I have not really made any quantum leaps in my circumstances over the last 30 years since I became 'successful'. I am still living in the same area, the same house, I've added two more on to it but it is still the same house.

You've bought up the rest of the street rather than move!

Well, they were quite small.

What are your ambitions in the material world?

I always have this vision of rescuing some ancient monastery which Cromwell didn't totally flatten and having it rebuilt by really good craftsmen. I am very interested in history still, despite having read it at Oxford. I am interested in that area of living history. I love good work, good craftsmanship and skill in any area and I would love to be able to be the cause of getting a group of craftsmen together to produce something of beauty.

What is the greatest pleasure you have had from your success?

Time, being able to afford time to pick and choose what I really want to do rather than being forced into it by circumstances. It's given me freedom. That freedom is not a freedom of material worth particularly, it's just a freedom to run my own life with minimum interference. I do what I do because I want to do it.

There are also other benefits which only come when you have achieved a certain status, and you are, in some cases, actually able to help people or affect something absolutely directly, which you would not have been able to do before.

An example in my case was as a result of the controversy if you like or the debate about the character I played in the film *A Fish Called Wanda*, who had a stammer. The question then arose whether a stammer should be portrayed on the screen. I was given the chance actually to help people who help stammerers and that's what I dearly wanted when my father was alive. I wanted someone to come along and help him and he'd obviously had various kinds of therapy and they hadn't worked.

I was put in touch with a therapist in London whom I liked very much and admired very much and they were starting a centre particularly to help children from any age, from about four to 14, which is the age where stammering can, if not be cured then certainly be alleviated. I said, 'If there's anything I can do, let me know,' and it's grown out of all proportion into a centre which is being called The Michael Palin Stammering Centre. And because of my name, it was able to attract publicity and help attract some money – along with other people – which has made that a success beyond their wildest dreams. It's up and running as a very efficient unit, and I would say that without my having had the chance to be in a major motion picture and to play a character who stammered, and an ability to attract publicity, that wouldn't have happened.

It's very often how things do happen, you'll stir something up and it forces you to give an account of yourself. I had to sort of think, 'Why did I play this character, did it give offence, and should I have done it?' – all that sort of thing, so in a sense because I talked it through and had a kind of debate with myself and others, that's how it got the publicity. So perhaps I am not so surprised, but it is certainly one thing about having the status of a successful person, and the money that goes with it, that you can help out in a particular area. I have been able to help out in other areas as well.

What other areas?

Well, I don't really talk about specific charities which I help, but I've put quite a bit of money into organizations for the homeless in London because I see people sleeping on the street and sleeping rough and generally I feel that most of the people there shouldn't be there, and if you have ever talked to them they are actually quite intelligent, sensible people who have just taken a wrong turning at some point. So if I have been able to help out at least they can be put in a hostel and given a chance to sort themselves out. That's one aspect of success.

You clearly do that because you want to do it, but do you think there is an obligation on people who have been successful to put something back into society?

If you believe in society, which I do, I think there is an obligation. I can't see any other way of behaving. If you've had some good luck and good fortune, I think it's important to share it in whatever way you can with the people around you. That is what life is – we are not an island, we are not separate individuals living vacuum-packed lives, we need all those people around us, or I feel we do anyway. If we can raise everybody's level of success or material welfare, then life will be that much better. I think it's a natural obligation.

If you could gather together in one room all the young people in the world who want to be as successful as you have become, what advice would you give them?

You have to be prepared to take on a task and see it through, that's vital even if sometimes it's not exactly what you want to do. Once you have decided, you have to follow through the consequences of that decision. If asked I would say to any group of people, 'Remember who you are, you are different from the person to the left, the person to the right, the person behind you and the person in front of you. There are things about you that are particular and are special, and you've got to find out what those are and you have always got to remember that this is something that only you can do.

But on top of that are there any core principles that can apply to a lot of people?

737

Well, again, slightly reiterating what I've said, 'Listen to people', I think listening is very important. You may think you know what you want, but one of the best things you can do is to find out from other people what they've done and how they've done it. Learn by example. The other thing is never to be too proud to go and do anything. You've actually got to go and get your feet dirty, your hands dirty, your whole body dirty if necessary, if you are going to find out what you can do, so never look down your nose at anything or anybody, especially anybody, because in the end they'll come back and kick you up the arse, just when you think you've got rid of them. And I suppose another main thing is you've got to be persistent, you've actually got to be able to say, 'Well that's a setback but I'm still going ahead.' You mustn't give up too early, well, you mustn't give up, ever.

When your time comes to leave this life, what would you like people to say about Michael Palin?

I was going to have on my gravestone, 'Michael Palin, he was good but not that good.'

NICK PARK

There is an air of perpetual surprise about the man who created Wallace and Gromit and went on to win an unprecedented three Hollywood Oscars for the ground-breaking animated films Creature Comforts, The Wrong Trousers *and* A Close Shave. *'I didn't think that somebody like me, from Preston, could get into films or television. I actually settled for the fact that animation would become my hobby.' Brought up in an artistic family, the middle of five children, his father was a professional photographer keen on woodwork, while his mother made all their clothes. 'We spent our time creating things out of papier mâché.' Hopeless at anything academic, he excelled at art, and wrote stories that made people laugh, but, he says, 'I don't know what I'd have done if I hadn't discovered my parents had a home-movie camera which had a single frame button on it.' He spent every spare second drawing, modelling and filming with that camera 'instead of playing with friends or watching TV'.*

When he was 14, a teacher got to hear about the films and showed them at school. 'They went down so well, I couldn't believe it.' The recognition he so badly wanted had begun. After that came art college and the big break, when he was invited to join Aardman Animations in Bristol. He talks here about the sacrifices during the six years it took to make A Grand Day Out, *including his time on the dole; and the 'incredible, frightening experience' of winning the first of his three Oscars. He explains why he resisted huge offers from Disney, Spielberg and Warner – 'It's important to work in Bristol rather than Hollywood, so we have this feeling we're making our films on our terms.' As for the rules for becoming a successful animator, 'It's dangerous to think there are any. You've got to start off copying other people, but you find your own style and uniqueness.' With his kind of animation, painstakingly making just two or three frames a day, 'You've got to go for it in one take. I like the spontaneity and improvisation that it brings – the make or break feeling.' There is no resting on laurels – 'As soon as I feel that I've reached an acceptable level, I get worried and think, "No, I've got to keep moving forward."' And above all, you've got to 'do what you do with integrity'.*

Nick Park, what is your definition of success?

My definition of success! The reason I find it difficult to answer is partly because, ultimately, I don't have a definition. I tend to try to avoid all definitions of success. If there's one that everybody agrees on it's probably wrong, and if there's a common idea of success out there, my normal reaction would be, 'I don't want it.' But for me personally, I would regard success, both as a human being and as a film-maker, as doing what I'm doing with integrity.

Is success related to a degree of achievement?

Yes. I think you could actually start to define success in terms of achieving a short-term goal, and achieving that goal successfully. For me, with making the Wallace and Gromit films, success was about whether I could pull that off and make each film work successfully. I have to somehow be convinced that it works. I'm glad that the films, so far, have been well received by the public and that's been an indication of their success, but I think if the films didn't work for me personally, then I couldn't consider them a success. One can do things that are popular and which are seen as successful in the eyes of the world, but unless I was convinced that I had done my best in it, for me it could not be seen as successful. It is also important that everything I do is done with integrity.

Did you set out to be a success or did success creep up and take you over?

I do find it odd to talk about success, because it's not something that's ever been in my vocabulary, especially with regard to my career. I think I come across to a lot of people as being very humble and self-effacing, but deep-down I am actually quite an ambitious person and I have been since I was a child. When I was younger I never had the concentration needed for maths and English, and all those academic subjects, the one thing I really did score on was art. I really excelled in it. I think it was partly a way of getting noticed.

Was that the only area in which you excelled?

I was utterly hopeless at anything academic. As I said, I failed miserably at maths and English, and although I enjoyed some of the subjects like French, geography and history, I didn't do very well at them. I couldn't write properly, I couldn't construct sentences and I couldn't put figures together. I just had a blindness towards academic subjects. It might be laziness, I don't know, but I know I did so badly that I had no confidence in them at all. But I was always recognized as an artist, I didn't even have to try, and when I was first making films – when I was 13 or thereabouts – it suddenly became something that made me feel very special. I didn't really tell anybody that I was doing it, it's always been the sort of thing I've let people find out for themselves. I don't know whether it's a result of my upbringing, but I've never really gone out to sell myself to anybody. I'd rather do things and let people see them, and that's just the way it's worked, and I feel very fortunate that that's the way it has worked.

You've talked about being both self-effacing and ambitious. Have there been times when those two were really struggling against each other within you?

Yes. I have had a bit of a dilemma. I've faced this tension all my life. I've always wanted to be noticed and because I was a rather shy and quiet person at school I wasn't really noticed very much, but being a film-maker and making cartoons elevated my standing in people's estimation. Despite the shyness, I think I always had a strong sense of drive towards art and a strong will to succeed. I remember as a child seeing a documentary about Walt Disney and how it started off with him drawing this little mouse character. At the time I was drawing my own characters in my school notepads. I used to daydream, as I suppose everybody does, about becoming the next great tennis player, or whatever. I used to think that one day I could have my characters known by the public, and what a thrill that would be. I dreamed about this a lot, going back to 11 or 12. But I didn't tell anybody. I kept it to myself – I think because I've just always thought that you're not supposed to sell yourself or boast.

What made you think that?

I don't know. I thought it was wrong, maybe it's something to do with coming from a Catholic family or guilt – I don't know. My family were never ones for pushing themselves. It was part of the whole ethos that comes from the culture of my own family.

To what extent has your family played a part in your success?

A great deal. I was brought up in a family with five children, of which I'm the middle one. Both my mother and father are artistic. My father has been a professional photographer – he's retired now – and he also does a lot of woodwork. My mother always used to make our clothes when we were children.

So one can see how those two things would have been passed onto you. The love of both would have gelled in you and given you your interest?

Yes. I don't remember being bored once as a child because there was always something to do on rainy days. There were always plenty of materials – paper, paints, everything. We just spent our time creating things out of *papier mâché* and all sorts of other things. We had a very active childhood. On television, I was always attracted to the creative programmes like *Vision On, Blue Peter,* and things like that. I used to get home from school and after doing my homework I would go straight into the attic to do some more filming. I always remember pushing. I used to think to myself, 'If I don't discipline myself and don't sacrifice myself to this, then I won't ever get anywhere with it.'

So a degree of sacrifice is an important part of a person's development?

Yes. I hear sports people talking about their commitment to training, and for me it was a similar kind of process. It would have been far easier for me to go off and play with my friends after school and what have you, but as I said before, I used to think to myself, 'If I don't work for this, then I won't get anywhere. And if I sit and watch television all evening I won't achieve anything' – that was when I was 12 or 13. I used to, quite painfully sometimes, pull myself away from the television and go upstairs and start drawing, modelling and filming with my cine camera. I made about half a dozen or more films whilst I was at school – each were a couple of minutes long.

Was that unusual for you to have that degree of determination so early? Can you identify the quality that gave you that?

I sometimes think that part of it might have been a way of trying to be recognized, because at school I wasn't. Back in those days you had to be good at sport, or academically good at something, to get some kind of recognition. And I think part of it was just that: me wanting to be recognized. But then again that's somewhat contradictory because I didn't tell anybody. I don't know quite what the answer is myself.

Why didn't you tell anybody about it? Were you afraid that people might think, 'Animation is for cissies,' or something like that?

Not at all. I just didn't think anybody would be interested, to tell you the truth. I admit, it was a very strange thing to do because I was the only person in our school out of 1,100 kids that did animation. There were no natural causes or influences, there wasn't an animation club or anything like that. I often wonder what I would have done if I hadn't discovered that my parents had a home-movie camera which had a single-frame button on it; I just happened to start experimenting with it. I was already drawing cartoons and watching Ray Harryhausen films on the television. I had a great fascination with cartoons, with drama or with anything performance-related. I really used to love reading my stories out in class at school, especially if they made people laugh.

From what sort of age were you writing these stories?

Well, this was at secondary school, between 11 and 16. If our homework was to write a story about a certain thing, I would usually try to put a strong element of comedy in it, which didn't always go down too well with the teachers. I once made the mistake of writing a limerick. We had to write a poem and I wrote a limerick about each of the teachers. We had this nun who was a very strict teacher – it was a Catholic school – and I remember her taking me aside to tell me off for writing these. She was trying to hold back her laughter while telling me off.

So it was a ticking-off, but you thought, 'Hang on, I'm getting the green light for this as well'?

That's right, yes. I remember other stories that I wrote which had the class in raptures, and that goes back to primary school. I remember one teacher reading my story out in class with tears of laughter running down her face. However, I never scored very well at English, because my grammar just wasn't very good, but I had the ideas – well, silly ideas. I loved that laughter, that's what spurred me on. I found receiving that kind of approval very satisfying.

And the idea of combining that approval with your pictures obviously evolved very rapidly?

It did, yes. It's funny though, art was not a popular subject at school, and was certainly not a subject you would have chosen if you wanted to achieve fame.

Was there a point where you thought to yourself, 'Well, I enjoy this and I'm good at it, but, frankly, I haven't a cat's chance in hell, so I'll go down another particular career route'?

No. I remember considering other things because I didn't think that somebody like me, from Preston, could actually get into the media, into television, and least of all into films. It was too much of a fantasy.

Why was it too much of a fantasy?

Well, because people from Preston didn't go into jobs like that. Maybe this is just a Northern thing, but you just thought that people in the South do that, you've got to live in London or Hollywood. I suppose regional television companies weren't so common in those days either, there was Granada in Manchester and that was the only one I'd ever really heard of. Plus, I always associated the media with glamour – I saw my first prospectus for a college course in film studies or television which showed a student holding a camera. I remember thinking that it just looked above me in terms of what I could do as a career. I actually settled for the fact that it would become a hobby.

My family, going back to my granny, had a philosophy that if you have a gift you should use it. That penetrated into all kinds of areas. It started when my closest friends knew about my hobby. One of them happened to mention it to my English teacher called Mr Kelly – this was in the fourth year. He insisted that I showed my films to the school, and I thought it was fantastic. But it was something I would never have volunteered to do at all. I only did it because I was pushed, but I was glad that I was.

Was that moment a catalyst in your life?

Yes, it was. The films were shown to half of my year and they went down so well I couldn't believe it – I was only about 14 and I'd only made about three or four very short films, which were so ropy and bad. Everyone was just so impressed by them. It was the start of me accepting the fact that something special was going on. Up till that moment I had always been so self-effacing and shy that I couldn't imagine being up there in front of other people and being looked up to for having a special gift. I was always far happier for that to remain a fantasy. I've found that in every stage of my life there's been a need to come to terms with the fact that this is a reality. I've always found that I looked up to the world around me and every step of my life has seen the world coming down to my level. I now realize that people are only people.

Tell me the story of your very first film, which got lost.

I used to draw cartoons in the back of my school notepads, and make flip-books. What you do is you get a notepad and you draw a character. You start at the back, because then it's easier to trace through, and you can then put the next piece of paper over the last one, and trace through, making it slightly different. Then lay the next piece of paper on that one, and trace that one and make it slightly different and so on. You're left with a progression of very slightly different drawings, and when you flick through it, you can see your drawings moving like a cartoon. It only lasts for about a second, depending on how many drawings you do, and I decided to make a film in that way. It took me about two weeks to make. It was my first-ever character, and I used to think that this would be the character that would make me famous. It was called Walter the Rat and he had a particular weakness for cider. The story was Walter the Rat walks on to the scene, picks up a bottle of cider, swigs it and falls over. It took me about two weeks to do. I filmed it all in single-frame, and sent it off to the labs – it never came back.

Is it frustrating that you can't really judge whether something is going to work until you've actually gone to the painstaking trouble of constructing a sequence, or do you know beforehand?

I owe a lot of my success to the fact that I started very young, because that's given me a lot of confidence. Students who haven't done animation before they get to college are often daunted by the equipment and the thought of doing it. They hear about how painstaking it is, and have a go at it in a frightened sort of way. It takes them a long time to get past that.

I must have been born with a camera in my hands, and that has really helped, because it's meant that I've gone at it in an aggressive way. Just the way Wallace's mouth moves is, if I can say it myself, quite daring. That's partly why Wallace and Gromit have got such a profile, because I've tried to be as daring as possible. I'm the kind of person who pushes himself. As soon as I feel that I've reached an acceptable level, I get worried and think, 'No, I've got to keep moving forwards.'

So because of your experience, you do know whether something's going to work?

Yes, because through experience I have the confidence that it's going to work. Another quality of this kind of animation is spontaneity, which is an intrinsic kind of quality that happens while you're working. You're working with a figure in front of the camera, filming frame by frame, and even though it's a very slow and painstaking process, you are producing a performance that you can't repeat twice. It's unlike a lot of other techniques – cel-drawn animation, for example, where you always have the chance to shoot something again or adjust the drawings. With this kind of animation you've got to go for it in one take. I like the spontaneity and improvisation that it brings, it's quite exciting this make-or-break feeling you have all the time. It's very much like a performance.

Do you have to take risks in order to be successful?

Yes. One of the things I hate most is blandness. That's my major challenge, the enemy I'm fighting all the time – I hope that no one can ever accuse me of being bland.

Why do you think that Wallace and Gromit are successful as characters?

It's very hard for me to answer this one, as I have such a hand in creating them, but I think they hit a nerve with people, they strike a chord.

One of your colleagues once said the films don't patronize children or pander to adults. Do you think that's part of it?

Yes. I know that they've become very commercially viable, but I do think of my audience, and I try to be aware of their needs – as to whether the film works or not. I'm constantly trying to think of ways I can communicate with them better and make them laugh more. But, when all is said and done, I think it's really myself that I have to please.

So a lot of your success depends on you having the same sense of humour as the viewing public?

Yes, but I don't know where that comes from, because I don't rationalize it. I don't calculate what the public want this year. I think what I am in touch with is what *I* used to like as a child and there are some things, I think, that don't change. I remember very clearly what I used to like on television and what I didn't like. This was my main reference point for ideas whilst I was at college. I used to think of the things I really liked, not in any rational way, but I would try to sieve those things out and make something of my own out of the best bits.

How much dedication is needed to be an animator? You once said that you nearly killed yourself on The Wrong Trousers.

You need an enormous amount of dedication.

Give me some idea of the sacrifices in your lifestyle that you might have to make, the hours of work put in, to be a successful animator.

Well, *A Grand Day Out* took me six years to make. It was very much a single-handed project and it was very hard to find people who would stay around long enough. I remember looking for help on the course at the National Film and Television School. I needed a lighting cameraman. Someone helped me for a few months, but it was very hard to find people who would be around long enough, they all kept graduating. I had to learn the craft of lighting myself and ended up having to do nearly everything myself, except for the sound, the music and, at the end, the editing. I made the film between the ages of 23 and 29. I was learning such a lot and growing up in such a lot of ways at that point. I went through such ups-and-downs, but funnily enough I never felt like giving up on it. I often got depressed. I was signing on the dole for some of the time and had very little money. I lived in Cricklewood, which was quite depressing – but I never actually felt like giving up on the film itself. The best thing that ever happened was when I was offered work in Bristol, with Aardman Animations, by Lord and Sproxton, who came to talk at the Film School one day. They saw my work, invited me back, and offered to help me finish the film as well. But even working professionally with a team requires an enormous amount of effort. We keep thinking that every job is going to get easier, yet we always end up working until midnight. We make a living from television commercials and independent films for Channel 4 and the BBC. They don't really pay, unless it's Wallace and Gromit now. But with television commercials there's always a deadline and we always end up working way into the night for weeks on end. There's never a way round it. Throwing more people on to it doesn't really make it quicker.

You talked about getting depressed in those early days on your first big film. How did you counter that? Do you have a technique, or is there anything you say to yourself?

It's an attitude that I haven't had to develop, it's just come naturally to me, and that is because I felt I was working on something that was very special and which people hadn't seen before, and that when it was finished it was going to knock people's socks off. I believed all the way through that it was going to be good. I did have some doubts, especially as I started to finish it – as I reached the stages where I couldn't change it any more. I'm terrible at committing myself to a particular idea. I always like things to stay open for as long as possible. You get all sorts of doubts when more people come on board and start to criticize it and help you to get it better. You can easily start to lose confidence in your own humour and your own ideas, because you've got so many people suggesting things from different angles.

Do you resent, in any way, having to surrender a degree of control, when other people come in to take over bits of the project, or do you say to yourself, 'However many people come in, I'm going to stay at the sharp end,' actually controlling and nudging and guiding wherever possible?

I do find it very difficult to delegate, especially with something like Wallace and Gromit. It goes back to my college days. I feel as though I've developed them myself from nothing to what they are now. They're my babies and I find it very hard to let go and trust other people with them, although now we have got some very good animators and model-makers who I have a lot more confidence in.

I've found it hard to come to terms with being a central figure. I've always been a struggling artist working on my own, and to go from that to having everybody wanting to do whatever I want was hard for me to get used to – actually giving people directions and trusting them. It took me a long time to trust other people, but it's worked really well, because this method of animation, unlike cartoon animation, doesn't have a tradition of a production-line technique, it's hand-made animation and each figure is animated by one person.

So you don't mind any more the fact that it is, as I think you almost put it, made in a more industrial way?

Industrial is perhaps too strong a word for it, but it's much more industrial than anything that's been done before. I don't want to spend another six years making a film – delegating is less painful.

What did you feel when you'd found that you'd won your first Oscar?

It was an incredibly frightening experience. I felt like a fish out of water there. I was incredibly thrilled, you know, just with the prestige value of being nominated. I was completely unknown at that time – about five or six years ago – and I suddenly had two finished films that were both nominated for an Oscar. It made a big splash for me, I felt really thrilled about it, but I didn't feel as though I belonged. I found having to go through all the stardom type things very frightening. On top of that, I was just so nervous, with my heart in my throat, that I thought 'I'm not going to get up to the stage if I do win. I'm going to faint or something, on the way up.'

Now that you've won it three times, are you more blasé about it?

I'm not sure if blasé is the right word, I hope not. I'm still very thrilled about the whole thing. I must admit last time was very different.

In what way?

Well, it's hard not to sound conceited or as if I expected it. I didn't expect it. I had to fight off any thoughts of expecting it. Lots of people say to you all the time, 'You're going to win, we think you're going to win' – and people who like the film are bound to say that. There are these contrasting emotions between knowing that you might have won and coping with the prospect of giving a speech in front of a billion people, and having to sit there and applaud somebody else, you've got to be ready for both at the same time, and I found myself so tense, trying to cope with being pulled in all those different directions, it's hard to try and keep it all in perspective in your own mind and say to yourself, 'If you don't win it doesn't matter, you've got two already.'

Your trio of Oscars have brought huge offers from Disney, from Spielberg, Warner Brothers, Fox, Turner. Why have you resisted those?

When they first came to us it was very thrilling. We've wanted to make feature films for a long time, long before anybody approached us, but we resisted the offers so that we could keep control of our ideas. When we go into a meeting with a large studio the first question is, 'Is it a musical?' We don't want to make a musical and we don't want to make a film for Hollywood. It seems like we will need a Hollywood-style budget because animation's so expensive, but we want to be in a situation where we're being commissioned to make our own film on our own terms. We've found a backer who's independent from Hollywood. His name is Jake Eberts. He was with Goldcrest Films many years ago, and he's come in with us to develop the film so that we can get it to a stage where we feel really happy with it, and then we can approach some of the studios and say, 'This is the film we want to make, do you want to come in with us?' That would be a far more ideal situation than if we had to make somebody else's film.

But you're not prepared to compromise for other markets and tweak your characters or your story-lines in order to satisfy other markets in different parts of the world? You want to do something that is intrinsically British?

Yes. We could go off to America and make a film there, but the people who we've been talking to, and that includes Disney and Steven Spielberg, seem to understand that Bristol's the right place for us to work – they'd be shooting themselves in the foot to take us over there. It's understandable, if someone's giving you a lot of money to make a film, that they want to have a say in how it's made. They're going to be concerned about the marketplace, they'll believe that they know it better than us, which is probably right. It's very hard for us to argue against them. I'm sure in the future that we're going to get into arguments about how old our lead characters are, whether they have American voices, etc. I'm sure we are going to have to fight that one.

But you will fight to do what you want?

Absolutely. We believe it's important that we make the films from Britain. It's important that we work in Bristol, just psychologically, so that we're not in Hollywood, so that we're separate and have this feeling that we're making what is our film on our terms.

And your success with the three Oscars has given you the bottle and the financial security to be able to say that?

Yes. The Oscars themselves are a mark of success. They certainly help in our talks with studios and when we talk finance with people. If you can put an Oscar, or three, on the table, not only do you have a signal of achievement from within the industry, but a product that is going to be recognized by the public worldwide.

You once said, 'I find marketing a moral dilemma.' What do you mean by that when it comes to marketing the characters from Wallace and Gromit?

First of all, I'm always a bit cautious of over-exposure. I can think of all the things I've got so tired of, simply because they are around us all the time. I'm nervous of Wallace and Gromit going down that track. I don't really want to give people the chance to get tired of them. Also, I suppose I feel like I'm more interested in making films than in merchandising characters, although I must admit that I've always longed to have characters that people know. At the same time, although our production company can survive off television commercials, it's good to have something else that can bring in money as well, that can allow us to make more films and to have more control over what we're doing. I'm not completely against merchandising, I just don't want to fill the world with rubbish. I don't want Wallace and Gromit to become a way of making a fast buck.

How do you come up with good ideas? What makes an idea for a good piece of animation click? What makes it successful?

I don't know. As far as I'm concerned, it's just whatever makes me laugh. I really have to feel it's good, deep-down; I have to measure things internally. I often need time to consider things, to feel really good about them, before I do anything. I think ideas have to mature. You think of something, you let it stand for a while, you turn it over in the back of your mind, and you suddenly come up with something else. You think of it in a slightly different way and you think, 'Yes, that's it.' But where ideas come from exactly, I don't know.

But are there any rules for making a successful animation film?

No. That's the danger. If there were rules you'd be able to do it again and again.

What do you regard as your biggest failures, and how did you recover from them?

In my career, I haven't really had any. I'm very lucky.

Has your personal life had to pay any price for your success?

Yes. Relationships might have worked out better, although I can't blame the film world for that. I think what's happened has happened for a reason. Even though I'm single, I've always been much more committed to work. I'd like to have met the right person and settled down, but I get quite dedicated and committed to the filming. I suppose I'm married to my work in many ways – although it's no substitute.

And you feel the degree of work that you take upon yourself has made it very difficult for someone who doesn't fully understand you to come alongside you?

I think so, yes. I've had relationships with very nice girls, but there has been a certain incompatibility because of the work, and because of the nature of the work.

Do you think that every successful person has some kind of a conflict at some stage, between their professional life and their personal life?

I think so. Being an artist is not a nine-to-five job. You can't stop at six o'clock, although I must admit that nowadays I treat my time as very important – I like to be alone, especially when I'm directing seven or eight units at once with a crew of 40, as on *A Close Shave*. I have some very good friends who are there when I need them, but they recognize that need as well. I suppose it's all about meeting the person who can cope with that.

Are there any heroes you admire as being at the pinnacle of success, either past or present?

I really don't have any heroes. There are people whom I admire, whose work I like. I love Van Morrison's music, for example. I can listen to that anytime and anywhere. I like the fact that he's a dreamer – that appeals to me very much. I like the fact that his work has a kind of spiritual element to it as well. That clicks with me.

Has religion been a part of your success?

Yes, I think it has. I was brought up as a Catholic, though I would consider myself a Christian now. I still attend a Catholic church, and an Anglican church. But throughout the making of *A Grand Day Out,* I lost my faith completely.

Why was that?

I don't know. It was a time when I needed to question everything. That was partly why it was such a depressing time.

You were depressed while you were making this great movie?

Yes. It was daunting. It was taking me years to make and I felt that my life was slipping away. Even though I believed in the film, I felt locked into it. I started to question a lot of what I'd been brought up with and experienced during my teenage years. Before I went to film school I had been so sure about my faith in God, but I suddenly felt as though I didn't belong anywhere, and very vulnerable.

But you've now come back on course, in that you've found a faith with which you're comfortable. Is that a comfort to you in your work?

It is. I don't believe in talking about God in my work, that's not the place for it, but I do hope that my faith comes through in some way. It helps me to keep things in perspective, because I'm sometimes very susceptible to the fame side of it all. For example, I spent two or three weeks in the States after the Oscars having meetings with big-studio executives, and whilst people are congratulating you all the time, slapping you on the back and telling you you're wonderful, it's easy to get taken in by it all. My faith helps me to keep my feet on the ground – maybe even to stay real.

What do you think are the greatest enemies of success?

Wanting success too badly. If I'd have set out to win an Oscar, or set out to target a particular audience, I don't think I would have done it. You may win that audience for a while, but if you're not being true to yourself, people can see through it.

I suppose that goes back to you talking about keeping your ambition under cover as it were?

Yes, if you're confident in a way that doesn't have any kind of grounding and if you try to sell yourself on that alone, then people will see through it.

What's the greatest pleasure you've had from your success?

The greatest pleasure! I suppose it's nice being invited to all sorts of things, and I've met lots of people that I wouldn't have met otherwise.

Do you think success has changed you in any way?

Not deep-down. I think I've got more used to success. I've learned a lot from it and I think I've learned how to handle it better. I now think that I've got a greater sense of who I am, but deep-down I hope that I'm not all that different. I still feel as though I'm growing in ways that anyone would wish to and the success I have achieved through films is just another experience in life, just another part of the process.

What advice would you give to any budding Nick Parks who sense that they want to make a career in animation?

There is far more technology around these days – computers, video cameras, which actually aren't all that good for animation, but I would say that if you can access this type of equipment, just experiment. Use the time and the imagination that you've got as much as you possibly can, and be as creative as possible. Apply for courses that do animation. Someone once said to me that the time I spent at college was never time wasted. That was really good advice. The time you can spend experimenting without commercial pressure is very valuable.

Is it becoming easier to be successful in animation?

I don't think it was ever easy. Looking back, if I'd have wanted to achieve success or make lots of money, I wouldn't have chosen animation. There are many animators whose work I admire, colleagues who were at college at the same time as me, but in some way Wallace and Gromit have stolen the limelight of the British animation scene. This has created a problem where the commercial world, and by that I mean the media, only want to know about those at the top or those who are in the limelight. Wallace and Gromit have had, to some extent, a negative effect on other people. I suppose this happened after the success of *Creature Comforts*. All the advertising agencies wanted Aardman to make their television commercials like Wallace and Gromit, but there are a lot of directors and animators in the company who have their own style and who, given the opportunity, could really shine. So in some ways achieving success has become more difficult. On the other hand, you could regard any publicity for British animation as a good thing for everybody – I'm not sure which is true.

But what advice would you give to anyone going into the profession, or working their way up the profession now – come up with a good idea, something that involves taking risks and which maybe produces something that is very different from other animation styles and techniques that are around?

Yes, although I realize that it's actually difficult to find originality just like that. Part of the process is finding your own style and uniqueness. To start off with you've got to copy other people, you learn from that, it's part of your development. That's what they did in the Renaissance. A painter would have many students who would copy what he was doing, and as they developed, they would start to develop their own style. I think that's the way you have to do it.

One final question, when your time comes to leave this life, what would you like people to say about you?

Well, it's funny, the things that people said about me after I'd won all those awards were the sort of things I only imagined people might say when I was dead.

Was there any particular phrase that made you think, 'That's how I'd like to be remembered'?

I suppose I'd like to be remembered for being innovative. I find it very hard to say something like this, it goes with what I've been saying all along – I find it very hard to say anything about myself. I don't know if I'm just being falsely modest, but I'd rather leave that sort of thing to other people.

MATTHEW PARRIS

At school he was never very good at writing, and 'only average' at English, yet he has become the most distinguished Parliamentary sketch-writer of his generation. He says 'a sense of the pantomime of politics is essential, but you must laugh with politicians, not always at them'. He confesses to being a plodder – 'in the field of hack writing, a degree of simple determination, conscientiousness and an ability to stick at things is terribly important'. For Matthew Parris, it wasn't always like that. His enormous self-confidence took a series of knocks as 'I failed at all but one of my various careers'. From Cambridge, where he abandoned his MA, he went into the Foreign Office, moving over to the Conservative research department, and then Mrs

Thatcher's office in Downing Street. He spent a few years as an MP, followed by a spell as presenter of the ITV current affairs programme Weekend World, *before being offered 'a section of* The Times *every day for a year as a teach-yourself journalism course'.*

He says his writing developed from things he wanted to say, and only later did he begin to develop writing skills as an end in themselves. Money was an incentive – 'Dr Johnson said nobody but a fool ever wrote for anything but money.' He discusses journalists' influence on the success of politicians, and advises them that 'the media are the winds, the currents, the rocks on which a political career can either sail or founder, so you must work with them and use them'. On the other hand, in outlining the qualities needed to be a successful MP, he warns 'you must avoid publicity'. He suggests it is often advisable to ignore conventional wisdom – 'You must always listen to the voice inside you that insists something is right, even if others say it is wrong.' Opportunity linked to character is 'the happy concurrence that brings success', so people from a difficult background can sometimes achieve enormous and unexpected success, while 'social or material standing, or the silver spoon in the mouth, often condemn people rather than bring them success'. He also knows people 'who would leave me floundering intellectually, but none of them have come to anything'. And, in a typical swipe at his fellow citizens, he describes Britons as 'an emotionally tangled and very ambitious people – if we can't succeed ourselves, then we take pleasure in trying to spoil the success of others'.

Matthew Parris, what is your definition of success?

I can't get away from the feeling that success is not just in one's own eyes, but also in the eyes of either the world at large, or people you love or respect. For me it would never be enough to set myself a goal, achieve it to my satisfaction and call myself a success in my own terms.

Which is the more important – the people you know and love, or the world at large?

Although I love the approval of those I know, I like to be generally regarded as good at what I do, and I look to those who do not know me as the people best able to offer an objective judgment of how well I'm doing.

Even though some of them may not be aware of all the circumstances surrounding something you write? Do you feel when you write that you are offering up something to the world that needs to be judged in its own right?

We must judge work objectively, without any great delving into the mind or problems of those who produce it. The work must be there after the person has gone, in isolation from the person, and be judged on its own merits. It's the thing itself that matters.

Do you think that those who judge success are uniformly objective?

There is no such thing as objectivity. The more people you have, the wider the view and the closer you get to some sort of common view.

To what extent do you think success is a product of background and upbringing?

Success is significantly determined by background and upbringing, but not always in the way that people think. People from what appears to be a difficult background with few special advantages or opportunities can sometimes achieve enormous and unexpected success. Social standing or material standing, or the silver spoon in the mouth often condemn people rather than bringing them success.

Is strength of character the core of anybody's success?

I think we have to look at success in different fields, and there may be kinds of genius which don't require strength of character, particularly on the creative side, but which call for other abilities, and may well go hand-in-hand with a weak or even degenerate character. But in many fields – certainly in the political field, and in the field of hack writing, which is what I do, I think a degree of simple determination, conscientiousness and an ability to stick at things is terribly important.

There really is no common standard, is there, for judging success when you are talking both about people who are successful through strength of character, and those who just happen to be in the right place at the right time?

There can be success that comes simply from good fortune. A statesman like Winston Churchill, for instance, could have been ludicrous as a politician in circumstances other than those which found his strength. There can also be the sort of success that comes from having some kind of genius or being given some kind of gift. You might have the most beautiful voice, you might have a wonderful talent for mimicry, you might have the gift of musical inspiration. Where gifts like that come from I don't know, but they are not the same thing as strength of character. They can't be dinned into a person and they won't be achieved by plodding. Perhaps more commonly, I think, success is achieved by effort. I have always regarded myself as a plodder. I may appear mercurial on the surface, but I'm not, actually. I just bang away at things until I get somewhere, and so do quite an extraordinary number of other people who have been successful. I look at my friends and colleagues who were at Cambridge with me. I'm quite bright, but I'm not a genius, and I knew a few who were really very, very clever, and who would just leave me floundering, intellectually. But none of them has come to anything. Sometimes, because of their intelligence, they have developed a sort of contempt for the standards by which the world operates and for success in worldly terms, and haven't even bothered to try because they don't respect the judgment of those less capable than themselves. They don't need the approval of such people. Those of us who are not so bright, who do need the approbation of people around us, sometimes work harder.

So you think there is a lot of unfulfilled potential out there, among people who don't wish to play the game?

The world is full of unfulfilled potential. There are people who simply haven't wanted to play the game. Those who have wanted to play the game and haven't been able to get into it by far exceed those who have played and won. I was born and brought up in ex-British colonies, places in which there was a small number of people – a few hundred thousand – who in every respect one accepted as being 'people', and a vast mass – millions – whom one didn't know, and whose language one didn't speak, and who weren't entirely part of the society. When I came to Britain at the age of 18, I found I had to make very few mental or social accommodations from my colonial experience to fit in with life in Britain.

This, too, was a country of some 54 million people whom one would never meet, with just a few hundred thousand people, mostly living in London, into whom one would keep bumping, whom one knew, or who knew people one knew, who went to the same dinner parties, who commissioned one to write things, and whom one commissioned to write things. There was a very small core of society with enormous privileges, and a very large number of people who quite often didn't get a look in. I can't believe that this is all a matter of merit. I don't believe I'm part of some pinnacle of a pyramid sustained by toiling masses of those with less competence than myself. I think it's a matter partly of opportunity.

And luck?

An enormous amount of luck comes into things. Everybody who has achieved success talks about their good fortune and everybody else thinks, 'How modest of them, it wasn't really good fortune, they must have earned it.' I don't believe that. Of course you must take advantage of luck, and of course those who succeed not only have had opportunities, but have taken them. Yet there are plenty of people who have never had opportunities, who have been knocked down really hard very early in life and have never got up again. They're just unlucky – it has nothing to do with merit. If I have one unhappiness, one great central unhappiness, with the political ideology to which I subscribe, Conservatism, it is its tendency to look at society as though we all started as players at the beginning of a game of Monopoly – on the same board, with the same money in the bank and the same chances from the Opportunity and Chance cards. A shake of the dice, and we're all off, and those who succeed do it by effort and intelligence and by playing the game well, and those who fail do so because they didn't put in the effort, have the intelligence or play the game well. Life isn't like that. We don't all start on the same board, or with the same money in the bank, we don't start with the same opportunities. I don't, as a Conservative, believe there's an awful lot we can do to change that, but what I can't bear is people who moralize about it – who vaunt their own success as some sort of reward for their own effort and who hold up the failure of other people as some kind of judgment on their lack of effort.

The key is opportunity, isn't it? I've talked to people who started from slums and have risen to be very successful in their particular field, and yet others who have been in the same position yet haven't had that degree of success. Can you say what it is that differentiates those two types of people?

It will be a mixture of chance and character. Chances come occasionally, and only to a few. How those chances are then seized depends on one's internal strengths. These come from family, and are not dependent on wealth or class or anything else. It's the happy concurrence of opportunity with character that brings success. It's quite fortuitous.

Are we dependent on a mentor as well?

Mentor is a rather grand word, and perhaps it doesn't quite describe the importance of having someone to look up to, and someone to encourage you. The two are not necessarily the same. One can have a great hero, it could be a sports star, a singer, a rock star, a famous politician, or just an older boy who lives on the same block and who seems like some kind of a god when you're younger. They may not know you, they may show no interest in you at all, and yet their example can be very important. Quite separately from that, there is the moral and emotional strength that comes from being given support and love and encouragement by another person. He or she may not be someone set above you in any way – it might be someone equal to you or even beneath you. And I think there's a difference between men and women here. All men have mothers, and mothers love their sons, perhaps with a sort of unqualified unconditional love. They can love their sons in a way which is different from the way they love anybody else. I don't think a daughter receives the same unconditional love from her mother as the son does. Daughters sometimes have a special bond with a father, but a father's affection for a daughter very often depends on her success, on the things he wants her to be, the kind of person he wants her to turn out as. That's not the case with mothers and sons. Whatever the son does, the mother will find a way of interpreting it as success. So many boys, from very early in their memories – and perhaps going back to before they had memories – have the unconscious knowledge of the complete and unconditional love of another person. I think this is what gives men their confidence, their arrogance, their recklessness, their extreme selfishness sometimes. I think it can create good and bad in people, and it can create extremes which are not so commonly found in women.

That is fascinating. What you're saying is that, if you accept that a mother's love and the relationship between mother and son is important, there is almost an in-built bias to make men more successful than women through that kind of encouragement?

Yes. There's an in-built bias which can project men towards peaks of success, and also towards peaks of failure and catastrophe. Women, on the whole, are likely to be more reliable than men. It's a generalization, of course, and it is certainly not to say that all men, or even most men, will reach those peaks, or that all women or most women can't, but if you look at very successful women, you'll very often find an extremely powerful and very much-loved father in the background who has perhaps provided for them what so many mothers have for so many sons.

And maybe there weren't any brothers in the family?

It may sometimes be the case that both the mother's and the father's love has been channelled to the daughter. There is often a special bond between father and daughter, but the circumstances of English family life mean that fathers spend much less time with daughters, and consequently there are fewer opportunities for contact and encouragement, so perhaps the fruits of that relationship don't so regularly come through.

When was the first time that you said to yourself – and this may be going way back into your early youth – 'I am successful, I am a success at something'?

When I was about two. As soon as I was able to articulate the thought that I was special. I think it must first have come from the conviction that I couldn't actually have been my parents' child. I don't know whether I thought I had been placed here by aliens or adopted, but I couldn't understand why I was surrounded by all these brothers and sisters who didn't quite appreciate my very special nature. I think a lot of people have this feeling as a child, and even throughout their lives, but it doesn't necessarily propel them anywhere. As far as I was concerned, however, as soon as I began to be successful at anything I took it as further evidence of my specialness. But even when I wasn't successful at things, I just thought the specialness hadn't yet been turned to any sort of practical advantage, and believed it would be sooner or later.

So you have always thought you were special?

Yes.

That shows a quite remarkable confidence. Is such confidence a factor in success?

Confidence is an immense factor in success, but it is often false confidence. I have always had a kind of recklessness based on the strange belief that somehow it's all going to be all right on the night for me, and I'm afraid that too often it has.

But what happens when it hasn't been all right on the night? When things haven't gone well, and your confidence has been exposed to a knock? How have you recovered from that?

You recover by stolidness, really. I have failed at all but one of my various careers. I didn't get my masters degree because I couldn't understand computers. I wasn't any good at all in the Foreign Office, which was my first job. I think Chris Patten would confirm that I didn't particularly distinguish myself in the Conservative research department in my second job. I failed sensationally working for Mrs Thatcher, writing rude replies to people who wrote to her which were later published in the newspapers. I wasn't actually a very successful back-bench MP, and I didn't really succeed as a television presenter. When I look back on all these things that I didn't turn out to be very good at I wonder how I kept my spirits up. I can't remember, I think I just kept plugging away.

Was it that feeling that you were special that kept you going?

I think one has some kind of internal belief that sooner or later it's all going to turn up trumps, that it's just a matter of time, and you just have to plug away until your undoubted talents are given the respect they are due.

How did you discover that you had talent as a writer? Was it a matter of someone giving you the opportunity, or did you push at the door until it finally opened?

I never actually wanted to be a writer. I was never very good at writing at school, I never used to win essay prizes and I was only averagely good at English. Journalism never occurred to me as a career. In fact it was ideas rather than writing that pushed me into journalism. I had things I wanted to say, and writing gave me the platform from which to say them. Once I was a Member of Parliament I found that people would occasionally print articles I wrote, mostly about transport policy, which interested me and still does, greatly. Then when I was a television presenter I found I could get the occasional column in *The Times*, voicing my thoughts on social policy. So the writing developed from having things to say. I found that, with practice, I wasn't a bad writer, and people started to give me a platform even before I had anything to say. Then I began to develop writing skills as an end in themselves. So now I start with the platform and the idea has to come next.

Presumably, as you are rising up the ladder of success, you need someone who is prepared to give you the opportunity to practise as a writer in public – because writing is a very public thing. But does it require a high degree of tolerance on the part of the people who are giving you work to allow you to ride through that 'training' period until you reach an adequate level?

That's absolutely right. I think there are some abilities in which an element of genius is central – perhaps singing, dancing, acting, music.

There are other abilities, like bricklaying or journalism, which are really just a hard slog. They involve skills anybody can learn and can develop with practice. But very few get the practice. My good fortune was to be asked by a man called Charles Wilson, who was editor of *The Times*, to write a parliamentary sketch and then to be left entirely alone for a year with a section of *The Times* in which to lay down 585 words every day.

It was as precise as that?

Yes, and there was almost no editorial interference. So I would write, and then the next day I would read what I had written in the newspaper, and I could see what worked and what didn't. Gradually I honed my skills. But how many people are offered a section of *The Times* as a teach-yourself-journalism course, and are paid handsomely for doing it? Money, too, has been an important incentive for me all along. Dr Johnson said that nobody but a fool ever wrote for anything but money. I admire, yet cannot entirely understand, people who haven't got publishers or readers, but who keep on writing to develop and test their own skills. I wouldn't write a word if there was nobody there to publish it or to pay me to do it. Occasionally I feel so strongly about an idea that I would want to write about it even if I weren't paid, but that's unusual. I write for money. Right from the start people have paid me to write, and you've no idea how encouraging it is for a writer to know that there's a space waiting in a newspaper for his piece and a cheque in the post to pay him for it.

Without that incentive would you have moved on to something else?

Yes. Oh, I certainly wouldn't have carried on writing if no one had paid me.

Do you share the view that we are peculiarly envious of success in Britain?

People say, 'Well, it's no good in Britain, because as soon as you begin to succeed, people will want to knock you down.' Why do people want to knock you down? Because we are emotionally tangled and, at root, very ambitious people. If we can't succeed ourselves, then we take pleasure in trying to spoil the success of others. It is actually the great drive for success, often frustrated, in Britain that results in this rather strange culture of sniping at those who have been successful. In our hearts we think we should be there, too. And so we carp at them.

Do you think that we ever could become more laid back about success and more understanding of it? And if we did, would it mean that Britain as a whole had a better chance of being a successful nation?

No. I think if we were to lower our expectations to something rather more in line with what, on the face of it, is our potential, we would just become another small, fading European power. Consider what Britain is – a small island, with few natural resources, no more human resources than many other countries, but look at the success we've achieved in the past, and are still achieving now. We punch way, way beyond our weight. That is, I think, because we are rather an emotionally tangled and quite a chippy people. So the last prescription we should be offered for greater success in the world is that we should relax and bother less about things.

But could we do better if we put success on a pedestal?

I think we do put success on a pedestal, and that's why we are so envious of it. The reason we don't like people standing on pedestals is that pedestals mean such a lot to us.

What do you regard as the most successful moments in your life? Perhaps those that, deep within yourself, gave you exceptional satisfaction.

When I was a boy at boarding school, I wasn't very good at sport or any of those physical pursuits in which boys vie with one another. I was generally regarded as rather a drip, and I was not especially popular. In the dormitory one night one of the popular boys who was very good at cricket started to feel sick. He was quite scared, and wanted to go to the ablution block. But it was dark and he was frightened to go on his own, and then everyone else got frightened too and no one wanted to go with him. So I said, 'I'll go with you.' It's hard to describe in retrospect, because nobody will understand why we were all so frightened, but we just were. So I walked with him. I felt very proud of myself because I had been braver than all the others. I have never forgotten that.

And presumably it changed the perception the others had of you?

It did, and that was the other reason I was proud. It wasn't only what I had done from my own point of view, but that I could see the others admired me for it. In fact I think that was the main reason it gave me such pleasure. I suffer, as many do, from insecurity. I think that it's all going to be taken away, everything's going to fall apart.

Do you think that every successful person has a degree of insecurity within them?

There may be types of success which, in a simple and uncomplicated way, stem from some enormous accomplishment or ability that you know you possess and which you know other people haven't got. That must be immensely relaxing and reassuring. But the rest of us live on our wits, on our confidence. We know that we have nothing to fear except fear, and that if our confidence breaks, then we will break, too. It's summed up by that wonderful song of B.B. King's, 'You Better Not Look Down or You Might Not Keep on Flying'.

Bertrand Russell, in one of his autobiographical essays, says that when he went up to Cambridge he thought, 'This is wonderful, I am going to meet the brightest, best and most intelligent young men in the world.' At the end of his first year, he reflected a little disappointedly that he didn't seem to have met them yet. At the end of his second year, he reflected that he and his friends *were* the brightest, best and most intelligent young men in the world. To me, such confidence as I've ever had has come not from any great belief in my own abilities, but from the growing realization that no one else is any cleverer than me, that they are all frauds as well, and that however undeserved my own success may be, the success of others is equally undeserved. So my own reassurance and self-confidence has come from a gradual understanding of the hollowness of other people's claims rather than from any serious belief in the solidity of my own.

So is there really no one to whom you unreservedly look up, whom you hero-worship, because everyone has got weaknesses – everyone is, to a certain extent, a fraud?

The people to whom I would unreservedly look up would be people like tightrope walkers in circuses, who can really do it, or people who can play a musical instrument, who have the most beautiful timbre to their voices, who have a gift. People who can plaster a ceiling, which I shall never be able to do, people who possess what you might call a solid skill or ability which is self-evident, and which does not depend on bravado or morale, or quick-wittedness. But when those of us who live by our wits, and on bravado, see others like ourselves – prime ministers, successful media people, broadcasters – who've achieved equal or greater success in the same field, we know that they are confidence tricksters too. Although we do look up to them, admiration is muted.

Who are your heroes in history, or indeed in the present? Who are the people to whom you look up and about whom you would say – notwithstanding all your caveats about fraudsters and so on – 'These are people I unreservedly admire because of what they have done, because of how successful they have been in one field or another'?

Two qualities inspire special respect in me. One is courage, valour. I'd admire anybody who has done anything really brave in history – be it in battle, in politics, in social reform. That's a quality for which I have complete admiration. The other is doggedness. Indeed, doggedness and valour are often entwined together. Sheer doggedness can be a terrific quality. I have a great admiration not so much for Henry VIII, or even – although she's admirable – Queen Elizabeth I, but for Henry VII, who was a most unattractive man – cold, apparently, and quite unlikeable. He didn't believe in great military victories, but he managed to settle most of the disputes in which England was involved. He settled the Wars of the Roses by marrying Elizabeth. He decided that the state needed to raise taxes because it needed money, he found ways of increasing revenue, and administered England better than it had been administered before. He was a patient, careful, circumspect, cautious, dogged administrator. Such people are almost never given their due in history – very few English schoolchildren would know who Henry VII was – and yet many of the glories of Elizabethan and Tudor England are in fact based on the fiscal foundations he laid down.

More generally, then, the kind of people you admire are those who can effect change, who can move the world forward in a beneficial way?

I admire people who push boundaries forward, who make changes, who reform, but I also admire those who lay the foundations which make that possible. Very often they are less acclaimed. We applaud those who, after some bridge in history has been crossed, establish the bridgehead, the first landmarks on the other side – the first towers, the first fortresses – and sometimes forget the people who built the bridge in the first place. There may, for example, be a great deal of admiration for Boris Yeltsin and rather less for Mikhail Gorbachev, even though Gorbachev is really the great man. We applaud Tony Blair for what he's done for the Labour Party, forgetting that it was Neil Kinnock who really laid the foundations for its modernization. We don't admire in the way that perhaps we should people like John Major, who patiently tried to build bridges between one era and another and achieved more than he has been given credit for. It is sometimes too easy to concentrate on the mountaineers and the sherpas who get to the peak and to forget the people who established the base camp. Because I am very much the kind of person who likes to be on the top peak, I always feel a terrific sense of indebtedness and admiration towards those who establish the base camps, and also the injustice of the lack of appreciation of their contribution.

What have you found to be the greatest enemies of success?

Laziness is the greatest enemy of success. I am afraid this is boring advice – it's just getting up a little before the others in the morning. The lie-ins, the laziness, the 'I won't bother with it' approach are the enemy. But there is another – not trusting your own judgment. Sometimes the things that have worked for me have come about as a result of backing my own hunches. Everybody has hunches, but on the whole we tend to disregard them and go by conventional wisdom. I've often had an instinct to ignore conventional wisdom, to persist with something even though the tenor of the times was against it. In doing so I have often found myself able to leap ahead of others a little bit.

A great enemy to success is waking up in the night, having an idea and feeling quite sure that its right, and then, the next morning, talking to other people, finding that no one else shares your view and suppressing your own understanding, and deferring to those around you. You must always listen to the voice inside you that insists that something is right even if others say that it's wrong.

Does success bring obligations?

I don't really understand the language of obligation very well. I feel obligations, but I don't know where they come from.

Do you have obligations to the rest of society? Do you have an obligation, if you are successful, not to be an island?

I'm disinclined to preach that if you are successful, you must repay your debt to society. I myself have always had a rather nagging conscience when it comes to giving other people a hand, so I do it because I want to do it. But I don't think everybody should do it. I can think of a couple of very, very clever and successful men and women, writers and others, who are completely selfish in their own lives. They don't reply to letters from young struggling artists, they don't give money to charity, don't do public speaking. Good luck to them. If they don't want to, if they want to indulge their own genius and carry on producing the things that they do well, then let them do so.

Has success changed you?

No, not really. I've become more confident – even more confident than I used to be – but I was already absurdly confident as a little boy. The biggest and most unwelcome change that success has produced in me – and I know this because friends say so – is that I have become more impatient with other people. There isn't time, I don't have time to listen, or I think I don't. I don't have time to lie on my back and stare at the ceiling, and the day becomes crowded with what I suppose to be obligations and things to be done. This busy life I have, far from arising out of energy or self-discipline, comes from a lack of self-discipline. If I had real energy and real self-discipline, I would see that there is a limit to the number of things that can be done in a day, and I would see that time to myself and time with other people was important. I would have the discipline to impose that on myself. It's a kind of self-indulgence to keep accepting new briefs and new obligations, running round getting tireder and tireder. It's not strong at all, it's weak. It's a weakness from which Mrs Thatcher critically suffered. In the last four of five years of her tenure as prime minister, when I knew her reasonably well as a boss, I could see that she was just very tired all the time. She wasn't getting enough sleep, she didn't have time to listen and she was impatient. It wrecked her performance as a politician and it brought her down. It was due not to an excess of energy, but to lack of self-discipline.

A question which brings together the two main arms of your career, as a politician and as a writer – ultimately, is political success a product of the press you get?

I think Enoch Powell's analogy about politicians and the sea really says it all. He said that politicians complaining about the media were like ships' captains complaining about the sea. Now, this image speaks to us on more than one level. First, of course, Enoch Powell is quite right, it's futile and silly for politicians to complain, because the sea – the media – is there, and the storms will occur, so there is no point in whining about it. But secondly, the sea, of course, is absolutely crucial to the captain. He cannot sail his ship without it, he must know where the currents are, from which direction the winds are coming, and where the rocks are. So it is with the press. The media are the winds, the currents, the rocks on which a political career can either sail or founder. You must, as far as you can, work with them and use them. If you don't know them, if you are unlucky with them, if you disregard them, you will founder. They are there – they are a fact of life, just as the voters are a fact of life in any democracy.

So there is no point in complaining about them even though there may be some inherent unfairnesses in what they write or say?

The press is inherently unfair, it's inherently deeply unfair.

Is that a flaw in society?

Again, there's no more point in calling the unfairness of the popular news media a flaw than there is in calling the existence of tornadoes in our weather systems a flaw – it occurs, and it will always occur.

But you can't change tornadoes – you can't stop them happening, at least, not yet – but you could change the media. Not necessarily through legislation, but through the types of people that come through the media, and the kind of things they want to do to help play a part in creating a better society. Or do you think that the media should never, ever try to do that? Is that too pompous an ambition?

You say you can change the media, but who do you mean by 'you'? I do believe that the media can be influenced. I think groundswells of indignation about things the media do can result in a change of course in the media. Like the sea, the press overreaches itself and, having overreached itself, it is repulsed by internal forces and by the reaction of readers, of viewers, of consumers, of those who work within it. It's much more useful to view it as one views a weather system than it is to see it as some kind of a car that you can steer. Weather systems are there, but we can take advantage of currents or shelter from them, we can protect ourselves from rain. There are all kinds of things we can do to live with weather systems, but we mustn't suppose that we can control them. All the media really are is the interflow, the interchange, through mechanized means, of thoughts, ideas, news, facts and opinion. But they combine to become a huge and eddying social force in which we play only a small part, and over which we have little immediate control by any act of will of our own.

Is it possible for any politician nowadays to remain successful for long, or is there a basic desire on the part of the media to seek out the weaknesses, the flaws, however slight, and use them to bring that person down?

There's nothing new in the tendency on the part of not just the populace, but also the media which minister to the populace, to build somebody up and then knock them down. You could see the same things happening in the 19th century, although the media were more timid in those days and took rather longer to bring people down. Nevertheless, people were destroyed by the same mixture of envy, desire for movement, story and plot as they are now. All that the very instant nature of the mass communications we have today has done to change things is to make all those forces perhaps more immediate, and therefore more violent in their effect, than they used to be. So now we build people up rather faster and we knock them down rather faster, too. The tendency of the media to look for flaws, and to try to unpick the success of politicians, is not in every respect a bad thing – it is to this that we owe the new vigilance that we have, for instance, about corruption in public life. But it is also to this that we owe some of the very unfair ways in which we have destroyed the achievements of politicians, or stopped politicians from pursuing good goals. I find it hard to say whether it is, on balance, good or bad.

Is it becoming more difficult for a politician to be successful for longer than a blip in history? Should anyone go into politics and expect to be consistently successful?

If you look at the way we talk and write about each other in the media, the answer would be an unqualified yes. But if you look at the endurance of political reputations over this century, it isn't clear to me that we are knocking people down any faster than we used to. Lloyd George lasted a long time, but so did Margaret Thatcher. Neil Kinnock went rather quickly, but so did Ramsay MacDonald. We have had plenty of flash-in-the-pan politicians in the past, and plenty who have gone on and on. John Major's was Prime Minister for nearly seven years, and he, Margaret Thatcher, Harold Wilson and Harold Macmillan before him are among the longer-serving premiers in our history. So before we hasten to say that they'll knock you down before you've got to the top in politics, we ought to observe that if that is the media's intention, they have not made too good a job of it.

What would you say are the ingredients first of a successful politician, and secondly of a successful parliamentary sketch-writer?

To be a successful politician, you need doggedness, persistence, circumspection and – this runs quite contrary to the conventional wisdom – you need to avoid publicity. Self-publicity has brought down far more politicians than it has ever elevated, and if you look at people who are consistently successful in public life in Britain, they tend to have been very dark horses for most of their careers.

But can you avoid publicity when the business of politics is increasingly played out on a minute-by-minute, blow-by-blow basis in a growing number of media outlets?

Yes, you can, because there are always plenty of people around you who will be looking for it. You can therefore stay in the shadows, and you're best advised to do so. Michael Portillo, for example, has destroyed himself by going too early for publicity. John Redwood probably has too. Whoever succeeds John Major in the Conservative Party will be somebody who has kept quiet for as long as possible. You don't want too much originality if you are to succeed in politics. Privately you can be as original as you like, but you must keep your originality to yourself. Don't surprise people with your thoughts.

And to be a successful parliamentary sketch-writer?

It has helped me that I understand it a little bit from the inside, but you must never describe it from an insider's point of view. You must always remember that your audience knows less about the goings-on at the House of Commons than they do about what's happening in *EastEnders*. You must laugh at it, but if you're there purely to throw stones at the political process, even if they're humorous stones, I don't think you'll in the end be very funny. It's much better if you sometimes laugh *with* politicians, not always at them, if you acknowledge that there is something there that's good, and that needs to be taken seriously, as well as much that is ludicrous and needs to be remarked upon. A sense of the pantomime of life, such as Charles Dickens had – a sense of the pantomime of politics – is essential, but Dickens did not lack a moral quality.

So you need scepticism rather than cynicism?

Scepticism is, I think, a healing and even a creative quality. Cynicism often in the end just reduces everything to ashes and won't produce an entertaining sketch.

If you could gather together all the young people who said, 'I want to be like Matthew Parris, I want to write his kind of columns,' what advice would you give them?

Rush out and do something different, something unusual. Try something ... I don't want to use the word 'brave', because I haven't been especially brave. Go sideways – don't just keep trying to crawl your way upwards, but look sideways.

Look for new opportunities?

No, I don't think sniffing around for opportunities is the right way of actually finding them. I think you should cultivate a sense of curiosity about the world, a sense of exploration. Try to explore, and try to discover new things, different things, new experiences, new places, different people. Take a gamble. And yet learn to persist, too, to plod. Seize moments and ideas, basic hunches, and yet plod for long stretches as well. Contradictory advice, I know.

One final question. When your time comes to leave this life, what would you like people to say about you?

I'd like people to say that I was the best in my generation at something. I don't especially mind what.

SHIMON PERES

'Experience is useless because it has already happened. Imagination is the great art of trying to forecast what will happen.' The words of a political visionary whose pursuit of long-term goals played a pivotal role in the historic 1993 Middle East Peace Agreement between Israel and the PLO. Such efforts haven't always brought him political rewards from a volatile electorate, bred in a territorial cockpit of violence, and often driven by an uneasy mix of fear, anger and hope. The potential of the 11-year-old boy with no proper education, who arrived from Poland with his parents in 1934, was soon spotted. He was elected to the leadership of Israel's youth movement 'because I tirelessly spoke to the people one-to-one, while rivals were spending all the time in meetings in headquarters'. By the time he reached 30 he was Director General of the Ministry of Defence, responsible for building up his country's armed forces.

A founder of the Israeli Labour Party, he fought four elections as its leader, failing to win a single outright victory. He served as Prime Minister of a national unity government in the mid-Eighties, but his 'unelectability' saw him being replaced by his old rival Yitzhak Rabin. Rabin made him Foreign Minister, and they patched up their differences in secret pursuit of the peace agreement. He took over the premiership briefly after Rabin's assassination, but lost it by just a few thousand votes in Israel's first direct elections for the post. The most important thing he's learned in politics is 'never give up. Success can come when you least expect it.' So 'trust the people', he says, 'and pay the price of some disappointments.' He talks here about the approach to the peace deal; about 'the third option' in any negotiation; the factors that prevented news of the talks leaking to the media; and why, when faced with a choice between his career and his family life, he has always chosen 'to serve something which was greater than myself'. He advises young politicians to never agree with the status quo. 'Ask what you can do to improve the life of your country, and of other people.' In politics, he sees only one way to measure success, and that is by the results, the record. 'You need a moral commitment, and the ability to fix your main goal and stick to it.' And in negotiations he warns, 'You must be careful not to be too successful – it may cost you a heavy price later.'

Shimon Peres, what is your definition of success?

Political success is different from success in a beauty contest or in a sports event, in politics there is just one way to measure success and that is by results. The record decides if it is success or not.

Can you achieve political success by the way that you attempt to achieve those results?

There is no special formula. There are no rules and regulations in politics. I think there should be two basic things in order to attain success. One, you must have a moral commitment, something which is larger than yourself, and the second is you must fix your main goal and stick to it. For the rest you have to manoeuvre, to create, to mobilize and to face a great deal of problems and quarrels. Somebody said you are as great as your quarrel, your fight. It's not simple, but the end result is the deciding factor.

And it is perfectly acceptable for that end result to take a considerable period of time - with some politicians it might take years?

Usually great things cannot be obtained overnight. Years and years and years. The lot of Moses is the fate of every politician, maybe not 40 years, maybe five or seven years, but if you are not ready to cross a desert you will never arrive at the Promised Land.

To what extent do you think success is a product of your background and upbringing?

I think you bring yourself up all your life. We are born with shortcomings, we will probably die with shortcomings and the problem is how much to invest in yourself in between the two. I think a person must have discipline, he must learn constantly without stopping, must struggle constantly without getting tired. The Lord gives you just part of the necessary ingredients, the rest you have to add from your own pocket and from your own heart.

What are the most important things that you have learned in the course of your political career?

Never give up. People often lose heart at the very last moment, on the verge of victory they think they have lost. If you know how to get over that last gap, you may win.

So success can come very suddenly, perhaps when you least expect it?

Not suddenly, but when you least expect it. When you think that all the chips are down, maybe that's the winning time.

When was the first moment that you said to yourself, 'I am successful at something, I have been successful'? It may be perhaps going back to when you were a teenager, when you were very young. When was the first time you said that?

I was a member of a youth movement in Israel from the age of about 16, and I was surprisingly elected as secretary of this movement without having any political connections or any family background. To this very day I don't know why they elected me, probably because I had a very heavy, deep voice or something like that. I had become one of the 12 members of the secretariat, 11 were more on the Marxist side, 11 preferred the wholeness of Israel more than a Jewish state, the 11 were more impressed by the imported socialism, so to speak, and were against the leader of our country at the time, Ben-Gurion. After three years working in the movement and to the surprise of everybody I got the majority and was elected secretary, that was the first success that I could really mark as a success and it came as a surprise to the whole nation.

Did it come as a surprise to you?

Not totally, because while the 11 were sitting all the time in meetings at the headquarters, I was moving around the country, tirelessly speaking to the people one-to-one, continuously making friends, convincing them of my views. I felt that I was winning them over.

Did that give you an appetite then for greater success, did that encourage you to drive on to do bigger and better things?

Rightly or wrongly, I felt all my life committed to an idea not to my personal success, but it showed me that if you work hard enough and devotedly you can achieve goals – goals that had looked impossible just two or three years previously and that nobody believed I would achieve. Since then I feel whenever I have a goal, never give up.

Is an important ingredient in achieving success that you have the ability to question yourself and what you do, to have doubts?

I cannot try to generalize, but when it comes to me I would say yes. The self-search, the self-criticism and the strength not to decide whom to blame, but to think what to correct is part of my way of life. I rarely blame other people, I rarely accuse other people. I think life is so short, why waste it on accusing people, I won't change them.

You have a reputation in Israel in some quarters of being something of a compromiser in your political career, do you feel that's an unfair judgment on you?

No. I see nothing wrong in compromises, but I don't compromise myself. I think you have to compromise on issues without compromising yourself. I don't give up my basic beliefs. To arrive somewhere, you have to gallop and go slow, you have to stop at the station and you have to put aside a stone. If you call that compromising, then yes it is a compromise, but do otherwise and you might break your neck.

But at the same time you have a goal so you are the kind of politician who believes in both, in compromising at times and having conviction at times, and it's a matter of deciding when you are tough and when you are the master of compromise?

No, I think that the goal is the strategy that compromises the tactic. It's a different sort of level.

Can pursuit of political success result in you trusting people too much?

Yes, it does, but better to pay this price than the price of not trusting them. All my life maybe I have paid the price of trusting people too much, but I have also gained a great deal because I trusted them. So let's be fair, by trusting them you extract from them the best they have. Then they go off, they fall in love, they change their minds, it's human – but if I was giving advice, it would be to trust people and pay the price of some disappointments.

I know that you go along with your great friend President Mitterrand's description of history as a galloping horse which you must jump on anywhere you can. Is politics on the whole really as erratic and unpredictable as that?

He says, when the galloping horse passes nearby your home, better mount and ride with it, otherwise it may gallop past and leave you where you are. This is a good description of certain opportunities. There is no single rule that governs the lives of people, or their politics. Politics is a human effort and there are supreme tests but, just as you cannot describe in simple terms human behaviour, you cannot describe in one way, or in simple terms, political behaviour.

Can you detach politics from your emotions? Are the most successful political decisions those which are cool and calculating with everything carefully weighed and measured, or could there be an inspiration or sudden decision which doesn't appear to have a great deal of logic about it at the time which is nevertheless the right thing to do politically?

You must make your mind a source of discipline on your emotions. On many occasions you have to control yourself. Emotions are not very productive, but imagination very much so. Life is made of two things, experience and imagination. Experience is useless because it has already happened, imagination is the great art of trying to forecast what will happen. I am very worried about people who are too preoccupied with experience. As Bernard Shaw said, experience is a collection of your mistakes. It is better to try and look ahead and don't be afraid to discover things that you haven't experienced. I would say that politics is also an adventure, it is a struggle with the unexpected, the impossible if you like. You must try to find the right course by using all your faculties. You must be careful not to convert imagination into fantasy and not to confuse the ground with the sky. You have to weigh very seriously in your own mind and heart what you think will happen or can happen, think it through and then see how to correct it. Most dreams are good thoughts and people are wrong in preferring to remember rather than to think or to dream. When it comes to dreams and memories, as far as I am concerned, memory is totally boring, dream is the only hope.

When you embarked on the peace process that led to the Oslo Accord, what at that stage was your assessment of your chances of success?

Quite great. In my own analysis, I thought that neither Rabin nor Arafat would have a better chance than on the basis that was suggested.

What were the factors that made you think that your chances of success were good?

I have learned in my life that there is something that I would call the third option. Usually people stand before a situation and say you have two options, either to do this or to do that. Neither of the two has a chance, it's the third option – the unknown one – where creativeness plays the most important part and gives you the real chance. I thought the Oslo agreement had the advantage of originality, of creativeness and of surprise, and, at the same time, of flexibility.

A key part in successfully completing that agreement was keeping the negotiations secret. How did you do that?

Basically because the number of people who were really fully in the picture were just two, Rabin and myself. Neither of us leaked, neither of us took issue with the other or tried to get the credit for his own side, which is what usually happens in politics, and we met without any note-takers. Rabin didn't tell his own group because, as he said very honestly, he didn't think that anything would come of it. For my part I worked with just a small group of people whom I trusted 100 per cent, they were loyal and extremely brilliant and much of the credit belongs to them and not to me. But then there were also surprises. Firstly the place, nobody expected Norway to be the centre of world affairs, such a beautiful country. Secondly, the Norwegian negotiators, they were a very small group and they played their part in a very discreet manner. Thirdly, it was unthinkable that we would negotiate with the PLO. The intelligence services of the world didn't pay much attention – thank heavens.

With hindsight, were there any flaws in the Oslo agreement?

Considering all the parties, considering all the difficulties, by and large my answer is no. It could have been a little bit better here, a little bit better there, but by and large no. In negotiations I think you must be careful not to be too successful, it may cost you a heavy price later. Perhaps the other side, the Palestinians, have occasionally been a little too successful. I was careful not to be.

No one has put that point before, you really believe it is possible to be too successful in achieving something?

Yes, then it won't work. It's like being born with two legs, but one leg is too high so you can hardly walk. Don't make one leg too high.

After the assassination of Yitzhak Rabin you said that boundless unending fear for the future filled your heart, is that still there?

Yes. It made Hamas a central part of our elections. We lost and a new government was elected, endangering all that we had achieved. What people called a success was for me a great sadness. It was a very difficult year. Rabin was assassinated before my eyes, it was a deep shock for me. Then there were four terrorist attacks, many people were killed. I went to each of the funerals, it was the most agonizing experience in my life, day after day. And the Hezbollah started to shoot and then the Right started to accuse, for me it was a world of deep chagrin.

How do you keep going in the face of all those things going wrong and indeed in the face of many death threats you've had yourself?

Basically I believe there is no person, no party, no ruler in a government that can stop the march of history. They can postpone it, they can derail it for a while. I think what I have proposed is the call of history, and if anyone tries to derail it, be it on his own head.

Who are your heroes, who are the people that you look up to, the giants, either past or present, whom you regard as being highly successful?

I was very impressed by David Ben-Gurion, the founder of our nation. I worked with him for 18 years. He was a man of immense courage and real talent with total devotion to his goal. He was my main hero, because of personal experience. In history there are many.

You and Yitzhak Rabin were life-long rivals and yet after his death, you spoke of the previous three years as being marked by a rare friendship, bereft of any self-interest, which stunned you both. How did it happen?

I think largely because I took a decision to give up all political battles and to devote myself to peace. I wanted to convince Yitzhak that I was no longer an active opponent and that the rivalry would stop for as long as the peace process could be continued. I told him that as long as we were negotiating for peace, he had no need to worry about me, but the minute he did anything to stop the process, my political opposition would resume.

A difficult thing for politicians to do?

I thought I was entitled to have my own right to select the rules and regulations. I have had so many advisers in my life, some of them a bit snobbish in their attitude, and I thought to myself, 'If they are so wise why aren't they doing better?' This time I decided to trust my own judgment.

Do you ever have to make a choice between your work and your home life?

Yes, but the choice was easily decided.

What did you choose?

To serve something which was greater than myself.

And would you give the same advice to anyone who wants to be successful, who is faced with the choice between their career and their family?

One hundred per cent. Suppose all your life you have had the best wine, so what? Suppose you went on vacation every year, so what? Suppose you combed your hair with the right oil, so what? At the end of your life, the Lord will call you back. You will ask yourself, or the Lord will, 'How many trees did you plant, how many children did you save, how much did you contribute to the way of life of your people and how well did you yourself behave as a human being?' Maybe I won't have the right answer to all the questions but I would like to be able to say, 'I am returning at the end of my life, honest to God and honest to myself.'

What do you think are the greatest enemies of success?

Fear, people are frightened.

And if they are frightened they don't have the courage to take difficult decisions?

They are too careful, unnecessarily so. They don't realize that to be careful is also dangerous.

Has success changed you at all? Are you the same person who came all the way from Poland at the age of 11?

In my eyes, yes. The last few years I have been subject to a great deal of admiration, which is most moving. Children come to our home and people send flowers. Wherever I go I am applauded and admired, it embarrasses me. Even if I go to the theatre in New York, the whole audience stands up and applauds me. I feel like asking, 'Do you really mean me?' But, basically, deep in my heart, I don't think I have changed. When I hear nice things said about me, I say, 'Aren't you exaggerating a little?'

If you could gather together in one room all the young people in the world who wanted to make a success of their lives, to be as successful as you have been as a politician, what advice would you give them?

Never agree with the status quo, never. But don't try to change the status quo in the wrong direction. Ask yourself what you can do to improve the life of your friends, the life of your country, the life of other people and don't think that only the Messiah can do it. Maybe he will come but he hasn't set a date and until he comes each of us must be a little Messiah, not by any claim but by belief, by the way we live. Think that you are not a devil, that you are not a killer, that you are not a nothing. Whatever force you have, concentrate it and make humanity, human life, human relations better and more peaceful.

No matter how good a country becomes, there's always room for change?

No country can become good enough to be satisfied with its goodness.

And never will?

I hope not. You know, as I believe that evil maybe doesn't have a frontier, so goodness doesn't have a frontier either. People will learn more, they will be more intelligent, they will be healthier, they will be cleaner, they will get better all the time. Compare this century with the previous century – we live longer, we are stronger, we are healthier, we are more educated. Things may again improve dramatically in the next century.

And you should pursue those ideas even though the voters might not deliver you the political success that you wish for?

I lost many elections, but I didn't lose any goal, it's strange. Whatever I believed in I achieved, even though I may sometimes have lost the election. I know of many people who have won elections and then didn't know what to do. For my part when I lost an election, I hope I knew what to do.

But when you lost that last election by just a handful of votes, that must have been a moment when potential success looked out of your grasp?

No, I never believe it's the end of the story, even today. You should always allow for the unexpected. They say quitters don't win and winners don't quit. Never quit.

So does that encourage you, the thought that even though you have lost and suffered what appeared at the time to be an incredible reverse, that something unexpected can come up in the political arena in the future, which would enable you to stage a comeback, as it were?

Yes. I have one enemy which is my age, but this enemy is more on my passport than in my bones. I still feel very energetic and able to work and to think. The punishment of age has not yet arrived at my court.

And yet you said you would retire as leader of the Labour Party?

Yes, because I didn't want people to think I was fighting for something personal. So they would leave me alone. I am sick and tired of them accusing me of having a personal agenda. In that respect the press is very unfair, they won't trust you unless they discover you have a personal agenda. If you want to be credible, say, 'I want to be rich, I want to be strong, I want to be successful.' That to them is very convincing. They won't believe me when I tell them that it's not a case of personal interest, money and power don't mean much to me, popularity doesn't mean much to me.

You say power doesn't mean much to you and yet power is what politics in some ways seems to be all about - to have the power to push through the changes that you want?

Power as a means, yes. You cannot have a light in your home without having a power station, but I wouldn't say that the power station is my purpose, my purpose is the light.

So we will be hearing more of Shimon Peres as the peace agreement develops in all kinds of different ways?

Maybe, I cannot assure you.

Is there a role that you feel you would like to play?

No, it depends on the circumstances.

But you are ready to be called back?

I haven't retired. I am fighting, I am going on, ready for every opportunity. I don't expect anybody to call me, I shall mobilize myself by my own will. I don't yet know which approach may be the best to try to improve the present situation.

If things became so bad, with perhaps another intifada *and maybe even worse, would you then come back for your country if you were asked?*

I shall come back even if I am not asked. While I was disappointed to lose the election by one-third of one per cent, I also understood that 49.7 per cent was quite an important support. I owe it to the people. I got thousands and thousands of letters, the most moving letters in my life, that said, 'Please go on, don't retire.'

When your time comes to leave this earth, what would you like people to say about you?

That here disappeared a person who was honest to God and honest to men. That's all.

FRANÇOIS PIENAAR

Few who witnessed the historic television pictures will easily forget the moving moment in June 1995 when sport cemented and enhanced the new post-apartheid South Africa. Their team, the Springboks, had just defied the pundits to win rugby's World Cup in front of an ecstatic home crowd of black and white faces. François Pienaar, their captain, watched in astonishment as his country's President, Nelson Mandela, walked across the pitch wearing what had been seen as a symbol of white supremacy – a Springbok jersey. The gesture meant infinitely more than the trophy Pienaar was about to receive, and was matched by his response. Asked how it felt to have 65,000 supporters behind him in the stadium, he replied, 'No, we had 43 million people behind us.' Those

who knew this young Presbyterian liberal would not have been surprised. Unquestionably his country's most influential sportsman, he had for years been quietly coaching disadvantaged youngsters from the black townships.

The youngest son of working-class parents, he worked his way to a law degree through a changing political climate which instilled his conviction that ability matters more than colour. Four words shape his attitude to both sport and life – discipline, dedication, desire and determination. He believes that you have to experience failure to grow, and describes here how he overcame a strong urge to quit the national side; and how a tour of New Zealand, widely seen in South Africa as a disaster, actually paved the way for the World Cup success. He reveals the technique for restoring team spirit when they thought they'd lost the World Cup: 'We addressed the worst fears of each member of the team – both as a player and as a human being.' He believes his passionate advocacy of professionalism in rugby later cost him his place in the Springbok team. Recently appointed player-coach for the ambitious English club, Saracens, he still harbours hopes of reclaiming his place in the South African side. This interview with the man once labelled 'the most destructive loose forward in rugby' probes his approach to winning the World Cup, and his views on both personal and team success. He also reveals an encouraging, catalytic moment at the tender age of eight when 'I felt like I was the best thing that ever touched a rugby ball.'

François Pienaar, what is your definition of success?

A successful person is a person that's consistently good at something. It's no use being good at something only once. You've got to be consistently good at something. Only then are you truly professional or truly successful.

Are you more successful if you've experienced failure?

You have to experience failure to grow, you have to experience it to become bigger. A wise person is not only someone who learns from another's mistakes, he definitely learns from his own.

Are there any things you regard as particular failures which you built upon to create success?

Yes, I've experienced failure. I've experienced highs and lows in my rugby, on both a provincial level and an international level. As a team I think our toughest assignment was in New Zealand in 1994. Many rated it as one of the worst tours ever, but if you looked afterwards at the percentage of games we won, we actually came out as one of the top touring sides.

People saw the whole tour as a failure because we didn't win a Test match. But we went to New Zealand without any experience whatsoever of their playing conditions, of their refereeing, of playing in front of their crowds. In fact when we played in Wellington, the wind blew so hard in front of the poles that our full-back couldn't even kick it over from the 22-metre line – that never happens in South Africa. Personally I saw that tour as a valuable learning experience, but a lot of people in South Africa saw it as a disaster, and when the team came back, many changes were made to the coaches, management and so on.

The following year, in the World Cup, we played against France in Durban in some of the worst conditions I've ever seen in South Africa but we weren't worried about the weather because we'd experienced New Zealand. If we hadn't had that tour, we wouldn't have been so successful in the World Cup. We had learned from that less successful tour and so, when we went on to the field at Durban, nobody spoke about the weather, just about beating France.

You've had criticism in your time. How do you cope with that?

I'll have criticism in the future as well. It's a simple fact that you can't please all the people all the time and that's what I live by. You can only please some of the people some of the time, especially in South Africa – they are very provincial-minded. I've always had the wind from the front, always, and I'll still have it. I cope with criticism by reminding myself that I've really broken all the records that I can break in South Africa, and that is enough for me.

Did you ever feel like giving up?

Never. I just felt like redirecting my energies. I changed my attitude and looked at the positive things that have come out of rugby, not the negative things. I don't read sections of newspapers dealing with rugby any more since many articles about me are written by those who, quite frankly, I don't respect as people who know the game. So when I read newspapers I avoid the section where I or the team might be mentioned.

Does that apply to the rest of the team as well?

No. A lot of the players, especially the younger guys, read newspapers because at that age you like to hear about yourself and read about yourself, but I try and get them away from it. The only way you can keep on track and keep growing as a player is to work on the positives of your game. The criticism will come, from the coach and from the other players, but it will be constructive criticism. Not the negative criticism that comes from those outside the game.

What do you reckon were the most successful moments of your life? Not on the sporting field but those that perhaps we don't know about, that aren't on public record.

Yes. When we went to New Zealand, the team was in really bad shape. We had no confidence. As I said, we were criticised severely in South Africa – we were actually in hiding the night before the first Test. But the way we planned, and I worked with the team throughout that tour, was a personal triumph – we eventually came away with a draw in the third Test and actually we should have beaten them – they were lucky to get the draw. When I came back I just felt so ecstatic about the way we'd developed. As a team captain and as a team player I felt I'd accomplished a great deal with the players.

And anything in your personal life, your early life perhaps. What was your first success? When did you first feel, 'I've been successful'?

Well, when I was eight years old, I played No.8. My Dad and my uncle came to watch me and they promised me a rand for every try that I scored, and a rand in those days was a hell of a lot of money. I scored eight tries for my team and I felt like I was the best thing that ever touched a rugby ball. That is the fondest memory I have from my childhood.

Do you need total control to obtain success? Have you got to be in charge, ruthlessly driving everything through or do you rely on others for success?

You have to rely on others because you don't have the vision yourself. That's why I said earlier that you have to learn from your mistakes and you have to learn from others. You don't live in the past but it's a fool who doesn't look back at his past, especially in a team game like ours. I listen to advice every day and I take advice because you can get into a rut and start believing that everything you say is the best. You need to judge yourself and you get the best judgment of your character when you listen to others.

Which is more difficult – team success or individual success?

They are different types of success. Individual success in a team game is easier than team success because you can play for yourself and be the best player on the park, but your game will be selfish. You may be regarded as a fantastic player, but the vision to play a central role in a successful team, to put the team in front of your personal aspirations – that is more difficult to achieve.

Is there a difference between planning for success and achieving it? You might, for example, sit down with your team and plan the way you want a game to develop, then the unexpected comes up, in a way that you hadn't thought about, and you've got to react instinctively to that, to reclaim the success that you were trying to achieve.

No, you always plan for the unexpected as well. You have Plan B as well as Plan A. That's what we did in the World Cup. We planned to win the World Cup. We didn't just go out and say, 'If we win this World Cup it will be fantastic,' we planned it and took it step by step. But we also planned for disaster, and for what would happen after disaster. The World Cup was in South Africa and South Africa is fierce when it comes to rugby, so if we lost the first game – which everybody thought we were going to do – what would we do after that? Would we just lie down or would we come back a better team and work from there? Your Plan B must also be a serious plan of action.

Was there any stage in the World Cup when you really felt that things were not going to plan and that you were in real danger of losing out?

Yes. When two of our players were suspended after the Canadian game. This was unfair and I still maintain that they were not treated in the right way. Video material shows that we just tried to play the game, whereas Canada came out and provoked us, they had everything to gain and nothing to lose. After that game our team spirit was very low, but we continued to train with the same commitment – though to be honest I felt we were going to lose the World Cup right there and then.

So how did you pick yourself up and recover from that?

We said before the World Cup that if something like that happened, we would need to sit down and discuss it, and we did. New players came into the side, and I used the new players to help pick up the team spirit. Chester Williams had missed out on the initial World Cup squad through injury and now, all of a sudden, he was back in the side – and his delight at being back in the side, I think, lifted the team. We had to get the team spirit back, because team spirit made the team. On paper we might not have had the best team of individuals, but we did have the best team as a unit. Had this been lost, we would not have been successful. That was the thing we had to work on. First of all, in dealing with this problem, we addressed the worst fears of each member of the team both as a player and as a human being. When these fears are in the open and everyone knows about them, they don't seem so much of a problem anymore. Ninety per cent of things that you worry about never actually happen.

There is a saying that you make your own luck. Do you believe that?

Yes, I do. This year, when we were in a bad patch, we were not successful – basically because we had lost the principles that we believed in – and people said we were unlucky. But it's not a lack of luck that makes you lose, it's the letting go of the principles by which you play.

Is luck an essential part of success?

You need breaks, but I think you make your own breaks.

Is there a difference, do you think, between sporting success and success in other fields, such as business and politics, or are there core similarities that run right through?

No, of course there are core similarities that run right through. I believe in the four Ds in life – discipline, dedication, desire and determination. They apply in sport and life in general.

Is there any person, big or small, in any profession, either living now or in history, whom you hugely admire as being at the pinnacle of success as you rate it?

Yes. President de Klerk and President Mandela for making the change in South Africa's government and for not resenting what had happened in the past. I really respect them as leaders. That to me was one of the biggest steps, and it's just a pity that President de Klerk is not getting the acclaim that he deserves because he took a step that could have gone either way.

Anybody outside politics?

I respect my coach tremendously for what he has taught me. He's taught me a hell of a lot of things but his way of handling situations and handling players is his biggest skill. He doesn't talk about it, but he's had cancer for 16 years, he fights through it and nobody ever knows about it. The success he's achieved as a human being, in his business and in rugby, is phenomenal. And the way he goes about it is an eye-opener. It's easy to get big-headed when you win the World Cup, it's easy to get big-headed when you are a top rugby player – it's the way that you handle it that makes you a better person.

And how does he handle it? How does he go about it?

The way he handled it when he was nothing, when he was just a nobody. The same way. He's down to earth, he's noble, he listens to people and he uses what he learns from people to overcome his weaknesses or to help him.

Is it becoming more or less difficult to achieve success in your particular field?

Much more difficult. What can you achieve after you've won the World Cup? People say when you have reached the top of a mountain there is only one way and that's down. Yes, you must go down but when you get to the bottom, I believe there will be another bigger mountain to be climbed. It may be in rugby, it may be in life. So success shouldn't be channelled only into one thing. I think quality of life is also very important to me.

Success arouses conflicting emotions in people. Some admire it tremendously, others feel very envious about other people's success. What do you say to those people who feel envy about success?

I don't think it's envy, I think it's jealousy more than envy. I believe people who are envious of another person will want to learn, whereas people who are jealous only criticize. Envious people are easy to work with because they listen to advice, jealous people see the wrong in the right. A great many people have been involved in the transition to professionalism in rugby, and there has been a lot of jealousy and suspicion. I was often depicted as the black sheep who was trying to ruin South African rugby, but if you speak to any rugby player or anybody else involved, you'll find that I only spoke my mind. I was always open and honest about it.

So was it a difficult time for you?

The most difficult time of my life, but if I look back I wouldn't have done anything different.

And how did you deal with the jealousy?

I'm still dealing with it, it's just that I listen to people that I respect, people that have given me advice and people that have guided me. You must have an alter ego and I've definitely got one. I've got a very close relationship with a coach and also with a family member who helps me, and I use them constantly to guide me and give me advice.

If you could gather all the young rugby players in the world – youngsters of 12, 14, 16, fanatical rugby fans – in one room and give them one piece of advice about how they could become as successful as you are, what would that be?

Never to stop dreaming. Because my success started in a dream and dreams can come true if you apply your mind. The way to go about it is never to lose your dream. If you lose your dream then you've got nothing to work for.

When your time comes to leave this Earth, what would you like them to say about you?

There's really no one thing I would like said about me. Perhaps just that I gave it my best.

There's nothing you would like to suggest – they must remember me for this or I hope they'll remember me ...

There's nothing that I would really like to suggest on the lines of 'I've done this and that'. No, I would like people to remember me for what I have given them, I hope I've given a lot of people a lot of pleasure. And if they remember me for the right things, it doesn't really matter what it is for because different people will remember different things. Players would remember differently from spectators and administrators, for example.

What would you expect your fellow team members to say?

I hope they would just respect me for all that I stood for, and for the fact that I never compromised the team for myself.

SIR CLIFF RICHARD

As a schoolkid, he walked on stage for the very first time to sing 'Ratty's Song' in Toad of Toad Hall, *and was 'terrified'. Within ten years he was in the charts, launched on a career which delivered 115 hits and 13 number ones across half a century. Then he invested £2 million of his own money to produce and star in the musical* Heathcliff, *which, despite generally poor reviews, played to full houses throughout Britain. So here he roundly attacks the critics for 'losing touch with what people want', and goes on to launch a remarkable assault on 240 radio stations across the country which have stopped playing his records (and those of Elton John and Tina Turner) because they think as artists they're too old. He courts controversy with the assertion*  *that 'one song from* Heathcliff – 'Gypsy Bundle' – *is, to me, better than anything that Blur or Oasis have done recently. It's a fantastic rock 'n' roll song, but the general public won't ever find out.' He says those top groups are 'not better, they're no different, and I want to be able to compete in that forum'.*

Born in India, he arrived in Britain at the age of seven, failed his eleven-plus and left school at 16. He describes here accidentally hearing an Elvis Presley record for the very first time. 'My first taste of wanting success was waking up and wanting to be Elvis.' His first group, the Quintones, split up when three of its members left for secretarial college; so he formed a new band, the Drifters, got a manager, signed for EMI, and began working the clubs. He talks revealingly about those early days as he tried to get his first break; tells how the song 'Living Doll' was changed to make it an instant number one hit; and his reaction to his first review in the New Musical Express – *'crude exhibitionism ... his violent hip-swinging was revolting ... hardly the kind of performance any parent could wish their child to witness'. From way back in the early days with his backing group the Shadows he's made a point of 'always surrounding myself with people who are right for what I'm doing. I'm not a loner, I trust in others, I lean on others.' A committed Christian, he thinks he's got his life in balance, unlike his hero Elvis 'who, despite his business and creative success, didn't find personal success'. Kept looking younger than his 58 years by a strict diet, he wants his success to continue, and 'one of the driving forces is that I can still do it'.*

Sir Cliff, what is your definition of success?

I've often met people in the street who I think are really successful because they can still smile at life, regardless of what they're going through personally. None of us ever knows when we see someone in the street whether they've got a tragedy to deal with. But the men or women who can actually get through life, smile and joke, and perhaps not have the obvious trappings of success like money and fame, they're the really successful people. But you obviously want to know what success means to me. For me, success has been being able to shop, for instance, without necessarily looking at the price tags – although I still do look at them. When I go out and I'm recognized by dozens of people on the street, that's also a sign of success, in that I've wheedled my way into people's minds and homes and hearts, some of them anyway. I think those things add up to success.

So you're talking about two kinds of success? Which of those two is the more important?

There's no doubt in my mind. You must be successful as a person. Think of Elvis. He was one of the most successful rock 'n' roll singers ever. He left behind a legacy that will always be Elvis. Yet as a man it didn't seem to me that he succeeded. Those of us who loved him will always feel saddened by the fact that he didn't seem to find personal happiness – didn't have a personal success. It was a business success, it was creative success, but he, the man, wasn't really successful.

So how have you managed to achieve that when he didn't? Are you a success as a man, do you think?

I'd like to think I am. None of us is immune to being let down or disappointed, or feeling saddened at times in life, but that's all part of living. On the whole I'm happy with what I am, and I'm happy with my relationships with friends and family, and in that respect I can only see myself as being a successful person because I'm not unhappy with life. And I still think that that is the most important thing. Most people think of success as being money, most people dream of being wealthy, of being famous. It's only when you actually get those things that you realize, yes, they are great, but unless they actually lead to you personally being happy, contented, surrounded by people that you love, it doesn't mean a light.

How did you avoid going down the particular path that Elvis went down?

I think I have my family support to thank. I feel I'm balanced – though I suppose this is a debatable point. My critics may say I'm not, but I feel I'm balanced and I feel that I owe all of that balance to a mother and father who were both enthusiastic and realistic as well. My mother was very, very pro me going into competitions and chasing success – the famous recording type of success.

Did she want fame for you? Was she ambitious for herself or did she transfer that ambition to you?

No, it was just for me, and she was very supportive. My father, on the other hand, although he was supportive, kept on saying, 'You've got to realize that, you know, you're giving this so much that if it doesn't happen, what are you going to do? Life will go on and you have to go on in it.' So I had this balance, on the one hand believing that I wanted this desperately and if I didn't make it I'd be disappointed, and on the other hand my dad was always there saying, 'Life is still there to be lived'. I feel that's now filtered through all my thoughts. If I lost it all overnight it would be desperately difficult to deal with, but I feel I would deal with it. I don't feel that pop music owns me. I manipulate it and use it to suit my wishes. I do whatever I want with it. My brief is to entertain and I do whatever I can to entertain this large minority group who like what I do – hence *Heathcliff*, hence all the records I make. My critics don't understand that. They don't understand that to be truly successful in the way that I've been successful takes hours and hours of thought, months of hard work and dedication and commitment to doing something that you know people want. My motivation, most of the time, is to say to myself that if I want to communicate to these people, they have to like me. And if they can love me, that makes communication all the better. Most people who communicate don't realize that if you're sitting in an audience listening to someone speak and you don't have any chemistry with them, you don't actually hear their message. It does not communicate. You're more likely to disagree with them than agree. I've discovered over the years, because of my Christian faith, that I want to present a positive approach to life – that's my main message, if I've got a message at all, and people have to like you. I'm amazed that so few people in the media have recognized that if you want to say anything or do anything that will send out messages in the right way, people have to like you.

How do you explain the different judgments that come on the one hand from the critics, and on the other hand from the ordinary members of the public who pack into Heathcliff *night after night? Where does the gap lie between those two judgments?*

I don't really know, other than it's obvious to me now that the critics have lost touch, they've lost touch with what the public want and don't understand what the public like. I haven't lost touch, otherwise I wouldn't be here any more. Maybe it's because they are too busy trying to force their own feelings about art or drama or dance or music upon the public, who quite often say, 'Well, that's fine for you, but it's not what we want, thank you very much.' Otherwise how could the critics have been so wrong about *Les Miserables, Cats, Phantom of the Opera* and *Starlight Express*? They disliked all of them and yet they're the longest-running musicals ever. They already hated *Heathcliff* even before we did it. They wrote their reviews long before I ever performed it. And what have we achieved? We have the biggest advance ever in the history of West End musicals. I don't worry myself to death thinking about the critics, they have to sort out their own art-form, as I'm trying to sort out mine. But they ought to be looking at themselves now and saying, 'We've somehow misunderstood this.'

Have the critics ever affected what you do? For instance, did you have doubts at the beginning with Heathcliff *when you suddenly found that so many people were saying you couldn't do it?*

Yes, I did succumb I'm afraid. I don't see how I can break away from being human. Five or six years ago, when I first mooted the idea, it was ridiculed. I heard people ridicule it on the radio. The press started to write all kinds of vitriolic, vicious things, and I couldn't understand why they would treat me this way. After all I'm supposed to be the Mr Nice Guy of pop, how could they be so horrible to someone who is basically Mr Nice Guy? But they did and it did affect me, because there was a time, about three years ago, when I thought, 'What am I doing?' Three years ago, just prior to when we were possibly going to open, I was on holiday in Portugal. I had sleepless nights, I used to wake up bathed in perspiration, and I thought, 'What am I doing?' All because they had planted in my mind this great doubt as to whether I could really pull this off.

But what did it do to you? Did it make you even more determined to succeed when you sorted out those initial doubts?

Yes. During that holiday, I'd mentioned to my friends that this was happening and they were very helpful. They said, 'Look, are you going to do it or not?' And I thought, 'Yes, I am.' From then onwards every single detestable thing I read goaded me on so that I was determined not to fail. I threw myself into it in a way that I've never thrown myself into anything before. It was to prove the press wrong – my whole performance is based on that. And it's helped me to forget being Cliff Richard. I have two hours of amnesia every day. I am Heathcliff for two hours a night. It's a fabulously liberating feeling, and I'm glad they goaded me on because I don't think I would have had quite the same guts to do what I'm doing if they hadn't.

What do you think is the secret of your 115 hits, your 13 number ones across five decades, with all the changes in the music scene that have taken place during those decades? Was there something about your attitude, your approach which actually made it possible for you to stay up with the trends, as it were?

I think my main attitude must have been right, which is that I treated rock and roll with a lot of respect. Even in the early days when we used to sing 'Rock and Roll is Here to Stay', we weren't sure that it was. How could we be sure? It was just a baby art-form, and yet we hoped that it would stay, and it has. One of the reasons why it's possible for someone like myself to have success over the decades is because rock 'n' roll doesn't seem to change very much. If you play an early Elvis Presley record and then you play a new Spice Girls record, there are technical differences – the technique of singing and the use of harmonies is different, even the instruments are different – but it still has this driving offbeat, bass, drums, guitars, keyboards, it's the same instrumentation. And I think that's the reason why, if you just keep an eye on what's happening and what the public like, you can still break through, even though you seem to be alienated from the art-form. I sometimes feel alienated because I can't get air play anymore. Now to me rock 'n' roll and radio go together, that is how it always was and it's how it always should be.

But you do get air play, I hear Cliff Richard records on Radio Two.

Yes, but Radio Two is not the mainstream for selling records, although it's the place where I now find myself at home. I listen to Radio Two, as I do the Melody station in London and most of the Gold stations, because they play across-the-board rock 'n' roll. Most stations that you tune into now play just one type of rock 'n' roll. There's nothing wrong with that type, it's just that all day long it drives me mad. As does the fact that they've now cut out people like myself and, to an extent, Elton John – the people who kicked it off for our country. We are still making good rock 'n' roll records. My records can be played alongside those of the Spice Girls. But the radio stations now, the 240 main radio stations in the country, will not play a Cliff Richard record. It has to be something to do with ageism. I think they think, Cliff is 57, we're aiming at a young age group. But it's not fair on the young group not to give them the choice, because age doesn't come into it when you're playing a CD. You play a CD and your ears tell you whether you like it or not. For instance, one of the songs from *Heathcliff* – 'Gypsy Bundle' – is, to me, better than anything that Blur or Oasis have done recently. It's a fantastic rock 'n' roll song, but the general public won't ever find out. I keep thinking to myself, 'Why are we being cut out of the competition?' It's not fair on the public and it's definitely not fair on those of us who can't get into the mainstream. We have to find a new way, because there's a massive audience out there that wants to hear people like myself and Elton and Tina Turner.

What's coming across very strongly is that after five decades you're still hungry for more success. What's the driving force that prevents you from saying, 'I've done jolly well over the last half century, I'm going to pack it in'?

I don't know whether I want more success. I want it to continue, and one of the main driving forces is that I can still do it. The awful thing in life is when somebody is capable of working and they're not allowed to. It must be awful when people are retired early, for instance. Their physical capabilities, their mental faculties are all completely in tune and ready to go, and yet somehow they don't work or can't get work. That is destructive for the person and for society. The same goes for an artist. If you were a painter, for instance, and you were still painting wonderful pictures and you couldn't get them shown anywhere, your career, your life's work would stop. That's the frustration – I still feel that I can compete with Oasis. Give me a concert stage and I'll out-Oasis them, or I'll try to anyway. If you fail it doesn't matter. The fact is that you were there competing and the public still have that choice. To me the choice is the important thing. So I'm driven on because I feel I can still do it. Rock 'n' roll is never going to change that much, and I can say that now really quite blatantly because bands like Blur and Oasis have openly come out and said, 'No Beatles, no me.' People are influenced. And they've not come up with anything new, just a name – Oasis, Blur. It's just a couple of new bands with younger members, people who are not as old as me. But they're not better, they're no different. They've definitely consolidated my feelings about rock 'n' roll not really changing that much. Individuals can use rock 'n' roll in the same way an artist uses paint. You can mix different colours and you can come up with different shades and hues that appear new, but they're not really. I don't think anything's ever going to be new again. It's just got to keep on being exciting. I keep coming back to painting, but it's the most obvious analogy. People have been putting paint on surfaces from cave walls to canvas for thousands of years, but they've been doing it over and over again using the same colours, painting the same subjects, the same trees, the same landscapes, the same faces, and yet the results are still exciting and new to look at. Rock 'n' roll's the same, it's a true art-form, and I want to be allowed to compete in that forum.

Let me take you back to your early days. You were born Harry Webb in India, you arrived in Britain at the age of seven. You failed the eleven-plus and you left school at 16. That's not necessarily an ideal start for someone who's going to have a successful career. What do you think your schooling did for you?

I was the top boy in my school before I took my eleven-plus. It was a foregone conclusion that I would pass and go on to the grammar school. My school, at that time, assessed me through my work throughout the year, and in that respect I was top boy. But when it came to sitting the exam, maybe it was nerves or whatever, I failed and ended up in a secondary modern school. I have read, since then, that some of us are not very good at taking exams, that was certainly the case as far as I was concerned. I hated that first morning at secondary school. Not only had I not gone to the grammar school, but when I got to the secondary modern in Cheshunt, there were three streams, A, B, and C, and I was in the lowest one, C. I was shattered. For a start I was going to have to go home and tell my father and mother. However, halfway through the morning this man came in and said, 'Is there an H. Webb here?' And I put my hand up, and he said, 'There's been a mistake.' And I thought, 'What's happening here? I'm going to the grammar school.' And he said, 'You shouldn't be in C, you should be in A.' Well, at least it was something. I felt so relieved. I suppose it was my first taste of success. I was taken out and put in the A-stream, and I stayed there right through school. I wasn't bad, but at 14 I heard Elvis.

How did you hear Elvis? What was the moment when you said, 'I want a career in pop'?

I can remember when I first heard Elvis. My friends and I were walking through Waltham Cross, and a car stopped outside a newsagent's. The driver obviously had gone in to buy cigarettes or a paper or something, but the car was still running and the radio was on. We heard Elvis singing 'Heartbreak Hotel', and before the DJ had been able to say what it was or anything, the man came back and drove off.

So it was in the early days and Elvis wasn't as big a name?

Oh, no, we hadn't even heard of him. We all went away and listened to Radio Luxembourg and the AFN until we finally heard who it was, and we thought, 'What a funny name, Elvis Presley.' We then became fans, and from that moment onwards I wanted desperately to be like Elvis. I used to dream of waking up and being Elvis. I guess my first taste of wanting success was way back then – the minute I heard Elvis I wanted to be like him. But I didn't think I'd make it. When I look back now, no one's ever sounded like Elvis other than impersonators, and it's all very well being an impersonator, but you're stuck being that person, you can't ever create something for yourself.

Did you consciously want to imitate Elvis? Did you want to be a British Elvis?

Yes, in the very early stages. I was quite happy, for instance, when the first press write-ups were on the lines of 'England's answer to Elvis'. I loved that. And if my photograph was taken and my lip was curled up and I looked a bit like Elvis, that used to make my day. But within a year of turning professional and having a semblance of success, I realized that not only was I not Elvis, I needed to find something of my own. And by chance we got to make a film and 'Living Doll' was in that film as a rock 'n' roll song. We thought it was rather a pseudo-sounding rock 'n' roll song, so we changed it and did a country version of it and that's the one that went to number one. Then it led me into other areas within the rock 'n' roll world.

Let me take you back to that moment when you first heard 'Heartbreak Hotel'. You decided that you wanted to be like Elvis – how did you set about achieving that?

Whatever I did, I wasn't looking ahead and saying, 'If I do this, that'll lead to this and that'll lead to an agent and that'll lead to success and a recording career.' I just did what I wanted to do at the time. We had a tight-knit group of friends at school and five of us got together and called ourselves The Quintones. We used to practise at lunch-hours, and just do harmonies, unaccompanied, *a cappella* stuff. Our teacher allowed our classroom to be like a club for us, and we just sang for our friends. It grew from that and we did a couple of youth clubs and that sort of thing. When we left school, that all broke down, but I still wanted to be a singer. Then I got involved in skiffle – that seemed to be the best opportunity because there weren't so many rock 'n' roll bands around. Skiffle music was very easy to play, it was home-baked and I just joined a group.

And were you working at this time as well?

I'd started working. My father got me a job in the place where he was working – I was just a glorified teaboy really. In the meantime I was going home at nights and singing, and we were playing in pubs by this point. It was during that time I met my drummer, a friend called Terry Smart, who had also been at my school but he was younger than me. One night we were talking and he said, 'Do you really like skiffle?' I said, 'Well, it's not my favourite, I like rock 'n' roll.' He said, 'So do I.' So we left the skiffle group and formed our own band. We called it The Drifters and then started playing a circuit of pubs, making the odd fiver and tenner at weekends. That led to coming into London, to the Two Is coffee bar, and playing in the basement in that hot sticky cellar. After a week we thought, 'Well this is it, we're not famous yet, so let's go.' Then we got the opportunity to play at a talent contest at the Gaumont, Shepherds Bush. The clever thing we did then was to say, 'We don't want to be part of the competition, we'll top the bill for you – give us top billing and we'll do it for nothing.' And we played and the kids went wild. So we played again the next month and this time we had an agent come and watch us and that's how we got a demo tape that we'd made to Norrie Paramor, who gave us an audition in his office. We plugged into the wall with our little 16-guinea amplifier and sang 'Move It', which Ian Samwell had written on the bus on the way to Norrie's office.

So you hadn't rehearsed it or practised it?

No, but we had the lyrics written out and we sang it to Norrie. And he said, 'Fabulous! We'll use that as the B-side to one of the other songs I've got.' So we made our first record. Of course, the rest is history, as they say.

But did you ever think, when you were in that hot sticky coffee bar, and things weren't happening, 'I've made a terrible mistake and I shouldn't really have gone down this route'? Any regrets at that point?

No, it was all too early on. I was only 17. At that stage my life stretched ahead of me, rock 'n' roll stretched ahead of me. I don't know that I'd consciously given myself any time limit. People are always saying to me, 'What advice would you give to young people starting off now?' First of all, be sure that you really love what you're doing, and then go for it. And second, give yourself a time limit, because it's a very destructive thing. You can go on too long, and I've seen people way beyond their sell-by dates still plugging away and not having a very happy time of it. If rock 'n' roll doesn't want you, then thumb your nose at it. Get on and do something else with your life.

So you're saying the break has got to come within a year, two years, three years, and if you're not getting that break then there's something wrong, so you ought to abandon it and think of doing something else?

I'd give it five years. I'm thinking about people who are perhaps in their late teens, early 20s. You can afford to go until 25. Your life's not going to disappear if you don't make it before then. Give yourself five years to actually fight the struggle through, doing your little gigs, sending your tapes around to record companies, doing auditions, and all of that. If something doesn't click, then after five years I would have thought it's pretty obvious that for whatever reason people are not taking to what you do, and as I say, I think you should thumb your nose at it. It's not the be-all and end-all of life.

We talked earlier about the criticism you have had with Heathcliff, *but way back in the early days the* New Musical Express *called your performance crude exhibitionism, and I quote: 'His violent hip-swinging was revolting, hardly the kind of performance on television any parent could wish their children to witness.' How did you react to that?*

I loved it, to be honest with you, because it was so untrue. I couldn't hip-swing. Elvis was the hip-swinger. This is another thing, journalists think they create things. In actual fact they just follow like sheep so often. We were desperate for an Elvis in this country and they latched on to me and they used terminology that people used about Elvis about me. I hip-swing now much more, but I couldn't do it then. I used to stand there and just shake a leg, and that was my limit. I got better at it as time went by, but that was my first-ever performance on television.

Do you think anybody in the early stages of success has to be prepared to take all kinds of criticism, some of it reasonable, but some unreasonable as well? What advice would you give them?

It's very hard to advise in this area because I can hardly take my own advice. It is really hard to ignore what the press say about you, because our humanity is such that we can't ignore it. I've spent two or three days in my home not going out because there's been some silly article that doesn't bear any resemblance to what I was trying to say in the interview, and I have thought to myself, 'I sound like an absolute berk.' Certainly if I was reading this about another artist I'd think, 'What a berk.' And so I'm embarrassed and I don't go out. But in the long term I have learned that you have to live with it. OK, stay indoors, as I do. If you're really embarrassed, stay indoors for a couple of days, people soon get over it. A newspaper article is one of the most forgettable things ever. And to me it's a terrible indictment on the art-form. If I was a journalist now I would be desperate to improve my art-form because most people say to me, if they've read something, 'Oh, we take it with a pinch of salt.' Well, I wouldn't like them saying that about my records. But it's true. So, if an artist is beginning, you have got to learn to deal with the fact that people will sometimes say kind things about you, but perhaps 60 per cent of the time it will not be so nice, and you've just got to do what you believe is right – that's all that really counts. And if it works, your audience won't listen to what anybody says about you because they've already made up their minds about whether they like what you do. It's not important what the critics think. It's only important what your fans think.

How dependent is your success on looks? How dependent is the success of any singing star on their looks?

I suppose for 90 per cent of singing stars, the way they look is important. But there's no rule because there are many singers who aren't particularly good-looking men or even women, and yet still have a charisma. Talent will still break through. But on the whole the public want to see something that they can aspire to. I receive mail from people saying, 'When we read that you're 57 and see you looking like that, it gives us hope.' There's just something there that says, 'Well, if he can do it, I can.' So the way one looks is important, and certainly from my point of view I've always attempted to keep the flab away. I'm told that I don't look my age, and if that's true then it's just good fortune. There's nothing you can do about ageing.

A special diet?

I've always dieted. Well, I've always had a regime of eating, that's perhaps a more correct way of putting it. I have a fairly small breakfast of just toast and coffee, I skip lunch and then I have dinner. So I'm a one-meal-a-day man. But I do supplement with vitamin pills. I was told a long time ago that if you cut a meal out, you're not going to get the vitamins that you would have had from that meal. So I take vitamins to make up for the food that I don't eat. That way I've managed to keep slim; I can get away with murder on stage, I suppose, by the fact that I don't look my age. And I think that it's been very, very helpful. For most people in my work it's not a necessity, but it's a big bonus.

The other thing that has marked your success is your position on drugs – you said very firmly, 'No drugs' – not much drink, and, of course, celibacy. Now was this all part of a plan for success or did they just happen?

No, they just happened. I mean they are all quirks of one's personality, I think. I never smoked. I was lucky with smoking because I had an aversion to cigarette smoke when I was very young. I couldn't bear to touch an ashtray. When I was a kid my father smoked quite heavily. My father would say, 'Pass me the ashtray,' and I would get my sister to do it. If I did have to pass him the ashtray I would have to go and wash my hands – I couldn't bear the smell of it. Now that aversion has gone, obviously, you couldn't live life without coming across people who smoke, and that's fine. But I've never wanted to smoke, and that kept me away from drugs because I didn't take that first smoke of pot. I know now that pot doesn't lead anywhere – other than to another joint I suppose – but it takes you under the umbrella of 'drugs'. I believe there's not been anyone on heroine who hasn't taken pot. Not that the pot led to it, but it's an interesting connection, that you're just taken into the drug world. And because I didn't smoke I didn't get into pot and I was not interested in drugs.

This is one thing that youngsters don't understand. They all think they know everything about life, as we all do when we are young, but we've got to hit them over the head over and over again saying, 'If you're 17, you know zilch compared to someone who's 27. And compared to someone who's 57, you know practically nothing. Therefore you've got to listen. When people are dead before they're 25, it's either a terrible accident or it's self-inflicted by drugs. And if drugs do that to you, why do you want to take them?' Everyone wants to live life to its fullest and to take anything that might damage that life is pointless to me.

How did you avoid the drugs thing? It's very difficult for young people now, whether they're in the pop scene or not, to avoid drugs. So how did you manage to do it?

I don't know. I just have never seen any value in it whatsoever. I don't want a false stimulation. I've often thought of it in connection with my faith. If Jesus was to walk into the room, I could offer him a glass of wine, but I wouldn't offer him a fag or cocaine. It's as simple as that. Some of the people that take drugs are the biggest environmentally green people ever. And I think to myself, 'How dare they?' If the planet is so wonderful and so green, why do we need this outside stimulation to enjoy a sunset, to be able to admire a tree? I love trees, and my garden is full of them. I go into my little three-quarter-acre of woodland and commune, and it's so therapeutic. I do some of my best praying surrounded by nature. Now which would you choose? I choose to live life and be in touch with reality all the time, and that's why I don't get drunk – I do drink but I don't get drunk. I want to be in control of my life.

Is religion a driving force that has been responsible for your success, or has it simply been there in the background riding shotgun to your career?

I think it was probably riding shotgun because, although I was successful before I became a Christian, I was never an atheist. When we were in India I went to a church school. It was almost like a meeting place, we Brits all went to some church or other on Sundays. So I had this churchy background. When my career started the Christianity took a step backwards, and it really was not part of my life at all, not until much later. But I will say this now, that it's formulated all my ideas. I gauge everything by what I know to be true from the Bible. It's amazing that the Bible is still relevant. The language is sometimes irrelevant, if you pick up the wrong Bible, but Christianity's not, because it's still about living. Only one man said, 'I have come that they may have life and have it in all its fullness.' If someone offers you that, that's what you want, you don't want to take cocaine when you've got life to have. So I gauge everything by it, it plays a major part in my career, because it plays the major part in my life. My career's a facet of my life, a part of my life, but everything is controlled by what I believe. I wouldn't do anything that I felt would bring dishonour upon God or embarrass myself, and I gauge it all by my faith.

In general terms, not necessarily for yourself, but in general terms, what are the main principles that make people successful?

I wouldn't have recognized it in myself, had you talked to me when I was 14, but there has to have been something within me, and surely within everybody who's actually made it to success in any form, in any way, in any place on this planet. There has to be something within you that drives you out beyond your friends, takes you out into the ether beyond where all the other – dare I say – normal people are. Because I don't think we are normal. The very fact that we chase success and put ourselves up in this position of great vulnerability means that we are strange in some respects. I try not to be strange, I'd like to think I'm a fairly normal person, but I have to agree that anybody who goes for success, if they make it, and particularly if they maintain it, has to have this core of something that drives them all the way. You have to have commitment and dedication. You have to have self-belief. You have to believe that you're good and you're right and that all the critics are wrong. You have to, otherwise you'd stop every time someone said, 'You're no good.'

And luck?

I never know how to use that word. Was it luck that we went to the Gaumont, Shepherds Bush and decided we'd top the bill and not participate in the competition? Was it luck that the next time we went back we invited an agent, and he happened to take a record we'd made to Norrie? Yes, it was fortunate, but we manipulated the luck. So I think luck is part and parcel of it, but it's too loose a word, it's too lank a word to be used in the context of what happened to me and happens to a lot of people. There are things that, when you look back, you think, 'Gosh, if I hadn't done that, would my career have even started?' But then if you actually analyse it, there was a reason why you did that in the first place.

Is there a downside to success?

There is only one downside, and that is that if you're recognizable, it means that whenever you leave your front door and close it behind you, you become vulnerable to the public. I don't want to separate myself from them, but quite often you have to.

Is that a price worth paying?

Yes, it is, because in the end this is where the money of success comes in. If I want to be on my own, I can afford to fly to my home in Portugal. I can afford to fly to America where they don't know me very well, and I can get away with walking down the street and not being recognized by anybody other than a chance Brit on tour.

What do you regard as your biggest failures and, more importantly, how did you recover from them?

I guess it wasn't my fault, but my father and I weren't that close when I was growing up. However in the last two years of his life we became really close, and I've always felt that the earlier relationship wasn't a failure exactly, but it was a disappointment. He would have loved *Heathcliff.* He would have loved the things that I've done since his death. Was that a failure? I don't know.

Do you think you will get married?

I don't know. I've never discarded the idea of marriage. I just assume that if I were to meet the person that I felt I couldn't live without, then I would get married. But at the moment I enjoy being single. And I'm being fair to myself and to my prospective partner, I guess. That's what I mean when I say it would change my approach to my career, because if I were to get married I would commit myself to that, and it would have to be more important than my career. It would have to be more important than my fans. Not that they would ever be unimportant, but this being in my life, this thing that had happened called marriage, would have to become a focal point and a priority. It would have to be, otherwise what hope would it have? Maybe that's the mistake a lot of people make, that the marriage doesn't become a priority anymore. Maybe it's because it's easier to get out of. I've always felt that it needs that prioritizing.

What advice would you give to young people who want to be as successful as you have become?

We're talking about amateurs, I guess, but they've really got to get some groundwork done. If you're a musician, keep practising. Whatever you're performing, you've got to give it 100 per cent. You need to perform often. It wasn't so easy for us because it was all so new. Nowadays you can play in pubs and clubs. Go and do it, just sing. Sing live with people and start gauging what they want. Don't force what you want upon them unless you've given them at least three songs that they want. Just learn the trade, but make sure that the first item on your brief is to entertain that crowd and make them feel good and happy to be in your presence. That will only come with experience. You've got to keep singing in different places and gain as many different experiences as possible.

What do you think are the greatest enemies of success?

Complacency. If you feel, 'That's it, I've done it. I've got my gold disc, I've made my movie, I've done my TV series,' then it's all over because there is nowhere else to go. The first time I got a gold disc I thought, 'Great, now then, what about the next one?' And it has to be like that, the goal always has to be slightly ahead of you. As much as you believe in yourself, you have to believe that you still haven't done it yet. You haven't made your best record, you haven't done your best performance, you haven't done your best TV show, they've all yet to come. I've still got loads of things to come that are going to be better than anything I've done in the past.

Does success bring obligations in its wake?

Yes. I think success has given me a lot of responsibility - a mantle that sometimes I don't like to wear. I've often felt that success has thrown my Christian faith into a public forum as well, and that's a terribly difficult mantle to wear, the fact that people suddenly have a particular expectation of you, 'Oh, he's the Christian.' Being bad on stage as Heathcliff is really a joy, because it's so much easier to be bad than it is to be good. Not only to act being a good person, but actually to be the someone that the public expect – they expect things of me that they wouldn't expect of anybody else. It's a mantle I don't like wearing, but because success gives you what it does, if you are a responsible human being you have to see that it is a position of great privilege, and with that privilege comes a responsibility. I don't bible-bash my fans otherwise they'd have stopped coming a long time ago, but I feel responsible. So, when I get the opportunity I offer them a positive approach to life, and I feel the Christian approach to life is the positive way. I can do that genuinely and they'll accept it because they respect me as a person. But the responsibility is there.

I do wish that rock 'n' roll would shoulder its responsibility more. When we did *Live Aid* I thought that that was going to be a major turning point because suddenly the pop world became responsible. It raised more than £50 million just from the concert that Bob Geldof miraculously organized. And I thought, 'That's it, we've grown up.' And then it slithered back – we're all human beings, I suppose.

Has success changed you at all?

Oh yes, I think so. When I've said in the past that success hasn't changed me, I think what I really meant was that I didn't feel corrupted by it, that I didn't feel spoiled by it – but changed, yes. I have a life that I couldn't have dreamed of. Even in my wildest dreams when I was first wanting to be like Elvis, I couldn't have dreamed that it would be like this. And so it's changed everything. Money changes you. Success has changed me, but I'd like to think it hasn't spoiled me.

And what's the greatest pleasure you've had from your success?

There have been many moments in my life when success has given me terrific pleasure. The pleasure of standing in front of an audience that obviously likes what you've done is almost second to none. But I suppose it is second to one other thing – being able to do things for people. I've been able to look after my family. We all say as children, 'Oh, mummy, I'll buy you a house one day, when I'm rich and my boat comes in.' Not everyone gets the chance to do that, but I could, and I did.

And when, on behalf of Tear Fund, the Evangelical Alliance Relief Fund, a relief organization, I've visited Uganda or Kenya or Nepal and seen a life that is so alien to ours, I've been able to do something for these places. We have poverty here, but if you were to take the most poverty-stricken person in Britain and put them in Uganda, they'd be like millionaires. It puts things in perspective. Not that we've got to become complacent about our problems here, not at all, but we should start thinking, 'I'm fortunate to be British, that I wasn't born in Uganda where the life expectancy is perhaps 40 years old.' There are villages where 80 per cent of the people have got AIDS, it's just horrific. Being able to do something for such people or attempt to touch them – that's also what success has given me. I'd never have done that, I don't think, if I hadn't been successful. I probably wouldn't have been interested in what was happening in Uganda.

When your time comes to leave this life, what would you like people to say about you?

Melody Maker had a review of one of my concerts – it's one of the rare times I got a fantastic review. It said, 'Rock 'n' roll and God' – it was about a gospel concert – 'work together well in the hands of someone who loves them both.' And I thought, That's fantastic, because rock and roll deals with the world, for me, and God deals with the spiritual side of man's nature, and I thought that was a fantastic thing to have as an epitaph.

DAME STELLA RIMINGTON

'The teachers at school,' she explains, 'thought I was not sound, so I didn't become head girl.' And when, after university, this then shy lady settled on a career as an historical archivist, 'If anyone at the time had told me I would end up as director general of MI5, I would have thought they had taken leave of their senses.' Not only was she the first woman to hold that post, but the first person in the job to have their name publicly revealed. She describes the effect of that, and the media reaction, on one of her two daughters – 'when she was in the house by herself and heard squeaking on the stairs, she wasn't sure who to be more afraid of – the IRA or the journalists'. She now concedes that 'that piece of publicity could have been managed better', but is in no doubt about the move to more openness being the right one – 'we risked losing the support of the public if we didn't explain ourselves better' and 'the media now understand better what are the parameters for openness'. Stella Rimington describes here how she was recruited to the security service as a clerical assistant when her diplomat husband was posted to India; how the end to sex discrimination removed the blocks to promotion; the switch of emphasis from 'defending the country against the Soviet bloc to the control of terrorism'; and the challenges for the security services in the future as the world changes.

She talks here about what makes a successful spy, although she feels that the word describes only a part of the job – 'the last sort of person we want is someone who thinks he's going to be James Bond'. MI5 looks for someone who is sound, reliable, has good intellectual grasp and behaves with honesty. They have to obey the rules, but must also be able to think on their feet, balance the risk and take responsibility for what they do – 'if they're out there on the street, out on their own, they can't ring up the boss and say: "What shall I do next?"' She concedes that because they now recruit people at a fairly young age 'it is not easy to judge whether people have got this rare combination of qualities'. She acknowledges 'a corporate sense of failure when a bomb goes off', but 'by definition, you can't have total prior intelligence'. She concedes, 'I suppose I became a target for terrorists, but I didn't think about it very much.' Now retired, her judgment is much in demand in the corporate sector, where she has joined the boards of BG and Marks & Spencer.

Dame Stella, what is your definition of success?

The definition of success is not something that I have ever really thought about. I suppose it is the achieving of something significant, and particularly something lasting, in the area of your own expertise. But I think one of the problems with success is that, in the public mind, it has become confused with some sort of public acclaim or public notoriety. So many people whom we regard as successes are people who've set out to achieve just that, for example, pop stars or actors, or even politicians, of course, who depend on public acclaim for their success. It is interesting to me that, looking down the list of people whom you are interviewing, I am probably the only public servant in a Whitehall sense, and I would say that there are many public servants who have achieved just as much success as I have, much more indeed, but because people haven't heard of them, they don't get included when you start listing successful people. The reason, I suppose, I'm included, is that I led an organization which by its nature people regard as interesting, because we're a nation of spy story readers. So it's extremely difficult to define success, but it has to be achieving something notable and lasting, but something which need not necessarily receive wide public acclaim.

Is success better if it is achieved out of the public eye in the Civil Service context you were talking about, and is it easier to achieve if you do it that way?

I don't think it's better, nor do I think it's easier. In many senses it's more difficult, because the kind of problems that you have to deal with in the public service are often extremely complex. I wouldn't want to denigrate the profession of being a pop star, but I suspect that if you're talented it's probably easier to achieve success in that sphere than it is in the complicated area of public business.

Do you think there is a very real difference then, between long-lasting success, success that you build up to over a period of time, and the kind of success that happens like a starburst?

I think that the long-lasting success takes more effort and it's often achieved as a result of a team effort, whereas the starburst type of success is very often an individual thing. Nobody in the public service achieves success except by combining their own efforts with those of a lot of other people as well.

Can you generalize and say what qualities are needed for people to be successful?

Obviously one needs the capacity for hard work, because I don't think success in any field is ever achieved without that. I think you've also got to have the ability to prioritize and to identify irrelevancies. When my children were young I found it was absolutely essential for me to be able to divide off my domestic life from my working life so that when I was at work I was not worrying about what might be going on at home, and when I was at home I was focusing on what was going on there and not worrying about what was going on at work. If you can't do that, you're never even going to start being a success.

How did you make that division, that split?

By ruthlessness, I suppose. It's very difficult and I think it's something that you can only learn to do gradually. As a mother, you have got to make sure that you're content with the domestic arrangements that you've put in place, but, inevitably, from time to time they break down. You have got to develop a kind of ruthlessness where you accept that if you are dividing your attention you are doing nobody any good. You are not being effective in what you are supposed to be doing at the time, you're just stressing yourself and probably everybody else around you.

And yet, in the nature of things, you could be involved in a considerable problem at work and suddenly a major family crisis breaks that demands your attention. Now given the job that you have, was it easy to switch from work to family, or did you actually have to say, 'Work has priority because of the nature of what I am doing'?

It's never easy to switch and, of course, crises do happen. I can remember one occasion when I was actively engaged on something quite pressing at work and the person who was looking after my daughter rang up to say that she had just been carted off to hospital. Obviously, my priority at that time was to go to hospital and be with my daughter. All you can do in those circumstances is work it out at the time. If you are working in a team situation, as I always have been, you have to rely on other people to step into the breach when there is a crisis. On that particular occasion I actually hadn't got any money in my purse and I had to borrow money for the taxi from my colleagues.

Do you think that every successful person has to make some sort of sacrifice as far as their personal or family life is concerned?

Yes, I think they do, but it isn't only the successful person who has to make the sacrifices. I think that there are sacrifices for the family as a whole. It may not be fashionable to say this, but for a woman those sacrifices are probably greater because, however much she tries to achieve this wonderful balancing act, she is inevitably torn between the demands of family and the demands of work. In working you are automatically making sacrifices, and I'm not sure whether I would ever have gone back to work after my first daughter was born if it hadn't been an economic necessity. About that time my husband, who was also in the public service, decided to leave and take up some other occupation but that didn't work out. So when my first daughter was born we were jolly short of money, and I felt I had no option but to go back to work. It was a real wrench and a drag and I was really torn at the time. I would happily have stayed at home and become the classic middle-class wife. The fact that I went back to work meant that I and my children had to make quite a lot of sacrifices. Those sacrifices became greater when I became director-general and was subject to a lot of press interest, which inevitably had its effect on them.

If you are a successful person in the public eye like that, is it particularly tough on your children and family?

It was particularly tough on my children, because of the intrusion into their private lives. When I was appointed director-general I was the first person in that position whose name was made known publicly, but for reasons of security we decided, at the time that announcement was made, that we wouldn't issue a photograph. That, for the press, was like a red rag to a bull and what happened, of course, was that lots of people tried to find out, and successfully found out, where I lived. They all came and camped outside the house trying to take photographs of me and, inevitably, of those members of my family who were living in the same house. So my younger daughter, who was doing her GCSEs at the time, was subject to this type of intrusion every time she opened the front door. What's more she knew that there was a security risk to this, and that these people camped outside the front door were, in a sense, threatening our safety. I had to be away quite a lot of the time and she, poor child, when she was in the house by herself and heard squeakings on the stairs, wasn't sure who to be more afraid of, the IRA or the journalists. The whole thing created a very uneasy situation for her which I felt extremely guilty about. As for my older daughter who was away at university, it rubbed off on her as well because she was pursued by journalists who had got hold of some completely fallacious story that she was a member of a far-left student organization. So yes, it had a big effect on them and I felt very much for them. I was extremely grateful that they rallied round in the way that they did.

Was it a price worth paying?

That's a difficult question to answer. You don't actually have any choice, that's the trouble. You enter into these things without being able to foresee the end result and all you can do is try to manage the situation as it unravels. I would hope that my successors wouldn't have to pay that price, but I think they, like myself, would feel that it was something that had to be put up with and was probably worth it in the end. We could have managed that initial piece of publicity better – that was a lesson that we learned, both me personally and corporately.

Do you regret that you were part of the learning curve as far as those excesses with the media were concerned?

No, I don't regret it. When I was first appointed, we took a decision corporately, and with ministers' agreement, that the time had come to be more open about what the service did. We needed to explain to people what the functions of the service were. A domestic security service very much depends on the support of the public and, with a lot of ill-informed and adverse comment in circulation, we risked losing that support if we didn't explain ourselves better. We actually took a policy decision to do it which, combined with the fact that I was the first woman in the post, inevitably meant that there would be a great deal of publicity focused on me personally. That was something I accepted and, in a sense, we exploited that situation. It helped us in what we were trying to do, which was to be more open.

Going back, was there anything in your childhood, in retrospect, that hinted at you becoming the director-general of MI5?

No, I don't think that there was. My chosen career path when I left university was quite different. I hadn't really got much idea what I wanted to do when I left university. I looked around for something that I thought might be more interesting than the average and I settled on the career of an historical archivist because I was quite interested in history and I didn't want a job just sitting in an office. You might think that being an historical archivist is a sort of dusty career spent in libraries and manuscript rooms, it isn't actually. In my first job, which was in the county archives in Worcester, I spent a lot of time driving round the county in a little van trying to persuade vicars and stately-home owners to deposit their historical archives in the county records office. So I got out and I met people. I met quite interesting people and I had the job of persuading some of them to do something they didn't want to do. It was at a time when lampshades made out of parchment were popular and a lot of people were getting good money selling their historical manuscripts to the lampshade makers. I had to persuade them that this was not the right thing to do in the long-term interests of history – they should deposit them in the records office. I set out on this career thinking it would be interesting, but it would also be intellectually stimulating because of the historical angle to it. I certainly didn't set out on a career in any sense geared to becoming director-general of MI5. I don't think I'd ever really heard of MI5. And if anybody had told me at that time that I would end up as the DG, I would have thought they had taken leave of their senses.

Would anyone whom you met at that time have looked at you and said, 'There goes a future director-general of MI5'?

I'm not sure that they would, because I think most people didn't know at that time what it took to be a director-general of MI5. I can remember when I was at school, I was nominated to be head girl. The process of choosing the head girl at the time was that the children had a vote and the teachers had a vote. I suspect that I was the children's candidate, I certainly wasn't the teachers' choice. Although I think I got most votes, the teachers thought I was not sound and so I didn't become head girl. If you'd asked them at the time they probably would not have thought that I was destined to be anything particularly significant.

Why didn't they think you were sound? Were you a trouble-maker?

I don't think I was a trouble-maker, but I was not particularly conformist and I liked to make my views heard.

Some people would say that if you weren't inclined to conform that would not have prepared you for a role in the Civil Service, because the view of the Civil Service is that you have to conform, you have to be part of this huge enormous team, and there are certain procedures and ways of behaving which require a degree of conformity.

The security service isn't part of the Civil Service and I have never really been in the Civil Service. From my job at the county archives, I joined the India Office Library which was attached, I suppose, to the Civil Service in that it was run by the Commonwealth Relations Office at the time, but I was in a very specialist area. Then I joined MI5 which is not formally part of the Civil Service although it is the Crown Service. As for conformity, it certainly is important for anybody who works in the Security Service to obey the rules. That is absolutely key. You must behave with honesty and you must obey all the rules. If you don't, then everything the service is about is negated. But, you must also be the kind of person who is able to take and balance risks. If your job is to gather intelligence, for example, on terrorism, and then use that information in order to prevent, in the most effective way, something unpleasant happening, you've got to be able to assess the risk of taking or not taking action at any given moment and balance that risk. If you merely want to follow the rules, intent on not causing any ructions, you are not going to be very good at the job. It's a job where individuals are given responsibility, they have got to be able to balance the risk and take the responsibility for what they do. So I don't think that what I described as my early personality necessarily conflicts with the requirements of the job I ended up doing.

So in a sense not conforming is a quality that one looks for in the Secret Service, but at the same time you have to play by the rules?

I think people who work in the Security Service have got to be individuals. The first and most important thing is that you must look for people who are honest, who understand the importance of not trying to bend the rules, of obeying the regulations. But you must also have people who are able to think on their feet, who can cope in a situation where they're out on the street, out on their own, where they can't ring up the boss and say, 'What shall I do next?' and whose judgment in those circumstances you are going to be able to rely on. You're looking for that element of individualism, of ability to take responsibility. But you've also got to have people who, as I say, are sound and reliable. You are looking for people who are able to assemble large quantities of information, to judge what they have, to prioritize and to sift the important from the unimportant. You are also looking for a considerable degree of intellectual grasp. If you are trying to recruit people at a fairly young age, as the Security Service largely does, it is not easy to judge whether people have got this quite rare combination of qualities.

Those are the qualities that make a good spy?

The word 'spy' is not one I would use. The Security Service tries to gather advance intelligence about threats to the country, but it also has to assess it and work out with others what action should be taken to prevent the harm that's intended. The word 'spy' implies that all you are doing is going out and covertly gathering information, but that's not the only skill which the Security Service officers deploy.

When you look round a room of people, all of them with different qualities, different attributes, can you tell fairly rapidly who is going to make a good member of the Security Service and who is not, or does it require detailed interviewing and observation of that person over a period of time before you can make that judgment?

The selection process consists of a number of interviews in different circumstances, and a number of tests in order to try to enable those doing the selecting to make that judgment. But it's not an easy judgment, particularly when people are still quite young. Of course, once people have come into the Service they have to be trained and they are on probation for two years. Some people who initially looked as though they would be suitable recruits turn out not to be, and others, who looked less promising initially, turn out to be extremely successful.

How do you identify them in the first place? How do you approach them?

The Security Service now has open recruiting and puts out literature like other Civil Service departments. If people are interested they can write in, they can read the booklet, they can decide whether they like the look of the job. There's a lot more information about work in the Security Service now than there ever was before.

Is it easy to spot someone who's already been recruited by a rival Security Service and is attempting to infiltrate your organization?

That's the skill of the counter-espionage officer, so I would like to think the Security Service was good at that.

Of course there wasn't open recruitment when you were recruited. How were you persuaded to join the Security Service?

Having started off as an historical archivist, I then got married and my husband was posted to the British High Commission in New Delhi as a First Secretary. I gave up work and went with him as a diplomatic wife. When we got to Delhi I found life without a job a bit boring. In those days the Security Service had a representative in New Delhi and he was looking for some locally engaged assistance. His eye lit on me and my eye lit on him and I joined him as a clerical assistant. When the time came for us to go back to London I said to myself, 'Do I want to go on being an historical archivist or does the work in MI5 look more interesting?' I decided MI5 looked more interesting so I applied for a full-time job and was recruited.

What was your first job in MI5?

I'd rather not talk in detail about what job I did at any given moment but suffice it to say that when I joined there was effectively a two-tier career. It was still the days when the men were the officers and the women were the other ranks. So women joining in those days could never have more than what in old Civil Service terms would have been called an executive class career. If you were a man, you could go straight into the administrative class. That changed quite rapidly, but when I joined I was really looking at a career in a supporting role. However, after a few years the effect of sex discrimination legislation, etc., and also pressure from the women in the service, persuaded the then powers-that-be that women and men must be treated equally. From then on my career went through all the areas in which the service was working. When I joined the Cold War was on and the major activity, which took more of the Service's effort than any other, was broadly to do with defending the country against the Soviet Union and its Warsaw Pact allies in various different ways. By the time I left, the Cold War was over and the weight of effort in the Service had swung overwhelmingly towards the control of terrorism.

Were you drawn to the Security Service by patriotism, by the thrill of the job, or what? What was it that made you feel that it was something that you wanted to do, to get involved in?

I think it was a combination of those things and a feeling that I've always had, that I wanted a job that was interesting, that would be interesting, unusual, exciting. In saying that I have to be a bit careful because the last sort of person one wants joining the Security Service is someone who thinks he is going to be James Bond. One is looking for people who genuinely understand that there is a serious job to do and are prepared to go about doing it in a serious way. But that said, I always found it a most fascinating, varied and interesting career. That's what I was hoping for when I joined, and I wasn't disappointed.

Success for most people in most professions means making a degree of sacrifice in one form or another. What is it like living in a world where you and the people you work with could be called on to make what you might call the ultimate sacrifice? Is it nerve-racking?

I don't think I recognise that as a description of the job. If you mean by ultimate sacrifice that you might get killed, that is only true for a very small proportion of the people who work in the Service, those people who are really at the sharp end of operations against terrorists, for example. For the most part that is not a risk which people in the Service face every day, and even for those who do that risk is reduced by what we call good tradecraft – assessing, analysing and balancing the risks. In my case, because of my high profile, I suppose I became a target for terrorists but I didn't think about it very much.

Why not, because a lot of people would?

I suppose it's because you just take it for granted in the circumstances you're in and you are confident that the risk is being assessed and appropriate action will be taken to protect you. You, personally, understand what the risk is and you know what the machinery is for dealing with that risk. You feel as confident as one ever can in those circumstances.

Did you ever feel like giving up?

I never felt like giving up, because I never had any specific goal. And anyway, I don't believe in giving up. I think you just have to plod on when times get hard.

Did you expect that being successful as the director-general of MI5 would lead to the jobs that you have now, the directorships of various companies?

No, I didn't really. I didn't know what it would lead to. I hoped it would lead to something interesting, but there wasn't any real precedent. I was the first director-general whose name was effectively a household name. Although the names of my predecessors had become known gradually, they didn't have that moment which I had when I was first appointed, when I suddenly became a public figure. There was no knowing what people would make of a retired director-general of the Security Service. I have found the various reactions quite interesting – some people aren't quite sure what the Security Service is all about, but they think it is perhaps just a bit dodgy, so better not to get involved. Other people take a completely different view and think that somebody who's been the head of the Security Service for a number of years and been through a period of great change has got something to contribute to other organizations that are experiencing change. Despite our policy of openness, I have been quite surprised by how many in senior public positions still have very little idea of what the Security Service does.

When you were in the hot seat, in the very nature of things you had rivals, rivals being other Security Services that are sometimes trying to frustrate what you do. Did you ever at any time sit back and think that success for you meant failure for somebody else?

Well, in the starkest terms, I suppose, if the KGB had a success in the Cold War, then it was a reversal for the Security Services of the West. And if the intelligence services were successful in getting prior information about a terrorist attack then it was failure for the terrorists. But in personal terms I don't think that's anything that I particularly reflected on. Apart from that stark contrast between the Eastern Bloc and the West in the days of the Cold War, the atmosphere in the world in which security services work is one of co-operation rather than rivalry. For example, the security services in Europe work extremely closely to combat terrorism. This is a broadly-based corporate effort with no professional rivalry.

Is it in any sense a game? Do you sometimes feel that you're there almost playing a board game and moving figures around the board with a kind of sense of detachment about it? And in fact do you have to think like that and separate the decision-making processes from any personal emotions you might feel about individuals involved?

I don't think that's any more true for my profession than it is for many others. Your description is rather John le Carré – the Smiley type of affair is not a very precise representation of what it is like in real life.

Who are your heroes? Who are the people you regard as being successful who you look up to, people either past or present?

The kind of people I admire are people who do things that they think are right even though they're not necessarily going to benefit personally. For example, I admire both F.W. de Klerk and Nelson Mandela for their willingness to compromise in the broader interests of their country. I admire John Major for putting Northern Ireland policy high up on his agenda even though, because it's such an extremely complex issue, the likelihood of his benefiting, personally or politically, was not very great. I admire Mikhail Gorbachev because he recognized the moment for making change and took action to try to make that change. I also admire people who turn adversity to advantage, like Frances Lawrence, the woman whose husband was murdered, for the way she has successfully turned this terrible tragedy in her own life into something which hopefully will benefit other people. Those are the kind of people I admire.

What do you say to those who envy success?

I think envy of success is probably the most damaging thing in a way. There are an awful lot of people around who are prepared to attack anybody who has any kind of success, and it usually is from envy. The only thing to do about such people is to ignore them and not allow them to get under your skin.

What do you think, apart from envy, are the greatest enemies of success?

Hubris, I suppose, self-satisfaction. If you sit down and say, 'I am a success,' then you won't be a success for very long. But I think that envy and the damaging kind of criticism that comes from it is probably the greatest enemy.

But is it also quite important never to be satisfied with what you are doing?

Yes, I think it is. One must always look at the next thing to be achieved, and I suspect that most successful people do that. That's why they're a success – they've got an inner striving which leads them on to the next thing, they are never 100 per cent satisfied with what they are doing.

Does success bring obligations in its wake?

Absolutely, without a doubt. I feel I have an obligation to other women who are trying to do the difficult thing of balancing their family life against their careers, and I feel that, if I can, I should offer them the benefit of my own experience. Whether it helps them or not depends on them. I take an interest in girls' education. I often get asked to give away the prizes at girls' schools and other things like that, and I try to accept as many of those invitations as I possibly can, because I think that it's very important for girls to have, as role models, people who have succeeded in all sorts of different walks of life. I think that it's important for them to see that you can succeed and not become some kind of harridan or peculiar shrivelled-up sort of person. You can remain a straightforward, recognizably ordinary person. Yes, there are certainly obligations. There are obligations not to say stupid things, as occasionally pop stars do. One must recognize that there are people who listen to what you say and possibly take their lead from you.

Has success changed you at all?

I think everybody always feels inside that they are still the same person that they were, because they have been living with themselves all the time. But I suppose it's changed me. I'm much more self-confident than I was. I was rather shy when I was younger. Even now I wouldn't say that I was the most self-confident of persons, I still get quite nervous when I'm going to speak in public or something like that.

Do you think that nervousness is an important ingredient in staying on edge as you move towards success?

Yes, I am sure it is. If you are too laid back, I don't think you perform as well as when you are a bit tense. The adrenaline flows and it makes you focus that bit more on what you're doing. I'm not as nervous as I used to be, without a doubt, but how else I've changed I don't know. I think I have always been a bit bossy and I probably still am a bit bossy, but whether I'm bossier than I was I don't know!

If you could gather together all the young people who admire what you have done, and are considering a career in the security services, what advice would you give them?

If the question is, 'Would I advise them to join the Security Service?' it would depend on who they were. I think the advice I would give to the young in general is, 'Keep an open mind, don't plan your life too rigidly. Be prepared to accept opportunities when they come along.' I would say, 'Look for a job that you think you will enjoy and you will get satisfaction out of, even if you don't think it's going to lead to fame and fortune. If you are interested in serving the country and you think that that will provide you with satisfaction, then go for a job in the Security Service or a job in the public service. But above all, keep an open mind, be prepared to make a change if the job you are doing doesn't seem to suit you. Keep flexible and look for something that will suit you.'

But if they do get into the security services, what is the biggest challenge and the biggest threat that those services face over the next decade or so, which they would have to deal with?

There are a lot of threats to the security of the state which they are going to have to deal with, but for the moment terrorism is at the top of the list. As far as I can see, that is going to go on being an extremely important area for quite a long time. It's very difficult, though, to foresee exactly where threats to the security of the state are going to come from and how they will change. None of us, for example, foresaw the end of the Cold War at precisely the time it happened. But the qualities needed are going to be broadly the same, whatever the threats they are working against. The important thing for them is to keep their sense of humour, to work hard and, even if you find occasionally the rules are a bore, accept that it's very important in a democracy that services like the Security Service are properly controlled and regulated.

Do you feel you've had to pay a strong personal price for your success? Do you feel that there is in fact a definite downside to success for everyone?

The downside for me has been upheaval in my private life caused by the necessity for security, set against the early activities of the press. One newspaper, for example, when I was first appointed, published a photograph of my house in a prominent position in its pages and that meant that I had to sell that house and move elsewhere. Effectively, I had to go underground in a way that was ironic really, when you consider that we were trying to be more open. All that has had an effect on my life from which I have not yet fully recovered – that is the price I have had to pay and the price that the rest of the family has had to pay as well.

When your time comes to leave this life, what would you like people to say about you?

I think I would like them to say that I'd behaved with dignity and grace and style, that I had not compromised my principles and the principles of public service for any personal gain, that I had not tried to achieve personal success at other people's expense, and had always acknowledged other people's contribution. I'd like them to say – but I don't think they will – that I'd never complained, and that's perhaps something that I've got to work on in the next period of my life.

MARY ROBINSON

She was called the world's most popular Head of State, with a formidable 93 per cent approval rating, but never placed great weight on popularity. Instead, the first woman to be President of Ireland judges success by 'the ability to identify a need for a change, and then effect some of that change'. She learned early on to 'stand firm, believe in yourself and not worry too much if you are criticised', when, as a member of the Senate, she introduced the first bill to legalise contraception in her overwhelmingly Catholic country, and received an avalanche of hate mail.

Mary Robinson grew up 'wedged between four brothers', and was encouraged by both parents 'to develop my full potential as a woman, and to have no barriers, no limits on what might be achieved'. From the age of seven she remembers wanting to redress imbalances, injustices and iniquities. She studied law at Trinity College Dublin and Harvard, before returning to TCD as Professor of Law and embarking on a brilliant, combative legal career. Her parents refused to attend her wedding to fellow lawyer Nick Robinson because he was a Protestant – although they were quickly reconciled. Basically shy when young, she tells here how she built up confidence by forcing herself to take part in debates, and of the time when she first realised 'I had the audience in my hands'. She recalls her initial 'total lack of interest' when approached to run for the Presidency, and why she changed her mind over the following few days. Her approach to the job was to 'work right up to the constitutional boundaries', developing the potential of the office. Her big crusade was for organisational success, seen in the growth of 'networking' in Ireland – local groups becoming more structured, and successfully tackling old problems like unemployment. She believes 'society will benefit greatly when there is a more even balance between the contributions of men and women'. After this interview took place, she decided not to stand for a second term as President, moving instead to a top, Geneva-based job with the United Nations as High Commissioner for Human Rights. Cynicism she sees as the great enemy 'because it can deflect people, undermining their commitment or values'. And her advice to young people is that 'the individual does matter, it is possible to effect change, it is important that people take on a responsibility to be involved in that kind of change'.

President Robinson, what is your definition of success?

I don't think I have worked out a neat definition. I have always thought of success as being able to change things, in whatever context.

Is there a difference between personal success and professional success?

Yes, possibly. Personal success has ultimately to do with being at peace with yourself, with what you are doing, having a sense of 'Well, I am on top of what I am doing, and I think it is working.' Professional success I suppose has more to do with being equipped and very focused, with having done your homework and applying yourself to the best of your ability. But, as I said, success is the ability to identify a need for change and then effect some of that change.

Is it possible to feel successful within yourself when the rest of the world, the critics, the media, are perhaps judging you not to be so successful?

Yes, I think I have had experience of that. You can be heavily criticized but know that what you've done has mattered, because it has brought about changes and was the right thing to have done. I learned quite early on, and I think it was a very important lesson, that you must sometimes stand firm, believe in yourself and not be too worried if you are much criticized.

So how do you ride that criticism? Is there a technique, a formula for doing it?

I think I found it very difficult the first time I was severely criticized. I remember that I wobbled and was affected by the criticism and very hurt by it. Then you build up what could be called scar tissue, a certain toughness, and again I'm glad I had to do that quite early in an elected public life.

What was the particular issue over which you felt scarred?

It was when I introduced family planning legislation in Ireland. I produced a Bill and I was taken aback by the criticism from both the public and the church authorities, who obviously mattered a lot in an Irish context, and also by the hate letters, because I wasn't accustomed to receiving 10, 20, 100 letters in a week which portrayed me as a terrible person from hell. Most of the vitriolic language was wrapped up in religious fervour and I found that I was feeling defensive, even walking down a street, as if everybody really was thinking that about me. Then I realized, 'I know that this is necessary, it is important, it may take a while, but I am at peace with myself and with what I am doing', and that ultimately was more important.

Did the strength of that criticism ever prompt any feelings of doubt that what you were doing was right?

I don't think so. If anything it firmed up my sense of resolve. Obviously it helped to have support from friends, particularly Nick. It was just before and in the early stages of our marriage, and his support was very important. Unfortunately he decided to tear up most of the letters, which I now regret, because he could see that I was affected and he felt that getting rid of the evidence would help.

Why do you regret that?

Because I think it was an important indicator of social change taking place and the difficulties of that period. I am an archivist at heart and I regret it when direct evidence is removed.

To what extent do you think your success is a product of your background and your upbringing?

I suppose to a considerable extent. I had a very happy supported childhood. I was lucky to grow up wedged between four brothers and to be encouraged by both parents to be myself, to develop my full potential as a girl, as a woman, and to have no barriers, no limits to what might be achieved. I don't know quite how they instilled this strong sense in me, but I know that I had a very real starting point, that I had as much potential to achieve what was in me as my brothers or anybody else in our age group.

And that was down to the attitude, the approach of your parents to you in all kinds of ways. What were the most seminal kinds of ways in which they influenced and shaped you as a lone sister amongst four brothers who presumably were fairly tough to live with?

I think it was very simple things. It was also the way they treated my brothers. For instance, we were all expected to do housework. In fact my brothers felt that I was the one who was favoured, being the only girl. There was an ease of relationship, I suppose, and the fact that no real distinction was drawn between my brothers and myself, while at the same time I was encouraged to bring out my strengths as a girl and a woman - not to try to be successful by trying to be male, but to see that it was possible to be female and successful. But it is hard to pin down exactly how that was promoted so consciously.

Was there always a sense of rivalry with your brothers?

Not rivalry in the sense that I felt particularly competitive. I certainly engaged in all the tomboy activities to keep up, and I held my own in that sense, but I realized that a lot of the goals and the changes that I wanted to bring about were outside that family context, so there wasn't any rivalry as such.

When was the first time, perhaps going back to your teens or even before, when you said to yourself, 'I have succeeded at something'?

I suppose there were early occasions of writing essays that were very highly regarded, or receiving praise for particular contributions.

How important is that praise?

I am not sure. I think it is possibly the other side to criticism. If anything, I have found that when I have known that something was important, that it was the right thing, but came up against a critical barrier, that was probably more of an influence. Quite often praise is misdirected. I have often been praised and thought, 'Well that's not really what I would consider worth praising,' and I think that was my reaction at quite a young age – feeling that you were being praised for the wrong reason. It's hard to explain, but I don't think it ever mattered as much as standing firm in the face of something more critical which attempts to stop you or to undermine a commitment to something. That was more likely to motivate me.

You went to Trinity College, Dublin, and because of the nature of that university at the time, you had to seek permission from the Catholic hierarchy to do that. Why did you go through that? Was there a touch of the rebel about you in the early days?

No. I followed my two older brothers to Trinity. My father had already sought permission for them, so in the family I think we regarded it as a joke, but in the context of the time it was important to my father that we should observe what was considered to be the necessary stage of seeking permission. It didn't cause any problems with my two older brothers, but by the time I came along it was a non-issue and indeed the ban had been removed when it came to my two younger brothers. We were at that time of transition when nobody really took it seriously.

But isn't there a hint of the rebel about Mary Robinson? You married a Protestant. Your parents didn't go to your wedding. Then you became a combative lawyer, fighting for the rights of women and the underprivileged, which was unconventional in Ireland in the '70s and '80s. Is there something inside you which wants to rail against certain things you believe passionately are wrong?

Yes, I think that although I grew up in a very supportive – sheltered if you like – and close family, I was always aware of being something of an outsider, observing and not being content with what I observed. I had from a very early stage what I can only describe as an inner sense of justice, and it has always been there. I have always been looking from whatever context at the wider circle and seeing issues there that are neither fair nor supportable and feeling that something should be done. But I think it is less rebelling than wanting to change, wanting to redress imbalances, injustices, inequities. I think that has been there since I was seven, eight, nine.

Do you think that in general outsiders, people who take an unconventional view of life rather than going along with the flow, have a better chance of being successful than those who choose to run with the herd?

I don't know. I certainly know that if I was characterizing myself I would say that I have that outside perspective and that it has been important.

Was it more or less difficult for you to be successful in that particular area of the law that you went into?

It is hard to know. I certainly found that going to the Harvard Law School and seeing that I could hold my own in that company – indeed with distinction at times – gave me a lot of confidence. When I came back to Ireland, I started to practise law in the summer of 1968, then very quickly began to tutor and later took up the professorship of law at Trinity. I had the confidence to seek out ways of both taking cases and writing about the areas of law in which I specialized, such as constitutional law. And I always tried to make the most of my academic work in practising law, and used my practising experience to make the teaching more interesting, with real anecdotal examples.

You talk about the importance of Harvard in giving you confidence and you said once that you are basically shy. A lot of successful people say that in their early days they were shy and it is almost as though that shyness encourages them to greater efforts than people who perhaps had a more natural confidence at a very early age. So how did you overcome your early shyness?

Well, certainly I was conscious of needing to become more confident, particularly in public and in public speaking, so I deliberately got involved in debates, and forced myself. I knew that I was going to dry up, and that I was going to have to get over this. I was very conscious of being observed in public and was going to have to cope with that, so I took part in *Irish Times* debates, debates in the King's Inns, I became Auditor of the Law Society. Now that was partly because I wanted to be able to voice the need for change in various ways, but also because I needed deliberately to build up my own confidence.

And that confidence came easily. Did there come a point where you broke through the confidence barrier so it was no longer a problem, so you didn't consciously have to summon up your strength and say, 'I must be confident'?

I think I can remember a particular point in an *Irish Times* debate in UCD, where suddenly I had the audience in my hands, and I got a sense of, I suppose, power from that, the power to influence an audience's listening that went beyond simply making good points in a debate – it was another dimension. I realized that that was a breakthrough. That same feeling has happened since, not always, not even frequently, but there are times when the audience is really listening and you can influence it by the power of communicating strongly what you really feel. From that point I had more confidence in a public sense, both in debate and, later, speaking from public platforms and in the Senate.

Have you always had a game plan for being successful? Was there a career path on which you set yourself with the particular ambition of achieving the presidency at the end, or was there an element of things simply happening, circumstances throwing you in certain directions?

Not a game plan. I really didn't look at life in terms of 'This is what I want to achieve personally'. It was more a matter of responding to circumstances and to this constant analysis of the need for change in whatever the circumstances were, when I was a student, when I was a young lawyer, when I was a law lecturer, when I was a member of the Senate. In each of those contexts there were issues that I found were worth engaging in and I didn't particularly view it as a matter of personal goals. I found great satisfaction from feeling that I could effect change and probe and control and be involved with others in trying to achieve change. I don't think I have ever looked ahead ten years and said, 'Where do I want to be?' That hasn't been the focus.

So when did the idea that you might run for the presidency first come into your mind?

I never contemplated it until I was approached very unexpectedly in February of 1990 and asked by a former Attorney-General in the Labour Party, John Rogers, if I would consider accepting a nomination from the Labour Party, which I had been a member of, but from which I had resigned about five years earlier over the Anglo-Irish agreement.

What did you think when he approached you?

I was completely surprised and my immediate reaction was one of total lack of interest or enthusiasm, because I was involved in the Irish Centre for European Law which had recently been set up, I had joined Chambers in London and I had a number of cases before the courts in Luxembourg and Strasbourg which were very interesting, and were the focus of my attention. But I recognized that the invitation to consider a nomination was an honour and therefore it would be impolite to say no immediately. John Rogers told me afterwards he could see from my face both surprise and, initially, a very negative response, so although I said I would take the weekend to consider, I think he felt that it was unlikely that I would say yes. But, during the weekend, I thought seriously for the first time about what the constitution provided for in a non-executive elected representative of the people, and I immediately found myself hugely interested in the potential of that. By the end of the weekend, even though with my track record I couldn't have any real expectation of being elected if I was nominated by the Labour Party, I was sufficiently engaged in wanting to make the case that there was a role and a resource in the presidency.

So initially you were attracted because, as you say, you wanted to make the case. When did you feel you could win?

That's quite hard to say. I felt that, even at a very early stage, there was so much enthusiasm that there was perhaps some possibility of winning. And then I suppose by early September I was influenced by other people saying to me, 'You must realize that this is winnable,' and from then on I think we were seized by a determination to win. By then the election was only a few weeks away.

When you realized you could win, did that lift your campaign to a different level?

I think that had been happening. There was certainly one moment – I think I was going to bed at night – when I did realize that not only was it winnable, but it was becoming more probable, and therefore we were talking about the next seven years. At that stage, probably for the first time, I recognized that we had already entered a new level of serious commitment and momentum.

And then you won. What did the girl from Ballina think about that? What went through your head at the moment of victory?

It is very hard to capture just how deeply emotional it was. I really did feel an extraordinary sense of personal emotion in response to the trust that had been placed in me. I will never forget how much I felt I must live up to this trust because I felt so overwhelmed by it. I was awed by the sense of being trusted to make this appointment what I had said it could be – a true reflecton of the thinking of a people from outside the political domain. I wanted to shape things in a way that would respond to the trust placed in me.

How close to politics can you go without jeopardizing your position or indeed the presidency itself?

I think it helps that I came to the position as somebody who had the training of a constitutional lawyer and an experience of political life. I am not saying that you have to have this background to be President, but because I was seeking to develop the potential of the office, I think it was a great help. I have been conscious of the constitutional framework and the boundaries, and I have a huge commitment to remain within those boundaries. I have no desire to stray either inadvertently or advertently beyond those boundaries, because that would be completely inappropriate, but it's a challenge to try to work right up to the boundary. I have been accused sometimes of perhaps glimpsing across, but I have always remained firmly within.

It would have been easier, would it not, to have adopted a more regal role if you like, as a figurehead, never tempted by the option of pushing the boundaries a little? Were you ever tempted by that prospect? Did you ever feel at any stage after you became President that 'It's all too much, I can't do what I wanted to do because I am not really in the political mainstream, therefore I simply ought to resign myself to being a figurehead as Presidents of the past have been'?

No, I think I was fortunate in being interested in becoming President in order to develop the resource of the office. I hadn't been interested in the abstract, I had never thought about it. When I became interested it was for the purpose of developing the potential and then using it within the modest context of its being a non-executive office. I have always been far more interested in staying within the constitutional framework but developing the potential, and I have never felt, as I am often asked, frustrated or prevented, because I knew beforehand precisely what the constitutional framework was. I didn't know and couldn't know exactly how it could be developed, and that was part of the excitement, part of the interest of it, part of the challenge.

Part of that development included incidents like the Loyalist women from Belfast's Sandy Row visiting you and you shaking Gerry Adams by the hand at a sensitive time. Does the kind of President that you want to be have to take some degree of risk?

Yes, I believe so, and it has to be very carefully and prudently done, because the office of representing the people outside politics is not a confrontational office and should not be divisive. It should be one that is as implicit as possible and yet also there has to be a certain willingness to give leadership and direction and, at times, this means taking carefully assessed risks.

Have you ever thought at any time, 'Maybe I'm going a little bit too far here'?

I don't think so. There have been times when I might have wished to find different words at a particular moment. Language is very important in this office, because what you say is closely noted by people – my words come back to me months and years afterwards. I have seen the way in which people can be influenced and how important it is to find the right words. There have been times when I have regretted that I didn't put something in a slightly different way, or put it better, but I haven't been conscious of actually doing something inappropriate.

You meet many women's organizations, a particular passion of yours, you call it networking. How important is that to the presidency?

It is important to me, in the style of presidency that I have adopted, to be very much in touch, and through being in touch to try to create a more inclusive society, so when I go to a small rural group or to an inner-city youth group, I can be part of a wider network, I can help them to form their own linkages. I am constantly, through the way I describe my interest in what they are doing, helping them to shape what they are doing. I have noticed that over the last six years the *ad hoc* single activities of local groups and organizations have become more structured. We have a very developed structure of area partnerships to address unemployment and I can see what a difference it is making in areas of high unemployment. I have a similar perspective on the women's organizations. I have seen networks developing which are a very important way of widening a circle, comparing experience and exchanging opportunities, being able to do together what would be difficult to achieve as a single small network of women. I have seen the links that have been formed between women's networks north and south on the island of Ireland, which has been very important, and there has been a growth, a structural development, which is quite significant. There has been a learning curve and perhaps we are seeing some of the evidence of that now in the participation by the Women's Coalition in the forum presently in Northern Ireland, and I would see that as being one manifestation of an increasing sophistication, an increasing harnessing of energies in a very focused way, and a taking up of challenges and developing of potential.

So you see yourself as a catalyst in this, stretching the political boundaries, stretching almost the meaning of politics, in terms of involving people more? You have actually said democracy is under scrutiny and you are interested in new ways of leadership. Now what do you mean by that? Is the successful politician of the future going to have to be a different animal from the kind of politician we have become used to over the last few decades?

Well, certainly I think it is recognized that there is a crisis in the normal shape of our democracies – electorates have become very disillusioned. We talk about democratic deficits, low polls, a dissatisfaction with the way in which people assess politics, which is at election time and through electing representatives. We talk about the extent to which those representatives are able to be in touch with and reflect the views and wishes of an electorate. I do believe it is necessary to widen and deepen the participation of the people in order to give them a deeper sense of democratic involvement, and this means bringing out all the strengths of the civil society. A lot of it I think is stronger if it is a bottom-up self-development. Certainly in the office I hold which is outside the political, it is possible to engage with a broader civil society and to encourage the kind of structural development that I have talked about, which involves statutory agencies, often central and local government bodies with voluntary organizations and groups. There is a very significant role for elected representatives in this process. In a sense it is for them to find that role, and part of it is to be aware of and to be linked into a lot of this local self-development. The more they are involved in and linked into it, the more they will represent the significance of it without trying to own it. I think it moves away from an idea of clientalism and dependency on the elected representative to be the voice. It is up to the elected representative to understand that people want to voice their own views and to be in touch with and, if you like, involved in a participatory way with the elected representative in that process.

So are there some tough decisions to be made by the successful politicians of the future? Do they have to accept that they may not have as much power in the same kind of way as they had in the past?

I think I would prefer not to predict for the politicians. What I do see is, I think, a healthy local empowerment and self-development and participation that is impatient of a process that isn't satisfactory in its level of participation.

You have been called the world's most popular head of state, with a 93 per cent approval rating. Can, and should, politicians be popular all the time?

I have never placed great emphasis or weight on popularity. I am in an office where I don't crunch on hard problems and policy options. I don't impose tax or refuse grants or whatever, so I am not as likely as political figures to undergo that kind of unpopularity. As to having support from a broader public, I think it has a certain significance in the office, because it seeks to be representative, not popular, but to be in touch with and relevant to people. That I think is important, but I will always recognize that it is more important to have that sense of being true to what I see as the trust placed in me and if necessary take risks that are appropriate and say things that may not be particularly popular. Popularity isn't the criterion.

Have you ever looked across the world and thought, 'Women could do better at politics than men'? That you as women could make a better fist of the world?

I have a deep consciousness that women have a contribution to make that goes beyond just having women in positions of responsibility. I hope we bring the strengths of a way of doing things, of a way of analysing institutional changes, which the world would greatly benefit from. Part of the proof of that, if you like, is the way in which women organize together in these networks and resource centres and structures. The institutional way of operating is very open and participatory and enabling, everybody is involved and able to make a contribution. These groups are not hierarchical, they don't exclude people from that kind of participation. So I feel strongly about, and have spoken publicly on a number of occasions about the development of the full potential contribution of women through a confidence in what we can bring to structures, to organization, to prioritizing, through having values that are more important to civil societies, because we have a more practical appreciation and experience to be brought to bear. Society will benefit greatly when there is a balance between men and women, a true balance, a more even balance in their respective contributions.

You have changed the presidency. Has the presidency changed you?

I think it particularly changed me at an earlier stage. I had developed a confidence in speaking through debating and the other measures that I mentioned earlier, but I had also guarded a great deal of myself and particularly my privacy, even when I was a member of the Senate, a lawyer and a campaigner for change on numerous issues. In interviews I tried to keep to public issues. When I was standing for the presidency and going forward I recognized that people had to know the person that they were going to trust and I had to open up much more. I found that quite difficult at the beginning when I realized also that our very private family was being put into a more public light.

How did you resolve the inevitable conflicts successful people have between their personal and professional lives? How did you balance the time needed to try to be good at both?

I have always been conscious of keeping the right balance, and for me that starts very much with the family. What I do is ensure first of all that the strength and warmth and communication of the family is there. And so, even though I was always involved in activities as a lawyer and as a member of the Senate, our children knew from their earliest years that they had priority, if need be, and I think that was the important message. It is very central to me, certainly, that that would be the case, and of course I was very fortunate to have the kind of friendship and support and criticism that Nick has always offered. He tells me the things I don't want to hear.

Is that important?

I think it is extremely important. I think that true friends are those who are open with their criticism, and I am fortunate enough to have a husband and some friends who do tell me to my face what I don't want to hear, and that is absolutely vital, particularly in an office like this where you tend to be put up on a pedestal. That's not to say that I appreciate what they say at the time – often we don't welcome the real, the important criticisms.

What do you think are the main qualities needed in general terms to be successful in life?

I am not sure that you can generalize because it comes back to what you see as being success. For me I think it has been the capacity for lateral thinking, the capacity to look at a situation, see perhaps how it might be changed and to identify how to go about that. It is a response to circumstances, to be able to effect change within those circumstances. More and more I see that doing this entails involving other people in the process.

And what qualities do you need when you come across those inevitable setbacks on the path to success? What qualities do you need to pull yourself back and re-enter the fray?

I think there is a need for resilience, a toughness within yourself that makes you determined to continue. I see the longer timescale as being very important. What may not be achievable immediately or in the short term must inevitably come about – that's how you look at it, because you see how necessary it is that it should. That is particularly true at the international level, looking at major international crises. The world is so ill-equipped and ill-prepared and doesn't have the right focus, and yet it must. That is what I mean about being involved in the need to effect change, and I would have a commitment to being part of the many voices wanting that change, knowing that it is not going to happen today or tomorrow, but knowing it must happen eventually if we are going to resolve issues of terrible inequality and inequity and correct unacceptable positions.

What do you think are the greatest enemies of success?

Cynicism, that sort of demoralizing, undermining attitude, is the great enemy, because it can deflect people, undermining their commitment or values. You need strength to resist that.

And if you could gather together in one room all the young people who want to effect the kind of change you are talking about, who want to be part of this process, what advice would you give them?

If they are already committed to change it would be to affirm that the individual does matter, that it is possible to effect change, that it is important that people do take on a responsibility to be involved in that kind of change. I believe there is a lot more individual commitment than we have estimated, and perhaps real leadership, at a political and an office-holding level such as I have, is to recognize those strengths, encourage them, affirm them, bring them out. Then they will find their own ways of effecting the change in a practical way.

When you time comes to leave this life, what would you like people to say about President Robinson?

That I had a commitment to bring about greater justice.

ANITA RODDICK

*Body Shop founder Anita Roddick – a wave of
unfettered enthusiasm and energy – has spent
most of her life challenging the way people think.
In setting up an eco-friendly beauty products
empire that straddles the world, she has been the
living embodiment of one of her most famous
advertising slogans – 'If you think you're too
small to be effective, try going to bed with a
mosquito.' This entrepreneurial daughter of
Italian immigrants has always marched to a
different drum beat. Rejected by drama college,
she trained as a teacher, but found the classroom
too limiting and took to the hippie trail, ending
up on Pacific Islands where living with 'pre-
industrial groups' gave her ideas for the massive
enterprise to come. But first, back in Sussex, she
opened an 'exhausting' café which 'taught her how to run a business'. Then, in
1976, she tried to raise a £4,000 bank loan to start the Body Shop, but was turned
down. 'The banks were useless at the start,' she says, 'and still are. It's easier for a
woman to raise money for her new kitchen cabinet, or even a car, than for a
business enterprise.' So her husband, Gordon, borrowed the money – and gave it to
her. Later, she could only raise money for expansion by giving away 50 per cent of
the company in return – a move that she now regrets. At the core of the Body Shop
concept were simple questions like 'Why can't you buy a smaller bottle of shampoo
and why can't you refill it?' Growth was rapid. In 1984, the company went public.*

*Financial success encouraged and funded her campaign for social change –
embracing human rights, the promotion of condoms, opposition to the Gulf War
and a Masters Degree course in 'Business and responsibility' at Bath University.
She measures her company each year 'by how brave we've been' – and needed lots
of bravery to deal with a potentially hugely damaging article attacking the Body
Shop's ethos and methods. She talks here of how she used 'reputation management'
to counter this 'corporate stalker', of how the allegations were challenged 'word for
word'; and of 'the intimacy approach', writing to every single shop to restore 'the
sense of family'. She regards her biggest current failure as 'not finding ways for my
ideas to be heard in my own company', which opens up the whole question of
whether large successful companies need a corporate discipline which doesn't
always sit easily with the entrepreneurial passions and ideas of the founder.*

Anita Roddick, what is your definition of success?

I want to define success by redefining it. For me it isn't that solely mythical definition – glamour, allure, power of wealth, and the privilege from care. Any definition of success should be personal because it's so transitory. It's about shaping my own destiny.

If you'd asked me this question 20 years ago, my definition of success would have been to have earned enough money to keep the kids fed. Ten years ago, it would have been to see how far the idea of The Body Shop could go. I would have measured it by how many people I employed, or how many stores were open, or whether we could open a store in another country. Now I would say that a measure of my success is that, in some way, I have managed to change the nature and function of business, to ensure that it becomes kinder and gentler, and to understand that business is more powerful than governments, and the huge responsibility that comes with that. So my definition of success today would be that I've managed to shape the new, challenging thinking on business.

What you're saying is that you start off in the very early stages, having relatively short-term materialistic ambitions, but as you're more successful you can then embrace wider concepts?

Yes, that's it in a nutshell, but when you're dealing with the question of success you have to deal with the personality of the people you're talking to. My entrepreneurial style is quite pathological. An entrepreneur is very enthusiastic and dances to a different drum beat, but never considers success as something which equates to personal wealth. That never enters our consciousness. We have incredible enthusiasm, and I think part of the success of any entrepreneur is energy. If one has that energy one can create a wonderful enthusiasm. Entrepreneurs have this real belief that their lives are about service and leadership.

What are the qualities that people need, to stand a reasonable chance of being successful?

That's a hard question to answer in a country, in a culture, where energy is so disarming and always dismissed. But you've got to be energetic. You've got to have a passion which comes from every tentacle of your body, and you've got to make that passion a reality. You constantly have to visualize the possible. I think if you have this passion for what you want to do, it creates a vision in your head which becomes the present. It's never something you aspire to, it *is* the present, and therefore you never see any problems. No entrepreneur that I've ever met has ever seen a problem.

Are you born with this passion, or can you learn it?

No. It's not inherent, it's a learned state. I think the environment that you grow up in is instrumental. If you look at most entrepreneurs, what do they have in common? Most of them have understood a sense of loss. They've been pushed out of childhood and rather than entering adulthood, they became providers. In my case my father died. We were an immigrant family in which every member *had* to work so we were always outside the stream. We never smelt the same as anybody, we stank of garlic, we never spoke the same, we were much more full of Italian *brio*, we were much more contradictory, we didn't have the sacred cows that other people had. When you march to a different drum beat, you look at things in a different way – you're never part of the throng.

Was being an outsider a factor in the sense that outsiders have to try harder than people who are part of the mainstream?

Definitely. And the immigrant background that I had instilled in me a sense that life was no more complicated than love and work. You had to work – even as a child – to earn enough money to keep the family going. We didn't have the constraints of class, we thought everything was possible, we didn't understand the class system here. And, as I mentioned before, we had energy and a secret ingredient, enthusiasm.

And when you left school you wanted to go into drama because you'd done drama at school. So at that stage, your future career was totally unformed, in fact it wasn't even in your mind, was it?

I suppose it's all about what shaped you as a child. My parents were Italian. My culture was the radio and the cinema. Because we didn't have television, we went to the cinema five days a week. It bred this desire to be up there on the golden screen. I can project my own individuality or fashion somebody else's identity, but my mum couldn't understand my wish to go into drama. She wanted to me to go into a profession, to be a teacher, a nurse or a secretary.

So you rebelled against her in applying for drama college?

I don't think I rebelled against her; I just thought I was good at it. My first element of success was winning a talent competition. At 14, I was having this major love affair with the dead James Dean. I wanted to read everything he had read. He read Strindberg, I read Strindberg. He read Ibsen, I read Ibsen. He was in love with this particular soliloquy, the madman soliloquy from a Charles Dickens novel, so I copied that as well. I dressed like a madman, wrapped in chains. For the performance I did what Stanislavsky, the great Russian director, did – I opened the curtain with my back to the audience, started with this great blood-curdling scream, and then acted like a maniac. It was so intensely exciting and I won. So I knew the power of theatre then and I don't think it's ever left me.

And did you feel you liked an audience?

I was comfortable with an audience. I had no sense of fear as long as I knew something about what I was doing. Even today, standing in front of 10,000 people, which I do occasionally to give a lecture or a talk, holds no fear for me at all.

You'd set your heart on a drama career, but you were turned down by the Central School of Speech and Drama. That was clearly a setback, how did you deal with that within yourself?

I thought, 'Where's my next audience?' If I wanted to make the most of my ability to project myself, the best thing in the world was to be a teacher. So there I was, a working-class kid going to a very middle-class teacher training college for three years, and then I became a teacher. I wanted to project myself on to the school room, and I did. It was hugely entertaining. For example, I dragged – this was in the 1960s so you could do that then – a group of kids who were studying O-level history on the First World War to France. We hitched there and slept in the trenches that still remained. We read Rupert Brooke poems. We acted out Joan Littlewood's *Oh! What a Lovely War.* I can't imagine any teacher being able to do that nowadays. But that was my style of teaching, it was all experiential.

You were clearly enjoying teaching, why did you stop?

I think it's about limitations – my limitation was the classroom. I was half a dozen years older than the kids I was teaching. The only difference between them and myself was that I was one side of the desk and they were the other.

One of the great things about the early 1960s was this new-found freedom to travel, especially as a working-class student. Student loans enabled students to travel, and travelling for me was like a university without walls, it always provided insights. I travelled to Paris and I lived in Paris, I worked for the United Nations in Geneva, I spent a year travelling around the Indian Ocean Islands and Pacific Islands, living with pre-industrial groups, fishing groups – that's when I first understood the power of community and a world beyond our Western notion, and the role women could play in it. It was education through experience, and it was where I got the ideas for The Body Shop.

Was The Body Shop in your mind at this stage?

No. I wanted to be a television director, a magnificent teacher, or whatever. I had no idea – all I wanted to do was to experience as much as I could.

So at this stage you were still uncertain as to what your future career would be? You were trying out lots of things and visiting all kinds of different places. You went on the hippie trail, but then you came back and started an Italian restaurant in Littlehampton.

Well, it was hardly an Italian restaurant. It started as a health-food café in Littlehampton, but after no time I realized we were going to go bankrupt. So we brought in a chip fryer, hamburgers and made pastas. I mean I remember one guy coming up and saying, 'Could I have a quick Lorraine and a glass of rosy wine?' But we had a sense of style – you cannot talk about success if you don't involve the words aesthetics and ethics, because to deny yourself the sense of delight and pleasure around whatever you do is to deny one of the great aspects of who you are as an individual. I styled everything, and the café looked like a wonderful Victorian celebration of Littlehampton at the turn of the century. We had music, but what's more, a real understanding of community – the only time I'd ever experienced that before was in a kibbutz. I embrace this wonderful notion that you can create communities and places where people's experiences are formed, where marriages or relationships are formed – and that can happen in cafés. It was the case in my mum's café and also in my café.

Was it a financial success?

Yes. And not only was it a financial success, it allowed my husband, Gordon, to go off for two years to ride this horse across South America. It allowed me the freedom to set up something which was going to be really small and controllable, The Body Shop, and it also gave me an enormous sense of understanding about how to run a business. Nobody, but nobody works as hard as somebody running a restaurant. I've never been more tired in my life, closing that café or that restaurant at night – at 11 o'clock, night after night. You go straight to bed and you can't get up in the morning because your legs are so damned exhausted. I can't understand how anybody wants to open up a restaurant!

So did you open up the first Body Shop to escape from the pressure of the restaurant?

Yes, I opened up The Body Shop because Gordon wanted to go away. I wanted a nice, easy, controllable nine-to-five, pick-up-the kids-from-school existence.

And what was the original concept of The Body Shop?

It was all about education through experience, and women are really good at this – understanding what they're interested in. During my years of travelling, I picked up so many ideas from people that I'd lived with – for example, in Tahiti the women wouldn't eat cocoa butter, they'd just rub it on their bodies and their skin was like silk. So my experiences with people from other cultures taught me things like that. I was also dissatisfied and dissatisfaction is a primary mover for energy. I used to go into a local chemist and only be able to buy this gallon of shampoo, and I used to think to myself, 'Why can't I have a small bottle? Why can't I refill it?' Simple questions like that. And the entrepreneur in me would say, 'Why not, why can't you?' That dissatisfaction gave me the energy to set it up.

And did you think, at that stage, 'This is the start of an empire'? You only had one shop, didn't you?

I never think big, I just think better, or more exciting. The nature of size is of no interest to me at all. The press say to me, 'You're opening up one shop every two days, and by the end of this century you'll have 2,000' – so what, the barometers of measurement for me are – is it better, is it more exciting? Until Gordon came back from the trip, it was just a livelihood. I just had this energy and opened up another shop and was fortunate enough to find somebody to loan me some money to do it.

And when you were trying to raise the money for the initial Body Shop, did you find the bank helpful?

Useless. And 20 years later they're still as bad. It is still easier for a woman to raise money for her new kitchen cabinet or even a car than it is for a business enterprise. It's seduction and that's wrong, because you're seduced into believing that the banks are really supportive of women. They're not, especially if the women are mothers. It's a very patriarchal system, not unlike the military. In 20 years, I have never met a bank manager who has the excitement and the *brio* of an entrepreneur. They're good housekeepers, they protect themselves.

After you opened your first shop and it was starting to make money, you decided to open a second. You went to the bank before anybody else to see if you could raise money? What was their reaction?

The first time I went, they said no to me, and so my husband went instead. They gave Gordon the money and he gave it to me. It's pathetic, but that's how it was. When I wanted to open up my second store, there was no way I was going to go to the bank. I'd only been trading for six months, we didn't know whether it was going to work. It could just be a fad, nobody had done this type of stuff before, and we didn't know whether it was going to work. So I had to find a private investor.

And you had to give away a slice of the business because of that.

I gave 50 per cent of it away. And that's been one of the biggest dilemmas for people reading the history of my company, 'How could you have done it?' Maybe I wouldn't be here talking today if I hadn't. I had no problem with it, because the accumulation of wealth is of no importance to me. Giving my wealth away, however, is of major importance to me – how I give it away, when I give it away, why I give away. So I had no problem with that, but, yes, 50 per cent is sitting in somebody else's pocket.

What was the trigger for the massive expansion of The Body Shop?

The trigger was self-financing. We didn't have any more money. Gordon came back and he said, 'We've got two stores, but how are we going to fund anybody else or anything else?' But luckily at that time people were coming along and saying, 'This is a good idea.' Women were coming to The Body Shop in Brighton and saying, 'I like this. I could do this. I could fill the bottles in the back, and hand-write the labels.' It was like a cottage industry, but it was fun. We had this intimacy, and we were thankful if anybody came along. It wasn't until a couple of years later that we started to embrace the concept of franchising. Then, anybody would come along, put the products in the back of their car, and sell them from barges and market stalls. So the business really defined itself about four or five years later when we suddenly realized we'd found something unique. We created this market, even though we didn't know what marketing was.

So there was an organic growth about the business to start with.

Naïvety was the thing that saved us. We didn't think that life was any more complicated than love and work. We could not take a moisture cream seriously. We didn't talk about our products as if they were the body and blood of Jesus Christ. We just had this wonderful idea that we had to tell stories, because the products were so bizarre. They had bits floating about in them. We used to tell people that there were black bits in the honey cleanser because the bees didn't clean their feet when they went back into the hive. We had grace, we didn't tell lies. We didn't know you were encouraged to tell lies, which is so often the case in our industry.

When did all this formulate into a business plan?

We started to get really serious about five or six years later, especially when we opened up in Covent Garden. There was this new shopping experience occurring in England, which didn't solely include the big retailers. We suddenly realized we'd got something going here and that we had to take it seriously. But the real benchmark was when we decided to go public. We had to plan for two or three years, we had to check everything. We started to employ financial directors, we had to have a strategy plan. We had to grow up, we had to be professional, we had to have strong financial direction.

Did other people come in to put you on the right track?

Yes. The people who came in to help us with the flotation were very cautious – they wanted us to do it much faster. And we were cautious. I don't know any entrepreneur that will ever take risks. We were very cautious and we did it. It took us two years to prepare ourselves for that.

You clearly have regrets about going public.

Yes. My entire company is full of paradoxes and that's the hard thing. We would never have been where we are today if we hadn't. It was the most magnificent form of speedy growth. It was so important in the 1980s to get recognition, because you could not get prime sites in retailing unless you had. Going public was a major step towards respectability, and for that I am thankful. It gave us freedom, it gave us the chance to invest in our huge manufacturing plant. However, although the constraints of going public are not that bad, they're constant. You never have time to reflect and pause and say, 'Are we having fun? Do we want to grow this year? Why don't we just have more fun with our employees? Why don't we do more social activism?' So you never have that real freedom to be able to take the identity of your company – which is, in essence, your own identity – and form it into something else. You're structured by the profit-and-loss sheet.

It's the bottom line the whole time.

Yes, and there is such a tyranny in the bottom line.

And yet, isn't that bottom line important? Apart from the fact that it determines the share price of your company, it actually dictates the extent to which you can use your profits to invest in expanding the business, and indeed to do all the other things that you want to do?

I agree with you, but you have to have a belief that your shareholders are *not* your financial investors. You have stakeholders, your employees, and I am more loyal to my employees than to any other group. You also have your customers, your suppliers. All of these peoples' livelihoods depend on you, so I want to equalize that level of responsibility to the importance of the financial investor.

Many of the investors are speculators. They only put a few pounds in our company for a nanosecond. When one talks about profit, one has to ask, 'Profit for whom?' How do my employees profit? How do the customers profit? Why do we only define profit as a financial profit? If we are to become visionaries in business, we are going to have to redefine words like profit. Does the environment profit by this obsession for growth? I'm now on that treadmill, how can I make my growth more responsible? How can I clean up the mess I create? How can I move towards sustainability? How can I move towards redefining the nature of business? It's a hard task to try and redefine that every day you're open for business.

Do you think that the business world is slowly moving towards accepting your ideas of this wider responsibility, rather than being slave to the shareholders and the dividends?

Yes, I think so. When I was talking at Harvard ten years ago, I got the feeling that I was an alien. We've now managed to shape a master's degree with Bath University on businesses and responsibility, which deals with the real taboo subjects of global economy, of human rights, of international change, of redefining the workplace as a spiritual endeavour and so on. Wittgenstein once said, 'Words create worlds.' We have to define it first, and then we have to have brave companies, and there are many, to put that definition into practice.

They have to be brave though?

Yes. Because the financial press only know one form of measurement – money and size. Redefining it is going to be a hard thing.

But given those pressures from the press on new people starting up in business or medium-sized companies that are struggling to get there financially, can't you understand why some business people may say, 'Anita's got some great ideas, but frankly they're not for us, or not for us yet'?

So be it. I think that's the part of being a leader. I think that's being a visionary leader. It's about being brave. I measure my company each year on how brave we have been.

How do you judge that?

The bravest thing we have ever done is to challenge one of the biggest multi-nationals in the world, Shell. Never in the history of business has one company challenged another company on a moral landscape. We challenged their environmental and human-rights practices with the Ogoni people in Nigeria, because there is no code of conduct to govern a corporation, especially a trans-national corporation. And we challenged them – along with the might of their PR people who are able to diminish the nature of human rights, their responsibility, and the racism that goes with it. In businesses, the only wars one fights are for market share. No one has ever stood in an arena of human rights and tried to redefine that. People will say, 'What in the hell has this got to do with skin and hair care?' My argument is, 'If we don't do this, who will?' That's being brave. Redefining the nature of the workplace is brave. In this country we are not good at bringing in child development centres which are attached to the workplace. The years under Mrs Thatcher left us with the notion that women support the male bread-winners. Get real! It's all about survival. The family has to be supported. The child has to be protected, and the workplace has to be the area for it, because the government has no interest in that subject.

Do you think that every successful business person has to accept some form of sacrifice about their personal life? Does there have to be a degree of dedication that drives you forward, that almost inevitably squeezes out the things you would like to do to have a totally fulfilling relationship with your partner?

I think, if you're a woman you see it differently because we've always juggled. We've juggled work with the kids, with our husbands. Traditionally we are the nurturers and the support for the male bread-winner. It's no big deal.

However, for men, the components of business are sexy. It's like fresh flesh. It's new ideas, a new force, a new discussion, and it embodies the male collegiate sense of relationships. And men do not discuss feelings. They will not stand up in a meeting and say, 'I'm going home to my kids,

I've spent too much time here.' Secondly, the workplace becomes a new community and that's another seduction, it compensates for the loss of community on a social scale. My neighbour is no longer the person who lives next door to me, it's the neighbour of interests. If only businesses weren't so seductive we'd spend more time with our partners. We live in a culture that measures us through work and diminishes the family. Until we stop measuring men or women as an entity of production, and start to measure people for the production of the human spirit, of which the family is important, we're always going to have this sacrifice.

As The Body Shop expanded and moved into America, you had a huge amount of praise and then, suddenly, there was this article in Business Ethics, *a small-circulation magazine of 14,000, which rocked you back on your heels. Now what was your reaction, a) when that article appeared? and b) what did you decide to do about it?*

Well, we had a corporate stalker! This is not just a man who wrote an article because he felt he had something to say. He was a man who wanted to challenge the very heart of our business. If my company was a woman he'd be up in front of the High Court. Even as we speak, he's trying to get articles in *The Guardian*. I don't know where he comes from, and I don't know the source of his income, all I know is his wife is vice-president of marketing for our biggest competitor in America.

It was the saddest time in my life because this article was placed in a friend's publication – we're all part of the Social Responsibility Movement in America – and she thought it was juicy enough and put it in because I reckon she needed to raise the circulation! The article was scathing, it was appalling. We tried to counteract the allegations made but we were seen as defensive. This huge web of assumptions was built around us, and we had to fight our way out of it.

What was more intriguing was what happened in England. We had 150 articles about us within a week – more than Bosnia. We had BBC TV, we had ITV, we had cameras, we had microphones. What were they looking for? Three gallons of shampoo that were leaked out into pipes in New Jersey. This is nothing compared to what goes on. It was the juiciest story they could find and we couldn't get our head around it. It was our darkest time because we lived on our radical reputation.

Did you see everything going down the tubes?

God, no. I just thought, 'Here we go again.'

Are you saying that if you're up there with your head above the business parapet you've got to expect to be attacked?

Absolutely. If you're challenging the notion of business as we do, if you're talking about redefinition of terminologies that are really uncomfortable – philosophical terminologies, spiritual terminologies – you're going to wear the biggest bull's eye on your back, because people will want to find anything about you that smacks of hypocrisy.

So how did you tackle it?

It was really interesting. We were camping out on the floor of our offices because our communication department had to be open 24 hours a day. We had to curb these stories which were going out internationally. I found intimacy was the only way to keep my sanity and my sense of reality. I wrote intimate faxes to every shop. It was like a diary of how I felt – how I had to rush out and get some pizzas, how we were camping out on the floor. I got letters back from our stores in Colorado, Taiwan, everywhere. That sense of being a family gave me great support. It was like grieving, and people were saying, 'Don't grieve, this is all right.'

That handles the emotional side, what did you do about the allegations?

We challenged them word for word, line by line. What was profoundly helpful for us, at that time, was the support that we had from Greenpeace, from Friends of the Earth, from Jonathan Porritt and Sara Parker. The people whose opinions we really valued were the people who understood the real essence of the values inherent in our company. We were amazed by the support.

Do you feel you've come through that now?

Yes. Now that people understand the pathology of the man who wrote the article. They understand where he comes from and what his agenda is.

Did you have a strategy for dealing with the media for countering all this? Because, as you say, there were articles, or news reports, which were fairly hostile?

Yes, we had a great strategy, but it didn't appear to do us any good. For the first time in our lives we had to do reputation management. And when you're coming from a company like ours, its whole brand is its reputation, and its values. We had to learn fast. We had to deal with the detail, the minutiae, because this man was going back 20 years, inventing scenarios and making assumptions. People hated the fact that we defended ourselves. We lost our credibility, because we had been too defensive, it looked as though we could not handle criticism. I'm still confused about it all three years later, and yet, to this day, I would defend my company in exactly the same way against such an obsessive person.

Do you think that personal publicity is a help or a hindrance? Should one person be hugely identified with a company in the way that you have been, and have you taken any steps to diminish that link?

That's a really good question. It's the nature of our society that everything is personalized, we have to put a person up on a pedestal. The dark side to all this is that the personal becomes the political, that every issue I deal with personally filters through to The Body Shop. And when you're a woman, and this is true, you're diminished because you're not listened to. I try to distance myself from that. But there are many more voices in the company than just mine.

Even with regard to long-term business interests?

Well, I don't know. The company is my baby. The company is brave because I want it to be brave and the people in the company are there to support that braveness. We attract some wonderful thinkers. The other side to that question is, are you going to get out and retire? The answer to that is, no. Nobody else will employ me! The Body Shop has become such an integral part of my identity, it's my blueprint.

Have you ever got to the stage where you thought, 'Things are so grim I've got to give up, I've got to go and try something else'?

My husband will say, 'When are we going to start having more fun again? When are we going to lighten up and be less tense?' The dilemma for me is that I don't know how to differentiate between enthusiasm and stress. I find it hard. My husband keeps on saying, 'Let's be a bit detached. We've got so many juicy projects, so much human rights campaigning to do.' But at the moment I don't feel I can do that, and when I do feel I can let go, then maybe I will. At the moment it's all so tense and vibrant.

You went through a phase when some of your franchisees got a bit twitchy. How did you deal with that?

Intimacy again. As with love and relationships, when they want to leave, the exit should be as magnificent and wonderful as the entry.

But can that make up for the bottom line which they were looking at for the profit margin?

No, but you can have a sense of care. A lot of them came in in the 1980s and achieved a huge amount of wealth. A lot of it just went out the door in the 1990s when reality checked in. I believe we should always try to buy back if they're unhappy, that has to be our mantra. But you cannot account for people's expectations.

You once said, 'It's obscene to die rich.' Do you believe that everybody who is successful has an obligation to put something back into society?

Yes. If we have influence and power, and if there is a media interest, for God's sake let's make sure that the words and the ideals that come out of our mouths are beyond our own self-aggrandizement. If you keep wealth, it's like water in a vase, it gets stale. There is no greater merit than in giving the whole damn stuff away. My kids are happy, my kids are well-adjusted. They have a notion of responsibility towards money, but they want to be part of a foundation into which we will put our money and give it away.

There are a lot of dark sides to success, but the light side of it is the ability to be opportunistic, and to be able to do things. Take Bosnia for example, what more can I do there than to be able to give money to the people I know to provide dozens of wheelchairs or fund the Human Rights Watch office in the Hague or in Croatia. The one thing I have in abundance is money, and I want to give it to that. I can't have another house or another pair of jeans – that's the joy of it all.

What do you regard as your biggest failure, and more importantly, how did you recover from it?

That's really hard, because I'm an optimist. I see all failures as an ability to shape things. I never see them as failures, they are just opportunities. My biggest failure at the moment is not finding ways to be heard in my own company. It's to do with how the company that I formed and shaped really doesn't match up to the company I started. It is big, it is powerful in terms of persuasion. It is very patriarchal. It has very much the culture of a company that manufactures and distributes. The creativity, the genie in the bottle that keeps on spurting out and vomiting out new ideas, and the speed of those ideas is really very hard for me. Often the ideas that I have are not heard.

But you're the boss.

No, I'm not. That's another great myth. I am a voice in the company. I, too, can get marginalized or be ignored.

But you're saying you don't have power.

I don't because it's a democratic process. There is this creative web over the company which shapes its identity. I've shaped its values, and that's an area that I have not given up, but shaping the business strategy is not just down to me. As an entrepreneur I said, 'We've got to reinvent.' But it's very hard to be heard because you have a Board that is very mechanistic and functional, but not necessarily visionary. It's a huge problem for me to look at the company, my baby, and say, 'Is this what I gave birth to?' You end up having to ambush your own company, to use guerrilla tactics to be heard. It's been a fantastically creative experience, but for the last two or three years I've had a sense of real diminishment in terms of being heard.

So although you have this fantastic. energy and you're constantly bubbling with ideas, there's got to be an element of control that says, 'Anita, you can't do this, you can't do that.' So although you might regard that as a failure, it is actually good for The Body Shop.

Well, you might say so, but I wouldn't. I would say that we should have redesigned the shops four years ago and not now. We should have extended the brand. There have been lots of discussions, but we're a company that is shaped by a very strong traditional presence, which has a different idea of how things should evolve.

Does luck play a part in success?

I'm not sure. Opportunism does. I don't understand luck. I don't think that I've been lucky.

Being in the right place at the right time, getting an early loan, finding a partner?

Is that luck? I don't know. In 1976 nobody could have spelt the word environmentalism. We just had an antenna out there and knew who were the forerunners in the planet. The real wisdom-seekers of the planet were the environmental groups, and we just listened, and still do – they give us direction. We're opportunistic. We see an opportunity and go with it, but I don't think luck plays any part in our success.

Are there any people, past or present, whom you really admire as being successful?

People that are successful in my eyes are not necessarily people who have been financially successful. I admire those people who have managed their lives and their work. People who have succeeded in business, but who still have a sense of familiarity with their children and with the community. Terence Conran, for example, seems to have a great time in his kitchen with lots of home-made vegetables, and looks really happy. It's all to do with family, the balance between that and work.

Is image important to success?

I think so. For me the image of the company is really important. What people perceive when they think about us. My image is really important. I don't want to be seen as a cosmetic diva, wearing high heels and hobbling around with 18 inches of make-up. I want to be seen as an activist and approachable.

What do you think are the greatest enemies of success?

Lethargy, assumption.

What do you mean by assumption?

That you don't learn from the past. The past should shape your thinking and your ability to reinvent yourself. Inability to do that is one of the greatest enemies to success – you need to be separate from the human condition. One of the great dangers of success, certainly if that success brings wealth, is that you're divorced from human suffering and the reality of our world planet, poverty. Wealth dehumanizes you. You can have anything you want. The true enemy to success, for me, is the inability to understand how the world is.

In pursuit of success, have you ever done anything you wish you hadn't done?

Yes. Being so open to the press. I always think they will take me as I am, with the honesty that I offer and there will not be any manipulation.

But there is an argument that says any publicity is good publicity?

Well, that's an argument I do not believe in because the consequences can be incredibly painful.

Let me put to you a quote from The Independent. *It talked about you and Gordon and said, 'You represent causes attractive to the liberal conscience, yet this goodness is used remorselessly to sell vanity products. You wash your hair in global concern and it is debatable whether the wizened peasants on the walls are dignified or patronized.' Now that's strong stuff, how do you react to that?*

We just think, 'Here's another journalist that's cashing in on cuteness.'

Responsibility and thoughtfulness are benchmarks for us. We have worked with tribal groups for ten years trying to shape relationships. We don't get customers coming in because of that. We did some focus groups in America, and 90 per cent of the customers come into the shop because 'they like the smell', 80 per cent because 'it was in the air'. They come in because they like the products, not because of social issues. For us, the work that we do behind the scenes, or in the stores, is about campaigning for human rights – it's an area that no other company wants to deal with.

But that helps your business concern as well, doesn't it?

It helps us shape a sense of empathy. I would guarantee that a huge percentage of our staff would walk out the door tomorrow if we were just like any other cosmetic company.

But when you get criticism like that, what's the inner mechanism you have inside you to deal with it?

First of all, it's the knowledge that you know the criticism is not true. The sense that what drives you forward is something beyond yourself, and that it has been the passion since day one. Secondly, the support from the people whose opinions you respect.

And they are better barometers than the media?

Oh yes, because the media have got to have a story that will sell – it has to be verbally cute or cynical.

If you could gather together all the young people in the world who look up to you as someone whom they would like to become, what advice would you give them?

First of all, keep it simple, ask questions – constantly ask questions. Look to people you admire and go straight to them and say, 'How do I do it, what advice can you give me?' We don't help in this country. We don't care about the young kids. I would encourage them to knock on the doors of people who could help them, with their skills or with their ideas. Secondly, if they want to set up their own companies, don't think 'business', think 'livelihoods'. We're being paralysed by the notion of setting up your own companies, or setting up your own businesses, forget that word. Think in terms of 'How can I have a livelihood that gives me independence, freedom of spirit, and where I don't have to rely on anybody for a job?'

It's got to mean your own company, hasn't it?

Well, it doesn't have to. The word company has all sorts of other connotations. Finding a skill or an interest, and then setting it up. Asking yourself what the world needs and what the world does not need. The world does not need another electric toothbrush, the world needs socially responsible services and products. Then say to yourself, 'How am I different from the person down the road that's doing this?' You just find out what your differences are and shout them from the rooftops. That's a simplistic equation, but you constantly need to ask questions, to research, to go into libraries, to ring up the editors of magazines or newspapers and just knock on doors.

When your time comes to leave this life, what would you like people to say about you?

She challenged with enthusiasm.

What about your husband's epitaph for you? He said it should be, 'Don't hang up yet, I haven't finished talking.'

He calls me the Great Blur, because he says, 'How does somebody with such short legs walk so fast?' You know that awful story of the person who died and was about to be buried and woke up again? I think I'd say, 'Check before you bury me.'

And what about your famous mosquito slogan?

Oh, yes! If you think you're too small to be effective, try going to bed with a mosquito!

LORD SAATCHI

'There is a point at which a child decides itself that it wants to succeed for its own reasons. Parents cannot make that click in the head happen.' For the man who, with his brother Charles, ran the first British company to get to the top of world advertising, that 'click' clearly happened early. One of four sons of a prosperous Jewish textile merchant who brought his young family to Britain from Iraq in 1946, Maurice Saatchi worked in 'an obsessive fashion' to obtain good marks at school and university. His analytical skills earned him a first-class degree from the London School of Economics. To his professor's disappointment, he opted for a career in business instead of research, launching Saatchi and Saatchi with Charles at the age of 24. He once described their business as 'more than a company – it's an attitude'. The aim was to combine size with that creative freshness which, at the time, was the hallmark of smaller companies. And people were the key: 'In an advertising company the assets go up and down in the lift.'

By 1986, they had 5 per cent of the world's advertising, with a host of major clients such as British Airways and Mars. But in 1994, moving steadily along the takeover trail – and even eyeing up the Midland Bank – they over-reached themselves. Over seven years, the share price had fallen from £50 to £1.50. In what Maurice calls 'the bitter harvest' of losing control, he fell victim to increasing shareholder criticism and plotting, and dramatically resigned as Chairman. He now puts the blame for that on 'a sense of arrogance' which led him to decline 'good advice from sensible people'. But within days, he had created a new company, M & C Saatchi, 'on a tide of strong emotion among employees and clients, the like of which I'd never seen before'. In 1996, heading for his fifth General Election as a guiding hand behind the Conservative Party's advertising, he was elevated to the House of Lords. Normally notoriously reticent about giving public interviews, he here opens up in more detail than ever before about the thinking and the influences that have shaped his remarkable career. He talks about the difference between selling products and political ideas, and, while admitting that it has become much harder to achieve success in advertising, he says there is no better industry to enter now, because it is based entirely on merit. 'There is no hierarchy – you can achieve top positions in your twenties.'

Lord Saatchi, what is your definition of success?

To make a ripple in the pond.

Why is it important to make a ripple?

It's an expression of an individual contribution.

Do you see it as a contribution to the economy, to society, or to what?

I don't think it makes very much difference what the field of endeavour happens to be. If you want to make a ripple there's only one way to do it, and that is to try to be the best there is in your chosen sphere, whether it is art or sport or politics or business. It only happens if you aim to be the best in your particular speciality.

So being the best ought to be a target for everyone who wants to be successful? It shouldn't be something that happens to you almost by accident – it should be a specific goal?

Yes. That is the only route I know to success in any field.

To what extent do you think your success is due to your background and your upbringing?

Freud attributes most of the misfortune or success of an adult life to early upbringing and the relationship between the child and the parents. So I think that is fundamental.

What was the nature of the relationship between you and your parents? Your father came over from Iraq in 1946 and set up home in North London. What kind of an upbringing did you and your brothers have?

It was oriented to hard work and doing the best you could. It's very striking – and I notice it now with my own children – that there is a point at which a child decides itself that it wants to succeed for its own reasons, for its own pride. Not every child comes to that point, but I imagine that the children who go on to be successful in later life have experienced a moment when it becomes important *to them* to do well. And that, surely, is a critical turning point in every person's life. To be successful in whatever is your chosen sphere, you must see a point B, know yourself to be at point A, and believe that you would be happier if you moved to point B. I think it goes on from there for the rest of your life.

Can your parents shepherd you on to that path or is it a path you have to decide to take yourself, at whatever age you decide to jump on to it?

I can only speak as a son and a father. My observation, in both roles, would be that it's a decision which an individual makes or doesn't make for himself.

But can parents help by creating the right environment?

There is no 'right' environment. I don't see that there's any particular merit or virtue in either of the two approaches. It's not necessary to have that linear A to B approach to achieve happiness in life. The people who decide to take that route believe they can see a point B where, they believe, they will be happy. But it's not necessarily an objective fact, and it's not necessarily the way to happiness for all people, or even most people. For example, Milan Kundera described happiness as a circle. He said it was a mistake to have a linear approach and to strive to reach point B. For him, happiness is the endless circular repetition of pleasurable acts, rather than something directional.

Do you think that happiness and success go hand in hand?

They are the same thing. Success *is* the achievement of happiness.

Just take me through your days at school, your qualifications, and going on to the London School of Economics, what you achieved there.

I was an intense schoolboy, always interested in achieving good grades. And I worked, I would say, in an obsessive fashion to earn those results at school and a good degree at university. I took it rather seriously.

After LSE you went to work for the Haymarket Group as business development manager, to the great disappointment of your professor at university who thought that you were poised to go into research.

Yes, well, my tutor, was a generous man. He was kind enough to say that I could have gone on to pursue an academic life.

So why didn't you?

Ironically, because the LSE was so inspiring. I enjoyed the economics course so much – the main specialization was in sociology and social psychology – that I wanted to apply what I'd learned. Of course, I didn't work all this out in the rational way I'm describing now.

So you then saw that you could apply that in business, though not necessarily, at that stage, in advertising?

No, at that stage advertising hadn't come into my life at all. It had just been a part of what I had studied, so I was interested in all forms of communication. I didn't know quite why, but I was fascinated by it, and I now realize that it was the result of the teaching I had at LSE. I spent two or three years with Haymarket. The job I had was to try to define new magazine launches or acquisitions which the company could make, and to pursue them, which we did vigorously. I enjoyed it immensely because I was working for people I admired.

But then you decided to switch to advertising. What was the catalyst for that?

Charles, who had been a great success in advertising at that time.

That was with the campaign of the pregnant man?

Yes. We discussed the possibility of starting an advertising agency ourselves. He had his perspective on the advertising world. I had a completely different perspective, from the point of view of a media owner. I felt sure there were all sorts of things that could be done better, as sure as only somebody of 24 could feel. So we agreed to have a go.

Were you a bit nervous about setting out on your own at the age of 24, and giving up a good job and a certain amount of financial security to do so?

Yes, I was. And also sad to leave Haymarket, where I had been very happy.

At what point did you begin to think, 'This is clicking, this is really going to work? It's something in which I'm going to spend my life'?

I think that took about six months. The fear of failure – which, of course, besets every new business as an ever-present threat – ended after only about six months, because the company was profitable from then on.

How did you achieve that? Was there an element of luck, or was it good planning?

It was huge good luck. We won some great clients. So we were paying our way as a new company, and we never really looked back.

But you were moving into an established market in which there were some very big names and you were, if you like, the cheeky upstart, the newcomer. That's quite a daunting prospect. What drove you to take that risk?

Soon after the company was set up – alarmingly soon, for many people, I would say – we decided that the company wasn't going to collapse and that we could do well. We had a touching degree of faith in the wisdom of what we were trying to do, and in the merits of it. So it had the feeling of a crusade. The crusade was a simple one, which was an important factor. As we saw the advertising industry at that time, clients faced a choice between small, probably very bright and creative young agencies on the one hand, and on the other, big, multi-national giants who were more reliable and disciplined and safe as suppliers of advertising, but who perhaps lacked the creative sparkle of the smaller and younger companies. So our purpose was to try to achieve the impossible – to have a big agency which would provide the stability that was important to both clients and employees, but somehow to combine size with being dynamic, youthful and innovative. We had a phrase for this. It was, 'It's good to be big, it's better to be good, but it's best to be both.' And we really worked at that, it was our credo throughout the company's history from that point, about six months after the foundation of the agency.

And what did you and your brother specifically bring to the table? Did you complement each other?

We were completely different. Charles was the creative one – he actually wrote advertisements and had ideas, and that, of course, is the only skill that matters in advertising. I was what is known as the 'suit', the one who carries the bag. Advertising agencies, basically, are composed of those two talents, of which the former is far more important.

A great many people, when they start off on their own, have some kind of mentor or mentors behind them. Did you have anyone like that, and do you think that every successful person, at some stage in their life, needs a mentor?

Everyone needs a hero.

Is there a difference?

Only in the sense that a mentor would be somebody you know personally and to whom you can talk. Whereas a hero could be anyone, alive or dead, who is your role model.

Certainly, I had heroes in advertising. I think probably the greatest was Bill Bernbach, who was the founder of an agency called Doyle Dane Bernbach. He had a particular approach to advertising which was based on creativity, and he changed the face of the industry. Prior to his arrival on the scene, advertising had been based very much on the concept of sheer salesmanship, of the doorstep variety, a hard, rational sell.

Bernbach's idea was that when the salesman calls at the door, it helps him to make the sale if you, the customer, actually *like* him. If you like him, you're more likely to like his product. This, of course, sounds quite straightforward now, but at the time, in the 1960s, it was a revolutionary concept. It led to the more emotional and image-based advertising that now probably accounts for the bulk of the industry's output around the world. He did that.

As the agency developed, did you have any maxims for what made a good advertising agency? I'm thinking of statements like 'Keep a tidy desk and phone the client every day.' Is that accurate?

I don't think we had maxims like that. But there was a powerful ethos and a strong shared sense of culture in the company which made it special. And I think it came from the original drive to achieve what, on the face of it, was impossible – namely, that elusive combination of size and creativity.

How important were people to the organization?

There is nothing else in an advertising agency, so that proverb about the assets going up and down in the lift is true. It's true of all specialized service companies. And the people we had in the company were the best in the industry, as it later turned out.

How did you pick them? How did you identify their qualities?

Several of them were there right at the beginning, and others came in the early years, the first five years, and stayed for many years thereafter. In terms of qualities, I don't think I can lay enough stress on that sense of purpose, of knowing why you were going to work and what you were trying to achieve, and the feeling that if you did achieve that, it would be very special. The knowledge that they were serving some greater goal was inspiring to people.

The process of finding the right people was by self-selection. Because the company did stand for something specific, and if you stand for something you will divide people. There will be those who are for you and others who are against you, so those who came into the company were the people who wanted to be a part of that crusade.

I think you have said that Saatchi's is more than a company, it's an attitude. Is loyalty an important part of that?

Loyalty to that concept, faith in that concept, I would regard as fundamental.

What makes a successful advertisement and a successful advertising campaign? Are there any clear core ingredients which they all must have?

Yes. Bertrand Russell, talking about happiness and how to achieve it, said that it requires 'the painful necessity of thought'. The advertisements which work are those which have been thought through with great precision, and which do not confuse the simple message they are trying to deliver. So deep thought, leading to simplicity of expression.

How much thought will go into creating a great five-word buzz phrase used by a company to sell a product?

Winston Churchill once wrote a letter to a friend which began, 'I wanted to write you a short letter, but I didn't have time.' That explains what I mean. To achieve simplicity, the short phrase you mentioned, requires much greater effort than a long and rambling sentence. Anyone can do that. These days audiences around the world are so sophisticated, so cynical, and so aware of being manipulated that only a thought-through, simply expressed, distilled argument is likely to cut through the barrage of information people are receiving every day.

Does the same principle apply to political advertising as well, or are there added dimensions to a political campaign?

The political campaign bears no resemblance to product or business campaigns.

You're not selling politicians in the same way as you would sell a commercial product like soap powder?

No, I think that is a misconception. My experience of politics is that it is a world apart. It has its own laws of gravity, it has its own time zones. It is completely different from business.

Are there any generalizations you can make about a political campaign? Is it true that the best political advertising campaigns are negative?

Not necessarily. If you look back and try to think of the most effective political messages in history, you would find short phrases of great simplicity and great power. For example, '*Liberté, Egalité, Fraternité,*' or '*Workers of the world unite, you have nothing to lose but your chains,*' or, '*I have a dream.*' These are not just slogans or soundbites, they encapsulate entire philosophies, whole political systems. Think of, '*One man, one vote,*' or, '*No taxation without representation.*' Or, '*Go West, young man.*' These are phrases which have changed the course of history. It is to that that one aspires, in a humble way, in mounting political campaigns.

So for you the best kind of politician would be one who speaks in soundbites?

I do take the view that if you can't express your argument in a short, crisp, simple way it may mean there's something wrong with your argument. I regard the search for simplicity as a test. It is not merely a discipline, it forces exactitude or it annihilates. It is the mark of a cause that is good that it can express itself in a short, powerful way. The best example I can give you is the way President Roosevelt persuaded a profoundly isolationist America to support Britain in its hour of greatest need. He invented a short phrase – two words – to do that, '*Lend Lease.*' And he had a simple way of expressing what that meant. He said to the American people, 'It's like this. Your neighbour's house is on fire and he comes to you and asks if he can have your hose. You say to him, "I will not give you my hose, but I will lend it to you. And after you've put out your fire you will return it to me."' The American public accepted Lend Lease on that basis. So that was a moment of great importance which turned on two words.

You built up the company over 25 years. It was incredibly successful, and then everything started to go wrong in the recession. The share price plummeted and you saw your world starting to collapse. What was your approach to that situation?

The company was a marvellous company, and, by then, a very big company as well, but the recession in advertising, which brought about the first drop in world advertising expenditure since the war, arrived at a most unfortunate moment for us. We had just completed some very large acquisitions, and the timing of the recession was exquisite in its inappropriateness. But I had no doubt that the company would continue to be successful.

And yet you were losing control of the company?

We had actually lost control of the company, but I don't think at that stage we quite realized how completely. During the years of growth, we had issued a large number of shares to finance acquisitions and our shareholding in the company had been diluted from a majority controlling interest to 1 or 2 per cent. I don't think we ever foresaw the bitter harvest of that loss of control.

Looking back, was there any way that you could have foreseen it, or were you carried along on this great wave of success that made you feel that you could almost do anything, that the world was your oyster – almost a sense of arrogance?

It wasn't 'almost' a sense of arrogance – it was exactly that.

What is your judgment on what went wrong in terms of your attitude?

We had very good advice from sensible people which we declined to take. That advice was that it was impossible to maintain what we had achieved in the previous 20 years – which was compound average growth in pre-tax profits, earnings per share and dividend per share of 32 per cent, and that beyond a certain size, it was inconceivable that we could continue to grow so much ahead of market growth. You can probably do that when you're quite small and you have a small market share, but we were, by then, the biggest agency in the world, and our share of world advertising was quite significant. So it defied logic to think that you could grow much more than the market, but we persisted in that belief.

Why did you do that? You were defying logic, you were defying the advice of experts.

Probably a habit of defying gravity had become ingrained. We would have been much better to have said to ourselves, 'Now this is a big mature company, and it will grow by a few percentage points more than the market, which means that perhaps it might grow by 10 per cent per annum, maybe a bit less.' That would have been a realistic, sensible goal, and we should have taken that advice.

Do you think there is a risk that every person who sets out to be successful will reach a point at which he is unable to take a realistic, objective view of his own position because it's been coloured so much by the treadmill of success he is on?

I'm certain that's the case. Don't they say that all political careers end in tears? I suppose it is true in all walks of life that it's a risk, but the alternative is to do nothing, and that's not a guaranteed route to happiness, either.

For years you didn't give interviews, and you still grant very, very few. Was it a part of your plan to create a mystique by not bowing to the normal convention of talking a lot in public about your business?

It did not begin in that way, but after a while we began to see that giving interviews was only likely to help our competitors and we didn't want to explain to the world our own view of what was making our company successful. We were sure we knew what we were doing and why, and we didn't particularly want to share that. That's how it began.

And yet wasn't part of your success the fact that people were writing about you?

I don't think they were writing about us because we didn't give interviews, I think they were writing about us because we did a lot of things, some of which were new, and broke new ground. There had not been a British company which had got to the top in world advertising, or anything like it. When we first went to America it was unheard of for a British company to acquire an American advertising agency. The industry had been completely dominated by American multi-national firms. So the idea that some British local company would come to Madison Avenue and try to buy it was considered bizarre. This sort of thing attracted attention.

You once said, 'Perception is reality.' Can successful advertising make people do anything, buy anything, even if deep-down they don't want to?

It depends how you define what people want. If you were to say that advertising sells people things they don't need, that would undoubtedly be true. You don't need a Hoover – you can clean a house with a broom and a dishcloth. You don't need an electric razor – you can shave with a cut-throat. So in the sense that advertising creates a demand for those kinds of innovation, it is not meeting needs, it is creating wants. But that is open to criticism only if you don't believe that the market, in trying to please the public, does so by producing better and better products and services. That's how it works. The jury is public opinion, and companies court public opinion by offering better products and services, and the jury then decides. This, to me, adds up to advancement, but if people prefer to stay with the broom they can do so.

What do you regard as your most successful advertising campaign?

I would say the work we've done over the years for British Airways. It has been a privilege to have been involved in what is certainly one of the great business success stories for decades, probably since the war. It's been a remarkable turnaround. And if the advertising played some small part in that, I would be very pleased.

What do you regard as your biggest failure, and how did you recover from it?

It must have been to allow control of Saatchi & Saatchi to pass out of our hands – particularly into the hands of people who didn't like the advertising business at all. And how did we recover from it? We haven't.

But you have gone some way towards doing so by starting a new company. When you lost control of Saatchi & Saatchi, did you think at any stage, 'I've made my pile, I'm giving up – I don't need to go back to the beginning and start up all over again.' What was it that drove you to set up your new company?

There is a saying in politics, which is that everything is driven by events. 'Events, dear boy, events,' was how Harold Macmillan explained what shaped his life, and I can only agree. The event of loss of control of the company was a traumatic one, but the events that followed were even more dramatic in that there was no opportunity to sit and think about alternatives. Events swept us along. It was, in fact, the only time in my life that I didn't have a point B which I knew I wanted to reach. It was a tide-in-the-affairs-of-man sensation, which I've never experienced before. Many people in the company, some of them people I'd worked with very closely, and a lot of young people, decided that they didn't want to stay with the old company under its new owner, and a lot of clients felt the same. And so this new company was born. It was created on a tide of strong emotion among employees and clients, the like of which I'd never seen before.

Was one of those feelings revenge?

There really wasn't time for the reflective questioning of motives and aims and purposes. It all happened in a matter of weeks and it felt right, so I didn't resist.

To what do you attribute that groundswell of feeling among both employees and clients? What was special about your operation that encouraged it?

I think people were just unhappy about the turn of events.

Would you say now that you need total control to maintain success?

Our new company is a partnership in which five people are equal partners, and the key people in each of our offices in each country are also big shareholders. This is a happy state of affairs. Of course, it's one that can only be achieved in a private company. Being in the public arena has many benefits, but one of the pitfalls is loss of control. It's still a price worth paying, though, and many people pay it.

A great many people feel that to be successful in business, you have to make a choice, at times, between family and work. How have you resolved that dilemma? Have you, at times, had to put your family on the back-burner in order to pursue your career?

Josephine and I devote specific time entirely to family, which is weekends. We go to Sussex and we don't see anyone. We don't entertain, and we don't go out. We have a very peaceful time.

Is it becoming more or less difficult to achieve success in the advertising field?

Far more difficult, I would say. When we began the industry still operated on a local basis, and around the world in different countries there were local agencies which were at or near the top of their industry. During the years in which we were building up Saatchi & Saatchi, the globalization of the advertising industry began. So that by the time we were the biggest agency in Britain, but had no overseas offices, we felt an endangered species. And we were right to feel insecure because that globalization has now occurred and the advertising business is now dominated by global advertisers who are interested in co-ordinating their campaigns across countries. This is very hard to do with a disparate collection of different local agencies in individual countries. So it's very hard to see how somebody could do quite the same today as we did. We always felt that a huge iron door was closing behind us and that we wanted to get through before it shut. I think it has now closed. So it would be much harder to achieve now what was possible through the 1970s and 1980s.

So, bearing in mind the different circumstances, what advice would you give to any young people now who are in the position you were in at Haymarket or when you were leaving the London School of Economics, whose feet are poised at the bottom of the ladder, and who really want to make as much a success of their lives, of their careers, as you have?

The first thing I would say is that they could not pick a better industry to enter than advertising, because it is an industry based entirely on merit. There is no hierarchy, there are no gradings based on seniority or age, so young people in their early twenties can achieve top positions in advertising – something that would be considered almost impossible in any other industry. That's because it's a very open world in which the man or woman with the idea is the best person in the room. You can get ahead with brains and determination. So the first advice I'd give that person is to have a go.

What do you think are the greatest enemies of success?

Self-satisfaction, by which I mean a feeling that you've done all you can.

And what are the core qualities you need to achieve success?

The click in the head of a child. That is an act of will.

Has success changed you at all?

Only in the direction of greater humility.

A lot of people might not be able to believe that.

It is true.

Humility rather than greater confidence, or both?

Humility, because you see the world flat-on, which is a source of strength and the root of happiness.

So no rosy glows?

No, because the rosy glow fades and then you're left with reality. You may as well face it flat-on from the beginning.

Did you?

No.

So that's the best bit of advice that you could give?

I think it is, yes.

What's the single greatest pleasure you have drawn from your successful career?

My life with Josephine and our family.

Your wife is a well-known novelist. Her first novel began with the phrase: 'Damaged people are dangerous, they know they can survive.' Are damaged people more likely to succeed than those who have not had some kind of traumatic experience?

That's the hard question which Josephine's book poses. I find the phrase compelling, and it's probably the reason the book was so successful. It's clearly true, but whether that means that you must have been damaged in some way in your childhood in order to be a successful person, I don't know. She was, I think, saying that damaged people are formidable because they have overcome the fear of failure and are therefore stronger. Whether this applies to success in the world, it's hard to say. There is a difference between survival and success.

Do you think that success brings obligations in its wake? Obligations of any kind, either to society as a whole, or to others?

Aside from the obvious obligations to society and community, there is an obligation to fulfil people's expectations – not to let people down if they have faith in you, if you've been lucky enough to win their faith. That is a profound responsibility.

Is criticism an inevitable part of success? If it is, how do you ride the attacks of critics and of those who are envious of what you've achieved?

In my own case I've been greatly helped by observing politicians and political leaders at times of great pressure. All political leaders have periods when the weight of criticism is immense and I've learned a lesson from watching how they stand up under that kind of pressure and don't crack, don't give in. There are many admirable qualities of politicians, but that's one of the most important. It's super-human at times.

I think you have to arrive at some deeper confidence in what you're trying to achieve. Of course, people say that the only thing politicians are interested in is clinging to power. That's not my experience of politicians. I think they do have a pastoral approach, and that most politicians believe that what they're trying to do is best for the people of this country. And it's that which keeps them going under criticism.

As for envy ... Harry Truman said that being bitter is for people who don't have something else to do. If you do feel envy it means you are a victim of the linear approach I described before, and have identified something you want. My best advice is to go and get it.

When your time comes to leave this life, what would you like people to say about you?

I'll try to answer that with a story. When Stanley Baldwin was Prime Minister he went to Oxford University to unveil a memorial to Scott of the Antarctic. In his speech he said an interesting thing, which was that Scott of the Antarctic was not a success. He did not reach the South Pole first, and died, tragically, in the attempt. Baldwin said that success alone is not enough, what is enough is to have a go. And that is what I believe. If you have a go, you're likely to lead a more interesting life, to meet more interesting people and to be a more interesting person yourself. So if I had to have a memorial I'd accept the one that Baldwin gave Scott of the Antarctic – that he had a go.

DAME CICELY SAUNDERS

Considered a bit naughty at school, she admits she did not make friends easily. Now, every day, Cicely Saunders has thousands of new 'friends' throughout the UK and beyond, because she started the modern hospice movement, one of the great British success stories of the last thirty years. People diagnosed with cancer or other life-threatening illnesses flock to this life raft of support services to receive a quality of care which also embraces their families, and which few can match. Prompted by an encounter with a remarkable patient, her contribution was to change the medical profession's approach to pain and symptom control, and, for the first time, put scientific rigour alongside friendship and a person-to-person relationship. 'Listen to the patient,' she says, 'you matter because you are you, and you matter to the last moment of your life.' She describes her approach as 'like putting a whole lot of elements into a kaleidoscope, and giving it a shake so that a new pattern of hospice care emerged'. As to why it should have been her – 'Ideas find people just as much as they find ideas. God or Providence or whatever showed me what I had to do, and then it was a question of getting on with it.'

She abandoned a degree course at Oxford to go into wartime nursing. A back operation forced her to give that up, so she went back to finish off her PPE course and became a medical social worker. Already committed to care of the dying, she was 33 when a surgeon pushed her into training to be a doctor. She realised that 'before I could get anybody to listen to my ideas, I had to demonstrate that I understood something they could recognize as acceptable medicine'. Six years later, armed with her new qualification and a mountain of research, her mission to convince a sceptical profession began in earnest. 'You win by showing there is a different way, and that there is something which is both challenging and rewarding.' More recently she helped form a National Hospice Council to cut through the rivalries between the various hospice charities so they could co-operate more and speak to government with one voice. She says, 'I never saw hospices as my children. It's always been a case of "come and talk to us, but go and do your own thing".' Looking briefly to the hospice movement's future, she adds, 'I do hope the standards will not drop, because it's difficult to balance the breadth of need and the depths of possibility.'

Dame Cicely, what is your definition of success?

Success is finding what you ought to do and managing to do it. I think ideas find people just as much as they find ideas, so it has something to do with being found, but then getting on with it.

So there is an element of luck?

I'd call it grace. Things came together to show me what I had to do, after I had, as it were, asked whatever you'd like to call it – God, or Providence, or whatever, 'What is it that I'm meant to do?' Three years later I knew, and then it was just a question of getting on with it.

And were there lots of early difficulties in doing that?

Yes, I had three years to begin with, just working as a volunteer nurse in one of the early homes to which I'd been sending dying patients. I was sure that what I had to do involved that group of patients, but I had to find out if I was suited to it. During those three years I just waited to see what the next step would be, until the surgeon for whom I was working pushed me into doing medicine. From then on it was hard work, and there were certainly difficulties, but I was much helped by the fact that my father told me not to worry about money. For a rather elderly medical student, starting at the age of 33, that was extraordinarily fortunate.

You said that you had to be sure you were suited to this work. A lot of people with a mission would carry on regardless without going through that particular checking process. Why did you feel you had to do it?

I suppose because in a way it was unexpected, and because I didn't really see any other way of being certain that I was on the right track. And it really was very exciting to find that I did fit in. And for that I owe an enormous debt of gratitude to both the patients and the staff of that home, St Luke's, and also to reading the old annual reports of the doctor who founded it in 1893. It was a whole process of discovery. I think you have to be ready to see whether you are on the right track, and to keep checking all the way along.

When you developed the concept of the modern hospice movement, the new kind of hospice ethos, what was different? What was so special about it? What changes did you feel had to take place within the medical system?

When I was looking after the patient who left me the founding gift for St Christopher's, there were three things he needed which he wasn't getting in a busy surgical ward. First of all he needed really good symptom control, better pain control, a real look at all the physical needs, but more than that, as a Jew from Poland with no family, dying at the age of 40, he also needed to look at himself and his life and be able to lay down that life with some degree of satisfaction, because he felt he'd done nothing. He had not married or had a family, and felt he had nothing to leave behind. His gift of £500 was a commission to open our home. In medicine then there was a lack of openness and communication, a lack of openness from person to person. Secondly, when he said, 'I want what is in your mind and in your heart,' he showed me that he needed the whole of the experience we could gain about pain, from scientific research to understanding how people felt, always given with the friendship of the heart. That was unusual, to put scientific rigour alongside friendship and a person-to-person relationship. Finally, after he died, having made peace with the God of his fathers, I had the real assurance that he'd come his own way in the freedom of the spirit. And so the other challenge was – what is it about people, the essential person, that goes on to the end of life and continues into whatever we think there is afterwards, and are we doing anything to help people find their own way? So that one person really gave me the keys, and all the other things – all the learning about research and home care and patients' families and all the rest of it – grew from there.

So he set you off on your great mission. How much opposition, or apathy, did you encounter within the medical profession?

Well, I was extremely lucky in that St Thomas's Hospital took me on as a medical student, with a push from the surgeon for whom I was working. He made a very important statement when I told him I thought I'd have to go back and try to nurse somehow, 'Go and read medicine – it's the doctors who desert the dying. There's so much more to be learned about pain, and you'll only be frustrated if you don't do it properly and they won't listen to you.' He was absolutely right. Before I could ever get anybody to listen to these ideas, I had to demonstrate that I understood something they could recognize as respectable medicine.

How difficult was it to win over all the people, or at least enough people, over time?

Well, you don't tackle the lot straight away. You talk first to the people who will respond. If I was going to do research, it wasn't going to be possible to do it at St Joseph's, so it was important that we had a place set up to do a demonstration. It therefore took the form of a series of invitations to come and talk to me. And I was able to go and see, for example, the chief medical officer of the Department of Health and say, 'We've got to do a comparative study between morphine and heroin, or diamorphine, I can show you a hospice full of patients pain-free and alert, but if I've got a magic drug that the rest of the world hasn't got, then that's no good. We've got to show that there is no clinically observable difference between morphine, available round the world – though not as widely as it should be – and heroin used in this particular way.' And of course that is exactly what we did show. So we won the people over through a series of introductions and meetings to tell them the story, having it clear enough in my own mind to be able to make it clear to them. There was no point in wasting time with people who were not interested to begin with. But through teaching rounds of students being brought, sometimes by their consultants at St Joseph's, we laid the foundations for St Christopher's.

It was a revolutionary task to change the thinking of the whole medical profession. Were you daunted by it in any way?

I wouldn't necessarily say it was the whole medical profession. I think you achieve things by looking at what is possible, step by step. I was very lucky in that, because I had done quite a lot of singing, I didn't find public speaking terribly difficult, and therefore I was able to go around – and, increasingly, I was asked to go around – talking about the nature and management of terminal pain. I didn't do fund-raising talks, I just took slides, showing people patients, telling stories and letting the patients do the work, quite honestly. It was the patients of St Joseph's who were the fund-raisers, founders and teachers of St Christopher's.

What kind of reports did you get at school?

Top of the form, or thereabouts, and 'Cicely should do better', except for music, which was always all right. I was pretty competent, but I was also thought to be naughty, and talked at the wrong moments, and did all the awkward things one does when one is unsure. But I wouldn't want to make too much of that.

Looking back on it, do you see yourself as a naughty child?

No, I was an unhappy child. I did not like school.

Is that unhappiness and, presumably, the sense of insecurity that comes from unhappiness, an important factor in your success, in your determination to drive through a project?

Yes, I think so. I finished up at Roedean as head of house, but I had a great feeling for the people who felt they didn't fit in. And I suppose that turning to doing something about dying patients – so often, certainly at that time, seen as failures – was really nothing to do with taking up a challenge, rather it was turning towards people who were in need, because I suppose I'd felt fairly needy myself. I wouldn't want to glamorize that. I really think I've gone on feeling safer and happier all my life, particularly when, having had a year at Oxford just before the war, which I did enjoy, I left to go nursing. From that moment on I became a popular person, the regular representative, and really I just felt I'd found my right place. So caring was obviously built in, but I hadn't previously had the opportunity to do it.

How did you get into nursing? And what made you think that nursing was going to be the right profession, because there were many you could have gone into?

Well, not in 1939–40, because it didn't seem to me that being at Oxford in wartime was the right thing for a girl to do. The sister of a friend of mine went off to train as a nurse, and suddenly it clicked in my mind. In wartime one has to do something which is of use, and nursing was the obvious thing, though my tutor said it was a mistake. I didn't want to simply go off and be a VAD, which was a Red Cross nurse. I wanted to train and do it properly. There were a lot of women who worked as Red Cross nurses, without training, through the war. They did terrific things, but ended up afterwards with no qualifications.

At what point did the connection with what was to become your modernization of the hospice movement take place? What was the key catalyst?

That came after I was invalided out of nursing, finished off a war degree at Oxford and became a medical social worker, having had my back operated on, which was the problem. It was David Tasmar, the patient I was talking about earlier, who was initially in the first ward I took over as a medical social worker – or lady almoner – at St Thomas's in July 1947, who was the catalyst.

I was in the surgical department, with a particular commitment to patients with cancer, and David was in this ward with an inoperable cancer. He was living in digs and working as a waiter, and when he was discharged and able to go back to work for about three or four months, I followed him up in out-patients, because I knew he was going to run into trouble. When he collapsed his landlady got on to me and I went to see him and followed him to the hospital to which he was admitted. That was the start of the history of the hospice movement, because that particular person, with his need, and with his potential – which, in fact, he considerably fulfilled, achieving a degree of satisfaction with himself and his life – is its real founder.

As you set about persuading the medical establishment and developing the concept of modern hospice care, were there any guiding principles that drove you forward to obtain the success you have achieved?

Quite honestly it was trusting in God to give me the opportunities, and at the same time working as hard as I possibly could. I was very lucky in that the professor of pharmacology at St Mary's gave me that clinical research fellowship, which made me look around, read around and just simply soak up information. And I was a voracious reader. Here and there were people who had written, anecdotally, about what they had done for dying patients, and there was a lot among the poets – Tolstoy's *The Death of Ivan Ilich* and things like that. The idea of the whole of the essential person being important to the moment of death came as much out of literature as it did from theology, although it did come from that as well. The fact that there were basic pain researchers, which I then came upon, was really very exciting.

I went out to America in 1963, and met up with quite a few pain researchers who were beginning to look at clinical pain, although at that time it was post-operative pain. I met one man who had written that the whole area of chronic pain simply hadn't been looked at. So obviously there was a gap, which was becoming more and more defined the more I read. But that had to go hand-in-hand with the commission, as it were, I'd had from David Tasmar. So, this scientific rigour, and the need to do something that could be really shown and proved, had to be combined with that commission.

I'm not basically a good researcher – I'm much more of an impresario – but we've had very good researchers. I've had some of the original ideas about what we needed to look at, but I didn't actually carry it all out myself. The need to look at the whole family came, I think, from what I'd learned in my social-worker days, and the idea of taking in bereavement, of family support before and after the patient's death, was developed. Doing this at home arose from my reading and from talking to district nurses – the first lecture I ever gave was to a group of district nurses. It was like putting a whole lot of elements into a kaleidoscope and giving it a shake so that the new pattern of the modern hospice emerged, with its emphasis on symptom control, with all the objective basis of research, with the commitment of teaching. In America I met a group of social workers called Cancer Care, who were supporting patients at home in New York. They were providing money for patients to have their own nurses, but they were also doing a lot of family support, much of it on the telephone. All these basic principles came together during the 1960s.

When we opened St Christopher's it was a very exciting, pioneering moment. But the real beginning was admitting our first four patients and our first small group of staff, and letting *them* tell us what their needs were, and then going on from there.

In those early days, did you ever have any doubts about the path you were taking? Did you ever think, 'I might be wrong about this'?

I suppose I was sure that God wanted me to do it, because when it started, on 24 June 1959, I really felt that He almost tapped me on the shoulder and said, 'Now you've got to get on with it.' I was reading what I read every morning, a little book of Bible readings. 'Commit thy way unto the Lord, and He shall bring it to pass.' And I thought, 'The moment has come.' I committed and He would help, and we'd get on with it.

From St Christopher's the hospice movement mushroomed. There are now over 200 hospices around Britain. As you watched and played a part in that development, did you feel every time a new hospice opened that it was an underlining of your earlier judgment?

I never saw the hospices as my children. It's always been a case of 'Come and talk to us, but go and do your own thing.' We never wanted a string of little St Christopher's all over the place. We never wanted to put even St Christopher's name on others, and certainly not my name. What was very important was that people took on board what we had learned in the way of the basic principles, but the interpretation had to be their own. And I have been just as excited at seeing what has happened around the world as I have been by what has happened in Britain. But it's been a question of the next generation all the time. At the beginning, while I was still doing clinical work, it was the patients and me, but otherwise it has been the rest of the team. So much of what has happened in the spread of hospices has been the work of other people – it's not been mine at all. It's just been nice to watch it. I do hope that the standards will not drop, because it's difficult to balance the breadth of need and the depth of possibility.

As you say, the difficulty when you've achieved something is maintaining that success, isn't it? Actually staying on the plateau you have reached without plunging back into a valley. So how are you doing that?

You have to hand the torch on. I am a sort of elder statesman now. I do a certain amount of writing and talking still, and I made two or three very exciting trips abroad last year, but what I am most pleased about is the developments being made by other people here and in other parts of the world. Our medical director has developed a professorial chair, and this particular chair, and the particular person who is filling it, and the way it combines St Christopher's and King's College Hospital, and King's College, the Strand, is absolutely fascinating. I'd never have done that. It wasn't my idea, it was his. The work our social work department is doing with families, and children and loss, wasn't mine, it was theirs. So I'm extraordinarily lucky in that they allow me to remain involved. I hope I just support. I'm still a networker, and I can give them introductions and start things up. That is brought about to some extent through the name of the hospice, but it's the next generation who are doing the exciting things.

Is that one of the secrets of continuing success? Knowing when the time has come to delegate, when you need to let go a little bit, but at the same time hold yourself in reserve, prepared to come in and crack the whip when necessary?

I don't crack the whip, and they wouldn't take any notice of me if I did! They're a very independent lot. As for advice, that comes out of discussion, really. I think what made it all so much easier for me was my commitment to my husband's care. Although I had known him for 30 years, initially his first wife was still alive in Poland, so we were only actually married for 15. He died last year, but for about ten years before that he suffered life-threatening illnesses and battled his way back. He was able to fight his way back to being able to paint and draw, but he needed a tremendous amount of care, so I had a huge commitment at home. And the last couple of years, the nights and the heaviness and so on, were not easy. I was pretty exhausted by the end. But we could work together at home, I knew that my husband was upstairs in the studio and that I was able to pay for somebody else to be with him when I couldn't – again, I'm very fortunate to have been able to do that – and I was with someone who, near the end of his life, was able to sit back and say, 'I am completely happy. I have done what I had to in my life, and now I'm ready to die.' And indeed he died in the most extraordinary peace, having done a really good portrait drawing three days earlier. He was at St Christopher's for the last six weeks. I hope I will be able to say the same sort of thing at the end of my life, but we'll have to wait and see.

Many of the patients in hospices are only weeks, months away from dying. They know that they are relatively close to death. Is there such a thing as a successful death?

Each person has to have his or her own death. The other day a patient, who was being brought up to the day centre by a volunteer driver said to one of our research people, 'The trees are so beautiful. Did I really have to have a terminal illness to know how beautiful they are?' That was a degree of illumination, really, at the end of her life, which was personal to her. Somebody else might stop grumbling for the first time in his or her life. Somebody else will be angry right to the end, for example about dying so young or leaving children behind. So you can't generalize about a 'successful' death. It has to be a person's own death, not one we think is right, and our approach has to be one of respect. What is it that this person is learning, trusting in, afraid of, or still needs to do? We must really try to be aware of that person, of his or her own relationships and culture and past and everything else, and of how this ending to life fits. David Tasmar's end of life did fit. He found somebody ready to listen as he talked it through, and he left something behind, thinking that perhaps this gift would help other people. He'd no idea how far it could go. I would say that his was a 'successful' death.

What is the special balm, almost, which the hospice movement appears to pour over people who are dying, and their relatives, creating this whole package of care which, according to more and more people, is of the highest quality available, the best in Britain today?

I think we have to be careful not to be sentimental about what is happening in hospices, and to realize how fortunate we are if we have a place with a staff complement that enables us to give people time, and nurses out in the community who have more time than the average district nurse. We must not sit back on our laurels and think that just because we can give attention people will feel a sense of self-worth. We have to be very aware of the people who are in general hospitals, people who don't have cancer – which is still the main hospice commitment, although we are increasingly looking at people with other illnesses. We must be aware of the long, slow deterioration of a lonely elderly person, for example. They need attention just as much as hospice people, and I think that's just as much of a challenge.

Are there any criteria that make a hospice successful?

When I went to the Queen to get my Order of Merit, she said, 'I've visited a lot of hospices, and they're all different, but they're all the same. How have you done it?' I'd never been asked that before, and I found myself saying, 'I think only because I've said to everyone, "Listen to your patients".' As I said, it's the patients who have told us what they needed, and if people feel they have attention, then they feel their importance is acknowledged. We are saying, 'You matter because you are you, and you matter to the last moment of your life. We'll do all we can, not only to help you die peacefully, but to live until you die.' That is something I said in a talk ages ago, which has been picked up and spread round as a sort of hospice commitment, I suppose. And I think that's the central point of the hospice movement, and can be done in a busy ward, by a palliative care nurse or doctor or a social worker.

But are there any other factors on top of that – practical ones, for instance? The contribution of so many volunteers? Could hospices be as successful as they are without volunteers, or other ingredients?

I don't think we could. Volunteers play an enormous part in it, particularly in this country and in the United States. Volunteers give you the extra space patients and families need – space to be themselves. We have hundreds of volunteers, and they're the most marvellous group, with a tremendous commitment. Their giving of themselves complements the professional giving of all the paid staff. It's a very important ingredient.

How important a part does religion play in your success?

It was extremely important. But when we started meeting five years before St Christopher's opened, and I invited everybody who was really interested, and who was going to be committed, there was a good atheist in our midst, so I knew we were going to be a community of the unlike. I think the nature of a spiritual commitment, which is much wider than just religious commitment, is important, but I have certainly never said that we all have to be the same.

What do you regard as your biggest failures, and how did you recover from them?

Well, I didn't do very well with my immediate successor. Because I saw things very clearly myself, I bulldozed people without realizing I was doing it, and I've had to learn that I can cut people off pretty smartly if I don't keep a hold on myself. I think my husband had an enormous amount to do with the fact that I don't really do that now.

How difficult was it for you to adopt a different approach?

When I moved from being medical director to chairman it was not an easy time, particularly as my husband was very ill shortly afterwards. An American Jewish psychiatrist from New York, who comes over and spends a week with us every year, was visiting, and he told me, 'You have got to go and find somebody to talk to outside this place.' That was very important. The person to whom I did go and talk – and talked for a long time – helped me to sort out a lot of things.

Was it difficult for you to let go of the reins, because, in a sense, the movement was your baby?

Yes, but that happens to everybody who has a family, doesn't it?

And to everyone who is successful as well? You have a project and you run with it, and then the time comes when you really do have to involve other people, embrace other people. It's a difficult thing to do, to control the development of success.

There was a stage when everything at St Christopher's was in files on the floor of my kitchen, and I was just working at home, very much on my own. My brother, who was a management consultant and who'd been at Harvard Business School, said, 'As a pioneer, you have to be somewhat of an autocrat. You can get advice, and so on, from all the people around, but they focus on you, and then go out from you.' I think scaling down that autocracy and creating a real management team was something that really only my successor could do, and St Christopher's was fortunate in that it had the right people at the right time. I think one of the problems of a pioneer is succession. Our present medical director and the young management team are really doing extremely well, and if I disappeared overnight, they would carry on. It would make no difference.

Would you say, in general terms, that if you really want to achieve something it's best done by an autocrat rather than by committee, where decision-making processes might be slow and ponderous?

I think what you need is an autocrat who appreciates the fact that, like everybody else, he or she has clay feet, and that he is extremely dependent on other people's advice, even if he doesn't necessarily take it. You must never stop listening to other people, including the people who are working for you. If you stop listening to the grass roots that is very dangerous.

In the late 1980s you perceived a weakness in the hospice movement in general, in that there were very powerful national charities at the top of the movement who were doing great things in their own right but were not working together as well as they could. So you set about establishing a National Hospice Council which would bring them all together. How difficult was that?

Well, I can't say I did it. It was just one of those things that happened. I wrote a letter to *The Times* when the nurses' salaries went up to say that I hoped the government would appreciate that some hospices were going to find this very difficult. Somebody sent me a generous cheque, and said, 'Any lobbying I can do for you, I will do for free.' This particular person was really the man behind the National Hospice Council. He set up a series of dinners at which I met people like the Minister for Health, and later the Secretary of State, and told them there needed to be a single voice, because government couldn't talk to all these mixtures. We were able to form this council, with an enormous amount of help from Eric Wilkes, another of the pioneers in the field – I'm not the only one about. But the person in the background, who has kept himself in the background and probably wouldn't want me to name him, was the catalyst – he was the one who quietly brought people together at the right moment and in the right way. And then we were lucky in appointing a quite brilliant executive director.

Were you surprised to see success taking place quietly and unobtrusively, without having to beat the drum and bang on the door in a public way?

It was fascinating to watch. It took about two years, and it's remarkable what the National Council has achieved in that time.

What were the main techniques used to set up the council?

Our benefactor was quite brilliant at bringing together a group of people, about eight or ten, at a round table and getting them to strike sparks off each other, and knowing who to put together for the next dinner. One or two key people had some really very good ideas. It gradually showed us that what Help the Hospices hadn't managed to do, to bring other charities together, could be achieved under a rather bigger umbrella.

In the charitable world in general, which is more important, the actual concept of the charity, the purpose of the charity or the raising of money?

Oh, it's the purpose. If you get it right, it'll happen – you have to get it right and then go for the money. The money will come if you can give a clear vision of something that really needs to be done, and can persuade people of it. To go and make the money first is the wrong way round.

But there are some people in the charitable sector who say that if you make fund-raising the number-one priority, you will raise more money, and therefore, you're more able to help the cause you have chosen.

If you're in a service charity, it's the work itself that is the main fund-raiser.

Are there any people, past or present, big or small, whose success you really admire? Who are your heroes?

Dame Julian of Norwich. Back in the days of the Black Death and the Hundred Years' War, she had a series of visions of the love of God which were translated into English at the beginning of this century. I have a number of translations. She spent 20 years meditating on her visions and praying about them as an anchoress attached to the St Julian Church in Norwich before she wrote them down. She took the time to get it right, and she produced something which speaks to us today in the most amazing way.

And have you any present-day heroes?

The people who just go off and do their own thing to help without recognition. Those who get recognition are not necessarily those who should be being given the credit. And people like Simon Weston, that boy who got so badly burned in the Falklands.

What do you think are the greatest enemies of success?

Pride, idolatry and self-inflation.

Do you think that success, in any field, brings with it obligations to the rest of society?

Everybody has his own obligation to society. We are all knots in a net, we all belong together. You can't just take yourself out and say, 'I will do my own thing with no commitment to anybody else.'

What is the single greatest pleasure you've had from your success?

Just seeing what's going on. Going to conferences and meeting people who are starting up hospices. I've been to Singapore, Japan, Hong Kong, Thailand, Korea, and seen people really excited about doing their own thing. A day of meeting people like that is a good day indeed.

If you could gather together in one room all the young people who have an idea, as you had, for changing a part of society – for changing one aspect, however small it might be – what advice would you give them?

See what appeals to you, something that might suit you, and listen. It's listening that tells you what to do. Listen not only to your inner self, but to what you see beyond yourself as true.

What advice would you give to those people who perhaps don't know a great deal about the hospice movement but would like to be involved, either as a helper or on the medical staff?

Don't put a halo around us – come and see us. See if there's an open day, or ring up and say, 'I am interested in being involved. Is there anything that somebody with my particular background can offer you?' And go and find out.

And what would you say to those potential patients who are frightened by the notion of hospices, because they still associate them with the old concept of the big, grey building up on the hill behind the trees where people go to die?

Talk to your own doctor, and think about home care first. If treatment is becoming less and less successful – and in fact has really come to an end – if you have problems with pain and symptoms, if you're worried about your family caring for you, and so on, consider the options with your doctor. Remember that we want to start in a person's home, and maybe that is all we will ever do. Hospice isn't just a building – it's an attitude, it's skills. It's as Schumacher said, going and seeing what people are doing and helping them to do it better.

One final question. When your time comes to leave this earth, what would you like people to say about you?

She was a trial sometimes, but she did what she could.

RAYMOND SEITZ

'One of the most intriguing things in history is
the combination of events and major characters.
It's someone who notices that the arrangement of
the stage has changed just enough so an
individual can make a difference.' Ray Seitz's
meticulously chosen imagery, easy manner and
finely tuned judgment explain President Bush's
'wholly unexpected' phone call asking him to
become the first career diplomat ever appointed as
American Ambassador to Britain. His three years
in the post were considered an unqualified
triumph, and it was only the arrival of a new
President that led to him quitting the service for
a move into international banking. Now Vice-
Chairman of Lehman Brothers, he is therefore
well placed to judge success in both his old and
new professions. 'Nobody goes into diplomacy for money. The rationalisation is that
you are serving a greater purpose – public good. It produces all sorts of vanities!
Success is the degree to which you have been able to provide a service, but it is
cloudy and ambiguous, you're participating in the next chapter of a book that
never, ever ends.' The financial world, however, he finds 'more precise and more
exacting. In banking, money is the yardstick, success is there for everyone to see –
and so is failure.'

Ray Seitz was brought up in a family who lived by 'a kind of Victorian ethic'
and had 'a certain disdain for material reward'. The concept of public service was
strong – his father commanded one of the American regiments that stormed ashore
in the D-Day landings. After toying briefly, at the age of eight, with an ambition to
be a singing cowboy, he set his sights on becoming a diplomat. After a history degree
from Yale and two years' teaching, he joined the US foreign service and worked his
way through a series of key postings to become a close adviser to two Secretaries of
State. He sees the hard part of diplomacy as understanding the limits – 'only then
can you really engage in trying to develop policies that serve the national interest'.
He agrees that diplomacy has now been overtaken by communications – 'the
responsibility is less defined than it used to be, and therefore it's more difficult to
have a sense of individual success'. Looking back, he sees 'a pattern made up of
life's little accidents', so, for him, personal success is 'an accumulation of events
that made my life more sensible, and therefore more fulfilling'.

Ray Seitz, what is your definition of success?

I suppose success is something that you experience at a certain age in your life when you can turn around and say, 'Well, it all made sense. Somehow it all came together.' Perhaps you can discover a pattern in your life that you can regard as fulfilling. In my own case, I take some satisfaction from looking back, even to the time when I was a boy, at things that happened along the way which seemed random. Now that I'm 54, I appreciate they weren't so random. They fit together. They produced something. There was an accumulation of events that made my life more sensible and, therefore, more fulfilling.

So you're saying you cannot make a real judgment of success until you have moved quite a way along the track of life. Are there not individual moments that are successful in their own right, whether they fit into a pattern or not?

It depends on what your ambitions are – in other words, whether you have set very specific goals for yourself. I've a good friend who set a specific financial goal for himself, which he thought would take most of his life to achieve. Yet he reached it by the time he was 30, and he has said to me ever since then that he was so ginned up about reaching that goal that, once he had attained it, he felt blank afterwards. For instance, I suppose there are certain people who are looking for an elective office or a financial reward of one kind or another, and therefore, it's measurable when they've arrived – 'I'm a professional athlete, I want to win the gold medal,' etc. I never had that, I never had a specific goal that I could have defined in that way. So my definition of success or my experience with success, really derives from looking backwards and saying, 'After all, it came together,' and that's what I find most satisfying.

What can you do to make it come together?

I suppose in diplomacy you can regard success, or the nature of success, as the degree to which you have been able to provide a service. The concept of public service was always very important in my family. But without any precision to it, it can be an amorphous thing too. You can, I suppose, wander through a diplomatic life and at the end of it say to yourself, 'You have provided a service because you were there and somebody else wasn't.' But I think it has to be a little more than that. Perhaps your work coincided with important external events, and you somehow found yourself in the middle of them – or on the fringe of them – but nonetheless participating in them and trying to contribute to their outcome in one fashion or another. The right place and the right time are important and wholly unpredictable.

And does it change, did the definition of success change when you moved from diplomacy into banking?

No, not particularly. But of course it's a new world, a world which is less amorphous than public service or diplomacy. The measurements are very precise. Even self-worth is sometimes measured against the standard of money. Money is a brutal thing and it's almost like getting scored on an exam. You get rank-ordered. The balance sheet of life in the banking world is very severe.

Diplomacy is cloudy and ambiguous – you never really know whether you've made any difference or not. And you flatter yourself that maybe you did a little bit or maybe you wrote this or said that, and it had some kind of impact. But you're also very aware of a long, long history of nations and peoples and conflict, and you have a very narrow sliver of it, you're participating in the next chapter of a book that never, ever ends.

You enter the financial world and it's more precise and more exacting. Success is there for everybody to see, and so is failure.

Which of the two definitions of success do you prefer?

Oh, I prefer the former, without any doubt. I think it all has to do with a sense of purpose. In diplomacy, for example, there was never any relationship between compensation and the work you did. In government service, you are paid at a certain level, and Congress makes sure it's not very much. And if Congress were tempted to make it more, the American people would object. So nobody goes into diplomacy for money. It's like politics. There's no neat unit of account to track you. You can look at one person, who is paid the same amount as you. He comes in at nine and leaves at five. Then look at somebody else who is consumed by the job, working late at night, flying off somewhere and often courting danger in one fashion or another – and every two weeks, the same cheque shows up for both. You hope it's enough to pay whatever your bills are, but the sum bears no relationship to what you are doing. In the world of banking, on the other hand, money is the yardstick, the definition.

In diplomacy you have to be able to say to yourself, 'There's a bigger purpose here – I'm doing this for a reason that is detached from material well-being or material reward.' And if you can feel that you are in fact serving that purpose, then it's a more sensible endeavour. But you have to create your own satisfaction.

A lot of diplomats say that if they had gone into the commercial world and if they had worked this hard, the material reward would have been much, much greater. I've said this also. But we didn't because we didn't want to. I suppose journalism is not all that different. The rationalization is that you are serving a bigger purpose, a greater purpose – public good. Now that may be frightfully conceited. It produces all sorts of vanities. And there are a lot of vanities in journalism and politics and diplomacy.

Is success a direct product of background, of upbringing?

Some of it. I have thought about that myself. There is so much serendipity in life. You try to think back to the small things that happened along the way, things which nudged you in this direction or that direction.

I don't think my interest in diplomacy or my wish to go into the foreign service was genetically coded, so I ask, 'What happened?' Did I read a book somewhere or see a movie? There are, by the way, very few great movies about diplomacy! What pushed me in that direction? Clearly, as much as anything, it's family, it's the way you were brought up, it's what you were exposed to around the house.

In my family there were two very strong things. One was public service, and in my immediate family that was expressed in the military, on both sides, my mother's and my father's. It was a very army family and it was a very patriotic family – you serve your nation. That's what you're there to do.

There are also judges in my family and I have an aunt who was a psychologist and a brilliant woman, who spent all her time in social service. Our family had a certain disdain for material reward, and lived by a kind of Victorian ethic. You read about the Victorian age and you wonder about the degree to which people actually believed what they said, but the succeeding generation believed what the preceding generation said and, certainly, that was the case in my family. If my father had been a minister, would I have gone into the ministry? Maybe I would have gone off as a missionary somewhere. But he was in the military. Serve your nation. And while I didn't choose the military route, there was certainly a sense in my family that the diplomatic and the military were two sides of the same coin.

So certainly the family, then I suppose education, and then, I suspect, your first brushes with a career, your first little encounters. Does that intrigue you or doesn't it? And also, to some degree, not knowing what else to do.

But those encounters are often accidental, purely by chance, so whether you achieve success in a particular career is often based on luck?

It's often based on luck. In my case my first encounter with diplomacy came through my family. I was about 15 or 16 and my father was stationed in Iran. He was head of a military aid operation and that tended to be a fairly diplomatic environment. It wasn't an army post – most of my time had been on army posts – and for a teenager it was unbelievably romantic – bazaars, different languages and all kinds of nationalities, all of which was exotic. I thought it was wonderful. And while the thought was probably somewhere in my mind, I think that experience in Iran and going to what, to me, were fascinating places – everything just snapped into place and it was then that I began to believe that this was what I wanted to do. I don't know whether anybody said to me, 'What do you want to do when you grow up?'

When I was eight or nine, I wanted to be a cowboy. And then I amplified that a little bit more by saying I wanted to be a singing cowboy, in the Roy Rogers vein. But between wanting to be a singing cowboy and wanting to go into the foreign service, I don't remember too many different stages. So I was lucky that I was familiar with the idea of public service and the military and international politics.

I'll tell you another thing, it's just things that pop into your mind. When I was about 18 or 19 and it was time to start thinking a little more seriously about what I wanted to do, I went to Omaha Beach in Normandy with my father and my stepmother – my mother had died much earlier. My father, when he was 35, was the commander of an American regiment that landed on Omaha Beach on the morning of 6 June. That visit was the first time I had seen those beaches. They were gentle and peaceful, and they resembled nothing that he remembered. It was a very emotional moment.

My father dealt with it pretty well, at least at the beginning, while walking along the beach. But we were choked up. That made a tremendous impression on me – the danger, the sacrifice and the sense of purpose, of dedication. He had gone into the army, he was being called upon by his nation to participate in this great historic event that could easily have cost him his life, and also the lives of many in his command. To me it was heroic and inspiring. So I might have arrived at the same conclusion intellectually, but again, I would never have had the internal inspiration if it hadn't been for this family experience.

By the time I was in university, I knew what I wanted to do and I didn't realize that was quite so unusual – to be 18 or 19 and be pretty sure you knew what you wanted to do. I hadn't arrived at that point by any practical and analytical route. It was just an accumulation of funny little things that happened.

Any regrets that you took the wrong decision?

No. Perhaps sometimes I was downcast or sometimes I'd say to myself, 'Well, should I get out of this game?' But the fact of the matter is, no. Some of that is because it ended nicely. I could turn around and say, 'All this did make sense, and it was wonderful.' This is retrospective, of course, but even along the way I found the work challenging. I thought the content was for the most part stimulating. I liked the action. People think diplomacy is a passive kind of thing, but that's not right. Diplomacy requires a lot of action. You're jumping on an aeroplane and going somewhere and trying to persuade people to do this or that, sometimes even your own people – and certainly in the United States the politics of diplomacy are a rough-and-tumble, rambunctious thing. I liked work, as well as the people I worked with.

Is having the right people around you an important contribution to success?

Oh, very much so. The sense of camaraderie and respecting the people you work with – and conversely the masses of people you work with that you don't respect. But on the whole I found I had friends in the foreign service who I thought were smart and dedicated and just good to be with – funny, a little fatalistic about things, who had a strong historical sense, and a kind of patriotism.

To what extent in achieving success must there be one person driving something through and to what extent is it a team effort?

I think in the world of governments it's got to be a joint effort. I wish one could say that you could have the diplomatic equivalent of Silicon Valley with a lot of really smart people – two or three smart kids in a garage developing some great idea. George Shultz used to say, 'Good ideas are not the problem in diplomacy'. We can all sit down and figure out the outlines of a Middle East settlement, for example, it's not beyond the genius of man to do that. What's hard is to get people to go along with whatever the good idea is. I've looked at peace plans for the Middle East for 30 years and they're all basically the same. There's no flash of brilliance, no flash of originality. The task is to try to line up the forces and the balances and the trade-offs that will permit a good idea to happen and to build the political context or the political framework or political support that can make it happen. Some of that requires luck, some of it you can push, some of it requires judgment, some of it is what you smell with your nose – all those little abstractions and intangibles. Sometimes it's successful and sometimes it's not. Maybe more often it's not. Good ideas are not the problem, getting them done is.

And isn't it also strong individuals like Peres and Arafat who are actually prepared to take risks in order to achieve this ultimate goal?

To me, one of the most intriguing things in history is the combination of events and the major characters, and you're quite right. It's Rabin or Sadat or someone who notices that the arrangement of the stage has changed just enough for an individual to make a difference, and this is a question as old as history – is it the event or is it the individual?

Mikhail Gorbachev is an intriguing example. Here was a man who, for whatever reason, was thrown upon the political shores of the Soviet Union at a time when the Soviet Union could have gone in a number of directions. He made a set of decisions whose implications I don't think he really firmly grasped. He didn't ride on the tide of history and he didn't control history, but the intersection of the man and history made things turn out a little differently. There is one decision that has always intrigued me. When the East Germans started to demonstrate in Dresden and Leipzig and East Berlin, Gorbachev decided to keep the Soviet troops in the barracks and to abandon the Honecker regime. The troops could have come out and changed everything. But he left the regime to its own fate, and as a result the face of Europe was changed. It made the East German regime unsustainable. It made German unification inevitable, which in turn made the withdrawal of Soviet forces from central Europe equally inevitable. Now, did he understand these great consequences would follow his decision? I doubt it, but he was deciding not to do something and that in turn loosed a variety of other events which we are still dealing with right now.

Had it gone the other way, what would have happened? Soviet tanks would have come out of the barracks and people would have been shot in the square in Leipzig. What would have happened then? I don't know.

Do you think that achieving any kind of successful change involves a degree of risk?

Yes, I think it does. I don't think you can analyse options with the confidence that option A produces this result and option B produces that result. At the end it's a risk, and almost surely it's not going to turn out the way you expected. You may have guessed it 80 per cent right or 20 per cent right, but you rarely understand it 100 per cent right. This is called the theory of unintended consequences. I think it's an intriguing question – for example, did Gorbachev know the momentous nature of the decision not to do something?

So the decision not to do something can be every bit as important as the decision actually to do something?

Absolutely. And at the end your instinct is the final bit of judgment. You can have all the analysis in the world, but it's instinct that tells you this one is better than that one.

All successful people have the right instinct?

Largely. I think largely.

Do all successful people have to have experienced some form of sacrifice or failure at some time in their lives? Does it help you become more successful if you've appreciated, known and overcome the downside?

In a classic profile that would be true. But I doubt whether it is generally true – 'Been so down it looks like up to me.' Maybe. I've read a couple of biographies recently, of George Patton and Douglas MacArthur, two great generals. Did they have setbacks? Well, yes. Were they disappointed? Yes. But on the whole they did what they wanted to do and were great soldiers – maybe frustrated at the end – but it's hard to identify some terrible setback in their careers. I would imagine athletes are much the same way too. If you were going to make a Hollywood movie, you'd have to have 'the setback', you'd have to have the guy who gets flattened, or he loses the race. But then he goes out and he trains even harder and he comes back, inspired by a woman no doubt, and he wins. That's Hollywood, but I don't think that's necessarily reality.

Were there moments in your life when you thought, 'I've failed here,' and how did you overcome that?

Once I was in a job where I felt I had responsibility but not the authority. That led to a lot of frustration and discontent. I didn't complain about it, or at least not that much. Nonetheless I sometimes felt dejected and a little humiliated. I seriously thought about leaving.

Why didn't you?

Because it slowly started to turn, it slowly started to change. I would like to say that that's because I made it change and I was patient enough to make it change. But I think it was more that outside actions influenced things, and the situation got better. It's one thing to think about resigning and quite another to contemplate what you would do instead. I think maybe that's a weakness. But it certainly made me more patient and things turned out all right.

What do you regard as your great successes, either professional ones or successes that the world generally doesn't know about?

That's an interesting question because it suggests having a specific goal and then achieving it. Inasmuch as I never had a specific goal, I perhaps never had that wonderful triumphal sense of success. I never plugged away at something and finally got there – like Gertrude Stein, 'there was no there there'. Maybe I should have had more defined goals, but I never did. So the majority of my flushes, if you will, were largely things that happened to me that made me say, 'This is great,' or 'I never expected this.' But that's quite a different reaction to having set out to achieve something and gotten there.

What were those kind of moments?

I think if I had to pick the most exciting moment in my career, it was the night I received a telephone call from President Bush asking me to be Ambassador in London. First it was a wonderful job, but second, I knew that a career person had never gone to London as Ambassador in more than 200 years. That position had always gone to a personal friend or political appointee of one kind or another – often very able people. It had never gone to a member of the career foreign service. That I was asked to do that job was wholly unexpected, and in a way it was the suddenness and sheer unpredictability that made it such a happy event. I suppose at that stage in my career I would not have been surprised to have been appointed Ambassador somewhere, but to be asked to be Ambassador in London would never have passed through my mind, even though I had served there twice before – in fact that was a reason why it was even less likely to happen. So when it did, and under such unusual circumstances, it just made me happy. That's quite different from triumphant.

Are there any people, big or small, past or present, whom you consider to have stood on the pinnacle of success? Who are the people you most admire?

Certainly my father, and not because I thought he was a great or an exceptional man, but because he was a courageous man, and courage and integrity to me are very closely related.

Another person I admired a lot is Abraham Lincoln. That may sound a little corny, but he was a tragic figure. The British say that the Americans really don't have a sense of irony, perhaps because they don't have the sense of tragedy. On the whole I think there is truth in that observation. But the American Civil War was a great tragedy, and I think Lincoln felt it so deeply, agonized about it so personally and overcame it so courageously that he stands out from other American leaders. He never lost that melancholy of war and death, and, of course, then he himself was killed. So I admire him not only for what he did and what he understood about the United States, but also because he was a Shakespearian character. He was a great man in the broadest and deepest sense. We've had very few of those.

Of people I've worked with, there are many that I admire, but the one I admire most, and certainly feel most affection for, is George Shultz. In some respects, he reminded me of my father. There is a man who could have gone off and made billions of dollars somewhere if he had wanted to, but he was brilliant, completely self-sacrificing, and had great integrity and dedication to service. I never saw him waver in any of that, and I worked with him very closely. I came to admire the integrity of the man. That, perhaps, is a very important definition of success – if you can go to bed at night, turn off the light and have those ten minutes before you're asleep and not feel ashamed. I think integrity is a vital part of feeling successful at the end of one's career.

Is it becoming more or less difficult to achieve success in the diplomatic world?

It's becoming much more difficult, largely because the role of diplomacy has changed so very much and, therefore, the individual's part in it is less responsible.

You mean you are being driven by some bureaucratic machine?

Yes. And diplomacy has been overtaken, as the cliché observation goes, by communications. The responsibility is less defined than perhaps it used to be, and therefore it's more difficult to have a sense of individual success. To be a diplomat, to be an American diplomat in the Cold War, was important, because you did feel that there was a great global struggle and that there were many dangers out there, and that there would be plenty of mistakes and plenty of misjudgments. There was a very great purpose to be served, however, so the context of what I and my colleagues were doing infused our jobs with considerable meaning. Individual success was less important. I think that same kind of meaning will be harder to find in years ahead. The stakes don't seem perhaps quite as high.

In America it is said that people don't envy success, they want it, whereas in this country there is a tendency to say, 'I want some of that' without maybe thinking how the person has achieved it. Why do you think success arouses conflicting emotions from admiration to envy?

Well, that's a question of social comparison. I think it is true that there were jealousies and resentments in British society, and probably still are, because people felt that society was very structured and that there were avenues that were denied to you by dint of your birth and nothing else. Your birth dictated what your possibilities were – education and so on. For a very long time they did, and you find a lot of people out there on the streets who say that they still do.

I think that's less true in the United States, but you can't rule it out entirely, certainly not if you are black. There are certain formulas for success – school, background, a variety of things. But all of that said, I think the United States is a much looser, less predictable or predetermined society.

What are the greatest attributes you can have for achieving success?

Dedication. That by definition almost means that other important things get lesser treatment. If you talk to someone successful, I don't think he would be wholly honest if he didn't say that, in the pursuit of a goal, some personal sacrifice in terms of family had not been made. There is almost inevitably a tension in that, it's built into the design, it's in the deal. Perhaps you could say that the measure of success is how you have been able to deal with those inevitable contradictions between career and family. Some people do it well, a lot of people don't. Trying to get that balance right – not being so consumed, not thinking about your own indispensability or your own particular distinctions – that's a very tough thing. It's one of those things where, 'If I knew then what I know now', you might look back and say you overdid it.

If you could gather together all the young people who are thinking about entering diplomacy, what advice would you give them for making a success of their careers?

Well, I would give them an answer that I think is probably true of diplomacy in general, but it's especially true of the American diplomatic process. They should spend a lot of time in Washington. If they are going into the foreign service to see the world and to have all sorts of exotic experiences, that's perfectly fine. But it's unlikely to yield the kind of success they might want. You have to spend time in Washington to understand the political process that produces foreign policy. Foreign policy is the product of domestic politics. You have to understand the unique politics of America, its vastness, its limits, its federal system. That's the hard part of diplomacy, understanding the limits, and only then can you really engage in trying to develop policies that serve the national interest. I think that's a very, very important part of it. It's something that was a particular part of my own career and I think it's indispensable to successful diplomacy.

What is the greatest pleasure that has come from the fruits of your success?

I have already mentioned one – the sense of fulfilment and that things sort of made sense – that is very pleasurable. The other is the sense of a family being proud of you and that's a validation. More unhappily, I regret my parents weren't alive to see how my career ended. That's natural. But my sister died seven or eight years ago, and she and I were very close. And I know she would have taken tremendous pleasure at the good things that have happened to me, and I am sorry that she couldn't be around so that I could give her that pleasure.

Could you have done what you have done without the support of your family?

If there is anything wrong with our discussion it's how strictly we have kept to career. There is so much of the personal side of one's life that plays a part in all of this, because of the decisions you make and sacrifices you impose on others – your immediate family, your children who are picked up and packed off to some place you've been told to go, and so forth. Without wanting to sound drippingly sentimental, Caroline, my wife, is very much a part of this, both in terms of what it imposes on her and in the sense of her own sacrifices along the way.

When I was an ambassador here, the best thing about the job was that we did it very much together and we obviously saw each other a lot. That doesn't mean we could talk to each other all the time. But we compared notes or reacted to people or situations together. She was very much a part of it.

To be really successful, do you have to have a strong partner on-side with you, a sounding board for advice, perhaps cutting through some of the sycophantic advice with which people can surround themselves?

Whether it's essential I don't know, but Caroline always gave me a sense of proportion about things. In my own experience she gave my job that ability to step back and laugh at all the silliness – there's an awful lot of silliness in life, a lot of absurdities. Humour is indispensable and, in a way, it is perhaps the best expression of proportion, of keeping things in balance.

When your time comes to leave this planet, what would you like people to say about you, how would you like to be remembered?

Well, I'll go back to Caroline on that one. There is a cemetery in South Carolina – she's from South Carolina – and there's an epitaph on one of the headstones which she always found amusing and I do too. It sounds just about right. I can't remember the woman's name on this headstone, but the epitaph reads, 'She hath done what she could.'

HELEN SHARMAN

'Astronaut Wanted – no experience necessary!' Helen Sharman heard that radio advertisement by accident as she station-hopped while her car was stuck at traffic lights. She describes here the last-minute decision to fill in the application form, and how, even after being called for an interview, she told only her mother and one colleague about it, because of worries that people might think she was gullible and had fallen for 'something stupid'. The 26-year-old girl from Sheffield was amazed when she eventually beat 13,000 other hopefuls to become one of two Britons sent for 18 months' special training in Moscow's Star City. She describes here how they broke down the gruelling programme into a series of separate goals to help them cope better; the  moment she learned she – and not her colleague, Timothy Mace – would become the first Briton in space; her thoughts during the re-entry into the earth's atmosphere, and how at first she found her subsequent fame difficult to handle.

Helen Sharman was brought up by strong-willed parents who encouraged her to be independent and make her own decisions in life. A bright pupil and a good linguist who nevertheless opted for a degree in chemistry, she then applied for many different types of work, eventually joining GEC to make cathode ray tubes. After three years, anxious to have more of an impact on the things she was doing 'instead of simply following instructions', she joined Mars confectionery – thus unwittingly spawning a welter of later tabloid headlines about 'the woman from Mars'. She likes being in control of her own life (but not other people's), and believes that coping with failures actually creates the will to keep going. She talks of the price that has to be paid for success; of the sacrifices of the long preparation period for the space flight, for which she 'gave up everything', but also of the things she learned which made it all worthwhile. Success for her wasn't, as people in the UK saw it, the actual getting into space: it was working on the experiments for which she had trained. With absolutely no experience in public speaking, she began a tour of British schools, and was suddenly filled with a belief she had found a real use for herself in communicating science. Now an accomplished broadcaster, she talks of luck, opportunity, principles, the need to have a focus – and tenacity. 'It doesn't matter what other people think, you've got to go with what you believe in.'

Helen Sharman, what is your definition of success?

I think success is achieving what you want to achieve, although many people regard your success as achieving what they would like to achieve. I believe very much it's doing something that you want to do.

And what happens when your definition of success, of how successful you've been, differs from society's at large?

I think you're very often questioned as to why you're doing things, or not doing them. And people seem to want answers. They want to understand why you don't wish to do what they would consider the norm. For example if you get to the age of 50 and you haven't had children people think that there's something wrong with you, rather than considering the possibility that you might have made that choice. I think that attitude goes across the board. And I was lucky, going into space was something that many people thought they would want to do. On the other hand I have asked others whether they would have done it had they had the same opportunity. And they have said no, they wouldn't. So, for them that wouldn't be success, although society sees that act of going into space as success.

What happens when your judgment of whether you are successful or not differs from that of society, which judgment do you run with?

I always run with my own – it is the only one I can ever really feel comfortable with. Although to be an accepted member of society as, I think, most of us want, one has to abide by some of society's rules. We don't commit murder, for instance. But when it comes down to making decisions as to what I would like to do within society's guidelines I go with what I want to do.

Going back to your early upbringing, how did that shape you as a person, to give you the opportunities for the kind of success that you've achieved?

I was brought up to be independent-minded and to make my own decisions in life. My mother and father were both very strong-willed and I was brought up to have a broad experience of life. I wasn't particularly mollycoddled, but on the other hand they looked after me to an extent that I didn't actually suffer any real dangers. I never felt driven, but looking back, certainly I was expected not to do nothing. They didn't expect me to do any one thing in particular, but I was encouraged to take up varied activities. For instance, when I was six I started to play the piano – something that I still love doing – and my parents were very keen that

I should do it. My father played, I showed a bit of an interest, so I was given the opportunity to go for lessons. They never quibbled about taking time to go with me to an athletics match, or whatever, with the school. But they never pushed me in any one direction, and I am very grateful. Even without this, I did perhaps react in a small way against what might have been expected of me. My father's a scientist, he did physics at university, and I wonder now why I chose chemistry. I liked physics, and I wonder if it was slightly a case of 'I can't possibly do exactly what my father did, I have to do something different and be my own person.' It was certainly not a conscious decision.

So a hint of a rebel there?

Maybe. Between the ages of 13 and 17 I was, in a way, a bit of a rebel at school in that although I did my schoolwork, I didn't like the way we were treated as schoolchildren. I thought this was terribly unfair and we ought to have our rights. I remember being told what to do, in no uncertain terms – things that I didn't believe I needed to do. And I didn't understand why I was being told to do them. It was just the system, it was designed to make things easier for other people.

But did that also make it easier for you to develop a sense of asserting what you wanted to do, because you were bouncing off this wall, as it were?

I think the school would have much preferred me to have kept quiet, because I didn't just tell them what I thought, I used to get the views of all my friends as well, and go in with this real strength behind me, and say, 'We have decided.' The teachers that I've met since remember me for that. I could get away with it because it didn't affect my schoolwork, but I think I was probably pushing them a little bit more than they really felt comfortable with.

But this idea of being a fighter, of fighting for what you wanted, started in those schooldays. How did you then carry it on, as you moved through your late teens and to university?

I always did just what I wanted to do, and I hope now, looking back, that I didn't put out too many people too much.

So talk me through the later stages of your education and into your first job.

After getting my chemistry degree, I didn't know what I wanted to do other than go into industry. I certainly didn't want to stay at university to do research. Somehow I knew there was more to life, I just wasn't quite sure what there was. I applied for many different types of jobs in which I could use my degree in some way. Some involved laboratory work, others were to do with actually making products, such as cosmetics. The one I eventually took was in the electronics industry with GEC, where I was involved in making cathode-ray tubes. I took that job because it offered variety – a bit of research, a bit of development, a bit of the production side, a bit of management. I enjoyed all of it.

And at that stage, what sort of career did you see developing ahead of you?

Only what I had been brought up to expect – that scientists became technologists in industry, and eventually technical directors, maybe even managing directors. I didn't know much more about industry than that. It's only by being out in the wide world that you realize that there's an awful lot more to it than you originally perceived. And the more you find out, the more you realize you are capable of. So you widen your horizons.

So there you were, having a job with a rough idea of where your career might lead you, and then suddenly your world changed.

After three years I went on to Mars Confectionery. I needed a change. I'd done a lot of things in my job, I'd learned a lot, but I wanted something more. I wanted to have more of an impact on the things I was doing, rather than just following instructions.

One particular evening I was driving from Slough, where Mars was, to my home in Surbiton, which in itself was unusual because I usually drove straight up to Birkbeck College in London where I was doing a part-time PhD. I would normally have been tuned in to listen to the traffic reports, but as I was just going home, I started flicking through the radio stations on the type of car radio that tunes to the next one on the dial, and as I flicked I caught, instead of some decent music that I was hoping for, the beginning of an advert, which was quite literally, 'Astronaut wanted, no experience necessary.' And it described an opportunity that I'd just never thought of before – for two people from Britain to go to Russia, train with the cosmonauts, and for one of them actually to launch into space, and do experiments on the space station.

But you'd never had an ambition to be an astronaut? You'd never thought, 'That's something I'd like to do'? It just came as a result of this radio advertisement?

No, I never knew of the opportunity before. I think this is one of the biggest problems in school life, generally – you only know what you're taught. You don't have much opportunity to find out more. So suddenly there I was with this idea that I'd never thought of before – being an astronaut. And I satisfied the criteria that they were asking for from the original applicants – age range 21-40, physically fit, possession of some sort of technical degree and the ability already to speak one or more foreign language. I thought, 'Yes, I could do that, but they'll never want me.' But then I thought, 'Why not? This would be a great opportunity.'

So was there a moment when you doubted whether you should apply? After your initial enthusiasm, did you sit back and think, 'Well, no, I'd never get that'?

The first thing that I did was call a telephone number that they gave out. There were a few questions on the phone, and then they sent a very complicated lengthy questionnaire, a job application form, really. And on the back were two completely blank pages for the reasons why you should be chosen to be Britain's astronaut. I thought, 'This is going to take me hours to fill in.' I was very busy trying to hold down a job and do some research in the evenings, so it lay around in my briefcase for days, if not weeks. Then one evening I was in Birkbeck College working on my degree and I had to wait while a piece of equipment cooled before I could use it. I went into the lab, turned on the cooler, went back to my desk to look out the papers from the previous day to decide what I was going to do that evening. And as I pulled everything out of my case, out came the application form, and the closing date was only about two days away. So that was the decision point. If I didn't do it then, I was going to miss the deadline. I actually thought, 'It's going to take me all evening to fill in this application form if I'm going to do it properly, and I could very usefully do some good research instead.' I was really getting into it, and I felt confident of getting some good results that night. I thought, 'The chances of me getting chosen are so remote, why bother? Why waste an evening? I'll carry on with my experiments.' I don't know what made me do it, but anyway I got up from the table, turned off the cooler, sat down, filled in the application form and posted it that evening from the post-box right outside the college, never really expecting to hear anything. And the strangest thing was that I just carried on life as normal, didn't really tell anybody else about it.

You didn't tell anyone you'd applied?

Only my mother. She was still living in Sheffield, and at the end of every week I'd give her a ring. She'd want to know what I'd done each day so when she got to Friday, I said, 'Oh, I applied to be an astronaut.' And she laughed, as one would. And I thought, 'Well, yes, I suppose it is a bit funny, isn't it?' So I didn't tell anybody else after that. Then not long afterwards, one morning after I had just got home from Mars after a shift of all-night work – which happened from time to time – and fallen asleep, the phone rang. It was somebody asking me to take part in the astronaut selection – would I be available on a particular date? I opened my diary, checked, said, 'Yes, that's fine,' wrote it in, put the phone down and went straight back to bed. I got up that evening thinking, 'That was a really weird dream.' But of course there it was in the diary, so when I went into work that night, I said to my colleague, 'I've just been asked to go along to this astronaut selection. Have you heard about it?' And he laughed. So again, I didn't tell anybody else for a while. I was worried that people might feel that I'd fallen for something stupid, that I was gullible. This can't possibly be real, why is she even thinking about wasting her time doing it? Even though I met all the necessary criteria, there were 13,000 others who had also applied, so why should it be me? So I thought, 'I'll go along to the selection. I'm bound to learn something, it'll be interesting.'

You thought that you could learn something from the selection process, even if you didn't get the job?

Very much so. I could learn more about the kind of qualities that were thought necessary to be an astronaut and I could find out something about the other people who'd applied. I don't think I ever expected to be chosen. And I find this very strange because I've heard a lot of people talk about achieving something, and they always say that you have to believe that not only can you do it, but that you will do it. You have to go in with this absolute confidence, yet I never had that absolute confidence. I knew I could do what was required, but I didn't believe that they would actually choose me, because so many other people were just as capable. I would have felt very arrogant if I'd believed that I was bound to be better than all those other thousands of people.

What happened after this first stage? There were 13,000 people around you, you were into the first leg of the selection process, how did it proceed from there?

There were medicals and psychologicals and then we all went home, and I thought, 'Well, that was interesting. I felt a bit tired on the treadmill, so maybe they won't choose me.' Then I received a letter a couple of weeks later to say would I come to the next round of medicals and psychologicals? And it really went on from there. We went to the Institute of Aviation Medicine in Farnborough where we were spun round in centrifuges and that at least felt as though we were doing something more relevant to space flight. It was at that stage that I read in the newspapers – this tells you how you much should believe what's in the newspapers – that the Soviets, as they were then, had asked that the two people selected should be of the same sex. They didn't mind whether they were male or female, but they had to be the same sex. At that stage there were 16 of us left and there were only two females, so I thought the chances of us both being selected were pretty slim. Again I decided I would just enjoy what I was doing, and learn from it. As it turned out that criterion wasn't deemed vital and a man – Timothy Mace, from the Army Air Corps – and I were chosen to go to Russia.

And then when you got to Russia there was more testing. How did that shake down?

In Russia we began serious training. They continued not so much to test as to prepare. They felt, for instance, that we could prepare ourselves for the sickness of space flight by experiencing some sort of motion sickness on Earth. So they would put us in spinning chairs. But we also had a lot more learning to do and both of us had to do all of the training. One of us would eventually fly, one would be back-up, but for most of the training we didn't know which one would be which.

Did you ever feel like giving up through all this?

Many times I felt like giving up, and I know Tim did as well. It was very hard. It was a commercial mission. The British Government did not have – and still does not want to have – anything to do with manned space flight, as such. The British management team was still seeking sponsors in Britain and there was no office or anything in Star City, a small village, north-east of Moscow. We were pretty much left on our own after we had been shown where we were going to live. The interpreter left and we were given a Russian teacher, from the university in Moscow, who didn't speak any English. Nobody in Star City spoke any English, and we felt rather isolated. The British Embassy was very helpful later on, but it was a long way away and we had no proper official links to it. Apart from the actual Russian language, communications were difficult. I had a telephone in my Star City flat, but I had to book a telephone call to the London office two or three hours in advance through a Russian operator, so when, in the beginning, I spoke none of the language this was not terribly easy. We felt very lonely.

How long were you there for?

Altogether for 18 months. After the first three or four it became a little easier because we could at least communicate with the other Russians and made friends with some of them. But even so, the communication links with the management team in Britain were very, very tenuous. And after three months the mission itself was in jeopardy because they hadn't raised the sponsorship that they needed. So for the next ten months Tim and I had to continue the training, because there was no time not to, knowing that at any time we could be called back to Britain and be looking for a job. If there was no money, there was no mission.

Which would have represented failure?

It would have represented failure for the mission, but not for me specifically, because I had been successful in my part of the training up till then. But finding that the project was in jeopardy made me realize how much I wanted to be there. Until then I wanted to go into space for three reasons – to experience a launch, to grow crystals in space, and to feel weightless. Now those reasons hadn't changed, and when the mission was in trouble, the Russian language was a barrier, communications with London were a problem and we really felt cut off, that end goal seemed a long way away. But as soon as the mission was threatened by financial issues, I realized how much I wanted it to happen. Suddenly, I very much wanted to stay in Russia. Rather than anticipating the worst, I became more focused on the things I was learning.

How did you recover from those moments when you felt like giving up? Was there something inside yourself, a kind of mechanism, that swung into action to counter these negative vibes?

I think it was, I suppose, really three things – first, the fact that Tim was there was very helpful – we supported each other very much in those first few months. Second, we broke down the 18 months training into sections, so that instead of solely looking forward to the final goal – a launch, and the things that we might be able to do in space – we took the attitude that if we passed the next exam, although we didn't much like doing exams, that at least was something we'd achieved. Then we could look forward to the next part of the training, and that was something else to aim for.

Does this mean that in order to counter the inevitable disappointments along any career, it's far better to have a series of short-term goals rather than one grand long-term goal at the end of the journey?

Yes. You need a general aim or purpose in life, you need to know what it is that you're hoping to achieve, but within that, to make it manageable, you can break it down, you can go on almost a day-by-day basis if you need to. In Russia Tim and I existed on a phase-by-phase or an exam-by-exam basis. To be honest, I think the third and over-riding element in countering the negative vibes was grim determination. We'd decided that, all in all, we wanted to be there – it wasn't all roses, it wasn't glamorous training to be an astronaut, but we were going to get through it, come hell or high water.

So for 18 months it was either you or Tim going into space, then you were told that you were the person who had been chosen. How were you told and what was your reaction?

It was actually three months before the launch. In February 1991 we were brought back to Britain for a few days. The first evening Tim and I were put up in a hotel in the centre of London, and one of the management team was to come to tell us, in our separate rooms, the joint decision made between the Soviets and the British management team. I think we literally drew straws, to see who was told first. I knew that Tim would love to go into space, and he would do a brilliant job. I knew that I wanted to go, and could do the job too. Overall, I wanted the decision to be me, but I knew that if it was, I would be very upset for Tim. And I was sure he would feel exactly the same.

I was the one to be told first. I almost couldn't believe it. My first thought, as soon as the person left my room, was that he was then going next door to see Tim, and my thoughts were with him. I went through what he would be going through as he was told that he'd been chosen to be backup. He still had a chance of flying, of course, if anything happened to me, but it was then much less likely.

How would you have reacted if it had gone the other way?

Very difficult to say. I was prepared, I think, for both decisions, whichever way it went. I would have been disappointed. I hope I would have acted in the way that Tim did. We were given five minutes and then they asked us to come downstairs for supper with the management team. Tim just patted me on the back and said something like, 'Great one, good for you.' In his disappointment, he was still able to say to me, 'I'm pleased for you.'

A very big thing to do. A lot of people, given the effort that had gone into it all, might not have been able to rise to the occasion in that way.

We knew that it wasn't quite all over, we still had exams to pass, medicals to go through. Even on the day of the launch, I could catch a cold or cut my finger and Tim would be the one to put on his space suit and fly, not me. He still had to continue with the training, so it wasn't a case of 'That's it, you're out, go home, get a job.' It was just that he was now part of the back-up team instead of the prime team. But even so, I'm sure he was disappointed.

I remember thinking that the most difficult thing for Tim would probably be returning to Britain and getting back to life in the Army Air Corps. It's a funny thing but society is such that people naturally expected the older male, who was military and a pilot, to be the first choice and the younger female, who just worked at a sweet factory, to be backup. It was probably more difficult for Tim to rejoin his colleagues and take up his old life again, than it would have been for me, just because of society's general attitude to these things.

Do you think that the stereotyping of different forms of success and of people's place in society is changing, and that people like you have more chance to be successful now than you would have had ten or fifteen years ago?

I think society is changing its attitudes very slowly, but this needn't be a barrier to success as long as you disregard those established views. Personally I have never worried about what society thinks, I've always just done what I wanted to do. When I think back right to choosing my A-level subjects at school at the age of 16, I decided I wasn't going to do languages, which I loved, I was going to study sciences, because they would be more difficult to pick up after school than a language would be. I remember my German teacher coming up to me and saying, 'Hey, don't you know you're going to be the only girl doing sciences?' And I thought, what a strange thing to say. I hadn't even considered it myself. And the only difference it made was that there was an odd number of people doing sciences, and of course being the girl I ended up doing experiments on my own, rather than with a partner. It really didn't matter.

You reached the top, you became an astronaut, you went up in the rocket, you spent eight days in space. Was there any time during those eight days when you didn't feel satisfied, when you felt, 'This is not worth all the effort that I've put into it,' and that there is ultimately a price to pay for success?

There's always a price to pay for success. However, my time in space was worth it. I think the price I paid was not really the frustrations and the hassles that we had in Russia, but that I gave up everything for those 18 months of training. I did very little other than train to be an astronaut. But it was a price I was willing to pay. At different stages in your life you have to assess situations like that. It was well worth it and I hope Tim, now, would look back on his training and say the same. He's probably making more use now of his space training than I am. But regardless of that, the things that you learn and the way that you think – not just technical knowledge, but the things you learn about yourself, and life – made it all worthwhile.

Did you ever think about the danger involved?

I often thought about the danger, not that I really knew exactly what it was in terms of the probability of failure. I knew that there were risks to be taken, that there was the risk of a catastrophic explosion during the launch, that there was a risk of burning up in the atmosphere coming back. But, to me, these were acceptable risks.

And yet they wouldn't have been acceptable to an awful lot of other people?

Well, I wonder. I think we all have our own limits. In my time I've driven a motorbike around London and enjoyed doing so. I did it because it was the best way to get to work and back. I didn't do it for the danger, I didn't do it for the thrill, I did it because it was a means to an end. Certainly I know people who think that that is too dangerous, and they wouldn't do it. Equally, there are some people who wouldn't want to go into space because of the dangers of not coming back. But again, I didn't go into space because of the thrill of doing something dangerous. Certainly I fancied the thrill of the launch – one of the reasons I applied was to experience the G-forces of the launch, but if I could have done that without the danger, then I would have much preferred to do so.

Suddenly you're in orbit and you've achieved the ultimate success, the dream, what's going through your mind at that point?

Perhaps the rest of Britain was looking upon my success as being the first Brit to get into space and I had done that. But for me, success was doing my job well, which meant getting on with my experiments, and that didn't start properly for another couple of days until we got to the space station. We spent two days just orbiting the Earth, occasionally increasing our height above the Earth's surface, doing what we call the housekeeping. We had to dry off our space suits because we had sweated a lot inside them – we had to stop them going mouldy. We had to check that the atmosphere was working correctly, that we weren't getting too much carbon dioxide, for instance, that the navigation systems were working, that we could talk to mission control. My real job didn't start for a couple more days.

So you were up there, you did your work, and then you came down again. Any hint of panic or concern during the descent?

There was no real panic or concern. We had things that went wrong pretty much throughout the space flight. During the launch we had an oxygen valve stick open, and had it remained stuck open, we would have had to blow a hole in the side of the space craft, because too much oxygen is a fire risk, and we'd have had to come back to Earth on the very next orbit – so I'd have got into space but I wouldn't have done any experiments. Fortunately, as soon as we got into the vacuum of space, that seemed to suck out whatever piece of dirt was stopping the valve from sealing properly. The valve closed, oxygen stopped coming in, and we were fine. On board the space station, the first night, we had a power failure. The lights went out and the fans circulating the air, which you need to stop you from suffocating in your own breath, stopped. We weren't expecting a power cut, but we knew how to cope with it, so it wasn't a panic. During the landing itself, nothing happened that shouldn't have happened. When the parachutes opened, they bounced us from side to side quite violently. We were moving through 40 or 50 degrees every half a second – quite a violent shaking – but that was something we were expecting.

When you came down, did you have a clear idea of how you were going to use your success as an astronaut?

When I landed on the Earth's surface, using it wasn't immediately in my mind, there were a lot of debriefings to go through. But finally, a couple of weeks later, when all that was finished, I came back to Britain and talked things over with the management team. I wanted to communicate aspects of the mission to people in Britain who would be able to use it – people in the aeronautical engineering industry, people who needed to know a bit more about the scientific disciplines. It was also intended that I would visit schools to help the children learn a bit more about science by focusing on something that they would all be interested in.

So there was a plan that you would become a kind of ambassador for science?

That was discussed, but it quickly became obvious that I was being pushed into areas where I felt uncomfortable. I shortly started out on my own.

But of course you were in a very unusual position, because being an astronaut is not a career to which you can rise – if I can put it this way – to ever greater heights. I mean you can't go from one mission to the next, to the next, to the next, you're an astronaut and then you're back looking for something to do. Did you ever feel that people were boxing you into a corner and that it was difficult for you then to develop other opportunities, or did the fact that you'd been an astronaut open doors that otherwise wouldn't have been there?

I think both are actually correct. In Britain, you're right, I couldn't be a career astronaut in the way that they can in the United States and Russia. But I knew, when I applied for this job, that, even if I was chosen, it was going to be a one-off chance. I was then in a position to decide what to do next with a clean slate. It's rare that that happens. Usually you're going from one job to another, taking a sort of baggage with you. In other ways it was difficult because people were trying to box me and push me in certain directions. There were agents approaching me to make money for them, for the management company and for me, but I wasn't in it for the money. I went into space for my own personal reasons, and I really believed that there were ways in which I should use that experience. I didn't want just to make money out of being a celebrity. I didn't feel right doing that.

But a lot of people would regard that as success.

Yes, but strangely, I didn't. There was no personal satisfaction in it, I suppose. I mean there was money, but then having money is not success. I had enough money – not a lot, but enough – and although there were ways of making a lot more, I knew I didn't need it and I wasn't prepared to go through some of the hoops that I was being asked to jump through to get it.

So once you'd decided you weren't going down that route, what were the alternatives, because you were there with a big label on you saying, 'Astronaut'?

I could easily just have gone back into industry, using the technical things I'd learned in Russia, and been a technologist, a technical manager or production manger, and I would have enjoyed that. But shortly after I came back, I had a very successful meeting with John Major, and he introduced me to a group of schools' science advisors from different parts of the country. We got together in London and I said, 'Look, I've got a load of ideas. I'm not a teacher, but I'd like somehow to put something back into the schools, can you help me?' And they very quickly organized a three-week tour of British schools for me. This is really what set me off. I knew that there was something there that I wanted to use, something I believed I should be using.

So I set off around the schools. I was more nervous than I'd been at any time in the space flight. I'd done no public speaking before and I was suddenly expected to stand up in front of large groups of people, and I was scared. I wasn't trained to do this, I was trained to be an astronaut, not trained to talk about it. I wasn't very good at it to start with and I didn't enjoy it very much, but I still knew that I should talk to groups of schoolchildren to put something back. The night before my first school visit I was up until two o'clock in the morning thinking what I was going to say to a group of ten-year-olds. I still hadn't really decided, but in the end I just thought I'm going to need some sleep, so I'll go to bed. I'll take along some slides, some pictures to show them, and just try and be as educational – whatever that means – as I can. And I had a great time because, of course, the children immediately indicated – by chattering, by turning round, picking their noses, doing anything that they thought was interesting – how much they understood of what I was telling them. The teachers gave me feedback as well, and by the time I came to do the second one, I was away and really enjoying myself. I was suddenly filled with the belief that I had found a real use for myself in communicating science. And the fact that I've been an astronaut gets me into places where perhaps I couldn't be otherwise.

Is there anything you would say to people who want to be successful in their chosen career, but are faced with that great bugbear of being simply too shy or too nervous about public speaking? How do you get over that barrier so that you feel at ease with the audience and it's not an ordeal every time you get up there?

I think, first of all you have to know what you're talking about, so it's a case of prepare, prepare, prepare. You can never prepare too much. But I really believe that had I not gone along to talk to schoolchildren – and I'm talking youngish children here, between the ages of 9 and 13 – I would not have enjoyed it, and I would never have been any good at it. The children taught me about listening to an audience and thinking about the audience. It wasn't just a case of what do I want to say, but what does the audience want to hear, and you need to be able to satisfy both parties.

Of course small children can be very cruel as well, can't they?

Yes, but in that respect I got immediate feedback. Adults sit quite politely, even if they're a bit bored, and they'll keep their eyes open most of the time. But children will chatter if they're bored or if they don't understand, it's immediately obvious, and that was a great lesson for me.

So to every successful person who's a bit shy, get out there and talk to a bunch of schoolchildren first before you get up on a platform?

I am confident now that you can communicate anything to anybody. If you find the right way, you can put anything across, and I think that was the lesson I learned. You have to think about how the individuals in your audience are going to be hearing you, but over and above that you've got to know your stuff and prepare what you're going to say. You can't just stand up and ad-lib for an hour. It doesn't even work for me now, and I've been doing it for five years.

But of course it all worked so well for you that you're now presenter for the BBC series Seeing Through Science, *you're doing more and more radio work. Do you sometimes look back to your early days and say, 'I never ever thought that I would end up a broadcaster'?*

I could never have imagined being a broadcaster or going into space. But I think life is very much about making use of opportunities, having an aim and living your life by your own principles, not other people's, and focusing on certain things. When I was at Mars, I was focused on my job. My aim in life then was to experience and use as much science as I could, because that's what I enjoyed, relating it to everyday life. Going into space was something that would help me do that. It wasn't moving away from my life's general purpose, although it was away from that particular focus. While you've got to be focused, there's got to be a balance between that and taking other opportunities that might arise. If you're too tunnel-visioned you're not going to see a great opportunity that might actually help you achieve your original aim.

What do you think are the greatest enemies of success?

Lack of tenacity. If you don't stick at trying to achieve what you're doing then you're never going to get there. And also, perhaps, listening to other people too much. You've got to take advice, but it's always a balance. I rely on other people for their stimulation, for ideas, as well as for advice on how I might go about something. At the end of the day you've got to go with what you really believe in, and then at least you will know whether you've been successful or not. It doesn't matter what other people think.

Who are your heroes? Who are the people you regard as being really successful, past or present, people who you admire, and why?

I greatly admire Yuri Gagarin, the first astronaut – cosmonaut, I suppose – the first person ever to do an orbit of the Earth. And I admire him not just because he was the first – although he had to be terrifically brave to do what he did – but to a large extent because of the things he had to cope with after he'd done that. He suddenly became a world celebrity, and I don't believe he necessarily wanted that and yet he was able to cope and fill the role of ambassador for space travel. He buckled down and did what he had to, while still continuing to be a cosmonaut, which was all he really wanted In fact, he was training for a second mission when he was killed.

If you could gather together all the young people who look up to Helen Sharman and say, 'I want to be like her,' what advice would you give them?

You've got to decide what it is you want to do first of all. Don't just be the best for the sake of being the best at something, but decide what it is you really want to do, that will give you personal satisfaction. Work out a way of achieving it and then just make it happen. Don't let people put you off, just keep on going, and if you really want to do it, I believe you can.

Opportunities are going to come up all through your life. Lives change direction much more quickly now than they ever have in the past. And what you want to do now might not be what you want to do in ten years' time. I think you've got to bear that in mind too.

When your time comes to leave this life, what would you like people to say about Helen Sharman?

I suppose in terms of people who only know me through what I've done, I don't really mind what they say, because I don't know them personally. I would like my friends and family, people who really know me, people I love, to be able to say, 'She was a nice person, she had her own beliefs, but she never used us to get what she wanted.' What the world says of me, by then, I really won't mind.

You wouldn't want the world at large to have this nice view of Helen Sharman? She was an achiever, she really did something, she saw it through, she got up there to be the first Briton in space. I mean that's surely how you'll be remembered.

It's nice to think that, and I wouldn't like to think that people were remembering me for anything bad, or because they thought I was a rotten person. Of course I'd like the rest of the world to say nice things about me, but it's the people who are nearest to me whose feelings about me are most important.

SIR GEORG SOLTI

The electrifying energy which this great conductor infused into orchestras and concert halls across the world flowed from his passionate belief that 'art is an eternal fight for something better'. He believed it was no good for a musician simply to reach a high standard and try to hold themselves there, because 'you either improve or fall down'. So, as his tastes changed, and he strove to keep up with every new development, he found that he became 'a different musician' every ten years or so. Britain received the full force of his legendary refusal to compromise after he was wooed from Germany to the Royal Opera House Covent Garden in 1959. He acknowledged that he was initially 'too revolutionary for some' as his determination that he – and nobody else – should decide the artistic policy rubbed some people up the wrong way. After 12 triumphant years in London, he concentrated on working with the Chicago Symphony Orchestra, producing a series of highly successful recordings.

In this, a rare interview just a few months before his death, Georg Solti talked about his early formative years; a 'caring and good' father who was a very unsuccessful businessman because 'he believed people would tell him the truth'; excellent piano tutoring at what was then one of the three best music schools in the world; the moment in his early teens when he suddenly realised he wanted to be a conductor; his two big breaks – the first as a pianist because two colleagues went down with 'flu, and the second as a conductor, which he obtained by pretending he was familiar with the orchestral score for Fidelio when he was not. He recalled going to Switzerland, just days before the Second World War, with 'no money, no friends, nothing'; how, after winning a music competition, he earned just enough to get by with concerts and 'illegal teaching'. More than half a century on, he tried not to allow the increasing physical handicaps of reaching his mid-80s to frustrate his drive and energy, even having his scores specially enlarged to combat difficulties with his eyesight. His only major disappointment in life was the many weeks spent away from his children while they were growing up. And his only resentment was being labelled by some early critics as an angry young man who could only do Wagner – 'It's a myth which has never been right, but the English love to put you down for something.'

Sir Georg, what is your definition of success?

I really don't know, because you can have success as a family and then you can have success within a group of colleagues, success as a musician. There are different sorts of success. I have success as a family in that I have two daughters whom I love and cherish. This I value more than any other kind of success in this world. Then I think I have a very good standing with my colleagues who generally accept me as a conductor. So I think I enjoy both these aspects of success.

What are the key qualities that you need for musical success?

I think you need three things – first of all talent, that's the beginning, you are born with it. Then, if you are industrious you can develop that talent and pursue the idea that you want to be good. You also need a certain amount of luck – not much, because I don't believe that luck in itself will make you successful. *You* make your luck. In my case perhaps just being alive is luck. I am very lucky that I didn't end up at Auschwitz. So, talent, industriousness (plus ambition) and luck – they are the ingredients.

To what extent is success a product of your background and upbringing?

I had an excellent musical education, probably the best that you could have between 1920 and 1930. I went to the Franz Liszt Academy in Budapest which was, at that point, the best music school in the world. This has changed now. Many of those from the Hungarian, Austrian, and German music schools went to America, so now America has the best music schools, not only the Juilliard, but others as well that are excellent, and that's why America has produced so many first-class musicians. But in my youth, in the 1920s, the music centres were Berlin, Vienna and Budapest.

What about your personal family background, your father, your mother? To what extent did they shape or condition your success?

My father came from a little Jewish family and he had nothing to do with music. He was a very unsuccessful businessman. He was too naïve and good-hearted and believed that people would tell him the truth but nobody ever did. In 1914, the State – the Austro-Hungarian Empire as it grandly called itself – invented something called the War Loan – there was later something similar in England. As a good patriot my father put all the money he had saved until 1914 into the War Loan because it had an interest rate higher than that of a bank. But when this five-year loan was completed in 1919, Hungary had been subject to the worst inflation and the money which he got back wouldn't even buy a tram ticket.

So you learned from your father's financial mistakes?

Yes. I always felt very sorry because he was such an unlucky man, and such a caring and good man. But I did learn never to sign state loans and I also learned to save money – work for it and don't spend it.

You trained as a pianist and then you decided that you wanted to move into conducting. Was it difficult for you to get the break into conducting? How did you persuade the Hungarian opera establishment to give you a chance to conduct?

I was very young when I decided I wanted to be a conductor, I was 13 or 14 years old, as young as that. I was at a concert conducted by Erich Kleiber and as I sat listening, lightning struck and from that moment I knew I wanted to be a conductor. I went home to my mother and said, 'Mama, I don't want to play a piano, I want to be a conductor,' and my very clever Jewish mother said, 'That's all right, my boy, go and practise now and we shall see what happens.' But I never gave up and when I was 18 I became a *repetiteur* or singing coach in the Budapest Opera. First of all I was unpaid, then a year later I got a proper salary. But the money didn't matter; what mattered was I learned my profession.

And then what was your big break that took you into conducting? What was your first big concert? Was it the Marriage of Figaro *back in 1938?*

I had only a single performance of *Figaro* on the fateful night of the *Anschluss* in 1938, in Budapest. The big break came in Salzburg. I arrived there in 1937, with a letter of recommendation from a friend who was president of the Friends of the Budapest Opera, asking the director of the Salzburg Festival to let me into the rehearsals – just to watch, nothing else. But there was a 'flu epidemic in Salzburg and when I presented my letter the fellow read it and said, 'Do you know *The Magic Flute*?' I said, 'Yes'. 'Could you come this afternoon and play the piano?' So at two o'clock I arrived at the rehearsal and started to play the piano.

And this was the lucky break, because people were ill with this 'flu epidemic?

Yes. Two of the pianists were ill, so they urgently needed a replacement. If somebody had told me Toscanini would come to this rehearsal, I'd have probably said, 'No, I don't dare!' But I didn't know this until I saw a little man walking on to the stage. I was down in the pit but I knew who he was, because I had seen him many times. I went on playing, what else could I do? He just looked down while conducting with one finger. Now I can follow anybody; I can follow *you* if you conduct. That's always a sign of a good musician, being able to follow somebody else. After the intermission he began to conduct normally, that little finger became five fingers or two hands. And then there was a break and he turned around, and for the first time he said, '*Bene.*' That was wonderful. I was in seventh heaven.

I also played *Fidelio*, I played *Falstaff*. During the rehearsals I played everything in the repertoire, interchanging with the other pianists. So I saw him every day.

But having had that praise from the Master, why not concentrate on piano? Why move into conducting?

I always wanted to conduct. Being a *repetiteur* was the first step towards becoming an opera conductor. I always wanted to conduct, not play the piano. Much later I came back to the piano. I have recently played a little again, but that's just for my enjoyment.

I went back to Budapest once the Festival finished and I got an engagement to return in 1938 – I was very proud. But I never went back because by then the Nazis had moved into Austria and occupied Vienna.

Did you feel, at that point, that all your hopes and all your dreams were dying? How did you keep your energy going? What made you keep hope alive?

I was in Switzerland when war broke out, I was stuck there. I had no money, nothing. But I began to practise the piano and I heard that there was an International Music Competition in Geneva every year. So in 1942, I went and won the first prize in piano. That helped me earn a little money, very modest sums, but it didn't matter, it kept me alive. I did some small concerts and a bit of teaching. As a refugee I wasn't really allowed to earn money, but towards the end of the war, 1944, I got permission – I should frame it – for five pupils. Of course nobody cared, whether it was five or seven or ten, so I had about ten and I earned enough to live on. Never for a second did I give up hope that one day – if I was still alive, which I wasn't so sure about! – I'd be a conductor. And so it happened.

What was the first major opportunity you had to be a conductor?

When I was in Zürich I heard through the grapevine about an ex-colleague, Edward Kilenyi. He and I had studied together in Dohnanyi's class and he had became the so-called Music Officer of Bavaria. I got a letter to him through a Swiss man who was going to Bavaria, and he came back with an answer, 'We need you, come!' This was only a few months after the end of the war and I was instructed to go to a particular border station between Switzerland and southern Germany near Lake Constance. A jeep would collect me. So I arrived at eight o'clock and waited for the jeep, but the jeep didn't come. I found out the last train going back to Zürich was at 9.30, so I decided to wait until then. At nine o'clock a jeep arrived, three young American soldiers got out, asked my name, and the Swiss let me through. They put me in an open jeep and I was driven through the night to Munich. I arrived the next morning at the Bavarian Opera House and was introduced by Kilenyi who said that I had been brought to help them. 'But we don't need him,' they said.

So you thought that your journey was for nothing?

Yes, but Kilenyi didn't give up, he said, 'I'll send you on to Stuttgart, there's a friend of mine, the Württemberg Officer of Music.' So I arrived in Stuttgart a day later. The journey wasn't as comfortable as the American jeep, I was on a German train without glass in the windows. It was a terrible journey during a cold winter – you cannot imagine!

But you were determined?

Absolutely. I arrived in Stuttgart and was introduced to the director and he said, 'Do you know *Fidelio?*' 'Ah, yes, I do,' I said – but I didn't. I knew the piano score but I had never seen the orchestra score.

You told a little white lie?

Yes, of course. And he said, 'Could you do it next week, we have a performance then?' 'Yes,' I said. So, I conducted *Fidelio* for the first time in my life, it was very exciting.

Were you nervous about that?

Very nervous. But never mind, a talented boy gets over the nervousness. So they offered me a contract, and they said I should go to see the Minister of Culture, Theodor Heuss. I was introduced to him and it all seemed very nice, but I said, 'Can I take the contract and look at it?' and went back to Zürich. When I arrived back there, the Bavarian Opera had heard about my success even though there were no newspapers and promptly sent me an invitation. Would I come and conduct *Fidelio* in Munich? I did and they engaged me immediately. So I had to apologise to Stuttgart and say, 'Sorry, I am not coming.'

There was a surprising end to this story 25 years later. I conducted a concert in Bonn at a state reception for President Sukarno of Indonesia. After the concert I was presented to Theodor Heuss who had become President of West Germany. He said to me, 'So you never regretted staying in Munich?' I said, 'Mr President, you still remember that?' 'Oh yes,' he said, 'I was very angry with you for not coming to Stuttgart.'

After many successful years in Germany, you were then presented with the option of either going to Covent Garden or to Los Angeles.

Yes. I wanted to do both. I conducted *Der Rosenkavalier* in London as a guest conductor in December 1959. Afterwards, Lord Drogheda, the chairman of the board who later became a great friend, said, 'We want to offer you the musical director job. You cannot say no, but we can't pay.'

Very British.

I said, 'I'm very sorry but I don't want it. I have had 15 years in opera (six in Munich, nine in Frankfurt) and I want to have a symphony orchestra now.' I also knew that I had a contract waiting for me in Los Angeles. He replied, 'Think it over, we can wait, we haven't got anybody else anyway.' So I went to Los Angeles, a place I had visited often over the years, and discussed it with my good friend Bruno Walter who lived there. 'I've got an offer from Covent Garden, but I don't want to do it,' I said. 'You *must*,' he replied, 'It is your duty, because if you don't do it, there will be a generation gap. You and Karajan are the only two left, you must do it.' So I did.

Do you think that every successful person needs a mentor?

Not a mentor really, what you need are friends. You need a friend to advise you and I have been very lucky. At Covent Garden I had Lord Drogheda who was a friend from the outset. I had a difficult relationship at first with David Webster, but later we became good friends and indeed he died a very close friend.

Could you have been as successful as you have been without that tremendous encouragement from Lord Drogheda?

I don't know. Maybe, because my ambition was enormous and I wanted to make it the best opera house in the world. That was my famous 'modest' statement at the first press conference: 'I want to make Covent Garden the world's best opera house.' And I did. When I left, *The Times* said, 'How right he was.'

Your first few years at Covent Garden were marked by what critics described as bullish performances, you had a certain temper they said. And one night an angry member of the audience hurled a cabbage on stage with the slogan, 'Solti must go.' How did you react to all that?

Actually it was just a very small clique who decided I was too German, because I believed, and still do, that an opera house is not a democratic institution. At an opera house somebody must decide what happens. One person has to decide the artistic policy, and nobody else. Of course, some people called me arrogant.

Do you think you were arrogant?

I was never arrogant. I have always been modest. A little example will help clarify the whole situation. I had a very good technical director, who has retired now. I had always been interested in all the elements of opera, what Wagner called the *Gesamtkunstwerk* – total work, not only music, but all the drama, acting, lighting and technical aspects. But this interest from a conductor was new for Covent Garden and this man hated me. He called me 'the Hungarian bastard'! But things changed and by the time I left ten years later, he called me George and I called him Bill. He said to me, 'I hated you, but now I am grateful, because you taught me that in opera everything matters.'

So for some of the critics I was, initially, too revolutionary. I was very hurt because I knew they were wrong, but I just went on working, working, trying to live with it. And I learned something. Never read any newspaper reviews.

You've stopped reading reviews?

Oh yes. Otherwise you commit suicide. Only read the good ones. I've a censor at home – my wife. If she says, 'Don't read it,' I don't read it. Or she might say, 'It's good, you can read it.'

Are the critics useful in the process of becoming successful, or are they superfluous?

They never killed anybody. And they can't actually *make* somebody. They have tried so often to build somebody up, to make a musical hero, but it never lasts. If the talent's not there, you'll never make it.

So talent will see you through?

Providing you are strong enough to live with the negative criticism. Sometimes it is very hard. I believe you must be strong and believe not only in yourself, but also in the direction in which an opera or a symphony orchestra is going.

Which is more important? The composer or the audience?

There is no question. The composer, of course. I never serve audiences, I try to serve a composer.

But you also test how far you can go with that composer's work – you do go to extremes at times?

I am testing myself, not the composer. One's taste changes. Every ten years I'm a different musician. That happens as long as you continue to work, and I'm still working all the time. You arrive at a new conception of an opera or symphony. Every year I lay aside many pieces, often for as long as ten years. Then I get a piece out again with a clean score. You can see one lying here – there's nothing written on it. Then I write my new conception on it. That's the only way to improve. Your talent continues to develop – it's natural, everybody's talent develops. In my case, this is very difficult because my taste is developing faster than my talent. My taste is developing enormously quickly, because I am interested in many things in this world – visual arts, theatre, books, television and much more.

Do people in the musical profession reach a level of success and then feel they have arrived? So that they are interested purely in maintaining themselves at that level, and not striving to do new things?

This is so. And the trouble is you cannot maintain a standard. You either improve or you fall back. You must keep striving for improvement. That applies to every musician, every artist, whatever he does – painting, sculpture, writing. Art is an eternal fight for something better. Composers are doing that all the time.

Do you think total control is important as far as every musician is concerned? Or is it just for the conductor? Are there musicians in the orchestra who can achieve a degree of total control while still working to a conductor?

Oh, yes – within their type of instrument. There are such wonderful instruments now – musical miracles. I can give you a small example. For the 50th Jubilee of the United Nations in 1995, I conducted a concert in Switzerland and invited probably the best musicians in the world. They all came because we called it 'Musicians for Peace', fighting for music not for wars. It was such a fantastic joy and every instrumentalist, or soloist, gave a performance which said, 'There you are, listen to that!'

Do you think music is a political force?

No, unfortunately not. During this century we have been through two World Wars, the Russian Revolution, millions and millions of people died for political and religious reasons. Some of them loved music, some of them did not. Hitler loved music, but it didn't prevent him from killing millions of people.

But some people believe, as I do, that good music lifts the spirit enormously. Music is a joy if you have the talent to listen. But you need to develop this talent, because you cannot listen to good music without spending a little time on it. Listen twice, three times a day to a symphony, alone at home, and suddenly you'll discover things which you never heard before.

How do you judge whether you have made a successful performance or not – do you judge it by the reaction of the audience?

No, no. I know it. I can feel when it is happening right, when things are coming through which I wanted. What is described as a successful performance is very nice for your own vanity, but, in my case, if I know it's not good, I'm not happy.

And in the course of producing that success, and achieving the total control that you talked about, is it necessary sometimes, as some people have said, to instil a certain amount of fear into the orchestra? Does it give the musicians an edge?

No, that is a myth. What gives them an edge is the joy of working with something good, achieving something. You can't scream at them, they'd walk out on you. They would go to union headquarters and say, 'We can't play with that monster.'

But they have occasionally said, 'He's too tough, he's too severe with us, he's too sharp.' Do you sometimes wonder whether your approach is the right one?

I have never had any difficulties with any orchestra, ever.

And you never had any doubts about your style?

No, not my style which, as I mentioned, is always developing. I suppose I did have some difficulty with two orchestras – I don't want to mention them by name but one was French and one English. They didn't understand at all what I wanted and became unpleasant and didn't listen to me at rehearsals.

How did you react to that?

Simple. I never went back.

Are there any core principles for achieving success, that go right through musicianship, or whatever your particular forte is in the world of music?

Talent is something essential, but it is not easy to define. I have a great sense of rhythmical talent, I have a talent for the dynamics of playing. I am interested in the extreme dynamics of *fortissimo* and *pianissimo*, not only middle dynamic *mezzo forte* playing. I'm not a *mezzo forte* musician. You also need something else, a talent for form, architectural talent.

Who are your heroes? Who are the people you regard as being the most successful people, either past or present whom you have met?

First of all, from the 18th and 19th centuries, my real heroes are probably Haydn, Mozart, Beethoven and Verdi. But there are others. My teacher, Bartok, was and is my hero because he was such a fantastic composer. He created something totally new, the *Volksmusik*, and put it into professional terms. He was a living legend. And he was extremely pure in political terms. He didn't allow his work to be performed in Germany after 1933, although he was very poor and he needed the royalties. He was not Jewish, yet he believed that it was an evil country and didn't want his music to be played there.

Is there anybody in the present whom you admire? Someone who is new, promising, up and coming?

Yes, there are many young talents. There are a few young talented conductors whom I think are excellent – about five of them. At any one time there always seems to have been about five first-class conductors, and we have five today.

That's about the number of people who bubble up to the top – about five or six?

About five to ten. There are the instrumentalists, too. We have a few wonderful piano players, friends of mine. Just recently a young Russian called Vengerov has emerged, a marvellous talent. And there are talented singers. I have just given a performance of *Don Giovanni*, a concert version, with young singers. It was a wonderful cast.

Are there enemies of success? What are they? What are the forces trying to pull you down?

The major enemies are becoming a megalomaniac, not wanting to work, thinking, 'I'm wonderful, I don't need to work.' These enemies are in yourself. I have never fallen prey to that fallacy – not yet.

Is there any one performance that you feel was, for you, the peak of success? As good as you could get it?

It's difficult to answer that. The Geneva concert, the World Orchestra for Peace, perhaps. I was so happy with the harmony within the musicians. I was afraid that having 85 stars together would cause problems – 'I want to sit *here*', 'I don't want to be *there*.' But there was none of that. Everybody enjoyed it. And it was a joy to hear such a sound. If you want to single out one performance, it's probably that one.

Has success changed you at all?

I don't think so. I am much more mellow nowadays than I was as a younger man. I am as enthusiastic about music as I have always been.

Do you think being angry as a young musician, is a formula for future success?

No, absolutely not. I was never angry, I just started to fight for music. Anger is if you say things like, 'I hate you.' I never said that, I said, 'It's not good enough.' That's not anger. But the English love to give you a particular label. I was an angry man who could only do Wagner. That's how I was seen in the beginning. I proved a thousand times that I can do Verdi, Mozart, Puccini, Strauss, whatever, but still, for some, I was the angry young man with his Wagner. It was never true.

So you have mellowed. Have you any frustrated ambitions, anything you would like to do, that you haven't been able to achieve?

Yes, I would love to have better eyesight and better hearing, because they're diminishing, that's a frustration.

In your mid-eighties do you still see future successes ahead? And what drives you on when most men might have thought of retiring?

Because I know one thing. I make much better music than ever before. Much better. And I want to produce that, though it's difficult with all the physical handicaps. For example, I have to enlarge my scores because I have trouble reading, my knee is hurting me, my back is hurting me – but I still love good music.

And if you could gather together all the young musicians who want to reach the top of their chosen profession, what advice would you give them?

Never give up, that's all.

What is the greatest pleasure that you have enjoyed from your success?

I don't know. It is a great joy to have my children around me and see them from time to time, and I know I can give them a reasonably secure existence. They are very musical, both of them. But they have trouble with a father who is a public figure. They don't like that. They want a father, not someone on a podium. It's a difficult life for them.

And have you ever been able to resolve that conflict between the pull of your professional work and the pull of the family?

No, unfortunately not. This is probably the only major disappointment in my life – that I had to travel so much between Chicago and London. When they were very little they came with me, but when they went to school, they couldn't. Then I tried to arrange my concerts for the school holidays, but I couldn't always do that. So I had many weeks away from them, which I could never make up.

I don't know whether I would do that again, knowing that two children were waiting for me at home, while their mother travelled with me. It was a choice, which maybe I wouldn't make today.

One final question. When your time comes to leave this earth, what would you like people to say about you?

I won't write my own obituary, somebody else can do that. Perhaps, 'He was a caring man, he tried to help his colleagues as much as he could.' I can't help the whole world because I have not got enough money for that. But I try to help young musicians all the time, sometimes financially.

And you think there is a firm obligation on anyone who is successful in any field to help and nurture young people?

Yes, I firmly believe that. Otherwise you are a monster, not a good human being.

REBECCA STEPHENS

*She admits now that she could – and should –
have made more of her earlier life. She chose not
to pursue any further studies after leaving
school, and spent ten years in interesting, but
limiting, journalistic work. But she is living
proof that the quantum leap forward which
many seek can come at any time. All that is
required, she believes, is the igniting of the spark
of desire, backed up by tenacity, a certain
resilience, a degree of talent and a willingness to
take risks. For Rebecca Stephens, that spark came
when she visited Mount Everest to report on an
expedition climbing the North-East ridge. There
and then she vowed to climb the highest
mountain in the world – and become the first
British woman to do so. Here, she talks about*

*how, from a standing start, it took four years for her to do it. She grew up in a
comfortable middle-class home, one of three sisters encouraged by their parents from
an early age to believe that everything was possible. The closest she'd come to
mountaineering as a child was a desire to climb to the top of hills.*

*Once her big ambition was locked in place she spent every spare holiday tackling
peaks like Mont Blanc. Even so, lack of experience led to her being turned down by
one Everest-bound expedition; and when she did find another with nine climbers
prepared to take a relative novice, the necessary sponsorship deal was only fixed up
three weeks before they were due to leave. It was a touch nerve-wracking, as she'd
had to give a full three months' notice for quitting her job as deputy editor of the
Resident Abroad magazine. But she is adamant that 'the closer you get to your
goal, the more risks you are prepared to take'. Another was frostbite in her little
finger at 20,000 feet. Would she have been prepared to lose it? 'The answer very
clearly was yes!' Then there was the gamble with the forecast storms when she was
only 12 hours from the summit. On returning to Britain she walked into a tidal
wave of media which unlocked a door – people, she says, are now prepared to listen
to her more. She has gone on to climb the highest peak in each of the world's seven
continents, so it is hardly surprising that she is much in demand as a lecturer on
motivation and teamwork. Now working on an ambitious project to encourage
young people to go out and explore for themselves, she stresses the need to review
goals continually: 'It's the moving forward that gives contentment and pleasure.'*

Rebecca Stephens, what is your definition of success?

My definition of success might actually be broader than one that you might hear on the street. I grew up thinking success was something that was achieved in professional terms or in financial terms, but now I don't see it like that at all. In fact I think those two areas, professionalism and finance, are very small factors – clearly they're important in that we have to live and feed ourselves, but what I'm really striving to achieve is a balance between my work and my social life and adventure, creativity and time to just potter around the house. That's the most difficult thing. Of course, everybody's definition of success will be different depending on what they want to do. Clearly there are some people who, more than anything else, want to make a lot of money, or to be a concert pianist, or win a Booker Prize or whatever it might be. It seems to me that money is often the thing by which our society measures success, but to me, if somebody makes a lot of money, but doesn't enjoy what they are doing, looks back at their life and thinks they've wasted it, that isn't success.

To what extent do you think that your success has been down to your background and your upbringing?

My background and upbringing had a lot to do with it. I will always thank my parents for saying, quite simply, 'If you want to do something, do it.' I remember very clearly as a student when there was an opportunity for me to go to Kenya to work on a farm for the summer, I told Mum, not really thinking that it was something that I could possibly do. But she said, 'You've got to go,' and I said, 'How can I?' She said, 'You get a job, you do this, and that, and you go,' and from that point I never looked back.

Did you always want to climb Everest? Was it an ambition from a very early age?

Not at all, not in the slightest. It wasn't something that occurred to me until I went to Everest as a journalist to report on another expedition in 1989 at the age of 27. Before that I had never climbed in my life. I'd skied a bit, just a week a year, and when I was small I gather that I liked getting to the top of hills – not that I ever took up climbing, but if we were on holiday in Dartmoor or Yorkshire, I'd look at the top of a hill and just go for it in a straight line, so I'm told, so perhaps a seed was sown.

But given that lack of experience, a lot of people might have said that your sudden ambition to climb Everest was a hugely unrealistic one.

Oh yes, a lot of people did say that.

And did they try to put you off?

I didn't really know about these people until afterwards, so the answer is no. Some people who knew me really well were pretty sure that I could do it, because, I suppose, they could see it was something that I wanted to do so badly. Although I do remember my editor saying to me, 'Oh, God, Rebecca, I hope next month you pass this mountaineering phase and want to bake bread or something,' but realistically it was three and a half years between the first time I went to Everest and the time I went back to climb it, which isn't very long. On that first trip to Everest, I was trying to work out *why* people wanted to climb this mountain. I certainly didn't at that time. I was very happy to spend time at high altitude wandering around from camp to camp just enjoying the scenery, enjoying the exercise and finding out a bit about the history of the place, which is extremely interesting and part of the reason I went back. But I thought people were mad to give up so much just to climb a mountain, the women in particular. I know this might sound a bit sexist, but there were four Frenchwomen there and I really thought that they might have more sense than to risk so much to climb a lump of rock. But through searching to find more to write about, I tried, in my own limited way, to climb up to a camp on the north-east ridge, which was at about 23,000 feet, and it was so immensely satisfying and so ... it's difficult to describe – it was reasonably easy at first when the weather was good, then the weather closed in and it was cold and as we climbed higher the air got thinner and it was just exhausting. But when I got there and could sit and appreciate the view and sense what I'd achieved, I felt more exhilarated than I'd ever felt in my life. So perhaps that was a turning point, perhaps that's when I looked up towards the summit and thought I'd like to come back. It was that which turned me to climbing.

Given that you didn't have any previous experience, was it easy to put together the necessary package of training?

What I learned watching other people climb was what it took for these people to get to the top. In actual fact, nobody got to the top from the north side that year, where I was, because the weather was lousy. Luck with the weather has a lot to do with it.

But you were also aware that you needed a great deal more training than you had in mountaineering in order to make that assault – how did you set about getting the necessary experience to enable yourself to have a go at Everest?

When I came back from that first trip I started climbing in my holidays. All my holidays between that first trip and the second trip to Everest were on mountains. I climbed Ben Nevis and Mont Blanc, met people doing that – and that's half the battle in any of these things, falling in with the right crowd – and I then went off to Mount Kenya and Kilimanjaro. I was building up a bit of confidence by now. Then I started trying to find a way to go to Everest. This would be expensive, obviously, but I thought that being a journalist I might be able to climb and write about it and get on a trip that way. I failed to do so, incidentally – I did apply to one group of people, a commercial expedition, but that didn't happen.

They turned you down?

Yes, because I didn't have enough experience, which was perfectly justified.

How did you react when they turned you down? Was it off-putting, did it make you think twice about what you were about?

Well, by that time I had already fallen in with another crowd who gave me the opportunity to go. I was with a team of ten climbers on the so-called British 40th Anniversary Everest Expedition. There were two leaders, one a guy called Peter Earl who, rather like me, saw the mountain and decided he wanted to climb it, despite the fact he had never climbed. And the other a guy called John Barry who had had a lot of climbing experience and who in turn gathered a team around him which comprised some extremely experienced mountaineers and some not so experienced, like me.

Did you at any time during those three and a half years have any doubt about the project on which you were embarked?

The simplest way to answer that is no. I wanted to go very badly. It seems that once you've stepped on a path – in my case, towards the mountain – then the further you walk along that path, the harder it is to step off.

Not even a twinge of doubt?

What I was going to say following that was that there were all sorts of doubts about whether we would be able to go, because we didn't have the money. Right up until the last minute we didn't have sponsorship. DHL, the sponsors, actually came on board only three weeks before we went. I was in a situation where I had to give up my job, and I thought, 'Here I am writing my resignation – I had to give three-months' notice – and there's a chance we might not even be going.' I was working as a journalist on a magazine called *Resident Abroad* which is an *FT* magazine for expatriates. It was a worrying time, though we had an underlying faith that something would turn up.

So if you take risks you have to be prepared to make sacrifices. Were you prepared to make every conceivable sacrifice necessary to achieve your goal?

How far do sacrifices go? That was one sacrifice, I suppose. It doesn't seem much in hindsight, but it felt it at the time. I'll tell you one thing that is interesting. When I was on the mountain, through carelessness really, I got a little bit of frostbite in my little finger – it was quite low on the mountain, just 20,000 feet. We came back down to 17,000 feet to the base camp that same day. It was beautifully sunny so we were lying out on the rocks soaking up the sunshine, and I looked at my hand and the little finger was a very unpleasant colour. When I woke up the next morning it had swollen and was badly blistered and I was frightened – this was my first experience of this sort of thing and I didn't know whether it was going to get worse or better and I thought, 'I've got frostbite at 20,000 feet – what's going to happen at 29,000 feet?' And through my mind ran the thought, 'Would I be prepared to lose this finger just to climb to the top, or two fingers?' And the answer, very clearly, was yes.

Really?

Yes. That surprises me now, but it's true. I wrote it in my diary and it's all there for me to read if ever I doubt how stupid I was. I would never think that sitting here in London, but, I suppose, the closer you get to your goal the more risks you're prepared to take.

You were prepared to lose a finger, two fingers. Would you have been prepared to lose your hand? In other words, is it a matter of degree?

I guess it is a matter of degree – yes. I don't think I would have been prepared to lose my hand but had you asked me that question on the South Col, just 12 hours from the top … No, I don't think I would have been prepared to lose my hand, at any time.

But you might have been prepared to take a risk with your hand?

I suppose so. In a sense you're taking a risk with your life, although I hasten to add you never really think you're going to die. The weather wasn't as good as it might have been when we were there. When we were at camp 2, thinking of going back up the mountain to the South Col, to camp 4, the weather forecast was for 55-knot winds. I was convinced that we'd get as far as the South Col and then just have to turn around and go back down the mountain again, forced back by the storm. Fortunately for us the forecast was as about as wrong as it's possible to be – on the South Col there was no wind at all. Nonetheless we still expected the storm to strike at some time and we knew that if it hit us while we were high on the mountain then we probably wouldn't make it down again. There was actually a thunderstorm in the valley *below* us when we were on the South Col – it just goes to show the scale of the mountain. We had no idea whether the storm might blow in our direction, or drift off elsewhere. We spent about an hour and a half deliberating, talking on the radio to the guys at camp 2 and base camp, trying to work out whether or not we should give it a go and make a bid for the summit. In the event, we went, of course, and the wind picked up just as we were coming down off the mountain to the South Col. We were lucky.

Do you have any inner technique for dealing with the inevitable setbacks, difficulties and failures that happen on the route to achieving an ambition?

I don't think it's any technique peculiar to me. At one point on Everest I felt crucified – there was a time I wanted to go and we didn't for various reasons, but 38 people, including Harry, from our team, and 37 from other expeditions, got to the top that day. More people reached the summit that day than on any other day in history and I thought, 'You don't get too many opportunities like that.' I handled it – or *didn't* handle it – by having a row! I was really upset. But having got over that I just thought, 'Well, that was that, you can't do anything about it now. You just have to make the best of the situation that you're in.'

So you can't dwell on that, you can't allow it to affect the way in which you move forward?

Absolutely not. I think all those feelings are completely useless, a waste of energy, unless you've learned something from them. There was no point in harbouring any ill feelings or thinking, 'Right, that's it – I'm off!' You have to reassess the situation and start again from where you are.

It took three and a half years from the ambition rising within you to achieve it – describe to me the moment when you got to the top and said, 'I've done it.'

The top is great. It's not the best bit, but I'll tell you about it first. As we were climbing along the summit ridge, I had this feeling inside me that we were going to stand on the top – whatever happened, whatever the weather threw at us – and when I say 'we' I mean myself and two Sherpas. For me it was fabulous, the Sherpas – neither of them had been to the top before – were overjoyed and almost childlike in their excitement, they grabbed the radio and told all their friends. That was wonderful, but incredibly short-lived. The other thing I have to say is that I was able to look down to Tibet from the summit and see where I'd been in 1989 and the glacier we'd walked along, where we'd camped, where the whole story started. That was wonderful.

But your feeling of triumph was short-lived?

It was extremely short-lived. In the back of your mind you're thinking, 'It's half-past twelve, we've got six hours' daylight left, we've got to get back down this mountain.' You know damn well that getting down is the most dangerous bit – you're tired, if you slip that's it, and you've only got so much oxygen left. It was cold and windy. Fear, I suppose, makes you turn around and go back down pretty much straight away.

So, hardly any time for exhilaration, and that exhilaration has to be firmly controlled because you're moving on to the next step, which is getting down?

Yes. In a sense the 'summit' is getting back down to the high camp on the South Col. Tcheri Zhambu was a third Sherpa who was going to climb with us and couldn't because he had a terrible cough. He had waited for us all day on the South Col, and had drinks ready and tried to feed us. I couldn't eat for some reason, despite the fact I was famished, and could barely drink. I certainly couldn't sleep because a storm came in and was bashing the tent – it was virtually flat on the ground by this stage, but I'd been on the South Col in a similar situation before, so I knew we would get down from there. Relatively speaking we were safe, and I spent all night lying there feeling, 'I've done it.' That was incredibly satisfying.

Looking back at your three and a half years and the aftermath of your achievement, what did you think of the media coverage of what you were doing?

It was quite extraordinary. I climbed Everest on the Monday, on the Tuesday we got down to base camp and on the Wednesday I was on the satellite telephone to DHL and radio stations and what-have-you, and DHL made it clear to me that on the following Saturday I was going to be at a press conference at the Royal Geographical Society in London. I said, 'You're joking!' I didn't think it was physically possible to get out in that time. It had taken us a couple of weeks to walk in. I was extremely disappointed because in the back of my mind I had been thinking of a particularly pleasant beach in Thailand that I could go to and relax. I just needed to build up my strength again and absorb the sunshine – we'd all been fantasizing about this. But we had to go back to London – the reality is that sponsorship is a business contract and you owe them, in a way. Without them it wouldn't have been possible. They organized a helicopter for us from Pheriche, about half a day's walk from base camp, and we flew to Kathmandu and straight back to London. An hour in the shower at some hotel and then we were at the RGS at this press conference. When we arrived at the airport, there were just hundreds of photographers and it was quite overwhelming. That side of it, in hindsight, didn't seem real.

Did you have to exercise a degree of control in dealing with the media? Did you just let rip or did you feel, 'Hang on a second, I can't lose my control here, I've got to be very calm and listen to the questions and think carefully about my answers'?

I did feel that very much. I didn't really let go, though I'm sure I probably made a couple of mistakes along the way. I was extremely aware of the fact that photographers in particular would want you to pose in the most ridiculous positions, and it wasn't difficult for me to say 'no' – I just felt something in my stomach that wouldn't let me do it, which was probably quite fortunate.

What were they wanting you to do?

Stand on one leg on an orange box with a rope slung round my neck and eyes up to the sky – just ghastly – or climb up the telegraph pole. But more seriously, one thing that was very difficult for me was the fact that in our team there were four of us – two Sherpas and Harry Taylor and myself – who got to the top. Harry Taylor climbed it a week before I did, without oxygen, and came back to England before me. I know there was some media coverage on him, but not much. The fact was, people wanted to know about me because I was a girl, it really was as simple as that as far as I could see. It was difficult because there were ten of us in the team and I was extremely aware of the fact that I couldn't have done it without any one of those people. Everybody was instrumental in my getting to the top. Having said that, the rest of the guys on the team were wonderfully generous about it all – except for a couple, but I understand that. In a sense you carry the guilt, but there wasn't really anything you could do about it, you know? What none of us realized was that DHL had hired public relations people while we were away who were gearing up the story. That's what happens if you take money off somebody else – you inevitably lose a bit of control.

You talked about the importance of the team. How do you get the balance right? This doesn't necessarily apply just to Everest, but to life in general. How do you get the balance right between having a driving ambition and pushing that through to a successful conclusion by exercising a high degree of control yourself and the dependence you have on other people who are helping you to make that possible?

I don't always take advice but I listen to it a lot. On the mountain, going back to that, I was always talking to the Sherpas and asking them, 'What do you think? Can we do this? Should we go today?' because I recognized that they knew much more than I did. It would be foolhardy to push through thinking you're right all the time. You need the energy and the will, but there's nothing wrong with using other people's expertise if it's there on offer. I'm just thinking of other examples. I'm working on a project at the moment – it's my idea, but when I look at a list of the expertise required to carry it out I realize I have none of it – design, accountancy, law – I don't have any of these skills, but I revel in trying to find the best people who do, and listening to every word they have to say. I'll still ask questions. I won't necessarily agree with them on everything. But I enjoy being with people who are more talented, brighter, more energetic than I am – always have done.

Has Everest been a catalyst in opening all kinds of other doors for you?

Yes, it has and I sometimes wonder at the logic of all that and how crazy it is, the way the world works. All I did was climb a hill really, it's as simple as that, lots of people – lots of my friends – could have climbed that hill. And yet it's unlocked the door into a big mansion that for some people will never be opened. You still have to walk along the corridors and explore the rooms, you still have to do that work yourself, but in a funny sort of way people are prepared to listen to you more. I don't know what goes through their minds, but in my own mind the biggest thing that's changed is my attitude to risk. I was extremely conservative, I was forced into a situation of taking a risk because climbing Everest was something I badly wanted to do and I couldn't give it up, and now I am positively prepared to take risks. I've still got a long way to go. I'm not talking about huge risks but at least *some* risk. I'm also prepared to pursue what I want to do with a belief that with luck it will work. And even if it doesn't, at least I've tried.

But having climbed the highest mountain in the world, there's nothing for you to do above that. How do you top that?

You're only saying that to be provocative. There's lots and lots to do. I'm talking round in circles about this project that I've got, but it's a much bigger project than Everest.

So what are you moving on to do?

I'd like to set up a centre of exploration which tells the story of explorers of the past, the Shackletons and the Scotts and the Mallorys and the Irvines. The idea is to inspire young people to *do* things, to look out, not in, to go out and explore for themselves. I started thinking about it when I came back from Everest. I realized that Hunt, Mallory, Irvine, Hillary, Tenzing, the people of old, were important to me – they were a part of the excitement, and I'd met lots of people who felt similarly. It just seemed to me that I'd had such fun through it all that to open other people's eyes would be a nice thing to do. But it's bigger than that as well. Where we are now has largely been shaped by our history of exploration and the things brought back – the scientific discoveries and the art and literature, all sorts of things. We shouldn't stop now. People say, 'What is there left to explore?' Well, there's space and there are the ocean beds, for the lucky few. And for the rest of us, there's still lots of fun to be had in the hills and on the sea. So that's what I'm aiming to do at the moment.

What do you think are the most important qualities you need, in general terms, to be successful?

The desire to do whatever it is, tenacity, a certain resilience, because it's not always a smooth path. In some chosen fields a degree of talent, obviously – not all of us could be a concert pianist, sadly. Intelligence comes in there somewhere as well, for some things, not all things.

Looking back over your whole life, what do you regard as your biggest failures, and more importantly, how did you recover from them?

I've failed in lots of things. I suppose my biggest failing is not fulfilling my potential. I may have done in one area, but I'm somebody who enjoys stretching myself and there are times when I didn't do so enough, because I was more interested in buying a flat or something. Once I was thinking of travelling and working overseas and I didn't because I had a boyfriend in London, which I suppose is all very natural, but I sometimes feel I could have made more of myself.

So was the sudden ambition to climb Everest part of your own internal reaction to a feeling that you hadn't really done the big things in life that you wanted to do, you hadn't seized the opportunities before?

There is absolutely no question in my mind that Everest satisfied a degree of ambition that I wasn't able to achieve where I was at the time. I had been working on a magazine for six years. I had got a lot out of it – it had enabled me to travel, to meet lots of people, to have a certain amount of responsibility for myself, and all these things I was looking for. But I suppose having been there for six years, what I never really felt I needed, but realize that I did in hindsight, was to satisfy this degree of ambition – 'Where am I going from here?' It wasn't clear to me at all and I suppose I was getting a little bit bored with things. Everest just came along and filled the gap.

What do you think is the downside of success once you've achieved it?

In my case I've had to get more worldly-wise, which in some ways is good, but in other ways is rather sad – you lose your naïvety.

Don't you want to lose your naïvety?

I don't suppose I do really. I quite like the fact that I've now got more understanding of how the world works, not that I have to any great extent, but certainly more than I had. But before, if I can try and explain, I was working for a magazine where, yes I wanted to travel and things like that, but really my aim was just the same as everybody else's in the office, in other words, to produce a magazine. And so in a way – maybe this is just a feminine thing, I don't know – I wasn't working in any atmosphere of conflict. My aim was the same as my boss's and all I needed from him was a pat on the back. When I came back from Everest, I realized that what people wanted from me was sometimes far from being good for me. Going back to that example of the photographers, what they wanted was an action picture for the newspaper, and I didn't want that, far from it, and so for the first time I found myself standing up and saying, 'Excuse me, just hold back.' On balance that's probably a good lesson to learn, but it's a hard lesson to learn.

Also, of course, you're up there and suddenly everybody has an opinion about you. You've just gone off and climbed a hill because you happen to have wanted to, and then the world and his wife says, 'Well, she should have done that,' or, 'She shouldn't have done that,' or, 'She didn't deserve that,' or whatever.

And many of these people have never met you?

No, they haven't met me.

What sort of criticism?

That I hadn't served a long enough apprenticeship, which is perfectly fair, I hadn't, but I didn't think there were any rules about these things. I got stronger – these things used to really hurt me and then after a while I toughened up and just wanted to knee them in the balls. So that's a hardening in my own personality that I don't really like, but it's survival, isn't it?

But that hardening actually needs to come after the initial success in order for you to tackle the public profile that you have and ride through to achieve further success?

Yes, probably. What I'm saying is that for the first time I realized that there were people out there who really didn't like me, just because I'd climbed a hill. That hardens you.

Are you talking about people in the media?

Not so much. As I say, this was all third-hand so it's difficult to be really clear about the reasons. I gather another reason was that, because of the sponsorship, there was publicity – too much publicity. I think there was a feeling – and actually rightly so – that all I did was climb Everest whilst in fact there are lots of people out there doing much, much more progressive, pioneering climbing. There's no question about that, that's absolutely true, but as I think I mentioned before, there wasn't actually much I could do about it.

Do you think success brings obligations in its wake?

Yes, I do feel that. In my own personal situation I'm invited to talk to schools a lot – I've probably done more in the past than I do now. It's quite difficult, because you almost need another parallel life to have the time to do it all. But I do some, and I think it's perfectly fair that I should be expected to do so.

But generally you have no problem with the idea that success requires you to put something back?

Not at all. I would rather give a little bit more than I take at the end of my life. But whether I feel you should give more if you've been successful, I'm not sure. It's obviously easier to give more if you're somebody people want. But I think, whatever I did in life, I would rather the balance swung a little more towards giving.

What is the greatest pleasure that you've had as a result of your success?

I've had lots of pleasures as a result of my success. I revel in the opportunities it gives me to meet interesting people. This museum – part of the joy is mixing with people from different walks of life. And I lecture about Everest too. Every time I do that I'm in a different situation, a business conference or school, or whatever, and that gives me enormous pleasure.

What do you say to young people who look up to you and say, 'I want to do something like that with my life'?

Well, the chances of their doing something in the same area are actually quite slim. If you ask most sensible people if they want to climb Everest, the answer's usually no. When I look back at my school years, I realize that I was persuaded to do subjects other than ones I might have chosen for myself. My problem was that I wanted to do a mix of art and science – maths, English and art – and the school didn't like that. I would say to those kids something that I wish I'd been told myself at their age – stuff them, you do the subjects or vocation or whatever it is that you really want to do, because if you don't want to do something you're never going to be good at it, it will bore you. And if what you want to do happens to be a high-risk job or high-risk activity, then give it a go anyway with all the passion you've got. If it doesn't work then it doesn't work, but you won't know if you don't try.

And what advice would you give in terms of seeking qualifications, in terms of applying for your first job, getting it and setting a goal and working towards it? What do you think they need to know?

That satisfaction comes from the fulfilment of potential, so never take the easy option. It's easy to say in hindsight. I know lots of people who wished they had studied harder and longer, and I feel it a bit myself. Even three years at that age seems forever. You want to get out, you want to get a job. And yet three years is nothing. Just a blink and it's gone. I'd say to anyone looking at various options, 'Go for the most difficult. Even if it takes six or seven years of studying, it will still seem only a blink in hindsight.'

When your time comes to leave this life, what would you like people to say about you?

God, you have thrown in a difficult one here. I would quite like to be seen as strong and somebody who had moral courage – I'm still working on that one incidentally.

JACKIE STEWART

Three times Formula One World Motor-racing Champion, Jackie Stewart left school at fifteen as 'a complete disaster'. Undiagnosed dyslexia had given him 'a humiliating time' – with pupils and teachers labelling him 'stupid, dumb and thick' because he couldn't read or recite the alphabet. At 58, that basic classroom mantra still eludes him, but his life is a formidable example of how an unpromising start is no real guide to a person's potential. 'Real success,' he says, 'is reaching your true potential – at whatever level that might be.' He discovered an aptitude for clay-pigeon shooting, and was in the British team by the time he was 19, narrowly missing selection for the 1960 Olympics. He would have made it to the 1964 Games had not motor-racing intervened.

Working as a mechanic in his father's garage, his preparation of cars for small race meetings impressed a wealthy patron, who rewarded him with a chance to drive. It was his big break. Over 11 years he won 26 out of 99 Formula One races, at a time when drivers were being killed and injured at a much greater rate than today. Risking the wrath of the sport's strong vested interests, he started what was to be a benchmark campaign for greater safety on the track.

When he retired from motor-racing at the age of 34, he was a multi-millionaire with a mansion in Switzerland, and a jet-setting lifestyle which continued as a chain of major international companies including Ford, Rolex and Moët and Chandon sought his advice and his name. He also returned to an early love, setting up the Jackie Stewart shooting school at Gleneagles Hotel. Then, 20 years later, he was back in Formula One, this time running (along with his son, Paul) the brand new Stewart Grand Prix team, backed by Ford. He never stops. Despite his dyslexia, he has taught himself to become an inspirational and hugely motivating public speaker. Most successful people, he believes, 'have difficulty managing the money and the power they suddenly acquire'. His solution is mind-management – the need to remove emotion from your business life because 'the heart is the most dangerous thing. Never,' he insists, 'allow the intoxication of the moment to take hold.' He believes that bad luck is created through lack of preparation – and draws on his own experience to offer advice on tackling life's inevitable setbacks.

Jackie Stewart, what is your definition of success?

Success could be recognized as the achievement of any individual's full potential. A remarkable number of people get some lesser form of success without doing that but real success is reaching your true potential, whatever God's gift to you was. Someone who can't read or write may be successful in reaching a level of achievement that would be much easier for someone else, but for that person their success is in reaching the ultimate limit within their capability.

And how important a factor is it that others recognize this?

I don't think other people's recognition is very important as long as the person himself knows that he could not have done a better job. There are many times when I may not have won a race but I did a good job and achieved as much as I could ever have done on that particular day. It is very egotistical to want public recognition of your success. It's not important because it's not success as such but other people's perception of your achievement or failure. It may be accurate, but it's often inaccurate.

So the essential judgment is to be true to yourself and to make a decision about whether you have succeeded inside yourself and not be swayed by what people outside might be saying about you?

Absolutely. My father used to always say, 'See yourself as others see you,' but in this case it might be more appropriate to say, 'You can kid a lot of people but you can't kid yourself.' You have to be bluntly honest with yourself in your own evaluation. But when I was younger and first won something, the recognition of that success was something that gave me great personal satisfaction because it was my first experience of being given credit for achieving anything.

Do you remember when that was?

It was when I was about 14 or 15, and I won my first clay pigeon shooting event. I became quite good at shooting, but I was dyslexic – and still am – and when you're at school and you can't read a simple passage from a book, you're abused by the sniggers and the coughing of your peers drawing attention to your inability. Such humiliation has a deep effect on a young person, so if you are at last recognized as being good at something, that means a great deal to you. Suddenly to get praise instead of abuse is very rewarding, but you've got to be very careful that it doesn't become intoxicating. People get intoxicated by their supposed success in every line of work, and I think it's terribly important to be able to see what your faults are. If you are really honest, your own criticism of your performance will be more focused than any other person's observations, and more useful in helping you to deliver at a higher level. I may have won some races or, in business, I may have achieved some deals that I know I worked really hard on but there are other occasions when I am aware that I didn't do a particularly good job, and I still achieved what others perceived as success. To me John McEnroe is a good example. John McEnroe had poor mind management, but incredible natural talent. The annoyance and the anger that he displayed so unattractively was in most cases aimed at himself; it was the frustration of not having played a shot as he had intended, giving the advantage to his opponent. His inability to achieve what he wanted to do frustrated him so much that if something else happened, a bad line call or something of that kind, he couldn't control that frustration any more. If in a competitive world you make mistakes you allow other people to gain the advantage.

But how do you control that frustration?

Mind management. To prepare me for the business world, the most important thing that I learned, both from my shooting and my motor racing, was to remove emotion. The heart is the most dangerous thing, you must never allow emotion to take hold.

But can you ever completely remove emotion? We are human beings after all.

Yes, but I think the really good performers clinically attack their performance to remove the little flaws that may not be obvious to the observer, to the critic, to the aficionado even. The right choice of words is important to a politician or in a business negotiation, and there is always room for improvement. On the race track someone like Frankie Dettori will have made mistakes and yet won races, but he knows he's made the mistake even though nobody else noticed. He was able to get away with it because the really good performers can succeed even on their off-days. Never allow the intoxication of the moment to take hold, you may have just broken the lap record but you haven't finished the race, you may have taken the meeting through to the stage of 'yes, in principle', and 'subject to contract', but if you don't see things through in a level-headed way the chances are the race will be lost or the deal will fall apart. Again, during business negotiations somebody might annoy you to a point where you get angry and, if you don't control your emotions in a very clinical fashion, you'll respond angrily. How many times have you said things in anger that later you regretted? In family situations, in human relationships, in many circumstances you can suddenly become so vulnerable to your own lack of control that a situation becomes irretrievable, your spontaneous response can destroy the deal, destroy the relationship, sometimes for ever. In motor racing if you get annoyed at making a mistake and letting someone pass you or if you get angry at another driver's aggressive behaviour, you'll probably drive off the road, so what's the point? As they say, 'Don't get mad, get even,' but you've got to have mind management not to get mad and you've got to position yourself strategically to get even or take advantage.

You talked earlier about your dyslexia – what was it like for you at school to be labelled as though you were an under-achiever, a no-hoper?

You were labelled stupid, dumb and thick because you couldn't read or recite the alphabet. Even today, if you gave me £10 million, I couldn't run through the alphabet. I don't know the words of the Lord's Prayer and I don't know the words of my own National Anthem although I've stood while it has been played at many victory ceremonies. The wiring system is not right up there: it's not a man-made problem in the sense that I didn't concentrate or pay attention at school, it's just something that occurs to some extent in one in ten young people, and more in boys than girls. The humiliation, the mental abuse, the lack of self-esteem that you experience leave their mark forever, more so in those days because dyslexia wasn't properly recognized by the teachers. I left school at 15 as a complete disaster, to the great relief of the school and much more to my own relief. It was a daily abuse, it was like somebody hitting you on the same spot everyday. When that happens the bruise gets bigger and the pain gets deeper.

There are so many young people still in that position today; they've got inferiority complexes, they're shy, they'll never look you in the eye, they'll avoid situations, they can't fill in a form. I couldn't fill in my driving test form and I still can't fill in any forms, I need secretaries to do that sort of thing for me. But I'm lucky, God gave me hands, eyes and co-ordination that allowed me first of all to shoot, which gave me back some self-respect, and then to drive racing cars which brought new confidence. On the other hand I don't know anything about the history of my country; I know my geography because I've been to places, and I can look at a map of the world and identify where I've been, but I still don't have a great knowledge of the English language. The language that I understand today has been learned from conversation rather than from reading. In talking about my shooting school or a feasibility study that I'm doing for a new shooting school, I'll mention 'topography'. Topography is a word I picked up from someone else's conversation and I asked what it meant. I liked the sound of the word and now I use it myself. The other day my mobile phone wasn't working very well and they told me it was because of 'topospherics', so now I will remember topospherics – that's a big one for me!

I do a lot of public speaking today, much of it in my work for Ford, but I always assume that the audience is as dumb as I am. I go to great lengths to paint as colourful, as pretty a picture of what I'm trying to illustrate in words so that they will understand me better, and I take longer to explain this than most other people. I have to be sure in my mind that they understand what I'm saying because I've suffered so much myself from not understanding the question or the instructions. Even today I went to the wrong room to meet you for this interview; because I'm dyslexic, numbers just don't mean anything to me and I got the hotel room number wrong. I have a busy schedule today and I spent 12 minutes – I made a note of how long it took me – to sort things out. So here I am late and frustrated because of my own inability. You never get over it, you only learn how to get round it, but on the positive side it has made me try harder.

I was going to ask you, are you more ambitious because you had to fight your way out of this desperately difficult start in life?

Because I'm fairly independent I'm not so worried about other people any longer, but to this day I still have something to prove to myself. I lost a deal the other day and I rescued it this morning at 6.00 a.m. because I can't give up, I don't want to give up, I've failed if I give up.

So the potential for success can come for two reasons – it can come through encouragement, through having a strong mentor or someone backing you, or it can come in your case through having an immense disadvantage and something within yourself saying I've got to fight to overcome this. Is that where ambition is born?

I think that's stronger than having a mentor behind you. You can ask other people for advice, you can go to some business guru and ask him what he would have done in similar circumstances, but then to some extent you're doing his deal. You've got to find your own way of achieving the success that you're after. It is important to be ambitious at whatever you want to do, and then you've got to find out how that can best be accomplished. Often it takes a long time to find out. Here I am at 57 years of age and still learning. Perhaps my strongest asset is my attention to detail. I say I'm the president of the menial task division. I need things to be clean, I need things to be tidy. In my office or even in this hotel, I'll always pick up a piece of paper that's lying on the floor. Now if I do that my staff will see that they should do it. If they don't, if they pass it and I pick it up they realize their mistake. The best way to help people understand what is important and what's not important is by example. If you look after the details, the chances are the bigger things will fall into place because it's all the little things that make up the big picture. You might think that, because of its size or bureaucracy, the Ford motor company's a giant, but Jack Nasser, who is now president of the company, doesn't think of it as a big company, he thinks of it as a conglomeration of small companies and he's right. A body doesn't die because the body as a whole has decayed; you discover there's an organ – a liver, a kidney, a heart, a brain – that's gone wrong, and if that organ is repaired and kept in good working order the chances are the body will function quite well.

How big a part do you think luck plays in success? Going right back to your early days, was it luck that took you into motor racing in the first place and was it luck that kept you on top?

I don't believe in bad luck, I believe in good luck. I believe that bad luck is created through lack of preparation, through lack of skills or talents, or poor judgment of people. If a young man gets into crime, it's not bad luck, he's chosen to mix with the wrong people and should have seen the dangers ahead. Another of my father's sayings was, 'If you fly with the crows, you are liable to be shot at.' If you go with the wrong group that's not bad luck, that's bad judgement. If I had been in a racing car that was badly prepared I probably wouldn't have won many races. It wasn't good luck that I chose the right teams to drive for, the right engineers, the right team manager, the right tyre man, engine man, suspension man, gear-box man. So it's not bad luck that the car breaks down at every race, there's a very good reason for it, either somebody hasn't tightened something up or the part was not good enough in the first place, designed poorly or manufactured badly. Good luck in most cases comes through the misfortune of others.

At the expense of others?

Yes, the poor performance of others in some cases. I have been lucky on occasions but usually it's been bad luck for someone else. When I retired from racing I gave most of my trophies away because I thought having them in a big room, all glittering and shining, was very self-serving – 'Look who I am and how clever I've been.' I didn't like it so I gave most of them away to people who'd helped me in my career. I've kept several. I kept the Princess Grace trophy from Monaco, I kept the American Grand Prix because it was a lovely punch bowl, and of my four wins in the Spanish Grand Prix I kept one in particular because, in that race, I came from sixth position and I won the race without ever passing a car, they all broke down or crashed. This was the perfect example of why you should never give up. I drove as well as I could on that day, but because of my car, my tyres, myself or whatever, I was never going to finish better than sixth. I kept that trophy, and I have it in my office as a reminder that you should never think you can't achieve something. You can still win through determination, through staying there. If you don't stay there trying your best, you're never going to do it; so you've got to stick with it, you've got to persevere, you've got to work at it. You should never, ever give up.

In motor racing, how much of success is down to the individual and how much is down to the team behind that individual?

There is an enormous dependency on the team. You've got to have the best car, the best chassis with the best engine and the best people. Damon Hill won the 1996 World Championship but, not taking anything from Damon, the Williams car and that team gave him the World Championship – I have no doubt in my mind at all. Schumacher was the best driver of 1996, he is the best driver in the world at the present time, but his car wasn't good enough, the team wasn't good enough, the package wasn't good enough. Now Ferrari have got the most expensive driver, the most expensive team manager, the most expensive designer, the most expensive test facility and the most expensive factory with the largest budget and they haven't won a World Championship for 17 years.

Have you ever felt like giving up? Have you ever felt like saying 'Right, I've done it all, that's it, I could happily coast through the rest of my life'?

Why would you want to give up? What is there to give up? My wife would like to spend more time with me, we would like to take longer holidays and have a more relaxed life, but I can't do that. I'm committed to several contracts that I went into with my eyes open, that I have to honour, and in any case I enjoy and get fulfilment from my work. I feel I've been put on this Earth to do whatever I should do, and the things that I'm driven to doing I want to do well.

From what you're saying there has been an element of sacrifice in your personal life. Do you think that every successful person has to sacrifice a slice of their family life?

Americans say there are no free lunches, you don't get the very best in life without paying for it in some form. We have been married for 34 years, so it hasn't been such a sacrifice that it's had a negative effect on our family life. We have two very healthy sons who are well-adjusted boys; they've been brought up well by their mother and I hope in some way by myself, and given a good example of how to behave in life. From the '60s through to the '90s we haven't had the problems that have affected so many families and their mother has had a great deal to do with that. Helen and I are still here, happy and together, despite a turbulent lifestyle and, for a while, the glamour and excitement of the Grand Prix circuit. But she didn't marry a racing driver, I was a clay pigeon shooter then and we've moved from one sphere to another and on to another. We're fairly well adjusted, we haven't allowed ourselves to become intoxicated either by the lifestyle or any of the benefits or privileges that our lifestyle brings. It's very important not to get carried away by this so-called success. Many people have difficulty managing the money and power that they suddenly acquire. You see some extraordinarily arrogant people who have had only a small degree of success, but the most successful people, the really big players, are the easiest in the world to deal with.

When you achieve sudden, fast success how do you keep your feet on the ground, what formula would you offer?

I think one of the advantages that I have had is that, as I have gone along, the people with whom I have had an important relationship have, almost exclusively, been more successful than me. They've either had a lot more money, a higher position, or more influence and power. It's easier for me to keep my feet on the ground in their company than if I had a bunch of court jesters around me, sycophants making me feel good, look good, pumping me up. I hate that. You're in danger of not seeing life as it really is, and then when you get into other company where you are not so big, you don't know how to handle it. I think it's a good lesson to try always to associate with people whom you respect and admire.

Let me take you back to the year when you spun off the track in the Belgian Grand Prix. You were trapped, you were soaked in petrol, you had a broken shoulder and a cracked rib. Some people might have said, 'That's enough, I'm out,' and yet you were back driving two months later. What was it inside you that made you want to get back on the track after an experience like that?

It's part of the business, it's what everybody else did, it was what was expected of you. The first time I got back in a car again my knees trembled on the pedals, but that's something you overcome. That's mind management. You say, 'Listen, you've done this all your professional life, there's nothing to stop you doing it again. Come on, let's get the act together.' Racing-team managers sometimes recognize that. I had an accident in South Africa in 1973, in qualifying. It was a big one, at 176 m.p.h., a brake problem. It could easily have got to me, so as soon as I was back in the pits Ken Tyrrell brought my team-mate in, put me into his car and told me to go out and re-qualify. It was the correct decision, you've got to get over that sort of experience quickly and recalibrate your mind. If you can't do that, then you're in the wrong business and it is time to stop.

What do you think are the most important qualities you need to be successful?

For me, attention to detail, mind management and trying constantly to have respect for other people.

And what would you say are the biggest enemies of success?

Ego, or self-adulation, over-confidence, and hiding from reality.

Who are the people you regard as being highly successful? Who are the people you admire, past or present?

His Majesty King Hussein of Jordan, because he's a real man, he has lived his life his way, he has done it in the face of considerable adversity. He's had something like 27 attempts on his life which he deals with very diligently but respectfully; he has achieved tremendous amounts for other people and done it in a responsible fashion and with dignity. He's a man whom women like as a man because he's a gentle man. I've never known a man with better manners, and yet so powerful in his own way; he has been personally responsible for so much of the re-shaping of the Middle East.

As a businessman Lord King took on an enormous bureaucratic nightmare in transforming British Airways into the world's favourite airline and a world leader. He's now a man of mature years with tremendous experience, a man of knowledge and dignity who came from modest beginnings and carries whatever he has been given, be it knighthood or peerage, with the same dignity. There are so many people I admire, people like Giovanni Agnelli, founder of the Fiat company, who has been able to shape a nation to some extent through the number of companies over which he has had an influence – banks, media, car makers, property. On a global basis he is a very major player. Then there's Roger Hill, the mechanic who brought me three World Championships. Roger Hill was probably better at what he did than I ever was at what I did, so he was a real achiever and reached far beyond his own expectations, beyond his own perception of his ability. I also admire Ken Tyrrell, he's over 70 years of age, he's still going on, his team isn't as successful today as it once was, but Ken's always kept his own principles, his own morals, his own commitments and his own integrity.

Is there a downside to success?

Not that I'm aware of. You lose some of the privacy that you may wish in life but, in my opinion, the privileges that you gain are far beyond those that you lose. If privacy is a concern it's usually because someone doesn't know how to deal with the situation and allows the problem to get out of proportion, to become exaggerated.

In pursuit of success have you ever done anything you wished you hadn't done?

There were times I might have behaved differently. But if I had my life to run again, I wouldn't change a lot.

Part and parcel of success is receiving criticism of one kind or another. How do you weather criticism? Is there a formula for doing that?

Objective criticism is very healthy and you've got to think about it but sometimes you've got to say, 'Listen, I can't do anything about it so let it go.'

You have had a very successful career, there is no need for you to work any more, and yet you are taking on the most difficult challenge in motor racing, which is starting your own team from scratch. Why go through all that hassle?

I really don't have an easy answer to it, but it doesn't occur to me that what anybody has done in the past has got anything at all to do with what one should do now or in the future. Business opportunities arrive, or crop up from time to time and one never really thinks about the downside, even though it may be there. My life has always been built on the basis that nothing is going to be easy – it's just a question of trying to reduce the downside elements: be it risk, discomfort or hassle.

I would not have done this at all had I not already had a son and a business in existence – which is what I had in Paul Stewart Racing. That business had to go somewhere to develop any further and this is the evolution of that. If we were going to go into motor racing in the big time, then Formula One was where we had to be. The combination of Paul's ambitions and the sudden possibility of Ford Motor Company being able to provide us with exclusive use of their Formula One factory engine for five years, was an opportunity that would probably not have come along again for a very long time.

But in the difficult formative stages of setting up the team, did you ever think, 'Why on earth am I doing this?'

There was the odd occasion when that happened, but it was a fast flash. Lenin said that there are no problems there are only solutions. Some of the obstacles have seemed insurmountable, but we have found our way round them – there have been very many moments of frustration and disappointment as well as elation and satisfaction.

Do you think it's becoming more or less difficult to achieve success in your profession?

I think it has probably become less difficult because there are more multinational corporations involved. More people need the services of someone who is moderately good at what they do, and if you're very good at what you do you're very much in demand. The scale of remuneration is higher than it's ever been. There's more opportunity today than there's ever been before.

Have you any frustrated ambitions?

No, I don't think I have. I know that I haven't done what I've yet to do. I know that there are more things in my life that I still have to do.

What kind of things?

I'd like to do something specifically in Scotland. At one time I had an ambiton to recreate a Scottish village somewhere that would be commercially attractive and viable, but that will have to wait because the Stewart Grand Prix team will take at least five or six years to establish itself properly.

Has success changed you at all?

I don't think so. Some of my values might have changed, but I don't think my basic values have. I can afford to buy things or invest in things today to a scale that I might never have previously been able to do, but I still know the value of money. I still keep thinking back to the days when I did not have a lot of money. When someone says, 'That's alright, we can do that. It will only cost us £1500,' I think, 'My God, £1500, that's an awful lot of money!' Others may say I've changed a lot, but from inside I don't feel I've ever changed.

What's the greatest pleasure that you have had from your successful career?

I think being able to fulfil the family unit in a comfortable, flexible, and enjoyable environment. At the end of the day your family is the most important thing in your life; that's where I get all my pleasure. Other things come and go, achievements in sport and such like, but at the end of the day you go back to your home, back to your family and they are the only ones you can really trust and rely on.

What do you say to those who envy success in others?

There's always some form of envy. The grass is always greener on the other side of the fence, but it's not always the way it looks. Nobody has everything for any length of time. Circumstances change and suddenly what was paradise can sometimes become a nightmare. I never take the good times for granted, because over the years I've seen so many ups and downs. There are very, very few people who live on a plateau. I always feel sorry for people who are envious and jealous.

What advice would you give to young people who want to succeed as you have succeeded?

To give total commitment to whatever they choose to do. There's no half-way mark, you just can't work at a level of mediocrity; it's got to be a total commitment, it's got to be an absolute focus, an absolute driven desire to succeed or achieve. Attention to detail is probably one thing I major on above all else. Try to eliminate all of the interruptions that may stop the success or achievement that you are aiming for. You have got to be on the ball all the time: to be pro-active; to be thinking ahead; to be looking at the potential downside risks, and if you don't address them, see them in reality, and try to plan around them. Above all you have to have integrity; without integrity you have nothing. It's no good trying to work a fast one, you get back what you put in and people who go for the short-cut, the cheap fix, will never make it long-term. They may make money, but they'll always be vulnerable, they will be found out, and they will lose in the end.

And what would you like people to say about you when your time comes to leave this life?

That I had integrity.

TERRY WOGAN

His gently disrespectful, self-deprecating humour has made him one of the most successful and popular broadcasters of his generation. The secret, he says, is to wing it, apply your own rules, rely on observation instead of a formal script, and throw away the safety net. Success in broadcasting is about the small gesture, the throwaway line; and whatever talent you have, television will find you out – nobody can make you better than you are. He explains his doubts about whether he would be able to repeat his success if he was starting out in Britain now. The elder son of middle-class parents who ran a grocery store, Terry Wogan was rather shy, withdrawn and introverted as a child. After going to a Jesuit-run school, he started a philosophy course, but 'couldn't be bothered to study', and became a bank clerk with no ultimate career goal. Four years later, he and at least 5,000 other hopefuls answered an advertisement for a newsreader/announcer on Irish radio. He is convinced it was his talent as a mimic that landed him the job.

Television followed, but he hankered after 'a bigger market', and eventually his demo tape rose to the top of the pile at BBC Radio, and programme offers followed rapidly. At 31, he was given his own breakfast show on Radio Two, pulling in huge audiences for 15 years, and hosting TV classics such as Come Dancing, Blankety Blank, Children in Need *and the* Eurovision Song Contest. *Extending his TV chat show to three nights a week forced a complete surrender to the demands of television, and when, many years later, that was taken off the air, he returned to the morning radio show that was his first love. He offers advice on nurturing talent and explains how he was mishandled and sacrificed by the BBC when his show was axed. Despite that he is adamant that he never recognises failure because 'you don't learn from it, it has nothing to teach you. You learn from success.' As for breaking into television now, his advice is to do it any way you can, even if it means making the tea! He explains that, because TV is much more niche-oriented, 'there's no pattern, no career path – it has to be in you'. He warns that fame and success on TV is brutal because the print media are 'so savage and vitriolic'. But the really important thing is to understand how transient success is, and never forget that 'the wind will blow away your footprints in the sands of time'.*

Terry Wogan, what is your definition of success?

It is whatever you mean by it – success as a person, or success in your chosen profession. Success in your chosen profession is, if you have any sense, largely due to luck and the ability to recognize an opportunity and take it when it occurs. Success as a person is a much more difficult thing to achieve and something that, perhaps, is unachievable, because the perfect person has never fully emerged – well, perhaps with one exception. So you try to be as good as you can, as decent as you can, as honest as you can, as straightforward as you can, as kind as you can, as gentle as you can. I think if, at the end of your life, you can look back and say you haven't too many things with which to reproach yourself, then perhaps you can be a success, and that is far more important than success or its corollary, fame. Both of those are overrated. As they always say, who talks with Napoleon now? Nobody.

Have you found at any time in your life an enormous conflict between work and family?

No, not at all, because I have never regarded work as being as important as my family.

Yet a lot of people would give up a slice of their family life in order to pursue a successful career.

I wouldn't. I have never lived to work, I work to live. I love what I do – I come into work every morning singing and whistling. The radio I really enjoy, television too, but I only love the doing of it. I never observe myself or listen to myself, because that's madness.

To what extent do you think that your success has been a direct product of your upbringing?

I think it has probably been the opposite. Nothing in my background, nothing in my upbringing.

What kind of a lad were you?

I was fairly timid. Strong and big, so I didn't get picked on.

Timid? Terry Wogan, timid?

Yes, I think I'm shy. It isn't a bad thing, and you get a lot of people in show business saying they are shy. Nobody ever says I am a show-off, do they?

In my education, my whole upbringing – which was middle-class, bourgeois, Irish, in a middle-class bourgeois Irish school – the worst sin was sex, and the second-worst sin was vanity. You had to be a team player, a conventional person and conform to the Jesuitical model. If you scored a try at rugby you ran back to the halfway line shamefaced. The captain might say, 'Well done,' but you certainly didn't thump the air with your fist, or anything like that. So how any of us came out of it with any self-esteem is beyond me, but we did. Maybe it was false pride.

You are a team player?

Yes, I suppose I am. That was the way I was brought up. As I'm always saying, if my father had been a doctor, my education and upbringing would have led me to become a doctor, but then luckily for me he wasn't, so I was able to go my own way. But there was no real rebellion in me. I am entirely conventional. Quite frankly, I don't know what I am doing in this business. I am just there, it just happened that way. In fact in our business there are a lot of people who are quite surprised to find themselves doing what they are doing on television and radio, because they are not extroverts. They are shy people who all their lives have been told by their mothers and fathers to push themselves a little bit further. 'You want to stop hiding, go on, get out,' you know. So they are behaving against type. It has been ingrained into them that being shy isn't awfully good, so they had better get out there and show off a bit.

So it's not a matter of overcoming the shyness, it is a matter of constantly fighting it?

Yes. I have a very low threshold of embarrassment. On the talk show, I used to get terribly embarrassed when people were excessively showing off, and I would never be a confrontational interviewer because if I embarrassed somebody, I would get embarrassed myself. I would never ask anybody a question that I wouldn't want asked of myself.

But are you shy in the sense that you are nervous when you find yourself in a public forum?

No, I'm not nervous.

You don't think the two go together to a certain extent?

I am not nervous at all any more. I spent 15 years being nervous on television in Ireland and initially here, but eventually I overcame that. Nervousness and shyness are not the same. As I say, I do get embarrassed very easily and that's probably a bit of a drawback if you are going to do a talk show, but on the other hand a talk show is supposed to be banal anyway – it is not an interview programme. This is where people get so mixed up between the two. You know, you get people advocating in the newspapers that talk shows should be presented by journalists. Journalists can't do talk shows – talk shows are done by comedians, celebrities and people like that. An interview programme should be presented by a journalist, perhaps, but that is a different thing. The Americans don't get them mixed up. Barbara Walters does interviews and Letterman and Lenno do talk shows. It is an entirely separate thing. Criticizing poor old Clive Anderson because he is not asking in-depth questions – what are we talking about? It's a talk show, it's on Sunday night at ten o'clock. It's not meant to have any great depth.

It's entertaining.

Exactly.

But was there a great sense of triumph way back in your early life when you said, 'Hey, I could really make a go of something, I'm really good at something'? Maybe a teacher giving you good marks in an exam, or scoring a try, or whatever?

Occasionally, yes, but I have always had that Irish combination of sentimentality and cynicism. I never attach too much importance to it. For example, when I won the Television Personality of the Year every year for ten years, I always knew it was because I was on television more often than anybody else. I was just there, so they voted for me, and they got used to voting for me, and that was that. I knew that when I ceased to do so much television I wasn't going to win it any more. It's transitory success, and I have always been able to look at it in a slightly dispassionate way. I am too much of a controlled person to let it take me over.

Does it help you to be successful if you are modest, either because you are born modest, or because you learn how to be modest?

We were trained to be modest. Modesty was the biggest single quality that was ingrained into us. You didn't boast, you didn't brag, you didn't show off. It may have been a major factor in my upbringing, but I don't know whether it is a major factor in being successful. The biggest factor in being successful is luck. That is what drives me mad. I meet captains of industry, fellows who are inordinately successful, and I admire them because they are successful in an area I know nothing about. I look at them and I am expecting sparks to come out of their ears. But in the main they are entirely unremarkable people. That sustains my belief that in business – banking, or in insurance – as in showbusiness, success depends an awful lot on being in the right place at the right time, on getting the opportunity when you are ready to take it, and on whatever you have to offer being relevant to that time. If I was trying to make it here now, I doubt I would be able to.

Really?

Yes. I haven't got the necessary qualities of confrontation. I am not sufficiently extrovert. I don't like comedy now, certainly on television, most successful comedy appears to be very acid, junior-common-room stuff, points-scoring, personal. That's not my kind of thing.

So what would the formula be? What would you say to young people entering the profession now who look at what you have achieved in your life and say, 'That's great, I want to be the next generation's Terry Wogan'? What qualities are needed for that?

I don't think you can be the next generation's Terry Wogan because Terry Wogan would be irrelevant in the next generation. Something else is required. Look at Chris Evans. He is, I suppose, enjoying the kind of attention and success that I enjoyed around about the mid-1970s – every article is about you, and all the rest of it. But he is a completely different kind of person, and what he has to offer is completely different. He has a greater capacity for work and application than I have, and he is possibly much more creative than I am. I admire him greatly. The other problem for him is of course that fame and success on television are now treated brutally – the print media are so savage and vitriolic that nobody has any chance of surviving longer than about two or three years before they are shot down in flames.

Is there any means of identifying what the qualities are in advance, and saying, 'Right, these are the things that I must do in order to become the equivalent of Terry Wogan'?

Well, I do get a lot of letters from young people saying, 'How do I get in?' Every second student wants to be in the media. I always feel so helpless, because there is no pattern, no career path. It has to be in you. I started in radio, which was a very good way to get into television at the time because it was national radio – there was no local radio, so everybody heard you. It's not a way in any more. You could be doing radio until hell froze over and you wouldn't get any television because nobody knows who you are any more. It's not a universal thing.

Is that because of the multiplicity of channels?

Yes. The whole thing has become very much more fragmented and youth is much more polarized from middle age and old age than it used to be. There is no universal programme on television – with the possible exception, maybe for a laugh, of the *Eurovision Song Contest* or the soap operas. It used to be *Morecambe and Wise, Blankety Blank,* all those programmes which everybody watched and which went right across the age groups. That doesn't happen any more. Television has become much more niche-orientated, much more compartmentalized. To a young person, I would say, get in there any way you can – make the tea – and then see what your opportunities are.

Regardless of how highly you might be qualified?

You can't throw a stone on a dusty road here without hitting somebody with a degree in media studies. It doesn't mean anything. The BBC used to run good schemes for trainees and that was a wonderful way in, but they don't do them any more. It is much more difficult to get in. If you are going to get in as a presenter, I would say, try to avoid naked ambition. Try and be a bit more subtle. Find out who is in a position to help you. Don't be too aggressive. If you achieve any degree of success, try and do it with modesty and with balance, and don't let it all go to your head and behave stupidly. With radio it's important to establish a rapport with your listener. It's important to talk to people rather than at them. And it's the same with television. You try and get through the tube to them with your eyes and with your attitude, but that's technique. It's something you can teach people. Otherwise, I think television and radio are something you can either do or you can't, and no amount of training is going to make you able to do it. You can reach a certain level with training, but if you don't have the talent, you won't go on and become a big star.

So how do you discover whether you can do it or not? How do you grab that opportunity from among the maybe tens of thousands of people who are seeking the same opportunity?

You can only grab the opportunity if it is offered to you, and once it is offered people will tell you whether you are going to make it or not. But the fact is there are loads of people on television who can't do it, so nobody's really defined what it is that makes somebody succeed.

Why do they get on to television if they can't do it?

Well, they're theatrical people, and they've been successful as comedians or whatever. They are still doing a stage act on television, their gestures and everything. These are very successful people, but they've never actually learned how to do television.

They've never realized that television and radio are very intimate media?

They are, and it's all about the small gesture and the throwaway line, about giving people credit for intelligence. The thing about television and radio is that you can't beat it home with a hammer. Film is the same. Americans can do film acting – in the main, British actors can't. Laurence Olivier was probably the worst film actor of his generation.

Come on, Terry.

He was a terrible actor on film, terrible – a dreadful ham. He was a wonderful stage actor. Our actors are still theatrically trained. That's why we don't do sitcoms as well as they do in America. We are over-acting and the thing is overwritten. And all the jokes are telegraphed.

Does it help to have a mentor, someone who picks you up at a certain stage in your career? Someone in authority who then runs with you? Have you had mentors?

Yes, everybody needs that. I have been very, very lucky. I keep coming back to luck, and it isn't out of a sense of false pride or modesty. You do need somebody. When I was working in the bank I answered an ad for a newsreader-announcer on Irish radio. All I had done up to then was to have got my exams, and I had been back to Belvedere in Dublin and done a year's philosophy course, which I abandoned, because I couldn't be bothered studying any more. I was only 17 anyway. I wasn't ready to go off to university for three years, I just wasn't ready, and I didn't fancy it. The only place I could have gone was to the arts. I wasn't going to go for a profession or anything like that, so there was no real incentive for me to do it. I had no ultimate aim. I knew I could get the exams, but I had never been particularly keen on study as such – reading, yes, but not studying. So I couldn't see a great future. I thought, to hell with it and joined the bank.

And yet at the time, university would have been the accepted career path for someone in your position.

Yes, it would, but I just thought, 'No, I can't be bothered.' So I went to join the bank, and about four years later I answered the ad in the newspaper. There were about 5,000 applications at least, maybe more, because there were no jobs in Ireland in the early 1960s.

So why did they pick you out of 5,000 or more?

Well, that's what I'd like to know. There would have been briefless lawyers applying, because the RTE was full of briefless lawyers, there would have been all sorts of people with firsts in English and all the rest of it, and they called me for an audition. I have never understood why. I suppose my ability to mimic got me through – I appeared to speak Gaelic well although I couldn't always understand it, and a bit of Italian, French and German, and I read the English all right. I got asked to do a training course, and that's where I met my first mentor, a man called Denis Meehan, who always had great faith in me. He gave me a job. And then I suppose the next most important person in my life would be Mark White, who was assistant head of the Gramophone Department at the BBC.

This was when?

This would be 1965, I suppose. Everybody wanted to get into radio. The pirates were going like steam-hammers, but everybody wanted to get into the BBC. The man in the Gramophone Department was getting tapes all the time, and one day he gets this tape which hasn't even been respooled. I'd forgotten to respool it before I sent it across. What a break for me! He got up from his desk, put it on the machine, respooled it – he must have thought, what kind of an eejit is this? – and played the thing, and then I got offered work by the BBC. So Mark was tremendously important to me.

Why did you want to work for the BBC?

It was a bigger market. I had achieved quite a lot of fame in Ireland. I was one of their first television newsreaders and then I did a quiz show. Then they had what they called the vertical plan, where we all hosted a separate day of the week. Friday was my day, and I hosted from whenever the station opened until it closed. I sent Mark another tape and got offered *Late Night Extra* and then I was asked to sit in for Jimmy Young, which I did for about a month. Then they offered me the afternoon show on Radio 1 and 2. The television came along slowly, the odd beauty contest – which I was never any good at – and *Come Dancing*, which I did for seven years. Even when I had finished people still thought Peter West was presenting it.

Jimmy Gilbert, who was the head of light entertainment at that time, and Bill Cotton seemed to like what I was doing introducing *A Song for*

Europe. I think between them they had decided to find something for me to do, because I appeared to have a certain potential or the public seemed to like me – I was winning all the awards on radio at that time. They found this thing *Blankety Blank*. It was the first time – possibly the only time – I was able to exactly translate my radio personality on to the television, because I was totally in charge. I could move as I wished and the camera followed me. I could make it up as I went along.

People home in on your self-deprecating humour, your ability to deflate pomposity. They suggest you are liked because you are disrespectful, anti-establishment.

But not too much. There is an acceptable level, you see. You have to be clever enough not to overstep the mark. What's the point of being an anarchist if you want to continue to work for the BBC? You can be slightly iconoclastic, but you can't be a complete anarchist because that's a contradiction in terms. Anyway, it's good-natured – it's not meant to destroy.

Do you ever feel you went over the top?

No, I always felt I had judgment with that. I still have, I hope. The limits are slightly fuzzier now. You can get away with a bit more.

Did you have to work at that, or was it the natural Terry coming through?

I didn't have to work at it. Paradoxically, I was much more restricted in Ireland on radio and television than I was over here. I found great freedom working for BBC Radio, and that's why I blossomed. That's why I blossomed on *Blankety Blank*. I was lucky to get the opportunities to do all those things, to loosen up, as it were.

You then had this phenomenal array of awards, a phenomenal number of decades at the top of British television and radio in one form or another, and then you got to the point where your chat show was axed, and the follow-up Friday Night with Wogan *was perhaps not as good as you or others would have liked.*

The axed thing … everything has to end, you know. Esther Rantzen did *That's Life* for 15 years, yet it finished and she's 'axed'.

Did it happen the way you would have liked it to happen?

No, it didn't, because it was mishandled by the BBC. They allowed themselves to be overtaken by events. They wanted me to continue until they could find something else. I wanted to finish about 18 months before we did, but they said no, we have nothing ready. They had 150 hours to fill and I felt I owed them a certain amount of loyalty. It was not my ambition to do *Wogan* until hell froze over. Even if it had been scheduled where it should have been – about 10.30 every evening, Monday to Friday – I wouldn't still be doing it now. It isn't American television, and my nature is not to go on and on, because you get very bored doing that.

The BBC began to prepare *Eldorado*. They tried to keep it out of the press, but eventually the press are going to find out you are building a village down in Spain, and besides, the person producing it wanted a bit of publicity, so in a sense I was sacrificed – it appeared as if it were not my timing, but the BBC's. The BBC wasted an asset – me. They allowed me to be demeaned, which was a big mistake from their point of view.

And then there were headlines implying that your career was at an end. How did you handle that?

I didn't allow it to get me down. I was annoyed at the sheer ineptitude of the BBC, and I still am, in retrospect. It was a disgraceful thing to do, in view of the service I had given them, the figures I had delivered year in year out. To allow what was then their major asset just to be blown away was absolutely ridiculous.

Is there any formula inside Terry Wogan for recovering from such a situation? It sounds as if you have had virtually no downsides to your career or to your life. Were you therefore less able to cope with this?

I'm an optimist, and I'd say I'm quite a steely person, and don't think I would ever let anything get me down for long. I knew that radio wanted me to go back as soon as this thing happened and I was happy to go back. If I'd had my way, I would have continued doing the radio while I was doing the television but you can't. The public need a break from you. Of course, it was a wonderful opportunity but as far as the rest went, not only did BBC Television mishandle *Wogan*, they mishandled the Friday-night thing as well. They should have allowed that to run. We tried to do something different with it, because I wanted to get away from the one-off talk show format – it's just death. I knew that ten years ago, when I took over from Parkinson. I did it for two or three seasons, and I thought, this is not worth doing because people are tired of it, they've seen all the personalities two or three times. Expectations are too high. If you only do it once a week you can't get any continuity.

Can a good presenter compensate for a bad format or a bad producer?

No.

Conversely, can a good producer lift a presenter to do more than he is capable of?

No, he can't. Television will find you out. Nobody can make you better than you are.

And yet a bad producer can inhibit you?

Yes, but in all cases it must be the combination of presenter and programme or presenters and programme. The format has to be right, the presenter has to be right. One won't work without the other. For example, you have the ridiculous situation where Anthea Turner was being paid enormous sums of money as a presenter because she presented the National Lottery. Fifteen million people weren't watching Anthea Turner, they were watching the National Lottery. This is not to decry her – and why shouldn't she get the benefit of it – but it's foolish thinking. It's the programme that is drawing the audience. When I gave up *Blankety Blank*, it was just as successful under Les Dawson, because the format was terrific. But the idea that you can take a presenter out of a successful format and put them into something else and they will be just as successful is flawed. Even somebody as terrific as Bruce Forsyth was taken away from *The Generation Game*. Michael Grade put him into *Bruce's Big Night* and it died.

If you were in management today what steps would you be taking to nurture successful talent for the future?

I would try not to be too influenced by the viewing figures. I would try and do what the old BBC did and say, right, I have faith in this person, I have faith in this idea, I have faith in this producer and these scriptwriters, and I am going to put in on the screen. If they don't like it the first time, I am going to look at it again and make it a bit better, but I am going to stick with it because I know what I am doing and I am going to have confidence in it. Our problem is, do we have anybody in charge who really knows what they are doing? That's another question which is probably futile speculation, so we'd have to assume that the people in charge do actually know what they are doing and have a feel for it. It's not necessarily true, but that's probably the case in any business in the world, and our business is so full of imponderables that you can't predict. There's no way of knowing what's going to succeed. You just have to try it. You won't know until the red light goes on and you look at the viewing figures the following morning.

What do you think are the ingredients of successful humour?

I was brought up on BBC Radio, listening to the Light Programme in my little hovel in Limerick. I didn't listen to Irish radio, I listened to things like *Take it From Here* and *The Goons* and *Much Binding in the Marsh*. That's my kind of humour and perhaps that's why I succeeded over here, because my sense of humour was much more anglicized. But nothing dates more than humour. When they repeated Tony Hancock's television series for the first time about ten years ago, I said to my son, sit down and look at this, this is really funny. The family didn't think it was at all funny. They sat there, Mum chatting, and the fact is, it wasn't. Even *Morecambe and Wise* doesn't seem quite as funny now. Not only does humour date, but television hasn't got any better. It's just got quicker, so your attention span, although you mightn't like to admit it, is shorter. You think, 'Oh, this sketch has gone on too long.' Ten years ago it didn't seem to go on too long, but now it does. I got the scripts for *It's That Man Again*. Now that programme and Tommy Handley kept the country alive and laughing during the war. You look at those scripts now. There isn't a funny line there. Nothing you could possibly laugh at.

When you go in to do a programme, do you go in with a pretty good idea of what jokes you are going to use, what lines of humour?

No.

You really genuinely wing the whole thing?

That's the way I work best. I'm not a comedian. I couldn't remember the lines of a joke. And I'm not an actor. I wouldn't want to remember lines and move to spots. That would make me so nervous, terrify me. I'm used to winging it, making it up as I go along, applying my own rules. I rely on observation, what I see around me. The more ridiculous aspects of life, or television – or listening to what people say. I recount this on the radio, and people react and take the idea into another dimension, or move it on laterally rather than vertically. Every morning I just walk in, pick up this huge pile of e-mail and faxes and letters, and make it up as I go along. Really, I believe in broadcasting without the net.

Living dangerously.

I believe in doing it live, because then I don't have to listen to it or look at it. I just go home and have my dinner. That is really the focus of my life.

Have you ever felt like giving up?

No, I'll pick my own time to give up. When I want to give up.

What are your biggest failures, and how did you recover from them?

I never recognize failure. You can't, because you don't learn from it at all – failure doesn't have anything to teach. You learn from success. I've had loads of things that haven't succeeded – television series that ran for a couple of seasons, or maybe only one. But they never marked me, particularly when I was younger. Perhaps they do as you get older – you can become too sensitive, but what you want to avoid is becoming an old curmudgeon. You find yourself telling people how things should be done, this is the way you do a talk show, and of course, you are out of date.

But isn't it very difficult to avoid being marked because of your position, because you are successful. If you make what other people perceive to be a mistake, if you go in the wrong direction, if you make the wrong choice, you are hammered by the critics in the most public way. Does that not get to you?

It does, of course, but with me it has been only in the last five or six years. I think that our print media have now become ridiculously vitriolic and antipathetic towards television. It has just become awful. People are not writing television criticism any more, they are writing feature articles.

For themselves?

Yes, and they are being offensive, awful to people.

Gratuitously so?

Oh yes, undoubtedly. It's done on a whim. It's writing to make a headline, and to hell with people's feelings.

Who are the people you really admire, past or present? Who are Terry Wogan's heroes, to whom you look up as the ultimate in success?

I haven't got many heroes. The historical figure is of course Alexander, you can always look at him and say, incredible. And Nelson, the architect of this country's success.

Anyone in the present?

Not really.

Why are Nelson and Alexander your heroes? They're generals leading their troops into the fray, aren't they?

Because they are so far away. Alexander's beyond criticism because nobody really knows anything about him. I mentioned Nelson because Trafalgar, in my opinion, was the most important battle ever fought by English forces, and as a result of it the Industrial Revolution was allowed to take place and the empire was built, since England was safe and could develop. So it was enormously successful, I think a more important battle than Waterloo. That's why I admire him. Of course, if he were alive today he would never have got to Trafalgar because his personal life would have been smeared all over the tabloids and he would have been dismissed. So you would have got some second-rater in charge, and probably lost Trafalgar.

But I'm not very good at heroes. When I was doing *Wogan*, I was never the kind of person who was a fan – only people like, say, James Stewart or June Allyson whom I used to see on the silver screen in my youth. I thought they were wonderful, and they turned out to be wonderful in real life as well. Otherwise very few. Your Gregory Pecks and people like that. I have no heroes who are politicians.

Any broadcasters? People whom you regard as being very successful.

Well, it's not so much a question of success. I tend to admire in people things that I can't do myself. As I said, I would admire Chris Evans's creativity and his bravery. I admire Bruce Forsyth for broadcasting without the net, taking chances, pushing it right up against the wire, as he used to do on *The Generation Game*, and be able to retrieve it when it looked as if it was going to fall into bad taste. Bob Monkhouse, just for getting out there and telling gags. I couldn't possibly do that. Anybody who does that has my undivided attention and admiration. Anybody, I suppose, who has succeeded in television, because it's such an incredibly difficult medium.

What do you think are the greatest enemies of success?

Lack of self-esteem. Lack of self-confidence. Bad luck. Lack of intelligence is probably the most important factor of them all. Intelligence is the biggest single factor in anything. That and luck. If you are a success, you ought to have enough intelligence to know how to cope with it. You cannot be a success without a certain amount of intelligence, whether it's native intelligence or intellectual ability.

You say a certain amount. You don't think you need a formidable intellect?

No. Some of the most successful people on television are some of the most deeply stupid people I have ever met, but they do have a native intelligence, an instinct for success. Let me qualify it a bit – instinct and intelligence.

What do you, as a successful performer, say to those whose business it is to criticize the successful?

I think you have to try to keep it on a less personal level. I think criticism in newspapers has become much too personal, it's now an exercise in showing off. This is not just true of television, it is true of theatrical criticism, football writing, sportswriting in general. Television criticism, and indeed radio criticism, has always seemed to me completely useless in any case, because people have already made up their minds about the thing when they've seen it. Theatre criticism is valid, because you read it before you see the show. If you happen to like a certain critic you will go by his judgment and say, 'Well, I won't go and see that show, because your man is usually right.' I once said to Sir David English when I went out to lunch with him, 'I don't see the validity of television criticism. I understand previews, but after the event people have made their own judgment.'

And if you didn't see it, it didn't matter.

Yes. He said, 'It works for us because if we get the right critic he reinforces the prejudices of most of our readers.' That's how it's done.

Do you think success brings any obligations to society?

I don't think I have any obligations to society. I pay my taxes, I behave decently. It brings obligations to your fellow man, but then everything does. The important thing is not to believe in it, to understand how transient it is and to be aware that the wind will blow away your footprints in the sands of time, and not to have false expectations. You know the way it is when you get into a television studio. 'Get Terry a cup of coffee. Is he all right? How's he doing? How is he today?' That's why you need a family to go back to, where you can go and make your own coffee, or where they haven't watched your show. My family never watch me on television at all, because I don't like watching it and they know it embarrasses me. We don't have a kind of adulatory, Daddy's-on-the-television thing – we've always had a fairly balanced life as far as that's concerned. There's neither praise nor blame. I come home, pour myself a drink and nobody fusses over me too much.

Has success changed you at all?

Yes, I am sure it has. It has probably made me more confident but not too much, I hope. But then, you never know yourself, you see. I have a view of myself – we all have a view of ourselves – which is slightly ̊roseate, particularly if we have been successful. But when you talk to your children, or you talk to your wife, you find it's not their view of you at all. They see a completely different person, and you say, 'Why, I'm not like that!' And that's important too, that you know that you are not as you think you are. I always think I can do everything without stress and that it doesn't take anything out of me to do television and radio till the cows come home, but my wife claims that it does in fact take a lot out of me.

Is that frank, honest opinion from those who are closest to you, and those you love, important in the fabric of success?

It is, of course. But the most important thing to have is a sense of humour. Lose that and you're dead. You need to be able to laugh at yourself and prick your own pomposity and look at the stupid incongruities. As I say, if I had been the most successful brain surgeon in the world, I might look at my success differently. If I had won a Nobel prize as a research physicist or scientist, I'd think that was worthwhile. But we're only talking about television and radio.

What would you like people to say about you when your time comes to leave this planet?

I think they'd probably put on the old tombstone, 'He looked as if he didn't know what he was doing.'